Segment Routing for Service Provider and Enterprise Networks

Florian Deragisch (CCIE #47970)

Leonir Hoxha (CCIE #49534)

Rene Minder (CCIE #8003)

Matthys "Thys" Rabe (CCIE #4237)

Kateel Vijayananda

Cisco Press

Hoboken, New Jersey

Segment Routing for Service Provider and Enterprise Networks

Florian Deragisch
Leonir Hoxha
Rene Minder
Matthys Rabe
Kateel Vijayananda

Published by:
Cisco Press

1 2024

Library of Congress Control Number: 2024945941

ISBN-13: 978-0-13-823093-7

ISBN-10: 0-13-823093-5

Warning and Disclaimer

Trademark Acknowledgments

Feedback Information

At Cisco Press, our goal is to create in-depth technical books of the highest quality and value. Each book is crafted with care and precision, undergoing rigorous development that involves the unique expertise of members from the professional technical community.

Readers' feedback is a natural continuation of this process. If you have any comments regarding how we could improve the quality of this book, or otherwise alter it to better suit your needs, you can contact us through email at feedback@ciscopress.com. Please make sure to include the book title and ISBN in your message.

We greatly appreciate your assistance.

Please contact us with concerns about any potential bias at https://www.pearson.com/report-bias.html.

GM K12, Early Career and Professional Learning: Soo Kang

Alliances Manager, Cisco Press: Caroline Antonio

Director, ITP Product Management: Brett Bartow

Managing Editor: Sandra Schroeder

Development Editor: Ellie C. Bru

Senior Project Editor: Mandie Frank

Copy Editor: Kitty Wilson

Technical Editors: Jakub Horn, Christian Schmutzer, Luc Andrew Burdet, Johan Gustawsson, Bram Van der Zwet

Editorial Assistant: Cindy Teeters

Designer: Chuti Prasertsith

Composition: codeMantra

Indexer: Timothy Wright

Proofreader: Barbara Mack

CISCO

Americas Headquarters	Asia Pacific Headquarters	Europe Headquarters
Cisco Systems, Inc.	Cisco Systems (USA) Pte. Ltd.	Cisco Systems International BV Amsterdam,
San Jose, CA	Singapore	The Netherlands

Cisco has more than 200 offices worldwide. Addresses, phone numbers, and fax numbers are listed on the Cisco Website at **www.cisco.com/go/offices**.

Cisco and the Cisco logo are trademarks or registered trademarks of Cisco and/or its affiliates in the U.S. and other countries. To view a list of Cisco trademarks, go to this URL: www.cisco.com/go/trademarks. Third party trademarks mentioned are the property of their respective owners. The use of the word partner does not imply a partnership relationship between Cisco and any other company. (1110R)

About the Authors

All the authors of this book are integral members of Cisco's professional services and product sales organizations. They have built extensive experience and expertise throughout their careers, working closely with service providers and enterprise customers to design, implement, transform, and optimize cutting-edge network solutions.

Florian Deragisch, CCIE #47970, is a Technical Leader, working with large service provider and carrier-grade enterprise customers. He joined Cisco in 2012 as part of a graduate program, where he discovered his passion for service provider designs and technologies. After gaining extensive exposure to MPLS-based networks and services, he embraced the evolution toward segment routing with his first SR-MPLS deployment in 2018. More recently, he has focused on the migration and deployment of L2VPN/L3VPN SRv6 services to build simple and highly scalable network architectures. He holds a master's degree in electrical engineering and information technology from the Swiss Federal Institute of Technology in Zurich and a Cisco Internetwork Expert certification (CCIE #47970). When not busy with work, he enjoys traveling to explore new places, cultures, and food.

Leonir Hoxha, CCIE #49534, has been with Cisco Systems since 2013, taking on various roles on the Professional Services team and later on the Pre-sales team—from troubleshooting to designing and implementing large-scale networks with a focus on service provider technologies, specifically MPLS services. In his current role as a Solutions Architect, he supports service providers and enterprise customers by understanding their requirements and providing cutting-edge solutions. An active speaker at Cisco Live conferences, he has delivered numerous sessions on segment routing across Europe, the United States, and Australia. He holds a bachelor's degree in computer science and a Cisco Internetwork Expert certification (CCIE #49534). In his free time, he enjoys electronic music, a nod to his first job as a DJ during his teenage years.

Rene Minder, CCIE #8003, is a Senior Program Advisor and Solution Architect with over 25 years of experience in the IT industry. He has been responsible for architecture and delivery in more than 70 customer engagements, evolving their networks and management infrastructures as well as the processes for developing, testing, and deploying them. He has led end-to-end IT architecture projects encompassing everything from portals offering service self-administration capabilities, to IT applications that automatically configure and test changes, to invoicing. His efforts have led to significant improvements in customer satisfaction, operational efficiency, and overall agility. He holds Lifetime Emeritus status for his Cisco Internetwork Expert certification (CCIE #8003).

Matthys "Thys" Rabe, CCIE #4237, a Lifetime Emeritus Cisco Certified Internetwork Expert (CCIE #4237), is a Technical Leader at Cisco Systems and holds a diploma in electrical engineering (telecommunications). With more than 25 years of experience in IP and MPLS operations with various service providers in South Africa and Switzerland, he has spent the past 10 years as a Technical Support Engineer focused on Swisscom. Prior to working at Cisco Systems, he was part of the Core IP Engineering team with a Swiss-based mobile provider. When he's not working, he enjoys fishing with his brothers in various southern African countries.

Kateel Vijayananda, is a solutions architect at Cisco Systems and has more than 30 years of experience in the networking industry. His expertise includes IPv6, IP services, design of large-scale networks for enterprise and service provider customers, and QoS assurance in IP networks. He has been with Cisco Systems since 2001, involved in several projects for service providers to deploy IP-based services using MPLS and segment routing. Before joining Cisco, he worked at Swisscom, a service provider in Switzerland, where he was responsible for developing MPLS VPN services. He is the co-author of the book *Developing IP-Based Services: Solutions for Service Providers and Vendors*. He holds a master's degree in computer science from the University of Maryland at College Park and a PhD in computer science from the Swiss Federal Institute of Technology at Lausanne (EPFL). In his spare time, he enjoys traveling and cooking.

About the Technical Reviewers

Jakub Horn has worked for more than 20 years at Cisco Systems and currently serves as a Principal Technical Marketing Engineer, specializing in cutting-edge technologies for service providers. Prior to this role, Jakub was a Network Consulting Engineer, delivering strategic solutions to global clients. His journey in tech began at IBM, where he honed his skills in networking and computer systems. Today, Jakub's expertise is centered on SRv6 technology, driving innovation in network architecture. As a passionate technologist, he continuously explores new advancements to shape the future of connectivity.

Christian Schmutzer is a Distinguished Engineer at Cisco Systems and has been with the company since 1998. Early in his career, he primarily worked on the design and deployment of large service provider backbones. He has been part of a business unit since 2005, serving as a technical subject matter expert for market-leading routing platforms such as the Cisco 7600 and ASR 9000. Since 2013, he has focused on packet/optical network architectures, future product definition, technology innovation, and leading customer deployments. He is the holder of several patents and the author of a series of IETF standards documents.

Bram van der Zwet is the Lead Architect for Network & Infrastructure at Swisscom, where he has been shaping the network architecture and technical strategy for Swisscom's IP and optical networks. His responsibilities extend to overseeing the physical infrastructure from Swisscom's IT and data centers down to the central offices in regional networks. He holds a degree from Delft University of Technology and is based in Bern, Switzerland. With more than 25 years of experience at Swisscom and a history of strategic roles driving innovation and excellence, he has become a key figure in the telecommunications industry.

Johan Gustawsson is a Senior Director within Cisco Data Center and Service Provider, focusing on driving the direction and strategy for routing and architectures. He has spent his entire career operating and building mass-scale networks, pioneering and driving market disruptions across routing and optical domains. Prior to joining Cisco, Johan was the Head of Network Architecture, Strategy, and Engineering at Arelion (formerly Telia Carrier), leading a globally distributed organization at the world's number-one-ranked Internet backbone. Johan holds a degree in Engineering from the KTH Royal Institute of Technology in Stockholm.

Luc André Burdet is a Senior Technical Leader in Engineering at Cisco, where he has been instrumental in driving innovation and strategic initiatives since May 2012. With more than 12 years of experience at Cisco, he focuses on advancing the company's engineering capabilities and leading key technical projects. He holds a master's degree from ETH Zürich and is based in Ottawa, Ontario. Luc André's technical expertise and leadership have established him as a pivotal figure in the networking industry, significantly contributing to Cisco's engineering excellence.

Acknowledgments

First and foremost, we would like to thank our main reviewers, Jakub Horn and Christian Schmutzer, for their meticulous reviews and invaluable feedback. Their dedication and attention to detail have significantly enhanced the quality of this book.

We also extend our thanks to Luc Andre Burdet for his expertise in the chapter focused on Layer 2 VPN technologies, and to Bram Van der Zwet and Johan Gustawsson for reviewing the chapters on business opportunities and organizational considerations. Your feedback has been instrumental in ensuring the accuracy and relevance of the information presented.

Special thanks to Marcel Witmer for all the support around PLE and integrated visibility and to Christian Schmutzer for his solid insight and input on PLE. We also appreciate Kaela Loffler and Ramiro Nobre for providing an overview on how micro-drops can influence overall service performance. Similarly, we would like to express our gratitude to Carmine Scarpitta and Ahmed Abdelsalam for their guidance on FRRouting's SRv6 implementation.

The authors had the pleasure of collaborating with Swisscom, a leading service provider based in Switzerland, on several aspects covered in this book. The insights gained from Swisscom's exposure to engineering, migrations, and operations have enriched the content, providing field perspectives that are invaluable for readers.

This book wouldn't have been possible without the support of many people on the Cisco Press team. Brett Bartow, Product Line Manager of the Pearson IT professional Group, was instrumental in sponsoring the book and driving it to execution. Sandra Schroeder, Managing Editor, was masterful with book graphics. Ellie Bru, Development Editor, has done a wonderful job in the technical review cycle; it has been a pleasure working with you. Mandie Frank, Senior Project Editor, thank you for leading the book to success through the production cycle. Kitty Wilson, Copy Editor, thank you for polishing up the book and making the content more shiny. Also, many thanks to the numerous Cisco Press unknown soldiers working behind the scenes to make this book happen.

We would like to express our deepest gratitude to our Cisco management for supporting and encouraging us in creating this book. Thank you to everyone who has contributed to this book. Your support and expertise have made this project possible.

Finally, we would like to extend our heartfelt thanks to our families. Your unwavering support, patience, and understanding have been our pillars of strength throughout the writing process. The countless hours spent away from you to work on this book have not gone unnoticed, and we are deeply grateful for your encouragement and understanding.

Contents at a Glance

Introduction   xx

Part I   **Introduction**

Chapter 1   MPLS in a Nutshell   1

Chapter 2   What Is Segment Routing over MPLS (SR-MPLS)?   33

Chapter 3   What Is Segment Routing over IPv6 (SRv6)?   103

Part II   **Segment Routing**

Chapter 4   Segment Routing in Detail   219

Chapter 5   Migrating to Segment Routing   353

Part III   **Service Design**

Chapter 6   L2VPN Service Deployment: Configuration and Verification Techniques   439

Chapter 7   L3VPN Service Deployment: Configuration and Verification Techniques   605

Chapter 8   Service Assurance   783

Chapter 9   High Availability and Fast Convergence   857

Part IV   **Business and Operational Considerations**

Chapter 10   Business Opportunities   997

Chapter 11   Organizational Considerations   1043

Appendix A   Reference Diagrams and Information 1109

Index   1115

Online Element:

Chapter 12   SRv6 Ecosystem Deployment Use Cases   1

Reader Services

Register your copy at www.ciscopress.com/title/ISBN for convenient access to downloads, updates, and corrections as they become available. To start the registration process, go to ciscopress.com/register and log in or create an account*. Enter the product ISBN 9780138230937 and click Submit. When the process is complete, you will find any available bonus content under Registered Products.

*Be sure to check the box that you would like to hear from us to receive exclusive discounts on future editions of this product.

For access to any available bonus content associated with this title, visit ciscopress.com/sr, sign in or create a new account, and register ISBN 9780138230937 by December 31, 2027.

Contents

Introduction   xx

Part I   **Introduction**

Chapter 1   **MPLS in a Nutshell   1**

How MPLS Operates   4

   MPLS Label Structure   6

   Control Plane and Data Plane   10

   Label Distribution Protocol (LDP)   11

   Label Allocation Mechanism   12

   MPLS Label Operations   14

   Traffic Forwarding Using Labels   15

   MPLS VPN Services Overview   16

   MPLS Traffic Protection   18

Challenges and Shortcomings of MPLS   19

   MPLS Label Space Limitation   20

   LSP and Summarization   21

   Inter-AS Limitations   21

   Lack of End-to-end QoS Control   21

   Configuration and Operational Complexity of MPLS/VPN and BGP   22

   RSVP-Based Traffic Engineering   22

   LDP–IGP Synchronization   24

   Load Balancing and Hashing   25

Beyond MPLS   28

Summary   30

References and Additional Reading   32

Chapter 2   **What Is Segment Routing over MPLS (SR-MPLS)?   33**

Problem Description and Requirements   40

Segment Routing over MPLS (SR-MPLS)   41

   Data Plane   41

   Segment Identifier (SID)   42

   SID Allocation   43

   IGP Prefix Segment (Prefix SID)   45

   IGP Adjacency Segment (Adjacency SID)   47

   BGP Prefix Segment (BGP Prefix SID)   49

BGP Peering Segments (BGP Peering SIDs)   50

Binding Segment (Binding SID)   52

IGP Extensions   53

IS-IS Extensions for Segment Routing (RFC 8667)   53

OSPF Extensions for Segment Routing (RFC 8665)   64

IGP Flexible Algorithm (Flex Algo) (RFC 9350)   73

MP-BGP Extensions   83

SR Prefix SID Extensions for BGP (RFC 8669)   85

BGP Link-State Extensions for SR (RFC 9085)   87

BGP Link-State Extensions for SR BGP Egress Peer Engineering (RFC 9086)   95

Summary   99

References and Additional Reading   100

Chapter 3   What Is Segment Routing over IPv6 (SRv6)?   103

Introduction   103

Segment Routing over IPv6 (SRv6)   103

IPv6 for SRv6 Recap   104

SRv6 Network Programming (RFC 8986)   107

SRv6 Segment Identifier (SID)   107

IPv6 Segment Routing Header (SRH) (RFC 8754)   123

Penultimate Segment Pop of the SRH   127

Ultimate Segment Pop of the SRH   129

Ultimate Segment Decapsulation   130

SRv6 Policy Headend Behaviors   132

SRv6 Policy Endpoint Behaviors   141

SRv6 Headend and Endpoint Behavior Overview   146

SRv6 Network Programming Extension: SRv6 uSID Instruction   147

uN Endpoint Variants   152

uA Endpoint Variants   156

SID Compression   161

Addressing Considerations   162

IPv6 Addressing   162

SRv6 Locator Addressing Scheme   165

Summarization   172

IGP Extensions   175

IS-IS Extensions for Segment Routing over IPv6 (RFC 9352)   175

MP-BGP Extensions 186

BGP Overlay Services on SRv6 (RFC 9252) 186

BGP Link-State Extensions for SRv6 (RFC 9514) 201

SR-Powered Network Evolution 205

MPLS Network Architecture: Control and Data Plane Overview 205

SR-MPLS Network Architecture: Control and Data
Plane Overview 207

SRv6 Network Architecture: Control and Data Plane Overview 209

Network Evolution at a Glance 210

SR-MPLS or SRv6 212

Benefits of Deploying Segment Routing 212

Hardware and Software Support 214

Feature Support 215

Summary 215

References and Additional Reading 217

Part II   **Segment Routing**

Chapter 4   **Segment Routing in Detail 219**

Link-State IGPs 221

IS-IS 221

IS-IS Levels 222

IS-IS Areas 222

IS-IS Router Types 222

IS-IS Routing 222

IS-IS Route Propagation and Leaking 223

IS-IS Overload Bit 223

OSPF 224

OSPF SPF Algorithm 224

OSPFv3 225

OSPFv3 Route Summarization 225

OSPFv3 Route Filtering 225

Segment Routing Baseline 225

SR-MPLS Baseline 226

Segment Routing Global Block (SRGB) 226

Segment Routing Local Block (SRLB) 227

SR-MPLS Addressing 227

SR-MPLS Configuration 228

SR-MPLS Verification   231

SRv6 Baseline   236

SRv6 uSID   236

SRv6 Addressing   237

SRv6 uSID Configuration   239

SRv6 uSID Verification   241

Segment Routing Control Plane (IGP)   243

SR-MPLS Control Plane   243

SR-MPLS IS-IS   244

SR-MPLS OSPF   250

SR-MPLS Anycast SID   254

SRv6 Control Plane   257

SRv6 IS-IS   257

SRv6 OSPF   301

Multiplane Topologies with Flex Algos   301

Components of SR Flex Algos   302

Flex Algo Use Cases Scenarios   304

SR-MPLS Configuration for Flex Algo Use Cases   322

Segment Routing Control Plane (BGP)   324

BGP Prefix SID   324

BGP Prefix SID Configuration   324

BGP Prefix SID Verification   327

Intra-AS BGP-LU with a BGP Prefix SID   328

Intra-AS BGP-LU Design   330

BGP Additional Path   331

Intra-AS BGP-LU Configuration   332

Intra-AS BGP-LU Verification   337

Data Forwarding from PE-1 to PE-3   341

Inter-AS BGP-LU   343

Inter-AS BGP-LU Design   343

Inter-AS BGP-LU Configuration   344

Inter-AS BGP-LU Verification   345

Data Forwarding from PE-1 to PE-5   349

Summary   350

References and Additional Reading   352

Chapter 5   Migrating to Segment Routing   353

Deployment Models   354

Migration Strategies   355

SR-MPLS Migration   358

SR-MPLS Reference Network Topology   358

Enabling SR-MPLS in an Existing Network (Coexistence)   358

Enabling SR-MPLS on P2, P3, and PE-3   360

Enabling and Preferring SR-MPLS on P1, P2, and PE-1   363

Building a New SR-MPLS Network   365

Enabling SRMS   365

Enabling LDP on the Border Node   372

Enabling the BGP Prefix SID in an SR-MPLS Network   376

BGP Proxy Prefix SID   383

SRv6 Migration   387

Building a New SRv6 Network Using an SRv6 IWG   389

Migration Use Case   391

Building a New SRv6 Network Using Inter-AS Option A   401

Migration Use Case   403

Building a New SRv6 Network Using Dual-Connected PE Devices   413

Migration Use Case   415

High Availability   425

Active-Active   425

Active-Backup   426

Load Sharing   426

Migration Paths from MPLS to SRv6   427

Flat MPLS Network   429

Unified MPLS Network   430

MPLS Network with Inter-AS Option C   431

Carrier Supporting Carrier MPLS Network   434

Summary   435

References and Additional Reading   437

Part III   Service Design

**Chapter 6   L2VPN Service Deployment: Configuration and
                Verification Techniques   439**

L2VPN (EVPN)   440

EVPN in Detail   442

EVPN Instance (EVI)   445

Ethernet Segment (ES)   447

Ethernet Tag ID   450

EVPN BGP Routes   452

EVPN E-LAN   472

SRv6 EVPN E-LAN Service Configuration and Verification   474

EVPN E-Tree   551

SRv6 EVPN E-Tree Service Configuration   552

EVPN E-Line   569

SRv6 EVPN E-Line (VPWS) Service Configuration   571

Summary   602

References and Additional Reading   602

Chapter 7   L3VPN Service Deployment: Configuration and Verification Techniques   605

L3VPN   606

SRv6 L3VPN Overlay Service   608

SRv6 L3VPN Full-Mesh Service   610

SRv6 L3VPN Hub-and-Spoke Service   636

SRv6 L3VPN Extranet Service   657

SR-MPLS L3VPN Overlay Service   677

SR-MPLS L3VPN Full-Mesh Service   688

SR-MPLS L3VPN Hub-and-Spoke Service   719

SR-MPLS L3VPN Extranet Service   752

Route Target Constraint   767

Route Target Constraint Configuration and Verification   771

Summary   780

References and Additional Reading   781

Chapter 8   Service Assurance   783

Transport   784

Segment Routing Data Plane Monitoring (SR-DPM)   788

SR-DPM Configuration and Verification   789

Path Tracing (PT)   798

Services   806

L2VPN Service Assurance   806

Ethernet Connectivity Fault Management (CFM)   808

ITU-T Y.1731 Performance Measurement   816

L3VPN Service Assurance   834

IPSLA and TWAMP   834

Summary   855

References and Additional Reading   855

Chapter 9   **High Availability and Fast Convergence**   **857**

BFD Failure Detection Mechanism   858

BFD BoB Configuration   865

BFD BoB Verification   868

BFD BLB Configuration   872

BFD BLB Verification   874

Topology-Independent Loop-Free Alternate (TI-LFA)   878

Link Protection Configuration   883

Link Protection Verification: SR-MPLS   885

Link Protection Verification: SRv6   902

Node Protection Configuration   914

Node Protection Verification: SR-MPLS   917

Node Protection Verification: SRv6   919

SRLG Protection Configuration   921

SRLG Protection Verification: SR-MPLS   923

SRLG Protection Verification: SRv6   931

Microloop Avoidance   935

BGP PIC Edge   943

BGP PIC Edge Configuration: SR-MPLS   948

BGP PIC Edge Verification: SR-MPLS   951

BGP PIC Edge Configuration: SRv6   962

BGP PIC Edge Unipath Verification: SRv6   970

BGP PIC Edge Multipath Verification: SRv6   981

Summary   995

References and Additional Reading   995

Part IV   **Business and Operational Considerations**

Chapter 10   **Business Opportunities**   **997**

Technological Opportunities and Benefits   999

Fewer Protocols   999

More QoS Options   1001

SR from the Access Network to the Data Center Network   1003

Traffic Engineering and Network Slicing   1005

Scale   1007

Routed Optical Networks   1008

Benefit 1: Simplified Long-Distance Connectivity   1008

Benefit 2: Easier and Cost-Effective Scaling   1009

Benefit 3: Simplified Redundancy   1009

Private Line Emulation   1011

Integrated Visibility   1017

Intent-Driven Configuration of Visibility Features   1018

Intent-/Model-Based Assurance   1019

High-Precision Probing   1020

Path Tracing   1023

New Hardware Generation   1025

CapEx Savings   1026

OpEx Savings   1030

Business Case Guidance   1032

Summary   1039

References and Additional Reading   1040

Chapter 11   Organizational Considerations   1043

Scenario 1: Replacing or Enhancing a Legacy Network with SR   1046

Knowledge   1046

Migration Strategy   1049

IT Evolution and Gap Awareness   1051

Scenario 2: Consolidating Networks and Services   1056

Domain Definitions   1056

Domain Architecture Blueprint   1059

Domain Responsibilities and Their Architectural Implications   1067

Domain Organization and Transformation   1074

Existing and New Processes   1083

Service Portfolio Consolidation   1083

Development and Release Methodology   1084

Process with a Clear Flow   1086

Environments   1089

*Domain Releases: A Symphony of Component Builds and
    Release Candidates   1096*

*Tooling: Embracing Automation for Environment and
    Process Efficiency   1097*

Tooling: Source of Truth   1098

Tooling: Binary Repository   1100

Tooling: Pipelines   1101

Change Management Across Domains   1104

Summary   1106

References and Additional Reading   1107

Appendix A   Reference Diagrams and Information   1109

SR-MPLS Reference Network   1109

SRv6 Reference Network   1111

SR Migration Reference Network   1112

Index   1115

Online Element:

Chapter 12   SRv6 Ecosystem Deployment Use Cases   1

SRv6 Open-Source Implementations   2

Linux Kernel   2

Free Range Routing (FRR)   7

Vector Packet Processor (VPP)   9

Software for Open Networking in the Cloud (SONiC)   13

SRv6 Open-Source Lab Deployment Examples   17

Linux SRv6 Deployment   18

Containerlab   20

Linux Underlay Connectivity   24

Linux IPv4 L3VPN Service   27

Linux IPv6 L3VPN Service   32

Linux IPv4/IPv6 L3VPN Service   34

Linux Point-to-Point L2VPN Service   36

VPP SRv6 Deployment   39

Basic VPP Setup   40

VPP Underlay Connectivity   43

VPP IPv4 L3VPN Service   45

VPP IPv6 L3VPN Service   54

VPP Point-to-Point L2VPN Service   57

SRv6 L3VPN Interoperability   61

Free Range Routing IPv4 L3VPN Service   62

Cisco Catalyst 8000V Edge IPv4 L3VPN Service   75

Summary   82

References and Additional Reading   83

Icons Used in This Book

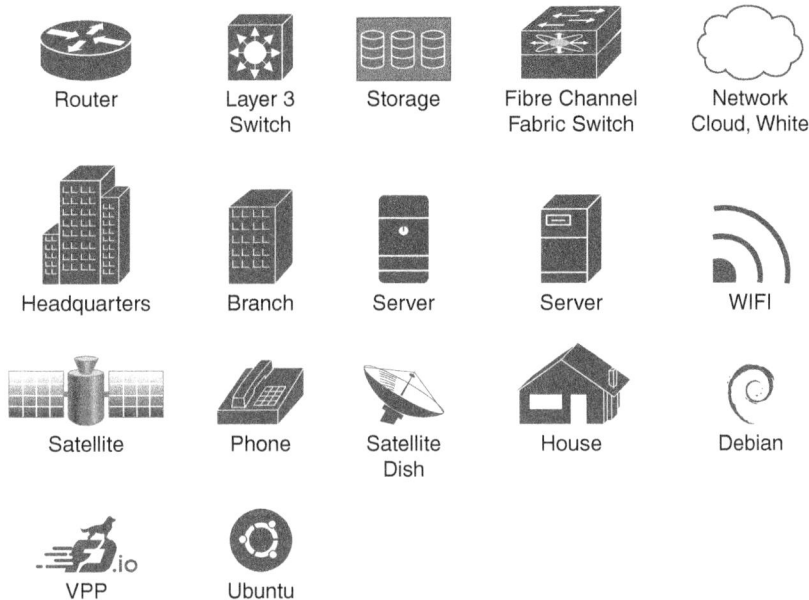

Router

Layer 3
Switch

Storage

Fibre Channel
Fabric Switch

Network
Cloud, White

Headquarters

Branch

Server

Server

WIFI

Satellite

Phone

Satellite
Dish

House

Debian

VPP

Ubuntu

Command Syntax Conventions

The conventions used to present command syntax in this book are the same conventions used in Cisco's Command Reference. The Command Reference describes these conventions as follows:

- **Boldface** indicates commands and keywords that are entered literally as shown. In actual output (not general command syntax), boldface indicates commands that are manually input by the user (such as a **show** command).

- Vertical bars (|) separate alternative, mutually exclusive elements.

- Braces { } indicate a required choice.

Introduction

Welcome to the future of MPLS and the realm of advanced networking technologies, where efficiency, scalability, and reliability are paramount. This book is your gateway to mastering segment routing (SR), a revolutionary technology that transforms IP data transport and network operations. From the foundational principles of MPLS to state-of-the-art implementations of SR over MPLS (SR-MPLS) and SR over IPv6 (SRv6), this book offers a comprehensive guide that bridges the gap between theory and practice.

The chapters cover the entire spectrum of SR, providing a holistic understanding of the technology. They feature practical examples for SR on both IOS XR and IOS XE platforms, ensuring that you have the knowledge to implement SR in different network environments.

This book also goes beyond technical details. It delves into the business opportunities and organizational implications of adopting SR, offering valuable insights into how SR can drive growth, improve customer experience, and streamline operations. Dedicated sections on the SRv6 ecosystem in data centers and cloud environments showcasing network functions virtualization (NFV) prepare you for the next wave of networking innovations.

Available online content enables you to gain hands-on practice and reinforce the theories covered. A business case template provides a tool to legitimize investments in SR technologies and calculate potential returns.

By the end of this book, you'll be equipped with the knowledge and tools to implement and manage SR technologies effectively, helping you stay ahead in this ever-evolving field.

What Sets This Book Apart

What distinguishes our book is its unique blend of content, offering readers an unparalleled experience that combines theoretical aspects of segment routing with hands-on experience from actual deployments.

- **Practical insights:** Drawing from real-world experiences, particularly our collaboration with Swisscom, this book provides real-world insights that bridge the gap between theory and practice. In this book you will find detailed configurations, design guidelines, and troubleshooting tips that are directly applicable to your work environment.

- **Step-by-step approach:** The content of this book is structured to guide you through a logical progression of information, from basic concepts to advanced implementations, making it suitable for both beginners and seasoned professionals. Each chapter builds on the previous one, providing a smooth learning curve.

- **Future-proofing:** With a dedicated section on the future of SRv6, featuring open-source SRv6 NFV implementations that can fit in data centers and cloud environments, this book prepares you for the next wave of networking innovations.

- **Interactive learning:** Downloadable content provides lab topology definitions, configurations, scripts, and templates to help you set up your own labs and experiment with them. Additionally, a lab guide is available, offering the option to run your lab in the cloud.

- **Beyond technology:** In addition to technical content, the business-oriented chapters outline the benefits of adopting SR and offer guidance in various areas to help leadership and teams smoothly transition to SR.

Goals and Methods

The primary goal of this book is to provide a thorough understanding of SR by offering detailed explanations, configuration examples, verification hints, and packet captures. It walks you through foundational concepts and practical implementations.

Two reference lab topologies, one for SR-MPLS and one for SRv6, are consistently referenced throughout the technical chapters. To make the learning process interactive and engaging, the downloadable lab support material enables you to set up your own lab so you can replicate and apply the described theory.

Who Should Read This Book?

This book is designed for network engineers, architects, and operators who are involved in the design, deployment, and management of modern networking infrastructures. It is also valuable for IT professionals, students, and researchers who wish to deepen their understanding of SR technologies. Business leaders and decision makers will find the chapters on new service opportunities and what to consider within an organization on the journey to SR particularly insightful.

How This Book Is Organized

The chapters in this book guide you from basic concepts to advanced implementations, ensuring a logical progression of information. A recap of MPLS is followed by an in-depth exploration of SR, detailed configurations, migration strategies, service assurance, and high availability. The final chapters provide a glimpse into the future of SRv6 in data centers and cloud environments, explore business opportunities that justify investment in this new technology, and offer non-technical thoughts to streamline the transition to SR.

This book is broken into 12 chapters and an appendix:

- **Chapter 1, "MPLS in a Nutshell":** This chapter provides an introduction to MPLS technology and its significance in modern networking as well as an overview of MPLS mechanisms and benefits.

- **Chapter 2, "What Is Segment Routing over MPLS (SR-MPLS)?":** This chapter provides a basic introduction to the general concepts of segment routing (SR) and explores SR-MPLS in the control plane and data plane.

- **Chapter 3, "What Is Segment Routing over IPv6 (SRv6)?":** This chapter explores SRv6 in the control plane and data plane and provides an overview of the evolution and simplification of SR-driven networks.

- **Chapter 4, "Segment Routing in Detail":** This chapter includes detailed information on configuration and verification of SR on Cisco devices and describes design guidelines and advanced features for SR networks.

- **Chapter 5, "Migrating to Segment Routing":** This chapter is a practical roadmap for migrating from MPLS to SR and presents strategies for greenfield and brownfield deployments.

- **Chapter 6, "L2VPN Service Deployment: Configuration and Verification Techniques":** This chapter provides an overview of customer-related L2VPN services implemented on an SRv6 underlay network. It includes basic configuration methodologies and service verifications.

- **Chapter 7, "L3VPN Service Deployment: Configuration and Verification Techniques":** This chapter provides an overview of customer-related L3VPN services implemented on SRv6 and SR-MPLS underlay networks. It includes basic configuration methodologies and service verifications.

- **Chapter 8, "Service Assurance":** This chapter presents procedures and processes for improving customer experience and satisfaction. It includes a discussion of tools and protocols for SLA monitoring and fault management in the transport network layer, as well as in the L2VPN and L3VPN service overlays.

- **Chapter 9, "High Availability and Fast Convergence":** This chapter introduces technologies and features for high availability and fast convergence in SR networks. It includes a detailed discussion of failure detection, path computation, and network convergence.

- **Chapter 10, "Business Opportunities":** This chapter describes the benefits of investing in SR and why network service providers should transition to this technology. It offers insights into how SRv6 can offer substantial opportunities and advantages over SR-MPLS as well as business case calculation guidance.

- **Chapter 11, "Organizational Considerations":** This chapter examines the impact of SR on organizational structures and processes and provides a guide to managing the transformation to a programmable SR network.

- **Chapter 12, "SRv6 Ecosystem Deployment Use Cases":** This online only chapter discusses the potential of SRv6 in data centers and cloud environments. It provides examples and interoperability scenarios involving open-source software.

- **Appendix A, "Reference Diagrams and Information":** This appendix describes the reference diagrams and information of the SR-MPLS, SRv6, and SR migration network topologies used throughout the book in a single location for the reader's convenience.

Downloadable Content

Readers can access downloadable content using the companion website as per the instructions below:

1. The user enters ciscopress.com/sr in his browser or clicks the hyperlink in the online book version.

2. The user completes the registration/login process.

3. The user confirms the already prepopulated ISBN number of the book and answers a proof-of-purchase challenge question, to access additional content.

4. The user clicks on the desired attachment.

The following attachments can be downloaded for use with this book:

- **SR-MPLS-Reference-Configuration-Lab.zip:** These files, which can be used across the entire book, include a reference diagram and configurations to deploy an SR-MPLS and services lab.

- **SRv6-Reference-Configurations-Lab.zip:** These files, which can be used across the entire book, include a reference diagram and configurations to deploy an SRv6 and services lab.

- **SRv6-Online-Lab-Guide.pdf:** This guide provides clear instructions on how to use an online lab, offering you the flexibility to run your SRv6 lab in the cloud.

- **SRv6-Migration-Lab.zip:** These files, which are meant to be used with Chapter 5, include a reference diagram and configuration for migration use cases.

- **SRv6-Linux-Lab.zip:** These files, which are meant to be used with Chapter 12, include a container-based lab topology definition and initialization script required to spin up the SRv6 Linux lab topology.

- **SRv6-VPP-Lab.zip:** These files, which are meant to be used with Chapter 12, include a bash script to spin up the SRv6 VPP topology, VPP instances, and startup configurations.

- **SRv6-Interop-Lab.zip:** These files, which are meant to be used with Chapter 12, include a Cisco CML topology definition and a running configuration of PE1 (IOS XR), P (IOS XE), and PE3 (IOS XE), as well as FRR settings and configuration for PE2 (FRR).

- **Segment-Routing-Business-Case-Template.xlsx:** This file, which is meant to be used with Chapter 10, includes a Microsoft Excel–based business case template to help you create your case for SR in your organization. Please review the provided sample data and update all cells that have a yellow background to reflect your specific information.

Note   This book contains references to the companion website in later chapters which leverage the previously listed downloadable content.

Chapter 1

MPLS in a Nutshell

Multiprotocol Label Switching (MPLS) is a well-established data transmission technology that is widely used among telecommunication companies, service providers, and enterprise networks. MPLS technology can transport protocols such as IP, Ethernet, ATM, SDH, and SONET. Any incoming data packet with source and destination IP addresses is encapsulated by appending a tag. This tag, in MPLS terminology, is a *label*. MPLS technology has become a vital component of modern networking infrastructure. It allows for efficient data transfer and management by providing a streamlined approach to packet forwarding. Using label forwarding instead of IP routing has also led to significant network performance and scalability improvements.

In the late 1990s, the first implementations of MPLS marked a significant advancement, making it possible to append tags to data packets and route them through a chain of nodes. MPLS was revolutionary because it enabled constant-length lookups on a 4-byte label, making packet forwarding much more efficient compared to the variable-prefix-length IP lookups used in traditional IP routing. Initially, MPLS used Tag Distribution Protocol (TDP) to attach labels to packets; it later evolved to use Label Distribution Protocol (LDP) for more sophisticated label management. MPLS can operate on a BGP-free core, significantly reducing the memory requirements for core routers. A BGP-free core means only the provider edge (PE) nodes use BGP, and the core (P) nodes are BGP free. The use of MPLS labels for forwarding enabled a wide variety of data types to be carried across a single network infrastructure. These innovations made MPLS a powerful tool for optimizing network performance and scalability.

With traditional MPLS technology, LDP labels need to follow whatever the interior gateway protocol (IGP) chooses as the best path. The advantage of MPLS is that no IP lookup is conducted on the transit nodes (core nodes); instead, only label-based forwarding is performed. The fact that a router does not have to do an IP lookup in the routing table but instead forwards the packets based on the label itself brought a lot of possibilities in terms of how packets are processed, resulting in higher performance of the router itself and, most significantly, offering differentiated services on top of the MPLS-based network.

MPLS is a shared network infrastructure used for a wide range of services. With it, there is no need for distinct physical network infrastructure to serve different services for end customers. Providing various services and solutions using a shared network infrastructure lowers the overall cost for network operators. Network operators can provide multiple services over MPLS networks for their end customers, making deployment of these services technically independent from the MPLS layer. Speaking of services, MPLS provides the possibility to offer services such as Internet services for private and public customers as well as virtual private network (VPN) services. From a high-level point of view, VPN services can be classified into the following categories:

- **Layer 3 VPN:** Known as L3VPN and described in RFC 2547

- **Layer 2 VPN:** Known as L2VPN and described in RFC 4664

- **Multicast VPN:** Known as mVPN and described in RFC 6513

L3VPN services offer an efficient way to provide any-to-any mesh connectivity at the IP address level. Each customer edge (CE) device attaches to a provider edge (PE) node, establishing IP-based neighborship through an IGP, Border Gateway Protocol (BGP), or static configuration. PE nodes connect to multiple CE devices and maintain separate routing tables for each customer using virtual routing and forwarding (VRF) instances. VRF instances ensure local routing table separation, while L3VPN enables deterministic connectivity among different VRF instances.

In an L3VPN setup, each PE node creates a unique VRF instance for every customer, ensuring isolation of each customer's routing information. The PE nodes receive IP prefixes from their connected CE devices and use Multiprotocol BGP (MP-BGP) to distribute these prefixes to other PE devices in the network. MP-BGP extends BGP to support multiple address families, enabling the PE nodes to handle both IPv4 and IPv6 prefixes as well as VPN-IPv4 and VPN-IPv6 prefixes.

The process begins when a CE router advertises its routes to the connected PE router. The PE router assigns a VPN label to each route and includes this label when advertising the route to other PE routers using MP-BGP. When a remote PE router receives these routes, it updates its VRF tables accordingly and distributes the prefixes to the appropriate CE devices.

L3VPN leverages MPLS to ensure that data packets follow the predetermined paths across the provider's network, ensuring quality of service (QoS) and optimizing resource utilization. MPLS labels are used to steer the packets through the provider network, enabling features such as traffic engineering and fast rerouting in the event of node or link failure.

VRF instances also enable the use of overlapping IP address spaces from different customers, eliminating the risk of IP address conflicts. This capability is beneficial for network operators hosting multiple customers with their own private IP address spaces.

L2VPN services extend Layer 2 connectivity across an MPLS network, enabling enterprises to link dispersed sites as if they were on the same LAN. Each CE device connects to a PE node, establishing point-to-point or multipoint Layer 2 connections to remote CE devices.

In traditional L2VPN solutions, PE nodes use pseudowires for point-to-point connections (Virtual Private Wire Service [VPWS]) and Virtual Private LAN Service (VPLS) for multipoint-to-multipoint Ethernet services. Pseudowires emulate direct links between CE devices by encapsulating Layer 2 frames into MPLS packets, which are then forwarded across the MPLS network. VPLS creates a full mesh network, providing any-to-any Layer 2 connectivity by replicating and forwarding Ethernet frames to the correct destinations.

From a network operator's perspective, implementing L2VPN involves configuring PE nodes to handle various customer connections. Each PE node maintains virtual forwarding instances (VFIs) for VPLS, which manage the customer-specific forwarding tables. These VFIs enable the PE nodes to handle Ethernet frames from multiple customers independently, ensuring that traffic from different customers remains isolated. The Layer 2 frames are encapsulated into MPLS labels and steered toward an egress PE node, where decapsulation takes place before the original frames are forwarded to the destination site or CE node. This book will delve into the next generation of L2VPN services: Ethernet VPN (EVPN).

mVPN with mLDP, as detailed in RFC 6513, optimizes multicast data distribution in MPLS networks. Between the PE and CE routers, protocols such as Protocol Independent Multicast (PIM) and Internet Group Management Protocol (IGMP) are used. Within the MPLS core, mLDP establishes multicast distribution trees. These trees, constructed as point-to-multipoint (P2MP) and multipoint-to-multipoint (MP2MP) label-switched paths (LSPs), enable efficient multicast traffic delivery. mLDP extends LDP to dynamically signal and create these LSPs, forming a scalable multicast routing framework. This approach eliminates the need for traditional GRE tunnels. By leveraging MPLS infrastructure, network operators can deliver multicast services within an MPLS VPN. mLDP simplifies the control plane by utilizing existing LDP mechanisms, seamlessly integrating with current MPLS deployments, and provides the capability to support large-scale multicast deployments across MPLS networks.

Apart from the VPN services, other use cases for MPLS are traffic engineering and traffic protection and restoration. Large service providers and enterprise networks need a scalable and more efficient way to achieve the same result with less effort and lower operational costs. Traffic engineering in MPLS allows network operators to control the flow of data through the network by optimizing the path that packets take. MPLS Traffic Engineering (MPLS TE) enables the creation of LSPs that can be dynamically adjusted based on current network conditions and policies. MPLS supports fast reroute (FRR) techniques that can switch traffic to a precalculated backup path in the event of a failure. This is important for maintaining service continuity, especially in networks that support critical services. Chapter 9, "High Availability and Fast Convergence," is dedicated to a traffic-protection methodology called Topology-Independent Loop-Free Alternate (TI-LFA) with segment routing. TI-LFA provides link and node protection in any topology, which is not the case with other legacy protection mechanisms.

MPLS is a technology that brings many benefits to modern networks, including:

- **Efficiency:** By pooling network resources, MPLS enables efficient utilization of both bandwidth capacity and network node capabilities. This means that critical and SLA-based applications can operate at maximum capacity without affecting other applications.

- **Reduced cost:** MPLS eliminates the necessity to operate dedicated routers and WAN circuits to suit various customers. It provides a more cost-effective way to manage and provision network services.

- **Improved scalability:** The P nodes do not use BGP because they are only involved in label forwarding and do not perform any IP lookups. BGP is used on the PE nodes to exchange customer routers. Therefore, the core devices remain BGP free.

- **Agility:** In traditional network models, it can be difficult to respond quickly to demands for new applications and services. MPLS, on the other hand, allows networks to grow, change, or be reduced without requiring new hardware or additional WAN circuits. This makes it easier to adapt to changing business needs and to onboard new customers in hours rather than days or weeks.

- **Improved reliability:** MPLS provides several mechanisms for fast rerouting of traffic in the event of link or node failures, which reduces downtime and improves service availability.

This introductory chapter provides an overview of MPLS technology. For those with experience in MPLS, it provides a logical path to understanding segment routing technology and Segment Routing over IPv6 (SRv6) throughout coming chapters. For those without experience in MPLS technology, it provides a solid foundation to understand MPLS fundamentals.

How MPLS Operates

Now that you have had a 30,000-foot overview of the MPLS technology, in the following sections of this chapter, we will examine the details of the MPLS label structure, how a label is allocated, and which protocol allocates a label. We will distinguish between the control plane and the data plane, and we will analyze label operations.

Figure 1-1 shows the device roles and their functions within an MPLS network domain.

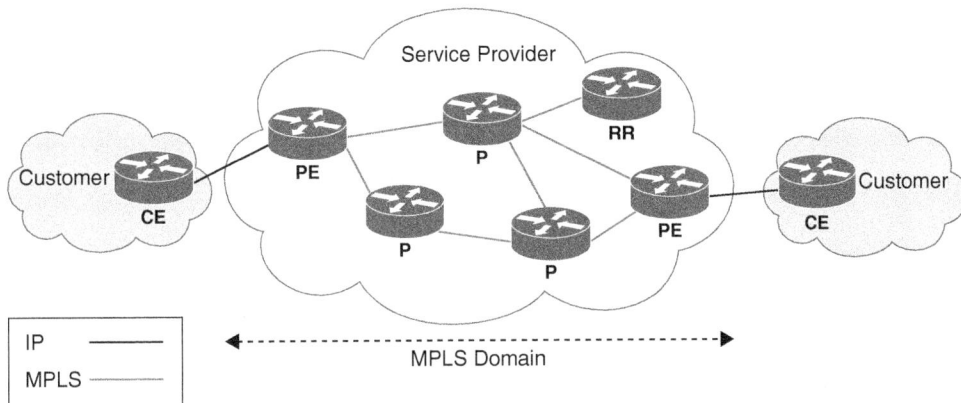

Figure 1-1   *MPLS Domains*

MPLS networks consist of several types of routers, each with a specific function:

- Provider (P) router, also known as label switch router (LSR):

  - All interfaces are MPLS enabled and participate in MPLS label switching. P routers are part of the transport across the MPLS backbone.

  - P node runs an IGP protocol such as OSPF or IS-IS (in the case of segment routing). With legacy MPLS, the LSR is also LDP enabled for label distribution and signaling.

  - P node does not run BGP peering internally or externally (so it has a BGP-free core), except when the P router also acts as BGP route reflector (RR)

  - Backbone routes are part of the global routing table and do not participate in any VRF.

  - An LSR does not contain any customer routes, but MPLS-encapsulated customer traffic is label forwarded on LSRs.

- Provider edge (PE) router, also known as label edge router (LER):

  - Core-facing interfaces are MPLS enabled, while customer-facing interfaces are IP or L2 enabled.

  - PE routers are border routers (ABRs/ASBRs) and contain knowledge of customer routes as well as MPLS backbone routes.

  - Customer routes are part of a VRF instance, and each VRF instance creates its own routing table separately from other VRF instances.

  - PE routers peer directly with CE routers via BGP, IGPs, or static routing.

  - BGP full mesh between PEs or PEs with RRs is mandatory to advertise and distribute customer routes to each other for end-to-end reachability.

- BGP route reflector (RR):

  - BGP RRs simplify the configuration of BGP peering sessions in large MPLS networks.

  - RRs act as central points for BGP route reflection in an MPLS network, reducing the number of BGP peering sessions required between PE routers.

  - In an MPLS network, BGP RRs are used to distribute IP routes and VPN routes among the PE routers.

- Customer edge (CE) router:

  - CE routers are located at the customer sites and are responsible for connecting a customer's LAN to the MPLS network. A CE typically has multiple Layer 3 interfaces and is connected to the PE router via a Layer 3 interface. A CE router is responsible for forwarding customer traffic to the PE router, which then encapsulates it to MPLS packets and adds the appropriate labels before forwarding them to the P router.

Overall, the roles of PE, P, and CE routers are crucial in the functioning of MPLS networks. A PE router connects customer sites to the MPLS network, a P router is responsible for transporting labeled packets across the network, and a CE router is responsible for connecting the customer's network to the service provider network. By dividing the responsibilities of these routers in this way, MPLS is able to efficiently transport traffic across large-scale networks while still maintaining security and privacy for each customer site.

MPLS enables the effective exchange of VPN routes using Multiprotocol Border Gateway Protocol (MP-BGP). Within an MPLS network, the core nodes are BGP free, whereas the PE nodes have BGP deployed, allowing for end-to-end customer routes transport. The provider network PEs can use MP-BGP to communicate and exchange customer routes dynamically, enhancing the scalability of routing and forwarding features of the underlying network infrastructure. Because MPLS operates on a BGP-free core network, BGP RRs are essential to support a large number of iBGP peering between PE devices. An RR reduces the iBGP peerings required for PE full mesh connectivity and IP/VPN/EVPN/mVPN route propagation over MPLS networks, where PE devices only peer with the RRs, and no direct peering between PE devices is required.

MPLS Label Structure

In traditional IP packet forwarding, each node independently analyzes the IP header to determine the next hop—a process known as per-hop routing. This involves an IP lookup in the routing table at each node along the path from source to destination. MPLS simplifies this by performing an IP lookup only at the LER. Subsequent nodes use label lookups, decoupling IP from the underlying transport in the core network.

An MPLS header is a 32-bit value inserted between the Layer 2 and Layer 3 headers of an IP packet by an ingress LER when the packet enters the MPLS network. The ingress LER adds a label to the packet to identify a specific LSP for packet forwarding across the network. Each LSR along the path looks up the label to determine the next LSR and swaps the label with a new one before forwarding the packet. This process continues until the packet reaches the egress LER. The path from the ingress LER, through the LSRs to the egress LER is known as the LSP.

To help you understand the MPLS header, Figure 1-2 provides a detailed overview, and the following list describes the fields in the header:

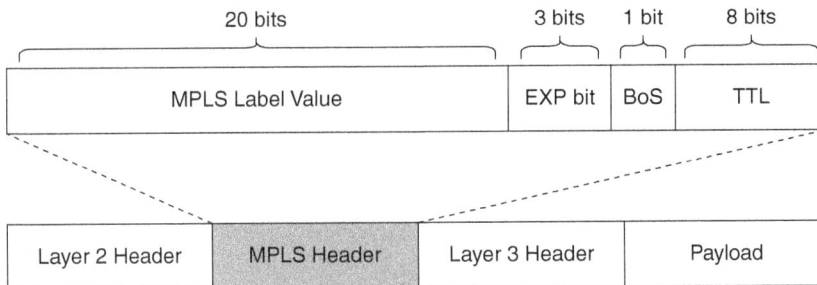

Figure 1-2 *MPLS Header*

- **MPLS Label Value:** This field consists of 20 bits. The label value range in this field starts from 0 and goes up to the maximum of 1,048,575, hence the limitation of ~1 million MPLS labels. The first 16 label values, from 0 to 15, are reserved for operational reasons and have a special meaning to an MPLS-enabled node, as specified in RFC 3032 and RFC 7274.

- **Experimental (EXP) bit:** This field consists of 3 bits. Initially, those bits were not used but were specified for later use as MPLS development advanced. Today, this field is used for QoS treatment on a packet.

- **Bottom of Stack (BoS):** This field consists of only 1 bit and two possible values: 0 or 1. If the value is 0, there is more than one label in the stack, and a node must continue processing the next label from the stack of labels. If the value is 1, it means the label is the last one (bottom) in the stack of labels, and the node must do an IP lookup or L2 Ethernet lookup afterward, but only if there is no additional label, such as a service label.

- **Time to Live (TTL):** This field provides the same function as a TTL field in an IP header: It helps avoid endless packet loops. Since intermediate MPLS nodes do not perform IP lookups, there is no way to check the TTL of an IP packet, so we need the TTL field in the MPLS header. For each hop a labeled packet travels, the TTL value decreases by one. The default TTL value is 255.

Packet forwarding using MPLS labels can be as simple as imposing a single label on top of an incoming packet or as complex as imposing a set of labels, where these set of labels are part of a label stack. A label stack (see RFC 3032) is a container that keeps MPLS labels in last-in, first-out (LIFO) order. In this case, a top label from the label stack, as shown in Figure 1-3, is processed first, and depending on the necessary MPLS label operation, the MPLS-enabled node processing the packet either forwards the labeled packet to an outgoing interface without any modification (top label swapped) or a more complex operation occurs, resulting in either a PUSH (adding an additional label) or POP (removing a label) operation.

As shown in Figure 1-3, the top label and any label below has a value of 0 in the BoS field, but the bottom label always has the value 1 and an instruction with the meaning that this is the last label in the stack. Once the last label from the stack is processed and popped, an IP lookup is commonly done as the last step to forward the packet to a next hop.

MPLS Label	EXP bit	BoS = 0	TTL	⇐ Top Label
MPLS Label	EXP bit	BoS = 0	TTL	...
MPLS Label	EXP bit	BoS = 1	TTL	⇐ Bottom Label

Figure 1-3 *MPLS Label Stack*

See the section "MPLS Label Operations," later in this chapter, for a detailed explanation of MPLS label operations.

We briefly mentioned the reserved label range (0–15), which has a special meaning for an MPLS-enabled node. As of this writing, only some of the reserved labels are officially assigned for any use:

- **IPv4 explicit null label (0):** The advantage of the explicit null label is that MPLS EXP bits are preserved throughout the MPLS network. When a PE node receives a labeled packet with an explicit null label, the label stack is stripped off, and IPv4 forwarding is performed. From a PHP (P) node perspective, it performs the swap operation, essentially replacing the top label with a null label, and the service label remains untouched. Figure 1-4 shows an example of the Explicit null label.

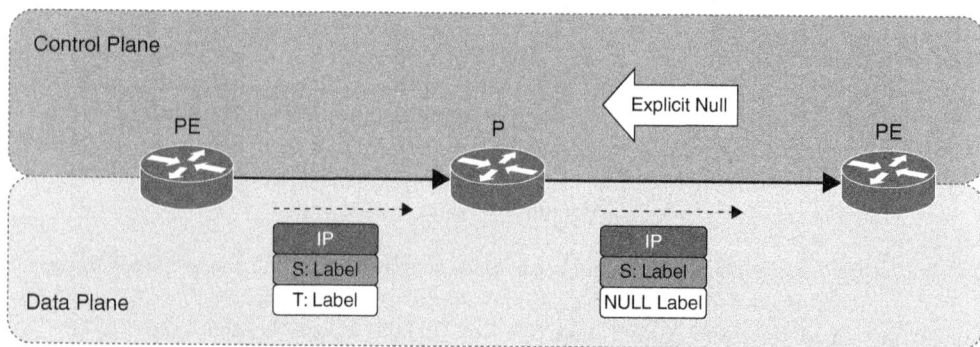

Figure 1-4 *IPv4 Explicit Null Label (0)*

- **Router alert label (1):** The label value 1 is assigned as the top label or anywhere in the label stack except as the bottom label. The router alert label does not hold any forwarding path information, and the primary purpose is to have the node examine the packet thoroughly before forwarding it to the next hop. A practical use case is an LSP ping, which intermediate nodes must process up to the destination. Once a node finishes the packet examination, the next label in the stack is checked for forwarding information. Before the labeled packet is put to the outgoing interface for forwarding to the next hop, the RA label (1) is added to the label stack as the top label.

- **IPv6 explicit null label (2):** The label value 2 is assigned to the last MPLS label in the stack, also known as the bottom label. It signals to the node that the label stack must be removed, and packet forwarding is now based on the IPv6 header. Much as with label value 0, the label stack is stripped off when the node receives a labeled packet with explicit null label value 2.

- **Implicit null label (3):** The label value 3 is assigned by an egress PE device to inform the directly connected P node to perform a POP operation whenever the P node forwards traffic to the egress PE device. This method is also called penultimate hop popping (PHP). Egress PE devices benefit from PHP because the incoming packet is unlabeled; the egress PE device performs only a simple IP lookup to forward the packet. Implicit null does not mean the incoming packet is always unlabeled (in the case of MPLS/VPN); it just means that the top label from the label stack is popped (removed). The advantage of implicit null is the performance of the PE router, which does not need to do a label lookup but only a single IP lookup. The disadvantage of implicit null is mainly related to QoS: If the transport label contains MPLS EXP bits for QoS, then this information is lost. Figure 1-5 shows an example of an MPLS VPN packet where the transport label is popped, and the service label remains until it reaches the egress PE router.

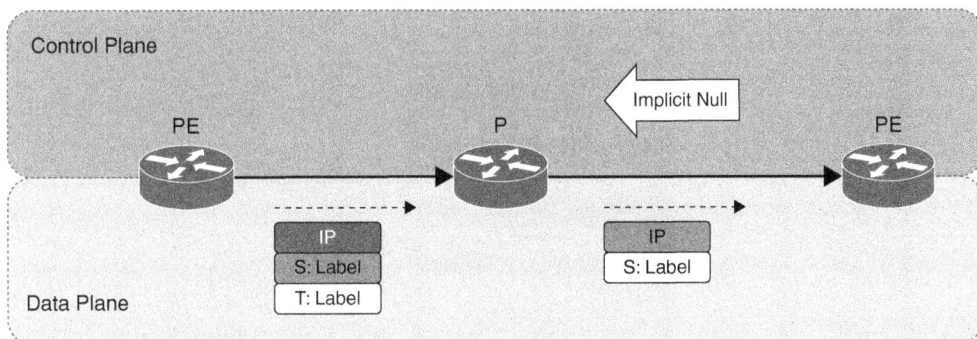

Figure 1-5   *Implicit NULL Label (3)*

Note   The MPLS reserved labels that are registered with IANA are listed at https://www.iana.org/assignments/mpls-label-values/mpls-label-values.txt.

Control Plane and Data Plane

To operate IP/MPLS networks, it is important to understand the difference between the control plane and the data plane (also known as the forwarding plane), especially in troubleshooting situations.

The control plane is crucial in establishing and managing a network, performing tasks such as topology discovery and assigning label values to be used by the network devices. The control plane of a network device is responsible for managing routing protocols, calculating optimal paths, maintaining routing tables, handling network topology updates, assigning MPLS labels, enforcing routing policies, and maintaining neighbor relationships. As shown in Figure 1-6, IGPs are part of the control plane, and network devices running the same IGP can distribute their IGP database (topology, nodes, links, and prefixes) to each other so that there is a common view of the network. Next, the network devices analyze the IGP database, pick all necessary prefixes from it, and populate the Routing Information Base (RIB) with destination addresses, the outgoing interfaces, and possibly the next-hop address. In the case of MPLS based on LDP, every routing entry in the RIB is assigned a label and stored in a separate database called the Label Information Base (LIB), which is also part of the control plane.

So you have seen that the network devices learn all necessary prefixes (IGP) and labels (LDP) and store them in their respective databases (RIB and LIB). Let us briefly look into the data plane. For a network device to forward IP or labeled packets, the forwarding information is written to the hardware itself. Any fixed router or line card of a modular router contains a Forwarding Information Base (FIB) table stored locally, which provides destination IP prefixes, next hops, and outgoing interfaces. Finally, label-based forwarding is done by looking up the forwarding information in the Label Forwarding Information Base (LFIB). The LFIB provides the incoming and outgoing label information with the respective outgoing interfaces to forward any labeled traffic. LDP feeds the LFIB with all the necessary label information.

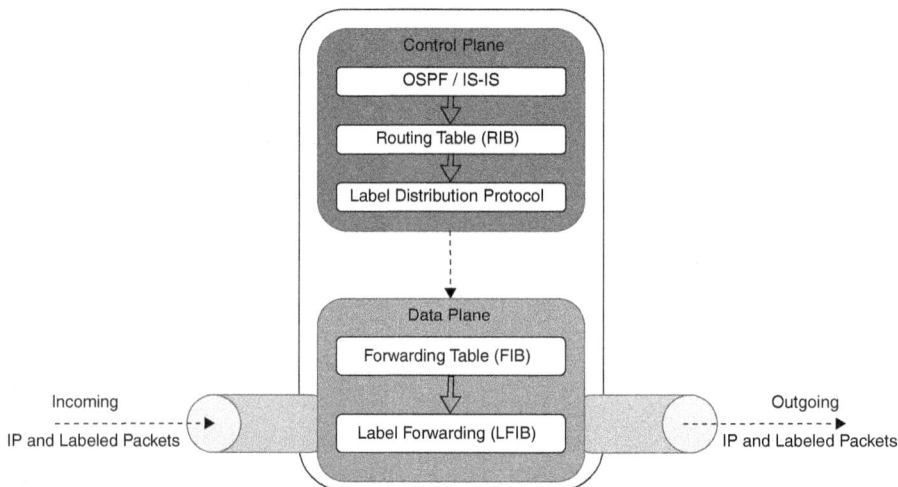

Figure 1-6 *Control Plane and Data Plane*

Label Distribution Protocol (LDP)

LDP enables PE and P nodes to automatically generate, distribute to peer devices, and request label-to-prefix binding information from peer devices in a network, thus facilitating the forwarding of data packets across the network, which is the fundamental aspect of MPLS networks. Using LDP, a node can discover peers and establish LDP sessions with them to exchange label binding information. LDP operates on a peer-to-peer basis, with each node in the network communicating with its neighbors to exchange label information. This enables PE and P nodes to distribute their local label bindings and establish an end-to-end label-switched path (LSP) throughout the MPLS network.

LDP uses two types of label distribution methods:

- **Downstream-on-demand:** This method is used when a node requires a label for a specific prefix. In this scenario, the requesting node sends a label request message to its neighbor, and the neighbor responds with a label mapping message.

- **Unsolicited downstream:** This method is used when a node has label information to share with its neighbors. In this scenario, the node sends a label mapping message to its neighbors, which they can then use to update their forwarding tables.

MPLS nodes use LDP to distribute labels along normally routed paths to support MPLS forwarding. The nodes create a label forwarding table from this information, which maps each incoming data packet to its corresponding label. MPLS forwarding differs from IP forwarding, where a device examines the destination address in the IP header and performs a route lookup. In MPLS forwarding, the nodes look at the incoming label, consult the LFIB, and forward the packet to the next hop. In MPLS networks, a group of packets assigned to a specific LSP are transported by being associated with a label mapping or binding that contains a label. This label serves as an identifier for the group of packets, which are collectively referred to as a forwarding equivalence class (FEC).

LDP was standardized by the Internet Engineering Task Force (IETF) in RFC 5036. As shown in Figure 1-7, neighbor discovery in LDP uses UDP port 646, and session establishment with the discovered neighbor uses TCP port 646. Nodes initiate the discovery phase by transmitting, at regular intervals, hello packets on UDP port 646 to the multicast address 224.0.0.2; they listen to this port for potential hello messages from other LDP nodes. This process allows all directly connected nodes to learn about each other and establish hello adjacencies. If two LDP speakers agree on the shared parameters, they establish neighbor adjacency by using TCP. An LDP ID, a unique identifier assigned to each node in the network, is typically assigned based on the node's IP address and included in all label distribution messages that the node exchanges. LDP neighbors initiate the exchange of label bindings using the already established TCP connection once the LDP adjacency is up and running—assuming that label allocation has already been completed independently by each node.

LDP can discover peers that are not directly connected if you provide a node with the IP address of one or more peers. The node sends targeted hello messages to UDP port 646 on each remote peer. If the targeted peer responds with a targeted hello message to the initiator, an LDP targeted adjacency is created, and session establishment can proceed. Targeted LDP sessions are used in specific scenarios such as for traffic protection, traffic engineering, and L2VPN point-to-point circuits, also known as pseudowires.

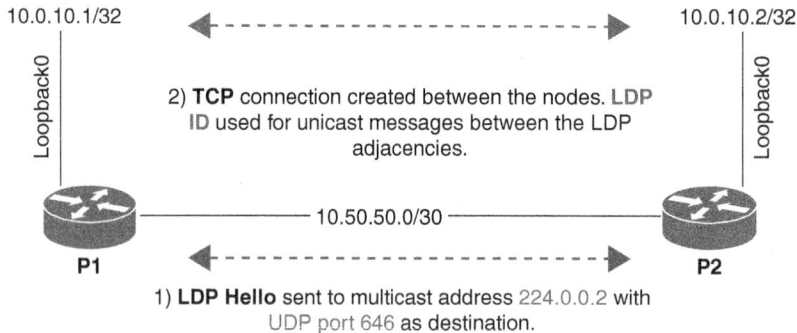

10.0.10.1/32   10.0.10.2/32

Loopback0

2) **TCP** connection created between the nodes. **LDP ID** used for unicast messages between the LDP adjacencies.

Loopback0

P1 —————————— 10.50.50.0/30 ——————————

P1   P2

1) **LDP Hello** sent to multicast address 224.0.0.2 with UDP port 646 as destination.

Figure 1-7   *LDP Adjacency*

In summary, LDP plays a critical role in legacy MPLS networks, as it automatically distributes labels to each node in the network, enabling the identification and routing of data packets. Nodes communicate with their neighbors in a peer-to-peer fashion to exchange label information through LDP. The label distribution process involves exchanging label mapping information, which is used to create a label forwarding table at each node. A node receives an incoming packet and looks up the corresponding label in its forwarding table before forwarding the packet to the next node in the chain.

Label Allocation Mechanism

An MPLS-enabled node must allocate labels to IP prefixes that are present in the routing table (RIB). When a node receives an incoming packet, it needs to determine how to forward it based on the information in the packet's label. The LDP label allocation process involves assigning a unique label to each prefix on a device level and distributing that label to all LSRs in the network. This process—such as label 25 assigned to prefix 10.0.10.1/32—is known as label mapping. If an incoming packet is not labeled, the intermediate LSR (P router) might drop the packet in case of MPLS/VPN traffic. The process of label mapping has local significance, meaning that any MPLS-enabled node allocates labels to IP prefixes independently of the other MPLS nodes.

The MPLS domain requires end-to-end label switching for any traffic entering until it reaches the egress PE device. The node generates a label and allocates it to an IP prefix, and it stores this information locally in the LIB. The LFIB, which is part of the data plane for MPLS traffic, also stores the same information. The responsibility for generating a label does not lie with an IGP. Instead, LDP, Resource Reservation Protocol (RSVP), and BGP are mechanisms that generate and distribute labels to other neighbors internally to the MPLS domain or external domains.

In summary, the label allocation process involves assigning a label for each prefix in the network domain and distributing these labels to all network nodes.

Label allocation and distribution with LDP was the standard for many years. Figure 1-8 provides a visual representation of this process.

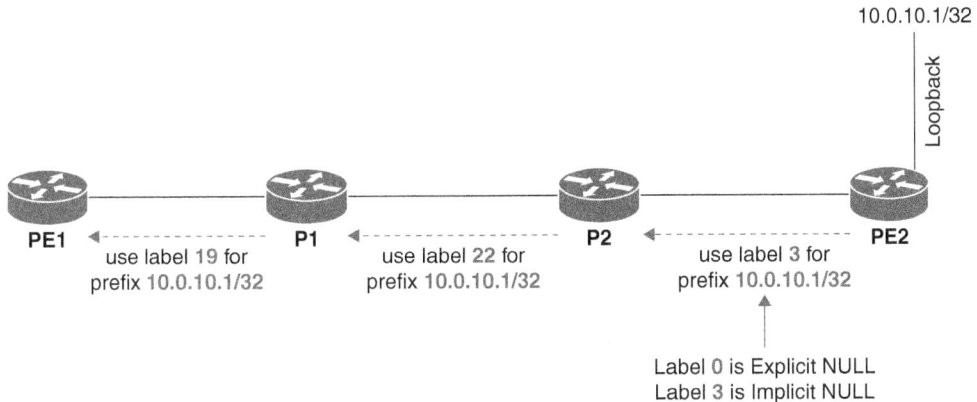

Figure 1-8 *Label Allocation*

This is the label allocation process that is occurring in Figure 1-8:

Step 1.   PE2 has a loopback interface configured with IP address 10.0.10.1/32. PE2 assigns a local label 3 (implicit null) to IP prefix 10.0.10.1/32. This is called a label mapping, and it is stored in the LIB (control plane). The same information is also stored in the LFIB (data plane).

Step 2.   PE2 uses LDP to propagate the label mapping (10.0.10.1 to 3) to all directly connected peers—in this case, to P2.

Step 3.   P2 receives the label mapping from step 2 and stores it in the LIB and LFIB. From P2's point of view, label 3 will be used as the outgoing label for 10.0.10.1

Step 4.   P2 assigns its own label for 10.0.10.1—in this case, label 22—to advertise it further to P1.

Step 5.   P1 receives label 22 for prefix 10.0.10.1, stores it in the LIB and LFIB as an outgoing label, and assigns an incoming label for prefix 10.0.10.1—in this case, label 19—and propagates it to PE1.

Step 6.   PE1 receives label 19 from P1 and stores it as an outgoing label in the LIB and LFIB.

To summarize, label allocation is performed when every node in the MPLS domain assigns a label to each prefix in the routing table independently of other nodes, making it locally significant. The node then dynamically propagates label mapping to other directly connected peers using LDP.

MPLS Label Operations

To process MPLS-encapsulated packets arriving on an ingress interface, a node needs to follow one of three predefined label operations (see Figure 1-9):

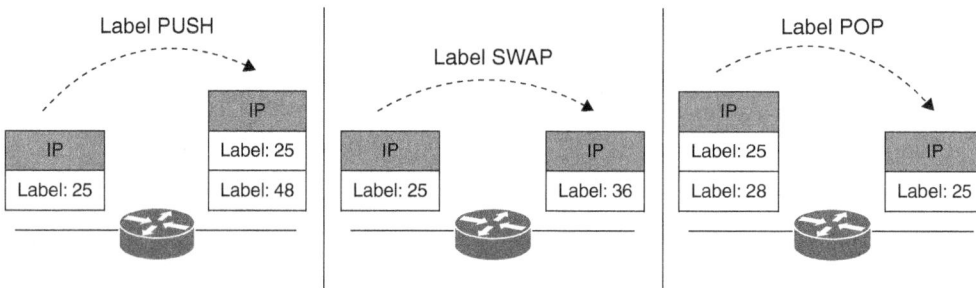

Figure 1-9   *MPLS Label Operations*

- **PUSH:** For any incoming packet, a label is added on top of the packet. If the incoming packet already has a label, an additional label is added on top of that label, thus creating a label stack. Usually, a PE node performs the PUSH operation. However, there are instances in which a P node also performs a PUSH operation during a failure event, when the fast reroute mechanism is activated.

- **SWAP:** For any incoming labeled packet, the node inspects the incoming label and swaps it with the outgoing label. SWAP operations are usually performed by P nodes.

- **POP:** For any incoming labeled packet, the node inspects the incoming label, pops (removes) the top label from the label stack, and forwards the packet. In cases where the top label is the last label, the node removes the label stack and forwards the packet based on a standard IP lookup—except when the label allocation mode on a PE node is set to per-prefix or per-CE, in which case no IP lookup is needed. The POP operation is usually performed by both PE and P nodes.

Apart from the label operations mentioned previously, in certain circumstance, an MPLS-enabled node can also push two or more labels on top of the label stack. This is especially important when using MPLS applications such as MPLS/VPN, traffic engineering, and FRR. In the case of MPLS/VPN, a node imposes one BGP label for the VPN prefix, also called a service label, and another label (LDP) for the transport prefix, also called transport label. In case of traffic engineering, where a strict end-to-end path is desired, the ingress PE node must push all the necessary labels in the label stack. In the case of FRR, if a node or a link in the path fails, the node must react immediately by rerouting the traffic through a backup path, and this is achieved by manipulating the original label stack of the labeled packet, essentially removing and adding more than one label on top of the packet.

Traffic Forwarding Using Labels

Traditional Layer 3 forwarding mechanisms require every router along the packet's path to extract all the necessary information from the Layer 3 header in order to forward the packet. The longest prefix match in the routing table is then performed based on the extracted data to determine the packet's next hop.

Usually, only the destination address field in the header is important. However, in some instances, other header fields are crucial. Therefore, each router must independently analyze the header as the packet passes through.

In MPLS label forwarding, the incoming packet's Layer 3 header analysis is performed once, at the ingress PE node. The Layer 3 header is transformed into an unstructured, fixed-length value called a *label*. Multiple headers can be mapped to the same label if they lead to the same selection of the next hop. Essentially, a label is assigned to each forwarding equivalence class (FEC) that includes a group of packets that are indistinguishable by the forwarding function.

The initial label choice does not need to be based entirely on the contents of the Layer 3 packet header. For instance, routing policies can influence forwarding decisions at subsequent hops. After a label is assigned, a short label header is added to the front of the Layer 3 packet, which is carried along with the packet across the network. At subsequent hops through each MPLS router in the network, labels are swapped, and forwarding decisions are made using the MPLS forwarding table lookup for the label carried in the packet header.

There is no need to reevaluate the packet header as it moves across the network. Because the label is of a fixed length and unstructured, the MPLS forwarding table lookup process is simple and fast.

Figure 1-10 illustrates label-based forwarding.

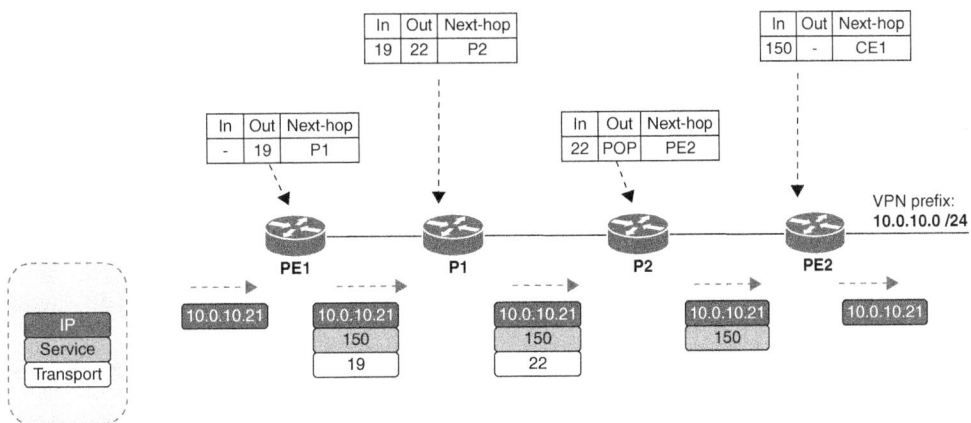

Figure 1-10   *Label-Based Forwarding*

A PE router normally has at least one CE node directly connected. The CE router advertises its own IP prefixes to the PE router dynamically, using a protocol such as BGP
or OSPF. Open Shortest Path First (OSPF) is a popular IGP used in large enterprise
networks. In contrast, BGP is more prevalent in large service provider networks. When
L3VPN is employed to serve customers, any protocol can be used as a VRF-aware
instance between the PE and CE nodes.

PE1 receives an IP packet from a VPN customer and performs an IP lookup based on
the destination IP address in the IP header of the incoming packet. Because this is a
VPN-based service, PE1 creates a label stack and imposes two labels on the label stack:
The bottom one is a BGP label 150, also called a service label, and the top label is the
transport label created by LDP. No label operation is performed on the bottom label
until it reaches the egress PE node—in this case PE2. The forwarding mechanism in the
MPLS transport is performed using the top label. After the label stack is imposed on the
IP packet, via a PUSH operation, PE1 forwards the data traffic to the next hop, which
is P1. At the ingress port of P1, the data traffic arrives with the top label 19. P1 checks
its own LFIB and recognizes the need to perform the SWAP operation, so it replaces
the label 19 with label 22 and forwards the labeled packet to P2 as the next hop via the
outgoing interface. P2 performs the POP operation to the incoming label 22 due to the
implicit null and forwards it via the outgoing interface to the next hop, PE2. PE2 checks
the incoming service label 150 and recognizes that this label has to be removed, so a POP
operation is performed, and the IP packet is routed normally to the CE node via a non-
labeled outgoing interface.

MPLS VPN Services Overview

To define a Multiprotocol Label Switching virtual private network (MPLS VPN), it is necessary first to understand the general concept of a VPN. A VPN is a network that utilizes
other public or private networks to provide private network services while operating on
an IP-based infrastructure. It comprises a group of sites that can privately communicate
with one another. VPN sites use a common routing table and operate as a network where
customers can connect to multiple sites using a shared MPLS provider core infrastructure. A site might have one or more CE nodes attached to one or more PE nodes.

MPLS VPNs operate at Layer 3 and adopt a peer model, allowing the service provider
and customer to exchange routing information at this layer. This peer model facilitates
data transmission between customer sites through the service provider's network without
customer intervention. Consequently, when a new site integrates into the MPLS VPN, the
PE to which the new site is connected is the only one that needs an update with the new
configuration for that particular VPN customer.

For completeness, Figure 1-11 shows the end-to-end MPLS VPN architecture from a
high-level point of view.

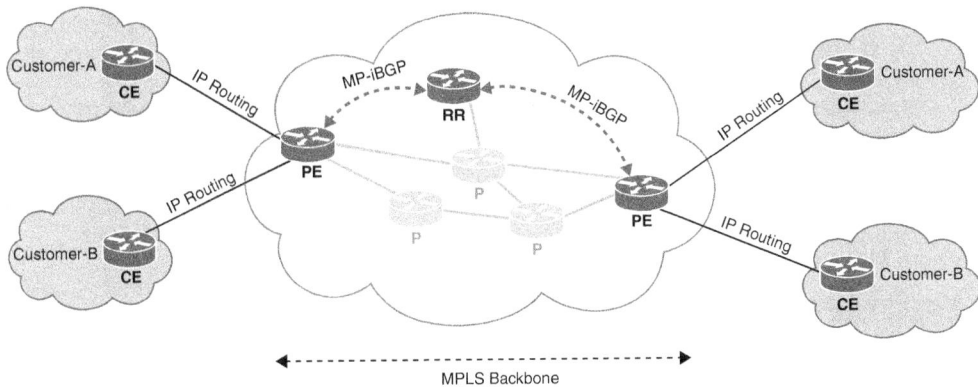

Figure 1-11 *MPLS VPN Architecture*

VRF is a technique used in MPLS VPNs to separate the routing tables of different customers at the same PE device. VRF maintains a separate routing table for each VPN customer, allowing for secure and efficient routing between sites.

An MPLS VPN consists of the following components:

- **VRF instances:** Each VRF instance represents a different VPN network. A VRF instance contains its own routing table, which is separate from the global routing table (GRT) of the PE router. This separation allows for secure routing between different VPNs.

- **MP-BGP:** This protocol is used for the distribution of VPN routes between the PE routers. Each PE router maintains a BGP session with other PE routers or a route reflector in the network. When a new VPN route is learned, it is advertised to other PE routers using BGP. BGP also allows for the exchange of VPN-related information, such as the route distinguisher (RD).

- **VPNv4/VPNv6 Address Family:** The VPNv4/VPNv6 address family is used for the distribution of VPN routes between the PE routers. Each VPN route contains an RD and a VPNv4/VPNv6 prefix. The VPNv4/VPNv6 prefix is a combination of the customer's IP prefix and the RD. The PE routers use the RD to distinguish between routes belonging to different VPNs. This essentially allows the same customer private IP addresses to exist in different VRF instances. In this case, IP address overlap does not cause an issue due to the different RD values appended.

- **Route distinguisher (RD):** The RD is a 64-bit value that is used to uniquely identify the VPN or customer prefix. An RD is appended to each IP Prefix which results in a 96-bit VPN route and allows the PE router to distinguish between routes that belong to different VPNs.

- **Route target (RT):** The RT is a 64-bit BGP extended community that is used to control the distribution of VPN routes within the MPLS VPN. The RT is assigned to each VPN route by the PE router at the ingress point of the VPN. The RT is used by the other PE routers to determine which VRF table to insert the VPN route into.

In summary, VRF is a key component of MPLS VPNs that enables separate and independent routing between different VPNs. The use of RDs and VPN-IPv4 addresses allows for the unique identification of VPN routes, and BGP is used to distribute VPN routes between PE routers. The RT is used to control the distribution of VPN routes within the MPLS VPN, ensuring that each VPN route is inserted into the correct VRF table.

MPLS Traffic Protection

MPLS FRR provides resiliency in the event of link or node failure by creating backup paths for each primary path, as shown in Figure 1-12. A primary path is the normal path that packets take across the network, and a detour backup path is available in case of failure on the primary path.

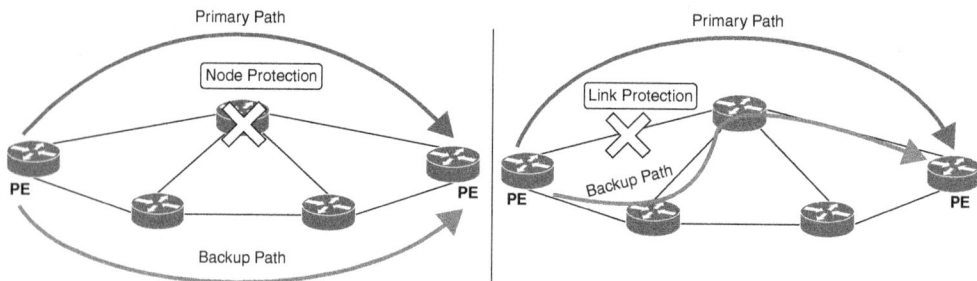

Figure 1-12   *MPLS Node and Link Protection*

Each prefix in the network has a backup path calculated by every router in the network. Let's briefly look at how routers calculate their backup paths:

Step 1.   To calculate a backup path, a router must determine the next-best available path to reach the destination prefix in the case of a primary path failure. This is done using the loop-free alternate (LFA) traffic protection technique. LFA finds a backup path that does not result in a forwarding loop and that is guaranteed to be loop free. However, it does not protect all possible topologies.

Step 2.   After calculating the backup path, the router generates a new label stack that represents the backup path and installs it into the router's forwarding table. The label stack has one or more labels, with the first label pointing to the next hop router on the backup path.

Step 3.   When a failure occurs on the primary path, the router swaps the primary path's label stack with the backup path's label stack. This action causes the packets to be forwarded along the backup path instead of the primary path. The label stack of the backup path includes the necessary node labels (PQ nodes) along the path to the destination prefix. When the packet reaches the next hop router on the backup path, the router pops the top label and forwards the packet to the following next hop router based on the label stack information.

Step 4.   The router switches back to the primary path by swapping the label stack of the backup path with the primary path's label stack after the primary path is restored. This process enables the packets to be forwarded along the primary path again.

In the realm of networking, FRR presents a temporary solution to minimize packet loss. The computation of backup path, however, may not guarantee sufficient bandwidth, leading to potential congestion on the alternate routes. It is crucial to note that the ingress router possesses complete knowledge of LSP policy constraints, making it the only entity capable of generating appropriate long-term alternate paths.

Apart from MPLS LFA (IGP and LDP), backup paths can also be created through RSVP sessions and, as with all RSVP sessions, require additional state and network overhead. Consequently, a node creates at most one backup path for every LSP that has FRR capability. Formulating multiple backup paths for each LSP leads to unnecessary overhead, without considerable additional benefits. Also, an important aspect of FRR technology is that it is considered a temporary solution to an intermittent network problem. A network operator should not rely permanently on a backup path. When a link or node fails, traffic from the primary path takes a detour toward a backup path, and it might happen that now the backup path is congested due to heavy traffic. This is the main reason traffic should always be routed back to the primary path after the primary path has recovered and links/nodes are stable enough to carry the original traffic.

Challenges and Shortcomings of MPLS

Although modern networks have widely adopted MPLS, which provides benefits such as traffic engineering, and virtual private networks (VPNs), it is important to be aware of some challenges and shortcomings. The following challenges are the most important:

- MPLS label space limitation

- LSP and summarization

- Inter-AS limitations

- RSVP-based traffic engineering

- LDP–IGP synchronization

- Load balancing and hashing

To give you a comprehensive understanding of these challenges, the following sections provide details.

MPLS Label Space Limitation

To understand the MPLS label space limitation, it is essential to understand how MPLS works.

Each packet entering the network is assigned a 20-bit number called an MPLS label, and this assignment process creates LSPs through the network. The ingress router assigns the labels that the network uses to forward the packets through the network. Once a packet reaches a core (P) router, the core router uses the label to determine the next hop for the packet. The core router then swaps the incoming label with the outgoing label and forwards the packet to the next hop.

The MPLS label space limitation is a challenge that arises because there is a finite number of labels that can be used in an MPLS network. The label space is limited to 2^{20} (1,048,576) labels, which may seem like a large number, but it can be easily exhausted in large networks—and this can cause several problems. One of the most significant problems is that it limits the scalability of the network when there may be requirements for additional nodes, links, or VPN prefixes. In large networks, the number of labels required can quickly exceed the available label space. When this happens, no new transport or service label can be generated, the network may become unstable, and packets may be dropped, leading to poor network performance.

Another problem caused by the label space limitation is that it can limit the number of VPN routes (L2VPN/L3VPN services) that can be supported in the network. VPNs can be created in MPLS networks in two ways: by assigning different labels to different VPNs (per-VRF label allocation mode) or by assigning different labels per prefix per VPN (per-prefix label allocation mode). When the label space is exhausted, it may not be possible to create new VPNs or assign labels to new customer prefixes, limiting the network's ability to support new customers or expand its services.

When the ASBR label allocation is on a per-prefix basis, even when the remote PE device is advertising a label per VRF instance (per-VRF label allocation), the egress ASBR allocates a label for each received prefix, resulting in faster label space depletion in the ASBR.

Similarly, at this writing, the global Internet routing table covers roughly 970,000 IPv4 and 200,000 IPv6 prefixes. Offering IPv4 Internet service as part of a VPN would be problematic using per-prefix label allocation since it would exhaust more than 90% of the available label space on the egress PEs providing this service.

Considering the limitations of MPLS label space, there is no real solution to this issue. However, a couple optimizations can be considered in managing label allocation in large-scale networks:

- Allocating labels on a per-VRF basis instead of per prefix can significantly decrease the number of required service labels.

- With label allocation for host only (/32) routes, LDP assigns labels only for loopback interfaces instead of for physical links.

- Assessing alternative inter-AS or intra-AS connectivity models can help you reduce label allocation.

LSP and Summarization

In an MPLS network, a network operator creates an LSP to define the path a packet should follow through the network. An LSP is a preconfigured path that connects a source node to a destination node, and each device along the path forwards the packet to the next device. The parameters used for creating LSPs include source and destination IP addresses.

MPLS LSPs face a challenge when summarized routes are advertised instead of more specific routes, such as /32 host routes. Sometimes network operators may want to advertise summarized routes to the rest of the network, and although this scenario may make sense in some instances from a network design perspective, it is not recommended in an MPLS environment. PE and P routers must know each other's /32 loopback addresses and potentially their physical interfaces to have a complete view of the underlay network. This allows each service node (PE node) to create an LSP with remote service node PEs and ensures appropriate end-to-end label forwarding.

Inter-AS Limitations

Inter-AS routing refers to the exchange of routing information and traffic between different ASs that are managed by same or different organizations or service providers. In an MPLS network, communication between ASs is facilitated by BGP. BGP as a standard protocol is used to exchange routing information between different ASs, while MPLS VPNs provide a way to extend a private network across multiple ASs using end-to-end LSPs.

However, MPLS IPv4 and IPv6 networks face several limitations when it comes to inter-domain routing, which can impact the performance and scalability of the network. The following sections examine some of these challenges and shortcomings.

Lack of End-to-end QoS Control

One of the main limitations of MPLS networks in inter-AS routing is the lack of end-to-end QoS control. MPLS networks provide QoS capabilities through DiffServ (Differentiated Services), which can be used to prioritize traffic and allocate network resources based on various criteria, such as traffic type, application, and user. However, these QoS mechanisms are limited to the boundaries of the MPLS network and do not extend to other ASs.

In inter-AS scenarios, traffic may traverse multiple ASs, each with its own QoS policies and capabilities. This can result in inconsistent QoS behavior across the network and affect the performance of delay-sensitive applications such as voice and video. To address this limitation, network operators must coordinate with other ASs to ensure that QoS policies are aligned and consistent across the entire traffic path.

Configuration and Operational Complexity of MPLS/VPN and BGP

A challenge in inter-AS routing using MPLS networks is the complexity of configuring BGP/MPLS VPNs. BGP/MPLS VPNs provide a way to extend a private network across multiple ASs using MPLS tunnels. However, configuring MPLS VPNs can be a complex and time-consuming process, particularly in large-scale networks with multiple ASs.

BGP/MPLS VPNs require careful planning and configuration to ensure that the routing information is exchanged correctly between ASs and that the MPLS tunnels are established and maintained properly. Moreover, changes in the network topology or routing policies may impact the BGP/MPLS VPN configuration, requiring network operators to constantly monitor and adjust the configuration. During network migrations or mergers, there is usually a high likelihood that this issue will rise, and a proper transport and services layer planning and design are mandatory.

Technical implementation differences might occur, which may result in different outcome. To address operational complexity, network operators can use automated network management and orchestration tools that can simplify network design, deployment, and management. Service providers can use tools such as network controllers, intent-based networking systems, and software-defined networking (SDN) platforms to automate network operations and reduce the risk of errors.

RSVP-Based Traffic Engineering

Resource Reservation Protocol Traffic Engineering (RSVP-TE) is a protocol used in MPLS networks for traffic engineering. Its primary function is to establish LSPs through the network, which are used to forward traffic from one point to another. RSVP-TE is an extension of RSVP.

One of the key features of RSVP-TE is its ability to signal traffic engineering tunnels. Traffic engineering tunnels are used to optimize network performance and avoid congested links. RSVP-TE uses tunnel signaling to create these traffic engineering tunnels.

When a traffic engineering tunnel is requested, RSVP-TE initiates a signaling process that involves the exchange of messages between the nodes in the network along the path of the tunnel. The nodes along the path reserve the necessary resources for the tunnel, and the tunnel is established. Once the tunnel is established, traffic is directed along the path of the tunnel.

RSVP-TE uses several different messages for signaling LSPs and traffic engineering tunnels. These messages include the Path message, which is used to advertise the path of the LSP or tunnel, and the Reservation message, which is used to reserve the necessary resources for the LSP or tunnel. RSVP-TE also uses other messages for error handling and other functions.

In addition to its signaling functions, RSVP-TE also provides support for traffic engineering metrics such as link utilization. This allows network operators to monitor and optimize network performance based on various traffic engineering criteria.

When a traffic engineering tunnel is established using RSVP-TE, it involves the signaling of an LSP through the underlay network. This LSP is used as the traffic engineering tunnel, and traffic is forwarded along this LSP according to the traffic engineering requirements.

The signaling of an RSVP-TE tunnel consists of:

- **RSVP-TE Path message:** The first step in tunnel signaling is the sending of an RSVP-TE Path message from the headend node of the tunnel to the tailend node. The Path message carries information about the source and destination of the tunnel, along with any traffic engineering requirements, such as bandwidth, latency.

- **Path message processing:** When the Path message reaches a node in the network, it is processed and forwarded to the next node along the path of the tunnel. During this processing, the node checks if it has enough resources to accommodate the tunnel, and if it does, it reserves the necessary resources for the tunnel. If there are insufficient resources, the node may send an RSVP-TE ResvErr message back to the headend node, indicating that the tunnel cannot be established.

- **RSVP-TE Resv message:** Once the necessary resources have been reserved, the tailend node sends an RSVP-TE Resv message back to the headend node, indicating that the tunnel has been established. The Resv message includes information about the path of the tunnel, along with any labels that have been assigned to the LSP.

- **Resv message processing:** When the Resv message reaches a node in the network, it is processed and forwarded to the previous node along the path of the tunnel. During this processing, the node installs any labels that have been assigned to the LSP and establishes an FEC for the LSP.

- **Tunnel forwarding:** Once the LSP has been established and labeled, traffic can be forwarded along the path of the tunnel using label swapping and forwarding. Each node along the path of the tunnel forwards traffic based on the labels assigned to the LSP, ensuring that traffic is directed along the path of the tunnel according to the traffic engineering requirements.

Throughout this process, each node in the network is responsible for signaling the next node in the path of the tunnel. This hop-by-hop signaling ensures that each node has the necessary resources reserved for the tunnel and that labels are correctly assigned to the LSP at each hop.

While RSVP-TE has been used in the past for traffic engineering, it has several limitations and drawbacks, which have led to its reduced popularity in modern networks. These are some of the limitations of RSVP-TE:

■ **Scalability:** RSVP-TE requires maintenance of LSP state information along the path, which can lead to scalability issues in large networks with a large number of LSPs.

■ **Complexity:** The RSVP-TE protocol is complex, which makes it difficult to deploy and maintain in large networks.

■ **Resource consumption:** The RSVP-TE protocol can consume significant network resources due to the need to maintain LSP state information and the requirement for end-to-end signaling.

Due to these limitations, RSVP-TE is not always the best choice for implementing traffic engineering in modern networks.

LDP–IGP Synchronization

MPLS LDP–IGP synchronization is a critical mechanism for ensuring reliable packet forwarding in an MPLS network. Before any MPLS traffic is forwarded, IGP and LDP must be in sync to avoid packet loss. Packet loss can occur if a node begins forwarding traffic using a new IGP adjacency before the LDP label exchange completes between the peers on that link. Similarly, if an LDP session closes, the device may continue to forward traffic using the link associated with the LDP peer, which can lead to packet loss.

To prevent these issues, MPLS LDP–IGP synchronization ensures that the LDP is fully established before the IGP path is used for traffic forwarding. This is accomplished by enabling LDP–IGP synchronization on each interface associated with an IGP OSPF or IS-IS process. Network operators can then prevent traffic blackholing and ensure reliable packet forwarding across their MPLS network.

When LDP–IGP synchronization is enabled on an interface, LDP checks whether any peer connected to the interface is reachable by looking up the peer's transport address in the routing table. If there's a routing entry (including longest match or default routing entry) for the peer, LDP assumes that LDP–IGP synchronization is required for the interface and notifies the IGP to wait for LDP convergence. However, LDP–IGP synchronization with peers requires that the routing table be accurate for the peer's transport address. If the routing table shows a summary route, a default route, or a statically configured route for the peer, it may not be the correct route for the peer. Thus, it's essential to verify that the route in the routing table can reach the peer's transport address to prevent traffic blackholing due to a missing label for that prefix.

Inaccurate routes in the routing table can cause issues with LDP session establishment, which causes the IGP to wait for LDP convergence unnecessarily for the sync hold-down time. This can lead to delays in forwarding traffic and potential packet loss.

A permanent solution to LDP–IGP synchronization issue is segment routing (SR) technology. With SR, when an IGP protocol advertises its own link-state database to other adjacent nodes, it also advertises SR-based labels (SIDs) at the same time. Thus, you end up with no delay in label distribution or in traffic forwarding due to IGP or LDP process initialization.

Load Balancing and Hashing

Many service providers see flat or even slightly decreasing revenues. Reducing costs while efficiently operating network devices and transmission links is crucial. Network capacity and redundancy are pillars of core transport networks which often rely on the following fundamental building blocks:

- Equal-cost multipath (ECMP)

- Link aggregation groups (LAGs) or link bundles

ECMP is a routing strategy in which a route is reachable via multiple best paths. As the name implies, those routes have to be equal to qualify, which in the scope of IGP means that the cumulative cost or metric along the path is the same. ECMP is common in highly symmetrical networks such as backbones where this kind of behavior is usually desired.

Aggregating several links into a single virtual interface (LAG or bundle) is another common strategy in backbone networks to facilitate smooth bandwidth extension. The virtual interface is treated as a large pipe, where each physical bundle member is considered equal, assuming that the transmission speed is the same. Some service providers refrain from using bundles because the members are not equal with respect to the distance in the underlying optical transport network. In order to be able to distinguish the interfaces, it may be preferrable to have several ECMP links instead of a single large pipe.

ECMP and LAG are often used in parallel to simplify capacity planning, flatten traffic bursts, and improve network availability in the event of node or link failures. ECMP load balancing and LAG hashing work identically on most routing platforms. The idea is that packets are evenly distributed across multiple paths or links. This is done by calculating an n-tuple hash, where several of the following fields are usually taken into account:

- Router ID

- Source and Destination MAC Address (L2)

- Source and Destination IP Address (L3)

- Source and Destination Port (L4)

- MPLS Label (or Flow Label, in the case of IPv6)

The exact fields and number of fields used for hashing depend on the traffic type and the underlying hardware architecture. It is important that packets belonging to the same flow are hashed along the same path. If they're not, per-packet load balancing may be required, which can lead to issues such as buffering and retransmissions on endpoints due to out-of-order packets or jitter or latency caused by different distances between available paths in the optical transport network.

Figure 1-13 shows some sample packets of different L2VPN and L3VPN services with two transport labels and a service label. It should become evident that extracting the proper Layer 2, Layer 3, or Layer 4 fields for MPLS services is nontrivial. On top of this, the presence of MPLS labels may lead to poor hashing diversity or even incorrect hashing parameters.

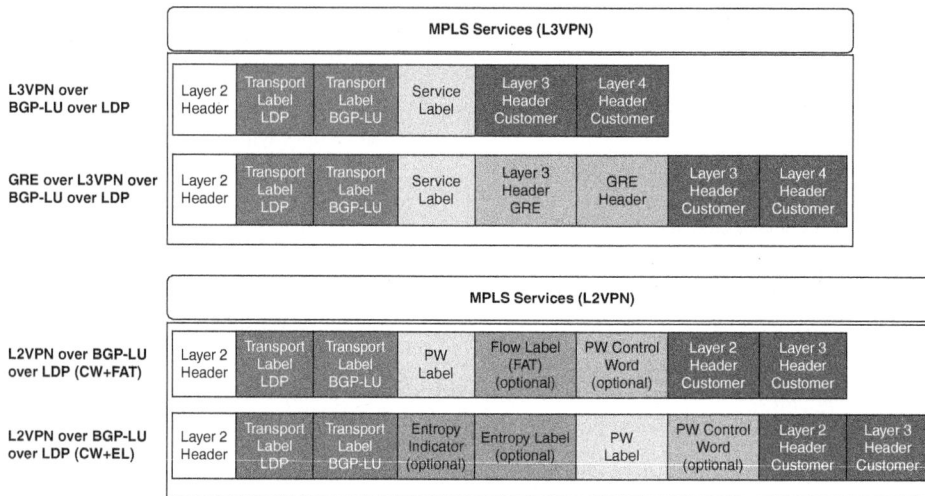

Figure 1-13   *Label Stack Example of MPLS Services*

There following RFCs describe improvements to the hashing of L2VPN/L3VPN MPLS services:

- RFC 6790: The Use of Entropy Labels in MPLS Forwarding

- RFC 4385: Pseudowire Emulation Edge-to-Edge (PWE3) Control Word for Use over an MPLS PSN

- RFC 6391: Flow-Aware Transport of Pseudowires over an MPLS Packet Switched Network

By default and depending on the platform capability, standard L3VPN provides good hashing results, except with services where the vast majority of fields are the same and the customer-specific information is hidden too deeply in the packet. GRE over L3VPN over BGP-LU over LDP is such a problematic service, where an overlay using GRE is spanned between two CE nodes over an L3VPN. With a multitude of customer services being transported through a single GRE tunnel, it would require a deeper packet inspection to be able to extract all customer-specific information. Lacking this inspection would result in poor hashing as there would be a single hash for all customers.

RFC 6790 defines the concept of an Entropy label, which is applicable to both L2VPN and L3VPN services and eliminates the need for deep inspection on transit routers. Instead, the ingress PE device extracts the relevant field of the service before the MPLS encapsulation takes place; then the device computes the hash and pushes the result as an additional label onto the stack. Transit routers no longer need to guess the underlying packet structure and can instead effectively load balance traffic by relying on the packet's MPLS label stack. For this to work, all devices in the path must support the Entropy label.

The inspection of L2VPN services is more challenging than the inspection of L3VPN services. As presented in the beginning of this chapter, the MPLS header does not specify the payload that follows after popping the Bottom of Stack (BoS) label. Instead, the router has to make an educated guess. In order not to sacrifice too much performance or too many network processor cycles, it is common to inspect the first nibble that follows the BoS label.

Example 1-1 shows an extract of an IPv4 L3VPN packet capture.

Example 1-1 *MPLS Packet Capture Extract (IPv4)*

```
Ethernet II, Src: RealtekU_12:7a:d0 (52:54:00:12:7a:d0), Dst: RealtekU_10:63:17
  (52:54:00:10:63:17)
MultiProtocol Label Switching Header, Label: 24012, Exp: 0, S: 0, TTL: 254
MultiProtocol Label Switching Header, Label: 24139, Exp: 0, S: 1, TTL: 254
Internet Protocol Version 4, Src: 10.0.0.1, Dst: 10.0.0.2
    0100 .... = Version: 4
<example shortened for brevity>
```

Note that the first nibble after the BoS label is 0100, which refers to an IPv4 header, whereas a nibble of 0110 would point to an IPv6 header. Other values would be treated as Layer 2 payload. This pragmatic approach falls apart as soon as MAC addresses start with 0x4 or 0x6, which causes the packet to be misinterpreted as an IP packet. The resulting load balancing would be nondeterministic and would most likely negatively impact the end-user experience of the service.

RFC 4385 defines the Ethernet control word, which solves the misinterpretation issue by inserting a 4-byte control word where the first nibble is 0000. In essence, ensures that transit routers do not falsely interpret the L2VPN pseudowire payload as IPv4 or IPv6 traffic and possibly extract source and destination IP addresses. For this to work, the ingress and egress PE devices have to agree on the usage of the control word.

The third improvement relates to multiple flows going over a single pseudowire. In this case, there may be one or more transport labels and a pseudowire label present (refer to Figure 1-13). Transit routers may not be able to inspect the Layer 2 information to distinguish the different flows. Instead, the P nodes compute the same hash for all flows, preventing proper load balancing. This problem description may sound familiar to the GRE use case introduced earlier. It can be solved by using the Entropy label as well.

There is yet another L2VPN-exclusive solution to this problem. RFC 6391 introduces an additional label in the MPLS label stack called the Flow label. The Flow label is imposed by the ingress PE node based on the relevant fields of the flow, which for an L2VPN could be source/destination addresses of Layer 2 and Layer 3 (if present). It is important to note that all packets belonging to the same flow must be transported using the same Flow label to guarantee that the same path is taken across the network for all packets belonging to the same flow. For this to work, ingress and egress PE devices have to agree on the usage of the Flow label.

> **Note**   The Entropy label is applicable to both L2VPN and L3VPN services and must be supported on all nodes in the path, whereas the Flow label is limited to L2VPN services but requires support on the PE nodes only.

Beyond MPLS

Many of the protocols and technologies that power the Internet today have their origin in the research and development conducted at the Defense Advanced Research Projects Agency (DARPA). The ARPANET, an early predecessor of the Internet, became operational in 1969, and the Internet Protocol suite (TCP/IP) was initially specified in 1973. Unsurprisingly, the native Internet Protocol (IP) lacks many of the requirements of modern networks, which evolved gradually over time and grew at an unprecedented pace. Consequently, existing protocols had to be augmented, and completely new protocols became necessary to fill gaps. The following use cases are examples:

- Exhaustion of IPv4 addressing space:

  - **Workaround:** Private IPv4 addresses (RFC 1918), Network Address Translation (NAT)

  - **Solution:** Internet Protocol version 6 (IPv6)

- Lack of virtual private network (VPN):

  - **Solutions:** MPLS VPN, DMVPN (GRE/IPsec), VXLAN

- Enhanced load balancing in the VPN context:

  - **Solutions:** Flow-Aware Transport (FAT) label (RFC 6391), Entropy label (RFC 6790), VXLAN UDP

- Lack of traffic engineering (TE):

  - **Solutions:** RSVP-TE, SR-TE

- Lack of service chaining:

  - **Solution:** Network service header (NSH) (RFC 8300)

MPLS is a mature technology and still heavily used in service provider and carrier-grade enterprise networks more than 20 years after its initial deployment. It overcomes several of the shortcomings of native IP routing, especially related to VPN services, but has its fair share of suboptimal traits, as discussed in the previous section. MPLS support in certain network areas, such as the access or data center network, has traditionally been rather limited. As of today, there is no de facto standard for a unified underlay data plane that connects endpoints in the access network, core, and data center.

In recent years, an increasing number of software-defined networking (SDN) solutions have come to market, marking a paradigm shift compared to how traditional networks are built, managed, and operated. SDN is a bit of a buzzword and means different things to different people. It is generally agreed that SDN is an approach to a network architecture that delivers a centralized and programmable network that is more flexible and easier to manage. The brain of the SDN architecture is a controller that enables centralized management and control, automation, and policy enforcement across both physical and virtual network elements. SDN solutions are often limited to a single network domain. For instance, Cisco's SDN portfolio includes the following solutions:

- **Data center:** Application Centric Infrastructure (ACI)

- **Wide-area network:** Software-Defined WAN (SD-WAN)

- **Campus:** Software-Defined Access (SD-Access)

- **Core:** Crosswork Network Controller (CNC)

Some third-party SDN solutions, especially in the field of SD-WAN, make bold claims around the demise of MPLS and position themselves as superior successors. This kind of marketing talk should be taken with a grain of salt. Comparing SD-WAN and MPLS is like comparing apples to oranges. One is an SDN solution that usually spans an overlay network over one or more transport networks, and the other is a packet-forwarding technique in the underlay transport network. In fact, many SD-WAN deployments rely on a mix of MPLS and low-cost broadband to interconnect the different sites.

It should become clear that MPLS is not the silver bullet to all network requirements and use cases. As a wise man once said, "The art of prophecy is very difficult, especially with respect to the future." However, looking into the crystal ball, it is almost certain that MPLS will remain an integral part of any service provider network in the foreseeable future. At the same time, promising new technology may cause major disruptions in the networking industry and become the MPLS successor: Segment Routing IPv6 (SRv6).

The details of SRv6 will be introduced Chapter 3, "What Is Segment Routing IPv6 (SRv6)?" but for now, it is just important to understand that SRv6 relies on the IPv6 data plane and not on MPLS. In a way, it is a step back to the roots (or the OSI model) and addresses many of the challenges and shortcomings of MPLS:

- Extensive IPv6 addressing space

- Virtual private networks (VPNs) using the IPv6 data plane

- Native load balancing, thanks to the IPv6 Flow label

- Traffic engineering using the IPv6 data plane

- Service chaining using the IPv6 data plane

At the same time, the potential of SRv6 goes much further and does not stop at replacing MPLS. Recall that MPLS support in some network domains is rather limited, and alternative overlay techniques such as VXLAN are heavily used (for instance, in the data center). Due to the IPv6 data plane of SRv6, there is an opportunity to unify the underlay end-to-end and use a single BGP-based control plane layer to provision services between the access and the data center network.

The journey to SRv6 is still at an early stage but continues to gain momentum. This book provides an in-depth approach to both theory and practice to be prepared for the transition from MPLS to SRv6 with or without an intermediate stop at SR-MPLS. Either way, the final destination of this network transition should be SRv6.

Summary

MPLS is a protocol that enables efficient forwarding of data packets across a network by assigning labels to the packets. Labels are used to identify paths through the network so packets can be quickly routed between nodes. MPLS operates at Layer 2.5, between the network layer (Layer 3) and the data link layer (Layer 2) of the OSI model.

MPLS has a label structure that consists of a 20-bit label value, a 3-bit Experimental (EXP) field, a 1-bit Bottom of Stack (BoS) indicator, and an 8-bit Time to Live (TTL) field. A label is inserted between the Layer 2 and Layer 3 headers of a packet. The Label Value field contains a unique identifier for the label, the EXP field is used to prioritize packets, and the TTL field is used to limit the lifespan of the packet, which also helps to break a routing loop in the core.

The control plane and the data plane are the two planes in MPLS. The control plane sets up the label-switched paths (LSPs) and manages the label distribution among routers. It exchanges label information between routers using Label Distribution Protocol (LDP) or Resource Reservation Protocol (RSVP). The data plane forwards the packets based on the labels assigned in the control plane.

LDP is used to distribute labels between routers in the network and is therefore a protocol that runs between MPLS-enabled routers. When a router receives a packet, it checks the label assigned to the packet and uses the label to forward the packet along the LSP. LDP also supports label stacking, where multiple labels can be assigned to a packet, allowing it to be routed through a more specific path, or follow a specific constraint.

When a packet enters an MPLS network, the router performs a label imposition (with a PUSH operation). As it traverses through the network, its label is swapped as it passes through each LSR. When it reaches its final destination, the label is removed (with a POP operation). Traffic forwarding using labels enables MPLS networks to quickly and efficiently forward traffic based on the labels assigned to each packet. Each node in the network maintains a label forwarding table that maps incoming labels to outgoing labels—essentially outgoing interfaces.

Traffic protection is a widespread use case for MPLS in the backbone and core networks. When combined with segment routing, the fast-reroute mechanism called TI-LFA is a key benefit for network operators using SR MPLS. TI-LFA is built explicitly to cover 100% traffic protection in the event of a node or link failure in an SR-enabled network. TI-LFA precalculates the backup path for any failure scenario, from any node in the network, so if a link failure is detected, the backup path takes over in less than 50 ms.

MPLS VPN services are a popular use case for MPLS, where VPN services are provided to customers over a shared service provider network. MPLS VPNs allow customers to securely connect their geographically dispersed sites by using virtual connections that are separate from the public Internet. The transport label is part of the MPLS forwarding in the core, whereas the service label is used to represent customer routes that are part of a VRF instance. Various categories of VPNs are available: L2VPN, L3VPN, and Multicast VPN (mVPN).

While MPLS has proven to be a reliable and scalable backbone solution for service providers and large enterprise networks, challenges and shortcomings limit its potential. One of the challenges of MPLS is its label space limitation. MPLS labels have a fixed length, which limits the number of labels that can be used in a network to 2^20.

Inter-AS limitations are another challenge of MPLS. MPLS was initially designed to work within a single administrative domain, which can make it difficult to connect networks from different domains. More recently, BGP Labeled Unicast was introduced to help with inter-AS, 6PE, unified MPLS, and CSC scenarios. BGP-LU is a key benefit for extending MPLS VPN services support over inter-AS domains.

RSVP-based traffic engineering is a method of controlling network traffic flows using MPLS, but it also has limitations. RSVP is a complex protocol that can be difficult to manage and scale, particularly in large networks. An RSVP-TE Path message is sent from the headend node to the tailend node, carrying info about tunnels source, destination, and traffic requirements. Each node along the path processes it, checks for resources, and either reserves them or sends a ResvErr message. The tailend node sends an RSVP-TE Resv message back to the headend node, indicating the establishment of the tunnel, and includes path and label information. RSVP-based traffic engineering can lead to inefficient use of network resources if not configured and managed properly by the network operator.

Service chaining complexities are another challenge of MPLS. Service chaining involves forwarding packets through a sequence of network functions or services, which can be complex to implement in MPLS networks. SRv6 has a far greater applicability for service chaining compared to MPLS technology.

In the long run, while MPLS has proven to be a reliable and scalable solution for transport networks for many years, network operators are adopting segment routing and SRv6 as the new standard deployment. Greenfield and brownfield deployments are both appropriate candidates for implementing SR MPLS or SRv6. In the case of SRv6, it can be used not only in traditional service provider architecture deployments but also in other areas, such as data centers, where it is necessary to push traffic through virtual machines, containers, and different virtual functions. The only requirement in that case is a plain IPv6 data plane without MPLS.

References and Additional Reading

- RFC 6790: The Use of Entropy Labels in MPLS Forwarding, www.rfc-editor.org/info/rfc6790

- RFC 4385: Pseudowire Emulation Edge-to-Edge (PWE3) Control Word for Use over an MPLS PSN, www.rfc-editor.org/info/rfc4385

- RFC 6391: Flow-Aware Transport of Pseudowires over an MPLS Packet Switched Network, www.rfc-editor.org/info/rfc6391

- RFC 1918: Address Allocation for Private Internets, www.rfc-editor.org/info/rfc1918

- RFC 8300: Using the Encapsulation for Lower-Layer Protocols (ELP) over TCP to Encapsulate Routing and Control Protocols, www.rfc-editor.org/info/rfc8300

- RFC 3032: MPLS Label Stack Encoding, www.rfc-editor.org/info/rfc3032

- RFC 7274: An Entropy Label Capability for MPLS Forwarding, www.rfc-editor.org/info/rfc7274

- RFC 2547: BGP/MPLS VPNs, www.rfc-editor.org/info/rfc2547

- RFC 4664: Framework for Layer 2 Virtual Private Networks (L2VPNs), www.rfc-editor.org/info/rfc4664

- RFC 6513: Multicast in MPLS/BGP IP VPNs, www.rfc-editor.org/info/rfc6513

- RFC 5036: LDP Specification, www.rfc-editor.org/info/rfc5036

Chapter 2

What Is Segment Routing over MPLS (SR-MPLS)?

We took a brief look at MPLS and its shortcomings in Chapter 1, "MPLS in a Nutshell." Now it is time to build a solid understanding of segment routing (SR) so you will be ready for the upcoming chapters, which cover high-level design, configuration, and verification of various transport- and service-related aspects of SR-enabled networks. This chapter introduces basic segment routing concepts by using an analogy and then goes into the theory behind the MPLS data plane encapsulation implementation. This chapter covers Segment Routing for MPLS (SR-MPLS), and Chapter 3, "What Is Segment Routing over IPv6 (SRv6)?" covers IPv6 (SRv6) data plane encapsulations. The terms, abbreviations, and acronyms introduced in this chapter are consistently used throughout the remainder of this book.

Before delving into the more technical specifications of segment routing, let's consider a simplified high-level analogy that serves as an example to explain underlying key concepts. The central processing unit (CPU) installed in an everyday device, such as a mobile phone, smart TV, laptop, or router is the brain of the system that controls other components, such as memory, hard disk, and a network interface card. The main task of the CPU is to execute program instructions in the form of machine code. Machine code is platform-specific binary code consisting of zeros and ones that is not human readable. Machine code for a given program is not portable between processor architectures; for example, ARM64 architecture-based machine code is not compatible with and cannot be run on x64 architecture-based devices and vice versa. You could think of it as two gingerbread recipes, one written in English and one in Bahasa Indonesian, each providing a list of instructions. While the Indonesian alphabet uses the same 26 letters as the English alphabet, a native English speaker will not be able to read or follow the recipe written in Bahasa Indonesian.

High-level programming languages such as Python, Java, C++, and Go allow programmers to write code that is independent of the underlying hardware architecture and human readable and that provides an abstraction layer to hide low-level hardware details. For instance, Example 2-1 shows a simple computer program that allocates a few variables, stores the sum of a + b in a variable, and sends the result to the standard output (that is, the user's screen in the terminal).

Example 2-1   *High-Level C++ Source Code*

```
#include <stdio.h>

int main(void){
    int a,b,c;
    a=1;
    b=2;
    c=a+b;
    printf("%d + %d = %d\n",a,b,c);
}
```

A compiler is a special program that translates high-level programming language source code into machine code that can be executed on a CPU. As an intermediate step, a compiler creates assembler code, which is one step away from machine code. Unlike machine code, assembler code is human readable and nicely shows the order of instructions that must be executed by the CPU to achieve the specified outcome of the high-level source code. Example 2-2 shows the same program from Example 2-1 but in assembler code.

Example 2-2   *Low-Level Assembler Source Code*

```
.LC0:
.string "%d + %d = %d\n"
main:
push rbp
mov rbp, rsp
sub rsp, 16
mov DWORD PTR [rbp-4], 1
mov DWORD PTR [rbp-8], 2
mov edx, DWORD PTR [rbp-4]
mov eax, DWORD PTR [rbp-8]
add eax, edx
mov DWORD PTR [rbp-12], eax
mov ecx, DWORD PTR [rbp-12]
mov edx, DWORD PTR [rbp-8]
mov eax, DWORD PTR [rbp-4]
mov esi, eax
mov edi, OFFSET FLAT:.LC0
mov eax, 0
call printf
mov eax, 0
leave
ret
```

The assembler program consists of a list of instructions whose machine code counterparts will be executed one by one by the CPU at runtime. A special CPU register, generally referred to as the program counter, stores the memory address of the current instruction. Upon completion, the program counter is incremented, and the next instruction is fetched from the updated memory address to be executed. In other words, the program counter keeps track of where the CPU is in the program execution—that is, where it is in the sequence of instructions.

Don't worry if you don't understand the assembler program. The details are not relevant. What is relevant is the fact that there are different instructions, such as **push, mov, sub,** and **add,** that seem to accept one or more parameters. The supported instructions vary between hardware architectures and CPU models. The instruction set architecture (ISA) defines which instructions can be used by a software program to control the CPU. Reading such a manual reveals that instructions have the following format:

```
label: mnemonic argument1, argument2, argument3
```

where:

- *label* is an identifier (not related to MPLS labels).

- *mnemonic* is a name for a class of instructions that have the same function.

- Arguments are mandatory or optional, depending on the mnemonic.

Example 2-2 shows a label called **main,** followed by **push** (*mnemonic*) and **rbp** (*argument1*). This instruction tells the CPU to store a special register on the stack, whereas the **add eax, edx** instruction takes two arguments to perform the addition of a + b in the source code. This simple program uses common instructions, but applications in the field of artificial intelligence (AI) and machine learning (ML) use more complex and specialized instructions. In principle, there are no limits on what kind of instructions a CPU can execute, as long as it is implemented in hardware and there is a practical benefit of implementing it. The length of an instruction may vary within an ISA, depending on the underlying hardware architecture.

Finally, executing the binary yields the output shown in Example 2-3.

Example 2-3 *Output of Program Execution*

```
cisco@ubuntu-server:~/Code$ ./program
1 + 2 = 3
cisco@ubuntu-server:~/Code$
```

At this point, you might wonder about the relevance of CPU instructions, program counters, and instruction formats in a segment routing book. The coming paragraphs shed light on the analogy and emphasize similarities between computer and segment routing architectures.

Segment routing (RFC 8402) leverages source routing, which allows the source node (ingress PE node) to steer a packet flow through the SR domain. This ability is a key difference from traditional MPLS-based networks, where ingress PE nodes lack such fine-grained control over the traffic path through the network when relying on LDP labels. Traffic engineering (TE) techniques enable the optimization of traffic distribution in MPLS networks at the cost of additional protocols such as Resource Reservation Protocol (RSVP) and network state information (TE tunnels) in the network, which is challenging to operate and negatively impacts the overall network scale. Segment routing significantly simplifies the network protocol stack by superseding signaling protocols like LDP or RSVP-TE.

Instead, SR extensions elevate the underlying link-state routing protocol, providing a comprehensive view of the network topology across the entire domain, to provide the same functionality that relied on multiple protocols in the past. The interior gateway protocol (IGP) advertises *segments*, which are essentially network instructions, throughout the network, which guarantees that every node within the domain has the same view. The flooding of segments enables the IGP to replace the previously mentioned signaling protocols and facilitates moving any tunnel state information from the network to the packet headers. A segment can have global significance within the network, such as instructing nodes in the SR domain to steer traffic to a specific node, or local significance, such as instructing a specific node to steer traffic across a specific interface.

Figure 2-1 shows the two supported data planes of the segment routing architecture. SR-MPLS reuses the MPLS data plane, whereas SR IPv6 (SRv6) relies on the IPv6 data plane.

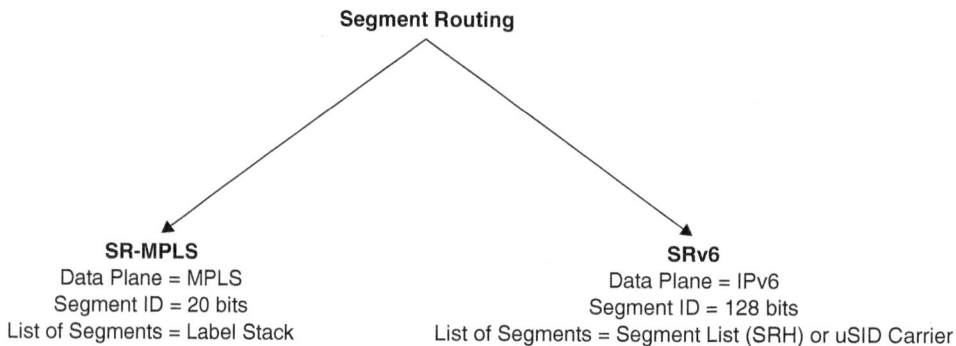

Segment Routing

SR-MPLS
Data Plane = MPLS
Segment ID = 20 bits
List of Segments = Label Stack

SRv6
Data Plane = IPv6
Segment ID = 128 bits
List of Segments = Segment List (SRH) or uSID Carrier

Figure 2-1 *Segment Routing Data Planes*

As previously mentioned, a segment represents a single instruction identified by a segment identifier (SID). The length of a SID depends on the underlying data plane. For SR-MPLS, the SID is 20 bits long and is written in the Label field of the MPLS header. In contrast, an SRv6 SID is a 128-bit identifier in the Destination Address field of the IPv6 header. As with the assembler program shown in Example 2-2, multiple ordered instructions can be expressed as a list of segments. A list of segments can be realized using multiple SIDs, which in the MPLS data plane results in a label stack. In the SRv6 data plane, a list of segments may be encoded using the segment routing header (SRH), a micro-SID (uSID) carrier, or a combination of both, depending on the SRv6 flavor and the number of segments. The fundamental terminology of segment routing is agnostic to the underlying data plane; the concept of a segment, SID, and list of segments applies to both encapsulation types.

> **Note** SRv6 terms and concepts, such as SRH and uSID, are explained in Chapter 3. The different segments in SR-MPLS are presented in more detail later in this chapter, in the section "Segment Routing for MPLS (SR-MPLS)."

You may have come across the term *network as a computer* in the context of segment routing, in reference to the network as a large distributed system where several devices work together to execute a network program consisting of a list of instructions or segments. All nodes within an SR domain must speak a common language to be able to interpret the segments correctly. SR can be applied to both the MPLS and IPv6 architectures, which means that nodes within an SR domain are not limited to networking devices if they understand the underlying data plane. This is especially true for IPv6, which is widely supported across a range of different networking nodes from the Internet of Things (IoT) in the industry to containers in the data center. Figure 2-2 shows an imaginary local weather station with sensors in three different locations and some services running in a data center (DC).

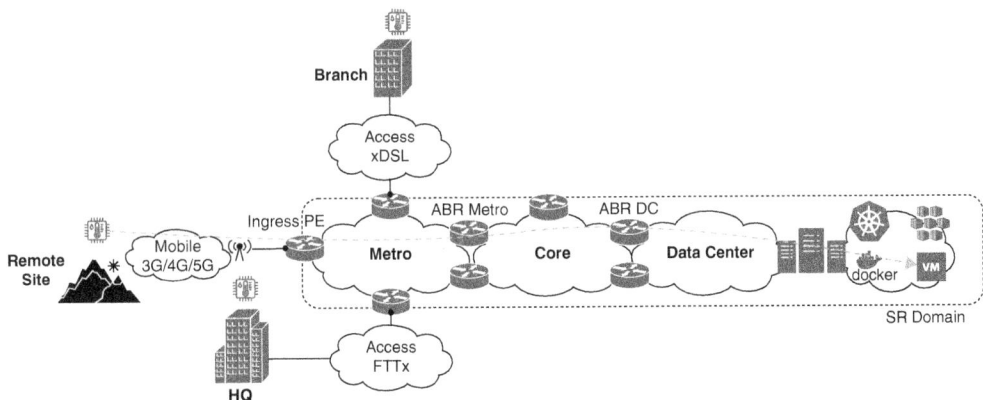

Figure 2-2 *Weather Station Network Topology*

The sensors connect to a local service provider (SP) using different access technologies. Each sensor measures temperature, humidity, and barometric pressure on a regular basis and transmits the data to a microservice hosted in a remote data center (on the right-hand side of the figure). The collected data is processed, stored, and evaluated every 24 hours to provide the weather forecast for the next seven days. It goes without saying that meteorology is far more complex than presented here, but this illustration will suffice for our example.

The SR domain in our example includes metro, core, and data center, up to and including the virtual machine or container, which means that segments could be executed by any of the nodes belonging to the SR domain. Within an SR domain, different roles can be distinguished:

- **Source/ingress node:** Handles the traffic as it enters the SR domain.

- **Transit node:** Handles the forwarding of traffic within the SR domain.

- **Endpoint/egress node:** Handles the traffic as it leaves the SR domain.

In traditional Layer 3 virtual private network (VPN) services, service provider and customer networks are isolated logically using virtual routing and forwarding (VRF) instances or access lists on the service edge to protect the SP infrastructure. Consequently, VRF instances or access lists are used to enforce the demarcation point of the SR domain. In our example, all three weather station sensors are isolated from the SP through VRF instances on the PE node, which means a network program can only be initiated by the ingress PE device receiving customer traffic.

Unlike in traditional software development, with segment routing there are no high-level network programming languages available. Instead, a network program is defined as an ordered list of segments, also known as an *SR policy*, that steers a packet flow along a desired path in the network. SR policies are source-routed policies identified through the tuple, such as headend, color, or endpoint. Headend and endpoint should be self-explanatory; the 32-bit color value identifies the intent or objective of the policy. The endpoint and color are used as identifiers to steer traffic into the corresponding SR policy. Examples of such an intent are low latency or MACsec encrypted paths from the headend to the endpoint. The source routing is crucial in moving the traffic engineering tunnel state from intermediate routers to the packet headers imposed by the ingress node through an SR policy.

Complementary information on how to implement such traffic engineering capabilities using the IGP is provided in the section "IGP Flexible Algorithm (Flex Algo) (RFC 9350)," later in this chapter. Example 2-4 shows an imaginary SR policy that defines a loose path from the ingress PE node (source node) to the container (endpoint node) hosting the weather application via two transit nodes. Note that there are two area border routers (ABRs) in the metro and the data center, which may result in equal-cost multipath routing (ECMP). If desired, a more restrictive path could be defined, such as using a specific ABR or only traversing the core over MACsec-encrypted links.

Example 2-4   *Network Program Pseudocode*

```
policy weather-app-policy
 1 goto ABR Metro
 2 goto ABR DC
 3 goto container weather-app
```

Figure 2-3 shows the ordered list of segments expressed in this pseudocode.

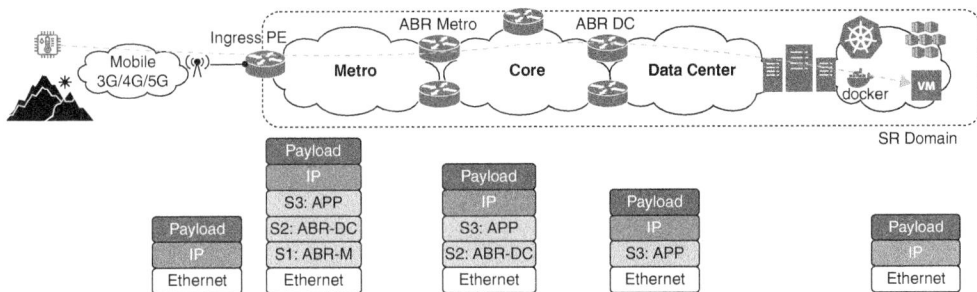

Figure 2-3   *Network Program Segment Routing Policy (SR-MPLS)*

The ingress PE node imposes one or more additional headers to encapsulate the original customer packet. Note that the exact headers depend on the underlying data plane, as discussed in detail in the section "Segment Routing for MPLS (SR-MPLS)," later in this chapter, and in Chapter 3. The additional encapsulation overhead is negligible in most cases and justified by the significant scalability gains in the backbone network achieved by transferring the tunnel state information from the network to the packet. In the case of SR-MPLS, the length of the list of segments decreases as the network program is executed. The first segment is executed by one of the ABR metro nodes. The metro ABR pops its own instruction from the stack and forwards the packet toward an ABR DC, which pops its own instruction and forwards the packet toward the weather-app container. Eventually, the packet reaches its destination, which in our example is the SR-aware weather-app container that decapsulates and processes the inner IP packet. Note that this example excludes a few details, such as penultimate hop popping (PHP) and the BGP service label for simplicity.

It should be becoming clear now that the execution of segments in a segment routing domain and the execution of instructions in computer architectures share several fundamental principles. In fact, those similarities are even more prominent with SRv6, as you will see in Chapter 3, which covers the Segments Left field of the SRH and the SRv6 SID format that are comparable to the program counter and instruction format, respectively.

The segment routing ecosystem encompasses a wide variety of Internet Engineering Task Force (IETF) standards and drafts across numerous working groups. The standardization process for segment routing has been progressing at an impressive pace, and most key drafts have become proposed standards. One exception worth highlighting here is the SRv6 compression drafts that are in the later stages of the standardization process. The successful mass-scale rollout of SR lead operators shows that there is no reason to delay the SR adoption.

Figure 2-4 displays a selection of the most important building blocks that make up segment routing (RFC 8402) and the segment routing policy architecture (RFC 9256).

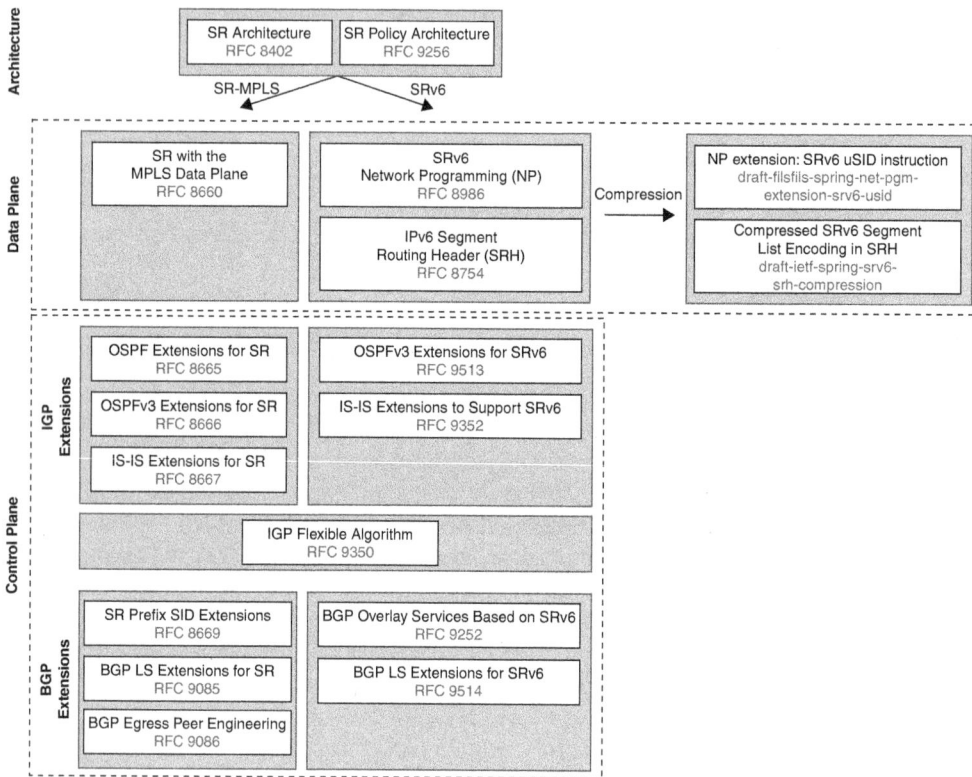

Figure 2-4 *Segment Routing Architecture*

Note Some of the official standards and draft titles have been shortened or modified in Figure 2-4 for better readability. This book covers many of the drafts and proposed standards in more detail, accompanying the somewhat dry theory with visual illustrations and packet captures.

Problem Description and Requirements

Before we delve into the details of segment routing, it is helpful to recall the problems and requirements segment routing aims to address and what it does not address. RFC 7855 takes into account many of the shortcomings of MPLS described in Chapter 1 and proposes a new network architecture based on source routing. These are the key take-aways in the RFC:

■ The SPRING architecture must be backward compatible. That is, SPRING-capable and non-SPRING-capable nodes must be able to interoperate for both MPLS and IPv6 data planes.

■ Existing MPLS VPN services must be deployable using the SPRING architecture without the need for additional signaling protocols.

- Fast reroute (FRR) computation and preprogramming are supported in any topology without the need for additional signaling protocols.

- FRR must support link and node protection, micro-loop avoidance, and shared risk constraints.

- Traffic engineering must be implemented without additional signaling protocols. The policy state should be part of the packet header instead of having states stored on midpoints and tailends per policy.

- Traffic engineering must support both strict and loose options, based on the distributed or centralized model.

- Egress peer engineering (EPE) allows the administrator of an autonomous system (AS) to select the exit point of the local AS based on the egress peering node, the egress interface, or a peering AS.

- Policies can be pushed through an SDN controller at the headend, which allows decoupling of the data and control planes.

The "SPRING Problem Statement and Requirements" effort led to the segment routing architecture standardization and guided other proposed standards of the SR ecosystem. The next section covers the SR-MPLS data and control plane in detail and introduces both IGP and BGP extensions that define the SR-MPLS solution.

Segment Routing over MPLS (SR-MPLS)

SR-MPLS brings the segment routing architecture to MPLS by leveraging the existing MPLS forwarding plane with no changes. In other words, SR-MPLS encapsulates packets into one or more MPLS headers and inherits common MPLS data plane operations, such as PUSH, SWAP, and POP, as well as PHP. The following sections introduce the fundamental building blocks of the SR-MPLS solution and provide visual representations to facilitate a smooth learning curve even for MPLS novices.

Data Plane

Because SR-MPLS reuses the MPLS data plane, the same data plane operations exist with slightly modified terminology (see Figure 2-5):

- **PUSH:** This operation inserts a segment at the top of the segment list. It is implemented as a PUSH operation of a label as the new topmost label in SR-MPLS.

- **NEXT:** This operation inspects the next segment of the segment list after completing the active segment. It is implemented as a POP operation of the top label in SR-MPLS.

- **CONTINUE:** This operation, where the active segment has not been completed yet and remains active, is implemented as a SWAP operation of the top label. Note that the SWAP operation will not change the label value if the segment routing label space is consistent across the SR domain.

The different SR label blocks are introduced in more detail in the section "SID Allocation," later in this chapter. Figure 2-5 shows the data plane operations for a node segment that forwards traffic across the SR domain to R0.

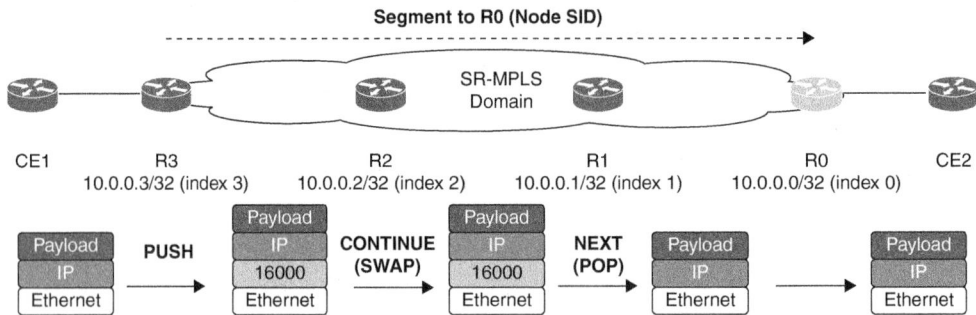

Figure 2-5   *SR-MPLS Data Plane Operations*

Segment Identifier (SID)

The terms *segment* and *segment identifier* (SID) are often used interchangeably. In theory, a *segment* is an instruction, whereas a *SID*, as the name implies, is an identifier, or, in the scope of SR-MPLS, an MPLS label value associated with a specific segment. In practice, this distinction is not crucial, but a common definition is beneficial when discussing segment routing with other peers.

Like CPU instructions, SR segments are not limited in what kind of instructions they are associated with. The scope of a segment can be globally or locally significant. In addition, a segment instruction may be transport related (a topological instruction) or service related (a service instruction). For example, forwarding a packet toward a specific adjacency is a locally significant topological instruction, whereas forwarding a packet toward a specific node is considered a globally significant topological instruction. Service instructions have a much wider scope than transport instructions and could in theory cover a wide range of networking functions (for example, QoS, NAT, FW).

The following segment (SID) types exist and are introduced in the upcoming sections:

- IGP Prefix Segment (Prefix SID)
  - Node Segment (Node SID)
  - Anycast Segment (Anycast SID)
- IGP Adjacency Segment (Adjacency SID)
  - Layer 2 Adjacency Segment (Layer 2 Adjacency SID)
  - Adjacency Segment (Adjacency SID)
- BGP Prefix Segment (BGP Prefix SID)

- BGP Peering Segment (BGP Peering SID)

    - BGP Peer Node Segment (PeerNode SID)

    - BGP Peer Adjacency Segment (PeerAdj SID)

    - BGP Peer Set Segment (PeerSet SID)

- Binding Segment (Binding SID) (which maps to an SR policy)

Figure 2-6 shows the grouping of the different segments in tree structures.

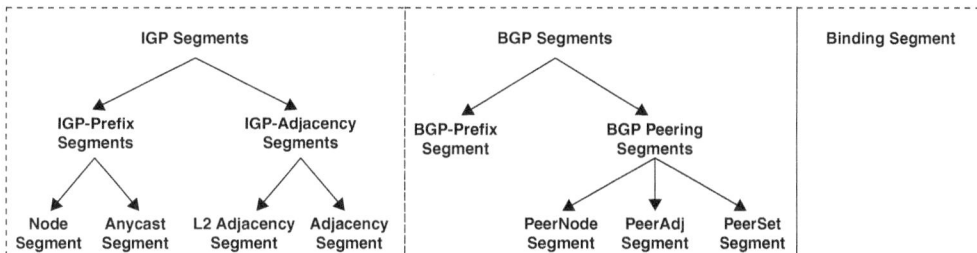

Figure 2-6 *Segment Routing Segments Overview*

SID Allocation

SR-MPLS reuses the existing MPLS data plane, which means that on each node, a range of labels is carved out from the existing MPLS label space for segment routing. Certain MPLS label space blocks are reserved for the special-purpose labels (0–15) or specific applications, and a large chunk of the label space is used for dynamic label allocation.

On Cisco devices, the label-switching database (LSD) manages locally allocated labels and assigns labels to its clients (MPLS applications). Examples of MPLS applications and protocols that need to allocate local labels include LDP, RSVP, BGP, and L2VPN.

Label collisions between different MPLS applications must be prevented for the protocols to work as expected. Label collisions are generally not a problem for dynamically allocated labels since the LSD ensures that each label is allocated only once. However, certain SIDs (such as Prefix SID) are statically defined by the operator, which opens the door for potential label collisions. To prevent label conflicts between statically and dynamically allocated labels, different label blocks must be allocated. Two new blocks have been allocated in the LSD for segment routing:

- Segment routing global block (SRGB)

- Segment routing local block (SRLB)

Figure 2-7 shows an example of the default label space carving in IOS XR that accommodates static SIDs, dynamic SIDs, and dynamic MPLS labels from other applications.

1,048,575   **MPLS Label Space**

Dynamic
SR Global Block
SR Local Block
MPLS Static
Special-Purpose

MPLS Applications (LDP, RSVP, BGP, L2VPN, etc)

-- 23,999

-- 15,999

-- 14,999

-- 15

0

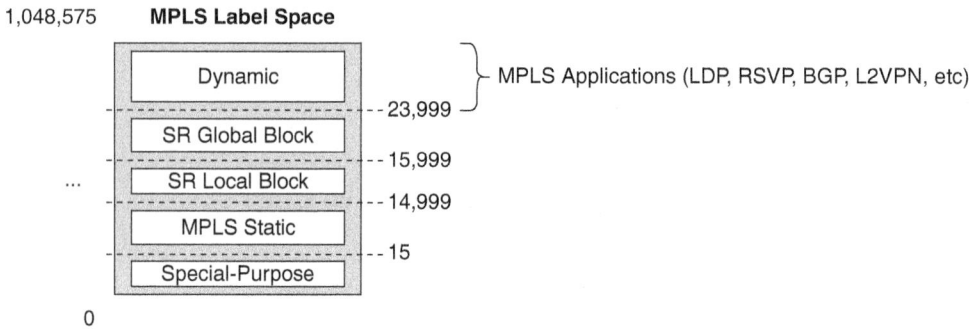

Figure 2-7 *Label-Switching Database (LSD) Label Allocation*

Note that the size and order of the SRLB, SRGB, and dynamic block may be configured differently. Generally, the blocks are not equal in size, and the vast majority of the label space is allocated to the dynamic block required for service scaling.

The following sections detail the SR block types.

Segment Routing Global Block (SRGB)

The SRGB is a dedicated block from the MPLS label space for globally significant segments. It is a local property of each node and identifies the locally reserved labels for global segments. Since the SRGB is a local property, different SRGBs could be configured on different nodes in the SR domain. In practice, this is not desirable because it unnecessarily complicates configuration, operation, and troubleshooting of the network. It is highly recommended to use the same SRGB throughout an SR domain. After all, simplicity is one of the key principles of the segment routing architecture.

Figure 2-8 shows an example of an SR domain using the same SRGB (16000–23999).

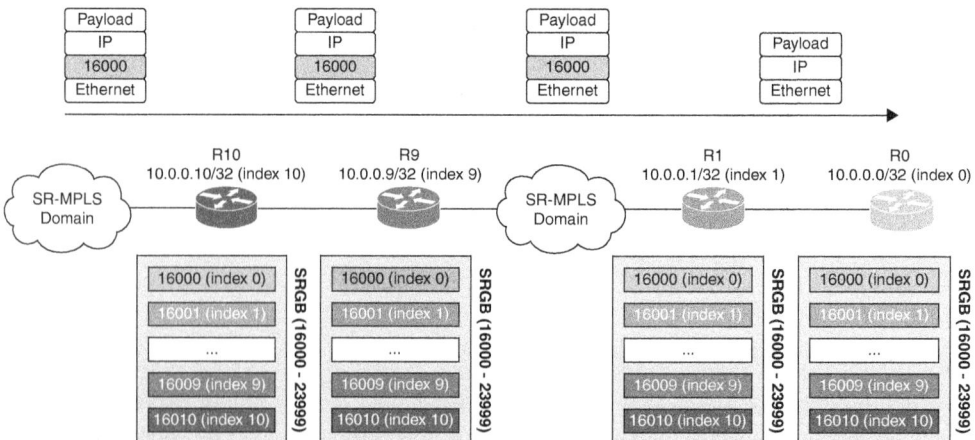

Figure 2-8 *Segment Routing Global Block*

Prefix SIDs are advertised as domain-wide unique indexes starting at 0. The absolute SID or MPLS label value is derived as follows:

Label value (SID) = SRGB base + SID index

For instance, the Node SID of R10's loopback is associated with the MPLS label 16010 (16000 + 10). The sample flow toward R0 in Figure 2-8 shows that the segment associated with R0's loopback0 prefix (10.0.0.0/32) is globally significant and maps to the same MPLS label (SID) on all nodes.

Segment Routing Local Block (SRLB)

The SRLB is a dedicated block from the MPLS label space for locally significant segments. It is a local property of each node and identifies the locally reserved labels for local segments. Much as with SRGBs, different SRLBs can be configured on different nodes in the SR domain. However, this is not recommended for the same reasons mentioned for SRGB.

Note   A local segment may be allocated either from the SRLB or the dynamic block, depending on how the SID was assigned. Manually configured local segments such as Adjacency SIDs, Layer 2 Adjacency SIDs or Binding SIDs (BSIDs) are taken from the SRLB, whereas dynamically allocated segments of the same segment types are usually coming from the dynamic space.

IGP Prefix Segment (Prefix SID)

A Prefix SID is generally globally significant and associated with an IP prefix and an instruction that is equivalent to forwarding the packet along the computed path of a given algorithm (such as Shortest Path First). The corresponding SID is distributed by the link-state IGP (IS-IS or OSPF) throughout the network as a globally unique index.

Note   Prefix SIDs are statically allocated within the SRGB by the operator and generally do not change.

The Node SID and Anycast SID are special types of Prefix SID:

- **Node SID:** This is a Prefix SID that is associated with a prefix that uniquely identifies a specific node in the domain, such as through loopback0. Node SIDs must be unique within the domain; that is, a Node SID cannot be associated with a prefix that exists on more than one device.

- **Anycast SID:** This is a Prefix SID that is associated with an anycast prefix in the domain. Anycast prefixes are usually advertised by two or more routers. Packets are forwarded along the computed path to reach the closest node (that is, the path with the lowest metric).

Figure 2-9 shows an example of a Node SID (16004) that is associated with the IGP-Node Segment of Router 4 (R4). Please note that only a single best path exists between R1 and R4. R1, the ingress node, imposes an MPLS label with a value of 16004 on the packet and forwards it along the shortest path toward R2. R2 performs penultimate hop popping (PHP) and forwards the packet to its destination.

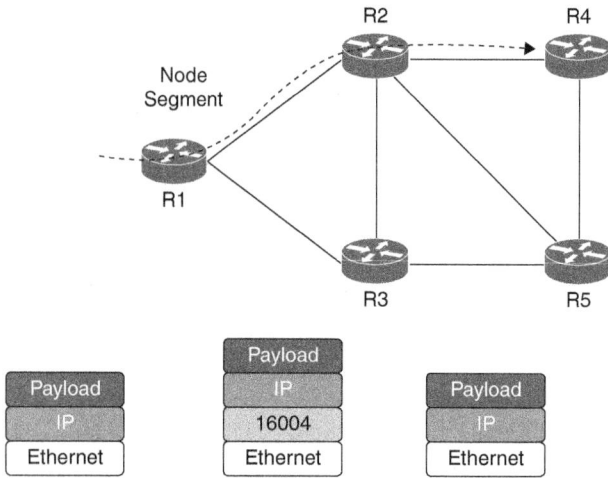

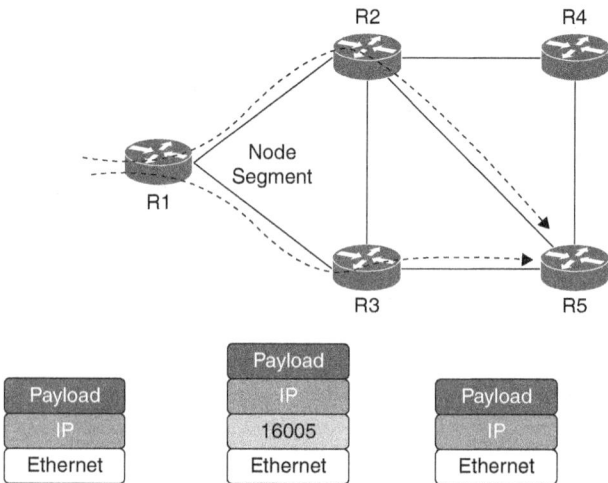

Figure 2-9   *Node SID (Single Path)*

Figure 2-10 shows an example of a Node SID (16005) that is associated with the IGP node segment of R5. Segment routing is ECMP aware and may leverage multiple paths. For instance, R1 may load balance different flows over different equal-cost paths. Note how the same MPLS label value of 16005 is used for both paths. R2 and R3 perform penultimate hop popping (PHP) and forward the packet to its destination.

Figure 2-10   *Node SID (ECMP)*

Figure 2-11 shows an example of an Anycast SID (16045) associated with the IGP anycast segment owned by R4 and R5. Note that traffic across the nodes of the anycast set may not be evenly distributed, depending on the shortest path between the ingress and egress nodes. In this example, R4 would receive one-third of the traffic, and R5 would receive two-thirds of the traffic.

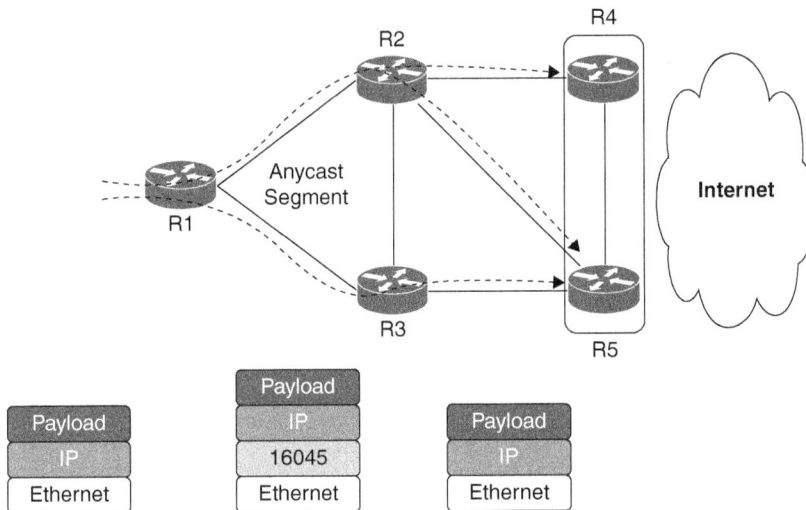

Figure 2-11   *Anycast SID*

IGP anycast segments are useful for redundant and symmetrical network topologies such as:

- Set of two area border routers interconnecting the same IGP domains

- Set of two autonomous system border routers connected to the same external networks (such as the Internet or Inter-AS Option C)

Refer to the section "IGP Extensions," later in this chapter, to learn more about the IGP control plane extension for all IGP SIDs.

IGP Adjacency Segment (Adjacency SID)

An Adjacency SID is generally locally significant and associated with a unidirectional adjacency from one node (local) to another (remote). Its instruction is equivalent to forwarding the packet out a specific outgoing interface. More than one Adjacency SID may be allocated per IGP adjacency to differentiate between protected and unprotected Adjacency SIDs. *Protected* means the SID is eligible for fast reroute protection in the event of a link failure. The corresponding SID is distributed by the link-state IGP (IS-IS or OSPF) throughout the network, usually as an absolute value instead of as an index.

Note Adjacency SIDs are allocated from a dynamic label pool by the node for each IS-IS adjacency. Adjacency SIDs are not persistent unless they are configured manually. Manually configured Adjacency SIDs are taken from the SRLB.

Figure 2-12 shows an example of a combination of a Node SID (16005) that is associated with the IGP node segment of R5 with a locally significant Adjacency SID (24045). A globally significant Adjacency SID can be used without an accompanying Node SID since all nodes within the domain would know how to execute this instruction. However, the example shows a locally significant Adjacency SID since they are more common.

R1, the ingress node, imposes two MPLS labels (16005 and 24045) on the packet and forwards it along the shortest path toward R2 or R3. R2 or R3 performs PHP and forwards the packet with the remaining label 24045 to R5. R5 recognizes the locally significant Adjacency SID 24045, pops the label, and forwards the packet out the interface associated with the Adjacency SID.

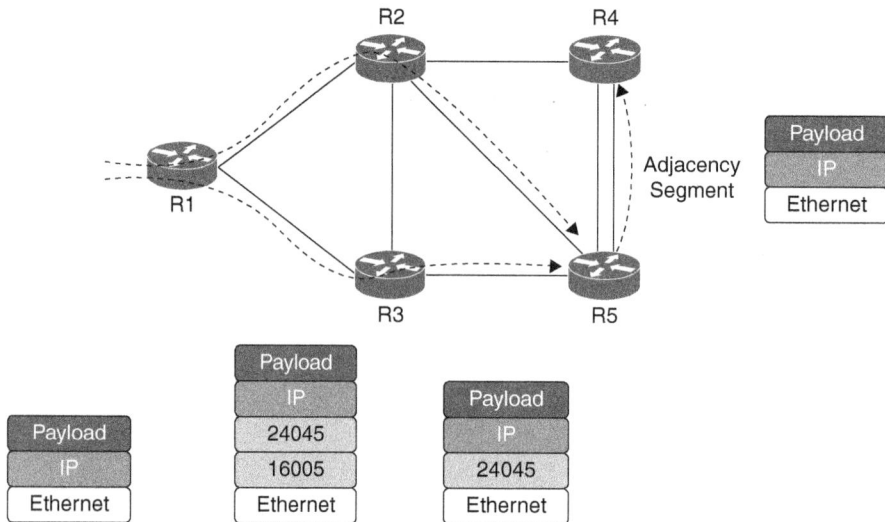

Figure 2-12 *Adjacency SID*

Figure 2-12 illustrates a pair of links between routers R5 and R4, with one potentially being more favorable in terms of reduced link delay or lower packet loss. To differentiate between individual adjacencies, some service providers chose not to create bundles or link aggregation groups (LAGs) in the past. Instead, they opted for equal-cost multipath routing between peers with multiple Layer 3 adjacencies. RFC 8668 (IS-IS) and RFC 9356 (OSPF) introduce the ability for the underlying IGP to advertise link attributes of individual bundle members within a bundle interface.

Figure 2-13 is largely identical to Figure 2-12 except for the fact that the two interfaces between R4 and R5 are now aggregated in a bundle. To steer traffic over a specific bundle member, the corresponding Layer 2 Adjacency SID (24245) must be imposed by the ingress PE R1 to make sure that R5 forwards the packet across the preferred bundle member.

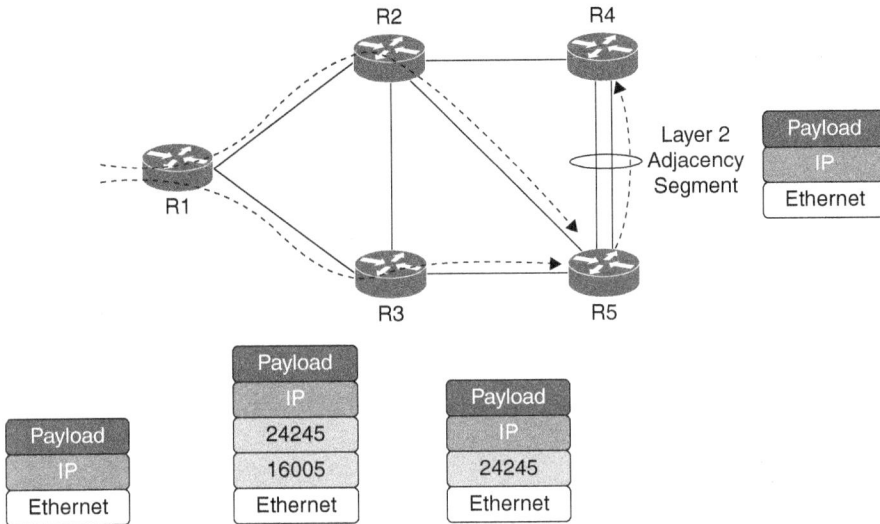

Figure 2-13 *Layer 2 Adjacency SID*

BGP Prefix Segment (BGP Prefix SID)

BGP Prefix SIDs are globally significant and associated to a BGP prefix with a Prefix SID attached. The instruction is equivalent to forwarding the packet along the computed path. The BGP Prefix SID extends the concept of an IGP Prefix SID into the BGP control plane.

The corresponding SID is advertised through BGP labeled unicast (IPv4 or IPv6) throughout the network, which consists of a single AS or multiple ASs, as a globally unique index.

Note BGP Prefix SIDs are statically allocated within the SRGB by the operator and generally do not change.

Figure 2-14 shows an example of a BGP Prefix SID (16005) that is associated with the BGP prefix 10.0.0.5/32, which belongs to R5's loopback. The example presents a common use case where two IGP domains (IGP 1 and IGP 2) are interconnected using BGP-LU (BGP Prefix SID). R5's Node SID (16005) is distributed within IGP 2 up to R3 but not leaked or redistributed into IGP 1. Instead, the SID is transported using the BGP Prefix SID that conveys SR information through the BGP control plane. R3 acts as ABR and inline route reflector (RR) performing BGP next-hop-self for all BGP UPDATE messages.

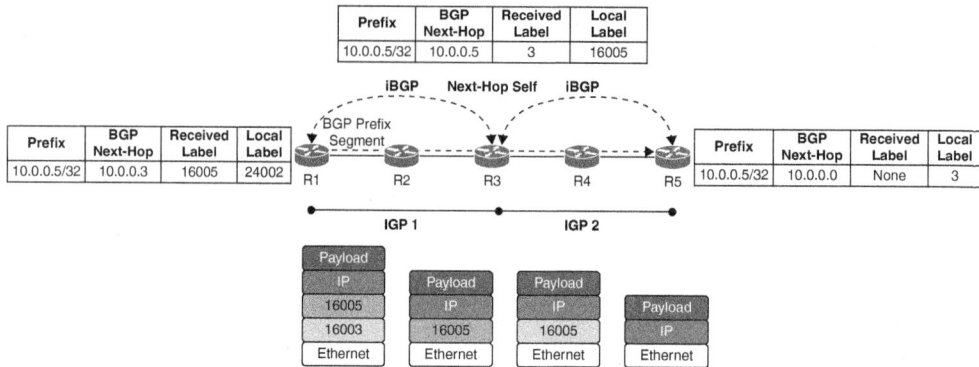

Figure 2-14 *BGP Prefix SID*

Initially, R5 advertises the implicit null label (3) in the NLRI of the BGP UPDATE message with a BGP Prefix SID label index value of 5. Since R3 performs BGP next-hop-self, it allocates a new local label based on the BGP Prefix SID information present in the BGP UPDATE message. R3 advertises the prefix of R5 with an updated BGP next- hop and label stack to R1.

R1 is now able to reach R5 with a recursive lookup:

- BGP Prefix SID of R5 (16005) with a BGP next hop pointing to R3

- IGP Node SID of R3 (16003)

R1 imposes the segment list (16003, 16005) and sends the packet to R2, which performs PHP for the IGP Node SID of R3. R3 performs PHP on the received BGP-LU label (implicit null) and changes from BGP Prefix SID to IGP Node SID to resolve the BGP next hop. The IGP Node SID of R5 is forwarded to R4, which performs PHP and delivers the packet to R5.

Refer to the section "SR Prefix SID Extensions for BGP (RFC 8669)," later in this chapter, to learn more about the BGP control plane extension for the BGP Prefix SID.

BGP Peering Segments (BGP Peering SIDs)

RFC 9087 documents the solution to the BGP Egress Peer Engineering (BGP-EPE) requirement mentioned earlier in this chapter, in the section "Problem Description and Requirements." It leverages a centralized SDN controller to program SR policies on ingress PE devices that steer packets across exit points (egress PE devices) of the local AS, where eBGP is used to interconnect different ASs. The exit point may be defined with varying levels of detail and may range from a certain AS up to a specific interface toward a specific BGP peer. New segments called BGP peering segments have been defined that are advertised across the network using the BGP Link-State (BGP-LS) address family.

Note BGP-EPE applies to the Internet use case in the global routing table (GRT), where packets are transported using unlabeled IPv4 or IPv6 encapsulation.

A BGP Peering SID is locally significant and associated with a BGP peering. Its instruction is equivalent to forwarding the packet toward a specific BGP peer or a set of peers that are considered equal. The BGP Peering SID paves the way for interdomain (inter-AS) source routing in the segment routing architecture within the GRT and relies on three different types of segments:

- **Peer node segment:** Forwards the packet to a specific BGP peer.

- **Peer adjacency segment:** Forwards the packet to a specific BGP peer over a specific interface.

- **Peer set segment:** Load balances the packet toward a set of BGP peers that are considered equal. The BGP peers may or may not be in the same AS.

Figure 2-15 provides a graphical representation of the different BGP peering segments.

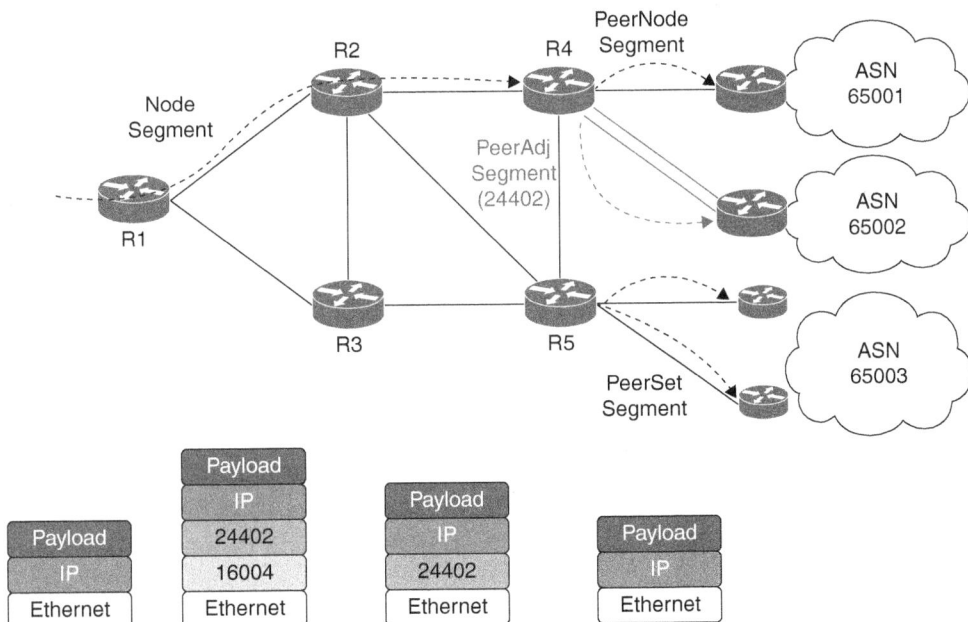

Figure 2-15 *BGP Peering SID*

Note that BGP egress engineering policies require two segments, which usually consists of a global node segment that points to the exit point of the domain (AS) and a local BGP segment that points to a BGP peer. Figure 2-15 shows the segment list (16004, 24402), which is equivalent to the instructions to reach R4 via the shortest path and forward the packet via a specific interface toward AS 65002.

See the section "BGP Link-State Extensions for SR BGP Egress Peer Engineering (RFC 9086)," later in this chapter, to learn more about the BGP control plane extension for the BGP Peering SIDs.

Binding Segment (Binding SID)

A Binding SID (BSID) is generally locally significant and associated with an SR policy. Its instruction is equivalent to steering traffic into an SR policy. The BSID can be used in static SR policies but is more commonly used in combination with a controller that has different means to discover SR policies and corresponding BSIDs, such as NETCONF, BGP-LS, and PCEP.

The headend of an SR policy instantiates a BSID per policy that can be used to steer traffic into the associated SR policy, which provides the following benefits:

- **Scalability:** BSIDs can be used to compress the label stack that allows for policies with very long segment lists. Different hardware platforms have different limits with respect to the maximum label stack depth, which may affect how many segments can be pushed by the source node or how many segments can be processed by a transit node. BSIDs can be used to stay within hardware platform limitations or reduce the encapsulation overhead.

- **Network opacity:** BSIDs effectively hide parts of the network topology by offering a path from one point of the network to another without specifying how it happens. Administrative authorities of a network may not want to disclose topology information to some of their customers.

- **Service independence:** BSIDs offer a stable anchor point in SR policies and hide network events in other parts of the network. For instance, a BSID may be used to steer traffic into an SR policy that follows the low-delay path between two metros. Any network event in the core, such as link or node failure or a new best path, is invisible to all headends using this BSID.

Figure 2-16 shows an example of a segment routing policy leveraging a BSID that is daisy-chained to other BSIDs. While this example may be a bit exaggerated, it clearly shows the power of BSIDs. The end-to-end policy counts 19 intermediate segments on the path toward Router 401. Many merchant silicon ASICs today struggle with more than eight labels in the label stack. Different hardware platforms have different limits, depending on the underlying network ASIC, which can be an operational challenge in networks with many different vendors or hardware models. The maximum SID depth (MSD) signals the maximum number of SIDs that are supported by a node or a link on a node. The MSD is a crucial parameter for segment routing deployments because it allows controllers or other entities to determine a priori if a certain SID stack can be supported across all network elements. MSD signaling is supported using IS-IS (RFC 8491), OSPF (RFC 8476), and BGP-LS (RFC 8814).

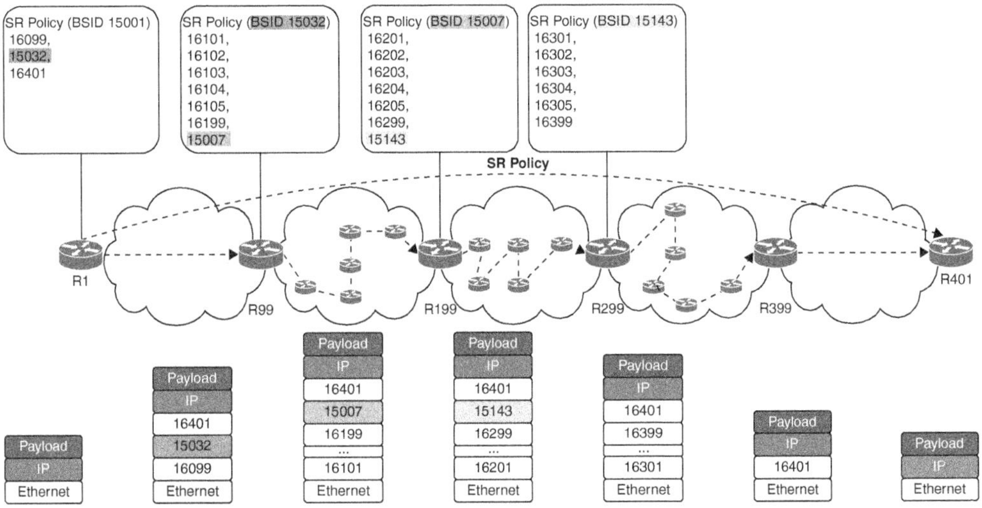

Figure 2-16 *Binding SID*

Assuming that the devices in Figure 2-16 support at most eight segments in the SID stack, the end-to-end policy can be segmented into multiple smaller policies. Several of those policies are daisy-chained into one another. For instance, the last SID of R99's policy (15007) belongs to a BSID on R199, which steers traffic into another policy, which, in turn, is steered into another policy on R299. Once traffic reaches R399, all previous segments will have been executed, and the final node segment of R401 is processed. By segmenting a very long policy into smaller policies and steering traffic from one policy into another by leveraging the BSID, it is possible to adhere to the MSD of eight segments in the example.

IGP Extensions

SR-MPLS reuses the existing MPLS data plane without any changes. The control plane, however, changes substantially. This section covers IGP extensions for IS-IS and OSPFv2, as well as IGP Flexible Algorithm, which complements the traffic engineering capabilities of the SR toolbelt. In the interest of brevity, it was decided to descope the OSPFv3 extensions for SR (RFC 8666) due to its similarities with OSPFv2.

The following sections are limited to discussing new type length value (TLVs) and sub-TLVs defined as part of the corresponding segment routing extensions RFCs. The packet captures provided support the visualization of the underlying control plane.

IS-IS Extensions for Segment Routing (RFC 8667)

IS-IS relies on link-state protocol data units (LSPs) to advertise routing information throughout the network. IS-IS LSPs contain a number of type length values (TLVs) and sub-TLVs, to provide a hierarchical, flexible, and easily extensible way of encoding routing information.

The IS-IS TLVs and sub-TLVs highlighted in Figure 2-17 have been registered with the Internet Assigned Numbers Authority (IANA) as part of RFC 8667 to facilitate the distribution of SR-specific information.

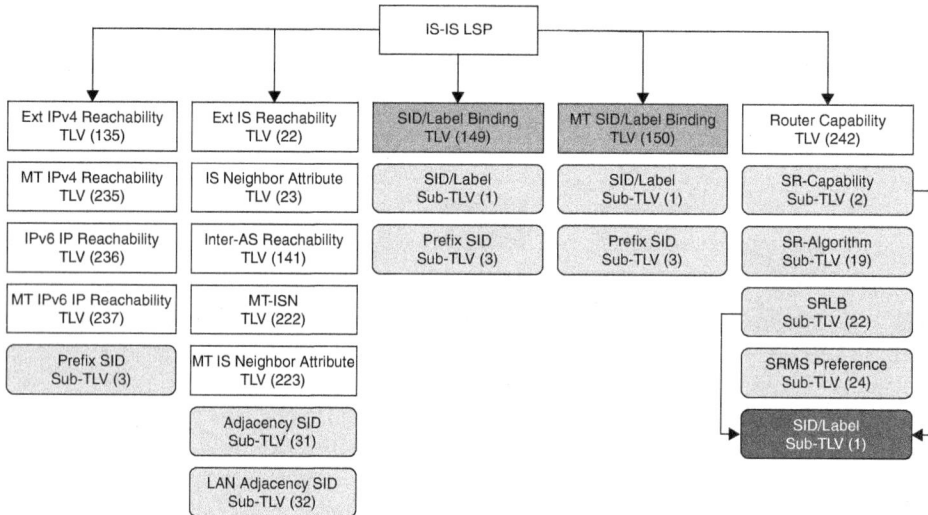

Figure 2-17   *IS-IS Extensions for SR-MPLS*

Note   IS-IS extensions for segment routing registered with IANA are available at https://www.iana.org/assignments/isis-tlv-codepoints/isis-tlv-codepoints.xhtml.

Segment Routing Capabilities

Segment routing capabilities in IS-IS are advertised using the Router Capability TLV, which has been augmented with the sub-TLVs presented in Table 2-1.

Table 2-1   *IS-IS Sub-TLVs for IS-IS Router Capability TLV (242)*

Value	Sub-TLV
2	Segment Routing Capability
19	Segment Routing Algorithm
22	Segment Routing Local Block (SRLB)
24	Segment Routing Mapping Server Preference (SRMS Preference)

Example 2-5 shows a packet capture of an IS-IS LSP with a Router Capability TLV (242) and a Segment Routing Capability sub-TLV (2). This sub-TLV is crucial to advertising the underlying data plane and SRGB.

Example 2-5 *IS-IS LSP with Segment Routing Capability Sub-TLV (2)*

```
IEEE 802.3 Ethernet
Logical-Link Control
ISO 10589 ISIS INTRA Domain Routing Information Exchange Protocol
ISO 10589 ISIS Link State Protocol Data Unit
<snip>
    LSP-ID: 0000.0000.0002.00-00
<snip>
    Router Capability (t=242, l=42)
        Type: 242
        Length: 42
        Router ID: 0x0a000002
        .... ...0 = S bit: False
        .... ..0. = D bit: False
        Segment Routing - Capability (t=2, l=9)
            1... .... = I flag: IPv4 support: True
            .0.. .... = V flag: IPv6 support: False
            Range: 8000
            SID/Label (t=1, l=3)
                Label: 16000
<snip>
```

The Segment Routing Capability sub-TLV consists of the following flags and fields:

- **MPLS IPv4 flag (I-flag):** Set on routers that can process SR-MPLS-encapsulated IPv4 packets.

- **MPLS IPv6 flag (V-flag):** Set on routers that can process SR-MPLS-encapsulated IPv6 packets.

- **Range:** Defines the number of entries in the SRGB.

- **SID/Label:** Defines the first value of the SRGB.

SID/Label and Range define the SRGB, which in our example starts at 16000 and ends at 23999, with a total of 8000 entries.

Example 2-6 shows a packet capture of an IS-IS LSP with a Router Capability TLV (242) and a Segment Routing Algorithm sub-TLV (19).

Example 2-6   *IS-IS LSP with Segment Routing Algorithm Sub-TLV (19)*

```
IEEE 802.3 Ethernet
Logical-Link Control
ISO 10589 ISIS INTRA Domain Routing Information Exchange Protocol
ISO 10589 ISIS Link State Protocol Data Unit
<snip>
    LSP-ID: 0000.0000.0002.00-00
<snip>
    Router Capability (t=242, l=42)
        Type: 242
        Length: 42
        Router ID: 0x0a000002
        .... ...0 = S bit: False
        .... ..0. = D bit: False
<snip>
        Segment Routing - Algorithms (t=19, l=3)
            Algorithm: Shortest Path First (SPF) (0)
            Algorithm: Strict Shortest Path First (SPF) (1)
            Algorithm: Unknown (128)
<snip>
```

The Segment Routing Algorithm sub-TLV shows all algorithms supported by a router and consists of the following flags and fields:

- **Algorithm:** Different metrics and constraints may be defined to compute the best path in the network based on the network operator's requirements. Two algorithms have been defined in RFC 8665:

  - **SPF algorithm (algorithm 0):** This is the well-known shortest path algorithm, which allows any transit node to overwrite the SPF computed at the source based on a local policy.

  - **Strict SPF algorithm (algorithm 1):** This is identical to algorithm 0 except that transit nodes cannot overwrite the SPF computed at the source.

Besides the well-known algorithms (0 and 1), the router in the example output supports algorithm 128, which has been defined by the operator. More details regarding custom algorithms are provided later in this chapter, in the section "IGP Flexible Algorithm (Flex Algo) (RFC 9350)."

Example 2-7 shows a packet capture of an IS-IS LSP with a Router Capability TLV (242) and an SRLB sub-TLV (22). Similarly to the Segment Routing Capability sub-TLV, it defines the starting point of the SRLB and its range.

Example 2-7   *IS-IS LSP with SRLB Sub-TLV (22)*

```
IEEE 802.3 Ethernet
Logical-Link Control
ISO 10589 ISIS INTRA Domain Routing Information Exchange Protocol
ISO 10589 ISIS Link State Protocol Data Unit
<snip>
    LSP-ID: 0000.0000.0002.00-00
<snip>
    Router Capability (t=242, l=42)
        Type: 242
        Length: 42
        Router ID: 0x0a000002
        .... ...0 = S bit: False
        .... ..0. = D bit: False
<snip>
        Segment Routing - Local Block (t=22, l=9)
            Flags: 0x00
            Range: 1000
            SID/Label (t=1, l=3)
                Label: 15000
<snip>
```

SID/Label and Range clearly define the SRLB, which in our example starts at 15000 and ends at 15999, with a total of 1000 entries.

A segment routing mapping server (SRMS) is required for SR–LDP interworking to provide a SID for an endpoint in the LDP domain. No additional functionality will be required to provide a label for an endpoint in the SR domain since LDP dynamically allocates a label for every route in the IGP by default. The interworking of SR and LDP, including migration steps, is covered in Chapter 5, "Migrating to Segment Routing."

The SRMS Preference sub-TLV (24) is optional and may be used to assign a preference (higher is better) to the SRMS advertisement in the presence of multiple mapping servers. In the absence of this sub-TLV, a default preference value of 128 will be assigned.

Segment Routing Identifiers (SIDs)

IS-IS advertises different types of SIDs associated with IGP prefix segments, IGP adjacency segments, and the binding segment. Table 2-2 shows the sub-TLV that is used to encode IGP Prefix SIDs:

Table 2-2   *IS-IS Sub-TLV for TLVs Advertising Prefix Reachability*

Value	Sub-TLV
3	Prefix-SID

The Prefix-SID sub-TLV may be present in the following TLVs:

- Extended IPv4 Reachability (TLV 135)

- Multi-Topology IPv4 Reachability (TLV 235)

- IPv6 IP Reachability (TLV 236)

- Multi-Topology IPv6 IP Reachability (TLV 237)

- SID/Label Binding TLV (149)

- Multi-Topology Binding TLV (150)

Example 2-8 shows a packet capture of an IS-IS LSP with an Extended IP Reachability
TLV (135) and a Prefix-SID sub-TLV (3). A Prefix-SID sub-TLV is associated with a prefix
advertised by a node.

Example 2-8   *IS-IS LSP with Prefix-SID Sub-TLV (3)*

```
IEEE 802.3 Ethernet
Logical-Link Control
ISO 10589 ISIS INTRA Domain Routing Information Exchange Protocol
ISO 10589 ISIS Link State Protocol Data Unit
<snip>
    LSP-ID: 0000.0000.0001.00-00
<snip>
    Extended IP Reachability (t=135, l=35)
        Type: 135
        Length: 35
        Ext. IP Reachability: 10.0.0.1/32
            Metric: 0
            0... .... = Distribution: Up
            .1.. .... = Sub-TLV: Yes
            ..10 0000 = Prefix Length: 32
            IPv4 prefix: 10.0.0.1
    <snip>
            subTLV: Prefix-SID (c=3, l=6)
                Code: Prefix-SID (3)
                Length: 6
                Flags: 0x40, Node-SID
                    0... .... = Re-advertisement: Not set
                    .1.. .... = Node-SID: Set
                    ..0. .... = no-PHP: Not set
                    ...0 .... = Explicit-Null: Not set
                    .... 0... = Value: Not set
                    .... .0.. = Local: Not set
                Algorithm: Shortest Path First (SPF) (0)
                SID/Label/Index: 0x00000001
<snip>
```

The Prefix-SID sub-TLV consists of the following flags and fields:

- **Re-advertisement flag (R-flag):** Set when the prefix is redistributed between different protocols or when it moves between IS-IS Level-1 and Level-2 (propagation and leaking).

- **Node-SID flag (N-flag):** Set when the Prefix-SID is a Node SID (that is, belongs to a router's loopback).

- **No Penultimate Hop Popping (PHP) flag (P-flag):** Set to disable the default PHP behavior.

- **Explicit NULL flag (E-flag):** Set to replace the Prefix-SID with the well-known explicit null value in the absence of PHP (with the P-flag set).

- **Value flag (V-flag):** Set to signal that the Prefix-SID carries a value instead of an index.

- **Local flag (L-flag):** Set to signal that the Prefix-SID value/index is locally significant instead of globally significant.

- **Algorithm:** As defined for the Segment Routing Algorithm sub-TLV.

- **SID/Label/Index:** This field may be a value or an index, depending on the V- and L-flags:

  - **V-flag and L-flag are equal to 0:** The field is a 4-byte index that defines the offset in the SRGB.

  - **V-flag and L-flag are equal to 1:** The field is a 3-byte local label (the 20 rightmost bits).

The packet capture in Example 2-8 shows that the IPv4 prefix 10.0.0.1/32 is assigned to a Node SID with an index of 1 for algorithm 0, which refers to Shortest Path First (SPF).

Table 2-3 shows the sub-TLV that is used to encode IGP Adjacency SIDs.

Table 2-3 *IS-IS Sub-TLVs for TLVs Advertising Neighbor Information*

Value	Sub-TLV
31	Adj-SID
32	LAN-Adj-SID

The Adj-SID sub-TLV may be present in the following TLVs:

- Extended IS Reachability (TLV 22)

- IS Neighbor Attribute (TLV 23)

- Inter-AS Reachability Information (TLV 141)

- Multi-Topology (MT) ISN (TLV 222)

- MT IS Neighbor Attribute (TLV 223)

Example 2-9 shows a packet capture of an IS-IS LSP with an Extended IS Reachability TLV (22) and an Adj-SID sub-TLV (31). Adj-SID sub-TLVs are associated with unidirectional IS-IS adjacencies advertised by a node.

Example 2-9   *IS-IS LSP with Adj-SID Sub-TLV (31)*

```
IEEE 802.3 Ethernet
Logical-Link Control
ISO 10589 ISIS INTRA Domain Routing Information Exchange Protocol
ISO 10589 ISIS Link State Protocol Data Unit
<snip>
    LSP-ID: 0000.0000.0001.00-00
<snip>
    Extended IS reachability (t=22, l=41)
        Type: 22
        Length: 41
        IS Neighbor: 0000.0000.0002.00
            IS neighbor ID: 0000.0000.0002.00
            Metric: 10
<snip>
            subTLV: Adj-SID (c=31, l=5)
                Code: Adj-SID (31)
                Length: 5
                Flags: 0x70, Backup, Value, Local Significance
                        0... .... = Outgoing Encapsulation: IPv4
                        .1.. .... = Backup: Set
                        ..1. .... = Value: Set
                        ...1 .... = Local Significance: Yes
                        .... 0... = Set: Not set
                        .... .0.. = Persistent: Not set
                Weight: 0x00
                .... 0000 0101 1101 1100 0000 = SID/Label/Index: 24000
<snip>
```

The Adj-SID sub-TLV consists of the following flags and fields:

- **Address-Family flag (F-flag):** Signals the forwarding encapsulation, where unset stands for IPv4 traffic and set for IPv6 traffic.

- **Backup flag (B-flag):** Set to signal the protection eligibility of an Adjacency SID through FRR in the event of a link failure.

- **Value flag (V-flag):** Set when the Adj-SID carries a value.

- **Local flag (L-flag):** Set when the Adj-SID is locally significant.

- **Set flag (S-flag):** Set when the Adj-SID refers to a set of adjacencies.

- **Persistent flag (P-flag):** Set when the Adj-SID is persistent across reloads/interface flaps (useful for static SR policies).

- **Weight:** Represents the weight used for load balancing purposes in the presence of parallel adjacencies with the same Adj-SID. A higher weight is preferred over a lower weight. For instance, two parallel adjacencies with weights of 1 and 3 will receive their share of traffic based on a 1:3 ratio, or 25%:75%.

In the packet capture shown in Example 2-9, you can see that the IPv4 IS-IS adjacency to neighbor 0000.0000.0002.00 is assigned the locally significant Adj-SID value of 24000, which is eligible for protection.

The LAN-Adj-SID sub-TLV is applicable to LAN networks with more than two IS-IS nodes and works similarly to the Adj-SID sub-TLV. It is rather uncommon to see LAN networks in service provider backbones.

SID/Label Binding

The SID/Label Binding TLVs, shown in Table 2-4, are required for a segment routing mapping server (SRMS) to advertise prefixes with their corresponding SIDs/labels.

Table 2-4   *IS-IS Top-Level TLVs*

Value	TLV
149	Segment Identifier/Label Binding
150	Multi-Topology Segment Identifier/Label Binding

Example 2-10 shows a packet capture of an IS-IS LSP with a SID/Label Binding TLV (149).

Example 2-10   *IS-IS LSP with a Segment Identifier/Label Binding TLV (149)*

```
IEEE 802.3 Ethernet
Logical-Link Control
ISO 10589 ISIS INTRA Domain Routing Information Exchange Protocol
ISO 10589 ISIS Link State Protocol Data Unit
<snip>
    LSP-ID: 0000.0000.0002.00-00
<snip>
    SID/Label Binding TLV (t=149, l=17)
        Type: 149
        Length: 17
        TLV Flags: 0x00
            0... .... = Flag F: Address Family: Not set
            .0.. .... = Flag M: Mirror Context: Not set
            ..0. .... = Flag S: Not set
            ...0 .... = Flag D: Not set
            .... 0... = Flag A: Attached: Not set
            .... .000 = Flag reserved: 0x0
```

```
Weight: 0
Range: 1
Prefix length: 32
Prefix: 10.0.0.254
SID/Label sub-TLV : Prefix SID
    SID/label sub-TLV type: Prefix SID (3)
    sub-TLV Flags: 0x00
        0... .... = Flag R: Re-advertisement: Not set
        .0.. .... = Flag N: Node-SID: Not set
        ..0. .... = Flag P: no-PHP: Not set
        ...0 .... = Flag E: Explicit-Null: Not set
        .... 0... = Flag V: Value: Not set
        .... .0.. = Flag L: Local: Not set
        .... ..00 = Flag reserved: 0x0
    sub-TLV Flags: 0x00
    Algorithm: 0
    SID/Label: 254
<snip>
```

The SID/Label Binding TLV consists of the following flags and fields:

- **Address-Family flag (F-flag):** Unset for IPv4 prefixes and set for IPv6 prefixes.

- **Mirror Context flag (M-flag):** Set if the SID relates to a mirrored context. (Refer to RFC 8402 for additional information on this use case.)

- **S-flag:** Unset if this TLV should not be leaked between IS-IS levels

- **D-flag:** Set when this TLV is leaked from Level 2 into Level 1, which prevents control plane loops.

- **Attached flag (A-flag):** May be set by the originator when the advertised prefixes and SIDs are directly connected to the originator. Must be cleared when the TLV is leaked to other areas/levels.

- **Range:** May be used to advertise a set of contiguous prefixes more efficiently, such as for grouping N prefixes into a single TLV instead of advertising Nx1 TLVs.

- **Prefix Length:** Prefix length in bits, such as 32 for an IPv4 loopback address.

- **Prefix:** Represents the prefix or forwarding equivalence class (FEC). For a Range value larger than 1, it marks the first prefix in a set of continuous prefixes.

The SID/Label binding in combination with the Prefix SID sub-TLV convey the relevant information that the IPv4 host route 10.0.0.254/32 is associated with SID index 254, which corresponds to an absolute value of 16254 when using an SRGB that starts at 16000.

Table 2-5 shows the sub-TLVs that may be present in the two SID/Label Binding TLVs. The Prefix SID sub-TLV was introduced earlier, in Table 2-2.

Table 2-5   *IS-IS Sub-TLVs for Segment Identifier/Label Binding TLVs*

Value	Sub-TLV
1	SID/Label
3	Prefix SID

The SID/Label sub-TLV may be present in the following TLVs:

- Segment Routing Capability sub-TLV (2)
- Segment Routing Local Block sub-TLV (22)
- SID/Label Binding TLV (149)
- Multi-Topology SID/Label Binding TLV (150)

Example 2-11 shows a packet capture of an IS-IS LSP with a SID/Label sub-TLV present in the Segment Routing Capability and Segment Routing Local Block sub-TLVs.

Example 2-11   *IS-IS LSP with SID/Label Sub-TLVs (1)*

```
IEEE 802.3 Ethernet
Logical-Link Control
ISO 10589 ISIS INTRA Domain Routing Information Exchange Protocol
ISO 10589 ISIS Link State Protocol Data Unit
<snip>
    LSP-ID: 0000.0000.0002.00-00
<snip>
    Router Capability (t=242, l=42)
        Type: 242
        Length: 42
        .... ...0 = S bit: False
        .... ..0. = D bit: False
        Segment Routing - Capability (t=2, l=9)
        Router ID: 0x0a000002
            1... .... = I flag: IPv4 support: True
            .0.. .... = V flag: IPv6 support: False
          Range: 8000
            SID/Label (t=1, l=3)
                Label: 16000
        Segment Routing - Local Block (t=22, l=9)
            Flags: 0x00
            Range: 1000
            SID/Label (t=1, l=3)
                Label: 15000
<snip>
```

The SID/Label sub-TLV, as the name implies, can either contain a SID (32-bit index) with a length of 4 bytes or an MPLS label (20-bit) with a length of 3 bytes.

In the packet capture shown in Example 2-11, you can see that the SID/Label for both SR Capability (SRGB) and SRLB points to MPLS labels of 16000 and 15000, respectively.

OSPF Extensions for Segment Routing (RFC 8665)

Router Information Opaque link-state advertisements (LSAs), Extended Prefix Opaque LSAs, and Link Opaque LSAs advertise the required SR parameters within the OSPF domain. Like IS-IS, OSPF also takes advantage of TLVs or sub-TLVs to encode the SR control plane information.

The OSPF TLVs and sub-TLVs highlighted in Figure 2-18 have been registered with the Internet Assigned Numbers Authority (IANA) as part of RFC 8665 to facilitate the distribution of SR-specific information.

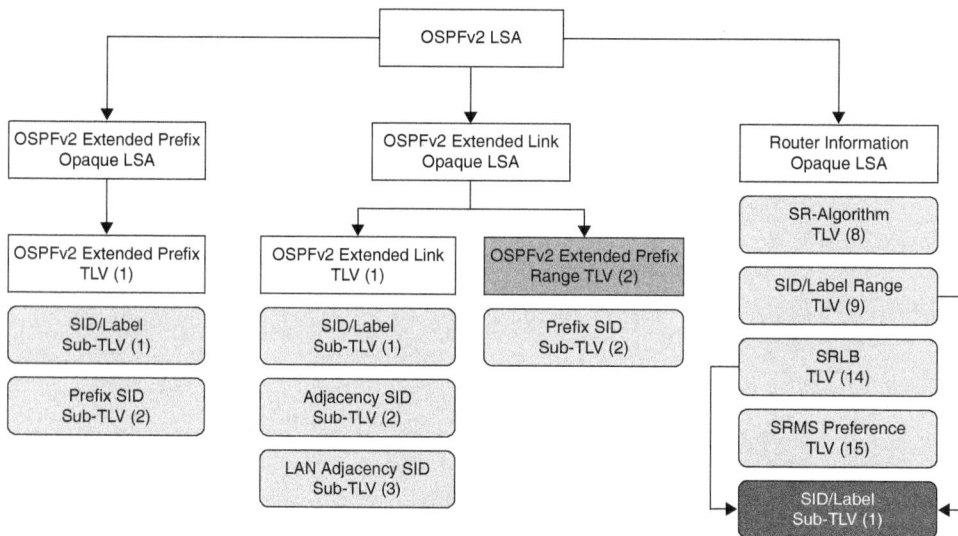

Figure 2-18 *OSPF Extensions for SR-MPLS*

Note OSPF extensions for segment routing that have been registered with IANA are listed at https://www.iana.org/assignments/ospf-parameters/ospf-parameters.xhtml#ri-tlv and. https://www.iana.org/assignments/ospfv2-parameters/ospfv2-parameters.xhtml.

Segment Routing Capabilities

Segment routing capabilities in OSPF are advertised using the Router Information Opaque LSA, which has been augmented with the TLVs presented in Table 2-6.

Table 2-6 *OSPF Router Information TLVs*

Value	TLV
8	Segment Routing Algorithm
9	SID/Label Range
14	Segment Routing Local Block (SRLB)
15	Segment Routing Mapping Server Preference (SRMS Preference)

Example 2-12 shows a packet capture of an OSPF LSA with a Segment Routing Algorithm TLV (8).

Example 2-12 *OSPF Opaque Router Information LSA with SR Algorithm TLV (8)*

```
Ethernet
Internet Protocol Version 4, Src: 192.168.0.0, Dst: 224.0.0.5
Open Shortest Path First
    OSPF Header
    LS Update Packet
        Number of LSAs: 1
        LSA-type 10 (Opaque LSA, Area-local scope), len 60
<snip>
            LS Type: Opaque LSA, Area-local scope (10)
            Link State ID Opaque Type: Router Information (RI) (4)
            Link State ID Opaque ID: 0
            Advertising Router: 10.0.0.1
<snip>
            Opaque Router Information LSA
<snip>
                SR-Algorithm
                    TLV Type: SR-Algorithm  (8)
                    TLV Length: 2
                    SR-Algorithm: Shortest Path First (0)
                    SR-Algorithm: Strict Shortest Path First (1)
<snip>
```

The Segment Routing Algorithm TLV shows all algorithms that are supported by a router. Besides the well-known algorithms (0 and 1), explained earlier in this chapter, in the section "Segment Routing Capabilities," no other algorithms have been defined by the operator. For more details regarding custom algorithms, see the section "IGP Flexible Algorithm (Flex Algo) (RFC 9350)," later in this chapter.

Example 2-13 shows a packet capture of an OSPF LSA with a SID/Label Range TLV (9). This TLV is crucial to advertising the SRGB.

Example 2-13   *OSPF Opaque Router Information LSA with SID/Label Range TLV (9)*

```
Ethernet
Internet Protocol Version 4, Src: 192.168.0.0, Dst: 224.0.0.5
Open Shortest Path First
    OSPF Header
    LS Update Packet
        Number of LSAs: 1
        LSA-type 10 (Opaque LSA, Area-local scope), len 60
<snip>
            LS Type: Opaque LSA, Area-local scope (10)
            Link State ID Opaque Type: Router Information (RI) (4)
            Link State ID Opaque ID: 0
            Advertising Router: 10.0.0.1
<snip>

            Opaque Router Information LSA
<snip>
                SID/Label Range  (Range Size: 8000)
                    TLV Type: SID/Label Range  (9)
                TLV Length: 12
                Range Size: 8000
                Reserved: 00
                SID/Label Sub-TLV  (SID/Label: 16000)
                    TLV Type: SID/Label (1)
                    TLV Length: 3
                    SID/Label: 16000
<snip>
```

The SID/Label Range TLV consists of the following field and sub-TLV:

■ **Range:** Defines the number of entries in the SRGB.

■ **SID/Label Sub-TLV (1):** Defines the first value of the SRGB.

SID/Label and Range define the SRGB, which in our example starts at 16000 and ends at 23999, with a total of 8000 entries. The SID/Label sub-TLV is discussed later in this chapter, in the section "Segment Routing Identifiers (SIDs)."

Example 2-14 shows a packet capture of an OSPF LSA with an SRLB TLV (14). Similarly to the previously described SID/Label Range TLV, it defines the starting point and range of the SRLB.

The SRLB TLV consists of the following field and sub-TLV:

■ **Range:** Defines the number of entries in the SRLB.

■ **SID/Label Sub-TLV (1):** Defines the first value of the SRLB.

Example 2-14   *OSPF Opaque Router Information LSA with SRLB TLV (14)*

```
Ethernet
Internet Protocol Version 4, Src: 192.168.0.1, Dst: 192.168.0.0
Open Shortest Path First
    OSPF Header
    LS Update Packet
        Number of LSAs: 14
<snip>
        LSA-type 10 (Opaque LSA, Area-local scope), len 84
<snip>
            LS Type: Opaque LSA, Area-local scope (10)
            Link State ID Opaque Type: Router Information (RI) (4)
            Link State ID Opaque ID: 0
            Length: 84
            Opaque Router Information LSA
<snip>
                SR Local Block  (Range Size: 1000)
                    TLV Type: SR Local Block (14)
                    TLV Length: 12
                    Range Size: 1000
                    Reserved: 00
                    SID/Label Sub-TLV  (SID/Label: 15000)
                        TLV Type: SID/Label (1)
                        TLV Length: 3
                        SID/Label: 15000
<snip>
```

SID/Label and Range clearly define the SRLB, which in our example starts at 15000 and ends at 15999, with a total of 1000 entries.

The SRMS Preference TLV (15) is optional and may be used to assign a preference (higher is better) to the SRMS advertisement in the presence of multiple mapping servers. In the absence of this sub-TLV, a default preference value of 128 will be assigned. The SRMS is covered in Chapter 5.

Segment Routing Identifiers (SIDs)

OSPF advertises different types of SIDs associated with IGP prefix segments, IGP adjacency segments, and the binding segment by using Extended Prefix or Extended Link Opaque LSAs. Table 2-7 shows the sub-TLVs that are used to encode IGP Adjacency SIDs:

Table 2-7   *OSPF Extended Link TLV Sub-TLVs*

Value	Sub-TLV
1	SID/Label
2	Adj-SID
3	LAN Adj-SID

The SID/Label sub-TLV may be present in the following TLVs:

- OSPFv2 Extended Prefix TLV (1)

- OSPFv2 Extended Link TLV (1)

- SID/Label Range TLV (9)

- SRLB TLV (14)

The SID/Label sub-TLV, as the name implies, can either contain a SID (32-bit index) with a length of 4 bytes or an MPLS label (20-bit) with a length of 3 bytes. Packet extracts in the section "Segment Routing Capabilities," earlier in this chapter, include the SID/Label sub-TLV for both SID/Label Range TLV and SRLB TLV.

The Adjacency SID sub-TLVs may be present in the Extended Link TLV.

Example 2-15 shows a packet capture of an OSPF LSA with an Adj-SID sub-TLV (2). Adj-SID sub-TLVs are associated with a unidirectional OSPF adjacency of the advertising node.

Example 2-15   *OSPF Extended Link Opaque LSA with Adj-SID Sub-TLV (2)*

```
Ethernet
Internet Protocol Version 4, Src: 192.168.0.1, Dst: 192.168.0.0
Open Shortest Path First
    OSPF Header
    LS Update Packet
<snip>
        LSA-type 10 (Opaque LSA, Area-local scope), len 80
<snip>
            Link State ID Opaque Type: OSPFv2 Extended Link Opaque LSA (8)
            Link State ID Opaque ID: 3
            Advertising Router: 10.0.0.1
<snip>
            OSPFv2 Extended Link Opaque LSA
                OSPFv2 Extended Link TLV  (Type: PTP      ID: 10.0.0.2
   Data: 192.168.0.0)
                    TLV Type: OSPFv2 Extended Link (1)
                    TLV Length: 56
                    Link Type: 1 - Point-to-point connection to another router
                    Reserved: 000000
                    Link ID: 10.0.0.2
                    Link Data: 192.168.0.0
                    Adj-SID Sub-TLV  (SID/Label: 24000)
                        TLV Type: Adj-SID (2)
                        TLV Length: 7
                            Flags: 0x60, (V) Value/Index Flag, (L) Local/Global Flag
                                0... .... = (B) Backup Flag: Not set
```

```
              .1.. .... = (V) Value/Index Flag: Set
              ..1. .... = (L) Local/Global Flag: Set
              ...0 .... = (G) Group Flag: Not set
              .... 0... = (P) Persistent Flag: Not set
        Reserved: 00
        Multi-Topology ID: 0
        Weight: 0
        SID/Label: 24000
<snip>
```

The Adj-SID sub-TLV consists of the following flags and fields:

- **Backup flag (B-flag):** Set to signal the protection eligibility of an Adjacency SID through FRR in the event of a link failure.

- **Value flag (V-flag):** Set when the Adj-SID carries a value as opposed to an index.

- **Local flag (L-flag):** Set when the Adj-SID is locally significant as opposed to globally significant.

- **Group flag (G-flag):** Set when the Adj-SID refers to a group of adjacencies and therefore may be used multiple times.

- **Persistent flag (P-flag):** Set when the Adj-SID is persistent across reloads/interface flaps (useful for static SR policies).

- **Multi-Topology ID:** Identifies the topology in the presence of multiple topologies. Ranges from 0 to 127, where 0 is reserved for the default topology.

- **Weight:** Represents the weight used for load balancing purposes in the presence of parallel adjacencies with the same Adj-SID. A higher weight is preferred over a lower weight. For instance, two parallel adjacencies with weights of 1 and 3 will receive their share of traffic based on a 1:3 ratio, or 25%:75%.

- **SID/Index/Label:** This field may be a value or an index, depending on the V- and L-flags:

  - **V-flag and L-flag are equal to 0:** The field is a 4-byte index that defines the offset in the SRGB.

  - **V-flag and L-flag are equal to 1:** The field is a 3-byte local label (the 20 rightmost bits).

In the packet capture shown in Example 2-15, you can see that the IPv4 OSPF adjacency to neighbor 10.0.0.2 is assigned the locally significant Adj-SID value 24000, which is not eligible for protection.

The LAN-Adj-SID is applicable to LAN networks with more than two OSPF nodes and works similarly to the Adj-SID. It is rather uncommon to see LAN networks in service provider backbones.

Table 2-8 shows the sub-TLVs that are used to encode IGP Prefix SIDs.

Table 2-8   *OSPF Extended Prefix TLV Sub-TLVs*

Value	Sub-TLV
1	SID/Label
2	Prefix-SID

The SID/Label sub-TLV was introduced in this chapter, in the section "Segment Routing Identifiers (SIDs)."

The Prefix-SID sub-TLV may be present in the following TLVs:

- OSPFv2 Extended Prefix TLV (1)

- OSPF Extended Prefix Range TLV (2)

Example 2-16 shows a packet capture of an OSPF LSA with a Prefix-SID sub-TLV (2). Prefix-SID sub-TLVs are associated with prefixes advertised by a node.

Example 2-16   *OSPF Extended Prefix Opaque LSA with Prefix-SID Sub-TLV (2)*

```
Ethernet
Internet Protocol Version 4, Src: 192.168.0.1, Dst: 192.168.0.0
Open Shortest Path First
    OSPF Header
    LS Update Packet
        Number of LSAs: 14
<snip>
        LSA-type 10 (Opaque LSA, Area-local scope), len 44
<snip>
            LS Type: Opaque LSA, Area-local scope (10)
            Link State ID Opaque Type: OSPFv2 Extended Prefix Opaque LSA (7)
            Link State ID Opaque ID: 1
            Advertising Router: 10.0.0.2
<snip>
        OSPFv2 Extended Prefix Opaque LSA
            OSPFv2 Extended Prefix TLV  (Type: Intra-Area
  Prefix: 10.0.0.2/32)
                TLV Type: OSPFv2 Extended Prefix (1)
                TLV Length: 20
                Route Type: Intra-Area (1)
                PrefixLength: 32
                Address Family: IPv4 Unicast (0)
                Flags: 0x40, (N) Node Flag
                Address Prefix: 10.0.0.2
                Prefix SID Sub-TLV  (SID/Label: 2)
                    TLV Type: Prefix SID (2)
                    TLV Length: 8
                    Flags: 0x00
```

```
                            .0.. .... = (NP) No-PHP Flag: Not set
                            ..0. .... = (M) Mapping Server Flag: Not set
                            ...0 .... = (E) Explicit-Null Flag: Not set
                            .... 0... = (V) Value/Index Flag: Not set
                            .... .0.. = (L) Local/Global Flag: Not set
                    Reserved: 00
                    Multi-Topology ID: 0
                    SR-Algorithm: Shortest Path First (0)
                    SID/Label: 2
<snip>
```

The Prefix SID sub-TLV consists of the following flags and fields:

- **No Penultimate Hop Popping (PHP) flag (NP-flag):** Set to disable the default PHP behavior.

- **Mapping Server flag (M-flag):** Set if the SID was advertised by a mapping server.

- **Explicit NULL flag (E-flag):** Set to replace the Prefix-SID with the well-known explicit null value in the absence of PHP (with the NP-flag set).

- **Value flag (V-flag):** Set to signal that the Prefix-SID carries a value instead of an index.

- **Local flag (L-flag):** Set to signal that the Prefix-SID value/index is locally significant instead of globally significant.

- **Multi-Topology ID:** Identifies the topology in the presence of multiple topologies. Ranges from 0 to 127, where 0 is reserved for the default topology.

- **Algorithm:** Different metrics and constraints may be defined to compute the best path in the network based on the network operator's requirements. Two algorithms have been defined in RFC 8665:

  - **SPF algorithm:** Well-known shortest path algorithm that allows any transit node to overwrite the SPF computed at the source based on a local policy.

  - **Strict SPF algorithm:** Identical to algorithm 0 except that transit nodes cannot overwrite the SPF computed at the source.

- **SID/Index/Label:** This field may be a value or an index, depending on the V- and L-flags:

  - **V-flag and L-flag are equal to 0:** The field is a 4-byte index that defines the offset in the SRGB.

  - **V-flag and L-flag are equal to 1:** The field is a 3-byte local label (the 20 rightmost bits).

In the packet capture shown in Example 2-16, you can see that the IPv4 prefix 10.0.0.2/32 is assigned to a Prefix-SID sub-TLV with an index of 2 for algorithm 0, which refers to SPF.

SID/Label Binding

The OSPF Extended Prefix Range TLV shown in Table 2-9 is required for a segment routing mapping server (SRMS) to advertise prefixes with their corresponding SIDs/labels.

Table 2-9   *OSPF Extended Link TLV*

Value	TLV
2	OSPF Extended Prefix Range

Example 2-17 shows a packet capture of an OSPF LSA with an OSPF Extended Prefix Range TLV (2). This TLV is useful when advertising a range of prefixes—for instance, in combination with an SRMS, where several contiguous prefixes belonging to the LDP domain have to be advertised within the SR domain.

Example 2-17   *OSPF Extended Prefix Opaque LSA with Extended Prefix Range TLV (2)*

```
Ethernet
Internet Protocol Version 4, Src: 192.168.0.1, Dst: 192.168.0.0
Open Shortest Path First
    OSPF Header
    LS Update Packet
        Number of LSAs: 14
<snip>
        LSA-type 10 (Opaque LSA, Area-local scope), len 48
<snip>
            LS Type: Opaque LSA, Area-local scope (10)
            Link State ID Opaque Type: OSPFv2 Extended Prefix Opaque LSA (7)
            Link State ID Opaque ID: 2
            Advertising Router: 10.0.0.2
<snip>
            OSPFv2 Extended Prefix Opaque LSA
                OSPFv2 Extended Prefix Range TLV   (Range Size: 1, Prefix:
    10.0.0.254/32)
                    TLV Type: OSPFv2 Extended Prefix Range (2)
                    TLV Length: 24
                    Prefix Length: 32
                    Address Family: IPv4 Unicast (0)
                    Range Size: 1
                    Flags: 0x00
                        0... .... = (IA) Inter-Area Flag: Not set
                    Reserved: 000000
                    Address Prefix: 10.0.0.254
                    Prefix SID Sub-TLV   (SID/Label: 254)
                        TLV Type: Prefix SID (2)
                        TLV Length: 8
                        Flags: 0x60, (NP) No-PHP Flag, (M) Mapping Server Flag
```

```
         .1.. .... = (NP) No-PHP Flag: Set
         ..1. .... = (M) Mapping Server Flag: Set
         ...0 .... = (E) Explicit-Null Flag: Not set
         .... 0... = (V) Value/Index Flag: Not set
         .... .0.. = (L) Local/Global Flag: Not set
     Reserved: 00
     Multi-Topology ID: 0
     SR-Algorithm: Shortest Path First (0)
     SID/Label: 254
<snip>
```

The OSPF Extended Prefix Range TLV consists of the following flags and fields:

- **Prefix Length:** Prefix length in bits (for example, 32 for an IPv4 loopback address).

- **Address-Family:** Unset for IPv4 prefixes.

- **Range Size:** May be used to advertise a set of contiguous prefixes more efficiently, such as to group N prefixes into a single TLV instead of advertising Nx1 TLVs.

- **Inter-Area flag (IA-flag):** Set for inter-area advertisement to be set by an ABR when advertising this TLV between areas.

- **Address Prefix:** Represents the prefix or forwarding equivalence class (FEC). For a range size value larger than 1, it marks the first prefix in a set of contiguous prefixes.

The Prefix SID sub-TLV (2) encodes the index 254 for prefix 10.0.0.254/32. The previous packet was originated by an SRMS, which you can tell by looking at the No-PHP and Mapping Server flags.

IGP Flexible Algorithm (Flex Algo) (RFC 9350)

Note   IGP Flexible Algorithm applies to both SR-MPLS and SRv6 but is covered in this section for convenience.

Traditionally, interior gateway protocols (IGPs) were quite limited in their capabilities to compute the best path for a given prefix through the network. The de facto standard for service provider networks is a metric-based Shortest Path First (SPF) algorithm to minimize the end-to-end metric between source and destination nodes. In most cases, the IGP metric is used for path computations; this is a static value set to achieve meaningful traffic forwarding across the network. A fundamental problem of this approach is the fact that the IGP topology and physical characteristics of the optical transport network (OTN) may be vastly different. Today's optical networks exhibit remarkable flexibility, enabling the configuration of virtually any arbitrary IP/MPLS topology on top of the underlying physical infrastructure of the optical network. Many service providers separate the optical and IP network teams into two different silos within the company, with limited exchange. Consequently, many network engineers consider the OTN as a black box, which may negatively impact the performance of upper layer protocols. Statically assigning IGP metrics is often challenging and can lead to unexpected behaviors, especially when experiencing network failures. The following are common IGP metric allocation methods:

- **Default metric or static metric:** The same metric is configured on all links, which minimizes the number of hops across the network. This approach works for highly symmetric networks, where the distance and bandwidth between two points of presence (PoPs) is comparable in the OTN for all interconnections.

- **Bandwidth-based metric:** Metrics are configured to achieve certain patterns of traffic flows across the network, providing a basic level of traffic engineering, usually preferring high-bandwidth links.

- **Latency-based metric:** IGP metrics are based on OTN distances or delay, which supposedly minimizes the latency across the network. Note that the OTN distance/delay may change when a backup path is activated due to a failure in the optical layer.

More complex use cases—for example, following an explicit path or avoiding certain links in the network—cannot be realized using baseline IGP functionality. Instead, traffic engineering must be deployed in the network, which comes at the cost of additional signaling protocols or tunneling states in the transport network in the case of RSVP-TE. Segment routing traffic engineering does not suffer from the same drawbacks as RSVP-TE, but it is more challenging to operate and troubleshoot compared to traditional IGP routing. RFC 9350 enhances link-state IGPs such as IS-IS and OSPF with the capability to compute constraints-based paths over the network. This new solution, called IGP Flexible Algorithm, can cover some basic traffic engineering use cases as part of the dynamic IGP path computation. As the name implies, it allows the creation of customized routing algorithms (flexible algorithms) to define specific forwarding behaviors based on different metrics or constraints. Essentially, IGP Flexible Algorithm enables network operators to segment a network into various topologies, each employing distinct Shortest Path First (SPF) computations to meet the specific needs of the services associated with a particular network slice.

IGP prefix segments are associated with tuples (prefix, topology, algorithm), and more than one segment may be associated with a prefix, as long as the tuple is unique. Multiple SIDs for a single prefix can be useful for achieving different forwarding behaviors across different paths to reach the same destination based on the algorithm.

Several algorithms are supported which can be pre-defined and supported by all devices by default or as defined by the operator. The idea of operator-defined algorithms is to alter the default metric-based shortest path calculation for segments. For instance, imagine that a service provider offers an end-to-end MACsec-encrypted path for its business services. Unfortunately, there are certain devices or links in the network topology that do not support MACsec. The operator could define a custom algorithm, also known as a flexible algorithm (or flex algo) to ensure that all business service traffic remains within the MACsec-capable network topology. The SPF algorithm minimizes the cost between the source and other nodes, only taking into account links and nodes that belong to the MACsec-capable network topology using such an operator-defined algorithm.

Figure 2-19 shows an example topology with different SPF trees calculated from R1's perspective, including a mix of unencrypted and encrypted paths. The default algorithm takes all nodes and links into account, whereas the operator-defined algorithm is limited to encrypted links.

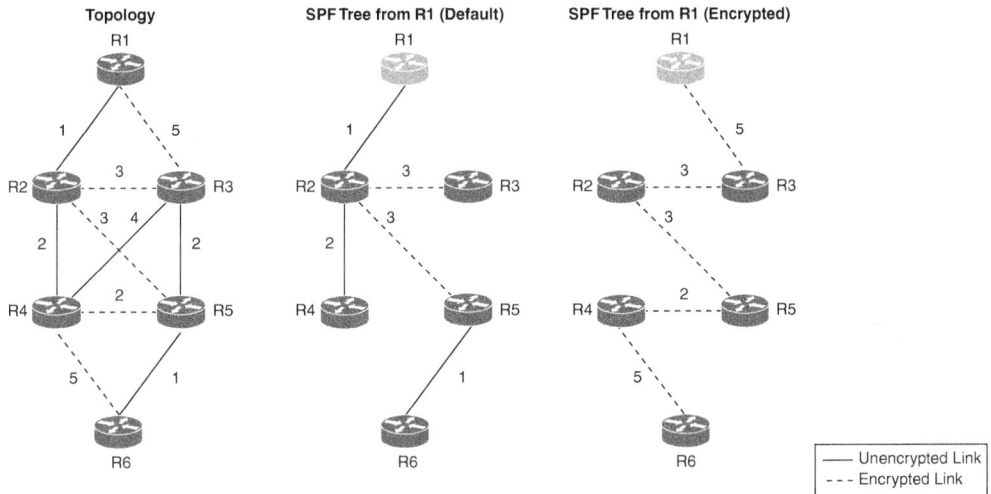

Figure 2-19 *Shortest Path Tree*

Two algorithms are part of the segment routing architecture by default:

- **Shortest Path First (SPF):** Forwards traffic along the IGP's SPF algorithm. Midpoints on the path may override the initially computed path based on local policies.

- **Strict Shortest Path First (Strict-SPF):** The same as SPF except that midpoints are instructed to honor the initial shortest path, basically ignoring local policies. The idea behind this restriction is that local policies may cause congestion or even lead to loops. FRR is allowed to alter the path.

Note   This section focuses on IS-IS extensions and refrains from repeating similar information for OSPF to reduce verbosity. The fundamentals are the same for both IS-IS and OSPF.

RFC 9350 defined the Flexible Algorithm Definition (FAD), which is a 3-tuple (triple) consisting of the following elements:

- Calculation type (for example, SPF or strict SPF)

- Metric type (for example, IGP metric, TE metric or delay)

- Set of constraints (for example, avoid certain links or SRLGs)

Note   As this book was being written, the IETF was working on an Internet Draft titled *Flexible Algorithms: Bandwidth, Delay, Metrics and Constraints* that proposes a generic per-flex algo metric to better distinguish different kinds of administrative metrics, such as jitter, reliability, or fiscal costs as per the network requirements.

The network operator assigns a unique identifier (flex algo) per FAD that must be consistent across the network on all devices participating in this algorithm. Generally, two or more network elements are assigned to advertise the FAD for redundancy reasons in case one of the designated nodes fails. Note that all devices in a network participate in algorithm 0 by default, whereas operator-defined flex algos may only be present on selected devices, as long as a contiguous end-to-end tree exists for an algorithm between source and destination. Finally, each Prefix SID is assigned a segment routing algorithm, which could be the default algorithm or an operator-defined flex algo. A single prefix may be associated with multiple Prefix SIDs and, consequently, multiple flex algos, if desired, to achieve different forwarding path selection behaviors.

Example 2-18 shows an IS-IS LSP for the prefix 10.0.0.1/32 with three Prefix SIDs belonging to three different algorithms. The Prefix SID of the default algorithm has a SID index of 1, whereas the flex algos 128 and 129 have indexes of 1001 (*0x3e9*) and 1101 (*0x44d*).

Example 2-18   *IS-IS LSP with Default Algo and Flex Algo Prefix SIDs*

```
IEEE 802.3 Ethernet
Logical-Link Control
ISO 10589 ISIS INTRA Domain Routing Information Exchange Protocol
ISO 10589 ISIS Link State Protocol Data Unit
<snip>
    LSP-ID: 0000.0000.0001.00-00
<snip>
    Extended IP Reachability (t=135, l=43)
        Type: 135
        Length: 43
        Ext. IP Reachability: 10.0.0.1/32
            Metric: 0
            0... .... = Distribution: Up
            .1.. .... = Sub-TLV: Yes
            ..10 0000 = Prefix Length: 32
          IPv4 prefix: 10.0.0.1
          SubCLV Length: 33
          subTLV: 32-bit Administrative Tag (c=1, l=4)
          subTLV: Prefix-SID (c=3, l=6)
              Code: Prefix-SID (3)
              Length: 6
            Flags: 0x40, Node-SID
```

```
            Algorithm: Shortest Path First (SPF) (0)
            SID/Label/Index: 0x00000001
        subTLV: Prefix-SID (c=3, l=6)
            Code: Prefix-SID (3)
            Length: 6
            Flags: 0x40, Node-SID
            Algorithm: Unknown (128)
            SID/Label/Index: 0x000003e9
        subTLV: Prefix-SID (c=3, l=6)
            Code: Prefix-SID (3)
            Length: 6
            Flags: 0x40, Node-SID
            Algorithm: Unknown (129)
            SID/Label/Index: 0x0000044d
<snip>
```

New IGP parameters have been registered with the Internet Assigned Numbers Authority (IANA) as part of RFC 9350 to facilitate the distribution of flex algo information.

Note IGP parameters for flex algo registered with IANA are listed at https://www.iana.org/assignments/igp-parameters/igp-parameters.xhtml. IS-IS extensions for flex algo registered with IANA are listed at https://www.iana.org/assignments/isis-tlv-codepoints/isis-tlv-codepoints.xhtml.

The IS-IS Flexible Algorithm Definition sub-TLV is advertised using the Router Capability TLV, as shown in Table 2-10. It has been enhanced with the algorithm type presented in Table 2-11. As its name implies, the role of the Flexible Algorithm Definition (FAD) sub-TLV is to distribute the FAD of all flex algos in the network.

Table 2-10 *IS-IS Sub-TLVs for IS-IS Router Capability TLV*

Value	Sub-TLV
26	Flexible Algorithm Definition (FAD)

The IS-IS FAD sub-TLV consists of the following flags and fields of interest:

- **Flex-Algorithm:** Flex algo (identifier) in the range 128–255.

- **Metric-Type:** Metric type to be used for the path calculation based on the values shown in Table 2-12.

- **Calc-Type:** IGP algorithm to be used for the path calculation (for example, SPF).

- **Priority:** Priority of the FAD in the range 0–255 (where the larger value takes precedence) acting as a tie-breaker in the event of contradicting definitions.

Table 2-11 *IGP Algorithm Type*

Value	Algorithm
128–255	Flexible

The IGP Flexible Algorithm specification distinguishes between the metric types shown in Table 2-12.

Table 2-12 *IGP Metric Type*

Type	Metric
0	IGP
1	Min Unidirectional Link Delay
2	Traffic Engineering Default

Example 2-19 shows a packet capture of an IS-IS LSP with a Router Capability TLV (242) and a Flexible Algorithm Definition sub-TLV (26). Note that any user-defined flex algo also creates an entry under the Segment Routing Algorithms sub-TLV. The example shows two user-defined flex algos, where Flexible Algorithm 128 uses unidirectional link delay as its metric type for the SPF calculations.

Example 2-19 *IS-IS LSP with FAD Sub-TLV (26)*

```
IEEE 802.3 Ethernet
Logical-Link Control
ISO 10589 ISIS INTRA Domain Routing Information Exchange Protocol
ISO 10589 ISIS Link State Protocol Data Unit
<snip>
    LSP-ID: 0000.0000.0002.00-00
<snip>
    Router Capability (t=242, l=71)
        Type: 242
        Length: 71
        Router ID: 0x0a000002
        .... ...0 = S bit: False
        .... ..0. = D bit: False
<snip>
        Segment Routing - Algorithms (t=19, l=4)
            Algorithm: Shortest Path First (SPF) (0)
            Algorithm: Strict Shortest Path First (SPF) (1)
            Algorithm: Unknown (128)
            Algorithm: Unknown (129)
<snip>
```

```
        Flexible Algorithm Definition (t=26, l=4)
            Flex-Algorithm: 128
            Metric-Type: Min Unidirectional Link Delay (1)
            Calculation-Type: Shortest Path First (SPF) (0)
            Priority: 128
<snip>
```

There are several sub-sub-TLVs for the FAD sub-TLV, as shown in Table 2-13. The role of these sub-sub-TLVs is to distribute the set of constraints belonging to a FAD.

Table 2-13   *IS-IS Sub-Sub-TLVs for Flexible Algorithm Definition Sub-TLV*

Type	Sub-Sub-TLV
0	Reserved
1	Flexible Algorithm Exclude Admin Group (FAEAG)
2	Flexible Algorithm Include-Any Admin Group
3	Flexible Algorithm Include-All Admin Group
4	Flexible Algorithm Definition Flags (FADF)
5	Flexible Algorithm Exclude SRLG (FAESRLG)

The three admin group sub-sub-TLVs share the same format, which includes the Extended Administrative Group (EAG) defined in RFC 7308, which relies on the concept of link colors. A *link color* refers to a specific bit in a bitstream that has a special meaning defined by the operator. For instance, the link color *blue* may refer to MACsec-enabled interfaces in the core and may be assigned bit 43, whereas the link color *red* may refer to microwave links and may be assigned bit 78. The EAG is flexible in size but must be a multiple of 4 bytes.

At a high level, the flex algo admin group sub-sub-TLVs express the following:

- **Flexible Algorithm Exclude Admin Group:** Defines which links should be excluded from the topology during the flex algo path computation (for example, microwave links).

- **Flexible Algorithm Include-Any Admin Group:** Defines which links should be included via an include any rule from the topology during the flex algo path computation (for example, MACsec OR low latency).

- **Flexible Algorithm Include-All Admin Group:** Defines which links should be included via an include all rule from the topology during the flex algo path computation (for example, MACsec AND low latency).

The Flexible Algorithm Definition flags (FADFs) are relevant to signal inter-area and external prefix calculation for a given flex algo. If all bits of the IS-IS FADF sub-TLV are 0, it may be omitted. Table 2-14 shows the FADF where bit 0 refers to the most significant bit.

Table 2-14 *IGP Flexible Algorithm Definition Flag*

Bit	Flag
0	Prefix Metric

Finally, the Flexible Algorithm Exclude SRLG sub-sub-TLV allows you to specify a shared risk link group (SRLG), which should be excluded from the topology during the flex algo path computation. This option is useful for defining disjointed paths between different flex algos where a link or node failure would affect only one flex algo but not both.

Example 2-20 shows a packet capture of an IS-IS LSP with a FAD sub-TLV (26) and a Flexible Algorithm Exclude Admin Group sub-sub-TLV (1).

Example 2-20 *IS-IS LSP with FAEAG Sub-Sub-TLV (1)*

```
IEEE 802.3 Ethernet
Logical-Link Control
ISO 10589 ISIS INTRA Domain Routing Information Exchange Protocol
ISO 10589 ISIS Link State Protocol Data Unit
<snip>
    LSP-ID: 0000.0000.0002.00-00
<snip>
        Flexible Algorithm Definition (t=26, l=26)
            Flex-Algorithm: 129
            Metric-Type: IGP Metric (0)
            Calculation-Type: Shortest Path First (SPF) (0)
            Priority: 128
            Flexible Algorithm Exclude Admin Group (t=1, l=20)
                Extended Admin Group[0]: 0x00000000
                Extended Admin Group[1]: 0x00000000
                Extended Admin Group[2]: 0x00000000
                Extended Admin Group[3]: 0x00000000
                Extended Admin Group[4]: 0x00000002
<snip>
```

Flexible Algorithm 129 was already included under the Segment Routing Algorithm sub-TLV shown in Example 2-19. That example shows that Flexible Algorithm 129 uses the IGP metric as its metric type but imposes a constraint for its SPF calculations to exclude a certain link color. The link color of the example corresponds to a configuration of an IOS XR device that uses bit position 129 to color links that should be avoided. IOS XR supports bit positions between 0 and 255 for link coloring, which explains why position 129 results in the EAG[4] value 0x2.

For comparison, Example 2-21 shows a packet capture for a flex algo where a certain type of link color should be included when calculating the end-to-end path. Note that this output also includes the Flexible Algorithm Definition flags and was extracted from a network running SRv6.

Example 2-21   *IS-IS LSP with FA I-A AG Sub-Sub-TLV (2) and FADF Sub-TLV (4)*

```
IEEE 802.3 Ethernet
Logical-Link Control   ·
ISO 10589 ISIS INTRA Domain Routing Information Exchange Protocol
ISO 10589 ISIS Link State Protocol Data Unit
<snip>
    LSP-ID: 0000.0000.0016.00-00
    Router Capability (t=242, l=57)
<snip>
        Flexible Algorithm Definition (t=26, l=29)
            Flex-Algorithm: 129
            Metric-Type: IGP Metric (0)
            Calculation-Type: Shortest Path First (SPF) (0)
            Priority: 100
            Flexible Algorithm Include-Any Admin Group (t=2, l=20)
                Extended Admin Group[0]: 0x00000000
                Extended Admin Group[1]: 0x00000000
                Extended Admin Group[2]: 0x00000000
                Extended Admin Group[3]: 0x00000000
                Extended Admin Group[4]: 0x00000002
            Flexible Algorithm Definition Flags (t=4, l=1)
    SRv6 Locator (t=27, l=108)
<snip>
```

The proliferation of segment routing deployments has led to the requirement to signal link attributes per application (for example, RSVP-TE, SR Policy, or LFA), where one or more applications may use the same or different attributes on a link. This initial functionality was introduced as part of RFC 8919 for IS-IS and RFC 8920 for OSPF and defines the following link attribute application identifiers:

- **Bit 0:** RSVP-TE (R-bit)

- **Bit 1:** Segment Routing Policy (S-bit)

- **Bit 2:** Loop-Free Alternate (F-bit)

A flex algo relies on link attributes to honor the set of constraints that are part of the FAD and considered during the path calculation. RFC 9350 introduces an additional bit for the flex algo application, as shown in Table 2-15.

Table 2-15   *Link Attribute Application Identifier*

Bit	Identifier
3	Flexible Algorithm (X-bit)

Example 2-22 shows an IS-IS LSP with link attributes belonging to the flex algo application for algorithm 129. The same pattern that was observed previously for the Extended Admin Group (EAG) under the Flexible Algorithm Definition shows up under the Application-Specific Link Attribute sub-TLV.

Example 2-22   *IS-IS LSP with Application-Specific Link Attributes sub-TLV (16)*

```
IEEE 802.3 Ethernet
Logical-Link Control
ISO 10589 ISIS INTRA Domain Routing Information Exchange Protocol
ISO 10589 ISIS Link State Protocol Data Unit
<snip>
    LSP-ID: 0000.0000.0016.00-00
<snip>
    Multi Topology IS Reachability (t=222, l=177)
        Type: 222
        Length: 177
        0000 .... .... .... = Reserved: 0x0
        .... 0000 0000 0010 = Topology ID: IPv6 routing topology (2)
        IS Neighbor: 0000.0000.0013.00
            IS neighbor ID: 0000.0000.0013.00
            Metric: 10
            SubCLV Length: 164
          subTLV: Link Local/Remote Identifiers (c=4, l=8)
          subTLV: Maximum link bandwidth (c=9, l=4)
          subTLV: Application-Specific Link Attributes (c=16, l=26)
                Code: Application-Specific Link Attributes (16)
                Length: 26
                0... .... = Legacy flag (L): Not set
                .000 0001 = SABM Length: 1
                0... .... = Reserved (R): Not set
                .000 0001 = UDABM Length: 1
                Standard Application Identifier Bit Mask: 0x10, FA bit (X)
                    0... .... = RSVP-TE bit (R): Not set
                    .0.. .... = Segment Routing Policy bit (S): Not set
                    ..0. .... = Loop-Free Alternate (LFA) bit (F): Not set
                    ...1 .... = Flexible Algorithm bit (X): Set
                User-Defined Application Identifier Bit Mask: 10
                subTLV: Extended Administrative Group (c=14, l=20)
                    Code: Extended Administrative Group (14)
                    Length: 20
                    Extended Admin Group[0]: 0x00000000
                    Extended Admin Group[1]: 0x00000000
                    Extended Admin Group[2]: 0x00000000
                    Extended Admin Group[3]: 0x00000000
                    Extended Admin Group[4]: 0x00000002
<snip>
```

The Flexible Algorithm Prefix Metric (FAPM) sub-TLV shown in Table 2-16 allows you to set a flex algo–specific metric to a prefix associated with this algorithm.

Table 2-16 *IS-IS Sub-TLV for TLVs Advertising Prefix Reachability*

Type	Sub-TLV
6	Flexible Algorithm Prefix Metric (FAPM)

The FAPM sub-TLV consists of the following fields:

- **Flex-Algorithm:** Specifies the flex algo (ranges from 128 to 255).

- **Metric:** Specifies the metric of the flex algo–specific prefix.

MP-BGP Extensions

BGP relies on BGP UPDATE messages to transfer its routing information to other peers within the same autonomous system (iBGP) or to external autonomous systems (eBGP). MP-BGP UPDATE messages are more convoluted than IGP link-state updates and are reiterated in this section. MP-BGP UPDATE messages have the generic format shown in Figure 2-20.

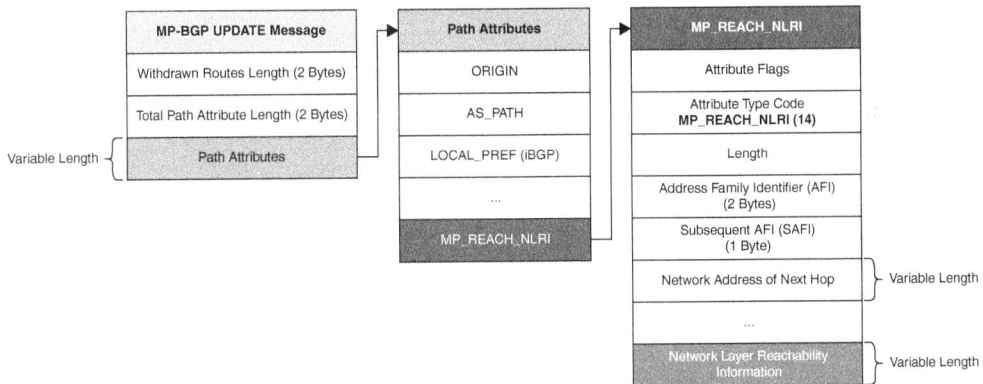

Figure 2-20 *MP-BGP UPDATE Message (Generic)*

BGP UPDATE messages include a variable number of path attributes, which are classified as follows:

- **Well-known mandatory:** Must be present and recognized by all BGP implementations.

- **Well-known discretionary:** May be present but must be recognized by all BGP implementations.

- **Optional transitive:** May be recognized by a BGP implementation but must be advertised to peers.

- **Optional non-transitive:** May be recognized by a BGP implementation but must only be advertised to peers if the attribute is recognized.

RFC 4760 introduces two new optional, non-transitive path attributes to extend BGP's capability to encode routing information of multiple network layer protocols (for example, L2VPN, L3VPN, BGP-LU, BGP-LS):

- Multiprotocol Reachable Network Layer Reachability Information (MP_REACH_NLRI)

- Multiprotocol Unreachable Network Layer Reachability Information (MP_UNREACH_NLRI)

Those attributes are used to carry sets of reachable or unreachable destinations and can be thought of as BGP containers for carrying routing information. BGP attributes such as MP_REACH_NLRI provide a flexible way to encode routing information, similar to how IGPs rely on TLVs. In fact, BGP also takes advantage of TLV for some address families, especially when advertising SR-related information.

The Address Family Identifier (AFI) and Subsequent Address Family Identifier (SAFI) fields identify the address family of the routing information encoded in the NLRI, as shown in Table 2-17.

Table 2-17 *Common BGP Address Families*

BGP Address Family	AFI	SAFI
IPv4 Unicast	1	1
IPv4 Multicast	1	2
IPv6 Unicast	2	1
IPv6 Multicast	2	2
IPv4 Labeled Unicast	1	4
IPv6 Labeled Unicast	2	4
IPv4 Labeled VPN Unicast	1	128
IPv6 Labeled VPN Unicast	2	128
Layer-2 VPN EVPN	25	70
Link-State	16388	71

Note   Address Family Identifier (AFI) and Subsequent Address Family Identifier (SAFI) values for Multiprotocol BGP registered with IANA are listed at https://www.iana.org/assignments/address-family-numbers/address-family-numbers.xhtml and https://www.iana.org/assignments/safi-namespace/safi-namespace.xhtml.

The following sections introduce segment routing (SR-MPLS) extensions to the BGP control plane required to advertise the BGP Prefix SID and link-state database between BGP speakers. Note that the following sections are limited to new TLVs and sub-TLVs defined as part of the corresponding segment routing extension RFCs. The displayed packet captures support the visualization of the underlying control plane.

SR Prefix SID Extensions for BGP (RFC 8669)

The BGP Prefix SID is a new optional, transitive BGP path attribute that takes advantage of TLVs to encode its information. The Label-Index TLV contained within the path attribute is only relevant for IPv4/IPv6 labeled unicast prefixes and is ignored for other address families.

The generic BGP UPDATE message format shown in Figure 2-20 changes slightly, as Figure 2-21 illustrates.

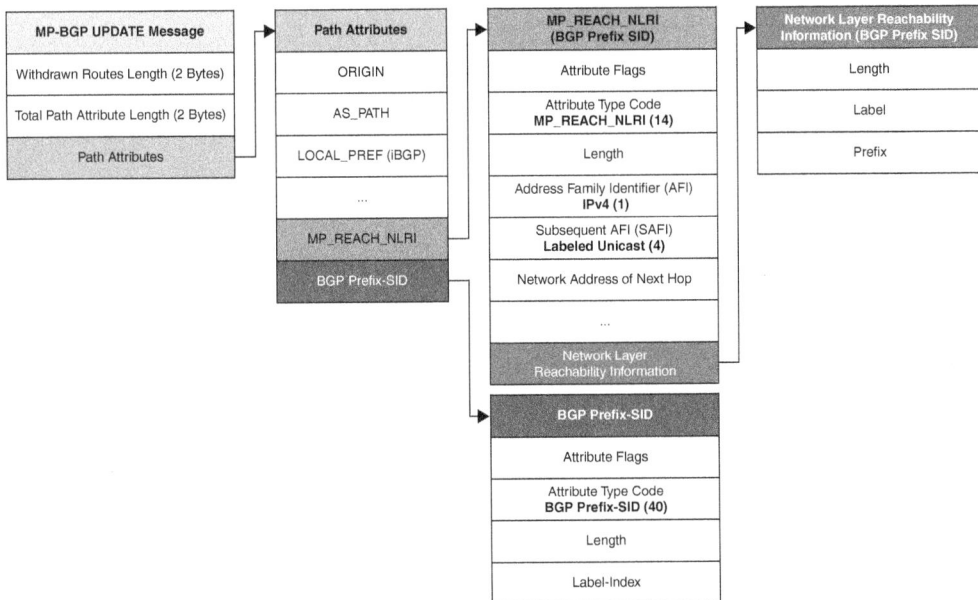

Figure 2-21   *BGP UPDATE Message Format (BGP Prefix SID)*

The newly defined BGP Prefix SID attribute is attached to a BGP labeled unicast prefix that stores the prefix and corresponding locally allocated label of the advertising BGP speaker.

New BGP path attributes and a new TLV have been registered with the Internet Assigned Numbers Authority (IANA) as part of RFC 8669 to facilitate the distribution of SR-specific information.

> **Note**   BGP extensions for segment routing registered with IANA are listed at https://www.iana.org/assignments/bgp-parameters/bgp-parameters.xhtml.

Table 2-18 shows the newly defined BGP Prefix SID path attribute, which contains the TLVs shown in Table 2-19.

Table 2-18   *BGP Path Attributes*

Value	Path Attribute
40	BGP Prefix SID

Table 2-19   *BGP Prefix SID TLV Types*

Value	TLV
1	Label-Index
3	Originator SRGB

Example 2-23 shows a packet capture of a BGP UDPATE message with the BGP Prefix SID attribute (40) and a Label Index TLV (1).

Example 2-23   *BGP UPDATE with Prefix-SID Attribute*

```
Ethernet
Internet Protocol Version 4, Src: 10.0.0.2, Dst: 10.0.0.1
Transmission Control Protocol, Src Port: 179, Dst Port: 16169
Border Gateway Protocol - UPDATE Message
<snip>
    Path attributes
        Path Attribute - MP_REACH_NLRI
            Flags: 0x90, Optional, Extended-Length, Non-transitive, Complete
            Type Code: MP_REACH_NLRI (14)
            Length: 17
            Address family identifier (AFI): IPv4 (1)
            Subsequent address family identifier (SAFI): Labeled Unicast (4)
            Next hop: 10.0.0.2
            Number of Subnetwork points of attachment (SNPA): 0
            Network Layer Reachability Information (NLRI)
                Label Stack=16003 (bottom) IPv4=10.0.0.3/32
                    MP Reach NLRI Prefix length: 56
                    MP Reach NLRI Label Stack: 16003 (bottom)
                    MP Reach NLRI IPv4 prefix: 10.0.0.3
        <snip>
```

```
Path Attribute - BGP Prefix-SID
        Flags: 0xc0, Optional, Transitive, Complete
            1... .... = Optional: Set
            .1.. .... = Transitive: Set
            ..0. .... = Partial: Not set
            ...0 .... = Extended-Length: Not set
            .... 0000 = Unused: 0x0
        Type Code: BGP Prefix-SID (40)
        Length: 10
        Label-Index: 3
            Type: Label-Index (1)
            Length: 7
            Reserved: 00
            Label-Index Flags: 0x0000
            Label-Index Value: 3
<snip>
```

The Label Index TLV consists of the 32-bit Label Index value, which represents the index of the SID. The Label Index TLV provides guidance to the receiving BGP speaker about which label should be allocated locally to this prefix when updating the next hop to a local loopback address before advertising it further. The outgoing label is always derived from the label field of the network layer reachability information (NLRI) contained within the BGP UPDATE message.

Example 2-23 shows that the prefix 10.0.0.3/32 is associated with the label 16003, which matches the content of the BGP Prefix SID with index 3. The advertising BGP speaker—possibly an inline route reflector—allocated the local label based on the *hint* stored in the BGP Prefix SID.

The Originator SRGB TLV is optional and could be used to propagate the SRGB of the prefix originator. However, it is preferrable to derive the SRGB from the local configuration.

BGP Link-State Extensions for SR (RFC 9085)

IGP topology visibility was traditionally restricted to a single domain, which limited the end-to-end view across multiple network domains. The segment routing architecture (RFC 8402) supports different modes of the control plane:

- **Distributed:** In the most common scenario, all nodes have the same end-to-end view of the network topology and can individually compute the best path. Ingress PE devices can steer traffic into an SR policy, which may contain one or more segments.

- **Centralized:** In the distributed scenario, nodes may not have the necessary link-state information to compute an end-to-end path. For instance, segmented networks with multiple domains or nodes requiring disjointed paths are unfeasible use cases with a distributed control plane. In those cases, an SR controller, commonly called a Path Computation Element (PCE), takes care of the path computation and signals the SR policy to the ingress PE device.

■ **Hybrid:** This is a mix of distributed and centralized control plane in which the SR controller is queried for destinations that lie outside the local domain. Destinations within the local domain are computed by the node itself. This approach takes some load off the controller, which is beneficial to the overall scale.

The BGP Link-State (BGP-LS) extension facilitates the exchange of IGP link-state and traffic engineering information using the BGP control plane, which is required for a centralized control plane scenario that relies on an SR controller. RFC 7752 introduced a new BGP network layer reachability information (NLRI) format (BGP-LS Link NLRI) that provides the flexibility to encode IGP topology information such as the following:

■ Nodes

■ Links

■ IP addresses

■ IGP and TE metric

By having one or more BGP-LS feeds per network domain, the entire end-to-end topology becomes visible. Potential consumers of those feeds are other routers or network controllers (PCE) that compute the path and signal the SR policy to the ingress PE nodes. Figure 2-22 shows a hierarchical network topology where each area border router injects the link-state information of its local domains into BGP and advertises it toward the PCE.

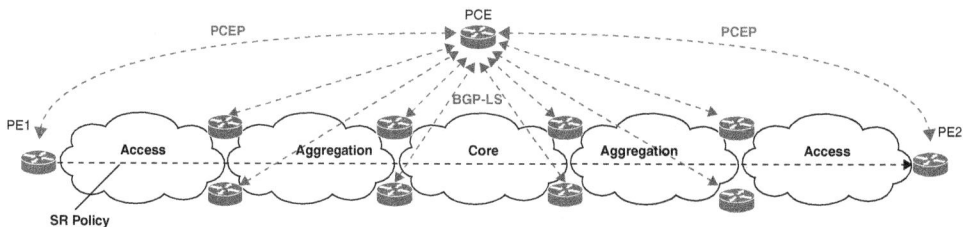

Figure 2-22   *BGP Link-State Control Plane*

Note that any node within a domain could be designated to inject its link-state information into BGP, but the ABRs are an obvious choice because they are redundant, attached to two domains, and generally run BGP. The combination of all feeds allows the central controller to compute an end-to-end path from PE1 to PE2 and signal the SR policy using the Path Computation Element Protocol (PCEP) to an ingress PE node.

Note BGP-LS extensions for segment routing registered with IANA are listed at https://www.iana.org/assignments/bgp-ls-parameters/bgp-ls-parameters.xhtml.

BGP-LS uses the TLVs presented in Table 2-20 to carry the IGP-equivalent topology information.

Table 2-20 *BGP-LS NLRI and Attribute TLVs*

TLV	Type	Description	IS-IS SR Extensions (RFC 8667)	OSPF SR Extensions (RFC 8665)
1034	Node	Segment Routing Capabilities	SR-Capabilities Sub-TLV (2)	SID/Label Range TLV (9)
1035	Node	Segment Routing Algorithm	SR-Algorithm Sub-TLV (19)	SR-Algorithm TLV (8)
1036	Node	Segment Routing Local Block	SR Local Block Sub-TLV (22)	SR Local Block TLV (14)
1037	Node	SRMS Preference	SRMS Preference Sub-TLV (19)	SRMS Preference TLV (15)
1099	Link	Adjacency SID	Adj-SID Sub-TLV (31)	Adj-SID Sub-TLV (2)
1100	Link	LAN Adjacency SID	LAN-Adj-SID Sub-TLV (32)	LAN Adj-SID Sub-TLV (3)
1158	Prefix	Prefix SID	Prefix-SID Sub-TLV (3)	Prefix-SID Sub-TLV (2)
1159	Prefix	Range	SID/Label Binding TLV (149)	OSPF Extended Prefix Range TLV (2)
1161	Node	SID/Label	SID/Label Sub-TLV (1)	SID/Label Sub-TLV (1)
1170	Prefix	Prefix Attribute Flags	Prefix Attribute Flags Sub-TLV (4)	Flags of OSPFv2 Extended Prefix TLV (1)
1171	Prefix	Source Router Identifier	IPv4/IPv6 Source Router ID Sub-TLV (11/12)	Prefix Source Router Address Sub-TLV (5)
1172	Link	L2 Bundle Member Attributes	L2 Bundle Member Attributes TLV (25)	L2 Bundle Member Attributes TLV (24)
1174	Prefix	Source OSPF Router-ID	N/A	Prefix Source OSPF Router-ID Sub-TLV (4)

Note   The following packet captures have been collected in an IS-IS topology. The output would look similar for OSPF.

Example 2-24 shows a packet capture of a BGP UDPATE message with the BGP-LS attribute (29) and SR Capability, SR Algorithm, and SR Local Block TLVs.

Example 2-24   *BGP UPDATE with BGP-LS Attribute (SR Capability, Algo and LB)*

```
Ethernet
Internet Protocol Version 4, Src: 10.0.0.3, Dst: 10.0.0.2
Transmission Control Protocol, Src Port: 43856, Dst Port: 179
Border Gateway Protocol - UPDATE Message
    Marker: ffffffffffffffffffffffffffffffff
    Length: 179
    Type: UPDATE Message (2)
    Withdrawn Routes Length: 0
    Total Path Attribute Length: 156
    Path attributes
        Path Attribute - MP_REACH_NLRI
            Flags: 0x90, Optional, Extended-Length, Non-transitive, Complete
            Type Code: MP_REACH_NLRI (14)
          Length: 52
          Address family identifier (AFI): BGP-LS (16388)
          Subsequent address family identifier (SAFI): BGP-LS (71)
          Next hop: 10.0.0.3
          Number of Subnetwork points of attachment (SNPA): 0
          Network Layer Reachability Information (NLRI)
              BGP-LS NLRI
<snip>
        Path Attribute - ORIGIN: IGP
        Path Attribute - AS_PATH: empty
        Path Attribute - LOCAL_PREF: 100
        Path Attribute - BGP-LS Attribute
            Flags: 0x80, Optional, Non-transitive, Complete
            Type Code: BGP-LS Attribute (29)
            Length: 83
            Link State
<snip>
                SR Capabilities
                    Type: 1034
                    Length: 12
                    Flags: 0x80, MPLS IPv4 flag (I)
                        1... .... = MPLS IPv4 flag (I): Set
```

```
                            .0. . . . . . . = MPLS IPv6 flag (V): Not set
                            ..00 0000 = Reserved: 0x00
                    Range Size: 8000
                    Type: 1161
                    Length: 3
                    . . . . 0000 0011 1110 1000 0000 = From Label: 16000
            SR Algorithm
                    Type: 1035
                    Length: 4
                    SR Algorithm: 0
                    SR Algorithm: 1
                    SR Algorithm: 128
                    SR Algorithm: 129
            SR Local Block
                    Type: 1036
                    Length: 12
                    Flags: 0x00
                    Range Size: 1000
                    Type: 1161
                    Length: 3
                    . . . . 0000 0011 1010 1001 1000 = From Label: 15000
<snip>
```

The SID/Label TLV, as the name implies, contains the value of the SID and is attached to the SR Capabilities and SR Local Block (SRLB) TLVs as a sub-TLV, as shown in Example 2-24.

The SR Capabilities, SR Algorithm, SRLB, and SRMS TLVs were presented earlier in this chapter, in the sections "IS-IS Extensions for Segment Routing (RFC 8667)" and "OSPF Extensions for Segment Routing (RFC 8665)," The SR node of the capture advertises the following SR parameters:

- **SRGB:** 16000–23999

- **SRLB:** 15000–15999

- **SR-MPLS:** With IPv4 encapsulation and algorithms 0, 1, 128, and 129

Note   Examples 2-5, 2-6, and 2-7 show the IS-IS TLVs that correspond to those in Example 2-24.

Example 2-25 shows a packet capture of a BGP UDPATE message with the BGP-LS attribute (29) and two Adjacency SIDs.

Example 2-25   *BGP UPDATE with BGP-LS Attribute (Adjacency SID)*

```
Ethernet
Internet Protocol Version 4, Src: 10.0.0.2, Dst: 10.0.0.3
Transmission Control Protocol, Src Port: 179, Dst Port: 43856
Border Gateway Protocol - UPDATE Message
    Marker: ffffffffffffffffffffffffffffffff
    Length: 331
    Type: UPDATE Message (2)
    Withdrawn Routes Length: 0
    Total Path Attribute Length: 308
    Path attributes
        Path Attribute - MP_REACH_NLRI
        Path Attribute - ORIGIN: IGP
        Path Attribute - AS_PATH: empty
        Path Attribute - LOCAL_PREF: 100
        Path Attribute - CLUSTER_LIST: 10.0.0.2
        Path Attribute - ORIGINATOR_ID: 10.0.0.3
        Path Attribute - BGP-LS Attribute
            Flags: 0x80, Optional, Non-transitive, Complete
            Type Code: BGP-LS Attribute (29)
            Length: 175
            Link State
<snip>
                Adjacency SID TLV
                    Type: 1099
                    Length: 7
                    Flags: 0x70, Backup Flag (B), Value Flag (V), Local Flag (L)
                        0... .... = Address-Family flag (F): Not set
                        .1.. .... = Backup Flag (B): Set
                        ..1. .... = Value Flag (V): Set
                        ...1 .... = Local Flag (L): Set
                        .... 0... = Set Flag (S): Not set
                        .... .0.. = Persistent Flag (P): Not set
                    Weight: 0
                    .... 0000 0101 1101 1100 0000 = SID/Label: 24000
                Adjacency SID TLV
                    Type: 1099
                    Length: 7
                    Flags: 0x30, Value Flag (V), Local Flag (L)
                        0... .... = Address-Family flag (F): Not set
                        .0.. .... = Backup Flag (B): Not set
                        ..1. .... = Value Flag (V): Set
                        ...1 .... = Local Flag (L): Set
```

```
                    .... 0... = Set Flag (S): Not set
                    .... .0.. = Persistent Flag (P): Not set
                Weight: 0
                .... 0000 0101 1101 1100 0001 = SID/Label: 24001
<snip>
```

The Adjacency SID and LAN Adjacency SID TLVs were presented earlier in this chapter, in sections "IS-IS Extensions for Segment Routing (RFC 8667)" and "OSPF Extensions for Segment Routing (RFC 8665)." The SR node of the capture advertises the following adjacency parameters:

- Locally significant and protected adjacency SID associated with MPLS label 24000

- Locally significant and unprotected adjacency SID associated with MPLS label 24001

The L2 Bundle Member Attributes TLV defined in RFC 8668 (IS-IS) and RFC 9356 (OSPF) provides bundle member visibility for Layer 3 bundle interfaces (LAGs). Prior to those RFCs, link attribute information was restricted to the Layer 3 interface associated with the IGP adjacency, which prevented operators from steering traffic flows over specific physical interfaces (bundle members). Such a requirement usually stems from the fact that not all bundle members are considered equal in a set of parallel links between two nodes. These are potential use cases:

- Bundle members may use different paths in the optical transport network (OTN), resulting in different latency.

- Operators may like to distribute certain traffic types across dedicated bundle members.

Besides link attributes related to bandwidth, loss, and delay, Adjacency SIDs are advertised per bundle member and allow more fine-grained traffic steering over bundle interfaces.

Example 2-26 shows a packet capture of a BGP UDPATE message with the BGP-LS attribute (29) and two Prefix SIDs and Prefix Attribute Flags and Source Router Identifier TLVs.

Example 2-26 *BGP UPDATE with BGP-LS Attribute (Prefix SIDs and others)*

```
Ethernet
Internet Protocol Version 4, Src: 10.0.0.2, Dst: 10.0.0.3
Transmission Control Protocol, Src Port: 179, Dst Port: 43856
<snip>
Border Gateway Protocol - UPDATE Message
    Marker: ffffffffffffffffffffffffffffffff
    Length: 184
    Type: UPDATE Message (2)
    Withdrawn Routes Length: 0
```

```
        Total Path Attribute Length: 161
        Path attributes
            Path Attribute - MP_REACH_NLRI
            Path Attribute - ORIGIN: IGP
            Path Attribute - AS_PATH: empty
            Path Attribute - LOCAL_PREF: 100
            Path Attribute - CLUSTER_LIST: 10.0.0.2
            Path Attribute - ORIGINATOR_ID: 10.0.0.3
            Path Attribute - BGP-LS Attribute
                Flags: 0x80, Optional, Non-transitive, Complete
                Type Code: BGP-LS Attribute (29)
                Length: 65
                Link State
<snip>
                        Prefix SID TLV
                            Type: 1158
                            Length: 8
                            Flags: 0x40, Node-SID (N)
                                0... .... = Re-advertisement (R): Not set
                                .1.. .... = Node-SID (N): Set
                                ..0. .... = No-PHP (P): Not set
                                ...0 .... = Explicit-Null (E): Not set
                                .... 0... = Value (V): Not set
                                .... .0.. = Local (L): Not set
                            Algorithm: 0
                            SID/Index: 2
                        Prefix SID TLV
                            Type: 1158
                            Length: 8
                            Flags: 0x40, Node-SID (N)
                                0... .... = Re-advertisement (R): Not set
                                .1.. .... = Node-SID (N): Set
                                ..0. .... = No-PHP (P): Not set
                                ...0 .... = Explicit-Null (E): Not set
                                .... 0... = Value (V): Not set
                                .... .0.. = Local (L): Not set
                            Algorithm: 128
                            SID/Index: 1002
<snip>
                        Prefix Attribute Flags TLV
                            Type: 1170
                            Length: 1
                            Flags: 0x20, Node (N)
                                0... .... = External Prefix (X): Not set
                                .0.. .... = Re-advertisement (X): Not set
```

```
                    ..1. .... = Node (N): Set
                    ...0 .... = ELC (E): Not set
            Source Router Identifier TLV
                Type: 1171
                Length: 4
                Router ID: 10.0.0.2
<snip>
```

Prefix SID TLVs were presented earlier in this chapter, in the sections "IS-IS Extensions for Segment Routing (RFC 8667)" and "OSPF Extensions for Segment Routing (RFC 8665)." The Prefix Attribute Flags and Source Router Identifier TLVs are derived from RFC 7684, RFC 9084 (OSPF), and RFC 7794 (IS-IS). The SR node of the capture advertises the following prefix parameters:

- Node SID index 2 belonging to algorithm 0

- Node SID index 1002 belonging to algorithm 128

- Source router 10.0.0.2

BGP Link-State Extensions for SR BGP Egress Peer Engineering (RFC 9086)

The BGP peering segments defined as part of the segment routing architecture are signaled using BGP-LS. RFC 9086 enhances the BGP-LS NLRI to encode BGP peering information (local and remote). Figure 2-23 shows the BGP UPDATE format of a BGP-LS prefix conveying Egress Peer Engineering (EPE) information.

Note that the structure shown here is vastly different from that of the previously documented BGP Prefix SID UPDATE messages, showcasing the flexibility of BGP.

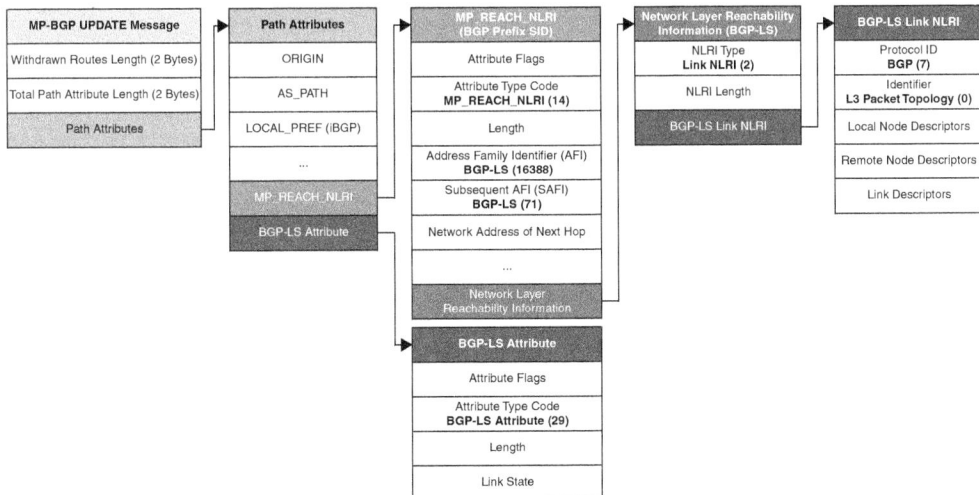

Figure 2-23 *BGP UPDATE Message Format (BGP Link State for EPE)*

New BGP-LS parameters have been registered with the Internet Assigned Numbers Authority (IANA) as part of RFC 9086 to facilitate the distribution of SR BGP-EPE information.

> **Note**   BGP-LS extensions for segment routing BGP-EPE registered with IANA are listed at https://www.iana.org/assignments/bgp-ls-parameters/bgp-ls-parameters.xhtml.

The introduction of a new protocol ID for BGP provides a clear marker for link-state information related to BGP, as opposed to traditional IGP topology information, as shown in Table 2-21.

Table 2-21   *BGP-LS Protocol ID*

Protocol ID	NLRI Information Source Protocol
7	BGP

BGP UPDATE messages with protocol ID 7 carry BGP peering information and corresponding segments, as listed in Table 2-22.

Table 2-22   *BGP-LS NLRI and Attribute TLVs*

TLV Code Point	TLV
512	Autonomous System (RFC 9552)
516	BGP Router ID
517	BGP Confederation Member
1101	PeerNode SID
1102	PeerAdj SID
1103	PeerSet SID

Example 2-27 shows a packet capture of a BGP UDPATE message with the BGP-LS attribute (29) and Autonomous Systems, BGP Router ID, and PeerNode SID TLVs:

Example 2-27   *BGP UPDATE with BGP-LS Attribute (BGP Router ID and others)*

```
Ethernet
Internet Protocol Version 4, Src: 10.0.0.3, Dst: 10.0.0.2
Transmission Control Protocol, Src Port: 62537, Dst Port: 179
Border Gateway Protocol - UPDATE Message
    Marker: ffffffffffffffffffffffffffffffff
   Length: 149
    Type: UPDATE Message (2)
    Withdrawn Routes Length: 0
```

```
    Total Path Attribute Length: 126
    Path attributes
        Path Attribute - MP_REACH_NLRI
            Flags: 0x90, Optional, Extended-Length, Non-transitive, Complete
            Type Code: MP_REACH_NLRI (14)
            Length: 94
            Address family identifier (AFI): BGP-LS (16388)
            Subsequent address family identifier (SAFI): BGP-LS (71)
            Next hop: 10.0.0.3
            Number of Subnetwork points of attachment (SNPA): 0
            Network Layer Reachability Information (NLRI)
                BGP-LS NLRI
                    NLRI Type: Link NLRI (2)
                    NLRI Length: 81
                    Link-State NLRI Link NLRI
                        Protocol ID: BGP (7)
                        Identifier: L3 packet topology (0)
                        Local Node Descriptors TLV
                            Type: 256
                            Length: 24
                            Autonomous System TLV
                                Type: 512
                                Length: 4
                                AS ID: 100 (0x00000064)
<snip>
                            BGP Router-ID TLV
                                Type: 516
                                Length: 4
                                BGP Router-ID: 10.0.0.3
                        Remote Node Descriptors TLV
                            Type: 257
                            Length: 24
                            Autonomous System TLV
                                Type: 512
                                Length: 4
                                AS ID: 200 (0x000000c8)
<snip>
                            BGP Router-ID TLV
                                Type: 516
                                Length: 4
                                BGP Router-ID: 172.16.1.1
                        Link Descriptors TLV
<snip>
```

```
Path Attribute - ORIGIN: IGP
Path Attribute - AS_PATH: empty
Path Attribute - LOCAL_PREF: 100
Path Attribute - BGP-LS Attribute
    Flags: 0x80, Optional, Non-transitive, Complete
    Type Code: BGP-LS Attribute (29)
    Length: 11
    Link State
        PeerNode SID TLV
            Type: 1101
            Length: 7
            Flags: 0xc0, Value flag (V), Local flag (L)
                1... .... = Value flag (V): Set
                .1.. .... = Local flag (L): Set
                ..0. .... = Backup flag (B): Not set
                ...0 .... = Persistent flag (P): Not set
            Weight: 0
            .... 0000 0101 1101 1100 0010 = SID/Label: 24002
<snip>
```

The BGP Router ID and BGP Autonomous System TLVs are self-explanatory. The peering segments consist of the following flags and fields, which should feel familiar by now from the IGP control plane extensions:

- **Value flag (V-flag):** Set when the Peering SID carries a value, as opposed to an index.

- **Local flag (L-flag):** Set when the Peering SID is locally significant, as opposed to globally significant.

- **Backup flag (B-flag):** Set to signal the protection eligibility of a Peering SID through FRR in the event of a link or node failure.

- **Persistent flag (P-flag):** Set when the Peering SID is persistent across reloads/ interface flaps (useful for static SR policies).

- **Weight:** Represents the weight used for load balancing purposes in the presence of parallel adjacencies with the same PeerAdj SID. A higher weight is preferred over a lower weight. For instance, two parallel adjacencies with weights of 1 and 3 will receive their share of traffic based on a 1:3 ratio, or 25%:75%.

- **SID/Label/Index:** This field may be a value or an index, depending on the V- and L-flags:

  - **V-flag and L-flag are equal to 0:** The field is a 4-byte index that defines the offset in the SRGB.

  - **V-flag and L-flag are equal to 1:** The field is a 3-byte local label (the 20 rightmost bits).

Summary

This chapter covers the theory behind the segment routing architecture as well as the underlying control and data plane for SR-MPLS. It presents a high-level analogy between the execution of software programs on a central processing unit (CPU) and network programs within a network cloud that is abstracted as a large computer. This analogy highlights many similarities and familiar concepts:

- Programs are broken down into smaller pieces called instructions that are executed one by one to achieve desired outcomes. Similarly, network programs consist of multiple instructions, which are called segments in the segment routing framework.

- Segments are associated with values called segment identifiers (SIDs) that rely on (20-bit) MPLS labels for SR-MPLS.

- Segments, like CPU instructions, can be associated with any kind of operation as long as it is feasible to implement in software or hardware.

This chapter also covers how SR, as defined in RFC 8402, supersedes existing legacy signaling protocols such as LDP and RSVP-TE and also significantly simplifies the network state and protocol stack through two key paradigm shifts:

- **Elevation of the IGP:** SR-MPLS extensions enable the IGP to advertise link-state IGP segments. Any path within the network can be represented using a sequence of node and adjacency segments.

- **Source routing:** An SR policy, structured as an ordered list of segments, facilitates source routing. By encoding the desired path as a list of segments at the ingress node, SR moves network state information from the network to MPLS headers using SIDs.

Segments can be classified as globally or locally significant, and it is possible to further distinguish between transport (topological instruction) and service-related (service instruction) operations. For instance, forwarding a packet toward a specific adjacency is a locally significant topological instruction, whereas forwarding a packet toward a specific node is considered a globally significant topological instruction. Service instructions generally cover a much wider scope of applications, such as Layer 2 or Layer 3 services, which could be extended to network virtualization functions (NFVs) handling Network Address Translation (NAT) or firewall functionality.

SR-MPLS reuses the MPLS data plane, which results in two additional carving entries of the 20-bit MPLS label space:

- **Segment routing global block (SRGB):** This is the label range for statically allocated globally significant SIDs.

- **Segment routing local block (SRLB):** This is the label range for statically allocated locally significant SIDs.

SR-MPLS instructions are built on top of IGP segments, BGP segments, and binding segments, which all evolve around topological instructions steering traffic across a path through the network. The VPN service layer information remains in control of the BGP control plane, which is not affected by SR-MPLS in the underlay.

The following segments are the most common in SR-MPLS deployments:

- **IGP prefix segment:** This segment is associated with an IP prefix and an instruction that is equivalent to forwarding a packet along the computed path of a given algorithm.

- **IGP adjacency segment:** This segment is associated with an instruction that is equivalent to forwarding a packet out a specific outgoing interface.

Subsequent sections covered segment routing control plane extensions for the MPLS data plane encapsulations in detail with packet capture extracts. You have seen that Type Length Values (TLVs) and sub-TLVs are heavily used in IS-IS, OSPF, and BGP segment routing extensions, providing a hierarchical, flexible, and easily extensible way of encoding routing information.

This chapter serves as a foundation for upcoming chapters, which focus on the configuration and verification of SR-MPLS. SR-MPLS is seen as a natural evolution of MPLS. You are encouraged to refer to this chapter for data plane details or as a reference for control plane extensions and relevant packet captures. Chapter 3 is the SRv6 equivalent of this chapter, following a similar structure.

References and Additional Reading

- RFC 8402: Segment Routing Architecture, https://datatracker.ietf.org/doc/html/rfc8402

- RFC 9256: Segment Routing Policy Architecture, https://datatracker.ietf.org/doc/rfc9256

Problem Description and Requirements

- RFC 7855: Source Packet Routing in Networking (SPRING) Problem Statement and Requirements, https://www.rfc-editor.org/rfc/rfc7855.txt

IGP-Adjacency Segment (Adjacency SID)

- RFC 8668: Advertising Layer 2 Bundle Member Link Attributes in IS-IS, https://datatracker.ietf.org/doc/html/rfc8668

- RFC 9356: Advertising Layer 2 Bundle Member Link Attributes in OSPF, https://www.rfc-editor.org/rfc/rfc9356.txt

BGP Prefix Segment (BGP Prefix SID)

- RFC 8669: Segment Routing Prefix Segment Identifier Extensions for BGP, https://www.rfc-editor.org/rfc/rfc8669.txt

- RFC 3107: Carrying Label Information in BGP-4, https://datatracker.ietf.org/doc/html/rfc3107

BGP Peering Segments (BGP Peering SIDs)

- RFC 9087: Segment Routing Centralized BGP Egress Peer Engineering, https://www.rfc-editor.org/rfc/rfc9087.txt

Binding Segment (Binding SID)

- RFC 8491: Signaling Maximum SID Depth (MSD) Using IS-IS, https://datatracker.ietf.org/doc/html/rfc8491

- RFC 8476: Signaling Maximum SID Depth (MSD) Using OSPF, https://www.rfc-editor.org/rfc/rfc8476.txt

- RFC 8814: Signaling Maximum SID Depth (MSD) Using the Border Gateway Protocol - Link State, https://www.rfc-editor.org/rfc/rfc8814.txt

IS-IS Extensions for Segment Routing (RFC 8667)

- RFC 8667: IS-IS Extensions for Segment Routing, https://datatracker.ietf.org/doc/html/rfc8667

OSPF Extensions for Segment Routing (RFC 8665)

- RFC 8665: OSPF Extensions for Segment Routing, https://www.rfc-editor.org/rfc/rfc8665.html

IGP Flexible Algorithm (Flex Algo) (RFC 9350)

- RFC 9350: IGP Flexible Algorithm, https://www.rfc-editor.org/rfc/rfc9350.html

- IETF Draft: Flexible Algorithms: Bandwidth, Delay, Metrics and Constraints, https://www.ietf.org/archive/id/draft-ietf-lsr-flex-algo-bw-con-12.txt

- RFC 8919: IS-IS Application-Specific Link Attributes, https://datatracker.ietf.org/doc/html/rfc8919

- RFC 8920: OSPF Application-Specific Link Attributes, https://datatracker.ietf.org/doc/html/rfc8920

MP-BGP Extensions

- RFC 4760: Multiprotocol Extensions for BGP-4, https://datatracker.ietf.org/doc/html/rfc4760

BGP Link-State Extensions for SR (RFC 9085)

- RFC 9085: Border Gateway Protocol - Link State (BGP-LS) Extensions for Segment Routing, https://www.rfc-editor.org/rfc/rfc9085.txt

- RFC 7752: North-Bound Distribution of Link-State and Traffic Engineering (TE) Information Using BGP, https://datatracker.ietf.org/doc/html/rfc7752

- RFC 7794: IS-IS Prefix Attributes for Extended IPv4 and IPv6 Reachability, https://datatracker.ietf.org/doc/html/rfc7794

- RFC 7684: OSPFv2 Prefix/Link Attribute Advertisement, https://datatracker.ietf.org/doc/html/rfc7684

- FC 9084, OSPF Prefix Originator Extensions, https://datatracker.ietf.org/doc/html/rfc9084

BGP Link-State Extensions for SR BGP Egress Peer Engineering (RFC 9086)

- RFC 9086: Border Gateway Protocol - Link State (BGP-LS) Extensions for Segment Routing BGP Egress Peer Engineering, https://www.rfc-editor.org/rfc/rfc9086.txt

- RFC 9552: Distribution of Link-State and Traffic Engineering Information Using BGP, https://www.rfc-editor.org/rfc/rfc9552.txt

Chapter 3

What Is Segment Routing over IPv6 (SRv6)?

Introduction

This chapter covers the theory behind the Segment Routing over IPv6 (SRv6) data plane encapsulation implementation. It provides valuable decision-making process inputs and outlines potential pitfalls when evaluating the network architecture evolution to Segment Routing over IPv6. In addition, the section "SR-Powered Network Evolution" describes the network evolution journey that began with the introduction of Segment Routing for MPLS (SR-MPLS) and ends with a converged SDN transport network based on SRv6.

Segment Routing over IPv6 (SRv6)

This section introduces SRv6, which shares many fundamental concepts with SR-MPLS. Although some operators might view SR-MPLS as a transitional step toward SRv6, this chapter shows that SRv6 is a superior solution that effectively addresses the challenges associated with MPLS discussed in the section "Challenges and Shortcomings of MPLS," in Chapter 1, "MPLS in a Nutshell." While SR-MPLS is already well established, a select number of compression-related SRv6 extensions are still in the process of being standardized as of this writing. The IETF has been advancing at an impressive pace, and all the major key drafts have been successfully standardized, achieving RFC status. This standardization marks a significant milestone in the evolution of SRv6, showcasing its readiness for widespread deployment and the promise of enhanced network efficiency.

Since SRv6 relies on the IPv6 data plane, it is crucial to have a solid understanding of IPv6 encapsulation and the IPv6 header. In fact, as you will see in this chapter, the vast majority of SRv6 use cases rely on IPv6 routing using an IPv6 header without any extension headers.

IPv6 for SRv6 Recap

Figure 3-1 shows the format of the IPv6 header, as specified in RFC 8200.

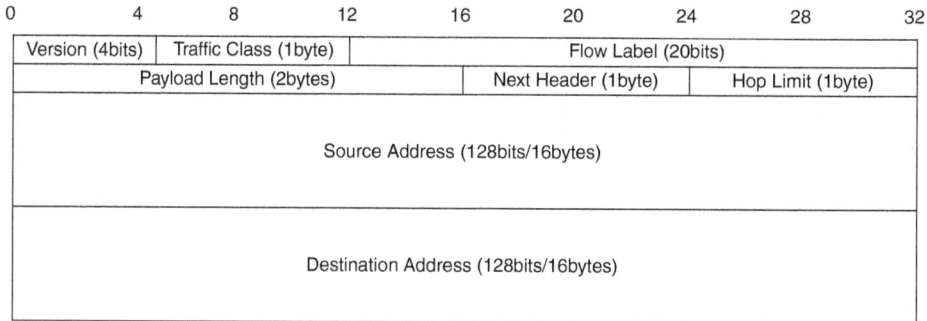

0	4	8	12	16	20	24	28	32

Version (4bits)	Traffic Class (1byte)	Flow Label (20bits)		
Payload Length (2bytes)		Next Header (1byte)	Hop Limit (1byte)	
Source Address (128bits/16bytes)				
Destination Address (128bits/16bytes)				

Figure 3-1 *IPv6 Header*

The IPv6 header consists of the following fields:

- **Version (4 bits):** Specifies the version of IP; set to 6 for IPv6.

- **Traffic Class (8 bits):** Used for traffic management (QoS) based on DSCP (6-bit) and ECN (2-bit).

- **Flow Label (20 bits):** Used for encoding entropy of the payload and subsequent flow hashing (load balancing).

- **Payload Length (16 bits):** Specifies the length of the payload following the IPv6 header.

- **Next Header (8 bits):** Identifies the header following the IPv6 header (for example, IPv4, IPv6, Ethernet, ICMP, TCP).

- **Hop Limit (8 bits):** Equivalent to the Time to Live (TTL) field of the IPv4 header.

- **Source Address (128 bits):** Identifies the source of the packet.

- **Destination Address (128 bits):** Identifies the destination of the packet.

Most of the fields are self-explanatory or easy to grasp. However, special attention should be paid to the Traffic Class, Flow Label, and Next Header fields.

The Traffic Class field is used for quality of service (QoS) marking, which involves Differentiated Services Codepoint (DSCP) and Explicit Congestion Notification (ECN). The 6-bit value of DSCP covers the decimal range from 0 to 63, which makes it possible to distinguish more than eight traffic classes. The 3-bit value of MPLS EXP in SR-MPLS is a significant limitation with SR-MPLS.

The Flow Label field facilitates efficient flow classification in combination with other IPv6 header fields, such as the Source Address and Destination Address fields. A sequence of packets belonging to the same Layer 3 flow are generally classified based on the 5-tuple of network addresses, transport protocol, and transport ports. Note that not all of those identifiers may exist in a flow, depending on the payload (for example ICMP), or they may be unavailable due to encryption or fragmentation. Layer 2 traffic flows usually take into account data link layer information for classification and may or may not include some of the higher-layer protocol information. Often, flow classification is not only vendor dependent but also platform dependent, with some devices supporting 7 or more-tuple flow classification, taking into account one or more MPLS labels.

The Flow Label field is a radical simplification for IPv6 compared to IPv4 or MPLS. Instead of cumbersomely inspecting a packet and trying to figure out where the relevant fields are located within the packet to extract the 5+-tuple, IPv6 uses a 3-tuple consisting of Source Address, Destination Address and Flow Label fields. Having all those fields at fixed positions within the IPv6 header simplifies the extraction of flow identifiers and consequently the hardware implementation of this process.

The Flow Label value is computed by the source node and not changed by transit nodes along the path. The source node in an SRv6 domain is usually an ingress PE device, which encapsulates the received packet coming from the edge into an outer IPv6 header with an optional segment routing header (SRH) extension header. The exact algorithm to compute the hash for the Flow Label value is implementation specific and may differ between vendors or platforms. However, depending on the type of service, different fields are considered, such as the following common identifiers:

- **Layer 2 VPN service:** Source and destination MAC addresses and source and destination IP addresses (IP payload only)

- **Layer 3 VPN service:** Source and destination IP addresses, transport protocol, and source and destination ports

This list is an example, and different implementations may consider additional fields. It is important to understand that the Flow Label value is computed only once in the network, at the source node, which is service aware; that is, Layer 2 or Layer 3 VPN services can be easily distinguished, and the tuple used for hashing can be extracted before additional encapsulation takes place. After the hash has been computed, it is written to the Flow Label field, which is, in turn, used by all transit nodes. In essence, the hard work of computing a proper hash needs to be performed only once by the source node, and all other nodes along the path can take advantage of this hash, which greatly reduces the complexity of flow classification to achieve proper load balancing for ECMP routing or LAG hashing.

Figure 3-2 shows an example of a traffic flow entering an SRv6 domain. The network is highly symmetric, with one core link relying on a link aggregation group (LAG). The ingress PE device encapsulates the received packet from the edge into an IPv6 header and populates the Flow Label field with the computed 20-bit hash (0xecfec). The packet entering the SRv6 domain is an IPv4 packet, as you can see from the Next Header field of the IPv6 header.

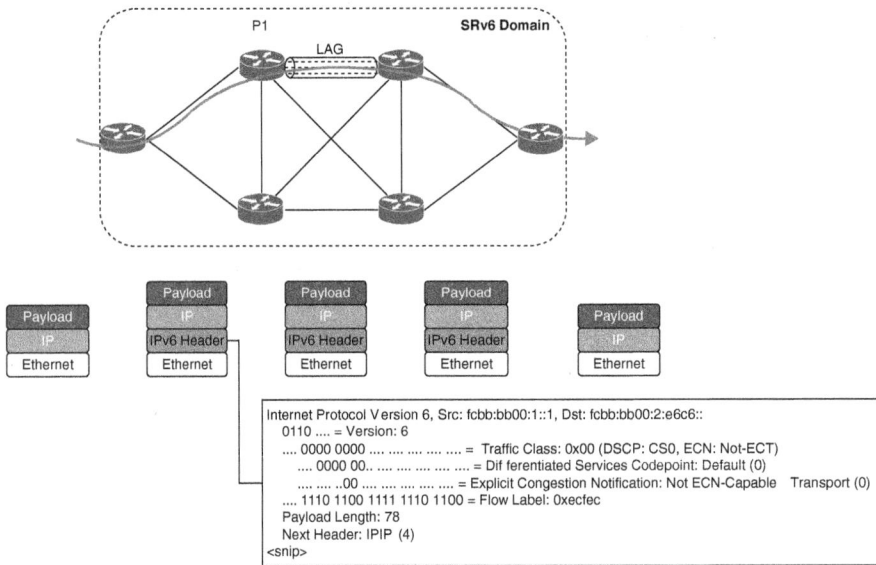

Figure 3-2 *IPv6 Flow Label and Capture*

Note   Many of the network figures related to MPLS/SR-MPLS in this book include an inner IP header with payload to emphasize the fact that MPLS sits between Layer 2 (the data link layer) and Layer 3 (the network layer) in the OSI model, which is why it is sometimes referred to as a Layer 2.5 networking protocol. SRv6 goes back to the roots of the OSI model and no longer relies on this shim layer. SRv6 network figures in this book are generally drawn with an inner payload only, unless the context asks for more detailed inner header information, such as IPv4/IPv6 or Ethernet.

The flow label must not change en route, and P1 classifies the flow based on the IPv6 source address, destination address, and flow label. P1 chooses the ECMP path and physical link of the LAG based on the hash of the IPv6 header, as shown in Figure 3-2.

The Next Header field identifies the upper layer protocol, which follows immediately after the IPv6 header. A key difference between IPv4 and IPv6 is the flexible support for extensions and options in IPv6, where *extension headers* are placed between the IPv6 header and upper layer protocols (for example, TCP or UDP).

Note   IP protocol numbers and IPv6 extension headers registered with IANA are listed at https://www.iana.org/assignments/protocol-numbers/protocol-numbers.xhtml and https://www.iana.org/assignments/ipv6-parameters/ipv6-parameters.xhtml#extension-header.

The routing header for an IPv6 extension is a central puzzle piece of the SRv6 solution as it allows the insertion of an optional segment routing header (SRH) after the IPv6 header.

The details of the SRH are introduced later in this chapter, in the section "IPv6 Segment Routing Header (SRH) (RFC 8754)."

SRv6 Network Programming (RFC 8986)

RFC 8986 lays the foundation of the segment routing architecture in the IPv6 data plane. Network instructions have to be encoded into the IPv6 header, which differs fundamentally from MPLS, where each instruction is represented by a label. Many fundamental concepts covered in Chapter 2, "What Is Segment Routing over MPLS (SR-MPLS)?" are the same for SRv6, though. An SRv6 SID is still associated with a segment, but instead of using an MPLS label, it is now represented as an IPv6 address. The IPv6 destination address in the outer IPv6 header is set to the SRv6 SID, which represents a network program, including a single instruction or an SR policy with a single segment. SRv6-unaware transit nodes forward an SRv6 SID based on the longest-prefix-match lookup on the IPv6 destination address. An IPv6 address associated with an SRv6 SID has a special format.

SRv6 Segment Identifier (SID)

SRv6 SIDs are 128-bit long IPv6 addresses that follow the format shown in Figure 3-3:

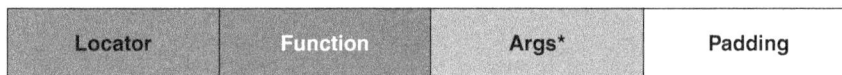

Locator	Function	Args*	Padding

Figure 3-3 *SRv6 SID Format*

- Locator:
  - Most significant bits
  - Routable part, which points to the parent node that instantiated the SID
  - Advertised through a link-state IGP (IS-IS or OSPF)
  - Should be unique within the SRv6 domain, except for SRv6 anycast locators
- Function:
  - Identifies a locally significant behavior of the parent node
- Arguments:
  - Least significant bits
  - One or more input arguments to the function (for example, service or flow information)
  - Optional

The length of the Locator (L), Function (F), and Arguments (A) fields are flexible as long as the total length is less than or equal to 128 bits. If the total length is less than 128 bits, the SID should be padded to 128 bits with zeros. As mentioned previously, the Arguments field is optional.

As shown in Figure 3-4, the Locator field may be expressed as two different fields: SID block (B) and Node ID (N). A common format for early SRv6 deployments was to allocate B::/48 for the SID block and B:N::/64 for the locator. In Cisco documentation, this is commonly referred to as *base format*. The section "SRv6 Locator Addressing Scheme," later in this chapter, discusses alternative locator assignments suited for large-scale deployments. For now, this basic split into SID Block, Node ID, and Function fields will suffice as an introduction to SRv6 SIDs.

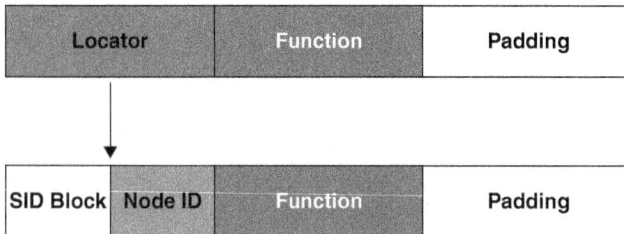

Figure 3-4   *SRv6 SID Format (Simplified)*

Let us look at the example presented in Figure 3-5:

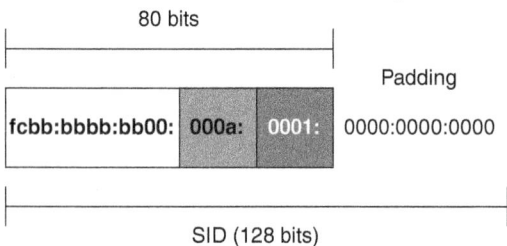

Figure 3-5   *SRv6 SID Format (Example)*

- A service provider allocates the SRv6 SID block—for example fcbb:bbbb:bb00::/48—from the unique local address (ULA) space for SRv6 locators in the network shared by all SRv6 nodes.

- Router 10 would be assigned the locator fcbb:bbbb:bb00:000a::/64 (L = 64 bits).

- Router 10 locally allocates function 0x0001 (F = 16 bits) without any arguments (A = 0 bits) for its SRv6 SID. The sum of L + F + A equals 80, which means that the remaining 48 bits must be padded with zero since SRv6 SIDs are 128-bit addresses.

- The resulting SRv6 SID associated with the segment to Router 10 equals fcbb:bbbb:bb00:a:1::.

Note   IPv6 addresses are expressed in hexadecimal, where 10 translates to 0xA and not 0x10, which would be 16.

For reachability and backward compatibility between SRv6-capable and IPv6-capable nodes, SRv6 nodes advertise the locator (for example, /64) as an IPv6 prefix in the link-state IGP, as shown in Figure 3-6. The locator prefixes act as aggregate prefixes for source and transit nodes to perform longest-prefix-match lookups on SRv6 SIDs and forward the packets accordingly.

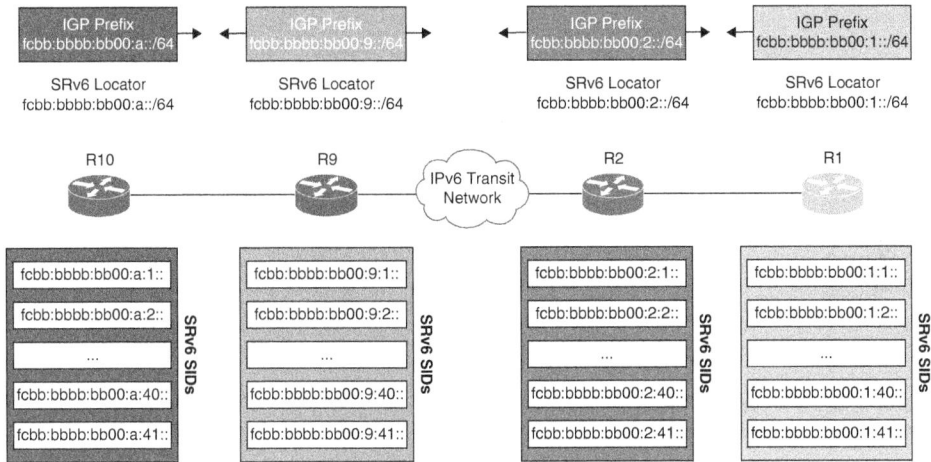

Figure 3-6 *SRv6 Locator and IGP Prefix*

Therefore, it is possible to provision SRv6 services over a native IPv6 network as long as the service edge is SRv6 capable. Obviously, certain SRv6 functionality, such as Topology Independent Loop-Free Alternate (TI-LFA) or traffic engineering, will not be available on native IPv6 transit nodes. This is discussed in more detail later in this chapter, in the section "IPv6 Segment Routing Header (SRH) (RFC 8754)." At this point, it may still be confusing how SRv6 SIDs can be used to provision services. A simplified analogy using familiar concepts from SR-MPLS will hopefully shed some light. Figure 3-7 shows the data plane encapsulation for both SR-MPLS and SRv6. It should be clear by now that SRv6 does not use labels, so how are transport and service identifiers encoded using a single IPv6 header?

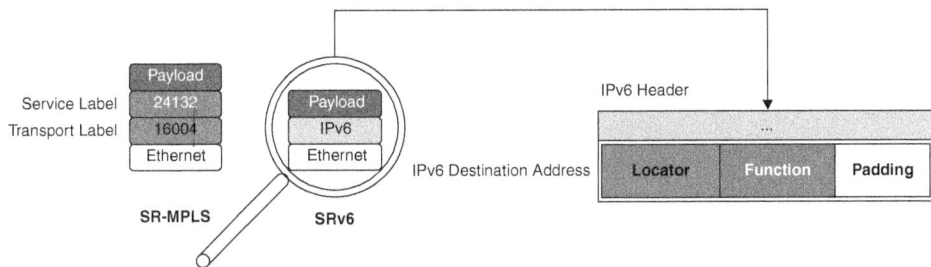

Figure 3-7 *SR-MPLS and SRv6 SID Analogy*

As described previously, the locator represents the routable part of the prefix, which points to the parent node. This resembles the loopback0 address of a node with the associated Prefix SID in the SR-MPLS space, whereas the function is a locally significant behavior of the parent node resembling a service label in the SR-MPLS space. In other words, a single SRv6 SID includes both globally significant information (locator) and locally significant information (function + arguments), which can encode the transport and service layers using a single SRv6 SID. The increased address space of IPv6 opens up new possibilities that have not been available with MPLS. Consequently, the types of SRv6 SIDs differ remarkably from those discussed in Chapter 2.

Routed and Non-Routed SRv6 SIDs

Routed and non-routed SIDs in SRv6 are what global and local SIDs are to SR-MPLS. An SRv6 SID is considered routed if it can be resolved via a less-specific route advertised in the routing protocol. An SRv6 SID that cannot be resolved via a route is considered non-routed.

For instance, let us assume that Router 10 advertises the following IPv6 prefix (locator) in the IGP and instantiates two SRv6 SIDs:

IGP prefix (locator)	**fcbb:bbbb:bb00:a::/64**
Routed SID	**fcbb:bbbb:bb00:a:123::**
Non-routed SID	**fcbb:bbbb:bb00:134::**

The routed SID is part of the /64 IGP prefix, whereas the non-routed SID is not. Conveniently, the IGP prefix represents the SRv6 locator of R10, which means that any SID following the locator-function-argument format will always be routed by design. An SRv6 SID that omits the node ID in the locator part would be an example of a non-routed SID.

A non-routed SRv6 SID has to be preceded by a routed SID to ensure that the packet ends up on the correct parent node before the non-routed SID is processed. You will see how multiple SRv6 SIDs can be encoded in additional IPv6 header information later in this chapter, in the sections "IPv6 Segment Routing Header (SRH) (RFC 8754)" and "SRv6 Network Programming Extension: SRv6 uSID Instruction." For simplicity, let us assume that two SRv6 SIDs are written in separate headers for the time being.

Figure 3-8 shows how a non-routed SID could be used in SRv6 by preceding a non-routed SID with a routed Prefix SID belonging to the parent node of the non-routed SID.

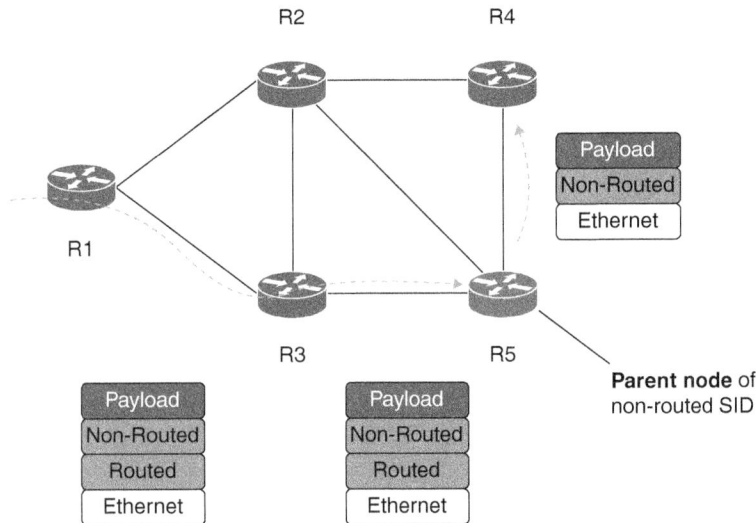

Figure 3-8   *Non-Routed SRv6 SID*

The following section discusses the most common endpoint behaviors in detail.

SRv6 Endpoint Behaviors

A few common SRv6 endpoint behaviors that are documented in RFC 8986 are listed in Table 3-1. Remember that any behavior could be associated to a SID as long as it is of practical use and can be implemented in software or hardware. The list presented here is not conclusive, and additional behaviors may be defined in the future, depending on the use cases. At first, the different behaviors may seem a bit cryptic, but there is a meaningful naming concept that is explained in the following list, using * as a wildcard character:

- **End.*:** End refers to an endpoint behavior.

- **End.*X:** The X refers to an xconnect (that is, cross-connect), which forces a packet out a specific interface.

- **End.*T:** The T refers to a table lookup.

- **End.D*:** The D refers to an IPv6 decapsulation of the inner IP packet or payload.

- **End.D*2, End.D*4, End.D*6, End.DT46:** The digit refers to the service:

  - **2:** L2VPN

  - **4:** IPv4 L3VPN

  - **6:** IPv6 L3VPN

  - **46:** IPv4/IPv6 L3VPN

- **End.DX2V, End.DT2U, End.DT2M:** The final letter refers to the Layer 2 lookup:

  - **V:** VLAN Lookup

  - **U:** MAC Lookup

  - **M:** Flooding

For instance, End.DX6 refers to an endpoint behavior with decapsulation and xconnect for an IPv6 L3VPN.

> **Note**   SRv6 endpoint behaviors for Segment Routing over IPv6 (SRv6) registered with IANA are listed at https://www.iana.org/assignments/segment-routing/segment-routing.xhtml.

Table 3-1   *SRv6 Endpoint Behaviors*

SRv6 Endpoint Behavior	Control Plane Signaling	Description
End	IGP/BGP-LS	Endpoint (SRv6 Prefix SID)
End.X	IGP/BGP-LS	Endpoint with L3 xconnect (SRv6 Adjacency SID)
End.T	IGP/BGP-LS	Endpoint with specific IPv6 table lookup
End.DX4	IGP/BGP-LS/BGP VPN	Endpoint with decapsulation and IPv4 xconnect (IPv4 L3VPN per-CE label allocation)
End.DX6	IGP/BGP-LS/BGP VPN	Endpoint with decapsulation and IPv6 xconnect (IPv6 L3VPN per-CE label allocation)
End.DT4	IGP/BGP-LS/BGP VPN	Endpoint with decapsulation and specific IPv4 table lookup (IPv4 L3VPN per-VRF label allocation)
End.DT6	IGP/BGP-LS/BGP VPN	Endpoint with decapsulation and specific IPv6 table lookup (IPv6 L3VPN per-VRF label allocation)
End.DT46	IGP/BGP-LS/BGP VPN	Endpoint with decapsulation and specific IPv4/IPv6 table lookup (IP L3VPN per-VRF label allocation)
End.DX2	BGP-LS/BGP VPN	Endpoint with decapsulation and L2 xconnect (point-to-point L2VPN)

SRv6 Endpoint Behavior	Control Plane Signaling	Description
End.DX2V	BGP-LS/BGP VPN	Endpoint with decapsulation and VLAN L2 table lookup (EVPN flexible xconnect)
End.DT2U	BGP-LS/BGP VPN	Endpoint with decapsulation and unicast MAC L2 table lookup (multipoint L2VPN [known unicast])
End.DT2M	BGP-LS/BGP VPN	Endpoint with decapsulation and L2 table flooding (multipoint L2VPN [broadcast, unknown-unicast, multicast])

Note   SRv6 headend behaviors and endpoint behaviors related to an SRv6 binding SID and are not included in this introductory section in order to flatten the learning curve. They are covered in later sections.

You should already know the following endpoint behaviors from SR-MPLS:

■ **End:** SRv6 instantiation of a Prefix SID

■ **End.X:** SRv6 instantiation of an Adjacency SID

The following sections discuss the most common endpoint behaviors in more detail. Note that except for the End behavior, all SID values in the examples are dynamically allocated and not tied to specific endpoint behaviors.

End Behavior

The endpoint (End) behavior, illustrated in Figure 3-9, is equivalent to a segment associated with a Prefix SID. Much as with SR-MPLS, the link-state IGP is responsible for the distribution of transport-related SIDs such as End within the network using TLVs, as documented in the section "IS-IS Extensions for Segment Routing over IPv6 (RFC 9352)".

R5 instantiates the End SID fcbb:bbbb:bb00:5:1:: (SID function 0x1) and floods its SRv6 locator information throughout the network. A source node in the SRv6 domain sends traffic to this SID, which follows the longest prefix match (/64 locator prefix) toward R5. SRv6 SIDs are locally significant and only known on the parent node that instantiated the SID. The locator or even larger aggregates are used to resolve the IPv6 destination address and forward traffic to its destination. The endpoint (End) behavior is fundamental for SRv6 TI-LFA or traffic engineering to steer traffic via specific nodes along the path.

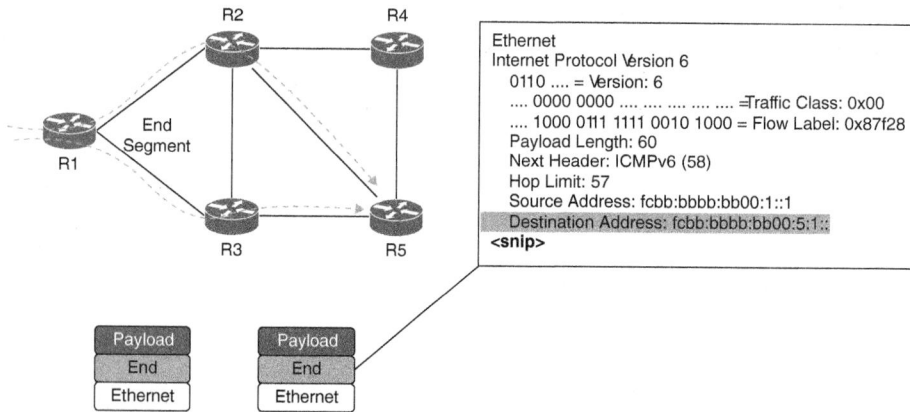

Figure 3-9 *SRv6 End Segment*

> **Note**   For the remainder of this book, we assume that the SID function 0x1 is associated with the SRv6 endpoint (End) behavior for base format deployments. The section "SRv6 Network Programming Extension: SRv6 uSID Instruction," later in this chapter, introduces the F3216 format, which uses a different value.

End.X Behavior

The endpoint with Layer 3 cross-connect (End.X) behavior shown in Figure 3-10 is equivalent to a segment associated with an Adjacency SID. Much as with the endpoint (End) behavior, the link-state IGP is responsible for the distribution of transport-related SIDs within the network using TLVs.

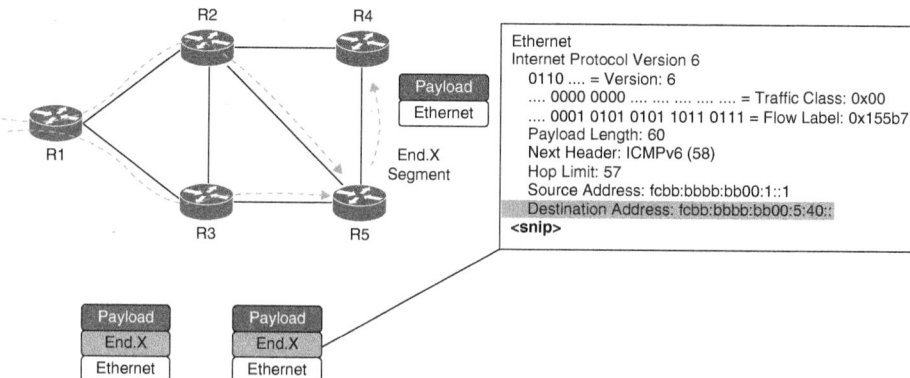

Figure 3-10 *SRv6 End.X Segment*

R5 instantiates the routed End.X SID fcbb:bbbb:bb00:5:40:: (SID function 0x40) for the adjacency toward R4 and floods this information throughout the network. A source node within the SRv6 domain may want to force traffic via the interface between R5 and R4 and encapsulates its payload into an outer IPv6 header with the destination address set to the End.X SID. The packet follows the longest prefix match (/64 locator prefix) up to R5, where it is processed and forwarded out the interface to R4. The endpoint with Layer 3 cross-connect behavior (End.X) is fundamental for SRv6 TI-LFA or traffic engineering to steer traffic via specific adjacencies along the path. The SRv6 instantiation of an Adjacency SID (End.X) only requires a single routable SRv6 SID, whereas with SR-MPLS, both a Node SID and an Adjacency SID are needed (refer to Figure 2-12).

SID Allocation Mode

Before looking at Layer 3 End.DX4/End.DX6 and End.DT4/End.DT6 endpoint behaviors, it makes sense to briefly revisit MPLS VPN label allocation modes to understand how they map to SRv6 SID allocation:

- **Per-prefix label allocation:** A VPN label is allocated for each prefix.

  - **Advantage:** Label diversity for hashing, forwarding performance (which is a lesser concern in modern hardware)

  - **Disadvantage:** Low scalability (for example, 1 million prefix [label] limit on PE or higher resource consumption in general)

- **Per-CE label allocation (equivalent to End.DX*):** A VPN label is allocated for each CE or next hop (PE/CE adjacency)

  - **Advantage:** High scalability, forwarding performance

  - **Disadvantage:** Limited label diversity for hashing

- **Per-VRF instance label allocation (equivalent to End.DT*):** A single VPN label is allocated for all prefixes in a VRF instance.

  - **Advantage:** High scalability

  - **Disadvantage:** Forwarding performance (additional IP lookup, which is a lesser concern in modern hardware), limited label diversity for hashing, negative side effects on convergence (BGP PIC edge)

It is noteworthy that no SRv6 counterpart exists for per-prefix label allocation. With the rise of merchant silicon not only in the core but also on the service edge and the ever-increasing RIB/FIB scale requirements in service provider networks, per-prefix label allocation became more and more unpopular. Per-CE node SID allocation is generally the preferable choice as it provides high scalability and fast convergence and does not suffer from the forwarding penalty introduced by the additional lookup of per-VRF allocation. The lack of label diversity for hashing is no longer an issue with SRv6, thanks to the IPv6 flow label.

End.DT4 Behavior

The endpoint with decapsulation and a specific IPv4 table lookup (End.DT4) behavior shown in Figure 3-11 is equivalent to an IPv4 L3VPN with per-VRF label allocation. Similar to SR-MPLS, BGP is responsible for the propagation of service-related SIDs, such as End.DT4 and End.DT6, within the network using TLVs, as documented in section "BGP Overlay Services on SRv6 (RFC 9252)." Transitioning from MPLS to SR-MPLS did not require changes in the BGP service control plane; however, the shift to SRv6 represents a significant evolution. In SRv6 environments, BGP now advertises a SID, which is a streamlined approach compared to the previous requirement of separate transport and service labels from distinct protocols within MPLS.

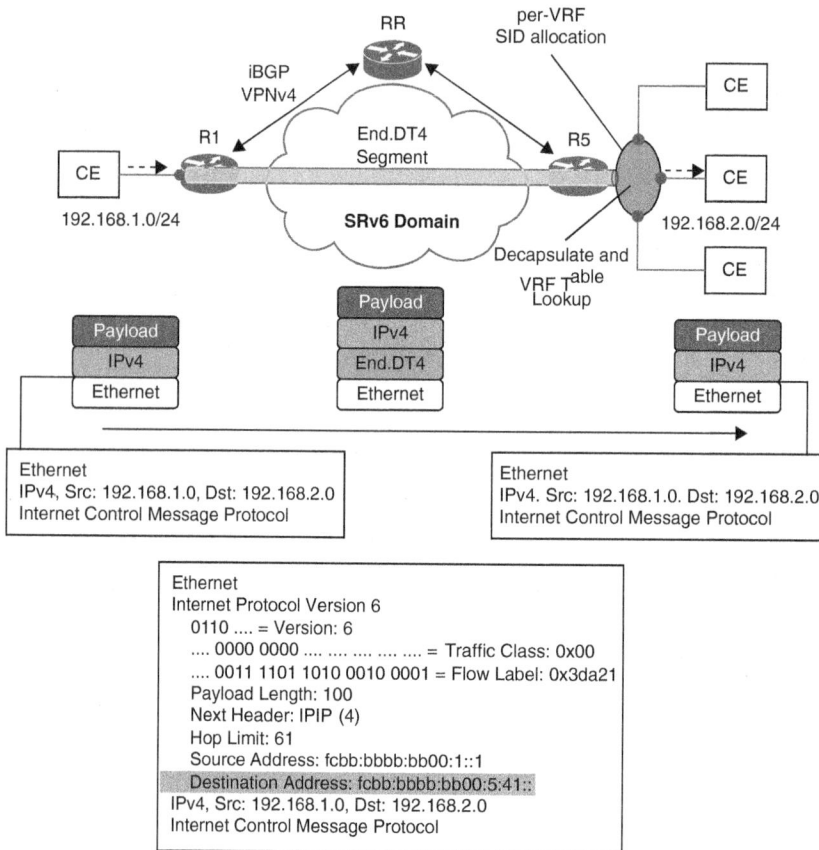

Figure 3-11   *SRv6 End.DT4 Segment*

R5 instantiates the End.DT4 SID fcbb:bbbb:bb00:5:41:: (SID function 0x41) for all pre-fixes in VRF1 and propagates this information in BGP (VPNv4 address family) via a route reflector to R1. R1 receives an ICMP packet from its local CE node, destined to a CE device attached to R5, performs a lookup, and encapsulates the ICMP payload into an outer IPv6 header. The packet follows the longest prefix match (/64 locator prefix) toward R5, where it is decapsulated, processed, and forwarded based on the FIB table associated with SID function 0x41 toward the CE with the destination address 192.168.2.0.

It is important to note that both PEs R1 and R5 must perform an IPv4 destination lookup on 192.168.2.0. Since R5 uses the same SID for all prefixes in VRF1, it requires one additional lookup to determine the egress interface and encapsulation information (adjacency). To reduce verbosity, we do not show an example for the End.DT6 behavior, which would be exactly the same except for these notable differences:

- Different SID on R5 (for example, fcbb:bbbb:bb00:5:42::, where the locator remains the same but the function changes)

- Different customer payload (for example, IPv6 instead of IPv4)

- Different Next Header field in the IPv6 header (for example, IPv6 (41) instead of IPv4(4))

Note   For the remainder of this book, we assume that the SID functions greater than 0x40 are associated with the SRv6 endpoint with decapsulation (End.D*) behavior for base format deployments. The section "SRv6 Network Programming Extension: SRv6 uSID Instruction," later in this chapter, introduces the F3216 format, which uses a different range.

End.DX4 Behavior

The endpoint with decapsulation and IPv4 cross-connect (End.DX4) behavior shown in Figure 3-12 is equivalent to an IPv4 L3VPN with per-CE device label allocation. Much as with the End.DT* behavior, with the End.DX4 behavior, BGP is responsible for the propagation of service-related SIDs such as End.DX4 and End.DX6 within the network using TLVs.

R5 instantiates the End.DX4 SID fcbb:bbbb:bb00:5:42:: (SID function 0x42) for a specific next hop (CE node) in VRF2 and propagates this information in BGP (using the VPNv4 address family) via a route reflector to R1. R1 receives an ICMP packet from its local CE device that is destined to a CE device attached to R5, performs a lookup, and encapsulates the ICMP payload into an outer IPv6 header. The packet follows the longest prefix match (/64 locator prefix) toward R5, where it is processed and forwarded toward the CE associated with SID function 0x42.

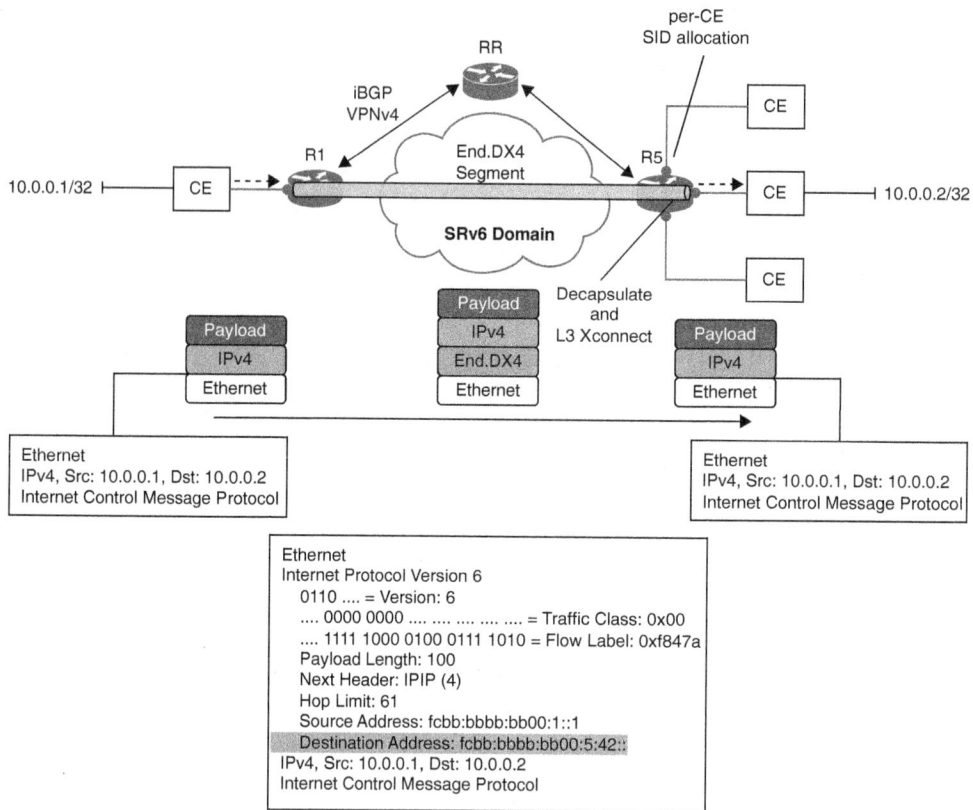

Figure 3-12 *SRv6 End.DX4 Segment*

It is important to note that the egress PE R5 does not need to perform an IPv4 destination lookup on 10.0.0.2 because R5 instantiates a unique SID per next hop (CE node) in VRF2. SID function 0x42 identifies the egress interface and encapsulation information (adjacency) to be used for packet forwarding. To reduce verbosity, we do not include an example for the End.DX6 behavior, which would be exactly the same as the End.DX4 behavior except for these notable differences:

- Different SID on R5 (for example fcbb:bbbb:bb00:5:43::, where the locator remains the same but the function changes)

- Different customer payload (for example, IPv6 instead of IPv4)

- Different Next Header field in the IPv6 header (for example IPv6 (41) instead of IPv4(4))

End.DX2 Behavior

The endpoint with decapsulation and Layer 2 cross-connect (End.DX2) behavior shown in Figure 3-13 is equivalent to EVPN Virtual Private Wire Service (VPWS). Much as with other endpoint with decapsulation behaviors, with the End.DX2 behavior, BGP is responsible for the propagation of service-related SIDs such as End.DX2 within the network using TLVs.

R5 instantiates the End.DX2 SID fcbb:bbbb:bb00:5:43:: (SID function 0x43) for a local Layer 2 access circuit attached to EVPN VPWS and propagates this information in BGP (using the EVPN address family) via a route reflector to R1. R1 has a local Layer 2 access circuit that belongs to the same EVPN VPWS. The EVPN VPWS is described in more detail in Chapter 6, "L2VPN Service Deployment: Configuration and Verification Techniques," in the section "EVPN E-Line." At a high level, EVPN VPWS can be thought of as a pipe running between the access circuits of R1 and R5 that does not require MAC learning or lookups due to the point-to-point nature of this service. R1 receives a packet from its local CE device that is destined to the destination MAC address (MAC 2) attached to a CE device behind R5 and encapsulates the payload into an outer IPv6 header.

Note that the customer Ethernet header and optional VLAN tags must be encapsulated for Layer 2 VPN services. A packet capture on an SRv6 transit node reveals that two Ethernet headers are present now, and the IPv6 Next Header field points to the inner Ethernet header (143). The packet follows the longest prefix match (/64 locator prefix) toward R5, where it is processed and forwarded toward the Layer 2 access circuit associated with SID function 0x43.

It is important to note that neither R1 nor R5 needs to perform a MAC destination look up on the inner Ethernet header. R1 forwards all traffic arriving on the Layer 2 access circuit toward the remote end of R5, and R5 can identify the egress Layer 2 access circuit based on the SID that was allocated for this EVPN VPWS. Keep in mind that the End.DX2 behavior can transport any upper layer protocols using a single SID (for example, IPv4 or IPv6), which is different from the Layer 3 VPN services described previously.

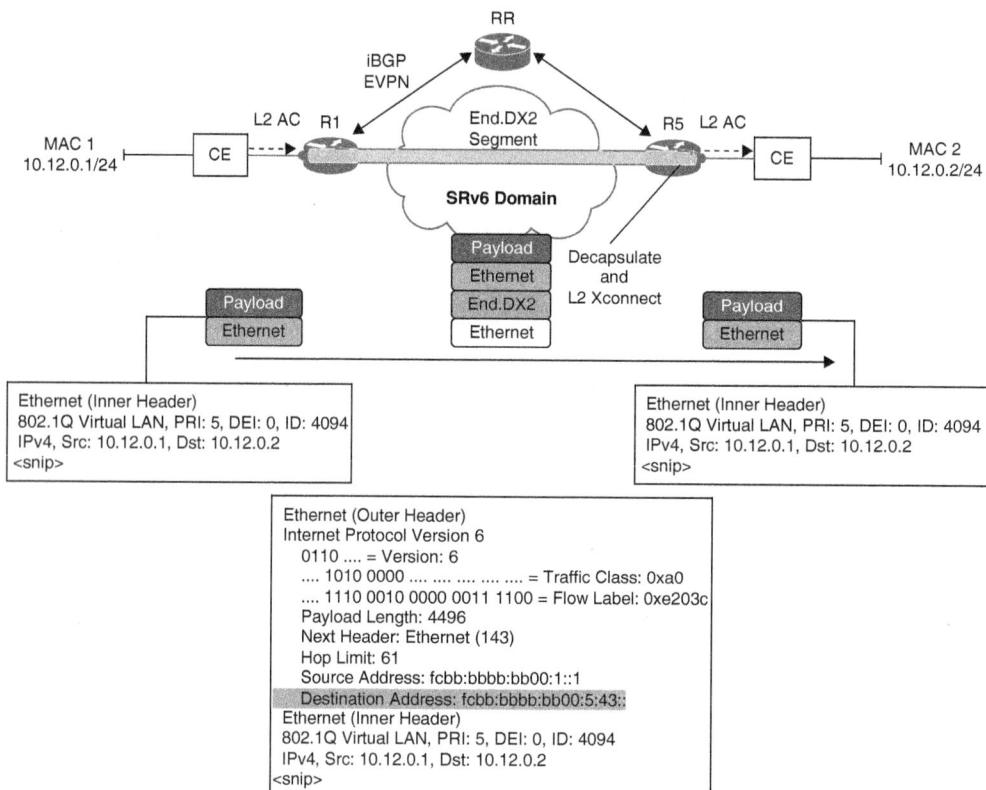

Figure 3-13 *SRv6 End.DX2 Segment*

End.DT2U Behavior

The endpoint with decapsulation and unicast MAC Layer 2 lookup (End.DT2U) behavior shown in Figure 3-14 is equivalent to an EVPN bridging service with unicast forwarding. Much as with other endpoint-with-decapsulation behaviors, with the End.DT2U behavior, BGP is responsible for the propagation of service-related SIDs such as End.DT2U within the network using TLVs.

R5 instantiates the End.DT2U SID fcbb:bbbb:bb00:5:44:: (SID function 0x44) for all MAC addresses belonging to the Layer 2 table and propagates this information in BGP (using the EVPN address family) via a route reflector to R1. R1 has a Layer 2 table associated with the same EVPN bridging service. The EVPN bridging service is described in more detail in Chapter 6, in the section "EVPN E-LAN." At a high level, it can be thought of as a large overlay switch that interconnects the access circuits of the member PE devices. As with a switch, MAC learning is required to populate the MAC address table required for forwarding. R1 receives a packet from its local CE device that is destined to the destination MAC address (MAC 2) attached to a CE device behind R5 and performs a MAC destination lookup. If the MAC 2 address is known on R1, R1 encapsulates the payload into an outer IPv6 header using the advertised SID of the egress PE device R5.

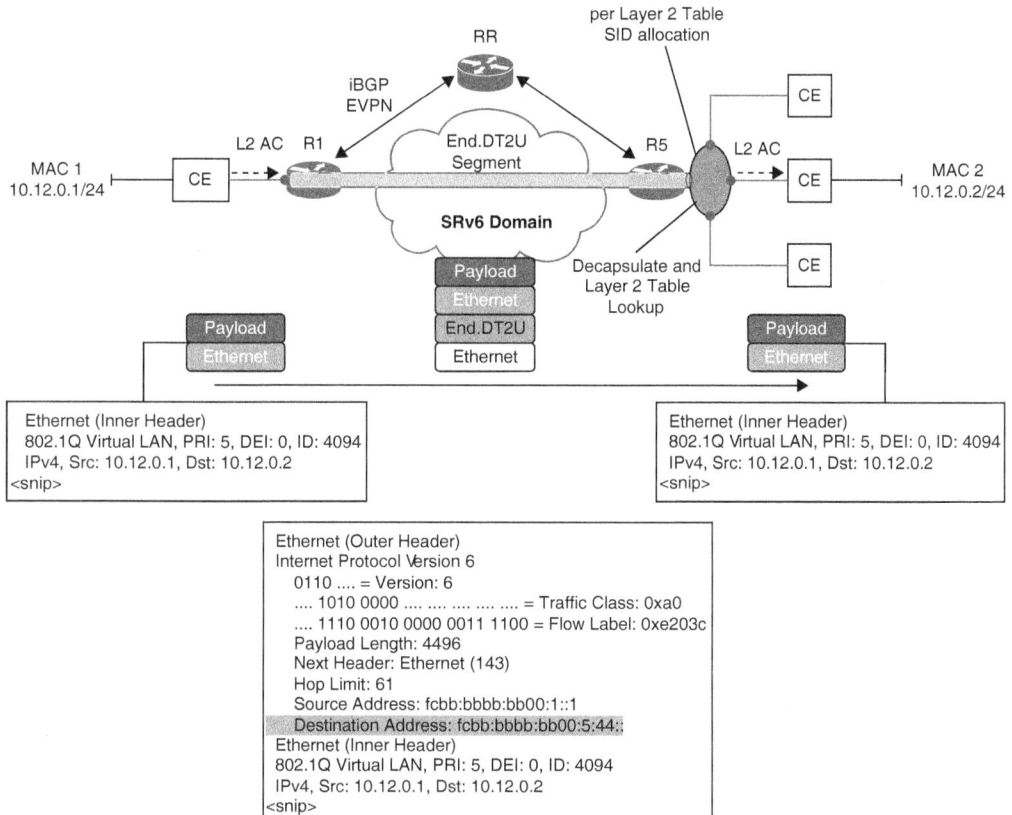

Figure 3-14 *SRv6 End.DT2U Segment*

Note that the customer Ethernet header and optional VLAN tags must be encapsulated for Layer 2 VPN services. A packet capture on an SRv6 transit node reveals that two Ethernet headers are present now, and the IPv6 Next Header field points to the inner Ethernet header (143). The packet follows the longest prefix match (/64 locator prefix) toward R5, where it is processed and forwarded based on the Layer 2 table associated with SID function 0x44 toward the CE device with the destination MAC 2 address.

It is important to note that both PE devices R1 and R5 must perform MAC destination lookups on MAC 2 addresses. Since R5 uses the same SID for all MAC addresses in the Layer 2 table associated with the SID, it requires one additional lookup to determine the egress interface and encapsulation information.

End.DT2M Behavior

The endpoint with decapsulation and Layer 2 table flooding (End.DT2M) behavior shown in Figure 3-15 is equivalent to an EVPN bridging service with BUM flooding. BUM includes the following traffic types:

- Broadcast

- Unknown unicast

- Multicast

Much as with other endpoint-with-decapsulation behaviors, with End.DT2M behavior, BGP is responsible for the propagation of service-related SIDs such as End.DT2M in the network using TLVs.

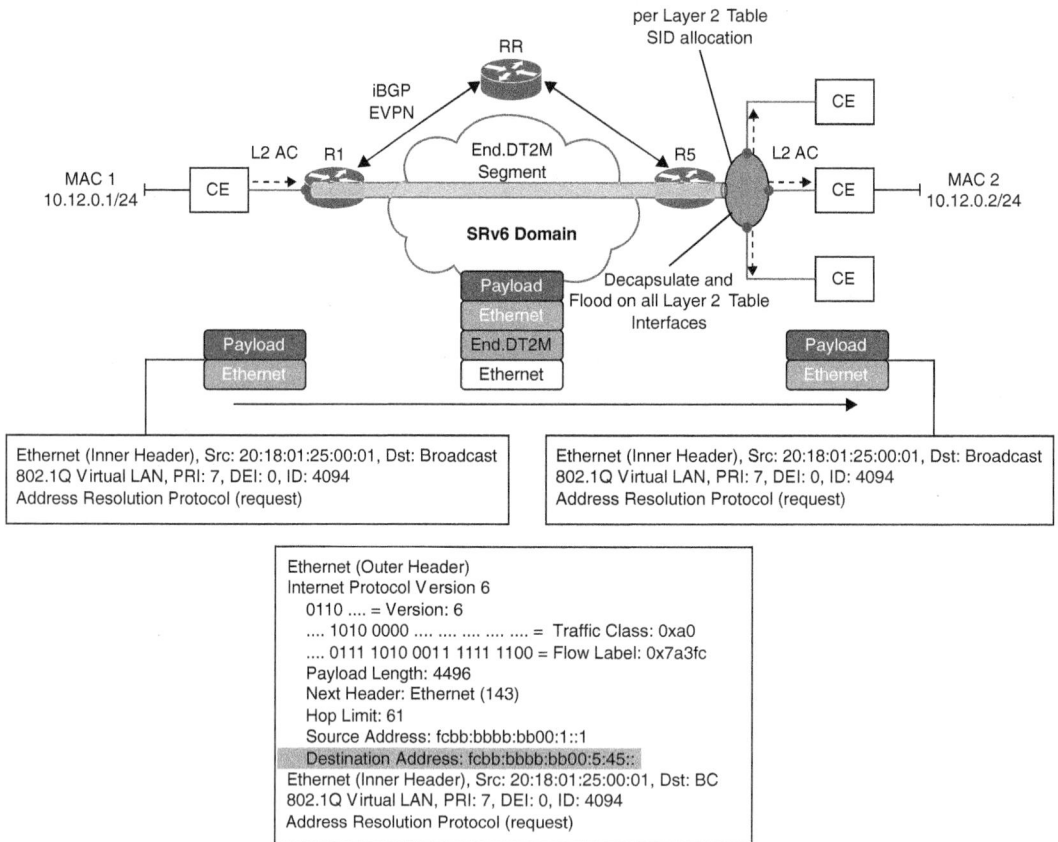

Figure 3-15 *SRv6 End.DT2M Segment*

R5 instantiates the End.DT2M SID fcbb:bbbb:bb00:5:45:: (SID function 0x45) for BUM traffic associated with the Layer 2 table and propagates this information in BGP (using an EVPN address family) via a route reflector to R1. R1 has a Layer 2 table that belongs to the same EVPN service. R1 receives from its local CE device a broadcast packet (ARP request) that should be replicated and sent to all egress PE devices and access circuits that belong to the same bridge domain. Ingress PE R1 performs a destination MAC address lookup and classifies the Ethernet broadcast address (ffff:ffff:ffff) as BUM traffic. Next, R1 has to replicate this packet for each egress PE device and encapsulates it into an outer IPv6 header using the advertised SID of the corresponding egress PE device. For simplicity, only a single egress PE device R5 is shown in Figure 3-15, but the principle is the same for additional egress PE devices. For each egress PE device participating in the broadcast domain, a replication of the original packet would have to be created, which would then be encapsulated into an outer IPv6 header with the corresponding End.DT2M SID of that egress PE device in the IPv6 destination address.

The packet follows the longest prefix match (/64 locator prefix) toward R5, where it is processed and flooded out all Layer 2 interfaces that belong to the Layer 2 table associated with the SID function 0x45. The intended recipient of the ARP request (MAC 2, 10.12.0.2) sends a response back to the originator (MAC 1, 10.12.0.1) enabling unicast connectivity between the two endpoints.

This overview covers the most common endpoint behaviors in many networks. This section omits endpoint behaviors related to SRv6 traffic engineering or SRv6 policy headend behaviors on purpose to reduce the complexity. Up to this point, a single SRv6 SID has been sufficient to realize simple Layer 2 or Layer 3 VPN services following the metric-based shortest path calculated by the IGP. Transit nodes in an SRv6 domain do not need to be SRv6 capable for basic longest prefix match forwarding of SRv6 SIDs. For many networks in both enterprise and service provider environments, this will suffice to do a like-for-like migration from MPLS to SRv6.

What about network operators that rely on traffic engineering? Traffic engineering (except with flex algos) generally requires more than one base format SID to be added to an SRv6 policy. At a glance, there seem to be two options to achieve this:

- Impose additional IPv6 (extension) headers.

- Encode multiple instructions in a single IPv6 destination address.

In fact, both of those options exist in the SRv6 framework and are introduced next.

IPv6 Segment Routing Header (SRH) (RFC 8754)

Advanced traffic engineering use cases require policies with more than one SRv6 SID, which is not possible to accommodate using a single IPv6 header. Adding an IPv6 header per SID would be inefficient and increase the packet overhead dramatically, which is why the IETF specified RFC 8754. The IPv6 segment routing header (SRH) shown in Figure 3-16 is a new routing extension header (Routing Type 4) that can carry multiple SIDs or instructions:

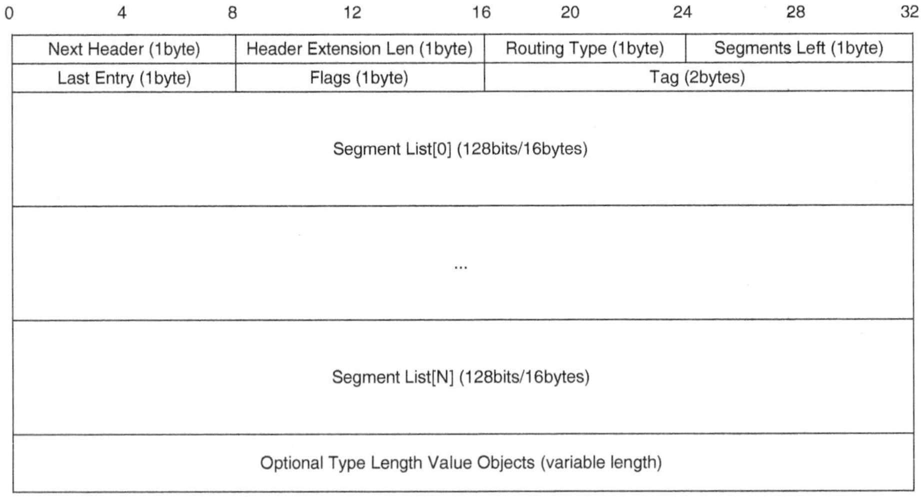

Figure 3-16 *IPv6 Segment Routing Header (SRH)*

The SRH consists of the following fields:

- **Next Header (8 bits):** Identifies the header following the SRH (for example, IPv4, IPv6, Ethernet, ICMP, TCP).

- **Header Extension Length (8 bits):** Specifies the length of the routing header (not including the first 8 bytes).

- **Routing Type (8 bits):** Specifies the routing type; set to 4 for SRH.

- **Segments Left (8 bits):** Identifies the remaining number of intermediate segments.

- **Last Entry (8 bits):** Serves as a zero-based index of the last segment that is used for SRH TLV detection and sanity checks.

- **Flags (8 bits):** Unused.

- **Tag (16 bits):** May be used for future use cases; set to zero when not used.

- **Segment List (128 bits):** Specifies a list of 128-bit IPv6 addresses (segments) in reverse order.

- **(Optional) Type Length Value (TLV) Objects (variable length):** May be used to provide metadata required for segments.

Some fields of the SRH may become relevant in the future but at this writing are not defined or are optional or not in widespread use. RFC 8754 defines two applications of the optional TLV Objects field:

- **Hashed Message Authentication Code (HMAC) TLV:** Provides authentication and integrity of the SRH.

  - **Authentication:** Ensures that the SRH has been generated by an authorized SRv6 node in the domain.

- **Integrity:** Ensures that the SRH has not been tampered with.

- **Padding TLVs:** Support two types of padding:

  - Pad1 (1 byte of padding)

  - PadN (N bytes of padding)

Figure 3-17 shows a graphical representation of the new terminology evolving around the segment routing header that is required to understand the description of data plane operations in this section.

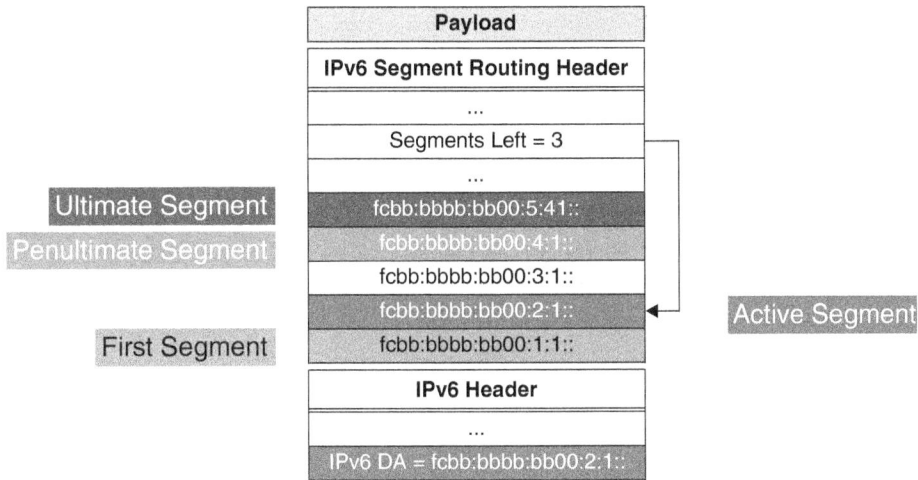

Figure 3-17 *SRv6 SRH Terminology*

The SRv6 source node adds the SRH and populates the fields based on the SRv6 policy. Figure 3-18 shows an example of an SRv6 policy with four segments in the segment list. SRv6 policies can be statically configured on a device or pushed through an external controller.

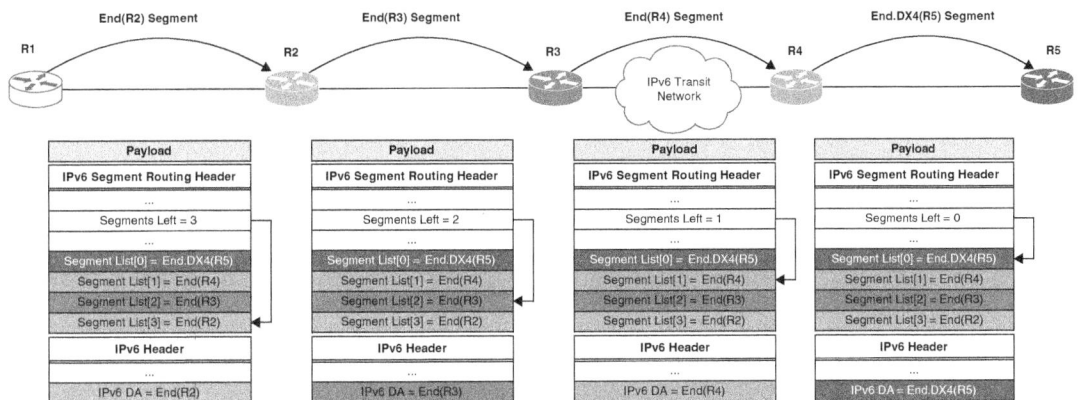

Figure 3-18 *SRv6 Policy with SRH*

The following SRv6 node types can be distinguished in the diagram:

- **Source node:** Device R1 steers traffic into an SRv6 policy.

  - SRv6 capable.

  - Encapsulates traffic into an IPv6 header with an optional SRH, including a segment list.

  - Sets the SRH last entry and the Segments Left field to N (number of segments minus 1 due to zero-based indexing).

  - Sets the IPv6 destination address to the first segment (segment list[N]).

Note   A reduced SRH (omitting the first segment that is already present in the IPv6 destination address) may be added by a source node in the event that preservation of the original SID list is not required for path backtracking purposes.

- **Transit node:** A device in the IPv6 transit network forwards SRv6 packets as plain IPv6 packets.

  - IPv6 capable.

  - Performs longest-prefix-match IPv6 routing.

  - Does not process any segments.

- **Endpoint node:** Devices R2 through R5 instantiated active segments in the IPv6 destination address.

  - SRv6 capable.

  - Performs longest-prefix-match IPv6 routing.

  - Processes locally instantiated segments.

Note   A device may take all three roles for different traffic flows or paths.

In the example shown in Figure 3-18, ingress PE R1 receives a payload from a CE device that is steered into an SRv6 policy, effectively encapsulating the customer packet into an outer IPv6 header. The policy includes four endpoint segments on R2, R3, R4, and R5. The source node R1 sets the Segments Left field to 3, copies the first segment located at segment list[3] into the IPv6 destination address, making it the active segment, and forwards the packet based on the longest prefix match.

R2 performs a longest-prefix-match lookup and has a locally instantiated SRv6 SID in the Forwarding Information Base (FIB) present for its endpoint behavior. The Segments Left field is decremented by one, and the segment located at segment list[2] is copied into the IPv6 destination address. Finally, the packet is forwarded to the new IPv6 destination address based on the longest prefix match.

The process is identical on R3 and R4. However, a native IPv6 network consisting of several hops that are not SRv6 capable interconnects R3 and R4. Since the active segment is always copied into the IPv6 destination address of the outer header, those transit nodes will be able to forward SRv6 traffic without any problems, following the longest prefix match route. In fact, the transit nodes will not even know that they are forwarding SRv6 traffic since they will not be able to distinguish SRv6 traffic from regular IPv6 traffic.

Eventually, the encapsulated payload arrives on the egress PE device R5, which performs a longest-prefix-match lookup and maps it to a FIB entry representing a locally instantiated SRv6 SID (End.DX4). The endpoint behavior processing in the presence of an SRH is all documented as part of RFC 8986, where in the case of End.DX4, the outer IPv6 header with all extension headers is removed and the exposed IPv4 packet is forwarded out the Layer 3 adjacency associated with the local End.DX4 SID.

With the addition of the segment routing header, various End, End.X, or End.T behaviors flavors can be distinguished:

- Penultimate Segment Pop (PSP) of the SRH

- Ultimate Segment Pop (USP) of the SRH

- Ultimate Segment Decapsulation (USD)

These flavors can be supported individually or in combination and are advertised as part of the SID in the link-state IGP. Endpoint flavors are configured by the network operator according to device platform capabilities.

Penultimate Segment Pop of the SRH

Figure 3-19 shows an example of a Penultimate Segment Pop (PSP) of the SRH, which is somewhat similar to penultimate hop popping (PHP) from MPLS. The device that copies the ultimate segment from the segment list into the IPv6 destination address and decrements the Segments Left field from 1 to 0 (R2) is called the *penultimate SR segment endpoint node*.

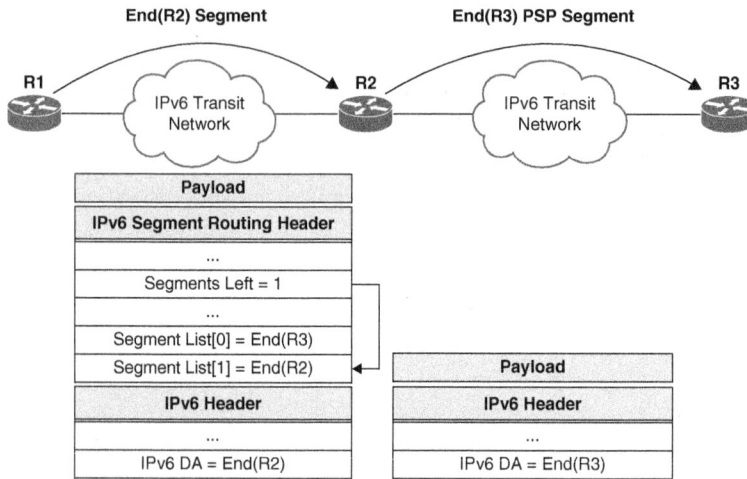

Figure 3-19   *SRv6 PSP of the SRH Endpoint Flavor*

The PSP-flavored End, End.X, and End.T behaviors modify their SRH processing to update the IPv6 header in order to remove the SRH.

At a high level, R2 performs the following steps:

Step 1.   Copies the value of the Next Header field from the SRH to the IPv6 header.

Step 2.   Reflects the new IPv6 header length (without the SRH).

Step 3.   Removes the SRH.

Step 4.   Forwards the packet toward the ultimate segment.

Note   Sanity checks and basic IPv6 header modifications such as IPv6 hop limit decrementation are ignored for pragmatic reasons in all PSP/USP/USD processing examples in this book.

PSP has the following benefits for the egress PE device (in this example, R3):

- Less complexity and overhead in the parsing and decapsulation of the packet
- Smaller network processor unit (NPU) cache required to access upper layer information (for example, IPv4 header required for End.DT4 processing)
- Simpler ASIC implementation
- Fewer NPU cycles required for segment processing, which may lead to higher performance (pps)

PSP may not be suitable for all deployments in the event that certain information from the SRH (for example, the Tag or optional TLV Objects fields) is required on the ultimate SR segment endpoint node.

Ultimate Segment Pop of the SRH

Figure 3-20 shows an example of a USP of the SRH. The device R3 is the ultimate SR segment endpoint node and removes the SRH.

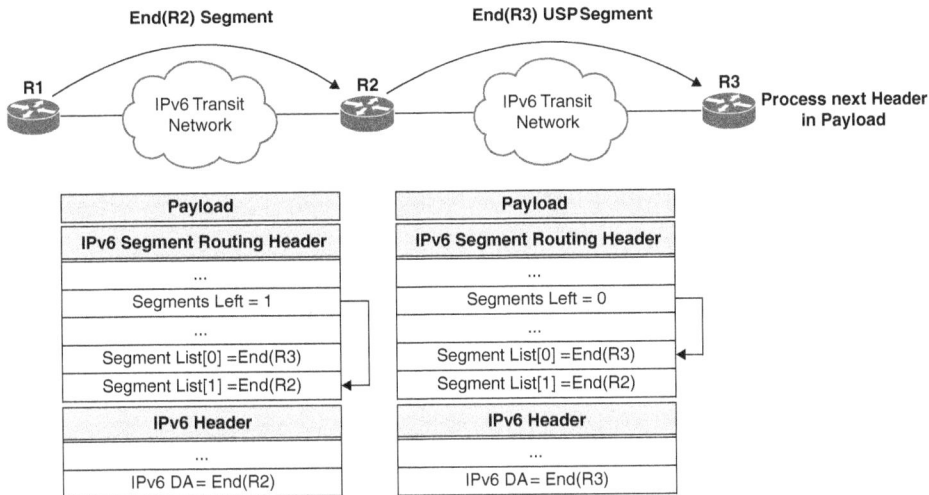

Figure 3-20 *SRv6 USP of the SRH Endpoint Flavor*

The USP-flavored End, End.X, and End.T behaviors modify their SRH processing to update the IPv6 header in order to remove the SRH before processing the upper layer header of the inner packet.

At a high level, R3 performs the following steps:

Step 1.   Copies the value of the Next Header field from the SRH to the IPv6 header.

Step 2.   Reflects the new IPv6 header length (without SRH).

Step 3.   Removes the SRH.

Step 4.   Processes the upper layer header of the inner packet.

The USP flavor is mainly useful in data center domains with highly specialized network interface cards (NICs) where packets with an SRH are destined for applications. The SRH should be removed before the packet is forwarded to the application. At the same time, information present in the Tag or optional TLV Objects fields may be required as additional input parameters for applications running in a virtualized or containerized environment. Another use case applies to network security where the operator may want to preserve the segment list of a packet for logging purposes or to only admit packets that passed through the firewall into a protected network environment.

Ultimate Segment Decapsulation

Figure 3-21 shows an example of an Ultimate Segment Decapsulation (USD) with an End segment. The device acting as the ultimate SR segment endpoint node (R3) removes the outer IPv6 header, including the optional SRH, and processes the upper layer headers accordingly.

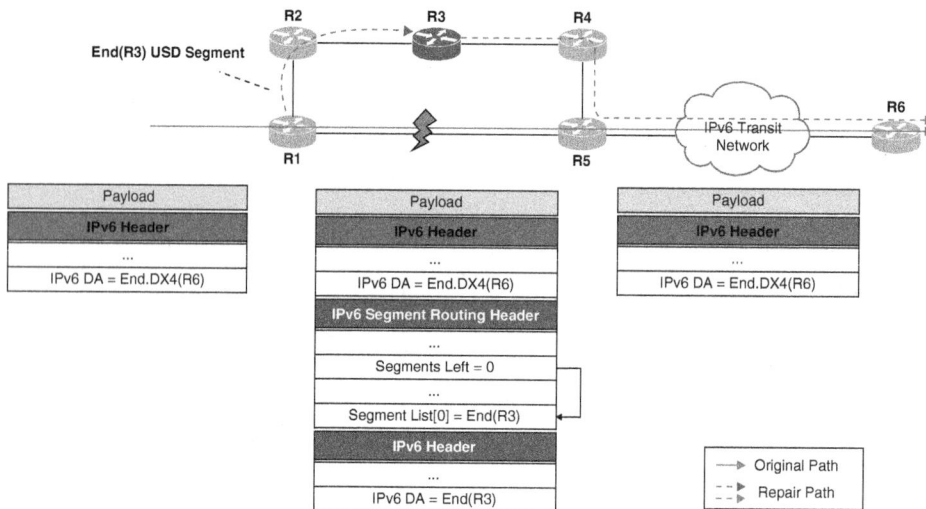

Figure 3-21   *SRv6 USD Endpoint Flavor*

USD is applicable to Topology Independent Loop-Free Alternate (TI-LFA), where the point of local repair (R1 in the example) steers the original packet into an SRv6 policy. Such a fast reroute policy, which may consist of one or more segments, reroutes traffic until the network converges to the identical post-convergence path. In the previous example, R1 needs to make sure that traffic is not routed back toward the failed link between R1 and R5. The backup path via a series of routers (R2, R3, and R4) requires a single segment backup path via R3 to prevent traffic from being routed back via the failed link. In theory, a single segment would not require the addition of an SRH, but for demonstration purposes, we assume that R1 would encapsulate the original packet into an IPv6 header with an SRH. R1 forwards the newly crafted packet out the interface connected to R2, from where it is delivered to R3. R3 performs USD for its End SID, which, in the case of an inner IPv6 packet, removes the IPv6 header with all its extension headers (for example, SRH) and performs an IPv6 lookup on the inner IPv6 destination address (End.DX4(R6)). From there, the End.DX4 SID of R6 follows the longest prefix match until it reaches R6, where it is processed.

Note   As you will learn going through the different SRv6 headend behaviors, there are two different options for steering SRv6 transit traffic into an SRv6 policy: H.Encaps* and H.Insert*. The TI-LFA example in Figure 3-21 deliberately uses the suboptimal H.Encaps implementation to showcase the USD endpoint flavor.

The original upper layer header processing of End, End.T, and End.X endpoint behaviors is modified to decapsulate and process the inner packet header:

End upper layer header processing:

- IF upper layer header equal to IPv4:
    - Remove the outer IPv6 header with all extension headers.
    - Forward the newly exposed packet based on the result of the IPv4 FIB lookup.
- ELSE IF upper layer header equal to IPv6:
    - Remove the outer IPv6 header with all extension headers.
    - Forward the newly exposed packet based on the result of the IPv6 FIB lookup.
- ELSE:
    - Process the upper layer header.

End.T upper layer header processing:

- IF upper layer header equal to IPv4:
    - Remove the outer IPv6 header with all extension headers.
    - Set the FIB table to the table associated with the End.T SID.
    - Forward the newly exposed packet based on the result of the IPv4 FIB lookup.
- ELSE IF upper layer header equal to IPv6:
    - Remove the outer IPv6 header with all extension headers.
    - Set the FIB table to the table associated with the End.T SID.
    - Forward the newly exposed packet based on the result of the IPv6 FIB lookup.
- ELSE:
    - Process the upper layer header.

End.X upper layer header processing:

- IF upper layer header equal to IPv4 or IPv6:
    - Remove the outer IPv6 header with all extension headers.
    - Forward the newly exposed packet out the L3 adjacency associated with the End.X SID.
- ELSE:
    - Process the upper layer header.

The use case and applications of the SRH evolving around SRv6 traffic engineering should be clearer now which allows introducing additional headend behaviors defined as part of RFC 8986 and its extensions that aim to steer traffic into an SRv6 policy.

SRv6 Policy Headend Behaviors

Table 3-2 lists various SR policy headend behaviors.

Table 3-2   *SRv6 Policy Headend Behaviors*

SRv6 Headend Behavior	Control Plane Signaling	Description
H.Encaps	IGP/BGP-LS	SRv6 headend with encapsulation in an SR policy (Layer 3 service)
H.Encaps.Red	IGP/BGP-LS	H.Encaps with reduced encapsulation (Layer 3 service)
H.Insert	IGP/BGP-LS	SRv6 headend with insertion of an SRv6 policy
H.Insert.Red	IGP/BGP-LS	H.Insert with reduced insertion of an SRv6 policy
H.Encaps.L2	BGP-LS	H.Encaps applied to received L2 frames (Layer 2 service)
H.Encaps.L2.Red	BGP-LS	H.Encaps.L2 with reduced encapsulation (Layer 2 service)

Endpoint behaviors are generally applicable to egress PEs, whereas headend behaviors are applicable to ingress PEs or intermediate nodes in the case of Point of Local Repair (PLR) for TI-LFA. As mentioned previously, PLR nodes may use the H.Encaps* or H.Insert* headend behavior to steer traffic into an SRv6 policy.

Ingress PE devices use the H.Encaps/H.Encaps.Red headend behavior for Layer 3 services (for example, End.DX4), whereas Layer 2 services (for example, End.DX2) depend on H.Encaps.L2/H.Encaps.L2.Red. A major difference between headend and previously introduced endpoint behaviors is the fact that the destination address of the received packet does not belong to the ingress node that steers the traffic into an SRv6 policy.

Note   Sanity checks and basic IPv6 header modifications such as IPv6 hop limit decrementation and IPv6 encapsulation details such as IPv6 Source Address, Payload Length, Traffic Class, Flow Label, and Next Header fields are ignored for pragmatic reasons in all SRv6 headend behavior examples in this book.

H.Encaps Behavior

Figure 3-22 shows the headend perspective of an IPv4 Layer 3 VPN service introduced earlier in Figure 3-12, with a SID associated with an End.DX4 segment on the egress PE

R5. The ingress PE R1 steers traffic into the SRv6 policy using the H.Encaps headend behavior, which is applicable to Layer 3 traffic in a VPN or the global routing table (GRT).

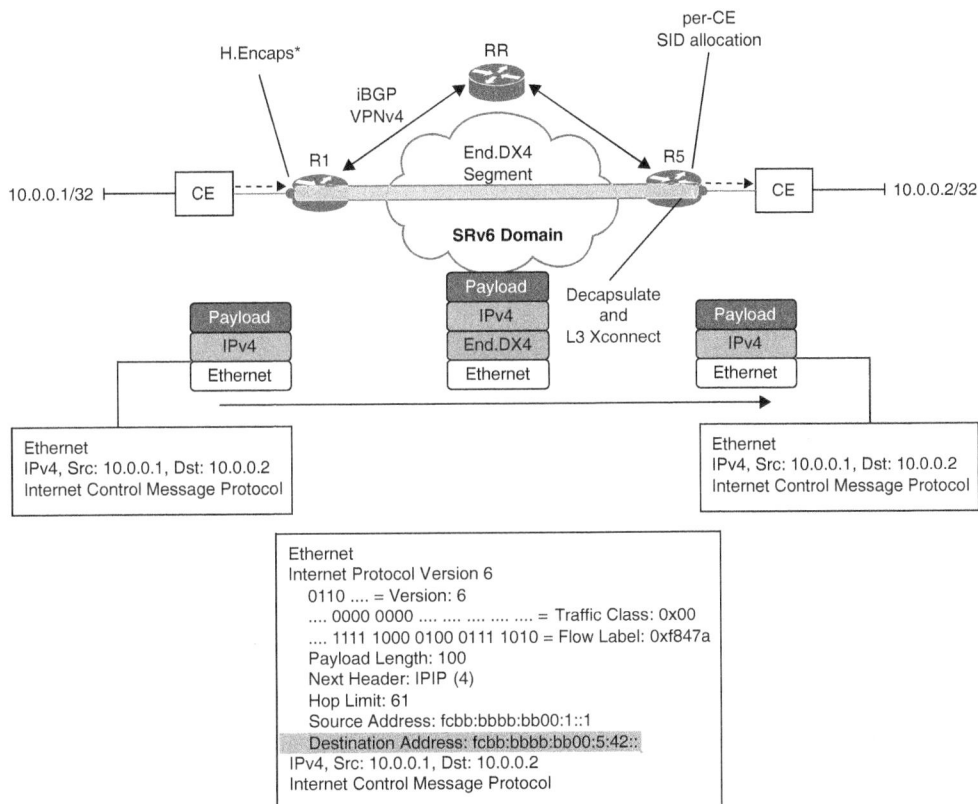

Figure 3-22 *SRv6 H.Encaps Behavior (without SRH)*

Ingress PE R1 receives an IP4 packet on the service edge, where the IP destination address lookup does not match with any local address. R1 performs a destination lookup in the routing table associated with the ingress interface, which could be a VRF instance or the GRT. In the example, the destination address is learned through BGP and was originated by R5. As explained previously, the BGP UPDATE message contains the relevant SID information to encapsulate the customer payload in an outer IPv6 header with an optional SRH (depending on the SRv6 policy). The example shows a simple Layer 3 VPN service with an SRv6 policy consisting of a single segment. Consequently, the SRH may be omitted if there is no requirement to encode meta information in the Flags, Tag, or TLV Objects fields of the SRH.

H.Encaps.Red Behavior

The previous example (refer to Figure 3-22) is very simple and covers Layer 3 services that do not rely on complex traffic engineering policies. A more complex use case is shown in Figure 3-23, which depicts a Layer 3 IPv6 customer overlay service with an SRH that needs to be transported across a service provider network using a specific SRv6 policy. The service and SRv6 policy consist of the following SIDs:

- Segment List[0] = fcbb:bbbb:bb00:5:44:: (End.DT6 of R5)

- Segment List[1] = fcbb:bbbb:bb00:4:1:: (End of R4)

- Segment List[2] = fcbb:bbbb:bb00:3:1:: (End of R3)

- Segment List[3] = fcbb:bbbb:bb00:2:1:: (End of R2)

Remember that the service SID for R5's End.DT6 behavior is dynamically allocated without a SID function-to-endpoint behavior mapping (where the function might be 0x44 and the behavior might be End.DT6).

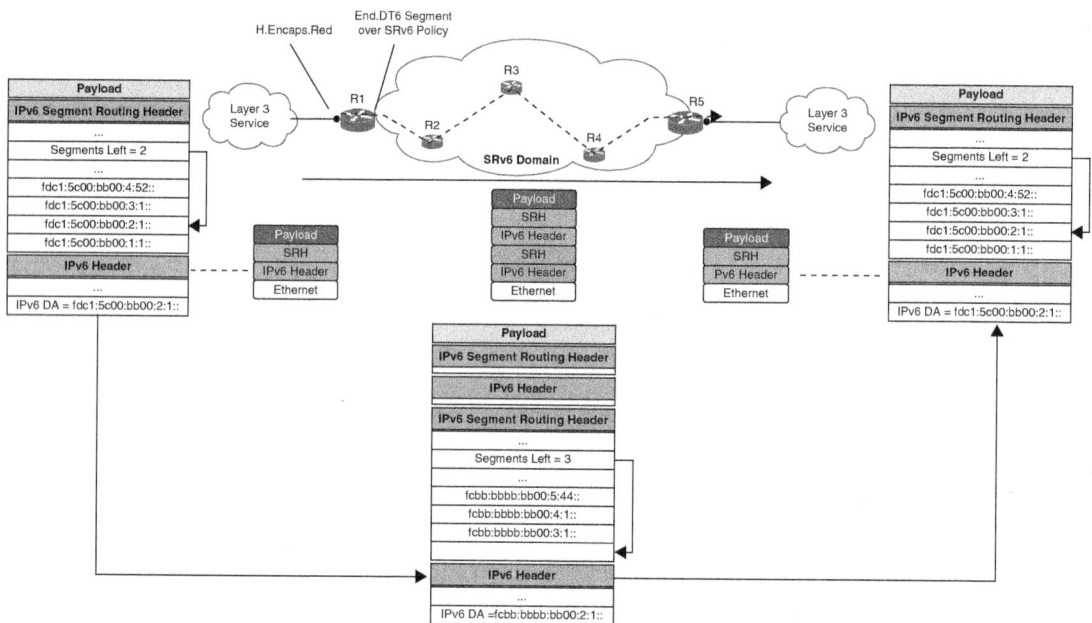

Figure 3-23 *SRv6 H.Encaps.Red Behavior (with SRH)*

The received customer payload on ingress PE device R1 is modified and encapsulated as follows:

- Create a new outer IPv6 header with SRH.

  - **IPv6 header:** Set the IPv6 destination address to the first segment of the SRv6 policy (End(R2)).

  - **SRH:** Encode the remaining SIDs of the policy as End(R3), End(R4), and End.

DT6(R5) into the SRH.

■ Encapsulate the customer payload into the new IPv6 outer header with the SRH.

Note The example in Figure 3-23 shows a customer payload consisting of an IPv6 header with an SRH. SRv6 offers transparent services, which means that the inner packet is not modified in any way. The inner packet could consist of a complex header structure (for example, customer SRv6 or GRE tunnel), which would not change the example in any way. The ingress PE device treats the packet being received from the customer edge as a payload that is encapsulated into an outer IPv6 header with or without an SRH (depending on the SRv6 policy).

The original packet is encapsulated into this new IPv6 header with an SRH and forwarded based on the IPv6 destination address of the outer IPv6 header's destination address (fcbb:bbbb:bb00:2:1::). Note that the first segment of the SRv6 policy (fcbb:bbbb:bb00:2:1::) is omitted from the SRH when using the H.Encaps.Red headend behavior since it is already included in the IPv6 destination address of the outer header and, therefore, somewhat redundant in the SRH. The reduced headend behavior therefore omits the first segment from the SRH, sets the last entry field to the number of segments minus 2, and keeps the Segments Left field at the number of segments minus 1, ensuring that the proper segment is executed next.

H.Encaps.L2 Behavior

Figure 3-24 shows the headend perspective of a Layer 2 VPN service introduced earlier (refer to Figure 3-13) with a SID associated with an End.DX2 segment on the egress PE device R5. The ingress PE device R1 steers traffic into the SRv6 policy using the H.Encaps.L2 headend behavior, which is applicable to point-to-point or multipoint Layer 2 VPN services. One of the key differences between H.Encaps and H.Encaps.L2 is the fact that H.Encaps encapsulates the Layer 2 payload (Layer 3 and above), whereas H.Encaps.L2 encapsulates the Layer 2 frame (Layer 2 and above).

Ingress PE device R1 receives an Ethernet frame on the service edge. Depending on the Layer 2 service, R1 performs a destination lookup in the MAC Layer 2 table associated with the ingress interface for multipoint services or steers traffic into a VPWS for point-to-point services. In the example, a point-to-point Layer 2 service that runs between R1 and R5 does not participate in MAC learning and consequently does not require a MAC lookup. The remote endpoint of the VPWS is learned through BGP and was originated by R5. As explained previously, the BGP UPDATE message contains the relevant SID information to encapsulate the customer Ethernet frame into an outer IPv6 header with the optional SRH (depending on the SRv6 policy). The example shows a simple Layer 2 VPN service with an SRv6 policy consisting of a single segment. Consequently, the SRH may be omitted if there is no requirement to encode meta information in the Flags, Tag, or TLV Objects fields of the SRH.

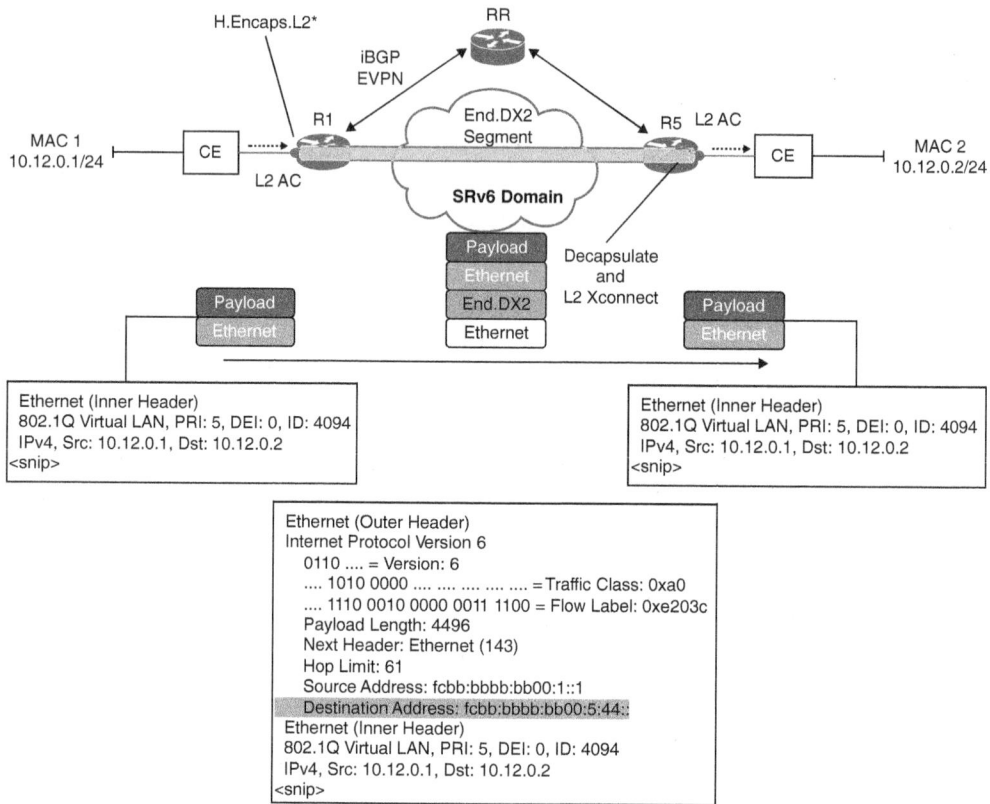

Figure 3-24   *SRv6 H.Encaps.L2 Behavior*

H.Encaps.L2.Red Behavior

The previous example covers Layer 2 services, which do not rely on complex traffic engineering policies. A more complex use case is shown in Figure 3-25, which illustrates a Layer 2 customer overlay service with an SRH that needs to be transported across a service provider network using a specific SRv6 policy. The service and SRv6 policy consist of the following SIDs:

- Segment List[0] = fcbb:bbbb:bb00:6:47:: (End.DT2U of R6)

- Segment List[1] = fcbb:bbbb:bb00:4:41:: (End.X of R4)

- Segment List[2] = fcbb:bbbb:bb00:3:1:: (End of R3)

- Segment List[3] = fcbb:bbbb:bb00:2:1:: (End of R2)

The received customer Layer 2 frame on ingress PE device R1 is encapsulated as follows:

- Create a new outer IPv6 header with SRH.

  - **IPv6 header:** Set the IPv6 destination address to the first segment of the SRv6 policy (End(R2)).

- **SRH:** Encode the remaining SIDs of the policy into the SRH as End(R3), End.X(R4), and End.DT2U(R6).

- **SRH:** Set the Next Header field to 143 (Ethernet).

- Encapsulate the customer Layer 2 frame (excluding preamble and FCS) into the new IPv6 outer header with SRH.

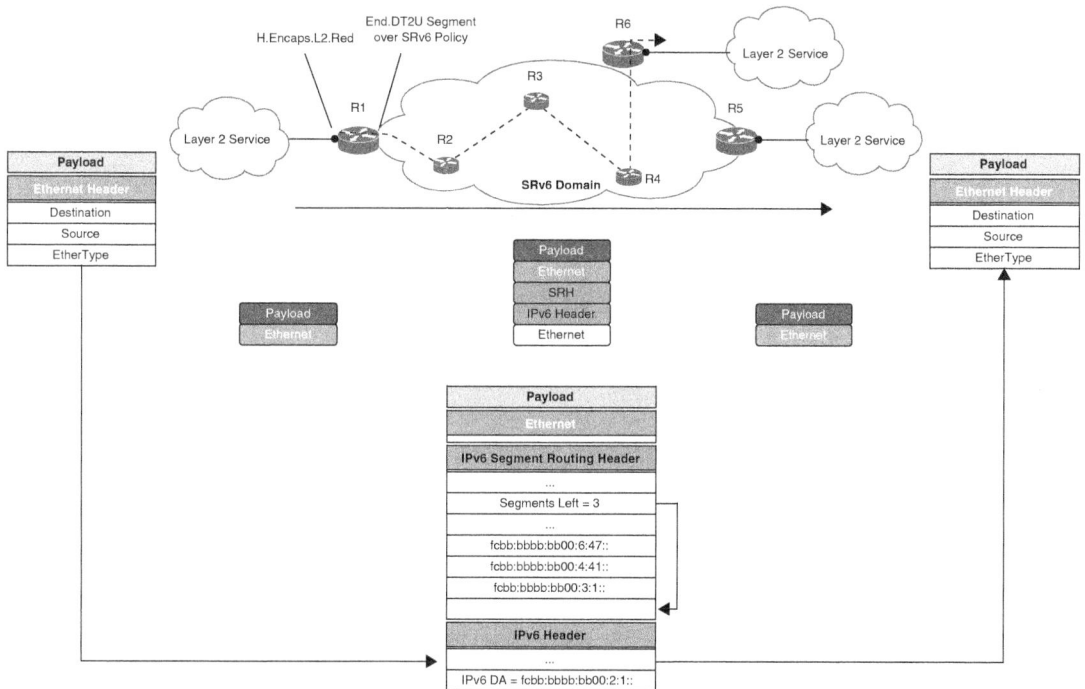

Figure 3-25 *SRv6 H.Encaps.L2.Red Behavior (with SRH)*

The original packet is encapsulated into an outer IPv6 header with an SRH and forwarded based on the IPv6 destination address of the outer header (fcbb:bbbb:bb00:2:1::). Again note that the first segment of the SRv6 policy (fcbb:bbbb:bb00:2:1::) is omitted from the SRH when using the H.Encaps.L2.Red headend behavior since it is already included in the IPv6 destination address of the outer packet and is therefore somewhat redundant in the SRH. The same principles discussed earlier regarding reduced headend behaviors apply here. Hopefully those examples are starting to feel somewhat repetitive to you because encapsulating and transporting services over an SRv6 network are mostly the same, no matter the type of service. The IPv6 and segment routing header provide the vessel to tunnel overlay services across the SRv6 domain, and the SIDs change depending on the service and SRv6 policy, but the end-to-end chain of encapsulation, forwarding, and decapsulation remains unchanged.

H.Insert Behavior

The remaining SRv6 headend behavior to be introduced is H.Insert, which steers traffic into an SRv6 policy, such as on nodes that suffer from local failures. Examples of such local failures could be a link failure affecting a local interface or a remote node failure, which looks like a link failure on the local node as far as the failure detection is concerned. Nodes suffering from local failures are commonly referred to as point of local repair (PLR) in the context of fast reroute, which is the primary application of the H.Insert headend behavior (see Figure 3-26).

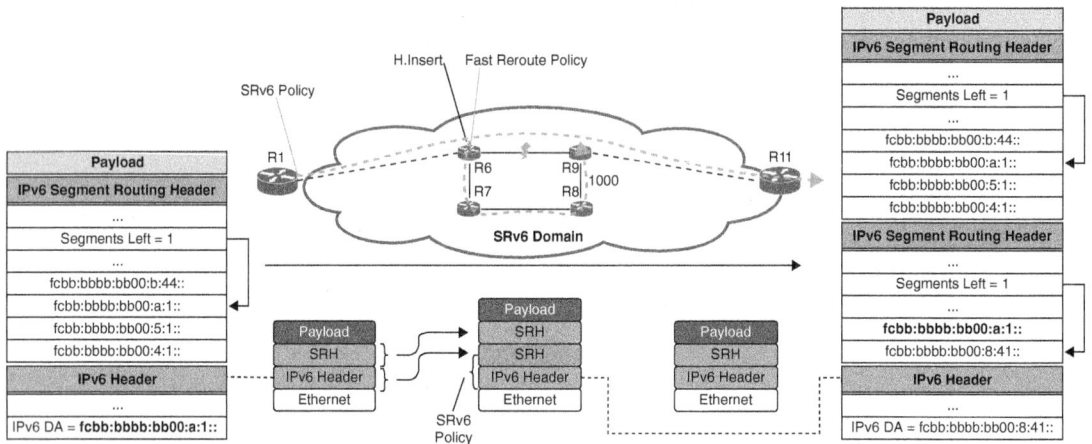

Figure 3-26   *SRv6 H.Insert Behavior (with SRH)*

The ingress PE device R1 shown in Figure 3-26 steers traffic into an SRv6 policy that consists of a traffic-engineered path across nodes R4, R5, and R10 (not shown in the diagram) with a Layer 2 or Layer 3 endpoint behavior on R11. Somewhere within the SRv6 domain is a square consisting of four devices where two devices (R8 and R9) are interconnected using a higher IGP metric (1000). By default, traffic flows across the direct link (R6 to R9) and avoids this high-metric link, as shown with the dashed line between ingress and egress PE devices. Suddenly, the preferred path becomes unavailable due to a core link failure, as shown in the diagram. The point of local repair (PLR) device, R6, must activate a backup path in hardware to reroute traffic around the network failure. The H.Insert headend behavior is a key building block for SRv6 Topology-Independent Loop-Free Alternate (TI-LFA), which is introduced in detail in Chapter 9, "High Availability and Fast Convergence," in the section "Topology-Independent Loop-Free Alternate (TI-LFA)." For now, it is sufficient to understand that backup paths are computed in advance—that is, before the failure happens in the network—and that those backup paths are preprogrammed in hardware, which allows for very fast convergence (sub 50 milliseconds). As the name Topology-Independent Loop-Free Alternate implies, the backup path must be loop free, meaning that traffic is not forwarded back to R6; in other words, traffic should not be routed back across the failed link. Without going into too much detail about TI-LFA, how far does traffic need to be rerouted to guarantee that it is not routed back across the failed link? The link between R8 and R9 has an IGP metric of 1000, which means that traffic destined to the IPv6 address fcbb:bbbb:bb00:a:1:: (End of R10) would be routed back toward the failed link from R7 to R6 or even from R8 to R7. Only once traffic reaches R9 would it be guaranteed that the backup path is loop free since it will not be rerouted back across the link between R6 and R9. Hence, the original packet received by R6 must be steered into a temporary fast reroute SRv6 policy until the network converges. This policy cannot steer traffic directly to R9 because it would follow the shortest path across the affected link between R6 and R9. Instead, traffic could be routed to R8 first, and from there across the high-metric link using its local Adjacency SID. Such a fast reroute SRv6 policy can be achieved using a single SID (for example, fcbb:bbbb:bb00:8:41::) based on the globally significant locator and the locally significant function part associated with the Adjacency SID (End.X) toward R9.

The H.Insert headend behavior steers traffic into the fast reroute SRv6 policy on the PLR R6, which ensures that traffic is forwarded using the backup path until the network converges. The fast reroute policy is inserted between the outer IPv6 header and the other optional SRH. The received packet on R6 is modified as follows:

- **Create a new SRH:** The SID list of the fast reroute policy End.X(R8) and the original IPv6 destination address are encoded into the new SRH.

- **Insert the new SRH:** The SRH containing the policy is inserted between the IPv6 header and the optional SRH of the original packet.

- **Modify the IPv6 header:** Set the IPv6 destination address to the new active segment fcbb:bbbb:bb00:8:41:: (End.X of R8).

The SRH inserted into the original packet contains both the fast reroute policy (fcbb:bbbb:bb00:8:41::) and the original IPv6 destination address (fcbb:bbbb:bb00:a:1::) of the received packet. Because the example shows the behavior for H.Insert and not H.Insert.Red, the first segment is included in the inserted SRH. Once the packet reaches R8, the Segments Left field is decremented from 1 to 0, the next segment (fcbb:bbbb:bb00:a:1::) is copied into the IPv6 destination address, and R8 may or may not perform Penultimate Segment Pop (PSP) before forwarding the packet to R9. If it does perform PSP, the packet received by R9 would have the same IPv6 destination address and SRH present as the packet received from R6 before the link failure happened. Eventually the network converges, and all devices agree that the only path between R6 and R9 goes via the high-metric link. At that point in time, no fast reroute SRv6 policy is required anymore, and traffic destined to the IPv6 address fcbb:bbbb:bb00:a:1:: can be forwarded by R6 toward R7 without the risk of traffic looping back.

When talking about backup paths in the context of TI-LFA, we can distinguish between zero-segment, single-segment, double-segment, and more backup paths. Zero-segment backup paths do not require any special fast reroute policy to achieve fast convergence, which is common in highly symmetric networks with equal cost multipathing (ECMP). In the presence of ECMP, one path backs up another path and vice versa without the need to insert an SRH. For single-segment backup paths, however, there will always be an SRH for both H.Insert and H.Insert.Red because the original IPv6 destination address must be stored in the segment list of the newly inserted SRH.

This section does not repeat this example for H.Insert.Red. See the section "End. B6.Insert.Red Behavior," later in this chapter, which covers a similar behavior showcasing a Binding SID.

SRv6 Policy Headend Behavior Comparison

Figure 3-27 compares the encapsulation headers of different SRv6 headend behaviors introduced in the previous paragraphs.

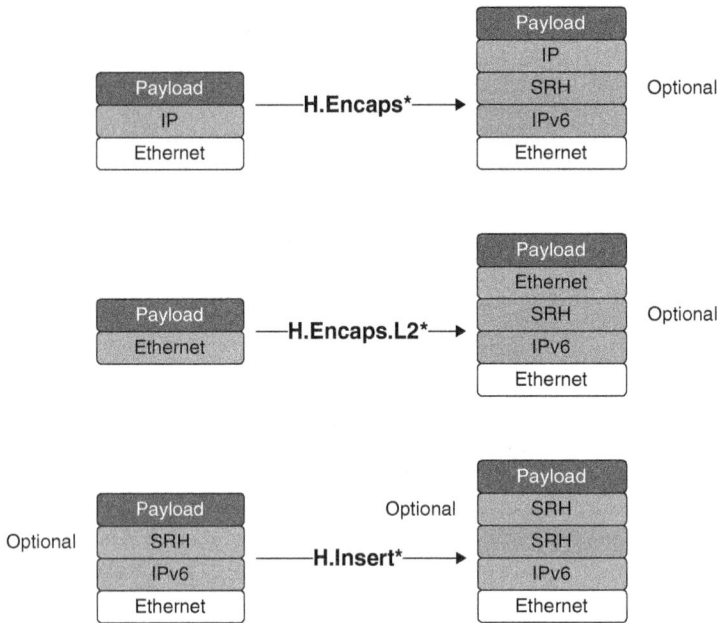

Figure 3-27   *SRv6 Headend Behaviors (Encaps and Insert)*

Different services and fast convergence applications require different headend behaviors:

- Layer 2 services require support for the H.Encaps.L2 or H.Encaps.L2.Red headend behaviors on the ingress PE.

- Layer 3 services require support for the H.Encaps or H.Encaps.Red headend behaviors on the ingress PE.

- TI-LFA fast reroute SRv6 policies require support for H.Encaps, H.Encaps.Red, H.Insert, or H.Insert.Red on the PLR.

Depending on the underlying hardware platform or software implementation, fast reroute SRv6 policies on the PLR may be realized using H.Encaps or H.Insert. The implementation of H.Insert is more challenging, which is why not all hardware platforms support it. While H.Insert is superior to H.Encaps for the application of TI-LFA due to the lower encapsulation overhead, one may argue that 50 ms of additional overhead during network events is negligible. It should be evident now why a native IPv6 transit network lacking SRH processing support limits the use of TI-LFA and SRv6 traffic engineering.

SRv6 Policy Endpoint Behaviors

Besides headend behaviors, different SRv6 policy endpoint behaviors exist, as shown in Table 3-3.

Table 3-3 *SRv6 Policy Endpoint Behaviors*

SRv6 Endpoint Behavior	Control Plane Signaling	Description
End.B6.Encaps	BGP-LS	Endpoint bound to SRv6 policy with encapsulation (SRv6 Binding SID)
End.B6.Encaps.Red	BGP-LS	Same as End.B6.Encaps but with reduced SRH (SRv6 Binding SID)
End.B6.Insert	BGP-LS	Endpoint bound to an SRv6 policy with SRH insertion (SRv6 Binding SID)
End.B6.Insert.Red	BGP-LS	Endpoint bound to an SRv6 policy with reduced SRH insertion (SRv6 Binding SID)

The previously introduced naming concept applies to transport- and traffic engineering–related policies alike, with the following additions:

- ***B6.***: B6 refers to an SRv6 Binding SID.

- ***Red:** Red refers to reduced, which means that the first SID of an SRv6 policy will be omitted from the SRH since it is already included in the IPv6 destination address of the outer IPv6 header.

- ***Encaps***: Encaps refers to encapsulation, which means traffic will be encapsulated into an outer IPv6 header with an optional SRH (depending on the policy).

- ***Insert***: Insert refers to insertion, which means that a new SRH will be added between the outer IPv6 header and other optional SRH of the received packet.

The End.B6.* (SRv6 Bindings SID) endpoint behaviors should already be familiar from SR-MPLS. There are two endpoint behaviors to steer traffic into an SRv6 policy: The End.B6.Encaps and End.B6.Insert endpoint behaviors. You use End.B6.Encaps to encapsulate the received packet into an outer IPv6 header with SRH (encaps), and you use End.B6.Insert to insert an additional SRH (insert) after the outer IPv6 header. These two behaviors are discussed in detail in the following sections.

Note Sanity checks and basic IPv6 header modifications such as IPv6 hop limit decrementation and IPv6 encapsulation details such as IPv6 Source Address, Payload Length, Traffic Class, Flow Label, and Next Header fields are ignored for pragmatic reasons in all SRv6 Binding SID examples in this book.

End.B6.Encaps Behavior

The endpoint behavior bound to an SRv6 policy with encapsulation is shown in Figure 3-28. Much like the SR-MPLS Binding SID, its application evolves around traffic engineering.

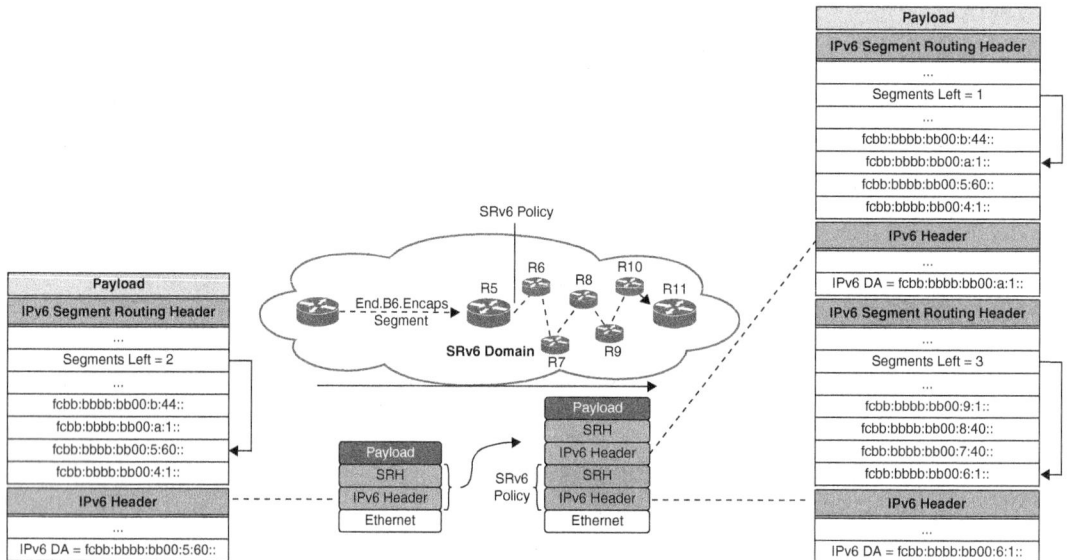

Figure 3-28   *SRv6 End.B6.Encaps*

R5 instantiates the End.B6.Encaps SID fcbb:bbbb:bb00:5:60:: (SID function 0x60) as the Binding SID (BSID) associated with an SRv6 policy consisting of the following SIDs:

■ Segment List[0] = fcbb:bbbb:bb00:9:1:: (End of R9)

■ Segment List[1] = fcbb:bbbb:bb00:8:40:: (End.X of R8)

■ Segment List[2] = fcbb:bbbb:bb00:7:40:: (End.X of R7)

■ Segment List[3] = fcbb:bbbb:bb00:6:1:: (End of R6)

R5 receives an IPv6 packet with an optional SRH where the IPv6 destination address matches a locally instantiated BSID. In the presence of a SRH, the Segments Left field is decremented, and the new active segment is copied into the IPv6 destination address. Next, a new IPv6 header with an optional SRH (depending on the SRv6 policy) is pushed to encapsulate the original packet. For example, the packet on R5 is modified and encapsulated as follows:

■ **SRH:** The Segments Left field changes from 2 to 1.

■ **IPv6 header:** Set the IPv6 destination address to the new active segment fcbb:bbbb:bb00:a:1:: (End of R10).

The new outer IPv6 header with SRH is inserted as follows:

- **IPv6 header:** Set the IPv6 destination address to the first segment of the SRv6 policy (End of R6).

- **SRH:** Encode the SID list End(R6), End.X(R7), End.X(R8), End(R9) into the SRH.

> **Note**   Depending on the SRv6 policy, an SRH may or may not be required. For instance, a policy that contains a single SID can be realized using an IPv6 header only where the SID is written into the IPv6 destination address. However, an SRH may still be desirable under certain circumstances to encode information into the Flags, Tag, or TLV Objects fields of the SRH (for example, HMAC or segment metadata).

The original packet is encapsulated into an outer IPv6 header with an SRH and forwarded based on the IPv6 destination address of the outer header (fcbb:bbbb:bb00:6:1::). Looking at the entire network program end-to-end, you can deduce that the packet likely belongs to a Layer 2 or Layer 3 VPN service over an SRv6 policy. The ultimate segment of the packet received by R5 (fcbb:bbbb:bb00:b:44::) could very well belong to an End.DT* or End.DX* behavior instantiated by R11. The remaining SIDs of the SRH segment list, except for the BSID of R5, seem to belong to End/End.X SIDs of R4 and R6 through R10, basically defining a rather strict traffic engineering path through the network.

End.B6.Encaps.Red Behavior

There is an optimization of the End.B6.Encaps behavior shown in Figure 3-29 that omits the first segment from the segment list of the SRH.

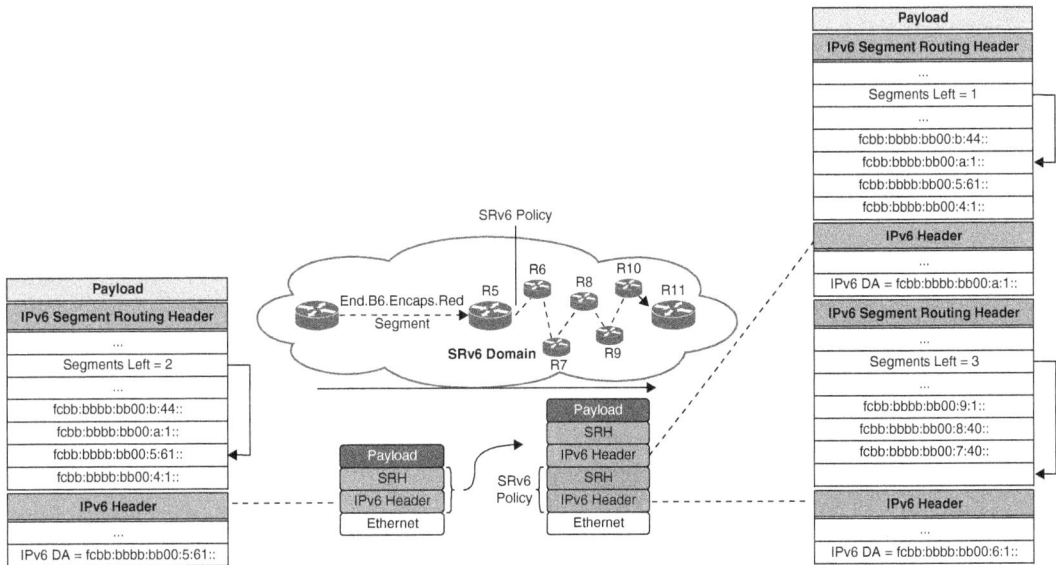

Figure 3-29   *SRv6 End.B6.Encaps.Red*

The endpoint behavior of End.B6.Encaps and End.B6.Encaps.Red is identical except for the newly imposed SRH that contains the SIDs of the SRv6 policy. The first segment of the SRv6 policy (fcbb:bbbb:bb00:6:1::) is somewhat redundant since it is included in both the IPv6 destination address and the SRH. The reduced endpoint behavior omits the first segment from the SRH, sets the last entry field to the number of segments minus 2 and keeps the Segments Left field at the number of segments minus 1 (in this case, 3), making sure that the proper segment (fcbb:bbbb:bb00:7:40::) is executed next.

Generally, reduced SRH endpoint behaviors are preferred since they result in less packet overhead, which is beneficial to the maximum supported end-to-end service payload size across the SRv6 domain. However, on a few occasions, a network operator may opt for unreduced endpoint behaviors to keep the complete SRv6 policy SID list in the SRH for compliance or monitoring purposes.

End.B6.Insert Behavior

Besides the encapsulation endpoint behaviors, there are insertion endpoint behaviors that, instead of encapsulating the original packet in an outer IPv6 header with an SRH, insert an SRH between the outer IPv6 header and an optional SRH of the original packet.

The endpoint behavior bound to an SRv6 policy (with insertion) is shown in Figure 3-30. Much like the SR-MPLS Binding SID, its application revolves around traffic engineering policies.

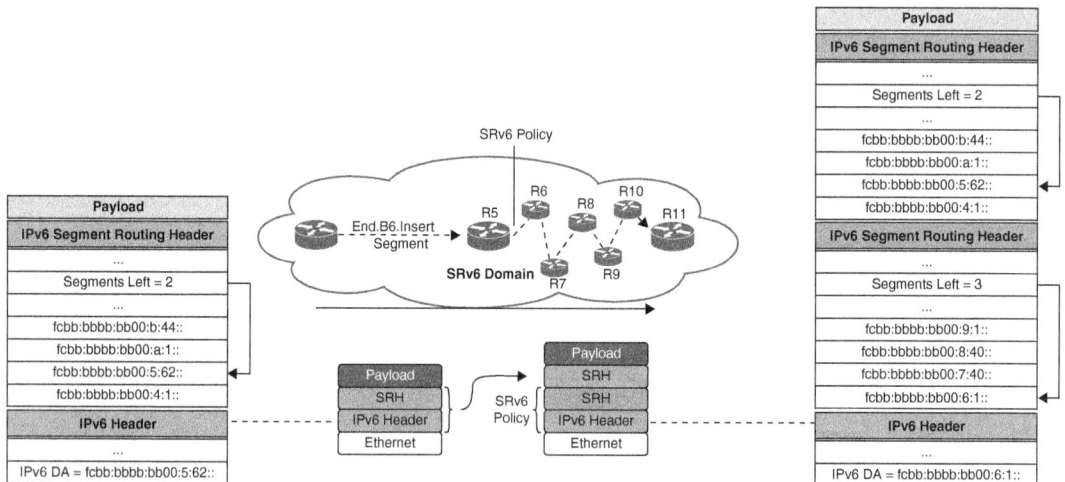

Figure 3-30 *SRv6 End.B6.Insert*

R5 instantiates the End.B6.Insert SID fcbb:bbbb:bb00:5:62:: (SID function 0x62) as the BSID associated with the previously introduced SRv6 policy consisting of the following SIDs:

- Segment List[0] = fcbb:bbbb:bb00:9:1:: (End of R9)

- Segment List[1] = fcbb:bbbb:bb00:8:40:: (End.X of R8)

- Segment List[2] = fcbb:bbbb:bb00:7:40:: (End.X of R7)

- Segment List[3] = fcbb:bbbb:bb00:6:1:: (End of R6)

R5 receives an IPv6 packet with an optional SRH where the IPv6 destination address matches the locally instantiated BSID. An SRH is inserted between the outer IPv6 header and the SRH of the received packet. For example, the packet on R5 is modified as follows:

- **Create a new SRH:** Encode the SID list of the policy End(R6), End.X(R7), End.X(R8), and End(R9) into the SRH.

- **Insert a new SRH:** Insert an SRH containing the policy between the IPv6 header and the optional SRH of the original packet.

- **Modify the IPv6 header:** Set the IPv6 destination address to the first segment of the SRv6 policy (End of R6).

An SRH is inserted into the original packet, which is forwarded based on the IPv6 destination address of the outer header (fcbb:bbbb:bb00:6:1::). Looking at the entire network program end-to-end, you can deduce that the packet likely belongs to a Layer 2 or Layer 3 VPN service over an SRv6 policy. The ultimate segment of the packet received by R5 (fcbb:bbbb:bb00:b:44::) could very well belong to an End.DT* or End.DX* behavior instantiated by R11. The remaining SIDs of the SRH segment list, except for the BSID of R5, seem to belong to End/End.X SIDs of R4 and R6 through R10, basically defining a rather strict traffic engineering path through the network.

End.B6.Insert.Red Behavior

An optimization of the End.B6.Insert behavior shown in Figure 3-31 omits the first segment from the segment list of the SRH.

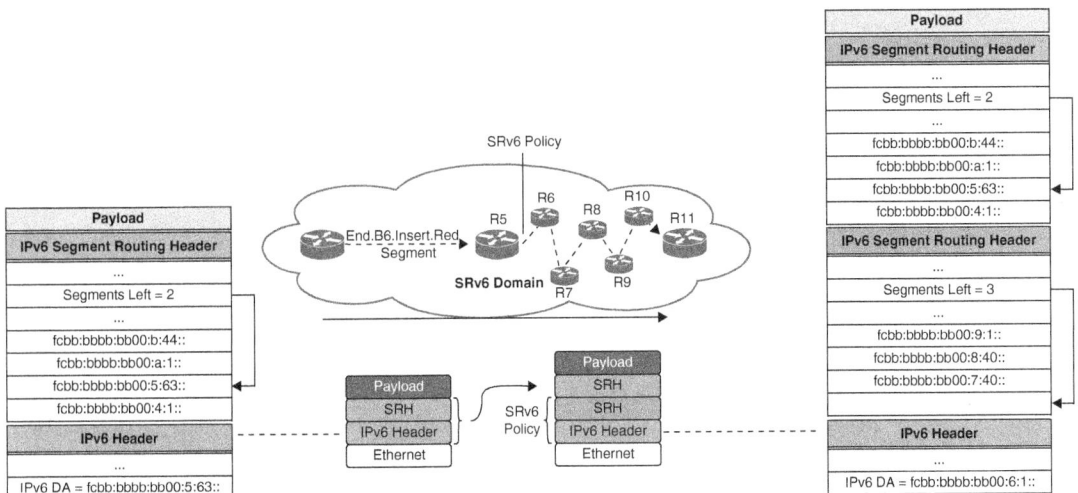

Figure 3-31 *SRv6 End.B6.Insert.Red*

The endpoint behavior of End.B6.Insert and End.B6.Insert.Red is identical except for the newly inserted SRH containing the SIDs of the SRv6 policy. The first segment of the SRv6 policy (fcbb:bbbb:bb00:6:1::) is somewhat redundant since it is included in both the IPv6 destination address and the SRH. The reduced endpoint behavior omits the first segment from the SRH, sets the last entry field to the number of segments minus 2, and keeps the Segments Left field set to the number of segments minus 1 (in this case, 3), ensuring that the proper segment (fcbb:bbbb:bb00:7:40::) is executed next.

SRv6 Policy Endpoint Behavior Comparison

Figure 3-32 compares the different endpoint behaviors bound to an SRv6 policy introduced in the previous paragraphs.

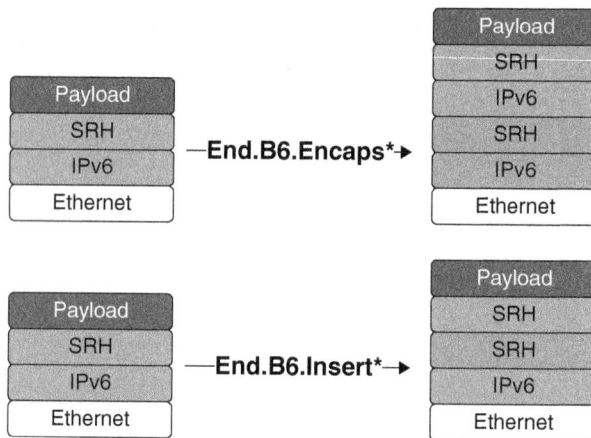

Figure 3-32   *Endpoint Bound to an SRv6 Policy (Encaps and Insert)*

Depending on the underlying hardware platform or software implementation, both or only one of the behaviors may be supported. As far as encapsulation overhead is concerned, the End.B6.Insert instruction is superior:

■ **End.B6.Encaps additional overhead:** IPv6 header (40 bytes) + SRH (8 bytes + 16 bytes per segment)

■ **End.B6.Insert additional overhead:** SRH (8 bytes + 16 bytes per segment)

SRv6 Headend and Endpoint Behavior Overview

You have seen that the segment routing header is a powerful addition to the SRv6 toolkit that facilitates various traffic engineering and TI-LFA use cases. It is worth highlighting that many common use cases, such as Layer 2 VPN or Layer 3 VPN services, can be realized using a single SID without the need to add an SRH. Even certain TI-LFA use cases (for example, zero-segment backup path) do not require an SRH, which is fairly common in highly symmetric networks. Native IPv6 transit networks would not limit the attachment of an SRv6 service edge but rather would restrict TI-LFA coverage, depending on the topology (for example, no support for single-segment backup paths), microloop avoidance, or SRv6 traffic engineering.

To help you reflect on the various headend and endpoint behaviors we have covered so far, Figure 3-33 illustrates the grouping of different SRv6 segments into a tree structure for your convenience. Most of those behaviors were discussed in the previous sections.

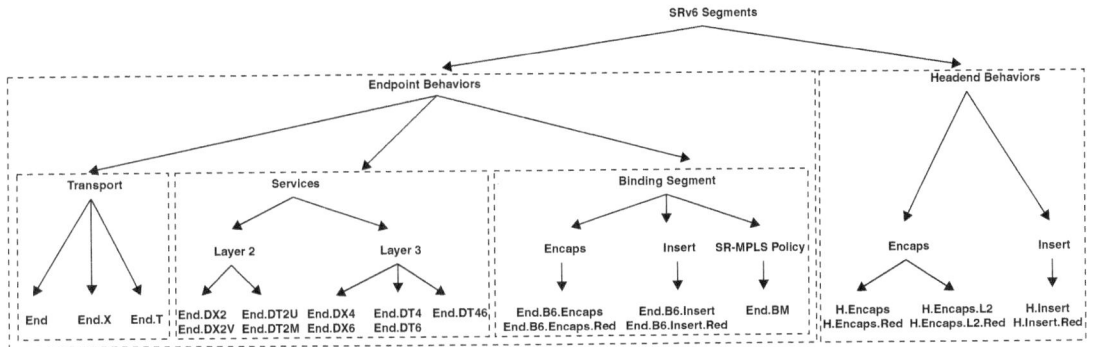

Figure 3-33   *Segment Routing over IPv6 Segments Overview*

The main drawback of the segment routing header is the additional overhead introduced per segment in the segment list. MPLS has a relatively low overhead of 32 bits (4 bytes) per SR-MPLS segment, whereas SRv6 introduces 40 bytes of overhead as part of the outer IPv6 header alone. Taking additional segments in an SRH into account increases the overhead by 8 bytes plus 16 bytes for each additional segment. Service provider networks with complex traffic engineering policies may face overhead of more than 100 bytes, which could become problematic for business service customers requiring a Layer 2 payload of 9000 bytes, depending on the backbone MTU settings. As briefly mentioned, instead of adding a segment routing header to encode multiple segments in a segment list, you can encode multiple instructions in a single IPv6 address.

SRv6 Network Programming Extension: SRv6 uSID Instruction

Note   The specification of the network programming extension SRv6 uSID instruction is still in draft state at this writing. Minor cosmetic changes are to be expected that may slightly impact this section.

Figure 3-34 shows an example of an SRv6 policy encapsulation that includes four segments in the segment list. The following inefficiencies are apparent:

■ The SRv6 SID block (for example, fcbb:bbbb:bb00::/48) is repeated for each SID.

■ SIDs are zero padded to 128 bits.

Payload
IPv6 Segment Routing Header
...
Segments Left = 3
...
fcbb:bbbb:bb00:4:41::
fcbb:bbbb:bb00:3:1::
fcbb:bbbb:bb00:2:1::
fcbb:bbbb:bb00:1:1::
IPv6 Header
...
IPv6 DA = fcbb:bbbb:bb00:1:1::

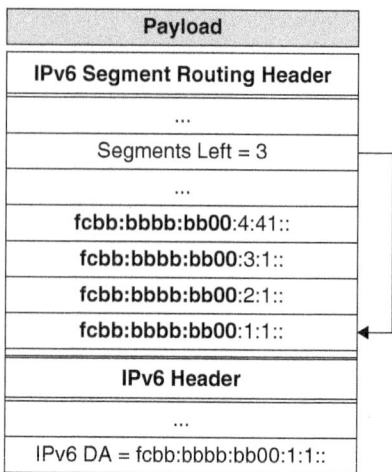

Figure 3-34   *SRv6 Policy with IPv6 Header and SRH*

The SRv6 micro SID (uSID) instruction extension to the SRv6 network programming framework is based on the Compressed SRv6 Segment List Encoding in the SRH specification and leverages the existing SRv6 control plane and SRH data plane encapsulation. It slightly extends the existing terminology and SRv6 endpoint behaviors. This section assumes an SRv6 uSID block of 32 bits with a uSID length of 16 bits, which is commonly referred to as F3216 format and results in a /48 locator using the SID structure shown in the section "SRv6 Network Programming (RFC 8986)," earlier in this chapter. A uSID locator consists of a 32-bit uSID block and a 16-bit uSID (node ID)—for instance, fcbb:bb00:0001::/48 for R1.

Figure 3-35 shows a graphical representation of the new terminology evolving around the uSID instruction extension:

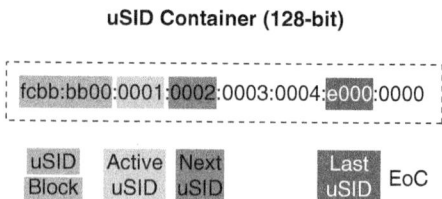

uSID Container (128-bit)

fcbb:bb00:0001:0002:0003:0004:e000:0000

| uSID Block | Active uSID | Next uSID | | Last uSID | EoC |

Figure 3-35   *SRv6 uSID Terminology*

- **Micro SID (uSID):** This is a flexible-length compressed SID (CSID) (for example, 16 bits long).

- **uSID block:** This is an operator-defined IPv6 address block to be used for uSID SID allocation (for example, fcbb:bb00::/32).

- **End of container (EoC):** This is a special delimiter uSID (0x0000) after the last uSID.

- **uSID/CSID container:** This is a 128-bit SRv6 SID that consists of the uSID block, one or more uSIDs, and optional EoC uSIDs.

- **Active uSID:** This is the first uSID after the uSID block.

- **Next uSID:** This is the uSID following the active uSID.

- **Last uSID:** This is the uSID at the end of the uSID container or before the initial EoC.

uSID containers may be written into the IPv6 destination address or as segments in the segment list of the SRH. Several new behaviors augment the existing SRv6 endpoint behaviors of the network programming model:

- **uN:** End behavior with NEXT-CSID

- **uA:** End.X behavior with NEXT-CSID

- **uDT*:** End.DT* behavior with NEXT-CSID

- **uDX*:** End.DX* behavior with NEXT-CSID

To create a mnemonic device, you may think of uN as *micro node* SID and uA as *micro adjacency* SID. The u stands for micro, which applies to Layer 2 and Layer 3 services as well. For instance, uDT4 refers to the End.DT4 with NEXT-CSID endpoint behavior.

> **Note**   This book uses Cisco and IETF terminology interchangeably when talking about SRv6 SID list compression. The uN and End(NEXT-CSID) endpoint behaviors are equivalent, as are the uA and End.X(NEXT-CSID) endpoint behaviors.

The SRv6 uSID endpoint behaviors are listed in Table 3-4.

Table 3-4   *SRv6 uSID Endpoint Behaviors*

uSID Endpoint Behavior	Control Plane Signaling	Description
uN	IGP/BGP-LS	Micro endpoint (SRv6 Prefix/Node SID)
uA	IGP/BGP-LS	Micro endpoint with L3 xconnect (SRv6 Adjacency SID)
uDX4	BGP VPN	Micro endpoint with decapsulation and IPv4 xconnect (IPv4 L3VPN per-CE label allocation)
uDX6	BGP VPN	Micro endpoint with decapsulation and IPv6 xconnect (IPv6 L3VPN per-CE label allocation)
uDT4	BGP VPN	Micro endpoint with decapsulation and specific IPv4 table lookup (IPv4 L3VPN per-VRF instance label allocation)

uSID Endpoint Behavior	Control Plane Signaling	Description
uDT6	BGP VPN	Micro endpoint with decapsulation and specific IPv6 table lookup
		(IPv6 L3VPN per-VRF instance label allocation)
uDT46	BGP VPN	Micro endpoint with decapsulation and specific IPv4/IPv6 table lookup
		(IP L3VPN per-VRF instance label allocation)
uDX2	BGP VPN	Micro endpoint with decapsulation and L2 xconnect
		(point-to-point L2VPN)
uDX2V	BGP VPN	Micro endpoint with decapsulation and VLAN L2 table lookup
		(EVPN flexible xconnect)
uDT2U	BGP VPN	Micro endpoint with decapsulation and unicast MAC L2 table lookup
		(multipoint L2VPN (known unicast))
uDT2M	BGP VPN	Micro endpoint with decapsulation and l2 table flooding
		(multipoint L2VPN [broadcast, unknown-unicast, multicast])

Note   SRv6 uSID endpoint behaviors registered with IANA are listed at https://www.iana.org/assignments/segment-routing/segment-routing.xhtml.

uSIDs can be classified as globally or locally significant and are allocated from different address spaces:

■ **Global Identifier Block (GIB):** Describes the address space available for globally significant uSIDs (global uSIDs).

■ **Local Identifier Block (LIB):** Describes the address space available for locally significant uSIDs (local uSIDs).

The uN endpoint behavior allocates a global uSID that can be used to steer traffic via the shortest path to a node, whereas multiple uN uSIDs in a uSID container can be used to steer traffic along a traffic engineered path consisting of several segments. Much as with SR-MPLS Node SIDs, multiple nodes may advertise the same uN SID (anycast), or a single node may advertise multiple uN SIDs (one per flex algo).

The uA endpoint behavior allocates a local uSID that can be used to steer traffic across a specific adjacency or a set of adjacencies. Much as with SR-MPLS Adjacency SIDs, since the uA uSID is locally significant, multiple nodes may advertise the same uA uSID, which is associated with a different local adjacency.

Note The concept of routed and non-routed SRv6 SIDs discussed in the section "Routed and Non-Routed SRv6 SIDs," earlier in this chapter, applies to uSIDs as well. In fact, it is common that globally significant (routed) uSIDs precede locally significant (non-routed) uSIDs in the control plane as far as IGP LSPs or BGP UPDATE messages are concerned, which is especially true for uA, uDT*, and uDX* endpoint behaviors.

Both uSID length and GIB/LIB address space carving are flexible, but for simplicity, here we follow the example provided by the SRv6 uSID instruction extension, which is what Cisco platforms follow at this writing.

Figure 3-36 shows an example of the 16-bit uSID address space that allows you to allocate the following numbers of global and local uSIDs:

■ **Global uSIDs:** The range 0x0000–0xDFFF includes 57,344 entries, where 0x0000 is reserved for the EoC.

■ **Local uSIDs:** The range 0xE000–0xFFFF includes 8192 entries.

Roughly 57,000 global uSIDs and 8000 local uSIDs are available. An operator assigns global uSIDs to network devices, and network devices generally allocate local uSIDs dynamically. A different uSID length or GIB/LIB allocation than the one used in this example would result in different numbers of global and local uSIDs.

The section "SRv6 Locator Addressing Scheme," later in this chapter, discusses aspects of uSID addressing and scaling in more details.

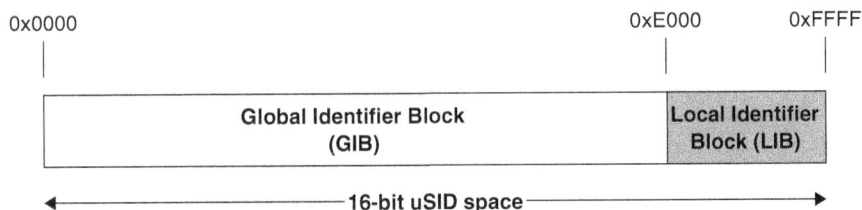

Figure 3-36 *SRv6 uSID GIB/LIB Carving (Example)*

This chapter has not yet introduced the NEXT-CSID flavor, which is applicable to the uN and uA endpoint behaviors. Remember that PSP/USD flavors are attached to the SID advertised in the IGP, whereas with the NEXT-CSID flavor, the device makes a local decision based on the result of the FIB lookup to distinguish between PSP/USD and NEXT-CSID. The following sections introduce the uN and uA endpoint variants.

uN Endpoint Variants

Figure 3-37 shows a logical representation of the uN endpoint behavior with two differ-ent FIB entries that are used to distinguish between the NEXT-CSID and other variants based on the longest-prefix match of the IPv6 destination address. In essence, they differ in matching the end of container (EoC) uSID 0x0000 after the local SRv6 locator. If the uN uSID is the last remaining uSID instruction in the uSID container, four different pro-cessing options may be applicable, based on the Segments Left field of the SRH or the absence of an SRH.

> **Note** The upcoming examples of uN and uA are based on the SRv6 uSID instruction draft; however, actual implementations may vary in complexity due to hardware optimizations.

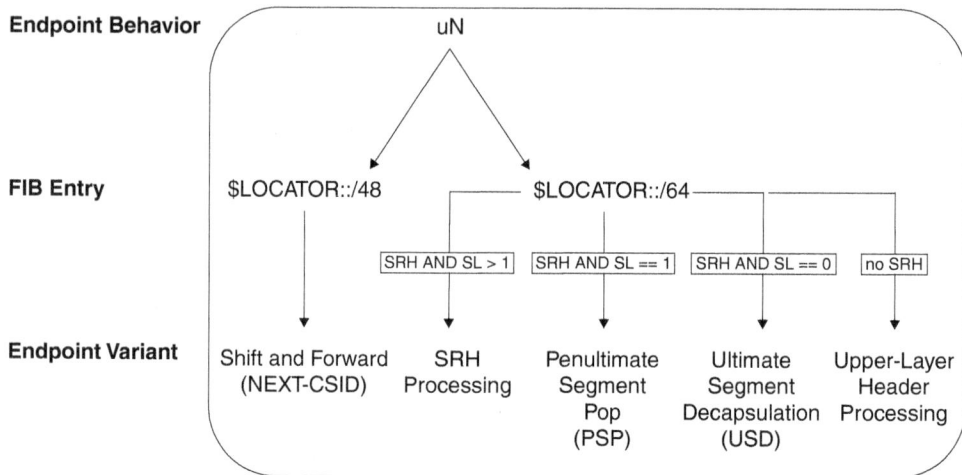

Figure 3-37 *uN Endpoint Variants (32-Bit uSID Block with 16-Bit uSID)*

Now let's look at some examples for uN endpoint behavior with different flavors (End with NEXT-CSID, PSP, and USD) based on a 32-bit uSID block and 16-bit uSID length. Please note that Ultimate Segment Pop (USP) of the SRH covers data center applications with specialized network interface cards and is excluded here on purpose.

Figure 3-38 shows a traffic flow with a uSID container in the IPv6 destination address with an optional SRH that is not relevant for this use case. The uSID container includes a small micro program that routes traffic via R2 to R3, where traffic is forwarded toward a specific next hop in a VPN.

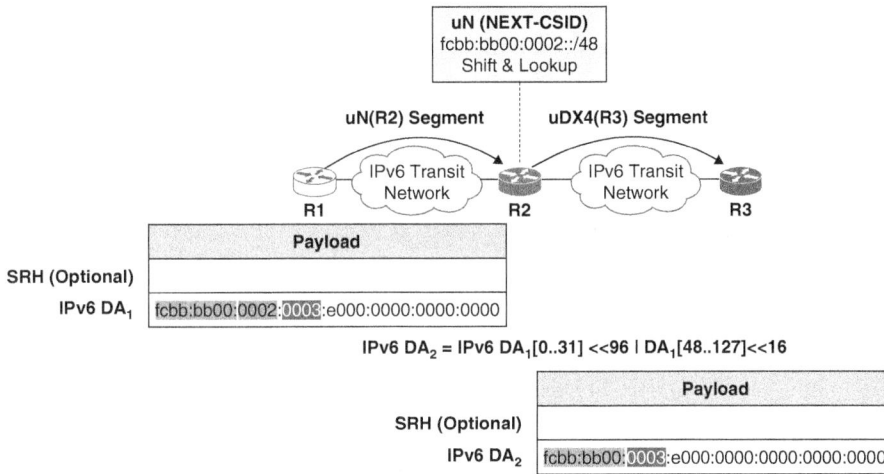

Figure 3-38   *uN(NEXT-CSID)*

R2 executes the uN(NEXT-CSID) endpoint behavior associated with a /48 FIB entry that performs a shift-and-lookup instruction. A partial left shift (<<) operation is performed on the original IPv6 destination address to shift by 16 bits (uSID length) before performing an IPv6 lookup on the new IPv6 destination address. The uSID block is not touched but all uSIDs after the active uSID are left shifted by 16 bits, which basically removes the active uSID from the uSID container, as shown in Figure 3-38. The new address is resolved using the locator of R3 and routed across an IPv6 transit network until it reaches R3. R3 recognizes the IPv6 destination address as a local SID pointing to a specific VPN adjacency.

Figure 3-39 shows a traffic flow with a uSID container in the IPv6 destination address and an additional uSID container in the SRH. The uSID containers include two micro programs: The first program routes the packet to R2 via R1, and the second program routes the packet from R3 to R8 via a series of hops. R2 executes the uN(PSP/USD) endpoint behavior associated with a /64 FIB entry.

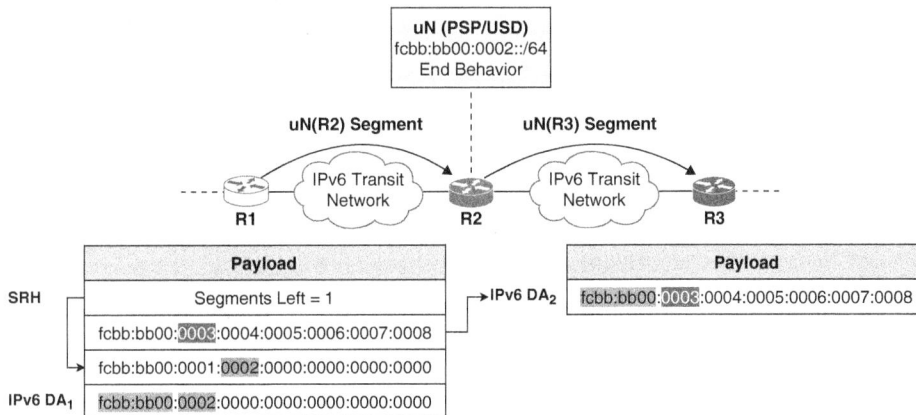

Figure 3-39   *uN(PSP/USD) SRH Processing with PSP*

Note the following:

- The uN (NEXT-CSID) FIB and uN (PSP/USD) entries look exactly the same except for the subnet mask.

- The FIB entries consist of the SRv6 locator matching different prefix lengths (/48 versus /64).

- The uN (PSP/USD) FIB entry includes the end of container uSID 0x0000, which marks the end of the micro program.

The packet reaching R2 is resolved using the uN(PSP/USD) /64 FIB entry, which performs the uN(PSP/USD) endpoint behavior. Since the Segments Left field in the SRH is decremented from 1 to 0, the SRH will be removed after the IPv6 header (IPv6 Destination Address, Next Header, Payload Length, and other fields, and so on) is updated during the SRH processing. The new address previously copied from the ultimate segment in the segment list is resolved using the locator of R3 and routed across an IPv6 transit network until it reaches R3. R3 recognizes the IPv6 destination address as a local uN SID matching a uN (NEXT-CSID) FIB entry, resulting in a shift-and-lookup instruction before the packet is forwarded toward the locator of R4. This process repeats until the packet reaches the owner of the last uSID 0x0008 (R8) in the IPv6 destination address.

Figure 3-40 shows a traffic flow with a uSID container in the IPv6 destination address and two additional uSID containers in the SRH. The uSID containers include three micro programs that route traffic to a series of nodes (R3 through R14) via R1 and R2. R2 executes the uN(PSP/USD) endpoint behavior associated with a /64 FIB entry.

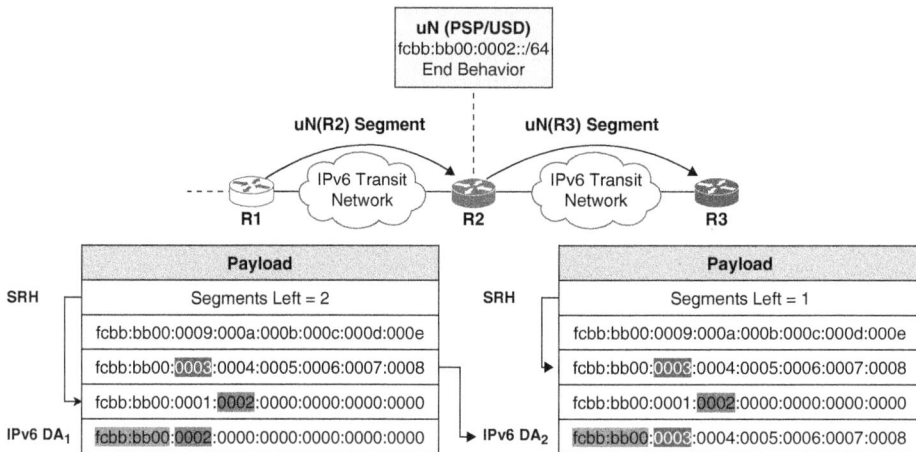

Figure 3-40   *uN(PSP/USD) SRH Processing*

The packet reaching R2 is resolved using the uN(PSP/USD) /64 FIB entry, which performs the uN(PSP/USD) endpoint behavior. Because the Segments Left field in the SRH is set to 2, regular SRH processing will take place. The IPv6 hop limit and SRH Segments Left field are decremented, and the new active segment is copied into the IPv6 destination address. The new address is resolved using the locator of R3 and routed across an IPv6 transit network until it reaches R3. R3 recognizes the IPv6 destination address as a local uN SID matching a uN(NEXT-CSID) FIB entry, resulting in a shift-and-lookup instruction before the packet is forwarded toward the locator of R4. This process repeats until the packet reaches the originator of the last uSID of the ultimate segment in the SRH, 0x000e (R14).

Figure 3-41 shows a traffic flow with a uSID container in the IPv6 destination address and a uSID container in the SRH that has been processed already. The uSID containers include two micro programs that route traffic to a series of nodes in a different domain until passing through R1 and R2.

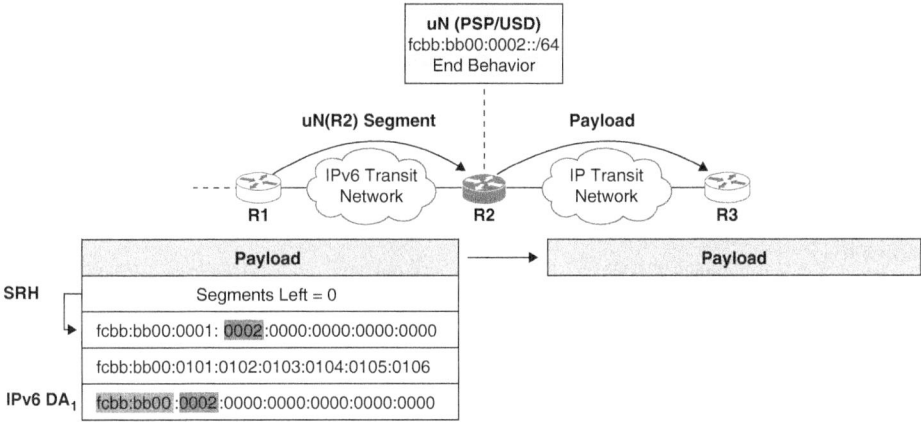

Figure 3-41   *uN(PSP/USD) SRH Processing with USD*

The packet reaching R2 is resolved using the uN(PSP/USD) /64 FIB entry that performs the uN(PSP/USD) endpoint behavior. Since the Segments Left field in the SRH is set to 0, Ultimate Segment Decapsulation (USD) will take place. Note the following:

- For the SRH to arrive with SL = 0, the penultimate segment endpoint node (for example, R6 in domain 1) could not have performed PSP.

- If the penultimate segment endpoint node performed PSP, the packet would arrive as an IPv6 in IPv6 packet in the case of an IPv6 payload where standard upper layer header processing as defined in RFC 8200 applies, which invokes the corresponding module to process the upper layer header (inner payload).

The processing depends on the upper layer header, but for an IPv4/IPv6 payload, the outer IPv6 header and all its extension headers are removed, and an IPv4/IPv6 FIB lookup is performed on the decapsulated packet. The payload in the example is an IPv4 or IPv6 payload where the prefix of the IP destination address is originated by R3. The new address is resolved and routed across an IP transit network until it reaches R3.

uA Endpoint Variants

Figure 3-42 shows a logical representation of the uA endpoint behavior with two different FIB entries to distinguish between the NEXT-CSID and other variants based on the longest-prefix match of the IPv6 destination address. Much as with the uN endpoint behavior, they differ in matching the end of container (EoC) uSID 0x0000 after a local uSID. If the uA uSID is the last remaining uSID instruction in the uSID container, four different processing options may be applicable, based on the Segments Left field of an SRH or the absence of an SRH.

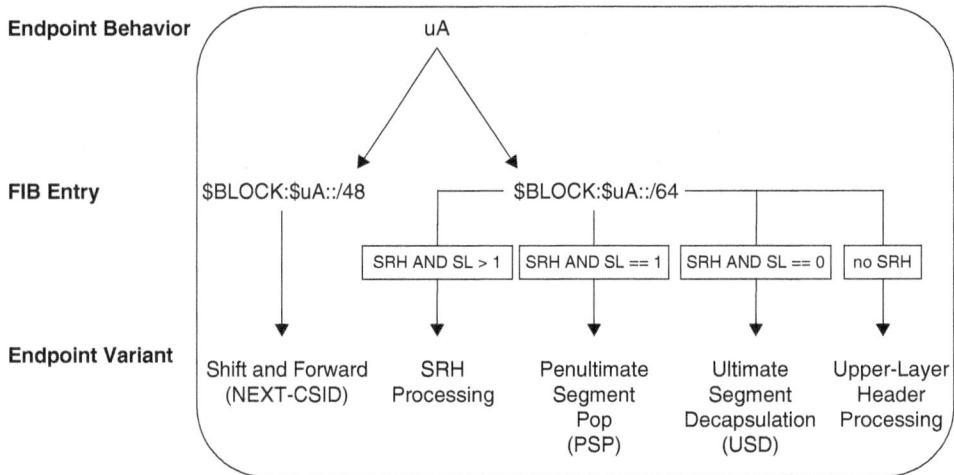

Figure 3-42   *uA Endpoint Variants (32-Bit uSID Block with 16-Bit uSID)*

uN uSIDs are global uSIDs, whereas uA uSIDs are local uSIDs. The IGP propagates uA SIDs as B:uN:uA::/64, which consists of two uSIDs that first provide the routing to the parent node (End with NEXT-CSID behavior) and then the cross-connect (End.X behavior). Refer to section "Routed and Non-Routed SRv6 SIDs," earlier in this chapter, to better understand the need for this. To increase hardware processing efficiency and avoid packet recirculation, it is common to install FIB entries that include both global and local uSIDs in a single entry. The following routes are needed for local IGP uSIDs (End or End.X), but the same principle applies to BGP services:

■ fcbb:bb00:0002:efaa::/64 (NEXT-CSID), where 0x0002 and 0xefaa relate to the global End uSID and a local End.X uSID of R2, respectively

■ fcbb:bb00:0002:efaa::/80 (PSP/USD), which is the same as the previous entry but with the additional end of container (EoC) uSID

Now let's look at a set of examples for uA endpoint behavior with different flavors (End.X with NEXT-CSID, PSP, and USD) based on 32-bit uSID block and 16-bit uSID length. Note that Ultimate Segment Pop of the SRH covers data center applications with specialized network interface cards and is excluded here on purpose.

Figure 3-43 shows a traffic flow with a uSID container in the IPv6 destination address with an optional SRH that is not relevant for this use case. The uSID container includes a small micro program that routes traffic via a specific egress interface of R2 toward R3, where traffic is forwarded toward a specific next hop in a VPN.

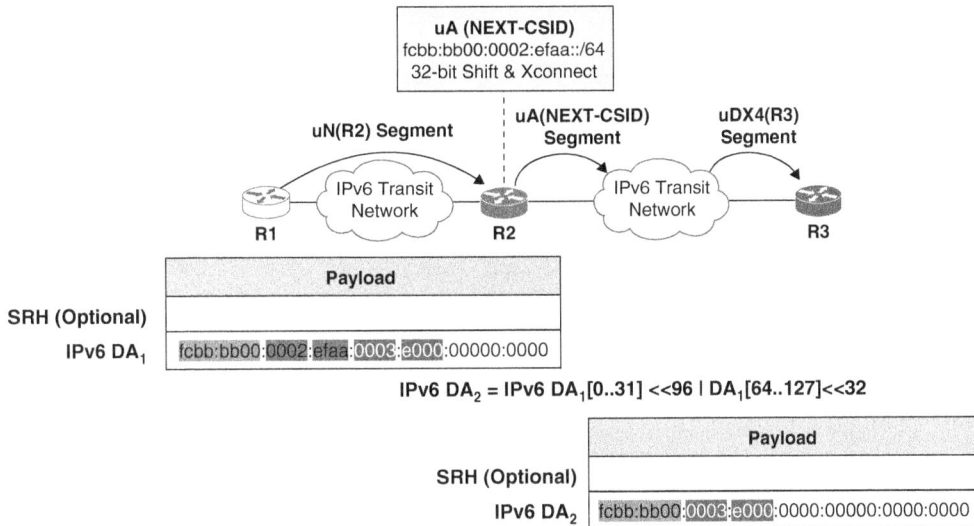

Figure 3-43 *uA(NEXT-CSID)*

R2 executes the uN (NEXT-CSID) endpoint behavior associated with a /48 FIB entry, which performs a shift-and-lookup instruction. A partial left shift (<<) operation is performed on the original IPv6 destination address to shift by 16 bits (uSID length) before performing an IPv6 lookup on the new IPv6 destination address. The new address is resolved using the local uA uSID (NEXT-CSID) endpoint behavior associated with a /48 FIB entry that performs a shift-and-xconnect instruction. Before performing the Layer 3 xconnect toward the egress interface associated with the local uA uSID, a partial left shift operation is performed on the intermediate IPv6 destination address to shift by 16 bits. As mentioned previously, for efficiency and simplicity, those two micro instructions are combined into a single instruction that performs a 32-bit left shift xconnect for packets that match a combined /64 FIB entry, as shown in Figure 3-43. The new IPv6 destination address is resolved using the locator R3 and routed across an IPv6 transit network until it reaches R3. R3 recognizes the IPv6 destination address as a local SID pointing to a specific IPv4 VPN adjacency (uDX4).

Figure 3-44 shows a traffic flow with a uSID container in the IPv6 destination address and an additional uSID container in the SRH. The uSID containers include two micro programs that route traffic to a series of nodes (R3–R8) via a specific egress interface on R2.

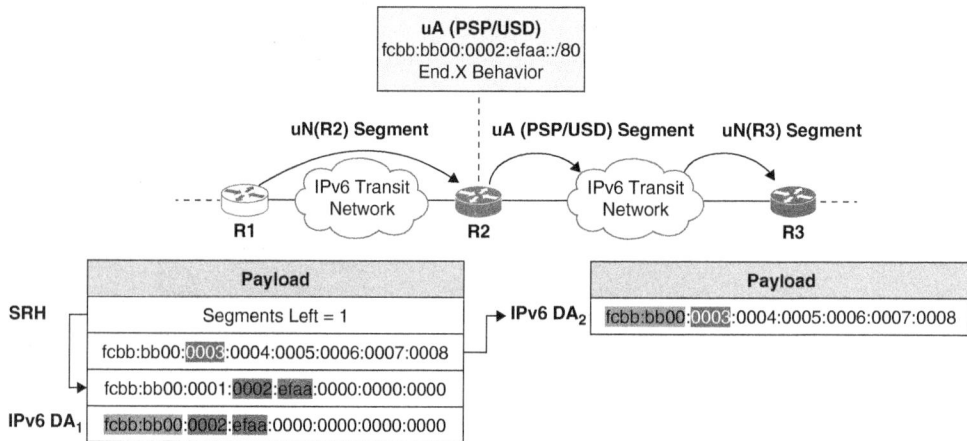

Figure 3-44   *uA(PSP/USD) SRH Processing with PSP*

R2 executes the uN (NEXT-CSID) endpoint behavior associated with a /48 FIB entry, which performs a shift-and-lookup instruction. A partial left shift (<<) operation is performed on the original IPv6 destination address to shift by 16 bits before performing an IPv6 lookup on the new IPv6 destination address. The new address is resolved using the local uA uSID (PSP/USD) endpoint behavior associated with a /64 FIB entry that performs the End.X instruction. As mentioned previously, for efficiency and simplicity, those two micro instructions are combined into a single instruction that performs the End.X behavior when matching the /80 FIB entry, as shown in Figure 3-44.

Since the Segments Left field in the SRH is set to 1, the SRH will be removed after the IPv6 header (IPv6 Destination Address, Next Header, and Payload Length fields) is updated during the SRH processing. R2 uses the Layer 3 adjacency associated with the End.X uSID to forward the packet without performing another lookup. The IPv6 transit network resolves the new IPv6 address that was previously copied from the ultimate segment in the segment list using the locator of R3 and routes traffic across until it reaches R3. R3 recognizes the IPv6 destination address as a local uN SID matching a uN (NEXT-CSID) FIB entry, resulting in a shift-and-lookup instruction before the packet is forwarded toward the locator of R4. This process repeats until the packet reaches the originator of the last uSID of the ultimate segment in the SRH, 0x0008 (R8).

Figure 3-45 shows a traffic flow with a uSID container in the IPv6 destination address and two additional uSID container in the SRH. The uSID containers include three micro programs that route traffic to a series of nodes (R3–R14) via R1 and a specific egress interface on R2.

R2 executes the uN (NEXT-CSID) endpoint behavior associated with a /48 FIB entry that performs a shift-and-lookup instruction. A partial left shift operation is performed on the original IPv6 destination address to shift by 16 bits before performing an IPv6 lookup on the new IPv6 destination address. The new address is resolved using the local uA uSID (PSP/USD) endpoint behavior associated with a /64 FIB entry that performs the End.X instruction. As mentioned previously, for efficiency and simplicity, those two micro instructions are combined into a single instruction that performs the End.X behavior when matching the /80 FIB entry, as shown in Figure 3-45.

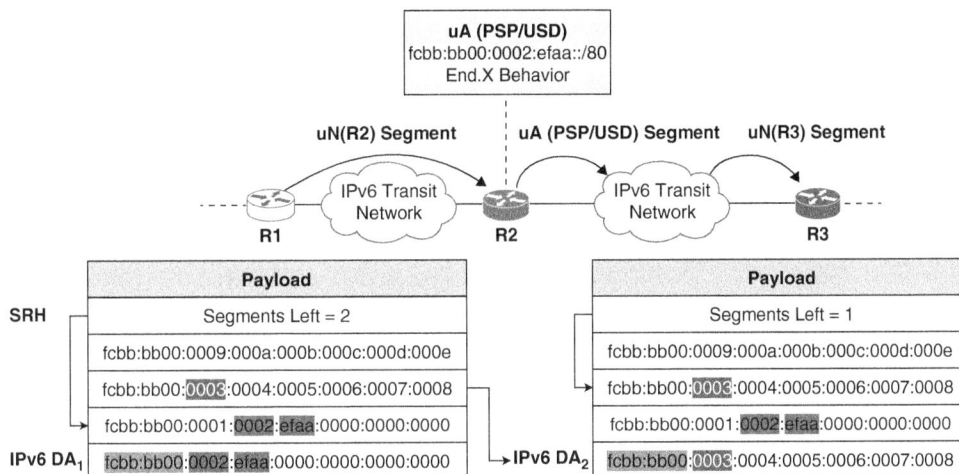

Figure 3-45   *uA(PSP/USD) SRH Processing*

Since the Segments Left field in the SRH is set to 2, regular SRH processing will take place. The Segments Left field in SRH is decremented by one, and the new active segment is copied into the IPv6 destination address. The new address is resolved using the locator of R3 and routed across an IPv6 transit network until it reaches R3. R3 recognizes the IPv6 destination address as a local uN SID matching a uN (NEXT-CSID) FIB entry, resulting in a shift-and-lookup instruction before the packet is forwarded toward the locator of R4. This process repeats until the packet reaches the originator of the last uSID of the ultimate segment in the SRH, 0x000e (R14).

Figure 3-46 shows a traffic flow with a uSID container in the IPv6 destination address and one uSID container in the SRH that has been processed already. The uSID containers include two micro programs that route traffic to a series of nodes in a different domain until passing through R1 and a specific egress interface on R2.

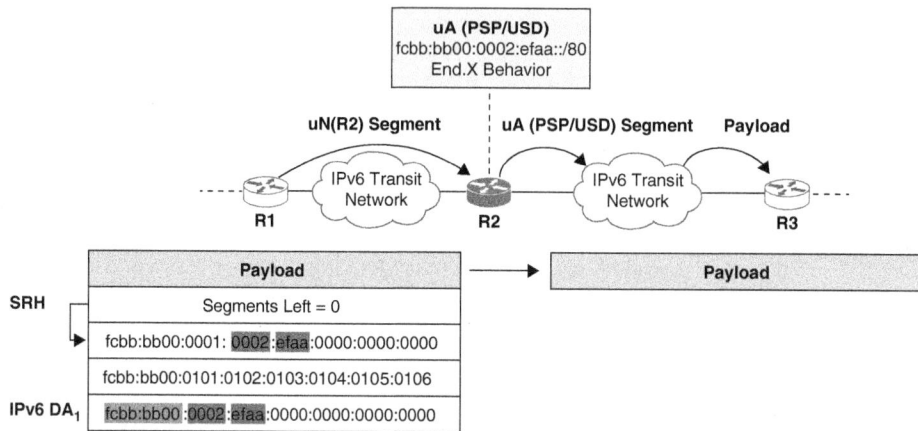

Figure 3-46 *uA(PSP/USD) SRH Processing with USD*

R2 executes the uN (NEXT-CSID) endpoint behavior associated with a /48 FIB entry that performs a shift-and-lookup instruction. A partial left shift operation is performed on the original IPv6 destination address to shift by 16 bits before performing an IPv6 lookup on the new IPv6 destination address. The new address is resolved using the local uA uSID (PSP/USD) endpoint behavior associated with a /64 FIB entry that performs the End.X instruction. As mentioned previously, for efficiency and simplicity, those two micro instructions are combined into a single instruction that performs the End.X behavior when matching the /80 FIB entry, as shown in Figure 3-46. Since the Segments Left field in the SRH equals 0, Ultimate Segment Decapsulation (USD) takes place. Note the following here:

- For the SRH to arrive with SL = 0, the penultimate segment endpoint node (for example, R6 in domain 1) could not have performed PSP.

- If the penultimate segment endpoint node performed PSP, the packet would arrive as an IPv6 in IPv6 packet in the case of an IPv6 payload, where standard upper layer header processing as defined in RFC 8200 applies, which invokes the corresponding module to process the upper layer header.

The processing depends on the upper layer, but for an IPv4/IPv6 payload, the outer IPv6 header and all its extension headers are removed, and the decapsulated packet is forwarded using the Layer 3 adjacency, as per End.X endpoint behavior. The payload in the example is an IPv4 or IPv6 payload where the prefix of the IP destination address is originated by R3. The packet is routed across an IP transit network until it reaches R3.

> **Note**   The concept of prepending a parent node's uN SRv6 uSID in front of a local SRv6 uSID is used for IGP uSIDs (for example, uA) and BGP service uSIDs (for example uDT* or uDX*) for Layer 2 and Layer 3 VPNs alike. It applies to both the control plane (IGP or BGP) and the data plane (RIB or FIB) and drives simplicity and efficiency.

SID Compression

The SRv6 uSID instruction extension claims the lowest encapsulation overhead among equivalent tunneling solutions. A fair apples-to-apples comparison is possible between compressed and uncompressed SRv6 SIDs, whereas SR-MPLS feels more like an orange due to the recursive lookups that yield one or more transport labels and a service label. On top of that, certain Layer 2 VPN services require additional labels for load balancing or hashing. SR-MPLS encapsulation overhead provides a reference. The following equations represent the encapsulation overhead in bytes for SR-MPLS, SRv6 SID, and SRv6 uSID:

$$SR - MPLS\ Encapsulation\ Overhead\ =\ 4 \times n$$

$$SRv6\ SID\ Encapsulation\ Overhead = \begin{cases} 0,\ if\ n = 0 \\ 40,\ if\ n = 1 \\ 40 + 8 + 16 \times (n - 1),\ if\ n > 1 \end{cases}$$

$$SRv6\ uSID\ Encapsulation\ Overhead = \begin{cases} 0,\ if\ n = 0 \\ 40,\ if\ 1 \le n \le 6 \\ 40 + 8 + 16 \times \left\lceil \dfrac{(n - 6)}{6} \right\rceil,\ if\ n > 6 \end{cases}$$

where n equals the number of segments

> **Note** A single uncompressed SID would not require an SRH, similar to how the first six uSIDs can be accommodated in an IPv6 header.

Figure 3-47 shows the encapsulation overhead, in bytes, in relation to the number of segments for all three encapsulation types.

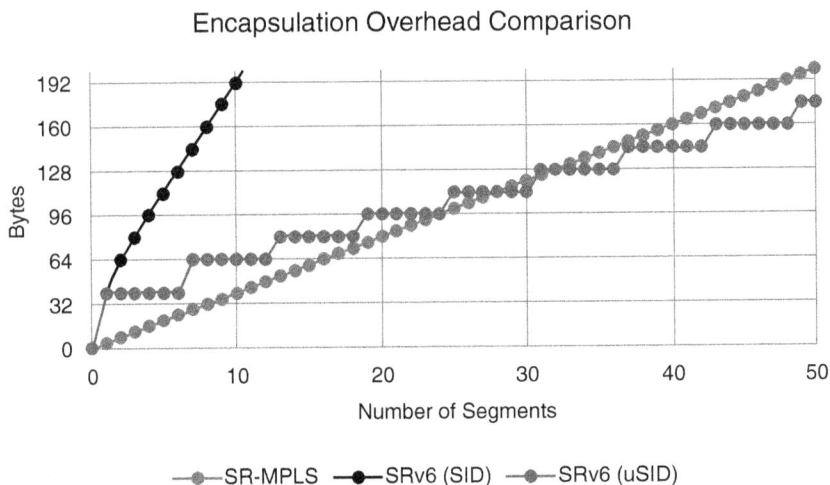

Encapsulation Overhead Comparison

— SR-MPLS   — SRv6 (SID)   — SRv6 (uSID)

Figure 3-47 *SR Encapsulation Overhead*

It comes as no surprise that SRv6 with uncompressed SIDs performs suboptimally with respect to encapsulation overhead. What is interesting, however, is that the SRv6 uSID starts with a large offset due to the IPv6 header size but grows very slowly. In fact, the SR-MPLS curve does not suffer from an offset but grows much faster, and the two curves have a first point of intersection at (24,96). For large number of segments ($n > 32$), SRv6 uSID outperforms SR-MPLS with respect to encapsulation overhead. However, it seems rather unlikely that operators require 30 or even 50 SIDs for their SR policies. The encapsulation overhead with up 10 SRv6 uSIDs adds up to 64 bytes, which should cover the vast majority of traffic engineering use cases in service provider networks without jeopardizing the promised end-to-end MTU of business customers.

Addressing Considerations

Proper addressing concepts are crucial for any network or service—including SRv6. Several fundamental design decisions must be made early on and will have long-lasting impacts on the SRv6 network. There are often trade-offs, and it is up to the operator to define the priorities accordingly. This section provides guidance on the most important aspects of SRv6 addressing and lists both advantages and disadvantages, where applicable.

IPv6 Addressing

At a high level, an operator configures the following addresses on an SRv6 router:

- SRv6 locator

- Loopback (control plane)

- Loopback (management plane)

- Transit links (infrastructure)

- Out-of-band management

This list is not exhaustive, and a network device may be managed through in-band methods, out-of-band methods, or both. As far as SRv6 is concerned, locators, control plane loopbacks (usually loopback0), and the transit links may have different scopes. IPv6 addressing scopes distinguish between global unicast addresses (GUAs), unique local addresses (ULAs) and link local addresses (LLAs), among others:

- **GUA:** Similar to IPv4 public address; allocated from the 2000::/3 subnet.

- **ULA:** Similar to IPv4 private address; allocated from the fc00::/7 subnet.

- **LLA:** Similar to IPv4 link-local address; allocated from the fe80::/10 subnet.

Note Recently, IANA approved a new IPv6 special-purpose address block 5f00::/16 for segment routing (SRv6) SIDs, as requested by the SRv6 segment identifiers in the IPv6 addressing architecture draft.

The SRv6 locator could use a SID block from the GUA or ULA space, each of which has advantages and disadvantages, as shown in Table 3-5.

Table 3-5   *SRv6 SID Block Addressing Considerations*

	Advantages	**Disadvantages**
Global unicast addresses	■ Routable over public infrastructure (for example, the Internet or the cloud) ■ IPv6 address collisions should not be a concern with a dedicated new block	■ A routable SID from the Internet may be a security concern ■ New IPv6 subnet allocation requests can take time and may even be declined by Internet registries ■ SRv6 SID block hardware platform restrictions may not be accommodated by Internet registries
Unique local addresses	■ Not accessible from the Internet ■ Preservation of public address space ■ Can accommodate addressing restrictions	■ Cannot be routed over public infrastructure ■ SID block could collide with existing addresses in the network

It is evident that advantages and disadvantages between the two options are reversed. For the vast majority of deployments, carving out a SID block from the ULA range will be the better choice. At this writing, certain SID block addressing restrictions on Cisco platforms are difficult to accommodate using GUA. Internet registries, such as RIPE, generally do not accept special requests such as "Bits X, Y, and Z must be zero in the newly allocated block." Other vendors may have similar platform restrictions that need to be considered when defining an SRv6 SID block. Routing SRv6 SID over public clouds (for example, the Internet) may be a future use case for a limited number of operators. However, the security implications of such a decision are wide ranging and must be considered carefully.

Note   Cisco recommends an SRv6 SID block allocation from the IPv6 unique local address (ULA) space.

Service providers configure loopback interfaces for various applications. It is quite common to see either a single loopback interface or separate loopback interfaces for control and management plane protocols. On Cisco IOS XR platforms, the SRv6 uSID locator prefix can be used to carve out a loopback interface address. The first 15 addresses of the locator are eligible for loopback addressing purposes (for example, LOCATOR::1/128–LOCATOR::F/128). Aggregating the loopback interface behind the aggregate (locator) reduces the number of routes in the IGP and streamlines the addressing and overall route summarization. Certain service providers may want to use a different address range for management-specific loopbacks, which facilitates a clear distinction between the SRv6 data plane and network management planes.

Internal infrastructure interfaces (transit links) are generally configured using addresses from the GUA or LLA (always present) space, each of which has advantages and disadvantages, as shown in Table 3-6.

Table 3-6   *Infrastructure Addressing Considerations*

	Advantages	Disadvantages
Global unicast addresses	■ Transit address is pingable from a remote neighbor ■ Interface information in traceroute could be coupled with DNS	■ More difficult configuration ■ Addresses must be documented/ maintained ■ Misconfiguration could result in duplicate addresses ■ More routes in the IGP
Link local addresses	■ Simple configuration (dynamically assigned) ■ No documentation required ■ Duplicate addresses should not be a problem ■ Fewer routes in the IGP	■ Transit address only pingable from a directly connected neighbor ■ Interface information in traceroute is not useful (though RFC 5837 resolves this impediment)

Again, advantages and disadvantages between the two options are reversed. There is no clear preference here, and one may be selected over the other based on the operator's priorities. Configuring link-local addresses is trivial and removes some of the deployment and maintenance complexity as far as infrastructure addresses are concerned. Without the inconvenience of unique global unicast addresses, the number of unique variables per device can be reduced drastically, potentially streamlining network automation.

There is a third option that has not been shown. Certain applications (for example, BFD over Bundle) may not be able to dynamically detect the peer device, which is an obvious requirement for the session to be established. Limitations are highly implementation specific and may differ between vendors or hardware platforms. However, one way to address such limitations is to statically configure link-local addresses instead of relying on dynamic allocation. The additional complexity could be limited by defining two static link-local addresses, such as fe80::1 and fe80::2. Routers located closer to the edge could be assigned fe80::1, whereas routers located closer to the core could be assigned fe80::2, or similar. Cross-links or core links would require a slightly adapted tie breaker logic.

Figure 3-48 shows a very small network and its corresponding addressing. The PE nodes (located closer to the edge) are configured with fe80::1, whereas the PE-facing links of the P nodes are configured with fe80::2. The intra-core/cross-links are configured with fe80::2 on the upper plane and fe80::1 on the lower plane. The core PoP on the left is considered more central and is assigned fe80::2 on the inter core links, whereas the other end is assigned fe80::1.

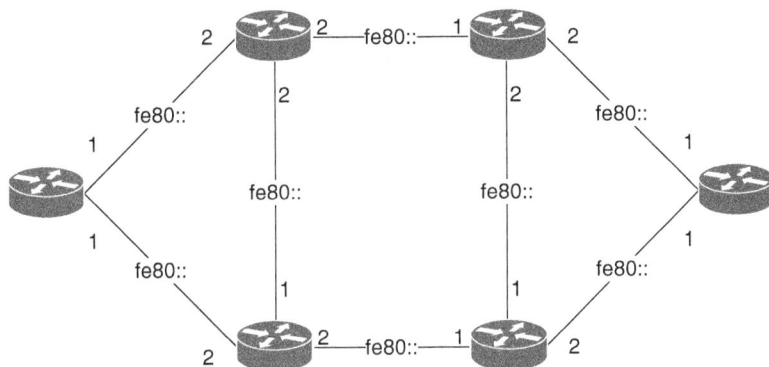

Figure 3-48 *Sample Topology with Statically Configured LLA*

Figure 3-48 is an example and may serve as an inspiration in the event that dynamically allocated LLAs are not feasible due to certain limitations.

SRv6 Locator Addressing Scheme

You can expect most network operators to deploy SRv6 uSID and select the ULA address space for carving out the SRv6 SID block. This section assumes an SRv6 uSID block of 32 bits with a uSID length of 16 bits. For simplicity, this section reuses the uSID GIB/LIB carving shown in Figure 3-36 that Cisco IOS XR platforms also support.

IANA has assigned the prefix fc00::/7 for unique local addresses (ULA), but as per RFC 4193, locally assigned prefixes require the least significant bit (L-flag) of the first octet to be 1. The RFC marks an L-flag of 0 as undefined, which operators may want to avoid when targeting RFC-compliant addressing. This leaves us with the prefix fd00::/8 to carve out the SRv6 SID block.

Note   This book uses both the fc00::/8 and fd00::/8 ULA spaces to carve out SID blocks. Both have been tested successfully on Cisco devices; however, fc00::/8 is not technically compliant with RFC 4193, and that may be relevant to you.

As mentioned previously, IPv6 ULA may already be in use in some service provider networks, so ideally operators should select a free range for SRv6 deployments. At this writing, certain temporary platform limitations and restrictions apply to the SRv6 SID block.

The SRv6 uSID block = PQRS:TUVW::/32, where:

-   PQRS:TU::/24 must be the same for all uSID blocks across the domain

-   VW must be smaller than 0x40 (that is, the 25th and 26th bits of the SID block must be zero)

Note   These limitations apply to certain Cisco hardware platforms and are expected to diminish over time. Nonetheless, feature limitations and restrictions are common, so you are advised to keep this in mind and consult platform-specific documentation before deploying SRv6. The presented platform limitations may very well become obsolete in the future but shall serve as an exercise on how to circumvent such restrictions in an addressing concept.

Note that the variables from the listed SID block are not in hexadecimal on purpose to prevent confusion. A suitable SRv6 uSID block that ticks all those boxes is, for instance, fdca:fe00::/32 for the default IGP algorithm 0 (metric-based SPF). The first 24 bits of the SID block must be the same across the SRv6 domain, which allows the operator to encode some information in the VW octet, such as the following:

- Flexible Algorithm

- Country, Metro, or Domain (which is useful for large scale deployments)

The number of flex algos and SRv6 routers in a network have an impact on the uSID block encoding. For the time being, we ignore this additional complexity. The sections "Small- and Medium-Scale Deployments" and "Large-Scale Deployments" introduce more advanced uSID block encodings. The remainder of this section relies on the uSID block fdca:fe00::/32.

In the SRv6 uSID F3216 format, SRv6 locators consists of the SID Block (B) and Node ID (N) fields, which for an SRv6 uSID block of 32 bits with a uSID length of 16 bits results in a /48 prefix length:

$$SRv6\ uSID\ Locator = B{:}N{::}/48$$

Note   The uSID carrier format notion can be expressed as Fbbuu, where bb and uu define the uSID block and uSID length, in bits. Besides F3216, other formats such as F4816 may be introduced in the future.

Operators can carve out and allocate the 16 bits of the Node ID (N) field as needed. The node ID acts as a global uN uSID where the IGP advertises different uN entries for the FIB to install those locally. As previously mentioned, in a 16-bit uSID space, there are approximately 57,000 global uSIDs and around 8,000 local uSIDs (starting with 0xE or 0xF). Running 57,000 devices in a single domain is not feasible and would not make any sense because it would negatively impact performance and convergence of the network. Instead, recommended architectures take advantage of hierarchical network designs with at most a few thousand devices per domain. Realistically, the following two node ID (N) encoding options exist for 16-bit uSID:

- **Option 1:** 0xDDNN (more domains and a smaller number of nodes per domain)

  - DD is 0x00–0xDF (domain IDs).

  - NN is 0x00–0xFF (node ID).

- Supports up to 224 domains with 256 nodes per domain.

- Total of 57,344 nodes.

- **Option 2:** 0xDNNN (fewer domains and a larger number of nodes per domain)

  - D is 0x0–0xD (domain IDs).

  - NNN is 0x000–0xFFF (node ID).

  - Supports up to 14 domains with 4096 nodes per domain.

  - Total of 57,344 nodes.

Option 1 (0xDDNN) is clearly the superior addressing option as it reduces the waste of global uSIDs and provides more flexibility. The first octet of the node ID (DD) in option 1 is often referred to as a *set* or *set ID*, where each set provides 256 node IDs (NN). In other words, a /40 summary holds up to 256 /48 prefixes (locators). Ultimately, SRv6 relies on the IPv6 data plane and its addresses, which means traditional IPv6 subnetting applies. Consequently, addressing is only limited by bit boundaries, and sets may be carved out differently. A logical IGP domain may reserve several sets if needed, as shown in Figure 3-49.

The core domain in Figure 3-49 is a relatively static environment where the number of devices will not change drastically over time. 500 devices with a /48 SRv6 locator require two sets (/40 subnets). Some of the metro networks, on the other hand, may grow over time, which is why the operator decided to allocate additional buffer for future growth. Metro 2, for instance, requires 1000 node IDs today and may grow to 1500 node IDs over time. 1500 /48 SRv6 locators require six sets (/40 subnets) to accommodate the future growth. Basically, with a node ID length of 1 byte, the number of required sets per domain equals the number of nodes divided by 256. It should be evident that massive summarization gains are possible in SRv6 with a proper addressing concept, which the section "Summarization," later in this chapter, discusses in more detail.

Up to this point, for the sake of simplicity, we have not considered flexible algorithms (flex algos). Operators may, however, want to define a few flex algos to cover the following use cases:

- Low latency

- Disjoint Plane A

- Disjoint Plane B

- MACsec encryption

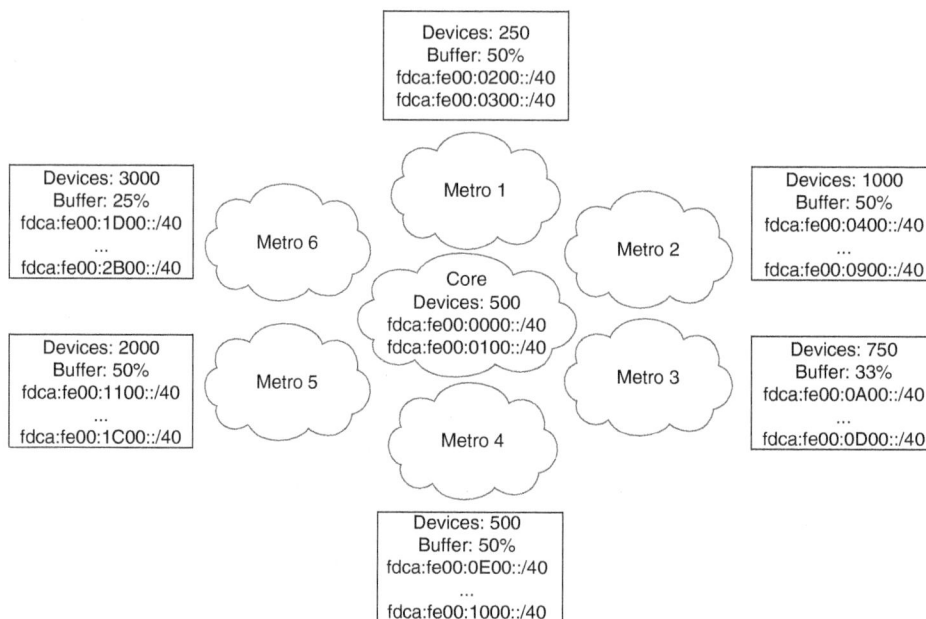

Figure 3-49 *SRv6 uSID Set Allocation Example*

Each flex algo requires a dedicated SRv6 locator per node to facilitate constraint-based IGP paths. SRv6 locators belonging to different algorithms can be allocated contiguously as follows:

- Core (500 devices)

  - Algo 0 (default)

    Sets: fdca:fe00:0000::/40 and fdca:fe00:0001::/40

  - Flex algo 128 (Disjoint Plane A)

    Sets: fdca:fe00:0002::/40 and fdca:fe00:0003::/40

  - Flex algo 129 (Disjoint Plane B)

    Sets: fdca:fe00:0004::/40 and fdca:fe00:0005::/40

  - Flex algo 130 (MACsec Encryption)

    Sets: fdca:fe00:0006::/40 and fdca:fe00:0007::/40

For a single domain, it may still be feasible to allocate sets contiguously but imagine adding a couple of metros to the mix, potentially with a highly asymmetric number of devices per flex algo. This book has not covered summarization in detail yet, but controlling mutual redistribution or route leaking between multiple domains can become very challenging to maintain. Luckily, there is a much better approach. Remember the unused VW octet at the beginning of this section? Instead of encoding the flex algo into the node ID of the SRv6 locator, which is a scarce resource, you can leverage the available octet (VW) that belongs to the SID block. The previous example contiguously assigns SRv6 locators for different flex algo changes to a contiguous allocation per flex algo instead:

- Core (500 devices)
  - Algo 0 (default)

    Sets: fdca:fe**00**:0000::/40 and fdca:fe**00**:0001::/40
  - Flex algo 128 (Disjoint Plane A)

    Sets: fdca:fe**01**:0000::/40 and fdca:fe**01**:0001::/40
  - Flex algo 129 (Disjoint Plane B)

    Sets: fdca:fe**02**:0000::/40 and fdca:fe**02**:0001::/40
  - Flex algo 130 (MACsec Encryption)

    Sets: fdca:fe**03**:0000::/40 and fdca:fe**03**:0001::/40

Encoding the flex algo into the SID block results in a much cleaner and symmetric allocation of SRv6 locators within a domain, which not only positively impacts route policy logic to control mutual redistribution or route leaking but also streamlines summarization. The next sections document SRv6 locator addressing for different scale requirements.

Small- and Medium-Scale Deployments

Allocating one SID block per algorithm works well for small- to medium-scale deployments that do not exceed 57,000 devices (global uSIDs). Small-scale deployments with fewer than 256 devices per domain require only a single /40 set for all of the SRv6 locators. Figure 3-50 shows an example of such a deployment with a core and two metro regions. Note that the SID block for each flex algo is identical across all domains, whereas the set (DD) changes for each domain. This approach supports addressing up to 256 node IDs (NN) per domain, which will suffice for many small-scale deployments.

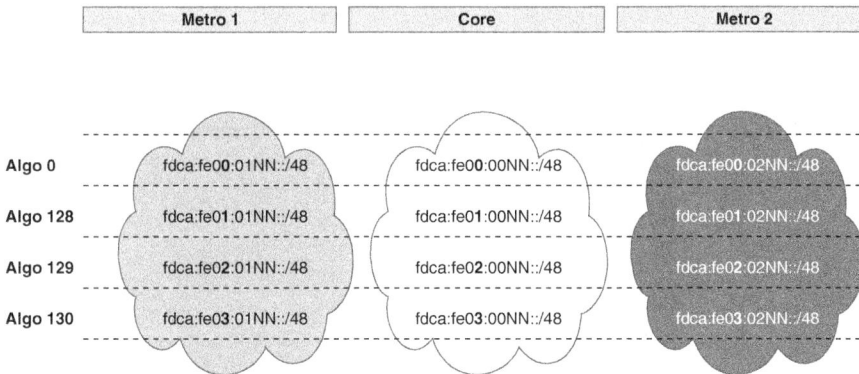

	Metro 1	Core	Metro 2
Algo 0	fdca:fe00:01NN::/48	fdca:fe00:00NN::/48	fdca:fe00:02NN::/48
Algo 128	fdca:fe01:01NN::/48	fdca:fe01:00NN::/48	fdca:fe01:02NN::/48
Algo 129	fdca:fe02:01NN::/48	fdca:fe02:00NN::/48	fdca:fe02:02NN::/48
Algo 130	fdca:fe03:01NN::/48	fdca:fe03:00NN::/48	fdca:fe03:02NN::/48

Figure 3-50 *SRv6 SID Block and Locator (Small-Scale Deployment)*

Larger networks with a few thousand devices per domain would require several /40 sets per domain, as shown in Figure 3-51. Extending this approach makes it possible to address up to 57,000 devices in total. However, in practice, there will always be some waste. For example, if Metro 50 required 262 node IDs, a large part of the second set would remain unallocated. Unallocated SIDs in a set cannot be used in other domains for summarization reasons, as you will see later, and are therefore effectively wasted. The "Summarization" section, later in this chapter, discusses summarization between different IGP domains that detail the reasons domains cannot recycle sets that are partially used in different domains. Wasted node IDs can be a concern for deployments where the total number of devices is close to 57,000 or for deployments with large numbers of metros and inefficient set utilization.

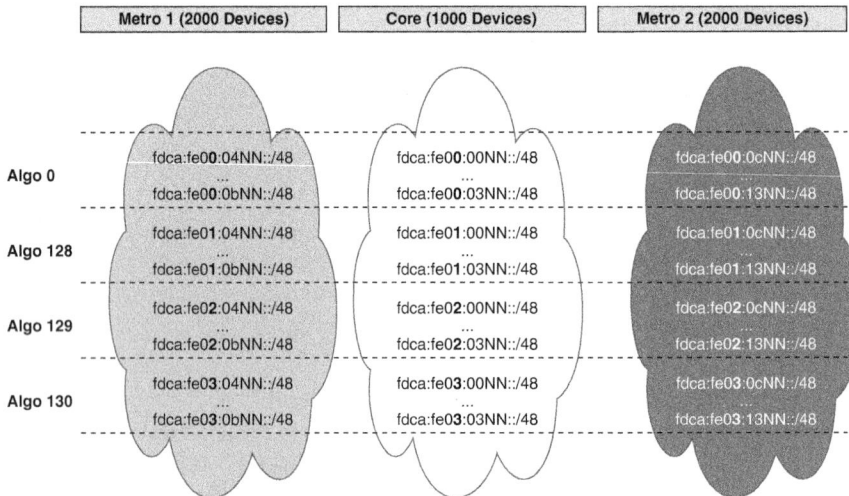

Figure 3-51 *SRv6 SID Block and Locator (Medium-Scale Deployment)*

Large-scale deployments beyond 57,000 devices require a different approach that allows scaling to millions of routers across an SRv6 domain.

Large-Scale Deployments

Large-scale deployments with more than 57,000 devices in an SRv6 domain require several SID blocks per flex algo. Honoring the previously mentioned platform limitation regarding the VW octet of the SID block, three flex algos (for example, Low Latency, Disjoint Plane A, and Disjoint Plane B) could result in the following SRv6 locator assignment:

- fdca:feVW:DDNN::/48, where:
  - V refers to the algorithm:

    0: Default algorithm

    1: Flex algo 128 (Low Latency)

    2: Flex algo 129 (Disjoint Plane A)

    3: Flex algo 130 (Disjoint Plane B)

  - W refers to a super domain:

    0–F: Region identifier

Note The SRv6 SID block and locator carving shown here is just an example. Architects and operators must take into account platform limitations, which may require a different logic than shown in the example.

Figure 3-52 shows a highly hierarchical large-scale deployment consisting of a super core and two super domains. An example of such a topology could be a transcontinental network, where each country is represented as a super domain that contains several in-country domains (metros) that are interconnected via some local core nodes belonging to the super core. A similar example could be made for very large countries.

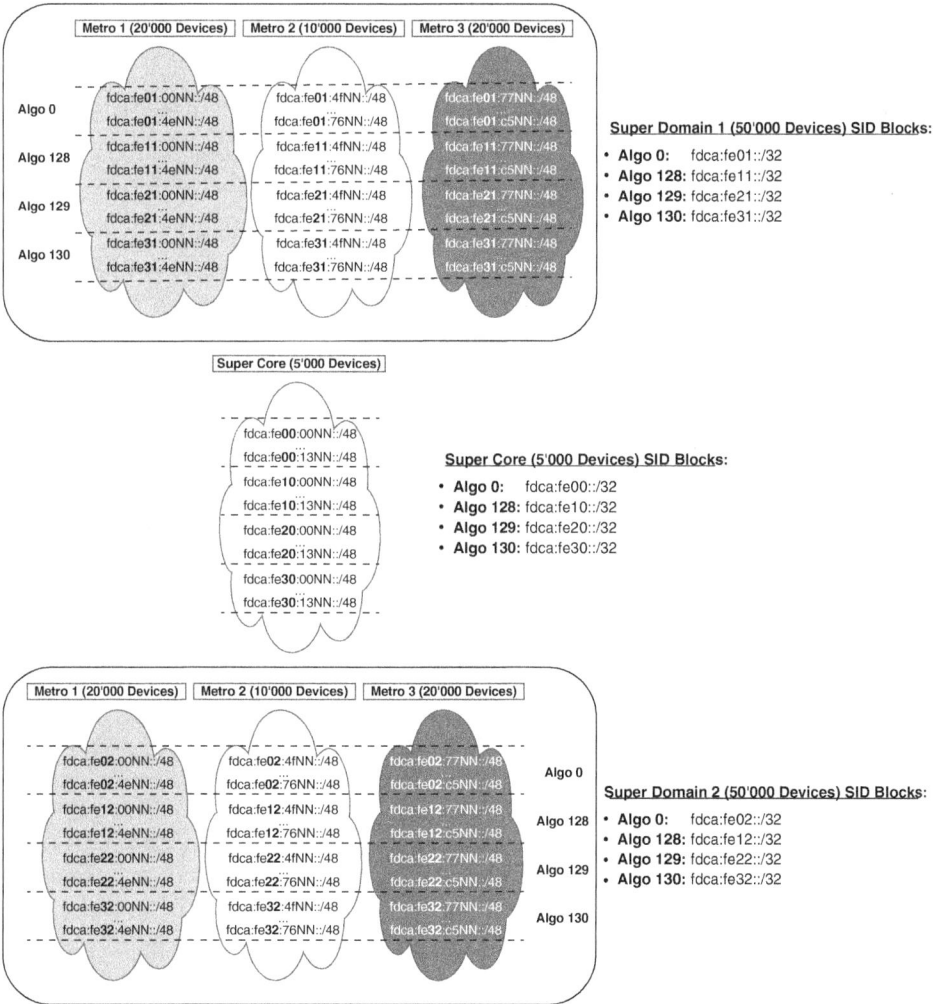

Figure 3-52 *SRv6 SID Block and Locator (Large-Scale Deployment)*

Such an allocation yields 16 super domains with up to 57,000 devices, totaling a maximum scale of 900,000 devices with 3 flex algos. At this writing, few enterprises or service providers would require more than 900,000 global uSIDs in their network. However, in the near future, the picture may change. Platform limitations may only apply to older networking ASICs (NPUs), whereas newer or upcoming generations of ASICs may or may not suffer from restrictions. How would the above address allocation change if the VW octet could utilize the full range of values? The answer depends on the requirements, such as the number of super domains or flex algos.

Let us look at the VW octet in more detail and discuss potential carving options (see Figure 3-53).

Algo   Super Domain

| VVVV | | WWWW | Up to 16 algos/domains |

| VV | | WWWWWW | Up to 4 algos with 64 domains |

| VVV | | WWWWW | Up to 8 algos with 32 domains |

Figure 3-53   *SRv6 SID Block Carving (Large-Scale Deployment)*

Splitting the VW octet into two equal nibbles (4 bits) for algorithm and super domain results in 16 domains with 16 algorithms. It seems rather unlikely that an operator would require 16 different algorithms in their network, which is why 4 bits for the algorithm will not make for an efficient use of the available addressing space. Instead, 2 bits or 3 bits is a better choice for the vast majority of networks. For instance, with 2 bits for the algorithm and 6 bits for the super domain, up to 64 super domains with four algorithms can be encoded in the SID block, resulting in a maximum scale of more than 3.6 million global uSIDs per flex algo.

Figure 3-54 shows an example of such a network deployment. Each domain assigns four different SID blocks (one per algorithm), with up to 57,000 global uSIDs each. A single super domain will consist of multiple subdomains, each allocated /40 sets, as needed per subdomain. The super domain ID-to-SID block mapping is straightforward for the first 16 super domains. Afterward, the super domain ID spills over into the V nibble, which complicates the reverse SID block-to-domain ID mapping a little bit, as you can observe for super domain IDs 62 and 63 in Figure 3-54.

Finally, when it comes to SRv6 SID block and locator carving, there is no one size fits all. Networks come in all sizes, shapes, and forms. Besides the network operator's requirement there may be network processor unit or software limitations that require consideration. The examples shown in the last few sections all rely on an SRv6 uSID block length of 32 bits with a uSID length of 16 bits. Other uSID flavors with different lengths may be possible, but the same principles apply.

Summarization

One of the biggest advantages of SRv6 is the massive benefits of summarization, where thousands of locators can be aggregated behind a single summary route. This section introduces summarization at the area or domain boundary in more detail and provides an overview of route aggregation advantages and disadvantages.

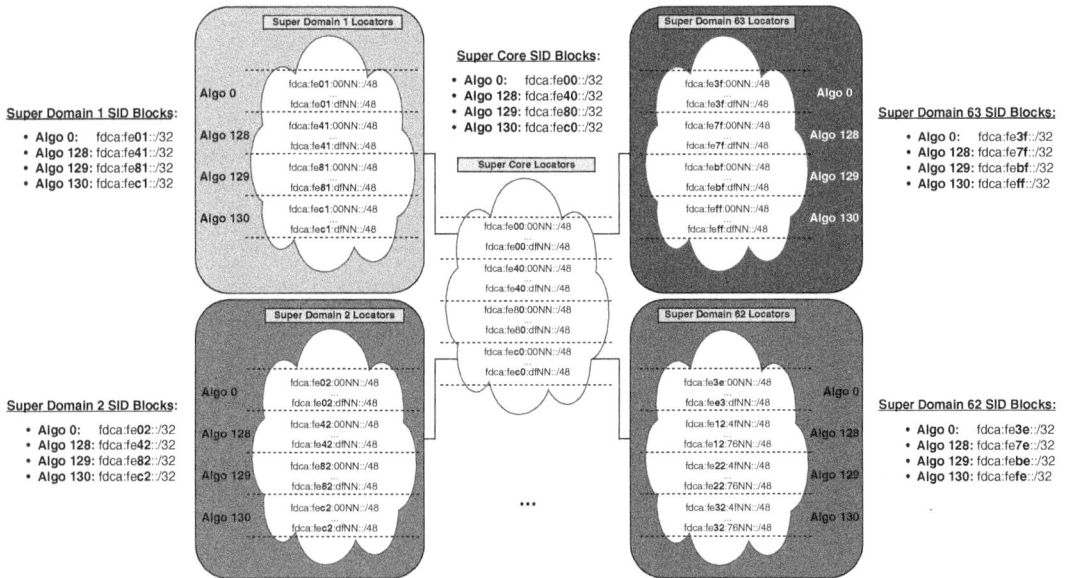

Figure 3-54   *SRv6 SID Block and Locator (Ultra-Large-Scale Deployment)*

The IPv6 data plane of SRv6 in combination with a meaningful addressing concept lays the foundation for large-scale summarization across the entire SRv6 domain. Thousands of SRv6 locators can be aggregated behind a handful of summary routes generated at the domain or metro boundaries. Figure 3-55 shows an imaginary network with different metro domains showcasing various aggregation strategies.

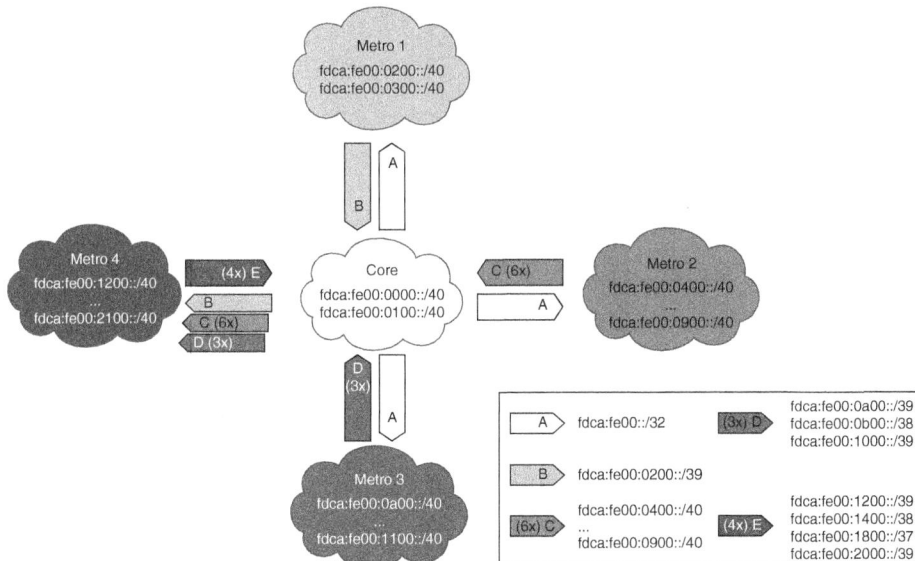

Figure 3-55   *SRv6 Route Summarization*

We can distinguish between the following metro connectivity directions:

- Inside connectivity to metro:

  - More specific routes must be propagated or redistributed into the core to ensure that the longest prefix match forwarding routes traffic toward the correct metro. The most basic summary consists of a /40 set aggregating 256 node IDs (locators). This strategy is applied to Metro 2 in this example, which generates and advertises six /40 sets toward the core network.

  - Larger metros may be able to generate one or even multiple larger summaries to aggregate more than 256 node IDs (locators) behind a single route, as shown for Metros 1, 3, and 4 in this example. Operators can strategically allocate multiple /40 sets for a single metro to facilitate clean summarization boundaries and allow for /39 aggregates or larger. Metro 4, for instance, which owns the sets from fdca:fe00:1200::/40 up to fdca:fe00:2100::/40 can be aggregated using two /39, a /38 and a /37 aggregate.

- Outside connectivity from metro:

  - Generate a fdca:fe00::/32 SID block summary route on the metro boundary for all external connectivity that summarizes up to 57,000 SRv6 locators behind a single aggregate. Such a large summary route massively reduces the number of external routes required for outside connectivity. This strategy was applied for Metros 1, 2, and 3 in the example network.

  - Metro 4 follows a different approach, where the metro boundary allows the aggregates learned from remote metros to be propagated or redistributed into the local metro. As a worst case, with a 32-bit SRv6 uSID block and 16-bit uSID length, where uSIDs beginning with 0xE or 0xF are reserved for local uSIDs, the maximum number of aggregates consists of up to 224 /40 sets across the entire /32 SID block. Each /40 set aggregates up to 256 node IDs (locators).

Summarization is highly beneficial for the overall IGP scale and performance but, of course, it comes at a cost:

- **Suboptimal routing:** Summarization results in a loss of end-to-end visibility for more specific routes. As a consequence, a forwarding decision that is based on an aggregate route may not be ideal and could result in a longer path with additional hops and possibly higher latency.

- **Wasted bandwidth for bogus traffic:** Summarization, especially in combination with default routes, could attract unwanted bogus traffic on the originator of the aggregate. Instead of dropping early, traffic is forwarded to the domain boundary where the discard route applies to drop bogus traffic. This should not be a problem with a proper aggregate for the SID block but it is something to keep in mind.

- **Risk of blackholing traffic:** Large summaries could lead to traffic blackholing if a certain sub-aggregate (for example, /40) within the aggregate (for example, /32) becomes temporarily unavailable on the originator of the summary route, which is usually a set of redundant area border routers (ABRs). Smaller aggregates are less likely to suffer from blackholing if they are propagated as learned from the core. The root cause of the blackholing could be a suboptimal design or a network failure.

- **Potential impact on BGP fast convergence:** Large summary routes (for example, /32 SID block) include not only the external address space of remote metros but also the address space of the local metro. A node failure within the local domain may not trigger BGP PIC edge failover to the backup path if a router is not notified about the node failure by BGP next hop tracking, since the /48 SRv6 locator of the service SID can still be resolved via the /32 aggregate.

Summarization in the SRv6 domain is a powerful tool that allows operators to aggregate thousands of SRv6 locators behind a few summary routes. It is important to note that summarization is not a silver bullet to all scale issues because the locators that belong to the local domain cannot be summarized. In other words, the number of aggregate routes is almost negligible in the great scheme of things. For example, an IGP domain with 2000 nodes will still learn 2000 local /48 locator prefixes per algorithm, which will always outweigh the number of remote /40 aggregates by several factors. Therefore, for simplicity and fast convergence, it is generally recommended to create a summary route per set (for example, /40). Furthermore, service scale becomes increasingly important as the number of devices in the transport network grows. To conclude, today's best practices related to IGP and BGP service scale are still applicable in the SRv6 world, and they may even be more crucial today than they once were, if you want to reap all the benefits of SRv6's scalability.

IGP Extensions

The following sections take you through the IGP extensions of SRv6. Note that the following sections are limited to new TLVs and sub-TLVs defined as part of the corresponding segment routing extensions RFCs. The displayed packet captures serve to support the visualization of the underlying control plane.

Also, in the interest of brevity, we decided to descope the OSPFv3 extensions for the SRv6 draft for several reasons. Currently, the number of service providers deploying IS-IS and OSPF is roughly evenly distributed. The migration to SRv6 presents an excellent opportunity to transition away from OSPF, as a new routing protocol (OSPFv3 or IS-IS) will be necessary for IPv6 support. It is anticipated that several operators will undertake a *ships in the night* migration, moving from OSPF to IS-IS during the SRv6 transition. Second, at the time of writing, IOS XR only supports IS-IS as the underlying IGP in SRv6 networks. Finally, the IS-IS and OSPFv3 extensions for SRv6 are somewhat similar, which allows you to get a head start with the content in the next section.

IS-IS Extensions for Segment Routing over IPv6 (RFC 9352)

The Internet Assigned Numbers Authority (IANA) registered the IS-IS TLVs and sub-TLVs highlighted in Figure 3-56 as part of RFC 9352 to facilitate the distribution of SRv6-specific information.

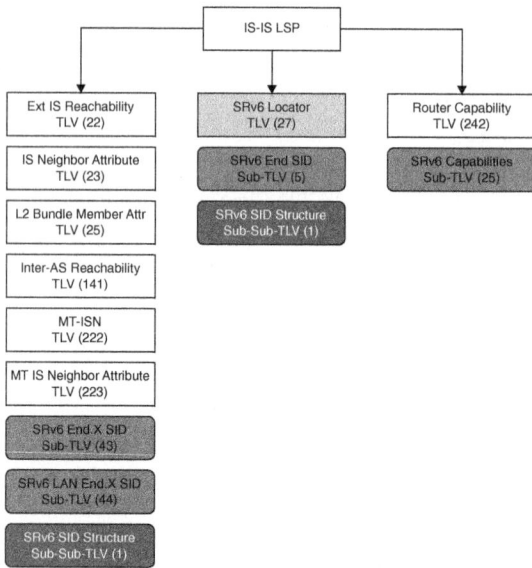

Figure 3-56 *IS-IS Extensions for SRv6*

Note   IANA lists the registered IS-IS extensions for Segment Routing over IPv6 at https://www.iana.org/assignments/isis-tlv-codepoints/isis-tlv-codepoints.xhtml.

Segment Routing over IPv6 Locator

A new IS-IS top-level TLV has been created to advertise SRv6 locator and corresponding End SID information in IS-IS, as presented in Table 3-7.

Table 3-7 *SRv6 IS-IS Top-Level TLV*

Type	TLV
27	SRv6 Locator

In addition, the IS-IS sub-TLVs for TLVs advertising prefix reachability have been modified to attach the sub-TLVs shown in Table 3-8 to the IS-IS SRv6 Locator TLV.

Table 3-8 *SRv6 Locator Sub-TLVs*

Type	Sub-TLV
1	32-bit Admin Tag
2	64-bit Admin Tag
4	Prefix Attribute Flags

Type	Sub-TLV
5	SRv6 End SID
11	IPv4 Source Router ID
12	IPv6 Source Router ID

Example 3-1 shows a packet capture of an IS-IS LSP with an SRv6 Locator TLV (27).

Example 3-1 *IS-IS LSP with SRv6 Locator TLV (27)*

```
IEEE 802.3 Ethernet
Logical-Link Control
ISO 10589 ISIS INTRA Domain Routing Information Exchange Protocol
ISO 10589 ISIS Link State Protocol Data Unit
<snip>
    LSP-ID: 0001.0000.0005.00-00
<snip>
    SRv6 Locator (t=27, l=182)
        Type: 27
        Length: 182
        0000 .... .... .... = Reserved: 0x0
        .... 0000 0000 0010 = Topology ID: IPv6 routing topology (2)
        Metric: 1
        Flags: 0x00
            0... .... = Down bit: Not set
            .000 0000 = Reserved: 0x00
        Algorithm: Shortest Path First (SPF) (0)
        Locator Size: 48
        Locator: fc00:0:105::
        SubCLV Length: 31
        subTLV: Prefix Attribute Flags (c=4, l=1)
            Code: Prefix Attribute Flags (4)
            Length: 1
            Flags: 0x00
                0... .... = X-Flag: Not set
                .0.. .... = R-Flag: Not set
                ..0. .... = N-Flag: Not set
                ...0 .... = E-Flag: Not set
                .... 0... = A-Flag: Not set
                .... .000 = Reserved: 0x0
        subTLV: SRv6 End SID (c=5, l=26)
            Code: SRv6 End SID (5)
            Length: 26
            Flags: 0x00
```

```
SRv6 Endpoint Function: End with NEXT-CSID, PSP & USD (48)
SID: fc00:0:105::
SubSubCLV Length: 6
   subsubTLV: SRv6 SID Structure (c=1, l=4)
       Locator Block Length: 32
       Locator Node Length: 16
       Function Length: 0
       Arguments Length: 80
<snip>
```

The SRv6 Locator TLV consists of the following flags, fields, and sub-TLVs:

- **R bits:** Bits reserved for future use cases.

- **Multi-Topology Identifier (MTID):** The IS-IS Multi-Topology ID (for example, 2 for IPv6 unicast routing topology).

- **Metric:** The SRv6 locator IS-IS metric.

- **Up/Down Bit (D-Flag):** Used to prevent routing loops in IS-IS when redistributing the SRv6 Locator TLV between different IS-IS processes at the same level or the same IS-IS process from Level 2 to Level 1. By setting the D-flag, the SRv6 Locator TLV cannot be redistributed back into Level 2 (or the original IS-IS process), effectively preventing routing loops.

- **Algorithm:** The IGP algorithm associated with the SRv6 Locator TLV (for example, Shortest Path First).

- **Locator Size:** The length of the SRv6 Locator TLV or prefix length (for example, /48 for uSID with 32-bit SID block and 16-bit uSID length).

- **Locator:** The SRv6 Locator TLV (for example, fc00:0:105::).

A series of optional sub-TLVs are commonly included in the Locator TLV, such as the Prefix Attribute Flags and SRv6 End SID sub-TLVs.

The Prefix Attribute Flags sub-TLV consists of the following flags:

- **External Prefix flag (X-flag):** Set for prefixes that were redistributed from a different protocol or different IS-IS process.

- **Re-Advertisement flag (R-flag):** Set for prefixes that were propagated between levels (for example, Level 2 to Level 1 or vice versa).

- **Node flag (N-flag):** Set for prefixes that uniquely identify the advertising node (for example, loopback address).

- **ELC flag (E-flag):** Set for host prefixes (for example, loopback address) to signal that all interfaces support entropy label capability. Not applicable to SRv6.

- **Anycast flag (A-flag):** Set for prefixes or a locator configured as anycast. Newly defined in RFC 9352.

The SRv6 End SID sub-TLV consists of the following flags:

- **Flags:** Reserved for future use cases

- **Endpoint Behavior:** Identifies the endpoint behavior associated with this SID, which in the case of the SRv6 End SID must be a variant of the End behavior (for example, End with NEXT-CSID and PSP/USD).

- **SID:** The advertised SID associated with the previously described endpoint behavior (for example, fc00:0:105::).

The SRv6 End SID must be allocated from the advertised locator. Example 3-1 shows an SRv6 locator (fc00:0:105::/48) with an identical SRv6 End SID. This is commonly the case for SRv6 uSID, where the node ID portion of the locator (for example, 0x105) is a uSID associated with the End (uN) behavior of the advertising node (for example, fc00:0:105::). The optional SRv6 SID Structure sub-sub-TLV shown in the packet capture of Example 3-1 is covered at the end of this section.

As discussed earlier in this chapter, not all devices within the backbone have to be SRv6 capable to transport services across the core. Legacy IPv6-capable devices ignore SRv6-specific TLVs and sub-TLVs, which is why SRv6 locators should be advertised as regular IPv6 prefixes for algorithms 0 and 1 to facilitate end-to-end connectivity over native IPv6 networks. Example 3-2 shows an IS-IS LSP with an IS-IS Multi-Topology Reachable IPv6 Prefixes TLV conveying the previously shown /48 SRv6 locator.

Example 3-2 *IS-IS LSP with SRv6 Locator IPv6 Reachability*

```
IEEE 802.3 Ethernet
Logical-Link Control
ISO 10589 ISIS INTRA Domain Routing Information Exchange Protocol
ISO 10589 ISIS Link State Protocol Data Unit
<snip>
    LSP-ID: 0001.0000.0005.00-00
<snip>
    Multi Topology Reachable IPv6 Prefixes (t=237, l=18)
        Type: 237
        Length: 18
        0000 .... .... .... = Reserved: 0x0
        .... 0000 0000 0010 = Topology ID: IPv6 routing topology (2)
        IPv6 Reachability: fc00:0:105::/48
```

```
      Metric: 1
      0... .... = Distribution: Up
      .0.. .... = Distribution: Internal
      ..1. .... = Sub-TLV: Yes
      Prefix Length: 48
      IPv6 prefix: fc00:0:105::
      SubCLV Length: 3
      subTLV: Prefix Attribute Flags (c=4, l=1): Flags:---
          Code: Prefix Attribute Flags (4)
          Length: 1
          Flags: 0x00
              0... .... = X-Flag: Not set
              .0.. .... = R-Flag: Not set
              ..0. .... = N-Flag: Not set
              ...0 .... = E-Flag: Not set
              .... 0... = A-Flag: Not set
              .... .000 = Reserved: 0x0
<snip>
```

You can think of this prefix, or a locator in general, as a summary route that aggregates more specific local SIDs behind it. Without such an aggregate route, transit devices will not know how to forward traffic with an SRv6 SID as IPv6 destination address to its destination, the SRv6 SID instantiator.

Note   Flex-Algo locators should not be advertised in Prefix Reachability TLV to prevent it from using the algorithm 0 forwarding plane.

Segment Routing over IPv6 Capabilities

SRv6 capabilities in IS-IS are advertised using the Router Capability TLV, which has been augmented with the sub-TLVs presented in Table 3-9.

Table 3-9   *SRv6 Capability Sub-TLV for IS-IS Router Capability TLV (242)*

Value	TLV
23	Node Maximum SID Depth (MSD)
25	SRv6 Capabilities

Example 3-3 shows a packet capture of an IS-IS LSP with a Router Capability TLV (242) and a Node Maximum SID Depth (MSD) sub-TLV (23). This sub-TLV is crucial to advertise the underlying platform capabilities concerning maximum SID depth.

Example 3-3 *IS-IS LSP with Node MSD Sub-TLV (23)*

```
IEEE 802.3 Ethernet
Logical-Link Control
ISO 10589 ISIS INTRA Domain Routing Information Exchange Protocol
ISO 10589 ISIS Link State Protocol Data Unit
<snip>
   LSP-ID: 0001.0000.0005.00-00
<snip>
    Router Capability (t=242, l=46)
        Type: 242
        Length: 46
        Router ID: 0x00000000
        .... ...0 = S bit: False
        .... ..0. = D bit: False
        Segment Routing - Algorithms (t=19, l=5)
        SRv6 Capability (t=25, l=2)
        Node Maximum SID Depth (t=23, l=10)
            MSD Type: Maximum Segments Left (41)
            MSD Value: 3
            MSD Type: Maximum End Pop (42)
            MSD Value: 3
            MSD Type: Maximum H.Insert (43)
            MSD Value: 3
            MSD Type: Maximum H.Encaps (44)
            MSD Value: 3
            MSD Type: Maximum End D (45)
            MSD Value: 4
<snip>
```

The Node Maximum SID Depth (MSD) sub-TLV consists of the following MSD Type fields:

■ **Maximum Segments Left (41):** Signals the maximum supported value of the Segments Left field of the SRH when performing the endpoint operation on the advertising node.

■ **Maximum End Pop (42):** Signals the maximum supported number of segments in the Segment List field of the SRH when performing the endpoint operation with PSP/USP on the advertising node.

■ **Maximum H.Insert (43):** Signals the maximum supported number of segments in the Segment List field of the SRH when performing the headend with insertion of an SRv6 policy.

■ **Maximum H.Encaps (44):** Signals the maximum supported number of segments that can be added to the Segment List field in the SRH when performing the H.Encaps operation on the advertising node.

■ **Maximum End D (45):** Signals the maximum supported number of segments in the Segment List field of the SRH when performing decapsulation (for example, End. DT*, End.DX*, End* with USD).

Note IGP MSD types registered with IANA are listed at https://www.iana.org/ assignments/igp-parameters/igp-parameters.xhtml#igp-msd-types.

Example 3-4 shows a packet capture of an IS-IS LSP with a Router Capability TLV (242) and an SRv6 Capability sub-TLV (25).

Example 3-4   *IS-IS LSP with SRv6 Capabilities Sub-TLV (25)*

```
IEEE 802.3 Ethernet
Logical-Link Control
ISO 10589 ISIS INTRA Domain Routing Information Exchange Protocol
ISO 10589 ISIS Link State Protocol Data Unit
<snip>
    LSP-ID: 0001.0000.0005.00-00
<snip>
    Router Capability (t=242, l=46)
        Type: 242
        Length: 46
        Router ID: 0x00000000
        .... ...0 = S bit: False
        .... ..0. = D bit: False
        Segment Routing - Algorithms (t=19, l=5)
        SRv6 Capability (t=25, l=2)
            Flags: 0x0000
                .0.. .... .... .... = OAM flag: Not set
                0.00 0000 0000 0000 = Unused: 0x0000
<snip>
```

The SRv6 Capability sub-TLV consists of the OAM Flag (O-Flag), which is set on routers that support OAM processing (for telemetry data collection and export), as defined in RFC 9259. All other bits are currently unused.

Segment routing algorithms and the Flexible Algorithm Definition (FAD) are advertised similarly to what you saw in the previous chapter, in the section "IS-IS Extensions for Segment Routing (RFC 8667)." Example 3-5 shows an advertising router that supports the SPF and strict SPF algorithms, as defined in RFC 8665. Besides these common algorithms, the device supports two customer-defined algorithms (flex algos) that rely on SPF calculation with varying metric types (delay and IGP metric). This should feel familiar because it is similar to the SR-MPLS examples in Chapter 2.

Example 3-5 *IS-IS LSP with SR Algorithm and FAD TLVs*

```
IEEE 802.3 Ethernet
Logical-Link Control
ISO 10589 ISIS INTRA Domain Routing Information Exchange Protocol
ISO 10589 ISIS Link State Protocol Data Unit
<snip>
    LSP-ID: 0001.0000.0005.00-00
<snip>
    Router Capability (t=242, l=46)
        Type: 242
        Length: 46
        Router ID: 0x00000000
        .... ...0 = S bit: False
        .... ..0. = D bit: False
        Segment Routing - Algorithms (t=19, l=5)
            Algorithm: Shortest Path First (SPF) (0)
            Algorithm: Strict Shortest Path First (SPF) (1)
            Algorithm: Unknown (128)
            Algorithm: Unknown (129)
<snip>
        Flexible Algorithm Definition (t=26, l=4)
            Flex-Algorithm: 128
            Metric-Type: Min Unidirectional Link Delay (1)
            Calculation-Type: Shortest Path First (SPF) (0)
            Priority: 128
        Flexible Algorithm Definition (t=26, l=4)
            Flex-Algorithm: 129
            Metric-Type: IGP Metric (0)
            Calculation-Type: Shortest Path First (SPF) (0)
            Priority: 128
<snip>
```

Segment Routing Identifiers (SIDs)

The SRv6 End.X SID sub-TLVs shown in Table 3-10 may be present in the following TLVs:

- Extended IS Reachability (TLV 22)

- IS Neighbor Attribute (TLV 23)

- Layer 2 Bundle Member Attributes (TLV 25)

- Multi-Topology (MT) ISN (TLV 222)

- MT IS Neighbor Attribute (TLV 223)

Table 3-10 *SRv6 IS-IS Sub-TLVs for TLVs Advertising Neighbor Information*

Value	Sub-TLV
43	SRv6 End.X SID
44	SRv6 LAN End.X SID

Example 3-6 shows a packet capture of an IS-IS LSP with an Extended IS Reachability TLV (222) and an SRv6 End.X SID sub-TLV (43). SRv6 End.X SID sub-TLV are associated with unidirectional IS-IS adjacencies advertised by a node. Note that the End.X SID is advertised as a subnet of the locator associated with the corresponding algorithm or topology.

Example 3-6 *IS-IS LSP with SRv6 End.X SID Sub-TLV (43)*

```
IEEE 802.3 Ethernet
Logical-Link Control
ISO 10589 ISIS INTRA Domain Routing Information Exchange Protocol
ISO 10589 ISIS Link State Protocol Data Unit
<snip>
    LSP-ID: 0001.0000.0005.00-00
<snip>
        Multi Topology IS Reachability (t=222, l=239)
            Type: 222
            Length: 239
            0000 .... .... .... = Reserved: 0x0
            .... 0000 0000 0010 = Topology ID: IPv6 routing topology (2)
        IS Neighbor: 0001.0000.0004.00
            IS neighbor ID: 0001.0000.0004.00
            Metric: 10
<snip>
            subTLV: SRv6 End.X SID (c=43, l=28)
                Code: SRv6 End.X SID (43)
                Length: 28
                Flags: 0x80, Backup flag
                    1... .... = Backup flag: Set
                    .0.. .... = Set flag: Not set
                    ..0. .... = Persistent flag: Not set
                Algorithm: Shortest Path First (SPF) (0)
                Weight: 0
                SRv6 Endpoint Function: End.X with NEXT-CSID, PSP & USD (57)
                SID: fc00:0:105:e006::
                SubSubCLV Length: 6
                    subsubTLV: SRv6 SID Structure (c=1, l=4)
```

```
                       Locator Block Length: 32
                       Locator Node Length: 16
                       Function Length: 16
                       Arguments Length: 64
<snip>
```

The SRv6 End.X SID sub-TLV consists of the following flags and fields:

- **Backup flag (B-flag):** Set to signal the protection eligibility of an End.X SID through fast reroute in the event of a link failure.

- **Set flag (S-flag):** Set when the End.X SID refers to a set of adjacencies.

- **Persistent flag (P-flag):** Set when the End.X SID is persistent across reloads/interface flaps (which is useful for static SR policies).

- **Weight:** Represents the weight used for load-balancing purposes in the presence of parallel adjacencies with the same End.X SID. A higher weight is preferred over a lower weight. For instance, two parallel adjacencies with weights of 1 and 3 will receive their share of traffic in a 1:3 ratio, or 25%:75%.

- **Endpoint Behavior:** Refers to the associated SRv6 endpoint behavior (for example, End.X with NEXT-CSID and PSP/USD).

- **SID:** Refers to the advertised SID (128 bits).

In the packet capture in Example 3-6, you can see that the SRv6 End.X SID to neighbor 0001.0000.0004.00 is assigned the locally significant Adj-SID value fc00:0:105:e006:: that is eligible for protection.

The SRv6 LAN End.X SID is applicable to LAN networks with more than two IS-IS nodes and works similarly to the previously introduced SRv6 End.X SID. It is rather uncommon to see LAN networks in service provider backbones.

An optional SRv6 SID Structure sub-sub-TLV listed in Table 3-11 may be attached to End/End.X sub-TLVs, as displayed in Example 3-1 and Example 3-6.

Table 3-11 *SRv6 IS-IS Sub-Sub-TLV for SRv6 SID Sub-TLVs*

Type	Sub-Sub-TLV
1	SRv6 SID Structure

This sub-sub-TLV is used to advertise the SID format throughout the network and consists of the following fields:

- Locator Block Length (SID Block)

- Locator Node Length (Node ID)

- Function Length

- Argument Length

As always, the length of a SID is less or equal to 128 bits, which is what the sum of all four fields must adhere to. The SID Structure sub-sub-TLV is not intended for the data plane to affect traffic forwarding but rather for the operations team to facilitate tracking, compliance checks, or security enforcement.

MP-BGP Extensions

The following sections will introduce SRv6 extensions to the BGP control plane required to advertise the BGP Prefix SID and link-state database between BGP speakers. Note that the following sections are limited to new TLVs and sub-TLVs defined as part of the corresponding segment routing extensions RFCs. The displayed packet captures serve to support the visualization of the underlying control plane.

BGP Overlay Services on SRv6 (RFC 9252)

SRv6 overlay services take advantage of the IP and Ethernet VPN control plane consolidation, relying solely on MP-BGP to propagate routing information between PE devices that belong to a common VPN. SRv6 service SIDs are commonly transported using BGP, as opposed to the IGP. Examples of service segments are endpoint behaviors with IPv6 decapsulation following table lookup (End.DT*) or xconnect (End.DX*) for both Layer 2 and Layer 3 services.

Nothing changes fundamentally in the overlay BGP control plane compared to legacy VPN services. Egress PE devices encode service-specific information in a BGP UPDATE message that is advertised to ingress PE devices that extract the required information in order to program the required outer IPv6 header encapsulation in hardware. Since the SRv6 data plane works differently from MPLS or SR-MPLS, the encoding of BGP UDPATE messages must be modified as well. This section highlights these changes and reiterates some of the service SIDs encountered earlier in this book.

Note   BGP extensions for Segment Routing over IPv6 registered with IANA are listed at https://www.iana.org/assignments/bgp-parameters/bgp-parameters.xhtml.

RFC 9252 augments the existing BGP Prefix SID attribute with two new TLVs, as shown in Table 3-12. At a high level, the BGP Prefix SID attribute serves three purposes for SRv6: It signals the support of BGP overlay services over SRv6, propagates the SID structure in use and, most importantly, includes the SRv6 service SID to be used by remote ingress PEs.

Table 3-12   *BGP Prefix-SID TLVs*

Value	TLV
5	SRv6 L3 Service
6	SRv6 L2 Service

The SRv6 L3 Service TLV encodes service-specific information for SRv6 and is equivalent to Layer 3 MPLS services:

- **IPv4 services:** End.DX4, End.DT4

- **IPv6 services:** End.DX6, End.DT6

- **Dual-stack services:** End.DT46

Figure 3-57 shows a BGP UPDATE message for an SRv6 SID related to a Layer 3 service. Note that the BGP Prefix SID attribute defined in Chapter 2 is now augmented to carry SRv6 SID information related to BGP services using different TLVs and sub-TLVs. Other attributes, such as the MP_REACH_NLRI, remain largely unchanged.

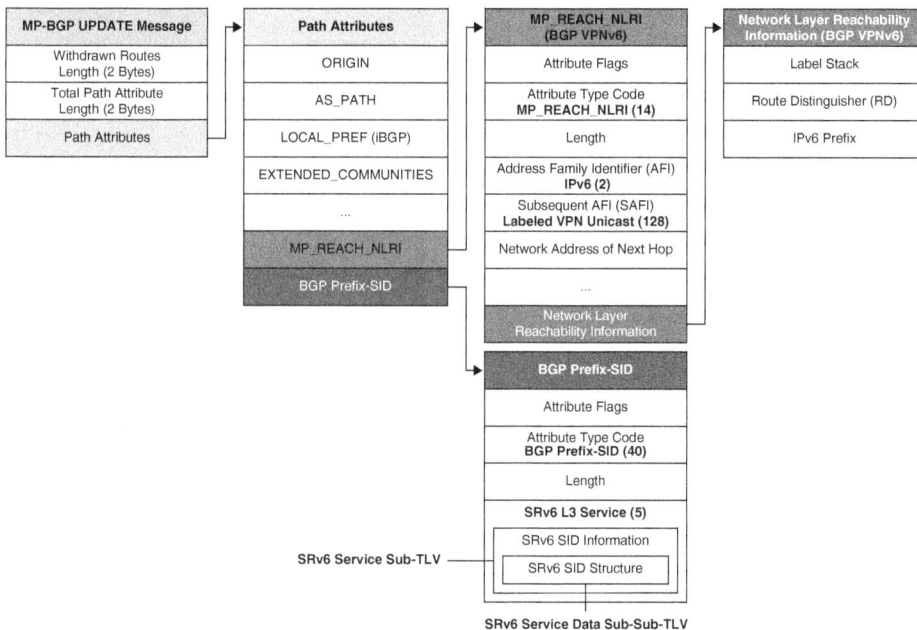

Figure 3-57   *BGP UPDATE Message Format (SRv6 L3 Service)*

The SRv6 L2 Service TLV encodes service-specific information for SRv6 and is equivalent to Layer 2 MPLS services:

- **Point-to-point services:** End.DX2, End.DX2V

- **Multipoint services:** End.DT2U, End.DT2M

Figure 3-58 shows a BGP UPDATE message for an SRv6 SID related to a Layer 2 service. The structure of the BGP UPDATE message looks very similar to the SRv6 L3 Service TLV example except that the EVPN NLRI differs considerably from the NLRI associated with BGP VPNv4/VPNv6 prefixes. Also, the content of the EVPN NLRI depends on the EVPN route type.

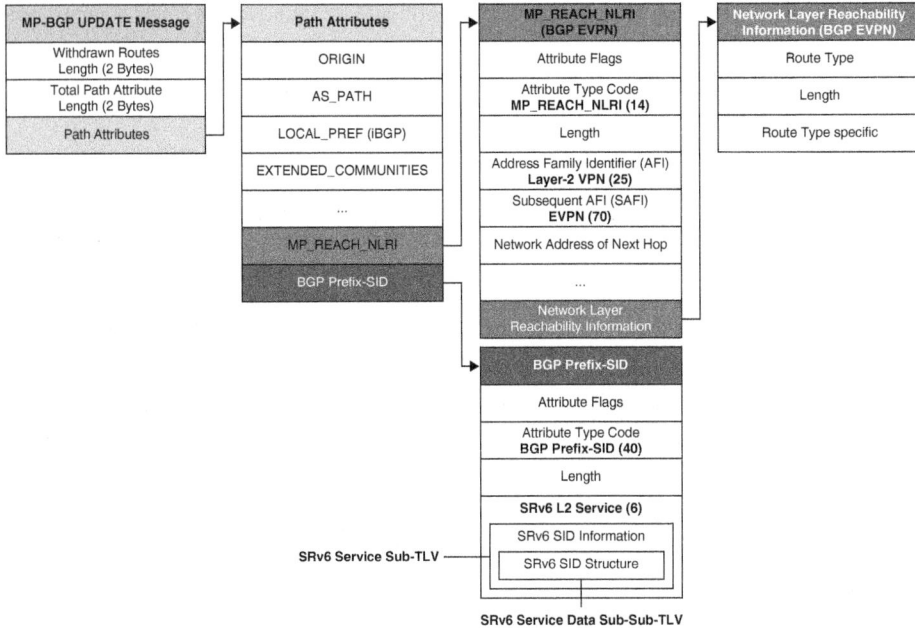

Figure 3-58   *BGP UPDATE Message Format (SRv6 L2 Service)*

The SRv6 Service TLV acts as a container for a variable number of additional sub-TLV and sub-sub-TLV shown in the previous diagrams. RFC 9252 defines a new SRv6 SID Information sub-TLV shown in Table 3-13.

Table 3-13   *SRv6 Service Sub-TLV*

Value	Sub-TLV
1	SRv6 SID Information

The SRv6 SID Information sub-TLV consists of the following relevant fields:

- **SRv6 SID Value:** Contains an SRv6 SID (locator portion or complete SID).

- **SRv6 Service SID Flags:** Undefined but may be useful for future use cases.

- **SRv6 Endpoint Behavior:** Contains the associated SRv6 endpoint behavior (as registered with IANA).

It is important to note that the SRv6 SID value may include a service SID or only a common part of the SRv6 SID, such as the locator. You'll learn the reason behind this shortly.

SRv6 Service Data sub-sub-TLV can be attached to the SRv6 SID Information sub-TLV to propagate properties of the SRv6 SID. RFC 9252 defines a new SRv6 Service Data sub-

sub-TLV, shown in Table 3-14, that is used to advertise the lengths of the various elements that make up a SID.

Table 3-14   *SRv6 Service Data Sub-Sub-TLV*

Value	TLV
1	SRv6 SID Structure Sub-Sub-TLV

The SRv6 SID Structure sub-sub-TLV consists of the following relevant fields:

- **Locator Block Length:** The bit length of the SID block

- **Locator Node Length:** The bit length of the node ID

- **Function Length:** The bit length of the function

- **Argument Length:** The bit length of the argument

- **Transposition Length:** The bit length of the part of the SID that has been shifted into the MPLS label field of the NLRI

- **Transposition Offset:** The bit length of the offset position of the part of the SID that has been shifted into the MPLS label field of the NLRI

The SID structure is highly dynamic because many of the fields are not fixed in length, as long as the sum of block, node, function, and argument length are equal to or smaller than 128 bits. Figure 3-59 shows an example of an SRv6 uSID deployment with a SID block length of 32 bits and uSID length of 16 bits.

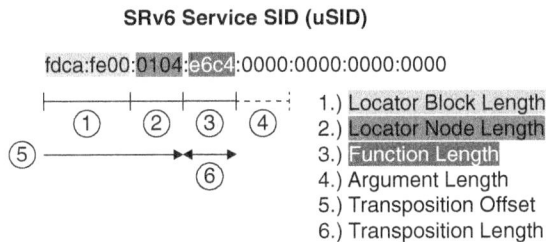

SRv6 Service SID (uSID)

fdca:fe00:0104:e6c4:0000:0000:0000:0000

1.) Locator Block Length
2.) Locator Node Length
3.) Function Length
4.) Argument Length
5.) Transposition Offset
6.) Transposition Length

Figure 3-59   *SRv6 SID Structure Overview*

Figure 3-59 has a locator block length of 32 bits with a node ID length of 16 bits. Remember that the SRv6 uSID locator from previous examples is a /48 prefix, which is the sum of the two elements. The function length in the example is 16 bits, with a variable argument length. The transposition length and offset may be a bit more confusing.

SRv6 BGP overlay services reuse most of the existing MP-BGP control plane and existing BGP attributes, such as the label field included in the MP_REACH_NLRI. However, SRv6 relies on the IPv6 data planes, which obsoletes the need for any label information in the BGP NLRI. Instead of a label, SRv6 BGP services can encode the SID function into the same 20-bit or 24-bit field (RFC 7432). In other words, the complete service SID can be split into two parts in the BGP UPDATE message:

- The SRv6 locator included in the SRv6 SID Information sub-TLV (for example, fdca:fe00:104::)

- The SRv6 function included in the Label field of the NLRI (for example, 0xe6c40)

In order to merge the two elements into the SRv6 service SID, the ingress PE device (receiving the update) must be told how to combine the different fields. The two transposition fields are basically an instruction manual on how to achieve this. For instance, the device should extract 16 bits of the 20-bit NLRI label field and append it to the SRv6 SID value starting from the 48th bit. The result of this operation will be the SRv6 service SID fdca:fe00:104:e6c4::.

You might wonder about the reason for this added complexity. It lies in the way how BGP works under the hood. BGP, unlike IS-IS, scales to millions of routes and has been heavily optimized for efficient packing, propagation, and processing of BGP UPDATE messages. Several prefixes or NLRI can be advertised in a single BGP UPDATE message; this is commonly called *update packing*. Only prefixes that share the same set of BGP path attributes are eligible for update packing, which includes attributes such as BGP standard and extended communities, AS PATH, BGP Prefix SID, and so on.

BGP update packing provides the following benefits:

- Less overhead per prefix allows you to pack more prefixes in a BGP UPDATE message and, consequently, more BGP UPDATE messages in a packet.

- Fewer packets required to advertise prefixes leads to better network utilization (less overhead).

- There are fewer packets to parse and process on the receiving device.

- Batch processing of packed prefixes sharing the same BGP attributes on receiving device (route policies)

As far as the SRv6 service SID is concerned, two different use cases can be distinguished.

- **End.DT***: A single SRv6 service SID is used for all prefixes (End.DT4/End.DT6) or MAC addresses (End.DT2U).

- **End.DX***: A single SRv6 service SID is used per next hop (End.DX4/End.DX6) or EVPN VPWS (End.DX2).

There is no issue with BGP update packing related to End.DT* endpoint behaviors because they use the same service SID for all IP prefixes that belong to a VRF table or MAC addresses that belong to a Layer 2 VLAN table. Therefore, the complete service SID could be included in the SRv6 SID Information sub-TLV. For End.DX* endpoint behaviors, however, the situation is different. A PE device with 1000 EVPN VPWS instantiates 1000 different service SIDs for the End.DX2 endpoint behavior, looking similar to the following:

- fdca:fe00:0001:e001::

- fdca:fe00:0001:e002::

- ...

- fdca:fe00:0001:e3e8::

If the entire SRv6 service SID were to be written into the BGP Prefix SID attribute, update packing would not be feasible because the SIDs are different, and consequently so are the BGP path attributes, which is a requirement for packing. A thousand BGP UPDATE messages would be required to propagate the control plane information of the 1000 EVPN VPWS sessions. It goes without saying that this approach is very inefficient. A much better approach is to include the common part of the SRv6 service SIDs, which is usually the locator, in the SRv6 Service TLV, and the variable part of the SRv6 service SID, which can be the function or argument, in the Label fields of the NLRI. This encoding, commonly called transposition scheme, facilitates efficient update packing for both BGP Layer 2 and Layer 3 overlay services over SRv6.

Note   The maximum BGP UPDATE message size equals 4096 bytes (per RFC 4271) or 65,535 bytes (per RFC 8654), which defines the upper limit of update packing per message.

Example 3-7 shows a packet capture of a BGP UPDATE message related to EVPN VPWS. It should be noted that multiple SRv6 service SIDs belonging to different EVPN VPWS are packed in a single UPDATE message. Those services share the same set of BGP path attributes, such as Origin, AS PATH, Local Preference, Extended Communities (for example, BGP Route Targets), and BGP Prefix SID. The SRv6 Service sub-TLV contains the SRv6 locator (fdca:fe00:1::) of the advertising device with the associated endpoint behavior for EVPN VPWS (End.DX2). The SID structure and transposition scheme conveyed in the SRv6 Service Data sub-sub-TLV specify an SRv6 locator length of 48 bits with a function length of 16 bits and no argument. The function part of the SRv6 service SID is encoded in the MPLS Label field of the EVPN NLRI. For instance, the EVPN VPWS service with the Ethernet Tag value 942031024 is associated with the MPLS Label value 944752, which is equivalent to 0xe6a70 in hexadecimal representation. Note that the function length is 16 bits, based on the SRv6 SID structure shown previously, which means the relevant function part is 0xe6a7. Following the transposition scheme yields the SRv6 service SID fdca:fe00:1:e6a7:: for this specific EVPN VPWS service.

As far as other EVPN VPWS services advertised by the same PE are concerned, all service-specific information is encoded within the EVPN NRLI. Fields like the Ethernet Tag ID and MPLS Label fields change between different services, but the common part of the SRv6 service SIDs (locator) remains the same for all services. The next EVPN NLRI encodes a different service with a, MPLS Label value of 0xe6a80 (944768), resulting in an SRv6 service SID of fdca:fe00:1:e6a8::. It should be clear by now how this would continue for additional services and why the complexity of the transposition scheme allows for efficient BGP update packing.

Example 3-7 *BGP UPDATE for SRv6 L2 Services*

```
Ethernet
Internet Protocol Version 6, Src: fdca:fe00:1::1, Dst: fdca:fe00:00ff::1
Transmission Control Protocol, Src Port: 48840, Dst Port: 179
Border Gateway Protocol - UPDATE Message
    Marker: ffffffffffffffffffffffffffffffff
    Length: 850
    Type: UPDATE Message (2)
    Withdrawn Routes Length: 0
    Total Path Attribute Length: 827
    Path attributes
        Path Attribute - MP_REACH_NLRI
            Flags: 0x90, Optional, Extended-Length, Non-transitive, Complete
            Type Code: MP_REACH_NLRI (14)
            Length: 750
            Address family identifier (AFI): Layer-2 VPN (25)
            Subsequent address family identifier (SAFI): EVPN (70)
            Next hop: fdca:fe00:1::1
                IPv6 Address: fdca:fe00:1::1
            Number of Subnetwork points of attachment (SNPA): 0
            Network Layer Reachability Information (NLRI)
                EVPN NLRI: Ethernet AD Route
                    Route Type: Ethernet AD Route (1)
                    Length: 25
                    Route Distinguisher: 10.0.0.1:30001
                    ESI: 00:00:00:00:00:00:00:00:00:00
                        ESI Type: ESI 9 bytes value (0)
                            ESI Value: 00 00 00 00 00 00 00 00 00
                            ESI 9 bytes value: 00 00 00 00 00 00 00 00 00
                    Ethernet Tag ID: 942031024
                    1110 0110 1010 0111 0000 .... = MPLS Label 1: 944752
                EVPN NLRI: Ethernet AD Route
                    Route Type: Ethernet AD Route (1)
                    Length: 25
                    Route Distinguisher: 10.0.0.1:30001
<snip>
                    Ethernet Tag ID: 942031025
                    1110 0110 1010 1000 0000 .... = MPLS Label 1: 944768
<snip>
```

```
            EVPN NLRI: Ethernet AD Route
    Path Attribute - ORIGIN: IGP
    Path Attribute - AS_PATH: empty
    Path Attribute - LOCAL_PREF: 100
    Path Attribute - EXTENDED_COMMUNITIES
    Path Attribute - BGP Prefix-SID
        Flags: 0xc0, Optional, Transitive, Complete
        Type Code: BGP Prefix-SID (40)
        Length: 37
        SRv6 L2 Service
            Type: SRv6 L2 Service (6)
            Length: 34
            Reserved: 00
            SRv6 Service Sub-TLVs
                SRv6 Service Sub-TLV - SRv6 SID Information
                    Type: SRv6 SID Information (1)
                    Length: 30
                    Reserved: 00
                    SRv6 SID Value: fdca:fe00:1::
                SRv6 SID Flags: 0x00
                SRv6 Endpoint Behavior: End.DX2 with NEXT-CSID (0x0041)
                Reserved: 00
                SRv6 Service Data Sub-Sub-TLVs
                    SRv6 Service Data Sub-Sub-TLV - SRv6 SID Structure
                        Type: SRv6 SID Structure (1)
                        Length: 6
                        Locator Block Length: 32
                        Locator Node Length: 16
                        Function Length: 16
                        Argument Length: 0
                        Transposition Length: 16
                        Transposition Offset: 48
<snip>
```

Example 3-8 shows a packet capture of a BGP UPDATE message related to an IPv6 Layer 3 VPN service. It should be noted that different IPv6 prefixes with the same SRv6 service SID belonging to a single VPN are packed in a single UPDATE message. All those prefixes share the same set of BGP path attributes, such as Origin, AS PATH, Local Preference, Communities (for example, BGP Route Targets), and BGP Prefix SID. The SRv6 Service sub-TLV contains the SRv6 locator (fdca:fe00:2::) of the advertising device with the associated endpoint behavior for IPv6 Layer 3 VPN with per-VRF instance SID allocation (End.DT6). The SID structure and transposition scheme conveyed in the SRv6 Service Data sub-sub-TLV specify an SRv6 locator length of 48 bits with a function length of 16 bits and no argument. Similarly to the previous EVPN VPWS example, the function part of the SRv6 service SID is encoded in the MPLS label field of the NLRI. For instance, the IPv6 Layer 3 VPN service with the BGP route distinguisher 10.0.0.2:0 is associated with the MPLS label value 1026528, which is equivalent to 0xfa9e0 in hexadecimal representation. As in the previous example, the function length is 16 bits based on the SRv6 SID structure included in the BGP Prefix SID, which means the relevant function part is 0xfa9e. Following the transposition scheme yields an SRv6 service SID of fdca:fe00:2:fa9e:: for this specific IPv6 Layer 3 VPN service.

For all End.DT* endpoint behaviors, prefixes (End.DT4 or End.DT6) or MAC addresses (End.DT2U) that belong to the same table (IP or Layer 2) are assigned the same SRv6 service SID. Example 3-8 shows several IPv6 prefixes that belong to the same IPv6 VPN and are assigned the same SID.

Example 3-8   *BGP UPDATE for SRv6 L3 (VPNv6) Services*

```
Ethernet
Internet Protocol Version 6, Src: fdca:fe00:ff::1, Dst: fdca:fe00:1::1
Transmission Control Protocol, Src Port: 179, Dst Port: 48840
Border Gateway Protocol - UPDATE Message
    Marker: ffffffffffffffffffffffffffffffff
    Length: 372
    Type: UPDATE Message (2)
    Withdrawn Routes Length: 0
    Total Path Attribute Length: 349
    Path attributes
        Path Attribute - MP_REACH_NLRI
            Flags: 0x90, Optional, Extended-Length, Non-transitive, Complete
            Type Code: MP_REACH_NLRI (14)
            Length: 217
            Address family identifier (AFI): IPv6 (2)
            Subsequent address family identifier (SAFI): Labeled VPN Unicast (128)
            Next hop:  RD=0:0 IPv6=fdca:fe00:2::1
                Route Distinguisher: 0:0
                IPv6 Address: fdca:fe00:2::1
            Number of Subnetwork points of attachment (SNPA): 0
            Network Layer Reachability Information (NLRI)
                Label Stack=1026528 (bottom) RD=10.0.0.2:0,
    IPv6=fd12:3456:789a:b000::/52
<snip>
                Label Stack=1026528 (bottom) RD=10.0.0.2:0, IPv6=fd12:3456:789a:1000
    :2000:3000:a:4/128
        Path Attribute - ORIGIN: INCOMPLETE
        Path Attribute - AS_PATH: 65501 65502 65503
        Path Attribute - LOCAL_PREF: 100
        Path Attribute - COMMUNITIES: 65501:100 65502:100 65503:100
        Path Attribute - EXTENDED_COMMUNITIES
```

```
    Path Attribute - CLUSTER_LIST: 10.0.0.254
    Path Attribute - ORIGINATOR_ID: 10.0.0.2
    Path Attribute - BGP Prefix-SID
       Flags: 0xc0, Optional, Transitive, Complete
       Type Code: BGP Prefix-SID (40)
       Length: 37
       SRv6 L3 Service
          Type: SRv6 L3 Service (5)
          Length: 34
          Reserved: 00
             SRv6 Service Sub-TLVs
                SRv6 Service Sub-TLV - SRv6 SID Information
                   Type: SRv6 SID Information (1)
                   Length: 30
                   Reserved: 00
                      SRv6 SID Value: fdca:fe00:2::
                   SRv6 SID Flags: 0x00
                   SRv6 Endpoint Behavior: End.DT6 with NEXT-CSID (0x003e)
                   Reserved: 00
                      SRv6 Service Data Sub-Sub-TLVs
                         SRv6 Service Data Sub-Sub-TLV - SRv6 SID Structure
                            Type: SRv6 SID Structure (1)
                            Length: 6
                            Locator Block Length: 32
                               Locator Node Length: 16
                               Function Length: 16
                               Argument Length: 0
                               Transposition Length: 16
                               Transposition Offset: 48
<snip>
```

Even though the example shows an End.DT6 (NEXT-CSID) or uDT6 endpoint behavior, the same example could be made for End.DX6 or uDX6 as well, in which case all prefixes belonging to the VRF instance that uses per-CE SID allocation could be packed in a single BGP VPN NLRI, as long as they share the same path attributes. Prefixes with a different BGP next hop (that is, coming from a different CE device), would have different service SIDs and consequently different values in the MPLS Label field.

Not every address family contains an MPLS Label field in its NLRI. For instance, native IPv4 or IPv6 unicast prefixes are defined by prefix and prefix length. Since there is no field that could be used to perform transposition, the entire SRv6 service SID is included in the BGP Prefix SID attribute for IPv4 or IPv6 services in the global routing table (GRT) over SRv6. This lack of transposition support is not an issue in the GRT because with per-VRF SID allocation (End.DT4/End.DT6), only a single SID would be required for all prefixes, or in the case of per-CE SID allocation (End.DX4/End.DX6), a single SID per next hop would be required.

Example 3-9 shows a BGP UPDATE message for an IPv4 unicast BGP overlay service over SRv6. Note that the transposition offset and length are set to zero, which means the complete service SID is included in the SRv6 Service sub-TLV (fdca:fe00:5:e004::). Only a single IPv4 prefix is shown in the NLRI, but nothing prevents efficient packing as long as a set of prefixes share the same BGP path attributes.

Example 3-9 *BGP UPDATE for SRv6 L3 (IPv4 Global Routing Table)*

```
Ethernet
Internet Protocol Version 6, Src: fdca:fe00:5::1, Dst: fcbb:bbbb:bb00:6::1
Transmission Control Protocol, Src Port: 51933, Dst Port: 179
Border Gateway Protocol - UPDATE Message
    Marker: ffffffffffffffffffffffffffffffff
    Length: 114
    Type: UPDATE Message (2)
    Withdrawn Routes Length: 0
    Total Path Attribute Length: 91
    Path attributes
        Path Attribute - MP_REACH_NLRI
            Flags: 0x90, Optional, Extended-Length, Non-transitive, Complete
            Type Code: MP_REACH_NLRI (14)
            Length: 26
            Address family identifier (AFI): IPv4 (1)
            Subsequent address family identifier (SAFI): Unicast (1)
            Next hop: fdca:fe00:5::1
                IPv6 Address: fdca:fe00:5::1
            Number of Subnetwork points of attachment (SNPA): 0
            Network Layer Reachability Information (NLRI)
                172.16.15.5/32
                    MP Reach NLRI prefix length: 32
                    MP Reach NLRI IPv4 prefix: 172.16.15.5
        Path Attribute - ORIGIN: IGP
        Path Attribute - AS_PATH: empty
        Path Attribute - LOCAL_PREF: 100
        Path Attribute - BGP Prefix-SID
            Flags: 0xc0, Optional, Transitive, Complete
            Type Code: BGP Prefix-SID (40)
            Length: 37
            SRv6 L3 Service
                Type: SRv6 L3 Service (5)
                Length: 34
                Reserved: 00
                SRv6 Service Sub-TLVs
```

```
            SRv6 Service Sub-TLV - SRv6 SID Information
                    Type: SRv6 SID Information (1)
                    Length: 30
                    Reserved: 00
                    SRv6 SID Value: fdca:fe00:5:e004::
                    SRv6 SID Flags: 0x00
                    SRv6 Endpoint Behavior: End.DT4 with NEXT-CSID (0x003f)
                    Reserved: 00
                    SRv6 Service Data Sub-Sub-TLVs
                        SRv6 Service Data Sub-Sub-TLV - SRv6 SID Structure
                            Type: SRv6 SID Structure (1)
                            Length: 6
                            Locator Block Length: 32
                            Locator Node Length: 16
                            Function Length: 16
                            Argument Length: 0
                            Transposition Length: 0
                            Transposition Offset: 0
<snip>
```

Similarly, Example 3-10 shows an example of a BGP UPDATE message for an IPv6 unicast BGP overlay service over SRv6. As for IPv4 unicast services, note that the transposition offset and length are set to zero, which means the complete service SID is included in the SRv6 Service sub-TLV (fdca:fe00:5:e005::). Only a single IPv6 prefix is shown in the NLRI, but nothing prevents efficient packing as long as a set of prefixes share the same BGP path attributes.

Example 3-10 *BGP UPDATE for SRv6 L3 (IPv6 Global Routing Table)*

```
Ethernet
Internet Protocol Version 6, Src: fdca:fe00:5::1, Dst: fcbb:bbbb:bb00:6::1
Transmission Control Protocol, Src Port: 51933, Dst Port: 179
Border Gateway Protocol - UPDATE Message
    Marker: ffffffffffffffffffffffffffffffff
    Length: 126
  Type: UPDATE Message (2)
  Withdrawn Routes Length: 0
  Total Path Attribute Length: 103
  Path attributes
      Path Attribute - MP_REACH_NLRI
          Flags: 0x90, Optional, Extended-Length, Non-transitive, Complete
          Type Code: MP_REACH_NLRI (14)
          Length: 38
```

```
Address family identifier (AFI): IPv6 (2)
Subsequent address family identifier (SAFI): Unicast (1)
Next hop: fdca:fe00:5::1
     IPv6 Address: fdca:fe00:5::1
Number of Subnetwork points of attachment (SNPA): 0
Network Layer Reachability Information (NLRI)
     fd02:15::5/128
          MP Reach NLRI prefix length: 128
          MP Reach NLRI IPv6 prefix: fd02:15::5
Path Attribute - ORIGIN: IGP
Path Attribute - AS_PATH: empty
Path Attribute - LOCAL_PREF: 100
Path Attribute - BGP Prefix-SID
     Flags: 0xc0, Optional, Transitive, Complete
     Type Code: BGP Prefix-SID (40)
     Length: 37
     SRv6 L3 Service
          Type: SRv6 L3 Service (5)
          Length: 34
          Reserved: 00
          SRv6 Service Sub-TLVs
               SRv6 Service Sub-TLV - SRv6 SID Information
                    Type: SRv6 SID Information (1)
                    Length: 30
                    Reserved: 00
                    SRv6 SID Value: fdca:fe00:5:e005::
                    SRv6 SID Flags: 0x00
                    SRv6 Endpoint Behavior: End.DT6 with NEXT-CSID (0x003e)
                    Reserved: 00
                    SRv6 Service Data Sub-Sub-TLVs
                         SRv6 Service Data Sub-Sub-TLV - SRv6 SID Structure
                              Type: SRv6 SID Structure (1)
                              Length: 6
                              Locator Block Length: 32
                              Locator Node Length: 16
                              Function Length: 16
                              Argument Length: 0
                              Transposition Length: 0
                              Transposition Offset: 0
<snip>
```

Similarly to locally significant SIDs related to the IGP (for example, End.X), SRv6 service SIDs instantiated for BGP overlay services over SRv6 must be routable from the ingress PE device to the egress PE device following the longest match prefix that usually resolves to the SRv6 locator of the egress PE device. To repeat the MPLS analogy made earlier, the SRv6 locator can be thought of as the MPLS transport label associated with the egress PE device's loopback, whereas the function part is equivalent to the MPLS service label associated with the service terminating on the egress PE device.

It is important to point out that with SRv6, the BGP transport session is fully decoupled from the data plane, which was not the case with MPLS. For instance, with MPLS and SRv6, the source of the BGP peering (TCP session) is set to become the BGP next hop address for all BGP UPDATE messages propagated by the BGP speaker (that is, the egress PE device). Under MPLS, the BGP next hop was usually set to a loopback address associated with an MPLS transport label. With SRv6, the BGP next hop may or may not be part of the SRv6 locator but could also be derived from a completely different IPv6 infrastructure block used for loopback addressing. In short, the BGP next hop for BGP overlay services over SRv6 is not used when programming outer IPv6 header encapsulation information of SRv6 service SIDs in hardware.

For your reference, Figure 3-60 shows the EVPN NLRI format of Layer 2 overlay services for the most common route types.

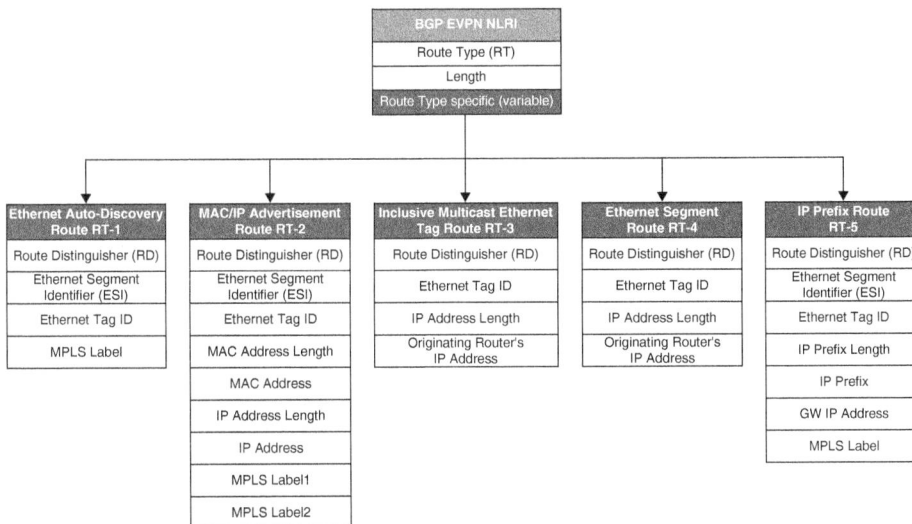

Figure 3-60 *Layer 2 Network Reachability Information (NLRI)*

EVPN is introduced in detail in Chapter 6, "L2VPN Service Deployment: Configuration and Verification Techniques" but for now it is sufficient to understand that EVPN builds on the following common route types with different applications and use cases:

- **Route Type 1:** Ethernet Auto-Discovery (AD) route

- **Route Type 2:** MAC/IP Advertisement route

- **Route Type 3:** Include Multicast Ethernet Tag route

- **Route Type 4:** Ethernet Segment route

- **Route Type 5:** IP Prefix route

Less common route types exist for more specialized multicast applications that are considered beyond the scope of this book:

- **Route Type 6:** Selective Multicast Ethernet Tag route

- **Route Type 7:** Multicast Membership Report Sync route

- **Route Type 8:** Multicast Leave Sync route

- **Route Type 9:** Per-Region I-PMSI A-D route

- **Route Type 10:** S-PMSI A-D route

- **Route Type 11:** Leaf A-D route

Note   BGP EVPN route types registered with IANA are listed at https://www.iana.org/assignments/evpn/evpn.xhtml.

Note that MPLS labels or SRv6 SID functions may be conveyed through the NLRI or path attributes applicable to specific route types. For instance, Route Type 3 lacks an MPLS label field in the EVPN NLRI but must carry a Provider Multicast Service Interface (PMSI) tunnel attribute, which is required to establish a tunnel between PE devices for BUM traffic. The PMSI Tunnel attribute contains an MPLS Label field that can be used to encode the function part of an SRv6 SID.

Multiple EVPN NLRIs may be advertised in a single MP_REACH_NLRI attribute for routes sharing the same BGP path attributes.

For your reference, Figure 3-61 shows the NLRI formats for different Layer 3 overlay services.

Layer 3 services are discussed in detail in Chapter 7, "L3VPN Service Deployment: Configuration and Verification Techniques," but for now it is sufficient to understand that the following Layer 3 services can be provisioned over SRv6:

- IPv4 unicast (global routing table)

- IPv6 unicast (global routing table)

- VPNv4 unicast

- VPNv6 unicast

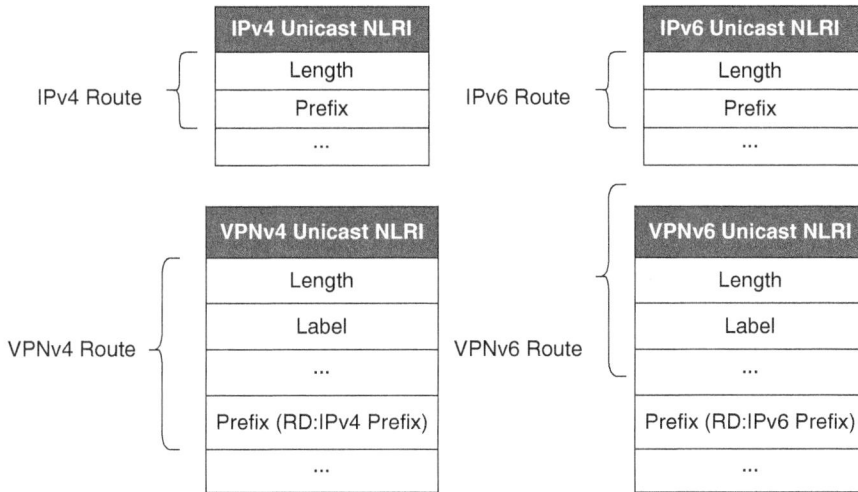

Figure 3-61   *Layer 3 Network Layer Reachability Information*

As shown previously, IPv4 and IPv6 unicast NLRI do not contain an MPLS Label field, which is why the complete SRv6 service SID must be included in the BGP Prefix SID attribute of the UPDATE message. VPNv4 and VPNv6 unicast, however, contain a label that allows to take advantage of the transposition scheme.

BGP Link-State Extensions for SRv6 (RFC 9514)

Similarly to the BGP link-state extensions for SR, BGP LS can be used to propagate SRv6 IGP topology information through BGP. This section takes you through the control plane enhancements required for SRv6. In essence, IGP TLV and sub-TLV information is encoded in the BGP LS NLRI and advertised to other BGP LS speakers.

A number of new BGP Link State (BGP-LS) parameters have been registered with the Internet Assigned Numbers Authority (IANA) as part of the BGP Link State Extension for SRv6 to facilitate the distribution of SRv6 topology information.

Note   BGP-LS extensions for Segment Routing over IPv6 registered with IANA are listed at https://www.iana.org/assignments/bgp-ls-parameters/bgp-ls-parameters.xhtml.

Table 3-15 shows a new SRv6 SID NLRI that was defined as part of the BGP Link State extension for SRv6 draft to augment the link-state NLRI.

Table 3-15   *BGP-LS NLRI*

Type	NLRI
6	SRv6 SID

The structure of this new NLRI is shown in Figure 3-62. The SRv6 SID NLRI consists of the Protocol ID, Identifier, Local Node, and SRv6 SID Descriptors fields. The SRv6 SID Descriptors field contains the newly defined SRv6 SID Information TLV, which you will see shortly.

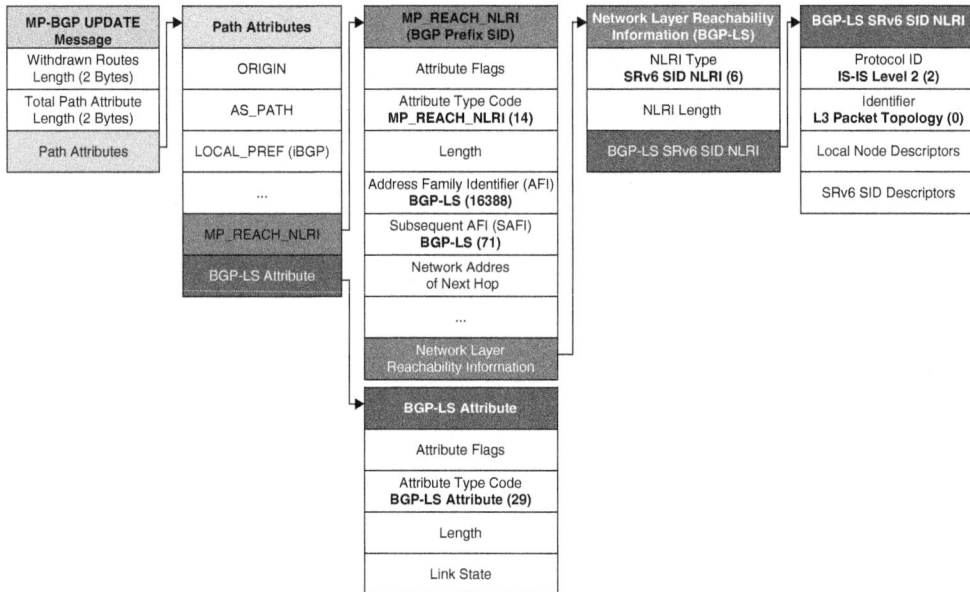

Figure 3-62   *BGP UPDATE Message Format (BGP-LS for SRv6)*

The mapping from IGP (IS-IS or OSPFv3) to BGP LS is shown in Table 3-16.

Table 3-16   *BGP-LS NLRI and Attribute TLVs*

TLV	Type	Description	IS-IS SRv6 Extensions (RFC 9352)	OSPFv3 SRv6 Extensions (RFC 9513)
518	SID	SRv6 SID Information	SRv6 End SID sub-TLV (5)	SRv6 End SID sub-TLV (1)
1038	Node	SRv6 Capabilities	SRv6 Capabilities sub-TLV (25)	SRv6 Capabilities TLV (20)
1106	Link	SRv6 End.X SID	SRv6 End.X SID sub-TLV (43)	SRv6 End.X SID sub-TLV (31)
1107	Link	IS-IS SRv6 LAN End.X SID	SRv6 LAN End.X SID sub-TLV (44)	N/A
1108	Link	OSPFv3 SRv6 LAN End.X SID	N/A	SRv6 LAN End.X sub-TLV (32)

TLV	Type	Description	IS-IS SRv6 Extensions (RFC 9352)	OSPFv3 SRv6 Extensions (RFC 9513)
1162	Prefix	SRv6 Locator	SRv6 Locator TLV (27)	SRv6 Locator TLV (42)
1250	SID	SRv6 Endpoint Behavior	SRv6 End SID sub-TLV (5)	SRv6 End SID sub-TLV (1)
1251	SID	SRv6 BGP Peer Node SID	N/A	N/A
1252	SID	SRv6 SID Structure	SRv6 SID Structure Sub-sub-TLV (1)	SRv6 SID Structure sub-TLV (30)

Example 3-11 shows a packet capture of a BGP UDPATE message with an SRv6 SID NLRI (6) that contains an SRv6 SID Information TLV. Furthermore, the BGP-LS attribute (29) includes the SRv6 Endpoint Behavior and SRv6 SID Structure TLV.

Example 3-11 *BGP UPDATE for BGP LS (SRv6)*

```
Ethernet
Internet Protocol Version 6, Src: fcbb:bbbb:bb00:6::1, Dst: fdca:fe00:5::1
Transmission Control Protocol, Src Port: 179, Dst Port: 21062
Border Gateway Protocol - UPDATE Message
    Marker: ffffffffffffffffffffffffffffffff
    Length: 440
    Type: UPDATE Message (2)
   Withdrawn Routes Length: 0
    Total Path Attribute Length: 417
    Path attributes
        Path Attribute - MP_REACH_NLRI
            Flags: 0x90, Optional, Extended-Length, Non-transitive, Complete
            Type Code: MP_REACH_NLRI (14)
            Length: 366
            Address family identifier (AFI): BGP-LS (16388)
            Subsequent address family identifier (SAFI): BGP-LS (71)
            Next hop: fdca:fe00:1::1
            Number of Subnetwork points of attachment (SNPA): 0
            Network Layer Reachability Information (NLRI)
                BGP-LS NLRI
                    NLRI Type: SRv6 SID NLRI (6)
                    NLRI Length: 65
                    Link-State NLRI SRv6 SID NLRI
                        Protocol-ID: IS-IS Level 2
                        Identifier: Unknown (100)
                        Local Node Descriptors TLV
```

```
                              SRv6 SID Descriptors TLV
                                SRv6 SID Information TLV
                                  Type: SRv6 SID Information TLV (518)
                                  Length: 16
                                  SID: fdca:fe00:1::
<snip>
        Path Attribute - ORIGIN: IGP
        Path Attribute - AS_PATH: empty
        Path Attribute - LOCAL_PREF: 100
        Path Attribute - CLUSTER_LIST: 172.16.20.16
        Path Attribute - ORIGINATOR_ID: 172.16.20.11
        Path Attribute - BGP-LS Attribute
            Flags: 0x80, Optional, Non-transitive, Complete
            Type Code: BGP-LS Attribute (29)
            Length: 16
            Link State
                SRv6 Endpoint Behavior TLV
                    Type: 1250 (SRv6 Endpoint Behavior TLV)
                    Length: 4
                    Endpoint Behavior: End with NEXT-CSID, PSP & USD (0x0030)
                    Flags: 0
                    Algorithm: 0
                SRv6 SID Structure TLV
                    Type: 1252 (SRv6 SID Structure TLV)
                    Length: 4
                    Locator Block Length: 32
                    Locator Node Length: 16
                    Function Length: 0
                    Argument Length: 0
<snip>
```

This packet capture presents the SRv6 SID fdca:fe00:1::, which is associated with the End instruction for algorithm 0. The SID structure is based on a 32-bit SID block with a 16-bit node ID resulting in a /48 SRv6 locator.

The signaling of BGP-EPE differs between SR-MPLS and SRv6 with respect to the BGP PeerNode and PeerSet SIDs that are advertised via the SRv6 BGP EPE PeerNode SID TLV. The SRv6 BGP PeerNode SID TLV is required for SRv6 SID NLRI related to BGP EPE functionality and must be included along with the End.X SIDs associated with BGP PeerNode or PeerSet.

SRv6 BGP PeerNode SID TLV contains the flags listed in Table 3-17, which are known from SRv6 End.X SIDs.

Table 3-17 *SRv6 BGP EPE SID Flags*

Bit	Flag
0	Backup (B-flag)
1	Set (S-flag)
2	Persistent (P-flag)

Besides those previously covered flags, the SRv6 BGP PeerNode SID TLV contains three relevant fields:

- **Weight:** Same as for SRv6 End.X SIDs

- **Peer AS Number:** Peer's BGP AS number

- **Peer BGP Identifier:** Peer's BGP Router ID

Now that we have concluded our exploration of the theoretical concepts on IGP and BGP extensions, we are ready to delve into practical applications and design-related scenarios.

SR-Powered Network Evolution

This section guides you through a network evolution, beginning with the introduction of SR-MPLS and advancing significantly with the advent of SRv6. For clarity, you will get a closer look of the control and data planes for each of the network evolution stages: MPLS, SR-MPLS, and SRv6.

MPLS Network Architecture: Control and Data Plane Overview

Legacy (LDP-based) MPLS networks today with over-the-top L2VPN and L3VPN services use some or all of the following control plane protocols:

- IGP (Interior Gateway Protocol)

- LDP (Label Distribution Protocol)

- RSVP-TE (Resource Reservation Protocol Traffic Engineering)

- BGP-LU (Border Gateway Protocol Labeled Unicast)

- BGP IPv4/IPv6/VPNv4/VPNv6 (Services)

Large-scale networks were built based on this foundation for many years, especially unified/seamless MPLS and inter-AS Option C topologies.

In the past, RSVP-TE was required to:

- Provide fast reroute (FRR) in the event of link or node failures in the core network.

- Improve overall link utilization of the network while avoiding congestion.

- Use static traffic engineering to minimize end-to-end delay for sensitive traffic (such as voice).

BGP-LU (RFC 3107) provided (inter-domain/inter-AS/inter-IPv6 island) connectivity for:

- Unified/Seamless MPLS

- Inter-AS Option C

- IPv6 Provider Edge (6PE)

Not all of the protocols mentioned here are present in every network.

Figure 3-63 shows an imaginary service provider that deployed Unified MPLS. Core and metro networks are isolated and run dedicated IGP processes to keep the databases separated. LDP dynamically allocates and advertises labels for host routes (loopbacks) within the local domain, whereas BGP-LU (RFC 3107) provides inter-domain connectivity between metro and core domains. The ABR act as inline Route Reflector (RR) and updates prefixes with next-hop-self when reflecting BGP UPDATES messages, which results in a label swap for the remote host routes (loopbacks). With BGP-LU in place, Provider Edge (PE) devices can establish a BGP session with the RR in the core domain for overlay services such as VPNv4, VPNv6 or Multicast VPN (MVPN).

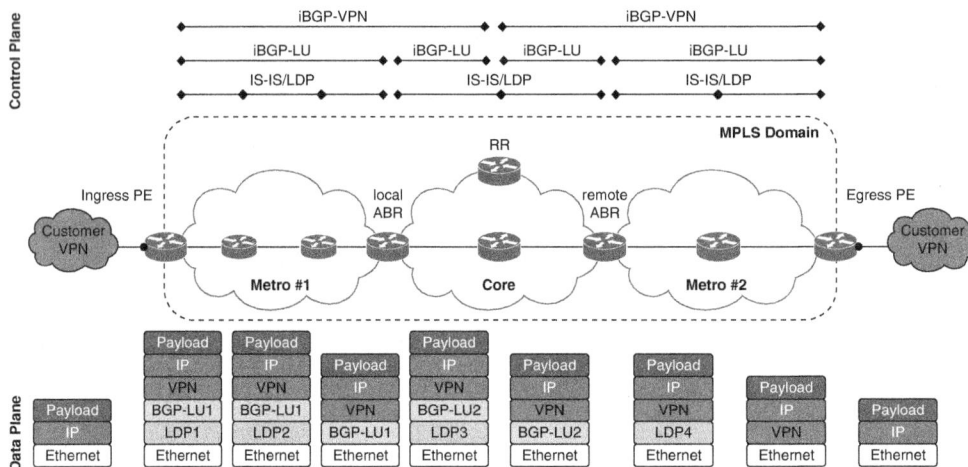

Figure 3-63 *Unified MPLS Control and Data Planes (MPLS)*

Now let's look at the label stack in more detail. Resolving an L3VPN over BGP-LU over IGP/LDP requires multiple recursions to build the MPLS label stack. This list describes the purposes of the VPN, BGP-LU, and LDP labels in Figure 3-63:

- The BGP VPNv4 Network Layer Reachability Information (NLRI) path attributes contain the following information:

  - Next Hop (egress PE loopback resolved through BGP-LU route)

  - Prefix (route distinguisher and service prefix)

  - Label Stack (service label)

- The BGP-LU Network Layer Reachability Information (NLRI) path attributes contain the following information:

  - Next Hop (ABR or egress PE loopback resolved through IGP/LDP)

  - Prefix (egress PE loopback)

  - Label Stack (second transport label)

- The IGP/LDP attribute contains the following information:

  - Loopback (ABR or egress PE loopback)

  - Labels (first transport label)

A VPNv4 BGP UPDATE message provides the service label at the top of the stack. The BGP next hop (NH) of this VPN prefix is resolved through a BGP-LU route, which adds the second transport label. Finally, the BGP next hop of the BGP-LU route is resolved through IGP/LDP, which adds the first transport label:

- Transport Label 1 (IGP/LDP)

- Transport Label 2 (BGP-LU)

- Service Label (BGP VPN)

Note MPLS labels are dynamically allocated by LDP, which explains why the first transport label changes on a hop-by-hop basis. The penultimate hop performs PHP, which is why the label stack decreases from three labels to two before every ABR and from two labels to one before the egress PE. The BGP-LU label changes on the ABR due to BGP next-hop-self, except for the remote ABR, which can reach the egress PE loopback directly through IGP/LDP. Finally, the service label does not change and remains the same end-to-end.

SR-MPLS Network Architecture: Control and Data Plane Overview

The first milestone when moving away from the legacy stack is the introduction of segment routing, which initiates an evolution and simplification in the protocol stack in service provider networks. Segment routing eliminates the need for LDP to advertise labels in MPLS networks. The IGP (IS-IS or OSPF) takes care of exchanging segment identifiers (SIDs) between routers in the network by using type length value (TLV) tuples. A SID or, in the case of SR-MPLS, a label value, is associated with a segment. Figure 3-64 shows the impact of moving from MPLS to SR-MPLS in the IGP. The underlying data plane remains largely the same and still relies on MPLS, but the labels, or rather SIDs, are now propagated through IGP extensions. LDP is no longer required in the transport of this network.

Note that the label stack of the MPLS packets in the data plane remains the same, except for one notable difference: The segments shown in Figure 3-64 are globally significant as opposed to the locally significant LDP labels, and they remain the same throughout the network. For instance, SR SID1 does not change on a hop-by-hop basis but is still subject to PHP.

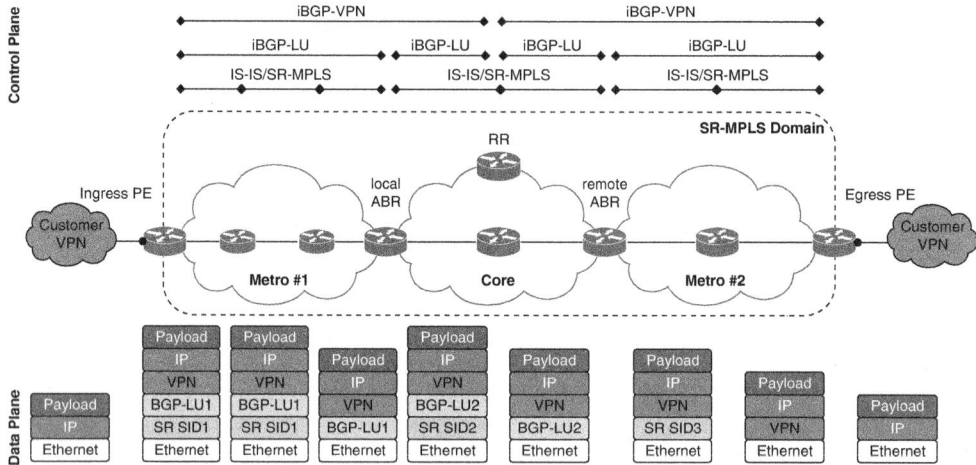

Figure 3-64   *Unified MPLS Control and Data Planes (SR-MPLS)*

Simultaneously, the concept of a SID was extended to BGP labeled unicast, where the definition of new BGP attributes enables BGP to transport BGP Prefix segment identifiers (BGP Prefix-SIDs). Figure 3-65 shows the subtle difference between dynamically allocated BGP-LU labels and BGP Prefix SIDs in the BGP control plane. The underlying data plane changes slightly because BGP Prefix SIDs are usually set by the source of the route (for example, egress PE device) and remain the same end-to-end, even if BGP next-hop-self operations take place along the way. The BGP Prefix SID attribute serves as a hint for intermediate BGP speakers (for example, ABRs) to allocate a specific local label when performing BGP next-hop-self.

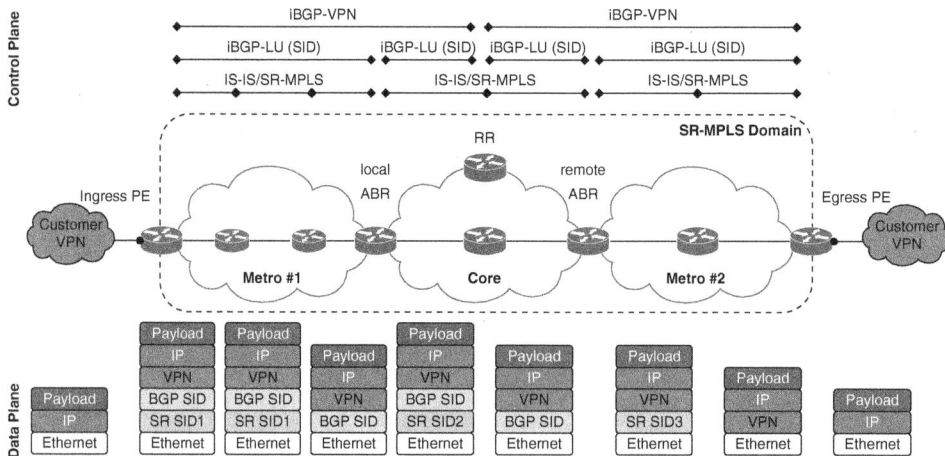

Figure 3-65   *Unified MPLS Control and Data Planes (SR-MPLS with BGP Prefix SID)*

With SR fully rolled out in the IGP and BGP control plane, it's worth highlighting the application of anycast SIDs again (refer to the section "BGP Prefix Segment (BGP Prefix SID)" in Chapter 2). IGP anycast segments can be leveraged in SR traffic engineering policies or when using the BGP Prefix SID, where redundant ABRs or ASBRs advertise the same SID for a given segment. Why would service providers want to deploy Anycast SIDs? Anycast SIDs can greatly simplify and improve the resiliency of SR policies. A node failure within a set would not invalidate the existing SR policy but would automatically reduce the number of members in the set. Upon recovery, the member would be added again and start attracting traffic. Network convergence benefits from Anycast SIDs as well because instead of relying on BGP Prefix Independent Convergence (BGP PIC) in the event of an ABR or ASBR node failure, the network relies on IGP convergence (TI-LFA) which is much faster, as you will see in Chapter 9, "High Availability and Fast Convergence."

IGP anycast segments cannot be used for services where the state between the members of the set differs, such as:

■ L2VPN/L3VPN services where the allocated service label is different on redundant PE devices

■ BGP-LU transport where the dynamically allocated transport label is different on redundant ABRs/ASBRs

■ Stateful network functions (for example, NAT or an IPsec gateway) where the state is not synchronized between redundant PE devices

Forwarding an L2VPN/L3VPN over an Anycast SID could result in partial blackholing of the traffic if it is sent to the wrong member of the set (that is, with the wrong service label).

Note   If service labels could be statically allocated on a set of routers on a per-VRF instance or per-CE basis for Layer 3 VPN or per VPWS or VPLS for Layer 2 VPN, it would open the door to L2VPN/L3VPN over anycast deployments, which is something that could be seen in the future.

SRv6 Network Architecture: Control and Data Plane Overview

Figure 3-66 illustrates the impact of SRv6 on the protocol stack. SRv6 uses IPv6 as its underlying data plane encapsulation, without any labels at all. Customer packets are encapsulated in an outer IPv6 header in most cases. The optional extension header, called the segment routing header (SRH), is needed only for specific use cases that require complex traffic engineering policies.

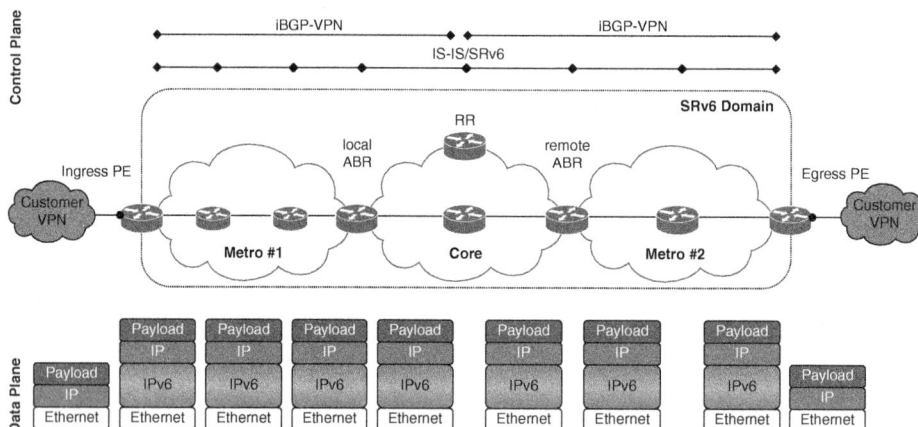

Figure 3-66   *Converged SDN Transport Network (SRv6/IPv6)*

A SID is a value associated with a segment, which in the case of SRv6 is a 128-bit value in the form of an IPv6 address. It is important to note that the MPLS label distinction between transport and service labels does not apply to SRv6 anymore. A single IPv6 address (SID) may contain both transport and service-related information. Therefore, intra-domain and inter-domain transport layer information, as well as service layer information all fuse into a single SRv6 SID. Figure 3-66 attempts to show the merging of transport and service into a single SID by using gradients.

Note   SRv6 has a major impact on network design and how different IGP domains or autonomous systems are interconnected. Unified MPLS, Inter-AS Option B/C, and, consequently, BGP labeled unicast are obsolete in SRv6 domains. As a result, the protocol stack with SRv6 is even leaner compared to SR-MPLS.

Network Evolution at a Glance

Figure 3-67 abstracts the three different stages previously outlined in the network evolution of service providers.

The initial protocol stack, labeled Unified MPLS or Inter-AS Option C, should be familiar to you from both real-life exposure and the previous sections.

The introduction of SR and SR-TE in the second protocol stack supersedes not only LDP but also RSVP. Traffic engineering (TE) forces traffic over a specific path, which can be defined dynamically or explicitly. Before SR-TE, the RSVP protocol was responsible for TE tunnel creation and maintenance. RSVP is a cumbersome signaling protocol, with each tunnel signaled from the source PE to the destination PE over all transit nodes, which means that each transit node has to create state information for each tunnel. Core P routers can have many transit tunnels, and RSVP state tables are resource intensive and difficult to troubleshoot. Similarly, legacy MPLS traffic engineering tunnels required for fast reroute (FRR) in the past are replaced with Topology-Independent Loop-Free Alternate (TI-LFA), which is covered in detail in Chapter 9, in the section "Topology-Independent Loop-Free Alternative (TI-LFA)."

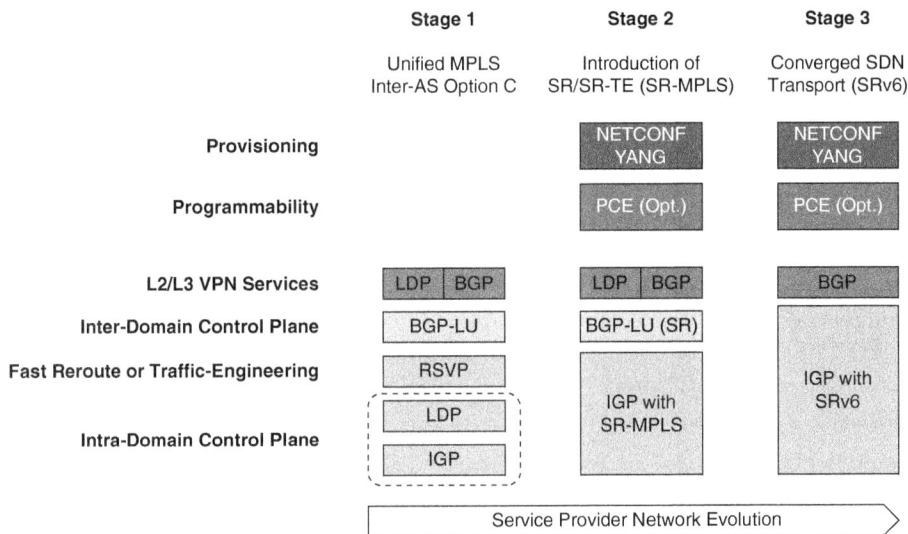

	Stage 1	Stage 2	Stage 3
	Unified MPLS Inter-AS Option C	Introduction of SR/SR-TE (SR-MPLS)	Converged SDN Transport (SRv6)
Provisioning		NETCONF YANG	NETCONF YANG
Programmability		PCE (Opt.)	PCE (Opt.)
L2/L3 VPN Services	LDP | BGP	LDP | BGP	BGP
Inter-Domain Control Plane	BGP-LU	BGP-LU (SR)	
Fast Reroute or Traffic-Engineering	RSVP	IGP with SR-MPLS	IGP with SRv6
Intra-Domain Control Plane	LDP / IGP		

Service Provider Network Evolution

Figure 3-67 *Service Provider Network Evolution*

BGP-LU has been the protocol of choice for inter-domain connectivity between isolated IGP domains. A special SDN controller or path computation element (PCE) containing the complete link-state database from all IGP domains could potentially replace this functionality. Routers generally have a limited view of the network, including only their local domain. Inter-domain connectivity without BGP-LU relies on Path Computation Element Communication Protocol (PCEP), which enables communication between a path computation client (PCC) and a path computation element (PCE). The controller calculates the path and returns a list of segments to the client, enabling it to reach remote egress PEs outside its local domain. The PCE is marked as optional in the diagram because it would only be required for inter-domain routing in the absence of BGP-LU or for advanced traffic path steering, such as disjoint paths, which require a centralized controller.

Note There are different flavors of the converged SDN transport network, and not all network deployments require traffic engineering or a controller. Large-scale deployments may even prefer to remain with BGP-LU for scalability reasons.

Example 3-12 shows a packet capture of an L3VPN service in an SR-MPLS network consisting of a transport label and a service label, as expected for L3VPN services in a flat IGP domain.

Example 3-12 *L3VPN over SR-MPLS Packet Capture*

```
Ethernet
MultiProtocol Label Switching Header, Label: 16011, Exp: 0, S: 0, TTL: 255
MultiProtocol Label Switching Header, Label: 24002, Exp: 0, S: 1, TTL: 255
Internet Protocol Version 4, Src: 10.101.0.101, Dst: 10.101.8.101
Internet Control Message Protocol
```

The third protocol stack depicted in Figure 3-67 marks the introduction of SRv6 in combination with Ethernet VPN (EVPN) as the next-generation solution for point-to-point and multipoint L2VPN services. EVPN is the de facto standard for L2VPN services today, not only addressing several limitations of the previous LDP-based legacy solutions but also relying on Border Gateway Protocol (BGP). Thanks to EVPN Layer 2, Layer 3 or hybrid services can be advertised using a single protocol (BGP) or even a single address family (EVPN) if desired. Ethernet VPN fundamentals and implementation specifics are covered in detail in Chapter 6, "L2VPN Service Deployment: Configuration and Verification Techniques."

Example 3-13 shows a packet capture of the same L3VPN service in an SRv6 network. The SRv6 capture no longer contains any MPLS labels but rather leverages a single IPv6 address (SID) to cover both transport and service.

Example 3-13 *L3VPN over SRv6 Packet Capture*

```
Ethernet
Internet Protocol Version 6, Src: fcbb:bb00:1::1, Dst: fcbb:bb00:2:e6c6::
Internet Protocol Version 4, Src: 10.101.0.101, Dst: 10.101.8.101
Internet Control Message Protocol
```

SR-MPLS is an evolution of the existing MPLS architecture, whereas SRv6 may be described as a revolution because it fundamentally simplifies the networking stack and changes how networks are built and interconnected.

SR-MPLS or SRv6

By now you should have a solid understanding of SR-MPLS and SRv6 fundamentals. The goal of this section is to highlight some of the questions that network operators will have to consider when evaluating a new segment routing deployment or potential migration scenarios from MPLS to SR-MPLS or SRv6.

Benefits of Deploying Segment Routing

First and foremost, what are the expected benefits of deploying segment routing in the network? It is always exciting for engineers to get their hands on new technology, but most network evolutions are driven by business cases. Table 3-18 summarizes the most common benefits of segment routing for both MPLS and IPv6 data plane implementations. SRv6 is the superior solution compared to SR-MPLS since it covers additional requirements, such as service chaining, without relying on additional signaling protocols and also has the potential to unify the underlying data plane (IPv6) from the access network up to the data center, allowing for streamlined network architectures. Last but not least, SRv6 runs on top of IPv6, where summarization yields massive scale gains, facilitating transport connectivity between tens of thousands of devices (or even more).

Table 3-18   *Segment Routing Benefits*

	SR-MPLS	SRv6
TI-LFA	Yes	Yes
Traffic engineering	Yes	Yes
Service chaining	No	Yes
Unified data plane	No	Yes
Summarization	No	Yes

TI-LFA and *traffic engineering* are common drivers to move from MPLS to SR-MPLS or SRv6 that are natively supported by segment routing through its IGP extensions. Topology-Independent Loop-Free Alternate (TI-LFA) is a powerful fast convergence feature that provides sub-50-millisecond convergence for transport-related link or node failures in the presence of a backup path in any network topology. The simplification of the network protocol stack and the reduction of network tunnel states is especially valid for traffic engineering deployments where the removal of RSVP can be considered a major milestone. Both of those benefits are applicable to SR-MPLS and SRv6.

With *service chaining*, different network functions can be daisy-chained in a flexible way to enforce the data path of a given service in an ordered sequence. Network functions virtualization (NFV) deployments such as virtual CPEs, firewalls, intrusion protection, Network Address Translation (NAT), and DDoS mitigation are common use cases. For instance, a service provider may want to offer different levels of business Internet access service to its customers. The bronze level of Internet access could include a chain with the NAT NFV, whereas silver Internet access could include a different chain with NAT and firewall NFVs. Finally, gold Internet access could include NAT, firewall, intrusion protection, and DDoS mitigation NFVs in its service chain. SRv6-aware NFVs allow operators to create service chains through segment lists, where each SID represents an NFV. This approach is both flexible and highly scalable since it does not require any state in the network.

SRv6 leverages the IPv6 data plane, which is supported across a wide portfolio of network domains and devices or even public clouds. Consequently, IPv6 has the potential to simplify and unify the data plane end-to-end. A common data plane from the access network to the data center not only simplifies the overall network architecture but also deployment, operation, and maintenance. IPv6 is commonly supported by off-the-shelf networking gear or less specialized networking ASICs, potentially resulting in lower purchasing costs. Overall, a unified data plane has a large cost-saving potential in both CapEx (capital expenditures) and OpEx (operating expenses).

With the departure from MPLS, SRv6 resurrects summarization in the transport layer of service provider networks. Besides the massive scale gains that are possible with IPv6, SRv6 also renders complex inter-AS Option B/C or unified MPLS deployments obsolete. BGP labeled unicast routes were taxing on low-cost or merchant silicon routers, which often required advanced filtering options to protect and harden devices from running out of resources due to resource-costly BGP-LU routes. The simplified data plane in combination with summaries aggregating hundreds or thousands of devices within a domain allows for a very lean transport network.

SRv6 brings several synergies to the table that allow network operators to simplify the end-to-end network architecture, including the underlying protocol stack for advanced use cases such as traffic engineering or service chaining, and also has the potential to drive hardware and software consolidation. The boundaries between traditional network silos are broken down and separate domains are joined into a single transport network, and services can be deployed between any two points in the network.

Hardware and Software Support

SR-MPLS can be considered an optional checkpoint on the journey to SRv6 because it is commonly supported by networking equipment running MPLS. Quite often a migration from MPLS to SR-MPLS is straightforward and may require only a software upgrade with an optional hardware profile activation. In other words, the existing installed base can be largely reused and would require a limited time investment as far as network readiness is concerned.

SRv6 is a different story. While the minimum requirement on the P nodes is to support IPv6 forwarding, the full benefits of SRv6, such as TI-LFA, flex algo, and traffic engineering, demand SRv6-aware devices across the transport layer. The service layer must be SRv6 aware, which not only includes PE but also RR devices. In other words, the bar to enable SRv6 in a network is considerably higher than for SR-MPLS. At this writing, all newer hardware generations of Cisco IOS XR and selected IOS XE/NX-OS platforms support SRv6.

Network operators that wish to deploy SRv6 in the future can be grouped and classified as follows:

- **Greenfield network:** Due to an upcoming hardware lifecycle in the network, it was decided to build a new cost- and energy-efficient high-capacity network to deploy SRv6 services from day one.

- **Brownfield network:** With partial SRv6/IPv6 support in the existing network, it was decided to reuse the existing transport layer and upgrade or refresh the existing service edge.

The migration approach for both options will vary greatly and will be presented in more detail in Chapter 5, "Migrating to Segment Routing."

Feature Support

Besides the fundamental SR-MPLS or SRv6 support, network operators will have to validate feature parity of the currently deployed services and features in the production network. Layer 3 VPN services are widely deployed and supported across both data planes. Layer 2 VPN or Multicast-related services and features, however, are more challenging. Chances are that some legacy Layer 2 VPN services cannot be migrated one-to-one to EVPN over SR-MPLS or SRv6 and require slight design modifications or even improvements. The EVPN ecosystem offers a wide range of flexible Layer 2 topologies that provide a future-proof migration path. Layer 2 migrations are non-trivial and may require dedicated features or network gateways to interconnect old and new. Similarly, Multicast or Multicast VPN support using IPv6 encapsulation is not as extensive as with IPv4 or MLDP in the transport layer at this writing.

Segment routing facilitates the deployment of a future-proof SDN-ready architecture. Even though an operator may only need a subset of the SR feature set today, this may change over time as new network applications and requirements emerge. The feature parity between MPLS, SR-MPLS, and SRv6 is given for the most fundamental services and features, whereas more advanced features will only be developed for segment routing (SR-MPLS and SRv6) or even exclusively for SRv6. For instance, path tracing, discussed in Chapter 8, "Service Assurance," was developed with a focus on SRv6 and may or may not be available in SR-MPLS in future IOS XR software releases.

Summary

The high-level analogy between the execution of software programs on a central processing unit (CPU) and network programs within a network cloud introduced in Chapter 2 is even more fitting for SRv6:

- An SRv6 segment is associated with a SID that is expressed as a 128-bit value (IPv6 address).

- CPU instructions must follow a certain format to adhere to the instruction set architecture of the underlying hardware platform.

- Similarly, the format of an SRv6 SID consists of locator, function, and argument parts.

- Whereas a special register (program counter) keeps track of the program execution for software programs, the Segments Left field of the segment routing header (SRH) fulfills a similar role for a network program (SRv6 policy).

SRv6 takes advantage of the extended address space of IPv6, where an SRv6 SID has a length of 128 bits, compared to the 20 bits of SR-MPLS. Consequently, the SRv6 SID format changes considerably and consists of locator, function, and argument parts. The locator portion represents the most significant bits and is routable toward the parent node, which instantiated the SID. The locator is comparable to the MPLS transport label, which forwards traffic toward a loopback address (BGP next hop), whereas the function portion identifies a locally significant behavior of the parent node and is comparable to the BGP service label in MPLS. It is important to note that a Layer 3 VPN service that requires transport and service labels in MPLS can be realized using a single SID (IPv6 address) in SRv6.

SRv6 segments can be classified into various headend or endpoint behaviors consisting of topological and service instructions. Even though SR-MPLS and SRv6 support different types of segments, there are a few universal segments that exist in both, such as the End (SRv6 instantiation of a prefix segment), End.X (SRv6 instantiation of an adjacency segment), and End.B6.Encaps (SRv6 instantiation of a Binding SID) endpoint behaviors. Other noteworthy endpoint behaviors are End.DX4/End.DX6 (IPv4/IPv6 L3VPN using per-CE SID allocation) and End.DT4/End.DT6 (IPv4/IPv6 L3VPN using per-VRF instance SID allocation).

A new type of IPv6 routing extension header called the segment routing header (SRH) was introduced to encode a list of SRv6 segments. Remember that a single segment can be encoded as part of the outer IPv6 header's destination address, but multiple segments require this new routing extension header. Three different SRH processing flavors can be distinguished for the End, End.X, and End.T endpoint behaviors:

- Penultimate Segment Pop (PSP) of the SRH is comparable to MPLS PHP, where the penultimate segment endpoint node removes the SRH after copying the ultimate segment from the SRH into the IPv6 destination address.

- Ultimate Segment Pop (USP) of the SRH, on the other hand, leaves the SRH removal to the ultimate endpoint node; it is comparable to the explicit null label in the MPLS space.

- Ultimate Segment Decapsulation (USD) decapsulates and processes the upper layer header.

The main drawback of encoding a list of segments in the SRH is the encapsulation overhead, which can easily exceed 100 bytes. The SRv6 uSID instruction extension proposes a solution to this problem by which several micro SID (uSID) instructions fit in a single 128-bit IPv6 address. A uSID is a flexible-length compressed SID (CSID) where multiple micro instructions share the same uSID block and can be written sequentially into a uSID container (128-bit SID). Common bit lengths for uSID deployments are a 32-bit uSID block and 16-bit uSIDs (F3216). Similar to the SRGB and SRLB for SR-MPLS, the uSID address space can be divided into a Global Identifier Block (GIB) and a Local Identifier Block (LIB).

You have learned about different addressing options concerning the SRv6 SID block and infrastructure links, as well as advantages and disadvantages of GUA and ULA for the SRv6 SID block and GUA and LLA for infrastructure addressing. You learned about three sample addressing concepts for deployments that differ in scale. An addressing concept that facilitates massive summarization gains is crucial to allow operators to scale beyond hundreds of thousands of SRv6 devices in a network.

You have seen that the differences between SR-MPLS and SRv6 extend beyond just data plane encapsulation and control plane extensions. SRv6 allows for much simpler network protocol stacks and architectures. For instance, BGP labeled unicast (BGP Prefix SID) is no longer needed to interconnect different IGP domains or autonomous systems when running SRv6 in the network.

This chapter compares SR-MPLS and SRv6, highlighting a set of common initial questions when considering an SR deployment. You learned about the benefits of the two SR data plane implementations and potential pitfalls related to software or hardware support.

This chapter provides a foundation for the upcoming chapters, which focus on the configuration and verification of SRv6. SR-MPLS can be seen as a natural evolution of MPLS, while SRv6 heralds a revolutionary shift that will transform the design and deployment of networks and services in the service provider and carrier-grade enterprise environments. You are encouraged to return to this chapter throughout the course of this book to look up data plane details and use it as a reference for control plane extensions and relevant packet captures.

References and Additional Reading

Segment Routing over IPv6 (SRv6)

- RFC 8200: Internet Protocol, Version 6 (IPv6) Specification, https://datatracker.ietf.org/doc/html/rfc8200

- RFC 2474: Definition of the Differentiated Services Field (DS Field) in the IPv4 and IPv6 Headers, https://datatracker.ietf.org/doc/html/rfc2474

- RFC 3168: The Addition of Explicit Congestion Notification (ECN) to IP, https://datatracker.ietf.org/doc/html/rfc3168

- RFC 6437: IPv6 Flow Label Specification, https://datatracker.ietf.org/doc/html/rfc6437

SRv6 Network Programming (RFC 8986)

- RFC 8986: Segment Routing over IPv6 (SRv6) Network Programming, https://www.rfc-editor.org/rfc/rfc8986.txt

IPv6 Segment Routing Header (SRH) (RFC 8754)

- RFC 8754: IPv6 Segment Routing Header (SRH), https://datatracker.ietf.org/doc/html/rfc8754

- IETF Draft: SRv6 NET-PGM extension: Insertion, https://www.ietf.org/archive/id/draft-filsfils-spring-srv6-net-pgm-insertion-09.txt

SRv6 Network Programming Extension: SRv6 uSID Instruction

- IETF Draft: Network Programming extension: SRv6 uSID instruction, https://www.ietf.org/archive/id/draft-filsfils-spring-net-pgm-extension-srv6-usid-16.txt

- IETF Draft: Compressed SRv6 Segment List Encoding, https://datatracker.ietf.org/doc/html/draft-ietf-spring-srv6-srh-compression

IS-IS Extensions for Segment Routing over IPv6 (RFC 9352)

- RFC 9352: IS-IS Extensions to Support Segment Routing over the IPv6 Data Plane, https://www.rfc-editor.org/rfc/rfc9352.html

- RFC 8491: Signaling Maximum SID Depth (MSD) Using IS-IS, https://datatracker.ietf.org/doc/html/rfc8491

BGP Overlay Services on SRv6 (RFC 9252)

- RFC 9252: BGP Overlay Services Based on Segment Routing over IPv6 (SRv6), https://www.rfc-editor.org/rfc/rfc9252.txt

BGP Link-State Extensions for SRv6 (RFC 9514)

- RFC 9514: Border Gateway Protocol - Link State (BGP-LS) Extensions for Segment Routing over IPv6 (SRv6), https://www.rfc-editor.org/rfc/rfc9514.txt

Chapter 4

Segment Routing in Detail

Chapter 3, "What Is Segment Routing over IPv6 (SRv6)?," introduces the concept of segment routing (SR) and provides background on the motivation for SR, advantages of SR, and IETF standardization efforts related to SR. As a quick recap, SR-MPLS relies on a stack of 20-bit entities called *MPLS labels*, and SRv6 uses one or more IPv6 addresses to forward an IP packet from the source to the destination. Although SR-MPLS and SRv6 use different transport mechanisms, the concept of using a link-state interior gateway protocol (IGP) like IS-IS, OSPF, or BGP only in the case of SR-MPLS to exchange SR-related information is the same for both SR-MPLS and SRv6. IGPs and BGP have been extended to facilitate this exchange.

This chapter provides a brief introduction to IS-IS, OSPFv2 to give you the necessary background to understand SR-MPLS and SRv6.

The section "Segment Routing Baseline" provides the configuration and the verification commands required to enable SR and the associated parameters on Cisco devices.

The section "Segment Routing Control Plane (BGP)" provides some design guidelines and configuration details to enable routing protocols like IS-IS, OSPF, and BGP to exchange SR-related information and to allow the router to forward packets in an SR network.

This chapter also discusses some other features that help improve the load balancing, high availability, scalability, convergence, and path steering capabilities of an SR network.

Anycast is a network addressing and routing method by which packets can be routed to a variety of different locations or nodes to provide load balancing and improve availability. In the SR architecture, an Anycast SID is assigned to an anycast prefix advertised by a set of routers (called an *anycast set*). An Anycast SID enforces the ECMP-aware shortest-path forwarding toward the closest node of the anycast set and helps provide load balancing. The anycast concept for SR-MPLS is explained in the section "SR-MPLS Anycast SID," and the anycast concept for SRv6 is explained in the section "SRv6 Anycast SID."

Scalability is a key requirement for large-scale service provider networks. Summarization at the area or domain border in an IGP addresses the scalability issue in an SRv6 network, explained in the section "SRv6 IS-IS Summarization".

Whereas summarization is the key to providing scalability in an SRv6 network, it cannot be used in an SR-MPLS network because summarization breaks the end-to-end label-switched path (LSP) in an SR-MPLS network. SR-MPLS relies on isolated IGP domains and BGP Labeled Unicast (BGP-LU) to provide scalability, as explained in the section "Intra-AS BGP-LU." The use of BGP-LU to provide scalability in SR-MPLS networks comes at certain costs, especially a second protocol in addition to the IGP to exchange SR-related information and a second MPLS label in the transport header to forward IP packets.

Although summarization at the border of an IGP domain in a hierarchical IGP network helps to build a scalable SRv6 network for Layer 3 and Layer 2 services, it introduces convergence issues for BGP-based multihoming services in SRv6 networks because summarization prevents the IGP from signaling the failure of devices in remote domains via the IGP and triggering BGP next hop tracking (NHT) that is required for BGP PIC. The limitation of BGP NHT in combination with summarization is addressed by Unreachable Prefix Announcement (UPA), wherein the unreachability of egress PE devices in remote domains is advertised by the IGP (see the section "Unreachable Prefix Announcement [UPA]").

IS-IS and OSPF use the SPF algorithm to calculate the shortest path to a destination based on the link metric that is advertised in the IGP. A flexible algorithm (flex algo) that allows the creation of multiple network topologies by exchanging various link attributes in the link state IGP helps meet requirements such as low latency and disjoint paths, as described in the section "Multiplane Topologies with Flex Algos."

In this chapter, you will see how routers can be configured to forward packets using SR technology. This chapter provides implementation details regarding SR on Cisco routers, including some design guidelines. It describes several components related to enabling, forwarding, and distributing SR-related information using an IGP like IS-IS or OSPF or an exterior gateway protocol like BGP. Several commands are provided to verify the configuration and the expected functionality outlined in Chapter 2 and Chapter 3.

An implementation depends on the choice of the operating systems (IOS XR or IOS XE) as well as the choice of IGP(IS-IS or OSPF), and differences in configurations on different operating systems and with different IGPs have been highlighted where relevant.

The data plane verification for reachability is done using **ping**, and **traceroute** is used to validate a path from the source to the destination in a network. In some cases, packet captures have used to validate MPLS labels and SRv6 SIDs. The information displayed for path verification includes the MPLS label in an SR-MPLS network and the IPv6 address of the intermediate nodes in the path for an SRv6 network.

Note   The SRv6 SID base format and SRv6 micro-SID (uSID) format are described in Chapter 3, in the section "SRv6 Segment Identifier (SID)." The uSID format is specified using the notation F*bbuu*, where *bb* is the size of the SRv6 block and *uu* is the length of the uSID. For example, F3216 is a format with a 32-bit uSID block and 16-bit uSIDs. All the configuration, verification, and data forwarding is done for F3216 format.

Link-State IGPs

A link-state IGP, as the name indicates, exchanges network topology information and constructs a map of the network connectivity in the form of a graph that shows which nodes are connected to which other nodes. Each node then independently calculates the shortest path from itself to every possible destination in the network by using the Dijkstra Shortest Path First (SPF) algorithm. There are three popular link-state IGPs for an IP network:

- Intermediate System-to-Intermediate System (IS-IS), described in RFC 1195

- Open Shortest Path First (OSPF), described in RFC 2328

- OSPFv3, described in RCC 2740

IS-IS

IS-IS is a link-state routing protocol that forms neighbor adjacencies to exchange information related to the network topology using link-state packets (LSPs). The information exchanged via the LSPs is used to create and maintain a link-state database, and the database information is used to run SPF algorithm to find the shortest path to each destination, based on the costs associated with the links and the networks. The best path is then installed in the routing table of the device.

IS-IS is a highly scalable routing protocol and is often deployed in large service provider network backbones. Network scalability can be achieved by using a hierarchical concept of levels, as illustrated in Figure 4-1, or logically separated isolated IS-IS processes with redistribution between the IS-IS processes on the autonomous systems border routers (ASBRs).

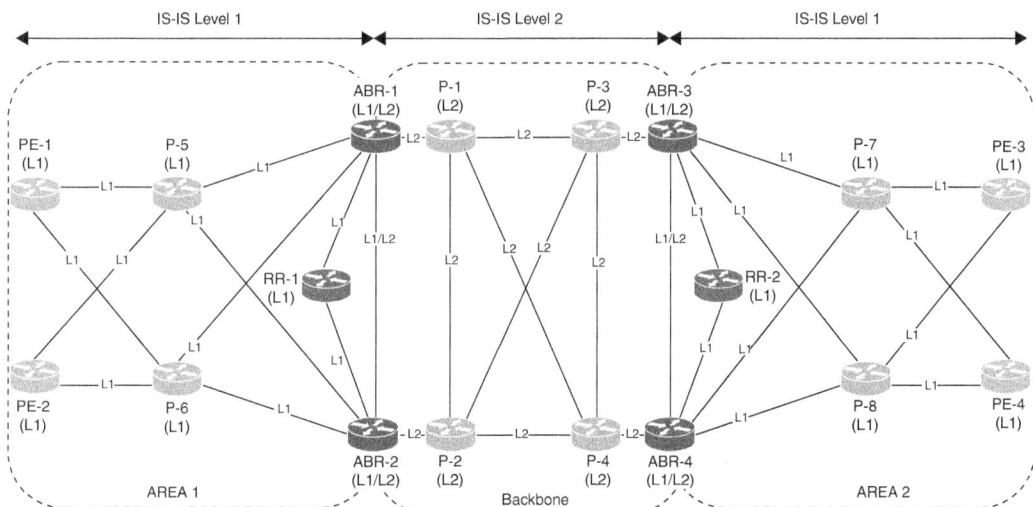

Figure 4-1 *IS-IS Areas and Levels*

IS-IS Levels

These are the IS-IS levels:

- **IS-IS Level 1:** All routers in Level 1 belong to the same area and share the same topology information. The Level 1 area must be contiguous (unlike with OSPF, where only Area 0 needs to be contiguous and other areas do not).

- **IS-IS Level 2:** All routers in Level 2 have access to the network reachability information for the entire network. This level forms the backbone and provides connectivity between different Level 1 areas. All routers in Level 2 must be contiguous (like Area 0 in OSPF).

IS-IS Areas

IS-IS uses *areas* to divide a network into logically separate domains in order to increase scalability and ease operation. While OSPF allows different interfaces of a router to belong to different OSPF areas, IS-IS assigns a router with all its interfaces to the same area. The backbone area is formed by all the IS-IS Level 2 routers. Links between routers in the same area can be in Level 1 or Level 2 or both, and links between routers in different areas are in Level 2 only.

IS-IS Router Types

IS-IS has three types of routers:

- **Level 1 routers:** A Level 1 router is an intra-area router. It only knows what the local area looks like and learns only the topology from its own area. It creates a Level 1 link-state database (LSDB) and SPF tree for the area. All routers in the same area form a Level 1 adjacency.

- **Level 2 router:** This is a backbone router that knows all intra-area and inter-area routes. It creates a Level 2 LSDB and SPF tree for the backbone.

- **Level 1–2 router:** This is a router that performs both roles. It creates separate Level 1 and Level 2 LSDBs and two SPF trees—one for each database. A Level 1–2 router, which is also referred to as an area border router (ABR), does the routing between the levels.

IS-IS Routing

Routing within an area is done by the Level 1 routers using the Level 1 LSDB. Level 2 routers (and Level 1–2 routers) exchange routing information to provide routing between areas. Routing information from Level 1 is propagated to Level 2 to provide routing between areas, and routing information from Level 2 is not propagated to Level 1 by default.

IS-IS Route Propagation and Leaking

In the context of SR, summarization is relevant only for SRv6 networks. In fact, it is not an option for SR-MPLS networks because summarization breaks the end-to-end LSP. Scalability in SR-MPLS network is provided by using BGP to exchange SR-related information across IGP domains.

By default, all routes from IS-IS Level 1 are propagated into IS-IS Level 2, which can significantly increase the Level 2 database. For example, in a network with 12 areas and 2500 devices per area, the Level 2 database would need to hold routing information for 30,000 network devices. Clearly, this is not scalable.

Summarizing routes from Level 1 to Level 2 on an ABR allows a reduction in the number of prefixes populating the Level 2 database, which improves scalability significantly.

Routers in Level 1 are not aware of the topology and network prefixes of other areas. The Level 1–2 routers provide reachability to other areas, using the attached bit in the LSP. The purpose of the attached bit is to indicate the presence of an ABR to all the Level 1 routers. When the attached bit in the LSP of a Level 1–2 router is set, a Cisco Level 1 router installs a default route pointing to the ABR in its routing table.

Level 1–2 routers also allow specific routes and summary routes to be leaked from Level 2 to Level 1. Propagating the routes in both directions between Level 1 and Level 2 without any filtering mechanisms may cause routing loops. For example, consider a route that has been propagated by the ABR from Level 2 into Level 1. Propagating this route back from Level 1 to Level 2 may result in a routing loop.

It is possible to prevent routing loops between levels by using a bit called the up/down bit (see RFC 3784, Section 4.1). The up/down bit is set to 0 when a route is first injected into IS-IS. If a route is advertised from Level 2 to Level 1, the bit is set to 1, indicating that the route has traversed down the hierarchy. ABRs do not advertise routes back from Level 1 into Level 2 when the up/down bit is set.

For more details about summarization, route leaking, and the attached bit, see the section "SRv6 IS-IS Summarization," later in this chapter.

IS-IS Overload Bit

An IS-IS router can set the overload bit (OL-bit) in its LSPs to signal other nodes within the network not to use its links when building their shortest path tree (SPT). The OL-bit only affects the use of the particular node as a transit node; networks advertised within the node's LSPs are still reachable (for example, the loopback addresses or redistributed networks).

Setting the overload bit on startup gives the router enough time to build the IS-IS LSDB and Forwarding Information Base (FIB) prior to the router being used as a transit node. Without the overload bit, a reloading router may inadvertently blackhole traffic due to an IS-IS adjacency being formed before the forwarding table has been programmed.

OSPF

The Open Shortest Path First (OSPF) protocol, defined in RFC 2328, is an IGP that is used to distribute routing information within a single autonomous system (AS).

OSPF SPF Algorithm

Similarly to IS-IS, OSPF uses a Shortest Path First (SPF) algorithm called the Dijkstra SPF algorithm to calculate the shortest path to every destination. The algorithm places each router at the root of a tree and calculates the shortest path to each destination, based on the cumulative cost required to reach that destination. Each router has its own view of the topology even though every router builds a shortest path tree using the same link-state database. The following sections describes the components involved in the creation of a shortest path tree.

Areas and Border Routers

The concept of areas in OSPF is similar to the concept of levels in IS-IS. An area is a logical grouping of contiguous networks and routers. All routers in an area have the same topology table but are not aware of routers in the other areas.

The backbone area (also known as Area 0 or Area 0.0.0.0) forms the core of an OSPF network and interconnects all nonzero areas in the OSPF domain. Routers that have interfaces in both the backbone area and at least one non-backbone area are called area border routers (ABRs) and are responsible for routing between OSPF areas. The backbone area must be contiguous and is responsible for distributing routing information between non-backbone areas.

OSPF areas are used to scale large networks by dividing the network into smaller, more manageable subnetworks. Each area has its own database, and routers in one area do not know about the topology of other areas. Inter-area routing is provided by the ABRs. This helps reduce the size of the link-state database (LSDB) and the complexity of the SPF calculation, which makes OSPF more efficient and scalable.

Each area in an OSPF network must connect to the backbone area, and all routers inside an area must have the same area ID to become OSPF neighbors. A router that connects an OSPF network to other external routing domains (for example, an EIGRP network) is called an autonomous system boundary router (ASBR).

OSPF LSAs

OSPF routers use link-state advertisements (LSAs) to exchange topology information. Each LSA contains routing and topology information to describe a part of an OSPF network. When two neighbors decide to exchange network information, they send each other a list of all LSAs in their respective topology databases. Each router then checks its topology database and sends a link-state request (LSR) message, requesting all LSAs not found in its topology table. The other router responds with a link-state update (LSU) that contains all the LSAs the other neighbor requested.

OSPFv3

Open Shortest Path First Version 3 (OSPFv3) is a link-state protocol that supports IPv6 (whereas OSPFv2 supports only IPv4). RFC 2740 discusses in detail the modifications made in OSPF to support IPv6. Some of them are highlighted here:

- The addressing semantics have been removed from OSPF packets and the basic LSAs. New LSAs have been created to carry IPv6 addresses and prefixes.

- OSPFv3 runs on a per-link basis instead of on a per-IP-subnet basis. Flooding scope for LSAs has been generalized.

- Authentication has been removed from OSPF, and the protocol instead relies on IPv6 Authentication Header and Encapsulating Security Payload.

- Option handling has been made more flexible.

- OSPFv3 forms neighbor adjacencies using IPv6 link-local addresses.

- OSPFv3 is enabled on a per-interface basis, whereas network commands are required with OSPF for IPv4.

OSPFv3 Route Summarization

Two types of summarizations are done on the ABRs: inter-area route summarization and external route summarization.

Inter-area route summarization is configured on ABRs to summarize routes between areas in an autonomous system. To take advantage of summarization and to minimize the number of summary routes, IP addresses assigned in an area must be contiguous.

External route summarization is specific to external routes that are injected into OSPFv3 using route redistribution. It is configured on ASBRs that are redistributing routes into OSPF.

OSPFv3 Route Filtering

The OSPF algorithm requires that every router in an area must see the same list of link-state advertisements. Otherwise, there is a serious risk that routing within the area will become unstable and perhaps generate loops. There is no way to filter the LSA information that is distributed to the routers in an area. However, because OSPF keeps the LSA database separate from the routing table, routes can be selectively installed in the routing table.

Inter-area route filtering is done on an ABR to selectively allow routes from other areas.

Segment Routing Baseline

This section discusses the configuration required to enable segment routing on a device and parameters related to segment routing, like the segment identifier (SID), which is described in the section "Segment Routing for MPLS (SR-MPLS)" in Chapter 2, "What Is Segment Routing over MPLS (SR-MPLS)?" We will look at both SR-MPLS and SRv6 and quickly recap SR concepts and SIDs for both SR-MPLS and SRv6.

SR-MPLS Baseline

Segment routing is a method of forwarding packets on a network based on the source routing paradigm. The source chooses a path and encodes it in the packet header as an ordered list of segments. (A segment is an identifier for any type of instruction.) For example, a topology segment identifies the next hop toward a destination. Each segment is identified by the segment ID (SID), which consists of a 20-bit integer.

IGP distributes two types of segments: prefix segments and adjacency segments. Each router (node) has at least one segment identifier (SID), and each link that is a part of the IGP has an Adjacency SID.

A Prefix SID is associated with an IP prefix and is manually configured from the segment routing global block (SRGB) range of labels and is distributed by IS-IS or OSPF. The prefix segment steers the traffic along the shortest path to its destination. A Node SID is a special type of Prefix SID that identifies a specific node. It is configured under the loopback interface, with the loopback address of the node as the prefix. A prefix segment is a global segment, so a Prefix SID is globally unique within the SR domain.

An adjacency segment is identified by an Adjacency SID, which represents a specific adjacency to a neighboring router. An Adjacency SID can be allocated dynamically from the dynamic label range or configured manually from the segment routing local block (SRLB) range of labels. The Adjacency SID is distributed by IS-IS or OSPF and is used to steer the traffic to a specific adjacency. An adjacency segment is locally significant and is unique relative to a specific router.

By combining Prefix (Node) and Adjacency SIDs in an ordered list, you can construct any path within a network.

The rest of this section focuses on how to configure and verify the operations of SR. The configuration is shown for IS-IS and OSPF on IOS XR and IOS XE devices. Let's quickly recap the SRGB, the SRLG, and addressing before moving on to configuration and verification.

Segment Routing Global Block (SRGB)

The segment routing global block (SRGB) is a range of labels that is reserved for SR global segments. A Prefix SID is advertised as a network-wide unique index or absolute value. The Prefix SID index points to a unique label within the SRGB range. The index is zero based, meaning that the first index is 0. The MPLS label assigned to a prefix is derived from the Prefix SID index plus the SRGB base. For example, with an SRGB range of 16000 to 23999, a prefix 10.0.1.1/32 with Prefix SID index of 1 is assigned the label value 16001. The Anycast SID, which has global significance, is also allocated a label from the SRGB.

To keep the configuration simple and straightforward, it is recommended to use the same SRGB on all the SR-enabled devices in the network. Using a heterogenous SRGB—that is, a different SRGB range of the same size across nodes—is also supported but is not recommended.

The default SRGB in IOS XR has a size of 8000 entries, starting from label value 16000. With this size, and assuming one loopback prefix per router, it is possible to assign Prefix SIDs to a network with 8000 devices.

In some situations, it is necessary to define a different SRGB range. This would be required, for example, when the default SRGB range is not large enough to accommodate all required Prefix SIDs or for SR interoperability between router implementations that use different default SRGB ranges.

Segment Routing Local Block (SRLB)

The segment routing local block (SRLB) is a range of label values preserved for the manual allocation of local segments, such as Adjacency SIDs, Layer 2 Adjacency SIDs, Binding SIDs (BSIDs), and BGP Peering SIDs. These labels are locally significant and are only valid on the nodes that allocate the labels.

A local segment is automatically assigned an MPLS label from the dynamic label range. In most cases, such as with TI-LFA backup paths and SR-TE explicit paths defined with IP addresses, this dynamic label allocation is sufficient. However, in some scenarios, it could be beneficial to manually allocate local segment label values to maintain label persistency (for example, with an SR-TE policy with a manual Binding SID that is performing traffic steering based on incoming label traffic with the Binding SID).

The default SRLB has a size of 1000, starting from label value 15000.

Figure 4-2 shows the default LSD label allocation. The initial block (0–14999) is reserved for special-purpose and static MPLS labels. The SRLB is allocated the range 15000 to 15999, and the SRBG is assigned 16000 to 23999. Dynamic MPLS labels are allocated from the range 24000 to 1048575.

SR-MPLS Addressing

As mentioned earlier, a Node SID is a special type of Prefix SID that identifies a specific node. It is configured under the loopback interface, with the loopback address of the node as the prefix. It uniquely identifies the node unless it is an Anycast SID. A network-wide scheme for allocating Node SIDs is required to ensure that each device gets a unique node SID. Adjacency SIDs are allocated from the SRLB and have local significance.

A SID can be configured as an absolute value or as an index to the SRGB or SRLB.

Special purpose and Static MPLS Labels	0
	14999
Reserved (SRLB)	15000
	15999
Reserved (SRGB)	16000
	23999
Dynamic Label Range	24000
	1048575

Figure 4-2 *LSD Label Allocation*

SR-MPLS Configuration

Figure 4-3 shows the steps for enabling SR-MPLS and the related parameters.

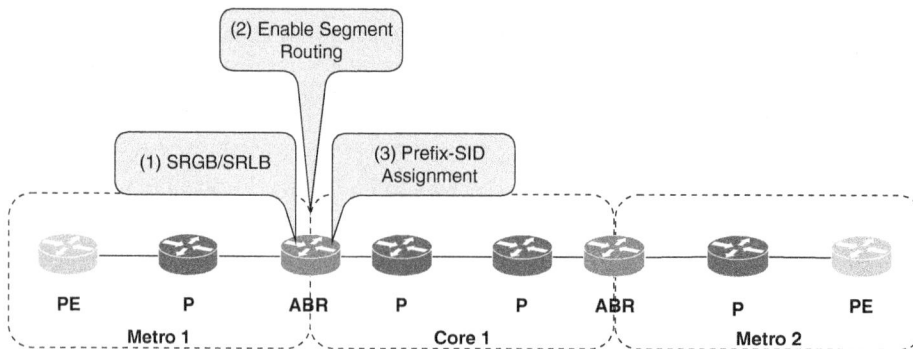

Figure 4-3 *SR-MPLS Configuration Steps*

The first step is optional and must be done when the default range of the SRGB has to be modified for interoperability reasons, as discussed in the section "Segment Routing Global Block (SRGB)." The configuration must be completed on all devices in the SR-MPLS network.

Step 1: Reconfiguring the SRGB/SRLB

Config 4-1 shows the command to set the start of the SRGB to 24000 and the size of the SRGB to 8000 on IOS XR and IOS XE devices. The SRGB starting value can be configured anywhere in the dynamic label range space (16000–1048575).

Config 4-1 *Reconfiguring the SRGB (IOS XR/IOS XE)*

```
segment-routing
 global-block 24000 31999
```

The local label allocation is managed by the label-switching database (LSD). An MPLS application must register as a client with the LSD to allocate labels. Most MPLS applications—such as LDP, RSVP, BGP (including BGP-LU, L2VPN, and L3VPN), IS-IS, OSPF (Adjacency SID), and SR-TE (Binding SID)—use labels allocated dynamically by the LSD. By default, the LSD allocates dynamic labels starting from 24000.

With SR-capable IOS XR software releases, the LSD preserves the default SRLB label range (15000–15999) and default SRGB label range (16000–23999), even if SR is not enabled. No labels are allocated from this preserved range. When SR is enabled with the default SRLB/SRGB, these label ranges are available and ready for use without a reboot. If an MPLS label range is configured and overlaps with the default SRLB/SRGB label ranges (for example, MPLS label range 15000–1048575), then the default SRLB/SRGB preservation is disabled and requires a reboot when SR is enabled.

Increasing the range of the SRGB from the default value (16000–23999) reduces the range of the dynamic labels available for other MPLS applications.

Note   Modifying an SRGB configuration is disruptive for traffic and may require a reboot if the new SRGB is already being used by other MPLS applications.

The SRLB can be reconfigured using the commands shown in Config 4-2. This configuration sets the start of the SRLB at 32000 and the end of the SRLB at 32999.

Config 4-2 *Reconfiguring the SRLB (IOS XR/IOS XE)*

```
segment-routing
 local-block 32000 32999
```

Step 2: Enable Segment Routing

Config 4-3 and Config 4-4 show the configurations for enabling segment routing on IOS XR devices for IS-IS and OSPF. For IS-IS, the command **segment-routing** is enabled under address-family IPv4, and for OSPF, **segment-routing** is enabled under area 0. Note that **segment-routing** can also be configured directly under the ospf process to enable it for all OSPF areas.

Config 4-3 *Enabling Segment Routing in IS-IS (IOS XR)*

```
router isis CORE1
 address-family ipv4 unicast
  segment-routing mpls
```

Config 4-4 *Enabling Segment Routing in OSPF (IOS XR)*

```
router isis CORE1
 address-family ipv4 unicast
  segment-routing mpls
```

In case of IOS XE, segment routing is directly enabled under the isis and ospf processes, as shown in Config 4-5 and Config 4-6.

Config 4-5 *Enabling Segment Routing in IS-IS (IOS XE)*

```
router isis CORE1
 segment-routing mpls
```

Config 4-6 *Enabling Segment Routing in OSPF (IOS XE)*

```
router ospf METRO2
 segment-routing mpls
```

Step 3: Assign the Prefix SID

The Node SID assigned to loopback0 from the SRBG must be unique in the SR-MPLS network and can be configured as an absolute value or as an index with respect to the start of the SRGB.

Before the Prefix SID can be assigned to a prefix (or interface), segment routing must be enabled under the routing process.

Config 4-7 and Config 4-8 show the configuration to assign a Node SID to loopback0. With IOS XR, the Prefix SID assignment is done under the routing process. The configurations show that the Prefix SID is specified as an absolute value (under IS-IS) or as an index (under OSPF).

Before the Prefix SID can be assigned to a prefix, segment routing must be enabled under the routing process.

Config 4-7   *Assigning the Prefix SID to Loopback0 in IS-IS (IOS XR)*

```
router isis CORE1
!
 interface Loopback0
  address-family ipv4 unicast
   prefix-sid absolute 16002
```

Config 4-8   *Assigning the Prefix SID to Loopback0 in OSPF (IOS XR)*

```
router ospf METRO2
 area 0
  interface Loopback0
   prefix-sid index 3001
```

Config 4-9 shows the Prefix SID assignment on for an IOS XE device. Here the Prefix SID is assigned to an IPv4 prefix (10.0.4.2/32) under the SR process. This is the IPv4 prefix assigned to the loopback interface. Since the configuration is done under the SR process, it the same for IS-IS and OSPF. As in the case of IOS XR, the Prefix SID can be specified as an absolute value or as an index to the SRGB.

Config 4-9   *Assigning the Prefix SID to Loopback 0 (IOS XE)*

```
interface Loopback0
 ip address 10.0.4.2 255.255.255.255

segment-routing mpls
 connected-prefix-sid-map
  address-family ipv4
   10.0.4.2/32 absolute 19002 range 1
  exit-address-family
```

SR-MPLS Verification

Figure 4-4 shows the verification steps you need to take after SR-MPLS is enabled on the routers. Although the figure shows the steps on only one device, the verification steps are valid for all devices in the SR-MPLS network.

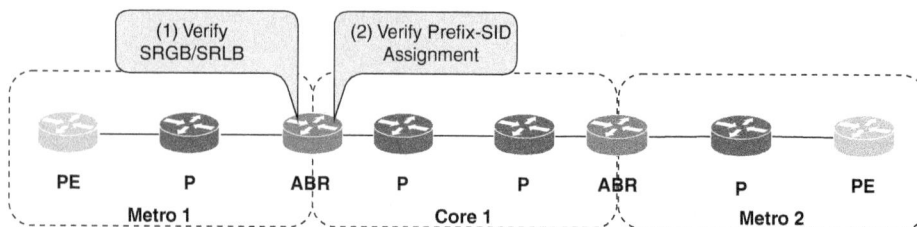

Figure 4-4 *SR-MPLS Verification Steps*

Step 1: Verify the SRGB and SRLB

SRGB and SRLG information is advertised in IS-IS and OSPF. This can be verified by using the IOS XR commands shown in Output 4-1 and Output 4-2. The output shows that the SRGB starts at 16000, and the range is 8000. The SRLB starts at 15000, and the size of the block is 1000.

Output 4-1 *Verifying the SRGB and SRLB for IS-IS (IOS XR)*

```
RP/0/0/CPU0:ABR-1#show isis database ABR-1.00-00 verbose


IS-IS CORE1 (Level-2) Link State Database
LSPID                    LSP Seq Num  LSP Checksum  LSP Holdtime/Rcvd  ATT/P/OL
ABR-1.00-00    * 0x00000084   0x2af5        971  /*               0/0/0
<snip>
  Hostname:        ABR-1
  Router Cap:      10.0.1.5 D:0 S:0
    Segment Routing: I:1 V:0, SRGB Base: 16000 Range: 8000
    SR Local Block: Base: 15000 Range: 1000
<snip>
```

Output 4-2 *Verifying the SRGB and SRLB for OSPF (IOS XR)*

```
RP/0/0/CPU0:PE-3#show ospf database opaque-area router-info self-originate

            OSPF Router with ID (10.0.4.1) (Process ID METRO2)

                Type-10 Opaque Link Area Link States (Area 0)
<snip>

   Router Information TLV: Length: 4
   Capabilities:
     Graceful Restart Helper Capable
```

```
      Stub Router Capable
      All capability bits: 0x60000000

   Segment Routing Algorithm TLV: Length: 2
      Algorithm: 0
      Algorithm: 1


   Segment Routing Range TLV: Length: 12
      Range Size: 8000


         SID sub-TLV: Length 3
         Label: 16000


   Node MSD TLV: Length: 2
         Type: 1, Value 10


   Segment Routing Local Block TLV: Length: 12
      Range Size: 1000


         SID sub-TLV: Length 3
         Label: 15000

<snip>
```

Output 4-3 and Output 4-4 shows the commands to verify the SRGB and SRLB on IOS XE devices. You can see that the SRGB starts at 16000, and the size is 8000. The SRLB starts at 15000, and the size of the block is 1000.

Output 4-3   *SRGB and SRLB Information in IS-IS (IOS XE)*

```
ABR-4#show isis database  ABR-4.00-00 verbose

Tag CORE1:

IS-IS Level-2 LSP ABR-4.00-00
LSPID                   LSP Seq Num  LSP Checksum  LSP Holdtime/Rcvd      ATT/P/OL
ABR-4.00-00    * 0x00001601    0xD22A               618/*           0/0/0
  Area Address: 49.0001
  NLPID:        0xCC
  Router CAP:    10.0.1.8, D:0, S:0
     Segment Routing: I:1 V:0, SRGB Base: 16000 Range: 8000
     Segment Routing Algorithms: SPF, Strict-SPF
     Segment Routing Local Block: SRLB Base: 15000 Range: 1000

<snip>
```

Output 4-4 *SRGB and SRLB Information in OSPF (IOS XE)*

```
ABR-4#show ip ospf database opaque-area  adv-router 10.0.4.2

            OSPF Router with ID (10.0.4.2) (Process ID 1)

                    Type-10 Opaque Area Link States (Area 0)

   <snip>

   LS age: 835
   Options: (No TOS-capability, DC)
   LS Type: Opaque Area Link
   Link State ID: 4.0.0.0
   Opaque Type: 4 (Router Information)
   Opaque ID: 0
   Advertising Router: 10.0.4.2
   LS Seq Number: 80000001
   Checksum: 0x6EE4
   Length: 76

<snip>

     TLV Type: Segment Routing Range
     Length: 12
       Range Size: 8000

         Sub-TLV Type: SID/Label
         Length: 3
           Label: 16000

     TLV Type: Segment Routing Node MSD
     Length: 2
       Sub-type: Node Max Sid Depth, Value: 13

     TLV Type: Segment Routing Local Block
     Length: 12
       Range Size: 1000

         Sub-TLV Type: SID/Label
         Length: 3
           Label: 15000
```

Step 2: Verify the Prefix SID Assignment

The Prefix SID assignment can be verified on IOS XR devices by using the commands shown in Output 4-5 and Output 4-6. With IS-IS, the command **show isis segment-routing label** shows that the Prefix SID 16002 has been assigned to loopback0 (10.0.1.2), and with OSPF, the command **show ospf sid-database** shows that Prefix SID index 3001 is assigned to 10.0.4.1.

Output 4-5 *Verifying the Prefix SID Assignment: IS-IS (IOS XR)*

```
RP/0/0/CPU0:P-2#show run int lo0

interface Loopback0
 ipv4 address 10.0.1.2 255.255.255.255

RP/0/0/CPU0:P-2#sh isis segment-routing label table

IS-IS CORE1 IS Label Table
Label          Prefix/Interface
----------     ----------------
16001          10.0.1.1/32
16002          Loopback0
<snip>
```

Output 4-6 *Verifying the Prefix SID Assignment: OSPF (IOS XR)*

```
RP/0/0/CPU0:PE-3#show ospf sid-database

SID Database for ospf METRO2 with ID 10.0.4.1

SID            Prefix/Mask
--------       ------------------
7              10.0.1.7/32
8              10.0.1.8/32
3001           10.0.4.1/32                  (L)
3002           10.0.4.2/32
3254           10.0.4.254/32
```

On IOS XE devices, the Prefix SID assignment is verified by using the command shown in Output 4-7. The output shows that Prefix SID 19002 has been assigned to prefix 10.0.4.2/32.

Output 4-7   *Verifying the Prefix SID Assignment (IOS XE)*

```
PE-4#show segment-routing mpls connected-prefix-sid-map ipv4


                PREFIX_SID_CONN_MAP ALGO_0


Prefix/masklen    SID Type Range Flags SRGB
    10.0.4.2/32 19002  Abs      1            Y
<snip>
```

SRv6 Baseline

This section delves into the basics of SRv6 uSID formats, addressing for SRv6 locators, and configuration and verification of SRv6 uSIDs on Cisco routers. The configuration is shown for IOS XR devices only.

SRv6 uSID

The SRv6 micro-SID (uSID) is an extension of the SRv6 architecture. It leverages the SRv6 network programming architecture to encode several SRv6 uSID instructions within a single 128-bit SID address (which is called a uSID carrier). The uSID format specifies the type of uSID supported in an SRv6 network. The format specification includes SRv6 block size and uSID length. F3216 is the default format—and the only format that is supported on Cisco devices at this writing. The details and benefits of SRv6 uSIDs are described in Chapter 3, in the section "SID Compression."

SRv6 uSID Allocation

The uSID architecture specifies both global and local uSIDs.

A global uSID provides reachability to a node and identifies a shortest path to a node in the SR domain. The uN is an example of a global SID defined in the uSID architecture. A node can have multiple global uSIDs from the same uSID block (for example, one uSID per IGP flex algo). Multiple nodes may share the same global uSID (Anycast SID). The global ID block (GIB) is the set of IDs available for global uSID allocation. The range of the GIB is from 0x0001 to 0xdfff. 0x0000 is reserved as it represent end of container (EoC). Figure 4-5 shows the default GIB size and range on a Cisco router.

A local uSID is associated with a local endpoint behavior, and it must therefore be preceded by a global uSID of the node. A local uSID identifies a local micro-instruction on the parent node. For example, it may identify a cross-connect to a direct neighbor over a specific interface or a VPN context. For example, if Router 1 with SRv6 locator fc00:0:1::/48 and Router 2 with SRv6 locator fc00:0:2::/48 are two different physical nodes of the uSID domain, and 0xe001 is a local uSID value, then fc00:0:1:e000::/64 and fc00:0:2:e000::/64 may bind two different behaviors. The local ID block (LIB) is the set of IDs available for local uSID allocation. The range of the LIB is from 0xe000 to 0xfeff on Cisco routers, as shown in Figure 4-5.

Wide LIB (W-LIB) is the extended set of IDs available for local uSID allocation. The extended set of IDs is useful when a PE with large-scale pseudowire termination requires more local uSIDs than provided from the LIB. The range of the W-LIB is 0x0ff00 to 0xffff on a Cisco router, as shown in Figure 4-5.

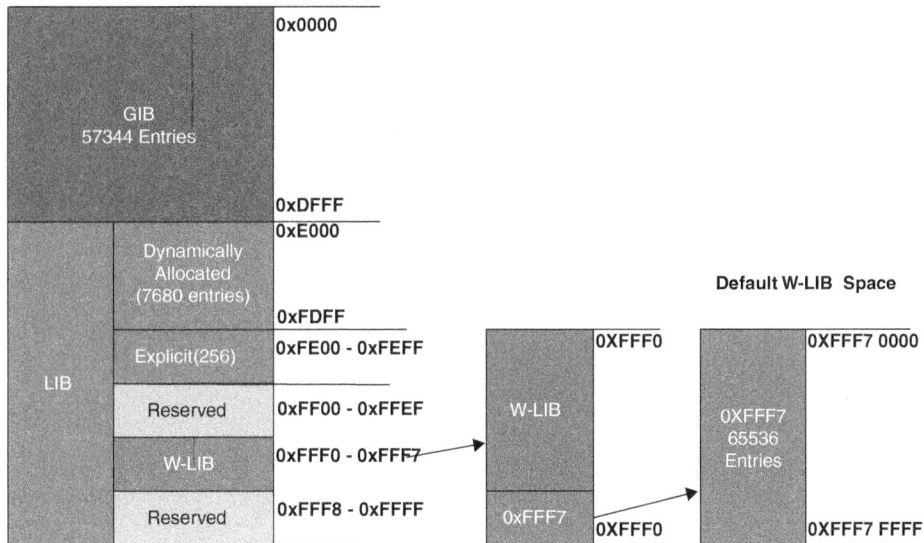

Figure 4-5   *Global ID Block (GIB), Local ID Block (LIB), and Wide LIB (W-LIB)*

SRv6 Addressing

On Cisco routers, the SRv6 locators must be allocated from the same base block (/24 IPv6 block) for the entire SRv6 domain. More details about SRv6 locator addressing can be found in Chapter 3, in the section "Addressing Considerations."

Interface Loopback0 Address

IPv6 addresses for the loopback0 interface can be allocated from the SRv6 locator that is advertised in IS-IS. Fifteen special addresses can be used for loopback addresses from the SRv6 locator range SRv6 locator::X/128, where the range of X is 0x1 to 0xF.

The advantage of allocating the IPv6 address of loopback0 based on the SRv6 locator is that the loopback0 interface does not need to be advertised in IS-IS.

> **Note**   The IPv6 address for loopback0 can also be allocated from a range that is independent of the SRv6 locator, as long as it is advertised in the IGP.

SRv6 uSID Locator Addressing Scheme Examples

Let's consider two examples for a multi-domain IS-IS network that allows for summarization per domain and supports at least two flex algos. The uSID locators are assigned from the IPv6 block PQRS:TU::/28. The uSID uses the F3216 format, thereby requiring that the uSID block size is 32 bits and the uSID locator is 48 bits.

Example 1: Fewer Domains, More Nodes per Domain

This example focuses on a network that has fewer domains and more nodes in each domain. The uSID locator for this example has the format *PQRS:TU0G:DNNN::/48*, where:

- *PQRS:TU*: Must be the same across the SRv6 domain.

- *G*: Set to 0x0 through 0xF (flex algo).

- *D*: Set to 0x0 through 0xD (domain ID). (E and F are reserved for local SIDs.)

- *NNN*: Set to 0x000 through 0xFFF (node ID).

This allocation scheme allows for 16 flex algos. Each flex algo can support 14 domains and 4096 nodes per domain, giving a total of $14 \times 4096 - 1 = 57,343$ nodes per flex algo. Remember that 0x0000 is reserved because it represents EoC.

Example 2: More Fewer Nodes per Domain

By carving out 8 bits for the domain identifier, we can increase the number of domains at the cost of nodes per domain. The uSID locator for this example has the format *PQRS:TU0G:DDNN::/48*, where:

- *PQRS:TU*: Must be the same across the SRv6 domain.

- *G*: Set to 0x0 through 0xF (flex algo).

- *DD*: Set to 0x00 through 0xDF (domain ID). (0xE0 through 0xFF are reserved for Local SIDs.)

- *NN*: Set to 0x0 through 0xFF (node ID).

This allocation scheme allows for 16 flex algos. Each flex algo can support 224 domains and 256 nodes per domain, giving a total of $224 \times 256 - 1 = 57,343$ nodes per flex algo. Keep in mind that 0x0000 is reserved because it represents EoC.

SRv6 uSID Locator Addressing Scheme in This Chapter

This chapter uses the IPv6 block fc00:0000::/32 and the SRv6 locator format fc00:000*G:DDNN*/48, where:

- **G:** Set to 0x0 through 0xF (flex algo), which allows for up to 16 flex algos:

  - **0:** Algo 0

  - **1:** Flex algo 128

  - **2:** Flex algo 129

  - **3:** Flex algo 130

- **DD:** Set to 0x00 through 0xDF (domain), which allows for up to 224 domains:

  - **00:** Core

  - **01:** Metro 1

  - **02:** Metro 2

- **NN:** Set to 0x00 though 0xFF (node ID). With this allocation, each domain can support up to 256 nodes, except for Domain 0, which can support 255 nodes because 0x0000 is reserved for EoC.

SRv6 uSID Configuration

Now that you have learned about uSIDs, their format, and the addressing schemes for SRv6 locators, you are ready to see how to enable SRv6 uSIDs and allocate an SRv6 locator on Cisco devices. Figure 4-6 shows the configuration steps for enabling SRv6 uSIDs and the related parameters. These steps must be completed on all the SRv6 devices in the SRv6 network.

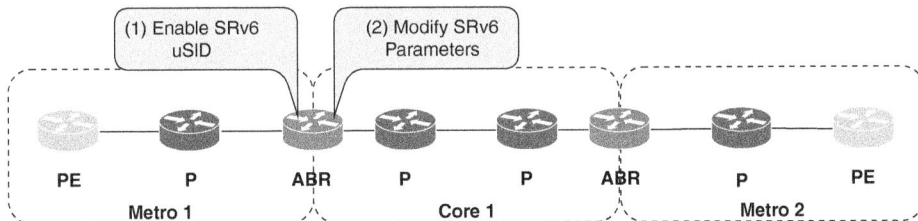

Figure 4-6   *SRv6 uSID Configuration Steps*

Step 1: Enable SRv6 uSIDs

The first step is to enable SRv6 on all the devices. The focus of this book is on uSIDs (f3216 format). The command **micro-segment behavior unode psp-usd** is used to enable the uSID behavior with PSP/USD. PSP (Penultimate Segment Pop) and USD (Ultimate Segment Decapsulation) are the SRv6 uSID endpoint behaviors, which are explained in Chapter 3, in the section "IPv6 Segment Routing Header (SRH) (RFC 8754)."

An SRv6 locator has a name and a /48 block assigned to it. Several locators can be enabled on a Cisco device.

Config 4-10 shows the configuration steps for enable the uSID (f3216) format on a device and assigning a fc00:0:1::/48 prefix to the locator with the name MAIN.

Config 4-10   *Enabling SRv6 (IOS XR)*

```
segment-routing
 srv6
  locators
   locator MAIN
    micro-segment behavior unode psp-usd
    prefix fc00:0:1::/48
```

Some hardware platforms require an additional hardware module command and a reload to enable SRv6 uSID (f3216). Config 4-11 shows the use of the **hw-module** command to enable SRv6 uSID functionality on NCS 540/NSC 5500 platforms. A reload is required after this command is run in order to enable SRv6 uSID functionality.

Config 4-11   *SRv6 uSID Hardware Profile (NCS540/NCS 5500)*

```
hw-module profile segment-routing srv6 mode micro-segment format f3216
```

Step 2: Modify SRv6 Parameters

Every SRv6 packet originating from a device requires a source IPv6 address. The source address is required when the destination or intermediate node needs to signal the source node about certain exception/error conditions. For example, when the hop limit of an IPv6 packet reaches 0 on a device, an ICMP time exceeded message is sent by the device to the source device using the source IPv6 address.

By default, the IPv6 address of the lowest loopback interface is used as the source address. The source address of the SRv6 packets originating from the device can be set as shown in Config 4-12.

Config 4-12   *Source Address Encapsulation (IOS XR)*

```
segment-routing
 srv6
  encapsulation
   source-address fc00:0:105::1
```

SRv6 uSID Verification

Figure 4-7 highlights the steps to verify the configuration related to SRv6 uSID.

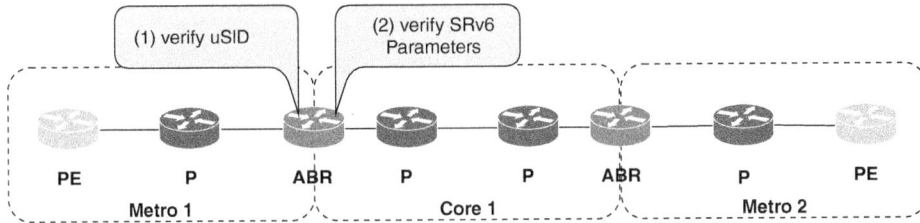

Figure 4-7 *Verifying the SRv6 uSID*

After enabling SRv6, the uSID- and SRv6-related parameters can be verified by using the command **show segment-routing srv6 manager**. This can be done on all the devices where SRv6 has been enabled. Output 4-8 has several sections that provide detailed information regarding SRv6 on the device:

- **Parameters:** This part of the output shows that SRv6 is enabled, and the operational mode is uSID with f3216 because the SID format is f3216. The uSID space is fc00::/24, the uSID LIB starts at 0xe000, and the source address for SRv6 encapsulation is fc00:0:1::1 (the loopback0 IPv6 address).

  Summary: This section shows the number of locators, the local SIDs that are configured, their operational state, and the status of local SID resources (maximum, free) for each uSID block. For the sake of brevity, information is shown for only one block.

- **Platform Capabilities:** This section indicates that TI-LFA and microloop avoidance are supported. The endpoint and headend behaviors (described in the section "SRv6 Headend and Endpoint Behavior Overview" in Chapter 3) are shown as a reference. The SRv6 parameters that are set on the outer IPv6 header during encapsulation— such as source address, hop limit, and the IPv6 traffic class—are displayed. Finally, information related to the maximum number of locators, maximum number of local SIDs, and SID hold time supported by the device are also listed in the output. The hold time for a SID refers to the duration for which the SID remains allocated after it is no longer in use.

Output 4-8   *SRv6 Parameters, Summary, and Platform Capabilities Information*

```
RP/0/RP0/CPU0:ABR-1#show segment-routing srv6 manager

Parameters:
  SRv6 Enabled: Yes
  SRv6 Operational Mode:
    Micro-segment:
      SID Base Block: fc00::/24
  Encapsulation:
    Source Address:
      Configured: fc00:0:101::1
      Default: fc00:0:101::1
    Hop-Limit: Default                                          Parameters
    Traffic-class: Default
  SID Formats:
    f3216 <32B/16NFA> (2)
      uSID LIB Range:
        LIB Start   : 0xe000
        ELIB Start  : 0xfe00
      uSID WLIB Range:
        EWLIB Start : 0xfff7
```

```
Summary:
  Number of Locators: 4 (4 operational)
  Number of SIDs: 32 (0 stale)
  Max SID resources: 9000
  Number of free SID resources: 8968
  OOR:
    Thresholds (resources): Green 450, Warning 270
    Status: Resource Available                                  Summary
        History: (0 cleared, 0 warnings, 0 full)
    Block fc00::/32:
        Number of SIDs free: 7672
        Max SIDs: 7680
        Thresholds: Green 384, Warning 231
        Status: Resource Available
            History: (0 cleared, 0 warnings, 0 full)
  <snip>
```

```
Platform Capabilities:
  SRv6: Yes
  TILFA: Yes
  Microloop-Avoidance: Yes
  Endpoint behaviors:
    End.DX6
    End.DX4
    End.DT6
    End.DT4
    End.DT46
    End.DX2
    End.DT2U
    End.DT2M
    End (PSP/USD)
    End.X (PSP/USD)
    uN (shift)
    uN (PSP/USD)
    uA (shift)
    uA (PSP/USD)
    uDX6
    uDX4
    uDT6
    uDT4
    uDT46
    uDX2                                                        Platform
    uDT2U                                                       Capabilities
    uDT2M
    uB6 (Insert.Red)
  Headend behaviors:
    T
    H.Insert.Red
    H.Encaps.Red
    H.Encaps.L2.Red
  <snip>

  Configurable parameters (under srv6):
    Ranges:
      LIB           : Yes
      WLIB          : Yes
    Encapsulation:
      Source Address: Yes
      Hop-Limit     : value=Yes, propagate=Yes
      Traffic-class : value=Yes, propagate=Yes
  Default parameters (under srv6):
    Encapsulation:
      Hop-Limit     : value=0, propagate=No
      Traffic-class : value=0, propagate=No
  Max Locators: 16
  Max SIDs: 9000
  SID Holdtime: 3 mins
```

Segment Routing Control Plane (IGP)

This section delves into how SR-related information is exchanged among devices in a network to provide an end-to-end SR path in the network. Information about the network topology and the relevant SR-related information is exchanged within an autonomous system using the existing routing protocols. SR relies on a small number of extensions to the IS-IS and OSPF protocols.

SR-MPLS Control Plane

There are two levels of configuration required to enable SR for a routing protocol instance. The top-level configuration enables segment routing globally, and configuration at the routing protocol level enables segment routing for a specific address family of a routing protocol instance.

Figure 4-8 shows the network that is used to explain the configuration and verification of SR-MPLS in this section.

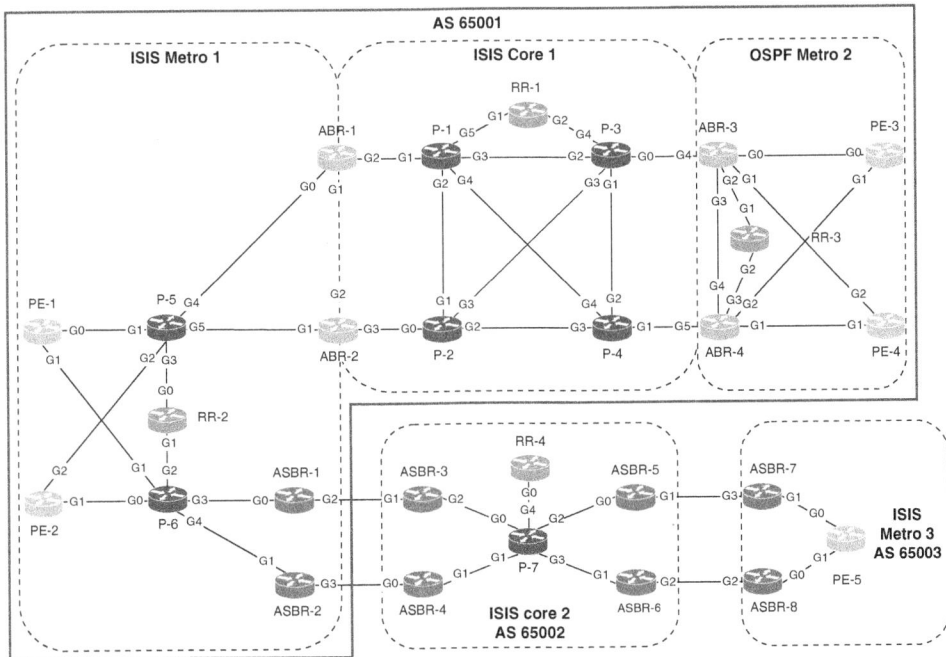

Figure 4-8   *SR-MPLS Network Topology*

The network has three autonomous systems:

■ AS 650001

  ■ Core 1 (IS-IS)

    □ Four P nodes (P-1, P-2, P-3, and P-4)

      ☐ One route reflector (RR-1)

   ■ Metro 1 (IS-IS)

      ☐ Two ABRs (ABR-1 and ABR-2)

      ☐ Two P nodes (P-5 and P-6)

      ☐ Two PE nodes (PE-1 and PE-2)

      ☐ Two ASBRs (ASBR-01 and ASBR-2)

      ☐ One route reflector (RR-2)

   ■ Metro 2 (OSPF)

      ☐ Two ABRs (ABR-3 and ABR-4)

      ☐ Two PE nodes (PE-3 and PE-4)

      ☐ One route reflector (RR-3)

■ AS 65002

   ■ Core 2 (IS-IS)

      ☐ One P node (P-7)

      ☐ Four ASBRs (ASBR-3, ASBR-4, ASBR-5, and ASBR-6)

      ☐ One route reflector (RR-4)

■ AS 65003

   ■ Metro 3 (IS-IS)

      ☐ Two ASBRs (ASBR-7 and ASBR-8)

      ☐ One PE node (PE-5)

These three BGP autonomous systems are used to illustrate intra-AS BGP-LU and inter-AS BGP-LU.

SR-MPLS IS-IS

Protocol extensions for IS-IS to support SR are described in Chapter 2, in the section "IS-IS Extensions for Segment Routing (RFC 8667)."

Each of the devices in the reference network has a loopback0 interface that is used for exchanging control plane information (BGP and IGP). The IPv4 address of the loopback0 interface has the format 10.0.D.N/32, where D represents the domain ID, and N represents the node ID. The Node SID is assigned based on the loopback0 IPv4 address.

The IS-IS NETID has the format 49.000D.000D.0000.000N.00, where D represents the domain ID, and N represents the node ID.

All devices in Core 1, Metro, Core 2, and Metro 3 are in IS-IS Level 2. Devices in Metro 2 are in OSPF Area 0.

Table 4-1 shows the allocation of loopback0 IPv4 addresses, IS-IS NSAP, and the SR-MPLS SID for all the devices in the SR-MPLS network shown in Figure 4-8.

Table 4-1 *IPv4 Loopback0, IS-IS NSAP, and SR-MPLS SID Allocation for an SR-MPLS Network*

Host Name	Domain	Domain ID	AS Number	Loopback0 10.0.D.N/32	IS-IS NSAP 49.00DD.00DD.0000.00NN.00	SR-MPLS SID
P-1	Core 1	1	65001	10.0.1.1/32	49.0001.0001.0000.0001.00	16001
P-2	Core 1	1	65001	10.0.1.2/32	49.0001.0001.0000.0002.00	16002
P-3	Core 1	1	65001	10.0.1.3/32	49.0001.0001.0000.0003.00	16003
P-4	Core 1	1	65001	10.0.1.4/32	49.0001.0001.0000.0004.00	16004
ABR-1	Core 1	1	65001	10.0.1.5/32	49.0001.0001.0000.0005.00 (Core 1)	16005
	Metro 1	3			49.0003.0003.0000.0007.00 (Metro 1)	16100 (ANYCAST)
ABR-2	Core 1	1	65001	10.0.1.6/32	49.0001.0001.0000.0006.00 (Core 1)	16005
	Metro 1	3			49.0003.0003.0000.0008.00 (Metro 1)	16100 (ANYCAST)
ABR-3	Core 1	1	65001	10.0.1.7/32	49.0001.0001.0000.0007.00 (Core 1)	16007
	Metro 2					
ABR-4	Core 1	1	65001	10.0.1.8/32	49.0001.0001.0000.0006.00 (Core 1)	16008
	Metro 2					
PE-1	Metro 1	3	65001	10.0.3.1/32	49.0003.0003.0000.0001.00	18001
PE2	Metro 1	3	65001	10.0.3.2/32	49.0003.0003.0000.0001.00	18002
P-5	Metro 1	3	65001	10.0.3.3/32	49.0003.0003.0000.0003.00	18003
P-6	Metro 1	3	65001	10.0.3.4/32	49.0003.0003.0000.0003.00	18004
ASBR-1	Metro 1	3	65001	10.0.3.5/32	49.0003.0003.0000.0005.00	18005
ASBR-2	Metro 1	3	65001	10.0.3.6/32	49.0003.0003.0000.0006.00	18006
RR-2	Metro 1	3	65001	10.0.3.254/32	49.0003.0003.0000.0254.00	18254
PE-3	Metro 2	4	65001	10.0.4.1/32	N/A	19001

Host Name	Domain	Domain ID	AS Number	Loopback0 10.0.D.N/32	IS-IS NSAP 49.00DD.00DD. 0000.00NN.00	SR-MPLS SID
PE-4	Metro 2	4	65001	10.0.4.2/32	N/A	19002
RR-3	Metro 2	4	65001	10.0.4.254/32	N/A	19254
P-7	Core 2	2	65002	10.0.2.1/32	49.0002.0002.0000.0001.00	17001
ASBR-3	Core 2	2	65002	10.0.2.2/32	49.0002.0002.0000.0002.00	17002
ASBR-4	Core 2	2	65002	10.0.2.3/32	49.0002.0002.0000.0003.00	17003
ASBR-5	Core 2	2	65002	10.0.2.4/32	49.0002.0002.0000.0004.00	17004
ASBR-6	Core 2	2	65002	10.0.2.5/32	49.0002.0002.0000.0005.00	17005
RR-4	Core 2	2	65002	10.0.2.254/32	49.0002.0002.0000.0254.00	17254
PE-5	Metro 3	5	65003	10.0.5.1/32	49.0005.0005.0000.0001.00	20001
ASBR-7	Metro 3	5	65003	10.0.5.2/32	49.0005.0005.0000.0002.00	20002
ASBR-8	Metro 3	5	65003	10.0.5.3/32	49.0005.0005.0000.0003.00	20003

SR-MPLS IS-IS Configuration

SR must be enabled under IS-IS to enable the advertisement of Prefix SIDs and Adjacency SIDs. Once SR is enabled under IS-IS, every Layer 3 adjacency in IS-IS is assigned an Adjacency SID. Config 4-13 and Config 4-14 show the configuration required to enable SR and assign a Prefix SID to loopback0 on IOS XR and IOS XE, respectively.

Config 4-13 *Enabling Segment Routing for IS-IS (IOS XR)*

```
router isis CORE1
address-family ipv4 unicast
  segment-routing mpls

interface Loopback0
  address-family ipv4 unicast
```

Config 4-14 *Enabling Segment Routing for IS-IS (IOS XE)*

```
segment-routing mpls
 connected-prefix-sid-map
  address-family ipv4
   10.0.1.1/32 index 1range 1
  exit-address-family
 !
```

SR-MPLS IS-IS Verification (IOS XR)

Output 4-9 shows the verification of several SR parameters advertised in the IS-IS LSP using the command **show isis database P-2.00-00 verbose**.

The Prefix SID, which is computed as the sum of the SRGB base (16000) and the Prefix SID index (2), is 16002.

One Adjacency SID is assigned and advertised for every Layer 3 adjacency in IS-IS. For the sake of simplicity, only one Adjacency SID is displayed in the output. Note that the Adjacency SID is advertised as an absolute value, without the index.

The start of the SRGB/SRLB and its range size are also advertised in IS-IS.

The maximum SID depth is shown to be 10.

Output 4-9   *Verifying the Prefix SID/Adjacency SID/SRGB/SRLB (IOS XR)*

```
RP/0/0/CPU0:P-2#show isis database P-2.00-00 verbose

IS-IS CORE1 (Level-2) Link State Database
LSPID                   LSP Seq Num  LSP Checksum  LSP Holdtime/Rcvd  ATT/P/OL
P-2.00-00     * 0x00001c49   0x6884        488  /*            0/0/0
  Area Address:   49.0001
  NLPID:          0xcc
  IP Address:     10.0.1.2
  Metric: 0          IP-Extended 10.0.1.2/32                              Node SID
    Prefix-SID Index: 2, Algorithm:0, R:0 N:1 P:0 E:0 V:0 L:0
    Prefix Attribute Flags: X:0 R:0 N:1

  Hostname:       P-2
  Metric: 10         IS-Extended P-1.00
    Interface IP Address: 192.168.1.3
    Neighbor IP Address: 192.168.1.2
    Link Maximum SID Depth:                                          Adjacency SID
      Label Imposition: 10
    ADJ-SID: F:0 B:0 V:1 L:1 S:0 P:0 weight:0 Adjacency-sid:24005

  Router Cap:     10.0.1.2 D:0 S:0
    Segment Routing: I:1 V:0, SRGB Base: 16000 Range: 8000
    SR Local Block: Base: 15000 Range: 1000
    SR Algorithm:                                                    SRGB/SRLB
      Algorithm: 0
      Algorithm: 1

    Node Maximum SID Depth:                                          SID Depth
      Label Imposition: 10
```

SR-MPLS IS-IS Verification (IOS XE)

Output 4-10 shows the verification of several SR parameters advertised in the IS-IS LSP using the command **show isis database P-1.00-00 verbose**.

The Prefix SID, which is computed as the sum of the SRGB base (16001) and the Prefix SID index (1), is 16001.

One Adjacency SID is assigned and advertised for every Layer 3 adjacency in IS-IS. For the sake of simplicity, only one Adjacency SID is displayed in the output. Note that the Adjacency SID is advertised as an absolute value, without the index.

The start of the SRGB/SRLB and its range size are also advertised in IS-IS.

The maximum SID depth is shown to be 16.

Output 4-10   *Verifying the Prefix SID/Adjacency SID/SRGB/SRLB (IOS XE)*

```
P-1#show isis database P-1.00-00 verbose

IS-IS Level-2 LSP P-1.00-00
LSPID                    LSP Seq Num  LSP Checksum  LSP Holdtime/Rcvd      ATT/P/OL
P-1.00-00      * 0x00001C27   0x752B                  600/*          0/0/0
  Area Address: 49.0001
  NLPID:        0xCC
```

```
  Router CAP:   10.0.1.1, D:0, S:0
    Segment Routing: I:1 V:0, SRGB Base: 16000 Range: 8000
    Segment Routing Algorithms: SPF, Strict-SPF
    Segment Routing Local Block: SRLB Base: 15000 Range: 1000
```
SRGB/SRLB

```
  Node-MSD
       MSD: 16
```
SID Depth

```
  Hostname: P-1
  Metric: 10        IS-Extended P-1.00
    Adjacency SID Value:21 F:0 B:0 V:1 L:1 S:0 P:0 Weight:0
    Interface IP Address: 192.168.1.4
    Neighbor IP Address: 192.168.1.5
    Admin. Weight: 10
    Physical BW: 1000000 kbits/sec
    Admin. Weight: 10
    Physical LINK BW: 1000000 kbits/sec
```
Adjacency SID

```
  IP Address:   10.0.1.1
  Metric: 0          IP 10.0.1.1/32
    Prefix-attr: X:0 R:0 N:1
    Prefix-SID Index: 1, Algorithm:SPF, R:0 N:1 P:0 E:0 V:0 L:0
```
Node-SID

SR-MPLS Reachability Verification

This section focuses on the verification of the reachability of Node SIDs in Metro 1 shown in Figure 4-9. The control plane used to exchange routing and SR information is discussed in the sections "SR-MPLS IS-IS," earlier in this chapter, and "SR-MPLS OSPF," later in this chapter.

A ping from PE-1 to PE-2 is used to show the reachability of Node SIDs of the SR-MPLS network. Figure 4-9 shows how a ping from PE-1 to PE-2 traverses the SR-MPLS network using the MPLS label(s) at each hop.

Output 4-11 shows that the ping from PE-1 to PE-2 is successful.

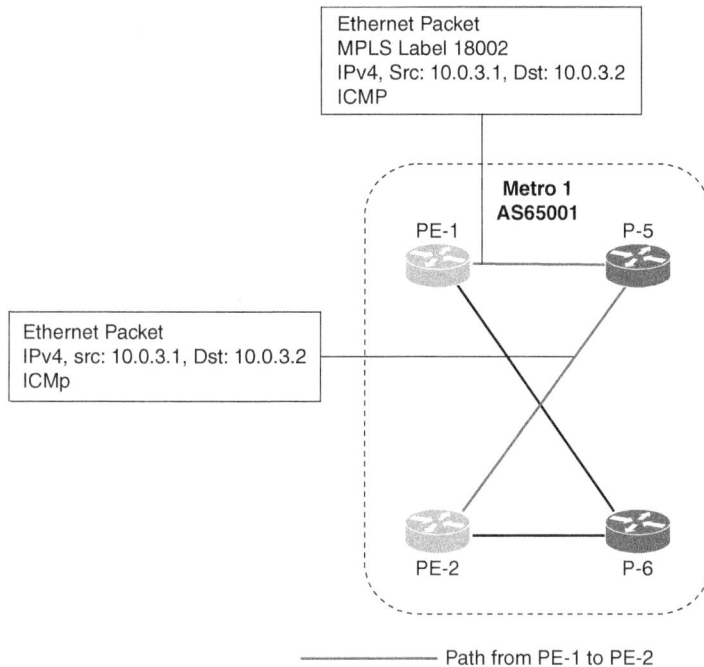

Figure 4-9 *Verifying Reachability of Node SIDs in the SR-MPLS Network: IS-IS*

Output 4-11 *Ping from PE-1 to PE-2*

```
RP/0/0/CPU0:PE -#ping 10.0.3.2 source lo0


Type escape sequence to abort.
Sending 5, 100-byte ICMP Echos to 10.0.3.2, timeout is 2 seconds:
!!!!!
Success rate is 100 percent (5/5), round-trip min/avg/max = 1/5/9 ms
```

The traceroute from PE-1 to PE-2 displayed in Output 4-12 validates the path shown in Figure 4-9. MPLS label 18002 is used for forwarding the packet on the link from PE-1 to P-5. Since P-5 is the penultimate hop from PE-1 to PE-2, P-5 pops the label and forwards the IPv4 packet to PE-2.

Output 4-12 *Traceroute from PE-1 to PE-2*

```
RP/0/0/CPU0:PE-1#traceroute 10.0.3.2 source lo0


Type escape sequence to abort.
Tracing the route to 10.0.3.2


 1  192.168.3.1 [MPLS: Label 18002 Exp 0] 19 msec  9 msec  0 msec <- P-5
 2  192.168.3.4 0 msec  *  0 msec <- PE-2
```

SR-MPLS OSPF

Protocol extensions for OSPF to support SR are described in Chapter 2, in the section "OSPF Extensions for Segment Routing (RFC 8665)."

OSPF is the IGP for Metro 2. All devices in Metro 2 are in OSPF Area 0.

SR-MPLS OSPF Configuration

SR must be enabled under OSPF to enable the advertisement of Prefix SIDs and Adjacency SIDs. Once SR is enabled under OSPF, Adjacency SIDs are allocated for every Layer 3 adjacency in OSPF. Config 4-15 and Config 4-16 show the configurations required to enable SR for OSPF and assign a Prefix SID to loopback0 on IOS XR and IOS XE devices. The Prefix SID is configured as an index in the case of IOS XR and as an absolute value for IOS XE to show that the Prefix SID can be configured either as an index or as an absolute value.

Config 4-15   *Enabling Segment Routing for OSPF (IOS XR)*

```
router ospf METRO2
 address-family ipv4 unicast
 area 0
  segment-routing mpls
  interface Loopback0
   prefix-sid index 3001
```

Config 4-16   *Enabling Segment Routing for OSPF (IOS XE)*

```
segment-routing
 connected-prefix-sid-map
  address-family ipv4
   10.0.4.2/32 absolute 19002 range 1
  exit-address-family

router ospf 1
 segment-routing mpls
```

SR-MPLS OSPF Verification (IOS XR)

Output 4-13 shows the verification of several SR parameters advertised in the OSPF LSP for IOS XR, using the command **show ospf database opaque-area self-originate**.

The Prefix SID, which is computed as the sum of the SRGB base (16000) and the Prefix SID index (3001), is 19001.

One Adjacency SID is assigned and advertised for every L3 adjacency in OSPF. For the sake of simplicity, only one Adjacency SID is displayed in the output. Note that the Adjacency SID is advertised as an absolute value, without the index.

The start of the SRGB/SRLB and its range size are also advertised in OSPF.

Output 4-13   *Verifying the Prefix SID/Adjacency SID/SRGB/SRLB (IOS XR)*

```
RP/0/RP0/CPU0:PE-3#show ospf data opaque-area self-originate

            OSPF Router with ID (10.0.4.1) (Process ID METR02)

                 Type-10 Opaque Link Area Link States (Area 0)

  LS age: 1624
 <snip>
    Segment Routing Algorithm TLV: Length: 2
       Algorithm: 0
       Algorithm: 1

    Segment Routing Range TLV: Length: 12
       Range Size: 8000

         SID sub-TLV: Length 3
          Label: 16000

    Node MSD TLV: Length: 2                          SRGB/SRLB/MSD
        Type: 1, Value 10

    Segment Routing Local Block TLV: Length: 12
       Range Size: 1000

         SID sub-TLV: Length 3
          Label: 15000

  LS age: 1624
 <snip>
    Extended Prefix TLV: Length: 20
       Route-type: 1
       AF        : 0
       Flags     : 0x40
       Prefix    : 10.0.4.1/32

       SID sub-TLV: Length: 8
         Flags    : 0x0
         MTID     : 0                                Node-SID
         Algo     : 0
         SID Index : 3001

  LS age: 1624
 <snip>
    Extended Link TLV: Length: 104
       Link-type : 1
       Link ID   : 10.0.1.7
       Link Data : 192.168.4.1

    Adj sub-TLV: Length: 7
       Flags    : 0x60
       MTID     : 0
       Weight   : 0
       Label    : 24001

    Local-ID Remote-ID sub-TLV: Length: 8
       Local Interface ID: 6
       Remote Interface ID: 3

    Remote If Address sub-TLV: Length: 4            Adjacency SID
       Neighbor Address: 192.168.4.0
```

SR-MPLS OSPF Verification (IOS XE)

Output 4-14 shows the verification of several SR parameters advertised in the OSPF LSP for IOS XE, using the command **show ospf database opaque-area self-originate**.

Output 4-14   *Verifying the Prefix SID/Adjacency SID/SRGB/SRLB (IOS XE)*

```
PE-4#show ip ospf database opaque-area self-originate

            OSPF Router with ID (10.0.4.2) (Process ID 1)

      Type-10 Opaque Area Link States (Area 0)


  LS age: 1808
<snip>
.-------------------------------------------------------------.
|   TLV Type: Segment Routing Range                           |
|   Length: 12                                                |
|     Range Size: 8000                                        |
|                                                             |
|     Sub-TLV Type: SID/Label                                 |
|     Length: 3                                               |
|       Label: 16000                                          |
|                                                             |
|   TLV Type: Segment Routing Node MSD              SRGB/SRLB/MSD
|   Length: 2                                                 |
|     Sub-type: Node Max Sid Depth, Value: 13                 |
|                                                             |
|   TLV Type: Segment Routing Local Block                     |
|   Length: 12                                                |
|     Range Size: 1000                                        |
|                                                             |
|     Sub-TLV Type: SID/Label                                 |
|     Length: 3                                               |
|       Label: 15000                                          |
'-------------------------------------------------------------'
  LS age: 1809
<snip>
.-------------------------------------------------------------.
|   TLV Type: Extended Prefix                                 |
|   Length: 20                                                |
|     Prefix   : 10.0.4.2/32                                  |
|     AF       : 0                                            |
|     Route-type: Intra                                       |
|     Flags    : N-bit                                        |
|                                                   Node-SID  |
|     Sub-TLV Type: Prefix SID                                |
|     Length: 8                                               |
|       Flags : None                                          |
|       MTID  : 0                                             |
|       Algo  : SPF                                           |
|       SID   : 3002                                          |
'-------------------------------------------------------------'
  LS age: 1813
<snip>
.-------------------------------------------------------------.
|   TLV Type: Extended Link                                   |
|   Length: 68                                                |
|   Link connected to : another Router (point-to-point)       |
|   (Link ID) Neighboring Router ID: 10.0.1.8                 |
|   (Link Data) Interface IP address: 192.168.4.5            |
|                                                             |
|     Sub-TLV Type: Adj SID                                   |
|     Length : 7                                              |
|       Flags  : L-Bit, V-bit                                 |
|       MTID   : 0                                  Adjacency SID
|       Weight : 0                                            |
|       Label  : 16                                           |
|                                                             |
|     Sub-TLV Type: Remote Intf Addr                          |
|       Remote Interface Address   : 192.168.4.4             |
|                                                             |
|     Sub-TLV Type: Local / Remote Intf ID                    |
|       Local Interface ID  : 7                               |
|       Remote Interface ID : 7                               |
'-------------------------------------------------------------'
```

The Prefix SID, which is computed as the sum of the SRGB base (16000) and the Prefix SID index (3002), is 19002.

One Adjacency SID is assigned and advertised for every L3 adjacency in OSPF. For the sake of simplicity, only one Adjacency SID is displayed in the output. Note that the Adjacency SID is advertised as an absolute value, without the index.

The start of the SRGB/SRLB and its range size are also advertised in OSPF.

SR-MPLS Reachability Verification

This section focuses on verifying the reachability of Node SIDs in the Metro 2 shown in Figure 4-10.

A ping from PE-3 to PE-4 is used to show the data forwarding capabilities of the SR-MPLS network. Figure 4-10 shows how a ping from PE-3 to PE-4 traverses the SR-MPLS network using the MPLS label(s) at each hop.

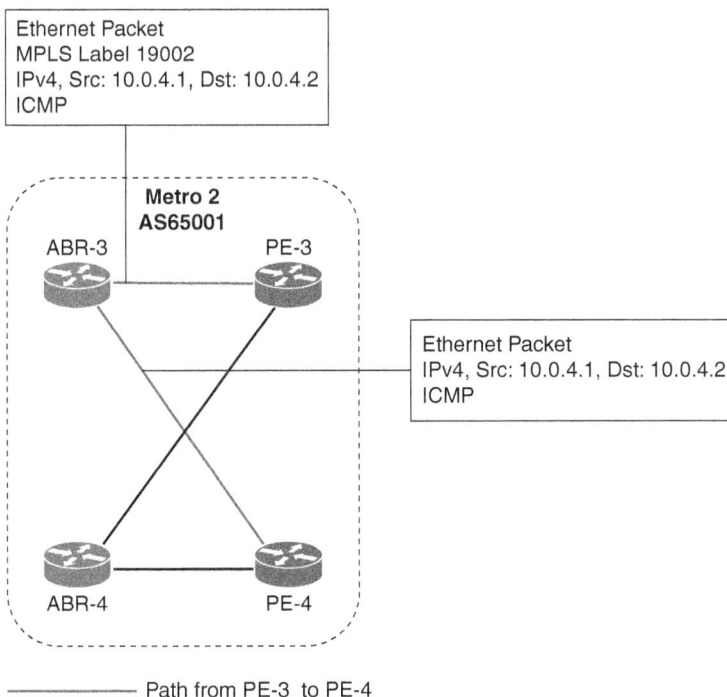

Figure 4-10   *Verifying Reachability of Node SIDs in the SR-MPLS Network: OSPF*

Output 4-15 shows that the ping from PE-3 to PE-4 is successful.

Output 4-15   *Ping from PE3 to PE-4*

```
RP/0/0/CPU0:PE-3#ping 10.0.4.2 source lo0

Type escape sequence to abort.
Sending 5, 100-byte ICMP Echos to 10.0.4.2, timeout is 2 seconds:
!!!!!
Success rate is 100 percent (5/5), round-trip min/avg/max = 9/11/19 ms
```

The traceroute from PE-3 to PE-4 displayed in Output 4-16 validates the path shown in Figure 4-10. MPLS label 18002 is used for forwarding the packet on the link from PE-1 to ABR-3. Because ABR-3 is the penultimate hop from PE-3 to PE-4, ABR-3 pops the label and forwards the IPv4 packet to PE-4.

Output 4-16   *Traceroute from PE-3 to PE-4*

```
RP/0/0/CPU0:PE-3#traceroute 10.0.4.2 source lo0

Type escape sequence to abort.
Tracing the route to 10.0.4.2

 1  192.168.4.0 [MPLS: Label 19002 Exp 0] 29 msec  19 msec  9 msec <- ABR-3
 2  192.168.4.7 19 msec  *  49 msec <- PE-4
```

SR-MPLS Anycast SID

An Anycast SID is a type of Prefix SID that identifies a set of nodes (anycast group) and is configured to advertise a shared prefix address and Prefix SID. Anycast routing enables the steering of traffic toward multiple advertising nodes. Packets addressed to an anycast address are forwarded to the topologically nearest node.

Figure 4-11 shows an autonomous system (AS 65001) with three domains. ABR-1 and ABR-2 are the area border routers between Metro 1 and Core 1. Traffic from Metro 1 to Metro 2 via Core 1 can be forwarded via ABR-1 or ABR-2 by using an anycast SID to provide redundancy and load balancing. More details about how to use an Anycast SID can be found in the section "SRv6 Anycast SID," later in this chapter.

SR-MPLS Anycast SID Configuration

An Anycast SID is configured by clearing the N-flag associated with a Prefix SID. For the configuration in this section, the Anycast SID (16100) is allocated to a prefix associated with a loopback. Loopback1 has the IP address 10.1.1.5/32 and the same IPv4 address, and Prefix SID is assigned to loopback1 on ABR-1 and ABR-2.

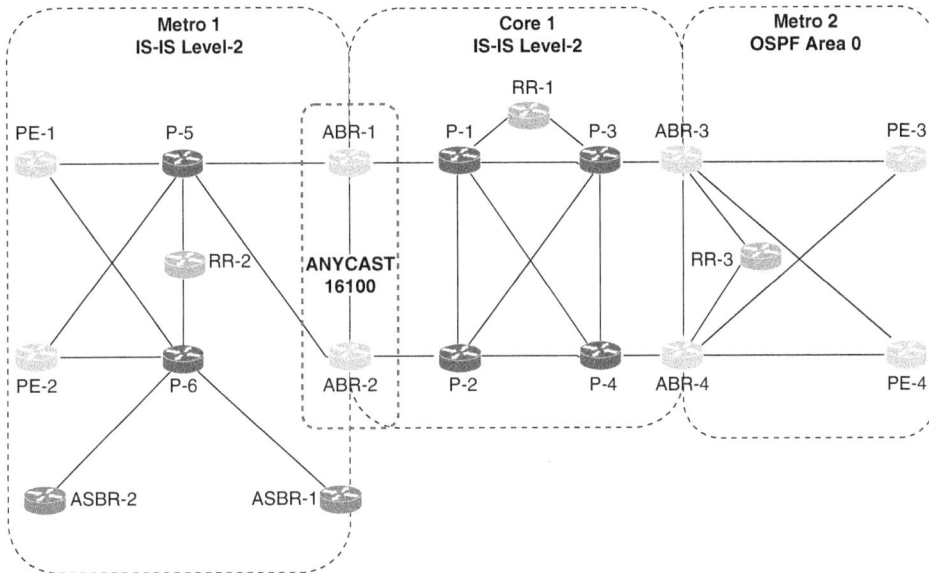

Figure 4-11 *Anycast SID on ABR-1 and ABR-2*

> **Note** The N-flag is set to indicate a Node SID. When the N-flag is clear, the SID represents a Prefix SID. An Anycast SID is a special subtype of Prefix SID.

ABR-1 is an IOS XR device where loopback1 is assigned the IP address 10.1.1.5/32 associated with the Anycast SID 16100. As mentioned before, an Anycast SID is configured by clearing the N-flag.

ABR-2 is an IOS XE devices. The steps to configure an Anycast SID involve assigning a Prefix SID (16100) to the IPv4 prefix (10.1.1.5) of interface loopback1. The n-flag of the prefix attribute is then cleared on interface loopback1 to indicate that the Prefix SID is an Anycast SID.

Config 4-17 and Config 4-18 show the configuration steps on IOS XR and IOS XE devices.

Config 4-17 *Configuring Anycast SID (IOS XR)*

```
interface Loopback1
 ipv4 address 10.1.1.5 255.255.255.255
 !

router isis CORE1
```

```
interface Loopback1
  prefix-attributes n-flag-clear
  address-family ipv4 unicast
   prefix-sid absolute 16100
  !
```

Config 4-18 *Configuring Anycast SID (IOS XE)*

```
interface Loopback1
 ip address 10.1.1.5 255.255.255.255
 isis prefix-attributes n-flag-clear level-1
 isis prefix-attributes n-flag-clear level-2
end

segment-routing mpls
 connected-prefix-sid-map
  address-family ipv4
   10.1.1.5/32 absolute 16100 range 1
  exit-address-family
```

SR-MPLS Anycast SID Verification

The advertisement of an anycast SID can be verified by checking the IS-IS LSP from ABR-1 and ABR-2. Output 4-17 shows that ABR-1 (an IOS XR device) advertises the prefix 10.1.1.5/32 in IS-IS with the Prefix SID index set to 100. The N-flag, which is part of the Prefix SID flag and prefix attribute flag, is clear, which means this SID is a Prefix SID and can be interpreted as an Anycast SID.

Note   RFC 8667 provides the following information about the Prefix SID flags and prefix attribute flags:

One the flags in the prefix-SID TLV is the N-Flag or Node-SID Flag. If set, then the prefix-SID refers to the router identified by the prefix. Typically, the N-Flag is set on prefix-SIDs that are attached to a router loopback address. The N-Flag is set when the prefix-SID is a Node-SID.

The Prefix Attribute Flags sub-TLV [RFC7794] also defines the N-Flag and R-Flag and with the same semantics of the prefix-SID flags. Whenever the Prefix Attribute Flags sub- TLV is present for a given prefix, the values of the N-Flag and R-Flag advertised in that sub-TLV MUST be used, and the values in a corresponding prefix-SID sub-TLV (if present) MUST be ignored.

Output 4-17 *Verifying the Advertisement of the Anycast SID (IOS XR)*

```
RP/0/0/CPU0:ABR-1#show isis database ABR-1.00-00 verbose

IS-IS CORE1 (Level-2) Link State Database
LSPID                     LSP Seq Num  LSP Checksum  LSP Holdtime/Rcvd  ATT/P/OL
ABR-1.00-00    * 0x000000f8   0x86d6        829  /*                0/0/0
  Area Address:    49.0001
  NLPID:           0xcc
  IP Address:      10.0.1.5
  <snip>
  Metric: 10          IP-Extended 10.1.1.5/32
    Prefix-SID Index: 100, Algorithm:0, R:0 N:1 P:0 E:0 V:0 L:0
    Prefix Attribute Flags: X:0 R:0 N:0
```

Output 4-18 shows that ABR-2 advertises the prefix 10.1.1.5/32 in IS-IS with the Prefix SID index set to 100 and the N-flag, which is shown as part of the Prefix-attr, is clear, indicating that this SID is an Anycast SID.

Output 4-18 *Verifying the Advertisement of the Anycast SID (IOS XE)*

```
ABR-2#show isis database ABR-2.00-00 version

IS-IS Level-2 LSP ABR-2.00-00
<snip>
  Hostname: ABR-2
<snip>
  Metric: 0           IP 10.1.1.5/32
    Prefix-attr: X:0 R:0 N:0
    Prefix-SID Index: 100, Algorithm:SPF, R:0 N:0 P:0 E:0 V:0 L:0
```

The section "SR-MPLS Anycast SID," earlier in this chapter, shows a use case where an Anycast SID is used for load balancing in an SR-MPLS network.

SRv6 Control Plane

This section provides the configuration and verification for enabling the IGP to propagate SRv6-related information. It focuses on the SRv6 control plane and how information is exchanged with other devices using IS-IS as the IGP. At this writing, IS-IS is the only IGP that supports SRv6 on IOS XR devices.

SRv6 IS-IS

IS-IS is a link-state routing protocol that relies on link-state protocol data units (LSPs) to advertise its routing information throughout the network. IS-IS LSPs contain many different Type Length Value (TLV) and sub-TLV fields, which provide a hierarchical, flexible, and easily extensible way of encoding routing information.

IS-IS extensions for SRv6 are described in RFC 9352. Details of the protocol extensions to IS-IS for SRv6 can be found in Chapter 3, in the section "IGP Extensions."

Figure 4-12 shows the SRv6 network that is used for validating the SRv6 configuration in this section.

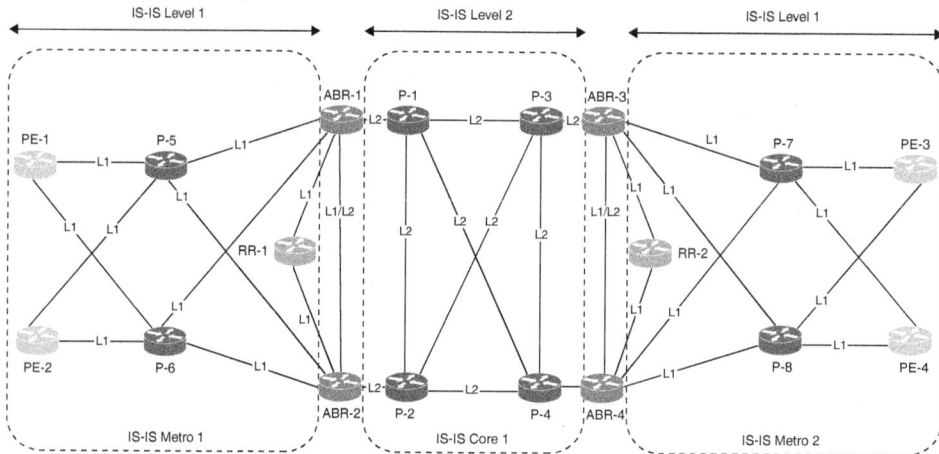

Figure 4-12   *SRv6 Network*

The network uses BGP AS 65000 and consists of the following:

- Core 1
  - Four P nodes (P-1, P-2, P-3, and P-4)
- Metro 1
  - Two ABRs (ABR-1 and ABR-2)
  - Two P nodes (P-5 and P-6)
  - Two PE nodes (PE-1 and PE-2)
  - One RR (RR-1)
  - Two CE nodes (CE-1 and CE-2)
- Metro 2
  - Two ABRs (ABR-3 and ABR-4)
  - Two P nodes (P-7 and P-8)
  - Two PE nodes (PE-3 and PE-4)

■ One RR (RR-2)

■ Two CE nodes (CE-3 and CE-4)

The IS-IS design for the SRv6 network shown in Figure 4-12 has the following features:

■ It uses the IS-IS multi-topology.

■ It is a hierarchy with Level 2 and Level 1 domains.

■ The core network is an IS-IS Level 2 domain.

■ The metro networks are in an IS-IS Level 1 domain.

■ Area border routers (ABRs) are Level 1–2 routers and provide connectivity between the metro networks and the core network.

■ IPv6 LLA is used for link addressing.

■ The SRv6 locator has the format fc00:000G:DDNN::/48, as described earlier, in the section, "SRv6 uSID Locator Addressing Scheme in This Chapter."

■ IS-IS NSAP NETID has the format 49.00DD.00DD.0000.00NN.00, where DD and NN are derived from the SRv6 locator.

■ The following domain IDs have been assigned for the SRv6 locators:

■ **Core:** 00

■ **Metro 1:** 01

■ **Metro 2:** 02

Table 4-2 provides the IS-IS NSAP, SRv6 locator, and IPv6 address of loopback0 for each of the devices in the SRv6 network.

Table 4-2 *IS-IS NSAP, SRv6 Locator, and Lo0 IPv6 Address Allocation for the SRv6 Network*

Host Name	IS-IS NSAP 49.00DD.00DD.0000.00NN.00	Loopback0 IPv6 Address	SRv6 Locator fc00:000GDDNN::/48
P-1	49.0000.0000.0000.0001.00	fc00:0000:0001::1/128	fc00:0000:0001::/48
P-2	49.0000.0000.0000.0002.00	fc00:0000:0002::1/128	fc00:0000:0002::/48
P-3	49.0000.0000.0000.0003.00	fc00:0000:0003::1/128	fc00:0000:0003::/48
P-4	49.0000.0000.0000.0004.00	fc00:0000:0004::1/128	fc00:0000:0004::/48
ABR-1	49.0001.0001.0000.0001.00	fc00:0000:0101::1/128	fc00:0000:0101::/48
ABR-2	49.0001.0001.0000.0002.00	fc00:0000:0102::1/128	fc00:0000:0102::/48
P-5	49.0001.0001.0000.0003.00	fc00:0000:0103::1/128	fc00:0000:0103::/48

Host Name	IS-IS NSAP 49.00DD.00DD.0000.00NN.00	Loopback0 IPv6 Address	SRv6 Locator fc00:000GDDNN::/48
P-6	49.0001.0001.0000.0004.00	fc00:0000:0104::1/128	fc00:0000:0104::/48
PE-1	49.0001.0001.0000.0005.00	fc00:0000:0105::1/128	fc00:0000:0105::/48
PE-2	49.0001.0001.0000.0006.00	fc00:0000:0106::1/128	fc00:0000:0106::/48
RR-1	49.0001.0001.0000.0007.00	fc00:0000:0107::1/128	fc00:0000:0107::/48
ABR-3	49.0002.0002.0000.0001.00	fc00:0000:0201::1/128	fc00:0000:0201::/48
ABR-4	49.0002.0002.0000.0002.00	fc00:0000:0202::1/128	fc00:0000:0202::/48
P-7	49.0002.0002.0000.0003.00	fc00:0000:0203::1/128	fc00:0000:0203::/48
P-8	49.0002.0002.0000.0004.00	fc00:0000:0204::1/128	fc00:0000:0204::/48
PE-3	49.0002.0002.0000.0005.00	fc00:0000:0205::1/128	fc00:0000:0205::/48
PE-4	49.0002.0002.0000.0006.00	fc00:0000:0206::1/128	fc00:0000:0206::/48
RR-2	49.0002.0002.0000.0007.00	fc00:0000:0207::1/128	fc00:0000:0207::/48

This section shows the steps involved in enabling IS-IS for SRv6 and the commands necessary to verify SRv6 functionality under IS-IS.

SRv6 IS-IS Configuration

Figure 4-13 shows the steps involved in configuring IS-IS for SRv6. Although the configuration steps are shown for only one device, they must be completed on all the devices that support SRv6. Because there are several types of devices with different roles (P, ABR, PE, and RR), the configuration is shown for one of each device type:

- **IS-IS Level 2 device:** P device

- **IS-IS Level 1–2 device:** ABR device

- **IS-IS Level 1 device:** PE device

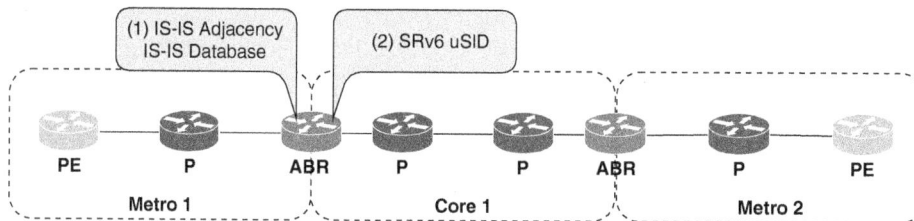

Figure 4-13 *IS-IS and SRv6 uSID Configuration*

The metric style is set to wide because this is a requirement for enabling SRv6. Config 4-19 shows the different parts of the configuration to enable IS-IS for SRv6. Loopback0 is for configuring the IPv6 address of loopbacl0 interface. The SRv6 locator is configured under segment-routing. Under router isis *<process name>*, the router type and NSAP are configured. IS-IS SRv6 is enabled under address-family iov6 unicast. Finally, the interface is included under IS-IS, and the type of the interface is also configured.

Config 4-19   *Configuring IS-IS*

```
interface Loopback0
  ipv6 address fc00:0:1::1/128
```
Loopback 0

```
segment-routing
  srv6
    encapsulation
      source-address fc00:0:1::1
    !
    locators
      locator MAIN
        prefix fc00:0:1::/48
```
SRv6 Locator

```
router isis CORE_1
  is-type level-2-only
  net 49.0000.0000.0000.0001.00
```
IS-IS Router Type and NSAP

```
address-family ipv6 unicast
  metric-style wide
  router-id Loopback0
  segment-routing srv6
    locator MAIN
```
IS-IS SRv6

```
interface GigabitEthernet0/0/0/0
  circuit-type level-2-only
  point-to-point
```
IS-IS Interface Configuration

These are the device-specific IS-IS parameters:

■ **P device in Core 1 (P-1):** P-1 in Core 1 is in IS-IS Level 2, and its IS-IS NETID is 49.0000.0000.0000.0001.00. Because P-1 is in IS-IS Level 2, the router type is set to level-2, and the circuit type is configured as level-2. The SRv6 locator MAIN is allocated the prefix fc00:0:1::/48 and is included in IS-IS under segment-routing. Finally, the IPv6 address of loopback0 is fc00:0:1::1/128, which is derived from the locator MAIN. The configuration for P-1 is shown in Config 4-20.

- **ABR device in Metro 1 (ABR-1):** ABR-1 in Metro 1 is in IS-IS Level 1–2, with the IS-IS NETID set to 49.0001.0001.0000.0001.00. Because ABR-1 is in IS-IS Level 1–2, the router type is set to level-1-2, and the circuit type is configured as level-1-2. The SRv6 locator MAIN is allocated the prefix fc00:0:101::/48 and is included in IS-IS under segment-routing. Finally, fc00:0:101::1/128 is assigned to the IPv6 address of loopback0. The configuration for ABR-1 is shown in Config 4-21.

- **PE device in Metro 1 (PE-1):** PE-1 in Metro 1 is in IS-IS Level 1, with the IS-IS NETID set to 49.0001.0001.0000.0005.00. Because PE-1 is in IS-IS Level 1, the router type is set to level-1, and the circuit type is configured as level-1. The SRv6 locator MAIN is allocated the prefix fc00:0:105::/48, which is included in IS-IS under segment-routing. The IPv6 address of loopback0 is assigned fc00:0:105::1/128. The configuration for PE-1 is shown in Config 4-22.

- **Route reflector device in Metro Domain 1 (RR-1):** The route reflector (RR) need not be a part of the SRv6 domain because it is not in the data forwarding path for any service that uses SRv6 as transport. This device needs IP connectivity to other devices to exchange control plane information via BGP. However, to keep the configuration simple and uniform, SRv6 is enabled on the RR. The configuration on the RR is like the configuration on PE-1.

Note   RR can use IPv4 or IPv6 for the BGP sessions with other BGP speakers in the network. Since IPv6 is already enabled for SRv6, it is logical for the RR to use IPv6 for the BGP sessions.

RR-1 in Metro 1 is in IS-IS Level 1, and its IS-IS NETID is 49.0001.0001.0000.0007.00. Because RR-1 is in IS-IS Level 1, the router type is set to level-1, and the circuit type is configured as level-1. The SRv6 locator MAIN is allocated the prefix fc00:0:107::/48 and is included in IS-IS under segment-routing. The loopback0 is assigned fc00:0:107::1/128 as its IPv6 address, which is derived from the SRv6 locator MAIN. The configuration for RR-1 is shown in Config 4-23.

Config 4-20   *Configuring IS-IS on P-1 (IOS XR)*

```
interface Loopback0
 ipv6 address fc00:0:1::1/128



segment-routing
 srv6
  locators
   locator MAIN
    prefix fc00:0:1::/48


```

```
router isis CORE_1
 is-type level-2-only
 net 49.0000.0000.0000.0001.00
 address-family ipv6 unicast
  metric-style wide
  router-id Loopback0
  segment-routing srv6
   locator MAIN

 interface GigabitEthernet0/0/0/0
  circuit-type level-2-only
  point-to-point
```

Config 4-21 *Configuring IS-IS on ABR-1 (IOS XR)*

```
interface Loopback0
 ipv6 address fc00:0:101::1/128


segment-routing
 srv6
  locators
   locator MAIN
    prefix fc00:0:101::/48

router isis METRO_1
 net 49.0001.0001.0000.0001.00
 is-type level-1-2
 address-family ipv6 unicast
  metric-style wide
  router-id Loopback0
  segment-routing srv6
   locator MAIN

 interface GigabitEthernet0/0/0/0
  circuit-type level-2-only
  point-to-point
```

Config 4-22 *Configuring IS-IS on PE-1 (IOS XR)*

```
interface Loopback0
 ipv6 address fc00:0:105::1/128
```

```
segment-routing
 srv6
  encapsulation
   source-address fc00:0:105::1
  !
  locators

   locator MAIN
    prefix fc00:0:105::/48

router isis METRO_1
 is-type level-1
 net 49.0001.0001.0000.0005.00
 address-family ipv6 unicast
  metric-style wide
  router-id Loopback0
  segment-routing srv6
   locator MAIN

 interface GigabitEthernet0/0/0/0
  point-to-point
 <snip>
```

Config 4-23   *Configuring IS-IS on RR-1 (IOS XR)*

```
interface Loopback0
 ipv6 address fc00:0:107::1/128



segment-routing
 srv6
  encapsulation
   source-address fc00:0:107::1
  !
  locators
   locator MAIN
    prefix fc00:0:107::/48

router isis METRO_1
 is-type level-1
 net 49.0001.0001.0000.0007.00
 address-family ipv6 unicast
  metric-style wide
 router-id Loopback0
  segment-routing srv6
```

```
   locator MAIN


  interface GigabitEthernet0/0/0/0
  point-to-point
<snip>
```

SRv6 IS-IS Verification

This section provides the commands and the relevant output to verify the IS-IS and SRv6 functionality. Figure 4-14 shows the steps for this verification, which are valid for all the devices in the SRv6 network.

The command to check IS-IS adjacency, **show isis adjacency**, helps to verify that the IS-IS configuration required to exchange the LSPs with the neighbors is correct. The command **show isis database level <n> <LSP ID>** is used to verify that the SRv6-related information is conveyed to all the IS-IS neighbors in the LSPs.

Verifying the SRv6 uSIDs helps to validate that the SRv6 end node behavior is correctly programmed on the device.

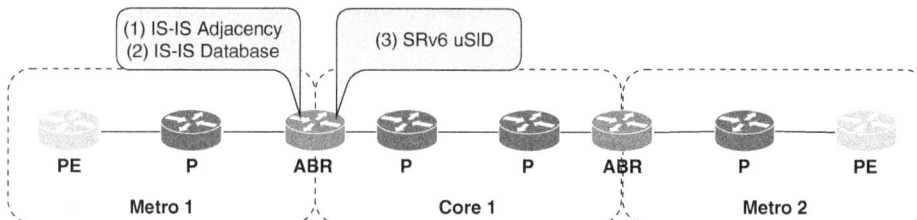

Figure 4-14   *Verifying IS-IS and SRv6 uSID*

Step 1: Verify IS-IS Adjacency

Output 4-19 shows that the command **show isis adjacency** is used to verify that IS-IS adjacencies (Level 1 and Level 2) on ABR-1 have been established. All the adjacencies in Level 2 and Level 1 are up. The output indicates the interface and the duration for which the adjacency has been established. Other information included in the output is related to the status of the BFD (IPv4 and IPv6) configured under the IS-IS process and the NSF capabilities of the device.

Output 4-19   *IS-IS Adjacencies on ABR-1*

```
RP/0/RP0/CPU0:ABR-1#show isis adjacency

IS-IS METRO_1 Level-1 adjacencies:
System Id      Interface         SNPA          State Hold Changed  NSF IPv4 IPv6
```

```
                                                                    BFD   BFD
ABR-2         Gi0/0/0/2              *PtoP*          Up    29   2w0d  Yes None None
P-5           Gi0/0/0/1              *PtoP*          Up    29   2w0d  Yes None None


RR-1          Gi0/0/0/4              *PtoP*          Up    21   2w0d  Yes None None


Total adjacency count: 3


IS-IS METRO_1 Level-2 adjacencies:
System Id     Interface             SNPA          State Hold Changed  NSF IPv4 IPv6
                                                                       BFD   BFD
ABR-2         Gi0/0/0/2              *PtoP*          Up    29   2w0d  Yes None None
P-1           Gi0/0/0/0              *PtoP*          Up    22   2w0d  Yes None None


Total adjacency count: 2
```

Step 2: Verify the IS-IS Database

The IS-IS database shows the SRv6 capability, SRv6 locator, SRv6 uSIDs, and IPv6 prefixes advertised by every device. The command **show isis database level 2 ABR-1.00-00 detail verbose** is used to show the information advertised by ABR-1 to its Level 2 neighbors. Output 4-20 has several sections and has been snipped to reduce the verbosity and to more clearly show the relevant parts of the output:

- **Link to neighbor and the Adjacency SIDs:** This part of the output provides info about the link and the Adjacency SIDs that are associated with this link, including information about the flex algo. Note that Adjacency SIDs are allocated for each flex algo.

- **SRv6 locator and Summary for algo 0:** The summary route for algo 0 is advertised as an IPv6 external route and does not contain the flex algo information. The SRv6 locator for algo 0 is also advertised as a prefix.

Step 3: Verify the SRv6 SIDs

Node SID

Output 4-21 shows the SRv6 uN allocated by the SID manager, which is advertised in IS-IS as an SRv6 locator.

Output 4-20 *Verifying SRv6 IS-IS*

```
RP/0/RP0/CPU0:ABR-1#show isis data level 2 ABR-1.00-00 detail  ver

IS-IS METRO_1 (Level-2) Link State Database
LSPID              LSP Seq Num  LSP Checksum  LSP Holdtime/Rcvd  ATT/P/OL
ABR-1.00-00     * 0x00000a34   0x9d36       848  /*            0/0/0
  Area Address:   49.0001
  LSP MTU:        1492
  NLPID:          0x8e
  MT:             IPv6 Unicast                            0/0/0
  Hostname:       ABR_M1_1
  Router Cap:     0.0.0.0 D:0 S:0

<snip>

  SRv6 Locator:   MT (IPv6 Unicast) fc00:0:101::/48 D:0 Metric: 1 Algorithm: 0     SRv6 Locator
    Prefix Attribute Flags: X:0 R:0 N:0 E:0 A:0                                     for base algo
    END SID: fc00:0:101:: uN (PSP/USD)
      SID Structure:
        Block Length: 32, Node-ID Length: 16, Func-Length: 0, Args-Length: 80

  Metric: 10       MT (IPv6 Unicast) IS-Extended P-1.00
    Local Interface ID: 3, Remote Interface ID: 3
    Physical BW: 1000000 kbits/sec
    Link Average Delay: 100 us
    Link Min/Max Delay: 100/100 us
    Link Delay Variation: 0 us
    Application Specific Link Attributes:
      L flag: 0, SA-Length: 1, UDA-Length: 1
      Standard Applications: 0x10 FLEX-ALGO
      User Defined Applications: 0x10
      Ext Admin Group:
        0x00000002
      Affinity: 0x00000002
      Link Min/Max Delay: 100/100 us
    END.X SID: fc00:0:101:e002:: B:1 S:0 P:0 uA (PSP/USD) Alg:0                      Link to Neighbor
      SID Structure:                                                                      and
        Block Length: 32, Node-ID Length: 16, Func-Length: 16, Args-Length: 64     Adjacency SIDS
    END.X SID: fc00:0:101:e003:: B:0 S:0 P:0 uA (PSP/USD) Alg:0
      SID Structure:
        Block Length: 32, Node-ID Length: 16, Func-Length: 16, Args-Length: 64
  Metric: 10       MT (IPv6 Unicast) IS-Extended ABR-2.00
    Local Interface ID: 5, Remote Interface ID: 5
    END.X SID: fc00:0:101:e000:: B:1 S:0 P:0 uA (PSP/USD) Alg:0
      SID Structure:
        Block Length: 32, Node-ID Length: 16, Func-Length: 16, Args-Length: 64
    END.X SID: fc00:0:101:e001:: B:0 S:0 P:0 uA (PSP/USD) Alg:0
      SID Structure:
        Block Length: 32, Node-ID Length: 16, Func-Length: 16, Args-Length: 64
```

Output 4-21 *uN Allocated by SRv6 SID Manager*

```
RP/0/RP0/CPU0:ABR-1#show segment-routing srv6 sid


*** Locator: 'MAIN' ***
SID                        Behavior         Context
  Owner           State RW
------------------------   ----------------  -------------------------------
  ------------------  -----  --
fc00:0:101::                 uN (PSP/USD)     'default':257
  sidmgr            InUse  Y
```

For every L3 adjacency, two routable Adjacency SIDs with PSP/USD behavior are
allocated as shown in Output 4-22. For the sake of simplicity, the Adjacency SID for only
one L3 adjacency (Gi0/0/0/2) is shown in the output. The protected Adjacency SID indicated by :P is platform dependent.

Output 4-22   *uA SID Allocated by SID Manager*

```
RP/0/RP0/CPU0:ABR-1#show segment-routing srv6 sid

*** Locator: 'MAIN' ***

SID                           Behavior         Context
  Owner                State RW
--------------------------    ----------------  ------------------------------- ----
  -------------- ----- --
<snip>
fc00:1:101:e000::             uA (PSP/USD)     [Gi0/0/0/2, Link-Local]:128:P
  isis-METRO_1        InUse Y
fc00:1:101:e001::             uA (PSP/USD)     [Gi0/0/0/2, Link-Local]:128
  isis-METRO_1        InUse Y
<snip>
```

The routable SIDs are advertised in IS-IS where fc00:0:101:e000 has the backup flag set to 1, indicating that this Adjacency SID is eligible for protection, as shown in Output 4-23.

Output 4-23   *uA SID Advertised in IS-IS*

```
RP/0/RP0/CPU0:ABR-1#show isis database level 1 ABR-1.00-00 det verbose

IS-IS METRO_1 (Level-1) Link State Database
LSPID                  LSP Seq Num  LSP Checksum  LSP Holdtime/Rcvd  ATT/P/OL
ABR-1.00-00       * 0x00000e9a   0x70b2         618 /*              0/0/0
<snip>
  Metric: 10        MT (IPv6 Unicast) IS-Extended ABR-2.00
    Local Interface ID: 6, Remote Interface ID: 5
    END.X SID: fc00:0:101:e000:: B:1 S:0 P:0 uA (PSP/USD) Alg:0
      SID Structure:
        Block Length: 32, Node-ID Length: 16, Func-Length: 16, Args-Length: 64
    END.X SID: fc00:0:101:e001:: B:0 S:0 P:0 uA (PSP/USD) Alg:0
      SID Structure:
        Block Length: 32, Node-ID Length: 16, Func-Length: 16, Args-Length: 64
<snip>
```

The output of the commands in this section is platform dependent. On some platforms the shift and PSP/USD endpoint entries are merged, and on others there are separate entries for shift and PSP/USD endpoints. This capability can be verified by using the command **show segment-routing srv6 manager internal**, as shown in Output 4-24, where you can see that the shift and PSP/USD endpoint entries are separate.

Output 4-24 *Platform Capability for Separate Shift and Non-Shift Endpoint Entries*

```
RP/0/RP0/CPU0:ABR-1#show segment-routing srv6 manager internal

<snip>
Platform Capabilities:
<snip>
  uSID Endpoint Entries:
    Local Only: Yes
    Global-Local Combo: Yes
    Separate Shift and Non-Shift: Yes
<snip>
```

Output 4-25 shows that Router1 has combined shift and PSP/USD endpoint entries.

Output 4-25 *Platform Capability for Combined Shift and Non-Shift Endpoint Entries*

```
Router1#show segment-routing srv6 manager internal

<snip>
  uSID Endpoint Entries:
    Local Only: Yes
    Global-Local Combo: Yes
    Separate Shift and Non-Shift: No
    Shift-Only Drop: No
<snip>
```

For every IS-IS adjacency, four Adjacency SIDs with shift and PSP/USD behavior are allocated and locally installed in the routing table. Two of these non-routable UAs are protected, and the other two are unprotected. However, these Adjacency SIDs are not routable and have only local significance to optimize forwarding operations. Note that the availability of protected non-routable UAs is platform dependent.

For the sake of simplicity, the Adjacency SID for only one L3 adjacency (Gi0/0/0/0) is shown in Output 4-26. The output shows that for every L3 adjacency, there are four Adjacency SID entries in the RIB. The output shows the network function (shift or PSP/USD) and outgoing interface where the packet is.

Output 4-26 *Non-Routable uA SIDs*

```
RP/0/RP0/CPU0:ABR-1#show route ipv6 local-srv6

<snip>
L    fc00:0:e000::/48, SRv6 Endpoint uA (shift)
       [0/0] via fe80::42:acff:fe15:7b02, 1w1d, GigabitEthernet0/0/0/2
```

```
L    fc00:0:e000::/64, SRv6 Endpoint uA (PSP/USD)
      [0/0] via fe80::42:acff:fe15:7b02, 1w1d, GigabitEthernet0/0/0/2
L    fc00:0:e001::/48, SRv6 Endpoint uA (shift)
      [0/0] via fe80::42:acff:fe15:7b02, 1w1d, GigabitEthernet0/0/0/2
L    fc00:0:e001::/64, SRv6 Endpoint uA (PSP/USD)
      [0/0] via fe80::42:acff:fe15:7b02, 1w1d, GigabitEthernet0/0/0/2
<snip>
```

SRv6 Reachability Verification

The previous sections show the configuration and verification of IS-IS for SRv6. This section shows the verification of the reachability of the Node SIDs and the routable Adjacency SIDs using a ping from PE-1 to PE-3.

Output 4-27 and Output 4-28 show the successful ping from PE-1 to the Node SID of PE-3 (fc00:0:205::) and to the Adjacency SID of PE-3 (fc00:0:205:e000::).

Output 4-27   *Node SID Reachability*

```
RP/0/RP0/CPU0:PE-1#ping ipv6 fc00:0:205::

Type escape sequence to abort.
Sending 5, 100-byte ICMP Echos to fc00:0:205::, timeout is 2 seconds:
!!!!!
Success rate is 100 percent (5/5), round-trip min/avg/max = 6/9/15 ms
```

Output 4-28   *Adjacency SID Reachability*

```
RP/0/RP0/CPU0:PE-1#ping ipv6 fc00:0:205::e000

Type escape sequence to abort.
Sending 5, 100-byte ICMP Echos to fc00:0:205::e000, timeout is 2 seconds:
!!!!!
Success rate is 100 percent (5/5), round-trip min/avg/max = 6/7/8 ms
```

SRv6 Anycast SID

An SRv6 anycast locator is a type of locator that is associated with a set of nodes (an anycast group) in an SRv6 network. Nodes in an anycast group are configured to advertise a shared anycast locator and associated uN SID. Anycast routing enables the routing of traffic toward multiple advertising nodes, and packets destined to an anycast address are forwarded to the topologically nearest node in the anycast group. One of the use cases for anycast in an SRv6 network is to advertise anycast uN SIDs at midpoints in the

SRv6 network, thereby making it possible to forward traffic to the topologically nearest exit point in the SRv6 network.

The following behaviors apply to an anycast locator:

- IS-IS does not program any advertise Adjacency SIDs associated with an anycast locator.

- SRv6 anycast locators can be assigned to flex algos.

Figure 4-15 shows the SRv6 network with Anycast SID configured on ABR-1 and ABR-2. The section "SRv6 Anycast SID Use Case," later in this chapter, explains the use case where Anycast SIDs are used to steer traffic from PE-1 to PE-3 via ABR-1 and ABR-2 for Layer 3 VPN services. The next two sections show how to configure and verify SRv6 anycast locators.

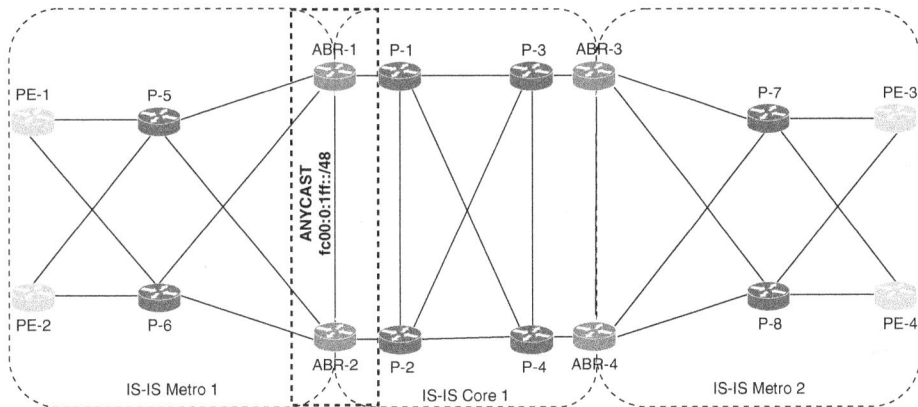

Figure 4-15 *Anycast SID on ABR-1 and ABR-2*

SRv6 Anycast SID Configuration

The anycast locator is configured on devices that belong to the anycast group. Config 4-24 shows the configuration of an SRv6 locator named ANYCAST and the command **anycast** used to indicate that the locator is an anycast locator.

Config 4-24 *Configuring Anycast SRv6 Locator on P-3 (IOS XR)*

```
segment-routing
 srv6
  locators
   locator ANYCAST
    micro-segment behavior unode psp-usd
    prefix fc00:0:1ff::/48
    anycast
```

SRv6 Anycast SID Verification

The command **show isis database level-1 ABR-1.00-01 detail verbose** is used to verify that the anycast flag is set for the SRv6 locator fc00:0:1ff::/48, as shown in Output 4-29. The A flag, which is part of the prefix attribute flags, is set to indicate that the locator fc00:0:1ff::/48 is an anycast locator.

Output 4-29   *Anycast Flag for SRv6 Locator fc00:0:1ff::/48*

```
RP/0/RP0/CPU0:ABR-2#show isis database level 1 ABR-1.00-01 detail verbose


IS-IS METRO_1 (Level-1) Link State Database
LSPID               LSP Seq Num  LSP Checksum  LSP Holdtime/Rcvd  ATT/P/OL
ABR-1.00-01         0x00000efb   0xb256          585  /1200          0/0/0
<snip>
  SRv6 Locator:    MT (IPv6 Unicast) fc00:0:1ff::/48 D:0 Metric: 1 Algorithm: 0
    Prefix Attribute Flags: X:0 R:0 N:0 E:0 A:1
    END SID: fc00:0:1ff:: uN (PSP/USD)
      SID Structure:
        Block Length: 32, Node-ID Length: 16, Func-Length: 0, Args-Length: 80
<snip>
```

SRv6 Anycast SID Use Case

Figure 4-16 shows the use case for anycast SID in the SRv6 network. The Anycast SID configured on ABR-1, and ABR-2 is used to forward traffic to the nearest exit point from the IS-IS domain Metro 1. An SRv6 traffic engineering policy uses the Anycast SID to steer traffic from PE-1 to PE-3 via ABR-1 and ABR-2.

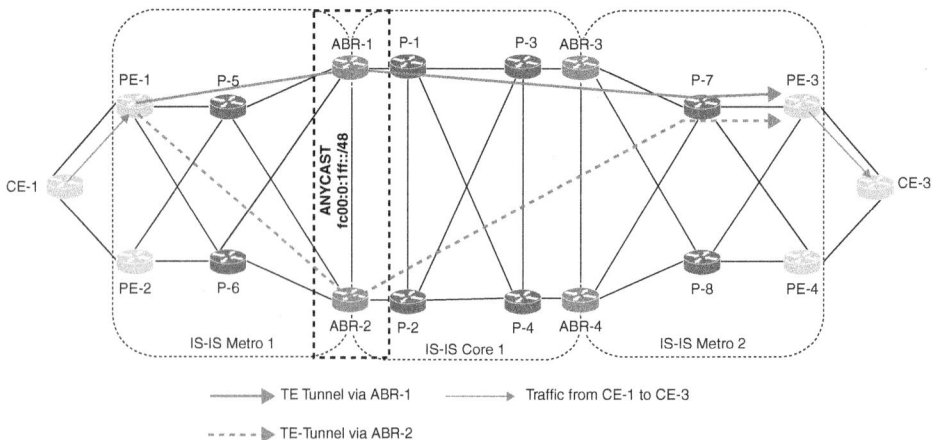

Figure 4-16   *Anycast Use Case for Layer 3 VPN Service*

Note Segment Routing for Traffic Engineering (SR-TE) uses a policy to steer traffic through the network. An SR-TE policy path is expressed as a list of segments. The concept of SR-TE for SR-MPLS and SRv6 networks is the same except in the notion of segments or SIDs.

Connectivity between CE-1 to CE-3 is provided using Layer 3 VPN services on PE-1 and PE-3. Traffic from CE-1 to CE-3 is forwarded via an SRv6 traffic engineering policy with explicit hops. The headend of the policy is PE-1, the destination is PE-3, and the first hop of the policy is the Anycast SID on ABR-1 and ABR-2. Once the traffic from CE-1 reaches PE-1, it is routed via the SRv6 policy to ABR-1 or ABR-2 (Anycast SID) and then to PE-3. PE-3 decapsulates the IPv6 header and forwards the IPv4 packet to CE-3.

The configuration required to steer traffic from CE-1 to CE-3 via the SRv6 TE tunnel has two parts:

- SR-TE policy definition on PE-1

- Traffic steering configuration on PE-3

Config 4-25 on PE-1 shows an SRv6 traffic engineering policy called ANYCAST that is configured with the following parameters:

- The destination is PE-3.

- The color is 1. The color parameter is helpful in traffic steering. Any BGP prefix with the color attribute set to 1 will forward the traffic via this SRv6 policy.

- An explicit path is specified by a segment list that includes the Anycast SID (fc00:0:1ff::) and the Node SID (fc00:0:203::) of ABR-3.

Config 4-26 shows the configuration for traffic steering on the egress PE-3, where the BGP attribute color is set to 1 for all the IPv4 routes of the VRF instance TEST using route-policy (COLOR_RP). When ingress PE-1 receives a BGP VPNv4 update for the IPv4 prefix vrf TEST with the color 1, it forwards all traffic destined for prefixes from the VRF instance TEST via the SRv6 ANYCAST policy.

Config 4-25 *SRv6-TE Policy and Traffic Steering Using Color on Ingress PE-1 (IOS XR)*

```
segment-routing
 traffic-eng
  segment-lists
   srv6
    sid-format usid-f3216
   !
   segment-list ANYCAST
```

```
   srv6
     index 10 sid fc00:0:1ff::
     index 20 sid fc00:0:203::
    !
  !
 !
policy ANYCAST
 srv6
   locator MAIN binding-sid dynamic behavior ub6-insert-reduced
  !
 color 1 end-point ipv6 fc00:0:205::1
 candidate-paths
  preference 100
    explicit segment-list ANYCAST
```

Config 4-26   *SRv6-TE Policy and Traffic Steering Using Color on Ingress PE-1 (IOS XR)*

```
extcommunity-set opaque ANYCAST
  1
end-set
!

route-policy COLOR_RP
  set extcommunity color ANYCAST
end-policy
!

vrf TEST
 rd 65000:1
 address-family ipv4 unicast
  import route-target
   65000:1
  !
  export route-policy COLOR_RP
  export route-target
   65000:1
```

Output 4-30 shows the verification of the SRv6-TE policy using the command **show segment-routing traffic-eng policy**. The output shows the following information:

■ The name of the policy is srte_c_1_ep_fc00:0:205::1.

■ The color of the policy is 1. This is same as the BGP attribute color of the VPN prefix 10.2.1.128/32. All BGP routes with color attribute 1 will be routed using this SR-TE policy.

- The destination is fc00:0:205::1.

- The operational status of the TE tunnel is up.

- The candidate path is an explicit list of segments (fc00:0:1ff::/48 and fc00:0:205::/48), as specified in the SR policy. The segment list ANYCAST is the candidate path, and its state is indicated as valid.

- The Binding SID is fc00:0:105:e00c:: with behavior End.B6.Insert.red.

This output confirms that all BGP prefixes that have color attribute set to 1 are routed using this SRv6-TE policy.

Output 4-30   *Verifying the SR-TE Tunnel Status and Attributes*

```
RP/0/RP0/CPU0:PE_M1_5#show segment-routing traffic-eng policy

SR-TE policy database
---------------------

Color: 1, End-point: fc00:0:205::1                                    Color

  Name: srte_c_1_ep_fc00:0:205::1                                     Name

  Status:
    Admin: up  Operational: up for 03:57:25 (since Jul  6 23:18:05.156) Status
  Candidate-paths:
  <snip>
    Explicit: segment-list ANYCAST (valid)
        Weight: 1, Metric Type: TE
        SID[0]: fc00:f:101::/48
                Format: f3216
                LBL:32 LNL:16 FL:0 AL:80
        SID[1]: fc00:0:205::/48                                       Explicit-Path
                Format: f3216
                LBL:32 LNL:16 FL:0 AL:80
    SRv6 Information:
      Locator: MAIN
      Binding SID requested: Dynamic
      Binding SID behavior: End.B6.Insert.Red

  Attributes:
    Binding SID: fc00:0:105:e00c::                                    Binding SID

  <snip>
```

On PE-1, Output 4-31 shows that the BGP prefix 10.2.1.128 advertised has the color attribute set to 1 and is reachable via the SRv6-TE policy with color 1.

Output 4-31   *Verifying the Color Attribute of BGP Prefix 10.2.1.128*

```
RP/0/RP0/CPU0:PE-1#show bgp vrf TEST 10.2.1.128


BGP routing table entry for 10.2.1.128/32, Route Distinguisher: 65000:1
<snip>
  Advertised to CE peers (in unique update groups):
    10.1.1.2
  200
    fc00:0:205::1 C:1 (bsid: fc00:0:105:e00c::) (metric 61) from fc00:0:107::1
    (172.19.0.19)
      Received Label 0xe00a0
      Origin IGP, metric 0, localpref 100, valid, internal, best, group-best,
  import-candidate, imported
      Received Path ID 0, Local Path ID 1, version 915
      Extended community: Color:1 RT:65000:1
      Originator: 172.19.0.19, Cluster list: 172.19.0.12, 172.19.0.21
      SR policy color 1, up, not-registered, bsid fc00:0:105:e00e::
<snip>
```

Output 4-32 shows the CEF entry for prefix 10.2.1.128 in the VRF instance TEST, which indicates that PE-1 routes the traffic via the Binding SID (fc00:0:105:e00c::/64), which corresponds to the Binding SID of the SRv6-TE policy. The recursive lookup for the Binding SID in CEF indicates that it is routed via fc00:0:1ff::, which is the Anycast SID of ABR-1 and ABR-2, and fc00:0:205::, which is the Node SID of ABR-3.

Output 4-32   *Verifying the CEF Entry for 10.2.1.128/32*

```
RP/0/RP0/CPU0:PE-1#show cef vrf TEST 10.2.1.128


10.2.1.128/32, version 164, SRv6 Headend, internal 0x5000001 0x30 (ptr 0x871c13b8)
  [1], 0x0 (0x0), 0x0 (0x899f3cc8)
<snip>

  via local-srv6-sid fc00:0:105:e00c::, 3 dependencies, recursive [flags 0x6000]
    path-idx 0 NHID 0x0 [0x86fdcd40 0x0]
    recursion-via-/64
    next hop VRF - 'default', table - 0xe0800000
    next hop fc00:0:105:e00c:: via fc00:0:105:e00c::/64
    SRv6 H.Encaps.Red SID-list {fc00:0:205:e00a::}
      SRv6 H.Insert.Red SID-list {fc00:0:1ff:: fc00:0:203::}
<snip>


RP/0/RP0/CPU0:PE-1#show cef ipv6 fc00:0:105:e00c::
fc00:0:105:e00c::/64, version 2914, SRv6 Endpoint uB6 (Insert.Red), internal
  0x1000001 0x200 (ptr <snip>
    next hop fe80::42:acff:fe15:8002/128
    SRv6 H.Insert.Red SID-list {fc00:0:1ff:: fc00:0:203::}
```

The outgoing packet on the link between PE-1 and P-4 that is shown in Output 4-33 indicates the IPv6 header and the segment routing header (SRH) inserted by PE-1. The IPv6 destination address corresponds to the Anycast SID, and the SRH contains the rest of the segment list to reach the destination PE-3. Note that the original destination IPv6 address for forwarding the packet to PE-3 (fc00:0:205:e00a) is also inserted into the SRH.

Output 4-33   *SRH Packet with IPv6 Destination Address and SRH*

```
Ethernet
Internet Protocol Version 6, Src: fc00:0:105::1, Dst: fc00:f:101::
    0110 .... = Version: 6
    .... 0000 0000 .... .... .... .... .... = Traffic Class: 0x00 (DSCP: CS0, ECN: Not-ECT)
    .... 0000 0000 0000 0000 = Flow Label: 0x00000
    Payload Length: 140
    Next Header: Routing Header for IPv6 (43)
    Hop Limit: 58
    Source Address: fc00:0:105::1
    Destination Address: fc00:f:101::                                    Destination IPv6 Address

    Routing Header for IPv6 (Segment Routing)
        Next Header: IPIP (4)
        Length: 4
        [Length: 40 bytes]
        Type: Segment Routing (4)
        Segments Left: 1                                                 Segment Routing Header
        Last Entry: 1
        Flags: 0x00
        Tag: 0000
        Address[0]: fc00:0:205:e00a::
        Address[1]: fc00:0:203::
Internet Protocol Version 4, Src: 10.1.1.1, Dst: 10.2.1.128
Internet Control Message Protocol
```

A ping from CE-1 to CE-3 is used to verify the data forwarding from CE-1 to CE-3, as shown in Output 4-34.

Output 4-34   *Ping from CE-1 to CE-3*

```
RP/0/RP0/CPU0:CE-1#ping 10.2.1.128

Type escape sequence to abort.
Sending 5, 100-byte ICMP Echos to 10.2.1.128 timeout is 2 seconds:
!!!!!
Success rate is 100 percent (5/5), round-trip min/avg/max = 8/9/11 ms
```

Figure 4-17 traces the path of the packet destined for CE-3 as it traverses the SRv6 network. Two flows are used to demonstrate the load balancing when using the Anycast SID. One flow is from CE-1 to CE-3, where the destination IP address is 10.1.200.128. The second flow is from CE-1 to CE-3, where the destination IP address 10.1.200.129. PE-1 is the ingress PE for both the flows.

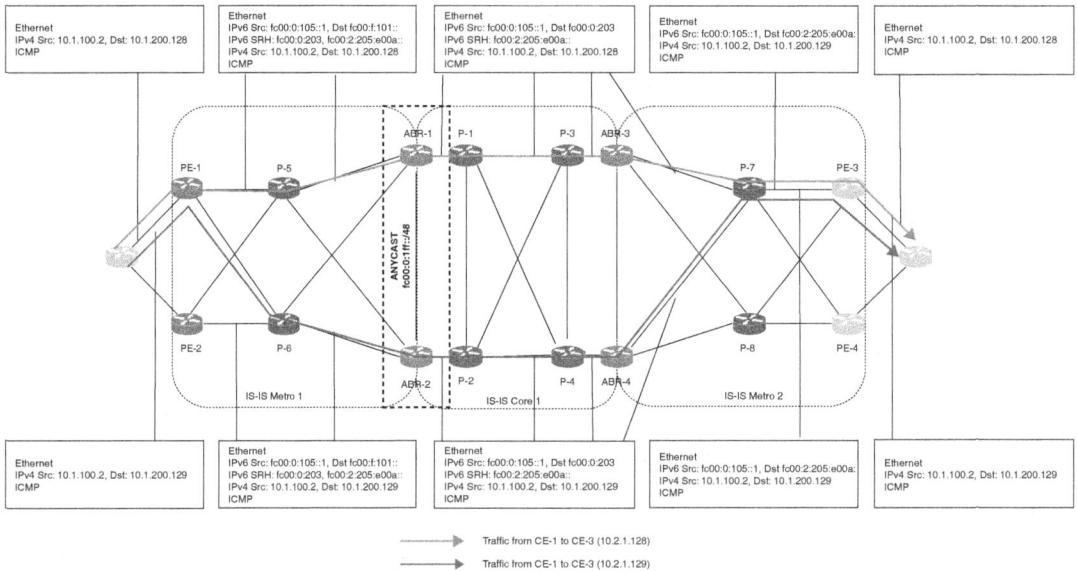

Figure 4-17 *Anycast Use Case: Data Plane Forwarding*

The routing table on PE-1, as shown in Output 4-35, indicates that both prefixes are reachable via fc00:0:105:e00c::, which is the Binding SID of the SRv6 policy.

Output 4-35 *RIB Entry for 10.02.1.128/32 and 10.2.1.129/32*

```
RP/0/RP0/CPU0:PE-1#show route vrf TEST 10.2.1.128


Routing entry for 10.2.1.128/32
<snip>
  Installed Jul  6 23:18:05.159 for 2d00h
  Routing Descriptor Blocks
    fc00:0:205::1, from fc00:0:107::1 via srv6-sid fc00:0:105:e00c:: (resolution len 64)
      Nexthop in Vrf: "default", Table: "default", IPv6 Unicast, Table Id:
0xe0800000
      Route metric is 0
  No advertising protos.


RP/0/RP0/CPU0:PE-1#show route vrf TEST 10.2.1.129


Routing entry for 10.2.1.129/32
<snip>
  Routing Descriptor Blocks
    fc00:0:205::1, from fc00:0:107::1 via srv6-sid fc00:0:105:e00c:: (resolution len 64)
      Nexthop in Vrf: "default", Table: "default", IPv6 Unicast, Table Id:
0xe0800000
      Route metric is 0
  No advertising protos.
```

The CEF entry displayed in Output 4-36 shows two SRv6 SID lists:

■ SRv6 H.Encaps.Red SID-list {fc00:0:205:e00a::}

■ SRv6 H.Insert.Red SID-list {fc00:0:1ff:: fc00:0:203::}

Output 4-36   *CEF Entry for 10.2.1.128/32 and 10.2.1.129/32*

```
RP/0/RP0/CPU0:PE-1#show cef vrf TEST 10.2.1.128


10.2.1.128/32, version 164, SRv6 Headend, internal 0x5000001 0x30 (ptr 0x871c13b8)
  [1], 0x0 (0x0), 0x0 (0x899f3cc8)
<snip>
   via local-srv6-sid fc00:0:105:e00c::, 3 dependencies, recursive [flags 0x6000]
    path-idx 0 NHID 0x0 [0x86fdcd40 0x0]
    recursion-via-/64
    next hop VRF - 'default', table - 0xe0800000
    next hop fc00:0:105:e00c:: via fc00:0:105:e00c::/64
    SRv6 H.Encaps.Red SID-list {fc00:0:205:e00a::}
      SRv6 H.Insert.Red SID-list {fc00:0:1ff:: fc00:0:203::}
<snip>



RP/0/RP0/CPU0:PE-1#show cef vrf TEST 10.2.1.129


10.2.1.129/32, version 165, SRv6 Headend, internal 0x5000001 0x30 (ptr 0x871c15a8)
  [1], 0x0 (0x0), 0x0 (0x899f3b38)
<snip>
   via local-srv6-sid fc00:0:105:e00c::, 3 dependencies, recursive [flags 0x6000]
    path-idx 0 NHID 0x0 [0x86fdcd40 0x0]
    recursion-via-/64
    next hop VRF - 'default', table - 0xe0800000
    next hop fc00:0:105:e00c:: via fc00:0:105:e00c::/64
    SRv6 H.Encaps.Red SID-list {fc00:0:205:e00a::}
      SRv6 H.Insert.Red SID-list {fc00:0:1ff:: fc00:0:203::}
<snip>
```

As a quick recap, H.Encaps.Red (S1) encapsulates the payload with an IPv6 header with the destination set to S1, and H.Insert.Red (S2,S3) inserts the current destination IPv6 address and S3 into the SRH and sets the destination address to S3. More details can be found in the section "IPv6 Segment Routing Header (SRH) (RFC 8754)" In Chapter 3.

Replacing S1 with fc00:0:205:e00a::, H.Encaps.Red {fc00:0:205:e00a::} results in the IPv4 payload encapsulated in an IPv6 packet with destination IPv6 address fc00:0:205:e00a::. Substituting S2 and S3 with fc00:0:1ff:: and fc00:0:203::, the subsequent H.Insert.Red {fc00:0:1ff:: fc00:0:203::} operation results in fc00:0:205:e00a:: and fc00:-:205::0 inserted to the SRH and fc00:0:1ff set as the destination IPv6 address. Output 4-37 shows this in the outgoing packet on PE-1.

Output 4-37   *Packet with SRH*

```
Ethernet
Internet Protocol Version 6, Src: fc00:0:105::1, Dst: fc00:0:205::
    0110 .... = Version: 6
    .... 0000 0000 .... .... .... .... .... = Traffic Class: 0x00 (DSCP: CS0, ECN: Not-ECT)
    .... 0000 0000 0000 0000 0000 = Flow Label: 0x00000
    Payload Length: 140
    Next Header: Routing Header for IPv6 (43)
    Hop Limit: 58
    Source Address: fc00:0:105::1
    Destination Address: fc00:0:205::                                       Destination IPv6 Address

    Routing Header for IPv6 (Segment Routing)
        Next Header: IPIP (4)
        Length: 4
        [Length: 40 bytes]
        Type: Segment Routing (4)
        Segments Left: 1
        Last Entry: 1                                                       Segment Routing Header
        Flags: 0x00
        Tag: 0000
        Address[0]: fc00:0:205:e00a::
        Address[1]: fc00:0:203::
Internet Protocol Version 4, Src: 10.1.1.1, Dst: 10.2.1.128
Internet Control Message Protocol
```

Since the IPv6 destination address for both the flows is fc00:0:1ff::, which is the Anycast SID of ABR-1 and ABR-2, one flow destined to 10.2.1.129/32 is sent to ABR-1, and the second flow destined to 10.2.1.129/32 is sent to ABR-2. This results in load balancing of the traffic, as shown in Figure 4-17.

ABR-1 and ABR-2 receive packets with the destination IPv6 address set to fc00:0:1ff:: and the SRH with two segments {fc00:0:205:e00a, fc00:0:205::}. On ABR-1 and ABR-2, fc00:0:1ff:: corresponds to the PSP/USD function (see Output 4-38).

Output 4-38   *RIB Entry for fc00:0:1ff:: on ABR-1 and ABR-2*

```
RP/0/RP0/CPU0:ABR-1#show route ipv6 fc00:0:1ff::

Routing entry for fc00:0:1ff::/64
  Known via "local-srv6 sidmgr", distance 0, metric 0, SRv6 Endpoint uN (PSP/USD),
  SRv6 Format f3216
  Installed May 30 05:38:26.135 for 5w4d
  Routing Descriptor Blocks
    directly connected
      Route metric is 0
  No advertising protos.
```

```
RP/0/RP0/CPU0:ABR-2#show route ipv6 fc00:0:1ff::


Routing entry for fc00:0:1ff::/64
  Known via "local-srv6 sidmgr", distance 0, metric 0, SRv6 Endpoint uN (PSP/USD),
  SRv6 Format f3216
  Installed May 30 05:38:17.575 for 5w2d
  Routing Descriptor Blocks
    directly connected
      Route metric is 0
  No advertising protos.
```

As a quick recap about PSP, endpoint behavior happens when the SRH segments left is 0. The new active segment is copied into the IPv6 destination address.

ABR-1 and ABR-2 execute a PSP (Penultimate Segment Pop)/USD (Ultimate Segment Decapsulation) behavior, and the new active segment (fc00:0:203::) in the SRH replaces the destination IPv6 address. The IPv6 hop limit and number of segments left in the SRH are decremented by 1. The packet with destination IPv6 address set to fc00:0:203:: and SRH with one segment {fc00:0:205:e00a} are forwarded by the rest of the nodes on the path to PE-3 without any changes.

On ABR-3, fc00:0:203::/64 corresponds to PSP/USD endpoint behavior (see Output 4-39). PE-3 does a PSP and replaces the IPv6 destination address with the new active segment in the SRH (fc00:0:205:e00a), updates the SRH (zero segments are left in SRH, meaning that the SRH is now deleted), and forwards the packet.

Output 4-39   *RIB Entry for fc00:0:205::/64 on PE-3*

```
RP/0/RP0/CPU0:PE-3#sh route ipv6 fc00:0:205::/64


Routing entry for fc00:0:205::/64
  Known via "local-srv6 sidmgr", distance 0, metric 0, SRv6 Endpoint uN (PSP/USD),
  SRv6 Format f3216
  Installed May 30 06:24:45.905 for 5w3d
  Routing Descriptor Blocks
    directly connected
      Route metric is 0
  No advertising protos.
```

The destination IPv6 address fc00:0:205:e00a:: corresponds to the uDT4 behavior on PE-3 (see Output 4-40). Now PE-3 decapsulates the IPv6 header and forwards the IPv4 packet toward CE-3.

Output 4-40   *RIB Entry for fc00:0:205:e00a:: on PE-3*

```
RP/0/RP0/CPU0:PE-3#show route ipv6 fc00:0:205:e00a::

Routing entry for fc00:0:205:e00a::/64
Known via "local-srv6 bgp-65000", distance 0, metric 0, SRv6 Endpoint uDT4,
SRv6 Format f3216
Installed May 30 06:26:17.194 for 5w2d
Routing Descriptor Blocks
  ::ffff:0.0.0.0 directly connected
    Nexthop in Vrf: "TEST", Table: "default", IPv4 Unicast, Table Id: 0xe0000002
    Route metric is 0
No advertising protos.
```

In the event of the failure of ABR-2, traffic that was flowing via ABR-2 is rerouted via ABR-1, as shown in Figure 4-18.

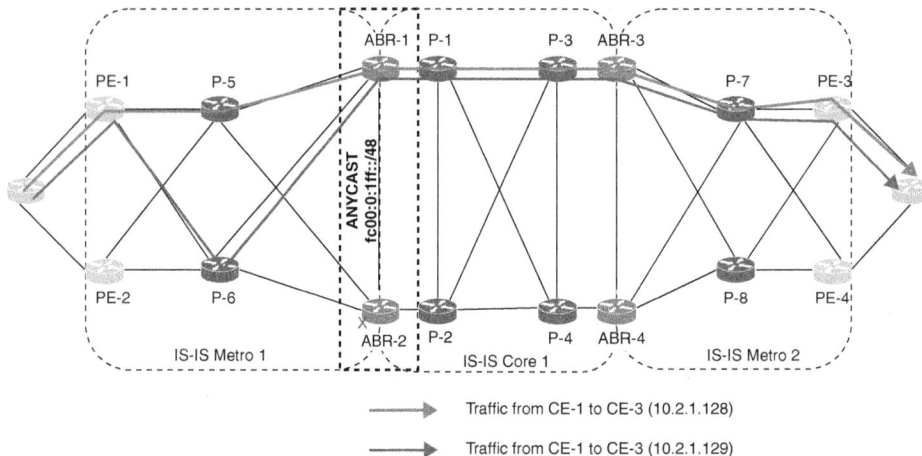

Figure from CE-1 to CE-3 (10.2.1.128)
Traffic from CE-1 to CE-3 (10.2.1.129)

Figure 4-18   *Anycast Use Case: Traffic Reroute via ABR-1*

SRv6 IS-IS Summarization

One of the main advantages of SRv6 technology is the scalability of the network in terms of number of devices in the network. SRv6 provides features and services like SR-MPLS but with much higher scalability in terms of the number of SRv6 devices. The key concept to scalability is the applicability of classless interdomain routing (CIDR) to SRv6 uSID networks.

A very large network with tens of thousands of devices cannot be built using a single IGP domain due to scalability side effects negatively affecting link-state databases and SPF calculations. The network must be split into multiple IGP domains either using the hierarchical structure of IGP protocols (IS-IS levels or OSPF areas) or using different IGP processes. However, redistributing all locators across all IGP domains would be beyond the capability of the IGP.

SRv6 offers a very elegant solution to this problem: summarization. With summarization, every ABR in an IGP domain propagates a few summary prefixes instead of the SRv6 locators of all the devices in an IGP domain. Unlike in an SR-MPLS network, summarization does not break the forwarding capabilities of SRv6 because the forwarding in an SRv6 network is based on the longest prefix lookup of the destination IPv6 address. An SRv6 device in an IS-IS Level 1 domain has complete visibility within the IS-IS Level 1 domain. Traffic destined to SRv6 devices in remote domains is routed to the nearest local ABR, which forwards it to the destination ABR.

There are different ways to implement summarization with or without a default route in the local domain. We will look at different choices when implementing summarization, highlighting the drawbacks of each choice and how the next choice overcomes some of the drawbacks of the previous choice.

Figure 4-19 shows summarization in an SRv6 network with two metros and one core network. The metro and core domains are allocated one or more fc00:0:*DD*::/40 IPv6 blocks, where *DD* represents the domain ID. The SRv6 locators in a domain are assigned from the allocated /40 block(s). Each metro generates one or more /40 summary routes toward the core domain, summarizing all the SRv6 locators in the metro. The forwarding from the source to the destination located in different IS-IS domains is based on the following:

- From the source to the local ABR, it is based on the default route advertised by the ABR in the local domain. This is optional and depends on the attach bit set by the ABR for the algo 0.

- From the local ABR to the remote ABR, it is based on the summary route advertised by the remote ABR.

- From the remote ABR to the destination, it is based on a device-specific route in the remote domain.

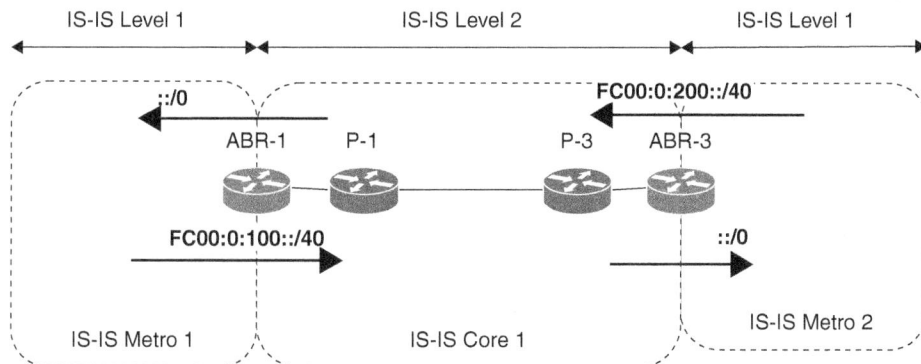

Figure 4-19 *Summarization in the SRv6 Network: Default Route*

While the default route simplifies the size of the routing table, it introduces additional problems. Hence, it not recommended to use the default route. These are the problems associated with default-route in the routing table:

- Traffic blackholing may occur. This means traffic for an unknown destination is routed via the default route to the ABR(s) and is dropped on the ABR when there is no specific route to the destination.

- By default, BGP sessions cannot be established when a remote BGP peer is reachable via the default route.

- BGP next hop tracking (NHT) cannot track the reachability of a remote BGP peer because it is always reachable via the default route.

Note   By default, BGP sessions cannot be established based on the default route in IOS XR.

Note   BGP next hop tracking is a feature that is event based and reduces the BGP convergence time by monitoring reachability of the BGP next hop.

The problems with the default route described previously can be remedied when the ABR advertises a summary covering all the SRv6 locators (fc00:0::/32) into IS-IS Level 1 instead of advertising the default route, as shown in Figure 4-20. Note that every IS-IS Level 1 device installs a default route pointing to the ABR when the attached bit is set by the ABR. The forwarding from the source to the destination located in different IS-IS domains is based on the following:

- From the source to the local ABR, it is based on the super summary route advertised by the local ABR

- From the local ABR to the remote ABR, it is based on the summary route advertised by the remote ABR.

- From the remote ABR to the destination, it is based on the device specific route in the remote domains.

Suppressing the default route solves the problem related to BGP sessions with devices in other metros. It does not solve the problem related to BGP NHT for BGP peers in the local metro and the remote metros, though, because the summary route prevents the BGP NHT from scheduling a next hop scan.

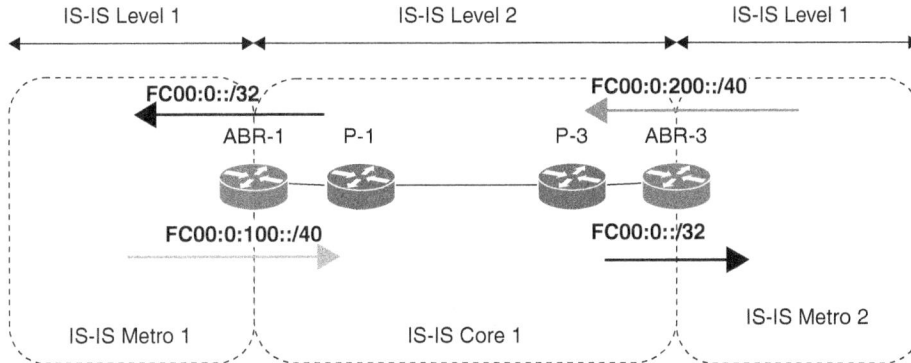

Figure 4-20   *Summarization in the SRv6 Network: Super Summary fc00:0::/32*

To overcome all the problems discussed so far, the ABR suppresses the advertisement of the default route and advertises the /40 summary(ies) (from all the remote metros) into IS-IS Level 1, as shown in Figure 4-21. The forwarding from the source to the destination located in a different IS-IS domain is based on the following:

- From the source to the local ABR, it is based on the summary route advertised by the local ABR.

- From the local ABR to the remote ABR, it is based on the summary route advertised by the remote ABR.

- From the remote ABR to the destination, it is based on the device specific route in the remote domains.

This solution addresses all the issues related to the default route except the BGP NHT for BGP peers in remote metros, which is addressed in the section "Unreachable Prefix Announcement (UPA)," later in this chapter.

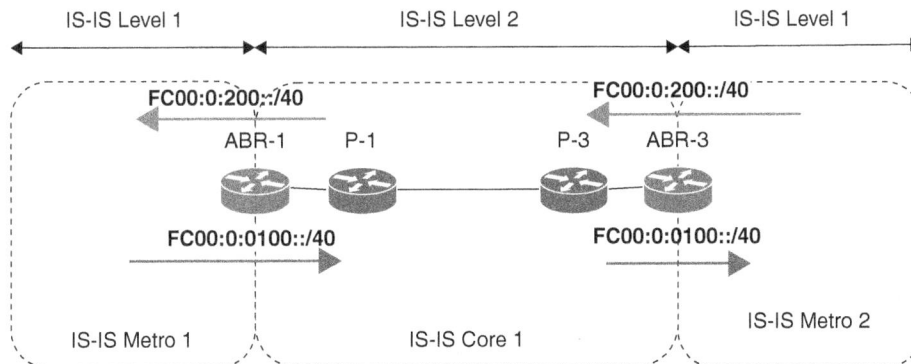

Figure 4-21   *Summarization in the SRv6 Network: Specific Summaries*

SRv6 IS-IS Summarization Configuration

Figure 4-22 shows the configuration steps for summarization, which are relevant only on the ABRs. This section provides the configuration for ABR-1 in Metro 1.

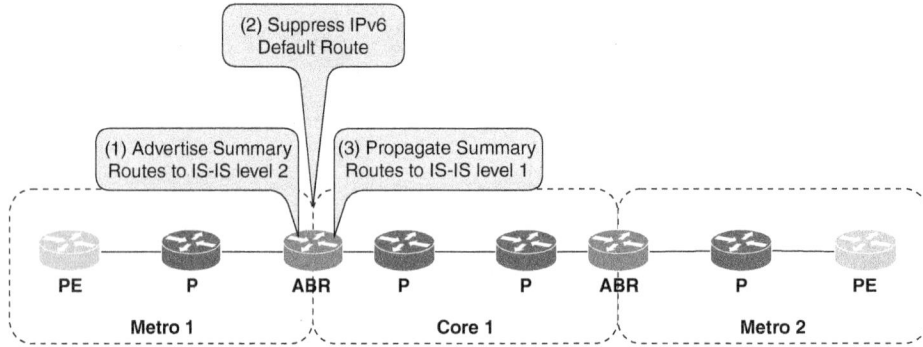

Figure 4-22 *Summarization: Configuration Steps*

The first step is to advertise the summary routes to IS-IS Level 2. Every ABR is configured to generate one or more summary routes toward the Level 2 core domain. In the event that a metro has multiple /40 IPv6 blocks due to a large number of devices, more than one summary route will be required. Config 4-27 shows the /40 summary route generated by the ABRs in Metro 1.

Config 4-27 *Summary Route Advertisement (IOS XR)*

```
router isis METRO_1
 address-family ipv6 unicast
    summary-prefix fc00:0:100::/40 level 2
```

The next step is to suppress the IPv6 default route. The ABRs suppress the advertisement of the default route. By default, the ABRs advertise the default route into IS-IS Level 1. The attached bit is unset to modify this behavior of the ABR, as shown in Config 4-28, and applied to all the ABRs.

Config 4-28 *Suppressing Default Route Generation (IOS XR)*

```
router isis METRO_1
 address-family ipv6 unicast
  attached-bit send never-set
```

The final step is to propagate the summary routes to IS-IS Level 1. ABRs selectively propagate routes from IS-IS Level 2 into IS-IS Level 1. By default, no routes from IS-IS Level 2 are advertised into IS-IS Level 1. Routes are leaked from IS-IS Level 2 to IS-IS Level

1 using a route policy with the following rules to allow the /40 summary routes from remote metros:

■ The prefix set IPV6_LOCAL_SUMMARY_PS is used to drop all summary routes that are local to this metro to prevent the local summary route from leaking back to the metro IS-IS Level 1.

■ The prefix set IPV6_L2_SUMMARY_PS is used to allow all /40 summary routes from remote metros.

Config 4-29 shows the route policy configuration to propagate routes from IS-IS Level 2 to Level 1, which is configured on all the ABRs in Metro 1.

Config 4-29   *Route Leaking from IS-IS Level 2 to IS-IS Level 1 (IOS XR)*

```
prefix-set IPV6_LOCAL_SUMMARY_PS
  fc00:0:100::/40 eq 40,
  fc00:1:100::/40 eq 40,
  fc00:2:100::/40 eq 40,
  fc00:3:100::/40 eq 40
end-set
!
prefix-set IPV6_L2_SUMMARY_PS
  fc00::/32 ge 40,
  fc00:1::/32 ge 40,
  fc00:2::/32 ge 40,
  fc00:3::/32 ge 40,
  fc00:f::/32 ge 40
end-set
!
route-policy IPV6_L2_TO_L1_RP
  if destination in IPV6_LOCAL_SUMMARY_PS then
    drop
  elseif destination in IPV6_L2_SUMMARY_PS then
    pass
  endif
end-policy

router isis METRO_1
 address-family ipv6 unicast
  propagate level 2 into level 1 route-policy IPV6_L2_TO_L1_RP
```

SRv6 IS-IS Summarization Verification

Figure 4-23 shows the steps required to verify that summarization has been configured properly and the routers are behaving as expected.

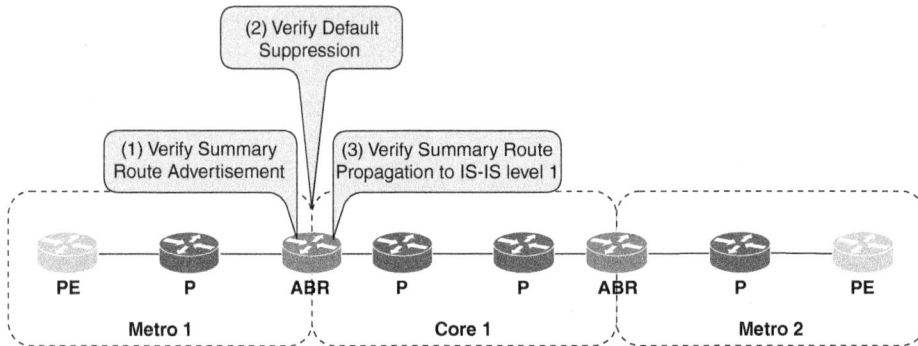

Figure 4-23 *Summarization: Verification Steps*

The first step is to verify the summary route advertisement. All the ABRs advertise summary routes for a metro as IPv6 external routes. The command **show isis database ABR-1.00-00 level 2 detail** is used for this verification (see Output 4-41).

Note   At this writing, IPv6 summary routes for the base algo (algo 0) are advertised as IPv6 external routes. IPv6 summary routes for flex algo N (N > 127) are advertised as SRv6 locators to include the algorithm number.

Output 4-41 *Summary Route Advertised by ABR-1*

```
RP/0/RP0/CPU0:ABR-1#show isis database ABR-1.00-00 level 2 detail

IS-IS METRO_1 (Level-2) Link State Database
LSPID                   LSP Seq Num  LSP Checksum  LSP Holdtime/Rcvd  ATT/P/OL
ABR-1.00-00        * 0x00001497   0xb8e7       853  /*              0/0/0
  Area Address:   49.0001
  LSP MTU:        1492
  NLPID:          0x8e
  MT:             IPv6 Unicast                              0/0/0
  Hostname:       ABR-1
  Router Cap:     0.0.0.0 D:0 S:0
  SRv6 Locator:   MT (IPv6 Unicast) fc00:0:101::/48 D:0 Metric: 1 Algorithm: 0
  Metric: 10         MT (IPv6 Unicast) IS-Extended P-1.00
  Metric: 10         MT (IPv6 Unicast) IS-Extended ABR-2.00
  Metric: 11         MT (IPv6 Unicast) IPv6-External fc00:0:100::/40
  Metric: 1          MT (IPv6 Unicast) IPv6 fc00:0:101::/48
```

ABR-1 inserts a discard route pointing to null0 for fc00:0:100::/40 to ensure that ABR-1 does not forward traffic for unknown destinations covered by fc00:0:100::/40. The command **show route ipv6 fc00:0:100::/40** is used to verify the discard route on the ABR as shown in Output 4-42.

Output 4-42   *Summary Route on ABR-1*

```
RP/0/RP0/CPU0:ABR-1#show route ipv6 fc00:0:100::/40


Routing entry for fc00:0:100::/40
  Known via "isis METRO_1", distance 115, metric 11 (summary), type manual summary
  Installed May  6 08:47:54.463 for 03:59:50
  Routing Descriptor Blocks
    directly connected, via Null0
      Route metric is 11
  No advertising protos.
```

The next step is to verify the default route suppression. Output 4-43 shows that the attached bit (ATT) is set in the LSP of ABR-1 before the command to suppress the default route advertisement, shown in Config 4-28, is configured on the router.

Note   The attached bit is shown under MT (which stands for multi-topology) for IPv6.

Output 4-43   *Attached Bit on ABR-1*

```
RP/0/RP0/CPU0:ABR-1#show isis database ABR-1.00-00 detail level 1


IS-IS METRO_1 (Level-1) Link State Database
LSPID                   LSP Seq Num  LSP Checksum  LSP Holdtime/Rcvd  ATT/P/OL
ABR-1.00-00           * 0x00001474   0x8f16            1088 /*           1/0/0
  Area Address:   49.0001
  LSP MTU:        1492
  NLPID:          0x8e
  MT:             IPv6 Unicast                                          1/0/0
<snip>
```

As a result of the attached bit in the LSP of the ABRs, every router in IS-IS Level 1 installs a default route in the routing table, pointing to the ABRs, which is verified in Output 4-44 for one of the routers (PE-1).

Output 4-44 *Default Route (::/0) on PE-1*

```
RP/0/RP0/CPU0:PE-1#show route ipv6 ::/0

Routing entry for ::/0
  Known via "isis METRO_1", distance 115, metric 20, candidate default path,
  type level-1
  Installed May  6 12:00:51.870 for 00:00:09
  Routing Descriptor Blocks
    fe80::42:acff:fe16:e402, from ::, via GigabitEthernet0/0/0/0, Protected
      Route metric is 20
    fe80::42:acff:fe16:e503, from ::, via GigabitEthernet0/0/0/2, Backup (Local-LFA)
      Route metric is 30
  No advertising protos.
```

After configuring the ABR(to suppress default routes, as shown in Config 4-28, the command **show isis database ABR-1.00-00 detail level 1**, as shown in Output 4-45, now indicates that the attached bit is cleared on ABR-1.

Output 4-45 *Attached Bit Cleared on ABR-1*

```
RP/0/RP0/CPU0:ABR-1#show isis database ABR-1.00-00 detail level 1

IS-IS METRO_1 (Level-1) Link State Database
LSPID                 LSP Seq Num  LSP Checksum  LSP Holdtime/Rcvd  ATT/P/OL
ABR-1.00-00        * 0x00001475   0x499b          1197 /*             0/0/0
  Area Address:   49.0001
  LSP MTU:        1492
  NLPID:          0x8e
  MT:             IPv6 Unicast                              0/0/0
<snip>
```

As a result, the routers in IS-IS Level 1 will not install the default route in the routing table. Output 4-46 from one of the routers (PE-1) shows that there is no default route.

Output 4-46 *No Default Route (::/0) on PE-1*

```
RP/0/RP0/CPU0:PE-1#sh route ipv6 ::/0

% Network not in table
```

The final step is to verify the summary route propagation to IS-IS Level 1. The ABRs are configured to leak routes from IS-IS Level 2 to Level 1. Only selected summary routes are leaked using a route policy. The IS-IS Level 1 LSP of the ABRs in Metro 2 now contains the summary route (fc00:0:100::/40) from Metro 1 as an IPv6 inter-area route. The LSP from ABR-3 now contains the IPv6 inter-area summary route, as shown in Output 4-47.

Output 4-47   *Summary Route (fc00:0:100::/40) Propagated by ABR-3*

```
RP/0/RP0/CPU0:ABR-3#show isis database ABR-4.00-00 level 1 detail


IS-IS METRO_2 (Level-1) Link State Database
LSPID                   LSP Seq Num  LSP Checksum  LSP Holdtime/Rcvd  ATT/P/OL
ABR-4.00-00             0x00001490   0x28cf          857 /1200          0/0/0
  Area Address:    49.0002
  LSP MTU:         1492
  NLPID:           0x8e
  MT:              IPv6 Unicast                              0/0/0
  Hostname:        ABR-4
  Router Cap:      0.0.0.0 D:0 S:0
  SRv6 Locator:    MT (IPv6 Unicast) fc00:0:101::/48 D:1 Metric: 31 Algorithm: 0
  SRv6 Locator:    MT (IPv6 Unicast) fc00:0:102::/48 D:1 Metric: 31 Algorithm: 0
  SRv6 Locator:    MT (IPv6 Unicast) fc00:0:202::/48 D:0 Metric: 1 Algorithm: 0
  Metric: 10       MT (IPv6 Unicast) IS-Extended ABR-3.00
  Metric: 10       MT (IPv6 Unicast) IS-Extended P-7.00
  Metric: 10       MT (IPv6 Unicast) IS-Extended P-8.00
  Metric: 10       MT (IPv6 Unicast) IS-Extended RR-2.00
  Metric: 41       MT (IPv6 Unicast) IPv6-Interarea fc00:0:100::/40
```

As a result of the summary route in the LSP from ABRs, all the IS-IS Level 1 routers install the summary route in the routing table, as shown in Output 4-48.

Output 4-48   *Summary Route (fc00:0:100::/40) on PE-3*

```
RP/0/RP0/CPU0:PE-3#sh route ipv6 fc00:0:100::/40

Routing entry for fc00:0:100::/40
  Known via "isis METRO_1", distance 115, metric 61, type inter-area
  Installed May  6 11:52:52.724 for 01:06:12
  Routing Descriptor Blocks
    fe80::42:acff:fe16:003, from ::, via GigabitEthernet0/0/0/0, Protected,
ECMP-Backup (Local-LFA)
      Route metric is 61
    fe80::42:acff:fe16:d302, from ::, via GigabitEthernet0/0/0/2, Protected,
ECMP-Backup (Local-LFA)
      Route metric is 61
  No advertising protos.
```

PE-3 uses this summary route to reach the PE device (PE-1) in Metro 1, which is verified by using the command **show route ipv6 fc00:0:105::,** as shown in Output 4-49.

Output 4-49   *PE-1 Reachable via the Summary Route*

```
RP/0/RP0/CPU0:PE-3#show route ipv6 fc00:0:105::

Routing entry for fc00:0:100::/40
  Known via "isis METRO_1", distance 115, metric 61, type inter-area
  Installed May  6 11:52:52.724 for 01:09:03
  Routing Descriptor Blocks
    fe80::42:acff:fe16:d003, from ::, via GigabitEthernet0/0/0/0, Protected,
  ECMP-Backup (Local-LFA)
      Route metric is 61
    fe80::42:acff:fe16:d302, from ::, via GigabitEthernet0/0/0/2, Protected,
  ECMP-Backup (Local-LFA)
      Route metric is 61
  No advertising protos.
```

The reachability from PE-3 to PE-1 can be verified by pinging the uN SID of PE-1, as shown in Output 4-50, and the uN SID should be reachable from all other SRv6 nodes in the network.

Output 4-50   *Reachability of PE-1 from PE-3*

```
RP/0/RP0/CPU0:PE-3#ping fc00:0:105::

Type escape sequence to abort.
Sending 5, 100-byte ICMP Echos to fc00:0:105::, timeout is 2 seconds:
!!!!!
Success rate is 100 percent (5/5), round-trip min/avg/max = 7/8/11 ms
```

Unreachable Prefix Announcement (UPA)

Summarization in SRv6 provides an elegant solution to increase network scalability because of the reduced level of information propagated between domains. However, it introduces several side effects, including suboptimal routing and convergence for BGP-based services.

Typically, BGP relies on a periodic scanner to validate the BGP next hop. Convergence is dependent in the periodicity of the scanner. BGP Prefix Independent Convergence (BGP PIC) is a technology that allows fast switchover, in a prefix-independent manner, to redundant paths in the event of an egress PE failure. In a nutshell, the ingress router PE-1 receives many prefixes from a primary egress router PE-3, and it receives the same set of prefixes from the secondary egress router PE-4. The ingress router PE-1 programs all primary paths into the hardware forwarding table. PE-1 also programs all paths from the secondary egress router PE-4 as backup paths. When the IGP of the ingress router PE-1 discovers the failure of the primary egress router PE-3, it invalidates all the BGP prefixes advertised by PE-3 based on BGP NHT and triggers an immediate switchover to the backup paths via PE-4. This is illustrated in Figure 4-24.

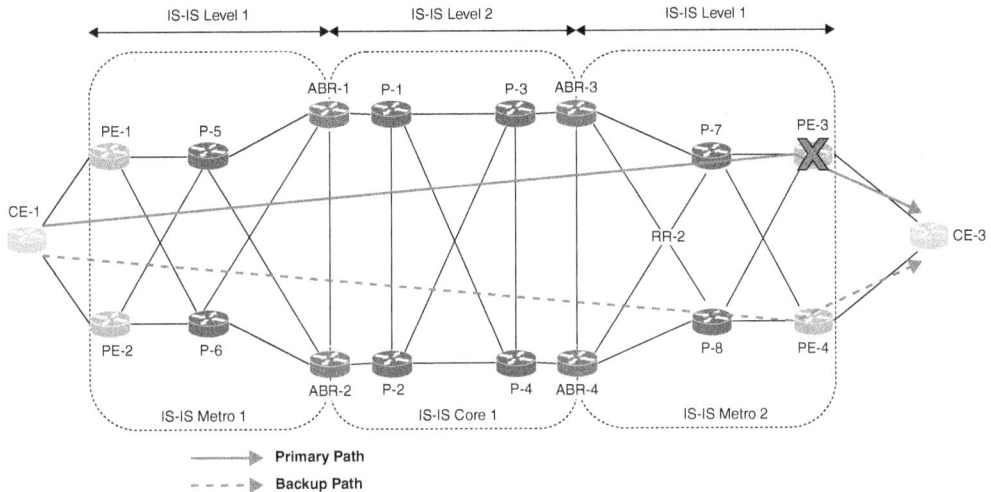

Figure 4-24   *BGP PIC Edge*

To trigger the switchover, PE-1 needs to be notified about the failure of the egress router PE-3. Normally, this notification comes from an IGP update in a single IGP domain or in multi-domain networks that do not use summarization. In such cases, the ingress PE triggers BGP PIC, and traffic restoration occurs very quickly (within a few seconds).

However, with summarization, PE-1 will never be notified about the failure of PE-3 because the failure of PE-3 is hidden by the summary route. Traffic restoration following an egress PE failure relies on BGP for convergence, which can occur in minutes.

The solution is the Unreachable Prefix Announcement (UPA). Essentially, a UPA is a regular IGP update that announces the unreachability of a prefix that is a component of the summary. An UPA informs the ingress PE about an egress PE failure and enables the ingress PE to trigger BGP NHT.

The unreachability property of the prefix is carried by using an "unreachable" metric, which is already part of the IS-IS protocol definitions. According to RFC 5308, any prefix advertised with a metric larger than MAX_V6_PATH_METRIC 0xfe000000 must not be considered during path computation and can be used for other purposes. Extensions to IS-IS and OSPF to support UPA are described in the IETF draft "draft-ietf-lsr-igp-ureach-prefix-announce-02."

Note   OSPF also supports UPA. According to RFC 2328, OSPF uses LSInfinity (0xffffff) to indicate that the destination described by an LSA is unreachable. RFC 2328 Section 14.1 describes the use of LSInfinity to indicate loss of prefix reachability.

Figure 4-25 shows how the UPA is generated/propagated/processed in a hierarchical IS-IS network. When ABR-3 and ABR-4 lose reachability to PE-3, they recognize that the locator of PE-3 is part of the summary prefix and generate a UPA for the locator of PE-3. The UPA is flooded to the rest of the network, and the IS-IS process of PE-1 receives and processes the UPA, which in turn triggers BGP PIC (based on BGP next hop tracking) for all BGP prefixes learned from PE-3. The route policy for propagating routes from IS-IS Level 2 to Level 1 on all the ABRs must be updated to allow UPAs, which are /48 prefixes from the SRv6 locator block.

UPAs are required only for PE devices that provide multihoming services. In Figure 4-26, PE-3 and PE-4 in Metro 2 are connected to CE-3 and provide L3VPN multihoming services. Convergence of the multihoming service depends on how quickly the remote PE nodes (PE-1 and PE-2) in Metro 1 detect when either PE-3 or PE-4 is unreachable.

PE-5 is another PE in Metro 2 that is connected to CE-5, and all the L3VPN services on PE-5 are single-homed.

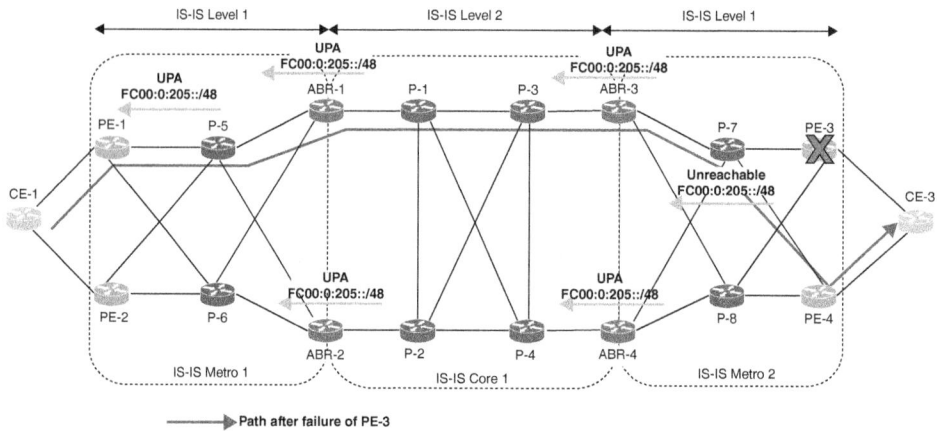

Figure 4-25   *UPA for PE-3 (fc00:0:205::/48)*

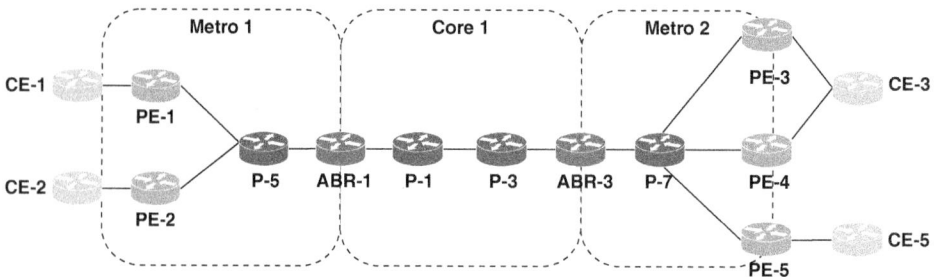

Figure 4-26   *PEs Offering Multihoming L3VPN Services*

In this scenario, ABR-3 must generate the UPA for PE-3 and PE-4 when they are not reachable. The UPA triggers BGP NHT on the remote PE nodes and help provide fast convergence (in less than a second) for the L3VPN multihoming service.

The behavior is different in the case of PE-5, where all the services will be unavailable when PE-5 is not reachable because there is no backup for PE-5. Services are restored when PE-5 is reachable and there is no need to generate a UPA for PE-5 when PE-5 becomes unreachable.

Selective generation of UPAs is achieved by tagging the SRv6 locators (on PE-3 and PE-4) that provide multihoming services. On ABR-1, the UPA is generated only for the SRv6 locators that are tagged.

Figure 4-27 shows the concept of selective generation of UPAs. When PE-3 has a node failure, the ABRs generated a UPA for PE-3. However, when PE-5 has a node failure, the ABRs do not generate a UPA.

Selective generation of UPAs helps improve the scalability of UPAs by reducing the number of UPAs that are generated by an ABR. Consider a metro network with several hundred PE devices, only a few of which offer multihoming services. The network topology is such that the failure of some aggregator devices results in several PE nodes becoming unreachable. Without this feature, the ABR generates a UPA for every PE that becomes unreachable. The UPAs are flooded throughout the network, and all PE devices (that are configured to process UPAs) must process the UPAs. By using this feature of selective advertisement of UPAs, it is possible to minimize the number of UPAs that are generated by the ABRs and reduce the number of UPAs that must be processed by remote PE nodes.

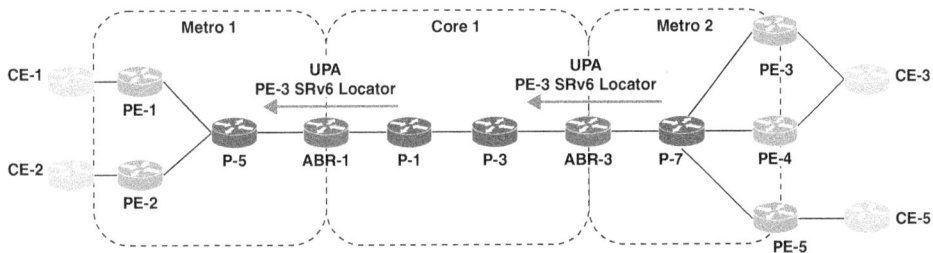

Figure 4-27   *Selective Generation of UPAs*

UPA Configuration

There are three steps involved in configuring a UPA, as shown in Figure 4-28.

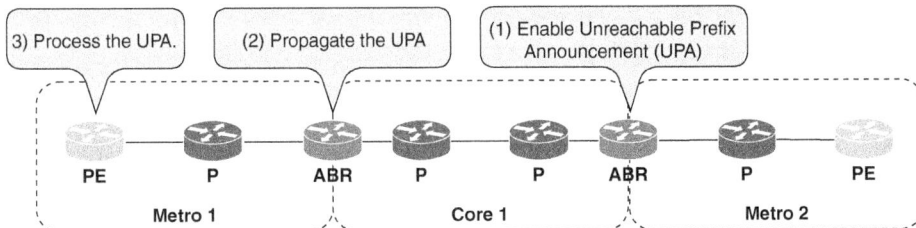

Figure 4-28   *UPA Configuration Steps*

The first step is to enable the UPA. The UPA is a /48 prefix and is generated for the loss of a specific route covered by the summary route. When a device is unreachable, the ABRs advertise the /48 UPA for the SRv6 in the IS-IS Level 2 LSP together with the summary route. The configuration shown in Config 4-30 allows the ABRs to generate the /48 UPA for a device when the ABR detects that it is unreachable.

Config 4-30   *UPA Announcement (IOS XR)*

```
router isis METRO_2
 address-family ipv6 unicast
  summary-prefix fc00:0:200::/40 level 2 adv-unreachable
```

Several parameters can be configured to refine the behavior of the UPA:

- **adv-metric:** This is the metric used when advertising a UPA. This parameter must match on the device (ABR) generating the UPA and the device (PE) processing the UPA. It is necessary to modify this parameter for interoperability reasons when the PE and ABR have different default values. The default value is 4261412865.

- **unreachable-component-tag:** This indicates that the UPA is generated only for selected prefixes. The prefixes are identified using tags.

- **adv-lifetime:** This is the lifetime of a UPA. When a PE with a large number of BGP routes fails, the remote PE (or route reflector) must invalidate (or withdraw) all the BGP routes from the failed PE. The UPA must be present until the remote PE (or route reflector) has processed the change in status of the failed PE. The default lifetime of a UPA is 180 seconds. In the event that the remote PE (or route reflector) requires more than 180 seconds, the lifetime of the UPA must be increased.

Note   There is no impact on router performance if the lifetime of the UPA is set to a large value in order to allow the BGP process to finish its task of invalidating (or withdrawing) the routes from the failed PE.

Config 4-31 shows that the lifetime of the UPA advertised by an ABR has been increased to 10 minutes. This parameter should be tuned based on the size of the BGP table.

Config 4-31   *Modifying the UPA Lifetime (IOS XR)*

```
router isis METRO_2
 address-family ipv6 unicast
  prefix-unreachable
   adv-lifetime 600
```

- **adv-maximum:** This is maximum number of UPAs that can be generated. Based on the default value, only 32 UPAs are generated by the ABR. It is important to avoid generating too many UPAs because a large number of UPAs can have a negative impact on stability. In a medium to large metro network, more than 32 PE nodes can become unreachable when an aggregator device (to which the PE nodes are connected) fails. It is necessary to change the adv-maximum setting to a larger value (based on the number of PE nodes) to permit UPAs to be generated for all devices that offer multihoming services. This helps the remote PE nodes to detect the failure of the primary PE and switch to the backup PE (via BGP PIC functionality).

Config 4-32 shows how to modify the maximum number of UPAs that are generated by an ABR.

Config 4-32   *Increasing the Maximum Number of UPAs (IOS XR)*

```
router isis METRO_2
 address-family ipv6 unicast
  prefix-unreachable
   adv-maximum 64
```

As described in section, "Unreachable Prefix Announcement (UPA)," UPAs are relevant only for PE nodes that offer multihoming services. In a large metro network, the number of UPAs that are generated by an ABR can be restricted by tagging the SRv6 locators of the PE nodes that offer multihoming services. Config 4-33 shows how the locators are tagged on a PE node.

Config 4-33   *Selectively Generating UPAs (IOS XR)*

```
router isis METRO_1
 address-family ipv6 unicast
  segment-routing srv6
   locator MAIN
    tag 1
```

The ABR then uses these tags to identify the prefixes for which the UPA has to be generated, as shown in Config 4-34. UPAs are generated only for the prefixes that are tagged with tag equal to 1.

Config 4-34   *Prefix Tagging for UPA Generation (IOS XR)*

```
router isis METRO_1
 address-family ipv6 unicast
  summary-prefix fc00:0:100::/40 level 2 adv-unreachable unreachable-component-tag 1
```

The second step is to propagate a UPA. The configuration shown in Config 4-35 allows the ABRs to leak /48 prefixes from IS-IS Level 2 to IS-IS Level 1. (The UPA is a /48 prefix.) The configuration prefix-set IPV6_L2_SUMMARY_PS is modified to allow /48 prefixes in addition to the /40 summary(ies) to propagate from IS-IS Level 2 to IS-IS Level 1. This configuration is done on all the ABRs.

Config 4-35 *Propagating UPAs from IS-IS Level 2 to Level 1 (IOS XR)*

```
prefix-set IPV6_L2_SUMMARY_PS
  fc00::/32 ge 40
end-set

route-policy IPV6_L2_TO_L1_RP
 if destination in IPV6_LOCAL_SUMMARY_PS then
    drop
  elseif destination in IPV6_L2_SUMMARY_PS then
    pass
  endif
end-policy

router isis METRO_1
 address-family ipv6 unicast
  propagate level 2 into level 1 route-policy IPV6_L2_TO_L1_RP
```

The third step is to process the UPA. Config 4-36 shows the configuration that is used to enable the processing of UPAs on PE nodes that depend on BGP PIC Edge for fast convergence.

Config 4-36 *Enabling UPA Processing (IOS XR)*

```
router isis METRO_1
 address-family ipv6 unicast
  metric-style wide
  prefix-unreachable
   rx-process-enable
```

UPA Verification

This section describes the steps to verify when UPAs are generated by ABRs in a metro network and propagated across the network to the remote metros and processed (and used) by PE devices.

There are three steps involved in verifying UPAs, as shown in Figure 4-29.

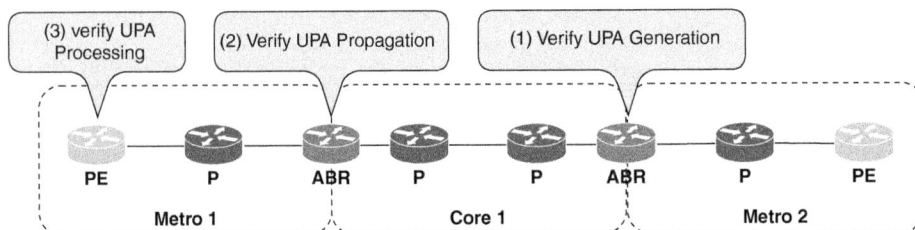

Figure 4-29 *UPA Verification Steps*

The first step is to verify that the UPA has been generated. On detecting the failure of the PE-3, the ABR in Metro 2 propagates a UPA via IS-IS Level 2. Output 4-51 verifies that the Level 2 LSP has the UPA for fc00:0:205::/48 with metric 4261412865. The command **show isis database level 2 ABR-3.00-00 detail** is used for this verification.

Output 4-51   *Verifying UPA Generation*

```
RP/0/RP0/CPU0:ABR-3#show isis database level 2 ABR-3.00-00 detail


IS-IS METRO_2 (Level-2) Link State Database
LSPID                    LSP Seq Num  LSP Checksum  LSP Holdtime/Rcvd  ATT/P/OL
ABR-3.00-00      * 0x0000155f   0xb369        1199 /*          0/0/0
  Area Address:   49.0002
  LSP MTU:        1492
  NLPID:          0x8e
  MT:             IPv6 Unicast                             0/0/0
  Hostname:       ABR-3
  <snip>
  Metric: 4261412865 MT (IPv6 Unicast) IPv6 fc00:0:205::/48
```

The second step is to verify that the UPA has been propagated. The ABR in the metro network receives the UPA and propagates it to all devices in IS-IS Level 1 via its Level 1 LSP. This verification, as shown in Output 4-52, uses the command **show isis database level 1 ABR-1.00-00 detail**.

Output 4-52   *UPA Propagation by ABR-1 to IS-IS Level 1*

```
RP/0/RP0/CPU0:ABR-1#show isis database level 1 ABR-1.00-00 detail


IS-IS METRO_1 (Level-1) Link State Database
LSPID                    LSP Seq Num  LSP Checksum  LSP Holdtime/Rcvd  ATT/P/OL
ABR-1.00-00      * 0x0000159f   0xae3b        1195 /*          0/0/0
  Area Address:   49.0001
  LSP MTU:        1492
  NLPID:          0x8e
  MT:             IPv6 Unicast                             0/0/0
  Hostname:       ABR-1
  <snip>
  Metric: 4261412865 MT (IPv6 Unicast) IPv6-Interarea fc00:0:205::/48
```

The third step is to verify the UPA processing. Output 4-53 shows that, before the failure of PE-3, the remote PE (PE-3) is reachable via the summary route fc00:0:200::/40.

Output 4-53 *Reachability of Remote PE PE-3 Before Failure*

```
RP/0/RP0/CPU0:PE-1#show route ipv6 fc00:0:205::

Routing entry for fc00:0:200::/40
  Known via "isis METRO_1", distance 115, metric 61, type inter-area
  Installed May  8 00:40:35.820 for 21:45:54
  Routing Descriptor Blocks
    fe80::42:acff:fe16:e402, from ::, via GigabitEthernet0/0/0/0, Protected,
ECMP-Backup (Local-LFA)
      Route metric is 61
    fe80::42:acff:fe16:e503, from ::, via GigabitEthernet0/0/0/2, Protected,
ECMP-Backup (Local-LFA)
      Route metric is 61
  No advertising protos
```

Upon receiving a UPA, a PE in the remote metro network installs this route in the routing table and triggers BGP PIC because of BGP NHT. Output 4-54 shows that PE-1 has processed the UPA and installed the route in its routing table. You know that fc00:0:205:: is now unreachable because the metric is 42949678294.

Output 4-54 *Processing and Installing a UPA on PE-1*

```
Routing entry for fc00:0:205::/48
  Known via "isis METRO_1", distance 254, metric 4294967294, unreachable prefix,
type inter-area
  Installed May  8 22:30:59.844 for 00:00:15
  Routing Descriptor Blocks
    directly connected, via Null0
      Route metric is 4294967294
  No advertising protos.
```

Output 4-55 shows an IS-IS LSP packet captured on the link between PE-1 and P-5 using Wireshark. The prefix fc00:0:205::/48 is advertised with the metric 4261412865.

Output 4-55 *IS-IS LSP Packet with a UPA for fc00:0:205::/48*

```
Frame 34: 1380 bytes on wire (11040 bits), 1380 bytes captured (11040 bits)
IEEE 802.3 Ethernet
Logical-Link Control
ISO 10589 ISIS InTRA Domain Routeing Information Exchange Protocol
ISO 10589 ISIS Link State Protocol Data Unit
    PDU length: 1363
    Remaining lifetime: 1200
```

```
LSP-ID: 0001.0000.0002.00-01
Sequence number: 0x00000c2e
Checksum: 0xfaee [correct]
[Checksum Status: Good]
Type block(0x03): Partition Repair:0, Attached bits:0, Overload bit:0, IS type:3
Multi Topology IS Reachability (t=222, l=229)
Multi Topology IS Reachability (t=222, l=239)
Multi Topology Reachable IPv6 Prefixes (t=237, l=252)
    Type: 237
    Length: 252
    0000 .... .... .... = Reserved: 0x0
    .... 0000 0000 0010 = Topology ID: IPv6 routing topology (2)
    IPv6 Reachability: fc00:0:205::/48
        Metric: 4261412865
        1... .... = Distribution: Down
        .0.. .... = Distribution: Internal
        ..1. .... = Sub-TLV: Yes
        Prefix Length: 48
        IPv6 prefix: fc00:0:205::
        SubCLV Length: 3
        subTLV: Prefix Attribute Flags (c=4, l=1): Flags:-R-
```

SRv6 OSPF

At this writing this chapter, there is no support for using OSPF as the IGP for exchanging information related to SRv6 on IOS XR.

Multiplane Topologies with Flex Algos

The SR architecture associates an SRv6 locator or Prefix SID to an algorithm that defines how the path is computed. Flexible Algorithm allows for user-defined algorithms where the IGP computes paths based on a user-defined combination of metric type and constraints. Many constraints may be used to compute a path over a network. A simple form of constraint may be to use a particular plane, and a more sophisticated form of constraint might include some extended metric, such as delay, as described in RFC 7810. Another use case could be to restrict the path and avoid links with certain affinities. Combinations of these are also possible. To provide maximum flexibility, the mapping between the algorithm value and its meaning can be defined by the user. When all the routers in the domain have a common understanding of the algorithm, the computation for the algorithm is consistent, and the traffic may not be subject to looping.

An operator can assign an SRv6 locator or a Prefix SID to a flex algo to realize forwarding beyond IGP metric-based SPF. As a result, a flex algo provides a traffic-engineered path that is automatically computed by the IGP to any destination that is reachable by the IGP.

Components of SR Flex Algos

This section describes the components that are required to support the SR flex algo functionality in IS-IS and OSPF:

Note This information applies for both SR-MPLS and SRv6. The difference between SR-MPLS and SRv6 is that SR-MPLS is based on the Prefix SID, and SRv6 is based on the SRv6 locator.

- **Flex algo definition:** An algorithm is a one-octet value. Values from 128 to 255 are reserved for user-defined values and are used for flex algo representation. The base algorithm (that is, the default IGP) is assigned the value 0. A definition of the flex algo includes its number, link affinities to include or exclude links, and the type of metric (that is, IGP metric, TE metric, link delay, and generic metric) used for calculating the shortest path to a destination.

- **Flex algo definition advertisement:** To guarantee loop-free forwarding for paths computed for a particular flex algo, all routers in the network must share the same definition of the flex algo. This is achieved by dedicated router(s) advertising the definition of each flex algo. Such an advertisement is associated with the priority to make sure that all routers agree on a single and consistent definition for each flex algo.

  The definition of a flex algo includes the algorithm number (128–255), metric type, and affinity constraints. At least one router in the area—and preferably two for redundancy—must advertise the flex algo definition. The valid definition must be advertised in order for the flex algo to be functional. When more than one router advertises the definition, the definition provided by the router with the highest priority is used by all routers. The default priority advertised by a router is 128. When the priority is the same, the router ID of the advertising router is the tiebreaker.

- **Flex algo link attribute advertisement:** Various link attributes may be used during flex algo path calculation. For example, include or exclude rules based on link affinities can be part of the flex algo definition, as defined in RFC 9350.

  Link attribute advertisements used during flex algo calculation must use the Application-Specific Link Attribute (ASLA) advertisements, as defined in RFC 8919 (for IS-IS) and RFC 8920 (for OSPF). In the case of IS-IS, if the L-flag is set in the ASLA advertisement, then legacy advertisements (that is, IS-IS Extended Reachability TLV) are used instead.

  The mandatory use of ASLA advertisements applies to the following link attributes:

  - Minimum Unidirectional Link Delay

  - TE Default Metric

- Administrative Group

- Extended Administrative Group

- Shared Risk Link Group

- **Flex algo SID advertisement:** The flex algo–specific SRv6 locator or SR-MPLS Prefix SID is advertised by the IGP. Each of the routers participating in the flex algo installs an MPLS labeled path in the MPLS forwarding table or an SRv6 locator in the IPv6 RIB to a specific destination, and that MPLS label or locator is then used to forward traffic on a flex algo path to the destination.

- **Calculation of flex algo path:** A router is capable of computing paths for multiple flex algos. A router must be configured to support a particular flex algo and must have a valid definition of the flex algo before that flex algo is used to compute the path to a destination.

  The following points are valid when computing the shortest path tree for a flex algo:

  - All nodes that do not support the flex algo will be pruned from the topology.

  - If the flex algo definition includes affinities that are excluded, then all links for which any such affinities are advertised will be pruned from the topology.

  - Routers use the metric that is part of the flex algo definition. If a metric is not advertised for a particular link, that link will be pruned from the topology.

  IS-IS and OSPF support Loop Free Alternate (LFA) paths, TI-LFA backup paths, and Microloop Avoidance paths for a particular flex algo. These paths are computed using the same constraints used in the calculation of the primary paths for the flex algo, and these paths use Prefix SIDs or SRv6 locators that are advertised specifically for the flex algo in order to enforce the backup or Microloop Avoidance path.

- **Installation of forwarding entries for flex algo paths:** The router installs the MPLS label that corresponds to the Prefix SID that it receives for a particular flex algo in the MPLS forwarding table. In the case of SRv6, the router installs the SRv6 locator that corresponds to the flex algo in the Routing Information Base and the Forwarding Information Base.

- **Flex algo prefix metric:** The flex algo Prefix Metric feature introduces a flex algo–specific prefix metric in the IS-IS and OSPF prefix advertisement, which provides a way to compute the best end-to-end flex algo optimized paths across multiple areas or domains.

Note   A prefix metric does not have any impact for SRv6 when the ABRs summarize the address block of the SRv6 locators.

Protocol extensions to support flex algos are described in Chapter 3, in the section "Segment Routing over IPv6 Capabilities."

Flex Algo Use Cases Scenarios

This section shows two use cases for flex algos: a low-latency path and disjoint paths. Each use case provides a description of the proposed solution using a flex algo, the configuration details, and the commands to verify the configuration. Traffic forwarding for these two use cases is demonstrated using **ping** and **traceroute**.

The configurations shown in this section use SRv6 as the transport mechanism. Similar configuration can be used for SR-MPLS. The section "SR-MPLS Configuration for Flex Algo Use Cases" provides the necessary configuration (without verification) for the low-latency path and disjoint paths.

Low-Latency Path Use Case

One of the common use cases for flex algos is a low-latency path between nodes in a network.

One solution, which is based on tuning the IGP based on the link latency, has its limitations in the sense that it is a static solution: Any change in the link latency will require a manual modification of the IGP metric. This manual solution is cumbersome and prone to errors due to humans involved.

A more elegant solution is to advertise the link latency as an attribute of the link and use this new link attribute to compute the (low-latency) path between two nodes in the network. This is achieved by defining a new flex algo that uses link delay as the metric. Every node that participates in this flex algo advertises a Prefix SID or an SRv6 locator for the new flex algo. All services that use this Prefix SID (SRv6 locator) for transport will use the low-latency path in the network.

Consider the network shown in Figure 4-30. All the links have the same IGP metric. The link delay is not same on all the links. The delay is measured in micro seconds (us) in this section. The following links have a delay of 500 us:

- PE-2 ←→P-5

- PE-1 ←→ P-6

- P-5 ←→ ABR-1

- P-1 ←→ P-3

- P-2 ←→ P-4

- P-8 ←→ ABR-4

- PE-3 ←→ P-8
- PE-4 ←→ P-7

The rest of the links have a delay of 100 us.

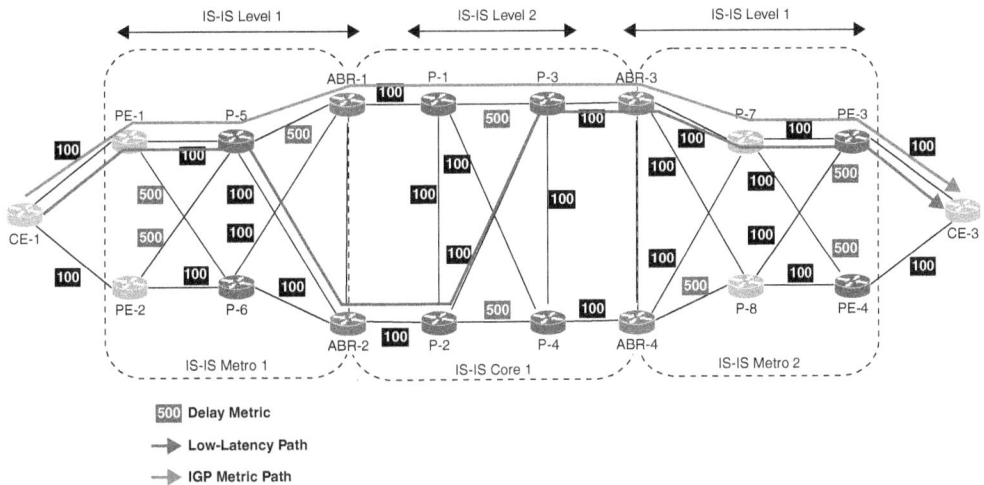

Figure 4-30 *Flex Algo Use Case: Low-Latency Path*

There are two equal-cost paths (based on the IGP metric) between PE-1 and PE-3 with an IGP cost of 70:

Path 1: PE-1—P-5—ABR-1—P-1—P-3—ABR-3—P-7—PE-3

Path 2: PE-1—P-5—ABR-2—P-12—P-3—ABR-3—P-7—PE-3

Path 1 has a latency of 1900 us, and from a latency perspective, this is not the best path. The best low-latency path is Path 2, which has a delay of 700 us.

Flex algo 128 is defined to use delay as a metric, and the link delay is advertised a part of the IGP. A separate SRv6 locator from the block fc00:1:DDNN::/48 must be allocated for flex algo 128 and is advertised in the IGP.

By using flex algo 128, it is possible to provide the fastest path (lowest delay) between CE-1 and CE-3.

Low-Latency Path Configuration

Figure 4-31 shows the three steps for configuring flex algos. Steps 1 and 2 must be done on all the devices that are part of the flex algo. Step 3, which shows the generation of the summary on the ABRs, is relevant only on the ABR devices that are part of the flex algo.

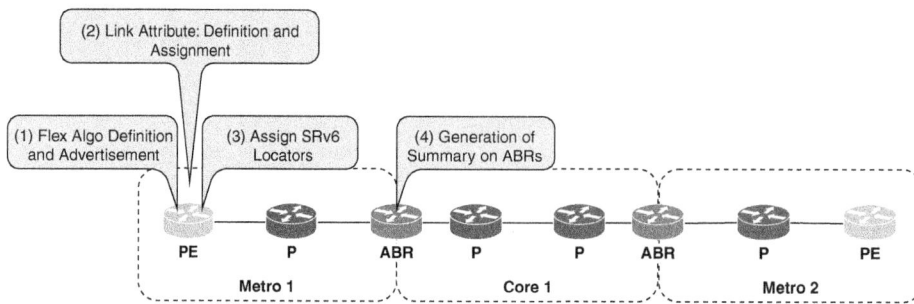

Figure 4-31   *Flex Algo Low-Latency Configuration Steps*

In step 1, the flex algo is defined on the device, and then the definition is advertised to the rest of the devices. The flex algo can be defined on multiple devices. The definition provided by the device with the highest priority is accepted by the rest of the devices. When more than one device has the same priority, the router ID is the tiebreaker. The default priority is 128. Config 4-37 shows the configuration for the definition and advertisement of flex algo 128, which uses delay as the metric type.

Config 4-37   *Defining and Advertising a Flex Algo (IOS XR)*

```
router isis METRO_1
 flex-algo 128
  metric-type delay
  advertise-definition
```

It is necessary to define and advertise the same flex algo on all devices that belong to an operator-defined algorithm to reduce the chances of misconfiguration.

Next, the link attributes are associated with the links that are used by the flex algo. In this case, flex algo 128 uses delay as a link attribute. If a link attribute is not defined for a link, then the link is not considered part of the IS-IS topology of the flex algo. The link delay can be statically assigned to a link, as shown in Config 4-38, or it can be dynamically measured using the Segment Routing Performance Measurement (SR PM) feature, based on Two-Way Active Measurement Protocol (TWAMP). A similar configuration is used to assign the delay to all the links.

Note   Network operators can use the SR PM feature to monitor network metrics like link delay, which uses the IP/UDP packet format defined in RFC 5357 (TWAMP-Light) for probes. TWAMP adds two-way or round-trip measurement capabilities and uses time stamps applied at the echo destination (reflector) to enable greater accuracy in measuring the delay.

More details about SR PM and TWAMP for link delay measurement can be found in Chapter 8, "Service Assurance."

Config 4-38   *Assigning Link Delay (IOS XR)*

```
performance-measurement
 interface GigabitEthernet0/0/0/0
  delay-measurement
   advertise-delay 100
  !
 !
 interface GigabitEthernet0/0/0/1
  delay-measurement
   advertise-delay 500
  !
 !
```

The third step is to associate an SRv6 locator with the flex algo, as shown in Config 4-39.

Config 4-39   *Assigning an SRv6 Locator to Flex Algo 128 (IOS XR)*

```
segment-routing
 srv6
  locators
   locator LowLatency
    micro-segment behavior unode psp-usd
    prefix fc00:1:101::/48
    algorithm 128
```

After an SRv6 locator is assigned to flex algo 128, this locator is advertised in IS-IS, as shown in Config 4-40.

Config 4-40   *Advertising the SRv6 Locator (IOS XR)*

```
router isis METRO_1
 address-family ipv6 unicast
  segment-routing srv6
   locator LowLatency
```

In the fourth step, the ABRs of a metro network generate a summary route for the SRv6 locators assigned to flex algo 128 for all devices in the metro network, as shown in Config 4-41.

Config 4-41 *Summary Route for Flex Algo 128 (IOS XR)*

```
router isis METRO_1
 address-family ipv6 unicast
  summary-prefix fc00:1:100::/40 level 2 algorithm 128 adv-unreachable
```

The prefix-set setting that prevents the leaking of the metro summary back into IS-IS Level 1 of the metro network is updated for flex algo 128, as shown in Config 4-42.

Config 4-42 *Using prefix-set to Prevent Leaking of the Metro 1 Summary in IS-IS Level 1 (IOS XR)*

```
prefix-set IPV6_LOCAL_SUMMARY_PS
 fc00:0:100::/40 eq 40,
 fc00:1:100::/40 eq 40
```

Low-Latency Path Verification

Figure 4-32 shows the steps for verifying the flex algo configuration. Although the figure shows the ABR, these commands can be used on all the devices where the flex algo is relevant. The verification of the summary advertisement is relevant to the ABRs.

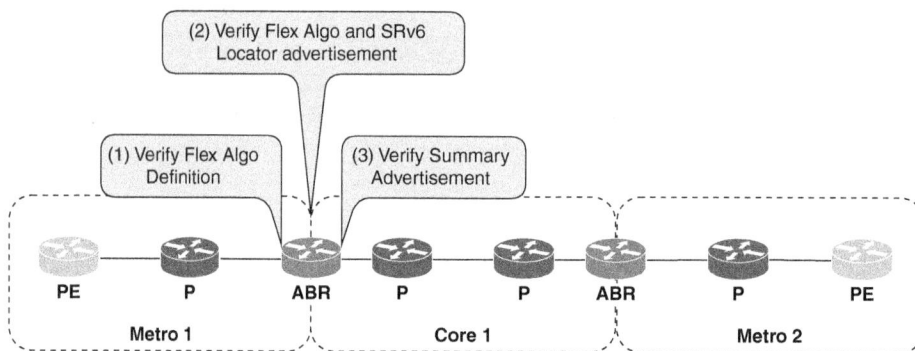

Figure 4-32 *Flex Algo Low-Latency Verification Steps*

The first step is to verify the flex algo definition. In this case, the command **show isis flex-algo 128** is used to verify the status of flex algo 128. The output has several parts, as shown in Output 4-56.

The flex algo definition indicates that all the routers have the same definition (Definition Equal to Local: Yes) and priority (128) for the flex algo. Since the priority is the same, the tiebreaker is the router ID. In IS-IS Level 2, the Definition Source is ABR-4. The metric-type, as per the definition, is Delay, and Prefix-metric is enabled for flex algo 128.

Status shows that flex algo 128 is defined and ready for use (Disabled: No) on ABR-1.

The Data Plane part of the output indicates that data forwarding for this flex algo is enabled for segment routing and disabled for IP.

Output 4-56   *Flex Algo 128 Enabled on ABR-1*

```
RP/0/RP0/CPU0:ABR_M1_1#show isis flex-algo 128

IS-IS METRO_1 Flex-Algo Database
Flex-Algo 128:
  Level-2:

    Definition Priority: 128
    Definition Source: ABR_M2_2.00
    Definition Equal to Local: Yes          Flex Algo Definition
    Definition Metric Type: Delay
    Definition Flex-Algo Prefix Metric: Yes


    Disabled: No                            Flex Algo Status

<snip>

  Data Plane Segemnt Routing: Yes           Data Plane
  Data Plane IP: No
```

The second step is to verify the flex algo and the SRv6 locator advertisement. The IS-IS LSP from PE-2, as shown in Output 4-57, uses the command **show isis database level 1 PE-2.00-00 verbose**, whose output indicates the following information about flex algo 128:

- Metric-Type is 1, which means flex algo 128 uses link delay as the metric.

- Alg-type is set to 1, which means the algorithm type is SPF.

- PE-2 advertised flex algo 128 with priority 128, which is the default value.

- The SRv6 locator for flex algo 128 is fc00:1:106::/48.

Output 4-57   *Flex Algo 128 Advertised by PE-2*

```
RP/0/RP0/CPU0:ABR-1#show isis database level 1 PE-2.00-00 verbose

IS-IS METRO_1 (Level-1) Link State Database
LSPID                 LSP Seq Num  LSP Checksum  LSP Holdtime/Rcvd  ATT/P/OL
PE-2.00-00         0x0000180c   0x2dae       730  /1200        0/0/0
  Area Address:    49.0001
```

```
   LSP MTU:        1492
   NLPID:          0x8e
   MT:             IPv6 Unicast                              0/0/0
   Hostname:       PE-2
   Router Cap:     0.0.0.0 D:0 S:0
     SR Algorithm:
<snip>
       Algorithm: 128
<snip>
     Flex-Algo Definition:
       Algorithm: 128 Metric-Type: 1 Alg-type: 0 Priority: 128
<snip>

   SRv6 Locator:    MT (IPv6 Unicast) fc00:1:106::/48 D:0 Metric: 1 Algorithm: 128
     Prefix Attribute Flags: X:0 R:0 N:0 E:0 A:0
     END SID: fc00:1:106:: uN (PSP/USD)
       SID Structure:
         Block Length: 32, Node-ID Length: 16, Func-Length: 0, Args-Length: 80
```

In step 3, the summary route for the SRv6 locators of flex algo 128 is advertised by the ABRs. Note that the summary route is advertised as an SRv6 locator because it is necessary to specify the flex algo associated with the summary route. The IPv6 External Route TLV does not have the capability to include the information regarding the flex algo. Output 4-58 shows the command **show isis database level 2 ABR-1.00-00 verbose** being used to verify that the summary route for flex algo 128 is advertised by ABR-1 as an SRv6 locator.

Output 4-58   *Summary Route for Flex Algo 128*

```
RP/0/RP0/CPU0:ABR-1#show isis database level 2 ABR-1.00-00 verbose



LSPID                   LSP Seq Num  LSP Checksum  LSP Holdtime/Rcvd  ATT/P/OL
ABR-1.00-00             0x00001931   0x54c1          932  /1200          0/0/0
  Area Address:    49.0001
  LSP MTU:         1492
  NLPID:           0x8e
  MT:              IPv6 Unicast                               0/0/0
  Hostname:        ABR-1
  Router Cap:      0.0.0.0 D:0 S:0
<snip>
   SRv6 Locator:    MT (IPv6 Unicast) fc00:1:200::/40 D:1 Metric: 401 Algorithm: 128
<snip>
```

Figure 4-33 shows the steps to verify the data plane forwarding for flex algo 128. PE-1 and PE-3 participate in flex algo 128.

After checking that a route to fc00:1:205:: (the SRv6 locator for flex algo 128 on PE-3 in Metro 2) has been installed on PE-1, a traceroute is used from PE-1 to trace the path with the shortest delay to PE-3.

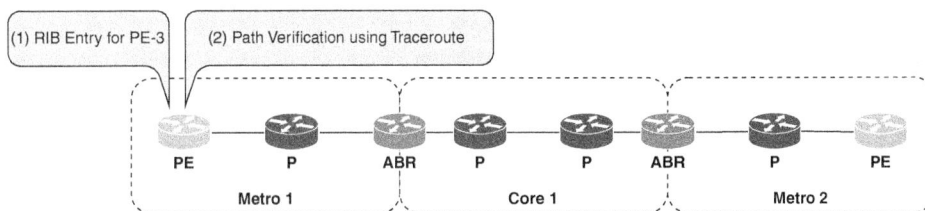

Figure 4-33   *Flex Algo Data Plane Verification*

The command **show route ipv6 fc00:1:205::** in Output 4-59 indicates that the RIB entry for PE-3 in Metro 2 is reachable via the summary route fc00:1:200::/40, the outgoing interface is Gigabit0/0/0/0, and the backup (local-LFA) interface is Gigabit0/0/0/2.

Output 4-59   *RIB Entry for the SRv6 Locator of PE-3 for Flex Algo 128*

```
RP/0/RP0/CPU0:PE-1#show route ipv6 fc00:1:205::

Routing entry for fc00:1:200::/40
  Known via "isis METRO_1", distance 115, metric 601, SRv6-locator (algo 128),
  type inter-area
  Installed May 14 11:23:03.378 for 14:11:55
  Routing Descriptor Blocks
    fe80::42:acff:fe16:e402, from ::, via GigabitEthernet0/0/0/0, Protected
      Route metric is 601
    fe80::42:acff:fe16:e503, from ::, via GigabitEthernet0/0/0/2, Backup (Local-LFA)
      Route metric is 1001
  No advertising protos.
```

Output 4-60 indicates that a traceroute from PE-1 to PE-3 using the SRv6 locator of flex algo 128 follows the low-latency path shown in Figure 4-33:

PE-1—P-5—ABR-2—P-2—P-3—ABR-3—P-7—PE-3.

Note that the traceroute uses the source address from algo 0 because the source address encapsulation is based on the loopback0 address, which is from algo 0.

Output 4-60   *Traceroute from PE-1 to PE-3 for the Low-Latency Path*

```
RP/0/RP0/CPU0:PE-1#traceroute ipv6 fc00:1:205::

Type escape sequence to abort.
Tracing the route to fc00:1:205::

1  fc00:0:103::1  2 msec  2 msec  2 msec  <--- P-5
2  fc00:0:102::1  3 msec  2 msec  3 msec  <--- ABR-2
3  fc00:0:2::1  4 msec  4 msec  3 msec  <-- P-2
4  fc00:0:3::1  5 msec  4 msec  4 msec  <--- P-3
5  fc00:0:201::1  8 msec  5 msec  7 msec  <-- ABR-3
6  fc00:0:203::1  7 msec  6 msec  9 msec  <-- P-7
7  fc00:0:205::1  5 msec  7 msec  8 msec  <-- PE-3
```

Disjoint Paths Use Case

Another possible use case for flex algos is to provide a disjoint path with no link/node overlap between two nodes in the network.

In a classical network without flex algos, this requirement can be fulfilled in several ways:

- Using static traffic engineering tunnels over disjoint paths

- Using dynamic traffic engineering tunnels where the paths are computed using an external controller (for example, SR-PCE)

- Dividing the network into two disjoint parts by running separate IGPs with non-overlapping links and nodes

Each of these methods has advantages and disadvantages. Some of the common disadvantages include the additional complexity and lack of resiliency due to failure of network nodes and links.

A flexible algorithm provides an elegant solution in certain topologies, using the existing IGP and creating two non-overlapping network topologies based on link attributes (affinity). Network links are marked using affinity bits, and the affinity is advertised as a part of the IGP. The flex algo makes use of this information to restrict the topology to the relevant affinity bit.

Figure 4-34 shows the use of a flex algo to provide disjoint paths in a network. This network provides a red path and a blue path; these two paths are disjoint and have no overlapping nodes or links. Links shown in the red plane are marked with affinity RED, while links shown in the blue plane are marked with affinity BLUE. Two flex algos (129 and 130) are defined, and these flex algos use SRv6 locators from different blocks, as shown in Figure 4-35.

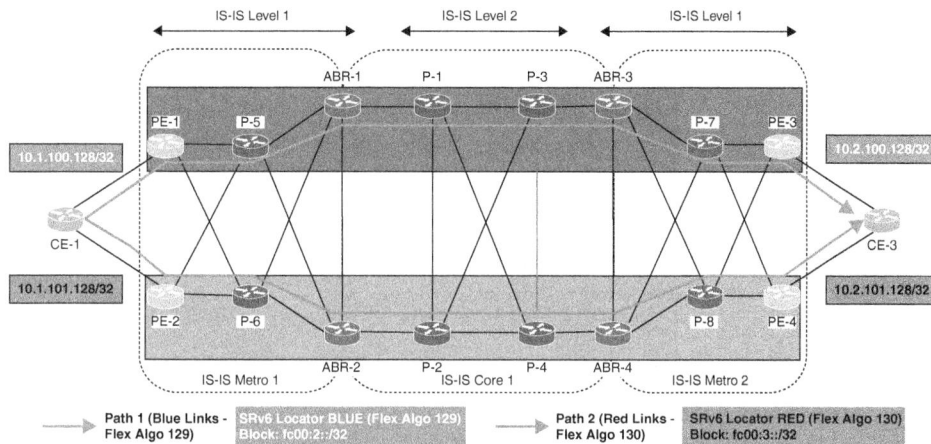

Figure 4-34 *Flex Algo Use Case: Disjoint Paths*

The next step is to assign these locators to an L3VPN service that requires disjoint paths. Two VRF instances (RED and BLUE) are used to distinguish between the blue path and the red path. VRF instance BLUE uses the blue path from PE-1 to PE-3 and from PE-3 to PE-1, and VRF instance RED uses the red path from PE-2 to PE-4 and from PE-4 to PE-2. The path allocation is achieved by assigning the SRv6 locator DisjointA to VRF instance BLUE and the SRv6 locator DisjointB to VRF instance RED.

Note It is not possible to provide redundancy for the blue and red paths in event of link or node failure.

CE-1 receives the routes for CE-3 from PE-1 and PE-2. When CE-1 sends the traffic destined for CE-3 to PE-1, this traffic uses the blue path in the SRv6 network. Similarly, when CE-1 sends the traffic destined for CE-3 to PE-2, the packets traverses the SRv6 network over the red path in the SRv6 network.

The blue and the red paths traverse the following devices in the SRv6 network:

- Blue path: PE-1—P-5—ABR-1—P-1—P-3—ABR-3—P-7—PE-3

- Red path: PE-2—P-6—ABR-2—P-2—P-4—ABR-4—P-8—PE-4

Disjoint Paths Configuration

Figure 4-35 shows the configuration steps for the disjoint paths use case with two flex algos: 129 and 130. Although the steps are shown for the ABR device, these steps must be completed on all devices that participate in flex algos 129 and 130.

The first step is to define and advertise flex algos 129 and 130, as shown in Config 4-43. These two flex algos are defined to use link affinity as link attributes, and these link affinities are defined using affinity maps. An affinity map is used to associate a name with a bit position, and each affinity map supports up to 32 bits. Affinity map BLUE is assigned bit position 1, and affinity map RED is assigned bit position 2.

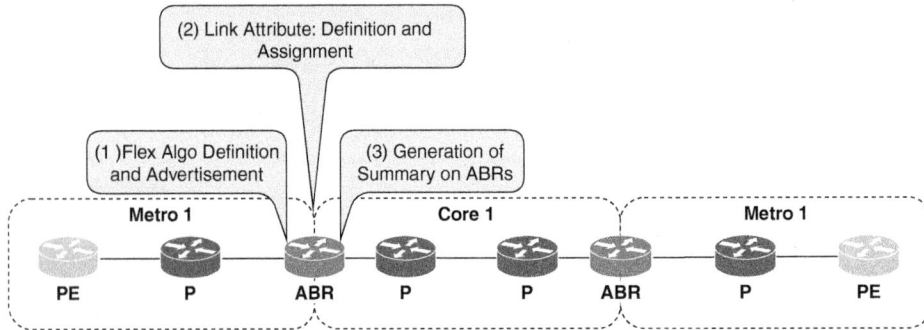

Figure 4-35   *Flex Algo Disjoint Paths Configuration Steps*

Config 4-43   *Defining and Advertising Flex Algos 129 and 130 (IOS XR)*

```
router isis METRO_1
affinity-map RED bit-position 2
affinity-map BLUE bit-position 1

flex-algo 129
 advertise-definition
 affinity include-all BLUE
 !
flex-algo 130
 advertise-definition
 affinity include-all RED
```

Config 4-44 shows the second step, which involves associating the link attributes to the links that are used by the flex algo. In this case, the link attribute is link affinity. If the link attribute is not defined for a link, then the link is not considered part of the IS-IS topology of the flex algo.

Config 4-44   *Assigning Link Affinity (IOS XR)*

```
router isis METRO_1

interface GigabitEthernet0/0/0/0
 affinity flex-algo BLUE
 !
 interface GigabitEthernet0/0/0/1
  affinity flex-algo RED
 !
```

The third step is to generate summary routes. Config 4-45 provides the necessary configuration commands to allow the ABRs of a metro network to generate a summary route for the SRv6 locators allocated to flex algos 129 and 130.

Config 4-45   *Summary Route for Flex Algos 129 and 130 (IOS XR)*

```
router isis METRO_1
 address-family ipv6 unicast
  summary-prefix fc00:2:100::/40 level 2 algorithm 129 adv-unreachable
  summary-prefix fc00:3:100::/40 level 2 algorithm 130 adv-unreachable
```

The prefix-set that prevents the leaking of the metro summary back into IS-IS Level 1 of the metro network is updated for flex algos 129 and 130, as shown in Config 4-46.

Config 4-46   *Using prefix-set for the Metro 1 Summary (IOS XR)*

```
prefix-set IPV6_LOCAL_SUMMARY_PS
  fc00:0:100::/40 eq 40,
  fc00:1:100::/40 eq 40,
  fc00:2:100::/40 eq 40,
  fc00:3:100::/40 eq 40
end-set
```

Disjoint Paths Verification

Figure 4-36 shows the steps to verify the configuration for the disjoint paths use case.

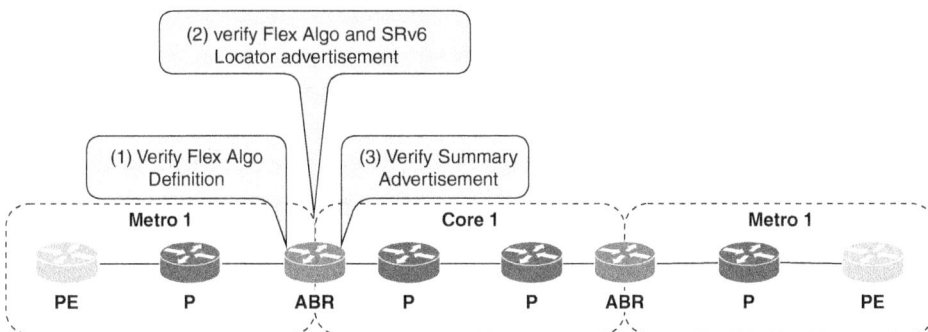

Figure 4-36   *Flex Algo Disjoint Paths Verification*

The first step is to verify the flex algo definition. The command **show isis flex-algo 129** is used to verify the status of flex algo 128. The output has several parts, as shown in Output 4-61.

The flex algo definition indicates that all the routers have the same definition (Definition Equal to Local: Yes) and priority (128) of the flex algo. Since the priority is the same, the tiebreaker is the router ID. In IS-IS Level 2, the Definition Source is ABR-4. The metric-type, as per the definition, is Delay, and Prefix-metric is enabled for flex algo 129.

The Link Affinity Attributes part indicates that flex algo 129 includes all links with affinity 0x00000002.

The flex algo status shows that flex algo 129 is defined and ready for use (Disabled: No) on ABR-1.

The Data Plane part of the output indicates that data forwarding for this flex algo is enabled for segment routing and disabled for IP.

Output 4-61 *Flex Algo 129 Enabled on ABR-1*

```
RP/0/RP0/CPU0:ABR_M1_1#sh isis flex-algo 129

IS-IS METRO_1 Flex-Algo Database
Flex-Algo 129:
  Level-2:

      Definition Priority: 128
      Definition Source: ABR_M2_2.00
      Definition Equal to Local: Yes        Flex Algo Definition
      Definition Metric Type: IGP
      Definition Flex-Algo Prefix Metric: No


      Exclude Any Affinity Bit Positions:
      Include Any Affinity Bit Positions:
      Include All Affinity Bit Positions:   1   Link Affinity Attributes
      Exclude SRLGs:


      Disabled: No                          Flex Algo Status

<snip>

    Data Plane Segemnt Routing: Yes
    Data Plane IP: No                       Data Plane
```

The second step is to verify the flex algo and SRv6 advertisement. Output 4-62 shows the IS-IS LSP from PE-1 in Metro 1 with the definition of flex algo 129. The definition includes the following information:

- Metric-Type is 0, which means the flex algo uses the IGP metric.

- Alg-type is 0, which means SPF is the algorithm type.

- Priority is 128.

- The link affinity is 0x00000002 with Include-all, indicating that all links with link affinity 0x00000002 are included in flex algo 129.

- The SRv6 locator for flex algo 129 is fc00:2:105::/48.

Output 4-62   *Flex Algo 129 Advertised by PE-1*

```
RP/0/RP0/CPU0:PE-1#show isis database level 1 PE-1.00-00 verbose


LSPID                   LSP Seq Num  LSP Checksum  LSP Holdtime/Rcvd  ATT/P/OL
PE-1.00-00              0x00000f81   0x117d           1056 /1200          0/0/0
  Area Address:    49.0001
  LSP MTU:         1492
  NLPID:           0x8e
  MT:              IPv6 Unicast                                     0/0/0
  Hostname:        PE-1
  Router Cap:      0.0.0.0 D:0 S:0
    SR Algorithm:
      Algorithm: 0
      Algorithm: 1
      Algorithm: 128
      Algorithm: 129
      Algorithm: 130
    Flex-Algo Definition:
      Algorithm: 128 Metric-Type: 1 Alg-type: 0 Priority: 128
    Flex-Algo Definition:
      Algorithm: 129 Metric-Type: 0 Alg-type: 0 Priority: 128
      Flex-Algo Include-All Ext Admin Group:
        0x00000002
<snip>
  SRv6 Locator:   MT (IPv6 Unicast) fc00:2:105::/48 D:0 Metric: 1 Algorithm: 129
    Prefix Attribute Flags: X:0 R:0 N:0 E:0 A:0
    END SID: fc00:2:105:: uN (PSP/USD)
      SID Structure:
        Block Length: 32, Node-ID Length: 16, Func-Length: 0, Args-Length: 80
<snip>
```

The third step is to verify the summary route advertisement. Output 4-63 shows that the summary routes for the SRv6 locators of flex algo 129 are advertised by the ABRs. Note that the summary routes are advertised as SRv6 locators for the same reason described earlier in this chapter, in the section "SRv6 IS-IS Verification."

Output 4-63   *Summary Route for Flex Algo 129 Advertised by ABR-1*

```
RP/0/RP0/CPU0:ABR-1#show isis database level 2 ABR-1.00-00 det

IS-IS METRO_1 (Level-2) Link State Database
LSPID                LSP Seq Num  LSP Checksum  LSP Holdtime/Rcvd  ATT/P/OL
ABR-1.00-00    * 0x0000199f   0x1942       1171 /*             0/0/0
  Area Address:    49.0001
  LSP MTU:         1492
  NLPID:           0x8e
  MT:              IPv6 Unicast                                  0/0/0
  Hostname:        ABR-1
  Router Cap:      0.0.0.0 D:0 S:0
<snip>
  SRv6 Locator:   MT (IPv6 Unicast) fc00:2:100::/40 D:0 Metric: 11 Algorithm: 129
<snip>
```

Output 4-64 shows that the RIB entry for PE-3 in Metro 2 for flex algo 129 is installed
on PE-1 and is reachable via the summary route fc00:2:200::/40.

Output 4-64   *RIB Entry for the SRv6 Locator of PE-3 for Flex Algo 129*

```
RP/0/RP0/CPU0:PE-1#show route ipv6 fc00:2:205::

Routing entry for fc00:2:200::/40
  Known via "isis METRO_1", distance 115, metric 61, SRv6-locator (algo 129), type
  inter-area
  Installed May 14 12:36:49.013 for 1d10h
  Routing Descriptor Blocks
    fe80::42:acff:fe16:e402, from ::, via GigabitEthernet0/0/0/0
      Route metric is 61
  No advertising protos.
```

Data Plane Forwarding

This section shows the steps for assigning a flex algo to a BGP L3VPN service and verifying the data plane forwarding when using flex algos.

Assigning a Flex Algo to a BGP L3VPN Service (VRF)

Each flex algo is assigned an SRv6 locator. This locator is then associated to the VRF
instance to be used for allocating the SRv6 SID to IP prefixes in the VRF instance.
Config 4-47 shows that on PE-3, the SRv6 locator BLUE (fc00:2:205::/48) is assigned to
flex algo 129, and VRF instance BLUE is assigned the SRv6 locator. Config 4-48 shows

that on PE-4, the SRv6 locator RED (fc00:3:206::/48) is assigned to flex algo 130, and VRF instance RED is assigned the locator RED.

Config 4-47   *Assigning a Flex Algo to VRF Instance BLUE on PE-3*

```
segment-routing srv6
  locators
   locator BLUE
    micro-segment behavior unode psp-usd
    prefix fc00:2:205::/48
    algorithm 129
    !
    !
router bgp 65000
 vrf BLUE
  rd auto
  address-family ipv4 unicast
   segment-routing srv6
    locator BLUE
    !
```

Config 4-48   *Assigning a Flex Algo to VRF Instance RED on PE-4*

```
segment-routing srv6
  locators

   locator RED
    micro-segment behavior unode psp-usd
    prefix fc00:3:206::/48
    algorithm 130
    !
router bgp 65000
 vrf RED
  rd auto
  address-family ipv4 unicast
   segment-routing srv6
    locator RED
```

Output 4-65 shows that the prefix 10.2.100.128/32 in VRF instance BLUE is assigned the SID fc00:2:205:e004::/64, which is based on the SRv6 locator assigned to flex algo 129.

Output 4-65   *SID Assigned to Prefix in the VRF Instance BLUE on PE-3*

```
RP/0/RP0/CPU0:PE-3#show bgp vrf BLUE 10.2.100.128/32

BGP routing table entry for 10.2.100.128/32, Route Distinguisher: 172.19.0.19:0
Versions:
  Process            bRIB/RIB  SendTblVer
  Speaker                 35        35
    SRv6-VPN SID: fc00:2:205:e004::/64  <-- SID assigned to IP prefix
  10.2.100.128/32
Last Modified: Jul 28 00:41:01.414 for 2w3d
Paths: (1 available, best #1)
  Advertised to PE peers (in unique update groups):
    fc00:0:207::1
  Path #1: Received by speaker 0
  Advertised to PE peers (in unique update groups):
    fc00:0:207::1
200
    10.2.100.2 from 10.2.100.2 (172.19.0.22)
      Origin IGP, metric 0, localpref 100, valid, external, best, group-best,
import-candidate
      Received Path ID 0, Local Path ID 1, version 35
      Extended community: RT:65000:100
      Origin-AS validity: (disabled)
```

Output 4-66 shows that the prefix 10.2.101.128/32 in VRF instance RED is assigned the SID fc00:3:206:e004::/64, which is based on the SRv6 locator assigned to flex algo 130.

Output 4-66   *SID Assigned to the Prefix in VRF Instance RED on PE-4*

```
RP/0/RP0/CPU0:PE-4#show bgp vrf RED 10.2.101.128/32

BGP routing table entry for 10.2.101.128/32, Route Distinguisher: 65000:101
Versions:
  Process            bRIB/RIB  SendTblVer
  Speaker                 31        31
    SRv6-VPN SID: fc00:3:206:e004::/64  <-- SID assigned to IP prefix
  10.2.101.128/32
Last Modified: Jul 28 00:41:01.424 for 2w3d
Paths: (1 available, best #1)
  Advertised to PE peers (in unique update groups):
    fc00:0:207::1
  Path #1: Received by speaker 0
  Advertised to PE peers (in unique update groups):
```

```
   fc00:0:207::1
200
   10.2.101.2 from 10.2.101.2 (172.19.0.22)
     Origin IGP, metric 0, localpref 100, valid, external, best, group-best,
import-candidate
     Received Path ID 0, Local Path ID 1, version 31
     Extended community: RT:65000:101
     Origin-AS validity: (disabled)
```

Verifying Data Plane Forwarding

Figure 4-37 shows the packet flow from CE-1 to CE-3. Traffic destined for 10.2.100.128/32 uses the links marked in blue (flex algo 129), and traffic to destination 10.2.101.128/32 traverses the links marked in red (flex algo 130).

Output 4-67 shows that a traceroute from PE-1 to PE-3 for the SRv6 locator of flex algo 129 (fc00:2:205::) is used to verify that the blue path shown in Figure 4-37 is used for traffic from CE-1 to CE-3:

> PE-1—P-5—ABR-1—P-1—P-3—ABR-3—P-7—PE-3

The traceroute uses the source address from algo 0 because the source address encapsulation is based on the loopback0 address, which is from algo 0. For the topology shown in Figure 4-37, there is no backup path for the blue path for certain failures. For example, when the link between ABR-1 and P-1 fails, there is no connectivity between CE-1 and CE-3 on the blue path.

Output 4-67   *Traceroute from PE-1 to PE-3 for the Blue Path*

```
RP/0/RP0/CPU0:PE-1#traceroute ipv6 fc00:2:205::

Type escape sequence to abort.
Tracing the route to fc00:2:205::

1  fc00:0:103::1 2 msec 1 msec 2 msec <-- P-5
2  fc00:0:101::1 3 msec 2 msec 3 msec <-- ABR-1
3  fc00:0:1::1 5 msec 3 msec 8 msec <-- P-1
4  fc00:0:3::1 4 msec 4 msec 5 msec <-- P-3
5  fc00:0:201::1 5 msec 5 msec 7 msec <-- ABR-3
6  fc00:0:203::1 7 msec 6 msec 9 msec <--P-7
7  fc00:0:205::1 6 msec 8 msec 7 msec PE-3
```

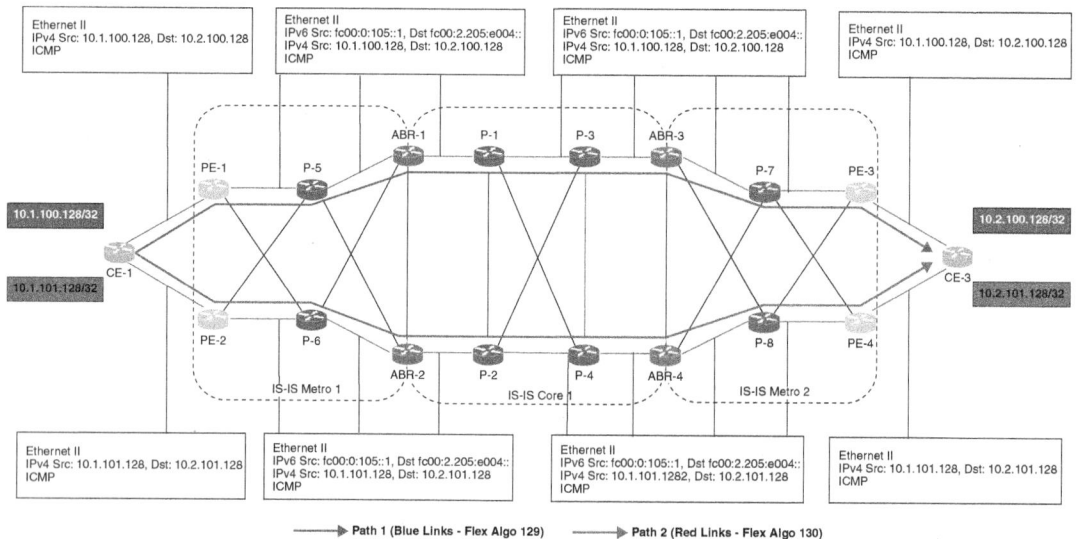

Figure 4-37   *Flex Algo Data Plane Verification*

Similarly, a traceroute from PE-2 to PE-4 for the SRv6 locator of flex algo 130 (fc00:3:206::) is used to verify that the red path shown in Figure 4-37 is used for the traffic from CE-1 to CE-3:

   PE-2 --- P-6 --- ABR-2 --- P-2 --- P-4 --- ABR-4 --- P-8 --- PE4

Output 4-68   *Traceroute from PE-2 to PE-4 for the Red Path*

```
RP/0/RP0/CPU0:PE-2#traceroute ipv6 fc00:3:206::

Type escape sequence to abort.
Tracing the route to fc00:3:206::

1  fc00:0:104::1 3 msec 2 msec 1 msec <-- P-6
2  fc00:0:102::1 3 msec 2 msec 2 msec <-- ABR-2
3  fc00:0:2::1 3 msec 3 msec 4 msec <-- P-2
4  fc00:0:4::1 4 msec 4 msec 4 msec <-- P-4
5  fc00:0:202::1 5 msec 5 msec 11 msec <-- ABR-4
6  fc00:0:204::1 6 msec 6 msec 5 msec <-- P-8
7  fc00:0:206::1 7 msec 5 msec 6 msec <--- PE-4
```

SR-MPLS Configuration for Flex Algo Use Cases

So far, we have looked at the configuration and verification of flex algo use cases for an SRv6 network. The same concepts are also valid for SR-MPLS.

The difference between SR-MPLS and SRv6 transport networks is in the transport identifier. In an SR-MPLS network, the transport identifier is the Node SID associated with the BGP next hop, while in an SRv6 network, the transport identifier is the SRv6 locator (uN behavior). Associating a transport mechanism to a flex algo is done in the control plane. In an SR-MPLS network, the Node SID is associated with a flex algo, while in an SRv6 network, the SRv6 locator is associated with a flex algo.

For the BGP-based services discussed in Chapter 7, "L3VPN Service Deployment: Configuration and Verification Techniques," the service label is associated with a transport identifier to transport Layer 3 VPN payload or Layer 2 VPN payload over an SR-MPLS or SRv6 network. The difference between the SR-MPLS and SRv6 networks is the mechanism to associate the service label and the transport identifier.

In an SR-MPLS network, the Node SID assigned to the BGP next hop of the BGP update determines the transport label. A Layer 3 VPN service or Layer 2 VPN service must use the BGP update source from a flex algo in order to use the path specified by the flex algo in the SR-MPLS network.

In an SRv6 network, the SRv6 locator advertised as a part of the BGP update is used as the transport identifier. A Layer 3 VPN service or Layer 2 VPN service must specify the SRv6 locator from a flex algo in order to use the path specified by the flex algo in the SRv6 network.

This section highlights the configuration differences between an SRv6 network and an SR-MPLS network for flex algos.

Config 4-49 shows the configuration for IS-IS and OSPF for both IOS XR and IOS XE devices. Interface loopback128 is assigned the IPv4 address 10.128.0.7/32 and the Prefix SID 16128. This Prefix SID is assigned to flex algo 128. In IOS XR, the Prefix SID is assigned to a flex algo under the IS-IS/OSPF router process, while in IOS XE, Prefix SID is assigned to a flex algo under connected-prefix-sid-map.

Config 4-49   *Assigning a Flex Algo to the Prefix SID (IOS XR/IOS XE)*

IOS-XR (IS-IS and OSPF)		IOS-XR (IS-IS and OSPF)	
``interface Loopback128
ipv4 address 10.128.0.7 255.255.255.255```	**Interface**	```interface Loopback128
ipv4 address 10.128.0.7 255.255.255.255```	**Interface**
``router isis CORE1
interface Loopback128
address-family ipv4 unicast
prefix-sid algorithm 128 absolute 16128```	**IS-IS**	```connected-prefix-sid-map
address-family ipv4 algorithm 128
10.128.0.7/32 absolute 16128 range 1
exit-address-family```	**prefix-sid-map**
``router ospf METRO2
area 0
interface Loopback128
prefix-sid algorithm 128 absolute 16128```	**OSPF**		

There are several ways to assign a flex algo to a BGP service. One way is to modify the BGP next hop for the service by using a route policy. In most cases, a service can be identified using the extended community route target. Config 4-50 shows a sample configuration where the BGP next hop is set to 10.128.0.7 (flex algo 128) for an L3VPN service that uses RT 65001:1. This route policy is then applied to the iBGP peers for VPNv4 updates.

Config 4-50 *Modifying the Next Hop Based on the Route Target (IOS XR)*

```
route-policy FA128_NEXTHOP_RP
  if extcommunity rt matches-any (65001:101) then
    set next-hop 10.128.0.7
  endif
end-policy

router bgp 65001
<snip>
 neighbor <iBGP Peer>
  address-family vpnv4 unicast
   route-policy FA128_NEXTHOP_RP
```

Segment Routing Control Plane (BGP)

Now that we have looked at the SRv6 control plane and data plane, we are ready to focus on how BGP is used in an SR-MPLS network to exchange SR-related information and provide scalability.

The IGP has been used to exchange SR-related information up to this point in this chapter. This section focuses on the exchange of SR-related information within an autonomous system and between autonomous systems using BGP to improve the scalability of an MPLS network.

BGP Prefix SID

Segments associated with a BGP prefix are known as BGP Prefix SIDs and are globally significant within an SR or BGP domain. The BGP Prefix SID identifies an instruction to forward the packet over the ECMP-aware best-path computed by BGP to the related prefix. RFC 8670 highlights some of the drawbacks related to ECMP that can be addressed using BGP Prefix SID. More details about BGP Prefix SID can be found in Chapter 2, in the section, "BGP Prefix Segment (BGP Prefix SID)."

BGP Prefix SID Configuration

Figure 4-38 shows the configuration steps required to enable and advertise BGP Prefix SIDs. This configuration must be done on all BGP speakers in the SR-MPLS network.

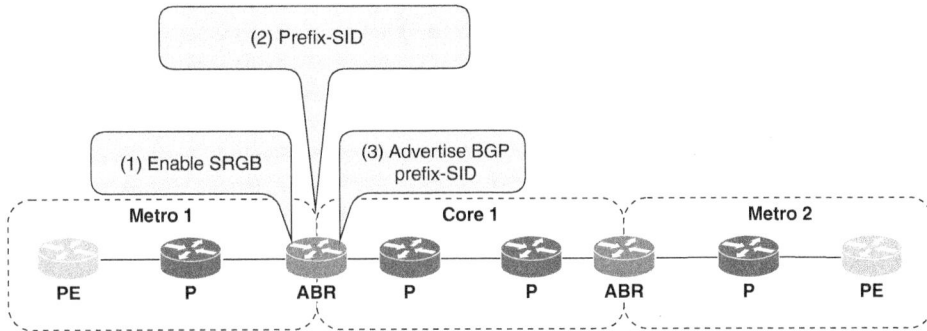

Figure 4-38 *BGP Prefix SID Configuration Steps*

Step 1: Enable SRGB

Each BGP speaker must be configured with an SRGB. Refer to section "SR-MPLS Baseline" for information about the SRGB configuration and verification.

Step 2: Configure the BGP Prefix SID

The BGP Prefix SID is manually configured from the segment routing global block (SRGB) range of labels. It provides the instruction regarding the label that should be allocated to the BGP prefix.

Config 4-51 and Config 4-52 show the configuration of a BGP Prefix SID on an IOS XR device and on an IOS XE device, respectively. In the case of IOS XR, the Prefix SID is assigned using a route policy that sets the SID index. For example, the prefix 10.0.4.1/32 is assigned the index 3001. Because the start of the SRGB is at 16000, the Node SID 19001 is associated with 10.0.4.1/32.

In the case of IOS XE, the BGP Prefix SID configuration is the same as the configuration of a Node SID for the IGP on an IOS XE device. In addition, segment routing is enabled for BGP under address-family ipv4 unicast.

Note that the Prefix SID is assigned to the IPv4 address of the BGP update source. Typically, this is the loopback0 interface. If the Node SID for loopback0 is also advertised in the IGP, then the Node SID and BGP Prefix SID must be set to the same value.

Config 4-51 *Configuring the BGP Prefix SID (IOS XR)*

```
route-policy SID($SID)
  set label-index $SID
end-policy

router bgp 65001
 address-family ipv4 labeled-unicast
  network 10.0.4.1/32 route-policy SID(3001)
```

Config 4-52 *Configuring the BGP Prefix SID (IOS XE)*

```
router bgp 65001
 address-family ipv4 unicast
  segment-routing
!
segment-routing mpls
 !
 connected-prefix-sid-map
  address-family ipv4
   10.0.4.2/32 absolute 19002 range 1
  exit-address-family
```

Step 3: **Advertise** the **BGP** Prefix SID

Config 4-53 and Config 4-54 show the configuration to enable the advertisement of the BGP Prefix SID for IOS XR and IOS XE, respectively. This configuration must be done on all BGP speakers.

On devices, address-family labeled-unicast is used to advertise the BGP Prefix SID.

In the case of IOS XE, the command **segment-routing mpls** is used to enable SR for BGP, and the command **send-label** allows BGP to send the BGP updates with labels (Prefix SID).

Note Unlike IOS XR, where address-family labeled-unicast is used for advertising the BGP Prefix SID, IOS XE uses address-family ipv4 unicast.

This configuration must be enabled for all route reflectors and route reflector clients.

Config 4-53 *Advertising the BGP Prefix SID (IOS XR)*

```
route-policy SID($SID)
  set label-index $SID
end-policy

router bgp 65001
 address-family ipv4 labeled-unicast
  network 10.0.4.1/32 route-policy SID(3001)
```

Config 4-54 *Advertising the BGP Prefix SID (IOS XE)*

```
route-policy SID($SID)
  set label-index $SID
end-policy

router bgp 65001
 address-family ipv4 labeled-unicast
  network 10.0.4.1/32 route-policy SID(3001)
```

BGP Prefix SID Verification

The verification of the BGP Prefix SID advertised by a device is validated in two steps, as shown in Figure 4-39. The verification can be done on all BGP-LU speakers in the SR-MPLS network.

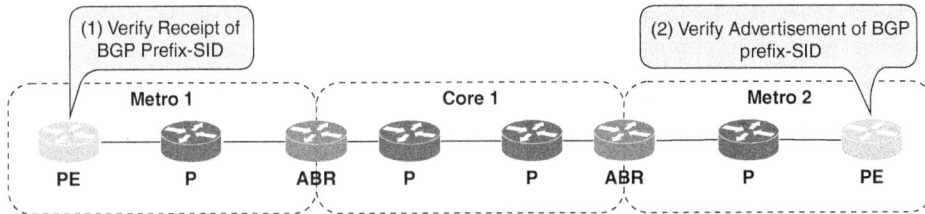

Figure 4-39 *BGP Prefix SID Verification Steps*

Step 1: Verify Receipt of the BGP Prefix SID

Output 4-69 shows the BGP entry for 10.0.4.2 sent by BGP neighbor PE-4 (10.0.4.2) via the route reflector (10.0.3.254). The received label is 19002, which corresponds to the Prefix SID assigned to 10.0.4.2 on PE-4, as shown in Output 4-70.

Output 4-69 *Verifying the BGP Prefix SID in the BGP Update (IOS XR)*

```
RP/0/0/CPU0:PE-1#show bgp ipv4 labeled-unicast 10.0.4.2


BGP routing table entry for 10.0.4.2/32
<snip>
Paths: (1 available, best #1)
  Not advertised to any peer
  Path #1: Received by speaker 0
  Not advertised to any peer
  Local
    10.1.1.5 (metric 20) from 10.0.3.254 (10.0.4.2)
      Received Label 19002
      Origin IGP, metric 0, localpref 100, valid, internal, best, group-best,
  labeled-unicast
      Received Path ID 1, Local Path ID 1, version 646
      Originator: 10.0.4.2, Cluster list: 10.0.3.254, 10.0.1.5, 10.0.1.254, 10.0.1.8
      Label-Index: 3002
```

Output 4-70 *Prefix SID Assigned to Prefix 10.0.4.2/32*

```
PE-4#show segment-routing mpls connected-prefix-sid-map local ipv4


               PREFIX_SID_CONN_MAP ALGO_0


  Prefix/masklen    SID Type Range Flags SRGB
    10.0.4.2/32 19002  Abs      1           Y
```

Step 2: Verify the Advertisement of the BGP Prefix SID

The same verification process is done on PE-4, which is an IOS XE device. Output 4-71 shows the BGP entry for 10.0.4.1/32 advertised by PE-3 (10.0.4.1) with the MPLS label 19001.

Output 4-71   *Verifying the BGP Prefix SID in the BGP Update (IOS XE)*

```
PE-4#show bgp ipv4 unicast 10.0.4.1/32

BGP routing table entry for 10.0.4.1/32, version 4538
Paths: (2 available, best #2, table default, RIB-failure(17))
Net local label from RIB
  Not advertised to any peer
  Refresh Epoch 1
  Local
    10.0.1.8 (metric 2) from 10.0.1.8 (10.0.1.8)
      Origin IGP, metric 0, localpref 100, valid, internal
      sr-labelindex 0xBB9
      Originator: 10.0.4.1, Cluster list: 10.0.1.8
      mpls labels in/out 19001/19001
      rx pathid: 0, tx pathid: 0
      Updated on Jun 14 2023 04:48:43 UTC
  Refresh Epoch 1
  Local
    10.0.1.7 (metric 2) from 10.0.1.7 (10.0.1.7)
      Origin IGP, metric 0, localpref 100, valid, internal, best
      sr-labelindex 0xBB9
      Originator: 10.0.4.1, Cluster list: 10.0.1.7
      mpls labels in/out 19001/19001
      rx pathid: 0, tx pathid: 0x0
      Updated on Jun 14 2023 04:48:36 UTC
```

Intra-AS BGP-LU with a BGP Prefix SID

The section "Segment Routing Control Plane (IGP)," earlier in this chapter, provides details about using an IGP to exchange Node SID information to provide an LSP between two PE devices in the IGP domain. The BGP Layer 3 and Layer 2 VPN services on the PE devices use the LSP to transport the service payload between PE devices.

The section "SRv6 IS-IS Summarization," earlier in this chapter, provides a solution—summarization—to scale the IGP for many devices. This solution is based on a hierarchy of IGP levels and involves the ABR advertising one or several summary routes representing all the devices in the IGP domain. While summarization helps to scale an SRv6 network that uses IPv6 addresses to forward packets, it breaks the end-to-end LSP path in an SR-MPLS network. An LSP to a PE device in the remote domain depends on the availability of the route to the PE device. Summarization at the ABR prevents the advertisement of the Node SIDs of the PE devices from the remote domain. We will look more closely at this problem with summarization by using the SR-MPLS network shown in Figure 4-40.

In the scenario, Metro 1, Core 1, and Metro 2 are in the same IGP domain. Metro 1 and Metro 2 are in IS-IS Level 1, Core 1 is in IS-IS Level 2, and ABR-1 and ABR-2 are the ABR routers summarizing the routes from Metro 1. PE-3 in Metro 2 does not receive the Node SID for PE-1 because of the summary route advertised by ABR-1 and ABR-2, which prevents PE-3 from establishing an LSP to PE-1. Therefore, summarization must not be used in an MPLS network.

Scalability in an MPLS network is achieved by splitting the network into several isolated IGP domains. Node SID advertisement between different domains is done using Border Gateway Protocol Labeled Unicast (BGP-LU). The solution to provide the scalability in an MPLS network relies on the use of BGP-LU sessions based on route reflectors (RRs) to facilitate the exchange of BGP Prefix SIDs between PE devices in the same AS but in different IGP domains.

With intra-AS BGP-LU, the routers (ABRs) that interconnect the IGP domains must be BGP-LU inline route reflectors with the next-hop-self setting to advertise the IPv4 prefix and the associated Prefix SID to the BGP neighbors.

The ABRs are inline route reflectors to scale the number of iBGP sessions in a large network with thousands of BGP speakers. One of the goals of an BGP-LU solution is to have a highly scalable end-to-end infrastructure. Thus, each IGP domain should be kept simple. Since all BGP sessions are iBGP, there is a need for a full mesh of peerings between all iBGP speakers within the AS, which results in a very large number of iBGP sessions. If the ABRs are route reflectors, the number of iBGP peerings is reduced to the number of BGP speakers in an IGP domain instead of between all BGP speakers of the complete AS.

BGP operates using recursive routing lookups to overcome the scalability limitations of an IGP. For the recursive lookup, BGP uses BGP next hop attached to each BGP route entry. Thus, for example, if PE-1 wants to send a packet to PE-3, then PE-1 does a routing lookup in its BGP routing table and finds a route to PE-3 and forwards the packet to the BGP next hop for PE-3. This next hop must be known by the underlying IGP. In order to ensure that the IGP has a route to the BGP next hop for PE nodes in remote domains, the ABR sets the next hop to self, thereby ensuring that the BGP next hop is within the local IGP domain.

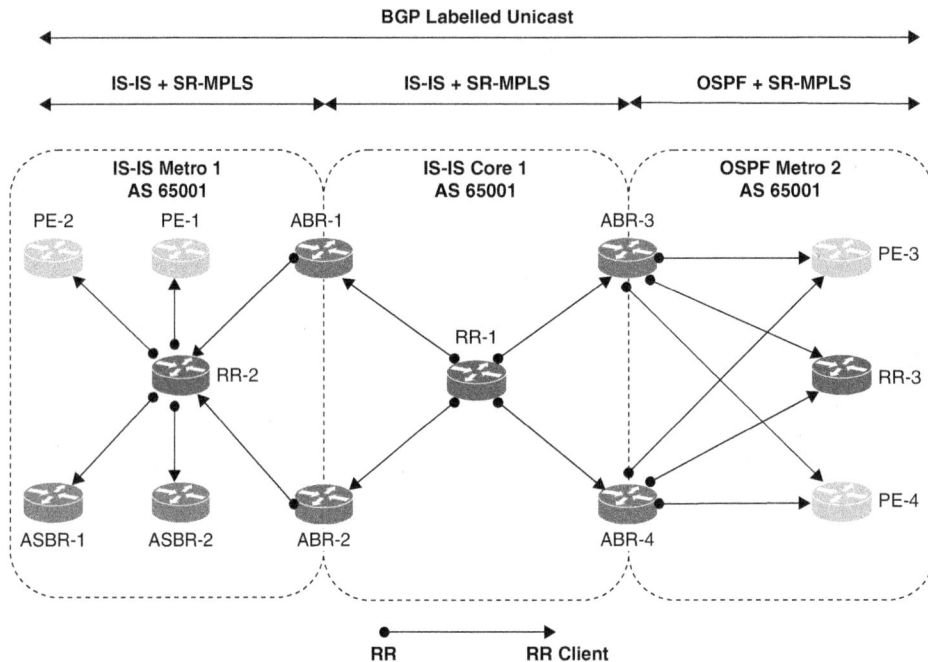

Figure 4-40   *BGP-LU Topology for AS65001*

Intra-AS BGP-LU Design

Figure 4-40 shows an SR-MPLS network with AS number 65001. The network is split into three domains, each with its own IGP; these domains are kept separate to provide scalability. The domain Core 1 provides connectivity between domains Metro 1 and Metro 2 using BGP-LU.

IS-IS is the IGP in the domains Core 1 and Metro 1, where all devices are in IS-IS Level 2 and the loopback0 interface of the devices is advertised in IS-IS. OSPF is the IGP in Metro 2, where all the devices are in Area 0. Segment routing is enabled for the IGPs to advertise the Node SIDs and the Adjacency SIDs.

ABR-1 and ABR-2 are inline route reflectors for Metro 1, and ABR-3 and ABR-4 are inline route reflectors for Metro 2. RR-1 is the route reflector for the BGP-LU connectivity between the ABRs in Core 1.

The ABRs participate in the IGP of the Core and Metro 1 and 2 domains to facilitate the BGP-LU sessions with the devices in the Core and Metro 1 and 2 domains.

AS border routers (ASBRs) provide connectivity to other autonomous systems. Details of the BGP-LU design and configuration for ASBRs can be found in the section "Inter-AS BGP-LU," later in this chapter.

BGP Additional Path

A BGP router advertises only the best path to its neighbors. When a better path is found, the router replaces the current path and advertises the better path to the neighbors. This replacement also happens when the current path is invalidated, such as due to failure of the router that advertised it.

The BGP Additional Path feature enables the advertisement of multiple paths for the same prefix. Additional Path is an extension to BGP, and it adds a unique path identifier to each path. The path ID works similarly to the route distinguisher (RD) in an MPLS VPN, except that the path IDs can be used in any BGP address family. This feature can only be used for iBGP, and there are three steps to implement it:

Step 1.   Enable routers to send and/or receive additional paths.

Step 2.   Define selection criteria on the router to determine which additional candidate paths should be selected other than the best path.

Step 3.   Advertise a set or sets of additional paths to each neighbor.

For the additional path selection, there are three options:

- **Best N:** This is the best path and the second-best path. The second-best path is chosen by eliminating the next best path and then selecting the next best path after that.

- **Group-best:** This is the set of paths that are the best paths from each AS.

- **All:** Every path that has a unique next hop can be used as an additional path.

Config 4-55 and Config 4-56 show the configuration for enabling the BGP Additional Paths features on IOS XR and IOS XE devices. BGP speakers must be configured to enable BGP Additional Paths wherever it is necessary.

In the case of IOS XR, the additional path send and receive capabilities are configured for the address family, and path section is done using a route policy.

In the case of IOS XE, the additional path send and receive capabilities are configured for each neighbor under the address family. The path section is configured for each neighbor using the command **neighbor <*IP Address*> advertise additional-paths all**.

Config 4-55   *Configuring the BGP Additional Paths Feature (IOS XR)*

```
route-policy BGP_ADD_PATH_RP
  set path-selection all advertise
end-policy

router bgp 65002
 bgp router-id 10.0.2.254
 address-family ipv4 unicast
  additional-paths receive
  additional-paths send
  additional-paths selection route-policy BGP_ADD_PATH_RP
```

Config 4-56   *Configuring the BGP Additional Paths Feature (IOS XE)*

```
router bgp 65002

 address-family ipv4 unicast
  neighbor 10.0.3.254 additional-paths send receive
  neighbor 10.0.3.254 advertise additional-paths all
```

Intra-AS BGP-LU Configuration

Config 4-57 and Config 4-58 show the IS-IS configuration related to SR for devices in Core 1 and Metro 1.

In IOS XR, the Prefix SID is assigned to loopback0 under the IS-IS process, and in IOS XE, the Prefix SID is set under segment-routing, using prefix-sid-map.

Config 4-57   *Configuring IS-IS in Core 1 and Metro 1 (IOS XR)*

```
router isis CORE1
is-type level-2-only
 address-family ipv4 unicast
  segment-routing mpls
interface Loopback0
  passive
  address-family ipv4 unicast
   prefix-sid absolute 16002
 !
 interface GigabitEthernet0/0/0/0
  circuit-type level-2-only
  point-to-point
  address-family ipv4 unicast
```

Config 4-58   *Configuring IS-IS in Core 1 and Metro 1 (IOS XE)*

```
interface GigabitEthernet1
ip router isis CORE1

router isis CORE1
 is-type level-2-only
 segment-routing mpls
 passive-interface Loopback0

segment-routing mpls
 connected-prefix-sid-map
  address-family ipv4
   10.0.1.1/32 absolute 16001 range 1
  exit-address-family
```

Config 4-59 and Config 4-60 show the configuration on ABR-1 (IOS XR) and ABR-2 (IOS XE) where SR is enabled to advertise the Prefix SIDs and the Adjacency SIDs. Prefix SIDs are assigned to the loopback0 and loopback1 interfaces. ABR-1 and ABR-2 participate in the Core 1 and Metro 1 IS-IS process to advertise the loopback0 and loopback1 interfaces in both the domains to establish BGP-LU sessions.

Note   Two loopbacks are used on the ABRs to implement the Anycast SID. The loopback0 interface is used for the BGP sessions, and the loopback1 interface is assigned the Anycast SID, which is used for load balancing. The n-flag is cleared to enable the Anycast SID for the loopback1 interface.

Config 4-59   *Configuring IS-IS on ABR-1 (IOS XR)*

```
interface GigabitEthernet1
ip router isis CORE1

router isis CORE1
 is-type level-2-only
 segment-routing mpls
 passive-interface Loopback0

segment-routing mpls
 connected-prefix-sid-map
  address-family ipv4
   10.0.1.1/32 absolute 16001 range 1
  exit-address-family
```

Config 4-60   *Configuring IS-IS on ABR-2 (IOS XE)*

```
interface GigabitEthernet1
ip router isis CORE1

router isis CORE1
 is-type level-2-only
 segment-routing mpls
 passive-interface Loopback0

segment-routing mpls
 connected-prefix-sid-map
  address-family ipv4
   10.0.1.1/32 absolute 16001 range 1
  exit-address-family
```

Config 4-61 and Config 4-62 show the OSPF configuration for IOS XR and IOS XE in Metro 2, where segment routing is enabled to advertise the Node SIDs and Adjacency SIDs.

In IOS XR, the Prefix SID is assigned to the loopback0 interface under the IS-IS process. In IOS XE, the Prefix SID for a prefix is set under segment-routing, using prefix-sid-map.

Config 4-61   *Configuring OSPF for Metro 2 (IOS XR)*

```
router ospf METRO2
 router-id 10.0.4.1
 segment-routing mpls
 network point-to-point
 address-family ipv4 unicast
 area 0
 segment-routing mpls
  interface Loopback0
   prefix-sid index 3001
  !
  interface GigabitEthernet0/0/0/0
  !
  interface GigabitEthernet0/0/0/1
```

Config 4-62   *Configuring OSPF for Metro 2 (IOS XE)*

```
segment-routing mpls
connected-prefix-sid-map
  address-family ipv4
    10.0.4.2/32 absolute 19002 range 1
  exit-address-family

interface Loopback0
 ip address 10.0.4.2 255.255.255.255
 ip ospf network point-to-point
 ip ospf 1 area 0

router ospf 1
 router-id 10.0.4.2
 segment-routing mpls
 passive-interface Loopback0
 network 192.168.4.4 0.0.0.1 area 0
 network 192.168.4.6 0.0.0.1 area 0
```

Like the ABRs in Metro 1, ABR-3 and ABR-4 participate in the IS-IS Core 1 process and the OSPF 1 process in Metro 2 to advertise the loopback0 interface in both the domains, as shown in Config 4-63 and Config 4-64.

Config 4-63   *Configuring OSPF and IS-IS on ABR-3 (IOS XR)*

```
router isis CORE1
address-family ipv4 unicast
  metric-style wide
  segment-routing mpls sr-prefer
 !
 interface Loopback0
  passive
  address-family ipv4 unicast
  prefix-sid absolute 16007
   !
 !
router ospf METRO2
 router-id 10.0.1.7
 network point-to-point
 address-family ipv4 unicast
 area 0
  interface Loopback0
   passive enable
   prefix-sid absolute 16007
```

Config 4-64   *Configuring OSPF and IS-IS on ABR-4 (IOS XE)*

```
segment-routing mpls
connected-prefix-sid-map
  address-family ipv4
   10.0.1.8/32 absolute 16008 range 1
  exit-address-family

router ospf 1
 router-id 10.0.1.8
 segment-routing mpls
 passive-interface Loopback0
 network 192.168.1.44 0.0.0.1 area 0
 network 192.168.4.2 0.0.0.1 area 0
 network 192.168.4.4 0.0.0.1 area 0
 network 192.168.4.42 0.0.0.1 area 0
 !
```

```
router isis CORE1
 net 49.0001.0001.0000.0008.00
 is-type level-2-only
 metric-style wide
 segment-routing mpls
 passive-interface Loopback0
```

Figure 4-41 shows the configuration steps for intra-AS BGP-LU:

Note   The BGP Prefix SID configuration must be done on all the BGP speakers.
The ABRs are inline RRs for the BGP-LU speakers in the metro network.

Step 1.   Configure the BGP Prefix SID. Refer to the section, "BGP Prefix SID
Configuration," earlier in this chapter, for information on how to configure
the BGP Prefix SIDs.

Step 2.   Configure the route reflector and clients.

Step 3.   Set next-hop-self on the ABRs.

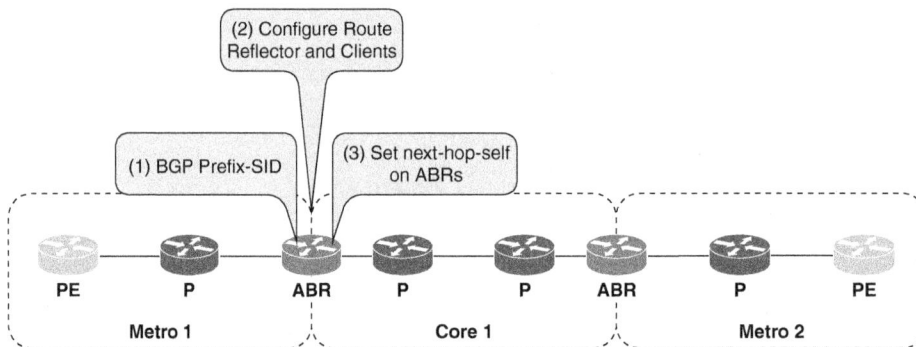

Figure 4-41   *Intra-AS BGP-LU Configuration Steps*

Config 4-65 and Config 4-66 show the BGP-LU configuration for an inline route reflector
(ABR-3) and route reflector client (PE-4) in Metro 1. The same configuration applies to
RRs and RR clients in Core 1 and Metro 2. The command **route-reflector-client** is used
to configure an iBGP neighbor as a route reflector client. The ABR sets the next hop to
itself because of the command **next-hop-self**.

On IOS XR devices, the additional command **ibgp policy out enforce-modifications** is
required to allow a route reflector to set next-hop-self for iBGP sessions, and on IOS XE,
the keyword **next-hop-self all** is required to set the next hop to self.

Config 4-65   *Configuring BGP-LU for the Route Reflector on Metro 1 (IOS XR)*

```
router bgp 65001
 bgp router-id 10.0.1.7
 ibgp policy out enforce-modifications
 address-family ipv4 unicast
  network 10.0.1.7/32 route-policy SID(7)
  allocate-label all
 !
neighbor 10.0.4.2
  remote-as 65001
  update-source Loopback0
  address-family ipv4 labeled-unicast
   route-policy PASS in
   route-reflector-client
   next-hop-self
  !
```

Config 4-66   *Configuring BGP-LU for the Route Reflector Client on Metro 1 (IOS XE)*

```
router bgp 65001
 neighbor 10.0.1.7 remote-as 65001
 neighbor 10.0.1.7 update-source Loopback0
 !
 address-family ipv4
  segment-routing mpls
  neighbor 10.0.1.7 activate
  neighbor 10.0.1.7 route-reflector-client
  neighbor 10.0.1.7 next-hop-self all
  neighbor 10.0.1.7 send-label
```

Intra-AS BGP-LU Verification

This section shows the commands and outputs to verify the advertisement of BGP Prefix SIDs between PE nodes located in Metro 1 and Metro 2. The BGP updates are traced from PE-3 in Metro 2 to PE-1 in Metro 1 and from PE-1 in Metro 1 to PE-3 in Metro 2. The commands and the output show the change in the BGP next hop as the BGP update traverses the ABRs in the network.

On IOS XR devices, the BGP-LU prefixes are advertised in the labeled unicast address family. The next hop is set to the ABR advertising these prefixes and is verified on the RR clients using the command **show bgp ipv4 labeled-unicast**.

On IOS XE devices, the BGP-LU prefixes are advertised in the ipv4 unicast address family, and the command **show bgp ipv4 unicast** is used to verify the next hop of the BGP-LU prefixes.

Figure 4-42 shows the BGP update for prefix 10.0.4.1 (loopback0 of PE-3) from PE-3 in Metro 2 to PE-1 in Metro 1. The BGP updates are sent in the following order:

1. PE-3 to ABR-3 and ABR-4

2. ABR-3/ABR-4 to RR-1

3. RR-1 to ABR-5 and ABR-6

4. ABR-6/ABR-6 to RR-2

5. RR-2 to PE-1

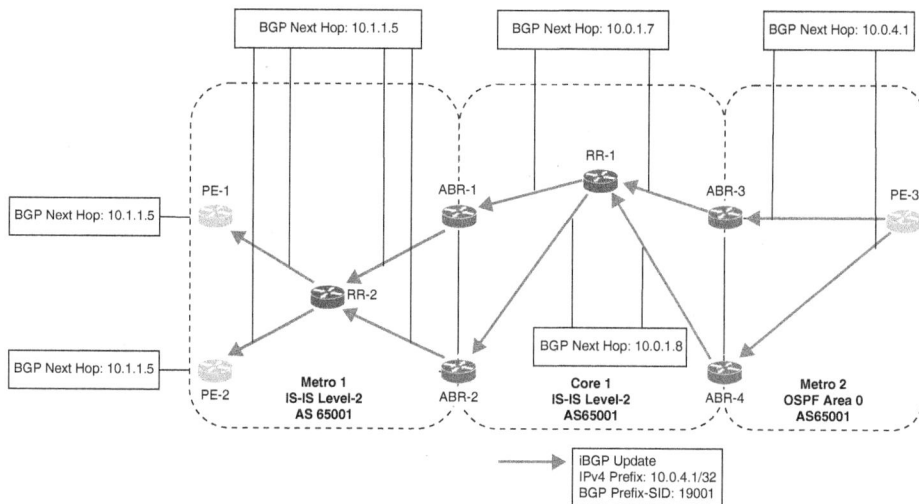

Figure 4-42   *BGP-LU Update for Prefix 10.0.4.1*

You need to verify the following:

■ The ABR modifies the BGP next hop to self before sending the BGP-LU updates to its BGP neighbors.

■ All other BGP-LU speakers do not modify the BGP next hop.

To avoid showing several outputs with similar verification, this section presents the verification steps for only the BGP prefix 10.0.4.1 advertised by PE-3, the change in BGP next hop is shown only for the update from ABR-3 to RR-1 in Core 1, and the label stack to forward the packets to PE-3 is shown only for ABR-1 and ABR-2

In Metro 2, the BGP-LU prefix 10.0.4.1/32 is advertised by PE-3 to ABR-3 and ABR-4. This can be verified on ABR-3 and ABR-4 for the BGP-LU prefix 10.0.4.1 as shown in Output 4-72 and Output 4-73.

Output 4-72 *Verifying the BGP Next Hop for BGP-LU Prefix 10.0.4.1 in Metro 2 on ABR-3 (IOS XR)*

```
RP/0/0/CPU0:ABR-3#show bgp ipv4 labeled-unicast 10.0.4.1

BGP routing table entry for 10.0.4.1/32
<snip>
  Local, (Received from a RR-client)
    10.0.4.1 (metric 2) from 10.0.4.1 (10.0.4.1)
      Received Label 3
      Origin IGP, metric 0, localpref 100, valid, internal, best, group-best,
  labeled-unicast
      Received Path ID 0, Local Path ID 1, version 433
      Label-Index: 3001
<snip>
```

Output 4-73 *Verifying the BGP Next Hop for BGP-LU Prefix 10.0.4.1 in Metro 2 on ABR-4 (IOS XE)*

```
ABR-4#sh bgp ipv4 unicast 10.0.4.1

BGP routing table entry for 10.0.4.1/32, version 5335
<snip>
  Local, (Received from a RR-client)
    10.0.4.1 (metric 2) from 10.0.4.1 (10.0.4.1)
      Origin IGP, metric 0, localpref 100, valid, internal, best
      sr-labelindex 0xBB9
      mpls labels in/out 19001/imp-null
      rx pathid: 0, tx pathid: 0x0
      Updated on Jun 17 2023 09:56:48 UTC

<snip>
```

On the IOS XR device ABR-3 and the IOS XE device ABR-4, the BGP next hop is 10.0.4.1, which corresponds to the loopback0 of PE-3.

ABR-3 sends the BGP update to RR-1 for prefix 10.0.4.1/32 with the modified BGP next hop to self, which corresponds to 10.0.1.7. Similarly, ABR-4 sends the BGP updates to RR-1 with the BGP next hop set to 10.0.1.8. RR-1 forwards the updates received from ABR-3 and ABR-4 to ABR-1 and ABR-2 without modifying the BGP next hop, which can be verified on ABR-1 and ABR-2 for the BGP-LU prefix 10.0.4.1 as shown in Output 4-74 and Output 4-75.

Output 4-74 *Verifying the BGP Next Hop for BGP-LU Prefixes in Core 1 on ABR-1 (IOS XR)*

```
RP/0/0/CPU0:ABR-1#show bgp ipv4 labeled-unicast 10.0.4.1

BGP routing table entry for 10.0.4.1/32
<snip>
  Path #1: Received by speaker 0
  Advertised IPv4 Labeled-unicast paths to peers (in unique update groups):
    10.0.3.254
  Local, (received & used)
    10.0.1.7 (metric 30) from 10.0.1.254 (10.0.4.1)
      Received Label 19001
      Origin IGP, metric 0, localpref 100, valid, internal, add-path,
labeled-unicast
      Received Path ID 0, Local Path ID 2, version 743
      Originator: 10.0.4.1, Cluster list: 10.0.1.254, 10.0.1.7
      Label-Index: 3001
  Path #2: Received by speaker 0
  Advertised IPv4 Labeled-unicast paths to peers (in unique update groups):
    10.0.3.254
  Local, (received & used)
    10.0.1.8 (metric 30) from 10.0.1.254 (10.0.4.1)
      Received Label 19001
      Origin IGP, metric 0, localpref 100, valid, internal, best, group-best,
labeled-unicast
      Received Path ID 1, Local Path ID 1, version 742
      Originator: 10.0.4.1, Cluster list: 10.0.1.254, 10.0.1.8
      Label-Index: 3001
```

Output 4-75 *Verifying the BGP Next Hop for BGP-LU Prefixes in Core 1 on ABR-2 (IOS XE)*

```
ABR-2#sh bgp ipv4 uni 10.0.4.1

BGP routing table entry for 10.0.4.1/32, version 959
Paths: (2 available, best #2, table default)
Net local label from SRGB
  Path advertised to update-groups:
     38
  Refresh Epoch 1
  Local, (received & used)
    10.0.1.8 (metric 30) from 10.0.1.254 (10.0.1.254)
      Origin IGP, metric 0, localpref 100, valid, internal, all
      sr-labelindex 0xBB9
      Originator: 10.0.4.1, Cluster list: 10.0.1.254, 10.0.1.8
      mpls labels in/out 19001/19001
```

```
    rx pathid: 0x1, tx pathid: 0x1
    Updated on Jun 30 2023 11:34:51 UTC
Path advertised to update-groups:
   38
Refresh Epoch 1
Local, (received & used)
  10.0.1.7 (metric 30) from 10.0.1.254 (10.0.1.254)
    Origin IGP, metric 0, localpref 100, valid, internal, best
    sr-labelindex 0xBB9
    Originator: 10.0.4.1, Cluster list: 10.0.1.254, 10.0.1.7
    mpls labels in/out 19001/19001
    rx pathid: 0x0, tx pathid: 0x0
```

Data Forwarding from PE-1 to PE-3

This section focuses on the data plane capability in the AS 65001 shown in Figure 4-43. The various control plane protocols used to exchange routing and SR information are discussed earlier in this chapter, in the sections "SR-MPLS IS-IS," "SR-MPLS OSPF," and "Intra-AS BGP-LU with a BGP Prefix SID."

A ping from PE-1 to PE-3 displays the data forwarding capabilities of the SR-MPLS network. Figure 4-43 shows how a ping from PE-1 to PE-3 traverses Metro 1, Core 1, and Metro 2, using MPLS labels at each hop.

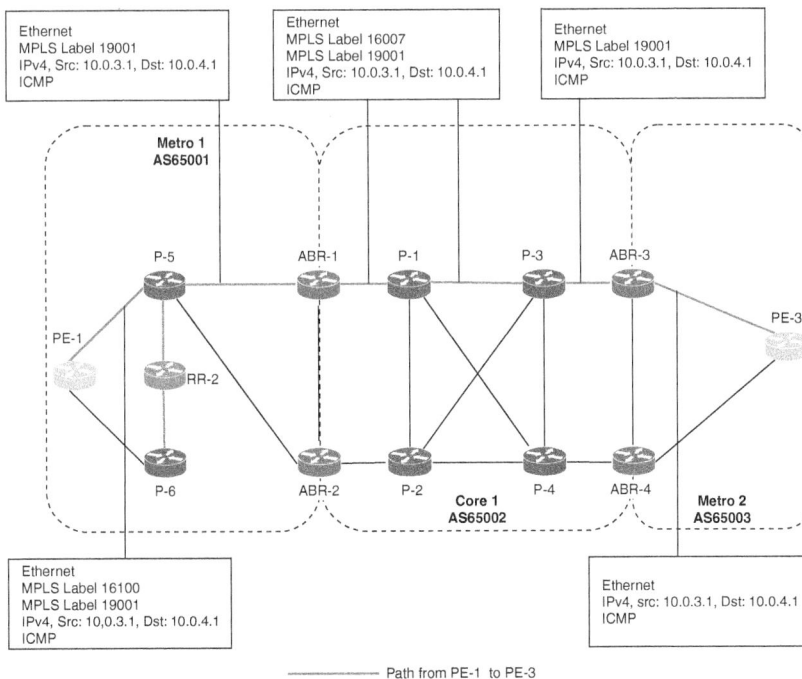

Figure 4-43   *Data Forwarding in the SR-MPLS Network*

Output 4-76 shows that the ping from PE-1 to PE-3 is successful.

Output 4-76   *Ping from PE-1 to PE-3 in SR-MPLS Network*

```
RP/0/0/CPU0:PE-1#ping 10.0.4.1 source lo0

Type escape sequence to abort.
Sending 5, 100-byte ICMP Echos to 10.0.4.1, timeout is 2 seconds:
!!!!!
Success rate is 100 percent (5/5), round-trip min/avg/max = 49/61/99 ms
```

The traceroute from PE-1 to PE-3 displayed in Output 4-77 validates the path shown in Figure 4-43. ABR-1 in Metro 1 is the next hop for PE-3 in Metro 2. PE-1 forwards the packet destined for PE-3 to P-5 with the MPLS labels 16100 and 19001. The outer label is 16100, which corresponds to the Anycast SID of ABR-1, and the inner MPLS label is 19001, which is the Prefix SID of PE-3.

Because P-5 is the penultimate hop to ABR-1, P-5 pops the outer label (16100) and forwards the packet to ABR-1, with 19001 as the topmost MPLS label.

> **Note**   Penultimate hop popping (PHP) behavior is explained in Chapter 1, "MPLS in a Nutshell."

Because ABR-3 is the next hop to reach PE-3 in Metro 2 for ABR-1, ABR-1 inserts the label 16007, which is the label for ABR-3, and forwards the packet to P-1. The packet that is forwarded by ABR-1 has a stack of labels, where 16007 is the outer label and 19001 is the inner label.

P-1 forwards the packet to P-3 without modifying the labels. Because P-3 is the penultimate hop to ABR-3, it pops the topmost label 16007 and forwards the packet to ABR-3 with the label 19001.

ABR-3 is the penultimate hop to PE-3 and pops the topmost label 19001 before forwarding the IPv4 packet to PE-3.

Output 4-77   *Traceroute from PE-1 to PE-3 in SR-MPLS Network*

```
RP/0/0/CPU0:PE-1#traceroute 10.0.4.1 source lo0

Type escape sequence to abort.
Tracing the route to 10.0.4.1

 1  192.168.3.1 [MPLS: Labels 16100/19001]  <- PE1 --- P-5 link
 2  192.168.3.9 [MPLS: Label 19001]  <- P-5 --- ABR-1 link
 3  192.168.1.0 [MPLS: Labels 16007/19001]  <- ABR-1 --- P-1 link
 4  192.168.1.5 [MPLS: Labels 16007/19001}  <- P-1 --- P-3 link
 5  192.168.1.39 [MPLS: Label 19001]  <- P-3 --- ABR-3 link
 6  192.168.4.1 49 msec  *  59 msec  <- ABR-3 --- PE-3 link
```

Inter-AS BGP-LU

The section "Intra-AS BGP-LU with a BGP Prefix SID," earlier in this chapter, provides details on the use of BGP-LU to scale the network within a single AS. The same concepts can be extended to provide connectivity between different autonomous systems using BGP-LU.

Inter-AS BGP-LU Design

Connectivity within an AS is provided using the intra-AS BGP-LU solution discussed earlier, in the section, "Intra-AS BGP-LU with a BGP Prefix SID." Autonomous system border routers (ASBRs) provide connectivity between different autonomous systems using eBGP-LU. The difference between iBGP-LU and eBGP BGP-LU is in the behavior of BGP next hop and the label for the BGP next hop. For iBGP-LU, the BGP next hop is modified only by the ABRs, and the BGP next hop is reachable using the SR label, whereas for eBGP-LU, the BGP next hop is always modified by the ASBRs, and the BGP next hop is reachable via the directly connected interface to ASBR. With IOS XR, a static route for the BGP next hop is required on an ASBR to provide an LSP to the BGP next hop.

Figure 4-44 shows the BGP-LU topology between AS 65001, 65002, and 65003:

- ASBR-1 and ASBR-2 are the ASBRs in AS 65001.

- ASBR-3, ASBR-4, ASBR-5, and ASBR-6 are the ASBRs in AS 65002. RR-4 is the route reflector for BGP-LU sessions between the ASBRs in AS 65002. Within AS 65002, the ASBRs are inline route reflectors and set the BGP next hop to self when advertising the BGP-LU prefixes to BGP speakers within the AS.

- ASBR-7 and ASBR-8 are the ASBRs in AS 65003.

In IOS XR, an LSP between the ASBRs in different autonomous systems is necessary to provide an end-to-end path between the autonomous systems. In Figure 4-44, ASBR-1 allocates a label for the interface address of ASBR-3 using a static host route (/32) and provides an LSP between AS 650001 and AS 65002.

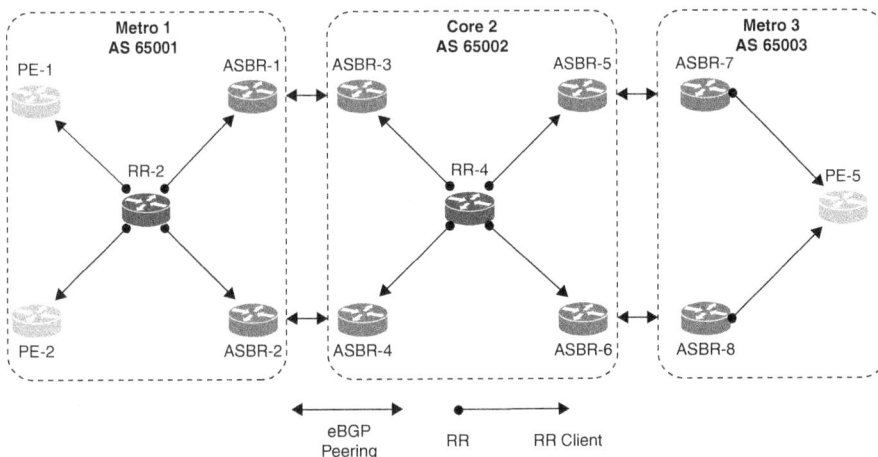

Figure 4-44 *BGP-LU Topology in BGP AS 65001, 65002, and 65003*

Inter-AS BGP-LU Configuration

This section details the configuration of the eBGP session to exchange SR-related information between the ASBRs shown in Figure 4-44. Config 4-67 and Config 4-68 show the configuration for ASBR-1 and ASBR-3, corresponding to the BGP-LU session between AS 65001 and AS 65002. The configuration on the rest of the ASBRs is similar. An eBGP session is enabled between ASBR-1 (in AS 65001) and ASBR-3 (in AS 65002) for the labeled-unicast address family.

On ASBR-1 (which is an IOS XR device), the eBGP session is established on the directly connected interface (192.168.50.1). A route policy is configured in both directions (in and out) to allow all prefixes.

Note   On the IOS XR device ASBR-1, a route policy is required for every eBGP neighbor to send and receive BGP updates. Otherwise, no BGP updates are sent, and all BGP updates received from the neighbor are dropped. The route policy PASS allows all updates to be sent and received without any filtering.

On the IOS XE device ASBR-3, an eBGP session is established on the directly connected interface (192.168.50.0). The command **segment-routing mpls** is used to enable BGP for SR. IPv4 labeled unicast is enabled for the neighbor 192.168.50.0 using the command **send-label** under the ipv4 address family.

Config 4-67   *BGP-LU Session on ASBR-1 (IOS XR)*

```
route-policy PASS
  pass
end-policy

router bgp 65001
neighbor 192.168.50.1
  remote-as 65002
  address-family ipv4 labeled-unicast
   route-policy PASS in
   route-policy PASS out
```

Config 4-68   *BGP-LU Session on ASBR-3(IOS XE)*

```
router bgp 65002
neighbor 192.168.50.0 remote-as 65001
 !
 address-family ipv4
  network 10.0.2.2 mask 255.255.255.255
  segment-routing mpls
  neighbor 192.168.50.0 activate
  neighbor 192.168.50.0 send-label
 exit-address-family
```

A static route for the eBGP neighbor (ASBR-3) is required on ASBR-1 to provide an LSP to ASBR-3. This is shown in Config 4-69. Note that this configuration is required only for IOS XR devices.

Config 4-69   *Static Route to ASBR-2 (IOS XR)*

```
router static
 address-family ipv4 unicast
  192.168.50.1/32 GigabitEthernet0/0/0/2
```

Inter-AS BGP-LU Verification

The section explains the commands required to verify the BGP-LU update between the ASBRs shown in Figure 4-45.

On an IOS XR device, the command **show bgp ipv4 labeled-unicast** is used to verify that the BGP-LU prefixes are received from the ASBR of the adjacent BGP AS. This command shows the next hop and the BGP Prefix SID associated with the BGP-LU prefix. The command **show cef <BGP-LU prefix>** shows the label stack used to forward the traffic to a specific BGP-LU prefix.

On an IOS XE device, the command **show bgp ipv4 unicast** is used to verify that the BGP-LU prefixes are received from the ASBR of the adjacent AS. This command shows the next hop and the BGP Prefix SID associated with the BGP-LU prefix. The command **show mpls forwarding labels <BGP-LU prefix-SID> details** shows the label stack used to forward the traffic to a specific BGP-LU prefix.

Figure 4-45 shows the BGP-LU updates for prefix 10.0.5.1 from PE-3 in AS 65003 to PE-1 in AS 65001 via AS 65002. The next hop is modified for eBGP updates, which is the expected eBGP behavior. Within an AS (for example, in AS 65002), ASBR-5 and ASBR-6 set the next hop to themselves when advertising prefixes within the AS.

The verification involves the following:

- The BGP next hop is modified to the outgoing interface when the ASBR advertises the routes to the remote ASBR. To avoid repeating the same verification steps for several ASBRs, the verification is done only for the BGP-LU update for 10.0.5.1 from ASBR-7 and ASBR-8 in AS 65003 to ASBR-5 and ASBR-6 in AS 65002.

- The ASBR sets the next hop to self when advertising the BGP-LU prefixes to other BGP speakers within the AS. This verification step is discussed earlier in this chapter, in the section, "Intra-AS BGP-LU Verification," for intra-AS BGP-LU and is not repeated in this section.

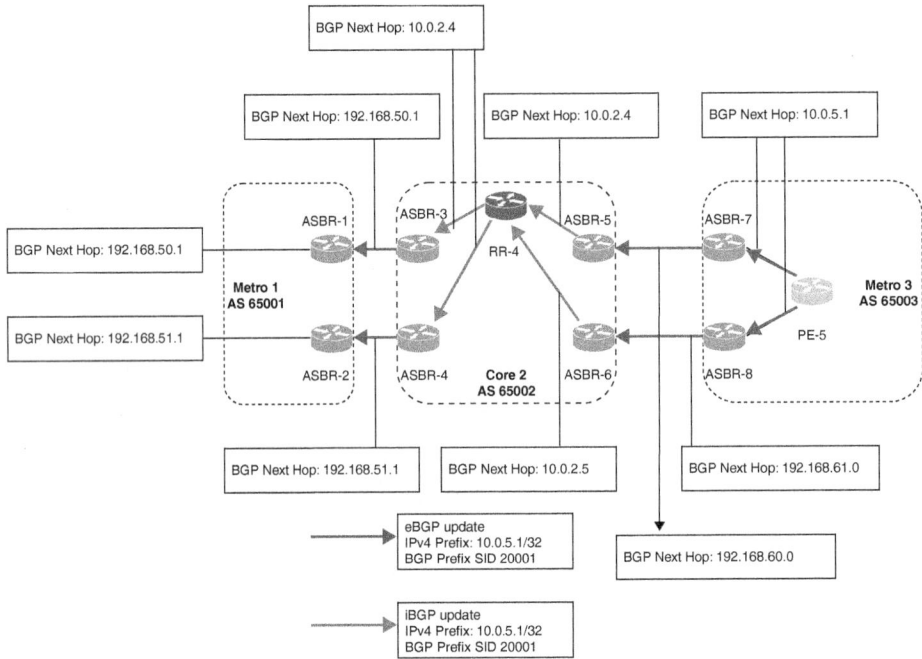

Figure 4-45   *BGP-LU Update for Prefix 10.0.5.1*

Table 4-3 provides the IP addresses of the loopbacks and links that help in verifying the BGP next hop for iBGP-LU and eBGP-LU updates.

Table 4-3   *IP Addressing for Links and Loopbacks in AS 65001, AS 65002, and AS 65003*

Network	Description
10.0.2.4/32	Loopback0 of ASBR-5
10.0.2.5/32	Loopback0 of ASBR-6
10.0.3.1/32	Loopback0 of PE-3
192.168.60.0/31	Link between ASBR-5 and ASBR-7
	ASBR-5: 192.168.60.1
	ASBR-7: 192.168.60.0
192.168.61.0/31	Link between ASBR-6 and ASBR-8
	ASBR-6: 192.168.61.1
	ASBR-8: 192.168.61.0

In AS 65003, the BGP-LU prefix 10.0.5.1/32 is advertised by PE-5 to ASBR-7 and ASBR-8. This can be verified on ASBR-7 and ASBR-8 as shown in Output 4-78 and Output 4-79.

On IOS XR device ASBR-8 and IOS XE device ASBR-7, the BGP next hop is 10.0.5.1, which corresponds to the loopback0 of PE-5. The label index is displayed in decimal (4001) on the IOS XR device, and the label index is displayed in hexadecimal (0xFA1) on the IOS XE device.

Output 4-78 *Verifying the BGP Next Hop for BGP-LU Prefix 10.0.5.1 on ASBR-8 (IOS XR)*

```
RP/0/0/CPU0:ASBR-8#show bgp ipv4 labeled-unicast 10.0.5.1

BGP routing table entry for 10.0.5.1/32
<snip>
  Local, (Received from a RR-client)
    10.0.5.1 (metric 10) from 10.0.5.1 (10.0.5.1)
      Received Label 3
      Origin IGP, metric 0, localpref 100, valid, internal, best, group-best,
  labeled-unicast
      Received Path ID 0, Local Path ID 1, version 18
      Label-Index: 4001
```

Output 4-79 *Verifying the BGP Next Hop for BGP-LU Prefix 10.0.5.1 on ASBR-7 (IOS XE)*

```
ASBR-7#show bgp ipv4 unicast 10.0.5.1

BGP routing table entry for 10.0.5.1/32, version 31
Paths: (1 available, best #1, table default, RIB-failure(17))
Net local label from RIB
  Advertised to update-groups:
     1
  Refresh Epoch 1
  Local, (Received from a RR-client)
    10.0.5.1 (metric 10) from 10.0.5.1 (10.0.5.1)
      Origin IGP, metric 0, localpref 100, valid, internal, best
      sr-labelindex 0xFA1
      mpls labels in/out 20001/imp-null
      rx pathid: 0, tx pathid: 0x0
```

In the next step, ASBR-7 sets the next hop to the outgoing interface before advertising the prefix 10.0.5.1 to ASBR-5, and ASBR-8 sets the next hop to the outgoing interface before sending the BGP update to ASBR-6. This can be verified on ASBR-5 and ASBR-6 as shown in Output 4-80 and Output 4-81.

On IOS XR device ASBR-5, the BGP next hop for the prefix 10.0.5.1 is 192.168.60.1, which is the address of the outgoing interface on ASBR-7. On IOS XE device ASBR-6, the BGP next hop for the prefix 10.0.5.1 is 192.168.61.1, which is the address of the outgoing interface on ASBR-8.

Output 4-80   *Verifying the BGP Next Hop for BGP-LU Prefix 10.0.5.1 on ASBR-5 (IOS XR)*

```
RP/0/0/CPU0:ASBR-5#show bgp ipv4 labeled-unicast 10.0.5.1


BGP routing table entry for 10.0.5.1/32
Versions:
  Process           bRIB/RIB  SendTblVer
  Speaker              5939        5939
    Local Label: 20001
Last Modified: Jun 30 11:11:19.235 for 01:12:55
Paths: (2 available, best #2)
<snip>
  Path #2: Received by speaker 0
  Advertised IPv4 Labeled-unicast paths to peers (in unique update groups):
    10.0.2.254
  65003
    192.168.60.1 from 192.168.60.1 (10.0.5.2)
      Received Label 20001
      Origin IGP, localpref 100, valid, external, best, group-best, labeled-unicast
      Received Path ID 0, Local Path ID 1, version 46
      Origin-AS validity: (disabled)
      Label-Index: 4001
```

Output 4-81   *Verifying the BGP Next Hop for BGP-LU Prefix 10.0.5.1 on ASBR-6 (IOS XR)*

```
ASBR-6#show bgp ipv4 unicast 10.0.5.1

BGP routing table entry for 10.0.5.1/32, version 8887
Paths: (2 available, best #2, table default)
<snip>
  Path advertised to update-groups:
     9
  Refresh Epoch 1
  65003
    192.168.61.1 from 192.168.61.1 (10.0.5.3)
      Origin IGP, localpref 100, valid, external, best
      sr-labelindex 0xFA1
      mpls labels in/out 20001/20001
      rx pathid: 0, tx pathid: 0x0
      Updated on Jun 30 2023 11:07:20 UTC
```

Data Forwarding from PE-1 to PE-5

This section focuses on the data plane connectivity from AS 65001 to AS 65003 via AS 65002, as shown in Figure 4-46. The various control plane protocols used to exchange routing and SR information are discussed earlier, in the section "Inter-AS BGP-LU Design." The data forwarding from AS 65001 to AS 65003 via AS 65002 is demonstrated using a ping from PE-1 to PE-5.

Figure 4-46 shows a ping from PE-1 to PE-5 that traverses the SR-MPLS network using an MPLS label or labels on each hop.

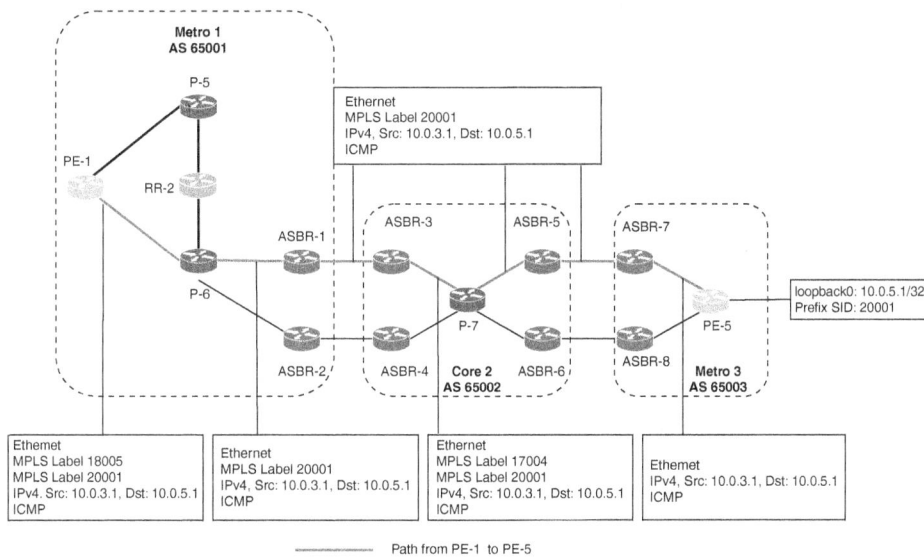

Figure 4-46 *Data Forwarding from AS 65001 to AS 65003 via AS 65002*

Output 4-82 shows that the ping from PE-1 to PE-5 is successful.

Output 4-82 *Ping from PE-1 to PE-5*

```
RP/0/0/CPU0:PE-1#ping 10.0.5.1 source  lo0

Type escape sequence to abort.
Sending 5, 100-byte ICMP Echos to 10.0.5.1, timeout is 2 seconds:
!!!!!
Success rate is 100 percent (5/5), round-trip min/avg/max = 59/95/149 ms
```

The traceroute from PE-1 to PE-5 displayed in Output 4-83 validates the path shown in Figure 4-46. In Metro 1, ASBR-1 is the next hop for PE-5. PE-1 forwards the packet destined for PE-5 to P-6 with the MPLS labels 18005 and 20001, where the outer label is 18005, which corresponds to the Prefix SID of ASBR-1, and the inner MPLS label is 20001, which is the Prefix SID of PE-5.

Because P-6 is the penultimate hop to ASBR-1, P-6 pops the outer label (18005) and forwards the packet to ASBR-1 with 20001 as the topmost MPLS label.

ASBR-1 forwards the packet to the next hop, which is ASBR-3.

Because ASBR-5 is the next hop to reach PE-5 in AS 65003, ASBR-3 inserts the label for ASBR-5 (17004) and forwards the packet to P-7, which is the penultimate hop to ASBR-5. P-7 pops the topmost label (17004) and forwards the packet with label 20001 to ASBR-5.

Because ASBR-7 is the next hop, ASBR-5 forwards the packet ASBR-7 without inserting any new label. ASBR-7, which is the penultimate hop to PE-5, pops the topmost label and forwards the IPv4 packet to PE-5.

Output 4-83   *Traceroute from PE-1 to PE-5*

```
RP/0/0/CPU0:PE-1#traceroute 10.0.5.1 source  lo0


Type escape sequence to abort.
Tracing the route to 10.0.5.1


 1  192.168.3.3 [MPLS: Labels 18005/20001] PE-1 --- P-6 link
 2  192.168.3.13 [MPLS: Label 20001] P-6 --- ASBR-1 link
 3  192.168.50.1 [MPLS: Label 20001] ASBR-1 --- ASBR-3 link
 4  192.168.2.1 [MPLS: Labels 17004/20001] ASBR-3 --- P-7 link
 5  192.168.2.4 [MPLS: Label 20001] P-7 --- ASBR-5 link
 6  192.168.60.1 [MPLS: Label 20001] ASBR-5 --- ASBR-7 link
 7  192.168.5.1 59 msec  *  49 msec ASBR-7 --- PE-5 link
```

Summary

This chapter covers the transport implementation details for SR-MPLS and SRv6 on Cisco devices.

It provides a brief introduction to IS-IS, OSPFv2, and OSPFv3, information on OSPF areas, IS-IS levels, and summarization that is relevant in the context of SR-MPLS and SRv6.

The section "Segment Routing Baseline" provides the configuration and verification commands required to enable SR and the associated parameters on Cisco devices. Some parameters, such as the SRGB, must be modified when the default SRGB is not the same on all the devices, which may be the case in a multi-vendor environment.

The section "Segment Routing Control Plane (IGP)" provides some design guidelines and configuration details to enable routing protocols like IS-IS, OSPF, and BGP to exchange SR-related information and to allow the router to forward packets in an SR network.

In addition to extending the IGP and BGP to facilitate exchange of SR-related information, this chapter presents some other features that help improve the load balancing, scalability, convergence, and path steering capabilities in an SR network.

Anycast is a network addressing and routing method that enables packets to be routed to a variety of different nodes and helps provide load balancing and improve availability. In the SR architecture, an Anycast SID is advertised by a set of routers representing the anycast set. The Anycast SID helps achieve load balancing by providing ECMP-aware shortest-path forwarding toward the closest node of the anycast set. The use case of anycast for high availability in an SR-MPLS network is demonstrated in the section "Intra-AS BGP-LU with a BGP Prefix SID," where the ABRs of Metro 1 advertise an Anycast SID for their BGP next hop and provide load balancing for traffic entering or exiting Metro 1. In an SRv6 network, the use case for load balancing with Anycast SIDs as well as SRv6 traffic engineering is presented in the section "SRv6 Anycast SID."

Scalability is a key requirement for large-scale service provider networks. The main scaling issues with link-state IGPs such as IS-IS and OSPF are the complexity of the link-state flooding and route calculation, as well as the size of the database, which contributes to the cost of route calculation and router memory consumption. One of the solutions to address the scalability of the IGP is summarization at the area or domain border in an IGP, which is explained for an SRv6 network in the section "SRv6 IS-IS Summarization." Three choices for summarization are presented, with each choice improving on the one before it. The default route is the first (but not recommended) of the three choices but has problems related to BGP connectivity and convergence. The second choice, which involves using a super summary (for example, fc00::/32), resolves the problem of BGP connectivity but does not address the BGP convergence for failure of egress PE nodes in the local and remote IGP metro networks. The third and the recommended choice, which depends on propagating the summary routes from remote metro networks, resolves the problem of BGP convergence for failure in the local domain but does not resolve the convergence issue for failures in the remote metro networks.

While summarization at the border of an IGP domain in a hierarchical IGP network helps to build a scalable SRv6 network, summarization prevents the IGP from signaling the failure of egress PE nodes in remote domains, and this signaling is required for triggering BGP NHT. The problem of BGP NHT failing to trigger with summarization in the event of an egress PE node failure is addressed by UPA, as explained in the section "Unreachable Prefix Announcement (UPA)." UPA addresses the BGP convergence problem due to summarization by announcing the unreachability of devices in remote domains via the IGP.

The section "Multiplane Topologies with Flex Algos," describes how a flex algo can meet requirements like low latency and disjoint paths by enabling the IGP to exchange several link attributes (such as link delay and affinity) and create multiple logical topologies of the network, each using a different link attribute. Uses cases for disjoint paths and a low-latency path are used to explain how flex algos can be used in an SRv6 network. For the sake of completeness, configuration details on enabling flex algos in an SR-MPLS network are been provided.

While summarization is the key to providing scalability in an SRv6 network, it cannot be used in an SR-MPLS network because summarization at the IGP domain border breaks the end-to-end LSP in an SR-MPLS network. The solution is to use BGP-LU to provide scalability in an AS within an SR-MPLS network, as explained in the section "Intra-AS BGP-LU with a BGP Prefix SID." The solution is based on allowing the ABRs of an IGP domain to advertise themselves as BGP next hops when advertising the BGP-LU prefixes. The section "Inter-AS BGP-LU" explains how BGP-LU can also be used to provide scalability when SR is used to provide connectivity between different autonomous systems.

References and Additional Reading

- RFC 2328: OSPF Version 2, https://www.ietf.org/rfc/rfc2328.txt

- RFC 2740: OSPFv3, https://datatracker.ietf.org/doc/html/rfc2740

- RFC 3784: Intermediate System to Intermediate System (IS-IS) Extensions for Traffic Engineering (TE), https://datatracker.ietf.org/doc/html/rfc3784

Segment Routing Control Plane

- IETF Draft: Compressed SRv6 Segment List Encoding in SRH, https://datatracker.ietf.org/doc/draft-ietf-spring-srv6-srh-compression

- IETF Draft: Network Programming extension: SRv6 uSID instruction, https://datatracker.ietf.org/doc/draft-filsfils-spring-net-pgm-extension-srv6-usid

- RFC 9352: IS-IS Extensions to Support Segment Routing over the IPv6 Data Plane - RFC 9352, https://datatracker.ietf.org/doc/rfc9352

- RFC 5302: Domain-Wide Prefix Distribution with Two-Level IS-IS, https://www.rfc-editor.org/rfc/rfc5302

- RFC 9350: IGP Flexible Algorithm, https://datatracker.ietf.org/doc/rfc9350

- RFC 5357: TWAMP, https://datatracker.ietf.org/doc/html/rfc5357

- IETF Draft: Unreachable Prefix Announcement, https://datatracker.ietf.org/doc/draft-ietf-lsr-igp-ureach-prefix-announce

- RFC 5120: Multi Topology (MT) Routing in Intermediate System to Intermediate Systems (IS-ISs), https://www.rfc-editor.org/rfc/rfc5120.txt

Segment Routing Control Plane (BGP)

- RFC 9252: BGP Overlay Services Based on Segment Routing over IPv6 (SRv6), https://datatracker.ietf.org/doc/html/rfc9252

- RFC 8670: BGP Prefix Segment in Large-Scale Data Centers, https://datatracker.ietf.org/doc/rfc8670

Chapter 5

Migrating to Segment Routing

Network operators face the ongoing challenge of staying competitive, which often requires proactively adopting new technologies. This brings us to the concept of *migration*, which involves shifting to newer technological landscapes. But what does migration really entail? It is a concept that is deceptively simple to state yet complex to execute.

At its core, migration involves moving from an existing network configuration to an enhanced, desired state. This journey unfolds a tapestry of complexity as it demands adaptations in hardware, software, configurations, IT systems, personnel, and business processes to accommodate the new technology. For network operators, especially those managing large-scale or diverse networks, the transformation is multifaceted and challenging. It can range from deploying entirely new infrastructures and overhauling networks to replacing outdated equipment, upgrading existing hardware, implementing new software solutions, and embracing novel protocols.

With the introduction of two segment routing (SR) technologies and their advantages in the previous chapters, this chapter provides a practical roadmap for implementing SR, whether you're starting afresh with a greenfield approach, or using a brownfield method, which involves integration with existing systems. This chapter presents simple steps to mitigate the risks associated with transitioning services from MPLS to SR.

This chapter covers the following topics:

- Deployment models and strategies for achieving connectivity between MPLS and SR networks during the migration phase, which is a critical period during which a network incrementally adopts SR

- Specifics of migrating from an LDP network to SR-MPLS and details of both deployment models and MPLS and SR interconnectivity options

- Three distinct strategies for migrating from MPLS to SRv6

- A roadmap for migration to an SRv6 network for four different MPLS networks

> **Note**   In this chapter, *MPLS* refers to both LDP and SR-MPLS, and *SR* denotes SR-MPLS and SRv6.

The migration process typically concerns the transition of customer edge (CE) or provider edge (PE) devices from one network environment to another. Although this chapter uses IPv4 to illustrate service migrations, the concepts are equally applicable to IPv6 services.

> **Note**   This chapter does not cover the decommissioning of legacy networks after a migration, although that is an important step.

Deployment Models

Greenfield network deployment refers to the installation of a network where previously there was none. This term is derived from the construction industry, where new development on previously undeveloped land is termed a *greenfield development*. An important advantage of greenfield deployment is the opportunity to implement cutting-edge technology solutions from the ground up, free from the constraints or dependencies of existing infrastructure, software, biases, or business processes. In the context of SR, a greenfield deployment refers to building a separate SR network and then migrating the services from the MPLS network to the SR network. During the migration phase, services may connect with both the SR and MPLS networks, and so interworking is essential to maintain seamless service connectivity across the networks. Implementing interworking might necessitate additional hardware and software, which can be phased out after the completion of the service migration.

In contrast to a greenfield deployment, a *brownfield deployment* involves an upgrade or expansion of an existing network. This type of deployment involves installation and configuration of new hardware or network technology that is designed to coexist with the legacy network. One benefit of brownfield development is the ability to enhance existing technology solutions within established business processes; in addition, an organization can avoid extra capital expenditure on new infrastructure by undertaking a brownfield development. However, brownfield projects also come with their own challenges, including the need for a comprehensive and accurate understanding of the existing network's limitations and issues with legacy infrastructure that can potentially slow the development process and inflate overall costs.

A brownfield deployment involves activating SR in the MPLS network. This process can be conducted in phases during several maintenance windows. Throughout these periods, SR and MPLS coexist within the network, which introduces increased complexity in terms of features and configurations. However, it also reduces the effort and mitigates risks typically associated with maintenance windows.

Migration Strategies

Transitioning the services to SR-MPLS or SRv6 in a network can be achieved through a multitude of viable methodologies, and this section illustrates several strategies. When embarking on a greenfield deployment and establishing a new SR core alongside metro and access layers, there are two principal strategies that stand out for migrating services from MPLS to SR network. The first strategy relies on the ability of the PE routers to simultaneously support MPLS and SR during the migration phase, and the second strategy depends on interworking.

Figure 5-1 illustrates the first strategy, which leverages an interworking gateway to sequentially transition the MPLS PE devices to the SR network in multiple maintenance windows. This strategy assumes that all the MPLS PE devices support SR.

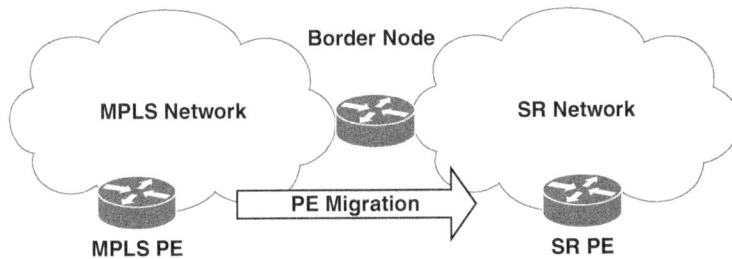

Figure 5-1 *Interworking Greenfield Strategy: Migrating PE Devices to a New SR Network*

In cases where the MPLS PE devices do not support SR, the CE devices can be migrated from the MPLS PE devices to the SR PE devices, as shown in Figure 5-2.

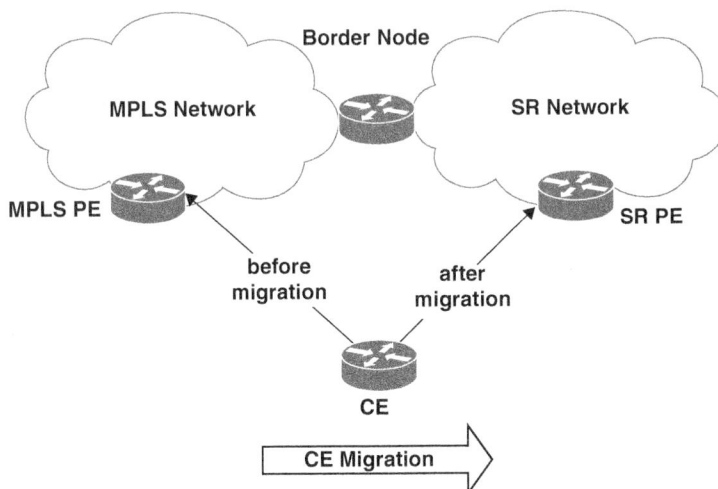

Figure 5-2 *Interworking Greenfield Strategy: Migrating CE Devices to the New SR Network*

Later sections of this chapter covering the interworking strategy involve the migration of PE devices or CE devices:

■ The section "Building a New SR-MPLS Network" covers migration from LDP to SR-MPLS, where a border node is the gateway between the LDP and SR-MPLS networks

■ The section "Building a New SRv6 Network Using an SRv6 IWG" covers migration from MPLS to SRv6 where an SRv6 interworking gateway (IWG) acts as the IWG between the MPLS and SRv6 networks, and the section "Building a New SRv6 Network Using Inter-AS Option A" presents a solution using ASBRs as IWGs between the two networks. The information on the migration of CE devices is also valid for the migration of PE devices.

Figure 5-3 shows the second strategy, where PE devices can be concurrently connected to both the MPLS and SR networks, thus removing the necessity for an interworking gateway between the two networks.

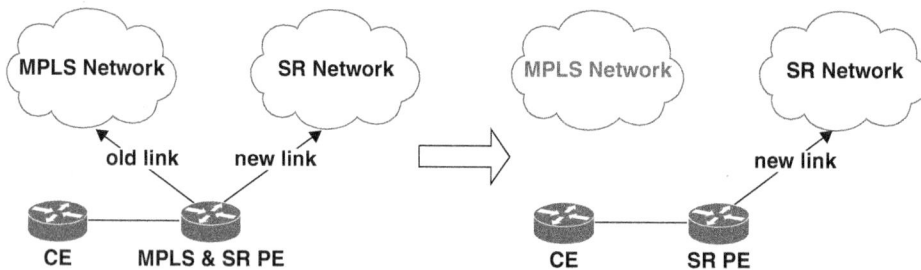

Figure 5-3 *Dual-Homed Greenfield Strategy : PE Devices Connected to the MPLS and SR Networks*

The PE devices must have sufficient port capacity, CPU, and memory to connect to the MPLS and SR networks simultaneously. The dual-homed strategy for migration from MPLS to SR is described in the section "SRv6 Network Using Dual-Connected PE Devices." The MPLS network can be decommissioned once all the MPLS PE devices have been migrated to the SR network.

A brownfield deployment uses a coexistence strategy, incorporating SR into the existing network as illustrated in Figure 5-4. This strategy entails activating SR in specific parts of the MPLS network and progressively expanding its scope in multiple migration windows.

For this approach to work, the existing network must be able to support SR. Throughout the transition phase, PE and P devices are configured to support MPLS and SR concurrently. When all the devices in the network are migrated to SR, the MPLS-related configuration can be removed from the network.

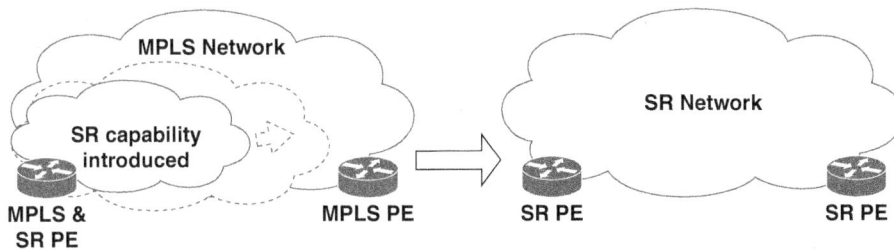

Figure 5-4 *Coexistence Brownfield Strategy: Enabling SR in an MPLS Network*

The coexistence strategy is discussed in the following sections:

■ LDP to SR-MPLS migration is presented in the section "Enabling SR-MPLS in an Existing Network (Coexistence)."

■ MPLS to SRv6 migration is explained in the section "SRv6 Network Using Dual-Connected PE Devices." Although this section shows the migration strategy for a greenfield deployment, it is also valid for a brownfield deployment.

Figure 5-5 shows another SRv6-specific brownfield strategy, which involves expanding the coverage of SRv6-based network services between PE devices connected to an existing IPv6 network.

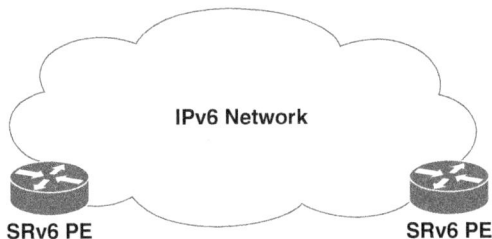

Figure 5-5 *IPv6 Backhaul Brownfield Strategy: SRv6-Based Services over an IPv6 Network*

Since the data packets from an SRv6 PE device are IPv6 packets with optional extension headers, they can be transported across any IPv6 network to facilitate SRv6-based service connectivity. However, this strategy comes with certain limitations, like the lack of TI-LFA and SRv6 traffic engineering in the native IPv6 network.

Note Migration of SRv6-based services using an existing IPv6 network is not covered in this chapter.

SR-MPLS Migration

Although LDP and SR-MPLS use the MPLS label to forward packets, the label distribution mechanism and the scope of the label are different for these networks. This section discusses the challenges of introducing SR-MPLS in an LDP network and the two methods to migrate from LDP to SR-MPLS: The first method involves the coexistence of LDP and SR-MPLS in the same network, and the second method uses the interworking capabilities of LDP and SR-MPLS with a segment routing mapping server and a border node.

SR-MPLS Reference Network Topology

Figure 5-6 shows the reference topology that is used in this section to describe the migration from LDP to SR-MPLS. In it, you can see that:

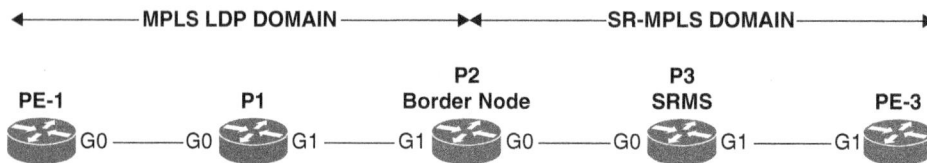

Figure 5-6   *LDP and SR-MPLS Reference Topology*

- PE-1 and P1 are LDP nodes supporting LDP.

- P2 is a border node supporting both LDP and SR-MPLS.

- P3 is the segment routing mapping server (SRMS).

- PE-3 supports SR-MPLS.

Enabling SR-MPLS in an Existing Network (Coexistence)

LDP and SR-MPLS can coexist in the same network as ships that cannot see each other at night because the label intervals used by MPLS LDP and SR-MPLS are separate. The coexistence means that SR-MPLS can be enabled on LDP nodes, and the separate label space for SR-MPLS and LDP allows nodes to operate in both domains at the same time without label collisions. The label-switched path between any two nodes in one direction uses either LDP labels or Prefix SIDs but not both.

In IOS-XR, the local label allocation is managed by the label-switching database (LSD), and MPLS applications must register as clients with the LSD to allocate labels. Most MPLS applications, including LDP, RSVP, L2VPN, BGP-LU, BGP-VPN, IS-IS, and OSPF, as well as segment routing for traffic engineering (SR-TE) use labels that are dynamically allocated by the LSD.

With SR-capable IOS-XR software releases, the LSD reserves the default label range 15000 to 15999 for the SR local block (SRLB) and 16000 to 23999 for the SR global block (SRGB), even if SR is not enabled. Allocation of the default SRLB/SRGB label range makes activation of SR possible without the need to reboot the device. When SR is enabled with the default SRLB/SRGB, the SRLB and SRGB are available and ready for use. By default, the LSD allocates dynamic labels starting from 24000.

When LDP and SR-MPLS are enabled on a router, two labels are assigned for a prefix, as shown in Figure 5-7, where all the nodes support MPLS LDP and SR-MPLS. The MPLS label table on PE-3 shows that two labels are allocated for every node in the network, and this is highlighted for the prefix 10.0.0.2/32.

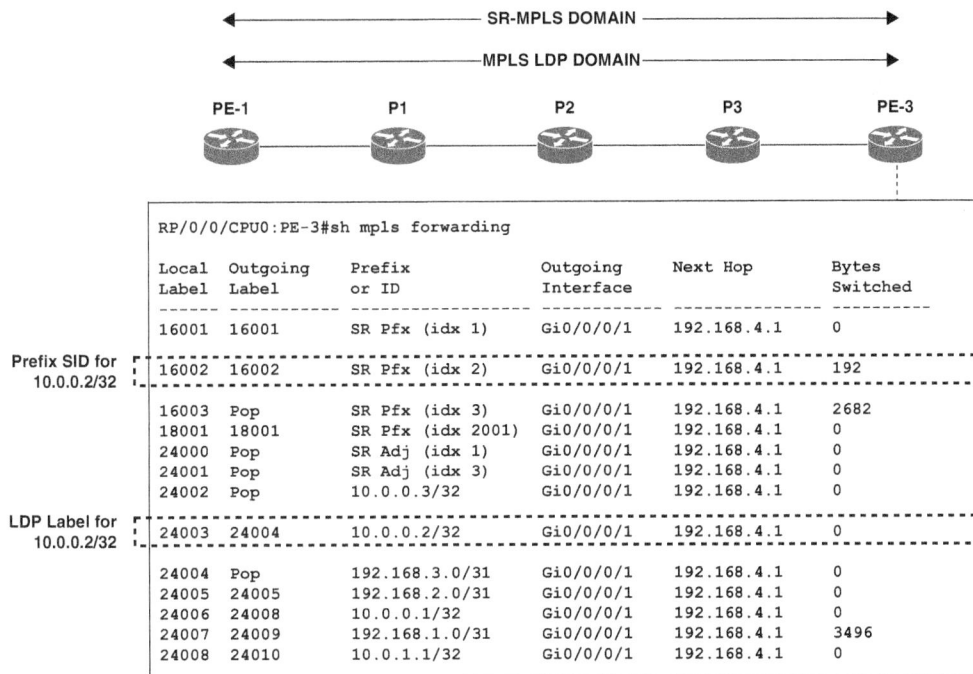

Figure 5-7 *LDP and SR-MPLS Coexistence*

The migration of the nodes from LDP to SR-MPLS can be done in a phased manner. Devices that are in the LDP and SR-MPLS domain can use either the LDP label or the Prefix SID for data forwarding and can be configured to prefer SR-MPLS over LDP.

Figure 5-8 shows an LDP network before the migration, where the MPLS label table on PE-3 uses MPLS labels from the dynamic range to reach all the devices in the network.

```
                    ◄──────────── MPLS LDP DOMAIN ──────────────►
```

Lo0: 10.0.1.1/32   Lo0: 10.0.0.1/32   Lo0: 10.0.0.2/32   Lo0: 10.0.0.3/32   Lo0: 10.0.1.3/32

```
  PE-1              P1                    P2                      P3              PE-3
```

```
┌─────────────────────────────────────────────────────────────────────────┐
│ RP/0/0/CPU0:PE-3#show mpls forwarding                                     │
│                                                                           │
│ Local  Outgoing    Prefix              Outgoing      Next Hop             │
│ Label  Label       or ID               Interface                         │
│ ------ ----------- ------------------- ------------  -----------          │
│ 24000  Pop         SR Adj (idx 1)      Gi0/0/0/1     192.168.4.1          │
│ 24001  Pop         SR Adj (idx 3)      Gi0/0/0/1     192.168.4.1          │
│ 24002  Pop         10.0.0.3/32         Gi0/0/0/1     192.168.4.1          │
│ 24004  24006       10.0.0.2/32         Gi0/0/0/1     192.168.4.1          │
│ 24005  24009       10.0.0.1/32         Gi0/0/0/1     192.168.4.1          │
│ 24006  24010       10.0.1.1/32         Gi0/0/0/1     192.168.4.1          │
└─────────────────────────────────────────────────────────────────────────┘
```

Dynamic Labels

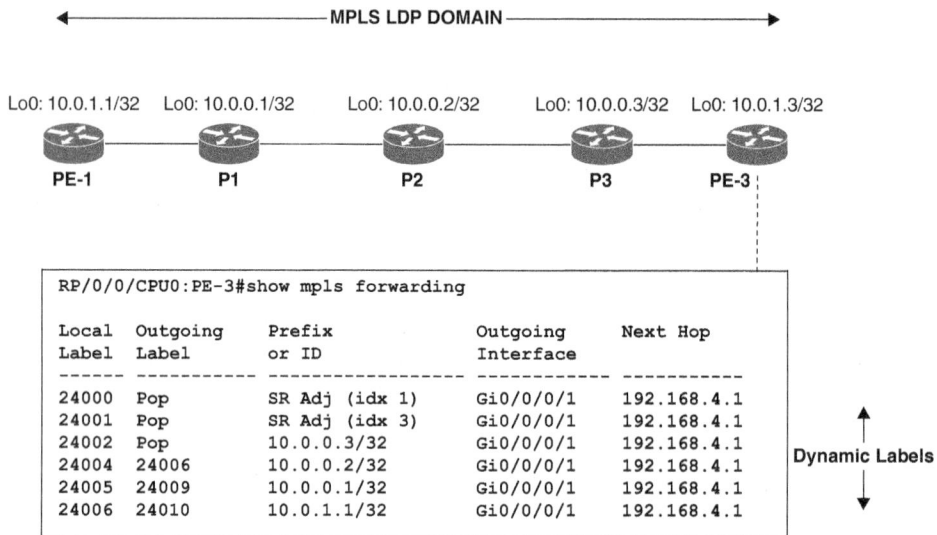

Figure 5-8   *MPLS LDP Network Before Migration*

Enabling SR-MPLS on P2, P3, and PE-3

At this point, SR-MPLS is enabled and preferred on P2, P3, and PE-3, as shown in Figure 5-9.

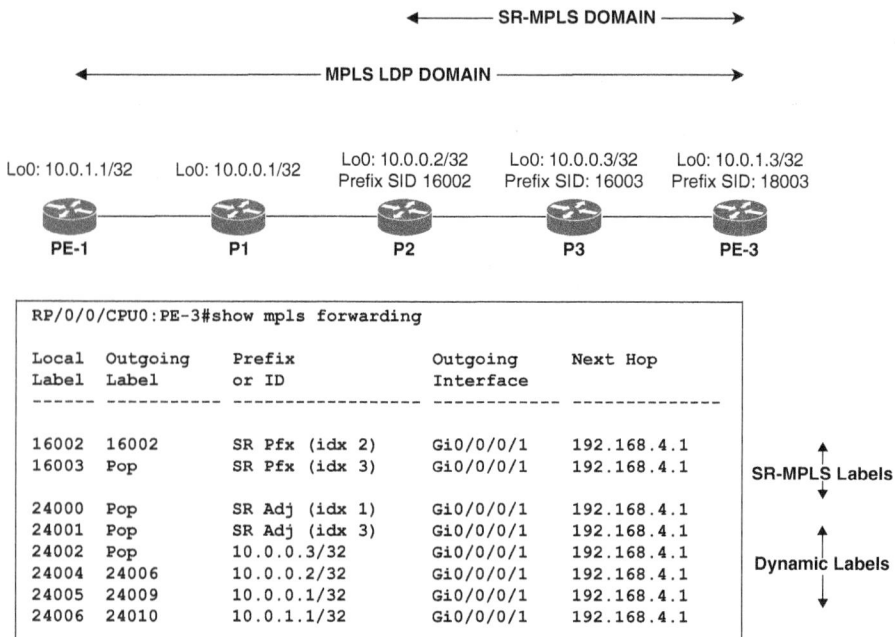

```
                                        ◄──────── SR-MPLS DOMAIN ────────►
```

```
                    ◄──────────── MPLS LDP DOMAIN ──────────────►
```

Lo0: 10.0.1.1/32   Lo0: 10.0.0.1/32   Lo0: 10.0.0.2/32   Lo0: 10.0.0.3/32   Lo0: 10.0.1.3/32
                                            Prefix SID 16002   Prefix SID: 16003   Prefix SID: 18003

```
  PE-1                  P1                    P2                  P3                  PE-3
```

```
┌─────────────────────────────────────────────────────────────────────────┐
│ RP/0/0/CPU0:PE-3#show mpls forwarding                                     │
│                                                                           │
│ Local  Outgoing    Prefix              Outgoing      Next Hop             │
│ Label  Label       or ID               Interface                         │
│ ------ ----------- ------------------- ------------  --------------       │
│                                                                           │
│ 16002  16002       SR Pfx (idx 2)      Gi0/0/0/1     192.168.4.1          │
│ 16003  Pop         SR Pfx (idx 3)      Gi0/0/0/1     192.168.4.1          │
│                                                                           │
│ 24000  Pop         SR Adj (idx 1)      Gi0/0/0/1     192.168.4.1          │
│ 24001  Pop         SR Adj (idx 3)      Gi0/0/0/1     192.168.4.1          │
│ 24002  Pop         10.0.0.3/32         Gi0/0/0/1     192.168.4.1          │
│ 24004  24006       10.0.0.2/32         Gi0/0/0/1     192.168.4.1          │
│ 24005  24009       10.0.0.1/32         Gi0/0/0/1     192.168.4.1          │
│ 24006  24010       10.0.1.1/32         Gi0/0/0/1     192.168.4.1          │
└─────────────────────────────────────────────────────────────────────────┘
```

SR-MPLS Labels

Dynamic Labels

Figure 5-9   *Network After Migration of P2, P3, and PE-3*

To prefer SR-MPLS, issue the command **segment-routing mpls sr-prefer**, as shown in
Config 5-1 and Config 5-2.

Config 5-1   *Preferring SR-MPLS over LDP(IOS-XR)*

```
!IS-IS
segment-routing
 global-block 16000 23999

router isis MPLS
address-family ipv4 unicast
  segment-routing mpls sr-prefer

!OSPF
segment-routing
 global-block 16000 23999

router ospf MPLS
 address-family ipv4 unicast
  segment-routing mpls sr-prefer
```

Config 5-2   *Preferring SR-MPLS over LDP (IOS-XE)*

```
!IS-IS
segment-routing mpls
 !
 set-attributes
  address-family ipv4
   sr-label-preferred

!OSPF
segment-routing mpls
 !
 set-attributes
  address-family ipv4
   sr-label-preferred
```

At this stage, the MPLS label table of PE-3 indicates that PE-3 uses the Prefix SIDs to
reach devices in the SR-MPLS domain, as shown in Output 5-1.

Output 5-1   *MPLS Label Table on PE-3(IOS-XR)*

```
RP/0/0/CPU0:PE3#show mpls forwarding

Local   Outgoing    Prefix            Outgoing      Next Hop        Bytes
Label   Label       or ID             Interface                     Switched
------  ----------  ----------------  ------------  --------------- -----------

16002   16002       SR Pfx (idx 2)    Gi0/0/0/1     192.168.4.1     0
16003   Pop         SR Pfx (idx 3)    Gi0/0/0/1     192.168.4.1     0
24000   Pop         SR Adj (idx 1)    Gi0/0/0/1     192.168.4.1     0
24001   Pop         SR Adj (idx 3)    Gi0/0/0/1     192.168.4.1     0
24002   Pop         10.0.0.3/32       Gi0/0/0/1     192.168.4.1     0
24004   24006       10.0.0.2/32       Gi0/0/0/1     192.168.4.1     0
24005   24009       10.0.0.1/32       Gi0/0/0/1     192.168.4.1     0
24006   24010       10.0.1.1/32       Gi0/0/0/1     192.168.4.1     0
```

Traffic between the SR-MPLS nodes uses label-switched path with the Prefix SID, as shown in Output 5-2.

Output 5-2   *Traceroute Between SR-MPLS Nodes*

```
RP/0/0/CPU0:PE-3#traceroute 10.0.0.2

Type escape sequence to abort.
Tracing the route to 10.0.0.2

 1  192.168.4.1 [MPLS: Label 16002 Exp 0] 29 msec  9 msec  9 msec ←--PE-3 to P3
 2  192.168.3.0 9 msec  *  59 msec ←--P3 to P2
```

The label-switched path from LDP nodes to the rest of the networks uses labels from the dynamic range, as shown in Output 5-3 and Output 5-4.

Output 5-3   *Traceroute from LDP Node PE-1 to SR-MPLS Node PE-3*

```
RP/0/0/CPU0:PE-1#traceroute 10.0.1.3

Type escape sequence to abort.
Tracing the route to 10.0.1.3

 1  192.168.1.1 [MPLS: Label 24000 Exp 0] 79 msec  59 msec  49 msec ←--PE-1 to P1
 2  192.168.2.0 [MPLS: Label 24005 Exp 0] 59 msec  49 msec  99 msec ←--P1 to P2
 3  192.168.3.1 [MPLS: Label 24006 Exp 0] 39 msec  139 msec  79 msec ←--- P2 to P3
 4  192.168.4.0 99 msec  *  59 msec ←--P3 to PE-3
```

Output 5-4 *Traceroute from SR-MPLS Node PE-3 to SR-MPLS Node P2*

```
RP/0/0/CPU0:PE-1#traceroute 10.0.0.2

Type escape sequence to abort.
Tracing the route to 10.0.0.2

  1  192.168.1.1 [MPLS: Label 24003 Exp 0] 69 msec  29 msec  49 msec ←--PE-1 to P1
  2  192.168.2.0 39 msec  *  9 msec ←--P1 to P2
```

Enabling and Preferring SR-MPLS on P1, P2, and PE-1

In the next step, the rest of the devices are migrated to SR-MPLS. This is shown in
Figure 5-10.

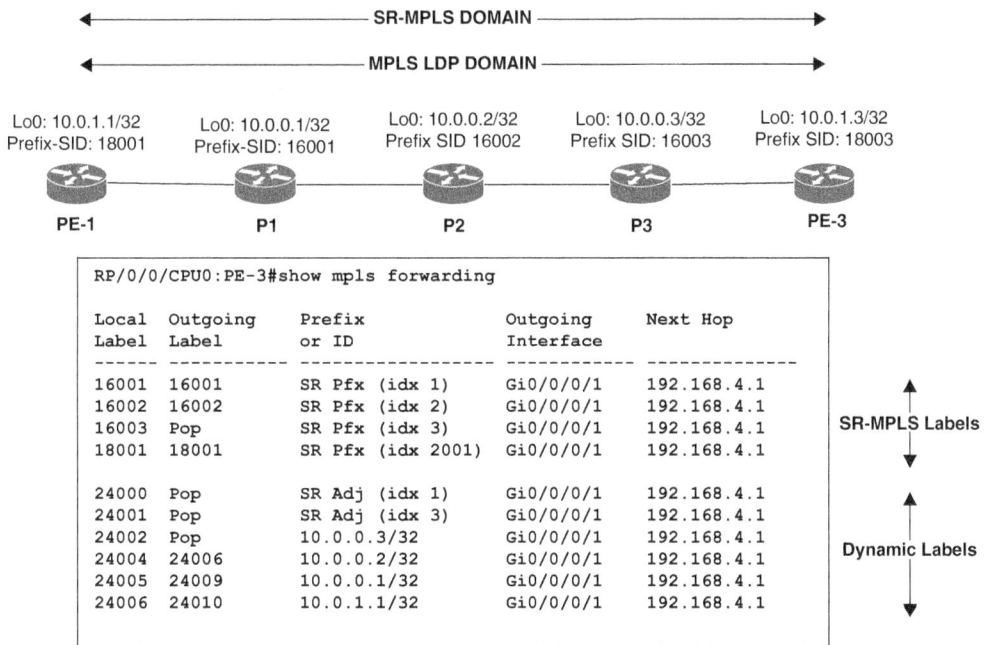

Figure 5-10 *All Devices Migrated to SR-MPLS*

The MPLS label table on PE-3 shows that it uses the labels from the dynamic range and
Prefix SIDs to reach all the devices in the network, as shown in Output 5-5.

Output 5-5 *MPLS Label Table on PE-3 (IOS-XR)*

```
RP/0/0/CPU0:PE-3#sh mpls forwarding

Local   Outgoing    Prefix              Outgoing       Next Hop          Bytes
Label   Label       or ID               Interface                        Switched
------  ----------  ------------------  ------------   ---------------   -----------
16001   16001       SR Pfx (idx 1)      Gi0/0/0/1      192.168.4.1       288
16002   16002       SR Pfx (idx 2)      Gi0/0/0/1      192.168.4.1       192
16003   Pop         SR Pfx (idx 3)      Gi0/0/0/1      192.168.4.1       3800
18001   18001       SR Pfx (idx 2001)   Gi0/0/0/1      192.168.4.1       384  <-- PE-1
24000   Pop         SR Adj (idx 1)      Gi0/0/0/1      192.168.4.1       0
24001   Pop         SR Adj (idx 3)      Gi0/0/0/1      192.168.4.1       0
24002   Pop         10.0.0.3/32         Gi0/0/0/1      192.168.4.1       0
24003   24004       10.0.0.2/32         Gi0/0/0/1      192.168.4.1       0
24004   Pop         192.168.3.0/31      Gi0/0/0/1      192.168.4.1       0
24005   24005       192.168.2.0/31      Gi0/0/0/1      192.168.4.1       0
24006   24008       10.0.0.1/32         Gi0/0/0/1      192.168.4.1       0
24007   24009       192.168.1.0/31      Gi0/0/0/1      192.168.4.1       3496
24008   24010       10.0.1.1/32         Gi0/0/0/1      192.168.4.1       0  <-- PE-1
```

The output highlights the two label entries from the dynamic label range and the Prefix
SID for PE-1.

The label-switched path between the nodes uses only Prefix SIDs, as shown in
Output 5-6 and Output 5-7.

Output 5-6 *Traceroute from PE-3 to P1*

```
RP/0/0/CPU0:PE-3#traceroute 10.0.0.1

Type escape sequence to abort.
Tracing the route to 10.0.0.1

 1  192.168.4.1 [MPLS: Label 16001 Exp 0] 69 msec  29 msec  9 msec  <-- P3
 2  192.168.3.0 [MPLS: Label 16001 Exp 0] 9 msec   9 msec  29 msec  <-- P2
 3  192.168.2.1 19 msec  *  29 msec  <-- P1
```

Output 5-7 *Traceroute from PE-3 to PE-1*

```
RP/0/0/CPU0:PE-3#traceroute 10.0.1.1

Type escape sequence to abort.
Tracing the route to 10.0.1.1
```

```
1  192.168.4.1 [MPLS: Label 18001 Exp 0] 29 msec  19 msec  29 msec ←-- PE-3 to P3
2  192.168.3.0 [MPLS: Label 18001 Exp 0] 39 msec  39 msec  19 msec ←-- P3 to P2
3  192.168.2.1 [MPLS: Label 18001 Exp 0] 19 msec  19 msec  19 msec ←-- P2 to P1
4  192.168.1.0 39 msec  *  149 msec ←-- P1 to PE-1
```

At this point, LDP can be disabled on all the devices, and the migration from LDP to SR-MPLS has been completed.

Building a New SR-MPLS Network

The previous section discusses the coexistence of LDP and SR-MPLS nodes in the same network, which does not require control plane connectivity between the LDP and SR-MPLS nodes. However, in the case of separate LDP and SR-MPLS networks, connectivity is not possible between the two networks because the label assignment is not complete for the LDP nodes in the SR-MPLS domain. LDP dynamically allocates labels for every IGP prefix by default, whereas SR-MPLS does a static allocation of Prefix SIDs only for the SR-MPLS nodes. Because the SR-MPLS nodes do not allocate labels for the LDP nodes, there is no label-switched path (LSP) between the SR-MPLS nodes and LDP nodes. Therefore, a segment routing mapping server (SRMS) is needed to allocate Prefix SIDs for the prefixes from the LDP domain and advertise this mapping to all the SR-MPLS nodes. A border node that runs both LDP and SR-MPLS does the label mapping between the dynamic labels and Prefix SID to provide connectivity between the two domains.

Figure 5-11 shows the MPLS and SR-MPLS domains interconnected using a border node and an SRMS in the SR-MPLS domain. The SRMS assigns the Prefix SIDs for the LDP nodes, and the border node does the label mapping between the two domains.

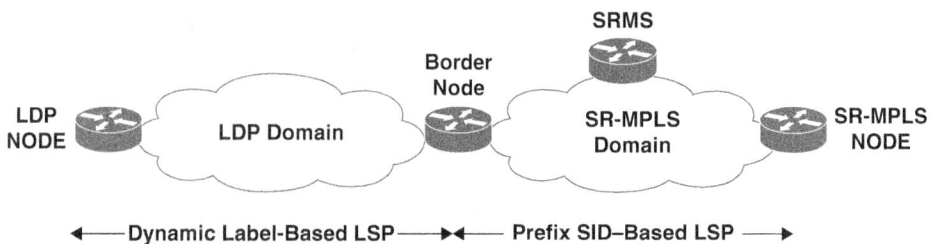

Figure 5-11 *Interworking Between the LDP and SR-MPLS Domains*

Interworking between the LDP and SR-MPLS domains can be enabled in two steps that are described in the following sections.

Enabling SRMS

The SRMS can be configured to assign Prefix SIDs for all the known nodes in the LDP network. There are two roles in providing the mapping functionality: segment routing mapping server (SRMS) and segment routing mapping client (SRMC). A node can act as an SRMS, an SRMC, or both.

The SRMS defines mapping entries for assigning SIDs to the LDP nodes, thereby creating a local SID-mapping policy that is then advertised to the SRMC via the IGP. Common sense dictates that the Prefix SIDs assigned to LDP nodes in the mapping policy must not overlap with the Prefix SID assignment for SR-MPLS nodes. The location of the SRMS in the network is not relevant. The role of the SRMS can be compared to the role of a BGP route reflector: It is a control plane mechanism, doesn't have to be in the data path, and must be resilient. As with a BGP route reflector, resiliency of an SRMS is provided by having more than one SRMS.

Mapping server advertisements are propagated between OSPF areas. In the case of IS-IS, the SRMS functionality supports the advertisement of Prefix SID mapping entries between IS-IS levels, thereby avoiding the need for a mapping server for each IS-IS level. The domain-wide option is used to advertise the Prefix SID mappings between IS-IS Level-2 and Level-1 routers. In the case of multiple IS-IS instances, a mapping server is required for each IS-IS instance.

The SRMC parses the mapping policy received from the SRMS and creates an active mapping policy that consists of non-overlapping mapping entries. At steady state, all nodes in the SR-MPLS network must have identical active mapping policies. When an SRMS is used, all nodes in an SR-MPLS network should be SRMCs to receive the prefix-to-SID mappings for the LDP nodes. This helps ensure a consistent active mapping policy on all the nodes in the SR-MPLS network.

The functionality of SRMS is illustrated in Figure 5-12, where P1 and PE-1 support only LDP, P3 and PE-3 support only SR-MPLS, P2 supports both LDP and SR-MPLS, and P3 is the SRMS.

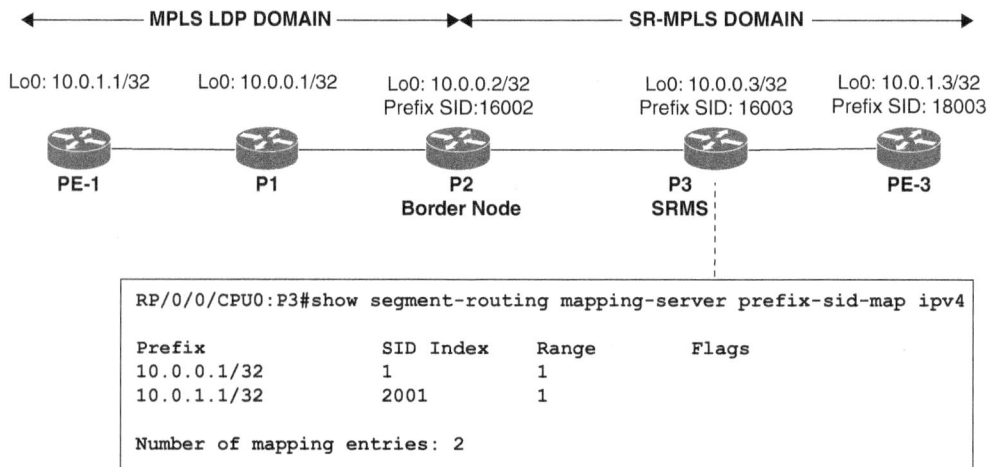

Figure 5-12   *SR-MPLS and LDP Interworking with Mapping Server*

Before the mapping server is enabled on P3, the label table on PE-3 has entries only for the SR-MPLS nodes as shown in Output 5-8.

Output 5-8   *MPLS Label Table without SRMS: PE-3 (IOS-XR)*

```
RP/0/0/CPU0:PE-3#show mpls forwarding

Local   Outgoing    Prefix              Outgoing      Next Hop         Bytes
Label   Label       or ID               Interface                      Switched
------  ----------- ------------------- ------------  --------------- ------------
16001   16001       SR Pfx (idx 1)      Gi0/0/0/1     192.168.4.1      0
16002   16002       SR Pfx (idx 2)      Gi0/0/0/1     192.168.4.1      0
16003   Pop         SR Pfx (idx 3)      Gi0/0/0/1     192.168.4.1      0
18001   18001       SR Pfx (idx 2001)   Gi0/0/0/1     192.168.4.1      0
```

The mapping server P3 assigns the SIDs from the SR-MPLS range to the prefixes in the LDP domain as shown in Output 5-9.

Output 5-9   *SRMS Mapping Policy: P3 (IOS-XR)*

```
RP/0/0/CPU0:P3#sh segment-routing mapping-server prefix-sid-map ipv4
Prefix              SID Index    Range        Flags
10.0.0.1/32         1            1
10.0.1.1/32         2001         1

Number of mapping entries: 2
```

This mapping is advertised to all the devices in the SR-MPLS domain.

PE-3 receives this mapping from P3 and updates its MPLS label table as shown in Output 5-10. The MPLS label table now includes entries for the LDP nodes as shown in Output 5-10.

Output 5-10   *MPLS Label with SRMS: PE-3 (IOS-XR)*

```
RP/0/0/CPU0:PE-3#show mpls forwarding

Local   Outgoing    Prefix              Outgoing      Next Hop         Bytes
Label   Label       or ID               Interface                      Switched
------  ----------- ------------------- ------------  --------------- ------------
16001   16001       SR Pfx (idx 1)      Gi0/0/0/0     192.168.1.1      0
16002   16002       SR Pfx (idx 2)      Gi0/0/0/0     192.168.1.1      0
16003   Pop         SR Pfx (idx 3)      Gi0/0/0/0     192.168.1.1      0
18001   18001       SR Pfx (idx 2001)   Gi0/0/0/0     192.168.1.1      0
```

Config 5-3 and Config 5-4 show how to enable the mapping server on IOS-XR and IOS-XE devices. In case of IOS-XR, the Prefix SID is specified as an index to the SRGB, while in IOS-XE, the Prefix SID can be specified as an index or absolute value. The prefixes to be mapped can also be specified as a range as shown for the prefixes 10.1.0.0/32 to 10.1.0.255/32.

Config 5-3   *SRMS (IOS-XR)*

```
router isis SR-MPLS
 address-family ipv4 unicast
  segment-routing prefix-sid-map advertise-local

segment-routing
 mapping-server
  prefix-sid-map
   address-family ipv4
    10.0.4.254/32 3254
    10.1.0.0/32 4000 range 255
```

Config 5-4   *SRMS (IOS-XE)*

```
router ospf SR-MPLS
 segment-routing prefix-sid-map advertise-local

segment-routing
 mapping-server
  prefix-sid-map
   address-family ipv4
    10.0.3.254/32 absolute 18254
```

The receipt and processing of the Prefix SID map on the SRMC from the SRMS is enabled by default on IOS-XR and IOS-XE.

Output 5-11 shows the command to verify the SRMS functionality on an IOS-XR device. The start of the Prefix SID index, the range, and the last prefix in an IP prefix block are included in the output.

Output 5-11   *Verifying SRMS Functionality on P3 (IOS-XR)*

```
RP/0/0/CPU0:P3#sh segment-routing mapping-server prefix-sid-map ipv4 detail

Prefix
10.0.0.1/32
```

```
    SID Index:       1
    Range:           1
    Last Prefix:     10.0.0.1/32
    Last SID Index: 1
    Flags:
10.0.1.1/32
    SID Index:       2001
    Range:           1
    Last Prefix:     10.0.1.1/32
    Last SID Index: 2001
    Flags:
Number of mapping entries: 2
```

Output 5-12 shows an OSPF LSA with an SRMS mapping policy entry, which includes the IP prefix, the range, and the starting Prefix SID to be allocated to the range.

Output 5-12   *OSPF LSA for an SRMS Mapping Policy Entry*

```
Ethernet II, Src: RealtekU_06:88:89 (52:54:00:06:88:89), Dst: IPv4mcast_05
  (01:00:5e:00:00:05)
Internet Protocol Version 4, Src: 192.168.4.40, Dst: 224.0.0.5
Open Shortest Path First
    OSPF Header
    LS Update Packet
        Number of LSAs: 11
<snip>
        LSA-type 10 (Opaque LSA, Area-local scope), len 48
<snip>
            OSPFv2 Extended Prefix Opaque LSA
                OSPFv2 Extended Prefix Range TLV  (Range Size: 1, Prefix:
  10.0.4.254/32)
                    TLV Type: OSPFv2 Extended Prefix Range (2)
                    TLV Length: 24
                    PrefixLength: 32
                    Address Family: IPv4 Unicast (0)
                    Range Size: 1
                    Flags: 0x00
                    Reserved: 000000
                    Address Prefix: 10.0.4.254
                    Prefix SID Sub-TLV  (SID/Label: 3254)
                        TLV Type: Prefix SID (2)
                        TLV Length: 8
                        Flags: 0x60, (NP) No-PHP Flag, (M) Mapping Server Flag
                            .1.. .... = (NP) No-PHP Flag: Set
                            ..1. .... = (M) Mapping Server Flag: Set
```

```
                            ...0 .... = (E) Explicit-Null Flag: Not set
                            .... 0... = (V) Value/Index Flag: Not set
                            .... .0.. = (L) Local/Global Flag: Not set
                        Reserved: 00
                        Multi-Topology ID: 0
                        SR-Algorithm: Shortest Path First (0)
                        SID/Label: 3254
        LSA-type 10 (Opaque LSA, Area-local scope), len 48
            .000 1110 0001 0000 = LS Age (seconds): 3600
            0... .... .... .... = Do Not Age Flag: 0
            Options: 0x20, (DC) Demand Circuits
            LS Type: Opaque LSA, Area-local scope (10)
            Link State ID Opaque Type: OSPFv2 Extended Prefix Opaque LSA (7)
            Link State ID Opaque ID: 3
            Advertising Router: 10.0.1.7
            Sequence Number: 0x8000001f
            Checksum: 0x5535
            Length: 48
            OSPFv2 Extended Prefix Opaque LSA
                OSPFv2 Extended Prefix Range TLV  (Range Size: 255,
    Prefix: 10.1.0.0/32)
                    TLV Type: OSPFv2 Extended Prefix Range (2)
                    TLV Length: 24
                    PrefixLength: 32
                    Address Family: IPv4 Unicast (0)
                    Range Size: 255
                    Flags: 0x00
                        0... .... = (IA) Inter-Area Flag: Not set
                    Reserved: 000000
                    Address Prefix: 10.1.0.0
                    Prefix SID Sub-TLV  (SID/Label: 4000)
                        TLV Type: Prefix SID (2)
                        TLV Length: 8
                        Flags: 0x60, (NP) No-PHP Flag, (M) Mapping Server Flag
                            .1.. .... = (NP) No-PHP Flag: Set
                            .1.. .... = (M) Mapping Server Flag:
    Set  <-- Received from SRMS
                            ...0 .... = (E) Explicit-Null Flag: Not set
                            .... 0... = (V) Value/Index Flag: Not set
                            .... .0.. = (L) Local/Global Flag: Not set
                        Reserved: 00
                        Multi-Topology ID: 0
                        SR-Algorithm: Shortest Path First (0)
                        SID/Label: 4000
```

Output 5-13 shows an IS-IS LSP with an SRMS mapping policy entry, which includes the IP prefix, the range, and the starting Prefix SID to be allocated to the range.

Output 5-13 *IS-IS LSP Showing an SRMS Mapping Policy Entry*

```
IEEE 802.3 Ethernet
Logical-Link Control
ISO 10589 ISIS InTRA Domain Routeing Information Exchange Protocol
ISO 10589 ISIS Link State Protocol Data Unit
<snip>
    SID/Label Binding TLV (t=149, l=17)
        Type: 149
        Length: 17
        TLV Flags: 0x00
        Weight: 0
        Range: 255
        Prefix length: 32
        Prefix: 10.1.0.0
        SID/Label sub-TLV : Prefix SID
            SID/label sub-TLV type: Prefix SID (3)
            Sub-TLV length: 6
            sub-TLV Flags: 0x00
            Algorithm: 0
            SID/Label: 4000
    SID/Label Binding TLV (t=149, l=17)
        Type: 149
        Length: 17
        TLV Flags: 0x00
        Weight: 0
        Range: 1
        Prefix length: 32
        Prefix: 10.0.4.254
        SID/Label sub-TLV : Prefix SID
            SID/label sub-TLV type: Prefix SID (3)
            Sub-TLV length: 6
            sub-TLV Flags: 0x00
            Algorithm: 0
            SID/Label: 3254
```

Verification of the prefix-to-SID mapping that is received from the SRMS is shown in Output 5-14, which indicates the Prefix SID index allocated to IP prefixes.

Output 5-14   *Verifying an Active Prefix-to-SID Mapping Policy on PE-3 (IOS-XR)*

```
RP/0/0/CPU0:PE-3#show isis segment-routing prefix-sid-map active-policy

IS-IS LDP-SR-MPLS active policy
Prefix              SID Index     Range         Flags
10.0.0.1/32         1             1
10.0.1.1/32         2001          1

Number of mapping entries: 2
```

Enabling LDP on the Border Node

The border node supports both LDP and SR-MPLS and provides the label mapping between the LDP and SR-MPLS domains that is required for forwarding traffic between the two domains.

For every label for prefix S1 advertised by the LDP neighbor, the border leaf installs the following in the MPLS label table:

■ A local label that corresponds to the Prefix SID associated with S1, as advertised by the SRMS.

■ An outgoing label that corresponds to the LDP label advertised by the LDP neighbor for prefix S1. If there is more than one LDP neighbor advertising the label for S1, then multiple entries are installed.

■ The outgoing interface that corresponds to the LDP neighbor.

This label mapping allows the border node to provide the SR-MPLS-to-LDP interworking. Traffic from the SR-MPLS nodes that is destined for LDP nodes is forwarded to the border nodes.

The label mapping for the LDP node 10.0.1.1/32 on border node P2 is illustrated in Figure 5-13.

P2 receives a remote label 24001 for the LDP node 10.0.1.1/32 from the LDP neighbor. The SRMS provides the Prefix SID assignment for 10.0.1.1/32, which can be verified in the active mapping policy on P2. P2 now creates an entry for 10.0.1.1/32 in the MPLS label table with Prefix SID 18001 as the local label and 24001 as the outgoing label that is used to forward traffic from the SR-MPLS nodes to LDP node PE-1.

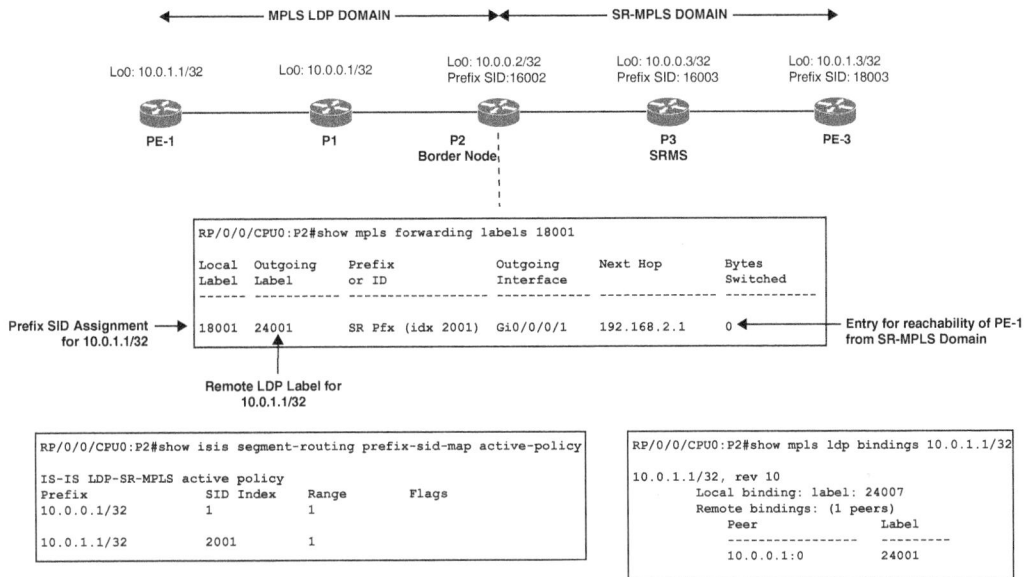

Figure 5-13 *Label Mapping for LDP Node PE-1 (10.0.1.1/32)*

For every prefix S2 that is advertised by the SR-MPLS-nodes, the border leaf installs the following in the MPLS label table:

- A local label that corresponds to the local LDP label assigned to prefix S2 by the border node.

- An outgoing label that corresponds to the Prefix SID associated with S2.

- The outgoing interface for the reachability of prefix S2. If there is more than one outgoing interface, multiple entries are installed.

This label mapping provides the LDP-to-SR-MPLS interworking. Traffic from the LDP nodes that is destined for SR-MPLS nodes is forwarded to the border nodes.

The label mapping for the SR-MPLS node 10.0.1.3/32 on border node P2 is illustrated in Figure 5-14.

P2 receives the Prefix SID 18003 for SR-MPLS node 10.0.1.3/32, as shown in the segment-routing label table. P2 assigns a local label 24005 for SR-MPLS node 10.0.1.3/32 that it advertises to its LDP neighbors. P2 now creates an entry for 10.0.1.3/32 in the MPLS label table with 24005 as the local label and the Prefix SID 18003 as the outgoing label. This entry is used to forward traffic from the LDP nodes to SR-MPLS node PE-3.

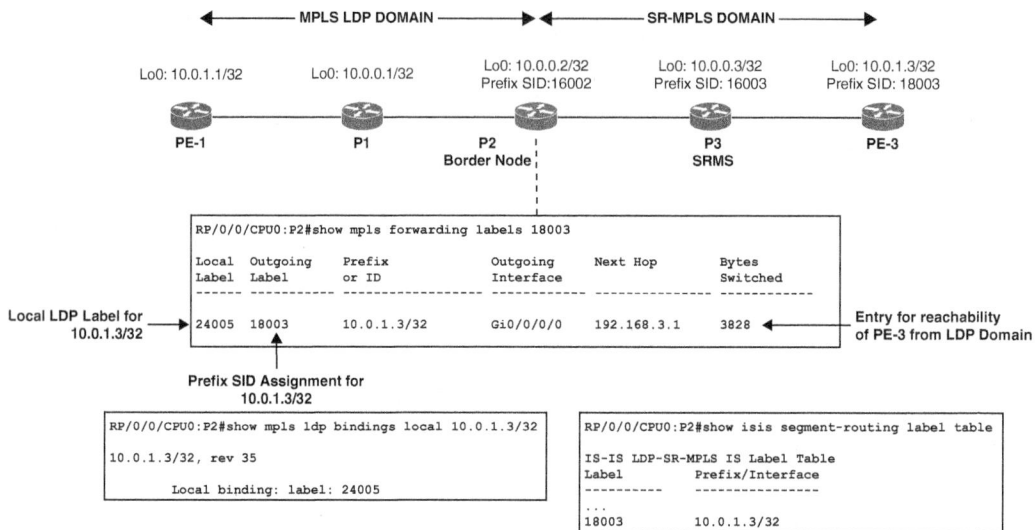

Figure 5-14   *Label Mapping on the Border Node for SR-MPLS Node 10.0.1.3/32*

Output 5-15 shows the MPLS label table on the border node P2.

Output 5-15   *MPLS Label Table on Border Node P2 (IOS-XR)*

```
P2#show mpls forwarding

Local   Outgoing      Prefix              Outgoing        Next Hop          Bytes
Label   Label         or ID               Interface                         Switched
------  -----------   ------------------  ------------    ---------------   -----------
16001   Pop           SR Pfx (idx 1)      Gi0/0/0/1       192.168.2.1       0 <--
   Entry for reachability of P1 from SR-MPLS Domain
16003   Pop           SR Pfx (idx 3)      Gi0/0/0/0       192.168.3.1       174
18001   24001         SR Pfx (idx 2001)   Gi0/0/0/1       192.168.2.1       0 <--
   Entry for reachability of PE-1 from SR-MPLS Domain
18003   18003         SR Pfx (idx 2003)   Gi0/0/0/0       192.168.3.1       0
24000   Pop           SR Adj (idx 1)      Gi0/0/0/0       192.168.3.1       0
24001   Pop           SR Adj (idx 3)      Gi0/0/0/0       192.168.3.1       0
24002   Pop           SR Adj (idx 1)      Gi0/0/0/1       192.168.2.1       0
24003   Pop           SR Adj (idx 3)      Gi0/0/0/1       192.168.2.1       0
24004   Pop           10.0.0.3/32         Gi0/0/0/0       192.168.3.1       0 <--
   Entry for reachability of P3 from LDP Domain
24005   18003         10.0.1.3/32         Gi0/0/0/0       192.168.3.1       0 <--
   Entry for reachability of PE-3 from LDP Domain
24006   Pop           10.0.0.1/32         Gi0/0/0/1       192.168.2.1       1198
24007   24001         10.0.1.1/32         Gi0/0/0/1       192.168.2.1       0
```

Figure 5-15 shows LDP-to-SR-MPLS interworking for the traffic flow from PE-1 to PE-3, where P2 provides the label mapping between the LDP and SR-MPLS domain for PE-3.

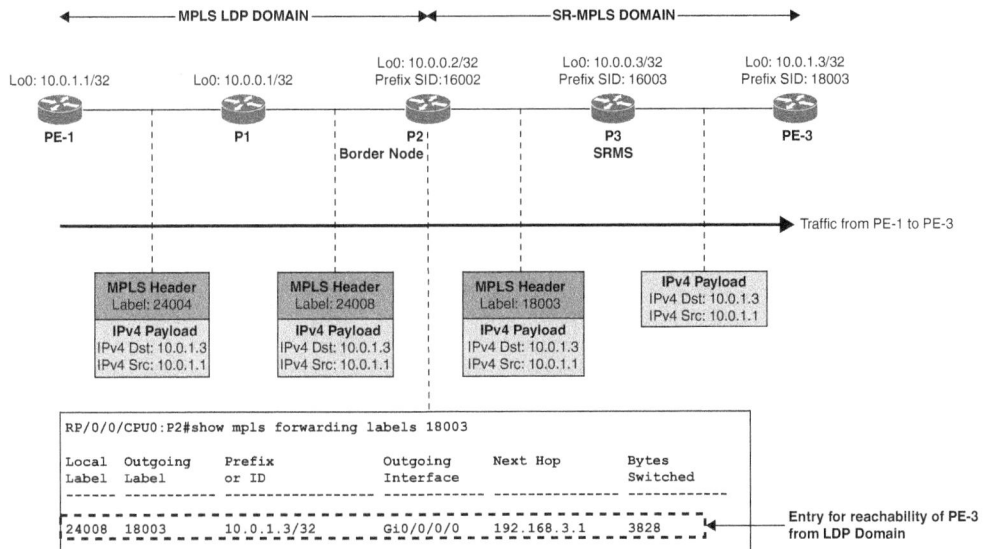

Figure 5-15   *LDP-to-SR-MPLS Interworking*

Output 5-16 shows a traceroute from PE-1 to PE-3. The label-switched patch from PE-1 to PE-3 uses the LDP labels until P2. P2 swaps the LDP label 24008 for the Prefix SID 18003. The rest of the label-switched path from P2 to PE-3 uses the Prefix SID 18003.

Output 5-16   *Traceroute from PE-1 to PE-3*

```
RP/0/0/CPU0:PE-1#traceroute ipv4 10.0.1.3

Type escape sequence to abort.
Tracing the route to 10.0.1.3

1  192.168.1.1 [MPLS: Label 24004 Exp 0] 49 msec   89 msec   69 msec ←--PE-1 to P1
2  192.168.2.0 [MPLS: Label 24008 Exp 0] 39 msec   59 msec   49 msec ←--P1 to P2
3  192.168.3.1 [MPLS: Label 18003 Exp 0] 159 msec  59 msec   59 msec ←--P2 to P3
4  192.168.4.0 59 msec  *   49 msec ←-- P3 to PE-3
```

Figure 5-16 shows SR-MPLS-to-LDP interworking is for the traffic flow from PE-3 to PE-1, where P2 provides the label mapping between the SR-MPLS and LDP domains for PE-1.

Output 5-17 shows a traceroute from PE-3 to PE-1. The label-switched patch from PE-3 to PE-1 uses the SR-MPLS Prefix SID until P2. P2 swaps the Prefix SID 18001 for the LDP label 24000. The rest of the label-switched path from P2 to PE-1 uses label from the dynamic range.

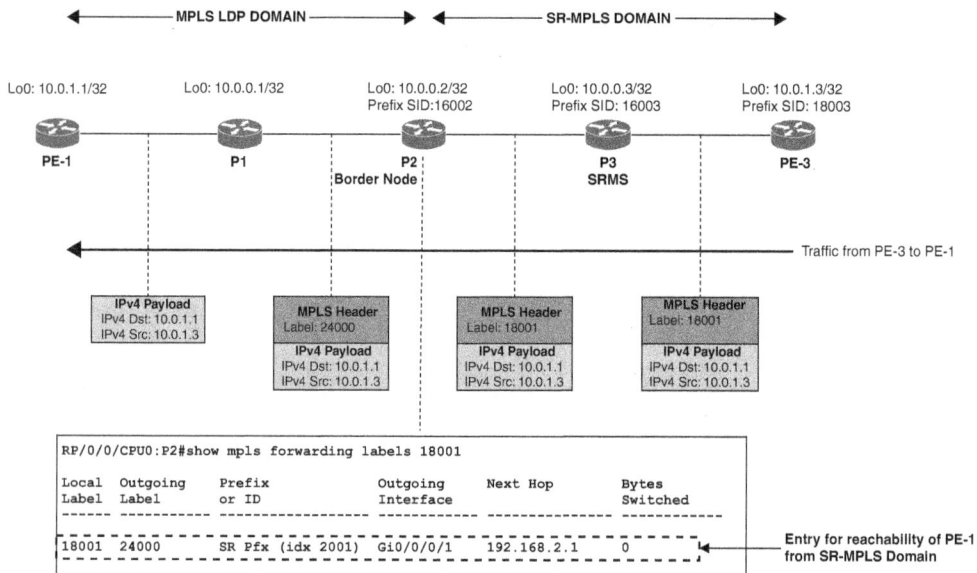

Figure 5-16   *SR-MPLS-to-LDP Interworking*

Output 5-17   *Traceroute from PE-3 to PE-1*

```
RP/0/0/CPU0:PE-3#traceroute ipv4 10.0.1.1

Type escape sequence to abort.
Tracing the route to 10.0.1.1

1  192.168.4.1 [MPLS: Label 18001 Exp 0] 89 msec  59 msec  49 msec ←-- PE-3 to P3
2  192.168.3.0 [MPLS: Label 18001 Exp 0] 49 msec  39 msec  89 msec ←-- P3 to P2
3  192.168.2.1 [MPLS: Label 24000 Exp 0] 79 msec  49 msec  49 msec ←-- P2 to P1
4  192.168.1.0 49 msec  *  69 msec ←-- P1 to PE-1
```

Enabling the BGP Prefix SID in an SR-MPLS Network

As you'll recall from the section "BGP Prefix Segment (BGP Prefix SID)" in Chapter 2, "What Is Segment Routing over MPLS (SR-MPLS)?" BGP Prefix SIDs are globally significant and are statically allocated by the operator in an SR-MPLS network. The network can benefit from enabling BGP Prefix SIDs through increased routing efficiency and network scalability. Assigning a unique identifier to each prefix makes it possible to optimize network paths more easily leading to reduced latency and better traffic engineering capabilities. In addition, BGP Prefix SIDs enhance the network's resiliency, as they allow for quick rerouting of traffic around points of failure without reliance on traditional signaling protocols. Overall, integrating BGP Prefix SIDs into an SR-MPLS network can significantly enhance the performance, manageability, and reliability of a service provider's infrastructure.

The BGP-LU speakers (BGP-SR nodes) in the SR-MPLS domain allocate BGP Prefix SIDs for all the SR-MPLS nodes and labels from the dynamic range for all the LDP nodes. The BGP-LU speakers in the LDP domain (BGP-LU nodes) allocate labels from the dynamic range for all the LDP and SR-MPLS nodes. This is explained as follows (see the reference network in Figure 5-17):

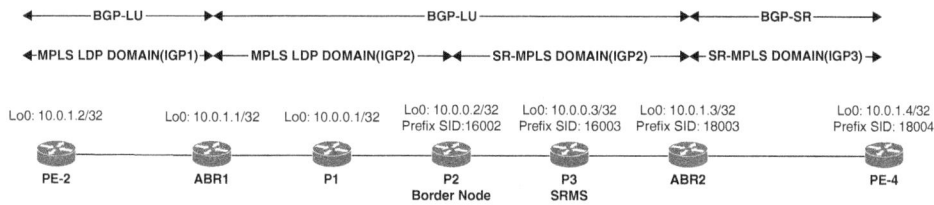

Figure 5-17 *BGP-SR and BGP-LU Interoperability*

- The BGP-LU nodes PE-2 and ABR1 are in the IGP1 domain, use LDP to allocate and distribute label information for IGP prefixes, and use BGP-LU to allocate and distribute label information for BGP prefixes.

- ABR1 is an inline route reflector for the BGP-LU domain.

- The BGP-LU nodes ABR1, P1, P2, P3 and ABR2 share the IGP2 domain and use BGP-LU to allocate and distribute labels for BGP prefixes. ABR1, P1, and P2 use LDP to allocate and distribute label information for IGP prefixes, and P2, P3, and ABR2 are in the SR-MPLS domain and use the IGP to distribute the Prefix SID information.

- ABR2 is an inline route reflector for the BGP-LU and BGP-SR domains.

- The BGP-SR nodes ABR2 and PE-4 are in the IGP3 domain, use BGP Prefix SIDs for BGP prefixes, and use BGP-LU to distribute BGP Prefix SID information.

The BGP-LU node ABR1 assigns the BGP label 24004 from the dynamic range for the loopback0 of BGP-LU node PE-2, as shown in Output 5-18. It also assigns the BGP label 24005 from the dynamic range for the loopback0 of BGP-SR node PE-4, as shown in Output 5-19.

Output 5-18 *BGP-LU Label Assigned to PE-2 on ABR1 (IOS-XR)*

```
RP/0/0/CPU0:ABR1#show bgp ipv4 labeled-unicast 10.0.1.2/32

BGP routing table entry for 10.0.1.2/32
Versions:
  Process           bRIB/RIB   SendTblVer
  Speaker              317          317
```

```
     Local Label: 24004 ←-- BGP Label assigned to PE-2
Last Modified: Jan 21 12:48:10.829 for 10:38:00
Paths: (1 available, best #1)
  Advertised to peers (in unique update groups):
    10.0.1.3
  Path #1: Received by speaker 0
  Advertised to peers (in unique update groups):
    10.0.1.3
  Local, (Received from a RR-client)
    10.0.1.2 (metric 10) from 10.0.1.2 (10.0.1.2)
      Received Label 3 ←-- BGP Label received from PE-2
      Origin IGP, metric 0, localpref 100, valid, internal, best, group-best,
labeled-unicast
      Received Path ID 0, Local Path ID 0, version 317
```

Although ABR1 receives the BGP Prefix SID for 10.0.1.4/32, it allocates a local label 24005 and advertises it to PE-2, as shown in Output 5-19.

Output 5-19   *BGP Label Assigned to PE-4 on ABR1 (IOS-XR)*

```
RP/0/0/CPU0:ABR1#show bgp ipv4 labeled-unicast 10.0.1.4/32

BGP routing table entry for 10.0.1.4/32
Versions:
  Process           bRIB/RIB  SendTblVer
  Speaker                58          58
     Local Label: 24005 ←-- BGP local label assigned to PE-4
Last Modified: Feb  2 03:35:21.859 for 1w3d
Paths: (1 available, best #1)
  Advertised IPv4 Labeled-unicast paths to peers (in unique update groups):
    10.0.1.2
  Path #1: Received by speaker 0
  Advertised IPv4 Labeled-unicast paths to peers (in unique update groups):
    10.0.1.2
  Local
    10.0.1.3 (metric 40) from 10.0.1.3 (10.0.1.3)
      Received Label 18004 ←-- BGP label received for PE-4
      Origin incomplete, metric 10, localpref 100, valid, internal, best,
group-best, labeled-unicast
      Received Path ID 0, Local Path ID 1, version 58
      Label-Index: 2004
```

The packet capture of the BGP updates from ABR1 to PE-2 shown in Output 5-20 confirms that ABR1 has allocated a local label 24005 even though a BGP Prefix SID is assigned for the prefix 10.0.1.4/32.

Output 5-20   *BGP Update for l0.0.1.4/32 from ABR1 to PE-2*

```
Internet Protocol Version 4, Src: 10.0.1.1, Dst: 10.0.1.2
Transmission Control Protocol, Src Port: 179, Dst Port: 58777
Border Gateway Protocol - UPDATE Message
    Marker: ffffffffffffffffffffffffffffffff
    Length: 96
    Type: UPDATE Message (2)
    Withdrawn Routes Length: 0
    Total Path Attribute Length: 73
    Path attributes
        Path Attribute - MP_REACH_NLRI
            Flags: 0x90, Optional, Extended-Length, Non-transitive, Complete
            Type Code: MP_REACH_NLRI (14)
            Length: 17
            Address family identifier (AFI): IPv4 (1)
            Subsequent address family identifier (SAFI): Labeled Unicast (4)
            Next hop: 10.0.1.1
            Number of Subnetwork points of attachment (SNPA): 0
            Network Layer Reachability Information (NLRI)
                Label Stack=24005 (bottom) IPv4=10.0.1.4/32  <-- Local Label
allocated for 10.0.1.14/32
                    MP Reach NLRI Prefix length: 56
                    MP Reach NLRI Label Stack: 24005 (bottom)
                    MP Reach NLRI IPv4 prefix: 10.0.1.4
<snip>
        Path Attribute - BGP Prefix-SID
            Flags: 0xc0, Optional, Transitive, Complete
            Type Code: BGP Prefix-SID (40)
            Length: 10
            Label-Index: 2004 <-- BGP Prefix-SID index
```

The BGP-SR node ABR2 assigns the BGP Prefix SID 24004 for the loopback0 of BGP-SR node PE-4, as shown in Output 5-21.

Output 5-21   *BGP-LU Label and Prefix SID Assigned to PE-2 on ABR2 (IOS-XR)*

```
RP/0/0/CPU0:ABR2#show bgp ipv4 labeled-unicast 10.0.1.4/32

BGP routing table entry for 10.0.1.4/32
Versions:
  Process           bRIB/RIB  SendTblVer
  Speaker                  6           6
```

```
   Local Label: 18004 <-- BGP prefix-SID assigned to PE-4
Last Modified: Jan 21 09:44:19.778 for 13:47:39
Paths: (1 available, best #1)
  Advertised to peers (in unique update groups):
    10.0.1.1
  Path #1: Received by speaker 0
  Advertised to peers (in unique update groups):
    10.0.1.1
  Local, (Received from a RR-client)
    10.0.1.4 (metric 10) from 10.0.1.4 (10.0.1.4)
      Received Label 3
      Origin IGP, metric 0, localpref 100, valid, internal, best, group-best,
labeled-unicast
      Received Path ID 0, Local Path ID 0, version 6
      Prefix SID Attribute Size: 10
      Label Index: 2004 <-- BGP label index for PE-4
```

Based on the BGP label assignment on the BGP-LU and BGP-SR nodes shown in Output 5-21, Table 5-1 shows the labels used for the LSPs between the BGP-LU and BGP-SR nodes shown in Figure 5-17.

Table 5-1   *Labels Used for LSP*

Headend Node	Endpoint Node	
	BGP-LU Node	**BGP-SR Node**
BGP-LU Node	Dynamic labels	Dynamic labels and BGP Prefix SID
BGP-SR Node	Dynamic labels	BGP Prefix SID

The LSP from the BGP-LU to a BGP-SR node (PE-2 > ASBR1 > P1 > P2 > P3 > ABR2 > PE-4) uses a combination of dynamic labels and BGP Prefix SIDs. The stitching between the dynamic labels and BGP Prefix SIDs for BGP-SR nodes is done by ABR1, which is the BGP-LU node that is closest to the BGP-SR domain. This is shown in Output 5-22, where the BGP-LU node ABR1 receives the BGP Prefix SID 18004 for PE-4 and assigns the local label 24005.

Output 5-22   *Label Stitching for BGP-SR Node PE-4 on ABR1 (IOS-XR)*

```
RP/0/0/CPU0:ABR1#show bgp ipv4 labeled-unicast 10.0.1.4/32

BGP routing table entry for 10.0.1.4/32
Versions:
  Process           bRIB/RIB  SendTblVer
  Speaker                 58          58
    Local Label: 24005 <-- BGP local label assigned to PE-4
```

```
Last Modified: Feb  2 03:35:21.859 for 1w3d
Paths: (1 available, best #1)
  Advertised IPv4 Labeled-unicast paths to peers (in unique update groups):
    10.0.1.2
  Path #1: Received by speaker 0
  Advertised IPv4 Labeled-unicast paths to peers (in unique update groups):
    10.0.1.2
  Local
    10.0.1.3 (metric 40) from 10.0.1.3 (10.0.1.3)
      Received Label 18004 <-- BGP label received for PE-4
      Origin incomplete, metric 10, localpref 100, valid, internal, best,
group-best, labeled-unicast
      Received Path ID 0, Local Path ID 1, version 58
      Label-Index: 2004
```

Since the interworking between BGP-LU and BGP-SR nodes for BGP prefixes does not require any additional devices or special configuration, migration from BGP-LU to BGP-SR can be done in a phased manner.

The path from PE-2 to PE-4 shown in Figure 5-18 includes the packet with the MPLS header and IP payload as it traverses every hop along the path.

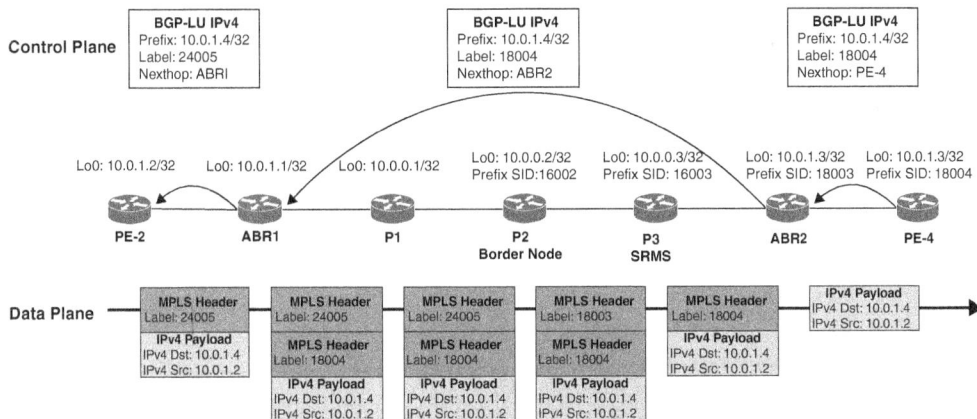

Figure 5-18   *Control and Data Plane Between PE-2 and PE-4*

The LSP from PE-2 to PE-4 uses the BGP label 24005 until ABR1 and uses two labels (24000 and 18004) until ABR2, where the outer label is the LDP label to reach ABR2 and the inner label is the BGP Prefix SID for PE-4. This is validated with a packet capture on the link between ABR1 and P1, as shown in Output 5-23.

Output 5-23   *Packet Captured on the Link Between ABR1 and P1*

```
Ethernet II
MultiProtocol Label Switching Header, Label: 24000, Exp: 0, S: 0, TTL: 1 <--
   MPLS label for ABR2
MultiProtocol Label Switching Header, Label: 18004, Exp: 0, S: 1, TTL: 1 <--
   BGP Prefix SID for PE-4
Internet Protocol Version 4, Src: 10.0.1.2, Dst: 10.0.1.4
User Datagram Protocol, Src Port: 46174, Dst Port: 33438
```

Output 5-24 shows a traceroute from PE-2 to PE-4.

Output 5-24   *Traceroute from PE-2 to PE-4*

```
RP/0/0/CPU0:PE-2#traceroute 10.0.1.4 source lo0


Type escape sequence to abort.
Tracing the route to 10.0.1.4

 1  192.168.6.0 [MPLS: Label 24005 Exp 0] 129 msec   99 msec   89 msec <--
 PE-2 to ABR1
 2  192.168.1.1 [MPLS: Labels 24000/18004 Exp 0] 119 msec   129 msec   169 msec <--
 ABR1 to P1
 3  192.168.2.0 [MPLS: Labels 24005/18004 Exp 0] 129 msec   99 msec   99 msec <--
 P1 to P2
 4  192.168.3.1 [MPLS: Labels 18003/18004 Exp 0] 89 msec   99 msec   89 msec <--
 P2 to P3
 5  192.168.4.0 [MPLS: Label 18004 Exp 0] 89 msec   229 msec   99 msec <--
 P3 to ABR2
 6  192.168.5.1 119 msec   *   89 msec <-- ABR2 to PE-4
```

Figure 5-19 shows the packet header with the labels as the packet traverses the path from PE-4 to PE-2.

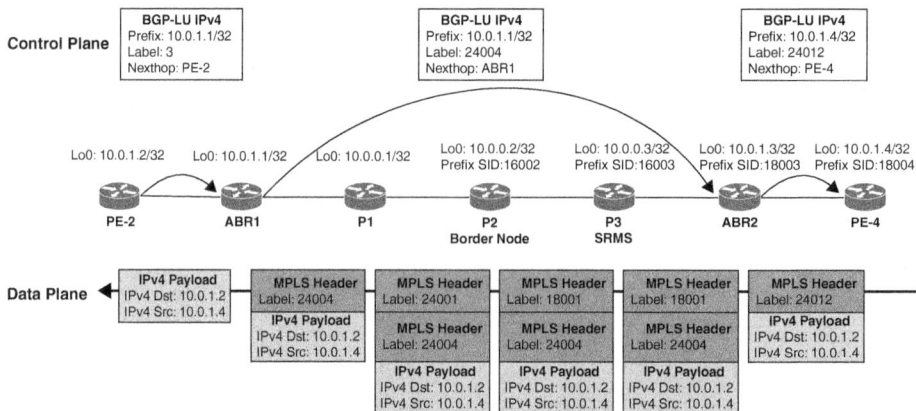

Figure 5-19   *Control Plane and Data Plane Between PE-4 and PE-2*

The LSP from PE-4 to PE-2 uses the BGP label 24012 until ABR2 and uses two labels (18001 and 24004) to reach ABR1, where the outer label is the Prefix SID to reach ABR2 and the inner label is the BGP-LU label allocated by ABR-1 for PE-2. This is validated with a packet capture on the link between ABR2 and P3, as shown in Output 5-25.

Output 5-25 *Packet Capture on the Link Between ABR2 to P3*

```
Ethernet II
MultiProtocol Label Switching Header, Label: 18001, Exp: 0, S: 0, TTL: 1 <---
   BGP Prefix SID for ABR1
MultiProtocol Label Switching Header, Label: 24004, Exp: 0, S: 1, TTL: 1 <---
   BGP-LU Label for PE-2
Internet Protocol Version 4, Src: 10.0.1.4, Dst: 10.0.1.2
User Datagram Protocol, Src Port: 20805, Dst Port: 33438
```

Output 5-26 shows a traceroute from PE-4 to PE-2.

Output 5-26 *Traceroute from PE-4 to PE-2*

```
RP/0/0/CPU0:PE-4#traceroute 10.0.1.2 source lo0


Type escape sequence to abort.
Tracing the route to 10.0.1.2


 1  192.168.5.0 [MPLS: Label 24012 Exp 0] 119 msec  89 msec  119 msec <----
    PE-4 to ABR2
 2  192.168.4.1 [MPLS: Labels 18001/24004 Exp 0] 109 msec  79 msec  89 msec <----
    ABR2 to P3
 3  192.168.3.0 [MPLS: Labels 18001/24004 Exp 0] 79 msec  109 msec  79 msec <----
    P3 to P2
 4  192.168.2.1 [MPLS: Labels 24001/24004 Exp 0] 79 msec  89 msec  89 msec <----
    P2 to P1
 5  192.168.1.0 [MPLS: Label 24004 Exp 0] 89 msec  89 msec  79 msec <---- P1 to ABR1
 6  192.168.6.1 89 msec  *  109 msec <---- ABR1 to PE-1
```

BGP Proxy Prefix SID

Using the BGP Prefix SID offers several advantages over dynamic label allocation, including deterministic transport label assignment, hardware resource optimization, and better convergence for unified MPLS/inter-AS Option C implementations in transport networks. However, there may be routers that do not support BGP Prefix SID, and an alternate approach may be required to assign BGP Prefix SIDs.

The BGP proxy Prefix SID feature makes it possible to attach BGP Prefix SID attributes for remote prefixes learned from BGP-LU nodes that are not SR capable and propagate them as SR prefixes. This allows an LSP toward non-SR nodes to use labels from the SRGB. The BGP proxy Prefix SID feature is implemented using a local SID-mapping policy that allows the user to configure SID-mapping entries to specify the Prefix SIDs for the prefixes. BGP uses this local SID-mapping policy to assign the Prefix SIDs for BGP-LU prefixes. BGP proxy Prefix SID is configured on the node that is connected to the BGP-LU and BGP-SR domains.

One use case for BGP proxy Prefix SID is an Anycast SID. The nodes that advertise an Anycast SID allocate the same SID for the prefix. In the case of non-SR nodes, there is no guarantee that LDP will allocate the same label for the prefix advertised by two nodes. In this case, the BGP proxy Prefix SID feature can be used to allocate the BGP Prefix SID to the prefix learned from the BGP-LU domain.

Figure 5-20 shows another use case for BGP proxy Prefix SID when there is mutual redistribution of prefixes between the BGP-LU and the IGP of the SR-MPLS domain.

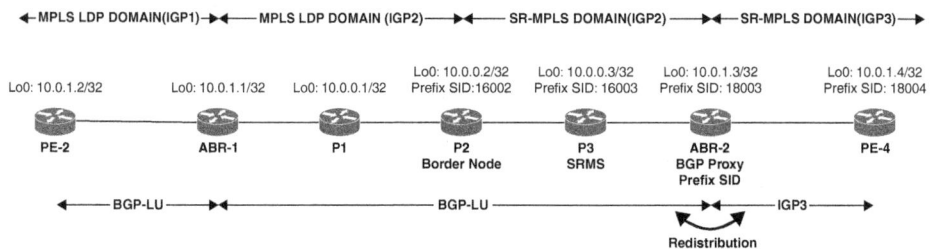

Figure 5-20 *Redistribution Between the BGP-LU and the SR-MPLS Domain*

ABR2 is connected to the BGP-LU domain and the SR-MPLS domain, and prefixes are redistributed between BGP and the IGP of the SR-MPLS domain. While BGP assigns labels to the prefixes from the SR-MPLS domain, labels are not assigned to the BGP-LU prefixes in the SR-MPS domain. As a result, there is a broken LSP from PE-4 to PE-2, where no labels are used from PE-4 to ABR2. This is shown in the traceroute from PE-4 to PE-2 in Output 5-27.

Output 5-27 *Traceroute from PE-4 to PE-2 Showing a Broken LSP from PE-4 to PE-2*

```
RP/0/0/CPU0:PE-4#traceroute 10.0.1.2 so lo0

Type escape sequence to abort.
Tracing the route to 10.0.1.2

 1  192.168.5.0 0 msec  0 msec  0 msec <--- No LSP from PE-4 to ABR2
 2  192.168.4.1 [MPLS: Labels 18001/24004 Exp 0] 139 msec  99 msec  129 msec
 3  192.168.3.0 [MPLS: Labels 18001/24004 Exp 0] 219 msec  129 msec  129 msec
 4  192.168.2.1 [MPLS: Labels 24001/24004 Exp 0] 109 msec  89 msec  79 msec
 5  192.168.1.0 [MPLS: Label 24004 Exp 0] 79 msec  79 msec  79 msec
 6  192.168.6.1 79 msec
```

BGP proxy Prefix SID is configured on ABR2 to assign Prefix SIDs to 10.0.1.2/32, as shown in Config 5-5.

Config 5-5 *BGP Proxy Prefix SID (IOS-XR)*

```
router bgp 65000
 address-family ipv4 unicast
  segment-routing prefix-sid-map

segment-routing
 global-block 16000 23999
 local-block 15000 15999
 mapping-server
  prefix-sid-map
   address-family ipv4
    10.0.1.2/32 2002
```

Now, when the BGP-LU prefixes are redistributed into the IGP, the Prefix SID information is also included in the LSP, as shown in Output 5-28.

Output 5-28 *Prefix SID Information Included in the IS-IS Update*

```
IEEE 802.3 Ethernet
Logical-Link Control
ISO 10589 ISIS InTRA Domain Routeing Information Exchange Protocol
ISO 10589 ISIS Link State Protocol Data Unit
<snip>
    Extended IP Reachability (t=135, l=55)
<snip>
        Ext. IP Reachability: 10.0.1.2/32
            Metric: 0
            0... .... = Distribution: Up
            .1.. .... = Sub-TLV: Yes
            ..10 0000 = Prefix Length: 32
            IPv4 prefix: 10.0.1.2
            SubCLV Length: 11
            subTLV: Prefix-SID (c=3, l=6) <-- Prefix SID information
                Code: Prefix-SID (3)
                Length: 6
                Flags: 0xa0, Re-advertisement, no-PHP
                Algorithm: Shortest Path First (SPF) (0)
                SID/Label/Index: 0x000007d2 <-- Prefix SID = 2002
            subTLV: Prefix Attribute Flags (c=4, l=1): Flags:X--
                Code: Prefix Attribute Flags (4)
                Length: 1
                Flags: 0x80, External Prefix
<snip>
```

This can also be verified in the IS-IS database information on PE-4, as shown in Output 5-29.

Output 5-29 *IS-IS Database Information on PE-4 (IOS-XR)*

```
RP/0/0/CPU0:PE-4#show isis database ABR2.00-00  det verbose

IS-IS BGP-PREFIX-SID (Level-2) Link State Database
LSPID              LSP Seq Num  LSP Checksum  LSP Holdtime  ATT/P/OL
ABR2.00-00         0x00000c54   0xcc1d        509           0/0/0
  Area Address:    49.0001
  NLPID:           0xcc
  IP Address:      10.0.1.3
  Metric: 0          IP-Extended 10.0.1.3/32
    Prefix-SID Index: 2003, Algorithm:0, R:0 N:1 P:0 E:0 V:0 L:0
    Prefix Attribute Flags: X:0 R:0 N:1
  Metric: 10         IP-Extended 192.168.5.0/31
    Prefix Attribute Flags: X:0 R:0 N:0
  Metric: 0          IP-Extended 10.0.1.2/32
    Prefix-SID Index: 2002, Algorithm:0, R:1 N:0 P:1 E:0 V:0 L:0
    Prefix Attribute Flags: X:1 R:0 N:0
<snip>
```

The data path from PE-4 to PE-2 now uses the label 18002 on the link between PE-4 and ABR2, as shown in Figure 5-21.

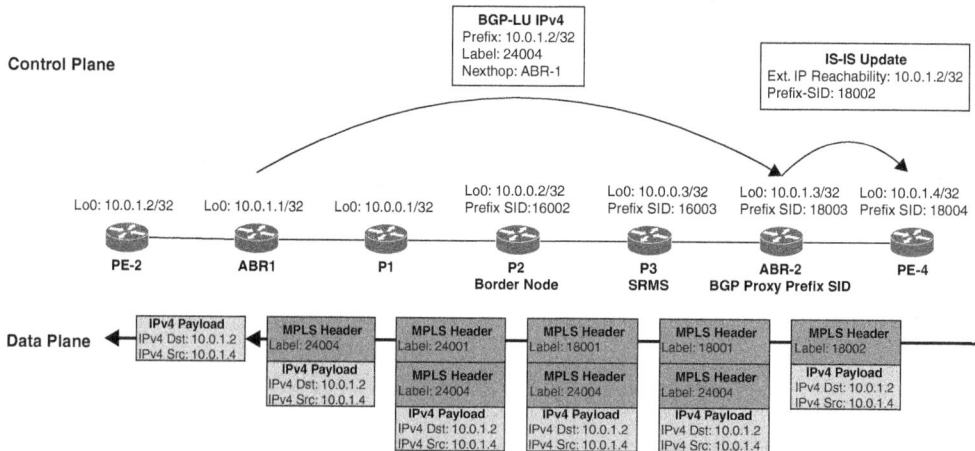

Figure 5-21 *Data Path from PE-4 to PE-2*

A traceroute displays the LSP from PE-4 to PE-2, as shown in Output 5-30.

Output 5-30   *Traceroute from PE-4 to PE-2*

```
RP/0/0/CPU0:PE-4#traceroute 10.0.1.2 so lo0


Type escape sequence to abort.
Tracing the route to 10.0.1.2


 1  192.168.5.0 [MPLS: Label 18002 Exp 0] 159 msec  239 msec  179 msec  <--
    PE-4 to ABR2
 2  192.168.4.1 [MPLS: Labels 18001/24004 Exp 0] 149 msec  129 msec  169 msec <--
    ABR2 to P3
 3  192.168.3.0 [MPLS: Labels 18001/24004 Exp 0] 159 msec  139 msec  179 msec <--
    P3 to P2
 4  192.168.2.1 [MPLS: Labels 24001/24004 Exp 0] 159 msec  169 msec  249 msec <--
    P2 to P1
 5  192.168.1.0 [MPLS: Label 24004 Exp 0] 149 msec  149 msec  119 msec  <--
    P1 to ABR1
 6  192.168.6.1 119 msec  <-- ABR1 to PE-2
```

The LSP from PE-4 to ABR2 uses the BGP label 18002, as allocated by ABR2, which is validated with a packet capture on the link between PE-4 and ABR2, as shown in Output 5-31.

Output 5-31   *Packet Capture on the Link Between PE-4 and ABR2*

```
Ethernet II, Src: 52:54:00:02:53:cf (52:54:00:02:53:cf), Dst: 52:54:00:19:2f:8c
  (52:54:00:19:2f:8c)
MultiProtocol Label Switching Header, Label: 18002, Exp: 0, S: 1, TTL: 255 <--
  BGP Prefix SID for 10.0.1.2/32
Internet Protocol Version 4, Src: 10.0.1.4, Dst: 10.0.1.2
Internet Control Message Protocol
```

We have now completed our discussion of migration from LDP to SR-MPLS, interoperability between BGP-LU and BGP-SR nodes, and the use of BGP proxy Prefix SID to facilitate communication between BGP-LU and BGP-SR nodes. The next section is focused on the challenges of migrating from MPLS to SRv6.

SRv6 Migration

The transport and service identifiers in the MPLS and SRv6 networks are different, which means it is necessary to provide interworking between the two domains. You have already seen two deployment models and strategies for migration from MPLS to SR. This section describes three different methods for migrating services from an MPLS network to an SRv6 network. The sections "Building a New SRv6 Network Using an SRv6 IWG" and "Building a New SRv6 Network Using Inter-AS Option A" describe two methods that are based on interworking between the two domains, and the section "SRv6 Network

Using Dual-Connected PE Devices" elaborates on the third method, which is based on coexistence of services in MPLS and SRv6 networks.

Note In this section, the term *MPLS* refers to both LDP-based MPLS and SR-MPLS. The illustrations and examples in this section use SR-MPLS in the MPLS domain, but they are also valid for MPLS LDP.

Figure 5-22 shows the reference topology that is used to illustrate the configuration and verification for the following SRv6 migration methods:

■ The Inter-AS Option A solution is based on the MPLS and SRv6 ASBRs.

■ IWG functionality is illustrated using an SRv6 IWG.

■ Dual-connected PE configuration and verification are shown with Dual-Connected PE device.

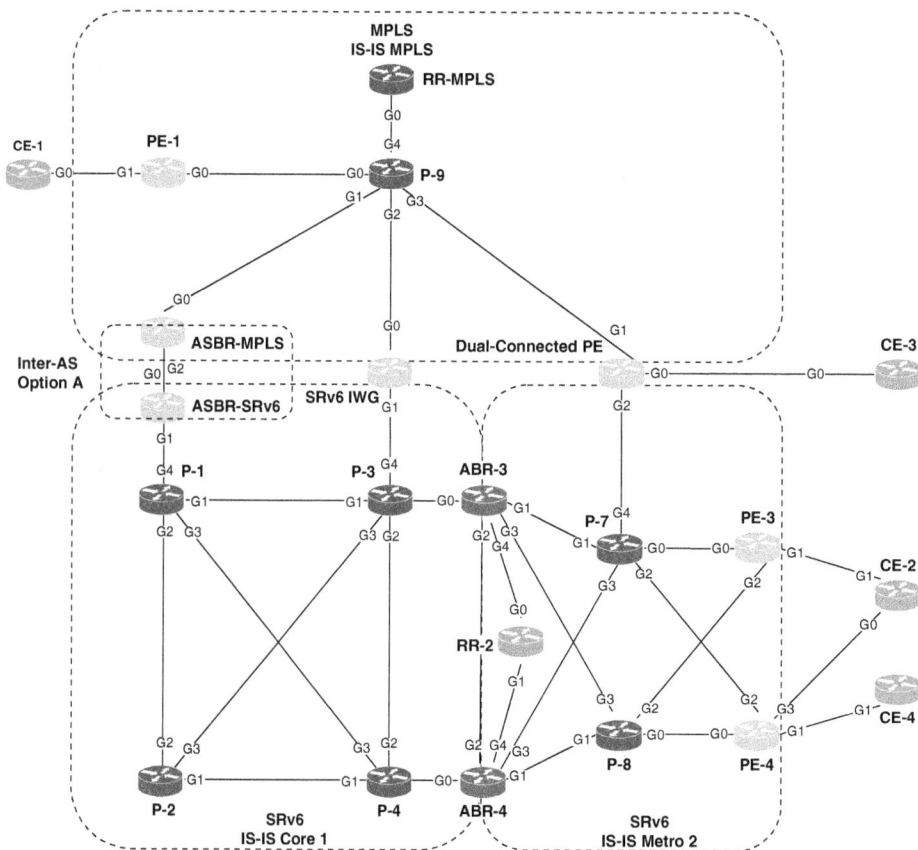

Figure 5-22 *SRv6 Reference Topology for SRv6 Migration Methods*

Building a New SRv6 Network Using an SRv6 IWG

An SRv6 interworking gateway (SRv6 IWG) facilitates the interworking for L3VPN services between MPLS and SRv6 domains by providing service continuity in the control plane and data plane, as shown in Figure 5-23.

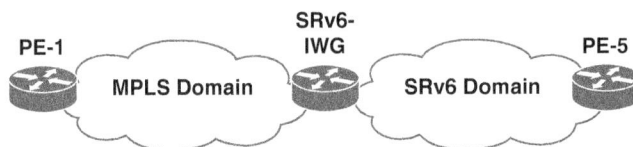

Figure 5-23   *An SRv6 IWG*

The SRv6 IWG provides interworking through re-origination of the BGP updates in the control plane and decapsulation/encapsulation of the packet headers when the packets traverse from one domain to the other. The SRv6 IWG allocates the MPLS service labels for VPNv4 prefixes learned from the SRv6 network and advertises them to the MPLS network. Similarly, the SRv6 IWG also allocates the SRv6 SIDs for VPNv4 prefixes learned from the MPLS network and advertises them to the SRv6 network.

The SRv6 IWG supports traffic forwarding from the MPLS to SRv6 domains by popping the MPLS VPN label and encapsulating the data packet with the appropriate IPv6 header before forwarding it to the SRv6 domain. In the other direction, the SRv6 IWG removes the IPv6 header, pushes the MPLS transport and service labels, and forwards the packet to the MPLS domain.

When the number of CE devices to be migrated is large, it is difficult to migrate all the CE devices in a single MW (Maintenance Window). The SRv6 IWG provides interworking between the two domains during the migration phase, facilitating a phased migration and mitigating the risks. The SRv6 IWG is required until all the CE devices have been migrated to the SRv6 domain.

In theory, an SRv6 IWG could provide interworking for L2VPN services like the L3VPN services. At this writing, SRv6 IWGs do not support interworking for L2VPN services between SRv6 and MPLS domains.

An SRv6 IWG is connected to the MPLS and SRv6 domains. Every VRF instance that requires connectivity between the two domains is configured on the SRv6 IWG and has two sets of route targets (RTs):

- **MPLS L3VPN RT (called the RT):** This is the RT used by the L3VPN service in the MPLS domain.

■ **SRv6 L3VPN RT (called the stitching RT):** This is the RT used by the L3VPN service in the SRv6 domain.

The RT and stitching RT of a VRF instance can be different, and the SRv6 IWG maps all the RTs of a VRF instance to the stitching RTs and vice versa, as shown in Figure 5-24.

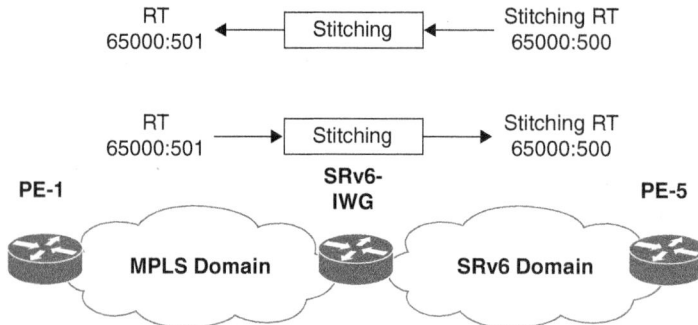

Figure 5-24   *RT Stitching on an SRv6 IWG*

The mapping can be explained with the configuration shown in Config 5-6 and Config 5-7, where the MPLS and SRv6 domains use different RTs for the same VRF instance.

Config 5-6   *RT Definition Across the MPLS Domain*

```
vrf ACME
 address-family ipv4 unicast
  import route-target
   65000:501
  !
  export route-target
   65000:501
```

Config 5-7   *RT Definition Across the SRv6 Domain*

```
vrf ACME
 address-family ipv4 unicast
  import route-target
   65000:500
  !
  export route-target
   65000:500
```

For the setup shown in Figure 5-24, the VRF instance on the SRv6 IWG is configured with a different RT and stitching RT, as shown in Config 5-8.

Config 5-8   *RT and Stitching RT on the SRv6 IWG*

```
vrf ACME
 address-family ipv4 unicast
  import route-target
   65000:501
   65000:500 stitching
  !
  export route-target
   65000:501
   65000:500 stitching
```

The SRv6 IWG imports the routes from the MPLS domain into the VRF instance and advertises it to the SRv6 domain with the SRv6 SID and the stitching RT. Similarly, when the SRv6 IWG imports a route received from the SRv6 domain into the VRF instance, it advertises it to the MPLS domain with the MPLS service label and the RT.

An SRv6 IWG works for VRF instances that have full mesh and hub and spoke topologies. It does not work for extranets and VRF instances with multiple export/import RTs, where it results in incorrect importing of routes into the VRF instance.

Migration Use Case

As explained at the beginning of this chapter, migration from MPLS to SRv6 requires interworking in the control and data planes. This section elaborates on the steps for migrating L3VPN services from the MPLS domain to the SRv6 domain using an SRv6 IWG, thereby facilitating the migration in several batches and minimizing the efforts and risks during the migration.

Figure 5-25 shows Site 1 and Site 2 connected over an MPLS network. The VRF ACME instance is used to provide the L3VPN services for the connectivity between the two sites. Site 1 has prefix 10.1.0.0/24 and will be referred to as prefix S1. Site 2 has prefix 10.2.0.0/24 and will be referred to as prefix S2.

Traffic from Site 1 to Site 2 over the MPLS network uses MPLS labels for data forwarding. The rest of this section explains the steps to migrate the two sites to the SRv6 network.

SRv6 IWG: Site 2 Migration

In the first step, Site 2 is migrated from PE-2 to PE-3. Figure 5-26 shows the tasks for preparing the SRv6 IWG for the migration, including enabling SR-MPLS and SRv6, establishing BGP VPNv4 sessions with the RRs in the MPLS and SRv6 domains, and configuring the ACME VRF instance.

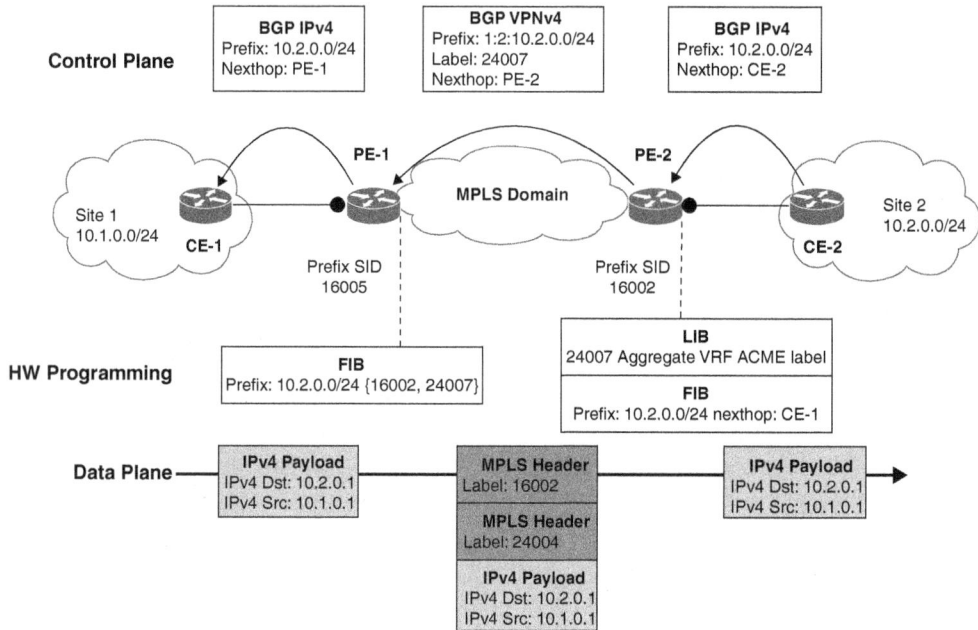

Figure 5-25 *SRv6 IWG Pre-Migration*

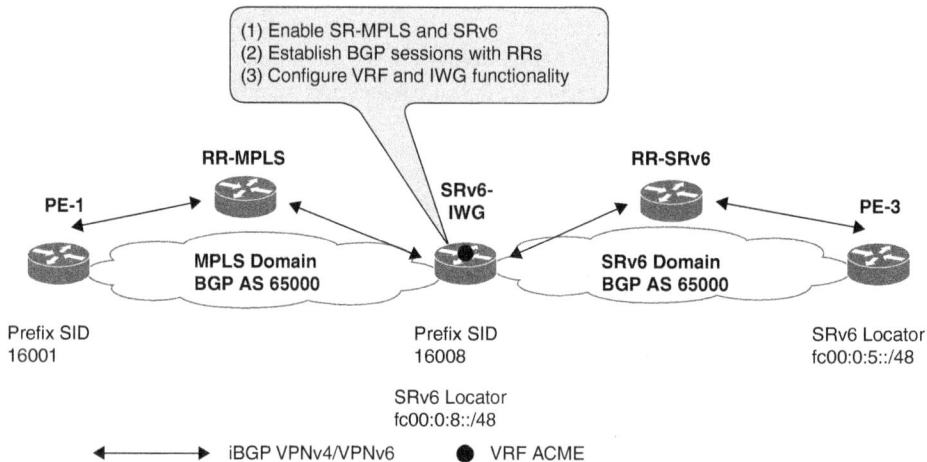

Figure 5-26 *SRv6 IWG Preparation*

SR-MPLS and SRv6 are enabled as shown in Config 5-9, where SRv6-IWG is assigned Prefix SID 16008 and SRv6 locator fc00:0:8::/48. Two separate IGPs are configured for the MPLS and SRv6 domains, and segment routing is enabled on both of the IGPs.

Config 5-9 *Enabling SR-MPLS and SRv6 on SRv6-IWG*

```
! SR-MPLS
segment-routing
 global-block 16000 23999

router isis MPLS
 address-family ipv4 unicast
  router-id Loopback0
  segment-routing mpls

 interface Loopback0
  address-family ipv4 unicast
   prefix-sid absolute 16008

! SRv6
segment-routing
 srv6
  locators
   encapsulation
    source-address fc00:0:8::1
   locator MAIN
    micro-segment behavior unode psp-usd
    prefix fc00:0:8::/48

router isis SRv6
 address-family ipv6 unicast
  metric-style wide
  router-id Loopback0
  segment-routing srv6
   locator MAIN
```

Config 5-10 shows the BGP configuration toward RR-MPLS and RR-SRv6.

Note Route reflectors are configured as route reflector clients of the SRv6 IWG. This is required to propagate the VPNv4 prefixes from one domain to the other.

Config 5-10 *SRv6 IWG BGP Session to RR-SRv6 and RR-MPLS*

```
! RR-MPLS
route-policy PASS
  pass
end-policy
```

```
router bgp 65000
 neighbor 10.0.0.3
  remote-as 65000
  description *** eBGP peering to RR-MPLS ***
  update-source Loopback0
  address-family vpnv4 unicast
   route-reflector-client

!RR-SRv6
route-policy PASS
  pass
end-policy

router bgp 65000
neighbor fc00:0:207::1
  remote-as 65000
  update-source Loopback0
  description *** iBGP peering to RR-SRv6 ***
  address-family vpnv4 unicast
   route-reflector-client
   encapsulation-type srv6
```

In the next step, the SRv6 IWG functionality is enabled for the ACME VRF instance using the configuration shown in Config 5-11.

Config 5-11   *SRv6: VRF Instance and IWG Configuration*

```
!
vrf ACME
 address-family ipv4 unicast
  import route-target
   65000:500 stitching <-- RT in SRv6 Domain
   65000:501 <-- RT in MPLS domain
  !
  export route-target
   65000:500 stitching
   65000:501
  !

router bgp 65000
 vrf ACME
  rd 1:8
  address-family ipv4 unicast
   mpls alloc enable <-- Allocate labels for IPv4 prefixes in VRF
   segment-routing srv6
```

```
neighbor 10.0.0.3
 remote-as 65000
 address-family vpnv4 unicast
  import re-originate stitching-rt <-- Import the VPNv4 routes from RR-SRv6
  advertise vpnv4 unicast re-originated <-- Advertise the re-originated VPNv4
 routes to RR-MPLS
 !
neighbor fc00:0:207::1
 use neighbor-group IBGP-M2-NG
 description *** iBGP peering to METRO_2 RR ***
 address-family vpnv4 unicast
  import stitching-rt re-originate <-- Import the VPNv4 routes from RR-MPLS
  encapsulation-type srv6
  advertise vpnv4 unicast re-originated stitching-rt <-- Advertise the
 re-originated VPNv4 routes to RR-SRv6
  !
 !
```

The RT and stitching RT are enabled for the VRF instance, BGP is enabled to allocate labels for IPv4 prefixes in the ACME instance, and BGP is configured to re-originate the VPNv4 routes from one domain to the other.

Note Although different RTs are used for the MPLS and SRv6 networks for this exercise to explain the role of the IWG, it is also possible for the RT and stitching RT to be one and the same.

Now Site 2 is migrated by moving CE-2 from PE-2 in the MPLS domain to PE-3 in the SRv6 domain. Config 5-12 shows the configuration on PE-3 for this activity.

Config 5-12 *Site 2 Migration on PE-3*

```
vrf ACME
 address-family ipv4 unicast
  import route-target
   65000:500
  !
  export route-target
   65000:500

route-policy PASS_RP
  pass
end-policy

router bgp 65000
 vrf ACME
 rd 1:3
```

```
address-family ipv4 unicast
 segment-routing srv6
  alloc mode per-ce
 !
 network 10.2.0.1/32
!
neighbor 10.2.103.1
 remote-as 65500
 address-family ipv4 unicast
  route-policy PASS_RP in
  route-policy PASS_RP out
```

Figure 5-27 shows the commands that are used to trace the advertisement of the prefix S2 from PE-3 to the SRv6 IWG and to PE-1 in the MPLS domain.

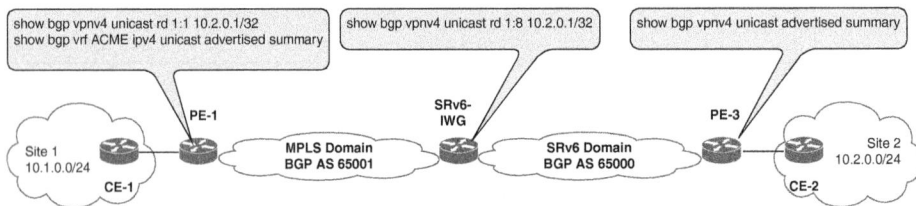

Figure 5-27 *SRv6 IWG Verification*

Output 5-32 shows that PE-3 advertises prefix S2 to SRv6-IWG via RR-SRv6 in the SRv6 domain.

Output 5-32 *BGP Advertisement on PE-3 (IOS-XR)*

```
RP/0/RP0/CPU0:PE-5#show bgp vpnv4 unicast advertised summary
Network            Next Hop        From           Advertised to
Route Distinguisher: 65000:1
Route Distinguisher Version: 52
 10.2.1.0/30       fc00:0:205::1   Local          fc00:0:207::1
 10.2.1.128/32     fc00:0:205::1   10.2.1.2       fc00:0:207::1
 10.2.1.129/32     fc00:0:205::1   10.2.1.2       fc00:0:207::1
Route Distinguisher: 65000:51001
Route Distinguisher Version: 62
 10.2.104.128/28   fc00:0:205::1   10.2.104.1     fc00:0:207::1
Route Distinguisher: 172.19.0.19:0
Route Distinguisher Version: 46
 10.2.100.0/30     fc00:0:205::1   Local          fc00:0:207::1
 10.2.100.128/32   fc00:0:205::1   10.2.100.2     fc00:0:207::1
Route Distinguisher: 172.19.0.19:1
Route Distinguisher Version: 71
 10.2.102.0/30     fc00:0:205::1   Local          fc00:0:207::1
 10.2.102.128/32   fc00:0:205::1   Local          fc00:0:207::1
```

```
Route Distinguisher: 1:3
Route Distinguisher Version: 509
10.2.0.1/32        fc00:0:205::1   10.2.103.1        fc00:0:207::1 <-- Prefix S2
  advertised to RR-SRv6
10.2.103.0/31      fc00:0:205::1   Local             fc00:0:207::1
10.2.103.128/28    fc00:0:205::1   10.2.103.1        fc00:0:207::1
```

Output 5-33 shows that SRv6-IWG has received prefix S2 with SRv6 SID fc00:0:5:e00d::
from RR-SRv6 and has re-originated prefix S2 with label 24002 and the RT 65000:501,
which is the RT for the ACME VRF instance in the MPLS domain, to RR-MPLS in the
MPLS domain.

Output 5-33 *Prefix S2 from the SRv6 Domain on SRv6-IWG (IOS-XR)*

```
RP/0/RP0/CPU0:SRv6-IWG#show bgp vpnv4 unicast rd 1:8 10.2.0.1/32 <-- Prefix S2

BGP routing table entry for 10.2.0.1/32, Route Distinguisher: 1:8
Versions:
  Process           bRIB/RIB   SendTblVer
  Speaker              1145         1145
    Local Label: 24002 <-- Label allocated to Prefix S2
    SRv6-VPN SID: fc00:0:8:e003::/64
Last Modified: Jan 20 13:05:07.971 for 00:00:56
Paths: (2 available, best #1)
  Advertised to peers (in unique update groups): <-- Advertised to RR-MPLS
    10.0.0.3
  Path #1: Received by speaker 0
  Advertised to peers (in unique update groups):
    10.0.0.3
  65500, (Received from a RR-client)
    fc00:0:205::1 (metric 31) from fc00:0:207::1 (172.19.0.19)
      Received Label 0xe00d0
      Origin IGP, metric 0, localpref 200, valid, internal, best, group-best,
  import-candidate, imported, re-originated
      Received Path ID 0, Local Path ID 1, version 1145
      Extended community: RT:65000:501 <-- Re-originated with RT for VRF ACME in
  MPLS domain
      Originator: 172.19.0.19, Cluster list: 172.19.0.21
      PSID-Type:L3, SubTLV Count:1
       SubTLV:
        T:1(Sid information), Sid:fc00:0:205::, Behavior:61, SS-TLV Count:1
        SubSubTLV:
         T:1(Sid structure):
      Source AFI: VPNv4 Unicast, Source VRF: default, Source Route
  Distinguisher: 1:3
```

PE-1 receives the update for prefix S2 from RR-MPLS, as shown in Output 5-34.

Output 5-34   *BGP Update for Prefix S2 on PE-1(IOS-XR)*

```
RP/0/RP0/CPU0:PE-1#show bgp vpnv4 unicast rd 1:1 10.2.0.1/32

BGP routing table entry for 10.2.0.1/32, Route Distinguisher: 1:1
Versions:
  Process           bRIB/RIB   SendTblVer
  Speaker              1233         1233
Last Modified: Jan 20 16:12:36.121 for 00:01:35
Paths: (1 available, best #1)
  Not advertised to any peer
  Path #1: Received by speaker 0
  Not advertised to any peer
  65000 65500
    10.0.0.8 (metric 20) from 10.0.0.3 (172.19.0.19) <-- Update from Prefix S2 from
RR-MPLS
    Received Label 24002 <-- Label for Prefix S2
    Origin IGP, metric 0, localpref 200, valid, internal, best, group-best,
import-candidate, not-in-vrf
    Received Path ID 0, Local Path ID 1, version 1233
    Extended community: RT:65000:501
    Originator: 172.19.0.19, Cluster list: 10.0.0.3, 172.19.0.25, 172.19.0.21
```

In the last step, PE-1 advertises prefix S2 to CE-1, as shown in Output 5-35.

Output 5-35   *BGP Advertisement on PE-1 (IOS-XR)*

```
RP/0/RP0/CPU0:PE-1#show bgp vrf ACME ipv4 unicast advertised summary

Network            Next Hop        From            Advertised to
Route Distinguisher: 1:1 (default for vrf ACME)
Route Distinguisher Version: 1029
10.1.0.9/32        10.3.103.2      10.0.0.3        10.3.103.3
10.1.103.128/28    10.3.103.2      10.0.0.3        10.3.103.3
10.1.103.144/28    10.3.103.2      10.0.0.3        10.3.103.3
10.1.103.240/28    10.3.103.2      10.0.0.3        10.3.103.3
10.2.0.1/32        10.3.103.2      10.0.0.3        10.3.103.3 <-- Prefix S2
    advertised to CE-1
10.2.103.0/31      10.3.103.2      10.0.0.3        10.3.103.3
10.2.103.128/28    10.3.103.2      10.0.0.3        10.3.103.3
10.3.103.0/31      10.3.103.2      10.0.0.3        10.3.103.3
10.3.103.2/31      10.3.103.2      Local           10.3.103.3
192.168.1.0/31     10.3.103.2      10.0.0.3        10.3.103.3
Processed 10 prefixes, 10 paths
```

After the verification that the prefixes are advertised from the SRv6 domain to the MPLS domain, the data path from Site 1 to Site 2 via the SRv6 IWG is validated, as shown in Figure 5-28.

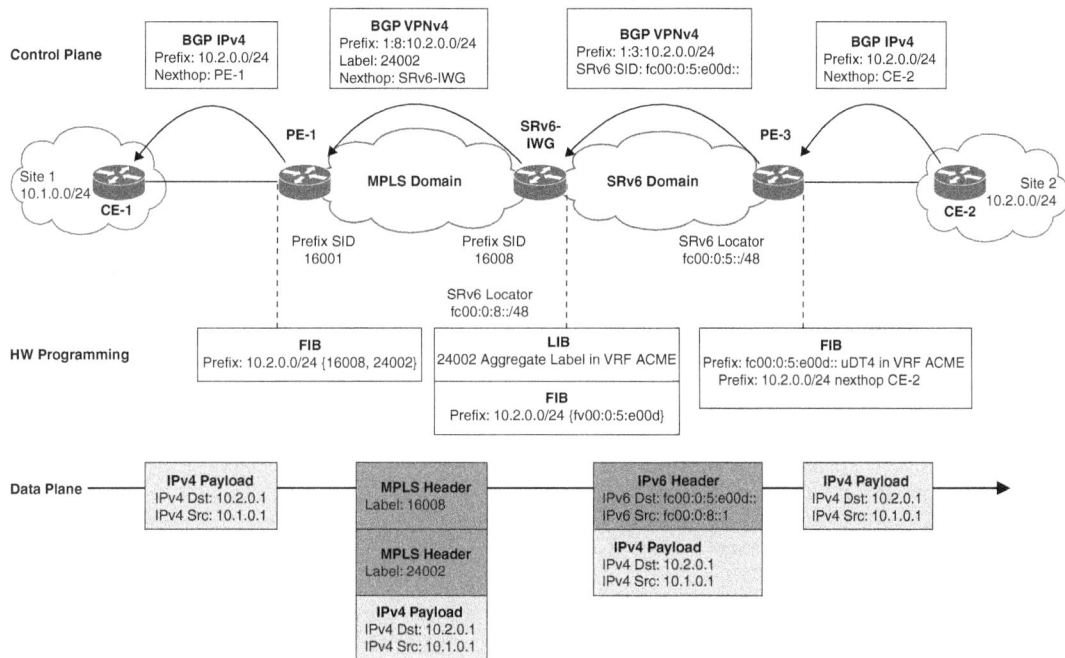

Figure 5-28   *Control Plane and Data Plane Between Site 1 and Site 2 After Migration of Site 2*

CE-1 forwards the IPv4 packet destined for CE-2 to PE-1, which encapsulates the IPv4 packet with the MPLS transport label (16008) and service label (24002), and forwards the packet to SRv6-IWG in the MPLS domain. SRv6-IWG decapsulates the MPLS service label 24002 and does a lookup in the ACME VRF instance because 24002 is an aggregate label. SRv6-IWG encapsulates the packet into an outer IPv6 header with the destination address fc00:0:5:e00d:: and forwards it in the SRv6 domain. On PE-3, fc00:0:5:e000:: corresponds to the uDT4 endpoint behavior with a lookup in the ACME VRF instance, which then forwards the packet to CE-2.

Output 5-36 shows the data forwarding verified using a ping from CE-1 to CE-2.

Output 5-36   *Ping from CE-1 to CE-2*

```
RP/0/RP0/CPU0:CE-1#ping 10.2.0.1 source 10.1.0.1

Type escape sequence to abort.
Sending 5, 100-byte ICMP Echos to 10.2.0.1 timeout is 2 seconds:
!!!!!
Success rate is 100 percent (5/5), round-trip min/avg/max = 5/6/7 ms
```

A traceroute from CE-1 to CE-2, as shown in Output 5-37, helps to validate the path. P-9 is a P node on the MPLS network that provides connectivity between PE-1 and SRv6-IWG.

Output 5-37   *Traceroute from CE-1 to CE-2*

```
RP/0/RP0/CPU0:CE-1#traceroute 10.2.0.1 source 10.1.0.1


Type escape sequence to abort.
Tracing the route to 10.2.0.1


 1   10.3.103.2 2 msec  1 msec  1 msec <-- CE-1 to PE-1
 2   10.1.0.0 [MPLS: Labels 16008/24002 Exp 0] 3 msec  2 msec  2 msec <-- PE-1 to P-9
 3   10.1.2.1 2 msec  2 msec  2 msec <-- P-9 to SRv6 IWG
 4   10.2.103.0 5 msec  6 msec  5 msec <-- PE-3 to CE-2
 5   10.2.103.1 6 msec  *  7 msec <-- CE-2
```

Data forwarding from CE-2 to CE-1 is verified using a ping, as shown in Output 5-38.

Output 5-38   *Ping from CE-2 to CE-1*

```
RP/0/RP0/CPU0:CE-2#ping 10.1.0.1 source 10.2.0.1
Type escape sequence to abort.
Sending 5, 100-byte ICMP Echos to 10.1.0.1 timeout is 2 seconds:
!!!!!
Success rate is 100 percent (5/5), round-trip min/avg/max = 7/8/12 ms
```

A traceroute from CE-2 to CE-1, as shown in Output 5-39, helps to the trace the path. An interesting observation is that the traceroute does not provide information about the path from PE-3 to SRv6-IWG in the SRv6 network.

Output 5-39   *Traceroute from CE-2 to CE-1*

```
RP/0/RP0/CPU0:CE-2#traceroute 10.1.0.1 source lo3


Type escape sequence to abort.
Tracing the route to 10.1.0.1


 1   10.2.103.0 2 msec  1 msec  1 msec <-- CE-2 to PE-3
 2   *  *  *    <-- Path through SRv6 Network
 3   10.1.2.0 [MPLS: Labels 16001/24007 Exp 0] 7 msec  6 msec  5 msec <-- SRv6 IWG
     to P-9
 4   10.1.0.1 [MPLS: Label 24007 Exp 0] 6 msec  6 msec  6 msec <-- P-9 to PE-1
 5   10.3.103.3 6 msec  *  7 msec <-- PE-1 to CE-1
```

SRv6 IWG: Site 1 Migration

In the next step, Site 1 is migrated from PE-1 to PE-4. The configuration on PE-4 for this migration step is like the configuration on PE-3 for Site 2 migration. Figure 5-29 shows the BGP updates between Site 2 and Site 1 after the migration.

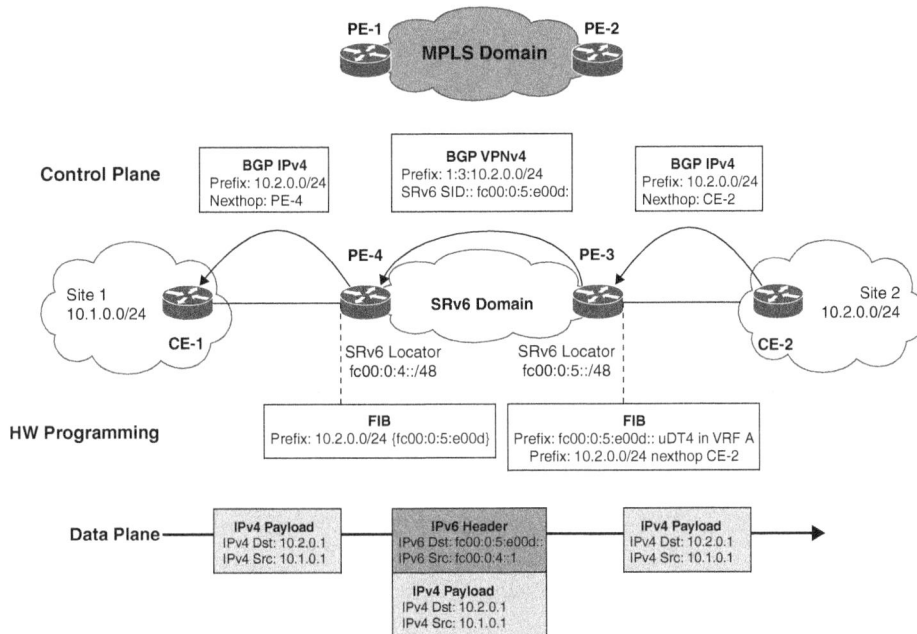

Figure 5-29 *Control Plane and Data Plane Between Site 1 and Site 2 After Migration of Site 1*

PE-3 now advertises prefix S2 with the SRv6 SID fc00:0:5:e00d::. PE-4 receives this BGP update and imports S2 into the ACME VRF instance and advertises prefix S2 to CE-1.

In the data plane, PE-4 now forwards traffic destined for Site 2 to PE-3. PE-3 removes the IPv6 header and forwards the IPv4 packet to CE-2.

Once all the sites have been migrated to SRv6, the SRv6 IWG can be removed from the network.

Building a New SRv6 Network Using Inter-AS Option A

This section focuses on using two ASBRs to provide interworking between MPLS and SRv6 domains. Unlike the SRv6 IWG, which supports interworking only for L3VPNs, this solution provides the interworking for L3VPN and L2VPN services using the well-known Inter-AS Option A interconnect using two ASBRs.

Note For the rest of this section, ASBR-MPLS refers to the ASBR in the MPLS domain, and ASBR-SRv6 refers to the ASBR in the SRv6 domain.

Figure 5-30 shows MPLS and SRv6 domains connected via ASBR-MPLS and ASBR-SRv6. The Layer 3 link is used for interworking for L3VPN services, and the Layer 2 link is used for the L2VPN services. The Layer 2 and Layer 3 links are logical links and can be implemented as subinterfaces on a physical link or a logical link. The Layer 3 link is terminated on a VRF instance, and the Layer 2 link is an attachment circuit (AC).

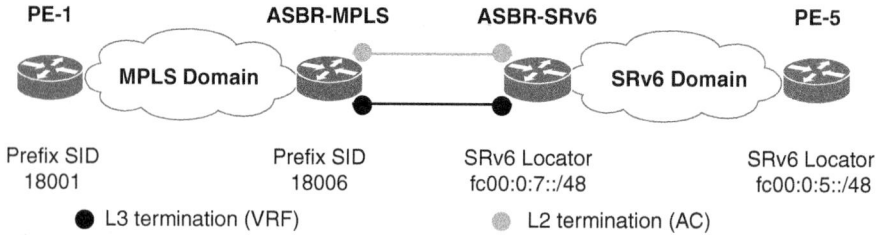

Figure 5-30 *Inter-AS ASBRs*

The ASBRs provide both transport and service termination before forwarding the packet to the ASBR in the other domain. The two ASBRs together emulate the role of the SRv6 IWG, as shown in Figure 5-31. ASBR-MPLS receives BGP updates from the MPLS domain and forwards them to ASBR-SRv6, which then sends the BGP updates to the SRv6 domain. In the data plane, ASBR-MPLS removes the MPLS service label and forwards the packet to ASBR-SRv6, which in turn inserts an outer IPv6 header and forwards the packet in the SRv6 domain. The roles of ASBR-MPLS and ASBR-SRv6 are reversed for traffic from the SRv6 domain to the MPLS domain.

There is a lot of similarity between the solutions with SRv6 IWGs and ASBRs because an SRv6 IWG combines the functionality of both of the ASBRs, as shown in Figure 5-31.

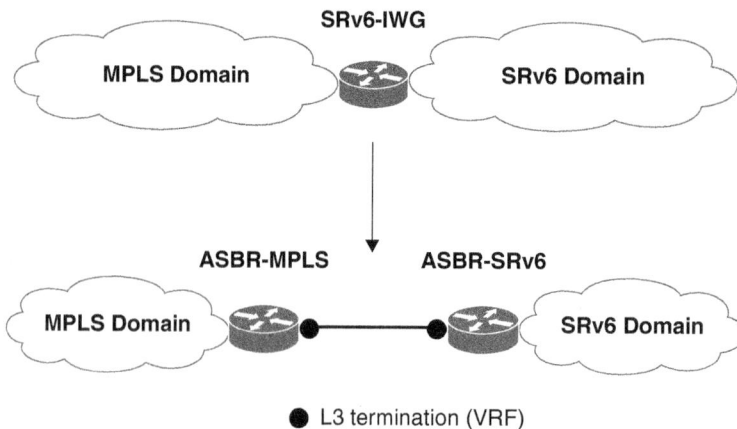

Figure 5-31 *Inter-AS ASBRs as an SRv6 IWG*

However, unlike the SRv6 IWG, the ASBRs can also provide interworking between the MPLS and SRv6 domains using a Layer 2 link between the ASBRs, as shown in Figure 5-32.

The EVPN VPWS service in a domain is terminated on the ASBR, and the Layer 2 link between the ASBRs provides the connectivity between the domains. The control and data planes of the two domains are independent of each other. In the data forwarding plane, L2 packets from CE-2 are encapsulated with an SRv6 header and forwarded in the SRv6 domain to ASBR-SRv6. ASBR-SRv6 removes the SRv6 header and forwards the L2 packet to ASBR-MPLS, which then encapsulates the L2 packet with MPLS labels and forwards the packets in the MPLS domain to PE-1. PE-1 removes the MPLS header and forwards the L2 packet to CE-1.

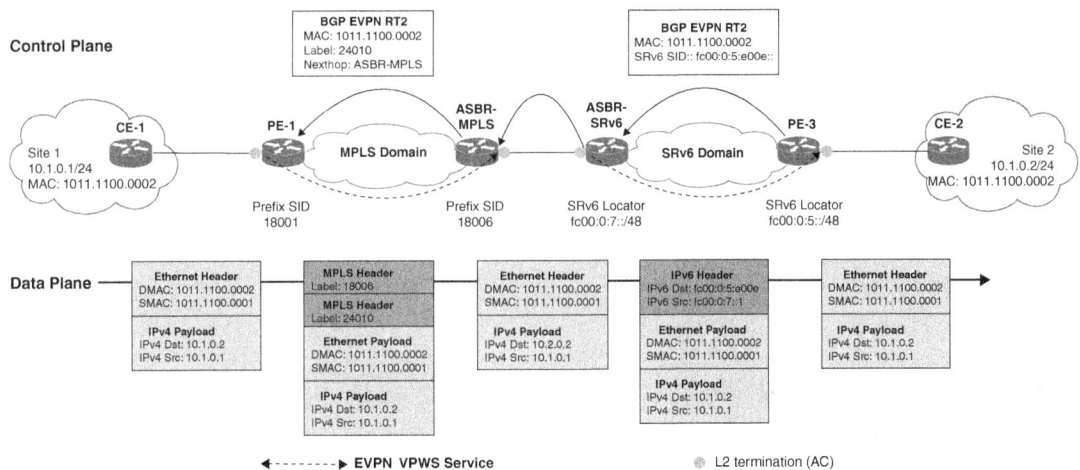

Figure 5-32 *Inter-AS Option-A: Control and Data Planes for L2VPN Services*

Migration Use Case

This section presents the steps for the migration of L3VPN services from MPLS to SRv6 using the interworking capability of ASBRs.

Figure 5-33 shows two sites connected over an MPLS network with details on the BGP updates and the data plane forwarding. These two sites must be migrated to the SRv6 network.

Inter-AS: Site 2 Migration

In the first step, Site 2 is migrated from PE-1 to PE-3. Figure 5-34 shows the configuration steps for preparing the ASBRs for the migration, including enabling SR-MPLS and SRv6, establishing BGP VPNv4 sessions with the RRs in the MPLS and SRv6 domains, and configuring the ACME VRF instance and eBGP sessions with the ASBRs in the other domain.

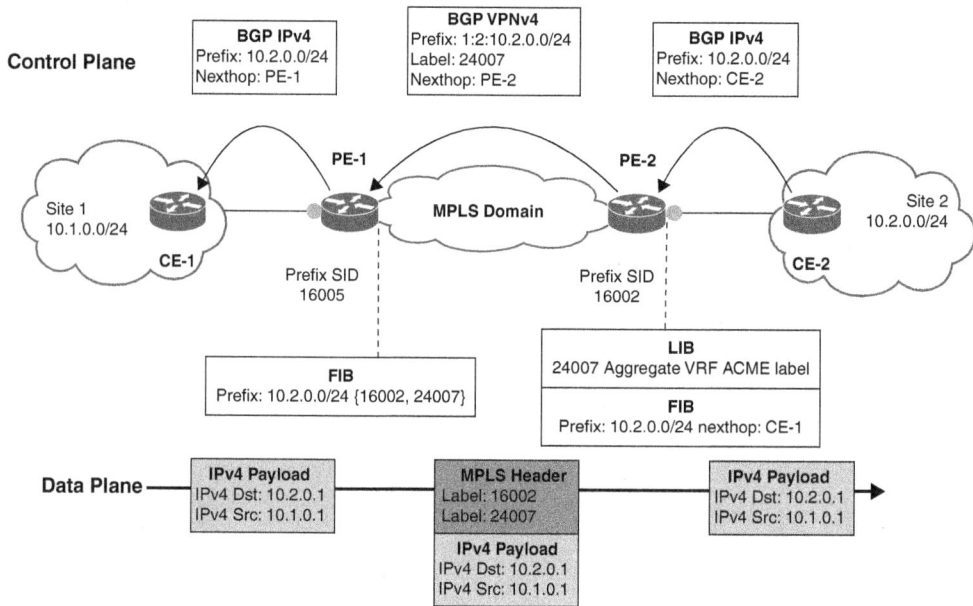

Figure 5-33 *Inter-AS Option A Pre-Migration*

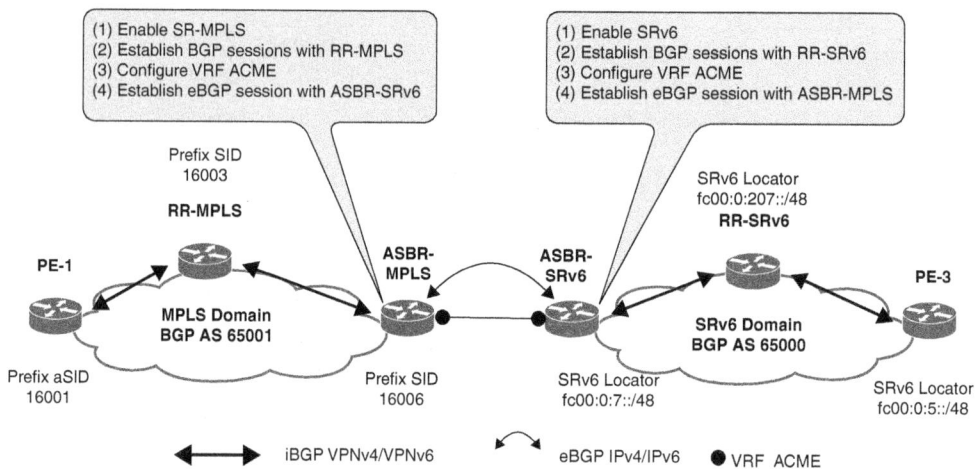

Figure 5-34 *ASBR Preparation*

Before starting the Inter-AS Option A related configuration, SR-related configuration must be completed on the ASBRs, as shown in Config 5-13.

Config 5-13 *SR-MPLS on ASBR-MPLS and SRv6 on ASBR-SRv6*

```
!ASBR-MPLS
segment-routing
 global-block 16000 23999

router isis MPLS
address-family ipv4 unicast
  segment-routing mpls

interface Loopback0
  address-family ipv4 unicast
    prefix-sid absolute 16006

!ASBR-SRv6
segment-routing
 srv6
  locators
   encapsulation
    source-address fc00:0:7::1
   locator MAIN
    micro-segment behavior unode psp-usd
    prefix fc00:0:7::/48

router isis SRv6
 address-family ipv6 unicast
  metric-style wide
  router-id Loopback0
  segment-routing srv6
   locator MAIN
```

Config 5-14 shows the configuration related to iBGP session with the route reflectors.

Config 5-14 *iBGP Sessions on ASBR-MPLS and on ASBR-SRv6*

```
!ASBR-MPLS
route-policy PASS
  pass
end-policy

router bgp 65001
 neighbor 10.0.0.3
  remote-as 65001
```

```
   description *** iBGP peering to RR-MPLS ***
   update-source Loopback0
   address-family vpnv4 unicast
 !
!ASBR-SRv6
route-policy PASS
  pass
end-policy

router bgp 65000
 neighbor fc00:0:207::1
   remote-as 65000
   update-source Loopback0
   description *** iBGP peering to RR-SRv6 ***
   address-family vpnv4 unicast
```

In the next step, the VRF instances are defined on the ASBRs, and the eBGP peering between the ASBRs is enabled to exchanged IPv4 prefixes, as shown in Config 5-15. On IOS-XR, a route policy is required for eBGP sessions to send and receive BGP updates.

Config 5-15 *Enabling VRF Instances and the eBGP Session for ASBR Functionality*

```
!ASBR-MPLS
vrf ACME
 address-family ipv4 unicast
  import route-target
   65000:501
  !
  export route-target
   65000:501
  !

route-policy PASS
  pass
end-policy

router bgp 65001
 vrf ACME
  rd 1:6
  address-family ipv4 unicast
  !
  neighbor 192.168.1.0
   remote-as 65000
   description eBGP Session to ASBR-SRv6
```

```
   address-family ipv4 unicast
    route-policy PASS in
    route-policy PASS out

!ASBR-MPLS
vrf ACME
 address-family ipv4 unicast
  import route-target
   65000:500
  !
  export route-target
   65000:500
  !

route-policy PASS
  pass
end-policy
!
router bgp 65000
 vrf ACME
  rd 1:7
  address-family ipv4 unicast
  !
  neighbor 192.168.1.1
   description eBGP Session to ASBR-MPLS
   remote-as 65001
   address-family ipv4 unicast
    route-policy PASS in
    route-policy PASS out
```

Now Site 2 is migrated by moving CE-2 from PE-2 in the MPLS domain to PE-3 in the SRv6 domain. Config 5-16 shows the configuration on PE-3 for this activity.

Config 5-16   *Site 2 Migration on PE-3*

```
vrf ACME
 address-family ipv4 unicast
  import route-target
   65000:500
  !
  export route-target
   65000:500
```

```
route-policy PASS_RP
  pass
end-policy

router bgp 65000
 vrf ACME
  rd 1:3
  address-family ipv4 unicast
   segment-routing srv6
    alloc mode per-ce
   !
   network 10.2.0.1/32
  !
  neighbor 10.2.103.1
   remote-as 65500
   address-family ipv4 unicast
    route-policy PASS_RP in
    route-policy PASS_RP out
```

Figure 5-35 shows the commands that are used to trace the advertisement of the prefix
S2 from PE-3 in the SRv6 domain to PE-5 in the MPLS domain via the ASBRs.

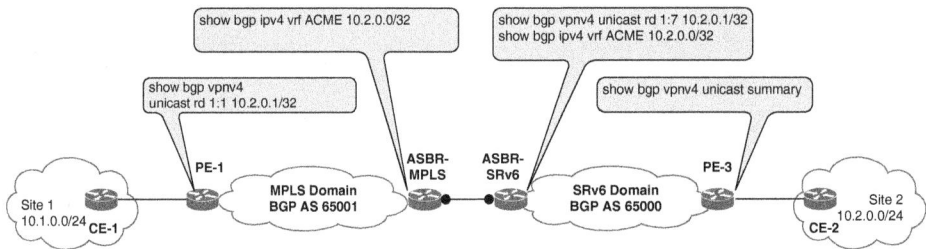

Figure 5-35　*Inter-AS ASBR Verification*

Output 5-40 validates that PE-3 has advertised prefix S2 to RR-SRv6.

Output 5-40　*Prefix S2 Advertised to RR-SRv6 on PE-3 (IOS-XR)*

```
RP/0/RP0/CPU0:PE-3#show bgp vpnv4 unicast advertised summary
Network           Next Hop        From            Advertised to

<snip>

Route Distinguisher: 1:3
Route Distinguisher Version: 515
```

```
10.2.0.1/32        fc00:0:205::1   10.2.103.1      fc00:0:207::1 <-- Prefix S2 is
   advertised to RR-SRv6

10.2.103.0/31      fc00:0:205::1   Local           fc00:0:207::1

10.2.103.128/28    fc00:0:205::1   10.2.103.1      fc00:0:207::1

Processed 11 prefixes, 11 paths
```

Now, looking at the update received by ASBR-SRv6, as shown in Output 5-41, we can see that PE-3 has advertised it with the SRv6 SID f00:0:205:e00d::.

Output 5-41 *Prefix S2 Received from RR-SRv6 on ASBR-SRv6 (IOS-XR)*

```
RP/0/RP0/CPU0:ASBR-SRv6#show bgp vrf ACME ipv4 unicast  10.2.0.1/32
Sat Jan 20 23:49:38.769 UTC
BGP routing table entry for 10.2.0.1/32, Route Distinguisher: 1:7
Versions:
  Process           bRIB/RIB  SendTblVer
  Speaker              396         396
Last Modified: Jan 20 13:13:06.311 for 10:36:32
Paths: (2 available, best #1)
  Not advertised to any peer
  Path #1: Received by speaker 0
  Not advertised to any peer
  65500
    fc00:0:205::1 (metric 41) from fc00:0:207::1 (172.19.0.19) <-- Prefix S2
   received from RR-SRv6
      Received Label 0xe00d0 <-- Function part of SRv6 SID
      Origin IGP, metric 0, localpref 200, valid, internal, best, group-best,
   import-candidate, imported
      Received Path ID 0, Local Path ID 1, version 393
      Extended community: RT:65000:500
      Originator: 172.19.0.19, Cluster list: 172.19.0.21
      PSID-Type:L3, SubTLV Count:1
       SubTLV:
        T:1(Sid information), Sid:fc00:0:205::, Behavior:61, SS-TLV Count:1 <--
   Locator part of SRv6 SID
         SubSubTLV:
          T:1(Sid structure):
      Source AFI: VPNv4 Unicast, Source VRF: default, Source Route
   Distinguisher: 1:3
```

Output 5-42 indicates that ASBR-ASRv6 has advertised prefix S2 to ASBR-MPLS.

Output 5-42 *Prefix S2 Advertised to ASBR-MPLS on ASBR-SRv6 (IOS-XR)*

```
RP/0/RP0/CPU0:ASBR-SRv6#show bgp vrf ACME ipv4 unicast advertised summary
Sun Jan 21 01:00:26.707 UTC
Network            Next Hop        From             Advertised to
Route Distinguisher: 1:7 (default for vrf ACME)
Route Distinguisher Version: 420
10.1.0.9/32        192.168.1.0     fc00:0:207::1    192.168.1.1
10.1.103.128/28    192.168.1.0     fc00:0:207::1    192.168.1.1
10.1.103.144/28    192.168.1.0     fc00:0:207::1    192.168.1.1
10.1.103.240/28    192.168.1.0     fc00:0:207::1    192.168.1.1
10.2.0.1/32        192.168.1.0     fc00:0:207::1    192.168.1.1 <-- Prefix S2
    advertised to ASBR-MPLS
10.2.103.0/31      192.168.1.0     fc00:0:207::1    192.168.1.1
10.2.103.128/28    192.168.1.0     fc00:0:207::1    192.168.1.1
10.3.103.0/31      192.168.1.0     fc00:0:207::1    192.168.1.1
```

In the last step of the BGP updates verification, Output 5-43 shows that PE-1 has received Prefix S2 from RR-MPLS with label 24008 and had advertised this prefix to CE-1.

Output 5-43 *Prefix S2 Advertised to CE-1 on PE-1 (IOS-XR)*

```
RP/0/RP0/CPU0:PE-1#show bgp vrf ACME ipv4 unicast 10.2.0.1/32

BGP routing table entry for 10.2.0.1/32, Route Distinguisher: 1:1
Versions:
  Process           bRIB/RIB  SendTblVer
  Speaker             1271        1271
Last Modified: Jan 21 02:17:56.121 for 00:00:03
Paths: (1 available, best #1)
  Advertised to CE peers (in unique update groups):
    10.3.103.3 <-- Advertised to CE-1
  Path #1: Received by speaker 0
  Advertised to CE peers (in unique update groups):
    10.3.103.3
  65000 65500
    10.0.0.6 (metric 20) from 10.0.0.3 (10.0.0.6) <- Prefix S1 received from RR-MPLS
      Received Label 24008 <-Label for Prefix S2
    Origin IGP, localpref 100, valid, internal, best, group-best,
import-candidate, imported
    Received Path ID 0, Local Path ID 1, version 1271
    Extended community: RT:65000:501
    Originator: 10.0.0.6, Cluster list: 10.0.0.3
    Source AFI: VPNv4 Unicast, Source VRF: default, Source Route Distinguisher: 1:6
```

Figure 5-36 shows the data path from Site 1 in the MPLS domain to Site 2 in the SRv6 domain via the ASBRs after verification that the prefixes are advertised from SRv6 to the MPLS domain.

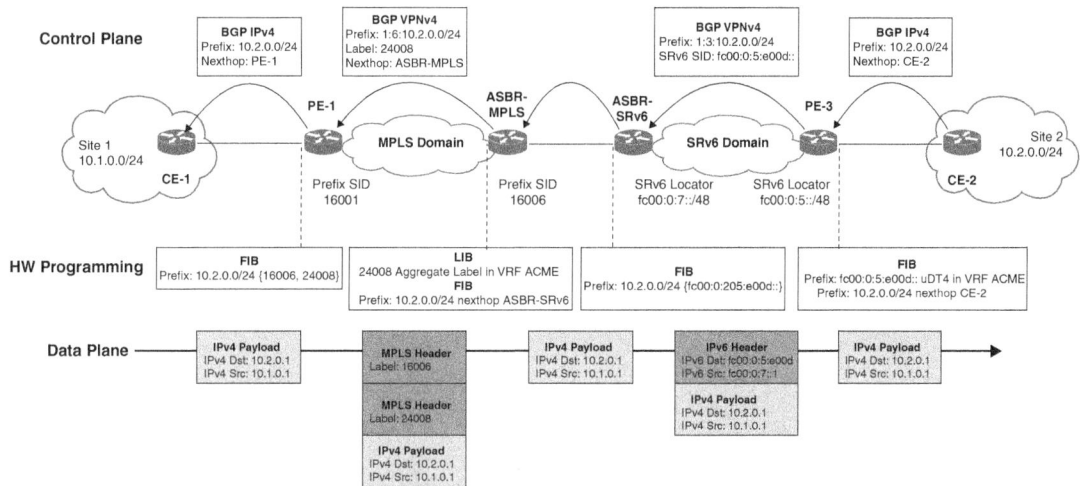

Figure 5-36 *Inter-AS Option A: Control Plane and Data Plane Between Site 1 and Site 2 After Migration of Site 2*

CE-1 forwards the IPv4 packet destined for CE-2 to PE-1, which encapsulates the IPv4 packet with the MPLS transport label (16006) and service label (24008), and forwards the packet to ASBR-MPLS in the MPLS domain. ASBR-MPLS decapsulates the MPLS service label 24008 and does a lookup in the ACME VRF instance and forwards the packet to ASBR-SRv6. ASBR-SRv6 encapsulates the packet into an outer IPv6 header with the destination address fc00:0:5:e00d:: and forwards it in the SRv6 domain. On PE-3, fc00:0:5:e000:: corresponds to the uDT4 endpoint behavior with a lookup in the ACME VRF instance, and PE-3 then forwards the packet to CE2.

Output 5-44 shows the data forwarding verification using a ping from CE-1 to CE-2.

Output 5-44 *Ping from CE-1 to CE-2*

```
RP/0/RP0/CPU0:CE-1#ping 10.2.0.1 source 10.1.0.1

Type escape sequence to abort.
Sending 5, 100-byte ICMP Echos to 10.2.0.1 timeout is 2 seconds:
!!!!!
Success rate is 100 percent (5/5), round-trip min/avg/max = 5/6/7 ms
```

A traceroute from CE-1 to CE-2, as shown in Output 5-45, helps to the trace the path. P-9 is a P node on the MPLS network that provides connectivity between PE-1 and ASBR-MPLS.

Output 5-45 *Traceroute from CE-1 to CE-2*

```
RP/0/RP0/CPU0:CE-1#traceroute  10.2.0.1


Type escape sequence to abort.
Tracing the route to 10.2.0.1


 1   10.3.103.2 2 msec  1 msec  1 msec <-- CE-1 to PE-1
 2   10.1.0.0 [MPLS: Labels 16006/24008 Exp 0] 4 msec  3 msec  3 msec <-- PE-1 to P-9
 3   10.1.1.1 [MPLS: Label 24008 Exp 0] 3 msec  3 msec  3 msec <-- P-9 to ASBR-MPLLS
 4   192.168.1.0 3 msec  3 msec  3 msec <-- ASBR-MPLS to ASBR-SRv6
 5   10.2.103.0 8 msec  9 msec  9 msec <-- PE-3
 6   10.2.103.1 9 msec  *  10 msec <-- CE-2
```

Data forwarding from CE-2 to CE-1 is verified using a ping, as shown in Output 5-46.

Output 5-46 *Ping from CE-2 to CE-1*

```
RP/0/RP0/CPU0:CE-2#ping 10.1.0.1 source 10.2.0.1
Type escape sequence to abort.
Sending 5, 100-byte ICMP Echos to 10.1.0.1 timeout is 2 seconds:
!!!!!
Success rate is 100 percent (5/5), round-trip min/avg/max = 7/8/12 ms
```

A traceroute from CE-2 to CE-1, as shown in Output 5-47, helps to the trace the path. An interesting observation is that the traceroute does not provide information about the path in the SRv6 network.

Output 5-47 *Traceroute from CE-2 to CE-1*

```
RP/0/RP0/CPU0:CE-2#traceroute 10.1.0.1 source lo3


Type escape sequence to abort.
Tracing the route to 10.1.0.1


 1   10.2.103.0 7 msec  1 msec  1 msec <-- CE-2 to PE-3
 2   192.168.1.0 6 msec  5 msec  4 msec <-- PE-3 to ASBR-SRv6
 3   192.168.1.1 6 msec  5 msec  5 msec <-- ASBR-SRv6 to ASBR-MPLS
 4   10.1.1.0 [MPLS: Labels 16001/24007 Exp 0] 8 msec  7 msec  7 msec <--
     ASBR-MPLS to P1
 5   10.1.0.1 [MPLS: Label 24007 Exp 0] 7 msec  7 msec  7 msec <-- P1 to PE-1
 6   10.3.103.3 8 msec  *  14 msec <-- PE-1 to CE-1
```

Inter-AS Option A: Site 1 Migration

Figure 5-37 shows the final step, where Site 1 is migrated from PE-1 to PE-4.

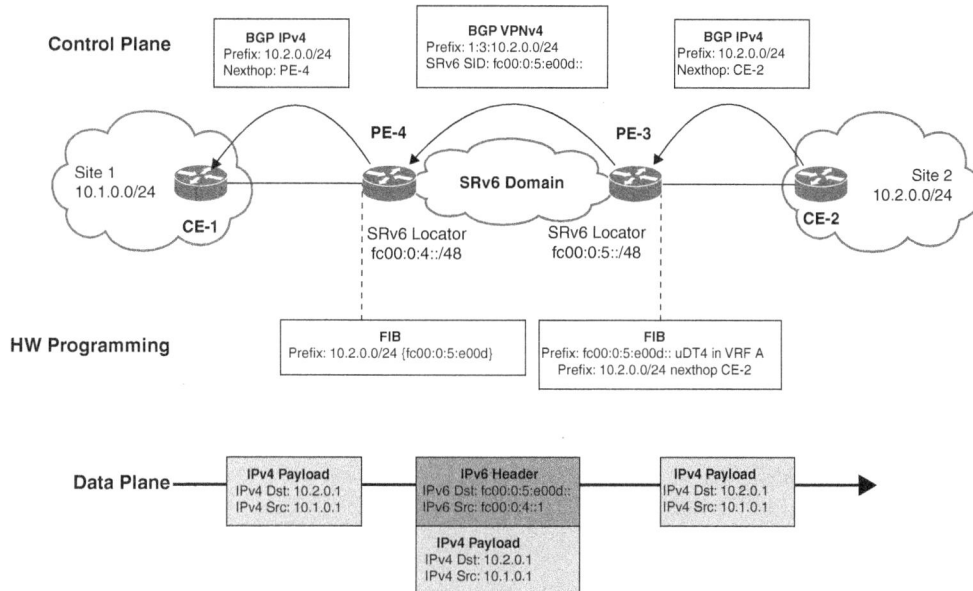

Figure 5-37 *Inter-AS Option A: Control Plane and Data Plane Between Site 1 and Site 2 After Migration of Site 1*

PE-3 now advertises prefix S2 with the SRv6 SID fc00:0:5:e00d::. PE-4 receives this BGP update and imports S2 into the ACME VRF instance and advertises prefix S2 to CE-1.

In the data plane, PE-3 now forwards traffic destined for Site 1 to PE-4. PE-4 removes the IPv6 header and forwards the IPv4 packet to CE-1.

When all the sites have been migrated to SRv6, the ASBRs can be removed from the network.

Building a New SRv6 Network Using Dual-Connected PE Devices

The two previous sections present solutions for interworking between MPLS and SRv6 domains using an SRv6 IWG or pairs of ASBRs. This section focuses on a solution where a dual-connected PE device is used to provide L3VPN services based on the coexistence of SRv6 and MPLS. The services in the MPLS and SRv6 domains are independent of each other. Hence, there is no need for interworking between the services in the two domains.

Figure 5-38 shows a dual-connected PE device that provides L3VPN services for the SRv6 and MPLS domains.

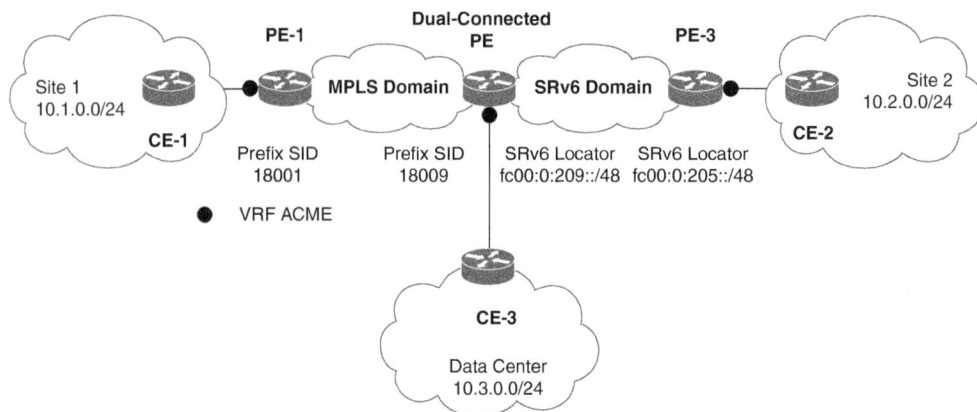

Figure 5-38 *Dual-Connected PE Devices: L3VPN Services*

Connectivity between Site 1 connected to PE-1 and the data center connected to the dual-connected PE device is provided by the ACME VRF instance in the MPLS domain. In the SRv6 domain, connectivity between Site 2 connected to PE-3 and the data center is also provided by the ACME VRF instance. However, there is no connectivity between Site 1 and Site 2.

The dual-connected PE device participates in the BGP control plane of the SRv6 and MPLS domains for the same VRF instance, allocates SRv6 SIDs and MPLS service labels to the IPv4/IPv6 prefixes, and advertises the VPNv4/VPNv6 prefixes in the SRv6 and MPLS domains. The VPNv4/VPNv6 prefixes are advertised to the MPLS domain with MPLS labels, and they are advertised with an SRv6 SID in the SRv6 domain. Separate route reflectors are required for each domain to distinguish between the VPNv4/VPNv6 prefixes from the MPLS and SRv6 domains on the dual-connected PE device.

Unlike with the SRv6 IWG and Inter-AS Option A, the dual-connected PE device can provide the connectivity for all L3VPN topologies, including extranet topologies. The dual-connected PE device does not forward the VPNv4 routes received from the MPLS domain to the SRv6 domain and vice versa. As a result, it can preserve the extranet L3VPN topology and avoid leaking routes between VRF instances.

The dual-connected PE device also supports L2VPN E-LAN and E-Line services for MPLS and SRv6. Figure 5-39 shows the dual-connected PE device providing E-LAN services between CE-1, CE-2, and CE-3, where CE-1 is connected to the MPLS PE device PE-1, CE-2 is connected to the SRv6 PE device PE-2, and CE-3 is connected to dual-connected PE device.

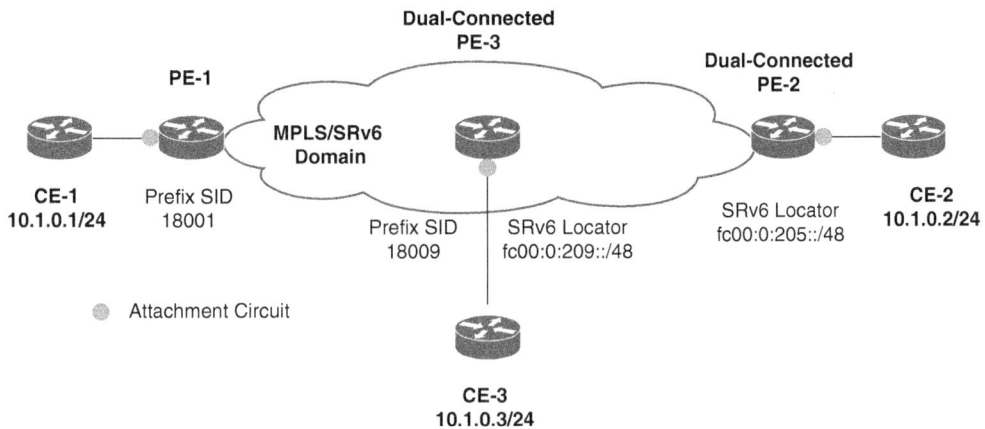

Figure 5-39 *Dual-Connected PE Devices: L2VPN E-LAN Services*

Note Migration from VPLS LDP and VPWS LDP to EVPN SRv6 using the dual-connected PE device is documented in the Cisco Live breakout session BRKSP-2468.

This section focuses on using the dual-connected PE devices for migrating L3VPN services from MPLS to SRv6 networks.

Migration Use Case

This section describes the steps to migrate Site 2 and Site 1 from MPLS to SRv6 for L3VPN services using the coexistence capability of dual-connected PE devices.

The SRv6 and MPLS transport networks can be separate or can be the same, as shown in Figure 5-40.

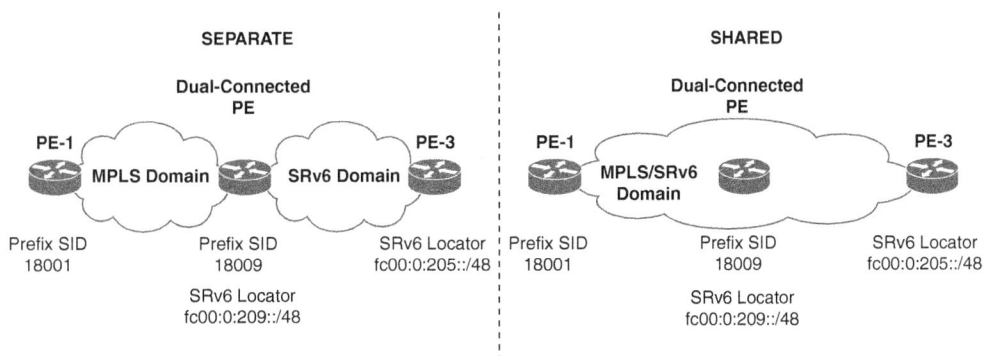

Figure 5-40 *Separate Versus Shared MPLS and SRv6 Networks*

With a separate-networks scenario, the dual-connected PE has at least one core link to the MPLS and SRv6 network, while with a same-network scenario, all the devices in the network must support both SRv6 and MPLS. The functioning of the dual-connected PE is the same for both cases. In this section, it is assumed that the SRv6 and MPLS networks are separate, meaning that dual-connected PE devices have separate links to the MPLS and SRv6 domains.

Figure 5-41 shows an MPLS network that provides L3VPN services with hub and spoke topology between Site 1, Site 2, and the data center. Two spoke sites, Site 1 and Site 2, subscribe to the services in the data center, which is the hub site. The prefix 10.1.0.0/24 from Site 1 is referred to as S1, the prefix 10.2.0.0/24 from Site 2 is referred to as Prefix S2, and the prefix 10.3.0.0/24 from the data center is referred to as S3. The steps for migrating the data center and Site 2 to SRv6 are illustrated in Figure 5-41.

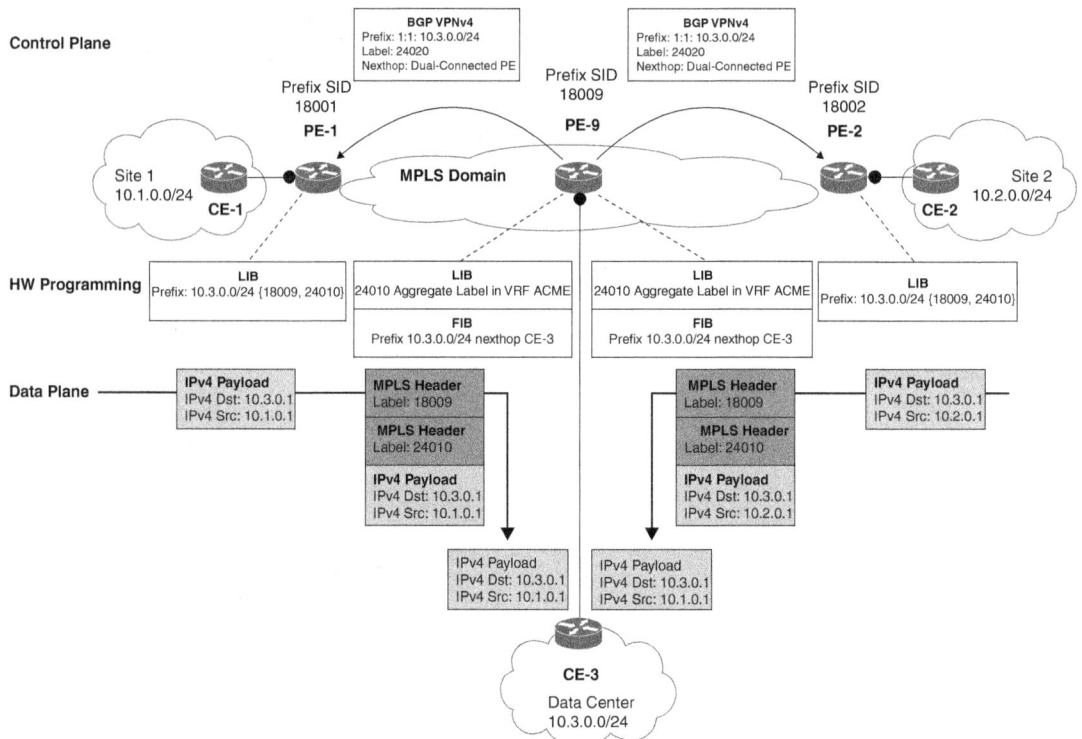

Figure 5-41   *Dual-Connected PE Devices: Pre-Migration*

Traffic from Site 1 to Site 2 over the MPLS network uses MPLS labels for data forwarding. The rest of this section explains the steps to migrate the two sites to the SRv6 network.

Dual-Connected PE Devices: Site 2 Migration

In the first step, Site 2 is migrated from PE-2 to PE-3. Before Site 2 is migrated, the Dual-Connected PE device must be prepared to enable the dual-connected PE device functionality. Figure 5-42 shows the configuration steps for preparing the dual-connected PE device, which involve enabling SRv6, establishing BGP sessions with the RR in the SRv6 domain, and enabling the dual-connected PE functionality.

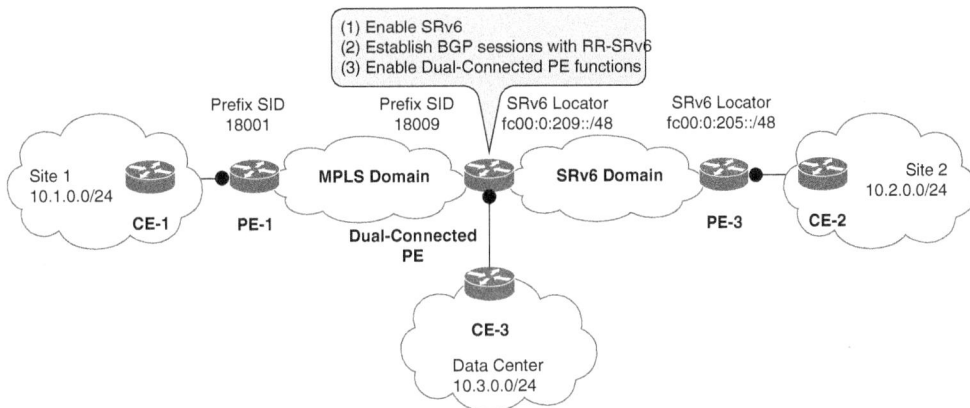

Figure 5-42 *Dual-Connected PE Device Preparation*

SRv6 is enabled on the dual-connected PE device as shown in Config 5-17, which provides the configuration to enable SRv6 on the dual-connected PE device.

Config 5-17 *Dual-Connected PE Devices: Enabling SRv6*

```
segment-routing
 srv6
  locators
   encapsulation
    source-address fc00:0:209::1
   locator MAIN
    micro-segment behavior unode psp-usd
    prefix fc00:0:209::/48

router isis SRv6
 address-family ipv6 unicast
  metric-style wide
  router-id Loopback0
  segment-routing srv6
   locator MAIN
```

Config 5-18 shows the second step: the BGP configuration toward RR-SRv6. The command **encapsulation-type srv6** is used to enable SRv6 encapsulation. By default, MPLS encapsulation is enabled.

Config 5-18   *Dual-Connected PE Devices: BGP Session to RR-SRv6*

```
router bgp 65000
 neighbor fc00:0:207::1
  remote-as 65000
  update-source Loopback0
  description *** iBGP peering to RR-SRv6 ***
  address-family vpnv4 unicast
   encapsulation-type srv6!
```

Dual-connected PE device functionality is enabled by configuring BGP to allocate MPLS labels and SRv6 SIDs for IPv4 prefixes in the ACME VRF instance as shown in Config 5-19.

Config 5-19   *VRF Instance for Dual-Connected PE Device Functionality*

```
vrf ACME
 address-family ipv4 unicast
  import route-target
   65000:500
  !
  export route-target
   65000:500
 !
router bgp 65000
 vrf ACME
  rd auto
  address-family ipv4 unicast
   mpls alloc enable
   segment-routing srv6
    alloc mode per-ce
```

Now Site 2 can be migrated by moving CE-2 from PE-2 in the MPLS domain to PE-3 in the SRv6 domain. Config 5-20 shows the configuration for this migration.

Config 5-20   *Site 2 Migration on PE-3*

```
vrf ACME
 address-family ipv4 unicast
  import route-target
   65000:500
  !
  export route-target
   65000:500
```

```
route-policy PASS_RP
  pass
end-policy

router bgp 65000
 vrf ACME
  rd auto
  address-family ipv4 unicast
   segment-routing srv6
    alloc mode per-ce
   !
   network 10.2.0.1/32
  !
  neighbor 10.2.103.1
   remote-as 65500
   address-family ipv4 unicast
    route-policy PASS_RP in
    route-policy PASS_RP out
```

Figure 5-43 shows the commands that are used to verify the functionality of the dual-connected PE device.

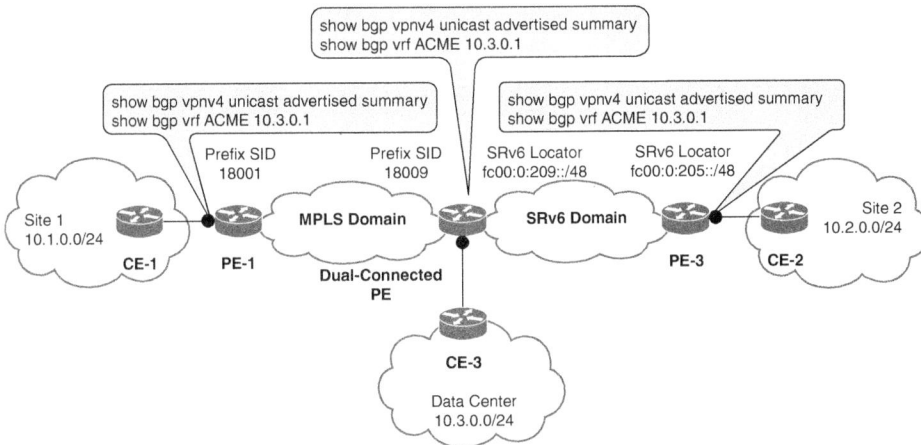

Figure 5-43 *Dual-Connected PE Device Verification*

The verification is done for the BGP update for prefix S3 from the dual-connected PE device to PE-1 in the MPLS domain and PE-3 in the SRv6 domain.

Output 5-48 highlights the output which shows that dual-connected PE device's prefix S3 has been allocated the label 24020 and SRv6 SID fc00:0:209:e004::, and it is advertised to RR-SRv6 and RR-MPLS.

Output 5-48   *Prefix S3 Advertised to PE-1 and PE-3 on Dual-Connected-PE (IOS-XR)*

```
RP/0/RP0/CPU0:Dual-Connected-PE#show bgp vrf ACME 10.3.0.1/32


BGP routing table entry for 10.3.0.1/32, Route Distinguisher: 1:1
Versions:
  Process              bRIB/RIB  SendTblVer
  Speaker                935        935
    Local Label: 24020  <-- Label assigned to Prefix S3
    SRv6-VPN SID: fc00:0:209:e004::/64  <-- SRv6 SID assigned to Prefix S3
    Gateway Array ID: 2, Resilient per-CE nexthop set ID: 1
Last Modified: Jan 21 06:43:56.241 for 22:15:02
Paths: (1 available, best #1)
  Advertised to PE peers (in unique update groups):
    fc00:0:207::1                        10.0.0.3  <-- Advertised ro RR-SRv6 and
RR-MPLS
  Path #1: Received by speaker 0
  Advertised to PE peers (in unique update groups):
    fc00:0:207::1                        10.0.0.3
  65009
    10.3.103.1 from 10.3.103.1 (10.1.0.9)
      Origin IGP, metric 0, localpref 100, valid, external, best, group-best,
import-candidate
      Received Path ID 0, Local Path ID 1, version 935
      Extended community: RT:65000:500 RT:65000:501
      Origin-AS validity: (disabled)
```

PE-1 receives prefix S3 from RR-MPLS and advertises it to CE-1, as shown in Output 5-49.

Output 5-49   *Prefix S3 from RR-MPLS on PE-1 (IOS-XR)*

```
RP/0/RP0/CPU0:PE-1#show bgp vrf ACME 10.3.0.1/32


BGP routing table entry for 10.3.0.1/32, Route Distinguisher: 10.0.0.1:2
Versions:
  Process              bRIB/RIB  SendTblVer
  Speaker                1327       1327
Last Modified: Jan 22 00:55:08.121 for 04:46:57
Paths: (1 available, best #1)
  Advertised to CE peers (in unique update groups): <-- Advertised to CE-1
    10.3.103.3
  Path #1: Received by speaker 0
  Advertised to CE peers (in unique update groups):
    10.3.103.3
  65000 65009
    10.0.0.9 (metric 20) from 10.0.0.3 (172.19.0.26) <-- Received from RR-MPLS
      Received Label 24020 <-- Label assigned to Prefix S3
```

```
        Origin IGP, metric 0, localpref 100, valid, internal, best, group-best,
    import-candidate, imported
        Received Path ID 0, Local Path ID 1, version 1327
        Extended community: RT:65000:500 RT:65000:501
        Originator: 172.19.0.26, Cluster list: 10.0.0.3
        Source AFI: VPNv4 Unicast, Source VRF: default, Source Route Distinguisher: 1:1
```

PE-3 receives prefix S3 from RR-SRv6 and advertises it to CE-3, as shown in Output 5-50.

Output 5-50 *Prefix S3 from RR-SRv6 on PE-3 (IOS-XR)*

```
RP/0/RP0/CPU0:PE-3#show bgp vrf FULL-500-VRF 10.3.0.1/32

BGP routing table entry for 10.3.0.1/32, Route Distinguisher: 172.19.0.19:2
Versions:
  Process           bRIB/RIB  SendTblVer
  Speaker                551         551
Last Modified: Jan 21 06:43:56.231 for 22:21:14
Paths: (1 available, best #1)
  Advertised to CE peers (in unique update groups): <-- Prefix S3 advertised to CE-3
    10.2.103.1
  Path #1: Received by speaker 0
  Advertised to CE peers (in unique update groups):
    10.2.103.1
  65009
    fc00:0:209::1 (metric 21) from fc00:0:207::1 (172.19.0.26) <-- Received from
RR-SRv6
      Received Label 0xe0040 <-- Function part of SRv6 SID assigned to prefix S3
      Origin IGP, metric 0, localpref 100, valid, internal, best, group-best,
    import-candidate, imported
      Received Path ID 0, Local Path ID 1, version 551
      Extended community: RT:65000:500 RT:65000:501
      Originator: 172.19.0.26, Cluster list: 172.19.0.21
      PSID-Type:L3, SubTLV Count:1
       SubTLV:
        T:1(Sid information), Sid:fc00:0:209::, Behavior:61, SS-TLV Count:1 <--
Locator part of SRv6 SID
         SubSubTLV:
          T:1(Sid structure):
      Source AFI: VPNv4 Unicast, Source VRF: default, Source Route Distinguisher: 1:1
```

After the verification that the prefixes are advertised from the dual-connected PE to PE-1 and PE-3, the data path from Site 1 and Site 2 to the data center in the SRv6 domain via the dual-connected PE is validated, as shown in Figure 5-44.

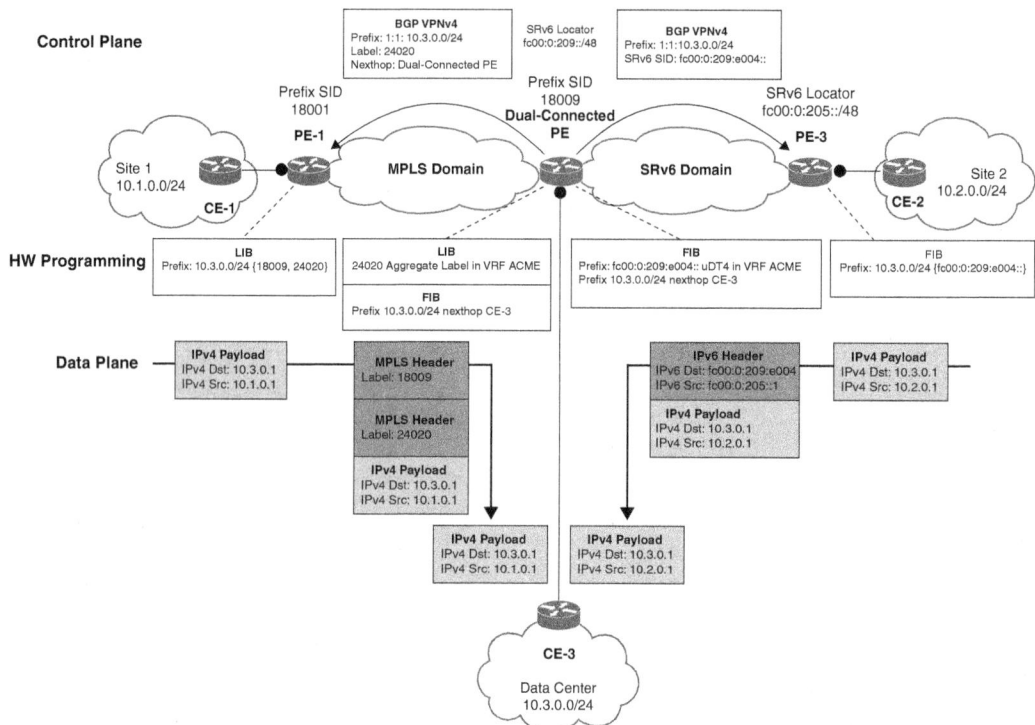

Figure 5-44 *Control Plane and Data Plane Between Site 1, Site 2, and the Data Center After Migration of Site 2*

CE-1 forwards the IPv4 packet destined for CE-3 to PE-1, which encapsulates the IPv4 packet with the MPLS transport label (18009) and service label (24020) and forwards the packet to the dual-connected PE device. The dual-connected PE device decapsulates the MPLS service label 24020, does a lookup in the ACME VRF instance, and then forwards the packet to CE-3.

CE-2 forwards the IPv4 packet destined for CE-3 to PE-3, which encapsulates the IPv4 packet with an IPv6 header where the destination address is fc00:0:209:e004:: and forwards it in the SRv6 domain. The dual-connected PE device receives the packet, decapsulates the IPv6 header, does a lookup in the ACME VRF instance because fc00:0:209:e004:: corresponds to uDT4 in the ACME VRF instance, and forwards the IPv4 packet to CE-3.

Output 5-51 shows the data forwarding verification using a ping from CE-1 to CE-3.

Output 5-51 *Ping from CE-1 to CE-3*

```
RP/0/RP0/CPU0:CE-1#ping 10.3.0.1 source lo0


Type escape sequence to abort.
Sending 5, 100-byte ICMP Echos to 10.3.0.1 timeout is 2 seconds:
!!!!!
Success rate is 100 percent (5/5), round-trip min/avg/max = 3/3/4 ms
```

A traceroute from CE-1 to CE-3, as shown in Output 5-52, helps to show the path through the network. P-9 is a P node on the MPLS network that provides connectivity between PE-1 and Dual-Connected-PE.

Output 5-52 *Traceroute from CE-1 to CE-3*

```
RP/0/RP0/CPU0:CE-1#traceroute 10.3.0.1 source lo0

Type escape sequence to abort.
Tracing the route to 10.3.0.1

 1  10.3.103.2 2 msec  1 msec  1 msec <-- CE-1 to PE-1
 2  10.1.0.0 [MPLS: Labels 16009/24020 Exp 0] 12 msec  4 msec  4 msec <-- PE-1 to P-9
 3  10.1.3.1 [MPLS: Label 24020 Exp 0] 5 msec  4 msec  4 msec <-- P-9 to
    Dual-Connected-PE
 4  10.3.103.1 5 msec  *  4 msec <-- Dual-Connected-PE to CE-3
```

Data forwarding from CE-2 to CE-3 is verified using a ping, as shown in Output 5-53.

Output 5-53 *Ping from CE-2 to CE-3*

```
RP/0/RP0/CPU0:CE-2#ping 10.3.0.1

Type escape sequence to abort.
Sending 5, 100-byte ICMP Echos to 10.3.0.1 timeout is 2 seconds:
!!!!!
Success rate is 100 percent (5/5), round-trip min/avg/max = 3/3/4 ms
```

A traceroute from CE-2 to CE-3, as shown in Output 5-54, helps to the trace the path.

Output 5-54 *Traceroute from CE-2 to CE-3*

```
RP/0/RP0/CPU0:CE-2#traceroute 10.3.0.1

Type escape sequence to abort.
Tracing the route to 10.3.0.1

 1  10.2.103.0 2 msec  1 msec  1 msec <-- CE-2 to PE-3
 2  10.3.103.0 3 msec  3 msec  3 msec <-- PE-3 to Dual-Connected-PE
 3  10.3.103.1 3 msec  *  4 msec <-- Dual-Connected-PE to CE-3
```

This section has shown the migration of Site 2 to PE-3, which is an SRv6 PE device. Since Site 2 does not require connectivity to sites connected to the MPLS domain, there is no need to enable dual-connected PE functionality on PE-3. If Site 2 requires connectivity to Site 1 and the data center, the dual-connected PE functionality must be enabled on PE-3.

Since the connectivity between two dual-connected PE devices can use the MPLS and SRv6 network, the dual-connected PE device can decide on the transport network for L3VPN and L2VPN services. This decision can be influenced using BGP attributes for the VPNv4, VPNv6, and L2VPN prefixes learned from RR-MPLS and RR-SRv6.

Dual-Connected PE Devices: Site 1 Migration

Figure 5-45 shows the final step, where Site 1 is migrated from PE-1 to PE-4.

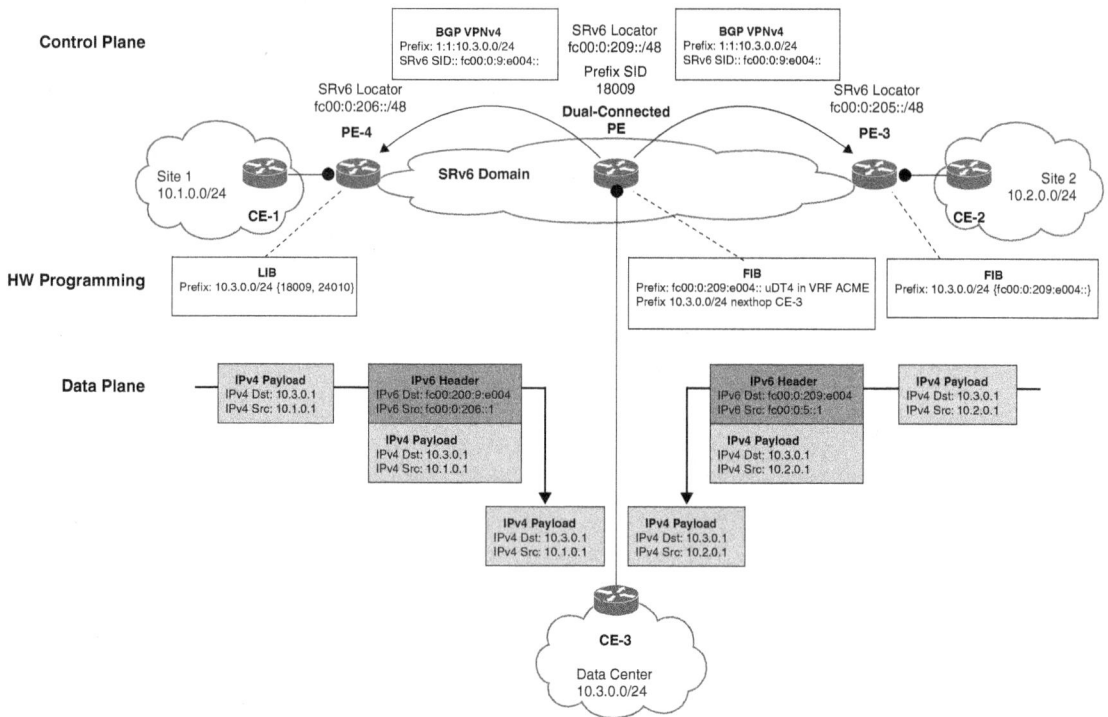

Figure 5-45 *Control Plane and Data Plane Between Site 1, Site 2, and the Data Center After Migration of Site 1*

PE-4 receives prefix S3 from the dual-connected PE device, imports it into the ACME VRF instance, and advertises it to CE-1.

In the data plane, PE-4 now forwards traffic destined for the data center to the dual-connected PE device, which removes the IPv6 header and forwards the IPv4 packet to CE-3.

When all the sites have been migrated to SRv6, the MPLS functionality in the network can be turned off.

High Availability

Devices like an IWG, an inter-AS ASBR, and a dual-connected PE device are critical for connectivity between the MPLS and SRv6 domains. The availability of these devices can be improved by introducing multiple devices.

This section uses IWGs to explain the concept of high availability for devices that provide the connectivity between MPLS and SRv6 domains.

An SRv6 IWG can provide the following modes of redundancy:

■ Active-active

■ Active-backup

■ Load sharing

Active-Active

In active-active mode, the SRv6 IWGs set the same BGP attributes for the prefixes before advertising them to all the PE devices in the MPLS and SRv6 domains. When a PE device uses all the available paths for data forwarding, it can distribute the load between the SRv6 IWGs.

Figure 5-46 shows the active-active mode of redundancy. SRv6 IWG1 and IWG2 advertise the prefix from Site 2 to the MPLS domain with the BGP local preference 100. PE-1 decides to install both the paths in the FIB. Now there are two ECMP paths via the two IWGs for the traffic from PE-1 to Site 2.

Similarly, there are two ECMP paths via the two IWGs for the traffic from PE-2 to Site 1 because the IWGs advertise the prefix from Site 1 with the same BGP local preference.

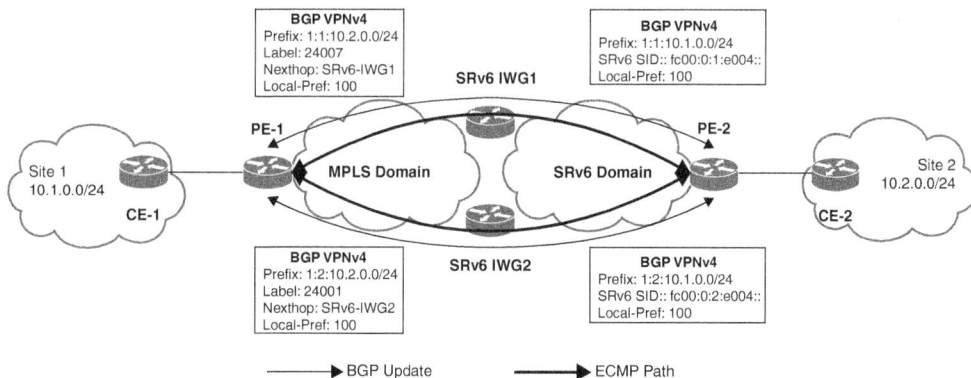

Figure 5-46 *SRv6 IWG Redundancy: Active-Active*

All the redundancy and load-balancing mechanisms that are applicable to L3VPN PE devices are also applicable to the SRv6 IWG.

Active-Backup

In active-backup mode, the SRv6 IWGs set different BGP attributes for the prefixes before advertising them to all the PE devices in the MPLS and SRv6 domains. PE devices forward traffic to the SRv6 IWG that advertises the prefix with the better BGP attribute.

Figure 5-47 shows the SRv6 IWG active-backup mode of redundancy. SRv6 IWG1 advertise the prefixes from the SRv6 domain with the BGP local preference 200, and SRv6 IWG2 advertises the same prefixes with the BGP local preference 100. PE-2 receives both of the BGP updates and installs the path via SRv6 IWG1 in the FIB and forwards the traffic via SRv6 IWG1. In the event of a failure of SRv6 IWG1, PE-2 forwards the traffic to SRv6 IWG2.

Active-backup paths for the traffic from the SRv6 domain to the MPLS domain is achieved in the same manner when the IWGs advertise the prefixes to the SRv6 domain with different BGP local preferences.

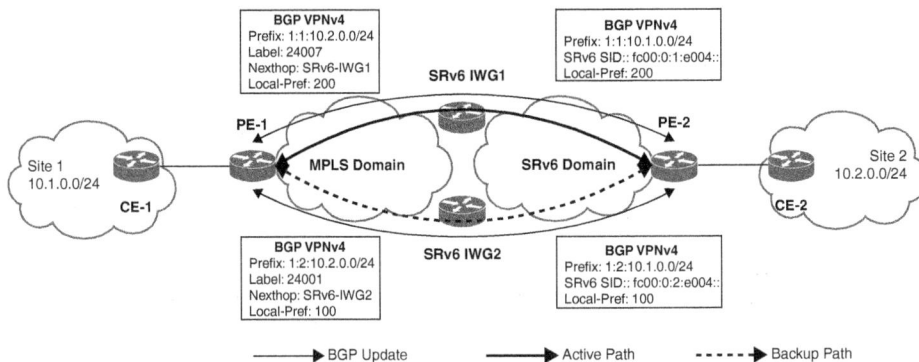

Figure 5-47   *SRv6 IWG Redundancy: Active-Backup*

Load Sharing

Every L3VPN service that requires interworking must be configured on the IWG, which can result in millions of VPNv4 routes on an IWG, which may then lead to scalability issues and exhaustion of hardware resource in the FIB.

Since the IWG re-originates the VPNv4 routes only for the VRF instances configured on the IWG, the VRF instances can be distributed across several groups of SRv6 IWGs, thereby reducing the number of the VPNv4 routes in each IWG.

Figure 5-48 shows two groups of SRv6 IWGs to provide load balancing. Each group has two IWGs to provide redundancy.

VRF ACME1 is configured on IWGs of Group 1, and VRF ACME2 is configured on IWGs of Group 2. This setup provides per-VRF instance load balancing between the two groups of SRv6 IWGs. Each group can have more than one IWG to provide redundancy.

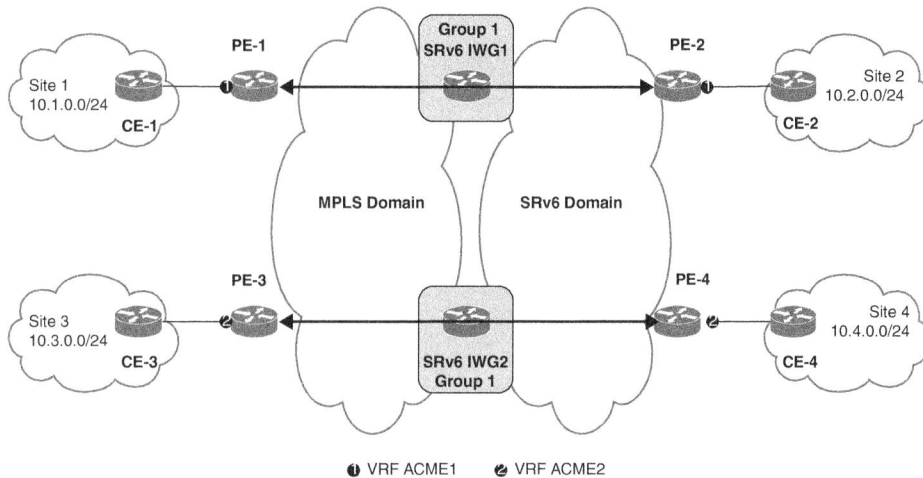

Figure 5-48   *SRv6 IWG Redundancy: Load Sharing per VRF*

Migration Paths from MPLS to SRv6

This section provides the high-level steps to migrate L3VPN and L2VPN services from four different types of MPLS networks to an SRv6 network using the methods described in the section "SRv6 Migration," earlier in this chapter.

Figure 5-49 shows a decision tree that can aid in the choice strategy when migrating from MPLS to SRv6.

When all the devices in the MPLS network support IPv6 and some or all PE devices support SRv6, coexistence is the preferred migration strategy. It is not mandatory for all the P devices to support SRv6 because data forwarding in an SRv6 network is based on IPv6. However, the inability of some P devices to support SRv6 comes with certain limitations, such as the lack of TI-LFA and SRv6 traffic engineering in the IPv6 network. After IPv6/SRv6 is enabled in the MPLS network, SRv6-capable PE devices are configured as dual-connected PE devices, and the sites connected to legacy MPLS PE devices are migrated to SRv6 PE devices. This strategy requires the introduction of a route reflector for SRv6 in the existing MPLS network. MPLS-related configurations can be removed from the network when all the service migration have been completed.

A new SRv6 network is required when some of the P devices do not support IPv6. Interworking is the preferred migration strategy once the new SRv6 network is deployed. As described in the section "Building a New SRv6 Network Using SRv6 IWG," SRv6 IWGs can be used to interconnect MPLS and SRv6 networks, and as described in the section "Building a New SRv6 Network Using Inter-AS Option A," ASBRs can also be used to interconnect these networks. PE devices capable of supporting SRv6 are moved to the SRv6 network, and the sites that are connected to legacy MPLS PE devices are migrated to PE devices in the SRv6 network in a phased manner. The MPLS network can be decommissioned once all the service migrations have been completed.

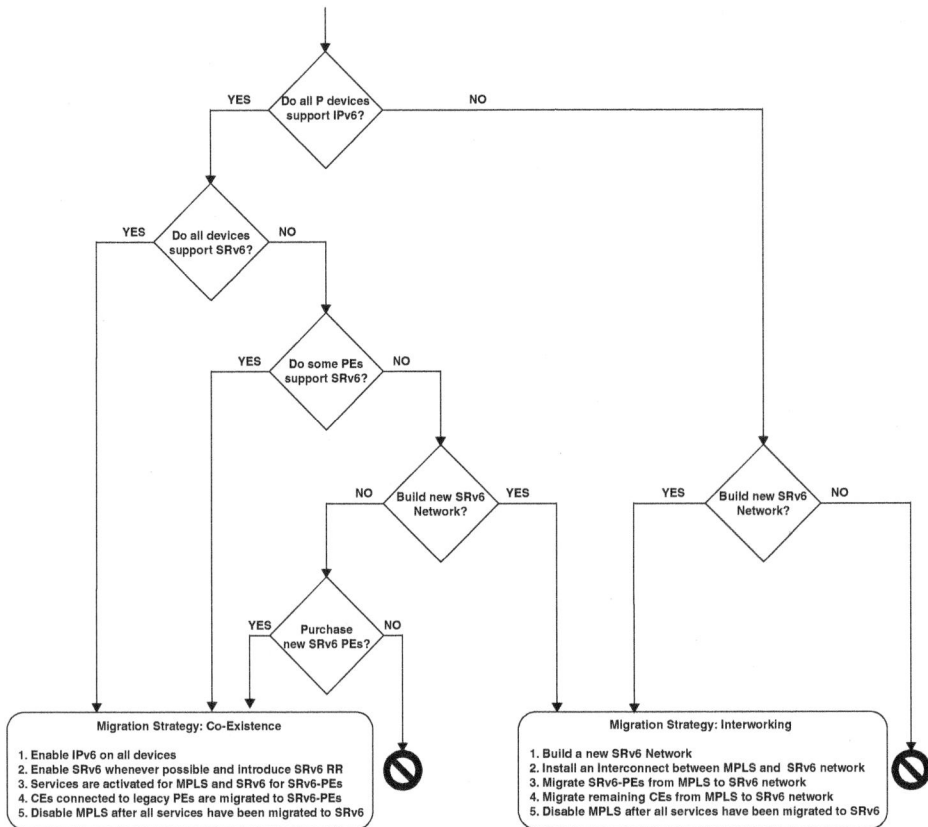

Figure 5-49   *Decision Tree for SRv6 Migration Strategy*

This section discusses migration from MPLS to SRv6 using coexistence and interworking for four different types of MPLS networks:

■ **Flat MPLS network:** This is an MPLS network with a single IGP domain with LDP or SR-MPLS for label assignment and distribution.

■ **Unified MPLS network:** This is an MPLS network with multiple IGP domains and one BGP domain. BGP-LU is used to assign and exchange labels for BGP prefixes. Each IGP domain can use LDP or SR-MPLS for label distribution.

■ **MPLS network with inter-AS Option C:** This is an MPLS network where multiple BGP ASs are connected using inter-AS Option C. Each BGP AS can be a flat or unified MPLS network.

■ **Carrier Supporting Carrier (CSC) MPLS network:** A CSC network enables one MPLS VPN-based service provider to allow other service providers to use its backbone network. The service provider that provides the backbone network to the other provider is called the backbone carrier. The service provider that uses the backbone network is called the customer carrier.

The target SRv6 network can have the same topology as the MPLS network, with one or more BGP ASs, or it can be simplified by using a single BGP AS. The migration steps described in the following sections assume that the topology and the number of BGP ASs of the SRv6 network is same as in the MPLS network.

Flat MPLS Network

Figure 5-50 shows the steps for migration from MPLS to SRv6 when all the devices in the MPLS network support IPv6 and some of the PE devices support SRv6.

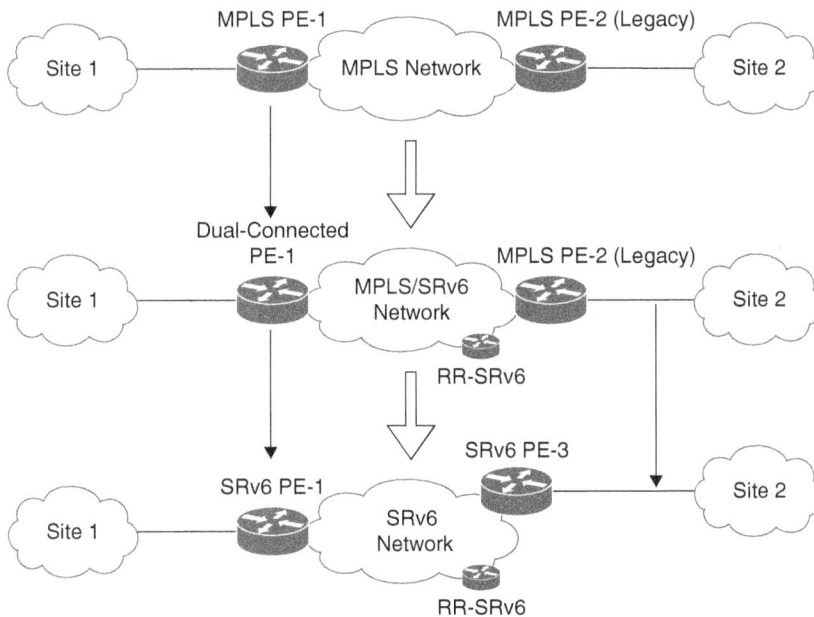

Figure 5-50 *Flat MPLS Network Migration: Coexistence*

Site 2 connected to a legacy MPLS PE device is migrated to SRv6 PE-3. MPLS-related configuration can be removed from the network when all the service migrations have been completed.

When some of the devices in the MPLS network do not support IPv6, a new SRv6 network is built and interconnected to the MPLS network, as shown in Figure 5-51. PE devices capable of supporting SRv6 and remaining sites that are connected to legacy PE devices are moved from the MPLS network to the SRv6 network in a phased manner.

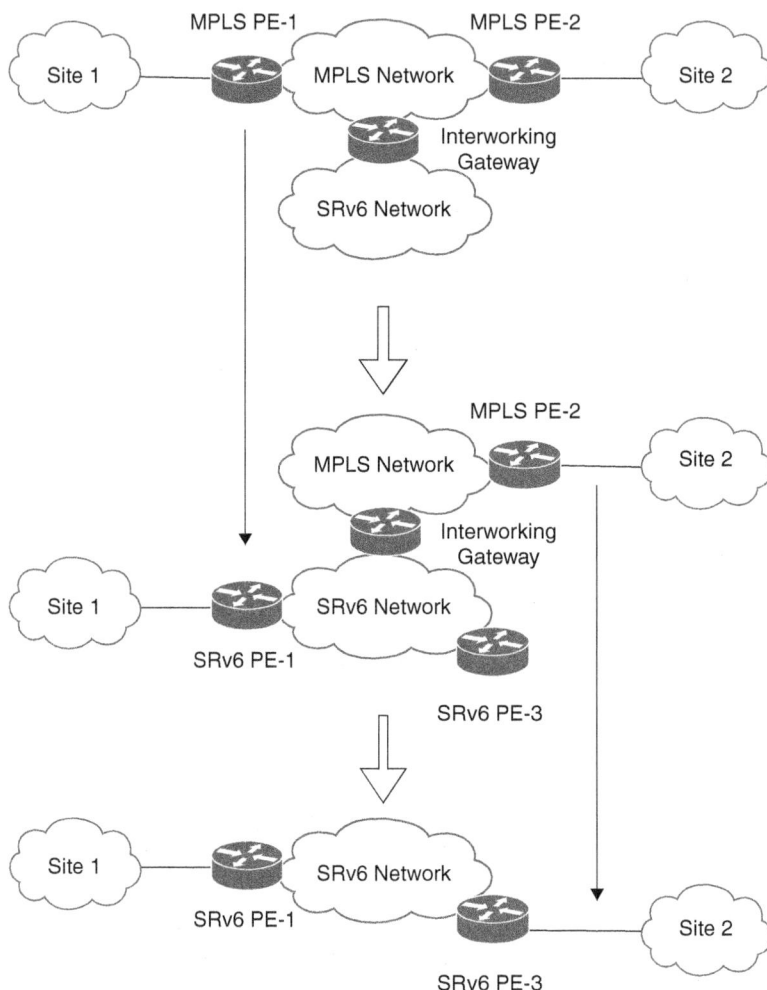

Figure 5-51 *Flat MPLS Network Migration Using an Interworking Gateway*

Unified MPLS Network

Figure 5-52 shows the steps for migrating a unified MPLS network using the Coexistence strategy. Enabling IPv6 or SRv6 in the MPLS network requires redistribution or propagation of IPv6 routes between the core and access networks with summarization and mechanisms to prevent loops due to mutual redistribution.

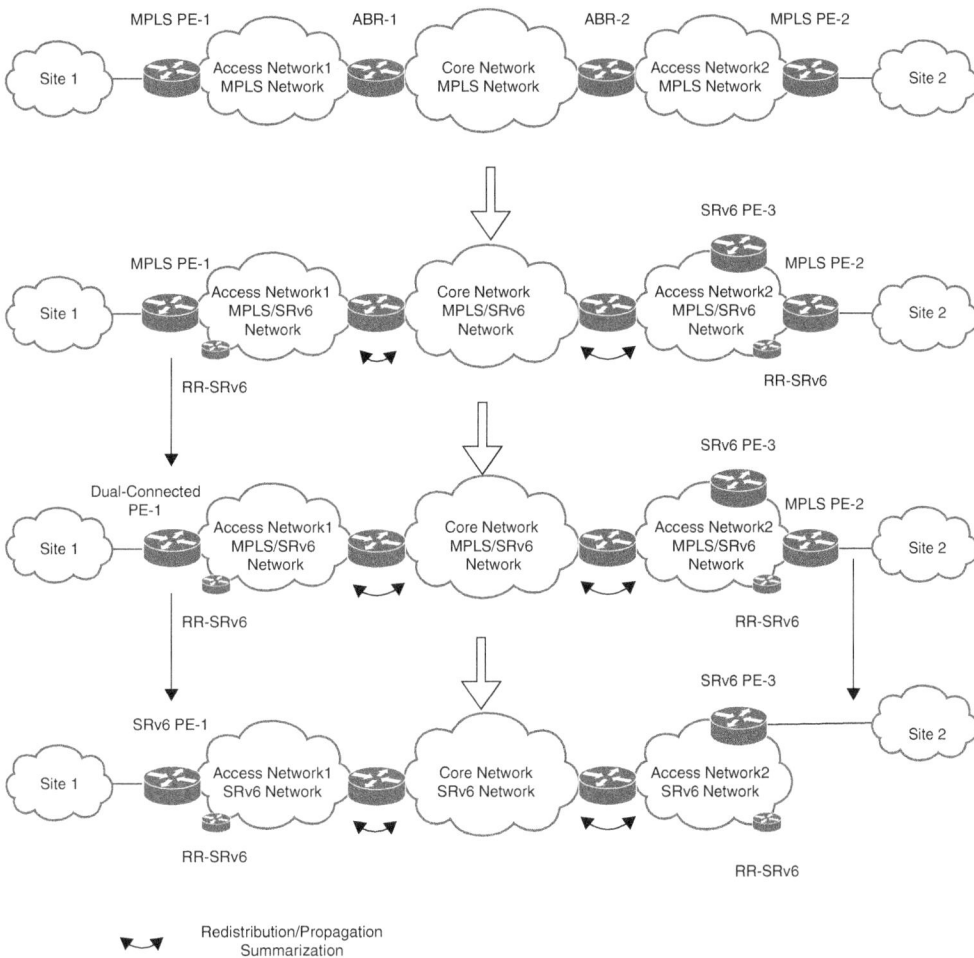

Figure 5-52 *Unified MPLS Network Migration: Coexistence*

Figure 5-53 shows the migration steps for a unified MPLS network using an interworking gateway between the MPLS and SRv6 networks. The interconnect between MPLS and SRv6 networks can be implemented using an SRv6 IWG or inter-AS Option A. Migration of the SRv6-capable PE devices or sites connected to legacy MPLS PE devices can be done in any order. The interconnect between the MPLS and SRv6 networks can be located either in the access or core network.

MPLS Network with Inter-AS Option C

Figure 5-54 shows the steps for migrating an MPLS network based on inter-AS Option C to SRv6 using the coexistence strategy. eBGP IPv6 sessions are required between the ASBRs to exchange IPv6 routes between the different BGP ASs. Redistribution of IPv6 routes between BGP and the IGP on the ASBRs with summarization and mechanisms to prevent loops due to mutual redistribution is required to provide end-to-end IPv6 connectivity between the different ASs. After SRv6 is configured on all the P devices and ASBRs, the dual-connected PE functionality is enabled on SRv6-capable PE devices, and the sites connected to the legacy MPLS PE devices are migrated to the SRv6 PE devices.

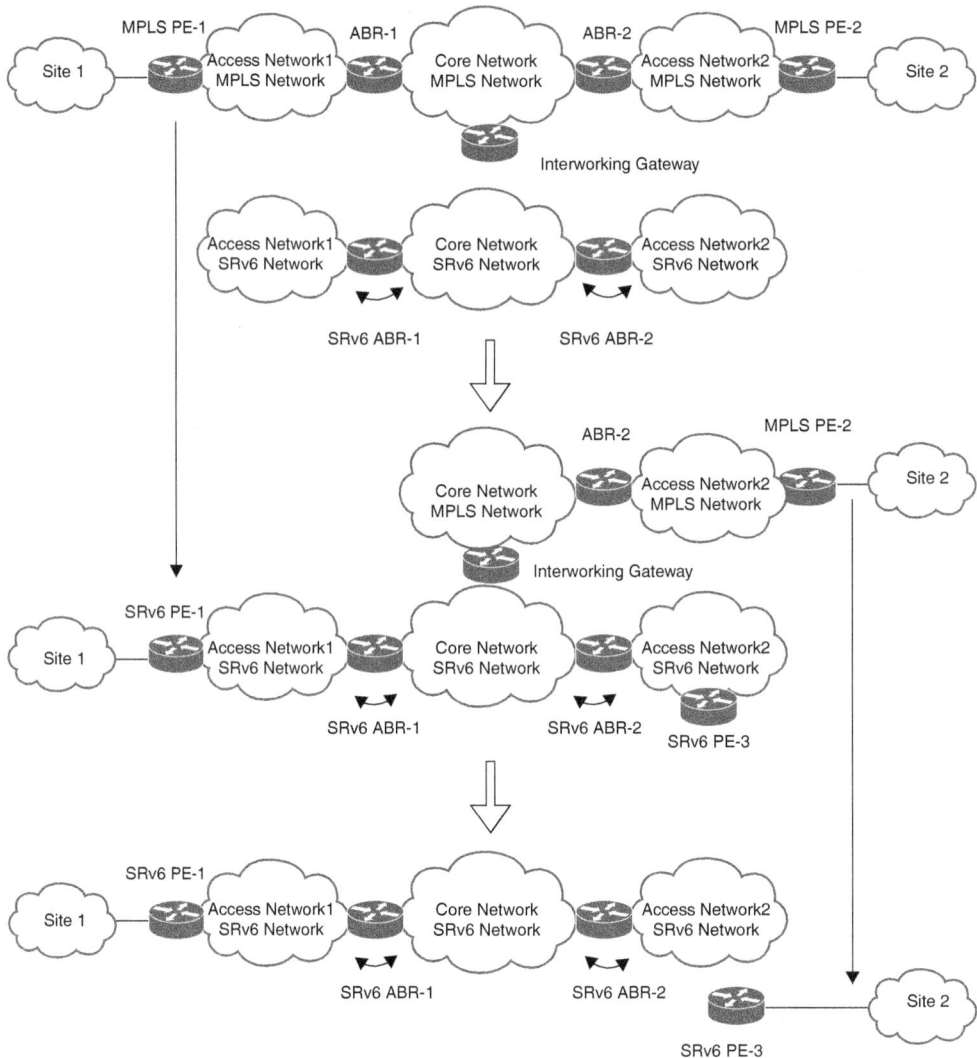

Figure 5-53 *Unified MPLS Network Migration: Interworking*

Figure 5-55 shows the steps for migrating an MPLS network with inter-AS Option C using an interworking gateway between the MPLS and SRv6 networks. The interconnecting gateway between the MPLS and SRv6 networks can be placed in one or more BGP ASs. Sites connected to the legacy MPLS PE devices are migrated to SRv6 PE devices, and MPLS PE devices capable of supporting SRv6 are moved to the SRv6 network.

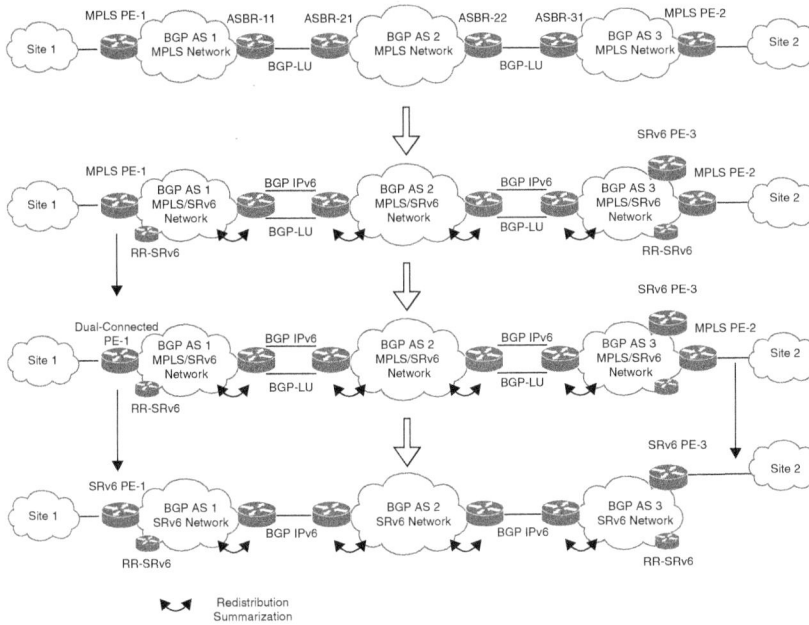

Figure 5-54 *Inter-AS Option C MPLS Network Migration: Coexistence*

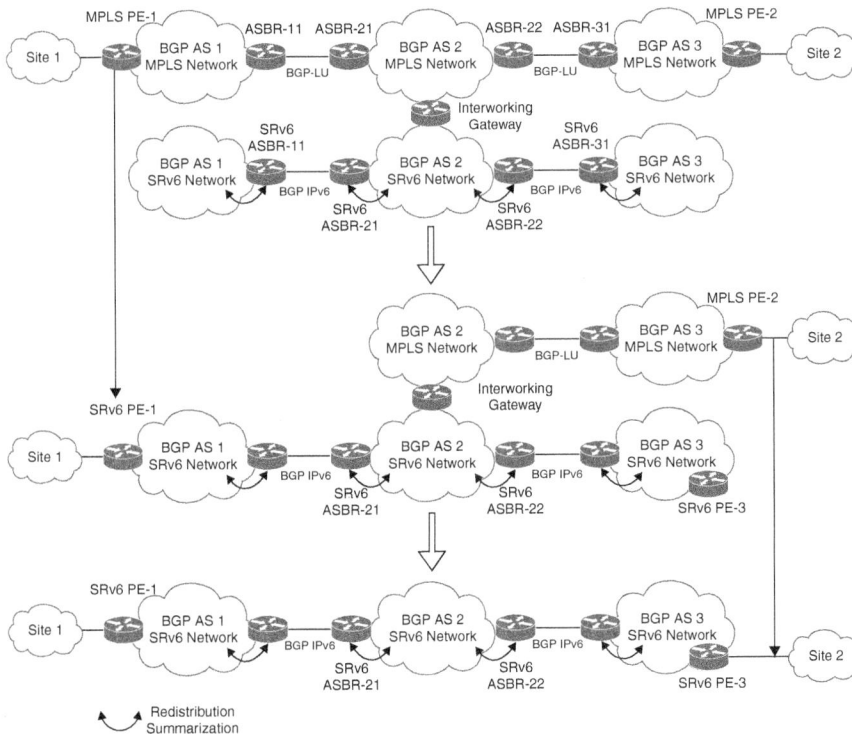

Figure 5-55 *Inter-AS Option C MPLS Network Migration: Interworking*

Carrier Supporting Carrier MPLS Network

Figure 5-56 shows the steps for migrating a CSC MPLS network to SRv6 using the coexistence strategy. CSC Site 1 and CSC Site 2 are customer carrier networks connected over the CSC core MPLS network, which is the backbone carrier network. eBGP IPv6 sessions are required between the CSC CE device and CSC PE device to exchange IPv6 routes between the CSC sites over the backbone carrier network. Redistribution of IPv6 routes between BGP and the IGP on the CSC CE devices with summarization and mechanisms to prevent loops due to mutual redistribution is required to provide end-to-end IPv6 connectivity between the different ASs. After SRv6 is configured on all the P and CSC CE devices in the CSC sites, the dual-connected PE device functionality is enabled on SRv6-capable PE devices in CSC Site 1 and CSC Site 2, and the sites connected to the legacy MPLS PE devices are migrated to the SRv6 PE devices. Note that there is no need to enable SRv6 in the backbone carrier network because the IPv6 traffic from the CSC sites is encapsulated with MPLS labels in the backbone carrier network.

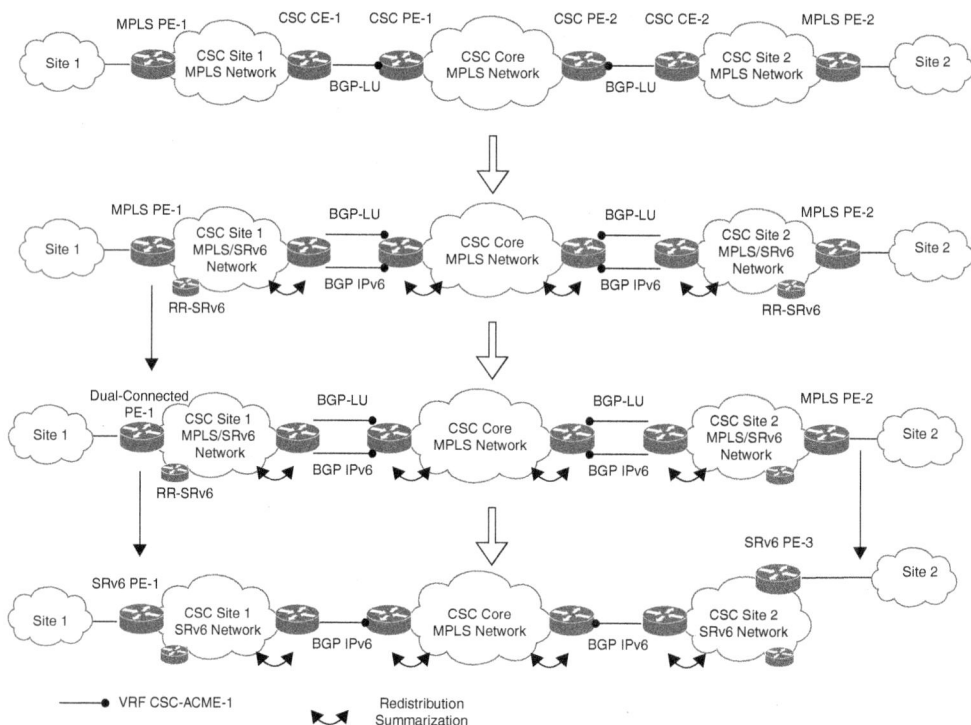

Figure 5-56 *CSC MPLS Network Migration: Coexistence*

Figure 5-57 shows the steps for migrating the CSC MPLS network using the interworking strategy.

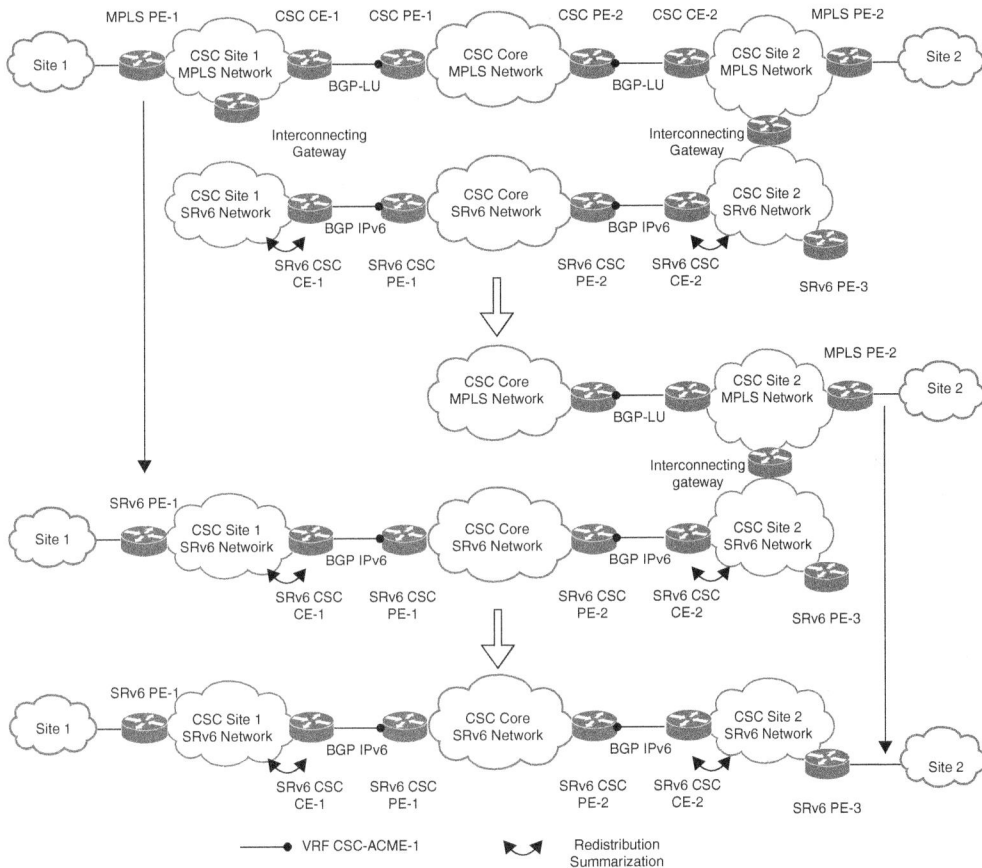

Figure 5-57 *CSC MPLS Network Migration: Interworking*

The interconnect between the MPLS and SRv6 networks can be provided between the CSC sites or the CSC core network. Sites connected to the legacy MPLS PE-2 in the CSC sites are connected to SRv6 PE-3; MPLS PE-1, which can support SRv6, is migrated to the SRv6 network.

Summary

The transition from MPLS to segment routing offers several benefits for service providers. However, as with any other technological advancement, this transition can present various challenges. This chapter outlines two deployment models and introduces several strategic approaches for the phased migration of L2VPN and L3VPN services from MPLS to SRv6 networks. The goal of these approaches is to minimize risks.

Table 5-2 provides a comparison of the different strategies based on the following criteria for the migration from LDP to SR-MPLS:

- **Deployment model:** A deployment may be either a greenfield deployment or a brownfield deployment.

- **Interworking/coexistence:** Does the method provide interworking or coexistence between MPLS and SRv6? Interworking requires that the MPLS and SR networks are separate, while coexistence assumes that all devices can support MPLS and SR.

- **Additional devices:** Are additional devices and interfaces needed, or will the functionality be integrated with the existing devices?

- **Service coverage:** Will the migration method cover L3VPN and L2VPN services?

- **Service topology:** What service topology will be used? Will it be a full mesh, hub and spoke, or extranet topology for L3VPN?

Table 5-2   *LDP to SR-MPLS: Comparison of the Migration Strategies*

Criterion	LDP and SR-MPLS	SRMS and Border Node
Deployment model	Brownfield	Greenfield
Interworking/coexistence	Coexistence	Interworking
Additional devices	None	Existing devices can be used as the border node and SRMS
Service coverage	L3VPN or L2VPN	L3VPN or L2VPN
L3VPN service topologies	All topologies	All topologies

Table 5-3 compares the different strategies for MPLS-to-SRv6 migration, considering the service topology as an additional criterion.

Table 5-3   *MPLS to SRv6: Comparison of Migration Strategies*

Criterion	IWG	Inter-AS Option A	Dual-Connected PE
Deployment model	Greenfield	Greenfield	Greenfield and brownfield
Interworking/coexistence	Interworking	Interworking	Coexistence
Additional devices	Requires at least one SRv6 IWG	Requires at least two ASBRs	Existing PE devices can be converted to use as dual-connected PE devices

Criterion	IWG	Inter-AS Option A	Dual-Connected PE
Service coverage	L3VPN (L2VPN is not supported at this writing.)	L3VPN or L2VPN	L3VPN or L2VPN
L3VPN service topologies	Limited coverage that is restricted to full mesh or hub and spoke	Limited coverage that is restricted to full mesh or hub and spoke	Supports all topologies, including extranets and hub and spoke

References and Additional Reading

SR-MPLS Migration

- RFC 8661: Segment Routing MPLS Interworking with LDP, https://datatracker.ietf.org/doc/html/rfc8661

- RFC 7432: BGP MPLS-Based Ethernet VPN, https://datatracker.ietf.org/doc/html/rfc7432

- RFC 4364: BGP/MPLS IP Virtual Private Networks (VPNs), https://datatracker.ietf.org/doc/html/rfc4364

SRv6 Migration

- IETF Draft: SRv6 and MPLS interworking, https://datatracker.ietf.org/doc/html/draft-agrawal-spring-srv6-mpls-interworking

- Migrate Your MPLS Network and Services to SRv6 with Simplicity - BRKSP-2468, https://www.ciscolive.com/on-demand/on-demand-library.html?zid=pp&search=BRKSP-2468#/session/1707505562433001pahG

Chapter 6

L2VPN Service Deployment: Configuration and Verification Techniques

In this chapter, we explore L2VPN overlay services established across the SRv6 transport underlay frameworks we've already examined. This chapter outlines fundamental approaches for configuration and methods for confirming the integrity of L2VPN service structures. Keep in mind that the content provided here does not delve extensively into L2VPN services. Instead, this chapter serves as a primer on the transition and deployment of well-established L2VPN technologies within SRv6 transport infrastructures.

If there is a requirement for Layer 2 connectivity, a service provider must set up an L2VPN service using technologies such as Virtual Private LAN Service (VPLS), Virtual Private WAN Service (VPWS), or the more recent advancement in L2VPN technology, Ethernet VPN (EVPN). These overlay services are then transported across a unified core transport network. Transport networks capable of handling L2VPN can offer Ethernet LAN (E-LAN), Ethernet Tree (E-Tree), or Ethernet Line (E-Line) services. In this setup, the service provider maps the incoming customer Layer 2 traffic into bridge domains or establishes point-to-point circuits. These bridge domains or point-to-point circuits are then interconnected across the transport network with other customer site Layer 2 bridge domains or point-to-point circuits. In this way, L2VPN services facilitate the extension of subnets from one end to the other, enabling the provision of managed services such as point-to-point, Internet connectivity, intranet, and extranet services to end customers. Figure 6-1 provides a high-level illustration of how L2VPN overlay services are transported over an SRv6 core network, which will be the primary focus of this chapter."

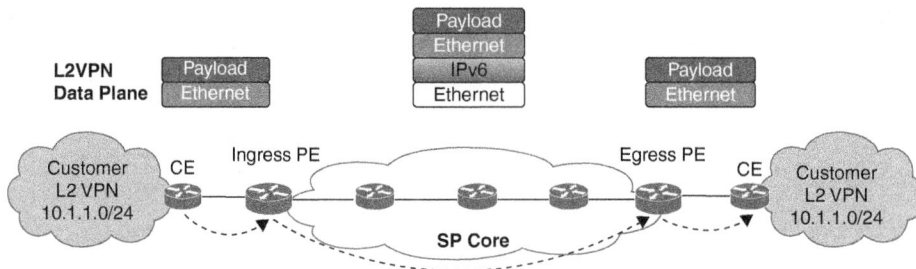

Figure 6-1   *L2VPN Connectivity Across an SRv6 Core Network*

L2VPN (EVPN)

The introduction of Multiprotocol Label Switching (MPLS) in RFC 3031, with its highly efficient and flexible data transportation capabilities through the use of MPLS labels, allowed for fast and efficient forwarding decisions without the need for complex IP lookups at each hop. MPLS is protocol agnostic, meaning it can transport packets of various network protocols, such as IP and Ethernet packets. This flexibility is a key part of MPLS's utility in creating sophisticated and scalable network services, including Layer 2 virtual private networks (L2VPNs).

MPLS L2VPN services provide a transport mechanism for Layer 2 frames between multiple customer sites across an MPLS backbone. These services essentially allow the extension of customer Layer 2 networks across geographically dispersed locations, making it possible to create a VPN that emulates a single LAN segment to the customer. L2VPNs are built using two main architectures: Virtual Private LAN Service (VPLS) and Virtual Private Wire Service (VPWS). VPLS provides a multipoint-to-multipoint service, emulating an Ethernet LAN, while VPWS offers point-to-point connectivity, similar to a traditional leased line. Both VPLS and VPWS are essentially transported across a core network through the use of MPLS pseudowires (PW). A pseudowire is simply an emulated point-to-point connection established across a packet-switched network (PSN) that uses Label Distribution Protocol (LDP) for setting up the pseudowire circuits.

Over the past 15 years, Ethernet VPN (EVPN) has begun to gain traction with service providers and large enterprises, and it is now seen as the logical evolution from the VPLS architecture for Layer 2 provisioning. Limitations that are inherent to VPLS lack of multipathing and multihoming capabilities, lack of multicast optimization and redundancy, among others are resolved through EVPN.

EVPN uses Border Gateway Protocol (BGP) to address these limitations via the control plane, whereas VPLS is inherently a data plane learning and forwarding solution. BGP as its control plane protocol provides more scalability than the flooding and learning mechanism used in VPLS. EVPN can handle a larger number of endpoints without suffering from the same level of complexity and resource consumption that VPLS might encounter due to network expansion. EVPN is able to multicast traffic more efficiently through the use of inclusive multicast Ethernet routes, eliminating the requirement to flood multicast traffic to all endpoints. VPLS, in contrast, typically floods multicast traffic across the entire Layer 2 domain. The multihoming capabilities inherent with EVPN enable single customer edge (CE) routers to connect to multiple provider edge (PE) devices for increased redundancy and load balancing. More granular traffic isolation through unique route targets (RTs) and route distinguishers (RDs) for different services is an additional benefit of EVPN. This is an improvement over VPLS, which typically relies on a single broadcast domain for all connected sites. EVPN uses BGP to advertise MAC addresses, leading to more optimal forwarding paths and faster convergence in the event of network failures. VPLS, on the other hand, relies on traditional MAC learning, which can be slower to converge. EVPN supports both Layer 2 VPN and Layer 3 VPN services, allowing for integrated routing and bridging in the same service instance. This provides greater flexibility in network design compared to VPLS. EVPN is therefore the superior option for Layer 2 VPN services, offering enhanced robustness, scalability, and flexibility over VPLS.

Metro Ethernet Forum (MEF) is an industry consortium that defines standards for carrier Ethernet services. Within the Metro Ethernet Forum 3.0 (MEF 3.0) umbrella standard, several subscriber and operator services standards are defined. One of them, MEF 6.3, is a specification that outlines various Ethernet services and attributes from the perspective of the subscriber. It defines the characteristics and types of Ethernet services that service providers can offer to their subscribers. Figure 6-2 provides a diagrammatic overview of these subscriber services.

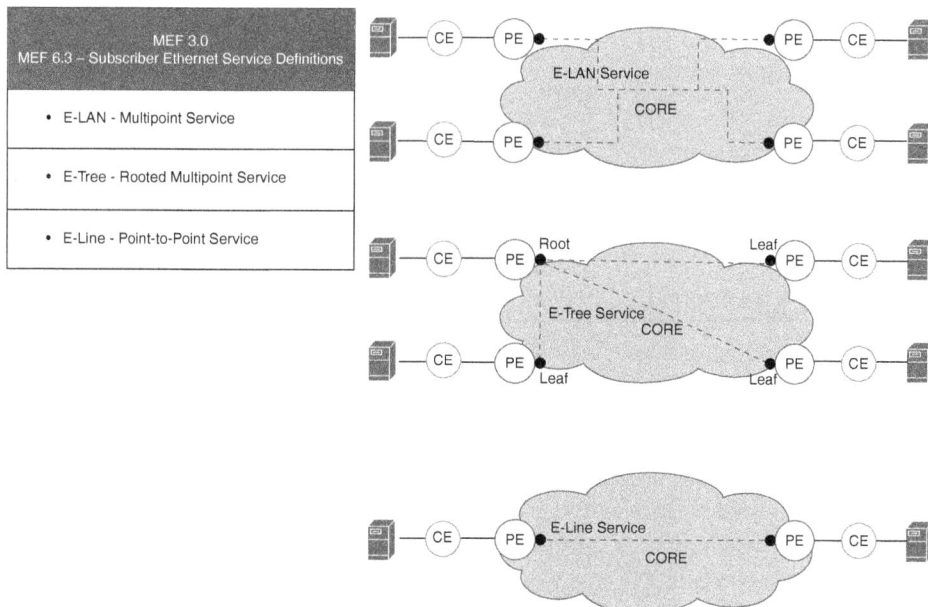

Figure 6-2 *MEF 6.3: Subscriber Ethernet Service Definitions*

Figure 6-3 illustrates how EVPN services map to the MEF 6.3 subscriber service definitions:

- **E-LAN service (multipoint-to-multipoint connection):** EVPN E-LAN interconnects multiple endpoints in a multipoint-to-multipoint fashion that allows for any-to-any connectivity between customer sites, similar to traditional Ethernet LAN services.

- **E-Tree service (rooted multipoint connection):** EVPN E-tree involves designating certain sites as "root" or "hub" sites and others as "leaf" sites, with traffic flowing from leaf to root and from root to leaf but not directly between leaf sites.

- **E-Line service (point-to-point connection):** EVPN VPWS can be used to create a virtual point-to-point Ethernet service. This is typically achieved by setting up an EVPN instance with only two endpoints to provide a dedicated Ethernet connection between two customer sites

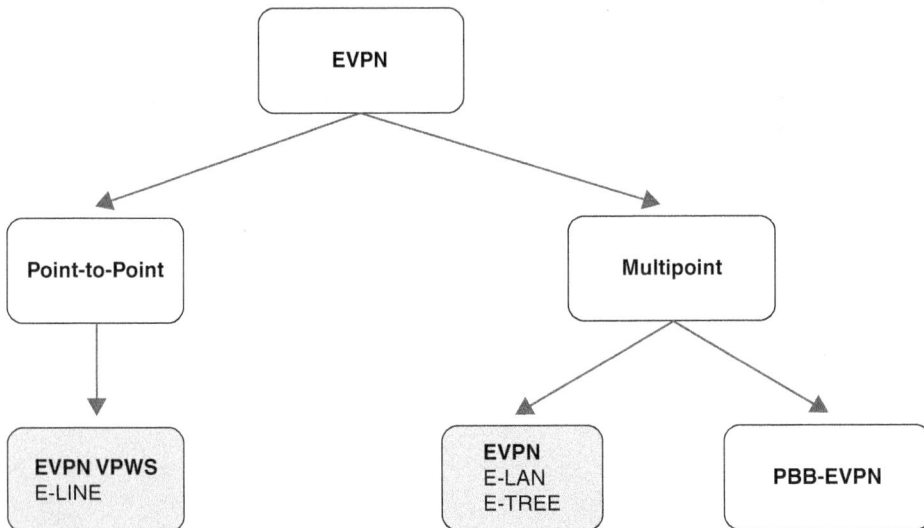

Figure 6-3 *EVPN Family: Next-Generation Ethernet Service Solutions*

EVPN in Detail

Ethernet VPN (EVPN) is a technology that provides Layer 2 VPN services over IP/MPLS transport networks and supports both unicast and multicast traffic, using BGP to distribute MAC/IP address reachability information. EVPN provides extensible and flexible multihoming VPN solutions for intra-subnet connectivity among tenant systems and end devices, which may be physical or virtual. EVPN provides E-LAN services and also allows for the provisioning of E-LINE services, with either port-active, single-active, or all-active multihoming with flow-based load balancing. EVPN VPWS simplifies pseudowire (PW) signaling and provides fast convergence upon node or link failure. The RFCs that define standards for EVPN include RFC 7432, RFC 8214, RFC 8365, and RFC 9135

Now let's look at the EVPN terminology used throughout this book and look at EVPN concepts in more detail. Let's start with some of the benefits of EVPN:

■ **All-active multihomed redundancy:** Figure 6-4 provides a visual representation of EVPN all-active capabilities. With VPLS, this was not possible, and Multi-Chassis LAG (MC-LAG) was used in an active/standby state for multihomed site connectivity.

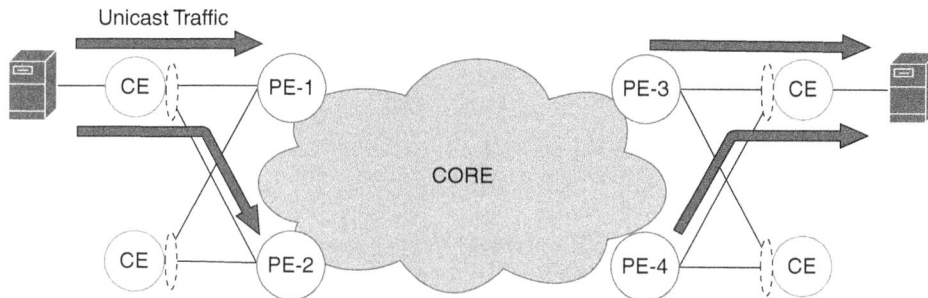

Figure 6-4   *EVPN All-Active Multihoming*

■ **Broadcast, unknown-unicast, and multicast (BUM) traffic loop avoidance:** L2 networks that use data plane learning and forwarding are prone to traffic loops caused by the flooding of traffic (BUM traffic) from the PE routers, whereas those that use EVPN use a split-horizon mechanism to prevent this traffic from being looped back. Figure 6-5 illustrates a multihomed PE router that is discarding BUM traffic originating from the CE router, effectively preventing traffic loops.

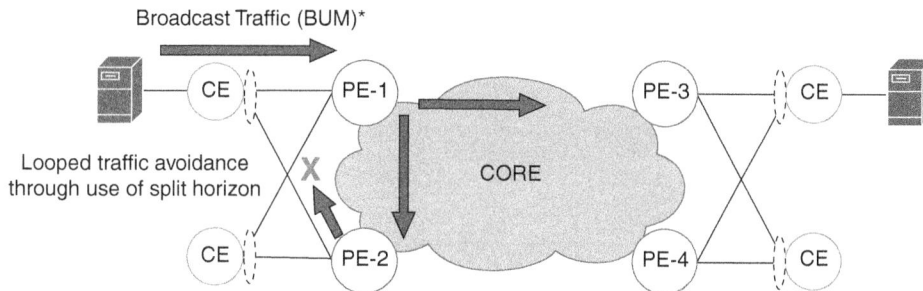

* BUM: Broadcast, unknown-unicast, and multicast

Figure 6-5   *EVPN Broadcast, Unknown-Unicast, and Multicast (BUM) Traffic Loop Avoidance*

■ **BUM traffic duplication avoidance:** EVPN multihomed sites that receive BUM traffic ingress from the core use a duplication avoidance mechanism known as a designated forwarder (DF) to prevent the CE device from receiving duplicate traffic, as illustrated in Figure 6-6. Data plane–based learning and forwarding networks (VPLS networks, for example) don't have this mechanism, and hence multihoming is not possible.

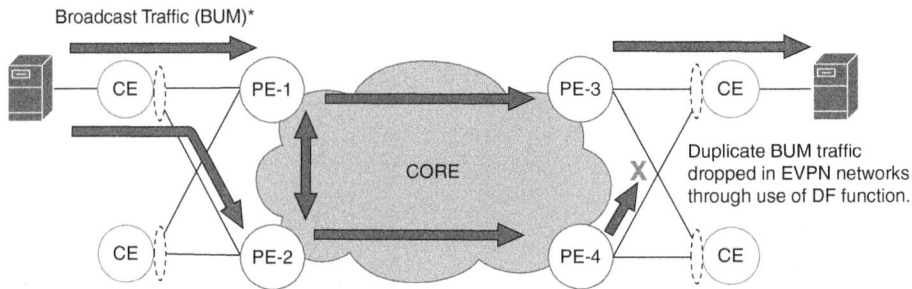

Figure 6-6   *EVPN Broadcast, Unknown-Unicast, and Multicast (BUM) Traffic Duplication Avoidance*

- **Load balancing through EVPN aliasing:** EVPN allows for traffic load balancing in the core. For example, when a PE router forwards traffic to a specific destination MAC address learned from a multihomed attached site, it can forward this traffic to both multihomed PE routers (see Figure 6-7), although it may only have learned the MAC address from one of the PE routers attached to the multihomed site. This is known as aliasing.

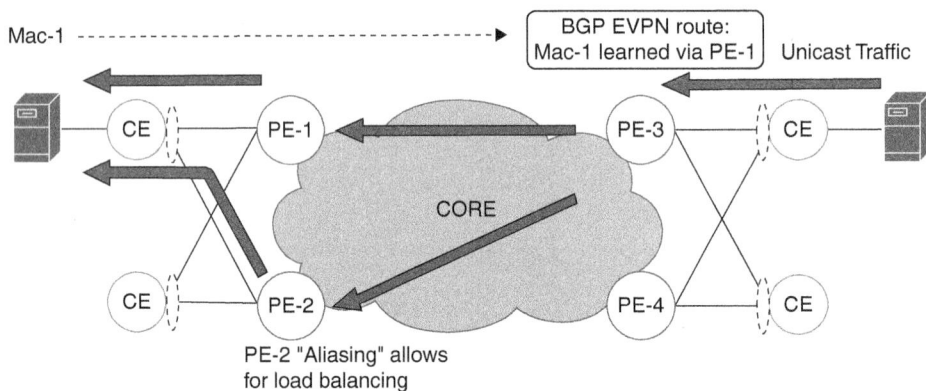

Figure 6-7   *EVPN Load Balancing via Aliasing*

Now let's look at some of the common terminology related to EVPN solutions and in use throughout this section:

- **Broadcast domain:** A broadcast domain is usually represented by a VLAN, and a VLAN is identified using a VLAN ID (VID).

- **EVPN instance (EVI):** An EVI is an instance of an EVPN that is present on multiple PE routers where the instance has been provisioned.

- **MAC VRF:** A MAC VRF instance is similar in concept to a VRF instance in L3VPN provisioned networks. A MAC VRF instance is a virtual routing table for L2 MAC addresses provisioned on PE routers.

■ **Ethernet segment (ES):** An ES is an Ethernet link (or site) that attaches a device or network to a PE router or multiple PE routers. These are the ES device and network types, which are covered in more detail later in this chapter, in the section "Ethernet Segment (ES)":

   ■ Single-homed device (SHD)

   ■ Multihomed device (MHD)

   ■ Single-homed network (SHN)

   ■ Multihomed network (MHN)

■ **Ethernet segment identifier (ESI):** An Ethernet segment has a unique 10-byte identifier known as an ESI.

■ **Ethernet tag ID:** The Ethernet tag ID is stored in a 4-byte field where 12 or 24 bits are used for VLAN, VPN ID, or EVI identification.

EVPN Instance (EVI)

An EVI (EVPN instance) is a logical entity that represents a unique Layer 2 broadcast domain within an EVPN. It is functionally similar to a VLAN in traditional Ethernet networking but designed to operate across a WAN.

Each EVI is associated with a unique identifier that distinguishes it from other EVIs in the same EVPN. This identifier allows for the segregation of traffic that belongs to different Layer 2 domains or customer networks. Within an EVI, the participating Ethernet segments can communicate with each other as if they were on the same local network, regardless of their physical location.

Figure 6-8 provides a graphical depiction of customer-provisioned EVIs on a PE router.

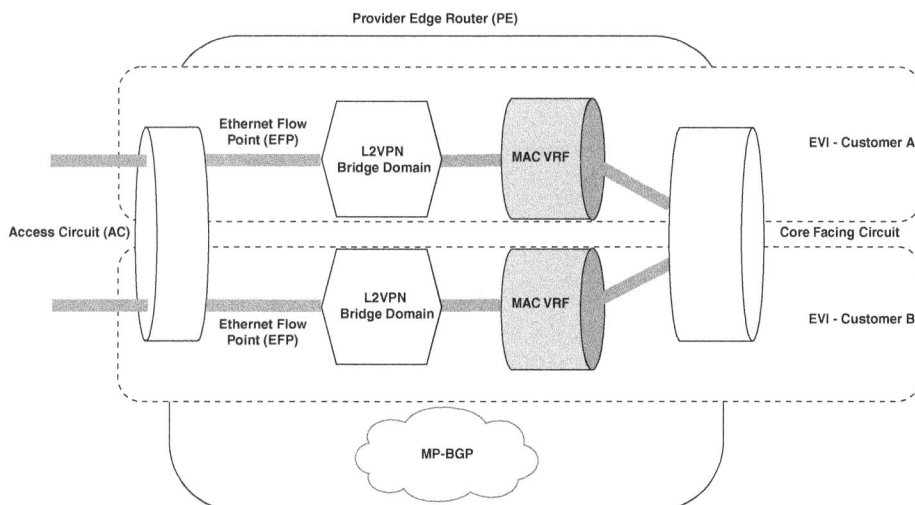

Figure 6-8   *EVPN Instances (EVIs) Provisioned on PE Routers*

An EVI encompasses all provider edge (PE) routers where it is configured and participating within an EVPN. An EVI is, in principle, a VPN identifier in the core network. Within a PE router, the EVI includes the MAC-VRF table, which is essentially the L2 MAC address routing table with a bridge domain component. The MAC-VRF table is similar in concept to an L3VPN VRF instance, which contains attached CE L3 routes; the MAC-VRF table contains the attached CE L2 routes. An EVI MAC-VRF table requires a unique route distinguisher (RD) for EVI identification and route targets (RTs) for allowing L2 MAC routes to be imported into an EVI. Output 6-1 provides an example of how these L2 MAC routes are displayed in a MAC-VRF table. You can see here that five MAC address entries have been imported into the bridge domain 200-BD on the router PE-1.

Output 6-1   *EVPN Route Type 2 MAC Route in Bridge Domain 200-BD on PE-1*

```
RP/0/RP0/CPU0:PE-1#show bgp l2vpn evpn bridge-domain 200-BD route-type 2
BGP router identifier 172.19.0.10, local AS number 65000
<snip>
Status codes: s suppressed, d damped, h history, * valid, > best
              i - internal, r RIB-failure, S stale, N Nexthop-discard
Origin codes: i - IGP, e - EGP, ? - incomplete
   Network          Next Hop          Metric LocPrf Weight Path
Route Distinguisher: 172.19.0.10:200 (default for vrf 200-BD)
Route Distinguisher Version: 2884
*>i[2][0][48][2011.1100.0001][0]/104
                    fc00:0:205::1                  100       0 i
*>i[2][0][48][2011.1100.0002][0]/104
                    fc00:0:205::1                  100       0 i
*>i[2][0][48][2011.1100.0003][0]/104
                    fc00:0:205::1                  100       0 i
*>i[2][0][48][2011.1100.0004][0]/104
                    fc00:0:205::1                  100       0 i
*>i[2][0][48][2011.1100.0005][0]/104
                    fc00:0:205::1                  100       0 i

Processed 5 prefixes, 5 paths
RP/0/RP0/CPU0:PE-1#
```

Now we're going to look at some terms that you'll encounter throughout the SRv6 EVPN service configuration and verification sections in this chapter.

The IOS XR software uses the Cisco Ethernet virtual circuit (EVC) framework for Layer 2 configurations to overcome some of the scaling and flexibility limitations imposed by traditional IEEE 802.1Q VLANs. The Cisco EVC framework align with MEF 6.3: Subscriber Ethernet Services Definitions, MEF 10.4: Subscriber Ethernet Service

Attributes, and MEF 11: UNI Requirements and is composed of the following building blocks:

- **Ethernet flow point (EFP):** An EFP is a Layer 2 logical subinterface that is used to classify traffic under physical or bundle (LAG) interfaces.

- **Ethernet virtual circuit (EVC):** An EVC is an end-to-end representation of a single instance of a Layer 2 service. An EFP is defined as an endpoint of an EVC within a node. As multiple EVCs can pass through one physical interface, the main purpose of an EFP configuration is to identify the traffic that belongs to a specific EVC on that interface and to apply the forwarding behavior and features specific to that EVC.

- **Bridge domain (BD):** A BD is an Ethernet broadcast domain that is internal to a node. The bridge domain decouples the VLAN from the broadcast domain and has a one-to-many mapping with an EFP for a specific EVC. EFPs that belong to the same bridge domain will receive traffic from other attached EFPs even if they are configured with different VLAN IDs.

- **Bridge group (BG):** A BG is purely a logical configuration entity that is used to group one or more bridge domains together.

An EVI can include one or multiple bridge domain, depending on the attached service interface types, which can be port based, VLAN based, or VLAN bundle based. You'll learn more about these EVPN VLAN service interface definitions later in this chapter, in the section "Ethernet Tag ID." The bridge domains into which the service interfaces are mapped are where Layer 2 frames are learned, based on source MAC addresses, and forwarded based on destination MAC addresses. At the bridge domain level, traffic forwarding is based on the standard data plane learning and forwarding model.

Ethernet Segment (ES)

The Ethernet segment (ES) is one of the major advantages that EVPN has over the older VPLS technology, as it allows for all-active multihoming, traffic load balancing, fast convergence, and seamless integration of Layer 2 and Layer 3. An ES is essentially a representation of a site connected to either a single PE router or multiple PE routers.

Figure 6-9 shows customer sites connected to PE routers. These connections together with the site form an ES, which can be either a single device or a complete network. As you learned earlier, these are the ES devices and network types:

- Single-homed device (SHD)

- Multihomed device (MHD)

- Single-homed network (SHN)

- Multihomed network (MHN)

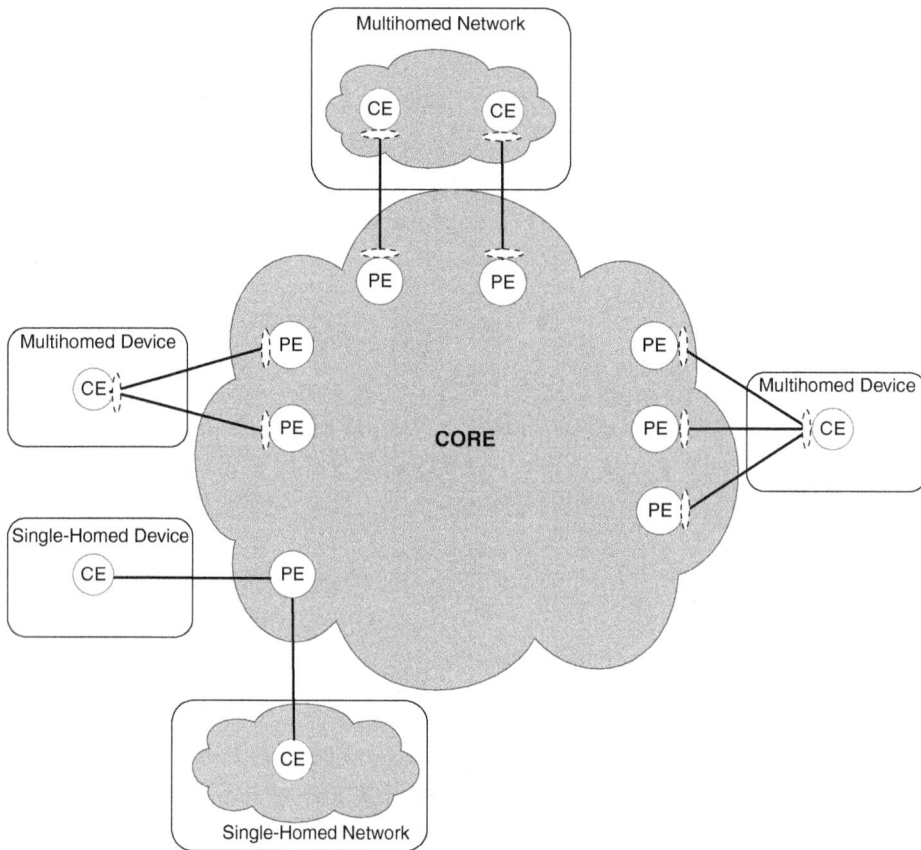

Figure 6-9   *EVPN Ethernet Segment Connectivity Overview*

A multihomed device/multihomed network (MHD/MHN) can be further refined based on redundancy or load-balancing modes, as shown in Figure 6-10.

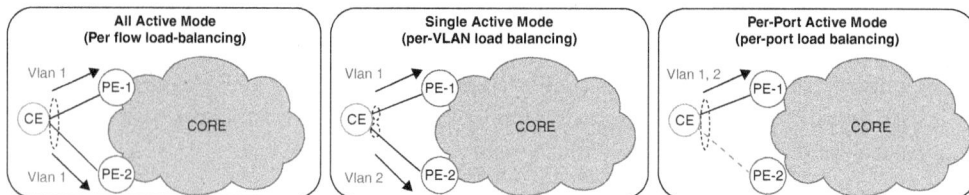

Figure 6-10   *EVPN Redundancy and Load-Balancing Modes*

■ **All active mode (per flow):** Device VLAN traffic is forwarded by all attached PE routers and is hashed per flow.

■ **Single active mode (per VLAN):** Device VLAN traffic is forwarded only by a single PE router and is hashed per VLAN

■ **Per-port active mode (per Port):** Device port is active on a single PE and traffic is hashed per port

A multihomed site is identified by a unique 10-byte global identifier known as an Ethernet segment identifier (ESI), which is used as part of the auto-discovery of these Ethernet segments as well as in the designated forwarder election (DF election) process described later in this chapter, in the section "EVPN Route Type 4: Ethernet Segment Route." The ESI comprises a network-wide unique nonzero value.

RFC 7432 specifies multiple ESI types and two reserved ESI identifiers and uses the format shown in Figure 6-11):

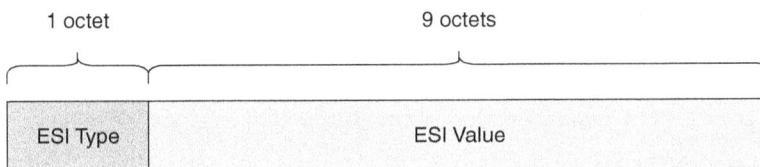

Figure 6-11   *EVPN Ethernet Segment Identifier Format*

■ **Type 0:** Indicates that this value is manually allocated by the service provider network operator.

  ■ **00.00.00.00.00.00.00.00.00:** Reserved ESI representing a single-homed site

  ■ **00.00.fc.00.01.02.00.00.00:** Example of manually configured ESI

■ **Type 1:** An auto-generated ESI created when using Link Aggregation Control Protocol (LACP) between PE routers and CE devices.

  ■ **01.aa.aa.aa.aa.aa.aa.bb.bb.00:**

    ☐ **0xaaaaaaaaaaaa:** 6-byte CE LACP system MAC address

    ☐ **0xbbbbbb:** 2-byte CE LACP port key

    ☐ **0x00:** 1 byte set to 0

■ **Type 2:** An auto-generated ESI when the PE and CE routers are interconnected via a switching device using Multiple Spanning Tree Protocol (MSTP).

  ■ **02.aa.aa.aa.aa.aa.aa.bb.bb.00:**

    ☐ **0xaaaaaaaaaaaa:** 6-byte root bridge MAC address

    ☐ **0xbbbb:** 2-byte root bridge priority

    ☐ **0x00:** 1 byte set to 0

- **Type 3:** An ESI type that can be manually allocated by the service provider network operator or auto-generated using the LAG interface or system LACP MAC address.

  - **03.aa.aa.aa.aa.aa.aa.bb.bb.bb:**

    - □ **0xaaaaaaaaaaaa:** 6-byte system MAC address

    - □ **0xbbbbbb:** 3-byte local discriminator

- **Type 4:** An ESI type that is router ID based and can be manually allocated by the service provider network operator or auto-generated.

  - **04.aa.aa.aa.aa.bb.bb.bb.bb.00:**

    - □ **0xaaaaaaaa:** 4-byte router ID

    - □ **0xbbbbbbbb:** 4-byte local discriminator

    - □ **0x00:** 1 byte set to 0

- **Type 5:** An ESI that is autonomous system (AS) based and can be manually allocated by the service provider network operator or auto-generated.

  - **05.00.00.aa.aa.bb.bb.bb.bb.00:** 2-byte AS

    - □ **0xaaaa:** 2-byte AS number, with 2 high-order bytes set to 0x00

    - □ **0xbbbbbbbb:** 4-byte local discriminator

    - □ **0x00:** 1 byte set to 0

  - **05.aa.aa.aa.aa.bb.bb.bb.bb.00:** 4-byte AS

    - □ **0xaaaaaaaa:** 4-byte AS number

    - □ **0xbbbbbbbb:** 4-byte local discriminator

    - □ **0x00:** 1 byte set to 0

- **Reserved ESI:** Known as the MAX-ESI.

  - **ff.ff.ff.ff.ff.ff.ff.ff.ff**

Ethernet Tag ID

As mentioned at the beginning of this chapter, the Ethernet tag ID is a 4-byte (32-bit) field with 12 bit or 24 bit used for VLAN, VPN ID, or EVI identification. The tag ID, known as the VLAN ID (VID), identifies a VLAN or broadcast domain, and one or more of these VLANs can exist within each EVPN. Each VLAN can be composed of different VLAN IDs, and the onus is on the PE router to provide VLAN ID translation at the access circuit facing the CE device. For the EVPN Route Type 1 per-ESI Ethernet A-D route, the Ethernet tag ID is set to the reserved MAX-ET 4294967295 (0xFFFFFFFF).

There are various types of EVPN VLAN service interfaces:

■ **EVPN VLAN-based service interface:** With the VLAN-based service interface, the EVI which is essentially a VLAN (broadcast domain) consisting of the VID, a single bridge domain, and the MAC VRF table. If the VIDs are different between the PE routers, VID translation occurs on the PE routers, as shown in Figure 6-12. The Ethernet Tag ID fields in all the EVPN routes (EVPN Route Types 1–4) are set to 0.

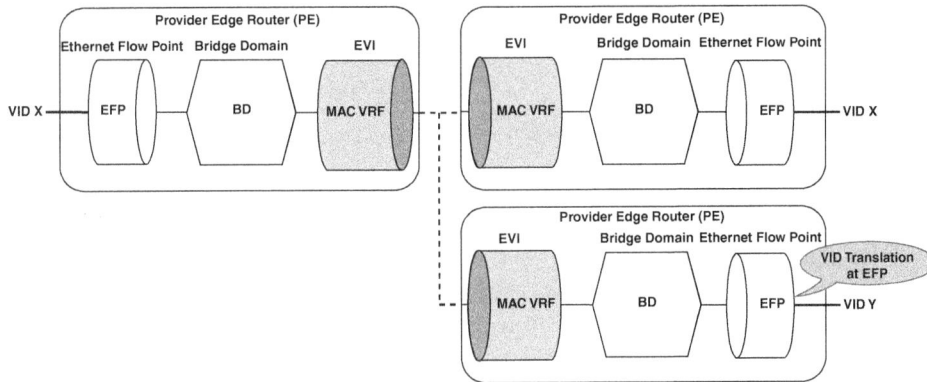

Figure 6-12 *EVPN VLAN-Based Service Interface*

■ **EVPN VLAN bundle service interface:** With the VLAN bundle service interface shown in Figure 6-13, the EVI contains multiple VLANs (that is, multiple broadcast domains) mapped to a single bridge domain, which is associated with the MAC VRF table. The implication is that while these multiple VLANs are sharing the single bridge domain, all MAC addresses should be unique. With this service, there is no VID translation. As with the VLAN-based service interface, the Ethernet Tag ID fields in all the EVPN routes are set to 0.

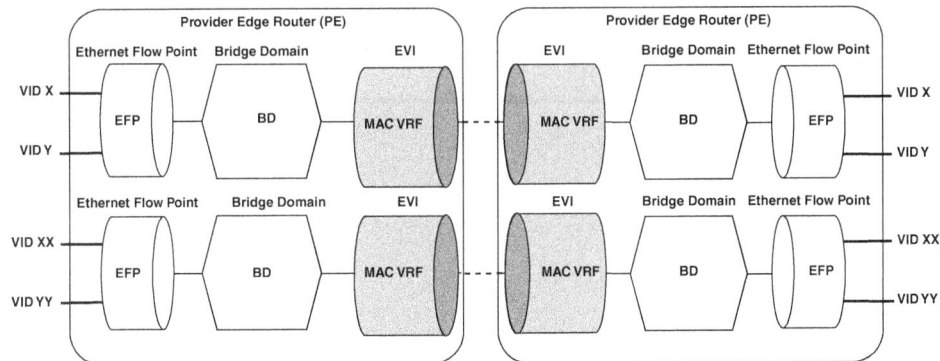

Figure 6-13 *EVPN VLAN Bundle Service Interface*

■ **EVPN port-based service interface:** With the port-based service interface shown in Figure 6-14, all VLANs on the interface belong to the same EVPN service. This service is similar to the EVPN VLAN bundle service interface.

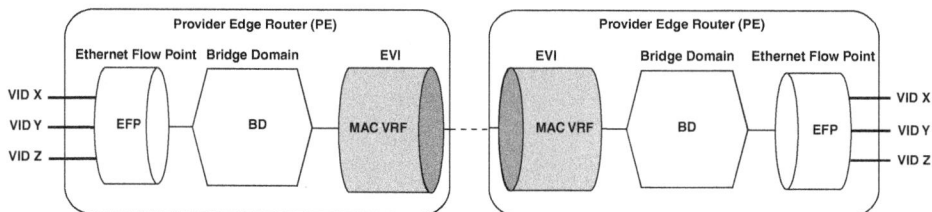

Figure 6-14 *EVPN Port-Based Service Interface*

■ **EVPN VLAN-aware bundle service interface:** With the VLAN-aware bundle service interface in Figure 6-15, the EVI contains multiple VLANs (that is, multiple broadcast domains), each VLAN is linked to its own bridge domain, and these bridge domains in turn are all associated with a single MAC VRF table. If the VLAN VIDs are the same, thus requiring no VID translation, the Ethernet Tag ID field in the EVPN routes will still be set to this common VLAN VID. However, if a VLAN has multiple VIDs set across the individual PE routers, necessitating VID translation, a common Ethernet Tag ID field will be set in the EVPN routes originated by the PE routers. On receipt of these EVPN routes, the receiving PE routes can associate the correct bridge domain with that VID and perform VLAN ID translation at egress toward the CE device.

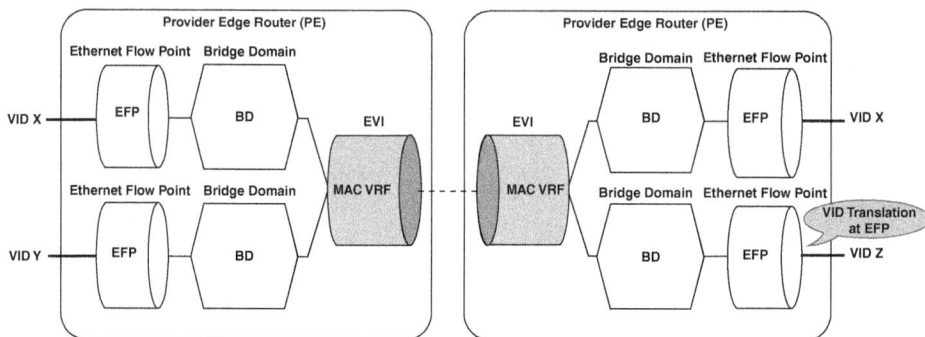

Figure 6-15 *EVPN VLAN-Aware Bundle Service Interface*

EVPN BGP Routes

The EVPN protocol overcomes many of the limitations of the L2VPN VPLS technology due to the fact that EVPN is based on the BGP control plane, whereas L2VPN VPLS is purely a data plane learning and forwarding solution.

Figure 6-16 illustrates a scenario in which a provider edge (PE) router acquires a source MAC address from an incoming Ethernet frame. Subsequently, the BGP control plane disseminates information about the reachability of this MAC address to all PE routers participating in the EVPN through a Route Type 2 MAC-IP advertisement route.

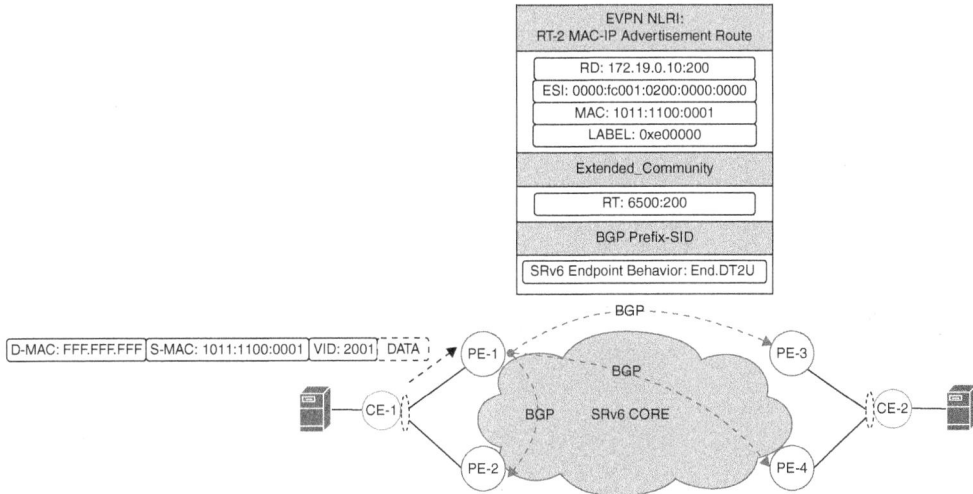

Figure 6-16 *EVPN BGP Route Type 2 MAC Reachability Advertisement*

EVPN Network Layer Reachability Information (NLRI) is encapsulated in BGP using BGP extensions with the address family identifier (AFI) 25 and subsequent address family identifier (SAFI) 70. Figure 6-17 shows the various NLRI types transported with BGP. These EVPN route types are briefly listed here, and additional details and packet captures are provided in the following sections.:

- **Route Type 1:** Ethernet auto-discovery (A-D) route

- **Route Type 2:** MAC-IP advertisement route

- **Route Type 3:** Inclusive multicast route

- **Route Type 4:** Ethernet segment route

Other route types are defined in IETF RFCs but are beyond the scope of this book:

- **Route Type 5:** IP prefix route

- **Route Type 6:** IGMP/MLD proxy route

- **Route Types 7 and 8:** IGMP/MLD join and leave synchronization

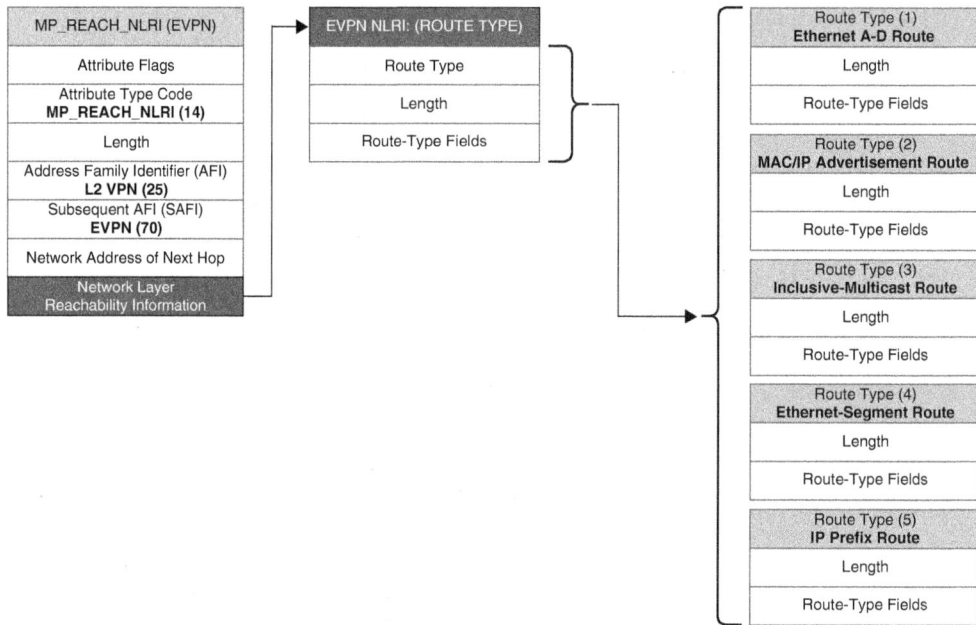

Figure 6-17 *EVPN BGP Route Types (RFC 7432)*

EVPN Route Type 1: Ethernet Auto-Discovery (A-D) Route

Note   The router configuration outputs and example packet captures used in this section were collected from the SRv6 reference network provided in Appendix A, "Reference Diagrams and Considerations."

EVPN NLRI Route Type 1 has into two variants:

- Per-ESI Ethernet A-D route
- Per-EVI Ethernet A-D route

These Ethernet A-D route types are used in both point-to-point and multipoint EVPN services to allow the following behaviors:

- **Split horizon (per-ESI Ethernet A-D route):** In an all-active multihomed attached device or network scenario, broadcast, unknown-unicast, and multicast (BUM) traffic received from the local Ethernet segment is forwarded by the ingress PE router to all remote PE routers participating in that EVPN. On receipt by the peer PE router attached to the same MHN/MHD, this BUM traffic is not forwarded back into the same Ethernet segment, thereby breaking a potential broadcast loop.

To achieve split horizon, the ingress non-designated forwarder PE router adds an encapsulating label in MPLS, known as the EVPN ESI filter label, to the BUM traffic to allow the peer PE router to identify and drop the BUM traffic, preventing those packets from reaching the Ethernet segment from where they originated. (For more information, see the section "EVPN Route Type 4: Ethernet Segment Route," later in this chapter.) The ESI filter label is included as part of the BGP extended communities attribute. Example 6-1 shows a BGP packet capture snippet from a port-active multihomed configuration with the single-active bit in the ESI filter label extended community set to 1 and the ESI filter label set to the MPLS label value 3 (implicit null).

Example 6-1   *EVPN Route Type 1 Packet Capture*

```
<snip>
        Path Attribute - EXTENDED_COMMUNITIES
            Type Code: EXTENDED_COMMUNITIES (16)
            Length: 24
            Carried extended communities: (3 communities)
                ESI MPLS Label: Single-Active redundancy, Label: 3 [Transitive EVPN]
                    Type: Transitive EVPN (0x06)
                    Subtype (EVPN): ESI MPLS Label (0x01)
                    …. …1 = Single active bit: Single-Active redundancy
                    MPLS Label: 48
                    [0000 0000 0000 0000 0011 …. = MPLS Label: 3]
<snip>
```

- **Fast convergence (per-ESI Ethernet A-D route):** For a local PE router to signal a failure condition in a local ES toward its remote PE router peers, that local PE router is required to withdraw the learned MAC address routes from its remote peers. Depending on the scale of these routes on the local PE router, this per-MAC address withdrawal from the MAC address table may lead to slow convergence. Therefore, to improve convergence, EVPN Route Type 1 is used for MAC mass withdrawal.

- **All-active or single-active ESI state (per-ESI Ethernet A-D route):** The ESI all-active or single-active (including port-active) configured state is signaled as part of this per-ESI Ethernet A-D route and is identified in the CLI output displayed in Output 6-2 as **Extended community: EVPN ESI Label:0x01:3**. This field is used together with the split-horizon label to indicate the redundancy mode:

  - **All-Active (0x00):** Ethernet segment split-horizon label (not shown)

  - **Single-Active (0x01):** Ethernet segment split-horizon Label 3 (see Output 6-2)

  This ESI all-active or single-active redundancy mode is also displayed in the packet capture shown in Example 6-1 within the extended community of the BGP UPDATE message.

To examine an EVPN Route Type 1 per-ESI Ethernet A-D route in more detail, you can issue the command **show bgp l2vpn evpn rd 172.19.0.10:1 [1][172.19.0.10:1][0000. fc00.0102.0000.0000][4294967295]/184**, as shown in Output 6-2.

Output 6-2   *EVPN per-ESI Ethernet A-D Route Route Type 1 Example on PE-2*

```
RP/0/RP0/CPU0:PE-2#show bgp l2vpn evpn rd 172.19.0.10:1 [1][172.19.0.10:1][0000.
  fc00.0102.0000.0000][4294967295]/184
BGP routing table entry for [1][172.19.0.10:1][0000.fc00.0102.0000.0000]
  [4294967295]/184, Route Distinguisher: 172.19.0.10:1
Versions:
  Process          bRIB/RIB  SendTblVer
  Speaker              336         336
Last Modified: Aug 27 09:32:27.489 for 4w5d
Paths: (1 available, best #1)
  Not advertised to any peer
  Path #1: Received by speaker 0
  Not advertised to any peer
  Local
    fc00:0:105::1 (metric 21) from fc00:0:107::1 (172.19.0.10)
      Received Label 0
      Origin IGP, localpref 100, valid, internal, best, group-best,
  import-candidate, not-in-vrf
      Received Path ID 0, Local Path ID 1, version 336
      Extended community: EVPN ESI Label:0x01:3 RT:65000:200 RT:65000:201
      Originator: 172.19.0.10, Cluster list: 172.19.0.12
RP/0/RP0/CPU0:PE-2#
```

The relevant values from this CLI output correspond with fields from the EVPN Route Type 1 per-ESI Ethernet A-D route packet capture in Example 6-2. They are highlighted and briefly described here:

- **Route Type:** Ethernet A-D Route Type 1

- **Route Distinguisher:** Unique RD 172.19.0.10:1 per PE router and Ethernet segment

- **ESI:** Ethernet segment identifier 00:00:fc:00:01:02:00:00:00:00

- **Ethernet Tag ID:** Reserved Ethernet Tag ID MAX-ET 4294967295 (0xFFFFFFFF)

- **MPLS Label:** 0

- **Path Attribute - EXTENDED_COMMUNITIES:**

  - **ESI MPLS labels Single active bit:** Indicates whether the all-active or single-active state is configured. In the packet capture, the single-active bit is set to 1 as this is from a single-active redundancy service. In an all-active scenario, the single-active bit would be set to 0.

- **ESI MPLS label, MPLS label:** Consists of three octets where the higher-order 20 bits is the label. This is the split-horizon label encapsulating the BUM traffic being forwarded to the peer ESI PE routers simultaneously with the received EVPN inclusive multicast label. The packet capture in Example 6-2 displays a value of 3 as it is set to implicit null. This capture is representative of a port-active service, and any BUM traffic forwarded to the peer PE router (ESI standby mode) will not require the split-horizon label. The EVPN inclusive multicast label is described later in this chapter, in the section "EVPN Route Type 3: Inclusive Multicast Route."

  □ **Route Target:** All EVI route targets

Example 6-2   *EVPN Route Type 1: Per-ESI Ethernet A-D Route Detailed Packet Capture (Single-Active)*

```
Border Gateway Protocol - UPDATE Message
    Path attributes
        Path Attribute - MP_REACH_NLRI
            Flags: 0x90, Optional, Extended-Length, Non-transitive, Complete
            Type Code: MP_REACH_NLRI (14)
            Length: 48
            Address family identifier (AFI): Layer-2 VPN (25)
            Subsequent address family identifier (SAFI): EVPN (70)
            Next hop: fc00:0:105::1
                IPv6 Address: fc00:0:105::1
            Number of Subnetwork points of attachment (SNPA): 0
            Network Layer Reachability Information (NLRI)
                EVPN NLRI: Ethernet AD Route
                    Route Type: Ethernet AD Route (1)
                    Length: 25
                    Route Distinguisher: 0001ac13000a0001 (172.19.0.10:1)
                    ESI: 00:00:fc:00:01:02:00:00:00:00
                        ESI Type: ESI 9 bytes value (0)
                        ESI Value: 00 fc 00 01 02 00 00 00 00
                        ESI 9 bytes value: 00 fc 00 01 02 00 00 00 00
                    Ethernet Tag ID: 4294967295
                    0000 0000 0000 0000 0000 .... = MPLS Label 1: 0
        Path Attribute - ORIGIN: IGP
        Path Attribute - AS_PATH: empty
        Path Attribute - LOCAL_PREF: 100
        Path Attribute - EXTENDED_COMMUNITIES
            Flags: 0xc0, Optional, Transitive, Complete
            Type Code: EXTENDED_COMMUNITIES (16)
            Length: 24
            Carried extended communities: (3 communities)
```

```
        ESI MPLS Label: Single-Active redundancy, Label: 3 [Transitive EVPN]
              Type: Transitive EVPN (0x06)
              Subtype (EVPN): ESI MPLS Label (0x01)
              .... ...1 = Single active bit: Single-Active redundancy
              MPLS Label: 48
              [0000 0000 0000 0000 0011 .... = MPLS Label: 3]
        Route Target: 65000:200 [Transitive 2-Octet AS-Specific]
              Type: Transitive 2-Octet AS-Specific (0x00)
              Subtype (AS2): Route Target (0x02)
              2-Octet AS: 65000
              4-Octet AN: 200
        Route Target: 65000:201 [Transitive 2-Octet AS-Specific]
              Type: Transitive 2-Octet AS-Specific (0x00)
              Subtype (AS2): Route Target (0x02)
              2-Octet AS: 65000
              4-Octet AN: 201
<snip>
```

■ **Aliasing (per-EVI Ethernet A-D route):** In an all-active multihomed attached device or network scenario, a MAC/IP address might only be learned through one of the ingress PE routers, leading to a situation where the remote EVPN PE routers only forward traffic to that specific PE router, resulting in uneven traffic flow to the MHN/MHD. Aliasing is therefore the ability for a PE router to signal to its remote EVPN PE peers that it has reachability to an attached ES even though it may not have learned certain MAC/IP addresses from the attached ES. This then allows the remote EVPN PE routers to effectively load balance traffic across the participating MHN/MHD PE routers. The combination of the per-ESI Ethernet A-D route with the single-active bit set to 0 in the BGP Ext-community flag fields (where 0 = all-active and 1 = single-active) together with the per-EVI Ethernet A-D route with the included aliasing MPLS labels are used for aliasing purposes. Traffic forwarding from the ingress EVPN PE routers toward the MHN/MHD will therefore use both the MPLS label from a Route Type 2 MAC route as well as the MPLS label from the per-EVI Ethernet A-D route to reach and load balance across both egress PE routers.

The command **show bgp l2vpn evpn rd 172.19.0.19:200 [1][0000.fc00.0102.0000.0000] [0]/120** from router PE-2 in Output 6-3 and its corresponding detailed EVPN Route Type 1 per-EVI Ethernet A-D route packet capture in Example 6-3 are highlighted and briefly described in the following list:

■ **Route Type:** Ethernet A-D Route Type 1

■ **Route Distinguisher:** Unique route distinguisher 172.19.0.10:200 per-PE router per EVI

- **ESI:** Ethernet segment identifier 00:00:fc:00:01:02:00:00:00:00

- **Ethernet Tag ID:** 0

- **MPLS Label:** Aliasing label set to 917504 (though the CLI command outputs this as 0xe00000 for the 20-bit label and the most significant 16 bits would be the SRv6 uSID 0xe000)

- **Path Attribute - EXTENDED_COMMUNITIES:**

  - **Route Target:** Per-EVI route target 65000:200

- **Path Attribute - BGP Prefix-SID:**

  - **SRv6 Endpoint Behavior:** End.DT2U with NEXT-CSID (0x0043) (This refers to the endpoint behavior with decapsulation and unicast MAC Layer 2 lookup [End. DT2U]. Refer to Chapter 3, "What Is Segment Routing over IPv6 (SRv6)?" for more details.

Output 6-3   *BGP Output for EVPN Route Type 1 per-EVI A-D Entry*

```
RP/0/RP0/CPU0:PE-2#show bgp l2vpn evpn rd 172.19.0.10:200
  [1] [0000.fc00.0102.0000.0000] [0]/120
BGP routing table entry for [1][0000.fc00.0102.0000.0000][0]/120,
  Route Distinguisher: 172.19.0.10:200
<snip>
Paths: (1 available, best #1)
  Not advertised to any peer
  Path #1: Received by speaker 0
  Not advertised to any peer
  Local
    fc00:0:105::1 (metric 21) from fc00:0:107::1 (172.19.0.10)
      Received Label 0xe00000
      Origin IGP, localpref 100, valid, internal, best, group-best,
import-candidate, not-in-vrf
      Received Path ID 0, Local Path ID 1, version 322
      Extended community: RT:65000:200
      Originator: 172.19.0.10, Cluster list: 172.19.0.12
      PSID-Type:L2, SubTLV Count:1
       SubTLV:
        T:1(Sid information), Sid:fc00:0:105::, Behavior:67, SS-TLV Count:1
         SubSubTLV:
          T:1(Sid structure):
RP/0/RP0/CPU0:PE-2#
```

Example 6-3   *EVPN Route Type 1: Per-EVI Ethernet A-D Route Detailed Packet Capture (Single-Active)*

```
Border Gateway Protocol - UPDATE Message
    Path attributes
        Path Attribute - MP_REACH_NLRI
            Flags: 0x90, Optional, Extended-Length, Non-transitive, Complete
            Type Code: MP_REACH_NLRI (14)
            Length: 48
            Address family identifier (AFI): Layer-2 VPN (25)
            Subsequent address family identifier (SAFI): EVPN (70)
            Next hop: fc00:0:105::1
                IPv6 Address: fc00:0:105::1
            Number of Subnetwork points of attachment (SNPA): 0
            Network Layer Reachability Information (NLRI)
                EVPN NLRI: Ethernet AD Route
                    Route Type: Ethernet AD Route (1)
                    Length: 25
                    Route Distinguisher: 0001ac13000a00c8 (172.19.0.10:200)
                    ESI: 00:00:fc:00:01:02:00:00:00:00
                        ESI Type: ESI 9 bytes value (0)
                        ESI Value: 00 fc 00 01 02 00 00 00 00
                        ESI 9 bytes value: 00 fc 00 01 02 00 00 00 00
                    Ethernet Tag ID: 0
                    1110 0000 0000 0000 0000 .... = MPLS Label 1: 917504
        Path Attribute - ORIGIN: IGP
        Path Attribute - AS_PATH: empty
        Path Attribute - LOCAL_PREF: 100
        Path Attribute - EXTENDED_COMMUNITIES
            Flags: 0xc0, Optional, Transitive, Complete
            Type Code: EXTENDED_COMMUNITIES (16)
            Length: 8
            Carried extended communities: (1 community)
                Route Target: 65000:200 [Transitive 2-Octet AS-Specific]
                    Type: Transitive 2-Octet AS-Specific (0x00)
                    Subtype (AS2): Route Target (0x02)
                    2-Octet AS: 65000
                    4-Octet AN: 200
        Path Attribute - BGP Prefix-SID
            Flags: 0xc0, Optional, Transitive, Complete
            Type Code: BGP Prefix-SID (40)
            Length: 37
            SRv6 L3 Service
                Type: SRv6 L2 Service (6)
```

```
            Length: 34
            Reserved: 00
            SRv6 Service Sub-TLVs
                SRv6 Service Sub-TLV - SRv6 SID Information
                    Type: SRv6 SID Information (1)
                    Length: 30
                    Reserved: 00
                    SRv6 SID Value: fc00:0:105::
                    SRv6 SID Flags: 0x00
                    SRv6 Endpoint Behavior: End.DT2U with NEXT-CSID (0x0043)
<snip>
```

The detailed EVPN Route Type 1 per-EVI Ethernet A-D Route packet capture in Example 6-4 is from an E-Line (VPWS) configured service. The differences between this route type and the E-LAN Route Type 1 per-EVI Ethernet A-D route are briefly described in the following list:

- **Route Type:** Ethernet A-D Route Type 1

- **Route Distinguisher:** Unique RD 172.19.0.10:300 per-PE router per EVI

- **ESI:** Ethernet segment identifier manually configured as 00:00:fc:00:01:03:00:00:00:00)

- **Ethernet Tag ID:** Configured l2vpn xconnect Service-ID 300300

- **MPLS Label:** Label set to 917680, (though the CLI command outputs this as 0xe00b00 for the 20-bit label and the most significant 16 bits would be the SRv6 uSID 0xe00b)

- **Path Attribute - EXTENDED_COMMUNITIES:**

  - **Layer 2 Attributes: Flags: 0x0002, P flag:** Set to 1 as this is a capture from an all-active multihomed PE router (See RFC 8214 for information on these control flag definitions.)

  - **Layer 2 Attributes: L2 MTU:** According to RFC 8214, "a received L2 MTU of zero means that no MTU checking against the local MTU is needed (This packet capture example is from a PE router where MTU checking is not explicitly configured, as indicated in the packet capture as 0.)

  - **Route Target:** Per-EVI route target 65000:300

- **Path Attribute - BGP Prefix-SID:**

  - **SRv6 Endpoint Behavior:** End.DX2 with NEXT-CSID (0x0041) refers to the endpoint behavior with decapsulation and Layer 2 cross-connect (End.DX2). (Refer to Chapter 3 for more details.)

Example 6-4   *EVPN Route Type 1: Per-EVI Ethernet A-D Route Detailed Packet Capture (E-Line All-Active)*

```
Border Gateway Protocol - UPDATE Message
    Path attributes
        Path Attribute - MP_REACH_NLRI
            Flags: 0x90, Optional, Extended-Length, Non-transitive, Complete
            Type Code: MP_REACH_NLRI (14)
            Length: 48
            Address family identifier (AFI): Layer-2 VPN (25)
            Subsequent address family identifier (SAFI): EVPN (70)
            Next hop: fc00:0:105::1
                IPv6 Address: fc00:0:105::1
            Number of Subnetwork points of attachment (SNPA): 0
            Network Layer Reachability Information (NLRI)
                EVPN NLRI: Ethernet AD Route
                    Route Type: Ethernet AD Route (1)
                    Length: 25
                    Route Distinguisher: 0001ac13000a012c (172.19.0.10:300)
                    ESI: 00:00:fc:00:01:03:00:00:00:00
                        ESI Type: ESI 9 bytes value (0)
                        ESI Value: 00 fc 00 01 03 00 00 00 00
                        ESI 9 bytes value: 00 fc 00 01 03 00 00 00 00
                    Ethernet Tag ID: 300300
                    1110 0000 0000 1011 0000 .... = MPLS Label 1: 917680
        Path Attribute - ORIGIN: IGP
        Path Attribute - AS_PATH: empty
        Path Attribute - LOCAL_PREF: 100
        Path Attribute - EXTENDED_COMMUNITIES
            Flags: 0xc0, Optional, Transitive, Complete
            Type Code: EXTENDED_COMMUNITIES (16)
            Length: 16
            Carried extended communities: (2 communities)
                Layer 2 Attributes: flags: 0x0002, L2 MTU: 0 [Transitive EVPN]
                    Type: Transitive EVPN (0x06)
                    Subtype (EVPN): Layer 2 Attributes (0x04)
                    Flags: 0x0002, P flag
                        0000 0000 000. .... = Reserved: 0x000
                        .... .... ...0 .... = CI flag: Not set
                        .... .... .... 0... = F flag: Not set
                        .... .... .... .0.. = C flag: Not set
                        .... .... .... ..1. = P flag: Set
                        .... .... .... ...0 = B flag: Not set
                    L2 MTU: 0
```

```
                        Reserved: 0000
                  Route Target: 65000:300 [Transitive 2-Octet AS-Specific]
                        Type: Transitive 2-Octet AS-Specific (0x00)
                        Subtype (AS2): Route Target (0x02)
                        2-Octet AS: 65000
                        4-Octet AN: 300
            Path Attribute - BGP Prefix-SID
                  Flags: 0xc0, Optional, Transitive, Complete
                  Type Code: BGP Prefix-SID (40)
                  Length: 37
                  SRv6 L3 Service
                        Type: SRv6 L2 Service (6)
                        Length: 34
                        Reserved: 00
                        SRv6 Service Sub-TLVs
                              SRv6 Service Sub-TLV - SRv6 SID Information
                                    Type: SRv6 SID Information (1)
                                    Length: 30
                                    Reserved: 00
                                    SRv6 SID Value: fc00:0:105::
                                    SRv6 SID Flags: 0x00
                                    SRv6 Endpoint Behavior: End.DX2 with NEXT-CSID (0x0041)
                                    Reserved: 00
<snip>
```

EVPN Route Type 2: MAC/IP Advertisement Route

One of the many advantages of EVPN over VPLS is control plane learning of MAC/IP addresses via BGP, and although the EVPN PE router does data plane learning for locally attached devices or networks, the remote MAC/IP addresses are learned via BGP.

The EVPN Route Type 2 MAC/IP advertisement route, shown in Output 6-4, is a specific route type that contains the actual MAC/IP route details and is similar in many ways to an L3VPN IP BGP route. This is relevant Route Type 2 MAC route information output from the command **show bgp l2vpn evpn rd 172.19.0.10:200 [2][0][48][1011.1100.0001] [0]/104** executed on router PE-2:

- **Advertised mac-address:** 1011.1100.0001

- **Route Distinguisher:** 172.19.0.10:200

- **Received Label:** 0xe00000, which in this example is the SRv6 uSID 0xe000

- **Extended community:** 0x0000 07d0 RT:65000:200, where 0x0000 07d0 is the VLAN ID 2000 of the attached access circuit and the attached route target 65000:200

- **EVPN ESI:** 0000.fc00.0102.0000.0000

- **Sid: fc00:0:105:::** Configured SRv6 locator of the originating PE router

- **Behavior: 67:** Refers to the SRv6 endpoint behavior End.DT2U

Output 6-4   *BGP Output for a Single EVPN Route Type 2 Entry*

```
RP/0/RP0/CPU0:PE-2#show bgp l2vpn evpn rd 172.19.0.10:200 [2][0][48][1011.1100.0001]
  [0]/104
BGP routing table entry for [2][0][48][1011.1100.0001][0]/104, Route Distinguisher:
  172.19.0.10:200
Paths: (1 available, best #1)
  Not advertised to any peer
  Path #1: Received by speaker 0
  Not advertised to any peer
  Local
    fc00:0:105::1 (metric 21) from fc00:0:107::1 (172.19.0.10)
      Received Label 0xe00000
      Origin IGP, localpref 100, valid, internal, best, group-best,
  import-candidate, not-in-vrf
      Received Path ID 0, Local Path ID 1, version 4084
      Extended community: Flags 0x10: SoO:172.19.0.10:200 0x060e:0000.0000.07d0
RT:65000:200
      Originator: 172.19.0.10, Cluster list: 172.19.0.12
      EVPN ESI: 0000.fc00.0102.0000.0000
      PSID-Type:L2, SubTLV Count:1
        SubTLV:
        T:1(Sid information), Sid:fc00:0:105::, Behavior:67, SS-TLV Count:1
          SubSubTLV:
          T:1(Sid structure):
RP/0/RP0/CPU0:PE-2#
```

In the detailed EVPN Route Type 2 MAC route packet capture in Example 6-5, the relevant values that correspond with the CLI outputs of Output 6-4 are highlighted and described in the following list:

- **Route Type:** MAC Advertisement Route Type 2

- **RD:** Unique RD 172.19.0.10:200 per-PE router per EVI

- **ESI:** Ethernet segment identifier 00:00:fc:00:01:02:00:00:00:00, from where this route originates

- **Ethernet Tag ID:** VLAN ID for VLAN-aware bundling service interface or set to 0, as in this example

- **MAC Address:** MAC address of the advertised route is 10:11:11:00:00:01

- **IP Address:** IP address, if applicable

- **MPLS Label:** EVPN label 917504 in the packet capture (though the CLI command outputs it in an SRv6 uSID format as 0xe00000)

- **Path Attribute - EXTENDED_COMMUNITIES:**

  - **Route Origin:** Route originating router

  - **EVPN attachment circuit:** VLAN identification 0x7d0 (2000)

  - **Route target:** Route target set as 65000:200

- **Path Attribute - BGP Prefix-SID:**

  - **SRv6 SID Value:** fc00:0:105:: as the configured SRv6 locator of the originating PE router

  - **SRv6 Endpoint Behavior:** SRv6 endpoint behavior of End.DT2U (0x0043) refers to the endpoint behavior with decapsulation and unicast MAC L2 table lookup

Example 6-5   *EVPN Route Type 2: MAC Route Detailed Packet Capture*

```
Border Gateway Protocol - UPDATE Message
    Path attributes
        Path Attribute - MP_REACH_NLRI
            Flags: 0x90, Optional, Extended-Length, Non-transitive, Complete
            Type Code: MP_REACH_NLRI (14)
            Length: 56
            Address family identifier (AFI): Layer-2 VPN (25)
            Subsequent address family identifier (SAFI): EVPN (70)
            Next hop: fc00:0:105::1
                IPv6 Address: fc00:0:105::1
            Number of Subnetwork points of attachment (SNPA): 0
            Network Layer Reachability Information (NLRI)
                EVPN NLRI: MAC Advertisement Route
                    Route Type: MAC Advertisement Route (2)
                    Length: 33
                    Route Distinguisher: 0001ac13000a00c8 (172.19.0.10:200)
                    ESI: 00:00:fc:00:01:02:00:00:00:00
                        ESI Type: ESI 9 bytes value (0)
                        ESI Value: 00 fc 00 01 02 00 00 00 00
                        ESI 9 bytes value: 00 fc 00 01 02 00 00 00 00
                    Ethernet Tag ID: 0
                    MAC Address Length: 48
                    MAC Address: 10:11:11:00:00:01 (10:11:11:00:00:01)
                    IP Address Length: 0
                    IP Address: NOT INCLUDED
                        [Expert Info (Note/Protocol): IP Address: NOT INCLUDED]
                            [IP Address: NOT INCLUDED]
                            [Severity level: Note]
```

```
                            [Group: Protocol]
                    1110 0000 0000 0000 0000 .... = MPLS Label 1: 917504
        Path Attribute - ORIGIN: IGP
        Path Attribute - AS_PATH: empty
        Path Attribute - LOCAL_PREF: 100
        Path Attribute - EXTENDED_COMMUNITIES
            Flags: 0xc0, Optional, Transitive, Complete
            Type Code: EXTENDED_COMMUNITIES (16)
            Length: 24
            Carried extended communities: (3 communities)
                Route Origin: 172.19.0.10:200 [Transitive IPv4-Address-Specific]
                    Type: Transitive IPv4-Address-Specific (0x01)
                    Subtype (IPv4): Route Origin (0x03)
                    IPv4 address: 172.19.0.10
                    2-Octet AN: 200
                EVPN Attachment Circuit: 0x0000 0x0000 0x07d0 [Transitive EVPN]
                    Type: Transitive EVPN (0x06)
                    Subtype (EVPN): EVPN Attachment Circuit (0x0e)
                    Raw Value: 0x0000 0x0000 0x07d0
                Route Target: 65000:200 [Transitive 2-Octet AS-Specific]
                    Type: Transitive 2-Octet AS-Specific (0x00)
                    Subtype (AS2): Route Target (0x02)
                    2-Octet AS: 65000
                    4-Octet AN: 200
        Path Attribute - BGP Prefix-SID
            Flags: 0xc0, Optional, Transitive, Complete
            Type Code: BGP Prefix-SID (40)
            Length: 37
            SRv6 L3 Service
                Type: SRv6 L2 Service (6)
                Length: 34
                Reserved: 00
                SRv6 Service Sub-TLVs
                    SRv6 Service Sub-TLV - SRv6 SID Information
                        Type: SRv6 SID Information (1)
                        Length: 30
                        Reserved: 00
                        SRv6 SID Value: fc00:0:105::
                        SRv6 SID Flags: 0x00
                        SRv6 Endpoint Behavior: End.DT2U with NEXT-CSID (0x0043)
<snip>
```

EVPN Route Type 3: Inclusive Multicast Route

The inclusive multicast Route Type 3 route is used for transporting BUM frames throughout the EVI, essentially allowing for BUM traffic that is ingress replicated by the PE router to be encapsulated with the received inclusive multicast Ethernet tag and then forwarded to each of the PE routers participating in the EVI.

The command **show bgp l2vpn evpn rd 172.19.0.10:200 [3][0][32][172.19.0.10]/80** displayed in Output 6-5 provides the following relevant EVPN Route Type 3 information for a specific EVI:

- **Route Distinguisher:** 172.19.0.10:200

- **Extended community:** Route target 65000:200

- **Provider Multicast Service Interface (PMSI) encapsulating MPLS Label:** Allocated SRv6 uSID 0xe00100

- **Sid fc00:0:105:::** The SRv6 locator of the originating PE router

- **Behavior: 68:** Refers to the SRv6 endpoint behavior End.DT2M

Output 6-5 *BGP Output for a Single EVPN Route Type 3 Entry*

```
RP/0/RP0/CPU0:PE-2#show bgp l2vpn evpn rd 172.19.0.10:200 [3][0][32][172.19.0.10]/80
BGP routing table entry for [3][0][32][172.19.0.10]/80, Route
Distinguisher: 172.19.0.10:200
Paths: (1 available, best #1)
  Not advertised to any peer
  Path #1: Received by speaker 0
  Not advertised to any peer
  Local
    fc00:0:105::1 (metric 21) from fc00:0:107::1 (172.19.0.10)
      Origin IGP, localpref 100, valid, internal, best, group-best,
import-candidate, not-in-vrf
      Received Path ID 0, Local Path ID 1, version 4017
      Extended community: RT:65000:200
      Originator: 172.19.0.10, Cluster list: 172.19.0.12
      PMSI: flags 0x00, type 6, label 0xe00100, ID 0xac13000a
      PSID-Type:L2, SubTLV Count:1
       SubTLV:
        T:1(Sid information), Sid:fc00:0:105::, Behavior:68, SS-TLV Count:1
         SubSubTLV:
          T:1(Sid structure):
RP/0/RP0/CPU0:PE-2#
```

From the detailed EVPN Route Type 3 inclusive multicast route packet capture in Example 6-6, the relevant values from this capture that correspond with the CLI output in Output 6-5 are highlighted and described in the following list:

■ **Route Type:** Inclusive multicast Route Type 3

■ **RD:** Unique RD 172.19.0.10:200 per-PE router per EVI

■ **Ethernet Tag ID:** VLAN ID for VLAN-aware bundling service interface; otherwise set to 0, as shown in the Example 6-6 packet capture

■ **Path Attribute - EXTENDED_COMMUNITIES:**

   ■ **Route target:** Route target 65000:200

■ **Path Attribute - PMSI_TUNNEL_ATTRIBUTE:**

   ■ **Tunnel Type: Ingress Replication (6):** Indicates that the ingress PE router will replicate every BUM frame and unicast these frames as separate unicast frames to the remote egress PE routers (See RFC 6514 for additional tunnel types used to establish the PMSI tunnel.)

   ■ **MPLS Label:** Multicast MPLS label 917584 (though the CLI command displays this as label 0xe00100)

   ■ **Tunnel Identifier:** According to RFC 6514, "when the Tunnel Type is set to Ingress Replication, the Tunnel Identifier carries the unicast tunnel endpoint IP address of the local PE that is to be this PE's receiving endpoint address for the tunnel"

■ **Path Attribute - BGP Prefix-SID:**

   ■ **SRv6 SID Value:** SRv6 locator of the originating PE router fc00:0:105::

   ■ **SRv6 Endpoint Behavior:** SRv6 endpoint behavior of End.DT2M refers to decapsulation and L2 flooding

Example 6-6   *EVPN Route Type 3: Inclusive Multicast Route Detailed Packet Capture*

```
Border Gateway Protocol - UPDATE Message
    Path attributes
        Path Attribute - MP_REACH_NLRI
            Flags: 0x90, Optional, Extended-Length, Non-transitive, Complete
            Type Code: MP_REACH_NLRI (14)
            Length: 40
            Address family identifier (AFI): Layer-2 VPN (25)
            Subsequent address family identifier (SAFI): EVPN (70)
            Next hop: fc00:0:105::1
                IPv6 Address: fc00:0:105::1
            Number of Subnetwork points of attachment (SNPA): 0
            Network Layer Reachability Information (NLRI)
                EVPN NLRI: Inclusive Multicast Route
```

```
                Route Type: Inclusive Multicast Route (3)
                Length: 17
                Route Distinguisher: 0001ac13000a00c8 (172.19.0.10:200)
                Ethernet Tag ID: 0
                IP Address Length: 32
                IPv4 address: 172.19.0.10
    Path Attribute - ORIGIN: IGP
    Path Attribute - AS_PATH: empty
    Path Attribute - LOCAL_PREF: 100
    Path Attribute - EXTENDED_COMMUNITIES
        Flags: 0xc0, Optional, Transitive, Complete
        Type Code: EXTENDED_COMMUNITIES (16)
        Length: 8
        Carried extended communities: (1 community)
            Route Target: 65000:200 [Transitive 2-Octet AS-Specific]
                Type: Transitive 2-Octet AS-Specific (0x00)
                Subtype (AS2): Route Target (0x02)
                2-Octet AS: 65000
                4-Octet AN: 200
    Path Attribute - PMSI_TUNNEL_ATTRIBUTE
        Flags: 0xc0, Optional, Transitive, Complete
        Type Code: PMSI_TUNNEL_ATTRIBUTE (22)
        Length: 9
        Flags: 0
        Tunnel Type: Ingress Replication (6)
        1110 0000 0000 0001 0000 .... = MPLS Label: 917520
        Tunnel ID: tunnel end point -> 172.19.0.10
            Tunnel type ingress replication IP end point: 172.19.0.10
    Path Attribute - BGP Prefix-SID
        Flags: 0xc0, Optional, Transitive, Complete
        Type Code: BGP Prefix-SID (40)
        Length: 37
        SRv6 L3 Service
            Type: SRv6 L2 Service (6)
            Length: 34
            Reserved: 00
            SRv6 Service Sub-TLVs
                SRv6 Service Sub-TLV - SRv6 SID Information
                    Type: SRv6 SID Information (1)
                    Length: 30
                    Reserved: 00
                    SRv6 SID Value: fc00:0:105::
                    SRv6 SID Flags: 0x00
                    SRv6 Endpoint Behavior: End.DT2M with NEXT-CSID (0x0044)
<snip>
```

EVPN Route Type 4: Ethernet Segment Route

Route Type 4 is used for multihomed Ethernet segment auto-discovery as well as the designated forwarder (DF) election procedure.

The PE routers filter routes based on the extended community ES import route type and therefore import only those Ethernet segment RT-4 routes that the PE router itself is connected to (in multihomed scenarios).

In a multihomed scenario, one of the attached PE routers is elected the designated forwarder (DF), and its function is to forward BUM traffic to the local attached Ethernet segment, thereby preventing duplicate BUM frames from reaching the Ethernet segment.

The EVPN Route Type 4 route details shown in the CLI command in Output 6-6 provide the following relevant information:

- **Route Distinguisher:** 172.19.0.10:0, which is associated with the global bridge domain into which this Route Type 4 has been imported (This global bridge domain or global MAC VRF table has a global scope on the router in that it stores routes that are not associated with the service-associated L2 bridge domains but rather stores the local and remote learned Route Type 4 Ethernet segment routes together with local Route Type 1 per-ESI Ethernet A-D routes.)

- **Extended community: EVPN ES Import:** The MAC portion of the ESI = 00fc.0001.0200

- **Extended community: DF Election:** 0:0x0028:0 for exchanging the DF election algorithm and capabilities

Output 6-6 *BGP Output for a Single EVPN Route Type 4 Entry*

```
RP/0/RP0/CPU0:PE-2#show bgp l2vpn evpn rd 172.19.0.10:0 [4][0000.
  fc00.0102.0000.0000][32][172.19.0.10]/128
BGP routing table entry for [4][0000.fc00.0102.0000.0000][32][172.19.0.10]/128,
Route Distinguisher: 172.19.0.10:0
Paths: (1 available, best #1)
  Not advertised to any peer
  Path #1: Received by speaker 0
  Not advertised to any peer
  Local
    fc00:0:105::1 (metric 21) from fc00:0:107::1 (172.19.0.10)
      Origin IGP, localpref 100, valid, internal, best, group-best,
import-candidate, not-in-vrf
      Received Path ID 0, Local Path ID 1, version 6500
      Extended community: EVPN ES Import:00fc.0001.0200 DF Election:0:0x0028:0
      Originator: 172.19.0.10, Cluster list: 172.19.0.12
RP/0/RP0/CPU0:PE-2#
```

From the detailed EVPN Route Type 4 Ethernet segment route in the packet capture displayed in Example 6-7, the relevant values from this capture that correspond with the CLI outputs in Output 6-6 are highlighted and briefly described in the following list:

- **Route Type:** Ethernet segment Route Type 4

- **Route Distinguisher:** Route distinguisher 172.19.0.10:0 for all Route Type 4 routes per PE router, in this case PE-1

- **ESI:** Ethernet segment identifier 00:00:fc:00:01:02:00:00:00:00

- **IPv4 Address:** Originating router IP address 172.19.0.10, used in determining a PE router's ordinal number and used in the modulo calculation to determine which router will be the designated forwarder

- **Path Attribute - EXTENDED_COMMUNITIES:**

  - **ES Import RT:** The ES import RT comprising of the 6-byte MAC address portion of the ESI 00:fc:00:01:02:00 limits these Ethernet segment Route Type 4 routes to PE routers that are connected to the same local attached Ethernet segment

  - **DF Election:** DF election and capabilities exchanged. The default DF election is based on the modulo election algorithm per ESI only via the EVPN Route Type 4 routes. The port-active modulo DF election is based on a modulus-based algorithm described in RFC 7432 and updated in RFC 8584. The index in the next hop IP list and sorted by IP address (lowest to highest) is based on the following:

    - ☐ $(V \bmod T) = J$

    - ☐ V: byte # [3:6] in the ESI (last 4 bytes of the ES import RT: 00.01.02.00)

    - ☐ T: Total number of PEs connected to the Ethernet segment

    - ☐ J: The PE to be elected as active

Example 6-7   *EVPN Route Type 4: Ethernet Segment Route Detailed Packet Capture*

```
Border Gateway Protocol - UPDATE Message
    Path attributes
        Path Attribute - MP_REACH_NLRI
            Flags: 0x90, Optional, Extended-Length, Non-transitive, Complete
            Type Code: MP_REACH_NLRI (14)
            Length: 46
            Address family identifier (AFI): Layer-2 VPN (25)
            Subsequent address family identifier (SAFI): EVPN (70)
            Next hop: fc00:0:105::1
                IPv6 Address: fc00:0:105::1
            Number of Subnetwork points of attachment (SNPA): 0
            Network Layer Reachability Information (NLRI)
                EVPN NLRI: Ethernet Segment Route
```

```
                     Route Type: Ethernet Segment Route (4)
                     Length: 23
                     Route Distinguisher: 0001ac13000a0000 (172.19.0.10:0)
                     ESI: 00:00:fc:00:01:02:00:00:00:00
                          ESI Type: ESI 9 bytes value (0)
                          ESI Value: 00 fc 00 01 02 00 00 00 00
                          ESI 9 bytes value: 00 fc 00 01 02 00 00 00 00
                     IP Address Length: 32
                     IPv4 address: 172.19.0.10
         Path Attribute - ORIGIN: IGP
         Path Attribute - AS_PATH: empty
         Path Attribute - LOCAL_PREF: 100
         Path Attribute - EXTENDED_COMMUNITIES
             Flags: 0xc0, Optional, Transitive, Complete
             Type Code: EXTENDED_COMMUNITIES (16)
             Length: 16
             Carried extended communities: (2 communities)
                  ES Import: RT: 00:fc:00:01:02:00 [Transitive EVPN]
                     Type: Transitive EVPN (0x06)
                     Subtype (EVPN): ES Import (0x02)
                     ES-Import Route Target: 00:fc:00:01:02:00 (00:fc:00:01:02:00)
                  DF Election: 0x0000 0x2800 0x0000 [Transitive EVPN]
                     Type: Transitive EVPN (0x06)
                     Subtype (EVPN): DF Election (0x06)
                     Raw Value: 0x0000 0x2800 0x0000
<snip>
```

As you have seen, the benefits of EVPN L2VPN technology are due to the EVPN control plane being based on BGP rather than the VPLS architecture's data plane learning and forwarding mechanism. The EVPN benefits discussed here illustrate the ability to provide traffic multipathing, site multihoming, BUM traffic optimization, and improved redundancy capabilities, all of which were not possible with VPLS. The following sections focus on EVPN E-LAN and E-Line service configuration and verification tasks.

EVPN E-LAN

EVPN E-LAN allows for the creation of geographically separated LAN networks as a simulated bridged domain via MPLS, SR-MPLS, or SRv6 core service provider networks. All LAN functionality, such as MAC address learning, MAC address aging, and BUM traffic forwarding, is addressed across these separated LAN segments as part of the simulated bridged domain.

The configuration and verification tasks for the EVPN E-LAN service are addressed in this section, but it would not be possible to address all the potential configuration variants. This section will, however, give you an understanding of how to configure these services across an SRv6 provisioned transport network.

Table 6-1 shows the EVPN route types typically used in both E-LAN and E-Tree subscriber services. (Recall that EVPN Route Type 5 routes and higher are beyond the scope of this book.)

Table 6-1 *EVPN (E-LAN and E-Tree) Route Types and Usage*

Type	Route Type Name	Route Use	EVPN
0x1	Ethernet auto-discovery (A-D) route	Used with Extended Community: EVPN ESI Filter Label: ■ MAC address mass withdrawal (fast convergence) ■ Split-horizon label advertisement ■ Aliasing (load balancing)	Used
0x2	MAC/IP advertisement route	Used with MAC mobility extended community Used with default gateway extended community ■ Advertising MAC address and MAC/IP binding (ARP) ■ MAC mobility	Used
0x3	Inclusive multicast route	Used with PMSI tunnel attribute Used for forwarding BUM traffic	Used
0x4	Ethernet segment route	Used with ES import extended community ■ Redundancy group discovery (ES connectivity discovery) ■ Designated forwarder election	Used

The network in Figure 6-18 is the SRv6 reference network used for the configuration and verification tasks required to build and verify the EVPN services. You can find additional details in the "SRv6 Reference Network" section of Appendix A.

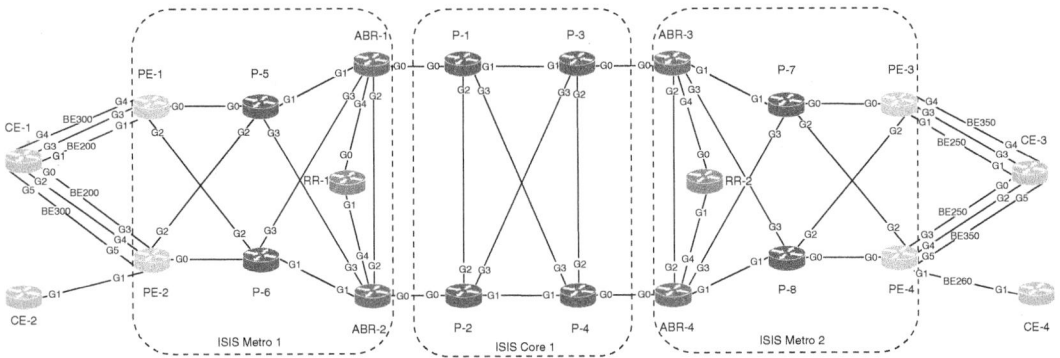

Figure 6-18   *SRv6 Reference Network*

SRv6 EVPN E-LAN Service Configuration and Verification

This section is divided into two sections: one on E-LAN port-active multihomed service configuration and verifications and one on E-LAN single-homed service configuration and verification tasks. It is important to take note of the documented flow of the service configuration and verification tasks throughout these sections in order avoid any confusion that may arise. Associated configuration and verification tasks are categorized as follows:

■ **Ethernet flow point:** Access circuit configuration and verification tasks

■ **EVI:** EVPN configuration and verification tasks

■ **Bridge domain:** L2VPN configuration and verification tasks

■ **BGP:** BGP configuration and verification tasks

Both the EVPN E-LAN and E-LINE services sections adhere to this structure.

EVPN E-LAN Port-Active Multihomed Service

As shown earlier, in Figure 6-8, with the port-active (per-port) multihomed service, a device port is active on a single PE, and this active/standby setup allows for traffic hashing per port. In this example, illustrated in Figure 6-19, the EVPN E-LAN service will be configured between the multihomed routers CE-1 and CE-3.

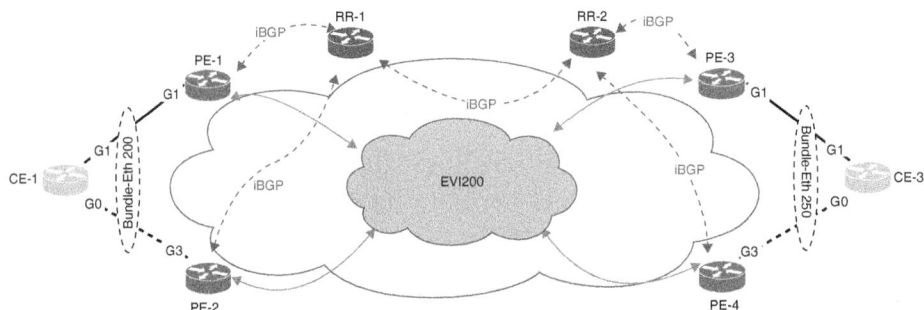

Figure 6-19   *EVPN E-LAN Port-Active MHD Reference Network*

EVPN E-LAN Port-Active MHD (Access Circuit) Configuration

The first of the configuration steps is the access circuit provisioning, as illustrated in Figure 6-20.

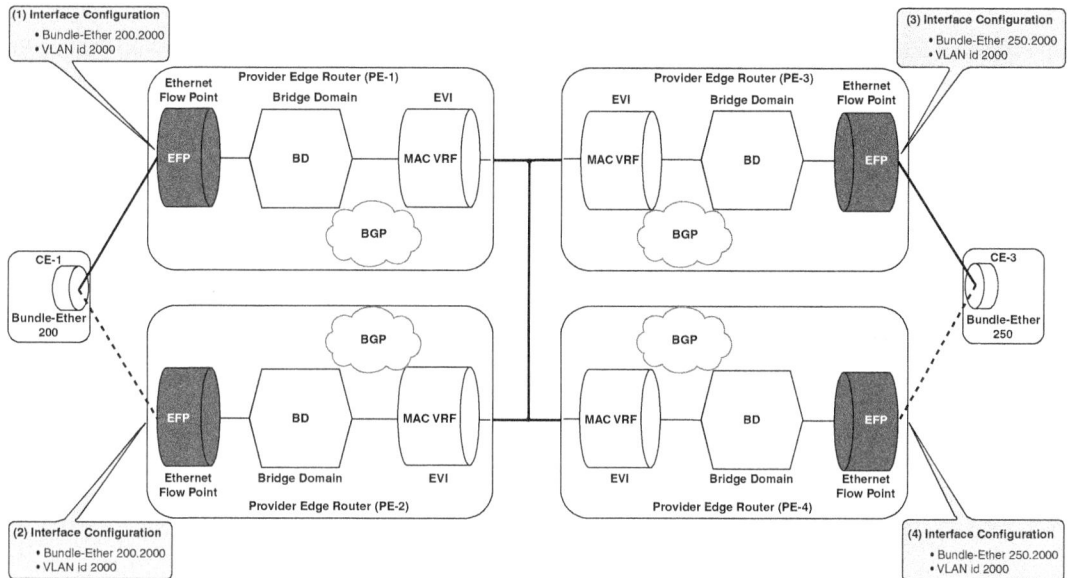

Figure 6-20   *EVPN E-LAN Port-Active MHD EFP (Access Circuit) Configuration Tasks*

The interface configuration tasks in Config 6-1 are the minimum required for router PE-1.

Config 6-1   *EVPN E-LAN Port-Active MHD EFP Configuration on PE-1*

```
!
interface Bundle-Ether200
 description Connected_to_CE-1
 lacp system mac 00fc.0001.0200
!
interface Bundle-Ether200.2000 l2transport
 encapsulation dot1q 2000
!
interface GigabitEthernet0/0/0/1
 description Connected_to_CE-1
 bundle id 200 mode active
 !
!
```

The interface configuration tasks in Config 6-2 are the minimum required for router PE-2.

Config 6-2   *EVPN E-LAN Port-Active MHD EFP Configuration on PE-2*

```
!
interface Bundle-Ether200
 description Connected_to_CE-1
 lacp system mac 00fc.0001.0200
!
interface Bundle-Ether200.2000 l2transport
 encapsulation dot1q 2000
!
interface GigabitEthernet0/0/0/3
 description Connected_to_CE-1
 bundle id 200 mode active
  !
```

The interface configuration tasks in Config 6-3 are the minimum required for router PE-3.

Config 6-3   *EVPN E-LAN Port-Active MHD EFP Configuration on PE-3*

```
!
interface Bundle-Ether250
 description Connected_to_CE-3
 lacp system mac 00fc.0002.0250
!
interface Bundle-Ether250.2000 l2transport
 encapsulation dot1q 2000
!
interface GigabitEthernet0/0/0/1
 description Connected_to_CE-3
 bundle id 250 mode active
  !
```

The interface configuration tasks in Config 6-4 are the minimum required for router PE-4.

Config 6-4   *EVPN E-LAN Port-Active MHD EFP Configuration on PE-4*

```
!
interface Bundle-Ether250
 description Connected_to_CE-3
 lacp system mac 00fc.0002.0250
!
interface Bundle-Ether250.2000 l2transport
 encapsulation dot1q 2000
!
interface GigabitEthernet0/0/0/3
 description Connected_to_CE-3
 bundle id 250 mode active
```

The LACP system MAC address used on both provider edge routers (PE-1 and PE-2) must be configured with the same MAC address in order to allow the CE router (CE-1) to receive this common LACP system ID from the interface bundle-ether 200 physical members. This applies similarly for the LACP system MAC address used on both provider edge routers (PE-3 and PE-4). Note that this LACP system MAC address can either be applied globally to the router or per the bundle-ether interface.

EVPN E-LAN Port-Active MHD EFP (Access Circuit) Verification

This section describes common and useful commands for verifying and troubleshooting the previously configured EVPN MHD E-LAN access circuits service configurations. Figure 6-21 provides an overview of the CLI commands used in this section.

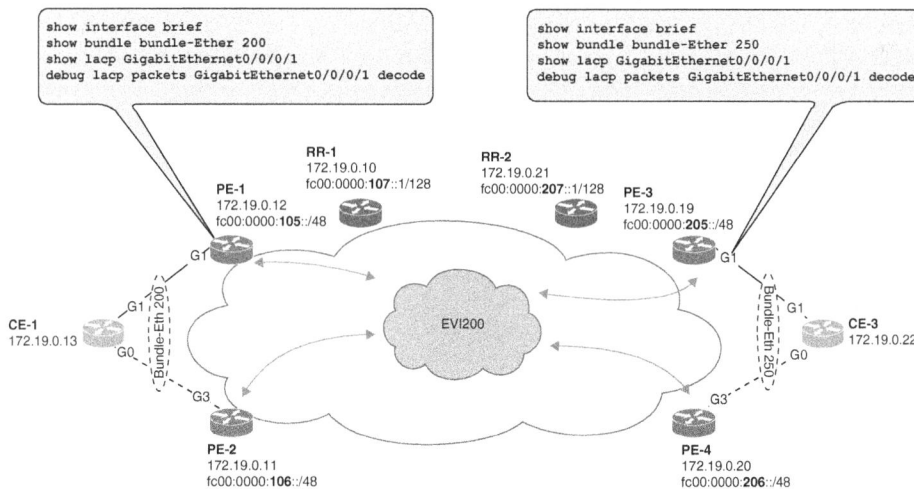

Figure 6-21 *EVPN E-LAN Port-Active MHD EFP (Access Circuit) Verification*

To verify the access circuit state for the port-active multihomed service EVI 200, you must verify the state on both PE-1 and PE-2 in IS-IS Metro 1 and on PE-3 and PE-4 in IS-IS Metro 2. The outputs in this section show examples of some useful basic verification commands.

On the PE router PE-1, the output from **show interfaces brief** in Output 6-7 confirms that the bundle-ether 200 and subinterface BE200.2000 interface/line protocol states are up/up.

Output 6-7 *Interface Output on PE-1*

```
RP/0/RP0/CPU0:PE-1#show interfaces brief

             Intf      Intf      LineP              Encap    MTU      BW
             Name      State     State              Type   (byte)   (Kbps)
      -------------------------------------------------------------------------
```

BE200	up	up	ARPA	1514	1000000
BE200.2000	up	up	802.1Q	1518	1000000
BE200.2001	up	up	802.1Q	1518	1000000
Lo0	up	up	Loopback	1500	0
Gi0/0/0/0	up	up	ARPA	9000	1000000
Gi0/0/0/1	up	up	ARPA	1518	1000000
Gi0/0/0/2	up	up	ARPA	9000	1000000

The command **show bundle bundle-Ether 200** in Output 6-8 provides more details on a per-bundle-ether interface basis; in this case, the bundle-ether 200 status is **Up** and **Active** on interface Gi0/0/0/1. Because bundle-ether 200 is part of the port-active multihomed service configured for EVI 200, bundle-ether 200 will be in active state on PE router PE-1, and on PE-2 it will be in standby mode at the port level. The designated forwarder (DF) election process determined which PE router's port was elected as active and which was placed in standby mode. Refer to the section "EVPN Route Type 4: Ethernet Segment Route" for a more detailed explanation of the DF election process.

Output 6-8   *Interface BE 200 Status on PE-1*

```
RP/0/RP0/CPU0:PE-1#show bundle bundle-Ether 200

Bundle-Ether200
  Status:                                    Up
  Local links <active/standby/configured>:   1 / 0 / 1
  Local bandwidth <effective/available>:     1000000 (1000000) kbps
  MAC address (source):                      001c.f93d.24d6 (Chassis pool)
  Inter-chassis link:                        No
  Minimum active links / bandwidth:          1 / 1 kbps
  Maximum active links:                      64
  Wait while timer:                          2000 ms
  Load balancing:
    Link order signaling:                    Not configured
    Hash type:                               Default
    Locality threshold:                      None
  LACP:                                      Operational
    Flap suppression timer:                  Off
    Cisco extensions:                        Disabled
    Non-revertive:                           Disabled
  mLACP:                                     Not configured
  IPv4 BFD:                                  Not configured
  IPv6 BFD:                                  Not configured


  Port                  Device          State       Port ID         B/W, kbps
  --------------------  --------------- ----------- --------------- ----------
  Gi0/0/0/1             Local           Active      0x8000, 0x0001  1000000
      Link is Active
```

The PE router's bundle-ether interface configurations are set to use the Link Aggregation Control Protocol (LACP) (IEEE 802.3ad). The outputs from the command shown in Output 6-9 executed on router PE-1 and Output 6-10 executed on PE-2 verify that the local interface and partner interface (CE-1 router) system IDs match on the two PE routers. In addition, interface Gi0/0/0/1 on PE-1 is in **Selected** and **Distrib** state, while Gi0/0/0/3 on PE-2 is in **Standby** and **Waiting** state, as expected based on the outcome of the DF election process.

Output 6-9   *Bundle-Ether 200: Member LACP State on PE-1*

```
RP/0/RP0/CPU0:PE-1#show lacp GigabitEthernet0/0/0/1


State: a - Port is marked as Aggregatable.
       s - Port is Synchronized with peer.
       c - Port is marked as Collecting.
       d - Port is marked as Distributing.
       A - Device is in Active mode.
       F - Device requests PDUs from the peer at fast rate.
       D - Port is using default values for partner information.
       E - Information about partner has expired.


Bundle-Ether200

  Port             (rate)  State   Port ID       Key    System ID
  ------------------ ------ -------- ------------- ------ ------------------------
Local
  Gi0/0/0/1           1s   ascdAF-- 0x8000,0x0001 0x00c8 0x8000,fc-00-00-01-02-00
  Partner             1s   ascdAF-- 0x8000,0x0001 0x00c8 0x8000,00-00-00-01-18-00

  Port                    Receive   Period Selection  Mux      A Churn P Churn
  ------------------ ---------- ------ ---------- --------- ------- -------
Local
  Gi0/0/0/1               Current   Fast   Selected   Distrib   None    None
```

Output 6-10   *Bundle-Ether 200: Member LACP State on PE-2*

```
RP/0/RP0/CPU0:PE-2#show lacp GigabitEthernet0/0/0/3


State: a - Port is marked as Aggregatable.
       s - Port is Synchronized with peer.
       c - Port is marked as Collecting.
       d - Port is marked as Distributing.
       A - Device is in Active mode.
       F - Device requests PDUs from the peer at fast rate.
       D - Port is using default values for partner information.
       E - Information about partner has expired.
```

```
Bundle-Ether200

  Port              (rate)  State   Port ID        Key    System ID
  ------------------ -------- ------- ------------- ------ ------------------------
Local
  Gi0/0/0/3          1s      a---AF-- 0x8000,0x0001 0x00c8 0x8000,fc-00-00-01-02-00
  Partner            1s      as--AF-- 0x8000,0x0002 0x00c8 0x8000,00-00-00-01-18-00


  Port                      Receive   Period Selection  Mux       A Churn P Churn
  ------------------ -------- -------- ------ ---------- --------- ------- -------
Local
  Gi0/0/0/3                  Current   Fast   Standby    Waiting   Churn   None
```

As shown in Config 6-5 and Config 6-6, a **lacp system mac 00fc.0002.2600** misconfiguration occurred between PE routers PE-3 and PE-4, where the interface bundle-ether 250 on PE-4 used the globally configured MAC address, while interface bundle-ether 250 on PE-3 had a directly configured MAC address. Technically this is not a misconfiguration, but both PE router system IDs must match when attached to a dual-homed device. The intent with the example configurations shown here is to use a per-bundle-ether MAC address rather than the global configured MAC address.

Config 6-5   *Bundle-Ether Interface Specific MAC Address Configuration on PE-3*

```
!
lacp system mac 00fc.0002.2500
!
interface Bundle-Ether250
 description Connected_to_CE-3
 lacp system mac 00fc.0002.0250
!
```

The configuration snippet in Config 6-6 from router PE-4 shows that bundle-ether 250 does not have a directly configured MAC address.

Config 6-6   *Bundle-Ether Interface Global MAC Address Configuration on PE-4*

```
!
lacp system mac 00fc.0002.2600
!
interface Bundle-Ether250
 description Connected_to_CE-3
!
```

Output 6-11 shows the result of the CLI command **show bundle bundle-Ether 250** on CE-3, which shows the **Partner System ID/Key do not match** error indication.

Output 6-11   *Bundle-Ether 250 System ID Error on CE-3*

```
RP/0/RP0/CPU0:CE-3#show bundle bundle-Ether 250

Bundle-Ether250
<snip>

  Port                    Device            State         Port ID         B/W, kbps
  -------------------     ---------------   -----------   -------------   ----------
  Gi0/0/0/0               Local             Configured    0x8000, 0x0002    1000000
      Partner System ID/Key do not match that of the Selected links
  ←--------------------Issue
  Gi0/0/0/1               Local             Active        0x8000, 0x0001    1000000
      Link is Active
```

In addition, the command **show lacp bundle-Ether 250** in Output 6-12 provides more details about the cause of the issue. In this case, the system IDs are mismatched.

Output 6-12   *Bundle-Ether 250 LACP System ID Error Verification on CE-3*

```
RP/0/RP0/CPU0:CE-3#show lacp bundle-Ether 250

<snip>
Bundle-Ether250

  Port                (rate)  State    Port ID        Key     System ID
  -------------------  ------  -------  -------------  ------  ------------------------
Local
  Gi0/0/0/0            1s      a---AF-- 0x8000,0x0002  0x00fa  0x8000,00-00-00-02-28-00
    Partner            1s      a---AF-- 0x8000,0x0002  0x00fa  0x8000,00-fc-00-02-26-00
  Gi0/0/0/1            1s      ascdAF-- 0x8000,0x0001  0x00fa  0x8000,00-00-00-02-28-00
    Partner            1s      ascdAF-- 0x8000,0x0001  0x00fa  0x8000,00-fc-00-02-02-50


  Port                        Receive     Period Selection  Mux        A Churn P Churn
  -------------------         ----------  ------ ----------  ---------  ------- -------
Local
  Gi0/0/0/0                   Current     Fast   Unselect    Detached   Churn   Churn
  Gi0/0/0/1                   Current     Fast   Selected    Distrib    None    None
```

After the configurations were aligned on both of the PE routers, the system ID mismatch was resolved. The **Partner is not Synchronized (Waiting, Standby, or LAG ID mismatch)** error shown in Output 6-13 indicates that the bundle-ether member interface Gi0/0/0/0 is in standby mode toward the router PE-4, while the member interface Gi0/0/0/1 is active toward the router PE-3.

Output 6-13   *Bundle-Ether 250 Partner Corrected System ID Match Verification on CE-3*

```
RP/0/RP0/CPU0:CE-3#show bundle bundle-Ether 250

Bundle-Ether250
  Status:                              Up
<snip>
  Port                 Device          State         Port ID          B/W, kbps
  -------------------- --------------- ------------- --------------- ----------
  Gi0/0/0/0            Local           Negotiating   0x8000, 0x0002    1000000
    Partner is not Synchronized (Waiting, Standby, or LAG ID mismatch)
  Gi0/0/0/1            Local           Active        0x8000, 0x0001    1000000
    Link is Active
RP/0/RP0/CPU0:CE-3#
```

After correcting the configuration, both the member interface LACP system IDs now match on router CE-3, as shown in Output 6-14.

Output 6-14   *Bundle-Ether 250 LACP System ID Match Verification on CE-3*

```
RP/0/RP0/CPU0:CE-3#show lacp bundle-Ether 250

<snip>
Bundle-Ether250

  Port           (rate) State   Port ID       Key    System ID
  -------------------- ------- ------------- ------ ------------------------
Local
  Gi0/0/0/0        1s  as--AF-- 0x8000,0x0002 0x00fa 0x8000,00-00-00-02-28-00
    Partner        1s  a---AF-- 0x8000,0x0002 0x00fa 0x8000,00-fc-00-02-02-50
  Gi0/0/0/1        1s  ascdAF-- 0x8000,0x0001 0x00fa 0x8000,00-00-00-02-28-00
    Partner        1s  ascdAF-- 0x8000,0x0001 0x00fa 0x8000,00-fc-00-02-02-50

  Port                 Receive     Period Selection  Mux        A Churn P Churn
  -------------------- ----------- ------ ---------- ---------- ------- -------
Local
  Gi0/0/0/0            Current     Fast   Selected   Attached   None    Churn
  Gi0/0/0/1            Current     Fast   Selected   Distrib    None    None
RP/0/RP0/CPU0:CE-3#
```

The debugging command **debug lacp packets GigabitEthernet0/0/0/1 decode** is extremely useful for troubleshooting LACP issues between two routers as its output provides detailed decoded LACP packet information both on ingress and egress from an interface. Output 6-15 shows the normal operating condition on router PE-3.

Output 6-15 *Debug LACP Interface Output Example on PE-3*

```
RP/0/RP0/CPU0:PE-3#debug lacp packets GigabitEthernet0/0/0/1 decode
<snip>
RP/0/RP0/CPU0:PE-3#RP/0/RP0/CPU0:May 14 07:07:01.671 UTC: BM-LOCAL[298]:
  GigabitEthernet0/0/0/1 (in) @ May 14 07:07:01.671: LACPDU. Actor: System ID
  0x8000, 00-00-00-02-28-00; Key 0x00fa; Port ID 0x8000, 0x0001; State 0x3f.
  Partner: System ID 0x8000, 00-fc-00-02-02-50; Key 0x00fa; Port ID 0x8000, 0x0001;
  State 0x3f. Collector: Max delay 65535. Cisco rate: Req tx rate 1000; Incoming tx
  rate 1000.
RP/0/RP0/CPU0:May 14 07:07:02.921 UTC: BM-LOCAL[298]: GigabitEthernet0/0/0/1 (out)
  @ May 14 07:07:02.920: LACPDU. Actor: System ID 0x8000, 00-fc-00-02-02-50; Key
  0x00fa; Port ID 0x8000, 0x0001; State 0x3f. Partner: System ID 0x8000, 00-00-00-
  02-28-00; Key 0x00fa; Port ID 0x8000, 0x0001; State 0x3f. Collector: Max delay
  65535. Cisco rate: Req tx rate 1000; Incoming tx rate 1000.
<snip>
```

On router PE-2, the output from **show interfaces brief** (see Output 6-16) confirms that the interface bundle-ether 200 and subinterface bundle-ether 200.2000 interface/line protocol states are down/down. This is the expected interface state, as interface bundle-ether 200 is configured as **evpn interface Bundle-Ether200 ethernet-segment load-balancing-mode port-active** on both router PE-1 and PE-2 and, as described earlier, the EVPN port-active multihoming per-port DF election process uses the modulo operation for determining which PE router will be active and which will be standby for the bundle-ether 200.

Output 6-16 *Interface Output on PE-2*

```
RP/0/RP0/CPU0:PE-2#show interface brief
```

Intf Name	Intf State	LineP State	Encap Type	MTU (byte)	BW (Kbps)
BE200	down	down	ARPA	1514	0
BE200.2000	down	down	802.1Q	1518	0
BE200.2001	down	down	802.1Q	1518	0
Lo0	up	up	Loopback	1500	0
Gi0/0/0/0	up	up	ARPA	9000	1000000
Gi0/0/0/1	up	up	ARPA	1500	1000000
Gi0/0/0/1.2000	up	up	802.1Q	1504	1000000
Gi0/0/0/2	up	up	ARPA	9000	1000000
Gi0/0/0/3	up	up	ARPA	1518	1000000

The command **show bundle bundle-Ether 200** displays the interface bundle-ether 200 status as **LACP OOS** and **Standby** on interface Gi0/0/0/3, as shown in Output 6-17. This is a result of the per-port DF election process between the routers PE-1 and PE-2, as described earlier.

> **Note**   Recent IOS XR releases also support hot standby for EVPN port-active where
> the main and subinterfaces on the standby bundle-ether interface remain in **Up** state,
> allowing for faster convergence from standby state to active state in the event of a failure
> or transition event. The bundle-ether interface status would be reflected as **EVPN Hot-**
> **Standby** as opposed to **LACP OoS (out of service)**.

Output 6-17   *Interface Bundle-Ether 200 Status LACP OOS on PE-2*

```
RP/0/RP0/CPU0:PE-2#show bundle bundle-Ether 200


Bundle-Ether200
  Status:                                    LACP OOS (out of service)
  Local links <active/standby/configured>:   0 / 1 / 1
  Local bandwidth <effective/available>:     0 (0) kbps
  MAC address (source):                      0018.1972.60eb (Chassis pool)
  Inter-chassis link:                        No
  Minimum active links / bandwidth:          1 / 1 kbps
  Maximum active links:                      64
  Wait while timer:                          2000 ms
  Load balancing:
    Link order signaling:                    Not configured
    Hash type:                               Default
    Locality threshold:                      None
  LACP:                                      Operational
    Flap suppression timer:                  Off
    Cisco extensions:                        Disabled
    Non-revertive:                           Disabled
  mLACP:                                     Not configured
  IPv4 BFD:                                  Not configured
  IPv6 BFD:                                  Not configured


  Port                  Device            State         Port ID         B/W, kbps
  --------------------  ---------------   -----------   --------------  ----------
  Gi0/0/0/3             Local             Standby       0x8000, 0x0001    1000000
      Link is in standby due to bundle out of service state
```

EVPN E-LAN Port-Active MHD EVPN Configuration

The second of the configuration steps is the EVPN EVI circuit provisioning, as displayed
in Figure 6-22.

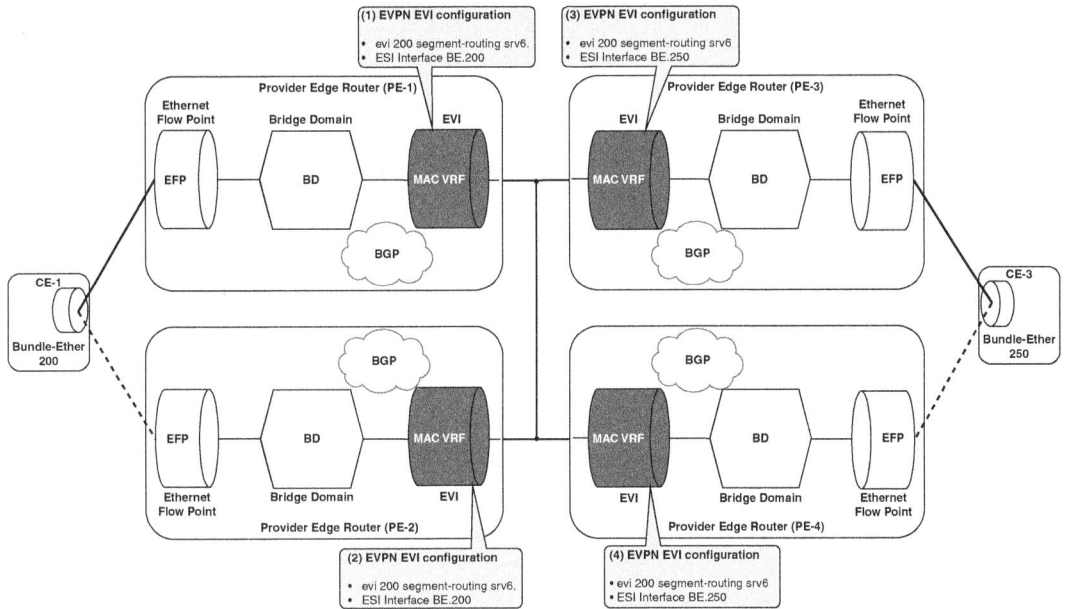

Figure 6-22 *EVPN E-LAN Port-Active MHD EVPN PE Configuration Tasks*

The EVPN configuration in Config 6-7 is sufficient for the EVPN portion of the E-LAN provisioning tasks on routers PE-1 and PE-2.

Config 6-7 *EVPN E-LAN Port-Active MHD EVPN Configurations on PE-1 and PE-2*

```
!
evpn
 evi 200 segment-routing srv6
  !
  advertise-mac
!
 interface Bundle-Ether200
  ethernet-segment
   identifier type 0 00.fc.00.01.02.00.00.00.00
   load-balancing-mode port-active
  !
segment-routing srv6
 locator MAIN
 !
```

Likewise, the EVPN configuration in Config 6-8 is sufficient for the EVPN portion of the E-LAN provisioning tasks for routers PE-3 and PE-4.

Config 6-8   *EVPN E-LAN Port-Active MHD EVPN Configurations on PE-3 and PE-4*

```
!
evpn
 evi 200 segment-routing srv6
  !
  advertise-mac
 !
 interface Bundle-Ether250
  ethernet-segment
   identifier type 0 00.fc.00.01.02.50.00.00.00
   load-balancing-mode port-active
  !
 segment-routing srv6
  locator MAIN
 !
```

Although these configurations are sufficient for the EVPN portion of the E-LAN provisioning tasks, it should be noted that the following parameters are auto-derived:

■ **EVI BGP route distinguisher (RD):** The auto-derived RD for EVI 200 on router PE-1 is **172.19.0.10:200** (ROUTER-ID:VPN-ID).

■ **EVI BGP route target (RT):** The auto-derived RD for EVI 200 on router PE-1 is **65000:200** (ASN:VPN-ID).

As described earlier in this chapter the ESI parameters themselves can be auto-derived, however in Config 6-7 and Config 6-8, these globally unique ESI identifiers were manually configured as **identifier type 0 00.fc.00.01.02.00.00.00.00** on routers PE-1 and PE-2 and configured as **identifier type 0 00.fc.00.01.02.50.00.00.00** on routers PE-3 and PE-4. Since this is a port-active multihomed service, the additional configuration **load-balancing-mode port-active** is required under the ES-facing bundle-ether interfaces.

Several optional configurations can also be considered for greater control. For example, it is possible to statically configure the route distinguisher as shown in Config 6-9, although auto-RD derivation is best practice to ensure network-wide route distinguisher uniqueness. Statically configuring the import/export route targets, on the other hand, gives you more flexibility and control over the import and export of routes either statically or via route policies.

The snippet in Config 6-10 is a typical example configuration that gives you some additional control and flexibility in allowing or dropping imported EVPN routes based on matching BGP communities.

Config 6-9   *EVPN E-LAN Port-Active MHD EVPN Configurations: Explicit RD and RT*

```
evpn
 evi 200 segment-routing srv6
  bgp
   rd 172.19.0.10:200
   route-target import 65000:200
   route-target export 65000:200
   !
  advertise-mac
<snip>
```

Config 6-10   *EVPN E-LAN Port-Active MHD EVPN Configurations: Import RT Route Policy*

```
!
community-set COMMUNITY_CS
  65000:1000
end-set
!
route-policy IMPORT_RP
  if community in COMMUNITY_CS then
    pass
  else
    drop
  endif
end-policy
!
evpn
 evi 200 segment-routing srv6
  bgp
   rd 172.19.0.10:200
   route-target import 65000:200
   route-target export 65000:200
   route-policy import IMPORT_RP
   !
  advertise-mac
   !
  !
```

Similarly, as shown in Config 6-11, the operator can set BGP communities on EVPN routes when they are exported.

Config 6-11   *EVPN E-LAN Port-Active MHD EVPN Configurations: Export RT Route Policy*

```
!
 route-policy EXPORT_RP($AS, $COM)
  set community ($AS:$COM) additive
 end-policy
!
evpn
 evi 200 segment-routing srv6
  bgp
   rd 172.19.0.10:200
   route-target import 65000:200
   route-target export 65000:200
   route-policy export EXPORT_RP(65000, 1001)
  !
  advertise-mac
  !
 !
```

There is an option to configure the SRv6 locator per EVI as opposed to having the SRv6 locator globally allocated to all EVIs. This is especially useful if multiple SRv6 locators are in use on the provider edge router. Config 6-12 shows a configuration example for a per-EVI SRv6 locator allocation.

Config 6-12   *EVPN E-LAN Port-Active MHD EVPN Configurations: Per-EVI SRv6 Locator*

```
evpn
 evi 200 segment-routing srv6
  bgp
   rd 172.19.0.10:200
   route-target import 65000:200
   route-target export 65000:200
  !
  advertise-mac
  !
  locator MAIN
<snip>
```

Provisioning of the Ethernet segment–associated LAG interface is a requirement for EVPN port-active mode, and an Ethernet segment Route Type 4 route creation is the result of this configuration. As mentioned previously, the ESI value is auto-generated when using Link Aggregation Control Protocol (LACP) between PE routers and CE devices. The ES import RT is auto-generated from the 6-octet portion of the 9-octet ESI value that corresponds to a MAC address. This import RT is used for limiting the Route Type 4 routes to PE routers that are connected to the same local attached Ethernet segment. Both attributes are operator configurable, as highlighted in the configuration snippet shown in Config 6-13.

Config 6-13 *EVPN E-LAN Port-Active MHD EVPN Configurations: Explicit ESI and ES Import RT*

```
evpn
 evi 200 segment-routing srv6
  bgp
   rd 172.19.0.10:200
   route-target import 65000:200
   route-target export 65000:200
  !
  advertise-mac
  !
  locator MAIN
 !
 interface Bundle-Ether200
  ethernet-segment
   identifier type 0 00.fc.00.01.02.00.00.00.00
   load-balancing-mode port-active
   bgp route-target 00fc.0001.0200
  !
<snip>
```

When deploying an EVPN port-active scenario, the default per-PE router active/standby ES determination is based on the DF election procedure, which is based on a modulus algorithm, as discussed in section "EVPN Route Type 4: Ethernet Segment Route." However, there may be a requirement to have more control over which PE router is active for a specific ES. In such a case, a preference-based DF election procedure may be deployed to allow the operator to select the active PE router based on a preference DF weight value. The **service-carving preference-based** configuration line in Config 6-14 allows the operator to select the active PE router based on the higher **weight** preference value.

Config 6-14 *EVPN E-LAN Port-Active MHD EVPN Configurations: Preference-Based Service Carving*

```
evpn
 evi 200 segment-routing srv6
  !
  advertise-mac
  !
 interface Bundle-Ether200
  ethernet-segment
```

```
      identifier type 0 00.fc.00.01.02.00.00.00.00
      load-balancing-mode port-active
      service-carving preference-based
       weight 1000
     !
  <snip>
```

Another optional but recommended configuration is the EVPN core isolation protection feature, which allows the core-facing interfaces to be associated with an Ethernet segment (ES), and in the event that all core interfaces go down (a PE router isolation event), EVPN will take down the Ethernet segment (ES) facing access interfaces. Locally attached CE devices will no longer make use of those specific member links in the impacted bundle-ether interfaces and will continue forwarding traffic via the alternate provider edge router. A configuration example for the core isolation protection feature is provided in Config 6-15.

Config 6-15   *EVPN E-LAN Port-Active MHD EVPN Configurations: Core Isolation Protection*

```
evpn
 evi 200 segment-routing srv6
  !
  advertise-mac
  !
  locator MAIN
 !
!
group 200
  core interface Gi0/0/0/0
  core interface Gi0/0/0/2
 !
 interface Bundle-Ether200
  ethernet-segment
   identifier type 0 00.fc.00.01.02.00.00.00.00
   load-balancing-mode port-active
   bgp route-target 00fc.0001.0200
  !
  core-isolation-group 200
 !
```

In highly scaled EVPN networks, slow BGP control plane convergence starts to become a reality especially during the recovery of a multihomed PE router after a failure. There are several configurable timers that can assist in improving convergence, especially during the recovery of a PE router configured with multihomed services. Table 6-2 mentions the configurable timer names and time ranges and the event types that trigger them.

Table 6-2 *EVPN E-LAN Port-Active MHD EVPN: Timers*

Sequence Event No.	Timer Name	Range of Timer	Event Trigger
1	startup-cost-in	30–86,400 sec	Node recovery
2	staggered-bringup-timer	0–300,000 msec	Interface recovery
3	peering	0–3600 sec	Interface recovery

The example configuration shown in Config 6-16 includes the following optional timer configurations:

- **startup-cost-in:** After the router has reloaded and actively begins to bring up its configured routing processes, the startup-cost-in timer is triggered and keeps the access circuit interfaces in a Down state. This allows the core-facing routing protocols to properly converge and stabilize in order to prevent a traffic blackholing occurrence. This timer is disabled by default, and the operator may need to configure this value as required based on network scale.

- **staggered-bringup-timer:** If there are multiple Ethernet segments, this timer will stagger the circuit state from Down to Up of each ES individually. This Ethernet segment bringup staggering process limits the BGP control plane load, thereby allowing the propagation and processing of critical EVPN Route Type 4 and Route Type 1 routes.

- **peering:** This peering timer allows the propagation of the EVPN Route Type 4 but delays the DF election procedure for the configured period. This allows for the remote PE router to process the Route Type 4 routes before commencing with the DF election procedure. This becomes especially relevant at high route scale, where there is a possibility that processing these Route Type 4 routes may be delayed.

Config 6-16 *EVPN Configurations: Adjustable Timers*

```
!
evpn
 staggered-bringup-timer 300000
 startup-cost-in 1200
 !
 timers
  peering 10
 !
```

EVPN E-LAN Port-Active MHD EVPN Verification

This section describes the common and useful commands displayed in Figure 6-23 that are used to verify and troubleshoot the previously shown EVPN MHD EVI service configuration.

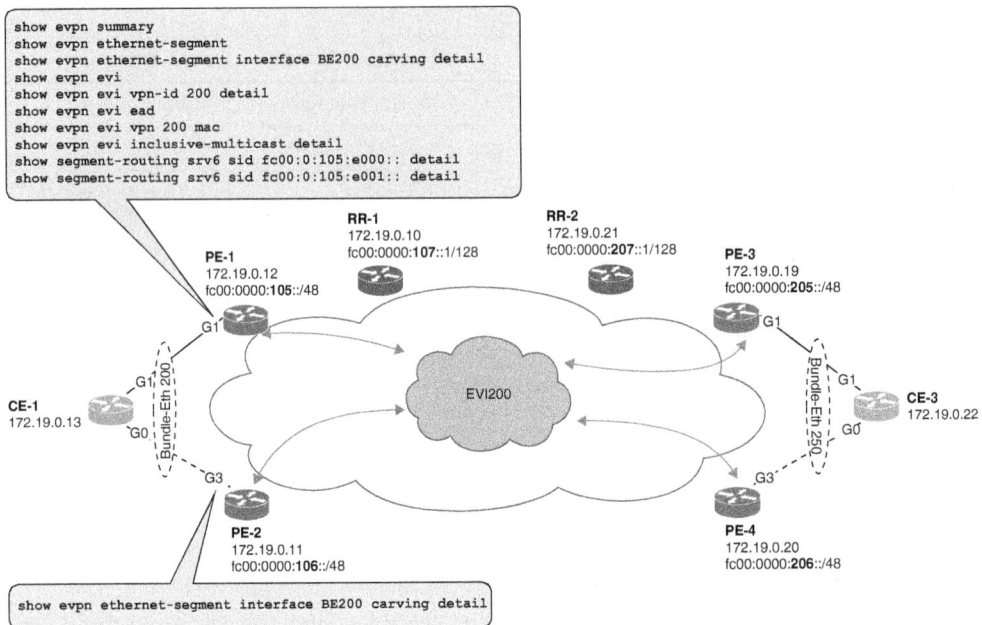

Figure 6-23   *EVPN E-LAN Port-Active MHD EVPN Verification*

To verify the EVPN component of the multihomed port-active service EVI 200, the commands described in this section provide the pertinent outputs. These outputs are collected from both PE-1 and PE-2 in IS-IS Metro 1. MAC addresses 1011.1100.0001–1011.1100.0005 originated from the router CE-1, while MAC addresses 2011.1100.0001–2011.1100.0005 originated from the router CE-3.

The command **show evpn summary** is useful for obtaining an overall summary view with regard to the EVPN status across all EVIs configured on the router. Some highlighted outputs from this command in Output 6-18 include the following:

■ **Number of EVIs:** Displays three EVIs. (200, 201, and 65535). Use the command **show evpn evi** (shown shortly, in Output 6-22) to provide an overview of the configured EVI VPN-IDs and their related bridge domains.

■ **Number of Local EAD Entries:** Displays two local Ethernet A-D entries on router PE-1. Use the command **show evpn evi ead local** to display the actual local Ethernet A-D details.

■ **Number of Remote EAD Entries:** Displays eight remote Ethernet A-D entries on router PE-1. Use the command **show evpn evi ead** (shown shortly, in Output 6-24) to display the actual remote Ethernet A-D details.

■ **Number of Local MAC Routes:** Displays five local MAC address entries that originated from router CE-1.

- **Number of Remote MAC Routes:** Displays five remote MAC address entries that originated from router CE-2. More details about these remote MAC addresses are shown shortly, in Output 6-25.

- **Number of Local IMCAST Routes:** Displays two local inclusive-multicast routes (RT-3) representing EVI 200 and EVI 201. Use the command **show evpn evi inclusive-multicast local** to display the details of these local inclusive multicast entries.

- **Number of Remote IMCAST Routes:** Displays six remote inclusive-multicast routes (RT-3) representing EVI 200 and EVI 201 on PE-2, PE-3. and PE-4. Use the command **show evpn evi inclusive-multicast** to display the details of both local and remote inclusive multicast details entries.

- **Number of ES Entries:** Displays one Ethernet segment (ES RT-4) on the PE router. Use the command **show evpn ethernet-segment** to get more details about the configured Ethernet segment on router PE-1.

Output 6-18   *EVPN E-LAN Port-Active MHD EVPN Summary Overview on PE-1*

```
RP/0/RP0/CPU0:PE-1#show evpn summary


----------------------------
Global Information
----------------------------
Number of EVIs                    : 3
Number of TEPs                    : 4
Number of Local EAD Entries       : 2
Number of Remote EAD Entries      : 8
Number of Local MAC Routes        : 5
            MAC                   : 5
      MAC-IPv4                    : 0
      MAC-IPv6                    : 0
Number of Local ES:Global MAC     : 1
Number of Remote MAC Routes       : 5
            MAC                   : 5
      MAC-IPv4                    : 0
      MAC-IPv6                    : 0
Number of Remote SYNC MAC Routes  : 0
Number of Local IMCAST Routes     : 2
Number of Remote IMCAST Routes    : 6
Number of Internal Labels         : 0
Number of single-home Internal IDs : 0
Number of multi-home Internal IDs : 1
Number of ES Entries              : 1
Number of Neighbor Entries        : 6
```

```
EVPN Router ID                  : 172.19.0.10
BGP ASN                         : 65000
PBB BSA MAC address             : 001c.f93d.24d0
Global peering timer            :       3 seconds
Global recovery timer           :      30 seconds
Global carving timer            :       0 seconds
Global MAC postpone timer       :     300 seconds [not running]
Global core de-isolation timer  :      60 seconds [not running]
EVPN services costed out on node : No
        Startup-cost-in timer   : Not configured
        EVPN manual cost-out    : No
        EVPN Bundle Convergence : No
RP/0/RP0/CPU0:PE-1#
```

The next step in the port-active multihomed service verification process is to view the Ethernet segments attached to the PE routers. The command **show evpn ethernet-segment** provides an overview of the Ethernet segments attached to a PE router. In Output 6-19, there is just the single configured Ethernet segment, ESI 0000. fc00.0102.0000.0000, with its interface bundle-ether 200 attached to PE-1.

Output 6-19   *EVPN E-LAN Port-Active MHD EVPN Ethernet Segment Overview on PE-1*

```
RP/0/RP0/CPU0:PE-1#show evpn ethernet-segment

Ethernet Segment Id      Interface                          Nexthops
------------------------ ---------------------------------- --------------------
0000.fc00.0102.0000.0000 BE200                              172.19.0.10
                                                            172.19.0.11
RP/0/RP0/CPU0:PE-1#
```

For more details on this Ethernet segment configured on the router PE-1, the command **show evpn ethernet-segment interface BE200 carving detail** in Output 6-20 provides detailed Ethernet segment output information for the interface bundle-ether 200. The highlighted outputs from this command include some useful operational data:

- **Interface name—BE200:** Output confirms that interface bundle-ether 200 is the main interface attached to the Ethernet segment 0000.fc00.0102.0000.0000.

- **State—Up:** Because this interface BE200 is configured for a multihomed port-active service, the ESI state is **Up** on router PE-1 and **Standby** on the peer router PE-2, as shown in Output 6-21.

- **ESI Type—0:** The output indicates that the ESI value is manually allocated via the router EVPN configuration

- **Value—0000.fc00.0102.0000.0000:** This is a user-provisioned 10-byte Ethernet segment identifier (ESI).

- **ES Import RT—00fc.0001.0200:** The ES import RT comprising of the 6-byte MAC address portion of the ESI limits these Ethernet segment Route Type 4 routes to the PE routers PE-1 and PE-2 connected to the same local Ethernet segment.

- **Topology:**

  - **Operational: MH:** The topology is configured and operating as a multihomed Ethernet segment. This state must match on the two PE routers.

  - **Configured: Port-Active:** The topology is configured and operating on both PE routers as port-active load-balancing attached to the multihomed Ethernet segment.

- **Peering Details: 2 Nexthops:** These two IP addresses are the "originating router IP" addresses obtained via the EVPN Route Type 4 entry, as described in section the "EVPN Route Type 4: Ethernet Segment Route" and used in the designated forwarder election algorithm

  - **172.19.0.10 [MOD:P:7fff:T]: MOD** refers to the default modulo-based DF election algorithm in use for this specific Ethernet segment. The **P** flag refers to whether non-revertive service carving is enabled: **P** indicates that it can be preempted, and a **DP** indicates "don't preempt." The next field is the hex value **0x7fff** (32767), which is the default service carving weight assigned to the ES on router PE-1, based on the outcome of the DF election algorithm. The final field is the **T** flag, which is used for signaling whether to use time synchronization (NTP or PTP) between peer PE routers. By default, when the DF role is transferred from one PE router to another, it takes 3 seconds (peering timer) to complete the process. During this time, there is a possibility of traffic loss. To improve the DF election process after a failure recovery, the router can use the Network Time Protocol (NTP) synchronization mechanism. This ensures that the clocks of peering routers are synchronized, allowing for more efficient DF role changes.

- **Service carving results:**

  - **Forwarders: 2:** Two EVIs' forwarders are configured (and forwarding) in this Ethernet segment.

  - **Elected: 2**

    - **SRv6 E: 200, 201:** As a result of the DF election (service carving) algorithm, both EVI 200 and 201 are elected and forwarding in the Ethernet segment.

- **Local SHG label: None:** No local split-horizon group label is allocated as this is a port-active service (MPLS label 3 Implicit NULL label).

- **Remote SHG labels: 0:** No split-horizon group label is received as this is a port-active service (MPLS label 3 Implicit NULL label).

Output 6-20   *EVPN Ethernet Segment Detail on PE-1*

```
RP/0/RP0/CPU0:PE-1#show evpn ethernet-segment interface BE200 carving detail

<snip>
Ethernet Segment Id        Interface                              Nexthops
----------------------     -------------------------------------  --------------------
0000.fc00.0102.0000.0000 BE200                                    172.19.0.10
                                                                  172.19.0.11
  ES to BGP Gates    : Ready
  ES to L2FIB Gates : Ready
  Main port           :
     Interface name : Bundle-Ether200
     Interface MAC  : 001c.f93d.24d6
     IfHandle       : 0x00000024
     State           : Up
     Redundancy     : Not Defined
  ESI type            : 0
     Value            : 0000.fc00.0102.0000.0000
  ES Import RT        : 00fc.0001.0200 (from ESI)
  Source MAC          : 0000.0000.0000 (N/A)
  Topology            :
     Operational     : MH
     Configured      : Port-Active
  Service Carving    : Auto-selection
     Multicast       : Disabled
  Convergence         :
  Peering Details     : 2 Nexthops
     172.19.0.10 [MOD:P:7fff:T]
     172.19.0.11 [MOD:P:00:T]
  Service Carving Synchronization:
     Mode            : NONE
     Peer Updates    :
            172.19.0.10 [SCT: N/A]
            172.19.0.11 [SCT: N/A]
  Service Carving Results:
     Forwarders      : 2
     Elected         : 2
            SRv6 E   :       200,       201
     Not Elected     : 0
  EVPN-VPWS Service Carving Results:
     Primary         : 0
     Backup          : 0
     Non-DF          : 0
  MAC Flushing mode : STP-TCN
   Peering timer     : 3 sec [not running]
  Recovery timer     : 30 sec [not running]
```

```
   Carving timer      : 0 sec [not running]
   HRW Reset timer    : 5 sec [not running]
   Local SHG label    : None
   Remote SHG labels : 0
   Access signal mode: Bundle OOS (Default)


RP/0/RP0/CPU0:PE-1#
```

The output of the command **show evpn ethernet-segment interface BE200 carving detail** on the Ethernet segment peer router PE-2, displayed in Output 6-21, provides similar output to what was displayed on PE-1, although in this case router PE-2 is the non-DF router for the Ethernet segment attached to interface bundle-ether 200. Notice the following in the output:

- **State: Standby:** Because this interface bundle-ether 200 is configured for multihomed port-active service, the ESI state is **Standby** on the router PE-2.

- **Service Carving Results:**

  - **Forwarders: 2:** Two EVIs' forwarders are configured (but not forwarding) in this Ethernet segment.

  - **Not Elected: 2**

    - **SRv6 NE: 200, 201:** As a result of the DF election (service carving) algorithm, EVI 200 and 201 are not elected and therefore are not in a forwarding state.

Output 6-21 *EVPN Ethernet Segment Detail on PE-2*

```
RP/0/RP0/CPU0:PE-2#show evpn ethernet-segment interface BE200 carving detail

<snip>
Ethernet Segment Id      Interface                          Nexthops
------------------------ ---------------------------------- --------------------
0000.fc00.0102.0000.0000 BE200                              172.19.0.10
                                                            172.19.0.11
  ES to BGP Gates   : Ready
   ES to L2FIB Gates : Ready
   Main port         :
      Interface name : Bundle-Ether200
      Interface MAC  : 0018.1972.60eb
      IfHandle       : 0x00000024
      State          : Standby
      Redundancy     : Not Defined
   ESI type          : 0
     Value           : 0000.fc00.0102.0000.0000
   ES Import RT       : 00fc.0001.0200 (from ESI)
 Source MAC         : 0000.0000.0000 (N/A)
```

```
Topology           :
    Operational    : MH
    Configured     : Port-Active
Service Carving    : Auto-selection
    Multicast      : Disabled
Convergence        :
Peering Details    : 2 Nexthops
    172.19.0.10 [MOD:P:00:T]
    172.19.0.11 [MOD:P:7fff:T]
Service Carving Synchronization:
    Mode           : NONE
    Peer Updates   :
            172.19.0.10 [SCT: N/A]
            172.19.0.11 [SCT: N/A]
Service Carving Results:
    Forwarders     : 2
    Elected        : 0
    Not Elected    : 2
            SRv6 NE :      200,      201
EVPN-VPWS Service Carving Results:
    Primary        : 0
    Backup         : 0
    Non-DF         : 0
MAC Flushing mode  : STP-TCN
Peering timer      : 3 sec [not running]
Recovery timer     : 30 sec [not running]
Carving timer      : 0 sec [not running]
HRW Reset timer    : 5 sec [not running]
Local SHG label    : None
Remote SHG labels : 0
Access signal mode: Bundle OOS (Default)

RP/0/RP0/CPU0:PE-2#
```

The command **show evpn evi** in Output 6-22 provides an overview of the configured EVI VPN IDs and their related bridge domains on the PE router.

Output 6-22   *EVPN EVI Summary on PE-1*

```
RP/0/RP0/CPU0:PE-1#show evpn evi

VPN-ID     Encap      Bridge Domain                Type
---------- ---------- ---------------------------- --------------------
200        SRv6       200-BD                       EVPN
201        SRv6       201-BD                       EVPN
65535      N/A        ES:GLOBAL                    Invalid
```

By verifying the details of a specific EVI with the **show evpn evi vpn-id 200 detail** command, as displayed in Output 6-23, you can obtain the following useful information:

■ **Unicast SID: fc00:0:105:e000:::** The SRv6 SID value is allocated to any locally learned MAC routes and propagated as EVPN Route Type 2 MAC routes via BGP.

■ **Multicast SID: fc00:0:105:e001:::** The SRv6 SID value is allocated and propagated as an EVPN Route Type 3 inclusive multicast route, allowing for ingress replicated BUM traffic from remote PE routers participating in the EVI to be encapsulated with the received inclusive multicast Ethernet label and forwarded to the advertising PE router.

■ **RD Auto: (auto) 172.19.0.10:200:** The route distinguisher is auto-derived.

■ **RT Auto: 65000:200:** The route target value is auto-derived, and the **Route Targets in Use** field indicates whether the auto-derived route targets are in use or manually configured.

Output 6-23   *EVPN EVI VPN-ID 200 Detail on PE-1*

```
RP/0/RP0/CPU0:PE-1#show evpn evi vpn-id 200 detail

VPN-ID     Encap      Bridge Domain               Type
---------- ---------- --------------------------- --------------------
200        SRv6       200-BD                      EVPN
   Stitching: Regular
   Unicast SID:  fc00:0:105:e000::
   Multicast SID:  fc00:0:105:e001::
 E-Tree: Root
 Forward-class: 0
 Advertise MACs: Yes
 Advertise BVI MACs: No
Aliasing: Enabled
 UUF: Enabled
 Re-origination: Enabled
 Multicast:
   Source connected   : No
   IGMP-Snooping Proxy: No
   MLD-Snooping Proxy : No
 BGP Implicit Import: Enabled
 VRF Name:
 Preferred Nexthop Mode: Off
 BVI Coupled Mode: No
 BVI Subnet Withheld: ipv4 No, ipv6 No
```

```
    Statistics:
       Packets            Sent                  Received
          Total           : 0                   0
          Unicast         : 0                   0
          BUM             : 0                   0
       Bytes              Sent                  Received
          Total           : 0                   0
          Unicast         : 0                   0
          BUM             : 0                   0
    RD Config: none
    RD Auto   : (auto) 172.19.0.10:200
    RT Auto   : 65000:200
    Route Targets in Use              Type
    ------------------------------    ---------------------
    65000:200                         Import
    65000:200                         Export

RP/0/RP0/CPU0:PE-1#
```

The command **show evpn evi ead** in Output 6-24 displays all local and remote learned EVPN Route Type 1 Ethernet A-D routes on router PE-1. The output provides a very good overview of all the auto-discovered Ethernet segments and their related EVIs. Let's consider the remote router PE-2 with next hop fc00:0:106::1 as an example. The following per-ESI Ethernet A-D route and per-EVI Ethernet A-D routes are learned:

- EVPN per-EVI Route Type 1 variant:

  - **VPN-ID—200:** VPN-ID refers to the user-provisioned EVI.

  - **Encap—SRv6:** This is confirmation that the encapsulation method is SRv6.

  - **Ethernet—Segment ID 0000.fc00.0102.0000.0000:** The ES ID is provisioned between the multihomed routers

  - **EtherTag—0x0:** This is set to 0.

  - **Nexthop—fc00:0:106::1:** This is the SRv6 locator of router PE-2.

  - **SID—fc00:0:106:e000:::** This is the aliasing SID. This is a port-active scenario, so the ingress router will not use this SID to load balance traffic toward the egress PE router.

- EVPN per-ESI Route Type 1 variant:

  - **VPN-ID—200:** VPN-ID refers to the user-provisioned EVI.

  - **Encap—SRv6:** This is confirmation that the encapsulation method is SRv6.

  - **Ethernet Segment ID—0000.fc00.0102.0000.0000:** This is the ES ID provisioned between the multihomed routers.

■ **EtherTag—0xffffffff:** This is set to the reserved Ethernet tag ID MAX-ET
  4294967295.

■ **Nexthop—fc00:0:106::1:** This is the SRv6 locator of router PE-2.

■ **Label—0:** Per-ESI Route Type 1 sets this label to 0.

Output 6-24 *EVPN Route Type 1 Ethernet A-D per-EVI Details*

```
RP/0/RP0/CPU0:PE-1#show evpn evi ead

VPN-ID  Encap  Ethernet Segment Id       EtherTag   Nexthop          Label     SID
-------  -----  ---------------------     ---------  --------------   ------    ----------------
200     SRv6   0000.fc00.0102.0000.0000  0x0        ::               0         fc00:0:105:e000::
                                                     fc00:0:106::1    IMP-NULL  fc00:0:106:e000::
200     SRv6   0000.fc00.0102.0000.0000  0xffffffff fc00:0:106::1    0
200     SRv6   0000.fc00.0202.5000.0000  0x0        fc00:0:205::1    IMP-NULL  fc00:0:205:e000::
                                                     fc00:0:206::1    MP-NULL   fc00:0:206:e004::
200     SRv6   0000.fc00.0202.5000.0000  0xffffffff fc00:0:205::1    0
                                                     fc00:0:206::1    0
201     SRv6   0000.fc00.0102.0000.0000  0x0        ::               0         fc00:0:105:e002::
                                                     fc00:0:106::1    IMP-NULL  fc00:0:106:e002::
201     SRv6   0000.fc00.0102.0000.0000  0xffffffff fc00:0:106::1    0
201     SRv6   0000.fc00.0202.5000.0000  0x0        fc00:0:205::1    IMP-NULL  fc00:0:205:e002::
                                                     fc00:0:206::1    IMP-NULL  fc00:0:206:e006::
201     SRv6   0000.fc00.0202.5000.0000  0xffffffff fc00:0:205::1    0
                                                     fc00:0:206::1    0
RP/0/RP0/CPU0:PE-1#
```

The output from the **show evpn evi vpn 200 mac** command shown in Output 6-25 displays both the local and remotely learned MAC routes with their next hops and SID attributes. Because the demonstration lab topology is based on SRv6 transport, the remote
MAC next hop is the remote PE router's originating IPv6 address, and the SID values are
obtained from the received EVPN Route Type 2 MAC routes. The next hop for the
locally learned MAC address routes point via the local interface Bundle-Ether200.2000.

Output 6-25 *EVPN Route Type 2 Local and Remote MAC Route per-EVI Details*

```
RP/0/RP0/CPU0:PE-1#show evpn evi vpn 200 mac

VPN-ID   Encap  MAC address      IP address    Nexthop                 Label    SID
--------  -----  -------------    -----------   --------------------    ------   ------------
200      SRv6   1011.1100.0001 ::              Bundle-Ether200.2000    0        fc00:0:105:e000::
200      SRv6   1011.1100.0002 ::              Bundle-Ether200.2000    0        fc00:0:105:e000::
200      SRv6   1011.1100.0003 ::              Bundle-Ether200.2000    0        fc00:0:105:e000::
200      SRv6   1011.1100.0004 ::              Bundle-Ether200.2000    0        fc00:0:105:e000::
200      SRv6   1011.1100.0005 ::              Bundle-Ether200.2000    0        fc00:0:105:e000::
```

```
200        SRv6   2011.1100.0001 ::       fc00:0:205::1      IMP-NULL fc00:0:205:e000::

200        SRv6   2011.1100.0002 ::       fc00:0:205::1      IMP-NULL fc00:0:205:e000::

200        SRv6   2011.1100.0003 ::       fc00:0:205::1      IMP-NULL fc00:0:205:e000::

200        SRv6   2011.1100.0004 ::       fc00:0:205::1      IMP-NULL fc00:0:205:e000::

200        SRv6   2011.1100.0005 ::       fc00:0:205::1      IMP-NULL fc00:0:205:e000::

RP/0/RP0/CPU0:PE-1#
```

The next step in the verification process is to display EVPN Route Type 3 inclusive multi-cast route details. The command **show evpn evi inclusive-multicast detail** in Output 6-26 displays both local and remote inclusive multicast routes for EVI 200. This output provides the inclusive multicast SID information from all the PE routers participating in EVI 200. Any local BUM traffic entering a PE router will use these SID values as a unicast destination address. For example, the router PE-2 has the inclusive multicast SID fc00:0:106:e001::, while PE-3 uses fc00:0:205:e001::, and PE-4 uses fc00:0:206:e005::.

Output 6-26   *EVPN Route Type 3 Inclusive Multicast Route Details*

```
RP/0/RP0/CPU0:PE-1#show evpn evi inclusive-multicast detail

VPN-ID     Encap EtherTag  Originating IP
---------- ------ ---------- ----------------------------------------
200        SRv6   0          172.19.0.10
   TEPid  : 0xffffffff
   PMSI Type: 6
   Nexthop: ::
   SR-TE Info: N/A
   SID    : fc00:0:105:e001::
   Source : Local
   E-Tree : Root
200        SRv6   0          172.19.0.11
   TEPid  : 0x05000001
   PMSI Type: 6
   Nexthop: 172.19.0.11
   SR-TE Info: N/A
   SID    : fc00:0:106:e001::
   Source : Remote
   E-Tree : Root
200        SRv6   0          172.19.0.19
   TEPid  : 0x05000003
   PMSI Type: 6
   Nexthop: 172.19.0.19
   SR-TE Info: N/A
   SID    : fc00:0:205:e001::
   Source : Remote
   E-Tree : Root
```

```
200        SRv6   0          172.19.0.20
   TEPid  : 0x05000002
   PMSI Type: 6
   Nexthop: 172.19.0.20
   SR-TE Info: N/A
   SID    : fc00:0:206:e005::
   Source : Remote
   E-Tree : Root
<snip>
RP/0/RP0/CPU0:PE-1
```

Finally, it is possible to verify additional details of the SIDs obtained in the previous outputs by using the **show segment-routing srv6 sid fc00:0:105:e000:: detail** command, as demonstrated in Output 6-27. This output confirms the allocated unicast SID function and behavior details:

- **SID: fc00:0:105:e000:::** This is the PE-1 router's SRv6 local SID.

- **Behavior: uDT2U:** This endpoint behavior is for traffic decapsulation and unicast MAC L2 table lookup.

- **Context: 200:0:** A context is for MAC or IP address isolation for example, a VRF instance in L3VPN setup or an EVI in a EVPN setup. In this case, the context refers to the EVPN provisioned EVI 200.

- **Owner: l2vpn_srv6:** This refers to the SID owner process. In this case, you can see that L2VPN owns the SID function. BGP or an IGP (IS-IS) can also be SID owners.

- **Locator: MAIN:** The SID was allocated from the configured SRv6 locator MAIN.

Output 6-27 *Segment Routing SRv6 SID Detail: Unicast SID*

```
RP/0/RP0/CPU0:PE-1#show segment-routing srv6 sid fc00:0:105:e000:: detail

*** Locator: 'MAIN' ***

SID                  Behavior     Context             Owner            State   RW
-------------------  -----------  ------------------  ---------------  -----   --
fc00:0:105:e000::    uDT2U        200:0               l2vpn_srv6       InUse   Y
  SID Function: 0xe000
  SID context: { evi=200, opaque-id=0 }
  Locator: 'MAIN'
  Allocation type: Dynamic
RP/0/RP0/CPU0:PE-1#
```

The **show segment-routing srv6 sid fc00:0:105:e001:: detail** command in Output 6-28 confirms the allocated multicast SID function and behavior details:

- **SID: fc00:0:105:e001:::** This is the PE-1 router SRv6 SID.

- **Behavior: uDT2M:** The endpoint behavior is for traffic decapsulation and L2 table flooding.

Output 6-28 *Segment Routing SRv6 SID Detail: Multicast SID*

```
RP/0/RP0/CPU0:PE-1#show segment-routing srv6 sid fc00:0:105:e001:: detail

*** Locator: 'MAIN' ***


SID                     Behavior      Context             Owner           State   RW
------------------      ------------  ------------------  -------------   -----   --
fc00:0:105:e001::       uDT2M         200:0               l2vpn_srv6      InUse   Y
 SID Function: 0xe001
  SID context: { evi=200, opaque-id=0 }
  Locator: 'MAIN'
  Allocation type: Dynamic
RP/0/RP0/CPU0:PE-1#
```

EVPN E-LAN Port-Active MHD L2VPN Configuration

The third configuration step is the L2VPN bridge domain provisioning, which will be linked to the EVPN EVI, as shown in Figure 6-24.

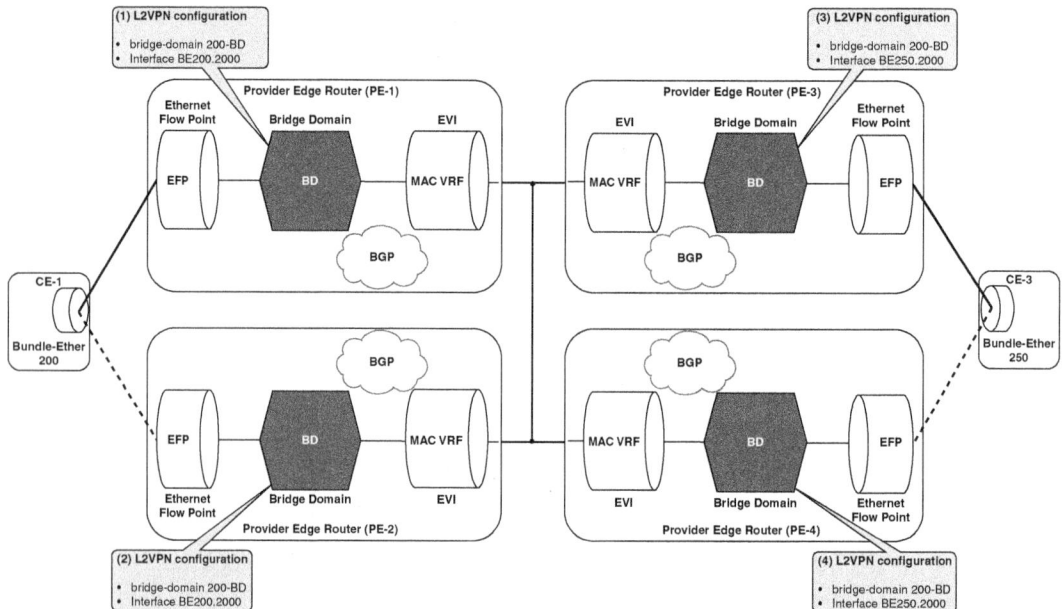

Figure 6-24 *EVPN E-LAN Port-Active MHD L2VPN PE Configuration Tasks*

Since the MAC learning between the Ethernet flow point (EFP) and the provider edge router is data plane driven, a bridge domain configuration is required to provide this multipoint service functionality. The bridge domain will then stitch the access circuit (EFP) to the EVPN EVI, as shown in the configurations in Config 6-17 for routers PE-1 and PE-2 and a similar configuration in Config 6-18 for routers PE-3 and PE-4.

Config 6-17   *EVPN E-LAN Port-Active MHD L2VPN PE Router Configurations on PE-1 and PE-2*

```
l2vpn
 bridge group ELAN-BG
  bridge-domain 200-BD
   interface Bundle-Ether200.2000
   !
   evi 200 segment-routing srv6
   !
```

Config 6-18   *EVPN E-LAN Port-Active MHD L2VPN PE Router Configurations on PE-3 and PE-4*

```
l2vpn
 bridge group ELAN-BG
  bridge-domain 200-BD
   interface Bundle-Ether250.2000
   !
   evi 200 segment-routing srv6
   !
```

Although these configurations are the minimum required for EVPN E-LAN service functionality, there are additional behaviors that can be configured by the operator, based on requirements to address data plane protection. It should be noted, however, that these optional commands are not only related to SRv6 but are also applicable to both MPLS and SR-MPLS environments.

A traffic storm is a traffic condition that occurs when ingress traffic is flooded into an L2VPN bridge domain. This traffic flooding can cause excessive traffic in that bridge domain and subsequently may cause a degradation in network performance. Storm control is a data plane feature that allows for rate limiting of BUM traffic, thereby minimizing any impact a traffic storm might have. The storm control rate limiters may be configured globally within a bridge domain or per access circuit interface; they monitor the incoming traffic rate on an interface and drop the traffic when the configured threshold level is reached. It should be noted that there is no impact to unicast traffic with a destination MAC address in the forwarding table. The configuration snippet in Config 6-19 has the traffic rates set to 10,000 packets per second (pps) for all BUM traffic types, but it could also be set to a kilobits-per-second (kbps) rate as well as for selected BUM traffic types only.

Config 6-19 *EVPN E-LAN Port-Active MHD L2VPN: Storm Control*

```
l2vpn
 bridge group ELAN-BG
  bridge-domain 200-BD
   interface Bundle-Ether200.2000
    storm-control unknown-unicast pps 10000
    storm-control multicast pps 10000
    storm-control broadcast pps 10000
   !
   evi 200 segment-routing srv6
   !
```

Other optional commands that may be used within the bridge domain are commands related to data plane protection and MAC security, as shown in Config 6-20:

- **mac limit maximum {MAX}:** This command sets a limit for learned MAC addresses before allowing an action to take place.

- **mac limit action {flood | no-flood | shut-down}:** This command causes action to be taken after the limit has been exceeded.

- **mac limit notification {both | none | trap}:** This is a notification action setting that can take place via an SNMP trap and/or syslog or no action.

- **mac secure logging:** With this command, if a known MAC address appears sourced from another access circuit, then log the event.

- **mac secure action {none | shutdown}:** The MAC secure **shutdown** option will shut down the interface after it exceeds a configured number of MAC moves within a specified move interval. If this is configured under the interface rather than globally within the L2VPN bridge domain, there is an additional option to restrict the MAC address and drop the violating packet and prevent it from being relearned.

- **mac secure shutdown-recovery-timeout {seconds}:** This command automatically recovers the MAC secure shutdown action after the specified timeout value.

Config 6-20 *EVPN E-LAN Port-Active MHD L2VPN: Data Plane Security*

```
l2vpn
 bridge group ELAN-BG
  bridge-domain 200-BD
   mac
    limit
     maximum 4000
     action no-flood
     notification both
    !
```

```
   secure
    logging
    action none
  !
 !
 interface Bundle-Ether200.2000
  storm-control unknown-unicast pps 10000
  storm-control multicast pps 10000
  storm-control broadcast pps 10000
  !
 evi 200 segment-routing srv6
  !
 !
!
```

EVPN E-LAN Port-Active MHD L2VPN Verification

This section describes the commands listed in Figure 6-25, which may be used to verify and troubleshoot an L2VPN service configuration.

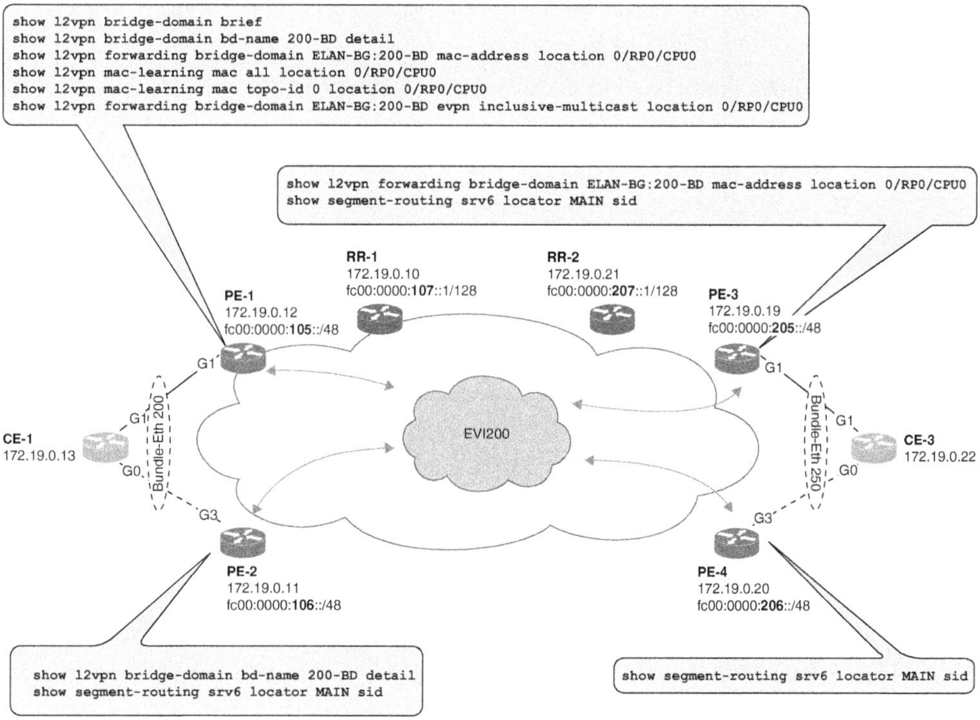

Figure 6-25 *EVPN E-LAN Port-Active MHD L2VPN Verification*

As described earlier in this chapter, in the section "EVPN Instance (EVI)," a bridge domain is an Ethernet broadcast domain that is internal to a node. MAC address learning between the Ethernet flow point (EFP) and the provider edge router is data plane driven, with the bridge domain itself providing this multipoint service functionality. The commands in this section verify the bridge domain state and trace the MAC addresses learned from router CE-1 (for example, 1011.1100.0001–1011.1100.0005) via the attached EFP to where these MAC addresses are ultimately learned on the remote CE router CE-3 across EVI 200.

The **show l2vpn bridge-domain brief** command provides a brief overview and the state of the configured bridge groups and which bridge domains are associated with these bridge groups. The relevant state information from Output 6-29 is as follows:

- **ID: 0:** This is the bridge domain ID number, which is useful for referencing the bridge domain in other commands.

- **State: up:** The admin down state is the state when the bridge domain has been configured as shutdown.

- **Num ACs/up: 1/1:** This is the number of associated access circuits as well as access circuits in the up state. As shown in the output, a single access circuit has been associated with each configured bridge domain 200-BD and 201-BD, and both are up.

- **Num PWs/up: 0/0:** Pseudowires are not applicable because the bridge domain is associated with EVPN EVIs.

- **Num PBBs/up:0/0:** Provider backbone bridging is not applicable in this case.

- **Num VNIs/up: 0/0:** VXLAN is not applicable in this case.

Output 6-29 *L2VPN Bridge Domain Brief State on PE-1*

```
RP/0/RP0/CPU0:PE-1#show l2vpn bridge-domain brief

Legend: pp = Partially Programmed.
Bridge Group:Bridge-Domain Name  ID    State   Num ACs/up   Num PWs/up    Num PBBs/
  up  Num VNIs/up
-------------------------------- ----  -------------- ------------ -------------- ----
  ------- -----
ELAN-BG:200-BD                    0     up       1/1          0/0          0/0     0/0
ELAN-BG:201-BD                    1     up       1/1          0/0          0/0     0/0
```

In order to display per-bridge domain detail information, you can use the command **show l2vpn bridge-domain bd-name 200-BD detail**, as shown in Output 6-30. The output of this command executed on PE-1 can be grouped into three main sections from which the bridge domain/EVPN/access circuit configured state together with status information can easily be obtained:

Note This is not a complete list of all status information from the command output.

- **bridge-domain: 200-BD:**

  - **bridge-domain state: up:** The bridge domain can also be in an admin down state if configured as shutdown.

  - **AC: 1 (1 up):** The associated access circuit interface bundle-ether 200.2000 is in the up state.

- **EVPN:**

  - **EVPN state: up**

  - **evi: 200 (SRv6):** EVPN EVI 200 is associated via the configuration to the bridge domain 200-BD.

- **Access circuits:**

  - **AC: Bundle-Ether200.2000, state is up:** Interface bundle-ether 200.2000 is in the up state.

  - **Type VLAN; Num Ranges: 1**

  - **VLAN ranges: [2000, 2000]:** The VLAN-ID associated with the access circuit. Interface bundle-ether 200.2000 is configured with **encapsulation dot1q 2000.**

Output 6-30   *L2VPN Bridge Domain 200-BD Detail State Output on PE-1*

```
RP/0/RP0/CPU0:PE-1#show l2vpn bridge-domain bd-name 200-BD detail

Legend: pp = Partially Programmed.
Bridge group: ELAN-BG, bridge-domain: 200-BD, id: 0, state: up, ShgId: 0, MSTi: 0
<snip>
  ACs: 1 (1 up), VFIs: 0, PWs: 0 (0 up), PBBs: 0 (0 up), VNIs: 0 (0 up)
  List of EVPNs:
    EVPN, state: up
      evi: 200 (SRv6)
     XC ID 0xfff01001
    Statistics:
      packets: received 0 (unicast 0), sent 0
      bytes: received 0 (unicast 0), sent 0
      MAC move: 0
  List of ACs:
    AC: bundle-ether 200.2000, state is up
      Type VLAN; Num Ranges: 1
      Rewrite Tags: []
      VLAN ranges: [2000, 2000]
  <snip>
```

Output 6-31 from router PE-2 indicates that the interface bundle-ether 200 is in a **down** state, which is expected because EVI 200 is a port-active multihomed service.

Output 6-31 *L2VPN Bridge Domain 200-BD Detail State on PE-2*

```
RP/0/RP0/CPU0:PE-2#show l2vpn bridge-domain bd-name 200-BD detail

Bridge group: ELAN-BG, bridge-domain: 200-BD, id: 0, state: up, ShgId: 0, MSTi: 0
<snip>
  ACs: 1 (0 up), VFIs: 0, PWs: 0 (0 up), PBBs: 0 (0 up), VNIs: 0 (0 up)
  List of EVPNs:
    EVPN, state: up
      evi: 200 (SRv6)
<snip>
  List of ACs:
    AC: Bundle-Ether200.2000, state is down (Segment-down)
      Type VLAN; Num Ranges: 1
      Rewrite Tags: []
      VLAN ranges: [2000, 2000]
<snip>
```

The next stage in verifying the L2VPN configured states is to display the MAC addresses learned via the bridge domain 200-BD on PE-1 through the command **show l2vpn forwarding bridge-domain ELAN-BG:200-BD mac-address location 0/RP0/CPU0**. In this example scenario, CE-1 has forwarded L2 traffic across the subinterface bundle-ether 200.2000 toward the PE router, and the output of this command displays five locally learned MAC addresses, as shown in Output 6-32.

Output 6-32 *L2VPN Forwarding Bridge Domain 200-BD Local Learned MAC Addresses on PE-1*

```
RP/0/RP0/CPU0:PE-1#show l2vpn forwarding bridge-domain ELAN-BG:200-BD mac-address
   location 0/RP0/CPU0
Mac Address    Type    Learned from/Filtered on   LC learned Age          Mapped to
------------   ------  ------------------------   ---------- -----------  ---------
   ----
1011.1100.0001 dynamic BE200.2000                 0/RP0/CPU  0d 0h 0m 27s N/A
1011.1100.0002 dynamic BE200.2000                 0/RP0/CPU  0d 0h 0m 27s N/A
1011.1100.0003 dynamic BE200.2000                 0/RP0/CPU  0d 0h 0m 27s N/A
1011.1100.0004 dynamic BE200.2000                 0/RP0/CPU  0d 0h 0m 27s N/A
1011.1100.0005 dynamic BE200.2000                 0/RP0/CPU  0d 0h 0m 26s N/A
RP/0/RP0/CPU0:PE-1#
```

The remote peer PE routers in EVI 200 display these MAC addresses as learned from the EVPN side as expected. Output 6-33 shows an example from the PE-3 router in IS-IS Metro 2.

Output 6-33 *L2VPN Forwarding Bridge Domain 200-BD: Remote Learned MAC Addresses on PE-3*

```
RP/0/RP0/CPU0:PE-3#show l2vpn forwarding bridge-domain ELAN-BG:200-BD mac-address
   location 0/RP0/CPU0
Mac Address     Type    Learned from/Filtered on  LC learned Age           Mapped to
--------------- ------  ------------------------  ---------- ------------- ---------
   ----
1011.1100.0001 EVPN     BD id: 0                  N/A        N/A           N/A
1011.1100.0002 EVPN     BD id: 0                  N/A        N/A           N/A
1011.1100.0003 EVPN     BD id: 0                  N/A        N/A           N/A
1011.1100.0004 EVPN     BD id: 0                  N/A        N/A           N/A
1011.1100.0005 EVPN     BD id: 0                  N/A        N/A           N/A
RP/0/RP0/CPU0:PE-3#
```

An alternate command to verify locally learned MAC addresses across all topology IDs (bridge domains) is **show l2vpn mac-learning mac all location 0/RP0/CPU0**, as shown in Output 6-34.

Output 6-34 *Alternate Command: L2VPN MAC Address Learning All Bridge Domains on PE-1*

```
RP/0/RP0/CPU0:PE-1#show l2vpn mac-learning mac all location 0/RP0/CPU0
Topo ID    Producer        Next Hop(s)       Mac Address       IP Address
---------- --------------- ----------------- ----------------- ---------------
0          0/RP0/CPU0      BE200.2000        1011.1100.0001
0          0/RP0/CPU0      BE200.2000        1011.1100.0002
0          0/RP0/CPU0      BE200.2000        1011.1100.0003
0          0/RP0/CPU0      BE200.2000        1011.1100.0004
0          0/RP0/CPU0      BE200.2000        1011.1100.0005
1          0/RP0/CPU0      BE200.2001        1022.2200.0001
1          0/RP0/CPU0      BE200.2001        1022.2200.0002
1          0/RP0/CPU0      BE200.2001        1022.2200.0003
1          0/RP0/CPU0      BE200.2001        1022.2200.0004
1          0/RP0/CPU0      BE200.2001        1022.2200.0005
RP/0/RP0/CPU0:PE-1#
```

Alternatively, if only the output of a single bridge domain is required (such as in Output 6-32), you can use the relevant topology ID rather than display the routes for all topologies. This topology ID was obtained previously with the command **show l2vpn bridge-domain brief** in Output 6-29. See the example shown in Output 6-35 from the router PE-1.

Output 6-35   *Alternate Command: L2VPN MAC Address Learning per Bridge Domain (Topo ID) on PE-1*

```
RP/0/RP0/CPU0:PE-1#show l2vpn mac-learning mac topo-id 0 location 0/RP0/CPU0
Topo ID    Producer        Next Hop(s)        Mac Address        IP Address
---------- --------------- ------------------ ------------------ ---------------

0          0/RP0/CPU0      BE200.2000         1011.1100.0001

0          0/RP0/CPU0      BE200.2000         1011.1100.0002

0          0/RP0/CPU0      BE200.2000         1011.1100.0003

0          0/RP0/CPU0      BE200.2000         1011.1100.0004

0          0/RP0/CPU0      BE200.2000         1011.1100.0005
RP/0/RP0/CPU0:PE-1#
```

The next output to be verified is the EVPN Route Type 3 inclusive multicast forwarding information, including the destination SRv6 SID associated with EVI 200 across all participating PE routers. Output 6-36 shows the **show l2vpn forwarding bridge-domain ELAN-BG:200-BD evpn inclusive-multicast location 0/RP0/CPU0** command, whose output displays the three next hop SIDs used when forwarding BUM traffic from the ingress router PE-1 into the EVI 200 in order for this traffic to reach each of the remote peer PE routers.

Output 6-36   *L2VPN Forwarding Inclusive-Multicast: Bridge Domain 200-BD on PE-1*

```
RP/0/RP0/CPU0:PE-1#show l2vpn forwarding bridge-domain ELAN-BG:200-BD evpn
    inclusive-multicast location 0/RP0/CPU0


Bridge-Domain Name    BD-ID XCID    TEP-id      Next Hop                  Label/VNI
------------------    ----- ------  ----------  --------------------      ---------

ELAN-BG:200-BD          0    0xfff01001 0x05000001 SRv6 SID fc00:0:205:e001::, fmt type: 2
                                       0x05000002 SRv6 SID fc00:0:206:e005::, fmt type: 2
                                       0x05000003 SRv6 SID fc00:0:106:e001::, fmt type: 2
```

Table 6-3 provides an overview of the EVPN Route Type 3 SIDs advertised within EVI 200 from the remote PE routers.

Table 6-3   *EVPN Route Type 3: Inclusive Multicast SIDs*

Router	SID	EVI	Endpoint Function	Comment
PE-2	fc00:0:106:e001	200	uDT2M	Endpoint with decapsulation and L2 table flooding EVPN (BUM)
PE-3	fc00:0:205:e001	200	uDT2M	Endpoint with decapsulation and L2 table flooding EVPN (BUM)
PE-4	fc00:0:206:e005	200	uDT2M	Endpoint with decapsulation and L2 table flooding EVPN (BUM)

The SRv6 local SID outputs from each of the peer PE routers confirm that the L2VPN inclusive multicast SIDs do indeed match those received on the router PE-1, as previously displayed in Output 6-36. The command **show segment-routing srv6 locator MAIN sid** executed on PE-2 provides confirmation (see Output 6-37).

Output 6-37   *SRv6 Local SIDs: uDT2M (Inclusive Multicast) Verification on PE-2*

```
RP/0/RP0/CPU0:PE-2#show segment-routing srv6 locator MAIN sid


SID                   Behavior      Context                 Owner             State   RW
-------------------   -----------   ---------------------   ---------------   -----   --
fc00:0:106::          uN (PSP/USD)  'default':262           sidmgr            InUse   Y
fc00:0:106:e000::     uDT2U         200:0                   l2vpn_srv6        InUse   Y
fc00:0:106:e001::     uDT2M         200:0                   l2vpn_srv6        InUse   Y
fc00:0:106:e002::     uDT2U         201:0                   l2vpn_srv6        InUse   Y
fc00:0:106:e003::     uDT2M         201:0                   l2vpn_srv6        InUse   Y
<snip>
RP/0/RP0/CPU0:PE-2#
```

The command **show segment-routing srv6 locator MAIN sid** executed on PE-3 in Output 6-38 provides confirmation from PE-3.

Output 6-38   *SRv6 Local SIDs: uDT2M (Inclusive Multicast) Verification on PE-3*

```
RP/0/RP0/CPU0:PE-3#show segment-routing srv6 locator MAIN sid


SID                   Behavior      Context                 Owner             State   RW
-------------------   -----------   ---------------------   ---------------   -----   --
fc00:0:205::          uN (PSP/USD)  'default':517           sidmgr            InUse   Y
fc00:0:205:e000::     uDT2U         200:0                   l2vpn_srv6        InUse   Y
fc00:0:205:e001::     uDT2M         200:0                   l2vpn_srv6        InUse   Y
fc00:0:205:e002::     uDT2U         201:0                   l2vpn_srv6        InUse   Y
fc00:0:205:e003::     uDT2M         201:0                   l2vpn_srv6        InUse   Y
<snip>
RP/0/RP0/CPU0:PE-3#
```

Finally, Output 6-39 provides local confirmation of the inclusive multicast SID advertised from router PE-4.

Output 6-39 *SRv6 Local SIDs: uDT2M (Inclusive Multicast) Verification on PE-4*

```
RP/0/RP0/CPU0:PE-4#show segment-routing srv6 locator MAIN sid

SID                    Behavior    Context                 Owner            State   RW
-------------------    ----------- ----------------------  ---------------  -----   --
<snip>
fc00:0:206:e004::      uDT2U       200:0                   l2vpn_srv6       InUse   Y
fc00:0:206:e005::      uDT2M       200:0                   l2vpn_srv6       InUse   Y
fc00:0:206:e006::      uDT2U       201:0                   l2vpn_srv6       InUse   Y
fc00:0:206:e007::      uDT2M       201:0                   l2vpn_srv6       InUse   Y
fc00:0:206:e008::      uDT2U       210:0                   l2vpn_srv6       InUse   Y
fc00:0:206:e009::      uDT2M       210:0                   l2vpn_srv6       InUse   Y
RP/0/RP0/CPU0:PE-4#
```

EVPN E-LAN Port-Active MHD BGP Configuration

The fourth configuration step is the BGP provisioning on all the PE routers, as shown in the high-level overview diagram in Figure 6-26. EVPN is transported in the BGP multiprotocol extensions and is identified via address family identifier (AFI) 25 (L2VPN) and subsequent address family identifier (SAFI) 70 (EVPN).

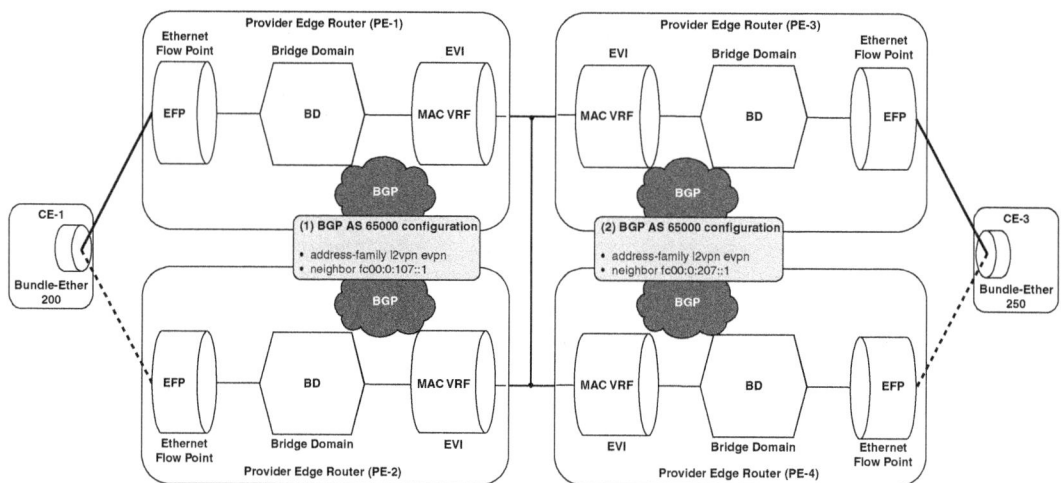

Figure 6-26 *EVPN E-LAN Port-Active MHD BGP Configuration Tasks*

The IPv6 peering addresses used for the BGP configuration are as follows:

- **PE-1:** fc00:0:105::1

- **PE-2:** fc00:0:106::1

- **RR-1:** fc00:0:107::1

- **PE-3:** fc00:0:205::1

- **PE-4:** fc00:0:206::1

- **RR-2:** fc00:0:207::1

The route reflectors are using BGP dynamic neighbor configuration via the summary route fc00:0:100::/40 for PE-1 and PE-2 in Metro 1 and using the summary route fc00:0:200::/40 for PE-3 and PE-4 in Metro 2. This BGP dynamic neighbor configuration allows BGP peering to a group of remote neighbors defined by a range of IP addresses. The implementation of BGP dynamic neighbors can significantly reduce the amount of CLI configuration used in larger-scale networks. The BGP dynamic neighbor configured router will be operating in TCP passive mode and will therefore "listen" for a TCP connection from a remote peer. RR-1 is configured for BGP dynamic neighbor peering via **neighbor fc00:0:100::/40** in Config 6-21. RR-1 also peers with RR-2 in Metro 2 via the standard neighbor peer configuration, **neighbor fc00:0:207::1.**

Config 6-21   *EVPN E-LAN Port-Active MHD BGP Configuration on RR-1*

```
router bgp 65000
 bgp router-id 172.19.0.12
 !
 address-family l2vpn evpn
 !
 neighbor-group IBGP-PE-NG
  remote-as 65000
  description *** iBGP peering to METRO-1 PE ***
  update-source Loopback0
  !
  address-family l2vpn evpn
   route-reflector-client
  !
 !
 neighbor-group IBGP-RR-NG
  remote-as 65000
  description *** iBGP peering to METRO-2 RR ***
  update-source Loopback0
  !
  address-family l2vpn evpn
  !
 !
 neighbor fc00:0:100::/40
  use neighbor-group IBGP-PE-NG
  description *** iBGP session to METRO-1 PE ***
 !
```

```
 neighbor fc00:0:207::1
  use neighbor-group IBGP-RR-NG
  description *** iBGP peering to METRO-2 RR ***
 !
```

Routers PE-1 and PE-2 peering with RR-1 in Metro 1 will have similar BGP configurations. The configuration in Config 6-22 is sufficient.

Config 6-22   *EVPN E-LAN Port-Active MHD BGP Configuration on PE-1 and PE-2*

```
router bgp 65000
 bgp router-id 172.19.0.10
 !
 address-family l2vpn evpn
 !
 neighbor-group IBGP-RR1-NG
  remote-as 65000
  description *** iBGP peering to METRO-1 RR ***
  update-source Loopback0
   !
   address-family l2vpn evpn
   !
 !
 neighbor fc00:0:107::1
  use neighbor-group IBGP-RR1-NG
  description *** iBGP peering to METRO-1 RR ***
 !
```

In Metro 2, RR-2 is similarly configured for BGP dynamic neighbor peering via **neighbor fc00:0:200::/40** in Config 6-23. RR-2 is also provisioned with the required standard neighbor peer configuration, **neighbor fc00:0:107::1**, to peer with RR-1 in Metro 1.

Config 6-23   *EVPN E-LAN Port-Active MHD BGP Configuration on RR-2*

```
router bgp 65000
 bgp router-id 172.19.0.21
 !
 address-family l2vpn evpn
 !
 neighbor-group IBGP-PE-NG
  remote-as 65000
  description *** iBGP peering to METRO-2 PE ***
  update-source Loopback0
   !
   address-family l2vpn evpn
```

```
    route-reflector-client
  !
 !
 neighbor-group IBGP-RR-NG
  remote-as 65000
  description *** iBGP peering to METRO-1 RR ***
  update-source Loopback0
  !
  address-family l2vpn evpn
  !
 !
 neighbor fc00:0:200::/40
  use neighbor-group IBGP-PE-NG
  description *** iBGP session to METRO-2 PE ***
 !
 neighbor fc00:0:107::1
  use neighbor-group IBGP-RR-NG
  description *** iBGP peering to METRO-1 RR ***
  !
```

And as with the PE configurations in Metro 1, both PE-3 and PE-4 will peer with RR-2 in Metro 2. The configuration in Config 6-24 is sufficient to bring up these peering sessions.

Config 6-24 *EVPN E-LAN Port-Active MHD BGP Configuration on PE-3 and PE-4*

```
router bgp 65000
 bgp router-id 172.19.0.19
 !
 address-family l2vpn evpn
 !
 neighbor-group IBGP-RR2-NG
  remote-as 65000
  description *** iBGP peering to METRO-2 RR ***
  update-source Loopback0
  !
  address-family l2vpn evpn
  !
 !
 neighbor fc00:0:207::1
  use neighbor-group IBGP-RR2-NG
  description *** iBGP peering to METRO-2 RR ***
  !
```

The BGP **address-family l2vpn evpn** configurations for both of the route reflectors, RR-1 and RR-2, as well as for the four PE routers is sufficient for the BGP EVPN control plane and allows the exchange of all EVPN route types required for the port-active multihomed service to operate correctly.

EVPN E-LAN Port-Active MHD BGP Verification

This section describes the commands shown in Figure 6-27 that are used to verify and troubleshoot the BGP **address-family l2vpn evpn** service configuration.

```
show bgp l2vpn evpn summary
show bgp vrf-db table all
show bgp vrf-db table 0xfd00ffff
show bgp vrf-db table 0xff0000c8
show bgp vrf-db table 0xff0000c9
show bgp l2vpn evpn bridge-domain 200-BD
show bgp l2vpn evpn rd 172.19.0.10:200
show bgp l2vpn evpn bridge-domain 200-BD received-sids wide
show bgp l2vpn evpn bridge-domain 200-BD [1][0000.fc00.0102.0000.0000][0]/120
show bgp l2vpn evpn bridge-domain 200-BD [1][0000.fc00.0102.0000.0000][4294967295]/120
show bgp l2vpn evpn bridge-domain 200-BD [2][0][48][2011.1100.0001][0]/104
show bgp l2vpn evpn bridge-domain 200-BD [3][0][32][172.19.0.19]/80
show bgp l2vpn evpn route-type ethernet-segment
show bgp l2vpn evpn rd 172.19.0.10:0 [4][0000.fc00.0102.0000.0000][32][172.19.0.11]/128
```

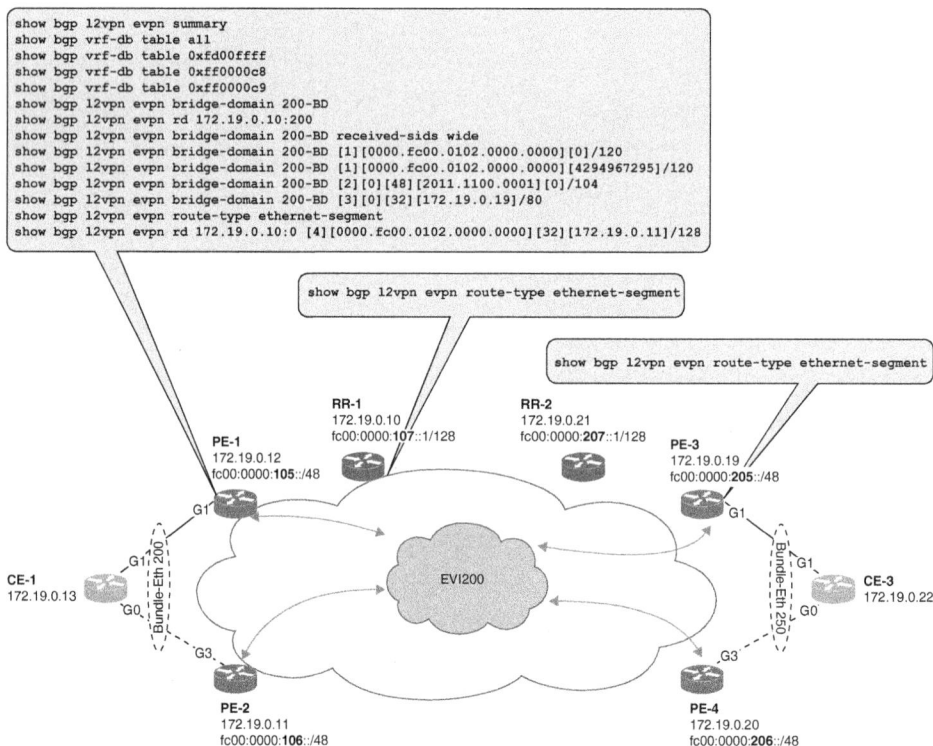

Figure 6-27   *EVPN E-LAN Port-Active MHD BGP Verification*

The final major component of the control plane verification steps is the BGP component. The router outputs are collected from the routers PE-1 and RR-1 in IS-IS Metro 1 and PE-3 and RR-2 in IS-IS Metro 2. The MAC addresses 1011.1100.0001–1011.1100.0005 originated from router CE-1, and MAC addresses 2011.1100.0001–2011.1100.0005 originated from the router CE-3.

The command **show bgp l2vpn evpn summary** in Output 6-40 provides an initial high-level overview of the router PE-1 BGP peering neighborship state with the route reflector RR-1. The BGP neighbor IPv6 address fc00:0:107::1 is the configured **update-source Loopback0** on RR-1. The **PfxRcd** column indicates the number of received prefixes from the route reflector RR-1. These include the EVPN RT-1, RT-2, RT-3, and RT-4 for this BGP address family, which equates to 21 accepted prefixes, of which 21 are best paths.

Output 6-40 *BGP AF L2VPN EVPN Summary Overview on PE-1*

```
RP/0/RP0/CPU0:PE-1#show bgp l2vpn evpn summary
BGP router identifier 172.19.0.10, local AS number 65000
BGP generic scan interval 60 secs
Non-stop routing is enabled
BGP table state: Active
Table ID: 0x0
BGP main routing table version 687
BGP NSR Initial initsync version 1 (Reached)
BGP NSR/ISSU Sync-Group versions 0/0
BGP scan interval 60 secs

BGP is operating in STANDALONE mode.


Process       RcvTblVer    bRIB/RIB   LabelVer  ImportVer  SendTblVer  StandbyVer
Speaker            687          687        687        687         687           0
Neighbor        Spk    AS MsgRcvd MsgSent    TblVer  InQ OutQ  Up/Down  St/PfxRcd
fc00:0:107::1     0 65000    4337     4048       687    0    0    2d18h         21

RP/0/RP0/CPU0:PE-1#
```

The **show bgp vrf-db table all** command in Output 6-41 provides the VRF database for all BGP-related L3VPN and EVPN instances. Each VRF is assigned a particular VRF ID. From this table, these IDs can be used to provide more details related to route target information for each of the EVPN instances.

Output 6-41 *BGP Provisioned Contexts Summary on PE-1*

```
RP/0/RP0/CPU0:PE-1#show bgp vrf-db table all
ID           REF    AF              VRF
0xe0000000   2      IPv4 Unicast    default
0xe0000001   7      IPv4 Unicast    BLUE
0xe0000002   6      IPv4 Unicast    TEST
0xe0000003   7      IPv4 Unicast    ANYCAST
0xe0800000   2      IPv6 Unicast    default
0xfd00ffff   6      L2VPN EVPN      ES:GLOBAL
0xff0000c8   9      L2VPN EVPN      200-BD
0xff0000c9   6      L2VPN EVPN      201-BD
RP/0/RP0/CPU0:PE-1#
```

By including these previously obtained IDs, as shown in Output 6-42, details of all the import route targets for the EVPN default VRF ES:GLOBAL are displayed. The EVPN

ES import route target is part of the BGP extended communities contained in the EVPN Route Type 4 route. This is the MAC address portion of the ESI, and in this example there is only a single Ethernet segment configured with ES import RT 00fc.0001.0200.

Output 6-42   *BGP EVPN Context ES:GLOBAL on PE-1*

```
RP/0/RP0/CPU0:PE-1#show bgp vrf-db table 0xfd00ffff
VRF-TBL: ES:GLOBAL (L2VPN EVPN)
  TBL ID: 0xfd00ffff
  RSI Handle: NULL
  Refcount: 6
  Import:
    RT-List: EVPN ES Import:00fc.0001.0200
    Stitching RT-List: EVPN ES Import:00fc.0001.0200
  Export:
    RT-List: { }
RP/0/RP0/CPU0:PE-1#
```

Similarly, for EVI 200, the command **show bgp vrf-db table 0xff0000c8** shown in Output 6-43 displays its applied route target import/export list. The export route target 65000:200 is included as part of the BGP extended communities contained in the EVPN Route Type 1 per-EVI Ethernet A-D route and the EVPN Route Type 2 MAC advertisement route.

Output 6-43   *BGP Provisioned Context 200-BD on PE-1*

```
RP/0/RP0/CPU0:PE-1#show bgp vrf-db table 0xff0000c8
VRF-TBL: 200-BD (L2VPN EVPN)
  TBL ID: 0xff0000c8
  RSI Handle: NULL
  Refcount: 9
  Import:
    RT-List: RT:65000:200
  Export:
    RT-List: RT:65000:200
RP/0/RP0/CPU0:PE-1#
```

For the second configured EVI, 201, the command **show bgp vrf-db table 0xff0000c9** shown in Output 6-44 displays its applied route target import/export list. The export route target 65000:201 is included as part of the BGP extended communities contained in the EVPN Route Type 1 per-EVI Ethernet A-D route and the EVPN Route Type 2 MAC advertisement route.

Output 6-44   *BGP Provisioned Context 201-BD on PE-1*

```
RP/0/RP0/CPU0:PE-1#show bgp vrf-db table 0xff0000c9
VRF-TBL: 201-BD (L2VPN EVPN)
  TBL ID: 0xff0000c9
  RSI Handle: NULL
  Refcount: 6
  Import:
    RT-List: RT:65000:201
  Export:
    RT-List: RT:65000:201
RP/0/RP0/CPU0:PE-1#
```

The command **show bgp l2vpn evpn bridge-domain 200-BD** and some variations there-of are probably the most widely used for BGP route verification. In Output 6-45, all the EVPN route types are displayed for the bridge domain 200-BD, which is part of EVI 200. Output 6-45 displays the following EVPN routes types imported into the EVI 200, and a few highlighted routes are discussed:

- **[1][0000.fc00.0102.0000.0000][0]/120 (EVPN Route Type 1):** This is a per-EVI Ethernet A-D route, locally originated and learned from remote PE routers.

- **[1][0000.fc00.0102.0000.0000][4294967295]/120 (EVPN Route Type 1):** This is a per-ESI Ethernet A-D route identifiable through the reserved MAX Ethernet tag ID 4294967295.

- **[2][0][48][1011.1100.0001][0]/104 (EVPN Route Type 2):** This is a MAC route locally learned via the Ethernet segment and attached router CE-1.

- **[2][0][48][2011.1100.0001][0]/104 (EVPN Route Type 2):** This is a MAC route remotely learned via the EVPN EVI 200 from the router PE-3.

- **[3][0][32][172.19.0.11]/80 (EVPN Route Type 3):** This is an inclusive multicast route learned from the router PE-2.

Output 6-45   *BGP L2VPN EVPN EVI 200 Routes on PE-1*

```
RP/0/RP0/CPU0:PE-1#show bgp l2vpn evpn bridge-domain 200-BD
BGP router identifier 172.19.0.10, local AS number 65000
<snip>

Status codes: s suppressed, d damped, h history, * valid, > best
              i - internal, r RIB-failure, S stale, N Nexthop-discard
Origin codes: i - IGP, e - EGP, ? - incomplete
  Network          Next Hop            Metric LocPrf Weight Path
Route Distinguisher: 172.19.0.10:200 (default for vrf 200-BD)
Route Distinguisher Version: 687
```

```
*>  [1][0000.fc00.0102.0000.0000][0]/120
                    0.0.0.0                            0 i
*  i                fc00:0:106::1             100      0 i
*>i[1][0000.fc00.0102.0000.0000][4294967295]/120
                    fc00:0:106::1             100      0 i
*>i[1][0000.fc00.0202.5000.0000][0]/120
                    fc00:0:205::1             100      0 i
*  i                fc00:0:206::1             100      0 i
*>i[1][0000.fc00.0202.5000.0000][4294967295]/120
                    fc00:0:205::1             100      0 i
*  i                fc00:0:206::1             100      0 i
*>  [2][0][48][1011.1100.0001][0]/104
                    0.0.0.0                            0 i
*>  [2][0][48][1011.1100.0002][0]/104
                    0.0.0.0                            0 i
*>  [2][0][48][1011.1100.0003][0]/104
                    0.0.0.0                            0 i
*>  [2][0][48][1011.1100.0004][0]/104
                    0.0.0.0                            0 i
*>  [2][0][48][1011.1100.0005][0]/104
                    0.0.0.0                            0 i
*>i[2][0][48][2011.1100.0001][0]/104
                    fc00:0:205::1             100      0 i
*>i[2][0][48][2011.1100.0002][0]/104
                    fc00:0:205::1             100      0 i
*>i[2][0][48][2011.1100.0003][0]/104
                    fc00:0:205::1             100      0 i
*>i[2][0][48][2011.1100.0004][0]/104
                    fc00:0:205::1             100      0 i
*>i[2][0][48][2011.1100.0005][0]/104
                    fc00:0:205::1             100      0 i
*>  [3][0][32][172.19.0.10]/80
                    0.0.0.0                            0 i
*>i[3][0][32][172.19.0.11]/80
                    fc00:0:106::1             100      0 i
*>i[3][0][32][172.19.0.19]/80
                    fc00:0:205::1             100      0 i
*>i[3][0][32][172.19.0.20]/80
                    fc00:0:206::1             100      0 i

Processed 18 prefixes, 21 paths
RP/0/RP0/CPU0:PE-1#
```

Output 6-46 shows an alternate version of this command, which displays the same EVPN route type information. In this case, the EVI selection is based on the use of the route distinguisher 172.19.0.10:200 in the command for displaying the routes imported into EVI 200.

Output 6-46   *BGP L2VPN EVPN RD 172.19.0.10:200 Routes on PE-1*

```
RP/0/RP0/CPU0:PE-1#show bgp l2vpn evpn rd 172.19.0.10:200
<snip>
Route Distinguisher: 172.19.0.10:200 (default for vrf 200-BD)
<snip>
*> [1][0000.fc00.0102.0000.0000][0]/120
                          0.0.0.0                              0 i
* i                       fc00:0:106::1            100          0 i
*>i[1][0000.fc00.0102.0000.0000][4294967295]/120
                          fc00:0:106::1            100          0 i
*>i[1][0000.fc00.0202.5000.0000][0]/120
                          fc00:0:205::1            100          0 i
* i                       fc00:0:206::1            100          0 i
*>i[1][0000.fc00.0202.5000.0000][4294967295]/120
                          fc00:0:205::1            100          0 i
* i                       fc00:0:206::1            100          0 i
*> [2][0][48][1011.1100.0001][0]/104
                          0.0.0.0                              0 i
<snip>
*>i[2][0][48][2011.1100.0001][0]/104
                          fc00:0:205::1            100          0 i
<snip>
*> [3][0][32][172.19.0.10]/80
                          0.0.0.0                              0 i
<snip>

Processed 18 prefixes, 21 paths
RP/0/RP0/CPU0:PE-1#
```

Following on from the command **show bgp l2vpn evpn bridge-domain 200-BD**, the command **show bgp l2vpn evpn bridge-domain 200-BD received-sids wide** in Output 6-47 displays all the EVPN route types imported into the EVI 200, with the addition of the received SID information. For example:

■ **[1][0000.fc00.0102.0000.0000][0]/120 (EVPN Route Type 1):** This is a per-EVI Ethernet A-D route, locally originated and received from router PE-2 with next hop fc00:0:106::1 and a received SID of fc00:0:106:e000::.

- **[2][0][48][2011.1100.0001][0]/104 (EVPN Route Type 2):** This is a MAC route received from router PE-3 with next hop fc00:0:205::1 and a received SID of fc00:0:205:e000::.

- **[3][0][32][172.19.0.19]/80 EVPN (Route Type 3):** This is an inclusive multicast route learned from the router PE-3 with next hop fc00:0:205::1 and a received SID of fc00:0:205:e001::.

Output 6-47 *BGP L2VPN EVPN EVI-200 Received SIDs on PE-1*

```
RP/0/RP0/CPU0:PE-1#show bgp l2vpn evpn bridge-domain 200-BD received-sids wide
BGP router identifier 172.19.0.10, local AS number 65000
<snip>


Status codes: s suppressed, d damped, h history, * valid, > best
              i - internal, r RIB-failure, S stale, N Nexthop-discard
Origin codes: i - IGP, e - EGP, ? - incomplete
   Network                              Next Hop         Received Sid
Route Distinguisher: 172.19.0.10:200 (default for vrf 200-BD)
Route Distinguisher Version: 837
*>  [1][0000.fc00.0102.0000.0000][0]/120        0.0.0.0          fc00:0:105::
*  i                                            fc00:0:106::1    fc00:0:106:e000::
*>i[1][0000.fc00.0102.0000.0000][4294967295]/120fc00:0:106::1   NO SRv6 Sid
*>i[1][0000.fc00.0202.5000.0000][0]/120        fc00:0:205::1    fc00:0:205:e000::
*  i                                            fc00:0:206::1    fc00:0:206:e000::
*>i[1][0000.fc00.0202.5000.0000][4294967295]/120fc00:0:205::1   NO SRv6 Sid
*  i                                            fc00:0:206::1    NO SRv6 Sid
*>  [2][0][48][1011.1100.0001][0]/104           0.0.0.0          fc00:0:105::
*>  [2][0][48][1011.1100.0002][0]/104           0.0.0.0          fc00:0:105::
*>  [2][0][48][1011.1100.0003][0]/104           0.0.0.0          fc00:0:105::
*>  [2][0][48][1011.1100.0004][0]/104           0.0.0.0          fc00:0:105::
*>  [2][0][48][1011.1100.0005][0]/104           0.0.0.0          fc00:0:105::
*>i[2][0][48][2011.1100.0001][0]/104            fc00:0:205::1    fc00:0:205:e000::
*>i[2][0][48][2011.1100.0002][0]/104            fc00:0:205::1    fc00:0:205:e000::
*>i[2][0][48][2011.1100.0003][0]/104            fc00:0:205::1    fc00:0:205:e000::
*>i[2][0][48][2011.1100.0004][0]/104            fc00:0:205::1    fc00:0:205:e000::
*>i[2][0][48][2011.1100.0005][0]/104            fc00:0:205::1    fc00:0:205:e000::
*>  [3][0][32][172.19.0.10]/80                  0.0.0.0          fc00:0:105:e001::
*>i[3][0][32][172.19.0.11]/80                   fc00:0:106::1    fc00:0:106:e001::
*>i[3][0][32][172.19.0.19]/80                   fc00:0:205::1    fc00:0:205:e001::
*>i[3][0][32][172.19.0.20]/80                   fc00:0:206::1    fc00:0:206:e001::


Processed 18 prefixes, 21 paths
RP/0/RP0/CPU0:PE-1#
```

The verification of individual BGP EVPN route types follows a similar command structure to the standard commands used to verify VPNv4 unicast individual route details. The command **show bgp l2vpn evpn bridge-domain 200-BD [1][0000. fc00.0102.0000.0000][0]/120** executed on router PE-1 is of the BGP EVPN Route Type 1 per-EVI Ethernet A-D route originated on both PE routers PE-1 and PE-2 for the Ethernet segment associated with the interface bundle-ether 200. Highlighted details from Output 6-48 are discussed in the following bullet points:

- **ESI:** This is the 10-byte Ethernet segment identifier 00:00:fc:00:01:02:00:00:00:00.

- **Local Label:** This is a local aliasing label represented as decimal 14680064. This field is 24 bits in length and transports the 16-bit uSID 0xe000 in the higher-order 20 bits of the MPLS Label field.

- **Received Label:** This is the received aliasing label 0xe00000 from router PE-2 represented in hexadecimal format. The 16-bit uSID 0xe000 is encoded in the higher-order 20 bits of the MPLS Label field.

- **Route Target:** This is per-EVI route target 65000:200.

- **Sid:fc00:0:105::, Behavior:67:** This is the local PE router SRv6 locator value fc00:0:105::, and the behavior 67 refers to the endpoint behavior End.DT2U with NEXT-CSID (0x0043). Refer to Chapter 2, "What Is Segment Routing over MPLS (SR-MPLS)?" for more details.

- **Sid:fc00:0:106::, Behavior:67:** This is the remote PE router SRv6 locator value fc00:0:106::, and the behavior 67 refers to the endpoint behavior End.DT2U with NEXT-CSID (0x0043).

- **Source Route Distinguisher:** This is source RD 172.19.0.11:200 inserted by the originating router PE-2.

Output 6-48 *BGP EVPN Route Type 1 Per-EVI Ethernet A-D Route Details on PE-1*

```
RP/0/RP0/CPU0:PE-1#show bgp l2vpn evpn bridge-domain 200-BD [1][0000.
  fc00.0102.0000.0000][0]/120
BGP routing table entry for [1][0000.fc00.0102.0000.0000][0]/120, Route
  Distinguisher: 172.19.0.10:200
Versions:
  Process           bRIB/RIB  SendTblVer
  Speaker              551          551
    Local Label: 14680064
Last Modified: May 21 01:17:30.115 for 1d03h
Paths: (2 available, best #1)
  Advertised to peers (in unique update groups):
    fc00:0:107::1
  Path #1: Received by speaker 0
  Advertised to peers (in unique update groups):
    fc00:0:107::1
```

```
Local
  0.0.0.0 from 0.0.0.0 (172.19.0.10)
    Origin IGP, localpref 100, valid, redistributed, best, group-best,
import-candidate, rib-install
    Received Path ID 0, Local Path ID 1, version 4
    Extended community: RT:65000:200
    PSID-Type:L2, SubTLV Count:1
     SubTLV:
      T:1(Sid information), Sid:fc00:0:105::, Behavior:67, SS-TLV Count:1
       SubSubTLV:
        T:1(Sid structure):
Path #2: Received by speaker 0
Not advertised to any peer
Local
  fc00:0:106::1 (metric 21) from fc00:0:107::1 (172.19.0.11)
    Received Label 0xe00000
    Origin IGP, localpref 100, valid, internal, import-candidate, imported,
rib-install
    Received Path ID 0, Local Path ID 0, version 0
    Extended community: RT:65000:200
    Originator: 172.19.0.11, Cluster list: 172.19.0.12
    PSID-Type:L2, SubTLV Count:1
     SubTLV:
      T:1(Sid information), Sid:fc00:0:106::, Behavior:67, SS-TLV Count:1
       SubSubTLV:
        T:1(Sid structure):
    Source AFI: L2VPN EVPN, Source VRF: default, Source Route
Distinguisher: 172.19.0.11:200
RP/0/RP0/CPU0:PE-1#
```

The detailed command output displayed in Output 6-49 is of the EVPN Route Type 1 per-ESI Ethernet A-D Route originated from the router PE-2. The relevant values from this output are as follows:

- **ESI:** This is the 10-byte Ethernet segment identifier 00:00:fc:00:01:02:00:00:00:00, as configured between the two PE routers PE-1 and PE-2.

- **Ethernet Tag ID:** This is the reserved MAX-Ethernet Tag ID 4294967295.

- **Received Label:** This is set to 0.

- **Extended community: ESI MPLS Label:** This consists of EVPN ESI Filter Label:0x01:3 with the redundancy mode bit set to 0x01 (Single-Active), MPLS split-horizon label with a value of 3, and the route targets RT:65000:200 RT:65000:201 for all EVIs associated with the Ethernet segment.

- **Source Route Distinguisher:** This is the source RD 172.19.0.11:1 inserted by the originating PE router PE-2.

Output 6-49 *BGP EVPN Route Type 1 per-ESI Ethernet A-D Route Details on PE-1*

```
RP/0/RP0/CPU0:PE-1#show bgp l2vpn evpn bridge-domain 200-BD [1][0000.
  fc00.0102.0000.0000][4294967295]/120
BGP routing table entry for [1][0000.fc00.0102.0000.0000][4294967295]/120,
  Route Distinguisher: 172.19.0.10:200
<snip>
Paths: (1 available, best #1)
  Not advertised to any peer
  Path #1: Received by speaker 0
  Not advertised to any peer
  Local
    fc00:0:106::1 (metric 21) from fc00:0:107::1 (172.19.0.11)
      Received Label 0
      Origin IGP, localpref 100, valid, internal, best, group-best,
import-candidate, imported, rib-install
      Received Path ID 0, Local Path ID 1, version 575
      Extended community: EVPN ESI Label:0x01:3 RT:65000:200 RT:65000:201
      Originator: 172.19.0.11, Cluster list: 172.19.0.12
      Source AFI: L2VPN EVPN, Source VRF: default, Source Route
Distinguisher: 172.19.0.11:1
RP/0/RP0/CPU0:PE-1#
```

As mentioned at the beginning of this section, the MAC addresses 1011.1100.0001–
1011.1100.0005 were originated by the router CE-1, while the MAC addresses
2011.1100.0001–2011.1100.0005 are from router CE-3. The **show bgp l2vpn evpn
bridge-domain 200-BD [2][0][48][2011.1100.0001][0]/104** command shown in
Output 6-50 provides information on an example EVPN Route Type 2 MAC address
route 2011.1100.0001 originated by the router CE-3:

- **Received Label 0xe00000:** The received label is 0xe00000, of which the most
  significant 16 bits are the SRv6 uSID 0xe000 attached to the MAC address route by
  the originating router PE-3.

- **Extended community:** Included within the BGP extended community attributes of
  the received route are the following:

  - **SoO:172.19.0.19:200:** Site of origin, a loop prevention mechanism

  - **0x0000.07d0:** Attachment circuit ID (4 octets) 0x0000.07d0 for the VLAN 2000
    configured on the subinterface bundle-ether 250.2000 on router PE-3

  - **RT:65000:200:** The route target associated with this specific Route Type 2 MAC
    route

- **EVPN ESI: 0000.fc00.0202.5000.0000:** This is the Ethernet segment identifier
  configured for the interface bundle-ether 250 on router PE-3.

- **BGP Prefix-SID:**

  - **Sid:fc00:0:205:::** SRv6 locator of the originating router PE-3

■ **Behavior:67:** SRv6 endpoint behavior (67) End.DT2U (0x0043), which is an
endpoint behavior with decapsulation and unicast MAC L2 table lookup

■ **Source Route Distinguisher:** Source RD 172.19.0.19:200 inserted by the
originating router PE-3

Output 6-50   *BGP EVPN Route Type 2 MAC Route Details on PE-1*

```
RP/0/RP0/CPU0:PE-1#show bgp l2vpn evpn bridge-domain 200-BD [2][0][48]
  [2011.1100.0001][0]/104
BGP routing table entry for [2][0][48][2011.1100.0001][0]/104, Route
  Distinguisher: 172.19.0.10:200
<snip>
Paths: (1 available, best #1)
  Not advertised to any peer
  Path #1: Received by speaker 0
  Not advertised to any peer
  Local
    fc00:0:205::1 (metric 61) from fc00:0:107::1 (172.19.0.19)
      Received Label 0xe00000
      Origin IGP, localpref 100, valid, internal, best, group-best,
import-candidate, imported, rib-install
      Received Path ID 0, Local Path ID 1, version 859
      Extended community: SoO:172.19.0.19:200 0x060e:0000.0000.07d0 RT:65000:200
      Originator: 172.19.0.19, Cluster list: 172.19.0.12, 172.19.0.21
      EVPN ESI: 0000.fc00.0202.5000.0000
      PSID-Type:L2, SubTLV Count:1
       SubTLV:
        T:1(Sid information), Sid:fc00:0:205::, Behavior:67, SS-TLV Count:1
         SubSubTLV:
          T:1(Sid structure):
      Source AFI: L2VPN EVPN, Source VRF: default, Source Route
  Distinguisher: 172.19.0.19:200
RP/0/RP0/CPU0:PE-1#
```

The next route type to be discussed is the EVPN Route Type 3 inclusive multicast route
received from router PE-3 and used for transmitting any BUM traffic to PE-3. These are
some details from Output 6-51:

■ **Extended community:** Included within the BGP extended community attributes of
the received route are the following:

■ **RT:65000:200:** The route target associated with this EVPN Route Type 3
inclusive multicast route

■ **Originator: 172.19.0.19:** This is the Router PE-3 originating router's router ID (RID).

■ **PMSI (provider multicast service interface):**

■ **flags 0x00, type 6:** Ingress Replication (6), indicating that the ingress router PE-1
will replicate all BUM frames and unicast them to the router PE-3

- **label 0xe00100:** The SID function attached to this inclusive multicast route by the originating router PE-3 to allow the unicast forwarding of any BUM traffic

  - **ID 0xac130013:** The unicast tunnel endpoint IP address 172.19.0.19 in hexadecimal notation for router PE-3

- **BGP Prefix-SID:**

  - **Sid: fc00:0:205:::** The SRv6 locator of the originating router PE-3

    - **Behavior: 68:** In contrast to the SRv6 endpoint behavior (67) for the Route Type 2 MAC route, the endpoint behavior (68) in this case is End.DT2M (0x0044), which is an endpoint with decapsulation and L2 flooding behavior (multicast).

- **Source Route Distinguisher:** The source RD 172.19.0.19:200 inserted by the originating router PE-3

Output 6-51 *BGP EVPN Route Type 3 Inclusive Multicast Route Details on PE-3*

```
RP/0/RP0/CPU0:PE-1#show bgp l2vpn evpn bridge-domain 200-BD [3][0][32]
  [172.19.0.19]/80
BGP routing table entry for [3][0][32][172.19.0.19]/80, Route
  Distinguisher: 172.19.0.10:200
Versions:
  Process           bRIB/RIB   SendTblVer
  Speaker              626          626
Last Modified: May 21 03:41:05.115 for 1d00h
Paths: (1 available, best #1)
  Not advertised to any peer
  Path #1: Received by speaker 0
  Not advertised to any peer
  Local
    fc00:0:205::1 (metric 61) from fc00:0:107::1 (172.19.0.19)
      Origin IGP, localpref 100, valid, internal, best, group-best,
import-candidate, imported
      Received Path ID 0, Local Path ID 1, version 626
      Extended community: RT:65000:200
      Originator: 172.19.0.19, Cluster list: 172.19.0.12, 172.19.0.21
      PMSI: flags 0x00, type 6, label 0xe00100, ID 0xac130013
      PSID-Type:L2, SubTLV Count:1
       SubTLV:
        T:1(Sid information), Sid:fc00:0:205::, Behavior:68, SS-TLV Count:1
         SubSubTLV:
          T:1(Sid structure):
      Source AFI: L2VPN EVPN, Source VRF: default, Source Route
  Distinguisher: 172.19.0.19:200
RP/0/RP0/CPU0:PE-1#
```

Up until this point in this verification section, the CLI commands have filtered all the BGP EVPN route types based on a bridge domain name or route distinguisher (RD) associated with a particular EVI. You can also take advantage of other useful and widely used BGP control plane verification commands, as listed in Output 6-52. These commands display the outputs of a selected EVPN route type, chosen either through the numerical value **<1-8>**, or through the route type name. When you use these commands, the displayed route entries include all route distinguishers in the BGP table. Be aware that in with large-scale networks, you may get large outputs.

Output 6-52   *BGP EVPN Route Type Commands*

```
RP/0/RP0/CPU0:PE-1#show bgp l2vpn evpn route-type ?
  <1-8>                Route type value
  ethernet-ad          Display EVPN Ethernet Advertisement routes
  ethernet-segment     Display EVPN Ethernet Segment routes
  igmp-join-synch      Display EVPN MCAST Join synch routes
  igmp-leave-synch     Display EVPN MCAST Leave synch routes
  inclusive-mcast      Display EVPN Inclusive Multicast routes
  ip-advertisement     Display EVPN IP Advertisement routes
  mac-advertisement    Display EVPN MAC Advertisement routes
  selective-mcast      Display EVPN Selective Multicast Ethernet Tag routes
```

You can display EVPN Route Type 4 Ethernet segment routes exchanged between peer multihomed PE routers by using with the **show bgp l2vpn evpn route-type ethernet-segment** command. The example in Output 6-53 shows an EVPN Route Type 4 for the Ethernet segment configured between PE-1 and PE-2.

Output 6-53   *BGP EVPN Route Type 4 Ethernet Segment Route Details on PE-1*

```
RP/0/RP0/CPU0:PE-1#show bgp l2vpn evpn route-type ethernet-segment
BGP router identifier 172.19.0.10, local AS number 65000
<snip>

Status codes: s suppressed, d damped, h history, * valid, > best
              i - internal, r RIB-failure, S stale, N Nexthop-discard
Origin codes: i - IGP, e - EGP, ? - incomplete
   Network          Next Hop            Metric LocPrf Weight Path
Route Distinguisher: 172.19.0.10:0 (default for vrf ES:GLOBAL)
Route Distinguisher Version: 573
*> [4][0000.fc00.0102.0000.0000][32][172.19.0.10]/128
                     0.0.0.0                                    0 i
*>i[4][0000.fc00.0102.0000.0000][32][172.19.0.11]/128
                     fc00:0:106::1                  100         0 i
Route Distinguisher: 172.19.0.11:0
Route Distinguisher Version: 532
```

```
*>i[4] [0000.fc00.0102.0000.0000] [32] [172.19.0.11]/128
                        fc00:0:106::1                 100      0 i

Processed 3 prefixes, 3 paths
RP/0/RP0/CPU0:PE-1#
```

The CLI command **show bgp l2vpn evpn route-type ethernet-segment** executed on router PE-3 in Output 6-54 displays the local Ethernet segment configured between PE-3 and PE-4. The noticeable difference between these two outputs executed on different PE routers (Output 6-53 and Output 6-54) is that they only display their actual attached Ethernet segments due to the ES import route target being based on the extracted 6-byte portion of the ESI type 0.

Output 6-54   *BGP EVPN Route Type 4 Ethernet Segment Route Details on PE-3*

```
RP/0/RP0/CPU0:PE-3#show bgp l2vpn evpn route-type ethernet-segment
BGP router identifier 172.19.0.19, local AS number 65000
<snip>

Status codes: s suppressed, d damped, h history, * valid, > best
              i - internal, r RIB-failure, S stale, N Nexthop-discard
Origin codes: i - IGP, e - EGP, ? - incomplete
   Network          Next Hop          Metric LocPrf Weight Path
Route Distinguisher: 172.19.0.19:0 (default for vrf ES:GLOBAL)
Route Distinguisher Version: 1366
*>  [4] [0000.fc00.0202.5000.0000] [32] [172.19.0.19]/128
                        0.0.0.0                               0 i
*>i[4] [0000.fc00.0202.5000.0000] [32] [172.19.0.20]/128
                        fc00:0:206::1                 100      0 i
Route Distinguisher: 172.19.0.20:0
Route Distinguisher Version: 1308
*>i[4] [0000.fc00.0202.5000.0000] [32] [172.19.0.20]/128
                        fc00:0:206::1                 100      0 i

Processed 3 prefixes, 3 paths
RP/0/RP0/CPU0:PE-3#
```

To get the full EVPN Route Type 4 Ethernet segment routes exchanged throughout the network, the route reflector can provide this view, as seen from RR-1 in Output 6-55, where both Ethernet segments 0000.fc00.0102.0000.0000 and 0000.fc00.0202.5000.0000 configured in the reference network are visible.

Output 6-55   *BGP EVPN Route Type 4 Ethernet Segment Route Details on RR-1*

```
RP/0/RP0/CPU0:RR-1#show bgp l2vpn evpn route-type ethernet-segment
BGP router identifier 172.19.0.12, local AS number 65000
<snip>


Status codes: s suppressed, d damped, h history, * valid, > best
              i - internal, r RIB-failure, S stale, N Nexthop-discard
Origin codes: i - IGP, e - EGP, ? - incomplete
   Network          Next Hop           Metric LocPrf Weight Path
Route Distinguisher: 172.19.0.10:0
Route Distinguisher Version: 300
*>i[4][0000.fc00.0102.0000.0000][32][172.19.0.10]/128
                      fc00:0:105::1                   100       0 i
Route Distinguisher: 172.19.0.11:0
Route Distinguisher Version: 41
*>i[4][0000.fc00.0102.0000.0000][32][172.19.0.11]/128
                      fc00:0:106::1                   100       0 i
Route Distinguisher: 172.19.0.19:0
Route Distinguisher Version: 338
*>i[4][0000.fc00.0202.5000.0000][32][172.19.0.19]/128
                      fc00:0:205::1                   100       0 i
Route Distinguisher: 172.19.0.20:0
Route Distinguisher Version: 258
*>i[4][0000.fc00.0202.5000.0000][32][172.19.0.20]/128
                      fc00:0:206::1                   100       0 i
Processed 4 prefixes, 4 paths
RP/0/RP0/CPU0:RR-1#
```

The verification details of an EVPN Route Type 4 Ethernet segment route are displayed in Output 6-56:

- **[0000.fc00.0102.0000.0000]:** This is the 10-byte Ethernet segment identifier 00:00:fc:00:01:02:00:00:00:00.

- **Extended community:** Included with the BGP extended community attributes of the received route are the following:

  - **EVPN ES Import:00fc.0001.0200:** This is the defined portion of the ESI (6 bytes), which limits the EVPN Route Type 4 routes being imported to only PE-1 and PE-2 that are connected to the same local attached Ethernet segment.

  - **DF Election:0:0x0028:0:** With the DF election and capabilities exchange, the default DF election is based on the modulo election algorithm per ESI. For more details, refer to the section "EVPN Route Type 4: Ethernet Segment Route," earlier in this chapter.

- **Source Route Distinguisher:** The route distinguisher 172.19.0.11:0 is from the ES:GLOBAL VRF instance and is inserted by router PE-2 in this case. The VRF instance ES:GLOBAL is similar in concept to a global bridge domain or global MAC VRF table. It has global scope in that it stores routes that are not associated with a single service each but that rather may span several bridge domains or cross-connects. This ES:GLOBAL VRF instance stores the local and remote learned Route Type 4 Ethernet segment routes together with local Route Type 1 per-ESI Ethernet A-D routes.

Output 6-56 *BGP EVPN Route Type 4 Ethernet-Segment Route Detail on PE-1*

```
RP/0/RP0/CPU0:PE-1#show bgp l2vpn evpn rd 172.19.0.10:0 [4][0000.
  fc00.0102.0000.0000][32][172.19.0.11]/128
BGP routing table entry for [4][0000.fc00.0102.0000.0000][32][172.19.0.11]/128,
  Route Distinguisher: 172.19.0.10:0
<snip>
Paths: (1 available, best #1)
  Not advertised to any peer
  Path #1: Received by speaker 0
  Not advertised to any peer
  Local
    fc00:0:106::1 (metric 21) from fc00:0:107::1 (172.19.0.11)
      Origin IGP, localpref 100, valid, internal, best, group-best,
import-candidate, imported, rib-install
      Received Path ID 0, Local Path ID 1, version 548
      Extended community: EVPN ES Import:00fc.0001.0200 DF Election:0:0x0028:0
      Originator: 172.19.0.11, Cluster list: 172.19.0.12
      Source AFI: L2VPN EVPN, Source VRF: default, Source Route
Distinguisher: 172.19.0.11:0
RP/0/RP0/CPU0:PE-1#
```

As mentioned earlier, the configuration examples in this section are the minimum required for a service to function correctly.

EVPN E-LAN Single-Homed Service

EVPN E-LAN single-homed service refers to either a single-homed device (SHD) or a single-homed network (SHN) attached to a provider edge router (PE), and as the name suggests, the device or network is single attached to the EVPN network. The following configurations are based on the setup shown in Figure 6-28, where the EVPN E-LAN single-homed service is configured between the routers CE-2 and CE-4.

The router CE-2 is attached to the router PE-2 in IS-IS Metro 1 via the physical interface Gi0/0/0/1, and the router CE-4 is attached to the router PE-4 in IS-IS Metro 2 via a link aggregation group (LAG) interface bundle-ether 260.

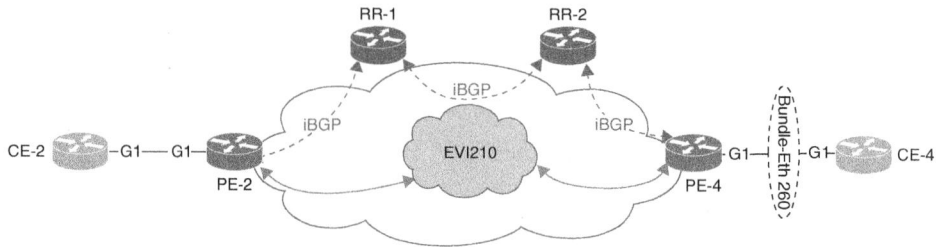

Figure 6-28 *EVPN E-LAN: SHD Reference Network*

EVPN E-LAN SHD EFP (Access Circuit) Configuration

The first of the configuration steps is the access circuit provisioning, as shown in Figure 6-29.

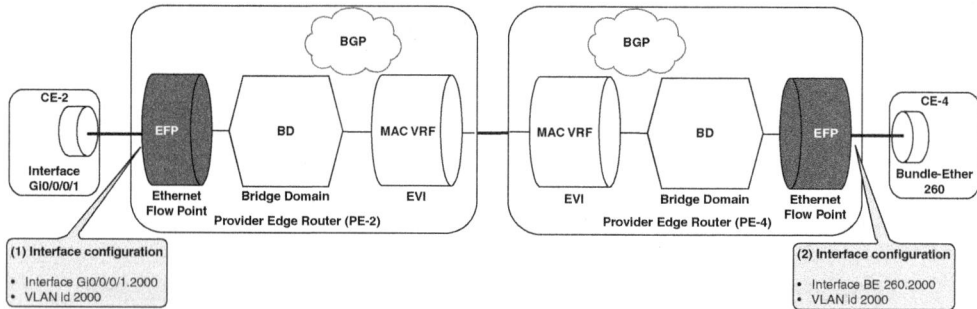

Figure 6-29 *EVPN E-LAN SHD EFP (Access Circuit) Configuration Tasks*

On the router PE-2, a physical interface GigabitEthernet0/0/0/1 is configured, as shown in Config 6-25.

Config 6-25 *EVPN E-LAN SHD EFP PE Router Configuration on PE-2*

```
!
interface GigabitEthernet0/0/0/1
 description Connected_to_CE-2
!

interface GigabitEthernet0/0/0/1.2000 l2transport
 encapsulation dot1q 2000
!
```

The EVPN E-LAN single-homed service access circuit on PE-4 is the bundle-ether 260 interface, as configured in Config 6-26.

Config 6-26 *EVPN E-LAN SHD EFP PE Router Configuration on PE-4*

```
!
interface Bundle-Ether260
 description Connected_to_CE-4
 lacp system mac 00fc.0002.0260
!
interface Bundle-Ether260.2000 l2transport
 encapsulation dot1q 2000
!
```

Although either physical or link aggregation group (LAG) interface configurations may be configured for a single-homed service, the interface bundle-ether 260 used in Config 6-26 requires that the EVPN ESI be set to ESI 0 00.00.00.00.00.00.00.00.00, as shown and explained shortly, in the EVPN configuration of PE-4 in Config 6-28.

EVPN E-LAN SHD EFP (Access Circuit) Verification

The same commands used in the section "EVPN E-LAN: Port-Active MHD EFP (Access Circuit) Verifications" are applicable in this section and therefore are not repeated here.

EVPN E-LAN SHD EVPN Configuration

The second of the configuration steps is EVPN EVI circuit provisioning, as illustrated in Figure 6-30.

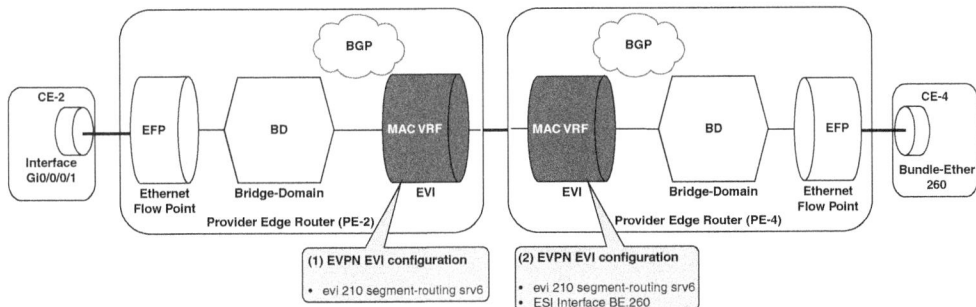

Figure 6-30 *EVPN E-LAN SHD EVPN PE Router Configuration Tasks*

The EVPN EVI configuration tasks in Config 6-27 are sufficient for router PE-2. There is no requirement to configure the ESI as 0 since a physical interface will always be 0.

Config 6-27   *EVPN E-LAN SHD EVPN PE Router Configurations on PE-2*

```
evpn
 evi 210 segment-routing srv6
  advertise-mac
  !
 !
 segment-routing srv6
  locator MAIN
  !
 !
```

The configurations in Config 6-28 for router PE-4 are sufficient for the EVPN EVI provisioning tasks, but as mentioned earlier, in the section "Ethernet Segment (ES)," the ESI is explicitly configured as ESI **0 00.00.00.00.00.00.00.00.00** due to the use of the bundle-ether 260 interface attached to router CE-4. Setting the Ethernet segment identifier (ESI) to 0 is done intentionally because this value is the designated ESI for a single-homed site. By default, a bundle-ether interface is automatically assigned a nonzero ESI, as it is typically presumed that the interface will be used in a multihomed configuration.

Config 6-28   *EVPN E-LAN SHD EVPN PE Router Configurations on PE-4*

```
evpn
 evi 210 segment-routing srv6
  advertise-mac
  !
 !
 interface Bundle-Ether260
  ethernet-segment
   identifier type 0 00.00.00.00.00.00.00.00.00
  !
 !
 segment-routing srv6
  locator MAIN
  !
```

EVPN E-LAN SHD EVPN Verification

Figure 6-31 provides a list of CLI commands that can be used to verify and troubleshoot an EVPN service configuration. This section describes the verification of the EVPN E-LAN SHD EVI service configuration.

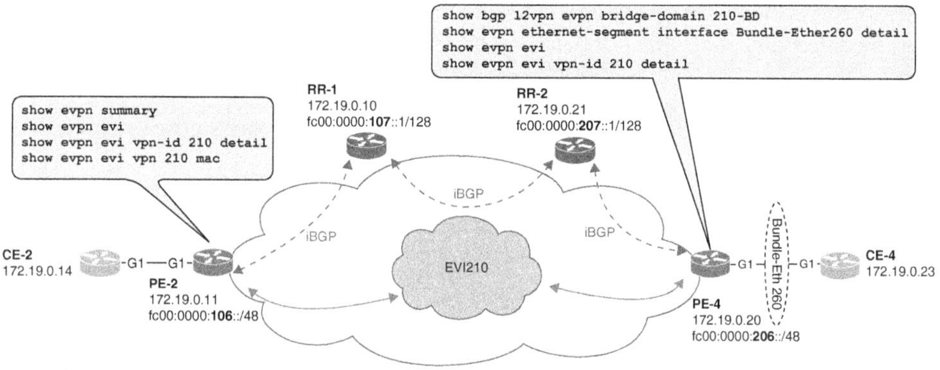

Figure 6-31 *EVPN E-LAN SHD EVPN Verification*

The commands in the earlier section "EVPN E-LAN Port-Active MHD EVPN Verification" are applicable for this section as well.

If the operator made a configuration mistake on the router PE-4 and did not explicitly configure the interface bundle-ether 260 with an **ethernet-segment identifier type 0 00.00.00.00.00.00.00.00.00**, a BGP EVPN Route Type 1 route will be propagated, consisting of an auto-generated ESI Type 1 based on SYSTEM-PRIORITY.CPE-LACP-SYSTEM-ID.CPE-LACP-PORT-KEY, as shown in Output 6-57. The output also indicates that the router PE-2 from IS-IS Metro 1 is not propagating a BGP EVPN Route Type 1 route, which is expected due to the use of a non-LAG interface Gi0/0/0/1 connected to CE-2 defaulting to ESI 0.

Output 6-57 *BGP Output for EVI 210 (Single-Homed Service) on PE-4*

```
RP/0/RP0/CPU0:PE-4#show bgp l2vpn evpn bridge-domain 210-BD


Status codes: s suppressed, d damped, h history, * valid, > best
              i - internal, r RIB-failure, S stale, N Nexthop-discard
Origin codes: i - IGP, e - EGP, ? - incomplete
   Network          Next Hop            Metric LocPrf Weight Path
Route Distinguisher: 172.19.0.20:210 (default for vrf 210-BD)
Route Distinguisher Version: 771
*> [1][0100.0000.0229.0001.0400][0]/120
                    0.0.0.0                                 0 i
<snip>
*>i[3][0][32][172.19.0.11]/80
                    fc00:0:106::1              100        0 i
*> [3][0][32][172.19.0.20]/80
                    0.0.0.0                                 0 i
RP/0/RP0/CPU0:PE-4#
```

Continuing with the ESI configuration error, Output 6-58 from PE-4 indicates that the interface bundle-ether 260 has not been manually configured as ESI 0 00.00.00.00.00.00.00.00.00 in the EVPN configuration and is therefore auto-generating an ESI Type 1 route. Since the intended router configuration is for a single-homed service, the configuration should be adapted to an explicitly configured ESI Type 0 behavior.

Output 6-58   *EVPN Output: I/F BE260, an Auto-Generated ESI Type 1 Route on PE-4*

```
RP/0/RP0/CPU0:PE-4#show evpn ethernet-segment interface Bundle-Ether260 detail
<snip>
Ethernet Segment Id      Interface                          Nexthops
----------------------   --------------------------------   --------------------
0100.0000.0229.0001.0400 BE260                              172.19.0.20
  ES to BGP Gates    : Ready
  ES to L2FIB Gates  : Ready
  Main port          :
     Interface name  : Bundle-Ether260
     Interface MAC   : 0025.846a.b6f9
     IfHandle        : 0x00000054
     State           : Up
     Redundancy      : Not Defined
  ESI type           : 1
     System-id       : 0000.0002.2900
     Port key        : 0104
  ES Import RT        : 0000.0002.2900 (from ESI)
  Source MAC         : 0000.0000.0000 (N/A)
  Topology           :
     Operational     : SH
     Configured      : All-active (AApF) (default)
  Service Carving    : Auto-selection
     Multicast       : Disabled
  Convergence        :
  Peering Details    : 1 Nexthops
     172.19.0.20 [MOD:P:00:T]
  Service Carving Synchronization:
     Mode            : NONE
     Peer Updates    :
            172.19.0.20 [SCT: N/A]
  Service Carving Results:
     Forwarders      : 1
     Elected         : 1
     Not Elected     : 0
  EVPN-VPWS Service Carving Results:
     Primary         : 0
     Backup          : 0
     Non-DF          : 0
```

```
  MAC Flushing mode : STP-TCN
  Peering timer     : 3 sec [not running]
  Recovery timer    : 30 sec [not running]
  Carving timer     : 0 sec [not running]
  HRW Reset timer   : 5 sec [not running]
  Local SHG label   : None
  Remote SHG labels : 0
  Access signal mode: Bundle OOS (Default)
RP/0/RP0/CPU0:PE-4#
```

To reiterate, a bundle-ether interface is by default in EVPN multihoming (MH) mode, and to enable EVPN single-homing (SH) mode, the ESI value (identifier type) must be set to 0. Output 6-59 from router PE-4 displays the Ethernet segment details after interface bundle-ether 260 is manually configured for ESI Type 0. The ESI is now displayed as N/A with Operational SH (single-homing), as is intended.

Output 6-59   *EVPN Output: I/F BE260, ESI Type 0 Verification on PE-4*

```
RP/0/RP0/CPU0:PE-4#show evpn ethernet-segment interface Bundle-Ether260 detail
<snip>


Ethernet Segment Id      Interface                          Nexthops
------------------------ ---------------------------------- --------------------
N/A                      BE260                              172.19.0.20
 ES to BGP Gates    : Ready
  ES to L2FIB Gates : Ready
  Main port         :
     Interface name : Bundle-Ether260
     Interface MAC  : 0025.b420.80d2
     IfHandle       : 0x00000144
     State          : Up
     Redundancy     : Not Defined
  ESI type          : Invalid
  ES Import RT       : 0000.0000.0000 (Incomplete Configuration)
  Source MAC        : 0025.b420.80cd (PBB BSA, no ESI)
  Topology          :
     Operational    : SH
     Configured     : All-active (AApF) (default)
  Service Carving    : Auto-selection
     Multicast      : Disabled

<snip>

RP/0/RP0/CPU0:PE-4
```

With the bundle-ether 260 interface being explicitly configured as ESI 0 00.00.00.00.00.00.00.00.00 on PE-4, the BGP EVPN Route Type 1 entry is no longer generated, as shown by the CLI command **show bgp l2vpn evpn bridge-domain 210-BD** in Output 6-60. The output displays the local and remote EVPN Route Type 3 inclusive multicast routes together with EVPN Route Type 2 MAC addresses learned as a result of customer traffic flowing between CE-2 and CE-4.

Output 6-60   *BGP Output for EVI 210 (Single-Homed Service) on PE-4*

```
RP/0/RP0/CPU0:PE-4#show bgp l2vpn evpn bridge-domain 210-BD
BGP router identifier 172.19.0.20, local AS number 65000
<snip>


Status codes: s suppressed, d damped, h history, * valid, > best
              i - internal, r RIB-failure, S stale, N Nexthop-discard
Origin codes: i - IGP, e - EGP, ? - incomplete
  Network          Next Hop          Metric LocPrf Weight Path
Route Distinguisher: 172.19.0.20:210 (default for vrf 210-BD)
Route Distinguisher Version: 192
*>i[2][0][48][1033.3300.0001][0]/104
                    fc00:0:106::1               100       0 i
<snip>
*> [2][0][48][2033.3300.0001][0]/104
                    0.0.0.0                               0 i
<snip>
*>i[3][0][32][172.19.0.11]/80
                    fc00:0:106::1               100       0 i
*> [3][0][32][172.19.0.20]/80
                    0.0.0.0                               0 i
Processed 12 prefixes, 12 paths
RP/0/RP0/CPU0:PE-4#
```

The command **show evpn evi** in Output 6-61 provides an overview of the configured EVI VPN-IDs and their related bridge domains on the router PE-4.

Output 6-61   *EVPN EVI Summary on PE-4*

```
RP/0/RP0/CPU0:PE-4#show evpn evi

VPN-ID     Encap      Bridge Domain                 Type
---------- ---------- ----------------------------- --------------------
200        SRv6       200-BD                        EVPN
201        SRv6       201-BD                        EVPN
205        SRv6       205-BD                        EVPN
210        SRv6       210-BD                        EVPN
65535      N/A        ES:GLOBAL                     Invalid
RP/0/RP0/CPU0:PE-4#
```

Through the use of the VPN ID obtained from the output in Figure 6-61, you can get additional information about EVI 210 with the command **show evpn evi vpn-id 210 detail**, as shown in Output 6-62:

- **Unicast SID: fc00:0:206:e006:::** This is the SRv6 SID value allocated to any locally learned MAC routes and propagated as EVPN Route Type 2 MAC routes via BGP

- **Multicast SID: fc00:0:206:e007:::** This is the SRv6 SID value allocated and propagated as an EVPN Route Type 3 inclusive multicast route, which allows for ingress replicated BUM traffic from remote PE routers participating in the EVI to be encapsulated with the received inclusive multicast Ethernet label and forwarded to the advertising PE router.

- **RD Auto : (auto) 172.19.0.20:210:** The route distinguisher is auto-derived.

- **RT Auto : 65000:210:** The route target's auto-derived value and the **Route Targets in Use** field shown in Output 6-62 indicate whether the auto-derived route targets are in use or whether they are manually configured.

Output 6-62 *EVPN EVI VPN-ID 210 Detail on PE-4*

```
RP/0/RP0/CPU0:PE-4#show evpn evi vpn-id 210 detail

VPN-ID     Encap      Bridge Domain                  Type
---------- ---------- ------------------------------ -------------------
210        SRv6       210-BD                         EVPN
   Stitching: Regular
   Unicast SID:  fc00:0:206:e006::
   Multicast SID:  fc00:0:206:e007::
   E-Tree: Root
   Forward-class: 0
   Advertise MACs: Yes
   Advertise BVI MACs: No
   Aliasing: Enabled
   UUF: Enabled
   Re-origination: Enabled
   Multicast:
    Source connected   : No
     IGMP-Snooping Proxy: No
     MLD-Snooping Proxy : No
   BGP Implicit Import: Enabled
   VRF Name:
   Preferred Nexthop Mode: Off
   BVI Coupled Mode: No
   BVI Subnet Withheld: ipv4 No, ipv6 No
```

```
Statistics:
  Packets            Sent                Received
    Total          : 0                   0
    Unicast        : 0                   0
    BUM            : 0                   0
  bytes              Sent                Received
    Total          : 0                   0
    Unicast        : 0                   0
    BUM            : 0                   0
RD Config: none
RD Auto   : (auto) 172.19.0.20:210
RT Auto   : 65000:210
Route Targets in Use              Type
------------------------------    --------------------
65000:210                         Import
65000:210                         Export

RP/0/RP0/CPU0:PE-4#
```

EVPN E-LAN SHD L2VPN Configuration

The third configuration step is the L2VPN bridge domain provisioning and linking of this bridge domain to the previously configured EVPN EVI 210, as shown in Figure 6-32.

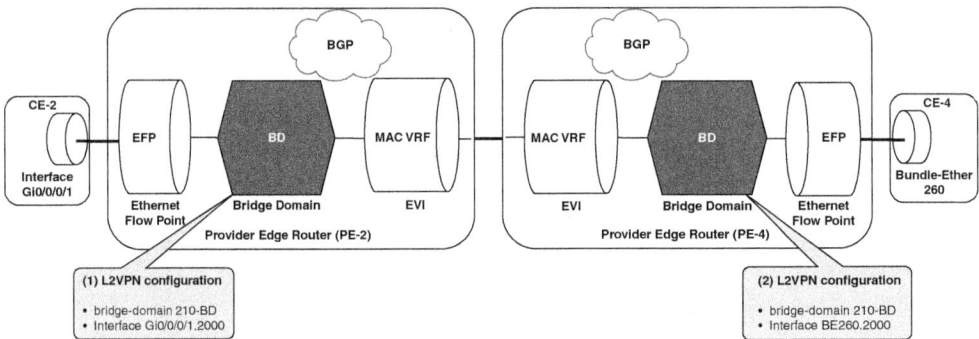

Figure 6-32   *EVPN E-LAN SHD L2VPN PE Router Configuration Tasks*

The L2VPN optional configurations used in the multihomed service provisioning from section "EVPN E-LAN Port-Active MHD L2VPN Configuration" can be reused for this single-homed service as these configurations will be similar. The L2vpn bridge domain configuration from router PE-2 in Config 6-29 links the subinterface GigabitEthernet0/0/0/1.2000 to EVI 210.

Config 6-29 *EVPN E-LAN SHD L2VPN PE Router Configuration on PE-2*

```
l2vpn
 bridge group ELAN-BG
  bridge-domain 210-BD
   interface GigabitEthernet0/0/0/1.2000
   !
   evi 210 segment-routing srv6
   !
```

The L2VPN bridge domain configuration for router PE-4 in Config 6-30 links the subinterface Bundle-Ether260.2000 to EVI 210.

Config 6-30 *EVPN E-LAN SHD L2VPN PE Router Configuration on PE-4*

```
l2vpn
 bridge group ELAN-BG
  bridge-domain 210-BD
   interface Bundle-Ether260.2000
   !
   evi 210 segment-routing srv6
   !
```

EVPN E-LAN SHD L2VPN Verification

Figure 6-33 provides a list of CLI commands that can be used to verify and troubleshoot the L2VPN service configuration. This section shows the use of some of these CLI commands in the verification steps.

The commands in the section "EVPN E-LAN Port-Active MHD L2VPN Verification" are also applicable for the following SHD L2VPN verification tasks.

The following commands can be used to verify the bridge domain state and trace the MAC addresses learned locally (2033.3300.0001–2033.3300.0005) from the router CE-4, and those learned from the remote router CE-2 across EVI 210 (1033.3300.0001–1033.3300.0005).

The **show l2vpn bridge-domain brief** command in Output 6-63 provides a brief overview of the state of the configured bridge groups and which bridge domains are associated with these bridge groups. The bridge domain of interest is the previously configured 210-BD.

```
show l2vpn bridge-domain brief
show l2vpn bridge-domain bd-name 210-BD detail
show l2vpn forwarding bridge-domain ELAN-BG:210-BD mac-address location 0/RP0/CPU0
show l2vpn forwarding bridge-domain ELAN-BG:200-BD evpn inclusive-multicast location 0/RP0/CPU0
show l2vpn mac-learning mac all location 0/RP0/CPU0
show l2vpn mac-learning mac topo-id <ID> location 0/RP0/CPU0
show segment-routing srv6 locator MAIN sid
```

RR-1
172.19.0.10
fc00:0000:**107**::1/128

RR-2
172.19.0.21
fc00:0000:**207**::1/128

iBGP

iBGP

iBGP

EVI210

CE-2
172.19.0.14

G1 — G1

PE-2
172.19.0.11
fc00:0000:**106**::/48

Bundle-Eth 260

G1

G1

CE-4
172.19.0.23

PE-4
172.19.0.20
fc00:0000:**206**::/48

```
show l2vpn bridge-domain brief
show l2vpn bridge-domain bd-name 210-BD detail
show l2vpn forwarding bridge-domain ELAN-BG:210-BD mac-address location 0/RP0/CPU0
show l2vpn forwarding bridge-domain ELAN-BG:210-BD evpn inclusive-multicast location 0/RP0/CPU0
show l2vpn mac-learning mac all location 0/RP0/CPU0
show l2vpn mac-learning mac topo-id <ID> location 0/RP0/CPU0
show segment-routing srv6 locator MAIN sid
```

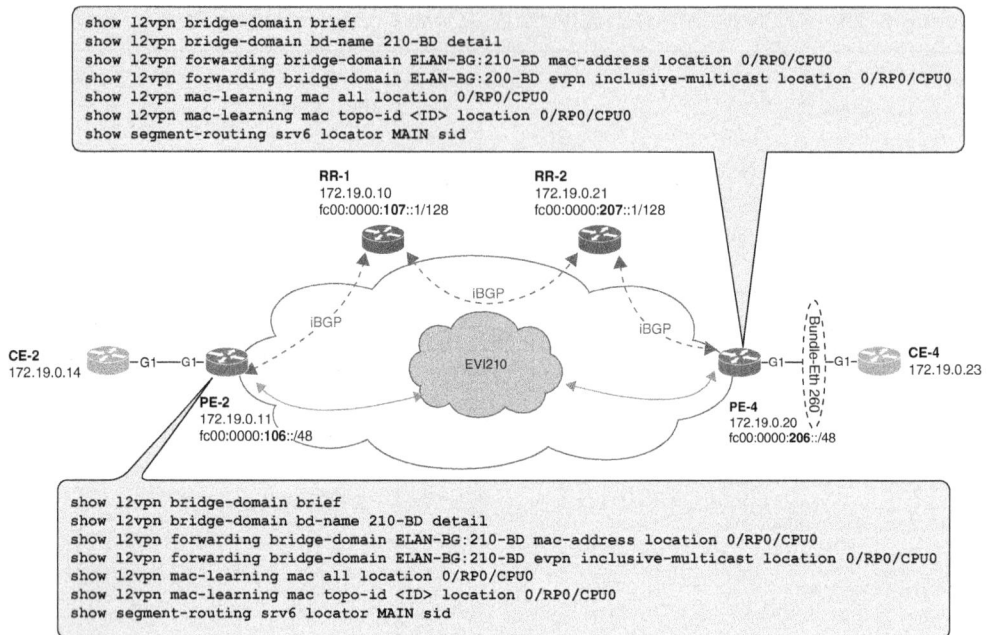

Figure 6-33   *EVPN E-LAN: SHD L2VPN Verification*

Output 6-63   *L2VPN Bridge Domain Brief State Output on PE-4*

```
RP/0/RP0/CPU0:PE-4#show l2vpn bridge-domain brief
Legend: pp = Partially Programmed.
Bridge Group:Bridge-Domain Name ID  State   Num ACs/up  Num PWs/up  Num PBBs/up  Num VNIs/up
------------------------------- --- ------  ----------- ----------- -----------  -----------
ELAN-BG:200-BD                   0  up      1/0         0/0         0/0          0/0
ELAN-BG:201-BD                   1  up      1/0         0/0         0/0          0/0
ELAN-BG:205-BD                   2  up      2/1         0/0         0/0          0/0
ELAN-BG:210-BD                   3  up      1/1         0/0         0/0          0/0
RP/0/RP0/CPU0:PE-4#
```

All PE routers associated with EVI 210 display MAC addresses learned both locally
and via the EVPN from the routers CE-2 and CE-4. They can be displayed as shown in
Output 6-64 from router PE-4. The MAC addresses 1033.3300.0001–1033.3300.0005
are learned from BD id: 3 across the EVPN from router CE-2, and the MAC addresses
2033.3300.0001–2033.3300.0005 are locally learned from subinterface BE260.2000, to
which router CE-4 is attached.

Output 6-64 *L2VPN Forwarding Bridge Domain 210-BD: Local and Remote MAC Addresses on PE-4*

```
RP/0/RP0/CPU0:PE-4#show l2vpn forwarding bridge-domain ELAN-BG:210-BD mac-address
   location 0/RP0/CPU0
Mac Address     Type    Learned from/Filtered on  LC learned Age              Mapped to
-------------- ------- ------------------------  ---------- ----------------- -----------
   ---
1033.3300.0001 EVPN    BD id: 3                  N/A        N/A               N/A
1033.3300.0002 EVPN    BD id: 3                  N/A        N/A               N/A
1033.3300.0003 EVPN    BD id: 3                  N/A        N/A               N/A
1033.3300.0004 EVPN    BD id: 3                  N/A        N/A               N/A
1033.3300.0005 EVPN    BD id: 3                  N/A        N/A               N/A
2033.3300.0001 dynamic BE260.2000                0/RP0/CPU   0d 0h 0m 51s     N/A
2033.3300.0002 dynamic BE260.2000                0/RP0/CPU   0d 0h 0m 51s     N/A
2033.3300.0003 dynamic BE260.2000                0/RP0/CPU   0d 0h 0m 50s     N/A
2033.3300.0004 dynamic BE260.2000                0/RP0/CPU   0d 0h 0m 50s     N/A
2033.3300.0005 dynamic BE260.2000                0/RP0/CPU   0d 0h 0m 49s     N/A
RP/0/RP0/CPU0:PE-4#
```

The command **show l2vpn forwarding bridge-domain ELAN-BG:210-BD mac-address location 0/RP0/CPU0** in Output 6-65 executed on router PE-2 displays the MAC addresses learned from the local CE-2 router via subinterface Gi0/0/0/1.2000 and the remote MAC addresses from BD id: 2 via the EVPN from router PE-4.

Output 6-65 *L2VPN Forwarding Bridge Domain 210-BD: Local and Remote MAC Addresses on PE-2*

```
RP/0/RP0/CPU0:PE-2#show l2vpn forwarding bridge-domain ELAN-BG:210-BD mac-address
   location 0/RP0/CPU0
Mac Address     Type    Learned from/Filtered on LC learned Age              Mapped to
-------------- ------- ------------------------ ---------- ----------------- ------------
1033.3300.0001 dynamic Gi0/0/0/1.2000           0/RP0/CPU   0d 0h 0m 56s     N/A
1033.3300.0002 dynamic Gi0/0/0/1.2000           0/RP0/CPU   0d 0h 0m 56s     N/A
1033.3300.0003 dynamic Gi0/0/0/1.2000           0/RP0/CPU   0d 0h 0m 56s     N/A
1033.3300.0004 dynamic Gi0/0/0/1.2000           0/RP0/CPU   0d 0h 0m 56s     N/A
1033.3300.0005 dynamic Gi0/0/0/1.2000           0/RP0/CPU   0d 0h 0m 55s     N/A
2033.3300.0001 EVPN    BD id: 2                 N/A        N/A               N/A
2033.3300.0002 EVPN    BD id: 2                 N/A        N/A               N/A
2033.3300.0003 EVPN    BD id: 2                 N/A        N/A               N/A
2033.3300.0004 EVPN    BD id: 2                 N/A        N/A               N/A
2033.3300.0005 EVPN    BD id: 2                 N/A        N/A               N/A
RP/0/RP0/CPU0:PE-2#
```

EVPN Route Type 3 inclusive multicast forwarding information for the bridge domain 210 associated with EVI 210 is shown in Output 6-66 on PE-4. The command **show**

l2vpn forwarding bridge-domain ELAN-BG:210-BD evpn inclusive-multicast location 0/RP0/CPU0 displays the next hop SID used when forwarding BUM traffic into the EVI 210 for this traffic to reach the remote peer PE router.

Output 6-66 *L2VPN Forwarding Inclusive Multicast: Bridge Domain 210-BD on PE-4*

```
RP/0/RP0/CPU0:PE-4#show l2vpn forwarding bridge-domain ELAN-BG:210-BD evpn
  inclusive-multicast location 0/RP0/CPU0
Bridge-Domain Name       BD-ID XCID       TEP-id     Next Hop              Label/VNI
------------------------------ ------ ---------- ---------- -------------------- --------
ELAN-BG:210-BD              3       0xfff01004 0x05000002 SRv6 SID fc00:0:106:e005::, fmt type: 2
RP/0/RP0/CPU0:PE-4#
```

Output 6-67 displays the VPN Route Type 3 inclusive multicast forwarding information for the bridge domain 210 associated with EVI 210 on router PE-2.

Output 6-67 *L2VPN Forwarding Inclusive-Multicast: Bridge Domain 210-BD on PE-2*

```
RP/0/RP0/CPU0:PE-2#show l2vpn forwarding bridge-domain ELAN-BG:210-BD evpn
  inclusive-multicast location 0/RP0/CPU0
Bridge-Domain Name       BD-ID XCID       TEP-id     Next Hop              Label/VNI
--------------------     ------ ---------- ---------- -------------------- ----------
ELAN-BG:210-BD              2       0xfff01003 0x05000003 SRv6 SID fc00:0:206:e007::, fmt type: 2
RP/0/RP0/CPU0:PE-2#
```

The SRv6 local SID output from router PE-4 displayed in Output 6-68 confirms that the L2VPN inclusive multicast SID matches fc00:0:206:e007::, displayed with the CLI command in Output 6-67 on router PE-2.

Output 6-68 *SRv6 Local SID: uDT2M (Inclusive-Multicast) Verification on PE-4*

```
RP/0/RP0/CPU0:PE-4#show segment-routing srv6 locator MAIN sid

SID                   Behavior       Context                    Owner          State  RW
--------------------  ------------   -------------------------  -------------  -----  --
fc00:0:206::          uN (PSP/USD)   'default':518              sidmgr         InUse  Y
fc00:0:206:e000::     uDT2U          200:0                      l2vpn_srv6     InUse  Y
fc00:0:206:e001::     uDT2M          200:0                      l2vpn_srv6     InUse  Y
fc00:0:206:e002::     uDT2U          201:0                      l2vpn_srv6     InUse  Y
fc00:0:206:e003::     uDT2M          201:0                      l2vpn_srv6     InUse  Y
fc00:0:206:e004::     uDT2U          205:0                      l2vpn_srv6     InUse  Y
fc00:0:206:e005::     uDT2M          205:0                      l2vpn_srv6     InUse  Y
fc00:0:206:e006::     uDT2U          210:0                      l2vpn_srv6     InUse  Y
fc00:0:206:e007::     uDT2M          210:0                      l2vpn_srv6     InUse  Y
fc00:0:206:e008::     uDX2           3000:3000                  l2vpn_srv6     InUse  Y
```

```
fc00:0:206:e009::    uA (PSP/USD)   [Gi0/0/0/0, Link-Local]:0:P   isis-METRO_2   InUse  Y
fc00:0:206:e00a::    uA (PSP/USD)   [Gi0/0/0/0, Link-Local]:0     isis-METRO_2   InUse  Y
fc00:0:206:e00b::    uA (PSP/USD)   [Gi0/0/0/2, Link-Local]:0:P   isis-METRO_2   InUse  Y
fc00:0:206:e00c::    uA (PSP/USD)   [Gi0/0/0/2, Link-Local]:0     isis-METRO_2   InUse  Y
RP/0/RP0/CPU0:PE-4#
```

Similarly, the **show segment-routing srv6 locator MAIN sid** output on router PE-2 displayed in Output 6-69 confirms that the L2VPN inclusive multicast SID matches fc00:0:106:e005::, displayed with the CLI command in Output 6-66 on router PE-4.

Output 6-69 *SRv6 Local SID: uDT2M (Inclusive Multicast) Verification on PE-2*

```
RP/0/RP0/CPU0:PE-2#show segment-routing srv6 locator MAIN sid
SID                   Behavior        Context                        Owner          State  RW
-------------------   -------------   ----------------------------   ------------   -----  --
fc00:0:106::          uN (PSP/USD)    'default':262                  sidmgr         InUse  Y
fc00:0:106:e000::     uDT2U           200:0                          l2vpn_srv6     InUse  Y
fc00:0:106:e001::     uDT2M           200:0                          l2vpn_srv6     InUse  Y
fc00:0:106:e002::     uDT2U           201:0                          l2vpn_srv6     InUse  Y
fc00:0:106:e003::     uDT2M           201:0                          l2vpn_srv6     InUse  Y
fc00:0:106:e004::     uDT2U           210:0                          l2vpn_srv6     InUse  Y
fc00:0:106:e005::     uDT2M           210:0                          l2vpn_srv6     InUse  Y
fc00:0:106:e006::     uA (PSP/USD)    [Gi0/0/0/2, Link-Local]:0:P    isis-METRO_1   InUse  Y
fc00:0:106:e007::     uA (PSP/USD)    [Gi0/0/0/2, Link-Local]:0      isis-METRO_1   InUse  Y
fc00:0:106:e008::     uA (PSP/USD)    [Gi0/0/0/0, Link-Local]:0:P    isis-METRO_1   InUse  Y
fc00:0:106:e009::     uA (PSP/USD)    [Gi0/0/0/0, Link-Local]:0      isis-METRO_1   InUse  Y
fc00:0:106:e00a::     uDX2            3000:3000                      l2vpn_srv6     InUse  Y
fc00:0:106:e00b::     uDT2U           205:0                          l2vpn_srv6     InUse  Y
fc00:0:106:e00c::     uDT2M           205:0                          l2vpn_srv6     InUse  Y
RP/0/RP0/CPU0:PE-2#
```

EVPN E-LAN SHD BGP Configuration

The fourth and final configuration step is the BGP provisioning on all the PE routers, as shown in Figure 6-34.

The E-LAN BGP configurations previously used for the multihomed service in the section "EVPN E-LAN Port-Active MHD BGP Configuration" can be reused for this single-homed service as these configurations are the same.

EVPN E-LAN SHD BGP Verification

This section describes some of the common and useful commands shown in Figure 6-35 that are used to verify and troubleshoot the BGP **address-family l2vpn evpn service** configuration.

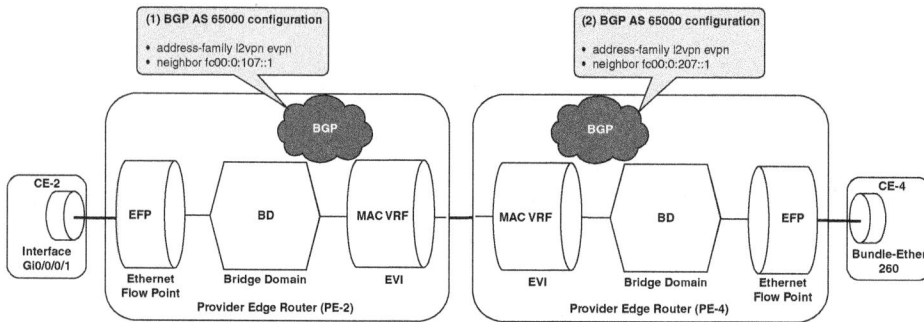

Figure 6-34 *EVPN E-LAN SHD BGP PE Router Configuration Tasks*

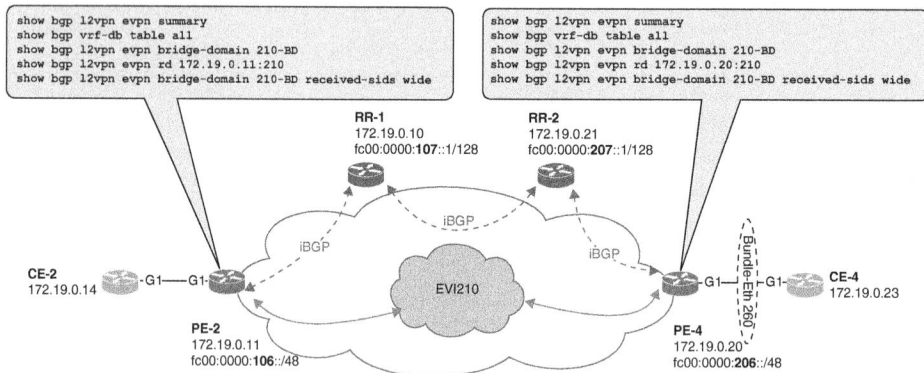

Figure 6-35 *EVPN E-LAN SHD BGP PE Router Verification*

The commands from the earlier section "EVPN E-LAN Port-Active MHD BGP Verification" are also applicable for the following SHD BGP verifications.

Output 6-70 and Output 6-71 display all the EVPN route types for the bridge domain 210-BD, which is part of the EVI 210 on both routers PE-2 and PE-4. The main difference compared to the multihomed port-active service is the lack of EVPN Route Type 1 routes since those are not required for the single-homed service. Output 6-70 from router PE-2 displays the following EVPN routes types imported into EVI 210:

- [2][0][48][1033.3300.0001][0]/104 (EVPN Route Type 2): The MAC route in example output from the MAC addresses learned locally via the subinterface Gi0/0/0/1.2000 from the router CE-2

- [2][0][48][2033.3300.0001][0]/104 (EVPN Route Type 2): The MAC route in example output from the MAC addresses remotely learned via the EVPN EVI 210 from the router PE-4 with next hop fc00:0:206::1

- [3][0][32][172.19.0.11]/80 (EVPN Route Type 3): The inclusive multicast route locally generated for EVI 210

- [3][0][32][172.19.0.20]/80 (EVPN Route Type 3): The inclusive multicast route learned from the router PE-4

Output 6-70 *BGP L2VPN EVPN EVI 210 Routes on PE-2*

```
RP/0/RP0/CPU0:PE-2#show bgp l2vpn evpn bridge-domain 210-BD
BGP router identifier 172.19.0.11, local AS number 65000
<snip>


Status codes: s suppressed, d damped, h history, * valid, > best
              i - internal, r RIB-failure, S stale, N Nexthop-discard
Origin codes: i - IGP, e - EGP, ? - incomplete
   Network          Next Hop            Metric LocPrf Weight Path
Route Distinguisher: 172.19.0.11:210 (default for vrf 210-BD)
Route Distinguisher Version: 1541
*> [2][0][48][1033.3300.0001][0]/104
                     0.0.0.0                                 0 i
*> [2][0][48][1033.3300.0002][0]/104
                     0.0.0.0                                 0 i
*> [2][0][48][1033.3300.0003][0]/104
                     0.0.0.0                                 0 i
*> [2][0][48][1033.3300.0004][0]/104
                     0.0.0.0                                 0 i
*> [2][0][48][1033.3300.0005][0]/104
                     0.0.0.0                                 0 i
*>i[2][0][48][2033.3300.0001][0]/104
                     fc00:0:206::1              100         0 i
*>i[2][0][48][2033.3300.0002][0]/104
                     fc00:0:206::1              100         0 i
*>i[2][0][48][2033.3300.0003][0]/104
                     fc00:0:206::1              100         0 i
*>i[2][0][48][2033.3300.0004][0]/104
                     fc00:0:206::1              100         0 i
*>i[2][0][48][2033.3300.0005][0]/104
                     fc00:0:206::1              100         0 i
*> [3][0][32][172.19.0.11]/80
                     0.0.0.0                                 0 i
*>i[3][0][32][172.19.0.20]/80
                     fc00:0:206::1              100         0 i


Processed 12 prefixes, 12 paths
RP/0/RP0/CPU0:PE-2#
```

Similarly, Output 6-71 from the router PE-4 displays the following EVPN routes types imported into the EVI 210:

■ **[2][0][48][1033.3300.0001][0]/104 (EVPN Route Type 2):** The MAC route in example output from the MAC addresses remotely learned via the EVPN EVI 210 from the router PE-2 with next hop fc00:0:106::1

- **[2][0][48][2033.3300.0001][0]/104 (EVPN Route-Type 2):** The MAC route in example output from the MAC addresses learned locally via the subinterface BE260.2000 from the router CE-4

- **[3][0][32][172.19.0.11]/80 (EVPN Route Type 3):** The inclusive multicast route learned from the router PE-2

- **[3][0][32][172.19.0.20]/80 (EVPN Route Type 3):** The inclusive multicast route locally generated for EVI 210

Output 6-71   *BGP L2VPN EVPN EVI 210 Routes on PE-4*

```
RP/0/RP0/CPU0:PE-4#show bgp l2vpn evpn bridge-domain 210-BD
BGP router identifier 172.19.0.20, local AS number 65000
<snip>
Route Distinguisher: 172.19.0.20:210 (default for vrf 210-BD)
Route Distinguisher Version: 252
*>i[2] [0] [48] [1033.3300.0001] [0]/104
                     fc00:0:106::1                    100        0 i
*>i[2] [0] [48] [1033.3300.0002] [0]/104
                     fc00:0:106::1                    100        0 i
*>i[2] [0] [48] [1033.3300.0003] [0]/104
                     fc00:0:106::1                    100        0 i
*>i[2] [0] [48] [1033.3300.0004] [0]/104
                     fc00:0:106::1                    100        0 i
*>i[2] [0] [48] [1033.3300.0005] [0]/104
                     fc00:0:106::1                    100        0 i
*>  [2] [0] [48] [2033.3300.0001] [0]/104
                     0.0.0.0                                     0 i
*>  [2] [0] [48] [2033.3300.0002] [0]/104
                     0.0.0.0                                     0 i
*>  [2] [0] [48] [2033.3300.0003] [0]/104
                     0.0.0.0                                     0 i
*>  [2] [0] [48] [2033.3300.0004] [0]/104
                     0.0.0.0                                     0 i
*>  [2] [0] [48] [2033.3300.0005] [0]/104
                     0.0.0.0                                     0 i
*>i[3] [0] [32] [172.19.0.11]/80
                     fc00:0:106::1                    100        0 i
*>  [3] [0] [32] [172.19.0.20]/80
                     0.0.0.0                                     0 i
Processed 12 prefixes, 12 paths
RP/0/RP0/CPU0:PE-4#
```

The command **show bgp l2vpn evpn bridge-domain 210-BD received-sids wide** in Output 6-72 from PE-2 displays all the EVPN routes types imported into EVI 210 with the addition of the received SID information:

■ **[2]|[0]|[48]|2033.3300.0001]|[0]/104 (EVPN Route Type 2):** The MAC route received from the router PE-4 next hop fc00:0:206::1 with a received SID of fc00:0:206:e006::

■ **[3]|[0]|[32]|172.19.0.19]/80 (EVPN Route Type 3):** The inclusive multicast route learned from the router PE-4 next hop fc00:0:206::1 with a received SID of fc00:0:206:e007::

Output 6-72 *BGP L2VPN EVPN EVI 210 Received SIDs on PE-2*

```
RP/0/RP0/CPU0:PE-2#show bgp l2vpn evpn bridge-domain 210-BD received-sids wide
BGP router identifier 172.19.0.11, local AS number 65000
<snip>
   Network                               Next Hop              Received Sid
Route Distinguisher: 172.19.0.11:210 (default for vrf 210-BD)
Route Distinguisher Version: 1541
*>  [2][0][48][1033.3300.0001][0]/104      0.0.0.0               fc00:0:106::
*>  [2][0][48][1033.3300.0002][0]/104      0.0.0.0               fc00:0:106::
*>  [2][0][48][1033.3300.0003][0]/104      0.0.0.0               fc00:0:106::
*>  [2][0][48][1033.3300.0004][0]/104      0.0.0.0               fc00:0:106::
*>  [2][0][48][1033.3300.0005][0]/104      0.0.0.0               fc00:0:106::
*>i[2][0][48][2033.3300.0001][0]/104      fc00:0:206::1         fc00:0:206:e006::
*>i[2][0][48][2033.3300.0002][0]/104      fc00:0:206::1         fc00:0:206:e006::
*>i[2][0][48][2033.3300.0003][0]/104      fc00:0:206::1         fc00:0:206:e006::
*>i[2][0][48][2033.3300.0004][0]/104      fc00:0:206::1         fc00:0:206:e006::
*>i[2][0][48][2033.3300.0005][0]/104      fc00:0:206::1         fc00:0:206:e006::
*>  [3][0][32][172.19.0.11]/80             0.0.0.0               fc00:0:106:e005::
*>i[3][0][32][172.19.0.20]/80             fc00:0:206::1         fc00:0:206:e007::

Processed 12 prefixes, 12 paths
RP/0/RP0/CPU0:PE-2#
```

As mentioned earlier, the configuration examples in this section are the minimum required for the service to function correctly.

EVPN E-Tree

In the earlier sections of this chapter, on EVPN E-LAN configuration and verification, one of the take-aways was that all sites within an EVI had full interconnectivity with each other. However, there are scenarios in which customers don't require full site connectivity for security or other reasons. Traditionally in standard MPLS L3VPN networks, such networks are designed as hub-and-spoke networks, with a main site (and possibly a second for redundancy) and multiple remote sites. The required communication flow is usually between the main site (hub) and the remote sites (spokes), and there is no inter-spoke communication.

In the EVPN scenario, this hub-and-spoke functionality is addressed using the EVPN E-Tree service, described in RFC 8317, through the provisioning of a rooted-multipoint Ethernet service over the core transport network based on MPLS, SR-MPLS, or, most recently, SRv6. This EVPN E-Tree service allows access circuits to be configured as a root site (hub) or a leaf site (spoke).

RFC 8317 defines three E-Tree scenarios, and as of this writing, Cisco IOS XR 7.8.1 currently supports only EVPN E-Tree Scenario 1 Option A for the SRv6 implementation:

> **Scenario 1: One leaf or root site(s) per PE:** With this scenario, a specific EVI configured on a PE router can either be a root site or a leaf site but not both. If there is a requirement for both root and leaf sites on the PE router, they need to be configured in different EVIs. Multiple leaf access circuits can be provisioned within the same EVI on the same PE router, and to prevent any inter-leaf traffic flows, split-horizon group (SHG) filtering needs to be configured. Scenario 1 Option A using two BGP route targets per EVI is the EVPN E-Tree option used for the E-Tree configuration tasks in this section.

SRv6 EVPN E-Tree Service Configuration

This section describes the configuration of an EVPN E-Tree service (see Figure 6-36) and is based on an SRv6 underlay network with a single configured port-active multihomed root site (root) attached to CE-1. There are two configured leaf sites: Leaf Site-1, attached to CE-3, which is a port-active multihomed site, and Leaf Site-2, attached to CE-4, which is a single-homed site.

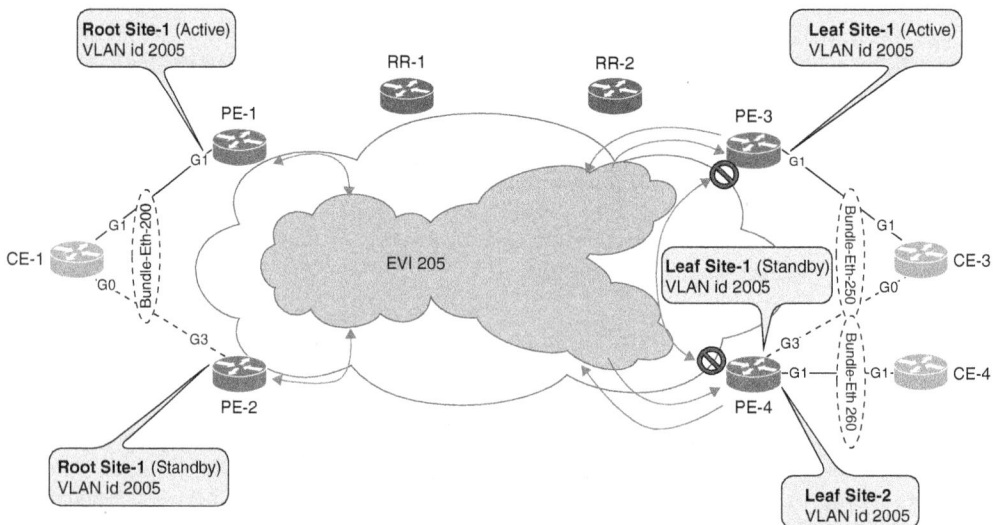

Figure 6-36   *EVPN E-Tree Port-Active MHD Reference Network*

EVPN E-Tree EFP (Access Circuit) Configuration

Figure 6-37 is a high-level representation of the access circuit configurations required for the EVPN E-Tree service.

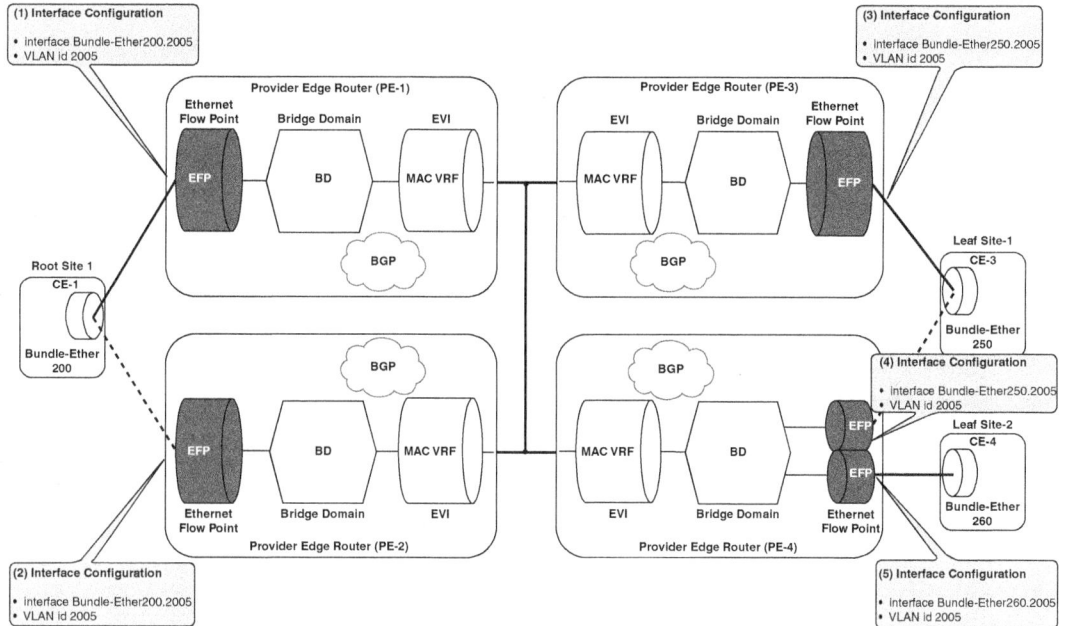

Figure 6-37   *EVPN E-Tree EFP (Access Circuit) Configurations*

These EFP (access circuit) configurations are similar to the EVPN E-LAN configuration tasks, although in the case of this EVPN E-Tree service, the configured EVI is 205, and the VLAN ID being used is 2005.

The following configs show the minimum configurations required across the four PE routers. Config 6-31 is the E-Tree root access circuit configuration on router PE-1 for the MHD router CE-1.

Config 6-31   *EVPN E-Tree Root EFP (Access Circuit) Configurations on PE-1*

```
!
interface Bundle-Ether200
 description Connected_to_CE-1
 lacp system mac 00fc.0001.0200
!
interface Bundle-Ether200.2005 l2transport
 description ETREE-ROOT_L2VPN_205-BD
 encapsulation dot1q 2005
!
```

```
interface GigabitEthernet0/0/0/1
 description Connected_to_CE-1
 bundle id 200 mode active
 !
```

Config 6-32 is the E-Tree root access circuit configuration on router PE-2 for the MHD router CE-1.

Config 6-32   *EVPN E-Tree Root EFP (Access Circuit) Configurations on PE-2*

```
!
interface Bundle-Ether200
 description Connected_to_CE-1
 lacp system mac 00fc.0001.0200
 !
interface Bundle-Ether200.2005 l2transport
 description ETREE-ROOT_L2VPN_205-BD
 encapsulation dot1q 2005
 !
interface GigabitEthernet0/0/0/3
 description Connected_to_CE-1
 bundle id 200 mode active
 !
```

Config 6-33 is the E-Tree Leaf Site-1 access circuit configuration on router PE-3 for the MHD router CE-3.

Config 6-33   *EVPN E-Tree Leaf Site-1 EFP (Access Circuit) Configurations on PE-3*

```
!
interface Bundle-Ether250
 description Connected_to_CE-3
 lacp system mac 00fc.0002.0250
 !
interface Bundle-Ether250.2005 l2transport
 description ETREE-LEAF-1_L2VPN_205-BD
 encapsulation dot1q 2005
 !
interface GigabitEthernet0/0/0/1
 description Connected_to_CE-3
 bundle id 250 mode active
 !
```

Config 6-34 is the E-Tree Leaf Site-1 access circuit configuration on router PE-4 for the MHD router CE-3.

Config 6-34 *EVPN E-Tree Leaf Site-1 EFP (Access Circuit) Configurations on PE-4*

```
!
interface Bundle-Ether250
 description Connected_to_CE-3
 lacp system mac 00fc.0002.0250
!
interface Bundle-Ether250.2005 l2transport
 description ETREE-LEAF-1_L2VPN_205-BD
 encapsulation dot1q 2005
!
interface GigabitEthernet0/0/0/3
 description Connected_to_CE-3
 bundle id 250 mode active
 !
```

Finally, Config 6-35 is the E-Tree Leaf Site-2 access circuit configuration on router PE-4 for the SHD router CE-4.

Config 6-35 *EVPN E-Tree Leaf Site-2 EFP (Access Circuit) Configurations on PE-4*

```
!
interface Bundle-Ether260
 description Connected_to_CE-4
 lacp system mac 00fc.0002.0260
!
interface Bundle-Ether260.2005 l2transport
 description ETREE-LEAF-2_L2VPN_205-BD
 encapsulation dot1q 2005
!
interface GigabitEthernet0/0/0/1
 description Connected_to_CE-4
 bundle id 260 mode active
 !
```

EVPN E-Tree EFP (Access Circuit) Verification

Figure 6-38 shows some common and useful commands that are used to verify and troubleshoot the configured EVPN E-Tree EFP (access circuit) configurations.

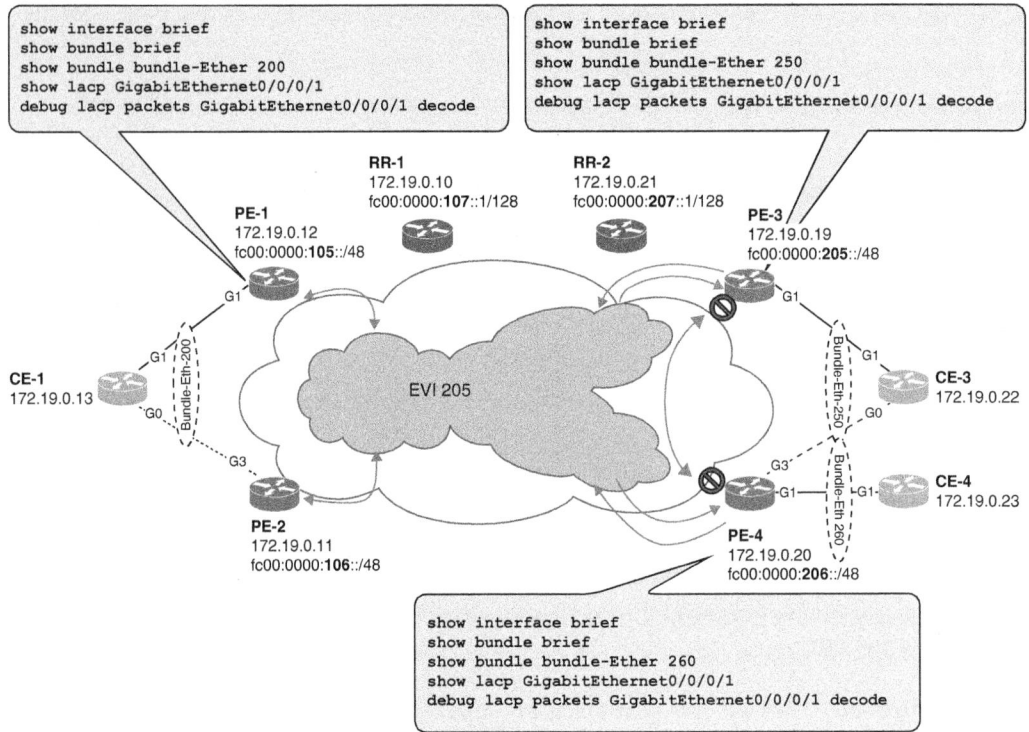

Figure 6-38   *EVPN E-Tree EFP (Access Circuit) PE Router Verification*

The same commands used earlier, in the section "EVPN E-LAN Port-Active MHD EFP (Access Circuit) Verification," are applicable for the EVPN E-Tree EFP (access circuit) verifications and therefore are not repeated here.

EVPN E-Tree: EVPN Configuration

The second part of the E-Tree configuration steps is the EVPN EVI circuit provisioning, as shown in Figure 6-39.

At this writing, EVPN E-Tree for SRv6 supports only the Scenario 1 Option A implementation (two BGP route targets per EVI). The minimum required root site configurations are displayed in Config 6-36, where the export route target is set as 65000:10205 and will be imported by the leaf sites as well as the root site of the peer PE router. The import route targets will be 65000:20205 exported from the leaf sites and 65000:10205 exported from the root site of the peer PE router.

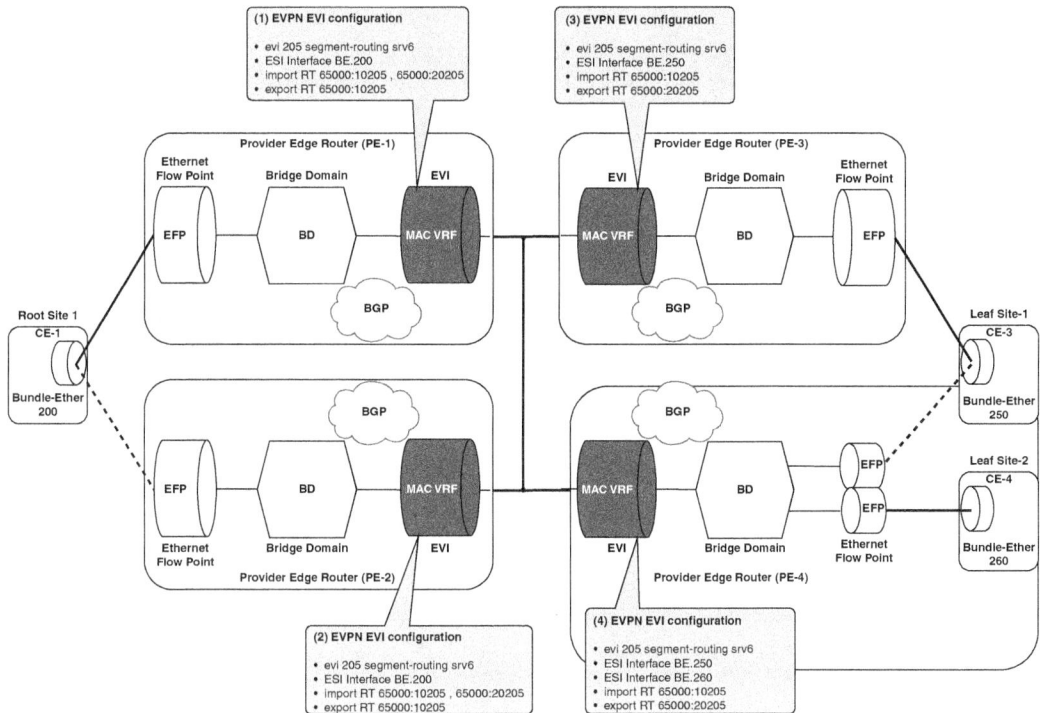

Figure 6-39 *EVPN E-Tree EVPN Configurations*

Config 6-36 *EVPN E-Tree EVPN Root Site Configurations on PE-1 and PE-2*

```
evpn
 evi 205 segment-routing srv6
  bgp
   route-target import 65000:10205 ←-------root site
   route-target import 65000:20205 ←-------leaf site
   route-target export 65000:10205 ←-------root site
  !
  description ETREE-ROOT_L2VPN_205-BD
  advertise-mac
  !
 !
interface Bundle-Ether200
  ethernet-segment
   identifier type 0 00.fc.00.01.02.00.00.00.00
   load-balancing-mode port-active
  !
 !
 segment-routing srv6
  locator MAIN
  !
```

The configuration for Leaf Site-1 on router PE-3 is displayed in Config 6-37, where the route target 65000:10205 is imported from the root site and route target 65000:20205 is the export route target to allow the leaf site routes to be imported by the root sites.

Config 6-37   *EVPN E-Tree EVPN Leaf Site Configurations on PE-3*

```
evpn
 evi 205 segment-routing srv6
  bgp
   route-target import 65000:10205 ◄---root site
   route-target export 65000:20205 ◄---leaf site
  !
  description ETREE-LEAF-1_L2VPN_205-BD
  !
  advertise-mac
  !
 !
interface Bundle-Ether250
  ethernet-segment
   identifier type 0 00.fc.00.02.02.50.00.00.00
   load-balancing-mode port-active
  !
 !
segment-routing srv6
  locator MAIN
 !
!
```

The configurations for Leaf Site-1 and Leaf Site-2 on router PE-4 are displayed in Config 6-38, where the route target 65000:10205 is imported from the root site, and route target 65000:20205 is the export route target to allow the leaf site routes to be imported by the root sites.

Config 6-38   *EVPN E-Tree EVPN Leaf Site Configurations on PE-4*

```
evpn
 evi 205 segment-routing srv6
  bgp
   route-target import 65000:10205 ◄---root site
   route-target export 65000:20205 ◄---leaf site
  !
  description ETREE-LEAF-1-2_L2VPN_205-BD
  !
  advertise-mac
  !
 !
```

```
interface Bundle-Ether250
 ethernet-segment
  identifier type 0 00.fc.00.02.02.50.00.00.00
  load-balancing-mode port-active
 !
!
interface Bundle-Ether260
 ethernet-segment
  identifier type 0 00.00.00.00.00.00.00.00.00
 !
!
segment-routing srv6
 locator MAIN
 !
```

The leaf sites will only receive routes from the root sites, and the root sites will receive routes both from leaf and other root sites.

EVPN E-Tree EVPN Verification

Figure 6-40 provides a list of CLI commands that can be used to verify and troubleshoot the EVPN T-Tree service configuration.

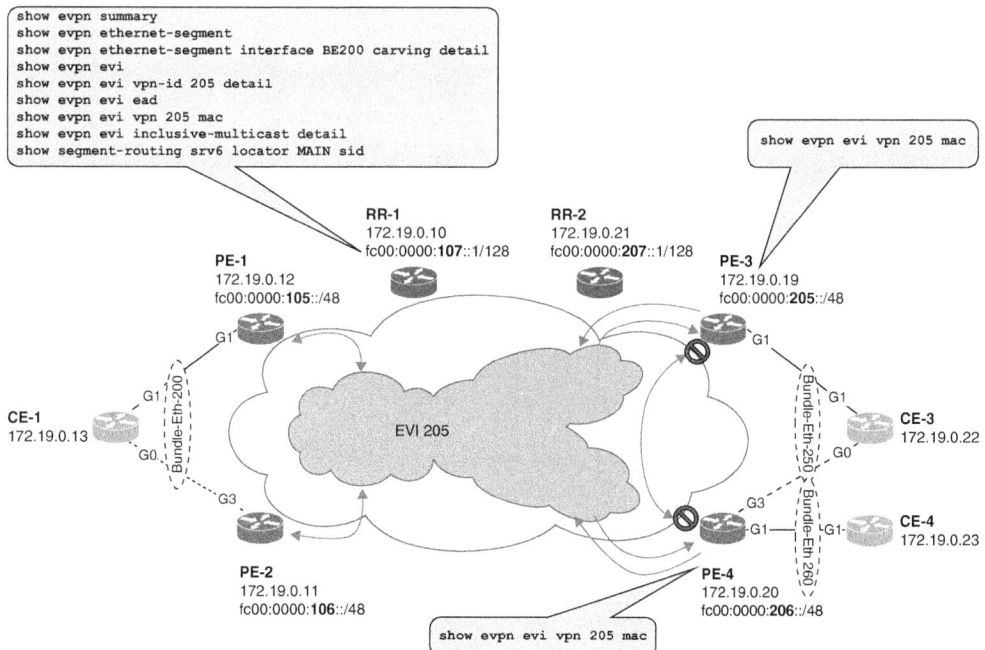

Figure 6-40 *EVPN E-Tree: EVPN Verification*

The commands in the earlier section "EVPN E-LAN Port-Active MHD EVPN Verification" are also applicable for the EVPN E-Tree verifications.

To demonstrate the use of the root and leaf site route targets, the command **show evpn evi vpn 205 mac** is used to verify the local and remote learned MAC routes in Output 6-73 from PE-1. The output includes MAC addresses 1055.5500.0001–1055.5500.0005 learned locally from root site router CE-1 and those learned remotely from Leaf Site-1 router CE-3 (2055.6600.0001–2055.6600.0005), as well as those from the Leaf Site-2 router CE-4 (2055.7700.0001–2055.7700.0005).

Output 6-73   *EVPN Route Type 2 Local and Remote MAC Routes for the Root Site on PE-1*

```
RP/0/RP0/CPU0:PE-1#show evpn evi vpn 205 mac

VPN-ID  Encap  MAC address     IP address  Nexthop                 Label     SID
-------  ------ --------------- ----------  ---------------------   ------    --------------
205     SRv6   1055.5500.0001  ::          Bundle-Ether200.2005    0         fc00:0:105:e009::
205     SRv6   1055.5500.0002  ::          Bundle-Ether200.2005    0         fc00:0:105:e009::
205     SRv6   1055.5500.0003  ::          Bundle-Ether200.2005    0         fc00:0:105:e009::
205     SRv6   1055.5500.0004  ::          Bundle-Ether200.2005    0         fc00:0:105:e009::
205     SRv6   1055.5500.0005  ::          Bundle-Ether200.2005    0         fc00:0:105:e009::
205     SRv6   2055.6600.0001  ::          fc00:0:205::1           IMP-NULL  fc00:0:205:e004::
205     SRv6   2055.6600.0002  ::          fc00:0:205::1           IMP-NULL  fc00:0:205:e004::
205     SRv6   2055.6600.0003  ::          fc00:0:205::1           IMP-NULL  fc00:0:205:e004::
205     SRv6   2055.6600.0004  ::          fc00:0:205::1           IMP-NULL  fc00:0:205:e004::
205     SRv6   2055.6600.0005  ::          fc00:0:205::1           IMP-NULL  fc00:0:205:e004::
205     SRv6   2055.7700.0001  ::          fc00:0:206::1           IMP-NULL  fc00:0:206:e004::
205     SRv6   2055.7700.0002  ::          fc00:0:206::1           IMP-NULL  fc00:0:206:e004::
205     SRv6   2055.7700.0003  ::          fc00:0:206::1           IMP-NULL  fc00:0:206:e004::
205     SRv6   2055.7700.0004  ::          fc00:0:206::1           IMP-NULL  fc00:0:206:e004::
205     SRv6   2055.7700.0005  ::           fc00:0:206::1          IMP-NULL  fc00:0:206:e004::
RP/0/RP0/CPU0:PE-1#
```

The command **show evpn evi vpn 205 mac** in Output 6-74 from PE-3 shows that the Leaf Site-2 MAC addresses 2055.7700.0001–2055.7700.0005 are not imported into the EVI, and the root site MAC addresses are imported.

Output 6-74   *EVPN Route Type 2 Local and Remote MAC Routes for Leaf Site 1 on PE-3*

```
RP/0/RP0/CPU0:PE-3#show evpn evi vpn 205 mac

VPN-ID  Encap  MAC address     IP address  Nexthop                 Label     SID
-------  ------ --------------- ----------  ---------------------   ------    --------------
205     SRv6   1055.5500.0001  ::          fc00:0:105::1           IMP-NULL  fc00:0:105:e009::
205     SRv6   1055.5500.0002  ::          fc00:0:105::1           IMP-NULL  fc00:0:105:e009::
```

```
205   SRv6   1055.5500.0003 ::        fc00:0:105::1          IMP-NULL fc00:0:105:e009::
205   SRv6   1055.5500.0004 ::        fc00:0:105::1          IMP-NULL fc00:0:105:e009::
205   SRv6   1055.5500.0005 ::        fc00:0:105::1          IMP-NULL fc00:0:105:e009::
205   SRv6   2055.6600.0001 ::        Bundle-Ether250.2005   0        fc00:0:205:e004::
205   SRv6   2055.6600.0002 ::        Bundle-Ether250.2005   0        fc00:0:205:e004::
205   SRv6   2055.6600.0003 ::        Bundle-Ether250.2005   0        fc00:0:205:e004::
205   SRv6   2055.6600.0004 ::        Bundle-Ether250.2005   0        fc00:0:205:e004::
205   SRv6   2055.6600.0005 ::        Bundle-Ether250.2005   0        fc00:0:205:e004::
RP/0/RP0/CPU0:PE-3#
```

On router PE-4, the command **show evpn evi vpn 205 mac**, shown in Output 6-75, indicates that the Leaf Site-1 MAC addresses 2055.6600.0001–2055.6600.0005 are not imported into the EVI, and the root site MAC addresses are imported.

Output 6-75   *EVPN Route Type 2 Local and Remote MAC Routes for Leaf Site-2 on PE-4*

```
RP/0/RP0/CPU0:PE-4#show evpn evi vpn 205 mac

VPN-ID   Encap   MAC address      IP address   Nexthop                Label    SID
-------  ------  --------------   ----------   --------------------   ------   --------------
205      SRv6    1055.5500.0001 ::             fc00:0:105::1          IMP-NULL fc00:0:105:e009::
205      SRv6    1055.5500.0002 ::             fc00:0:105::1          IMP-NULL fc00:0:105:e009::
205      SRv6    1055.5500.0003 ::             fc00:0:105::1          IMP-NULL fc00:0:105:e009::
205      SRv6    1055.5500.0004 ::             fc00:0:105::1          IMP-NULL fc00:0:105:e009::
205      SRv6    1055.5500.0005 ::             fc00:0:105::1          IMP-NULL fc00:0:105:e009::
205      SRv6    2055.7700.0001 ::             Bundle-Ether260.2005   0        fc00:0:206:e004::
205      SRv6    2055.7700.0002 ::             Bundle-Ether260.2005   0        fc00:0:206:e004::
205      SRv6    2055.7700.0003 ::             Bundle-Ether260.2005   0        fc00:0:206:e004::
205      SRv6    2055.7700.0004 ::             Bundle-Ether260.2005   0        fc00:0:206:e004::
205      SRv6    2055.7700.0005 ::             Bundle-Ether260.2005   0        fc00:0:206:e004::
RP/0/RP0/CPU0:PE-4#
```

Next, we will look at preventing per-bridge domain inter-site traffic forwarding since local bridge domain inter-site connectivity cannot be prevented using route targets.

EVPN E-Tree L2VPN Configuration

The third configuration step is the L2VPN bridge domain provisioning and the linking of this bridge domain to the previously configured EVPN EVI 205, as shown in Figure 6-41.

As mentioned earlier, the leaf sites will only receive routes from the root sites, and the root sites will receive routes from both leaf sites and other root sites. However, on router PE-4, the bridge domain 205-BD has two leaf sites directly attached, where inter-site traffic forwarding can occur. Therefore, all leaf site access circuits attached to the same bridge domain must be configured to join a split-horizon group (SHG), as you will see shortly, in Config 6-41. A bridge domain split-horizon group is a mechanism used in Layer 2 virtual private networks to enhance security and prevent network loops. The split-horizon group technique within a bridge domain ensures that packets received on a particular access circuit are not forwarded out another access circuit belonging to the same SHG within a single bridge domain. Aside from the split-horizon group configuration, the remainder of the E-Tree L2VPN configurations on both root sites in Config 6-39 and leaf sites are the same as the E-LAN L2VPN configurations discussed previously.

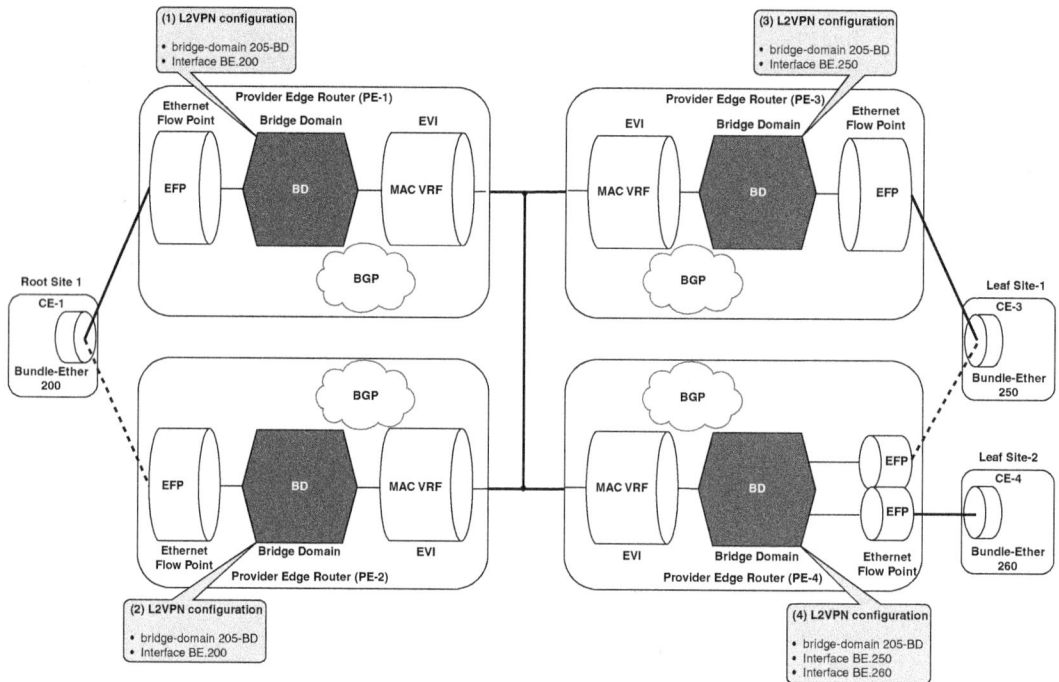

Figure 6-41 *EVPN E-Tree L2VPN Configuration Overview*

Config 6-39 *EVPN E-Tree L2VPN Root Site Configuration on PE-1 and PE-2*

```
l2vpn
 bridge group ELAN-BG
  bridge-domain 205-BD
   description ETREE-ROOT_L2VPN_205-BD
   interface Bundle-Ether200.2005
   !
   evi 205 segment-routing srv6
   !
```

The bridge domain configuration for Leaf Site-1 on router PE-3 is shown in Config 6-40.

Config 6-40 *EVPN E-Tree Leaf Site L2VPN Configuration on PE-3*

```
l2vpn
 bridge group ELAN-BG
  bridge-domain 205-BD
   description ETREE-LEAF-1_L2VPN_205-BD
   interface Bundle-Ether250.2005
   !
   evi 205 segment-routing srv6
   !
```

The bridge domain and split-horizon group configuration for Leaf Site-1 and Leaf Site-2 on router PE-4 is shown in Config 6-41.

Config 6-41 *EVPN E-Tree Leaf Site L2VPN Configuration on PE-4*

```
l2vpn
 bridge group ELAN-BG
  bridge-domain 205-BD
   description ETREE-LEAF-1-2_L2VPN_205-BD
   interface Bundle-Ether250.2005
    split-horizon group
   !
   interface Bundle-Ether260.2005
    split-horizon group
   !
   evi 205 segment-routing srv6
   !
```

EVPN E-Tree L2VPN Verification

Figure 6-42 provides a list of CLI commands that can be used to verify and troubleshoot the L2VPN service configuration.

The output of the CLI command **show l2vpn bridge-domain bd-name {bridge-domain-name} detail** has already been discussed in detail in the section "EVPN E-LAN Port-Active MHD L2VPN Verification," and the additional E-Tree split-horizon group configuration is verified on router PE-4 as shown in Output 6-76. The output displays that the leaf-site access circuits are configured into a split-horizon group, thereby preventing any inter–leaf site traffic flows. The output has been shortened for brevity, with emphasis on the state of the access circuits attached to bridge domain 205-BD as well as whether the split-horizon group is enabled on these access circuits and for both subinterface bundle-ether 250.2005 and bundle-ether 260.2005, this is indeed the case.

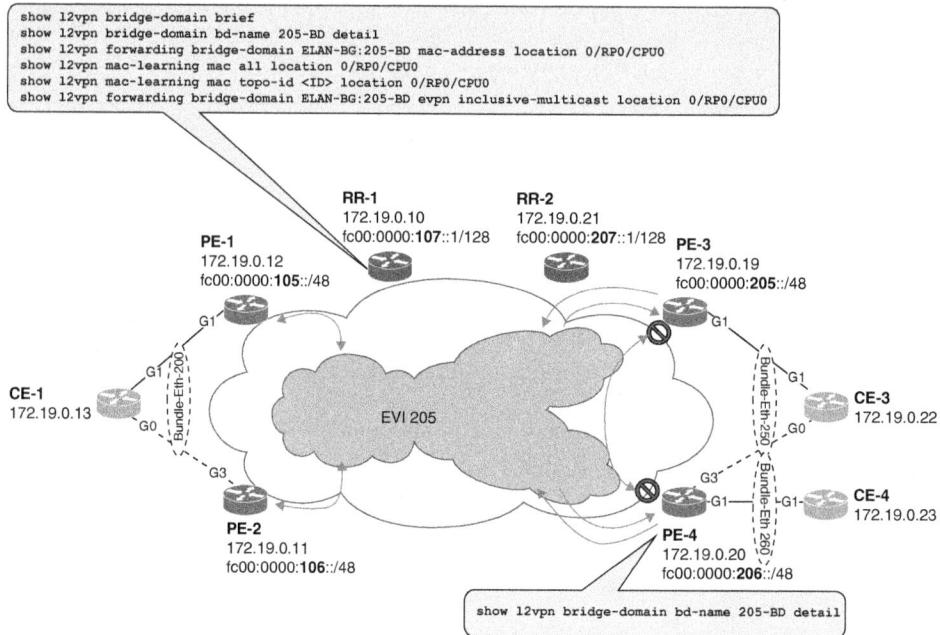

Figure 6-42   *EVPN E-Tree L2VPN PE Router Verification*

Output 6-76   *L2VPN Bridge Domain 205-BD Detail State on PE-4*

```
RP/0/RP0/CPU0:PE-4#show l2vpn bridge-domain bd-name 205-BD detail

<snip>
  List of ACs:
    AC: Bundle-Ether250.2005, state is down (Segment-down)
      Type VLAN; Num Ranges: 1
      Rewrite Tags: []
      VLAN ranges: [2005, 2005]
      MTU 1504; XC ID 0xfffc0003; interworking none; MSTi 2
      MAC learning: enabled
      Flooding:
        Broadcast & Multicast: enabled
        Unknown unicast: enabled
      MAC aging time: 300 s, Type: inactivity
      MAC limit: 4000, Action: none, Notification: syslog
      MAC limit reached: no, threshold: 75%
      MAC port down flush: enabled
      MAC Secure: disabled, Logging: disabled
      Split Horizon Group: enabled
<snip>
```

```
   AC: Bundle-Ether260.2005, state is up
     Type VLAN; Num Ranges: 1
     Rewrite Tags: []
     VLAN ranges: [2005, 2005]
     MTU 1504; XC ID 0xfffc0005; interworking none; MSTi 2
     MAC learning: enabled
     Flooding:
        Broadcast & Multicast: enabled
        Unknown unicast: enabled
     MAC aging time: 300 s, Type: inactivity
     MAC limit: 4000, Action: none, Notification: syslog
     MAC limit reached: no, threshold: 75%
     MAC port down flush: enabled
     MAC Secure: disabled, Logging: disabled
     Split Horizon Group: enabled
<snip>
```

EVPN E-Tree BGP Configuration

The PE router configurations in the examples from Config 6-22 and Config 6-24 are sufficient for the BGP control plane, and there is no change for an EVPN E-Tree service configuration.

EVPN E-Tree BGP Verification

This section describes some common and useful commands that are used to verify and troubleshoot the BGP address-family L2VPN EVPN service configuration (see Figure 6-43).

The commands in the earlier section "EVPN E-LAN Port-Active MHD:BGP Verification" are also applicable for the EVPN E-Tree BGP verifications.

In this reference network, the MAC routes are learned from the following CE routers: router CE-1 at the root site (1055.5500.0001–1055.5500.0005), router CE-3 at Leaf Site-1 (2055.6600.0001–2055.6600.0005), and router CE-4 at Leaf Site-2 (2055.7700.0001–2055.7700.0005).

The command **show bgp vrf-db table all** outputs the VRF database for all BGP-related L3VPN and EVPN instances. Each VRF instance will be assigned a particular VRF ID. From this table, these IDs can be used to provide more details related to route target information for each of the EVPN instances.

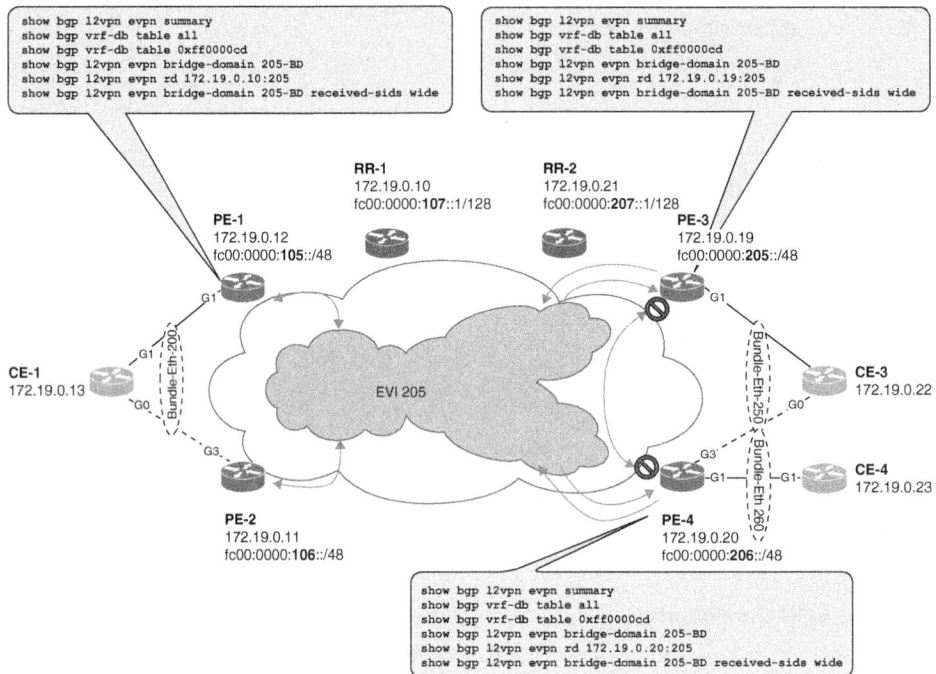

Figure 6-43   *EVPN E-Tree BGP Router Verification*

Output 6-77 displays the route target import/export list for the root site in EVI 205. The route targets are included as part of the BGP extended communities contained in the BGP EVPN Route Type 1 per-EVI Ethernet A-D routes and the BGP EVPN Route Type 2 MAC advertisement routes:

- **Import RT list:** 65000:10205, 65000:20205

- **Export RT list:** 65000:10205

Output 6-77   *BGP Provisioned Context 205-BD RT Details for the Root Site on PE-1*

```
RP/0/RP0/CPU0:PE-1#show bgp vrf-db table 0xff0000cd


VRF-TBL: 205-BD (L2VPN EVPN)
  TBL ID: 0xff0000cd
  RSI Handle: NULL
  Refcount: 9
 Import:
    RT-List: RT:65000:10205, RT:65000:20205
  Export:
    RT-List: RT:65000:10205
RP/0/RP0/CPU0:PE-1#
```

Output 6-78 shows the route target import/export list for Leaf Site-1 in EVI 205 on PE-3:

- **Import RT list:** 65000:10205

- **Export RT list:** 65000:20205

Output 6-78 *BGP Provisioned Context 205-BD RT Details for Leaf Site-1 on PE-3*

```
RP/0/RP0/CPU0:PE-3#show bgp vrf-db table 0xff0000cd

VRF-TBL: 205-BD (L2VPN EVPN)
  TBL ID: 0xff0000cd
  RSI Handle: NULL
  Refcount: 6
  Import:
    RT-List: RT:65000:10205
  Export:
    RT-List: RT:65000:20205
RP/0/RP0/CPU0:PE-3#
```

Output 6-79 shows the route target import/export list for Leaf Site-1 and Leaf Site-2 in EVI 205 on PE-4:

- **Import RT list:** 65000:10205

- **Export RT list:** 65000:20205

Output 6-79 *BGP Provisioned Context 205-BD RT Details for Leaf Site-1 and Leaf Site-2 on PE-4*

```
RP/0/RP0/CPU0:PE-4#show bgp vrf-db table 0xff0000cd

VRF-TBL: 205-BD (L2VPN EVPN)
  TBL ID: 0xff0000cd
  RSI Handle: NULL
  Refcount: 6
  Import:
    RT-List: RT:65000:10205
  Export:
    RT-List: RT:65000:20205
RP/0/RP0/CPU0:PE-4#
```

The command **show bgp l2vpn evpn bridge-domain 205-BD** in Output 6-80 (which has been shortened for brevity) displays all the EVPN route types for the EVI 205 (bridge domain 205-BD) on the root site router PE-1 and verifies that the EVPN Route Type 2 routes from both leaf sites are imported correctly.

Output 6-80   *BGP L2VPN EVPN Bridge Domain 205-BD Routes for the Root Site on PE-1*

```
RP/0/RP0/CPU0:PE-1#show bgp l2vpn evpn bridge-domain 205-BD
BGP router identifier 172.19.0.10, local AS number 65000
<snip>
   Network            Next Hop          Metric LocPrf Weight Path
Route Distinguisher: 172.19.0.10:205 (default for vrf 205-BD)
Route Distinguisher Version: 1472
*> [1][0000.fc00.0102.0000.0000][0]/120
                       0.0.0.0                            0 i
* i                    fc00:0:106::1              100     0 i
*>i[1][0000.fc00.0102.0000.0000][4294967295]/120
                       fc00:0:106::1              100     0 i
*>i[1][0000.fc00.0202.5000.0000][0]/120
                       fc00:0:205::1              100     0 i
* i                    fc00:0:206::1              100     0 i
*>i[1][0000.fc00.0202.5000.0000][4294967295]/120
                       fc00:0:205::1              100     0 i
* i                    fc00:0:206::1              100     0 i
*> [2][0][48][1055.5500.0001][0]/104
                       0.0.0.0                            0 i  <--local
<snip>
*>i[2][0][48][2055.6600.0001][0]/104
                       fc00:0:205::1              100     0 i  <--import leaf site-1
<snip>
*>i[2][0][48][2055.7700.0001][0]/104
                       fc00:0:206::1              100     0 i  <--import leaf site-2
<snip>
*> [3][0][32][172.19.0.10]/80
                       0.0.0.0                            0 i
*>i[3][0][32][172.19.0.11]/80
                       fc00:0:106::1              100     0 i
*>i[3][0][32][172.19.0.19]/80
                       fc00:0:205::1              100     0 i
*>i[3][0][32][172.19.0.20]/80
                       fc00:0:206::1              100     0 i

Processed 23 prefixes, 26 paths
RP/0/RP0/CPU0:PE-1#
```

Output 6-81 (which has been shortened for brevity) shows all the EVPN route types for EVI 205 (bridge domain 205-BD) on the router PE-3, and the only imported EVPN Route Type 2 routes are those imported from the root site.

Output 6-81   *BGP L2VPN EVPN Bridge Domain 205-BD Routes for the Leaf Site on PE-3*

```
RP/0/RP0/CPU0:PE-3#show bgp l2vpn evpn bridge-domain 205-BD


BGP router identifier 172.19.0.19, local AS number 65000
<snip>
Route Distinguisher: 172.19.0.19:205 (default for vrf 205-BD)
Route Distinguisher Version: 159
*>i[1][0000.fc00.0102.0000.0000][0]/120
                       fc00:0:105::1            100       0 i
* i                    fc00:0:106::1            100       0 i
*>i[1][0000.fc00.0102.0000.0000][4294967295]/120
                       fc00:0:105::1            100       0 i
* i                    fc00:0:106::1            100       0 i
*> [1][0000.fc00.0202.5000.0000][0]/120
                       0.0.0.0                            0 i
*>i[2][0][48][1055.5500.0001][0]/104
                       fc00:0:105::1            100       0 i  <--import root site
<snip>
*> [2][0][48][2055.6600.0001][0]/104
                       0.0.0.0                            0 i  <--local
<snip>
*>i[3][0][32][172.19.0.10]/80
                       fc00:0:105::1            100       0 i
*>i[3][0][32][172.19.0.11]/80
                       fc00:0:106::1            100       0 i
*> [3][0][32][172.19.0.19]/80
                       0.0.0.0                            0 i


Processed 16 prefixes, 18 paths
RP/0/RP0/CPU0:PE-3#
```

As mentioned earlier, the configuration examples in this section are the minimum required for a service to function correctly. They provide sufficient detail to allow the successful deployment of these services across an SRv6 transport network. The provisioning of these EVPN services across an SR-MPLS transport network is not covered in this book, but these provisioning tasks are similar to the ones described previously for an SRv6-based transport network.

EVPN E-Line

Today's EVPN E-Line (VPWS) services have their origin in the Any Transport over MPLS (AToM) services widely used by service providers since the early 2000s. By using AToM over their MPLS backbone networks, service providers can offer point-to-point services, also sometimes known as Virtual Private Wire Service (VPWS), to their end customers.

EVPN technology today offers the same point-to-point (VPWS) services as the AToM technologies, but with the advantages of an the EVPN solution applied to these point-to-point services (see RFC 8214):

■ There are no MPLS LDP pseudowires (PW) that need to be established end-to-end.

■ Multihoming capabilities (all-active, single-active, and port-active) are supported for load balancing and redundancy. With VPLS services, the only way to achieve similar redundancy is by using Multi-Chassis LAG (MC-LAG).

■ BGP is used for PE discovery and signaling.

■ EVPN VPWS requires only a subset of EVPN route types to advertise Ethernet segment and access circuit reachability.

   ■ EVPN per-EVI Ethernet A-D Route Type 1 routes are used to advertise point-to-point service ID.

   ■ EVPN per-ES Ethernet A-D Route Type 1 routes are used for fast convergence for link or node failure.

   ■ With the E-Line service, ingress traffic from the Ethernet segment can only be forwarded to a single ES destination, and so no MAC address lookup is required, removing the requirement for EVPN Route Type 2 routes.

   ■ EVPN Ethernet segment Route Type 4 routes are used for Ethernet segment auto-discovery between PE routers attached to multihomed devices.

The overview in Table 6-4 shows the EVPN route types typically used in for E-Line subscriber services.

Table 6-4   *EVPN (E-Line) BGP Route Types and Usage*

Type	Route Type Name	Route Use	E-Line
0x1	Ethernet auto-discovery (A-D) route	Used with the Extended Community: EVPN ESI Filter label	Used
		■ **MAC address mass withdrawal (fast convergence):** E-Line mass withdrawal	
		■ **Split-horizon label advertisement:** Not applicable for E-Line	
		■ **Aliasing (load balancing):** Not applicable for E-Line	

Type	Route Type Name	Route Use	E-Line
0x2	MAC/IP advertisement route	Used with MAC Mobility Extended Community	Not used
		Used with Default Gateway Extended Community	
		▪ Advertising MAC address and MAC/IP binding (ARP)	
		▪ MAC Mobility	
0x3	Inclusive multicast route	Used with PMSI Tunnel attribute	Not used
		▪ Used for forwarding BUM traffic	
0x4	Ethernet segment route	Used with ES-Import Extended Community	Used
		▪ **Redundancy group discovery:** The same as ES connectivity discovery	
		▪ **Designated forwarder election:** No DF election for E-Line	

SRv6 EVPN E-Line (VPWS) Service Configuration

The EVPN E-Line Service (VPWS) configuration in this section is an all-active multihomed service that is configured between the routers CE-1 and CE-3, as shown in Figure 6-44.

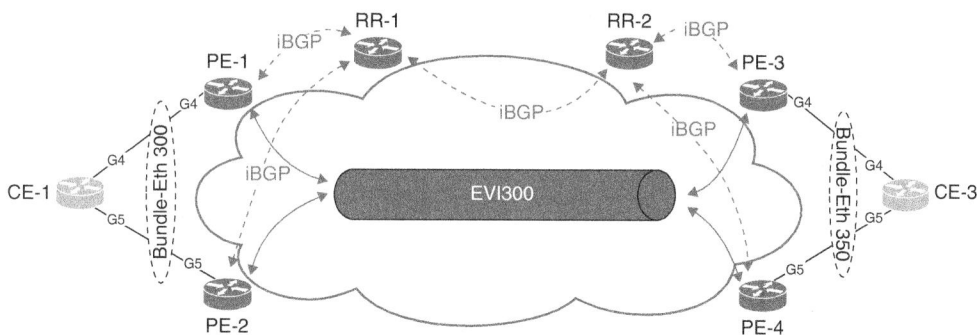

Figure 6-44 *EVPN E-Line All-Active Reference Network*

EVPN E-Line All-Active EFP (Access Circuit) Configuration

Figure 6-45 is a high-level representation of the PE routers and the required access circuit configurations required to successfully complete the configuration in this section.

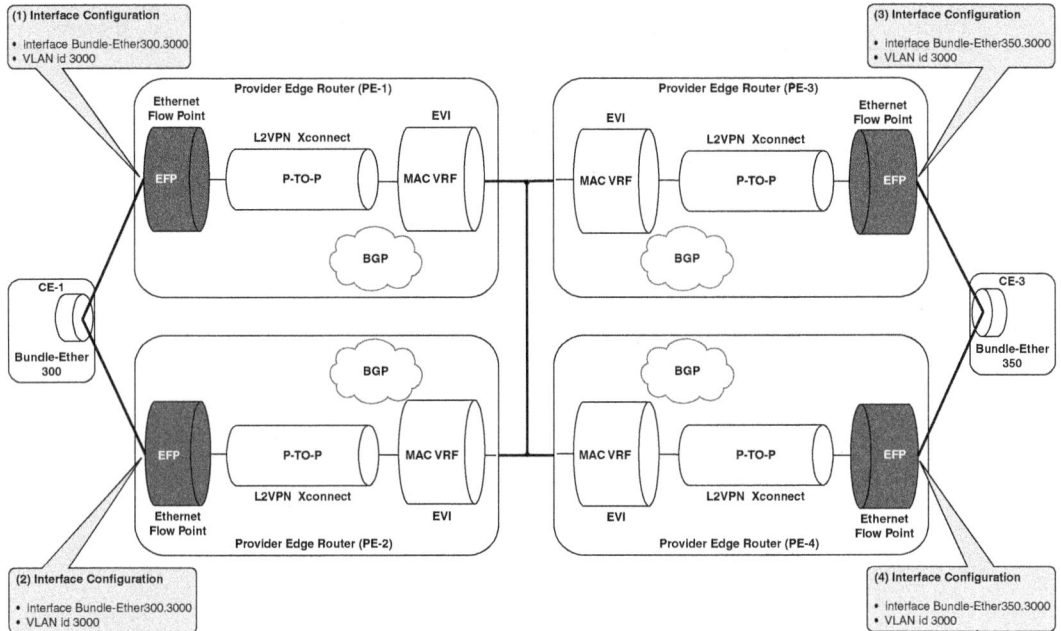

Figure 6-45 *EVPN E-Line All-Active EFP (Access Circuit) Configuration Tasks*

The LACP system MAC address used on both provider edge routers (PE-1 and PE-2) must be configured with the same LACP system MAC address in order to allow router CE-1 to receive this common LACP system ID from the interface bundle-ether 300 physical members. Config 6-42 shows the configuration of bundle-ether 300 on router PE-1.

Config 6-42 *EVPN E-Line All-Active PE Router Configuration on PE-1*

```
!
interface Bundle-Ether300
 description Connected_to_CE-1
 lacp system mac 00fc.0001.0300
!
interface Bundle-Ether300.3000 l2transport
 encapsulation dot1q 3000
!
interface GigabitEthernet0/0/0/4
 description Connected_to_CE-1
 bundle id 300 mode active
!
```

Config 6-43 shows the configuration of bundle-ether 300 on router PE-2.

Config 6-43   *EVPN E-Line All-Active PE Router Configuration on PE-2*

```
!
interface Bundle-Ether300
 description Connected_to_CE-1
 lacp system mac 00fc.0001.0300
!
interface Bundle-Ether300.3000 l2transport
 encapsulation dot1q 3000
!
interface GigabitEthernet0/0/0/5
 description Connected_to_CE-1
 bundle id 300 mode active
!
```

The configuration is similar for the LACP system MAC address used on both provider edge routers (PE-3 and PE-4). Note that this LACP system MAC address can either be applied globally to the router or per the bundle-ether interface, as configured in Config 6-44 on router PE-3.

Config 6-44   *EVPN E-Line All-Active PE Router Configuration on PE-3*

```
!
interface Bundle-Ether350
 description Connected_to_CE-3
 lacp system mac 00fc.0002.0350
!
interface Bundle-Ether350.3000 l2transport
 encapsulation dot1q 3000
!
interface GigabitEthernet0/0/0/4
 description Connected_to_CE-3
 bundle id 350 mode active
!
```

Config 6-45 shows the configuration of bundle-ether 350 on router PE-4.

Config 6-45   *EVPN E-Line All-Active PE Router Configuration on PE-4*

```
!
interface Bundle-Ether350
 description Connected_to_CE-3
 lacp system mac 00fc.0002.0350
!
```

```
interface Bundle-Ether350.3000 l2transport
 encapsulation dot1q 3000
!
interface GigabitEthernet0/0/0/5
 description Connected_to_CE-3
 bundle id 350 mode active
!
```

EVPN E-Line All-Active EFP (Access Circuit) Verification

Figure 6-46 shows some common and useful commands that can be used to verify and troubleshoot the EVPN E-Line EFP (access circuit) configurations.

Verifying the access circuit state for the all-active multihomed E-Line service EVI 300 must be carried out on the PE routers PE-1 and PE-2 in IS-IS Metro 1 as well as the PE routers PE-3 and PE-4 in IS-IS Metro 2. This step uses the same verification commands shown earlier, in the section "EVPN E-LAN Port-Active MHD EFP (Access Circuit) Verification."

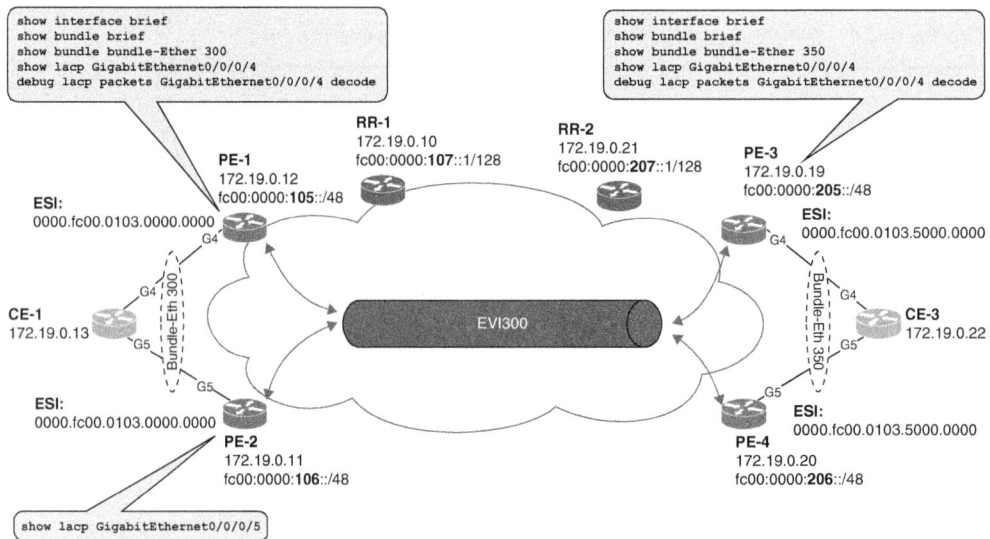

Figure 6-46 *EVPN E-Line All-Active EFP (Access Circuit) Verification*

On the router PE-1, the output from **show interfaces brief** in Output 6-82 confirms that the bundle-ether 300 and subinterface BE300.3000 interface/line protocol states are **up/ up** together with their LAG member interface Gi0/0/0/4.

Output 6-82 *show interfaces brief Output on PE-1*

```
RP/0/RP0/CPU0:PE-1#show interfaces brief

            Intf       Intf     LineP         Encap  MTU      BW
            Name       State    State          Type (byte)  (Kbps)
-----------------------------------------------------------------------
           BE200        up        up          ARPA   1514   1000000
      BE200.2000        up        up         802.1Q  1518   1000000
      BE200.2001        up        up         802.1Q  1518   1000000
      BE200.2005        up        up         802.1Q  1518   1000000
           BE300        up        up          ARPA   1514   1000000
      BE300.3000        up        up         802.1Q  1518   1000000
             Lo0        up        up       Loopback  1500         0
       Gi0/0/0/0        up        up          ARPA   9000   1000000
       Gi0/0/0/1        up        up          ARPA   1518   1000000
       Gi0/0/0/2        up        up          ARPA   9000   1000000
       Gi0/0/0/3        up        up          ARPA   1514   1000000
   Gi0/0/0/3.400        up        up         802.1Q  1518   1000000
   Gi0/0/0/3.402        up        up         802.1Q  1518   1000000
   Gi0/0/0/3.404        up        up         802.1Q  1518   1000000
       Gi0/0/0/4        up        up          ARPA   1518   1000000

RP/0/RP0/CPU0:PE-1#
```

The command **show bundle bundle-Ether 300** in Output 6-83 provides more details on a per-bundle-ether interface basis. In this case, the bundle-ether 300 status is **up** and **active** on interface Gi0/0/0/4. The interface bundle-ether 300 is part of the all-active multihoming service configured for EVI 300 and will be in active state on routers PE-1 and PE-2.

Output 6-83 *Interface Bundle-Ether 300 Status on PE-1*

```
RP/0/RP0/CPU0:PE-1#show bundle bundle-Ether 300

Bundle-Ether300
  Status:                                   Up
  Local links <active/standby/configured>:  1 / 0 / 1
  Local bandwidth <effective/available>:    1000000 (1000000) kbps
  MAC address (source):                     0025.8378.00f9 (Chassis pool)
  Inter-chassis link:                       No
  Minimum active links / bandwidth:         1 / 1 kbps
  Maximum active links:                     64
  Wait while timer:                         2000 ms
Load balancing:
  Link order signaling:                     Not configured
  Hash type:                                Default
  Locality threshold:                       None
```

```
 LACP:                                Operational
   Flap suppression timer:            Off
   Cisco extensions:                  Disabled
   Non-revertive:                     Disabled
 mLACP:                               Not configured
 IPv4 BFD:                            Not configured
 IPv6 BFD:                            Not configured


 Port                 Device          State       Port ID         B/W, kbps
 -------------------- --------------- ----------- --------------- ----------
 Gi0/0/0/4            Local           Active      0x8000, 0x0002   1000000
      Link is Active
RP/0/RP0/CPU0:PE-1#
```

The PE router's bundle-ether interface is configured to use Link Aggregation Control
Protocol (LACP) (IEEE 802.3ad), and the output from the command **show lacp
GigabitEthernet0/0/0/4** shown in Output 6-84 from router PE-1 verifies that the Local
interface and Partner interface (CE router) system IDs will match on PE-1 and PE-2.

Output 6-84 *Interface Bundle-Ether 300 Member Interface LACP States on PE-1*

```
RP/0/RP0/CPU0:PE-1#show lacp GigabitEthernet0/0/0/4
State: a - Port is marked as Aggregatable.
       s - Port is Synchronized with peer.
       c - Port is marked as Collecting.
       d - Port is marked as Distributing.
       A - Device is in Active mode.
       F - Device requests PDUs from the peer at fast rate.
       D - Port is using default values for partner information.
       E - Information about partner has expired.


Bundle-Ether300


  Port             (rate) State   Port ID        Key    System ID
 -------------------- -------- ------------- ------ ------------------------
Local
  Gi0/0/0/4           1s  ascdAF-- 0x8000,0x0002 0x012c 0x8000,00-fc-00-01-03-00
  Partner             1s  ascdAF-- 0x8000,0x0004 0x012c 0x8000,00-00-00-01-18-00


  Port                 Receive    Period Selection  Mux       A Churn P Churn
 -------------------- ---------- ------ ---------- --------- ------- -------
Local
  Gi0/0/0/4           Current    Fast   Selected   Distrib   None    None
RP/0/RP0/CPU0:PE-1#
```

The output from the command **show lacp GigabitEthernet0/0/0/5** shown in Output 6-85 executed on PE-2 confirms that the Local interface and Partner interface (CE) system IDs do indeed match on the two PE routers. Both interface Gi0/0/0/4 on PE-1 and interface Gi0/0/0/5 on PE-2 are in the **Selected** and **Distrib** state, as expected.

Output 6-85   *Interface Bundle-Ether 300 Member Interface LACP States on PE-2*

```
RP/0/RP0/CPU0:PE-2#show lacp GigabitEthernet0/0/0/5
State: a - Port is marked as Aggregatable.
       s - Port is Synchronized with peer.
       c - Port is marked as Collecting.
       d - Port is marked as Distributing.
       A - Device is in Active mode.
       F - Device requests PDUs from the peer at fast rate.
       D - Port is using default values for partner information.
       E - Information about partner has expired.


Bundle-Ether300


  Port            (rate)  State    Port ID       Key     System ID
  -------------------     --------  ------------- ------  -------------------------
Local
  Gi0/0/0/5        1s     ascdAF-- 0x8000,0x0002 0x012c 0x8000,00-fc-00-01-03-00
  Partner          1s     ascdAF-- 0x8000,0x0003 0x012c 0x8000,00-00-00-01-18-00


  Port                    Receive    Period Selection  Mux       A Churn P Churn
  -------------------     ---------- ------ ---------- --------- ------- -------
Local
  Gi0/0/0/5               Current    Fast   Selected   Distrib   None    None
RP/0/RP0/CPU0:PE-2#
```

Verifications can be conducted using the previous commands on the interface bundle-ether 350 and LAG members on both Metro 2 PE routers PE-3 and PE-4 to confirm that their operating state is as expected.

EVPN E-Line All-Active EVPN Configuration

The second configuration step is EVPN circuit provisioning, as shown in Figure 6-47.

Much like the EVPN E-LAN port-active multihomed configurations, the configurations in Config 6-46 and Config 6-47 are sufficient for the EVPN portion of the E-Line provisioning tasks. Both routers PE-1 and PE-2 use a manually configured ESI, as shown in Config 6-46 with **identifier type 0 00.fc.00.01.03.00.00.00.00**.

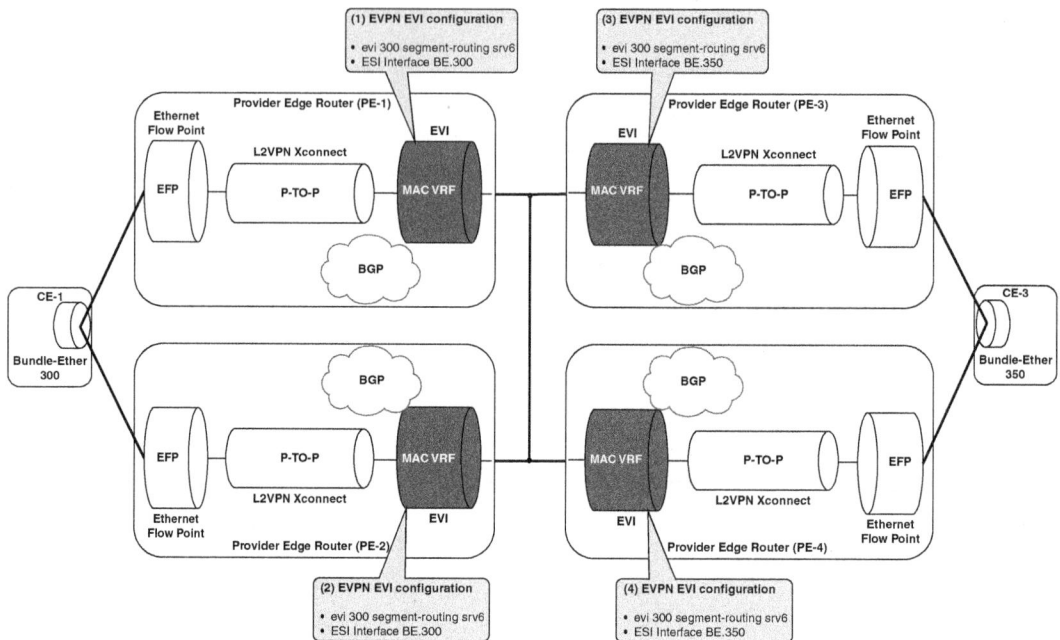

Figure 6-47   *EVPN E-Line All-Active EVPN Configuration Tasks*

Config 6-46   *EVPN E-Line All-Active EVI Router Configuration on PE-1 and PE-2*

```
evpn
 !
 evi 300 segment-routing srv6
 !
 interface Bundle-Ether300
  ethernet-segment
   identifier type 0 00.fc.00.01.03.00.00.00.00
  !
 !
 segment-routing srv6
  locator MAIN
 !
 !
```

Both routers PE-3 and PE-4 use a manually configured ESI, as shown in Config 6-47 with **identifier type 0 00.fc.00.01.03.50.00.00.00.**

Config 6-47 *EVPN E-Line All-Active EVI Router Configuration on PE-3 and PE-4*

```
evpn
 !
 evi 300 segment-routing srv6
 !
 interface Bundle-Ether350
  ethernet-segment
   identifier type 0 00.fc.00.01.03.50.00.00.00
  !
 !
 segment-routing srv6
  locator MAIN
 !
!
```

In the case of this EVPN E-Line all-active configuration, the default configuration behavior for load-balancing-mode is all-active, and it therefore does not have to be explicitly provisioned.

The EVPN E-Line service by default advertises an MTU of 0 and ignores MTU mismatches. However, the L2 MTU can be advertised, and MTU mismatches can be enforced explicitly. The optional configuration in Config 6-48 of **transmit-l2-mtu** and **enforce-mtu-match** may be done under the EVPN VPWS EVI to enforce the transmission and matching of the local/remote access circuit MTUs.

Config 6-48 *EVPN E-Line Access Circuit MTU Transmission and Enforcement*

```
evpn
 evi 300 segment-routing srv6
  transmit-l2-mtu
  enforce-mtu-match
  !
<snip>
```

Additional optional configurations that can also be considered are discussed in the earlier section "EVPN E-LAN Port-Active MHD EVPN Configuration."

EVPN E-Line All-Active EVPN Verification

Figure 6-48 shows common commands that are useful for verification and troubleshooting of the EVPN E-Line EVI service configuration.

This section shows relevant outputs from some useful commands that can be used to verify the EVPN component of the all-active multihomed service EVI 300. These outputs are collected from routers PE-1 and PE-2 in IS-IS Metro 1 and routers PE-3 and PE-4 in IS-IS Metro 2.

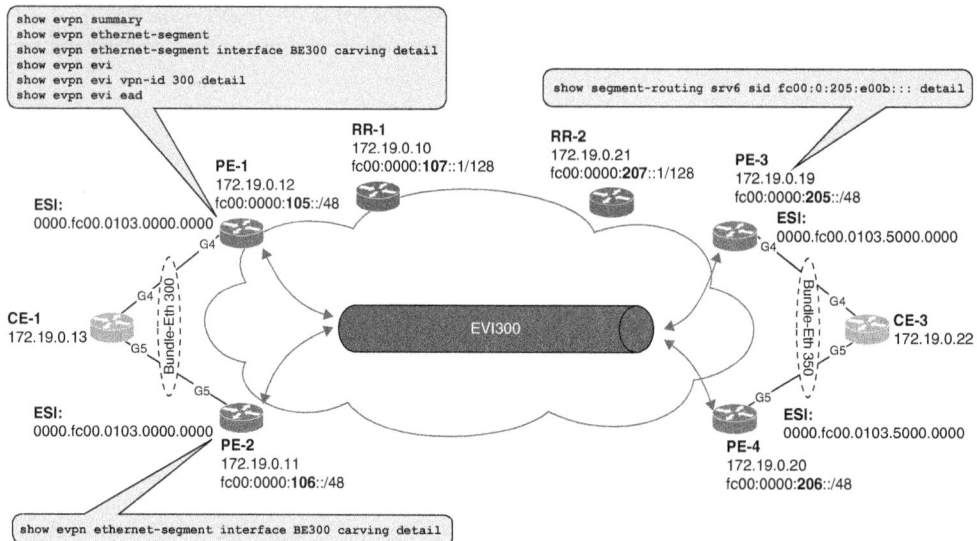

Figure 6-48   *EVPN E-Line All-Active EVPN Verification*

The command **show evpn ethernet-segment** provides an overview of the Ethernet segments attached to a PE router. In Output 6-86, there are two configured Ethernet segments, ESI 0000.fc00.0102.0000.0000 and 0000.fc00.0103.0000.0000, with interfaces bundle-ether 200 and bundle-ether 300 attached between PE-1 and PE-2.

Output 6-86   *EVPN Ethernet Segment Overview on PE-1*

```
RP/0/RP0/CPU0:PE-1#show evpn ethernet-segment

Ethernet Segment Id       Interface                      Nexthops
----------------------    ------------------------------ --------------------
0000.fc00.0102.0000.0000 BE200                           172.19.0.10
                                                         172.19.0.11
0000.fc00.0103.0000.0000 BE300                           172.19.0.10
                                                         172.19.0.11
RP/0/RP0/CPU0:PE-1#
```

For more details on the Ethernet segment related to the EVPN E-Line service configured on router PE-1, the command **show evpn ethernet-segment interface BE300 carving detail** in Output 6-87 provides detailed information for the bundle-ether 300 interface. The highlighted outputs from this command include some useful operational data:

- **Interface name: BE300:** The output confirms that interface bundle-ether 300 is the main interface attached to the Ethernet segment 0000.fc00.0103.0000.0000.

- **State: Up:** Because interface BE300 is configured for all-active multihomed service, the ESI state is **Up** on router PE-1 as well as on the peer router PE-2.

- **ESI Type: 0:** This indicates that the ESI value is manually configured by the operator.

- **Value: 0000.fc00.0103.0000.0000:** This indicates that the 10-byte ESI is manually provisioned by the user.

- **ES Import RT: 00fc.0001.0300:** The ES import RT comprising of the 6-byte MAC address portion of the ESI limits these Ethernet segment Route Type 4 routes to the PE routers PE-1 and PE-2 that are connected to the same local Ethernet segment.

  - **Operational : MH:** The topology is configured and operating as a multihomed Ethernet segment. This state must match on both PE routers.

  - **Configured : All-active (AApF):** This is the default configuration, and it is operating on both PE routers as all-active per-flow load balancing attached to the multihomed Ethernet segment.

- **Peering Details: 2 Nexthops:** These two IP addresses are the originating router IP addresses obtained via the EVPN Route Type 4 entry, as described earlier, in the section "EVPN Route Type 4: Ethernet Segment Route":

  - **172.19.0.10 [MOD:P:7fff:T]**

  - **172.19.0.11 [MOD:P:00:T]**

- **Service Carving Results:**

  - **Forwarders: 1:** One EVI forwarder is configured (EVI 300) in this Ethernet segment.

  - **Elected: 0**

- **EVPN-VPWS Service Carving Results:**

  - **Primary: 1:** Both PE ESI peer routers are set as primary. According to RFC 8214, "If set to 1 in multihoming Single-Active scenarios, this flag indicates that the advertising PE is the primary PE. MUST be set to 1 for multihoming All-Active scenarios by all active PE(s)."

  - **EVI:ETag P : 300:300300:** This is the P-bit advertised by the primary PE. EVI = 300 and ETag = 300300, which is provisioned l2vpn xconnect Service-ID. In a port-active multihomed configuration, a B-bit flag setting indicates that the originating PE router is the backup PE router. For example, it would appear as **EVI:ETag B : 300:300203.**

Output 6-87   *EVPN Ethernet Segment Detail on PE-1*

```
RP/0/RP0/CPU0:PE-1#show evpn ethernet-segment interface BE300 carving detail
<snip>


Ethernet Segment Id      Interface                        Nexthops
------------------------ -------------------------------- --------------------
0000.fc00.0103.0000.0000 BE300                            172.19.0.10
                                                          172.19.0.11
```

```
ES to BGP Gates  : Ready
ES to L2FIB Gates : Ready
Main port         :
   Interface name : Bundle-Ether300
   Interface MAC  : 0025.8378.00f9
   IfHandle       : 0x00000064
   State          : Up
   Redundancy     : Not Defined
ESI type          : 0
   Value          : 0000.fc00.0103.0000.0000
ES Import RT       : 00fc.0001.0300 (from ESI)
Source MAC        : 0000.0000.0000 (N/A)
Topology          :
   Operational    : MH, All-active
   Configured     : All-active (AApF) (default)
Service Carving   : Auto-selection
   Multicast      : Disabled
Convergence       :
Peering Details   : 2 Nexthops
   172.19.0.10 [MOD:P:7fff:T]
   172.19.0.11 [MOD:P:00:T]
Service Carving Synchronization:
   Mode           : NONE
   Peer Updates   :
            172.19.0.10 [SCT: N/A]
            172.19.0.11 [SCT: N/A]
Service Carving Results:
   Forwarders     : 1
   Elected        : 0
   Not Elected    : 0
EVPN-VPWS Service Carving Results:
   Primary        : 1
      EVI:ETag P   : 300:300300
   Backup         : 0
   Non-DF         : 0
MAC Flushing mode : STP-TCN
Peering timer     : 3 sec [not running]
Recovery timer    : 30 sec [not running]
Carving timer     : 0 sec [not running]
HRW Reset timer   : 5 sec [not running]
Local SHG label   : None
Remote SHG labels : 0
Access signal mode: Bundle OOS (Default)

RP/0/RP0/CPU0:PE-1#
```

The command **show evpn evi** in Output 6-88 provides an overview of the configured EVI VPN IDs and their related bridge domains (E-LAN) or VPWS services configured on a PE router.

Output 6-88 *EVPN EVI Summary on PE-1*

```
RP/0/RP0/CPU0:PE-1#show evpn evi

VPN-ID      Encap        Bridge Domain                  Type
----------  ----------   -----------------------------  --------------------
200         SRv6         200-BD                         EVPN
201         SRv6         201-BD                         EVPN
205         SRv6         205-BD                         EVPN
300         SRv6         VPWS:300                       VPWS (vlan-unaware)
65535       N/A          ES:GLOBAL                      Invalid
RP/0/RP0/CPU0:PE-1#
```

With the command **show evpn evi**, it is possible to verify the details of the specific VPWS EVI, as displayed in Output 6-89, and obtain the following useful information:

- **Unicast SID: <no SIDs>:** EVPN E-Line (VPWS) does not advertise an EVPN Route Type 2 route.

- **Multicast SID: < no SIDs >:** EVPN E-Line (VPWS) does not advertise an EVPN Route Type 3 route.

- **Advertise MACs: No:** EVPN E-Line (VPWS) does not advertise an EVPN Route Type 2 route.

- **Ignore MTU Mismatch: Enabled:** By default, a mismatched MTU will be ignored. This will be set to **Disabled** if **enforce-mtu-match** is configured.

- **Transmit MTU Zero: Enabled:** By default, an MTU of 0 will be transmitted. This will be set to **Disabled** if **transmit-l2-mtu** is configured.

- **RD Auto : (auto) 172.19.0.10:300:** The route distinguisher is auto-derived.

- **RT Auto : 65000:300:** The route target's auto-derived value is 65000:300, and the **Route Targets in Use** field shown in Output 6-89 indicates whether auto-derived RTs are in use or whether they are manually configured.

Output 6-89 *EVPN EVI VPN-ID 300 Detail on PE-1*

```
RP/0/RP0/CPU0:PE-1#show evpn evi vpn-id 300 detail

VPN-ID      Encap        Bridge Domain                  Type
----------  ----------   -----------------------------  --------------------
300         SRv6         VPWS:300                       VPWS (vlan-unaware)
```

```
      Stitching: Regular
      Unicast SID:  <no SIDs>
      Multicast SID:  <no SIDs>
      E-Tree: Root
      Forward-class: 0
      Advertise MACs: No
      Advertise BVI MACs: No
      Aliasing: Enabled
      UUF: Enabled
      Re-origination: Enabled
      Multicast:
        Source connected   : No
        IGMP-Snooping Proxy: No
        MLD-Snooping Proxy : No
      BGP Implicit Import: Enabled
      VRF Name:
      Preferred Nexthop Mode: Off
      Ignore MTU Mismatch: Enabled
      Transmit MTU Zero: Enabled
      BVI Coupled Mode: No
      BVI Subnet Withheld: ipv4 No, ipv6 No
       Statistics:
        Packets          Sent                Received
          Total          : 0                 0
          Unicast        : 0                 0
          BUM            : 0                 0
        Bytes            Sent                Received
          Total          : 0                 0
          Unicast        : 0                 0
          BUM            : 0                 0
      RD Config: none
      RD Auto   : (auto) 172.19.0.10:300
      RT Auto   : 65000:300
      Route Targets in Use          Type
      ----------------------------- --------------------
      65000:300                     Import
      65000:300                     Export

RP/0/RP0/CPU0:PE-1#
```

The command **show evpn evi ead** in Output 6-90 displays all local and remote learned EVPN Route Type 1 Ethernet A-D routes. This output provides a very good overview of all the auto-discovered Ethernet segments and their related EVIs. Let's take the output from router PE-2 as an example. The following per-ESI Ethernet A-D route and per-EVI Ethernet A-D routes from PE-3 and PE-4 in Metro 2 are displayed:

- Per-EVI Ethernet A-D Route Type 1:

  - **VPN-ID: 300:** The configured EVPN E-Line EVI 300 service

  - **Ethernet Segment Id: 0000.fc00.0103.5000.0000:** ESI configured on PE-3 and PE-4

  - **EtherTag: 0x4950c:** The configured VPWS Service ID 300300

  - **Next-Hop: fc00:0:205::1 / fc00:0:206::1:** The BGP next hop IPv6 source address for PE routers PE-3 and PE-4

  - **SID: fc00:0:205:e00b:: / fc00:0:206:e00d:::** SRv6 SIDs for PE routers PE-3 and PE-4

- Per-ESI Ethernet A-D Route Type 1:

  - **VPN-ID: 300:** The configured EVPN E-Line EVI 300 service

  - **Ethernet Segment Id: 0000.fc00.0103.5000.0000:** ESI configured on PE-3 and PE-4

  - **EtherTag: 0xffffffff:** The reserved MAX-Ethernet tag ID 4294967295

  - **Next-Hop: fc00:0:205::1 / fc00:0:206::1:** The BGP next hop IPv6 source address for PE routers PE-3 and PE-4

  - **SID: 0 / 0:** N/A

Output 6-90   *EVPN Route Type 1 Ethernet A-D per-EVI Details on PE-2*

```
RP/0/RP0/CPU0:PE-2#show evpn evi ead

VPN-ID  Encap  Ethernet Segment Id        EtherTag   Nexthop         Label    SID
-------  -----  -------------------------  ---------  --------------  -------  ------------------
<snip>
300     SRv6   0000.fc00.0103.0000.0000   0x4950c    ::              IMP-NULL fc00:0:106:e00d::
                                                     fc00:0:105::1   IMP-NULL fc00:0:105:e00b::
300     SRv6   0000.fc00.0103.0000.0000   0xffffffff fc00:0:105::1   0
300     SRv6   0000.fc00.0103.5000.0000   0x4950c    fc00:0:205::1   IMP-NULL fc00:0:205:e00b::
                                                     fc00:0:206::1   IMP-NULL fc00:0:206:e00d::
300     SRv6   0000.fc00.0103.5000.0000   0xffffffff fc00:0:205::1   0
                                                     fc00:0:206::1   0
3000    SRv6   0000.0000.0000.0000.0000   0xbb8      ::              IMP-NULL fc00:0:106:e008::
                                                     fc00:0:206::1   IMP-NULL fc00:0:206:e008::
RP/0/RP0/CPU0:PE-2#
```

Verification of the SIDs obtained in Output 6-90 can be done locally on the originating PE router with the **show segment-routing srv6 sid fc00:0:205:e00b:: detail** command, as demonstrated in Output 6-91:

- **SID: fc00:0:205:e00b:::** The PE-3 router SRv6 locator and function

- **Behavior: uDX2:** Endpoint behavior with decapsulation and L2 cross-connect

- **Context: 300:300300:** A context for MAC or IP address isolation, such as for a VRF instance in an L3VPN configuration or an EVI in an EVPN configuration; in this case, the context refers to the EVPN provisioned EVI 300 and the service ID (Eth-Tag) 300300

- **Owner: l2vpn_srv6:** The SID owner process; in this case, it refers to the L2VPN that owns the SID function. BGP or an IGP (IS-IS) can also be SID owners.

- **Locator: MAIN:** SID allocated from the configured SRv6 locator **MAIN**

Output 6-91   *Segment Routing SRv6 SID Detail: EVPN Route Type 1 SID on PE-3*

```
RP/0/RP0/CPU0:PE-3#show segment-routing srv6 sid fc00:0:205:e00b:: detail

*** Locator: 'MAIN' ***


SID                      Behavior      Context                 Owner           State   RW
----------------------   -----------   ---------------------   -------------   -----   --
fc00:0:205:e00b::        uDX2          300:300300              l2vpn_srv6      InUse   Y
  SID Function: 0xe00b
  SID context: { evi=300, eth-tag=300300 }
  Locator: 'MAIN'
  Allocation type: Dynamic
  Created: May 31 03:13:14.511 (4d00h ago)
RP/0/RP0/CPU0:PE-3#
```

EVPN E-Line All-Active L2VPN Configuration

The third configuration step is the L2VPN cross-connect (xconnect) provisioning, which will be linked to the EVPN EVI, as displayed in Figure 6-49.

The EVPN E-Line (VPWS) L2VPN configuration in Config 6-49 displays the xconnect instance **300-PTP** with the configured EVI ID 300 and service ID 300300. The access circuit, subinterface bundle-ether 300.3000, is bound to the VPWS instance **300-PTP** on both PE-1 and PE-2 The service ID 300300 will be matched on each far-end access circuit when belonging to the same service network.

Config 6-50 displays the opposite end of the xconnect instance **300-PTP** with the configured EVI ID 300 and service ID 300300. The access circuit, subinterface bundle-ether 350.3000, is bound to the VPWS instance **300-PTP** on both PE-3 and PE-4.

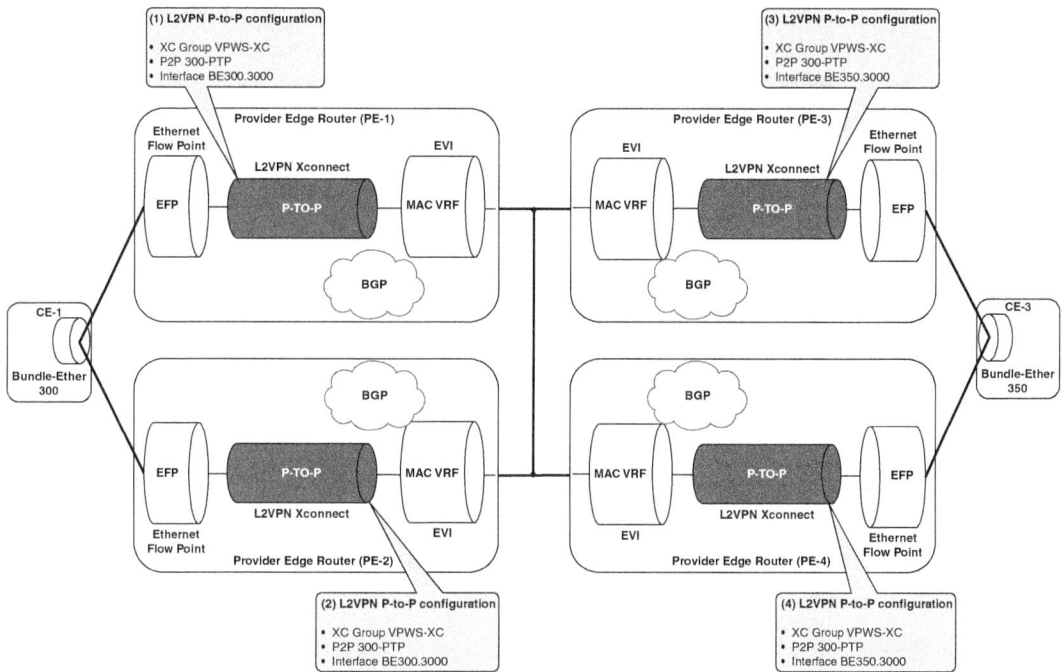

Figure 6-49 *EVPN E-Line All-Active L2VPN Configuration Tasks*

Config 6-49 *EVPN E-Line All-Active L2VPN Router Configurations on PE-1 and PE-2*

```
l2vpn
 xconnect group VPWS-XC
  p2p 300-PTP
   interface Bundle-Ether300.3000
   neighbor evpn evi 300 service 300300 segment-routing srv6
   !
```

Config 6-50 *EVPN E-Line All-Active L2VPN Router Configurations on PE-3 and PE-4*

```
l2vpn
 xconnect group VPWS-XC
  p2p 300-PTP
   interface Bundle-Ether350.3000
   neighbor evpn evi 300 service 300300 segment-routing srv6
   !
```

If multiple E-Line service instances are required between the same two PE routers, the operator could provision them by using a single EVI ID and a single import/export route target. The E-Line instances will be differentiated through the use of the unique service

IDs, as shown in Config 6-51. Each of the multiple per-EVI Ethernet A-D routes received by the ingress PE router will include a SID representing both the EVI and the E-Line service ID. Traffic reaching the egress PE router can then be identified based on this SID and forwarded out the correct egress access interface.

Config 6-51 *EVPN E-Line All-Active L2VPN Router Configurations: Multiple VPWS Instances*

```
l2vpn
 xconnect group VPWS-XC
  p2p 300-PTP
   interface Bundle-Ether300.3000
    neighbor evpn evi 300 service 300300 segment-routing srv6
    !
   !
  p2p 301-PTP
   interface Bundle-Ether300.3001
    neighbor evpn evi 300 service 300301 segment-routing srv6
    !
   !
  p2p 302-PTP
   interface Bundle-Ether300.3002
    neighbor evpn evi 300 service 300302 segment-routing srv6
    !
   !
```

EVPN E-Line All-Active L2VPN Verification

This section describes common and useful commands that can be used to verify and troubleshoot the previously configured EVPN E-Line all-active L2VPN service configuration (see Figure 6-50).

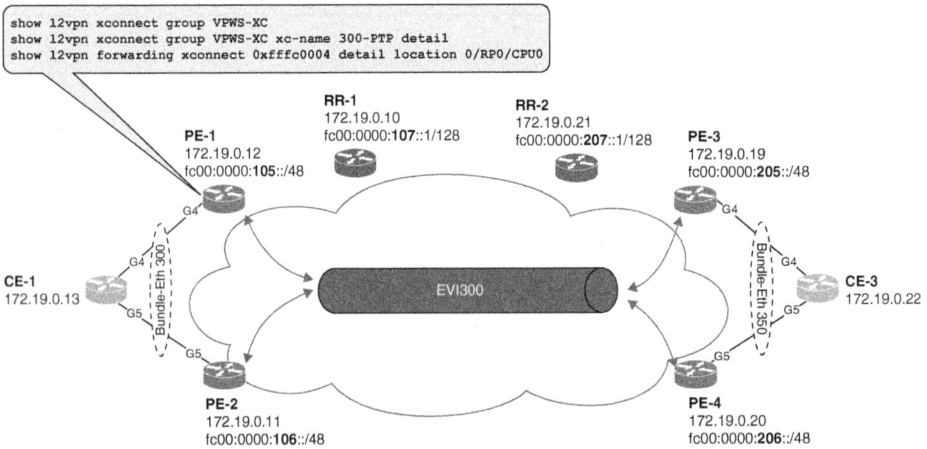

Figure 6-50 *EVPN E-Line All-Active L2VPN Verification*

To get an overview of the configured EVPN E-Line (VPWS) services and their states, the command **show l2vpn xconnect group VPWS-XC**, as shown in Output 6-92, provides summarized output of these VPWS services on a PE router. This output is divided into three parts:

- **XConnect:**

    - **Group: VPWS-XC:** User-configured xconnect group name

    - **Name: 300-PTP:** User-configured point-to-point xconnect service

    - **ST: UP:** State of the VPWS point-to-point xconnect service

- **Segment 1:**

    - **Description: BE300.3000:** L2 access circuit subinterface configured for this specific point-to-point xconnect service

    - **ST: UP:** State of the L2 access circuit between the PE and CE routers

- **Segment 2:**

    - **Description: EVPN 300,300300,::ffff:10.0.0.1:** EVI 300 and service ID 300300 with the IID ::ffff:10.0.0.1, which is an internal ID and is used to bind the L2 and the L3 forwarding chain. The IID is allocated by the ingress PE router and associates the egress PE router or routers to the EVI. The ingress PE router's Forwarding Information Base (FIB) L3 routing information will therefore resolve the IID toward the egress PE router's IGP locator SID. The IID can point to multiple next hops and thus enables equal-cost multipathing (ECMP).

    - **ST: UP:** State of the EVPN EVI between the local PE and remote PE routers

Output 6-92   *EVPN E-Line L2VPN Xconnect Group Overview on PE-1*

```
RP/0/RP0/CPU0:PE-1#show l2vpn xconnect group VPWS-XC
Legend: ST = State, UP = Up, DN = Down, AD = Admin Down, UR = Unresolved,
        SB = Standby, SR = Standby Ready, (PP) = Partially Programmed,
        LU = Local Up, RU = Remote Up, CO = Connected, (SI) = Seamless Inactive


XConnect                 Segment 1                    Segment 2
Group      Name     ST   Description          ST      Description              ST
------------------------ ----------------------- ---------------------------------
VPWS-XC    300-PTP  UP   BE300.3000           UP      EVPN 300,300300,::ffff:10.0.0.1
                                                                               UP
------------------------ ----------------------- ---------------------------------
RP/0/RP0/CPU0:PE-1#
```

The next step in the verification tasks is to delve into a specific point-to-point xconnect service, as shown in Output 6-93 for the configured xconnect service 300-PTP:

- **Group VPWS-XC, XC 300-PTP, state is up:** User-configured xconnect group and point-to-point service with its current state.

- **MTU 1504:** Interface MTU of 1518 bytes minus 14 bytes for the Ethernet header

- **XC ID 0xfffc0004:** Xconnect ID, which is used in the **show l2vpn forwarding xconnect** command in Output 6-94

- **Ignore MTU mismatch: Disabled:** User has configured **enforce-mtu-match** in order to keep the service state **Down** when mismatched MTUs are exchanged.

- **Transmit MTU zero: Disabled:** User has configured **transmit-l2-mtu** to ensure that interface MTUs can be matched.

- **SRv6: uDX2::** Endpoint behavior with decapsulation and L2 xconnect

- **Local: fc00:0:105:e00b:::** Local PE-1 router SRv6 locator and function

- **Remote: fc00:0:205:e00b:: / fc00:0:206:e00d:::** Remote all-active multihomed PE-3 and PE-4 router SRv6 locators and functions

- **SRv6 Headend: H.Encaps.L2.Red:** Ingress PE router encapsulates a received L2 frame into an IPv6 packet with an SRH (reduced-length SRH). The first SID is placed into the destination address field of the outer IPv6 header.

Output 6-93 *EVPN E-Line L2VPN Xconnect Group Point-to-Point Detail on PE-1*

```
RP/0/RP0/CPU0:PE-1#show l2vpn xconnect group VPWS-XC xc-name 300-PTP detail

Group VPWS-XC, XC 300-PTP, state is up; Interworking none
  AC: Bundle-Ether300.3000, state is up
    Type VLAN; Num Ranges: 1
    Rewrite Tags: []
    VLAN ranges: [3000, 3000]
    MTU 1504; XC ID 0xfffc0004; interworking none
    Statistics:
      packets: received 0, sent 0
      bytes: received 0, sent 0
      drops: illegal VLAN 0, illegal length 0
  EVPN: neighbor ::ffff:10.0.0.1, PW ID: evi 300, ac-id 300300, state is up
  ( established )
    XC ID 0xfff80001
    Encapsulation SRv6
    Encap type Ethernet
    Ignore MTU mismatch: Disabled
    Transmit MTU zero: Disabled
    Reachability: Up
```

```
    SRv6              Local                          Remote
    ---------------   ----------------------------   --------------------------
    uDX2              fc00:0:105:e00b::              fc00:0:205:e00b::
                                                     fc00:0:206:e00d::
    AC ID             300300                         300300
    MTU               1518                           1518
    Locator           MAIN                           N/A
    Locator Resolved  Yes                            N/A
    SRv6 Headend      H.Encaps.L2.Red                N/A
  Statistics:
    packets: received 0, sent 0
    bytes: received 0, sent 0
RP/0/RP0/CPU0:PE-1#
```

By using the xconnect id **XC ID 0xfffc0004** from Output 6-93, it is possible to obtain traffic forwarding statistics for the configured xconnect point-to-point service for both segments with the **show l2vpn forwarding xconnect 0xfffc0004 detail location 0/RP0/ CPU0** command, as shown in Output 6-94.

Output 6-94   *EVPN E-Line L2VPN Xconnect Point-to-Point Forwarding Detail on PE-1*

```
RP/0/RP0/CPU0:PE-1#show l2vpn forwarding xconnect 0xfffc0004 detail location 0/RP0/
  CPU0
Local interface: Bundle-Ether300.3000, Xconnect id: 0xfffc0004, Status: up
  Segment 1
    AC, Bundle-Ether300.3000, status: Bound
    Statistics:
      packets: received 0, sent 0
      bytes: received 0, sent 0
  Segment 2
    SRv6 EVPN, Internal ID: ::ffff:10.0.0.1, evi: 300, ac-id: 300300, status: Bound
    Control word disabled
    Statistics:
      packets: received 0, sent 0
      bytes: received 0, sent 0
RP/0/RP0/CPU0:PE-1#
```

EVPN E-Line All-Active BGP Configuration

The fourth and final configuration step is the BGP provisioning on all the PE routers, as shown in Figure 6-51.

The routers PE-1 and PE-2 peering with RR-1 in Metro 1 have similar BGP configurations, as shown in Config 6-52.

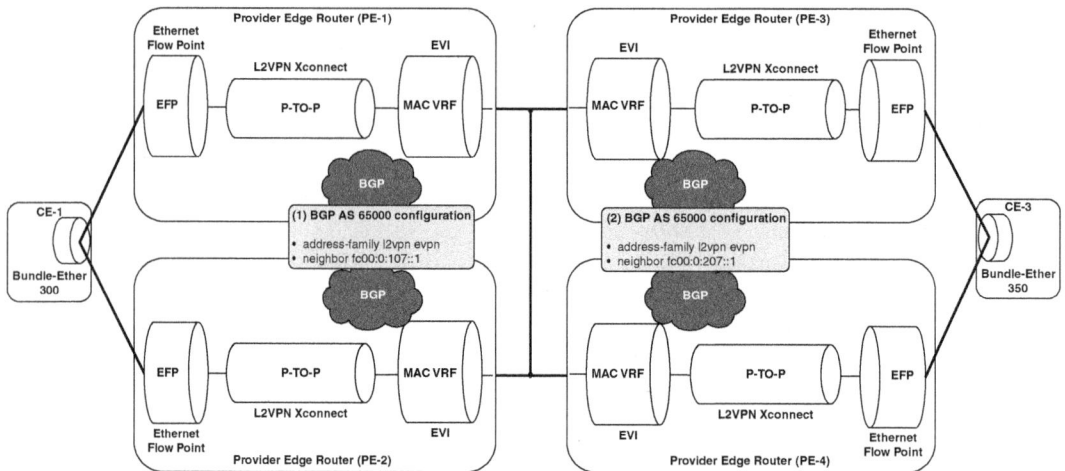

Figure 6-51   *EVPN E-Line All-Active BGP Configuration Tasks*

Config 6-52   *EVPN E-Line All-Active BGP PE Router Configurations on PE-1 and PE-2*

```
router bgp 65000
 bgp router-id 172.19.0.10
 !
 address-family l2vpn evpn
  !
 neighbor-group IBGP-RR1-NG
  remote-as 65000
  description *** iBGP peering to METRO-1 RR ***
  update-source Loopback0
  !
  address-family l2vpn evpn
  !
 !
 neighbor fc00:0:107::1
  use neighbor-group IBGP-RR1-NG
  description *** iBGP peering to METRO-1 RR ***
  !
```

Similarly, in Metro 2, the routers PE-3 and PE-4 peering with RR-2 have similar BGP
configurations, as shown in Config 6-53.

Config 6-53   *EVPN E-Line All-Active BGP PE Router Configurations on PE-3 and PE-4*

```
router bgp 65000
 bgp router-id 172.19.0.19
 !
```

```
address-family l2vpn evpn
!
neighbor-group IBGP-RR2-NG
 remote-as 65000
 description *** iBGP peering to METRO-2 RR ***
 update-source Loopback0
 !
 address-family l2vpn evpn
 !
!
neighbor fc00:0:207::1
 use neighbor-group IBGP-RR2-NG
 description *** iBGP peering to METRO-2 RR ***
 !
```

Note There are no differences between these BGP configurations and the EVPN E-LAN BGP configurations you have already seen. The BGP **address-family l2vpn evpn** configurations are sufficient for the BGP EVPN control plane and allow the exchange of all EVPN route types required for the EVPN E-Line all-active service.

EVPN E-Line All-Active BGP Verification

This section describes some common and commands that are useful for verifying and troubleshooting the BGP **address-family l2vpn evpn** configuration for this EVPN E-Line all-active service (see as shown in Figure 6-52).

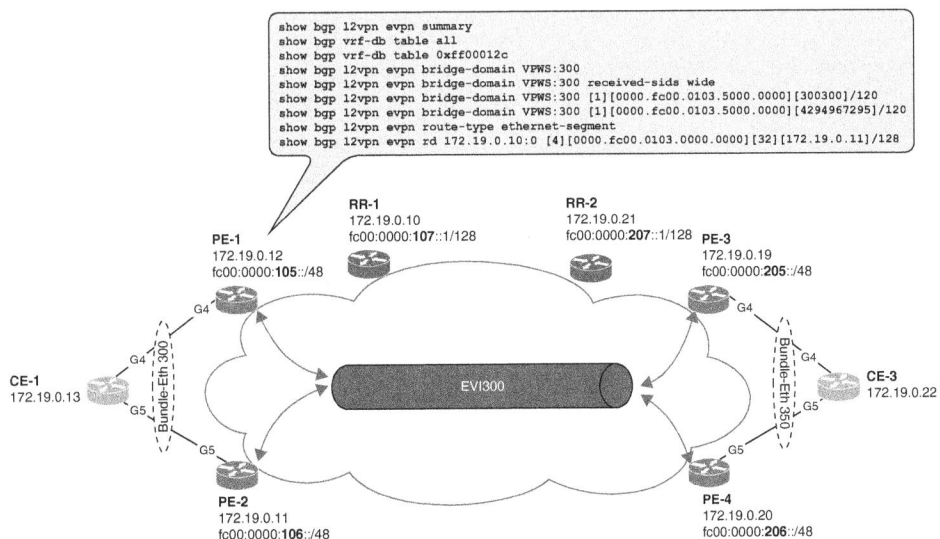

Figure 6-52 *EVPN E-Line All-Active BGP Verification*

The EVPN E-Line BGP verification commands are the same as the commands for the various EVPN E-LAN services, and any differences in the outputs are mentioned in this section. From the **show bgp vrf-db table all** output in Output 6-95, you can see that the VRF ID 0xff00012c for the xconnect point-to-point service 300-PTP is obtained and can be used to provide more details related to route target information for the EVPN instances.

Output 6-95 *BGP Summary Overview for Provisioned Contexts on PE-1*

```
RP/0/RP0/CPU0:PE-1#show bgp vrf-db table all
ID              REF     AF              VRF
0xe0000000      2       IPv4 Unicast    default
0xe0000001      7       IPv4 Unicast    BLUE
0xe0000002      7       IPv4 Unicast    TEST
0xe0000003      7       IPv4 Unicast    ANYCAST
0xe0800000      2       IPv6 Unicast    default
0xfd00ffff      10      L2VPN EVPN      ES:GLOBAL
0xff0000c8      7       L2VPN EVPN      200-BD
0xff0000c9      7       L2VPN EVPN      201-BD
0xff0000cd      9       L2VPN EVPN      205-BD
0xff00012c      6       L2VPN EVPN      VPWS:300
RP/0/RP0/CPU0:PE-1#
```

Output 6-96 displays the route target import/export list for EVI 300. The route target 65000:300 is included as part of the BGP extended communities contained in the BGP EVPN Route Type 1 per-EVI Ethernet A-D route.

Output 6-96 *BGP Provisioned Context VPWS:300 Details on PE-1*

```
RP/0/RP0/CPU0:PE-1#show bgp vrf-db table 0xff00012c

VRF-TBL: VPWS:300 (L2VPN EVPN)
  TBL ID: 0xff00012c
  RSI Handle: NULL
  Refcount: 6
  Import:
    RT-List: RT:65000:300
  Export:
    RT-List: RT:65000:300
RP/0/RP0/CPU0:PE-1#
```

With the command **show bgp l2vpn evpn bridge-domain VPWS:300** in Output 6-97, the relevant EVPN VPWS route types are displayed for the configured EVI 300 xconnect service. Note that it is possible to use the **bridge-domain** option in the command; refer to Output 6-88, where the command **show evpn evi** obtains the bridge domain details for this VPWS service. Alternatively, if the route distinguisher is known, the command **show bgp l2vpn evpn rd 172.19.0.10:300** provides the same output.

The noticeable difference between the output of this command and the output of the E-LAN service command **show bgp l2vpn evpn bridge-domain 200-BD** is that there are no Route Type 2 and Route Type 3 routes learned with the E-Line service. The only EVPN route types imported into the VPWS:300 context are Route Type 1 routes:

- **[1][0000.fc00.0103.0000.0000][300300]/120 (EVPN Route Type 1):** The per-EVI Ethernet A-D route with Ethernet tag ID 300300 (service ID) is both locally originated and learned from ES peer PE router PE-2.

- **[1][0000.fc00.0103.0000.0000][4294967295]/120 (EVPN Route Type 1):** The per-ESI Ethernet A-D route is identifiable through the reserved MAX-Ethernet tag ID 4294967295 and learned from the ES peer router PE-2.

- **[1][0000.fc00.0103.5000.0000][300300]/120 (EVPN Route Type 1):** The per-EVI Ethernet A-D route with Ethernet tag ID 300300 (service ID) is learned from remote peers PE-3 and PE-4.

- **[1][0000.fc00.0103.5000.0000][4294967295]/120 (EVPN Route Type 1):** The per-ESI Ethernet A-D route is identifiable through the reserved MAX-Ethernet tag ID 4294967295 and learned from remote peers PE-3 and PE-4.

Output 6-97 *BGP L2VPN EVPN Bridge Domain VPWS:300 Routes on PE-1*

```
RP/0/RP0/CPU0:PE-1#show bgp l2vpn evpn bridge-domain VPWS:300
BGP router identifier 172.19.0.10, local AS number 65000
BGP generic scan interval 60 secs
Non-stop routing is enabled
BGP table state: Active
Table ID: 0x0
BGP main routing table version 472
BGP NSR Initial initsync version 1 (Reached)
BGP NSR/ISSU Sync-Group versions 0/0
BGP scan interval 60 secs


Status codes: s suppressed, d damped, h history, * valid, > best
              i - internal, r RIB-failure, S stale, N Nexthop-discard
Origin codes: i - IGP, e - EGP, ? - incomplete
   Network            Next Hop            Metric LocPrf Weight Path
Route Distinguisher: 172.19.0.10:300 (default for vrf VPWS:300)
Route Distinguisher Version: 471
*> [1][0000.fc00.0103.0000.0000][300300]/120
                      0.0.0.0                                0 i
* i                   fc00:0:106::1            100          0 i
*>i[1][0000.fc00.0103.0000.0000][4294967295]/120
                      fc00:0:106::1            100          0 i
*>i[1][0000.fc00.0103.5000.0000][300300]/120
                      fc00:0:205::1            100          0 i
```

```
* i                    fc00:0:206::1                    100        0 i
*>i[1] [0000.fc00.0103.5000.0000] [4294967295]/120
                       fc00:0:205::1                    100        0 i
* i                    fc00:0:206::1                    100        0 i


Processed 4 prefixes, 7 paths
RP/0/RP0/CPU0:PE-1#
```

The command **show bgp l2vpn evpn bridge-domain VPWS:300 received-sids wide** in
Output 6-98 displays the EVPN Route Type 1 routes imported into EVI 300 with the
addition of the received SID information:

- **[1][0000.fc00.0103.0000.0000][300300]/120 (EVPN Route Type 1):** The per-EVI
  Ethernet A-D route is both locally originated and received from the ES peer PE
  router PE-2 with the next hop fc00:0:106::1 and the SID fc00:0:106:e00d::.

- **[1][0000.fc00.0103.5000.0000][300300]/120 (EVPN Route Type 1):** The per-
  EVI Ethernet A-D route is received from the remote peer routers PE-3 and PE-4
  with next hops fc00:0:205::1 and fc00:0:206::1 together with their received SIDs
  fc00:0:205:e00b:: and fc00:0:206:e00d::.

Output 6-98   *BGP L2VPN EVPN EVI 300 Received SIDs on PE-1*

```
RP/0/RP0/CPU0:PE-1#show bgp l2vpn evpn bridge-domain VPWS:300 received-sids wide
BGP router identifier 172.19.0.10, local AS number 65000
<snip>

Status codes: s suppressed, d damped, h history, * valid, > best
              i - internal, r RIB-failure, S stale, N Nexthop-discard
Origin codes: i - IGP, e - EGP, ? - incomplete
   Network                              Next Hop          Received Sid
Route Distinguisher: 172.19.0.10:300 (default for vrf VPWS:300)
Route Distinguisher Version: 471
*>  [1] [0000.fc00.0103.0000.0000] [300300]/120  0.0.0.0        fc00:0:105::
* i                                     fc00:0:106::1          fc00:0:106:e00d::
*>i[1] [0000.fc00.0103.0000.0000] [4294967295]/120fc00:0:106::1  NO SRv6 Sid
*>i[1] [0000.fc00.0103.5000.0000] [300300]/120  fc00:0:205::1   fc00:0:205:e00b::
* i                                     fc00:0:206::1          fc00:0:206:e00d::
*>i[1] [0000.fc00.0103.5000.0000] [4294967295]/120fc00:0:205::1  NO SRv6 Sid
* i                                     fc00:0:206::1          NO SRv6 Sid


Processed 4 prefixes, 7 paths
RP/0/RP0/CPU0:PE-1#
```

We can examine in more detail a Route Type 1 per-EVI Ethernet A-D route originated from the routers PE-3 and PE-4 with the command **show bgp l2vpn evpn bridge-domain VPWS:300 [1][0000.fc00.0103.5000.0000][300300]/120**, as shown in Output 6-99, where the following details are highlighted:

- **[0000.fc00.0103.5000.0000][300300]:** This reflects the 10-byte Ethernet segment identifier 00.00.fc.00.01.03.50.00.00.00 and the Ethernet tag ID 300300.

- **Received Label 0xe00b00:** The most significant 16 bits of the received label 0xe00b00 are the SRv6 uSID 0xe00b from router PE-3.

- **Received Label 0xe00d00:** The most significant 16 bits of the received label 0xe00d00 are the SRv6 uSID 0xe00d from router PE-4.

- **Extended community: EVPN L2 ATTRS:0x02:1518 RT:65000:300:**

  - **0x02: P flag:** Set to 1 as this output is from an all-active multihomed setup

  - **1518:** Remote interface L2 MTU size explicitly configured to be advertised

  - **RT:65000:300:** Route target advertised with the route (BGP AS number and EVI)

- **Sid:fc00:0:205::, Behavior:65:** This is the remote PE-3 locator value fc00:0:205::, and the behavior (65) refers to End.DX2 with NEXT-CSID (0x0041).

- **Sid:fc00:0:206::, Behavior:65:** This is the remote PE-4 locator value fc00:0:206::, and the behavior (65) refers to End.DX2 with NEXT-CSID (0x0041).

- **Source Route Distinguisher:** The source route distinguishers 172.19.0.19:300 and 172.19.0.20:300 are inserted by the originating PE routers PE-3 and PE-4.

Output 6-99 *BGP EVPN Route Type 1 per-EVI Ethernet A-D Route Details on PE-1*

```
RP/0/RP0/CPU0:PE-1#show bgp l2vpn evpn bridge-domain VPWS:300 [1][0000.
  fc00.0103.5000.0000][300300]/120
BGP routing table entry for [1][0000.fc00.0103.5000.0000][300300]/120,
  Route Distinguisher: 172.19.0.10:300
Versions:
  Process           bRIB/RIB   SendTblVer
  Speaker                 414          414
Last Modified: Jun  4 01:41:38.735 for 2d08h
Paths: (2 available, best #1)
  Not advertised to any peer
  Path #1: Received by speaker 0
  Not advertised to any peer
  Local
    fc00:0:205::1 (metric 61) from fc00:0:107::1 (172.19.0.19)
      Received Label 0xe00b00
      Origin IGP, localpref 100, valid, internal, best, group-best,
  import-candidate, imported, rib-install
```

```
    Received Path ID 0, Local Path ID 1, version 404
    Extended community: EVPN L2 ATTRS:0x02:1518 RT:65000:300
    Originator: 172.19.0.19, Cluster list: 172.19.0.12, 172.19.0.21
    PSID-Type:L2, SubTLV Count:1
     SubTLV:
      T:1(Sid information), Sid:fc00:0:205::, Behavior:65, SS-TLV Count:1
       SubSubTLV:
       T:1(Sid structure):
      Source AFI: L2VPN EVPN, Source VRF: default, Source Route
Distinguisher: 172.19.0.19:300
Path #2: Received by speaker 0
Not advertised to any peer
Local
  fc00:0:206::1 (metric 61) from fc00:0:107::1 (172.19.0.20)
    Received Label 0xe00d00
    Origin IGP, localpref 100, valid, internal, import-candidate, imported,
rib-install
    Received Path ID 0, Local Path ID 0, version 0
    Extended community: EVPN L2 ATTRS:0x02:1518 RT:65000:300
    Originator: 172.19.0.20, Cluster list: 172.19.0.12, 172.19.0.21
    PSID-Type:L2, SubTLV Count:1
     SubTLV:
      T:1(Sid information), Sid:fc00:0:206::, Behavior:65, SS-TLV Count:1
       SubSubTLV:
        T:1(Sid structure):
      Source AFI: L2VPN EVPN, Source VRF: default, Source Route
Distinguisher: 172.19.0.20:300
RP/0/RP0/CPU0:PE-1#
```

The command output displayed in Output 6-100 is of the EVPN Route Type 1 per-ESI Ethernet A-D route originated from the remote PE routers PE-3 and PE-4. These are the relevant values from this output:

- **[0000.fc00.0103.5000.0000][4294967295]:** This reflects the 10-byte Ethernet segment identifier 00.00.fc.00.01.03.50.00.00.00 and the reserved MAX-Ethernet tag ID 4294967295.

- **Received Label:** This is set to 0.

- **Extended community: EVPN ESI Label:0x00:3 RT:65000:300:** This consists of the EVPN ESI Filter label 0x00:3 with the redundancy mode bit = 0x0 (all-active), MPLS split-horizon label with a value of 3, and the route target RT:65000:300 for the EVI associated with the Ethernet segment.

- **Source Route Distinguisher:** The source route distinguishers 172.19.0.19:2 and 172.19.0.20:2 are inserted by the originating PE routers PE-3 and PE-4.

Output 6-100 *BGP EVPN Route Type 1 per-ESI Ethernet A-D Route Details on PE-1*

```
RP/0/RP0/CPU0:PE-1#show bgp l2vpn evpn bridge-domain VPWS:300 [1][0000.
  fc00.0103.5000.0000][4294967295]/120
BGP routing table entry for [1][0000.fc00.0103.5000.0000][4294967295]/120, Route
  Distinguisher: 172.19.0.10:300
Versions:
  Process           bRIB/RIB  SendTblVer
  Speaker              419          419
Last Modified: Jun  4 01:41:38.735 for 2d09h
Paths: (2 available, best #1)
  Not advertised to any peer
 Path #1: Received by speaker 0
 Not advertised to any peer
  Local
    fc00:0:205::1 (metric 61) from fc00:0:107::1 (172.19.0.19)
      Received Label 0
      Origin IGP, localpref 100, valid, internal, best, group-best,
 import-candidate, imported, rib-install
      Received Path ID 0, Local Path ID 1, version 398
      Extended community: EVPN ESI Label:0x00:3 RT:65000:300
      Originator: 172.19.0.19, Cluster list: 172.19.0.12, 172.19.0.21
      Source AFI: L2VPN EVPN, Source VRF: default, Source Route
 Distinguisher: 172.19.0.19:2
 Path #2: Received by speaker 0
 Not advertised to any peer
  Local
    fc00:0:206::1 (metric 61) from fc00:0:107::1 (172.19.0.20)
      Received Label 0
      Origin IGP, localpref 100, valid, internal, import-candidate,
 imported, rib-install
      Received Path ID 0, Local Path ID 0, version 0
      Extended community: EVPN ESI Label:0x00:3 RT:65000:300
      Originator: 172.19.0.20, Cluster list: 172.19.0.12, 172.19.0.21
      Source AFI: L2VPN EVPN, Source VRF: default, Source Route
 Distinguisher: 172.19.0.20:2
RP/0/RP0/CPU0:PE-1#
```

As mentioned at the start of this section, EVPN Route Type 1 and Route Type 4 are the only EVPN route types exchanged for EVPN E-Line services. The EVPN Route Type 4 Ethernet segment routes exchanged between the peer multihomed PE routers are displayed in Output 6-101 for all Ethernet segments configured between PE-1 and PE-2. The EVPN Route Type 4 for the EVPN E-Line service configuration is highlighted in the output for ESI 0000.fc00.0103.0000.0000.

Output 6-101 *BGP EVPN Route Type 4 Ethernet segment Route Details on PE-1*

```
RP/0/RP0/CPU0:PE-1#show bgp l2vpn evpn route-type ethernet-segment
BGP router identifier 172.19.0.10, local AS number 65000
<snip>


Status codes: s suppressed, d damped, h history, * valid, > best
              i - internal, r RIB-failure, S stale, N Nexthop-discard
Origin codes: i - IGP, e - EGP, ? - incomplete
  Network           Next Hop          Metric LocPrf Weight Path
Route Distinguisher: 172.19.0.10:0 (default for vrf ES:GLOBAL)
Route Distinguisher Version: 472
*> [4][0000.fc00.0102.0000.0000][32][172.19.0.10]/128
                    0.0.0.0                                0 i
*>i[4][0000.fc00.0102.0000.0000][32][172.19.0.11]/128
                    fc00:0:106::1                 100      0 i
*> [4][0000.fc00.0103.0000.0000][32][172.19.0.10]/128
                    0.0.0.0                                0 i
*>i[4][0000.fc00.0103.0000.0000][32][172.19.0.11]/128
                    fc00:0:106::1                 100      0 i
Route Distinguisher: 172.19.0.11:0
Route Distinguisher Version: 55
*>i[4][0000.fc00.0102.0000.0000][32][172.19.0.11]/128
                    fc00:0:106::1                 100      0 i
*>i[4][0000.fc00.0103.0000.0000][32][172.19.0.11]/128
                    fc00:0:106::1                 100      0 i

Processed 6 prefixes, 6 paths
RP/0/RP0/CPU0:PE-1#
```

Verification details of the EVPN Route Type 4 Ethernet segment route imported from the peer router PE-2 are displayed in Output 6-102:

- **[0000.fc00.0103.0000.0000]:** This reflects the 10-byte Ethernet segment identifier 00:00:fc:00:01:03:00:00:00:00.

- **Extended community:** The following are included within the BGP Extended community attributes of the received route:

  - **EVPN ES Import:00fc.0001.0300:** The ES import RT comprising of the 6-byte MAC address portion of the ESI limits these Ethernet segment Route Type 4 routes to the PE routers PE-1 and PE-2 that are connected to the same local Ethernet segment.

■ **DF Election:0:0x0008:0:** In an E-Line all-active multihomed service, the designated forwarder (DF) election procedure is not applicable because all active PE routers handle traffic as unicast, which means they all forward the traffic onto the Ethernet segment (ES).

■ **Source Route Distinguisher:** Source RD 172.19.0.11:0 is inserted by the originating router PE-2.

Output 6-102 *BGP EVPN Route Type 4 Ethernet Segment Route Detail on PE-1*

```
RP/0/RP0/CPU0:PE-1#show bgp l2vpn evpn rd 172.19.0.10:0 [4][0000.
  fc00.0103.0000.0000] [32] [172.19.0.11]/128
BGP routing table entry for [4][0000.fc00.0103.0000.0000][32][172.19.0.11]/128,
  Route Distinguisher: 172.19.0.10:0
Versions:
  Process           bRIB/RIB  SendTblVer
  Speaker                 56          56
Last Modified: Jun  3 23:02:05.735 for 3d08h
Paths: (1 available, best #1)
  Not advertised to any peer
  Path #1: Received by speaker 0
  Not advertised to any peer
  Local
    fc00:0:106::1 (metric 21) from fc00:0:107::1 (172.19.0.11)
      Origin IGP, localpref 100, valid, internal, best, group-best,
  import-candidate, imported, rib-install
      Received Path ID 0, Local Path ID 1, version 56
      Extended community: EVPN ES Import:00fc.0001.0300 DF Election:0:0x0008:0
      Originator: 172.19.0.11, Cluster list: 172.19.0.12
      Source AFI: L2VPN EVPN, Source VRF: default, Source Route
  Distinguisher: 172.19.0.11:0
RP/0/RP0/CPU0:PE-1#
```

In this section, we have briefly examined EVPN as a Layer 2 VPN technology and various terminologies related to the protocol. We examined the EVPN protocol behavior through packet captures of actual control traffic data frames and looked at the configuration and verification steps of various EVPN service types provisioned across an SRv6 transport network. These services included the E-LAN port-active multihomed service, E-LAN single-homed service, E-Tree service, and an E-Line all-active multihomed service. In Chapter 7, the focus will be on L3VPN services provisioned over both SRv6 and SR-MPLS transport networks.

Summary

This chapter provides a concise introduction to EVPN technology, which is used to deploy Layer 2 VPN services. You have seen that EVPN is a sophisticated VPN technology that overcomes several shortcomings associated with Virtual Private LAN Service (VPLS) in the context of Layer 2 VPNs, such as:

■ The absence of multihoming capabilities and the resulting lack of load balancing

■ The reliance on the less-efficient "flooding and learning" approach for MAC address discovery and dissemination

■ The limited scalability of VPLS compared to EVPN, which leverages the BGP control plane protocol

■ Suboptimal management of broadcast, unknown-unicast, and multicast (BUM) traffic

■ The inability to combine routing and bridging within a single service instance

This chapter also covers the configuration and validation of SRv6 EVPN E-LAN and E-Line services and how to set up the following EVPN offerings over an SRv6 backbone:

■ E-LAN port-active multihomed service

■ E-LAN single-homed service

■ E-Tree service

■ E-Line all-active multihomed service

It is important to be aware that the tasks described here were performed on Cisco IOS-XR routers running XR Version 7.8.2, which does not support the E-LAN all-active multihomed service feature.

References and Additional Reading

L2VPN (EVPN)

■ RFC 7432 BGP MPLS-Based Ethernet VPN, https://datatracker.ietf.org/doc/rfc7432

■ RFC 8214 Virtual Private Wire Service Support in Ethernet VPN, https://datatracker.ietf.org/doc/rfc8214

■ RFC 8365 A Network Virtualization Overlay Solution Using Ethernet VPN (EVPN), https://datatracker.ietf.org/doc/rfc8365

■ RFC 9135 Integrated Routing and Bridging in Ethernet VPN (EVPN), https://datatracker.ietf.org/doc/rfc9135/

- RFC 9062 Framework and Requirements for Ethernet VPN (EVPN) Operations, Administration, and Maintenance (OAM), https://datatracker.ietf.org/doc/rfc9062/

- MC-LAG Multi-Chassis Link Aggregation, https://community.cisco.com/t5/service-providers-knowledge-base/asr9000-xr-multichassis-lag-or-mc-lag-mclag-guide/ta-p/3133825

EVPN in Detail

- RFC 7432: BGP MPLS-Based Ethernet VPN 7.1 Ethernet Auto-discovery Route, https://datatracker.ietf.org/doc/rfc7432/

- RFC 7432: BGP MPLS-Based Ethernet VPN 8.5. Designated Forwarder Election, https://datatracker.ietf.org/doc/rfc7432/

- IETF Draft: Network Programming extension: SRv6 uSID instruction, https://datatracker.ietf.org/doc/html/draft-filsfils-spring-net-pgm-extension-srv6-usid-14

- RFC 8214: Virtual Private Wire Service Support in Ethernet VPN section 3.1.EVPN Layer 2 Attributes Extended Community regarding these control flag definitions, https://datatracker.ietf.org/doc/rfc8214

- RFC 6514: BGP Encodings and Procedures for Multicast in MPLS/BGP IP VPNs, https://datatracker.ietf.org/doc/rfc6514

- IETF Draft: AC-Aware Bundling Service Interface in EVPN, https://datatracker.ietf.org/doc/draft-ietf-bess-evpn-ac-aware-bundling

- IETF Draft: Fast Recovery for EVPN Designated Forwarder Election, https://datatracker.ietf.org/doc/html/draft-ietf-bess-evpn-fast-df-recovery-09

- IETF Draft: EVPN Multi-Homing Extensions for Split Horizon, Filtering https://datatracker.ietf.org/doc/draft-ietf-bess-evpn-mh-split-horizon/

- RFC 9252: BGP Overlay Services Based on Segment Routing over IPv6 (SRv6), https://datatracker.ietf.org/doc/rfc9252/

EVPN E-Tree

- RFC 8317: Ethernet-Tree (E-Tree) Support in Ethernet VPN (EVPN) and Provider Backbone Bridging EVPN (PBB-EVPN), https://datatracker.ietf.org/doc/rfc8317/

EVPN E-Line

- RFC 8214: Virtual Private Wire Service Support in Ethernet VPN, https://datatracker.ietf.org/doc/rfc8214/

L3VPN Service Deployment: Configuration and Verification Techniques

In Chapter 6, "L2VPN Service Deployment: Configuration and Verification Techniques," we explored the setup of L2VPN overlay services using SRv6 transport networks. This chapter shifts focus to the implementation of L3VPN overlay services that leverage both SRv6 and SR-MPLS frameworks. We will cover a range of L3VPN network designs, detailing fundamental setup procedures and methods for confirming service functionality. It is important to recognize that the content presented here serves as an overview of L3VPN service provisioning and validation over SR-MPLS and SRv6 transport networks rather than an exhaustive exploration of L3VPN technologies.

Most service providers today offer L3VPN services, and many enterprises use these services internally, so these services are well understood and ubiquitous. In most current deployments today, Multiprotocol Label Switching (MPLS) is the transport technology of choice to provide scalable, secure, and highly flexible IP-based VPN services. L3VPN services allow customer edge (CE) devices and provider edge (PE) devices to exchange IP routes. These service provider PE devices maintain multiple separated customer Layer 3 routing tables in virtual routing and forwarding (VRF) instances, preventing traffic leaking from one customer VPN into another customer VPN. These customer VRF instances are interconnected across the transport network and imported into remote VRF instances, allowing inter-site connectivity.

Figure 7-1 offers a conceptual depiction of the transportation of L3VPN overlay services across SRv6 and SR-MPLS core networks, which is the primary focus of this chapter.

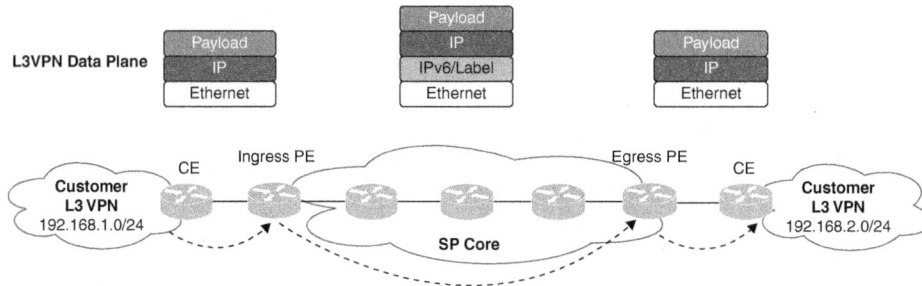

Figure 7-1   *L3VPN Connectivity Across an SRv6/SR-MPLS Core Network*

The following sections concentrate on the provisioning and verification of L3VPN services using SRv6 and SR-MPLS transport networks.

L3VPN

Layer 3 VPN (L3VPN) services are well-known and mature IP- and MPLS-based virtualization services deployed both by service providers and enterprises that enable the creation of VPNs. These virtual services, or VRF instances, allow for the separation and virtualization of routing information between the VPNs. L3VPN services allow service providers to offer multiple services to customers, such as full-mesh, hub-and-spoke, or extranet VPN networks with additional value-added services on top of these networks, such as additional network resiliency, traffic engineering, quality of service (QoS), and operations, administration, and maintenance (OAM). L3VPN services allow customer networks or devices to connect with service providers at Layer 3 by peering with the provider edge (PE) routers, usually via a routing protocol, such as BGP or an IGP (for example, OSPF, RIP). The PE routers forward these routes via BGP as the control plane protocol over a core network based on an MPLS, SR-MPLS, or SRv6 transport infrastructure to the remote PE routers, which in turn advertise these routes to the remote customer sites.

The following sections are not intended as a deep-dive into various L3VPN features, service configurations, and troubleshooting options. Rather, they discuss the provisioning of basic L3VPN services over both SRv6 and SR-MPLS transport networks. This chapter examines both L3VPN configuration and verification services for full-mesh, hub-and-spoke, and extranet VPN services both over SRv6 and SR-MPLS transport networks, as illustrated in Figure 7-2.

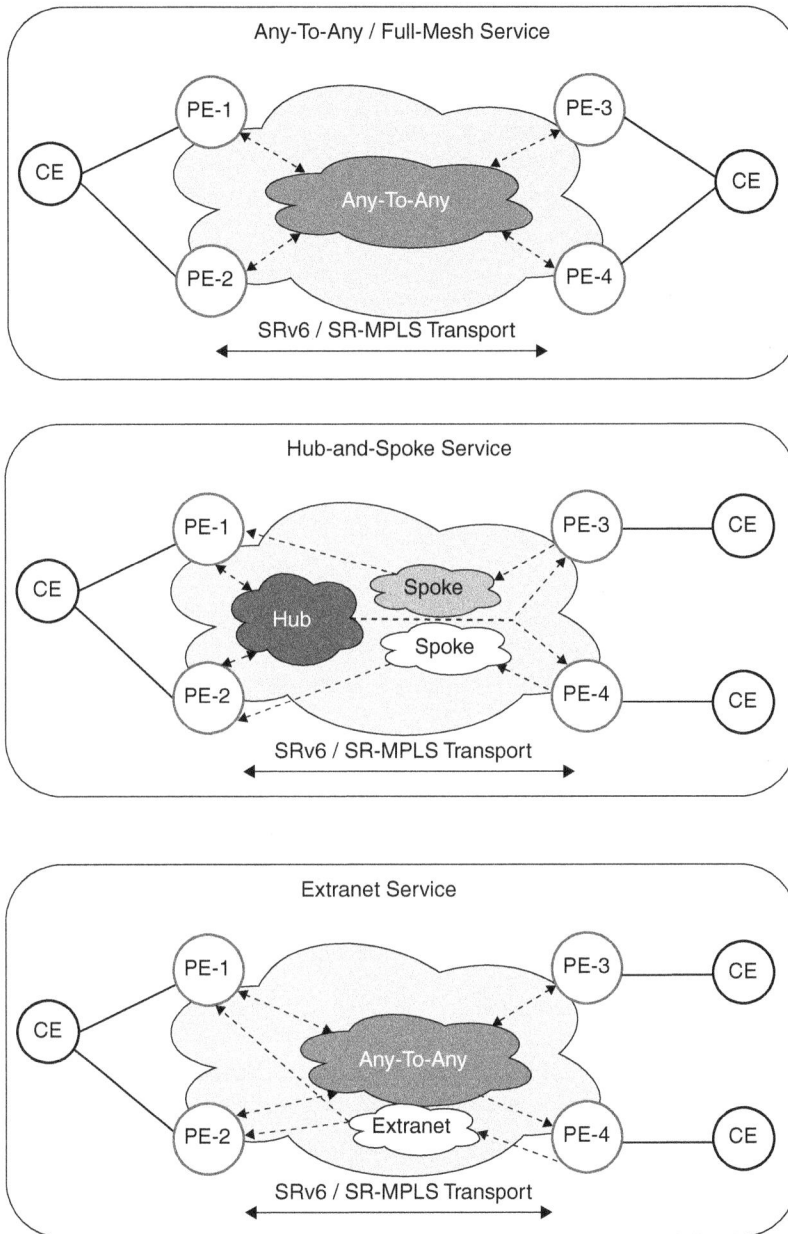

Figure 7-2 *L3VPN VPN Service Types*

SRv6 L3VPN Overlay Service

As mentioned at the beginning of the section, L3VPN is an overlay service with a BGP control plane and an underlay network based on either MPLS, SR-MPLS, or SRv6 transport services. PE routers advertise service prefix reachability to their peer PE routers, and based on the configured overlay services, these prefixes are installed in the FIB of said routers, allowing for inter-site connectivity and service availability.

> **Note**   With the Routing Information Base (RIB), every control plane protocol (IS-IS, BGP, OSPF, and so on) builds its own routing tables based on its best-path metrics and processes. From these tables, a global route table is built based on a default administrative distance allocated to each routing protocol.
>
> The Forwarding Information Base (FIB) includes Layer 3 routing information derived from the RIB as well as the Layer 2 adjacency details for frame encapsulation and forwarding.

This section discusses the L3VPN overlay service, which uses an SRv6 network as its underlay transport. For more comprehensive details on this topic, see RFC 9252.

Next, we'll look at a packet capture in which a single BGP packet is split into two distinct sections, presented in Example 7-1 and Example 7-2. Within these examples, there is a focus on two significant BGP path attributes, which will be mentioned regularly in the subsequent parts of this chapter.

Example 7-1 shows the Network Layer Reachability Information (NLRI) and has following important information highlighted:

- **Path Attribute - MP_REACH_NLRI:** NLRI within the MP_REACH_NLRI BGP attribute is modified to set the label field value to the SRv6 SID function:

  - **Network Layer Reachability Information (NLRI) BGP Prefix:** BGP prefix details are provided.

  - **Label Stack: 917664 (bottom):** The service label is 917664 (0xe00a0). Its most significant 16 bits, 0xe00a, is the SRv6 SID function and is equivalent to the service label in an L3VPN MPLS scenario. The verification sections later in this chapter highlight these service SID outputs and discuss them in more detail.

  - **Route Distinguisher: 65000:1:** This is the configured route distinguisher for the VRF instance.

  - **MP Reach NLRI IPv4 prefix: 10.1.1.0:** This is the IPv4 prefix being transported in the captured packet (AFI = 1, SAFI = 128).

Example 7-1 *SRv6 BGP Path Attribute: MP_REACH_NLRI Detailed Packet Capture*

```
<snip>
Border Gateway Protocol - UPDATE Message
    Path attributes
        Path Attribute - MP_REACH_NLRI
            Flags: 0x90, Optional, Extended-Length, Non-transitive, Complete
            Type Code: MP_REACH_NLRI (14)
            Length: 45
            Address family identifier (AFI): IPv4 (1)
            Subsequent address family identifier (SAFI): Labeled VPN Unicast (128)
            Next hop:  RD=0:0 IPv6=fc00:0:105::1
                Route Distinguisher: 0:0
                IPv6 Address: fc00:0:105::1
            Number of Subnetwork points of attachment (SNPA): 0
            Network Layer Reachability Information (NLRI)
                BGP Prefix
                    Prefix Length: 118
                    Label Stack: 917664 (bottom)
                    Route Distinguisher: 65000:1
                    MP Reach NLRI IPv4 prefix: 10.1.1.0
        Path Attribute - ORIGIN: INCOMPLETE
        Path Attribute - AS_PATH: empty
        Path Attribute - MULTI_EXIT_DISC: 0
        Path Attribute - LOCAL_PREF: 100
        Path Attribute - EXTENDED_COMMUNITIES
        Path Attribute - BGP Prefix-SID
<snip>
```

Example 7-2 shows the BGP Prefix SID and has the following important information highlighted:

- **BGP Path Attribute - BGP Prefix-SID:** This attribute is extended to transport the SRv6 SID information through the inclusion of the SRv6 Service TLV:

  - **SRv6 SID Information** This TLV encodes Service SID information for SRv6-based L3 services and is equivalent to the MPLS label in an L3VPN MPLS scenario. This TLV applies to SRv6 endpoint behaviors such as DX4/DX6/DT4/DT6.

  - The SRv6 Services TLV may include the SRv6 SID Information sub-TLV (1):

    □ **SRv6 SID Value: fc00:0:105:::** This is the egress PE router SID SRv6 locator.

    □ **SRv6 Endpoint Behavior: End.DT4 with NEXT-CSID:** This refers to the endpoint behavior and is the actual decapsulation and specific IPv4 table lookup behavior.

    □ **SRv6 Service Data Sub-Sub-TLV:** This is additional information about the SID structure.

Example 7-2   *SRv6 BGP Path Attribute: BGP Prefix SID Detailed Packet Capture*

```
<snip>
Border Gateway Protocol - UPDATE Message
    Path attributes
        Path Attribute - MP_REACH_NLRI
        Path Attribute - ORIGIN: INCOMPLETE
        Path Attribute - AS_PATH: empty
        Path Attribute - MULTI_EXIT_DISC: 0
        Path Attribute - LOCAL_PREF: 100
        Path Attribute - EXTENDED_COMMUNITIES
        Path Attribute - BGP Prefix-SID
            Flags: 0xc0, Optional, Transitive, Complete
            Type Code: BGP Prefix-SID (40)
            Length: 37
            SRv6 L3 Service
                Type: SRv6 L3 Service (5)
            Length: 34
            Reserved: 00
            SRv6 Service Sub-TLVs
                SRv6 Service Sub-TLV - SRv6 SID Information
                    Type: SRv6 SID Information (1)
                    Length: 30
                    Reserved: 00
                    SRv6 SID Value: fc00:0:105::
                    SRv6 SID Flags: 0x00
                    SRv6 Endpoint Behavior: End.DT4 with NEXT-CSID (0x003f)
                    Reserved: 00
                    SRv6 Service Data Sub-Sub-TLVs
                        SRv6 Service Data Sub-Sub-TLV - SRv6 SID Structure
                            Type: SRv6 SID Structure (1)
<snip>
```

SRv6 L3VPN Full-Mesh Service

This section describes the configuration and verification tasks in a standard L3VPN full-mesh overlay service across an SRv6 transport network. These tasks are based on the reference network shown in Figure 7-3, which shows the CE-1 router dual-homed to PE-1 and PE-2 and CE-2 single attached to the router PE-2 in IS-IS Metro 1. Similarly, in IS-IS Metro 2, the CE-3 router is dual-homed to PE-3 and PE-4, and CE-4 is single attached to the router PE-4. In addition, the dual-attached routers CE-1 and CE-3 are set up in a unipath active/standby scenario via their respective PE routers using BGP local preference, with the active path set to a BGP local preference of 200 and the standby path set to a BGP local preference of 150. To improve convergence times in the event of the active

PE–CE link failing, BGP Prefix Independent Convergence (BGP PIC) Edge has also been configured. With regard to SRv6 locator allocations, the following is configured:

- Network 10.1.103.128/28 (CE-1) uses the SRv6 locator MAIN with per-CE allocation mode via PE-1 and PE-2.

- Network 10.1.103.144/28 (CE-2) uses the SRv6 locator LowLatency with per-VRF allocation mode via PE-2 and applied through the route policy PREFIX_LOCATOR_ RP.

- Network 10.2.103.128/28 (CE-3) uses the SRv6 locator MAIN with per-CE allocation mode via PE-3 and PE-4.

- Network 10.2.103.144/28 (CE-4) users the SRv6 locator LowLatency with per-VRF allocation mode via PE-4 and applied through the route policy PREFIX_LOCATOR_ RP.

SRv6 L3VPN Full-Mesh Configuration

Figure 7-3 provides some of the relevant details (VRF instance name, import/export RT, IP network range, route policy names, and so on) used in the configurations for both CE and PE routers.

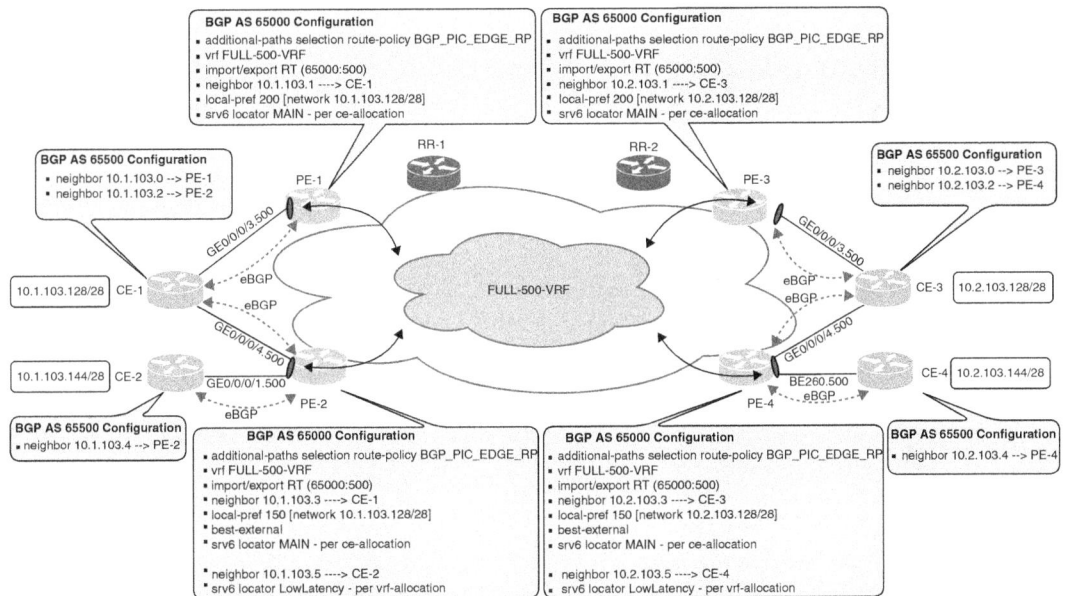

Figure 7-3 *SRv6 L3VPN Full-Mesh Configuration Tasks*

Config 7-1 shows the provisioned L3VPN service configuration used in the reference network for the VRF instance FULL-500-VRF on router PE-1.

Config 7-1   *SRv6 L3VPN Full-Mesh Configuration on PE-1*

```
!/* FULL-MESH VRF */
vrf FULL-500-VRF
 address-family ipv4 unicast
  import route-target
   65000:500
  !
  export route-target
   65000:500
  !
 !
!
!/* INTERFACE TO CE-1 */
interface GigabitEthernet0/0/0/3
 description Connected_to_CE-1
!
interface GigabitEthernet0/0/0/3.500
 vrf FULL-500-VRF
 ipv4 address 10.1.103.0 255.255.255.254
 encapsulation dot1q 500
!
!/* ROUTE-POLICIES */
route-policy PASS_RP
  pass
end-policy
!
route-policy BGP_LOC-PREF_RP($LP)
  set local-preference $LP
end-policy
!
route-policy PIC_EDGE_RP
  set path-selection backup 1 install
end-policy
!
!/* BGP CONFIGURATION */
router bgp 65000
 bgp router-id 172.19.0.10
 address-family vpnv4 unicast
  vrf all
   segment-routing srv6
    locator MAIN
    alloc mode per-vrf
   !
  !
```

```
  additional-paths selection route-policy PIC_EDGE_RP
 !
 neighbor-group IBGP-RR1-NG
  remote-as 65000
  description *** iBGP peering to METRO-1 RR ***
  update-source Loopback0
  address-family vpnv4 unicast
  !
 !
 neighbor fc00:0:107::1
  use neighbor-group IBGP-RR1-NG
  description *** iBGP peering to METRO-1 RR ***
 !
 vrf FULL-500-VRF
  rd auto
  address-family ipv4 unicast
   segment-routing srv6
    alloc mode per-ce
   !
  !
 neighbor 10.1.103.1
   remote-as 65500
  address-family ipv4 unicast
    route-policy BGP_LOC-PREF_RP(200) in
    route-policy PASS_RP out
    as-override
   !
  !
 !
!
!/* SRv6 CONFIGURATION */
segment-routing
 srv6
  encapsulation
   source-address fc00:0:105::1
  !
  locators
  <snip>
   locator MAIN
    micro-segment behavior unode psp-usd
    prefix fc00:0:105::/48
   !
   locator LowLatency
```

```
    micro-segment behavior unode psp-usd
    prefix fc00:1:105::/48
    algorithm 128
   !
  !
 !
```

Config 7-2 shows the provisioned L3VPN service configuration used for the VRF instance FULL-500-VRF on router PE-2.

Config 7-2   *SRv6 L3VPN Full-Mesh Configuration on PE-2*

```
!FULL-MESH VRF */
vrf FULL-500-VRF
 address-family ipv4 unicast
  import route-target
   65000:500
  !
  export route-target
   65000:500
  !
 !
!
!INTERFACE TO CE-2 */
interface GigabitEthernet0/0/0/1
 description Connected_to_CE-2
!
interface GigabitEthernet0/0/0/1.500
 vrf FULL-500-VRF
 ipv4 address 10.1.103.4 255.255.255.254
 encapsulation dot1q 500
!
!INTERFACE TO CE-1 */
interface GigabitEthernet0/0/0/4
 description Connected_to_CE-1
!
interface GigabitEthernet0/0/0/4.500
 vrf FULL-500-VRF
 ipv4 address 10.1.103.2 255.255.255.254
 encapsulation dot1q 500
!
!ROUTE-POLICIES */
route-policy PASS_RP
  pass
end-policy
!
```

```
route-policy BGP_LOC-PREF_RP($LP)
  set local-preference $LP
end-policy
!
route-policy PIC_EDGE_RP
  set path-selection backup 1 install
end-policy
!
route-policy PREFIX_LOCATOR_RP
  if destination in (10.1.103.144/28) then
    set srv6-alloc-mode per-vrf locator LowLatency
  else
    set srv6-alloc-mode per-ce
  endif
end-policy
!
!BGP CONFIGURATION */
router bgp 65000
 bgp router-id 172.19.0.11
 address-family vpnv4 unicast
  vrf all
   segment-routing srv6
    locator MAIN
    alloc mode per-vrf
   !
  !
  additional-paths selection route-policy PIC_EDGE_RP
 !
 neighbor-group IBGP-RR1-NG
  remote-as 65000
  description *** iBGP peering to METRO-1 RR ***
  update-source Loopback0
  address-family vpnv4 unicast
  !
 !
 neighbor fc00:0:107::1
  use neighbor-group IBGP-RR1-NG
  description *** iBGP peering to METRO-1 RR ***
 !
 vrf FULL-500-VRF
  rd auto
  address-family ipv4 unicast
   advertise best-external
   segment-routing srv6
```

```
     alloc mode route-policy PREFIX_LOCATOR_RP
    !
   !
  neighbor 10.1.103.3
   remote-as 65500
   address-family ipv4 unicast
    route-policy BGP_LOC-PREF_RP(150) in
    route-policy PASS_RP out
    as-override
   !
  !
  neighbor 10.1.103.5
   remote-as 65500
   address-family ipv4 unicast
    route-policy PASS_RP in
    route-policy PASS_RP out
    as-override
   !
  !
 !
!
!SRv6 CONFIGURATION */
segment-routing
 srv6
  encapsulation
   source-address fc00:0:106::1
  !
  locators
  <snip>
   !
   locator MAIN
    micro-segment behavior unode psp-usd
    prefix fc00:0:106::/48
   !
   locator LowLatency
    micro-segment behavior unode psp-usd
    prefix fc00:1:106::/48
    algorithm 128
   !
  !
 !
!
```

Config 7-3 shows the configuration for the VRF instance FULL-500-VRF on router PE-3 in IS-IS Metro 2.

Config 7-3 *SRv6 L3VPN Full-Mesh Configuration on PE-3*

```
!/* FULL-MESH VRF */
vrf FULL-500-VRF
 address-family ipv4 unicast
  import route-target
   65000:500
  !
  export route-target
   65000:500
  !
 !
!
!/* INTERFACE TO CE-3 */
interface GigabitEthernet0/0/0/3
 description Connected_to_CE-3
!
interface GigabitEthernet0/0/0/3.500
 vrf FULL-500-VRF
 ipv4 address 10.2.103.0 255.255.255.254
 encapsulation dot1q 500
!
!/* ROUTE-POLICIES */
route-policy PASS_RP
  pass
end-policy
!
route-policy BGP_LOC-PREF_RP($LP)
  set local-preference $LP
end-policy
!
route-policy PIC_EDGE_RP
  set path-selection backup 1 install
end-policy
!
!/* BGP CONFIGURATION */
router bgp 65000
 bgp router-id 172.19.0.19
 address-family vpnv4 unicast
  vrf all
   segment-routing srv6
```

```
    locator MAIN
     alloc mode per-vrf
    !
   !
   additional-paths selection route-policy PIC_EDGE_RP
  !
 neighbor-group IBGP-M2-NG
  remote-as 65000
  description *** iBGP peering to METRO-2 RR ***
  update-source Loopback0
  address-family vpnv4 unicast
  !
 !
 neighbor fc00:0:207::1
  use neighbor-group IBGP-M2-NG
  description *** iBGP peering to METRO-2 RR ***
  !
 vrf FULL-500-VRF
  rd auto
  address-family ipv4 unicast
   segment-routing srv6
    alloc mode per-ce
   !
  !
  neighbor 10.2.103.1
   remote-as 65500
   address-family ipv4 unicast
    route-policy BGP_LOC-PREF_RP(200) in
    route-policy PASS_RP out
    as-override
   !
  !
 !
!/* SRv6 CONFIGURATION */
segment-routing
 srv6
  encapsulation
   source-address fc00:0:205::1
  !
  locators
  <snip>
   locator MAIN
```

```
    micro-segment behavior unode psp-usd
    prefix fc00:0:205::/48
   !
   locator LowLatency
    micro-segment behavior unode psp-usd
    prefix fc00:1:205::/48
    algorithm 128
   !
  !
 !
```

Finally, Config 7-4 shows the service configuration for the VRF instance FULL-500-VRF on router PE-4 in IS-IS Metro 2.

Config 7-4   *SRv6 L3VPN Full-Mesh Configuration on PE-4*

```
!/* FULL-MESH VRF */
vrf FULL-500-VRF
 address-family ipv4 unicast
  import route-target
   65000:500
  !
  export route-target
   65000:500
  !
 !
!
!/* INTERFACE TO CE-4 */
interface Bundle-Ether260
 description Connected_to_CE-4
 lacp system mac 00fc.0002.0260
!
interface Bundle-Ether260.500
 vrf FULL-500-VRF
 ipv4 address 10.2.103.4 255.255.255.254
 encapsulation dot1q 500
!!
!/* INTERFACE TO CE-3 */
interface GigabitEthernet0/0/0/4
 description Connected_to_CE-3
!
interface GigabitEthernet0/0/0/4.500
```

```
 vrf FULL-500-VRF
 ipv4 address 10.2.103.2 255.255.255.254
 encapsulation dot1q 500
!
!/* ROUTE-POLICIES */
route-policy PASS_RP
  pass
end-policy
!
route-policy BGP_LOC-PREF_RP($LP)
  set local-preference $LP
end-policy
!
route-policy PIC_EDGE_RP
  set path-selection backup 1 install
end-policy
!
route-policy PREFIX_LOCATOR_RP
  if destination in (10.2.103.144/28) then
    set srv6-alloc-mode per-vrf locator LowLatency
  else
    set srv6-alloc-mode per-ce
  endif
end-policy
!
!/* BGP CONFIGURATION */
router bgp 65000
 bgp router-id 172.19.0.20
 address-family vpnv4 unicast
  vrf all
   segment-routing srv6
    locator MAIN
    alloc mode per-vrf
   !
  !
  additional-paths selection route-policy PIC_EDGE_RP
 !
 neighbor-group IBGP-M2-NG
  remote-as 65000
  description *** iBGP peering to METRO-2 RR ***
  update-source Loopback0
```

```
 address-family vpnv4 unicast
  !
 !
 neighbor fc00:0:207::1
  use neighbor-group IBGP-M2-NG
  description *** iBGP peering to METRO-2 RR ***
  !
 vrf FULL-500-VRF
  rd auto
  address-family ipv4 unicast
   advertise best-external
   segment-routing srv6
    alloc mode route-policy PREFIX_LOCATOR_RP
   !
  !
  neighbor 10.2.103.3
   remote-as 65500
   address-family ipv4 unicast
    route-policy BGP_LOC-PREF_RP(150) in
    route-policy PASS_RP out
    as-override
   !
  !
  neighbor 10.2.103.5
   remote-as 65500
   address-family ipv4 unicast
    route-policy PASS_RP in
    route-policy PASS_RP out
    as-override
   !
  !
 !
!
!/* SRv6 CONFIGURATION */
segment-routing
 srv6
  encapsulation
   source-address fc00:0:206::1
  !
  locators
  <snip>
   locator MAIN
```

```
    micro-segment behavior unode psp-usd
    prefix fc00:0:206::/48
   !
  locator LowLatency
    micro-segment behavior unode psp-usd
    prefix fc00:1:206::/48
    algorithm 128
   !
  !
 !
!
```

We will focus on the configurations on the router PE-1 in Config 7-1 and router PE-2 in
Config 7-2; PE-3 and PE-4 are similar in concept. We can break them down further for
explanatory purposes:

■ The L3VPN full-mesh VRF configuration tasks require the configuration of a VRF
instance FULL-500-VRF, together with the required import/export route targets,
and assignment of the PE–CE interfaces into the specific VRF instance. With the
full-mesh service, the import and export route targets will be set to the same value,
65000:500, as indicated in Config 7-5.

Config 7-5   *SRv6 L3VPN Full-Mesh Configuration: VRF and Interface Configuration*

```
vrf FULL-500-VRF
 address-family ipv4 unicast
  import route-target
   65000:500
  !
  export route-target
   65000:500
  !
 !
interface GigabitEthernet0/0/0/3.500
 vrf FULL-500-VRF
 ipv4 address 10.1.103.0 255.255.255.254
 encapsulation dot1q 500
 !
```

■ The segment routing SRv6 configuration is discussed in more detail in Chapter 4,
"Segment Routing in Detail," in the section "SRv6 uSID Configuration," but we
talk about this briefly in this section because the two SRv6 locators MAIN and
LowLatency are required as part of the service configurations (see Config 7-6). Later

in this chapter, the SRv6 locator MAIN is used for the CE-1 and CE-3 prefix SIDs, and the prefix SIDs for the routers CE-2 and CE-4 are based on the SRv6 locator LowLatency, which is the flex algo 128 for low-latency path calculation. For more details on flex algo, see the section "Multiplane Topologies with Flex Algos" in Chapter 4.

Config 7-6 *SRv6 L3VPN Full-Mesh Configuration: SRv6 Configuration*

```
segment-routing
 srv6
  encapsulation
   source-address fc00:0:105::1
  !
  locators
  <snip>
   locator MAIN
    micro-segment behavior unode psp-usd
    prefix fc00:0:105::/48
   !
   locator LowLatency
    micro-segment behavior unode psp-usd
    prefix fc00:1:105::/48
    algorithm 128
   !
```

■ To enable the L3VPN service for SRv6, the locator and SID allocation mode is configured under the router bgp 65000 configuration. In Config 7-7, from router PE-2, the SRv6 locator MAIN with per-VRF allocation mode is configured under the VPNv4 address family for all VRF instances. The SRv6 locator MAIN and per-VRF allocation mode are applied to any VRF instance not explicitly configured with a locator.

■ The VRF instance FULL-500-VRF assigns the SRv6 locator based on the route policy PREFIX_LOCATOR_RP:

   ■ It matches the IPv4 network route 10.2.103.144/28, which originates from CE-4.

   ■ It sets the SRv6 prefix SID from the SRv6 locator LowLatency, the low-latency flex algo 128.

   ■ It sets the allocation mode to per-VRF, which is the same as the per-VRF label allocation mode in MPLS.

   ■ If a learned route does not match, then the SRv6 prefix SID is allocated from the SRv6 locator **MAIN** with the allocation mode being set to per-CE, the same as the per next hop MPLS label allocation mode

- Because the reference network in Figure 7-3 is configured in a unipath active/standby scenario for the links between CE-1 and CE-3 and their respective PE routers, BGP Best-External and BGP PIC Edge are also configured to allow for faster convergence in the event that the active path fails:

  - An ingress route learned across the eBGP neighborships CE-1–PE-1 and CE-3–PE-3 is matched with the route policy BGP_LOC-PREF_RP(200), and the BGP local preference is set to 200.

  - An ingress route learned across the eBGP neighborships CE-1–PE-2 and CE-3–PE-4 is matched with the route policy BGP_LOC-PREF_RP(150), and the BGP local preference is set to 150.

  - Since the paths to these routes are now preferred via the path with the higher BGP local preference of 200, PE-2 and PE-4 withdraw their paths toward CE-1 and CE-3, respectively.

  - Configuring advertise best-external under the router BGP VRF instance on both PE-2 and PE-4 means that these customer routes will be advertised and no longer withdrawn, and with the additional-paths selection route-policy PIC_EDGE_RP configuration on both PE-1 and PE-3, the paths via the standby path will be added to the router FIB entries as a backup path.

Config 7-7   *SRv6 L3VPN Full-Mesh Configuration: BGP Configuration on PE-2*

```
router bgp 65000
 bgp router-id 172.19.0.11
 address-family vpnv4 unicast
  vrf all
   segment-routing srv6
    locator MAIN
    alloc mode per-vrf
   !
  !
  additional-paths selection route-policy PIC_EDGE_RP
 !
 !
 vrf FULL-500-VRF
  rd auto
  address-family ipv4 unicast
   advertise best-external
   segment-routing srv6
    alloc mode route-policy PREFIX_LOCATOR_RP
   !
  !
```

```
   neighbor 10.1.103.3
    remote-as 65500
    address-family ipv4 unicast
     route-policy BGP_LOC-PREF_RP(150) in
     route-policy PASS_RP out
     as-override
    !
   !
   neighbor 10.1.103.5
    remote-as 65500
    address-family ipv4 unicast
     route-policy PASS_RP in
     route-policy PASS_RP out
     as-override
    !
   !
  !
route-policy PREFIX_LOCATOR_RP
  if destination in (10.2.103.144/28) then
    set srv6-alloc-mode per-vrf locator LowLatency
  else
    set srv6-alloc-mode per-ce
  endif
end-policy
!
```

SRv6 L3VPN Full-Mesh Verification

Now we're ready to walk through service verification, using service commands to confirm that this L3VPN full-mesh service is configured and functioning correctly.

As indicated in Figure 7-4, the verification tasks in this section focus on the subnets originated from the CE routers CE-3 and CE-4 into the VRF instance FULL-500-VRF. The same verification commands can be applied in the opposite direction, for subnets originated from CE-1 and CE-2.

Output 7-1, derived from PE-1, confirms that the subnets originated from both CE-3 and CE-4 are observed:

- **Subnet 10.2.103.128/28 (CE-3):** This is the first path from next hop fc00:0:205::1 with BGP local preference 200.

- **Subnet 10.2.103.128/28 (CE-3):** This is the second path from next hop fc00:0:206::1 with BGP local preference 150.

- **Subnet 10.2.103.144/28 (CE-4):** This is a single path from next hop fc00:0:206::1 with the default BGP local preference 100.

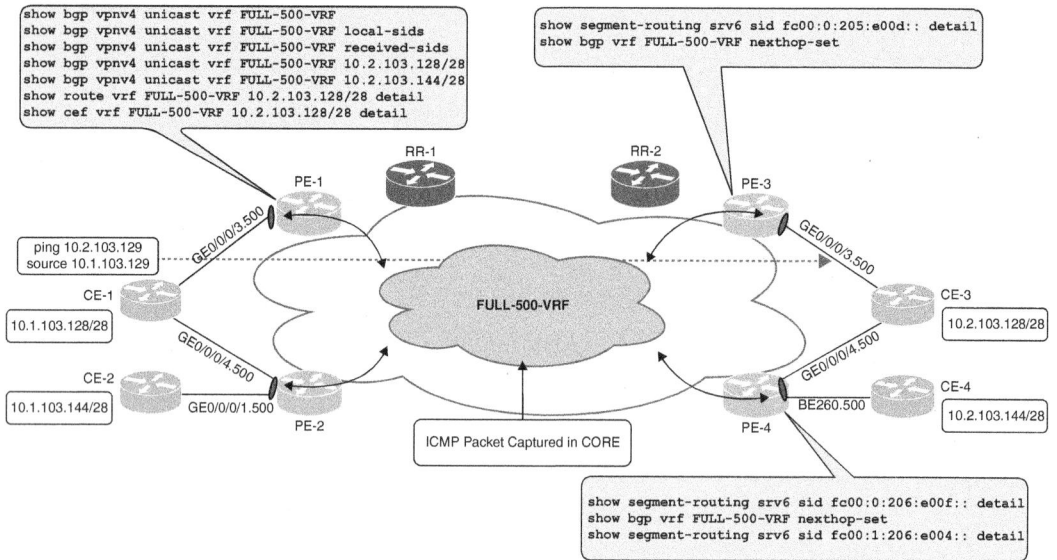

Figure 7-4   *SRv6 L3VPN Full-Mesh Verification Tasks*

Output 7-1   *SRv6 L3VPN Full-Mesh Configuration: BGP VPNv4 RIB on PE-1*

```
RP/0/RP0/CPU0:PE-1#show bgp vpnv4 unicast vrf FULL-500-VRF
BGP router identifier 172.19.0.10, local AS number 65000
<snip>
Route Distinguisher: 172.19.0.10:3 (default for vrf FULL-500-VRF)
Route Distinguisher Version: 691
*>  10.1.103.128/28    10.1.103.1            0    200    0 65500 i
* i                    fc00:0:106::1         0    150    0 65500 i
*>i10.1.103.144/28     fc00:0:106::1         0    100    0 65500 i
*>i10.2.103.128/28     fc00:0:205::1         0    200    0 65500 i
* i                    fc00:0:206::1         0    150    0 65500 i
*>i10.2.103.144/28     fc00:0:206::1         0    100    0 65500 i


Processed 4 prefixes, 6 paths
RP/0/RP0/CPU0:PE-1#
```

Output 7-2 and Output 7-3 provide similar output to Output 7-1, but in this case, the local SIDs, allocation mode, and locator information are displayed for all subnets in the VRF instance FULL-500-VRF.

For example, in Output 7-2 the subnet 10.1.103.128/28 (CE-1) is allocated the SID fc00:0:105:e00d:: with per-CE allocation mode and from the SRv6 locator MAIN. The other subnets in this output are not local to the VRF instance, and therefore, no local SIDs are allocated.

Output 7-2   *SRv6 L3VPN Full-Mesh Configuration: BGP VPNv4 RIB Local SIDs on PE-1*

```
RP/0/RP0/CPU0:PE-1#show bgp vpnv4 unicast vrf FULL-500-VRF local-sids
BGP router identifier 172.19.0.10, local AS number 65000
<snip>
   Network              Local Sid                              Alloc mode   Locator
Route Distinguisher: 172.19.0.10:3 (default for vrf FULL-500-VRF)
Route Distinguisher Version: 897
*> 10.1.103.128/28     fc00:0:105:e00d::                      per-ce       MAIN
* i                    fc00:0:105:e00d::                      per-ce       MAIN
*>i10.1.103.144/28     NO SRv6 Sid                            -            -
*>i10.2.103.128/28     NO SRv6 Sid                            -            -
* i                    NO SRv6 Sid                            -            -
*>i10.2.103.144/28     NO SRv6 Sid                            -            -


Processed 4 prefixes, 6 paths
RP/0/RP0/CPU0:PE-1#
```

In Output 7-3, the subnets 10.2.103.128/28 (CE-3) and 10.2.103.144/28 (CE-4) have the SIDs fc00:0:205:e00d::, fc00:0:206:e00f::, and fc00:1:206:e004:: allocated by their respective PE routers in Metro 2.

Output 7-3   *SRv6 L3VPN Full-Mesh Configuration: BGP VPNv4 RIB Received SIDs on PE-1*

```
RP/0/RP0/CPU0:PE-1#show bgp vpnv4 unicast vrf FULL-500-VRF received-sids
BGP router identifier 172.19.0.10, local AS number 65000
<snip>
   Network              Next Hop                    Received Sid
Route Distinguisher: 172.19.0.10:3 (default for vrf FULL-500-VRF)
Route Distinguisher Version: 897
*> 10.1.103.128/28     10.1.103.1                  NO SRv6 Sid
* i                    fc00:0:106::1               fc00:0:106:e00f::
*>i10.1.103.144/28     fc00:0:106::1               fc00:1:106:e004::
*>i10.2.103.128/28     fc00:0:205::1               fc00:0:205:e00d::
* i                    fc00:0:206::1               fc00:0:206:e00f::
*>i10.2.103.144/28     fc00:0:206::1               fc00:1:206:e004::


Processed 4 prefixes, 6 paths
RP/0/RP0/CPU0:PE-1#
```

If we analyze the BGP route 10.2.103.128/28 from the router CE-3 in more detail, we see that the command in Output 7-4 displays the following relevant information:

■ **Paths: (2 available, best #1):** The output confirms that the subnet is available across two paths, and the first path is the preferred one.

- **Path #1:**

  - **fc00:0:205::1 (metric 61) from fc00:0:107::1 (172.19.0.19):** PE-3 is the BGP next hop fc00:0:205::1 with BGP router ID 172.19.0.19.

  - **Received Label 0xe00d0:** The received label is 0xe00d0, and the most significant 16 bits of this label is the SRv6 uSID 0xe00d from router PE-3.

  - **Sid:fc00:0:205:::** This is the PE-3 remote node SID (uN) from the configured SRv6 locator MAIN.

  - **Behavior:61:** The endpoint behavior is End.DX4 with NEXT-CSID (0x003D) because of the configuration srv6-alloc-mode per-ce, which has similar behavior to the per-CE label allocation mode.

- **Path #2:**

  - **fc00:0:206::1 (metric 61) from fc00:0:107::1 (172.19.0.20):** PE-4 is the BGP next hop fc00:0:206::1 with BGP router ID 172.19.0.20.

  - **Received Label 0xe00f0:** The received label is 0xe00f0, and the most significant 16 bits of this label is the SRv6 uSID 0xe00f from router PE-4.

  - **Sid:fc00:0:206:::** This is the PE-4 remote node SID (uN) from the configured SRv6 locator MAIN.

  - **Behavior:61:** The endpoint behavior is End.DX4 with NEXT-CSID (0x003D) because of the configuration srv6-alloc-mode per-ce, which has similar behavior to the per-CE label allocation mode.

Output 7-4 *SRv6 L3VPN Full-Mesh Configuration: BGP VPNv4 RIB for 10.2.103.128/28 on PE-1*

```
RP/0/RP0/CPU0:PE-1#show bgp vpnv4 unicast vrf FULL-500-VRF 10.2.103.128/28
BGP routing table entry for 10.2.103.128/28, Route Distinguisher: 172.19.0.10:3
<snip>
Paths: (2 available, best #1)
  Advertised to CE peers (in unique update groups):
    10.1.103.1
  Path #1: Received by speaker 0
  Advertised to CE peers (in unique update groups):
    10.1.103.1
  65500
    fc00:0:205::1 (metric 61) from fc00:0:107::1 (172.19.0.19)
      Received Label 0xe00d0
      Origin IGP, metric 0, localpref 200, valid, internal, best, group-best,
  import-candidate, imported
      Received Path ID 0, Local Path ID 1, version 683
      Extended community: RT:65000:500
      Originator: 172.19.0.19, Cluster list: 172.19.0.12, 172.19.0.21
      PSID-Type:L3, SubTLV Count:1
```

```
      SubTLV:
        T:1(Sid information), Sid:fc00:0:205::, Behavior:61, SS-TLV Count:1
          SubSubTLV:
            T:1(Sid structure):
        Source AFI: VPNv4 Unicast, Source VRF: default, Source Route
    Distinguisher: 172.19.0.19:3
  Path #2: Received by speaker 0
  Not advertised to any peer
  65500
      fc00:0:206::1 (metric 61) from fc00:0:107::1 (172.19.0.20)
      Received Label 0xe00f0
      Origin IGP, metric 0, localpref 150, valid, internal, backup, add-path,
    imported
      Received Path ID 0, Local Path ID 4, version 690
      Extended community: RT:65000:500
      Originator: 172.19.0.20, Cluster list: 172.19.0.12, 172.19.0.21
      PSID-Type:L3, SubTLV Count:1
        SubTLV:
          T:1(Sid information), Sid:fc00:0:206::, Behavior:61, SS-TLV Count:1
            SubSubTLV:
              T:1(Sid structure):
        Source AFI: VPNv4 Unicast, Source VRF: default, Source Route
    Distinguisher: 172.19.0.20:2
  RP/0/RP0/CPU0:PE-1#
```

The second subnet being verified is the BGP route 10.2.103.144/28 from the router CE-4. Output 7-5 displays similar information to the route 10.2.103.128/28 from the router CE-3 (refer to Output 7-4) but with a different endpoint behavior, as highlighted in the output:

■ **Behavior:63:** The endpoint behavior is End.DT4 with NEXT-CSID (0x003F) because of the configuration srv6-alloc-mode per-vrf on router PE-4.

Output 7-5 *SRv6 L3VPN Full-Mesh Configuration: BGP VPNv4 RIB for 10.2.103.144/28 on PE-1*

```
RP/0/RP0/CPU0:PE-1#show bgp vpnv4 unicast vrf FULL-500-VRF 10.2.103.144/28

BGP routing table entry for 10.2.103.144/28, Route Distinguisher: 172.19.0.10:3
Versions:
  Process           bRIB/RIB  SendTblVer
  Speaker                691         691
Last Modified: Jun 13 23:05:45.735 for 4d02h
Paths: (1 available, best #1)
```

```
Advertised to CE peers (in unique update groups):
  10.1.103.1
Path #1: Received by speaker 0
Advertised to CE peers (in unique update groups):
  10.1.103.1
65500
  fc00:0:206::1 (metric 61) from fc00:0:107::1 (172.19.0.20)
    Received Label 0xe0040
    Origin IGP, metric 0, localpref 100, valid, internal, best, group-best,
import-candidate, imported
    Received Path ID 0, Local Path ID 1, version 691
    Extended community: RT:65000:500
    Originator: 172.19.0.20, Cluster list: 172.19.0.12, 172.19.0.21

    PSID-Type:L3, SubTLV Count:1
     SubTLV:
      T:1(Sid information), Sid:fc00:1:206::, Behavior:63, SS-TLV Count:1
        SubSubTLV:
         T:1(Sid structure):
      Source AFI: VPNv4 Unicast, Source VRF: default, Source Route
  Distinguisher: 172.19.0.20:2
RP/0/RP0/CPU0:PE-1#
```

Output 7-6 shows the RIB details for the subnet 10.2.103.128/28 originated from the router CE-3 and confirms the relevant details of this learned subnet, including the fact that it has a standby path via PE-4 due to the application of the BGP PIC Edge configuration:

- **Number of pic paths 1:** Subnet 10.2.103.128/28 has a backup BGP PIC Edge path via router PE-4.

- **fc00:0:205::1, from fc00:0:107::1:** PE-3 is the BGP next hop fc00:0:205::1.

   - **SRv6 Headend: H.Encaps.Red [f3216], SID-list {fc00:0:205:e00d::}:** This indicates H.Encaps with reduced encapsulation, where the first SID is copied into the Destination Address field of the outer IPv6 header.

- **fc00:0:206::1, from fc00:0:107::1, BGP backup path:** PE-4 is the BGP next hop fc00:0:206::1.

   - **SRv6 Headend: H.Encaps.Red [f3216], SID-list {fc00:0:206:e00f::}:** This indicates H.Encaps with reduced encapsulation, where the first SID is copied into the Destination Address field of the outer IPv6 header.

More details of H.Encaps with reduced encapsulation can be found in Chapter 3, "What Is Segment Routing over IPv6 (SRv6)?" in the section "IPv6 Segment Routing Header (SRH) (RFC 8754)."

Note that the RIB information for the subnet 10.2.103.144/28 follows the same format as that for 10.2.103.128/28 in Output 7-6 but without the backup path.

Output 7-6 *SRv6 L3VPN Full-Mesh Configuration: RIB Details for 10.2.103.128/28 on PE-1*

```
RP/0/RP0/CPU0:PE-1#show route vrf FULL-500-VRF 10.2.103.128/28 detail

Routing entry for 10.2.103.128/28
  Known via "bgp 65000", distance 200, metric 0
  Tag 65500
  Number of pic paths 1 , type internal
  Installed Jun 13 23:05:45.411 for 4d02h
 Routing Descriptor Blocks
    fc00:0:205::1, from fc00:0:107::1
      Nexthop in Vrf: "default", Table: "default", IPv6 Unicast, Table Id:
  0xe0800000
      Route metric is 0
      Label: None
      Tunnel ID: None
      Binding Label: None
      Extended communities count: 0
      Source RD attributes: 0x0001:44051:1245187
      NHID:0x0(Ref:0)
      SRv6 Headend: H.Encaps.Red [f3216], SID-list {fc00:0:205:e00d::}
    fc00:0:206::1, from fc00:0:107::1, BGP backup path
      Nexthop in Vrf: "default", Table: "default", IPv6 Unicast, Table Id:
  0xe0800000
      Route metric is 0
      Label: None
      Tunnel ID: None
      Binding Label: None
      Extended communities count: 0
      Source RD attributes: 0x0001:44051:1310722
      NHID:0x0(Ref:0)
      SRv6 Headend: H.Encaps.Red [f3216], SID-list {fc00:0:206:e00f::}
<snip>
RP/0/RP0/CPU0:PE-1#
```

To view the router FIB table, the command **show cef vrf FULL-500-VRF 10.2.103.128/28 detail** in Output 7-7 displays the output of the same target subnet 10.2.103.128/28 as mentioned previously for Output 7-6. This is the relevant information in this output:

- **via fc00:0:205::/128:** Router PE-3 is the BGP next hop fc00:0:205::1.

  - **next hop fc00:0:205::/128 via fc00:0:200::/40:** The BGP next hop is learned via the summarized network route for the IS-IS Metro 2 subnet in the global routing table.

  - **SRv6 H.Encaps.Red SID-list {fc00:0:205:e00d::}:** This indicates H.Encaps with reduced encapsulation, where the first SID is copied into the Destination Address field of the outer IPv6 header.

The egress traffic to the destination subnet on CE-3 (10.2.103.128/28) will be load balanced across the core-facing interfaces, as shown here:

- ☐ 0   Y   **GigabitEthernet0/0/0/0**   **fe80::42:acff:fe15:7f03**

- ☐ 1   Y   **GigabitEthernet0/0/0/2**   **fe80::42:acff:fe15:8002**

- ■ **via fc00:0:206::/128:** Router PE-4 is the BGP next hop fc00:0:206::1 and is the backup path.

  - ■ **next hop fc00:0:206::/128 via fc00:0:200::/40:** The BGP next hop is learned via the summarized network for the IS-IS Metro 2 subnet in the global routing table.

  - ■ **SRv6 H.Encaps.Red SID-list {fc00:0:206:e00f::}:** This indicates H.Encaps with reduced encapsulation, where the first SID is copied into the Destination Address field of the outer IPv6 header.

The FIB information for the subnet 10.2.103.144/28 would be presented in the same manner as the 10.2.103.128/28 subnet's details in Output 7-7, except it would not have a backup path.

Output 7-7   *SRv6 L3VPN Full-Mesh Configuration: FIB Details for 10.2.103.128/28 on PE-1*

```
RP/0/RP0/CPU0:PE-1#show cef vrf FULL-500-VRF 10.2.103.128/28 detail
10.2.103.128/28, version 221, SRv6 Headend, internal 0x5000001 0x30 (ptr 0x871bf2b8)
 [1], 0x0 (0x0), 0x0 (0x89ab72b8)
Updated Jun 13 23:05:45.413
Prefix Len 28, traffic index 0, precedence n/a, priority 3
 gateway array (0x89cf47e8) reference count 1, flags 0x102010, source rib (7), 0
 backups
             [1 type 3 flags 0x48441 (0x87e94368) ext 0x0 (0x0)]
 LW-LDI[type=0, refc=0, ptr=0x0, sh-ldi=0x0]
 gateway array update type-time 1 Jun 13 11:50:39.919
LDI Update time Jun 13 11:50:39.919

 Level 1 - Load distribution: 0
 [0] via fc00:0:205::/128, recursive

  via fc00:0:205::/128, 14 dependencies, recursive [flags 0x6000]
   path-idx 0 NHID 0x0 [0x86fdfba0 0x0]
   next hop VRF - 'default', table - 0xe0800000
   next hop fc00:0:205::/128 via fc00:0:200::/40
   SRv6 H.Encaps.Red SID-list {fc00:0:205:e00d::}
   Load distribution: 0 1 (refcount 1)

   Hash  OK  Interface                Address
   0     Y   GigabitEthernet0/0/0/0   fe80::42:acff:fe15:7f03
   1     Y   GigabitEthernet0/0/0/2   fe80::42:acff:fe15:8002
```

```
     via fc00:0:206::/128, 14 dependencies, recursive, backup [flags 0x6100]
  path-idx 1 NHID 0x0 [0x86fdfba0 0x0]
  next hop VRF - 'default', table - 0xe0800000
  next hop fc00:0:206::/128 via fc00:0:200::/40
  SRv6 H.Encaps.Red SID-list {fc00:0:206:e00f::}

RP/0/RP0/CPU0:PE-1#
```

A useful final step is to verify the actual SID details on the egress PE routers for the IP subnets 10.2.103.128/28 (CE-3) and 10.2.103.144/28 (CE-4) as there are behavior differences between these two.

Output 7-8, from PE-3, begins with the command **show segment-routing srv6 sid fc00:0:205:e00d:: detail**, which confirms the endpoint behavior uDX4 for subnet 10.2.103.128/28 received from CE-3 due to the configuration srv6-alloc-mode per-ce that sets the per-CE label allocation mode via the route policy PREFIX_LOCATOR_RP:

- **SID: fc00:0:205:e00d:::** This is the SRv6 SID that is allocated.

- **Behavior: uDX4:** This is the endpoint behavior with decapsulation and IPv4 cross-connect.

- **Context: 'FULL-500-VRF':1:** Due to the srv6-alloc-mode per-ce configuration, the IPv4 frames will be forwarded directly to nh-set-id=1 (no IPv4 lookup) in the VRF instance FULL-500-VRF. Output 7-9 shows this next hop set for the SID fc00:0:205:e00d:: together with the IP next hop address 10.2.103.1 on interface Gi0/0/0/3.500 of router CE-3.

- **Locator: 'MAIN':** The SID is allocated from the SRv6 locator MAIN as per the configuration under the BGP address family vpnv4 unicast.

Output 7-8   *SRv6 L3VPN Full-Mesh Configuration: SRv6 SID fc00:0:205:e00d on PE-3*

```
RP/0/RP0/CPU0:PE-3#show segment-routing srv6 sid fc00:0:205:e00d:: detail

*** Locator: 'MAIN' ***

SID                  Behavior     Context              Owner              State    RW
-----------------    -----------  -------------------  ------------------ -----    --
fc00:0:205:e00d::    uDX4         'FULL-500-VRF':1     bgp-65000          InUse    Y
  SID Function: 0xe00d
  SID context: { table-id=0xe0000004 ('FULL-500-VRF':IPv4/Unicast), nh-set-id=1 }
  Locator: 'MAIN'
  Allocation type: Dynamic
  Created: Jun 13 23:02:58.443 (4d02h ago)
RP/0/RP0/CPU0:PE-3#
```

The CLI command **show bgp vrf FULL-500-VRF nexthop-set** in Output 7-9 is useful for determining the next hop details for the SID fc00:0:205:e00d:: on Router PE-3.

Output 7-9   *SRv6 L3VPN Full-Mesh Configuration: BGP Next Hop Set on PE-3*

```
RP/0/RP0/CPU0:PE-3#show bgp vrf FULL-500-VRF nexthop-set

 Resilient per-CE nexthop set, ID 1
 Number of nexthops 1, Label 0, Flags 0x2100
 SRv6-VPN SID: fc00:0:205:e00d::/64
 Format: 2
 Nexthops:
 10.2.103.1
 Reference count 2,
RP/0/RP0/CPU0:PE-3#
```

The command **show segment-routing srv6 sid fc00:1:206:e004:: detail** in Output 7-10 obtained from PE-4 displays the SID details for the second subnet 10.2.103.144/28, which was received from CE-4 in VRF instance FULL-500-VRF, with the difference being that the allocation mode is per-VRF. These are the relevant details:

■ **SID: fc00:1:206:e004:::** This is the SRv6 SID that is allocated.

■ **Behavior: Endpoint behavior uDT4:** This is the endpoint with decapsulation and IPv4 table lookup.

■ **Context: 'FULL-500-VRF':** Due to the srv6-alloc-mode per-VRF behavior being applied by the route policy PREFIX_LOCATOR_RP, an IPv4 table lookup is required to forward the traffic to the destination 10.2.103.144/28.

■ **Locator: 'LowLatency':** The SRv6 SID is allocated based on the route policy PREFIX_LOCATOR_RP:

■ It matches IPv4 network 10.2.103.144/28, originating from CE-4.

■ It sets the SRv6 prefix SID from the SRv6 locator LowLatency, the low-latency flex algo 128.

Output 7-10   *SRv6 L3VPN Full-Mesh Configuration: SRv6 SID fc00:1:206:e004 on PE-4*

```
RP/0/RP0/CPU0:PE-4#show segment-routing srv6 sid fc00:1:206:e004:: detail

*** Locator: 'LowLatency' ***

SID                   Behavior       Context              Owner              State   RW
----------------      -----------    ------------------   ------------------ -----   --
fc00:1:206:e004::     uDT4           'FULL-500-VRF'       bgp-65000          InUse   Y
  SID Function: 0xe004
```

```
SID context: { table-id=0xe0000003 ('FULL-500-VRF':IPv4/Unicast) }
Locator: 'LowLatency'
Allocation type: Dynamic
Created: Jun 13 23:05:45.367 (2w3d ago)
RP/0/RP0/CPU0:PE-4#
```

Finally, the connectivity between the router CE-1 and the router CE-3 is confirmed by initiating an end-to-end IPv4 ping, as demonstrated in Output 7-11.

Output 7-11 *SRv6 L3VPN Full-Mesh Configuration: End-to-End ICMP Verification on CE-1*

```
RP/0/RP0/CPU0:CE-1#ping 10.2.103.129 source 10.1.103.129
Type escape sequence to abort.
Sending 5, 100-byte ICMP Echos to 10.2.103.129 timeout is 2 seconds:
!!!!!
Success rate is 100 percent (5/5), round-trip min/avg/max = 8/8/11 ms
RP/0/RP0/CPU0:CE-1#
```

In addition, a packet was captured in the reference network, where it is possible to verify the encapsulating IPv6 frame with the destination address fc00:0:205:e00d:: of router PE-3 and source IPv6 address fc00:0:105::1 of router PE-1. Enclosed within this frame is the ICMP message from the source IP address 10.1.103.129 (from CE-1) to the destination IP address 10.2.103.129 (to CE-3), as shown in the Example 7-3.

Example 7-3 *SRv6 L3VPN Full-Mesh Configuration: End-to-End ICMP Packet Capture*

```
<snip>
Internet Protocol Version 6, Src: fc00:0:105::1, Dst: fc00:0:205:e00d::
    0110 .... = Version: 6
    Payload Length: 100
    Next Header: IPIP (4)
    Hop Limit: 60
    Source Address: fc00:0:105::1
    Destination Address: fc00:0:205:e00d::
Internet Protocol Version 4, Src: 10.1.103.129, Dst: 10.2.103.129
    0100 .... = Version: 4
    .... 0101 = Header Length: 20 bytes (5)
    Differentiated Services Field: 0x00 (DSCP: CS0, ECN: Not-ECT)
    Total Length: 100
    Identification: 0x0cd8 (3288)
    Time to Live: 254
    Protocol: ICMP (1)
    Header Checksum: 0xccbb [validation disabled]
```

```
   [Header checksum status: Unverified]
   Source Address: 10.1.103.129
   Destination Address: 10.2.103.129
Internet Control Message Protocol
   Type: 8 (Echo (ping) request)
<snip>
```

SRv6 L3VPN Hub-and-Spoke Service

This section describes the configuration and verification tasks for a typical L3VPN hub-and-spoke service overlay network and its SRv6 transport network. L3VPN hub-and-spoke service deployments are widely used in MPLS networks and are therefore well understood. In an L3VPN hub-and-spoke service, the idea is that there is generally no spoke-to-spoke communication, and if there is, then it must transit via a hub site. The hub-to-spoke communication topology is achieved through the use of import and export route target values, as you'll see in this section. Figure 7-5 shows the two most commonly used hub-and-spoke configuration options:

- **Option 1 hub site:** A single PE–CE interface and a single VRF instance

- **Option 2 hub site:** Two PE–CE interfaces or subinterfaces and two VRF instances (one for import and one for export only)

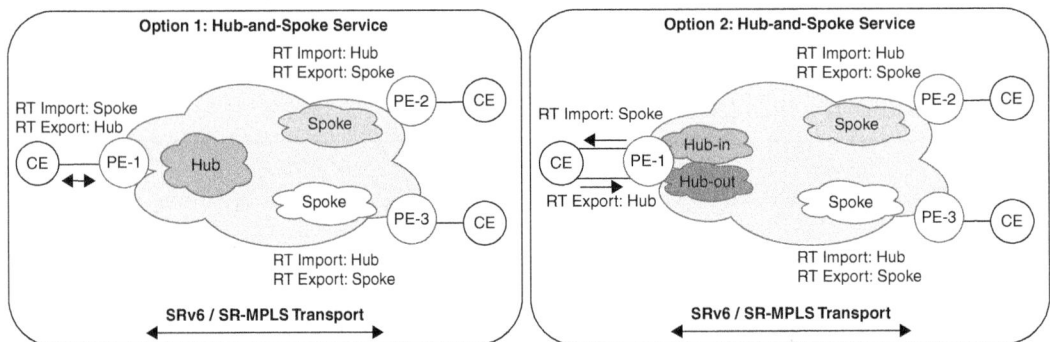

Figure 7-5   *L3VPN Hub-and-Spoke Configuration Options*

SRv6 L3VPN Hub-and-Spoke Configuration

The hub-and-spoke service illustrated in Figure 7-6 is based on the single PE–CE inter-face and single VRF instance hub site option (per PE router). In IS-IS Metro 1, the hub site consists of the CE-1 router being dual-homed to PE-1 and PE-2; in IS-IS Metro 2, the Spoke Site 1 router CE-3 is single attached to PE-3, and the Spoke Site 2 router CE-4 is single attached to PE-4. As you saw earlier in this chapter, the dual-attached hub site router CE-1 is set up in a unipath active/standby scenario via the routers PE-1 and PE-2 using a BGP local preference, with the active path set to a BGP local preference of 200 and the standby path set to a BGP local preference of 150. To improve convergence times in the event that the active PE–CE link fails, the BGP PIC Edge feature is also configured.

This hub-and-spoke service is configured based on the following listed SRv6 locator allocations, import/export RTs' and VRF instances:

- Hub site network 10.1.104.128/28 (CE-1) uses the SRv6 locator MAIN with per-CE allocation mode via PE-1 and PE-2.

- The hub site VRF instance is HUB-510-H1-VRF, with export route target 65000:510 and import route targets 65000:5100 and 65000:510.

- Spoke Site 1 network 10.2.104.128/28 from CE-3 uses the SRv6 locator MAIN with per-VRF allocation mode via PE-3.

- The Spoke Site 1 VRF instance is SPOKE-510-S1-VRF, with export route target 65000:5100 and import route target 65000:510.

- Spoke Site 2 network 10.2.104.144/28 from CE-4 uses the SRv6 locator MAIN with per-VRF allocation mode via PE-4.

- The Spoke Site 2 VRF instance is SPOKE-510-S2-VRF, with export route target 65000:5100 and import route target 65000:510.

In the reference network shown in Figure 7-6, communication is possible between the spoke sites only via the central hub site router CE-1, facilitated by the hub site advertising a default route toward the two spoke sites.

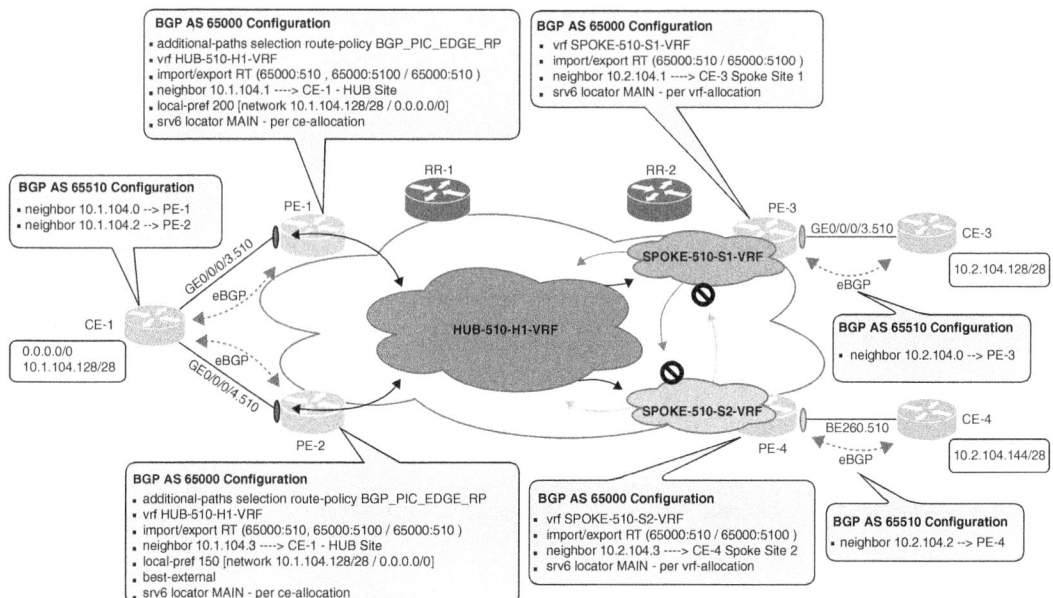

Figure 7-6 *SRv6 L3VPN Hub-and-Spoke Configuration Tasks*

Config 7-8 show a typical hub-and-spoke service configuration on router PE-1. The hub site VRF instance HUB-510-H1-VRF is configured on both routers, PE-1 and PE-2. The attached hub site router, CE-1, is originating a default route toward the spoke sites, thereby allowing them to communicate with each other via CE-1.

Config 7-8 *SRv6 L3VPN Hub-and-Spoke Configuration: Hub Site Configuration on PE-1*

```
!/* HUB VRF */
vrf HUB-510-H1-VRF
 address-family ipv4 unicast
  import route-target
   65000:510
   65000:5100
  !
  export route-target
   65000:510
  !
 !
!/* INTERFACE TO CE-1 */
interface GigabitEthernet0/0/0/3
 description Connected_to_CE-1
!
interface GigabitEthernet0/0/0/3.510
 vrf HUB-510-H1-VRF
 ipv4 address 10.1.104.0 255.255.255.254
 encapsulation dot1q 510
!
!/* ROUTE-POLICIES */
route-policy PASS_RP
  pass
end-policy
!
route-policy BGP_LOC-PREF_RP($LP)
  set local-preference $LP
end-policy
!
route-policy PIC_EDGE_RP
  set path-selection backup 1 install
end-policy
!
!/* BGP CONFIGURATION */
router bgp 65000
 bgp router-id 172.19.0.10
```

```
 address-family vpnv4 unicast
  vrf all
   segment-routing srv6
    locator MAIN
    alloc mode per-vrf
   !
  !
  additional-paths selection route-policy PIC_EDGE_RP
 !
!
 vrf HUB-510-H1-VRF
  rd 65000:510
  address-family ipv4 unicast
   segment-routing srv6
    alloc mode per-ce
   !
  !
  !
  neighbor 10.1.104.1
   remote-as 65510
   address-family ipv4 unicast
    route-policy BGP_LOC-PREF_RP(200) in
    route-policy PASS_RP out
    as-override
   !
```

Config 7-9 shows the hub site configuration on router PE-2.

Config 7-9   *SRv6 L3VPN Hub-and-Spoke Configuration: Hub Site Configuration on PE-2*

```
!/* HUB VRF */
vrf HUB-510-H1-VRF
 address-family ipv4 unicast
  import route-target
   65000:510
   65000:5100
  !
  export route-target
   65000:510
  !
 !
```

```
!/* INTERFACE TO CE-1 */
interface GigabitEthernet0/0/0/4
 description Connected_to_CE-1
!
interface GigabitEthernet0/0/0/4.510
 vrf HUB-510-H1-VRF
 ipv4 address 10.1.104.2 255.255.255.254
 encapsulation dot1q 510
!
!/* ROUTE-POLICIES */
route-policy PASS_RP
  pass
end-policy
!
route-policy BGP_LOC-PREF_RP($LP)
  set local-preference $LP
end-policy
!
route-policy PIC_EDGE_RP
  set path-selection backup 1 install
end-policy
!
!/* BGP CONFIGURATION */
router bgp 65000
 bgp router-id 172.19.0.11
 address-family vpnv4 unicast
  vrf all
   segment-routing srv6
    locator MAIN
    alloc mode per-vrf
   !
  !
  additional-paths selection route-policy PIC_EDGE_RP
 !
!
 vrf HUB-510-H1-VRF
  rd 65000:511
  address-family ipv4 unicast
   advertise best-external
   segment-routing srv6
    alloc mode per-ce
   !
  !
```

```
  neighbor 10.1.104.3
   remote-as 65510
   address-family ipv4 unicast
    route-policy BGP_LOC-PREF_RP(150) in
    route-policy PASS_RP out
    as-override
   !
```

Config 7-10 shows the configuration for the Spoke Site 1 attached via the router PE-3. The Spoke Site 1 router CE-3 is attached via the VRF instance SPOKE-510-S1-VRF.

Config 7-10 *SRv6 L3VPN Hub-and-Spoke Configuration: Spoke Site 1 Configuration on PE-3*

```
!/* Spoke 1 VRF */
vrf SPOKE-510-S1-VRF
 address-family ipv4 unicast
  import route-target
   65000:510
  !
  export route-target
   65000:5100
  !
 !
!/* INTERFACE TO CE-3 */
interface GigabitEthernet0/0/0/3
 description Connected_to_CE-3
!
interface GigabitEthernet0/0/0/3.510
 vrf SPOKE-510-S1-VRF
 ipv4 address 10.2.104.0 255.255.255.254
 encapsulation dot1q 510
!
!/* ROUTE-POLICIES */
route-policy PASS_RP
  pass
end-policy
!
!
route-policy PIC_EDGE_RP
  set path-selection backup 1 install
```

```
end-policy
!
!/* BGP CONFIGURATION */
router bgp 65000
 bgp router-id 172.19.0.19
 address-family vpnv4 unicast
  vrf all
   segment-routing srv6
    locator MAIN
    alloc mode per-vrf
   !
  !
  additional-paths selection route-policy PIC_EDGE_RP
 !
 vrf SPOKE-510-S1-VRF
  rd 65000:51001
  address-family ipv4 unicast
  !
  neighbor 10.2.104.1
   remote-as 65510
   address-family ipv4 unicast
    route-policy PASS_RP in
    route-policy PASS_RP out
    as-override
   !
```

Config 7-11 shows the configuration for the Spoke Site 2 attached via the router PE-4. The Spoke Site 2 router CE-4 is attached via the VRF instance SPOKE-510-S2-VRF.

Config 7-11   *SRv6 L3VPN Hub-and-Spoke Configuration: Spoke Site 2 Configuration on PE-4*

```
!/* Spoke 2 VRF */
vrf SPOKE-510-S2-VRF
 address-family ipv4 unicast
  import route-target
   65000:510
  !
  export route-target
   65000:5100
  !
 !
```

```
!/* INTERFACE TO CE-4 */
interface Bundle-Ether260
 description Connected_to_CE-4
!
interface Bundle-Ether260.510
 vrf SPOKE-510-S2-VRF
 ipv4 address 10.2.104.2 255.255.255.254
 encapsulation dot1q 510
!
!/* ROUTE-POLICIES */
route-policy PASS_RP
  pass
end-policy
!
route-policy PIC_EDGE_RP
  set path-selection backup 1 install
end-policy
!
!/* BGP CONFIGURATION */
router bgp 65000
 bgp router-id 172.19.0.20
 address-family vpnv4 unicast
  vrf all
   segment-routing srv6
    locator MAIN
    alloc mode per-vrf
   !
  !
  additional-paths selection route-policy PIC_EDGE_RP
 !
 vrf SPOKE-510-S2-VRF
  rd 65000:51002
  address-family ipv4 unicast
  !
  neighbor 10.2.104.3
   remote-as 65510
   address-family ipv4 unicast
    route-policy PASS_RP in
    route-policy PASS_RP out
    as-override
   !
  !
 !
!
```

These L3VPN hub-and-spoke service overlay configurations are essentially the same as those of the L3VPN full-mesh service configurations, with the main difference being the way the import and export route target values are configured. Essentially, the routes exported from the hub site VRF instance with a BGP route target set to 65000:510 will only be imported by the other hub site VRF instance attached PE router or the spoke site VRF instance attached PE routers. The routes exported by the spoke site VRF instances with BGP route target set to 65000:5100 will only be imported by the PE routers where the hub site VRF instances are attached. Config 7-12 shows the configuration for the hub site, and Config 7-13 shows the configuration for a spoke site.

Config 7-12   *SRv6 L3VPN Hub Site: VRF Instance Configuration*

```
vrf HUB-510-H1-VRF
 address-family ipv4 unicast
  import route-target
   65000:510
   65000:5100
  !
  export route-target
   65000:510
```

Config 7-13   *SRv6 L3VPN Spoke Site: VRF Instance Configuration*

```
vrf SPOKE-510-S2-VRF
 address-family ipv4 unicast
  import route-target
   65000:510
  !
  export route-target
   65000:5100
```

Be aware that in this reference network example, the spoke sites can communicate with one another via the hub site router CE-1. The requirement for the spoke site traffic to reach the hub site CE router before being routed back to the other spoke site router is usually due to the use of centralized firewalls or NAT services. The SRv6 allocation mode must therefore be configured as alloc mode per-ce for the hub site VRF instances; otherwise, the hub PE router itself will do an IP lookup and forward the traffic to the destination spoke site CE router.

Output 7-12 shows the expected behavior: The traceroute from Spoke Site 2 router CE-4 to Spoke Site 1 router CE-3 reaches the hub site CE-1 router before being routed back to Spoke Site 1 router CE-3.

Output 7-12 *SRv6 L3VPN Hub-and-Spoke Configuration: Spoke-to-Spoke Traceroute (alloc mode per-ce)*

```
RP/0/RP0/CPU0:CE-4#traceroute 10.2.104.129 source 10.2.104.145
Type escape sequence to abort.
Tracing the route to 10.2.104.129

 1  10.2.104.2 2 msec  2 msec  1 msec
 2  10.1.104.0 9 msec  8 msec  8 msec  ←---------Hub Site PE-1
 3  10.1.104.1 9 msec  13 msec  9 msec  ←---------Hub Site CE-1
 4  10.1.104.0 10 msec  9 msec  9 msec  ←---------Hub Site PE-1
 5  10.2.104.0 16 msec  16 msec  16 msec  ←-------Spoke Site 1 PE-3
 6  10.2.104.1 17 msec  *  20 msec  ←------------Spoke Site 1 CE-3
RP/0/RP0/CPU0:CE-4#
```

If the default SRv6 allocation mode alloc mode per-vrf is used or configured, then the hub site router PE-1 will do an IP lookup and forward the traffic directly on to the Spoke Site 1 router CE-3. You can see this behavior from the traceroute initiated from Spoke Site 2 router CE-4 in Output 7-13; the traceroute reaches the hub site PE-1 router before being routed back on toward the Spoke Site 1 router CE-3.

Output 7-13 *SRv6 L3VPN Hub-and-Spoke Configuration: Spoke-to-Spoke Traceroute (alloc mode per-vrf)*

```
RP/0/RP0/CPU0:CE-4#traceroute 10.2.104.129 source 10.2.104.145
Type escape sequence to abort.
Tracing the route to 10.2.104.129

 1  10.2.104.2 2 msec  1 msec  1 msec
 2  10.1.104.0 8 msec  8 msec  7 msec  ←---------Hub Site PE-1
 3  10.2.104.0 14 msec  14 msec  14 msec  ←------Spoke Site 1 PE-3
 4  10.2.104.1 22 msec  *  19 msec  ←-----------Spoke Site 1 CE-3
RP/0/RP0/CPU0:CE-4#
```

SRv6 L3VPN Hub-and-Spoke Configuration Verification

Now let's look at some basic commands you can use to verify the newly provisioned L3VPN hub-and-spoke service.

As shown in Figure 7-7, the verification tasks focus mostly on the subnets originated into both the spoke VRF instances, SPOKE-510-S1-VRF and SPOKE-510-S2-VRF, from the routers CE-3 and CE-4, respectively, and then imported into the hub site via the VRF instance HUB-510-H1-VRF on router PE-1.

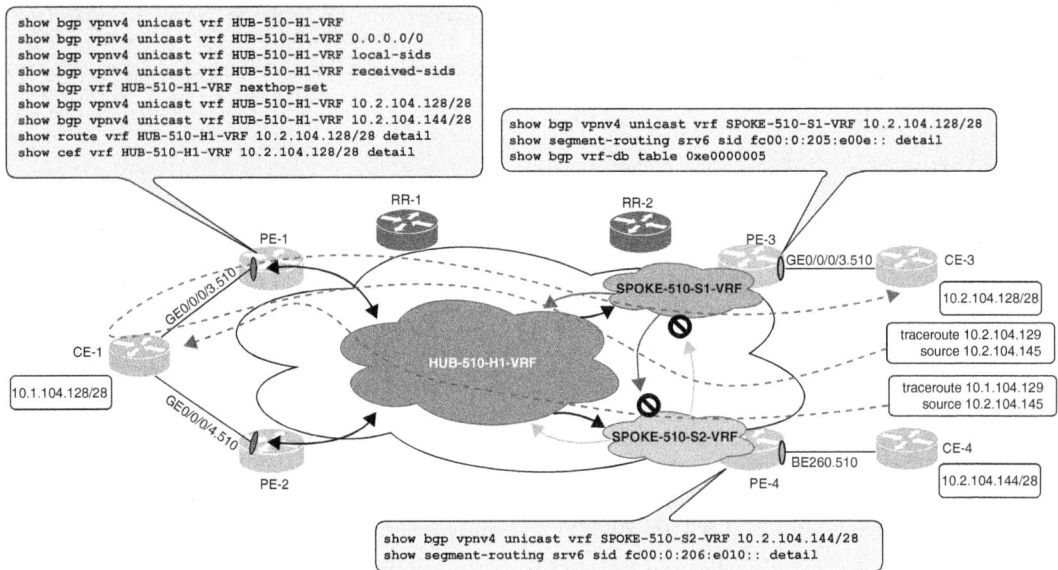

```
show bgp vpnv4 unicast vrf HUB-510-H1-VRF
show bgp vpnv4 unicast vrf HUB-510-H1-VRF 0.0.0.0/0
show bgp vpnv4 unicast vrf HUB-510-H1-VRF local-sids
show bgp vpnv4 unicast vrf HUB-510-H1-VRF received-sids
show bgp vrf HUB-510-H1-VRF nexthop-set
show bgp vpnv4 unicast vrf HUB-510-H1-VRF 10.2.104.128/28
show bgp vpnv4 unicast vrf HUB-510-H1-VRF 10.2.104.144/28
show route vrf HUB-510-H1-VRF 10.2.104.128/28 detail
show cef vrf HUB-510-H1-VRF 10.2.104.128/28 detail
```

```
show bgp vpnv4 unicast vrf SPOKE-510-S1-VRF 10.2.104.128/28
show segment-routing srv6 sid fc00:0:205:e00e:: detail
show bgp vrf-db table 0xe0000005
```

```
show bgp vpnv4 unicast vrf SPOKE-510-S2-VRF 10.2.104.144/28
show segment-routing srv6 sid fc00:0:206:e010:: detail
```

Figure 7-7   *SRv6 L3VPN Hub-and-Spoke Verification Tasks*

These are the routes of interest from the router PE-1 perspective:

■ **Subnet 0.0.0.0/0:** This is the first path from external next hop 10.1.104.1 (CE-1) with BGP local preference 200.

■ **Subnet 0.0.0.0/0:** This is the second path from next hop fc00:0:106::1 (PE-2) with BGP local preference 150.

■ **Subnet 10.1.104.128/28:** This is the first path from external next hop 10.1.104.1 (CE-1) with BGP local preference 200.

■ **Subnet 10.1.104.128/28:** This is the second path from next hop fc00:0:106::1 (PE-2) with BGP local preference 150.

■ **Subnet 10.2.104.128/28:** This is the single path from next hop fc00:0:205::1 (PE-3).

■ **Subnet 10.2.104.144/28:** This is the single path from next hop fc00:0:206::1 (PE-4).

Output 7-14 shows the RIB verification command **show bgp vpnv4 unicast vrf HUB-510-H1-VRF** executed on router PE-1. Both the routes from the local hub site router CE-1 are observed, via eBGP as well as via the iBGP path from router PE-2. In addition, both of the spoke site routes are also visible from the PE-3 and PE-4 routers.

Output 7-14 *SRv6 L3VPN Hub-and-Spoke Configuration: BGP VPNv4 RIB on PE-1*

```
RP/0/RP0/CPU0:PE-1#show bgp vpnv4 unicast vrf HUB-510-H1-VRF
BGP router identifier 172.19.0.10, local AS number 65000
<snip>
Route Distinguisher: 65000:510 (default for vrf HUB-510-H1-VRF)
Route Distinguisher Version: 744
*> 0.0.0.0/0          10.1.104.1                  200     0 65510 i
* i                   fc00:0:106::1               150     0 65510 i
*> 10.1.104.128/28    10.1.104.1            0     200     0 65510 i
* i                   fc00:0:106::1         0     150     0 65510 i
*>i10.2.104.128/28    fc00:0:205::1         0     100     0 65510 i
*>i10.2.104.144/28    fc00:0:206::1         0     100     0 65510 i


Processed 4 prefixes, 6 paths
RP/0/RP0/CPU0:PE-1#
```

Output 7-15 and Output 7-16, both from router PE-1, provide details of the local SIDs, received SIDs, allocation mode, and locator information for all the subnets in the VRF instance HUB-510-H1-VRF.

In Output 7-15, the default route as well as subnet 10.1.104.128/28 from router CE-1 are allocated the SID fc00:0:105:e00e:: with per-CE allocation mode from the SRv6 locator MAIN. The other subnets in this output are not local to the VRF instance, and therefore no local SIDs are allocated.

Output 7-15 *SRv6 L3VPN Hub-and-Spoke Configuration: BGP VPNv4 RIB Local SIDs on PE-1*

```
RP/0/RP0/CPU0:PE-1#show bgp vpnv4 unicast vrf HUB-510-H1-VRF local-sids
BGP router identifier 172.19.0.10, local AS number 65000
<snip>
  Network           Local Sid                      Alloc mode   Locator
Route Distinguisher: 65000:510 (default for vrf HUB-510-H1-VRF)
Route Distinguisher Version: 880
*> 0.0.0.0/0         fc00:0:105:e00e::              per-ce       MAIN
* i                  fc00:0:105:e00e::              per-ce       MAIN
*> 10.1.104.128/28   fc00:0:105:e00e::              per-ce       MAIN
* i                  fc00:0:105:e00e::              per-ce       MAIN
*>i10.2.104.128/28   NO SRv6 Sid                    -            -
*>i10.2.104.144/28   NO SRv6 Sid                    -            -


Processed 4 prefixes, 6 paths
RP/0/RP0/CPU0:PE-1#
```

Output 7-16 shows the output of the command **show bgp vpnv4 unicast vrf HUB-510-H1-VRF received-sids**, where the spoke site subnets 10.2.104.128/28 from CE-3 and 10.2.104.144/28 from CE-4 have the SIDs fc00:0:205:e00e:: and fc00:0:206:e010:: allocated by their respective PE routers in Metro 2. The hub site CE-1 default route and subnet 10.1.104.128/28 received from PE-2 are allocated the SID fc00:0:106:e010::.

Output 7-16   *SRv6 L3VPN Hub-and-Spoke Configuration: BGP VPNv4 RIB Received SIDs on PE-1*

```
RP/0/RP0/CPU0:PE-1#show bgp vpnv4 unicast vrf HUB-510-H1-VRF received-sids
BGP router identifier 172.19.0.10, local AS number 65000
<snip>
   Network           Next Hop                        Received Sid
Route Distinguisher: 65000:510 (default for vrf HUB-510-H1-VRF)
Route Distinguisher Version: 880
*> 0.0.0.0/0         10.1.104.1                      NO SRv6 Sid
*  i                 fc00:0:106::1                   fc00:0:106:e010::
*> 10.1.104.128/28   10.1.104.1                      NO SRv6 Sid
*  i                 fc00:0:106::1                   fc00:0:106:e010::
*>i10.2.104.128/28   fc00:0:205::1                   fc00:0:205:e00e::
*>i10.2.104.144/28   fc00:0:206::1                   fc00:0:206:e010::


Processed 4 prefixes, 6 paths
RP/0/RP0/CPU0:PE-1#
```

As mentioned earlier in this chapter, in the section "SRv6 L3VPN Hub-and-Spoke Configuration," there is a requirement for the inter-spoke site traffic to reach the hub site router CE-1 along the traffic forwarding path; to achieve this, the SRv6 allocation mode must be configured as alloc mode per-ce for the hub site VRF instances. This behavior is verified in Output 7-17 for the route 0.0.0.0/0 on the router PE-1. Note this important information:

- **SRv6-VPN SID: fc00:0:105:e00e::/64:** This is the allocated SID for default route learned from hub site router CE-1, and it is also verified with the command **show bgp vpnv4 unicast vrf HUB-510-H1-VRF local-sids.**

- **Gateway Array ID: 3, Resilient per-CE nexthop set ID: 3:** This is verification that per-CE next hop allocation mode is in use and verification of the next hop IP address of CE-1. Output 7-18 shows this verification via the command **show bgp vrf HUB-510-H1-VRF nexthop-set.**

- **Paths: (2 available, best #1):** The output confirms that the subnet is available across two paths, and the first path is the preferred one.

  - **Path #1:**

    □ **10.1.104.1 from 10.1.104.1 (172.19.0.13):** CE-1 is the eBGP next hop

10.1.104.1 with BGP router ID 172.19.0.13, so this an eBGP path.

☐ **localpref 200, valid, external, best:** BGP local preference is set to 200 for all routes learned over this eBGP path, and it is the best path for the route 0.0.0.0/0.

■ **Path #2:**

☐ **fc00:0:106::1 (metric 21) from fc00:0:107::1 (172.19.0.11):** PE-2 is the BGP next hop fc00:0:106::1 with a BGP router ID 172.19.0.11.

☐ **Received Label 0xe0100:** The received label is 0xe0100, and the most significant 16 bits of this label is the SRv6 uSID 0xe010 from router PE-2.

☐ **Extended community: RT:65000:510:** PE-1 imports this route into the VRF instance HUB-510-H1-VRF.

☐ **Sid:fc00:0:106:::** This is the PE-2 remote node SID (uN) from the configured SRv6 locator MAIN.

☐ **Behavior:61:** The endpoint behavior is End.DX4 with NEXT-CSID 0x003D because of the configuration srv6-alloc-mode per-ce, with behavior similar to that of the per-CE label allocation mode.

Output 7-17 *SRv6 L3VPN Hub-and-Spoke Configuration: BGP VPNv4 RIB for 0.0.0.0/0 on PE-1*

```
RP/0/RP0/CPU0:PE-1#show bgp vpnv4 unicast vrf HUB-510-H1-VRF 0.0.0.0/0
BGP routing table entry for 0.0.0.0/0, Route Distinguisher: 65000:510
Versions:
  Process           bRIB/RIB  SendTblVer
  Speaker                744         744
    SRv6-VPN SID: fc00:0:105:e00e::/64
    Gateway Array ID: 3, Resilient per-CE nexthop set ID: 3
Last Modified: Jun 24 22:56:17.735 for 01:12:33
Paths: (2 available, best #1)
  Advertised to peers (in unique update groups):
    fc00:0:107::1
  Path #1: Received by speaker 0
  Advertised to peers (in unique update groups):
    fc00:0:107::1
  65510
    10.1.104.1 from 10.1.104.1 (172.19.0.13)
      Origin IGP, localpref 200, valid, external, best, group-best, import-candidate
      Received Path ID 0, Local Path ID 1, version 744
      Extended community: RT:65000:510
  Path #2: Received by speaker 0
  Not advertised to any peer
  65510
```

```
fc00:0:106::1 (metric 21) from fc00:0:107::1 (172.19.0.11)
  Received Label 0xe0100
  Origin IGP, localpref 150, valid, internal, backup, add-path, imported
  Received Path ID 0, Local Path ID 3, version 744
  Extended community: RT:65000:510
  Originator: 172.19.0.11, Cluster list: 172.19.0.12
  PSID-Type:L3, SubTLV Count:1
   SubTLV:
    T:1(Sid information), Sid:fc00:0:106::, Behavior:61, SS-TLV Count:1
     SubSubTLV:
      T:1(Sid structure):
    Source AFI: VPNv4 Unicast, Source VRF: default, Source Route
  Distinguisher: 65000:511
RP/0/RP0/CPU0:PE-1#
```

The VRF instance HUB-510-H1-VRF BGP next hop set verification shown in Output 7-18 indicates that the locally allocated uSID 0xe00e will use the endpoint behavior End.DX4 because the SRv6 allocation mode is configured as alloc mode per-ce. The next hop IP address used to forward egress traffic toward router CE-1 is 10.1.104.1, which is the link address configured on router CE-1.

Output 7-18   *SRv6 L3VPN Hub-and-Spoke Configuration: BGP Next Hop Set on PE-1*

```
RP/0/RP0/CPU0:PE-1#show bgp vrf HUB-510-H1-VRF nexthop-set

Resilient per-CE nexthop set, ID 3
Number of nexthops 1, Label 0, Flags 0x2100
SRv6-VPN SID: fc00:0:105:e00e::/64
Format: 2
Nexthops:
10.1.104.1
Reference count 2,
RP/0/RP0/CPU0:PE-1#
```

The first remote subnet to be verified is the BGP route 10.2.104.128/28, originated from the Spoke Site 1 router CE-3 in Output 7-19, which displays the following relevant information:

■ **Paths: (1 available, best #1):** There is only a single path for the subnet from CE-3.

  ■ **Path #1:**

    □ **fc00:0:205::1 (metric 61) from fc00:0:107::1 (172.19.0.19):** PE-3 is the BGP next hop fc00:0:205::1 with a BGP router ID 172.19.0.19.

    □ **Received Label 0xe00e0:** The received label is 0xe00e0, and the most significant 16 bits of this label is the SRv6 uSID 0xe00e from router PE-3 for the

VRF instance SPOKE-510-S1-VRF, confirmed via the command **show bgp vpnv4 unicast vrf HUB-510-H1-VRF received-sids** (refer to Output 7-16).

☐ **Extended community: RT:65000:5100:** This is the export route target configured on the VRF instance SPOKE-510-S1-VRF and imported into the hub site VRF instance HUB-510-H1-VRF.

☐ **Sid:fc00:0:205:::** This is the PE-3 remote node SID from the configured SRv6 locator MAIN.

☐ **Behavior:63:** The endpoint behavior is End.DT4 with NEXT-CSID 0x003F because of the configuration srv6-alloc-mode per-vrf.

Output 7-19 *SRv6 L3VPN Hub-and-Spoke Configuration: BGP VPNv4 RIB for 10.2.104.128/28 on PE-1*

```
RP/0/RP0/CPU0:PE-1#show bgp vpnv4 unicast vrf HUB-510-H1-VRF 10.2.104.128/28
BGP routing table entry for 10.2.104.128/28, Route Distinguisher: 65000:510
Versions:
  Process           bRIB/RIB  SendTblVer
  Speaker                724         724
Last Modified: Jun 22 11:43:51.735 for 2d13h
Paths: (1 available, best #1)
  Not advertised to any peer
  Path #1: Received by speaker 0
  Not advertised to any peer
  65510
    fc00:0:205::1 (metric 61) from fc00:0:107::1 (172.19.0.19)
      Received Label 0xe00e0
      Origin IGP, metric 0, localpref 100, valid, internal, best, group-best,
import-candidate, imported
      Received Path ID 0, Local Path ID 1, version 724
      Extended community: RT:65000:5100
      Originator: 172.19.0.19, Cluster list: 172.19.0.12, 172.19.0.21
      PSID-Type:L3, SubTLV Count:1
       SubTLV:
        T:1(Sid information), Sid:fc00:0:205::, Behavior:63, SS-TLV Count:1
         SubSubTLV:
         T:1(Sid structure):
      Source AFI: VPNv4 Unicast, Source VRF: default, Source Route
  Distinguisher: 65000:51001
RP/0/RP0/CPU0:PE-1#
```

The second remote subnet to be verified is the BGP route 10.2.104.144/28, originated from the Spoke Site 2 router CE-4, via the command in Output 7-20, which displays the following relevant information:

■ **Paths: (1 available, best #1):** There is only a single path for the subnet from CE-4.

- ■ **Path #1:**

  - □ **fc00:0:206::1 (metric 61) from fc00:0:107::1 (172.19.0.20):** PE-4 is the BGP next hop fc00:0:206::1 with a BGP router ID 172.19.0.20.

  - □ **Received Label 0xe0100:** The received label is 0xe0100, and the most significant 16 bits of this label is the SRv6 uSID 0xe010 from PE-4 for the VRF instance SPOKE-510-S2-VRF, as confirmed via the command **show bgp vpnv4 unicast vrf HUB-510-H1-VRF received-sids** (refer to Output 7-16).

  - □ **Extended community: RT:65000:5100:** This is the export route target configured on the VRF instance SPOKE-510-S2-VRF and imported into the hub site VRF instance HUB-510-H1-VRF.

  - □ **Sid:fc00:0:206:::** This is the PE-4 remote node SID from the configured SRv6 locator MAIN.

  - □ **Behavior:63:** The endpoint behavior is End.DT4 with NEXT-CSID (0x003F) because of the configuration srv6-alloc-mode per-vrf.

Output 7-20   *SRv6 L3VPN Hub-and-Spoke Configuration: BGP VPNv4 RIB for 10.2.104.144/28 on PE-1*

```
RP/0/RP0/CPU0:PE-1#show bgp vpnv4 unicast vrf HUB-510-H1-VRF 10.2.104.144/28
BGP routing table entry for 10.2.104.144/28, Route Distinguisher: 65000:510
Versions:
  Process           bRIB/RIB  SendTblVer
  Speaker              722         722
Last Modified: Jun 22 11:42:50.735 for 2d14h
Paths: (1 available, best #1)
  Not advertised to any peer
  Path #1: Received by speaker 0
  Not advertised to any peer
  65510
    fc00:0:206::1 (metric 61) from fc00:0:107::1 (172.19.0.20)
    Received Label 0xe0100
      Origin IGP, metric 0, localpref 100, valid, internal, best, group-best,
  import-candidate, imported
      Received Path ID 0, Local Path ID 1, version 722
      Extended community: RT:65000:5100
      Originator: 172.19.0.20, Cluster list: 172.19.0.12, 172.19.0.21
      PSID-Type:L3, SubTLV Count:1
      SubTLV:
       T:1(Sid information), Sid:fc00:0:206::, Behavior:63, SS-TLV Count:1
        SubSubTLV:
         T:1(Sid structure):
      Source AFI: VPNv4 Unicast, Source VRF: default, Source Route Distinguisher:
  65000:51002
RP/0/RP0/CPU0:PE-1#
```

The next verification step is to verify the subnet 10.2.104.128/28 from the Spoke Site 1 router CE-3 to confirm relevant RIB details for this learned subnet. Output 7-21 displays the following relevant information for this route:

- **fc00:0:205::1, from fc00:0:107::1:** PE-3 is the active BGP next hop fc00:0:205::1.

  - **SRv6 Headend: H.Encaps.Red [f3216], SID-list {fc00:0:205:e00e::}:** This indicates H.Encaps with reduced encapsulation, where the first SID is copied into the Destination Address field of the outer IPv6 header.

Note   For more details about H.Encaps with reduced encapsulation, refer to the section "IPv6 Segment Routing Header (SRH) (RFC 8754)" in Chapter 3.

Output 7-21   *SRv6 L3VPN Hub-and-Spoke Configuration: RIB Details for 10.2.104.128/28 on PE-1*

```
RP/0/RP0/CPU0:PE-1#show route vrf HUB-510-H1-VRF 10.2.104.128/28 detail

Routing entry for 10.2.104.128/28
  Known via "bgp 65000", distance 200, metric 0
  Tag 65510, type internal
  Installed Jun 22 11:43:51.281 for 2d12h
  Routing Descriptor Blocks
    fc00:0:205::1, from fc00:0:107::1
      Nexthop in Vrf: "default", Table: "default", IPv6 Unicast, Table Id:
0xe0800000
      Route metric is 0
      Label: None
      Tunnel ID: None
      Binding Label: None
      Extended communities count: 0
      Source RD attributes: 0x0000:65000:51001
      NHID:0x0(Ref:0)
      SRv6 Headend: H.Encaps.Red [f3216], SID-list {fc00:0:205:e00e::}
  Route version is 0x3 (3)
  No local label
  IP Precedence: Not Set
  QoS Group ID: Not Set
  Flow-tag: Not Set
  Fwd-class: Not Set
  Route Priority: RIB_PRIORITY_RECURSIVE (12) SVD Type RIB_SVD_TYPE_REMOTE
  Download Priority 3, Download Version 19
  No advertising protos.
RP/0/RP0/CPU0:PE-1#
```

The **show cef vrf HUB-510-H1-VRF 10.2.104.128/28 detail** command in Output 7-22 displays the FIB output of the same target subnet 10.2.104.128/28 mentioned previously (refer to Output 7-21). The relevant information from this output is as follows:

■ **via fc00:0:205::/128:** Router PE-3 is the active BGP next hop fc00:0:205::1.

   ■ **next hop fc00:0:205::/128 via fc00:0:200::/40:** The BGP next hop is learned via the summarized network for the IS-IS Metro 2 subnet in the global routing table.

   ■ **SRv6 H.Encaps.Red SID-list {fc00:0:205:e00e::}:** This indicates H.Encaps with reduced encapsulation, where the first SID is copied into the Destination Address field of the outer IPv6 header.

The egress traffic to the destination subnet on CE-3 (10.2.104.128/28) will be load balanced across the core-facing interfaces, as shown here:

   ☐ 0   Y   GigabitEthernet0/0/0/0   fe80::42:acff:fe15:7f03

   ☐ 1   Y   GigabitEthernet0/0/0/2   fe80::42:acff:fe15:8002

Output 7-22   *SRv6 L3VPN Hub-and-Spoke Configuration: FIB Details for 10.2.104.128/28 on PE-1*

```
RP/0/RP0/CPU0:PE-1#show cef vrf HUB-510-H1-VRF 10.2.104.128/28 detail
10.2.104.128/28, version 19, SRv6 Headend, internal 0x5000001 0x30 (ptr 0x871be558)
  [1], 0x0 (0x0), 0x0 (0x899f3c78)
 Updated Jun 22 11:43:51.284
 Prefix Len 28, traffic index 0, precedence n/a, priority 3
 gateway array (0x89cf40a8) reference count 3, flags 0x2010, source rib (7), 0
 backups
              [1 type 3 flags 0x48441 (0x87e94f08) ext 0x0 (0x0)]
 LW-LDI[type=0, refc=0, ptr=0x0, sh-ldi=0x0]
 gateway array update type-time 1 Jun 11 07:32:49.563
LDI Update time Jun 11 07:32:49.575


 Level 1 - Load distribution: 0
 [0] via fc00:0:205::/128, recursive


   via fc00:0:205::/128, 16 dependencies, recursive [flags 0x6000]
    path-idx 0 NHID 0x0 [0x86fdfba0 0x0]
    next hop VRF - 'default', table - 0xe0800000
    next hop fc00:0:205::/128 via fc00:0:200::/40
    SRv6 H.Encaps.Red SID-list {fc00:0:205:e00e::}


   Load distribution: 0 1 (refcount 1)


   Hash  OK  Interface                 Address
   0     Y   GigabitEthernet0/0/0/0    fe80::42:acff:fe15:7f03
   1     Y   GigabitEthernet0/0/0/2    fe80::42:acff:fe15:8002
RP/0/RP0/CPU0:PE-1#
```

Output 7-23 shows verification of the SID details on the egress Spoke Site 1 router PE-3 for the IP subnet 10.2.104.128/28 (CE-3). In this output, alloc mode per-vrf has been configured for the VRF instance SPOKE-510-S1-VRF, and there is no Gateway Array ID: entry as there is in Output 7-17 for the hub site PE routers. Output 7-23 shows the following important information:

- **SRv6-VPN SID: fc00:0:205:e00e::/64:** This is the allocated SID for the 10.2.104.128/28 route learned from spoke site router CE-3.

- **Paths: (1 available, best #1):** The output confirms that the subnet is single attached.

- **Path #1:**

  - **10.2.104.1 from 10.2.104.1 (172.19.0.22):** CE-3 is the eBGP next hop 10.2.104.1 with a BGP router ID 172.19.0.22, so this is an external path.

Output 7-23 *SRv6 L3VPN Hub-and-Spoke Configuration: BGP VPNv4 RIB for 10.2.104.128/28 on PE-3*

```
RP/0/RP0/CPU0:PE-3#show bgp vpnv4 unicast vrf SPOKE-510-S1-VRF 10.2.104.128/28


BGP routing table entry for 10.2.104.128/28, Route Distinguisher: 65000:51001
Versions:
  Process           bRIB/RIB   SendTblVer
  Speaker              1347         1347
    SRv6-VPN SID: fc00:0:205:e00e::/64
Last Modified: Jun 22 11:46:03.905 for 2d14h
Paths: (1 available, best #1)
  Advertised to peers (in unique update groups):
    fc00:0:207::1
  Path #1: Received by speaker 0
  Advertised to peers (in unique update groups):
    fc00:0:207::1
  65510
    10.2.104.1 from 10.2.104.1 (172.19.0.22)
      Origin IGP, metric 0, localpref 100, valid, external, best, group-best,
  import-candidate
      Received Path ID 0, Local Path ID 1, version 1347
      Extended community: RT:65000:5100
RP/0/RP0/CPU0:PE-3#
```

For the Spoke Site 1 router PE-3, Output 7-24 displays the SID details for the subnet 10.2.104.128/28 from CE-3 attached to the VRF instance SPOKE-510-S1-VRF and confirms the endpoint behavior uDT4 due to use of the configuration srv6-alloc-mode per-vrf. The output shows the following important information:

- **SID: fc00:0:205:e00e:::** This is the SRv6 SID that is allocated.

- **Behavior: uDT4:** This is the endpoint behavior with decapsulation and IPv4 lookup.

- **Context: 'SPOKE-510-S1-VRF':** *Context* in this output refers to the configured VRF instance SPOKE-510-S1-VRF with table ID 0xe0000005.

- **Locator: 'MAIN':** The SID was allocated from the configured SRv6 locator MAIN.

Output 7-24   *SRv6 L3VPN Hub-and-Spoke Configuration: SRv6 SID fc00:0:205:e00e on PE-3*

```
RP/0/RP0/CPU0:PE-3#show segment-routing srv6 sid fc00:0:205:e00e:: detail

*** Locator: 'MAIN' ***


SID           Behavior          Context              Owner               State RW
--------------------------  ----------------  --------------------------------  ----
         ------------  -----  --
fc00:0:205:e00e::   uDT4   'SPOKE-510-S1-VRF'       bgp-65000           InUse  Y
  SID Function: 0xe00e
  SID context: { table-id=0xe0000005 ('SPOKE-510-S1-VRF':IPv4/Unicast) }
  Locator: 'MAIN'
  Allocation type: Dynamic
  Created: Jun 22 06:55:11.788 (2d19h ago)
RP/0/RP0/CPU0:PE-3#
```

Additional details of this VRF instance SPOKE-510-S1-VRF can be verified via the entry table-id=0xe0000005 and used with the command **show bgp vrf-db table 0xe0000005**, which provides details about both of the route targets, as shown in Output 7-25.

Output 7-25   *SRv6 L3VPN Hub-and-Spoke Configuration:* **show bgp vrf-db** *Details on PE-3*

```
RP/0/RP0/CPU0:PE-3#show bgp vrf-db table 0xe0000005

VRF-TBL: SPOKE-510-S1-VRF (IPv4 Unicast)
  TBL ID: 0xe0000005
  RSI Handle: 0x485f4ec0
  Refcount: 7
  Import:
    RT-List: RT:65000:510
  Export:
    RT-List: RT:65000:5100
RP/0/RP0/CPU0:PE-3#
```

Finally, connectivity between the Spoke Site 2 router CE-4 and Spoke Site 1 router CE-3 can be verified through an end-to-end traceroute like the one shown earlier, in

Output 7-12 to confirm inter-spoke site reachability via the hub site router CE-1. The verification commands for Spoke Site 2 are similar to those for Spoke Site 1 and are therefore not included here. These commands are by no means all that can be used for verification of these services but should be sufficient for explanation purposes.

SRv6 L3VPN Extranet Service

This section describes the configuration and verification tasks for an L3VPN extranet overlay service traversing an SRv6 transport network. In the previous two L3VPN examples, both the L3VPN full-mesh and hub-and-spoke service sites belonged to the same entity (company, enterprise, or department), which can be described as an *intranet*. However, communications between different VPNs maybe required, such as to an external intercompany service or shared-service VPN—and usually with limited access to a subset of networks; these VPNs can be referred to as *extranets*. A site can therefore be associated with more than one VPN; that is, it can be associated to both its intranet VPNs and one or more extranet VPNs. As with the L3VPN hub-and-spoke service, communication is achieved through the use of import and export route target values. In addition, export map or import map policies may be used for more advanced extranet access control.

SRv6 L3VPN Extranet Configuration

The extranet example network in Figure 7-8 is based on the previous two L3VPN intranets, where, from the perspective of the L3VPN hub-and-spoke VPN, there is the requirement that the Spoke Site 2 router CE-4 in Metro 2 be able to communicate with a subnet attached to the router CE-1 in the L3VPN full-mesh service in Metro 1. To recap, the CE-1 router is attached to the VRF instance FULL-500-VRF, which is dual-homed to PE-1 and PE-2. The dual-attached CE router CE-1 is set up in a unipath active/standby scenario via the PE routers using BGP local preference, with the active path set to a BGP local preference of 200 and the backup link set to a BGP local preference of 150. BGP PIC Edge has also been configured to improve convergence when the more preferred PE–CE link fails. The SRv6 locator allocations are as follows:

- Networks 10.1.103.128/28 and 10.1.103.240/28 (from CE-1) use the SRv6 locator MAIN with per-CE allocation mode via PE-1 and PE-2.

- Only the subnet 10.1.103.240/28 is to be exported to the VRF instance on router PE-4 for the Spoke Site 2 router CE-4 in Metro 2.

- The VRF instance on router PE-4 for the Spoke Site 2 router CE-4 will therefore import this additional extranet subnet 10.1.103.240/28 into its routing table.

- CE-1 in the L3VPN full-mesh service will learn only the subnet 10.2.104.144/28 from the extranet.

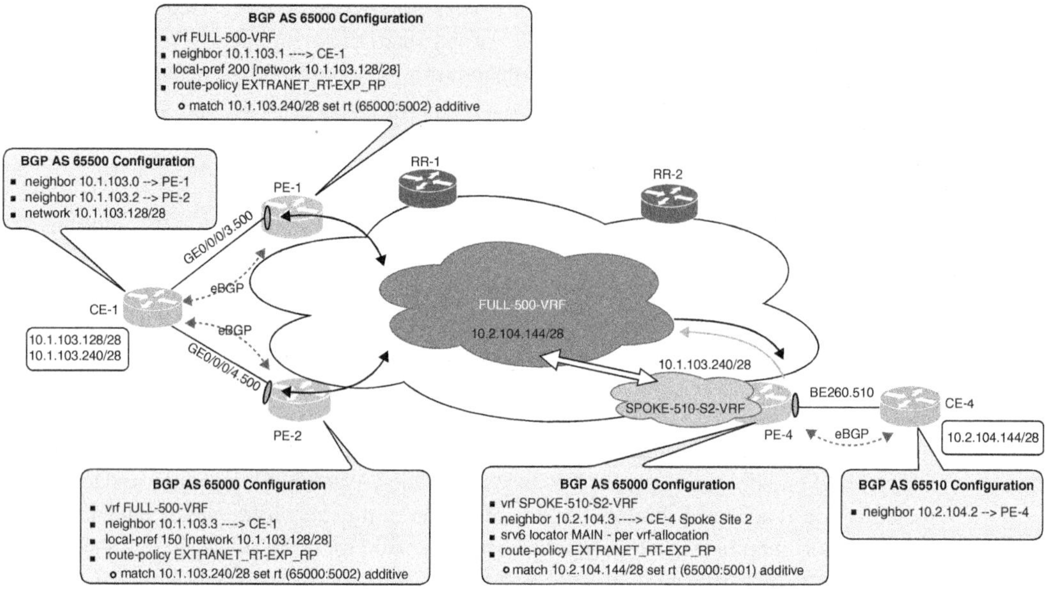

BGP AS 65000 Configuration
- vrf FULL-500-VRF
- neighbor 10.1.103.1 ----> CE-1
- local-pref 200 [network 10.1.103.128/28]
- route-policy EXTRANET_RT-EXP_RP
  - match 10.1.103.240/28 set rt (65000:5002) additive

BGP AS 65500 Configuration
- neighbor 10.1.103.0 --> PE-1
- neighbor 10.1.103.2 --> PE-2
- network 10.1.103.128/28

BGP AS 65000 Configuration
- vrf FULL-500-VRF
- neighbor 10.1.103.3 --> CE-1
- local-pref 150 [network 10.1.103.128/28]
- route-policy EXTRANET_RT-EXP_RP
  - match 10.1.103.240/28 set rt (65000:5002) additive

BGP AS 65000 Configuration
- vrf SPOKE-510-S2-VRF
- neighbor 10.2.104.3 ----> CE-4 Spoke Site 2
- srv6 locator MAIN - per vrf-allocation
- route-policy EXTRANET_RT-EXP_RP
  - match 10.2.104.144/28 set rt (65000:5001) additive

BGP AS 65510 Configuration
- neighbor 10.2.104.2 --> PE-4

Figure 7-8   *SRv6 L3VPN Extranet Configuration Tasks*

The snippet in Config 7-14 illustrates only the relevant L3VPN extranet configurations, where the route policy EXTRANET_RT-EXP_RP matches the 10.1.103.240/28 subnet to be exported and sets the export route target to 65000:5002. Note the usage of additive in the route policy EXTRANET_RT-EXP_RP, which allows the route target to be set in addition to the route target 65000:500 for the subnet 10.1.103.240/28, effectively allowing it to be imported into the other L3VPN full-mesh sites for the VRF instance FULL-500-VRF. Excluding additive would result in route target 65000:500 being replaced with 65000:5002 and the route not being imported in the VRF instance FULL-500-VRF on the other PE routers.

Config 7-14   *SRv6 L3VPN Extranet Additional Configurations on PE-1 and PE-2*

```
!
vrf FULL-500-VRF
 address-family ipv4 unicast
  import route-target
   65000:500
   65000:5001
  !
  export route-policy EXTRANET_RT-EXP_RP(EXTRANET_EXP_PS, 65000, 5002)
  export route-target
   65000:500
  !
 !
!
```

```
prefix-set EXTRANET_EXP_PS
  10.1.103.240/28
end-set
!
route-policy EXTRANET_RT-EXP_RP($PS, $AS, $COM)
  if destination in $PS then
    set extcommunity rt ($AS:$COM) additive
  endif
end-policy
!
```

In Output 7-26, the output of the command **show bgp vpnv4 unicast vrf FULL-500-VRF 10.1.103.240/28** executed on PE-4 in Metro 2 shows that both route targets (65000:500 and 65000:5002) are included with the received subnet 10.1.103.240/28 as a result of the route policy EXTRANET_RT-EXP_RP on both the ingress routers PE-1 and PE-2.

Output 7-26 *SRv6 L3VPN Extranet: BGP VPNv4 RIB for 10.1.103.240/28 on PE-4*

```
RP/0/RP0/CPU0:PE-4#show bgp vpnv4 unicast vrf FULL-500-VRF 10.1.103.240/28
BGP routing table entry for 10.1.103.240/28, Route Distinguisher: 172.19.0.20:2
Versions:
  Process           bRIB/RIB  SendTblVer
  Speaker               967          967
Last Modified: Jun 28 22:01:52.955 for 13:07:43
Paths: (2 available, best #1)
  Advertised to CE update-groups (with more than one peer):
    0.2
  Path #1: Received by speaker 0
 Advertised to CE update-groups (with more than one peer):
    0.2
  65500
    fc00:0:105::1 (metric 61) from fc00:0:207::1 (172.19.0.10)
      Received Label 0xe00d0
      Origin IGP, metric 0, localpref 200, valid, internal, best, group-best,
  import-candidate, imported
      Received Path ID 1, Local Path ID 1, version 961
      Extended community: RT:65000:500 RT:65000:5002
      Originator: 172.19.0.10, Cluster list: 172.19.0.21, 172.19.0.12
      PSID-Type:L3, SubTLV Count:1
       SubTLV:
       T:1(Sid information), Sid:fc00:0:105::, Behavior:61, SS-TLV Count:1
         SubSubTLV:
          T:1(Sid structure):
      Source AFI: VPNv4 Unicast, Source VRF: default, Source Route
  Distinguisher: 172.19.0.10:3
```

```
Path #2: Received by speaker 0
Not advertised to any peer
65500
  fc00:0:106::1 (metric 61) from fc00:0:207::1 (172.19.0.11)
    Received Label 0xe00f0
    Origin IGP, metric 0, localpref 150, valid, internal, backup, add-path,
imported
    Received Path ID 1, Local Path ID 2, version 967
    Extended community: RT:65000:500 RT:65000:5002
    Originator: 172.19.0.11, Cluster list: 172.19.0.21, 172.19.0.12
    PSID-Type:L3, SubTLV Count:1
     SubTLV:
       T:1(Sid information), Sid:fc00:0:106::, Behavior:61, SS-TLV Count:1
       SubSubTLV:
         T:1(Sid structure):
      Source AFI: VPNv4 Unicast, Source VRF: default, Source Route
  Distinguisher: 172.19.0.11:2
RP/0/RP0/CPU0:PE-4#
```

Output 7-27 shows the same command executed again on router PE-4 but this time, the route policy EXTRANET_RT-EXP_RP has additive set only on router PE-2 and removed on the route policy on router PE-1. As a result, that the route 10.1.103.240/28 from PE-1 does not have the route target 65000:500 set, and it is therefore not imported into the VRF instance FULL-500-VRF. There is now only one path available for the route 10.1.103.240/28 via router PE-2.

Output 7-27   *SRv6 L3VPN Extranet: BGP VPNv4 RIB for 10.1.103.240/28 on PE-4*

```
RP/0/RP0/CPU0:PE-4#show bgp vpnv4 unicast vrf FULL-500-VRF 10.1.103.240/28
BGP routing table entry for 10.1.103.240/28, Route Distinguisher: 172.19.0.20:2
Versions:
  Process           bRIB/RIB    SendTblVer
  Speaker              970         970
Last Modified: Jun 29 11:22:05.955 for 00:00:15
Paths: (1 available, best #1)
  Advertised to CE update-groups (with more than one peer):
    0.2
  Path #1: Received by speaker 0
  Advertised to CE update-groups (with more than one peer):
    0.2
65500
  fc00:0:106::1 (metric 61) from fc00:0:207::1 (172.19.0.11)
    Received Label 0xe00f0
    Origin IGP, metric 0, localpref 150, valid, internal, best, group-best,
import-candidate, imported
```

```
      Received Path ID 1, Local Path ID 1, version 970
      Extended community: RT:65000:500 RT:65000:5002
      Originator: 172.19.0.11, Cluster list: 172.19.0.21, 172.19.0.12
      PSID-Type:L3, SubTLV Count:1
       SubTLV:
        T:1(Sid information), Sid:fc00:0:106::, Behavior:61, SS-TLV Count:1
         SubSubTLV:
          T:1(Sid structure):
      Source AFI: VPNv4 Unicast, Source VRF: default, Source Route Distinguisher:
  172.19.0.11:2
RP/0/RP0/CPU0:PE-4#
```

Config 7-15 shows the relevant extranet configurations for router PE-4, where the route policy EXTRANET_RT-EXP_RP matches the 10.2.104.144/28 subnet to be exported and sets the export route target to 65000:5001. In this case, additive is included, as this route is still required to be imported into the hub site VRF instance of the previously configured hub-and-spoke service.

Config 7-15 *SRv6 L3VPN Extranet: Additional Configurations on PE-4*

```
!
vrf SPOKE-510-S2-VRF
 address-family ipv4 unicast
  import route-target
   65000:510
   65000:5002
   !
  export route-policy EXTRANET_RT-EXP_RP(EXTRANET_EXP_PS, 65000, 5001)
  export route-target
   65000:5100
   !
 !
!
prefix-set EXTRANET_EXP_PS
  10.2.104.144/28
end-set
!
route-policy EXTRANET_RT-EXP_RP($PS, $AS, $COM)
  if destination in $PS then
    set extcommunity rt ($AS:$COM) additive
  endif
end-policy
 !
```

These configurations demonstrate that a fundamental L3VPN extranet service using SRv6 for transport shares similarities with service configurations that rely on MPLS or SR-MPLS as the underlying transport mechanism.

SRv6 L3VPN Extranet Verification

Now let's discuss some basic commands used to verify the newly provisioned L3VPN extranet service. Figure 7-9 provides an overview of the commands used to verify this L3VPN extranet service. Router CE-4 (Spoke Site 2) is attached to router PE-4 and accesses the VRF instance SPOKE-510-S2-VRF (hub-and-spoke service) and requires access to an extranet service subnet 10.1.103.240/28, which is attached to the CE-1 router. The CE-1 router is attached to the VRF instance FULL-500-VRF, dual-homed to PE-1 and PE-2, and originates the extranet subnet 10.1.103.240/28 with an additional route target community to allow importation into the VRF instance SPOKE-510-S2-VRF at PE-4.

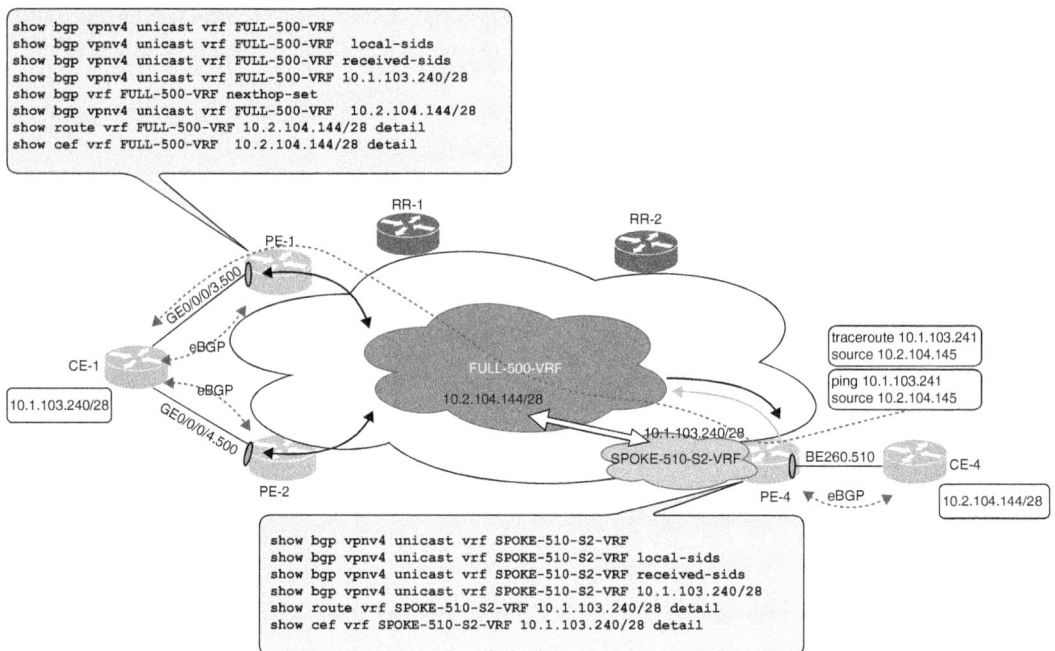

```
show bgp vpnv4 unicast vrf FULL-500-VRF
show bgp vpnv4 unicast vrf FULL-500-VRF  local-sids
show bgp vpnv4 unicast vrf FULL-500-VRF received-sids
show bgp vpnv4 unicast vrf FULL-500-VRF 10.1.103.240/28
show bgp vrf FULL-500-VRF nexthop-set
show bgp vpnv4 unicast vrf FULL-500-VRF  10.2.104.144/28
show route vrf FULL-500-VRF 10.2.104.144/28 detail
show cef vrf FULL-500-VRF  10.2.104.144/28 detail
```

```
traceroute 10.1.103.241
source 10.2.104.145
```

```
ping 10.1.103.241
source 10.2.104.145
```

```
show bgp vpnv4 unicast vrf SPOKE-510-S2-VRF
show bgp vpnv4 unicast vrf SPOKE-510-S2-VRF local-sids
show bgp vpnv4 unicast vrf SPOKE-510-S2-VRF received-sids
show bgp vpnv4 unicast vrf SPOKE-510-S2-VRF 10.1.103.240/28
show route vrf SPOKE-510-S2-VRF 10.1.103.240/28 detail
show cef vrf SPOKE-510-S2-VRF 10.1.103.240/28 detail
```

Figure 7-9　*SRv6 L3VPN Extranet Verification Tasks*

The subnet 10.1.103.240/28 from the local router CE-1 and subnet 10.2.104.144/28 from CE-4 are the focus of the following verifications:

- **Subnet 10.1.103.240/28 (CE-1):** This is the first path from external next hop 10.1.103.1 (CE-1) with BGP local preference 200.

- **Subnet 10.1.103.240/28 (CE-1):** This is the second path from next hop fc00:0:106::1 (PE-2) with BGP local preference 150.

■ **Subnet 10.2.104.144/28 (CE-4):** This is the single path from next hop fc00:0:206::1 (PE-4).

Output 7-28 shows the command **show bgp vpnv4 unicast vrf FULL-500-VRF** executed on router PE-1 with the subnets of interest highlighted for this extranet service.

Output 7-28   *SRv6 L3VPN Extranet: BGP VPNv4 RIB on PE-1*

```
RP/0/RP0/CPU0:PE-1#show bgp vpnv4 unicast vrf FULL-500-VRF
BGP router identifier 172.19.0.10, local AS number 65000
<snip>
Status codes: s suppressed, d damped, h history, * valid, > best
              i - internal, r RIB-failure, S stale, N Nexthop-discard
Origin codes: i - IGP, e - EGP, ? - incomplete
   Network            Next Hop            Metric LocPrf Weight Path
Route Distinguisher: 172.19.0.10:3 (default for vrf FULL-500-VRF)
Route Distinguisher Version: 881
*> 10.1.103.128/28    10.1.103.1               0    200    0 65500 i
*  i                  fc00:0:106::1            0    150    0 65500 i
*>i10.1.103.144/28    fc00:0:106::1            0    100    0 65500 i
*> 10.1.103.240/28    10.1.103.1               0    200    0 65500 i
*  i                  fc00:0:106::1            0    150    0 65500 i
*>i10.2.103.128/28    fc00:0:205::1            0    200    0 65500 i
*  i                  fc00:0:206::1            0    150    0 65500 i
*>i10.2.103.144/28    fc00:0:206::1            0    100    0 65500 i
*>i10.2.104.144/28    fc00:0:206::1            0    100    0 65510 i

Processed 6 prefixes, 9 paths
RP/0/RP0/CPU0:PE-1#
```

Details of the local SIDs, received SIDs, allocation mode, and locator information for all the subnets in the VRF instance FULL-500-VRF are displayed in Output 7-29 and Output 7-30.

The subnet of interest, 10.1.103.240/28 (CE-1 extranet service), is allocated the SID fc00:0:105:e00d:: with per-ce allocation mode from the SRv6 locator MAIN on router PE-1, as highlighted in Output 7-29.

Output 7-29   *SRv6 L3VPN Extranet: BGP VPNv4 RIB Local SIDs on PE-1*

```
RP/0/RP0/CPU0:PE-1#show bgp vpnv4 unicast vrf FULL-500-VRF local-sids
BGP router identifier 172.19.0.10, local AS number 65000
<snip>
   Network            Local Sid                       Alloc mode   Locator
Route Distinguisher: 172.19.0.10:3 (default for vrf FULL-500-VRF)
Route Distinguisher Version: 881
```

```
*> 10.1.103.128/28      fc00:0:105:e00d::                           per-ce      MAIN
* i                     fc00:0:105:e00d::                           per-ce      MAIN
*>i10.1.103.144/28      NO SRv6 Sid                                 -           -
*> 10.1.103.240/28      fc00:0:105:e00d::                           per-ce      MAIN
* i                     fc00:0:105:e00d::                           per-ce      MAIN
*>i10.2.103.128/28      NO SRv6 Sid                                 -           -
* i                     NO SRv6 Sid                                 -           -
*>i10.2.103.144/28      NO SRv6 Sid                                 -           -
*>i10.2.104.144/28      NO SRv6 Sid                                 -           -


Processed 6 prefixes, 9 paths
RP/0/RP0/CPU0:PE-1#
```

Output 7-30 shows the output of the command **show bgp vpnv4 unicast vrf FULL-500-VRF received-sids**, where the spoke site subnet 10.2.104.144/28 from CE-4 has been allocated the SID fc00:0:206:e010:: by PE-4. Note that the output also displays 10.1.103.240/28 from CE-1 with the allocated SID fc00:0:106:e00f:: from PE-2. This is due to the BGP PIC Edge configuration mentioned previously and is the backup path for the subnet 10.1.103.240/28.

Output 7-30   *SRv6 L3VPN Extranet: BGP VPNv4 RIB Received SIDs on PE-1*

```
RP/0/RP0/CPU0:PE-1#show bgp vpnv4 unicast vrf FULL-500-VRF received-sids
BGP router identifier 172.19.0.10, local AS number 65000
<snip>
   Network               Next Hop                    Received Sid
Route Distinguisher: 172.19.0.10:3 (default for vrf FULL-500-VRF)
Route Distinguisher Version: 881
*> 10.1.103.128/28      10.1.103.1                   NO SRv6 Sid
* i                     fc00:0:106::1                fc00:0:106:e00f::
*>i10.1.103.144/28      fc00:0:106::1                fc00:1:106:e004::
*> 10.1.103.240/28      10.1.103.1                   NO SRv6 Sid
* i                     fc00:0:106::1                fc00:0:106:e00f::
*>i10.2.103.128/28      fc00:0:205::1                fc00:0:205:e00d::
* i                     fc00:0:206::1                fc00:0:206:e00f::
*>i10.2.103.144/28      fc00:0:206::1                fc00:1:206:e004::
*>i10.2.104.144/28      fc00:0:206::1                fc00:0:206:e010::


Processed 6 prefixes, 9 paths
RP/0/RP0/CPU0:PE-1#
```

To more carefully analyze the BGP route 10.1.103.240/28, which is the extranet subnet to be imported into Spoke Site 2 that originated from router CE-1, we use the command **show bgp vpnv4 unicast vrf FULL-500-VRF 10.1.103.240/28**, which displays the following relevant information (see in Output 7-31):

■ **Paths: (2 available, best #1):** The output confirms that the subnet is available across two paths, and the first path is the preferred one.

  ■ **Path #1:**

    □ **SRv6-VPN SID: fc00:0:105:e00d::/64:** This is the allocated SID for the extranet route learned from router CE-1 (and is also verified in Output 7-29).

    □ **Gateway Array ID: 1, Resilient per-CE nexthop set ID: 1:** This is verification that per-CE next hop allocation mode is in use, and the next hop IP address is 10.1.103.1 on CE-1, as verified with the command **show bgp vrf FULL-500-VRF nexthop-set** in Output 7-32.

    □ **10.1.103.1 from 10.1.103.1 (172.19.0.13):** CE-1 is the eBGP next hop 10.1.103.1 with the BGP router ID 172.19.0.13.

    □ **Extended community: RT:65000:500 RT:65000:5002:** Both route targets (full-mesh RT 65000:500 and extranet RT 65000:5002) are included in the BGP route as configured in VRF instance FULL-500-VRF and applied via the export route policy EXTRANET_RT-EXP_RP.

  ■ **Path #2:**

    □ **fc00:0:106::1 (metric 21) from fc00:0:107::1 (172.19.0.11):** PE-2 is the BGP next hop fc00:0:106::1 with the BGP router ID 172.19.0.11.

    □ **Received Label 0xe00f0:** The received label is 0xe00f0, and the most significant 16 bits of this label is the SRv6 uSID 0xe00f. Output 7-30 confirms that this uSID matches the SRv6 uSID allocated on router PE-2

    □ **Sid:fc00:0:106:::** This is the PE-2 remote node SID from the configured SRv6 locator MAIN.

    □ **Behavior:61:** The endpoint behavior is End.DX4 with NEXT-CSID (0x003D) because of the configuration srv6-alloc-mode per-ce, which has similar behavior to the per-CE label allocation mode.

Output 7-31 *SRv6 L3VPN Extranet: BGP VPNv4 RIB for 10.1.103.240/28 on PE-1*

```
RP/0/RP0/CPU0:PE-1#show bgp vpnv4 unicast vrf FULL-500-VRF 10.1.103.240/28
BGP routing table entry for 10.1.103.240/28, Route Distinguisher: 172.19.0.10:3
Versions:
  Process           bRIB/RIB   SendTblVer
  Speaker              875          875
```

```
      SRv6-VPN SID: fc00:0:105:e00d::/64
      Gateway Array ID: 1, Resilient per-CE nexthop set ID: 1
Last Modified: Jun 30 05:35:45.735 for 22:32:39
Paths: (2 available, best #1)
  Advertised to peers (in unique update groups):
    fc00:0:107::1
  Path #1: Received by speaker 0
  Advertised to peers (in unique update groups):
    fc00:0:107::1
  65500
    10.1.103.1 from 10.1.103.1 (172.19.0.13)
      Origin IGP, metric 0, localpref 200, valid, external, best, group-best,
  import-candidate
      Received Path ID 0, Local Path ID 1, version 871
      Extended community: RT:65000:500 RT:65000:5002
  Path #2: Received by speaker 0
  Not advertised to any peer
  65500
    fc00:0:106::1 (metric 21) from fc00:0:107::1 (172.19.0.11)
      Received Label 0xe00f0
      Origin IGP, metric 0, localpref 150, valid, internal, backup, add-path,
  imported
      Received Path ID 0, Local Path ID 2, version 875
      Extended community: RT:65000:500 RT:65000:5002
      Originator: 172.19.0.11, Cluster list: 172.19.0.12
      PSID-Type:L3, SubTLV Count:1
       SubTLV:
        T:1(Sid information), Sid:fc00:0:106::, Behavior:61, SS-TLV Count:1
         SubSubTLV:
          T:1(Sid structure):
      Source AFI: VPNv4 Unicast, Source VRF: default, Source Route
  Distinguisher: 172.19.0.11:2
RP/0/RP0/CPU0:PE-1#
```

The VRF instance HUB-500-VRF BGP next hop set verification from Output 7-32 verifies that the locally allocated uSID 0xe00d is using the endpoint behavior End.DX4 as
a result of the SRv6 allocation mode configured as alloc mode per-ce. The next hop IP
address used to forward egress traffic toward the router CE-1 is 10.1.103.1, which is the
link address configured on router CE-1.

Output 7-32 *SRv6 L3VPN Extranet: BGP Next Hop Set on PE-1*

```
RP/0/RP0/CPU0:PE-1#show bgp vrf FULL-500-VRF nexthop-set

Resilient per-CE nexthop set, ID 1
Number of nexthops 1, Label 0, Flags 0x2100
SRv6-VPN SID: fc00:0:105:e00d::/64
Format: 2
Nexthops:
10.1.103.1
Reference count 2,
RP/0/RP0/CPU0:PE-1#
```

The next route to be examined is the Spoke Site 2 CE-4 subnet 10.2.104.144/28 originated from the VRF instance SPOKE-510-S2-VRF on PE-4 (see Output 7-33). Because the router CE-4 is single attached to router PE-4, there is only a single path available. The relevant details for this route are as follows:

- Path #1:

  - **fc00:0:206::1 (metric 61) from fc00:0:107::1 (172.19.0.20):** PE-4 is the BGP next hop fc00:0:206::1 with the BGP router ID 172.19.0.20.

  - **Received Label 0xe0100:** The received label is 0xe0100, and the most significant 16 bits of this label is the SRv6 uSID 0xe010. Output 7-30 confirms that this label matches the SRv6 SID allocated on router PE-4.

  - **Extended community: RT:65000:5001 RT:65000:5100:** Both route targets; hub-and-spoke service route target 65000:5100 and the extranet service route target 65000:5001 are included in the BGP route as configured in the VRF instance SPOKE-510-S2-VRF and applied via the export route policy **EXTRANET_ RT-EXP_RP** on router PE-4.

  - **Sid:fc00:0:206:::** This is the PE-4 remote node SID from the configured SRv6 locator MAIN.

  - **Behavior:63:** The endpoint behavior is End.DT4 with NEXT-CSID (0x003F) because of the configuration srv6-alloc-mode per-vrf.

Output 7-33 *SRv6 L3VPN Extranet: BGP VPNv4 RIB for 10.2.104.144/28 on PE-1*

```
RP/0/RP0/CPU0:PE-1#show bgp vpnv4 unicast vrf FULL-500-VRF  10.2.104.144/28
BGP routing table entry for 10.2.104.144/28, Route Distinguisher: 172.19.0.10:3
<snip>
Paths: (1 available, best #1)
  Not advertised to any peer
```

```
Path #1: Received by speaker 0
Not advertised to any peer
65510
  fc00:0:206::1 (metric 61) from fc00:0:107::1 (172.19.0.20)
    Received Label 0xe0100
    Origin IGP, metric 0, localpref 100, valid, internal, best, group-best,
import-candidate, imported
    Received Path ID 0, Local Path ID 1, version 881
    Extended community: RT:65000:5001 RT:65000:5100
    Originator: 172.19.0.20, Cluster list: 172.19.0.12, 172.19.0.21
    PSID-Type:L3, SubTLV Count:1
    SubTLV:
      T:1(Sid information), Sid:fc00:0:206::, Behavior:63, SS-TLV Count:1
      SubSubTLV:
       T:1(Sid structure):
    Source AFI: VPNv4 Unicast, Source VRF: default, Source Route
Distinguisher: 65000:51002
RP/0/RP0/CPU0:PE-1#
```

Next to be verified is the route information on router PE-1 for the subnet 10.2.104.144/28 from the Spoke Site 2 router CE-4 to confirm the relevant RIB details of this learned subnet. The output of the command **show route vrf FULL-500-VRF 10.2.104.144/28 detail** in Output 7-34 shows the following relevant information for this route:

- **fc00:0:206::1, from fc00:0:107::1:** PE-4 is the BGP next hop fc00:0:206::1.

  - **SRv6 Headend: H.Encaps.Red [f3216], SID-list {fc00:0:206::e010::}:** This indicates H.Encaps with reduced encapsulation, where the first SID is copied into the Destination Address field of the outer IPv6 header.

Output 7-34 *SRv6 L3VPN Extranet: RIB Details for 10.2.104.144/28 on PE-1*

```
RP/0/RP0/CPU0:PE-1#show route vrf FULL-500-VRF 10.2.104.144/28 detail

Routing entry for 10.2.104.144/28
  Known via "bgp 65000", distance 200, metric 0
  Tag 65510, type internal
  Installed Jun 30 05:38:53.062 for 23:20:36
  Routing Descriptor Blocks
    fc00:0:206::1, from fc00:0:107::1
      Nexthop in Vrf: "default", Table: "default", IPv6 Unicast, Table Id:
0xe0800000
      Route metric is 0
```

```
      Label: None
      Tunnel ID: None
      Binding Label: None
      Extended communities count: 0
      Source RD attributes: 0x0000:65000:51002
      NHID:0x0(Ref:0)
      SRv6 Headend: H.Encaps.Red [f3216], SID-list {fc00:0:206:e010::}
   Route version is 0x1 (1)
<snip>
RP/0/RP0/CPU0:PE-1#
```

The FIB information displayed via the command **show cef vrf FULL-500-VRF 10.2.104.144/28 detail** in Output 7-35 shows the router PE-1 FIB output for the target subnet 10.2.104.144/28. The relevant information from this output is as follows:

- **via fc00:0:206::/128:** Router PE-4 is the BGP next hop fc00:0:206::1.

  - **next hop fc00:0:206::/128 via fc00:0:200::/40:** The BGP next hop is learned via the summarized network for the IS-IS Metro 2 subnet in the global routing table.

  - **SRv6 H.Encaps.Red SID-list {fc00:0:206:e010::}:** This indicates H.Encaps with reduced encapsulation, where the first SID is copied into the Destination Address field of the outer IPv6 header.

    The egress traffic to the destination subnet on CE-4 (10.2.104.144/28) will be load balanced across the PE-1 core-facing interfaces, as shown here:

    - 0   Y   **GigabitEthernet0/0/0/0   fe80::42:acff:fe15:7f03**

    - 1   Y   **GigabitEthernet0/0/0/2   fe80::42:acff:fe15:8002**

Output 7-35 *SRv6 L3VPN Extranet: FIB Details for 10.2.104.144/28 on PE-1*

```
RP/0/RP0/CPU0:PE-1#show cef vrf FULL-500-VRF  10.2.104.144/28 detail
10.2.104.144/28, version 302, SRv6 Headend, internal 0x5000001 0x30 (ptr 0x871be368)
  [1], 0x0 (0x0), 0x0 (0x899f3c28)
 Updated Jun 30 05:38:53.064
 Prefix Len 28, traffic index 0, precedence n/a, priority 3
  gateway array (0x89cf4700) reference count 2, flags 0x2010, source rib (7), 0
  backups
                [1 type 3 flags 0x48441 (0x87e95448) ext 0x0 (0x0)]
  LW-LDI[type=0, refc=0, ptr=0x0, sh-ldi=0x0]
  gateway array update type-time 5 Jun 26 22:58:12.589
 LDI Update time Jun 22 07:08:05.958
```

```
 Level 1 - Load distribution: 0
 [0] via fc00:0:206::/128, recursive


  via fc00:0:206::/128, 16 dependencies, recursive [flags 0x6000]
   path-idx 0 NHID 0x0 [0x86fdfba0 0x0]
   next hop VRF - 'default', table - 0xe0800000
   next hop fc00:0:206::/128 via fc00:0:200::/40
   SRv6 H.Encaps.Red SID-list {fc00:0:206:e010::}


  Load distribution: 0 1 (refcount 1)


  Hash  OK  Interface                Address
  0     Y   GigabitEthernet0/0/0/0   fe80::42:acff:fe15:7f03
  1     Y   GigabitEthernet0/0/0/2   fe80::42:acff:fe15:8002

RP/0/RP0/CPU0:PE-1#
```

The Spoke Site 2 router CE-4 access to the extranet service subnet 10.1.103.240/28 is
described in the following outputs. Output 7-36 from PE-4 displays this subnet learned
from Metro 1 with next hops from PE-1 and from PE-2. The subnet 10.2.104.144/28 from
router CE-4 is learned via the PE–CE eBGP neighborship with a next hop of 10.2.104.3.
Be aware that the following outputs are similar to those executed on the router PE-1; they
are repeated here in order to provide the service verification view from router CE-4's
perspective.

Output 7-36   *SRv6 L3VPN Extranet: BGP VPNv4 RIB on PE-4*

```
RP/0/RP0/CPU0:PE-4#show bgp vpnv4 unicast vrf SPOKE-510-S2-VRF
BGP router identifier 172.19.0.20, local AS number 65000
<snip>
   Network          Next Hop            Metric LocPrf Weight Path
Route Distinguisher: 65000:51002 (default for vrf SPOKE-510-S2-VRF)
Route Distinguisher Version: 991
*>i0.0.0.0/0          fc00:0:105::1                200      0 65510 i
* i                   fc00:0:106::1                150      0 65510 i
*>i10.1.103.240/28    fc00:0:105::1           0   200      0 65500 i
* i                   fc00:0:106::1           0   150      0 65500 i
*>i10.1.104.128/28    fc00:0:105::1           0   200      0 65510 i
* i                   fc00:0:106::1           0   150      0 65510 i
*> 10.2.104.144/28    10.2.104.3              0            0 65510 i


Processed 4 prefixes, 7 paths
RP/0/RP0/CPU0:PE-4#
```

Details of the local SIDs, received SIDs, allocation mode, and locator information for the subnets in VRF instance SPOKE-510-S2-VRF are shown in Output 7-37 and Output 7-38.

The local subnet of interest is 10.2.104.140/28 from the router CE-4, which is allocated the SID fc00:0:206:e010:: with per-vrf allocation mode from the SRv6 locator MAIN, displayed in Output 7-37.

Output 7-37   *SRv6 L3VPN Extranet: BGP VPNv4 RIB Local SIDs on PE-4*

```
RP/0/RP0/CPU0:PE-4#show bgp vpnv4 unicast vrf SPOKE-510-S2-VRF local-sids
BGP router identifier 172.19.0.20, local AS number 65000
<snip>
   Network            Local Sid                              Alloc mode   Locator
Route Distinguisher: 65000:51002 (default for vrf SPOKE-510-S2-VRF)
Route Distinguisher Version: 991
*>i0.0.0.0/0          NO SRv6 Sid                            -            -
* i                  NO SRv6 Sid                            -            -
*>i10.1.103.240/28    NO SRv6 Sid                            -            -
* i                  NO SRv6 Sid                            -            -
*>i10.1.104.128/28    NO SRv6 Sid                            -            -
* i                  NO SRv6 Sid                            -            -
*> 10.2.104.144/28    fc00:0:206:e010::                      per-vrf      MAIN


Processed 4 prefixes, 7 paths
```

And in Output 7-38, the extranet subnet 10.1.103.240/28 from router CE-1 has been allocated the SIDs fc00:0:105:e00d:: by PE-1 and fc00:0:106:e00f:: by PE-2.

Output 7-38   *SRv6 L3VPN Extranet: BGP VPNv4 RIB Received SIDs on PE-4*

```
RP/0/RP0/CPU0:PE-4#show bgp vpnv4 unicast vrf SPOKE-510-S2-VRF received-sids
BGP router identifier 172.19.0.20, local AS number 65000
<snip>
   Network            Next Hop               Received Sid
Route Distinguisher: 65000:51002 (default for vrf SPOKE-510-S2-VRF)
Route Distinguisher Version: 991
*>i0.0.0.0/0          fc00:0:105::1          fc00:0:105:e00e::
* i                  fc00:0:106::1          fc00:0:106:e010::
*>i10.1.103.240/28    fc00:0:105::1          fc00:0:105:e00d::
* i                  fc00:0:106::1          fc00:0:106:e00f::
*>i10.1.104.128/28    fc00:0:105::1          fc00:0:105:e00e::
* i                  fc00:0:106::1          fc00:0:106:e010::
*> 10.2.104.144/28    10.2.104.3             NO SRv6 Sid


Processed 4 prefixes, 7 paths
RP/0/RP0/CPU0:PE-4#
```

We can view the BGP route 10.1.103.240/28 (the imported extranet subnet) that originated from the router CE-1 in more detail on router PE-4 with the command **show bgp vpnv4 unicast vrf SPOKE-510-S2-VRF 10.1.103.240/28**. Output 7-39 shows that it provides the following relevant information:

■ **Paths: (2 available, best #1):** The output confirms that the subnet is available across two paths, and the first path is the preferred one due to BGP local preference 200.

  ■ **Path #1:**

    □ **fc00:0:105::1 (metric 61) from fc00:0:207::1 (172.19.0.10):** PE-1 is the BGP next hop fc00:0:105::1 with the BGP router ID 172.19.0.10.

    □ **Received Label 0xe00d0:** The received label is 0xe00d0, and the most significant 16 bits of this label is the SRv6 uSID 0xe00d. Output 7-38 confirms that this SRv6 SID matches the local originating SID on router PE-1.

    □ **Extended community: RT:65000:500 RT:65000:5002:** Both route targets (full-mesh route target 65000:500 and extranet route target 65000:5002) are included in the BGP route as configured in VRF instance FULL-500-VRF and applied via the export route policy EXTRANET_RT-EXP_RP on router PE-1.

    □ **Sid:fc00:0:105:::** This is the PE-1 remote node SID from the configured SRv6 locator MAIN.

    □ **Behavior:61:** The endpoint behavior is End.DX4 with NEXT-CSID (0x003D) because of the configuration srv6-alloc-mode per-ce, which has similar behavior to the per-CE label allocation mode.

  ■ **Path #2:**

    □ **fc00:0:106::1 (metric 61) from fc00:0:207::1 (172.19.0.11):** PE-2 is the BGP next hop fc00:0:106::1 with the BGP router ID 172.19.0.11.

    □ **Received Label 0xe00f0:** The received label is 0xe00f0, and the most significant 16 bits of this label is the SRv6 uSID 0xe00f. Output 7-38 confirms that this SRv6 uSID matches the local originating SID on router PE-2.

    □ **Extended community: RT:65000:500 RT:65000:5002:** Both route targets (full-mesh route target 65000:500 and extranet route target 65000:5002) are included in the BGP route as configured in VRF instance FULL-500-VRF and applied via the export route policy EXTRANET_RT-EXP_RP on router PE-2.

    □ **Sid:fc00:0:106:::** This is the PE-2 remote node SID (uN) from the configured SRv6 locator MAIN.

    □ **Behavior:61:** The endpoint behavior is End.DX4 with NEXT-CSID (0x003D) because of the configuration srv6-alloc-mode per-ce, which has similar behavior to the per-CE label allocation mode.

Output 7-39 *SRv6 L3VPN Extranet: BGP VPNv4 RIB for 10.1.103.240/28 on PE-4*

```
RP/0/RP0/CPU0:PE-4#show bgp vpnv4 unicast vrf SPOKE-510-S2-VRF 10.1.103.240/28
BGP routing table entry for 10.1.103.240/28, Route Distinguisher: 65000:51002
Versions:
  Process           bRIB/RIB  SendTblVer
  Speaker                986         986
Last Modified: Jun 30 05:35:44.955 for 23:28:37
Paths: (2 available, best #1)
  Not advertised to any peer
  Path #1: Received by speaker 0
  Not advertised to any peer
  65500
    fc00:0:105::1 (metric 61) from fc00:0:207::1 (172.19.0.10)
      Received Label 0xe00d0
      Origin IGP, metric 0, localpref 200, valid, internal, best, group-best,
  import-candidate, imported
      Received Path ID 1, Local Path ID 1, version 980
      Extended community: RT:65000:500 RT:65000:5002
      Originator: 172.19.0.10, Cluster list: 172.19.0.21, 172.19.0.12
      PSID-Type:L3, SubTLV Count:1
       SubTLV:
        T:1(Sid information), Sid:fc00:0:105::, Behavior:61, SS-TLV Count:1
          SubSubTLV:
           T:1(Sid structure):
      Source AFI: VPNv4 Unicast, Source VRF: default, Source Route
  Distinguisher: 172.19.0.10:3
  Path #2: Received by speaker 0
  Not advertised to any peer
  65500
    fc00:0:106::1 (metric 61) from fc00:0:207::1 (172.19.0.11)
      Received Label 0xe00f0
      Origin IGP, metric 0, localpref 150, valid, internal, backup, add-path,
  imported
      Received Path ID 1, Local Path ID 4, version 986
      Extended community: RT:65000:500 RT:65000:5002
      Originator: 172.19.0.11, Cluster list: 172.19.0.21, 172.19.0.12
      PSID-Type:L3, SubTLV Count:1
       SubTLV:
        T:1(Sid information), Sid:fc00:0:106::, Behavior:61, SS-TLV Count:1
          SubSubTLV:
           T:1(Sid structure):
      Source AFI: VPNv4 Unicast, Source VRF: default, Source Route
  Distinguisher: 172.19.0.11:2
RP/0/RP0/CPU0:PE-4#
```

Verification of the extranet subnet 10.1.103.240/28 on router PE-4 via the command **show route vrf SPOKE-510-S2-VRF 10.1.103.240/28 detail** in Output 7-40 shows that this route has two paths, one via PE-1 and the other via PE-2. These are the relevant details:

■ **fc00:0:105::1, from fc00:0:207::1:** PE-1 is the active path, with BGP next hop fc00:0:105::1.

   ■ **SRv6 Headend: H.Encaps.Red [f3216], SID-list {fc00:0:105:e00d::}:** This indicates H.Encaps with reduced encapsulation, where the first SID is copied into the Destination Address field of the outer IPv6 header.

■ **fc00:0:106::1, from fc00:0:207::1, BGP backup path:** PE-2 is the backup path with BGP next hop fc00:0:106::1.

   ■ **SRv6 Headend: H.Encaps.Red [f3216], SID-list {fc00:0:106:e00f::}:** This indicates H.Encaps with reduced encapsulation, where the first SID is copied into the Destination Address field of the outer IPv6 header.

Output 7-40   *SRv6 L3VPN Extranet: RIB Details for 10.1.103.240/28 on PE-4*

```
RP/0/RP0/CPU0:PE-4#show route vrf SPOKE-510-S2-VRF 10.1.103.240/28 detail

Routing entry for 10.1.103.240/28
  Known via "bgp 65000", distance 200, metric 0
  Tag 65500
  Number of pic paths 1 , type internal
  Installed Jun 30 05:35:45.326 for 23:29:21
  Routing Descriptor Blocks
    fc00:0:105::1, from fc00:0:207::1
      Nexthop in Vrf: "default", Table: "default", IPv6 Unicast, Table Id:
0xe0800000
      Route metric is 0
      Label: None
      Tunnel ID: None
      Binding Label: None
      Extended communities count: 0
      Source RD attributes: 0x0001:44051:655363
      NHID:0x0(Ref:0)
      SRv6 Headend: H.Encaps.Red [f3216], SID-list {fc00:0:105:e00d::}
    fc00:0:106::1, from fc00:0:207::1, BGP backup path
      Nexthop in Vrf: "default", Table: "default", IPv6 Unicast, Table Id:
0xe0800000
      Route metric is 0
      Label: None
      Tunnel ID: None
      Binding Label: None
```

```
      Extended communities count: 0
      Source RD attributes: 0x0001:44051:720898
      NHID:0x0(Ref:0)
      SRv6 Headend: H.Encaps.Red [f3216], SID-list {fc00:0:106:e00f::}
  Route version is 0x14 (20)
<snip>
RP/0/RP0/CPU0:PE-4#
```

The CEF (FIB) information displayed via the command **show cef vrf SPOKE-510-S2-VRF 10.1.103.240/28 detail** in Output 7-41 displays the router PE-4 FIB output for the target extranet subnet 10.1.103.240/28. The relevant information from this output is as follows:

■ **via fc00:0:105::/128:** Router PE-1 is the active BGP path via next hop fc00:0:105::1.

   ■ **next hop fc00:0:105::/128 via fc00:0:100::/40:** The BGP next hop is learned via the summarized network for the IS-IS Metro 1 subnet in the global routing table.

   ■ **SRv6 H.Encaps.Red SID-list {fc00:0:105:e00d::}:** This indicates H.Encaps with reduced encapsulation, where the first SID is copied into the Destination Address field of the outer IPv6 header.

   The egress traffic to the destination subnet on CE-1 10.1.103.240/28 will be load balanced across the PE-4 core-facing interfaces, as shown here:

   □ **0   Y   GigabitEthernet0/0/0/0   fe80::42:acff:fe15:6902**

   □ **1   Y   GigabitEthernet0/0/0/2   fe80::42:acff:fe15:6803**

■ **via fc00:0:106::/128:** Router PE-2 is the backup BGP path via the next hop fc00:0:106::1.

   ■ **next hop fc00:0:106::/128 via fc00:0:100::/40:** The BGP next hop is learned via the summarized network for the IS-IS Metro 1 subnet in the global routing table.

   ■ **SRv6 H.Encaps.Red SID-list {fc00:0:106:e00f::}:** This indicates H.Encaps with reduced encapsulation, where the first SID is copied into the Destination Address field of the outer IPv6 header.

Output 7-41   *SRv6 L3VPN Extranet: FIB Details for 10.1.103.240/28 on PE-4*

```
RP/0/RP0/CPU0:PE-4#show cef vrf SPOKE-510-S2-VRF 10.1.103.240/28 detail

10.1.103.240/28, version 86, SRv6 Headend, internal 0x5000001 0x30 (ptr 0x872d9108)
  [1], 0x0 (0x0), 0x0 (0x89a7ccb0)
 Updated Jun 30 05:35:45.329
 Prefix Len 28, traffic index 0, precedence n/a, priority 3
  gateway array (0x89ea0278) reference count 4, flags 0x102010, source rib (7), 0
  backups
```

```
                    [1 type 3 flags 0x48441 (0x87874848) ext 0x0 (0x0)]
  LW-LDI[type=0, refc=0, ptr=0x0, sh-ldi=0x0]
  gateway array update type-time 1 Jun 12 12:28:37.766
 LDI Update time Jun 12 12:28:37.766


  Level 1 - Load distribution: 0
  [0] via fc00:0:105::/128, recursive

  via fc00:0:105::/128, 17 dependencies, recursive [flags 0x6000]
   path-idx 0 NHID 0x0 [0x870f5898 0x0]
   next hop VRF - 'default', table - 0xe0800000
   next hop fc00:0:105::/128 via fc00:0:100::/40
   SRv6 H.Encaps.Red SID-list {fc00:0:105:e00d::}


   Load distribution: 0 1  (refcount 1)

   Hash  OK  Interface            Address
   0     Y   GigabitEthernet0/0/0/0   fe80::42:acff:fe15:6902
   1     Y   GigabitEthernet0/0/0/2   fe80::42:acff:fe15:6802

  via fc00:0:106::/128, 17 dependencies, recursive, backup [flags 0x6100]
   path-idx 1 NHID 0x0 [0x870f5898 0x0]
   next hop VRF - 'default', table - 0xe0800000
   next hop fc00:0:106::/128 via fc00:0:100::/40
   SRv6 H.Encaps.Red SID-list {fc00:0:106:e00f::}

RP/0/RP0/CPU0:PE-4#
```

The ICMP ping in Output 7-42 confirms that the extranet service on router CE-1 is reachable from the spoke site router CE-4.

Output 7-42 *SRv6 L3VPN Extranet: Ping Verification of Extranet Service IP 10.1.103.241 on CE-4*

```
RP/0/RP0/CPU0:CE-4#ping 10.1.103.241 source 10.2.104.145

Type escape sequence to abort.
Sending 5, 100-byte ICMP Echos to 10.1.103.241 timeout is 2 seconds:
!!!!!
Success rate is 100 percent (5/5), round-trip min/avg/max = 8/9/11 ms
RP/0/RP0/CPU0:CE-4#
```

The traceroute from the loopback interface IP 10.2.104.145/32 on CE-4 to the loopback interface IP 10.1.103.241/32 on CE-1 shown in Output 7-43 confirms that the extranet service on router CE-1 is reachable from the spoke site router CE-4 and that the expected path is via the PE-1–CE-1 link 10.1.103.0/31.

Output 7-43   *SRv6 L3VPN Extranet: Traceroute Verification of Extranet Service IP 10.1.103.241 on CE-4*

```
RP/0/RP0/CPU0:CE-4#traceroute 10.1.103.241 source 10.2.104.145


Type escape sequence to abort.
Tracing the route to 10.1.103.241

 1  10.2.104.2 2 msec  1 msec  1 msec ←---------Spoke-Site VRF PE-4
 2  10.1.103.0 9 msec  8 msec  8 msec ←--------Hub-Site VRF PE-1
 3  10.1.103.1 10 msec  *  10 msec ←-----------Hub-Site VRF CE-1
RP/0/RP0/CPU0:CE-4#
```

In this section we have discussed L3VPN as an overlay service with a BGP control plane transported across an underlay network based on SRv6. We have described the configuration and verification tasks required for the provisioning of the following basic service types:

- **L3VPN full-mesh service:** Every site within the VPN network can communicate directly with every other site, creating a fully interconnected mesh topology.

- **L3VPN hub-and-spoke service:** The central hub site connects to various spoke sites. In this topology, all communication between the spoke sites typically goes through the hub site, which acts as a central point of transit and allows control and management of network traffic flows

- **L3VPN extranet service:** An extranet service allows secure communication between organizations by allowing specific external partners, customers, or vendors to access designated resources or services within a company's private network while maintaining separation from other parts of a company's internal network.

Next, we will explore the L3VPN service types in the context of an underlying network that uses Segment Routing with Multiprotocol Label Switching (SR-MPLS).

SR-MPLS L3VPN Overlay Service

In the L3VPN configuration tasks you've seen so far in this chapter, the focus has been on the provisioning of various L3VPN overlay services with SRv6 as the underlay transport network. This section focuses on setting up and verifying L3VPN overlay services, using the SR-MPLS transport reference network illustrated in Figure 7-10. For convenience in comparing configurations and command outputs with the network diagram, this figure with additional details is also available in Appendix A, "Reference Diagrams/ Information," in the section "SR-MPLS Reference Network." For details on how to provision the SR-MPLS transport service, refer to the section "SR-MPLS Configuration" in Chapter 4.

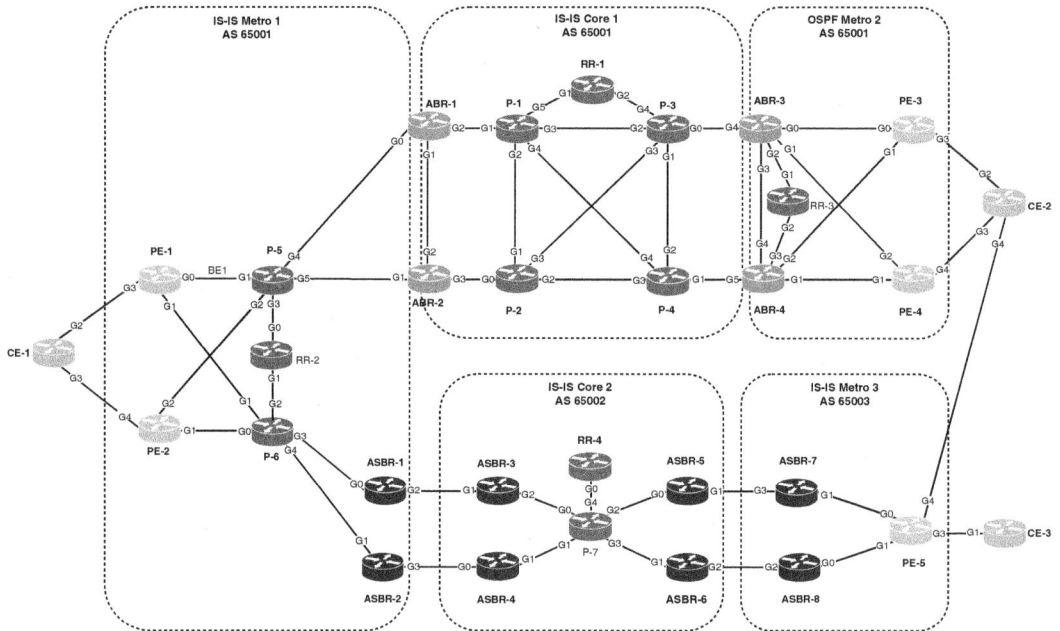

Figure 7-10   *SR-MPLS Reference Network*

In Figure 7-11, the BGP VPNv4 peerings between the various metro region PE routers and route reflectors are shown for reference purposes. Reachability between the PE routers located within the various domains is via BGP labeled unicast, which enables the exchange of the BGP Prefix SIDs between these routers. Refer to the section "Segment Routing Control Plane (BGP)" in Chapter 4, which discusses the provisioning of these Prefix SIDs in detail.

Note   Route reflector design and best practices are beyond the scope of this book.

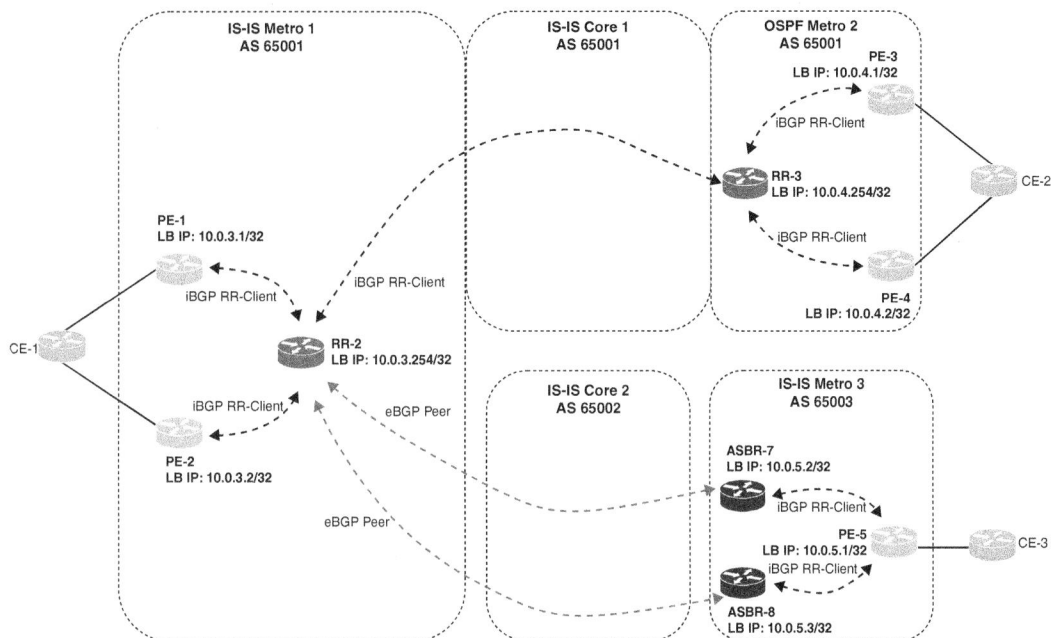

Figure 7-11 *SR-MPLS Reference Network: VPNv4 Address-Family Route Reflectors*

In Metro 1 (AS 65001), both the PE-1 and PE-2 routers are configured as route reflector clients of RR-2 for the BGP VPNv4 address family. Config 7-16 shows these router-specific configurations for router PE-1.

Config 7-16 *SR-MPLS: Metro 1 PE iBGP VPNv4 Peering to RR-2 on PE-1 (IOS XR)*

```
!
router bgp 65001
 bgp router-id 10.0.3.1
 <snip>
 !
 address-family vpnv4 unicast
 !
 neighbor-group IBGP-M1-NG
  remote-as 65001
  description *** iBGP peering to RR ***
  update-source Loopback0
  address-family vpnv4 unicast
  !
 !
 neighbor 10.0.3.254
  remote-as 65001
  use neighbor-group IBGP-M1-NG
  description *** iBGP session to METRO-1 RR ***
 !
```

Config 7-17 shows BGP VPNv4 address family configurations for router PE-2.

Config 7-17   *SR-MPLS: Metro 1 PE iBGP VPNv4 Peering to RR-2 on PE-2 (IOS XE)*

```
!
router bgp 65001
 bgp router-id 10.0.3.2
 bgp log-neighbor-changes
 neighbor 10.0.3.254 remote-as 65001
 neighbor 10.0.3.254 update-source Loopback0
 !
!
 address-family vpnv4
  neighbor 10.0.3.254 activate
  neighbor 10.0.3.254 send-community both
 exit-address-family
 !
!
```

Config 7-18 shows Metro 1-specific BGP VPNv4 address family configurations for router RR-2.

Config 7-18   *SR-MPLS: Metro 1 RR-2 iBGP VPNv4 Peering to PE-1 and PE-2 on RR-2 (IOS XR)*

```
!
router bgp 65001
 bgp router-id 10.0.3.254
<snip>
 !
 address-family vpnv4 unicast
  !
 neighbor-group IBGP-M1-NG
   remote-as 65001
   description *** iBGP peering to METRO-1 PE ***
   update-source Loopback0
   address-family vpnv4 unicast
    route-reflector-client
 !
 neighbor 10.0.3.1
   remote-as 65001
   use neighbor-group IBGP-M1-NG
   description *** iBGP session to METRO-1 PE ***
   !
 !
```

```
neighbor 10.0.3.2
 remote-as 65001
 use neighbor-group IBGP-M1-NG
 description *** iBGP session to METRO-1 PE ***
 !
!
```

RR-3 is a route reflector client of RR-2 between Metro 2 and Metro 1, but it is still within the same BGP autonomous system (AS 65001). Config 7-19 shows the RR-2 configuration toward RR-3.

Config 7-19 *SR-MPLS: Metro 1 RR-2 iBGP VPNv4 Peering to RR-3 on RR-2 (IOS XR)*

```
!
router bgp 65001
 bgp router-id 10.0.3.254
 <snip>
 !
 address-family vpnv4 unicast
 !
neighbor-group IBGP-RR-NG
  remote-as 65001
  description *** iBGP peering to RR ***
  update-source Loopback0
  address-family vpnv4 unicast
   route-reflector-client
  !
!
 neighbor 10.0.4.254
  use neighbor-group IBGP-RR-NG
  description *** iBGP session to RR in Metro 2 ***
 !
!
```

Config 7-20 shows the IOS XE–based RR-3 BGP VPNv4 address family configuration toward RR-2.

Config 7-20 *SR-MPLS: Metro 2 RR-3 iBGP VPNv4 Peering to RR-2 on RR-3 (IOS XE)*

```
!
router bgp 65001
 bgp router-id 10.0.4.254
 neighbor 10.0.3.254 remote-as 65001
```

```
  neighbor 10.0.3.254 update-source Loopback0
 !
 address-family vpnv4
  neighbor 10.0.3.254 activate
  neighbor 10.0.3.254 send-community both
 exit-address-family
  !
 !
```

Config 7-21 shows that in Metro 2 (AS 65001), both the PE-3 and PE-4 routers are configured as route reflector clients of RR-3 for the BGP VPNv4 address family.

Config 7-21   *SR-MPLS: Metro 2 RR iBGP VPNv4 Peering to PE-3 and PE-4 on RR-3 (IOS XE)*

```
 !
 router bgp 65001
  bgp router-id 10.0.4.254
  <snip>
  neighbor 10.0.4.1 remote-as 65001
  neighbor 10.0.4.1 update-source Loopback0
  neighbor 10.0.4.2 remote-as 65001
  neighbor 10.0.4.2 update-source Loopback0
  !
 !
  address-family vpnv4
   neighbor 10.0.4.1 activate
   neighbor 10.0.4.1 send-community both
   neighbor 10.0.4.1 route-reflector-client
   neighbor 10.0.4.2 activate
   neighbor 10.0.4.2 send-community both
   neighbor 10.0.4.2 route-reflector-client
  exit-address-family
   !
```

Config 7-22 shows the router PE-3 BGP VPNv4 address family configuration toward RR-3.

Config 7-22   *SR-MPLS: Metro 2 PE iBGP VPNv4 Peering to RR-3 on PE-3 (IOS XR)*

```
 !
 router bgp 65001
  bgp router-id 10.0.4.1
  <snip>
```

```
 !
 address-family vpnv4 unicast
 !
 neighbor-group IBGP-RR-NG
  remote-as 65001
  description *** iBGP peering to RR ***
  update-source Loopback0
  address-family vpnv4 unicast
  !
 !
neighbor 10.0.4.254
  remote-as 65001
  use neighbor-group IBGP-RR-NG
  description *** iBGP session to METRO-2 RR ***
  update-source Loopback0
 !
```

Config 7-23 shows the BGP VPNv4 address family configuration for the IOS XE–based router PE-4 toward RR-3.

Config 7-23 *SR-MPLS: Metro 2 PE iBGP VPNv4 Peering to RR-3 on PE-4 (IOS XE)*

```
 !
router bgp 65001
 bgp router-id 10.0.4.2
 bgp log-neighbor-changes
 neighbor 10.0.4.254 remote-as 65001
 neighbor 10.0.4.254 update-source Loopback0
 !
 !
 address-family vpnv4
  neighbor 10.0.4.254 activate
  neighbor 10.0.4.254 send-community both
 exit-address-family
 !
```

Config 7-24, Config 7-25, and Config 7-26 show the eBGP VPNv4 peerings between RR-2 in Metro 1 (AS 65001) and the ASBR-7 and ASBR-8 routers in Metro 3 (AS 65003). Take note of the egress route policy SET_VPNV4_MED_RP(150) configured on RR-2, which matches a VPNv4 route BGP local preference value (150) (non-transitive) and sets a higher MED value (150) to allow selection of a preferred path based on the lower MED value (50) for router PE-5 in Metro 3. The output of the command **show bgp vpnv4**

unicast vrf SPOKE-410-S2-VRF 10.1.10.144/28 in Output 7-44 shows these MED attributes for the learned BGP VPNv4 route 10.1.10.144/28 in the VRF instance SPOKE-410-S2-VRF on router PE-5.

Config 7-24   *SR-MPLS: Metro 1 eBGP VPNv4 Peering to ASBR-7 and ASBR-8 on RR-2 (IOS XR)*

```
!
route-policy SET_VPNV4_MED_RP($LP)
  if local-preference eq $LP then
    set med $LP
  else
    set med 50
  endif
end-policy
!
router bgp 65001
 bgp router-id 10.0.3.254
 <snip>
 !
 address-family vpnv4 unicast
 !
 neighbor-group EBGP-RR-NG
  remote-as 65003
  ebgp-multihop 255
  description *** eBGP peering to Metro 3 ASBR ***
  update-source Loopback0
  address-family vpnv4 unicast
   route-policy PASS in
   route-policy SET_VPNV4_MED_RP(150) out
   next-hop-unchanged
  !
 !
 neighbor 10.0.5.2
  use neighbor-group EBGP-RR-NG
  description *** eBGP session to RR in Metro 3 ASBR ***
 !
 neighbor 10.0.5.3
  use neighbor-group EBGP-RR-NG
  description *** eBGP session to RR in Metro 3 ASBR ***
 !
```

Config 7-25 shows the eBGP VPNv4 address family configuration for the IOS XE–based router ASBR-7 toward RR-2 in Metro 1.

Config 7-25 *SR-MPLS: Metro 3 eBGP VPNv4 Peering to RR-2 on ASBR-7 (IOS XE)*

```
!
router bgp 65003
 bgp router-id 10.0.5.2
 bgp log-neighbor-changes
 neighbor 10.0.3.254 remote-as 65001
 neighbor 10.0.3.254 ebgp-multihop 255
 neighbor 10.0.3.254 update-source Loopback0
 !
 address-family vpnv4
  neighbor 10.0.3.254 activate
  neighbor 10.0.3.254 send-community both
  neighbor 10.0.3.254 next-hop-unchanged
 exit-address-family
 !
```

Config 7-26 shows the eBGP VPNv4 address family configuration for the router ASBR-8 toward RR-2 in Metro 1.

Config 7-26 *SR-MPLS: Metro 3 eBGP VPNv4 Peering to RR-2 on ASBR-8 (IOS XR)*

```
!
router bgp 65003
 bgp router-id 10.0.5.3
 <snip>
 !
 address-family vpnv4 unicast
 !
 neighbor 10.0.3.254
  remote-as 65001
  ebgp-multihop 255
  update-source Loopback0
  address-family vpnv4 unicast
   route-policy PASS in
   route-policy PASS out
   next-hop-unchanged
  !
```

The router PE-2 is the active path to CE-1 using the BGP local preference 200. This is matched by the egress route policy SET_VPNV4_MED_RP(150) configured on RR-2. This policy sets the MED value to 50 to allow a preferred path to be selected based on this lower MED value in Metro 3 (AS 65003). In order to explain the behavior of this configured route policy, Output 7-44 shows that router PE-2 with BGP router ID 10.0.3.2 is the best path for the VPNv4 route 10.1.10.144/28, and router PE-1 with BGP router ID 10.0.3.1 is the backup path.

Output 7-44   *SR-MPLS: BGP VPNv4 RIB for 10.1.10.144/28 on PE-5*

```
RP/0/0/CPU0:PE-5#show bgp vpnv4 unicast vrf SPOKE-410-S2-VRF 10.1.10.144/28
BGP routing table entry for 10.1.10.144/28, Route Distinguisher: 65003:410
Versions:
  Process           bRIB/RIB  SendTblVer
  Speaker                299         299
Last Modified: Aug  9 05:56:15.362 for 1d21h
Paths: (2 available, best #2)
  Not advertised to any peer
  Path #1: Received by speaker 0
  Not advertised to any peer
  65001 65400
    10.0.3.1 (metric 10) from 10.0.5.2 (10.0.5.2)
      Received Label 24008
      Origin IGP, metric 150, localpref 100, valid, internal, backup, add-path,
  imported
      Received Path ID 0, Local Path ID 2, version 296
      Extended community: SoO:65400:1 RT:65001:400 RT:65001:4002
      Source AFI: VPNv4 Unicast, Source VRF: default, Source Route
  Distinguisher: 65001:401
  Path #2: Received by speaker 0
  Not advertised to any peer
  65001 65400
    10.0.3.2 (metric 10) from 10.0.5.2 (10.0.5.2)
      Received Label 21
      Origin IGP, metric 50, localpref 100, valid, internal, best, group-best,
  import-candidate, imported
      Received Path ID 0, Local Path ID 1, version 299
      Extended community: SoO:65400:1 RT:65001:400 RT:65001:4002
      Source AFI: VPNv4 Unicast, Source VRF: default, Source Route
  Distinguisher: 65001:402
RP/0/0/CPU0:PE-5#
```

In Metro 3 (AS 65003), the router PE-5 is configured as a route reflector client of both ASBR-7 and ASBR-8 for the BGP VPNv4 address family, as shown in Config 7-27, Config 7-28, and Config 7-29.

Config 7-27   *SR-MPLS: Metro 3 iBGP VPNv4 Peering to PE-5 on ASBR-7 (IOS XE)*

```
!
router bgp 65003
 bgp router-id 10.0.5.2
 <snip>
```

```
 neighbor 10.0.5.1 remote-as 65003
 neighbor 10.0.5.1 update-source Loopback0
!
 address-family vpnv4
  neighbor 10.0.5.1 activate
  neighbor 10.0.5.1 send-community both
  neighbor 10.0.5.1 route-reflector-client
 exit-address-family
  !
```

Config 7-28 shows the iBGP VPNv4 address family configuration for the router ASBR-8 toward the router PE-5.

Config 7-28 *SR-MPLS: Metro 3 iBGP VPNv4 Peering to PE-5 on ASBR-8 (IOS XR)*

```
 !
router bgp 65003
 bgp router-id 10.0.5.3
 <snip>
  !
 address-family vpnv4 unicast
  !
 neighbor 10.0.5.1
   remote-as 65003
   update-source Loopback0
   !
   address-family vpnv4 unicast
    route-reflector-client
 !
```

Config 7-29 shows the iBGP VPNv4 address family configuration for the router PE-5 toward both of the ASBR routers.

Config 7-29 *SR-MPLS: Metro 3 iBGP VPNv4 Peering to ASBR-7 and ASBR-8 on PE-5 (IOS XR)*

```
router bgp 65003
 bgp router-id 10.0.5.1
 <snip>
  !
 address-family vpnv4 unicast
  !
```

```
 neighbor 10.0.5.2
  remote-as 65003
  update-source Loopback0
  !
  address-family vpnv4 unicast
  !
 !
 neighbor 10.0.5.3
  remote-as 65003
  update-source Loopback0
  !
  address-family vpnv4 unicast
 !
```

Having successfully implemented the BGP VPNv4 configurations across all three metros, we now proceed to the initial phase of configuring and verifying the various L3VPN services, starting with the full-mesh service setup.

SR-MPLS L3VPN Full-Mesh Service

This section covers the configuration tasks and service verifications for an L3VPN full-mesh service overlay network provisioned across an SR-MPLS transport network.

The configuration tasks, as shown in Figure 7-12, involve a customer router CE-1 that is dual-homed to the routers PE-1 and PE-2 in IS-IS Metro 1, a customer router CE-2 that is dual-homed to the routers PE-3 and PE-4 in the OSPF Metro 2, and the customer router CE-3, which is single attached to the router PE-5 in IS-IS Metro 3. Provisioning this L3VPN full-mesh service involves configuring the following:

- The VRF instance provisioned on all PE routers for this service is named FULL-400-VRF.

- Network 10.1.10.128/28 originates from router CE-1 in a unipath active/standby scenario via the PE routers PE-1 and PE-2 using BGP local preference, the active path is set to a BGP local preference of 200 via PE-2, and the backup path is set to a BGP local preference of 150 via PE-1.

- Network 10.2.10.128/28 originates from router CE-2 in a unipath active/standby scenario as well via the PE routers PE-3 and PE-4 using a BGP local preference, with the active path is set to a BGP local preference of 200 via PE-3 and the backup path is set to a BGP local preference of 150 via PE-4.

- Network 10.3.10.128/28 is originated from the router CE-3 and single attached to the PE-5 router.

SR-MPLS L3VPN Full-Mesh Configuration

Figure 7-12 provides some of the relevant details (VRF instance name, import/export RT, IP network range, route policy names, and so on) used in the configurations for all the CE and PE routers.

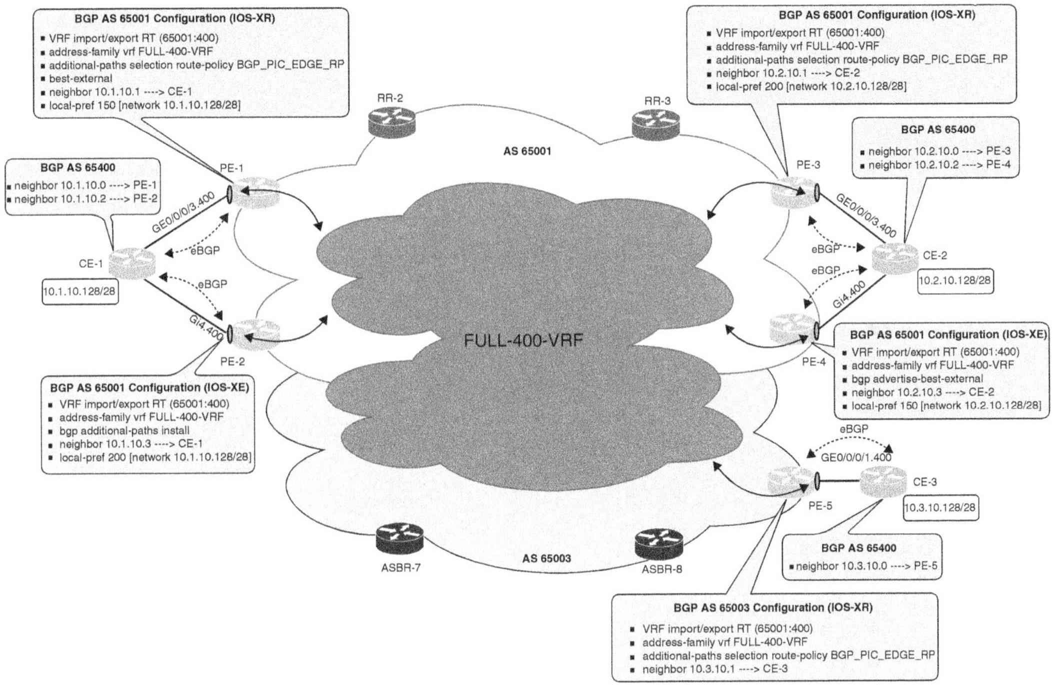

Figure 7-12 *SR-MPLS L3VPN Full-Mesh Configuration Tasks*

First, let's examine PE router configuration examples for the full-mesh service FULL-400-VRF connecting the CE routers CE-1, CE-2, and CE-3. Config 7-30 shows the relevant service configuration on the IOS XR–based Metro 1 router PE-1.

Config 7-30 *SR-MPLS L3VPN Full-Mesh Configuration on PE-1 (IOS XR)*

```
!
vrf FULL-400-VRF
 address-family ipv4 unicast
  import route-target
   65001:400
  !
  export route-target
   65001:400
  !
 !
!
```

```
interface GigabitEthernet0/0/0/3
 description Connected_to_CE-1
 cdp
!
interface GigabitEthernet0/0/0/3.400
 description Connected_to_CE-1
 vrf FULL-400-VRF
 ipv4 address 10.1.10.0 255.255.255.254
 encapsulation dot1q 400
!
route-policy SID($SID)
  set label-index $SID
end-policy
!
route-policy PASS_RP
  pass
end-policy
!
route-policy BGP_LOC-PREF_RP($LP)
  set local-preference $LP
end-policy
!
route-policy BGP_PIC_EDGE_RP
  set path-selection backup 1 install
end-policy
!
router bgp 65001
 bgp router-id 10.0.3.1
 address-family ipv4 unicast
  maximum-paths ibgp 2
  network 10.0.3.1/32 route-policy SID(2001)
  allocate-label all
 !
 address-family vpnv4 unicast
  additional-paths selection route-policy BGP_PIC_EDGE_RP
 !
neighbor-group IBGP-RR-NG
  remote-as 65001
  description *** iBGP peering to RR ***
  update-source Loopback0
  address-family ipv4 labeled-unicast
  !
```

```
 address-family vpnv4 unicast
  !
 !
 neighbor 10.0.3.254
  remote-as 65001
  use neighbor-group IBGP-RR-NG
  description *** iBGP session to METRO-1 RR ***
  !
 vrf FULL-400-VRF
  rd 65001:401
  address-family ipv4 unicast
   advertise best-external
  !
  neighbor 10.1.10.1
   remote-as 65400
   address-family ipv4 unicast
    route-policy BGP_LOC-PREF_RP(150) in
    route-policy PASS_RP out
    as-override
    site-of-origin 65400:1
  !
```

Config 7-31 shows the relevant service configuration on the IOS XE–based router PE-2 in Metro 1.

Config 7-31   *SR-MPLS L3VPN Full-Mesh Configuration on PE-2 (IOS XE)*

```
!
ip vrf FULL-400-VRF
 rd 65001:402
 route-target export 65001:400
 route-target import 65001:400
!
interface GigabitEthernet4
 description Connected_to_CE-1
 no ip address
 negotiation auto
 cdp enable
!
interface GigabitEthernet4.400
 description Connected_to_CE-1
 encapsulation dot1Q 400
 ip vrf forwarding FULL-400-VRF
 ip address 10.1.10.2 255.255.255.254
!
```

```
router bgp 65001
 bgp router-id 10.0.3.2
 bgp log-neighbor-changes
 neighbor 10.0.3.254 remote-as 65001
 neighbor 10.0.3.254 update-source Loopback0
 !
 address-family ipv4
  network 10.0.3.2 mask 255.255.255.255
  segment-routing mpls
  neighbor 10.0.3.254 activate
  neighbor 10.0.3.254 additional-paths receive
  neighbor 10.0.3.254 send-label
  maximum-paths ibgp 2
 exit-address-family
 !
 address-family vpnv4
  neighbor 10.0.3.254 activate
  neighbor 10.0.3.254 send-community both
 exit-address-family
 !
address-family ipv4 vrf FULL-400-VRF
  bgp additional-paths install
  neighbor 10.1.10.3 remote-as 65400
  neighbor 10.1.10.3 activate
  neighbor 10.1.10.3 as-override
  neighbor 10.1.10.3 soo 65400:1
  neighbor 10.1.10.3 route-map BGP_LOC-PREF_RP in
 exit-address-family
 !
route-map BGP_LOC-PREF_RP permit 10
 set local-preference 200
 !
```

Config 7-32 shows the relevant service configuration on the IOS XR–based router PE-3
in Metro 2.

Config 7-32   *SR-MPLS L3VPN Full-Mesh Configuration on PE-3 (IOS XR)*

```
!
vrf FULL-400-VRF
 address-family ipv4 unicast
  import route-target
   65001:400
  !
```

```
  export route-target
   65001:400
  !
 !
!
interface GigabitEthernet0/0/0/3
 description Connected_to_CE-2
 cdp
!
interface GigabitEthernet0/0/0/3.400
 description Connected_to_CE-2
 vrf FULL-400-VRF
 ipv4 address 10.2.10.0 255.255.255.254
 encapsulation dot1q 400
!
route-policy SID($SID)
  set label-index $SID
end-policy
!
route-policy PASS_RP
  pass
end-policy
!
route-policy BGP_LOC-PREF_RP($LP)
  set local-preference $LP
end-policy
!
route-policy BGP_PIC_EDGE_RP
  set path-selection backup 1 install
end-policy
!
router bgp 65001
 bgp router-id 10.0.4.1
 address-family ipv4 unicast
  maximum-paths ibgp 2
  network 10.0.4.1/32 route-policy SID(3001)
  allocate-label all
 !
 address-family vpnv4 unicast
  additional-paths selection route-policy BGP_PIC_EDGE_RP
 !
neighbor-group IBGP-RR-NG
  remote-as 65001
```

```
  description *** iBGP peering to RR ***
  update-source Loopback0
  address-family vpnv4 unicast
  !
 !
 neighbor 10.0.1.7
  remote-as 65001
  update-source Loopback0
  address-family ipv4 labeled-unicast
  !
 !
 neighbor 10.0.1.8
  remote-as 65001
  update-source Loopback0
  address-family ipv4 labeled-unicast
  !
 !
 neighbor 10.0.4.254
  remote-as 65001
  use neighbor-group IBGP-RR-NG
  description *** iBGP session to METRO-2 RR ***
  update-source Loopback0
 !
 vrf FULL-400-VRF
  rd 65001:403
  address-family ipv4 unicast
  !
  neighbor 10.2.10.1
   remote-as 65400
   address-family ipv4 unicast
    route-policy BGP_LOC-PREF_RP(200) in
    route-policy PASS_RP out
    as-override
    site-of-origin 65400:2
 !
```

Config 7-33 shows the service configuration on the IOS XE–based router PE-4 in Metro 2.

Config 7-33 *SR-MPLS L3VPN Full-Mesh Configuration on PE-4 (IOS XE)*

```
!
ip vrf FULL-400-VRF
 rd 65001:404
 route-target export 65001:400
 route-target import 65001:400
!
interface GigabitEthernet4
 description Connected_to_CE-2
no ip address
 negotiation auto
 cdp enable
!
interface GigabitEthernet4.400
 description Connected_to_CE-2
 encapsulation dot1Q 400
 ip vrf forwarding FULL-400-VRF
 ip address 10.2.10.2 255.255.255.254
!
router bgp 65001
 bgp router-id 10.0.4.2
 bgp log-neighbor-changes
 neighbor 10.0.1.7 remote-as 65001
 neighbor 10.0.1.7 update-source Loopback0
 neighbor 10.0.1.8 remote-as 65001
 neighbor 10.0.1.8 update-source Loopback0
 neighbor 10.0.4.254 remote-as 65001
 neighbor 10.0.4.254 update-source Loopback0
 !
 address-family ipv4
  network 10.0.4.2 mask 255.255.255.255
  segment-routing mpls
  neighbor 10.0.1.7 activate
  neighbor 10.0.1.7 send-label
  neighbor 10.0.1.8 activate
  neighbor 10.0.1.8 send-label
  maximum-paths ibgp 2
 exit-address-family
 !
 address-family vpnv4
  neighbor 10.0.4.254 activate
  neighbor 10.0.4.254 send-community both
 exit-address-family
 !
```

```
address-family ipv4 vrf FULL-400-VRF
  bgp advertise-best-external
  neighbor 10.2.10.3 remote-as 65400
  neighbor 10.2.10.3 activate
  neighbor 10.2.10.3 as-override
  neighbor 10.2.10.3 soo 65400:2
  neighbor 10.2.10.3 route-map BGP_LOC-PREF_RP in
exit-address-family
!
route-map BGP_LOC-PREF_RP permit 10
 set local-preference 150
!
```

Finally, Config 7-34 shows the service configuration from on the Metro 3 router PE-5, which is an IOS XR–based router.

Config 7-34   *SR-MPLS L3VPN Full-Mesh Configuration on PE-5 (IOS XR)*

```
!
vrf FULL-400-VRF
 address-family ipv4 unicast
  import route-target
   65001:400
  !
  export route-target
   65001:400
  !
 !
!
interface GigabitEthernet0/0/0/3
 description Connected_to_CE-3
 cdp
!
interface GigabitEthernet0/0/0/3.400
 description Connected_to_CE-3
 vrf FULL-400-VRF
 ipv4 address 10.3.10.0 255.255.255.254
 encapsulation dot1q 400
!
route-policy SID($SID)
  set label-index $SID
end-policy
!
route-policy PASS_RP
  pass
```

```
end-policy
!
route-policy BGP_PIC_EDGE_RP
  set path-selection backup 1 install
end-policy
!
router bgp 65003
 bgp router-id 10.0.5.1
 address-family ipv4 unicast
  maximum-paths ibgp 2
  network 10.0.5.1/32 route-policy SID(4001)
  allocate-label all
 !
 address-family vpnv4 unicast
  additional-paths selection route-policy BGP_PIC_EDGE_RP
!
 neighbor 10.0.5.2
  remote-as 65003
  update-source Loopback0
  address-family ipv4 labeled-unicast
  !
  address-family vpnv4 unicast
  !
  address-family l2vpn evpn
  !
 !
 neighbor 10.0.5.3
  remote-as 65003
  update-source Loopback0
  address-family ipv4 labeled-unicast
  !
  address-family vpnv4 unicast
!
 vrf FULL-400-VRF
  rd 65003:401
  address-family ipv4 unicast
  !
  neighbor 10.3.10.1
   remote-as 65400
   address-family ipv4 unicast
    route-policy PASS_RP in
    route-policy PASS_RP out
    as-override
!
```

The L3VPN full-mesh VRF configuration tasks involve the configuration of the VRF instance FULL-400-VRF, with the required import/export route targets and assignment of the PE–CE interfaces to the specific VRF instances. Config 7-35 shows an example for an IOS XR–based router.

Config 7-35 *SR-MPLS L3VPN Full-Mesh Configuration: IOS XR VRF Instance and Interface Configuration*

```
!
vrf FULL-400-VRF
 address-family ipv4 unicast
  import route-target
   65001:400
  !
  export route-target
   65001:400
  !
 !
!
interface GigabitEthernet0/0/0/3
 description Connected_to_CE-1
 cdp
!
interface GigabitEthernet0/0/0/3.400
 description Connected_to_CE-1
 vrf FULL-400-VRF
 ipv4 address 10.1.10.0 255.255.255.254
 encapsulation dot1q 400
!
```

Config 7-36 shows a VRF configuration snippet for an IOS XE–based router.

Config 7-36 *SR-MPLS L3VPN Full-Mesh Configuration: IOS XE VRF Instance and Interface Configuration*

```
!
ip vrf FULL-400-VRF
 rd 65001:402
 route-target export 65001:400
 route-target import 65001:400
!
interface GigabitEthernet4
 description Connected_to_CE-1
 no ip address
!
```

```
interface GigabitEthernet4.400
 description Connected_to_CE-1
 encapsulation dot1Q 400
 ip vrf forwarding FULL-400-VRF
 ip address 10.1.10.2 255.255.255.254
!
```

The VRF instance FULL-400-VRF in the SR-MPLS network shown in Figure 7-12 is configured as a unipath active/standby scenario for the PE–CE links between CE-1 and CE-2 and their respective PE routers. The BGP PIC Edge and BGP best-external features are also configured to allow for faster convergence in the event that the active path fails:

- An ingress route learned across the eBGP neighborships CE-1–PE-2 and CE-2–PE-3 is matched with the route policy BGP_LOC-PREF_RP, and the BGP local preference is set to 200.

- An ingress route learned across the eBGP neighborships CE-1–PE-1 and CE-2–PE-4 is matched with the route policy BGP_LOC-PREF_RP, and the BGP local preference is set to 150.

- In Config 7-37 for the IOS XR router PE-1, BGP PIC Edge is enabled explicitly together with the BGP best-external feature. This setup is configured to prevent the withdrawal of the eBGP path to the subnet 10.1.10.128/28 learned from CE-1 upon receipt of the preferred path via PE-2.

Config 7-37   *SR-MPLS L3VPN Full-Mesh Configuration: BGP PIC Edge and BGP Best External on PE-1 (IOS XR)*

```
!
route-policy BGP_PIC_EDGE_RP
  set path-selection backup 1 install
end-policy
!
route-policy BGP_LOC-PREF_RP($LP)
  set local-preference $LP
end-policy
!
router bgp 65001
 !
 address-family vpnv4 unicast
  additional-paths selection route-policy BGP_PIC_EDGE_RP
 !
 vrf FULL-400-VRF
```

```
 rd 65001:401
 address-family ipv4 unicast
  advertise best-external
 !
 neighbor 10.1.10.1
  remote-as 65400
  address-family ipv4 unicast
   route-policy BGP_LOC-PREF_RP(150) in
   route-policy PASS_RP out
   as-override
   site-of-origin 65400:1
!
```

BGP PIC Edge on the IOS XE router PE-2 is configured explicitly as shown in
Config 7-38 via the command **bgp additional-paths install**. Be aware that the command
bgp advertise-best-external will implicitly enable BGP PIC Edge as configured on the
router PE-4 in Config 7-33.

Config 7-38   *SR-MPLS L3VPN Full-Mesh Configuration: BGP PIC Edge Configuration
on PE-2 (IOS XE)*

```
!
router bgp 65001
 !
 address-family ipv4 vrf FULL-400-VRF
  bgp additional-paths install
  neighbor 10.1.10.3 remote-as 65400
  neighbor 10.1.10.3 activate
  neighbor 10.1.10.3 as-override
  neighbor 10.1.10.3 soo 65400:1
  neighbor 10.1.10.3 route-map BGP_LOC-PREF_RP in
 exit-address-family
!
route-map BGP_LOC-PREF_RP permit 10
 set local-preference 200
!
```

A final topic for this discussion is the BGP label allocation mode for L3VPN configurations. The BGP PIC Edge and BGP best-external configuration has an impact on the BGP label allocation feature. There are three BGP label allocation modes:

- **Per-prefix label allocation mode:** A label is allocated for every prefix received from the attached CE routers. The disadvantage is that this allocation mode is not very efficient when router resources are limited. This is the default mode in IOS XE and IOS XR.

- **Per-VRF label allocation mode:** A label is allocated per VRF instance for all locally originated routes and routes learned from the CE router. Although this is an efficient label allocation mode, it requires an IP lookup for incoming labeled packets to allow them to be forwarded on to their destinations.

- **Per-CE label allocation mode:** A label is allocated per next hop (CE router) within a VRF instance. This is an efficient label allocation mode, as it uses fewer labels than the per-prefix label allocation mode and has the added advantage of not requiring an IP next hop lookup for incoming MPLS-labeled IP frames.

Keep in mind the following with regard to label allocation modes and the BGP PIC Edge/ BGP best-external feature:

- On an active PE router with BGP PIC Edge, per-CE label allocation mode is not supported, although in IOS XR it is currently supported and is known as resilient per-CE label allocation. The per-VRF allocation mode may result in transient loops due to IP lookups.

- On a backup PE router with BGP best-external, per-CE label allocation mode is supported, and per-VRF allocation mode may result in transient loops following a PE–CE active path failure until BGP convergence has occurred.

- Both BGP PIC Edge and BGP best-external are fully supported with per-prefix label allocation mode.

Next, let's discuss some useful service verification commands for confirming that the L3VPN full-mesh service is configured and functioning correctly.

SR-MPLS L3VPN Full-Mesh Verification

The verification tasks in this section focus on the subnet 10.2.10.128/28 advertised into the VRF instance FULL-400-VRF by router CE-2. These same verification commands (IOS XR and IOS XE) can be applied for subnets originated from CE-1 and CE-3 as well. Figure 7-13 provides an overview of the commands used on the various PE routers.

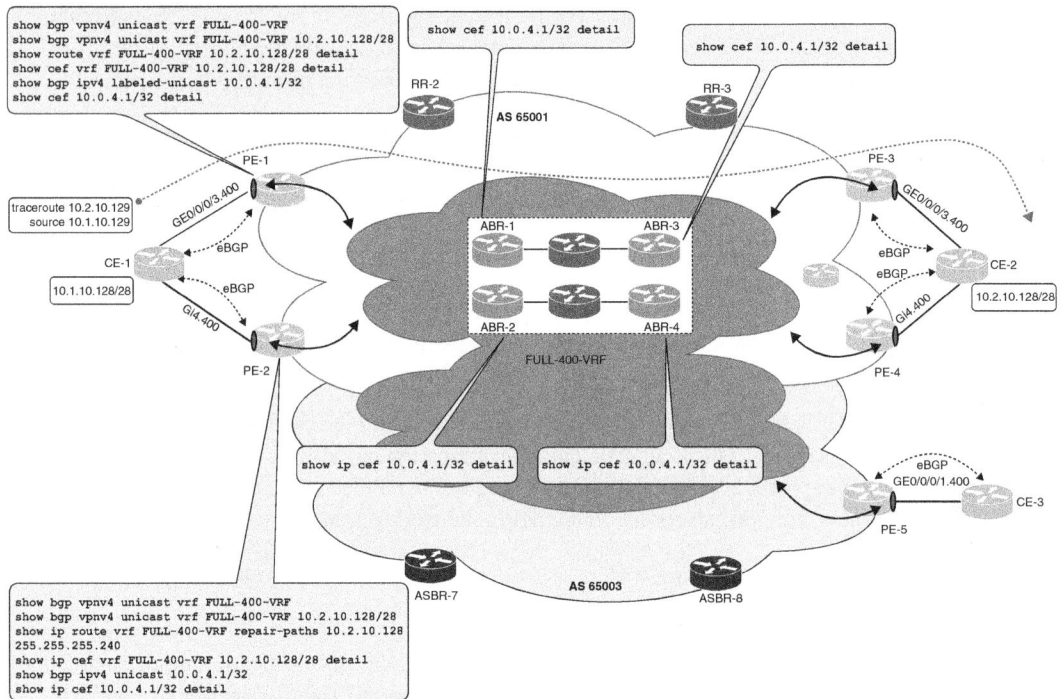

Figure 7-13 *SR-MPLS L3VPN Full-Mesh Verification Tasks*

In the outputs from the command **show bgp vpnv4 unicast vrf FULL-400-VRF** in Output 7-45 and Output 7-46 executed on routers PE-1 and PE-2, all the subnets originated from the customer CE routers are observed with the IP subnet 10.2.10.128/28 being the focus of the verification commands:

- **Subnet 10.2.10.128/28 (CE-2):** This is the first path from next hop 10.0.4.1 with BGP local preference 200.

- **Subnet 10.2.10.128/28 (CE-2):** This is the second path from next hop 10.0.4.2 with BGP local preference 150.

Output 7-45 *SR-MPLS L3VPN Full-Mesh Configuration: BGP VPNv4 RIB on PE-1 (IOS XR)*

```
RP/0/0/CPU0:PE-1#show bgp vpnv4 unicast vrf FULL-400-VRF

<snip>


Status codes: s suppressed, d damped, h history, * valid, > best
              i - internal, r RIB-failure, S stale, N Nexthop-discard
Origin codes: i - IGP, e - EGP, ? - incomplete
  Network          Next Hop          Metric LocPrf Weight Path
```

```
Route Distinguisher: 65001:401 (default for vrf FULL-400-VRF)
*>i10.1.10.128/28      10.0.3.2               0    200      0 65400 i
*                      10.1.10.1              0    150      0 65400 i
*>i10.2.10.128/28      10.0.4.1               0    200      0 65400 i
* i                    10.0.4.2               0    150      0 65400 i
*>i10.3.10.128/28      10.0.5.1                    100      0 65003 65400 i


Processed 3 prefixes, 5 paths
RP/0/0/CPU0:PE-1#
```

Output 7-46 shows the command **show bgp vpnv4 unicast vrf FULL-400-VRF** executed on router PE-2.

Output 7-46 *SR-MPLS L3VPN Full-Mesh Configuration: BGP VPNv4 RIB on PE-2 (IOS XE)*

```
PE-2#show bgp vpnv4 unicast vrf FULL-400-VRF
BGP table version is 114, local router ID is 10.0.3.2
Status codes: s suppressed, d damped, h history, * valid, > best, i - internal,
              r RIB-failure, S Stale, m multipath, b backup-path, f RT-Filter,
              x best-external, a additional-path, c RIB-compressed,
              t secondary path, L long-lived-stale,
Origin codes: i - IGP, e - EGP, ? - incomplete
RPKI validation codes: V valid, I invalid, N Not found

     Network          Next Hop         Metric LocPrf Weight Path
Route Distinguisher: 65001:402 (default for vrf FULL-400-VRF)
 *bi  10.1.10.128/28   10.0.3.1               0    150      0 65400 i
 *>                    10.1.10.3              0    200      0 65400 i
 *bi  10.2.10.128/28   10.0.4.2               0    150      0 65400 i
 *>i                   10.0.4.1               0    200      0 65400 i
 *>i  10.3.10.128/28   10.0.5.1                    100      0 65003 65400 i
PE-2#
```

Output 7-47 shows the command **show bgp vpnv4 unicast vrf FULL-400-VRF 10.2.10.128/28** executed on PE-1 and displays the following relevant information:

- **Paths: (2 available, best #1):** The output confirms that the subnet is available across two paths, and the first path is the preferred one.
  - **Path #1:**
    - **10.0.4.1 (metric 20) from 10.0.3.254 (10.0.4.1):** PE-3 is the BGP next hop 10.0.4.1 and is learned via BGP labeled unicast.
    - **Received Label 24002:** Router PE-3 has allocated a VPNv4 label 24002 for the route 10.2.10.128/28 from CE-2.

☐ **localpref 200, valid, internal, best:** The BGP local preference attribute 200 ensures that this path via PE-3 is the best path for traffic forwarding.

☐ **Extended community: SoO:65400:2 RT:65001:400:** Site-of-origin and route targets are applied to the subnet via PE-3.

■ **Path #2:**

☐ **10.0.4.2 (metric 20) from 10.0.3.254 (10.0.4.2):** PE-4 is the BGP next hop 10.0.4.2 and learned via BGP labeled unicast.

☐ **Received Label 18:** Router PE-4 has allocated a VPNv4 label 18 for the route 10.2.10.128/28 from router CE-2.

☐ **localpref 150, valid, internal, backup, add-path:** A BGP local preference attribute of 150 is applied to the subnet via PE-4 together with the BGP PIC Edge configuration on router PE-1. additional-paths selection route-policy BGP_PIC_EDGE_RP ensures that this path via PE-4 is the backup path and improves convergence in the event of a failure on PE-3.

☐ **Extended community: SoO:65400:2 RT:65001:400:** Site-of-origin and route targets are applied to the subnet via PE-4.

Output 7-47 *SR-MPLS L3VPN Full-Mesh Configuration: BGP VPNv4 RIB for 10.2.10.128/28 on PE-1 (IOS XR)*

```
RP/0/0/CPU0:PE-1#show bgp vpnv4 unicast vrf FULL-400-VRF 10.2.10.128/28
BGP routing table entry for 10.2.10.128/28, Route Distinguisher: 65001:401
Paths: (2 available, best #1)
  Not advertised to any peer
  Path #1: Received by speaker 0
  Not advertised to any peer
  65400
    10.0.4.1 (metric 20) from 10.0.3.254 (10.0.4.1)
      Received Label 24002
      Origin IGP, metric 0, localpref 200, valid, internal, best, group-best,
import-candidate, imported
      Received Path ID 0, Local Path ID 1, version 25
      Extended community: SoO:65400:2 RT:65001:400
      Originator: 10.0.4.1, Cluster list: 10.0.3.254, 10.0.4.254
      Source AFI: VPNv4 Unicast, Source VRF: default, Source Route
Distinguisher: 65001:403
  Path #2: Received by speaker 0
  Not advertised to any peer
  65400
```

```
   10.0.4.2 (metric 20) from 10.0.3.254 (10.0.4.2)
     Received Label 18
     Origin IGP, metric 0, localpref 150, valid, internal, backup, add-path,
   imported
     Received Path ID 0, Local Path ID 3, version 56
     Extended community: SoO:65400:2 RT:65001:400
     Originator: 10.0.4.2, Cluster list: 10.0.3.254, 10.0.4.254
     Source AFI: VPNv4 Unicast, Source VRF: default, Source Route
   Distinguisher: 65001:404
RP/0/0/CPU0:PE-1#
```

Output 7-48 shows the output of the command **show bgp vpnv4 unicast vrf FULL-400-VRF 10.2.10.128/28** on the IOS XE PE router PE-2. It displays similar information as the output from PE-1 for the BGP VPNv4 route 10.2.10.128/28:

- **Paths: (2 available, best #2, table FULL-400-VRF):** The output confirms that the subnet is available across two paths, and the second path is the preferred one.

  - **Path #1:**

    - **imported path from 65001:404:10.2.10.128/28:** A route with the route distinguisher 65001:404 is imported into the VRF instance.

    - **10.0.4.2:** The next hop PE-4 in the global routing table is learned via BGP labeled unicast.

    - **localpref 150, valid, internal, backup/repair:** A BGP local preference attribute of 150 applied to the subnet via PE-4 together with the BGP PIC Edge configuration **bgp additional-paths install** on router PE-2 ensures that this path via PE-4 is the backup/repair path in the event of a failure on PE-3.

    - **Extended Community: SoO:65400:2 RT:65001:400:** Site-of-origin and route targets are applied to the subnet via PE-4.

    - **mpls labels in/out nolabel/18:** Router PE-4 has allocated a VPNv4 label 18 for the route 10.2.10.128/28 from router CE-2.

  - **Path #2:**

    - **imported path from 65001:403:10.2.10.128/28:** A route with the route distinguisher 65001:403 is imported into the VRF instance.

    - **10.0.4.1:** Next hop PE-3 in the global routing table is learned via BGP labeled unicast.

    - **localpref 200, valid, internal, best:** The BGP local preference attribute 200 ensures that this path via PE-3 is the best path for traffic forwarding.

☐ **Extended Community: SoO:65400:2 RT:65001:400:** Site-of-origin and route targets are applied to the subnet via PE-3.

☐ **mpls labels in/out nolabel/24002:** Router PE-3 has allocated a VPNv4 label 24002 for the route 10.2.10.128/28 from router CE-2.

Output 7-48   *SR-MPLS L3VPN Full-Mesh Configuration: BGP VPNv4 RIB for 10.2.10.128/28 on PE-2 (IOS XE)*

```
PE-2#show bgp vpnv4 unicast vrf FULL-400-VRF 10.2.10.128/28
BGP routing table entry for 65001:402:10.2.10.128/28, version 109
Paths: (2 available, best #2, table FULL-400-VRF)
  Additional-path-install
  Advertised to update-groups:
     24
  Refresh Epoch 1
  65400, imported path from 65001:404:10.2.10.128/28 (global)
    10.0.4.2 (metric 20) (via default) from 10.0.3.254 (10.0.3.254)
      Origin IGP, metric 0, localpref 150, valid, internal, backup/repair
      Extended Community: SoO:65400:2 RT:65001:400
      Originator: 10.0.4.2, Cluster list: 10.0.3.254, 10.0.4.254 ,
recursive-via-host
      mpls labels in/out nolabel/18
      rx pathid: 0, tx pathid: 0
      Updated on Jul 18 2023 11:43:39 UTC
  Refresh Epoch 1
  65400, imported path from 65001:403:10.2.10.128/28 (global)
    10.0.4.1 (metric 20) (via default) from 10.0.3.254 (10.0.3.254)
      Origin IGP, metric 0, localpref 200, valid, internal, best
      Extended Community: SoO:65400:2 RT:65001:400
      Originator: 10.0.4.1, Cluster list: 10.0.3.254, 10.0.4.254 ,
recursive-via-host
      mpls labels in/out nolabel/24002
      rx pathid: 0, tx pathid: 0x0
      Updated on Jul 18 2023 11:43:39 UTC
PE-2#
```

Figure 7-14 provides an overview of the BGP VPNv4 route 10.2.10.128/28 from the router CE-2 propagated via both PE routers in Metro 2 (PE-3 and PE-4).

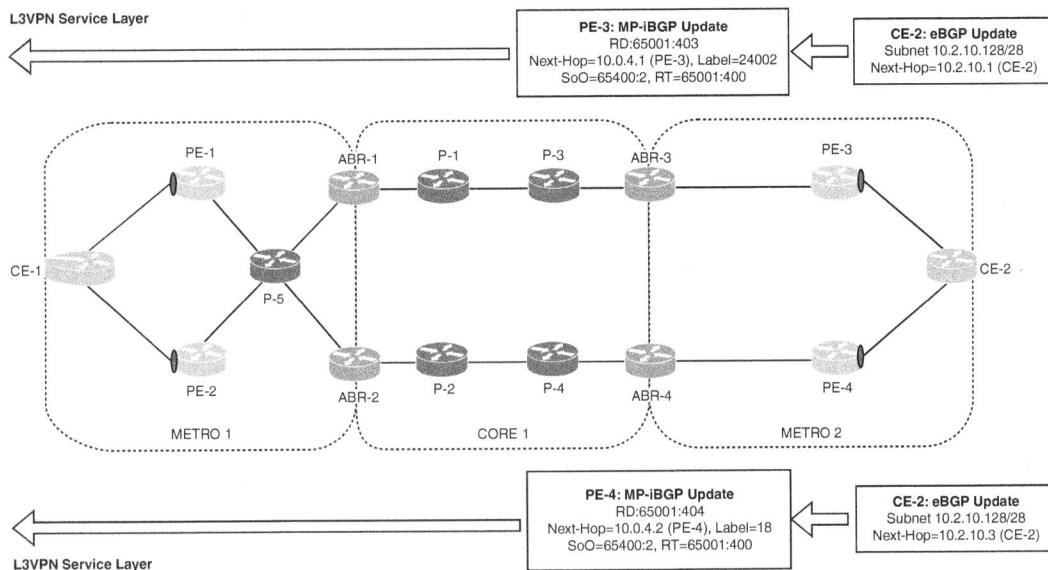

Figure 7-14 *SR-MPLS L3VPN Full-Mesh Configuration: L3VPN Service Layer Overview on 10.2.10.128/28*

Output 7-49 shows the output of the command **show route vrf FULL-400-VRF 10.2.10.128/28** detail executed on router PE-1. As you can see, it provides the RIB entry for the subnet 10.2.10.128/28 and confirms the relevant details of this learned subnet, including the fact that it has a backup path via PE-4 due to the BGP PIC Edge configuration:

■ **Number of pic paths 1, type internal:** Subnet 10.2.10.128/28 has a backup BGP PIC Edge path.

■ **10.0.4.1, from 10.0.3.254:** This is the active BGP path via router PE-3 with next hop 10.0.4.1.

■ **Label: 0x5dc2 (24002):** Router PE-3 has allocated a VPNv4 label 24002 for the route 10.2.10.128/28 from router CE-2.

■ **10.0.4.2, from 10.0.3.254, BGP backup path:** This is the backup BGP path via router PE-4 with next hop 10.0.4.2.

■ **Label: 0x12 (18):** Router PE-4 has allocated a VPNv4 label 18 for the route 10.2.10.128/28 from router CE-2.

Output 7-49   *SR-MPLS L3VPN Full-Mesh Configuration: RIB Details for 10.2.10.128/28 on PE-1 (IOS XR)*

```
RP/0/0/CPU0:PE-1#show route vrf FULL-400-VRF 10.2.10.128/28 detail

Routing entry for 10.2.10.128/28
  Known via "bgp 65001", distance 200, metric 0
  Tag 65400
  Number of pic paths 1 , type internal
  Installed Jul 16 07:52:54.263 for 4d20h
  Routing Descriptor Blocks
    10.0.4.1, from 10.0.3.254
      Nexthop in Vrf: "default", Table: "default", IPv4 Unicast, Table Id: 0xe0000000
      Route metric is 0
      Label: 0x5dc2 (24002)
      Tunnel ID: None
      Binding Label: None
      Extended communities count: 1
        SoO:65400:2
      Source RD attributes: 0x0000:65001:403
      NHID:0x0(Ref:0)
    10.0.4.2, from 10.0.3.254, BGP backup path
      Nexthop in Vrf: "default", Table: "default", IPv4 Unicast, Table Id: 0xe0000000
      Route metric is 0
      Label: 0x12 (18)
      Tunnel ID: None
      Binding Label: None
      Extended communities count: 1
        SoO:65400:2
      Source RD attributes: 0x0000:65001:404
      NHID:0x0(Ref:0)
  Route version is 0xb (11)
<snip>
RP/0/0/CPU0:PE-1#
```

For the IOS XE–based router PE-2, the command **show ip route vrf FULL-400-VRF repair-paths 10.2.10.128 255.255.255.240** in Output 7-50 provides the RIB details for the subnet 10.2.10.128/28:

- **10.0.4.1 (default), from 10.0.3.254, recursive-via-host:** This is the active BGP path via router PE-3 with next hop 10.0.4.1, and because BGP PIC Edge is configured on PE-2, recursion via a summary or default route is disabled, and iBGP next hops are resolved via host routes.

- **MPLS label: 24002:** Router PE-3 has allocated a VPNv4 label 24002 for the route 10.2.10.128/28.

- **[RPR]10.0.4.2 (default), from 10.0.3.254, recursive-via-host:** The BGP repair path is via next hop 10.0.4.2 (PE-4), and because BGP PIC Edge is configured on PE-2, recursion via a summary or default route is disabled, and iBGP next hops are resolved via host routes (in a process known as host recursion).

- **MPLS label: 18:** Router PE-4 has allocated a VPNv4 label 18 for the route 10.2.10.128/28.

Output 7-50 *SR-MPLS L3VPN Full-Mesh Configuration: RIB Details for Repair Path 10.2.10.128 on PE-2 (IOS XE)*

```
PE-2#show ip route vrf FULL-400-VRF repair-paths 10.2.10.128 255.255.255.240


Routing Table: FULL-400-VRF
Routing entry for 10.2.10.128/28
  Known via "bgp 65001", distance 200, metric 0
  Tag 65400, type internal
  Last update from 10.0.4.1 05:09:33 ago
  Routing Descriptor Blocks:
  * 10.0.4.1 (default), from 10.0.3.254, 05:09:33 ago, recursive-via-host
      opaque_ptr 0x7FE1A6F68158
      Route metric is 0, traffic share count is 1
      AS Hops 1
      Route tag 65400
      MPLS label: 24002
      MPLS Flags: MPLS Required
    [RPR]10.0.4.2 (default), from 10.0.3.254, 05:09:33 ago, recursive-via-host
      opaque_ptr 0x7FE1A6F68678
      Route metric is 0, traffic share count is 1
      AS Hops 1
      Route tag 65400
      MPLS label: 18
      MPLS Flags: MPLS Required
PE-2#
```

Output 7-51 shows the output of the command **show cef vrf FULL-400-VRF 10.2.10.128/28 detail** on router PE-1 to view the FIB details for the target subnet 10.2.10.128/28. The relevant information from this output is as follows:

- **via 10.0.4.1/32, recursive:** Router PE-3 is the active BGP path with next hop 10.0.4.1.

   - **recursion-via-/32:** IOS XR always recurses via /32 for labeled paths (that is, VPNv4 next hops).

   - **next hop 10.0.4.1/32 via 19001/0/21:** Next hop 10.0.4.1 (on PE-3) is learned via BGP labeled unicast label 19001.

- **next hop 192.168.3.1/32 Gi0/0/0/0   labels imposed {16100 19001 24002}:** This is a full label stack, with an IGP path via next hop 192.168.3.1/32 (on P-5) and SR-MPLS Anycast SID 16100 assigned to ABR-1 and ABR-2.The next hop 10.0.4.1 (on PE-3) with BGP labeled unicast label 19001. The BGP VPNv4 label is 24002. (Refer to the section "SR-MPLS Anycast SID" in Chapter 4 for more details on the Anycast SID).

- **via 10.0.4.2/32, 2 dependencies, recursive, backup:** Router PE-4 is the backup BGP path with next hop 10.0.4.2.

  - **recursion-via-/32:** IOS XR always recurses via /32 for labeled paths (that is, VPNv4 next hops).

  - **next hop 10.0.4.2/32 via 19002/0/21:** Next hop 10.0.4.2 (on PE-4) is learned via BGP labeled unicast, with label 19002.

  - **next hop 192.168.3.1/32 Gi0/0/0/0   labels imposed {16100 19002 18}:** This is a full label stack, with an IGP path via next hop 192.168.3.1/32 (on P-5) and SR-MPLS Anycast SID 16100 assigned to ABR-1 and ABR-2. The next hop 10.0.4.2 (on PE-4) with the BGP labeled unicast label 19002. The BGP VPNv4 label is 18.

Output 7-51   *SR-MPLS L3VPN Full-Mesh Configuration: FIB Details for 10.2.10.128/28 on PE-1 (IOS XR)*

```
RP/0/0/CPU0:PE-1#show cef vrf FULL-400-VRF 10.2.10.128/28 detail

10.2.10.128/28, version 216, internal 0x5000001 0x0 (ptr 0xa1415918) [1], 0x0 (0x0),
  0x208 (0xa19d00b8)
 Updated Jul 16 07:52:54.283
 Prefix Len 28, traffic index 0, precedence n/a, priority 3
  gateway array (0xa134e6c4) reference count 1, flags 0x102038, source rib (7), 0
  backups
                [1 type 1 flags 0x48441 (0xa17725d8) ext 0x0 (0x0)]
  LW-LDI[type=0, refc=0, ptr=0x0, sh-ldi=0x0]
  gateway array update type-time 1 Jul 16 07:52:54.283
 LDI Update time Jul 16 07:52:54.283
   via 10.0.4.1/32, 3 dependencies, recursive [flags 0x6000]
    path-idx 0 NHID 0x0 [0xa17cbcec 0x0]
    recursion-via-/32
    next hop VRF - 'default', table - 0xe0000000
    next hop 10.0.4.1/32 via 19001/0/21
      next hop 192.168.3.1/32 Gi0/0/0/0    labels imposed {16100 19001 24002}
   via 10.0.4.2/32, 2 dependencies, recursive, backup [flags 0x6100]
    path-idx 1 NHID 0x0 [0xa17cb918 0x0]
    recursion-via-/32
    next hop VRF - 'default', table - 0xe0000000
```

```
   next hop 10.0.4.2/32 via 19002/0/21
     next hop 192.168.3.1/32 Gi0/0/0/0    labels imposed {16100 19002 18}


   Load distribution: 0 (refcount 1)


   Hash  OK  Interface                Address
     0    Y   recursive                19001/0
RP/0/0/CPU0:PE-1#
```

Similarly, to view the router PE-2 (IOS XE) FIB details of the target subnet 10.2.10.128/28, Output 7-52 shows the use of the command **show ip cef vrf FULL-400-VRF 10.2.10.128/28 detail** and provides the following relevant information:

- **recursive via 10.0.4.1 label 24002:** Router PE-3 with next hop 10.0.4.1 has allocated a VPNv4 label 24002 for the route 10.2.10.128/28.

    - **recursive via 10.1.1.5 label 19001-(local:19001):** This is the BGP path to 10.0.4.1 (on PE-3) with the BGP labeled unicast label 19001 and the next hop 10.1.1.5.

    - **nexthop 192.168.3.5 GigabitEthernet2 label 16100-(local:16100):** This is the IGP path via next hop 192.168.3.5 (on P-5) and SR-MPLS Anycast SID 16100 assigned to ABR-1 and ABR-2.

- **recursive via 10.0.4.2 label 18, repair:** The backup/repair path via PE-4 with next hop 10.0.4.2 has allocated a VPNv4 label 18 for the route 10.2.10.128/28.

    - **recursive via 10.1.1.5 label 19002-(local:19002):** This is the BGP path to 10.0.4.2 (on PE-4) with the BGP labeled unicast label 19002 and next hop 10.1.1.5.

    - **nexthop 192.168.3.5 GigabitEthernet2 label 16100-(local:16100):** This is the IGP path via next hop 192.168.3.5 (on P-5) and SR-MPLS Anycast SID 16100 assigned to ABR-1 and ABR-2.

Output 7-52   *SR-MPLS L3VPN Full-Mesh Configuration: FIB Details for 10.2.10.128/28 on PE-2 (IOS XE)*

```
PE-2#show ip cef vrf FULL-400-VRF 10.2.10.128/28 detail
10.2.10.128/28, epoch 0, flags [rib defined all labels]
  recursive via 10.0.4.1 label 24002
    recursive via 10.1.1.5 label 19001-(local:19001)
      nexthop 192.168.3.5 GigabitEthernet2 label 16100-(local:16100)
  recursive via 10.0.4.2 label 18, repair
    recursive via 10.1.1.5 label 19002-(local:19002)
      nexthop 192.168.3.5 GigabitEthernet2 label 16100-(local:16100)
  PE-2#
```

Reachability to the service PE routers in the SR-MPLS reference network in Figure 7-11 occurs via domain-wide unique BGP Prefix SIDs, advertised as indexes or absolutes value by the BGP labeled unicast address family.

Figure 7-15 provides an L3VPN service layer overview of the BGP VPNv4 route 10.2.10.128/28 from the router CE-2 propagated via both PE routers in Metro 2 (PE-3 and PE-4) together with the BGP labeled unicast transport layer overview for next hop reachability (BGP Prefix SIDs) of the PE routers in Metro 2 (PE-3 and PE-4).

Note   The SR-MPLS transport layer is excluded from the diagram in Figure 7-15.

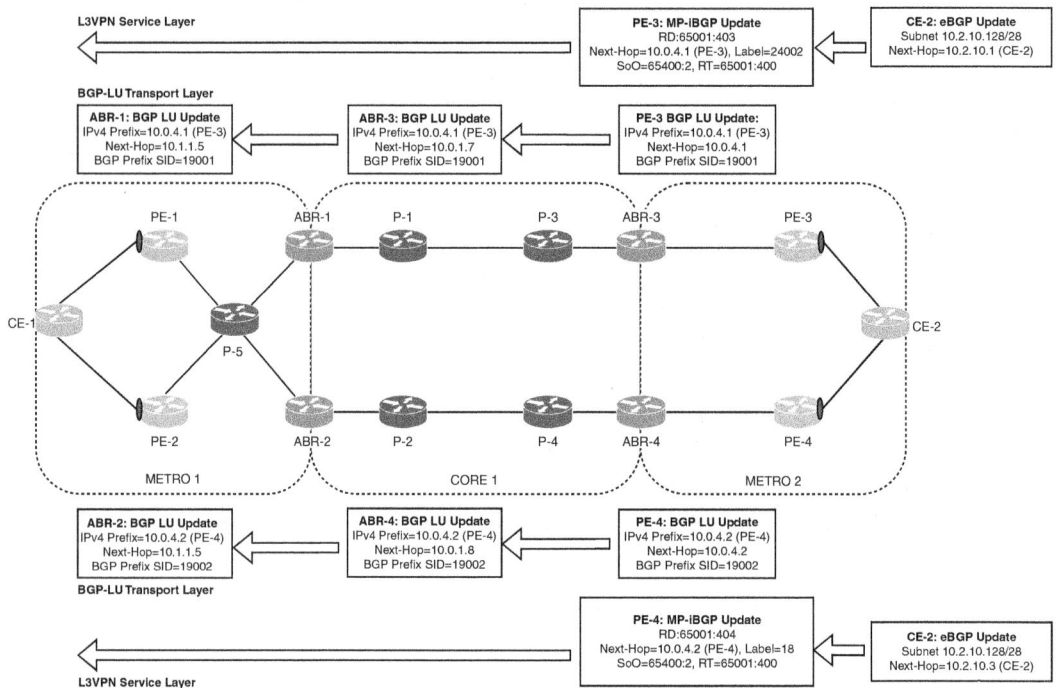

Figure 7-15   *SR-MPLS L3VPN Full-Mesh Configuration: BGP LU Transport Overview on 10.0.4.1/32 and 10.0.4.2/32*

Output 7-53 shows the output of the command **show bgp ipv4 labeled-unicast 10.0.4.1/32**, which provides the BGP labeled unicast route information of the next hop route 10.0.4.1/32 for the BGP subnet 10.2.10.128/28 executed on router PE-1. The relevant details from this output are as follows:

■ **Paths (1 available, best #1):**

   ■ **10.1.1.5 (metric 20) from 10.0.3.254 (10.0.4.1):** This is the BGP labeled unicast path to 10.0.4.1 (on PE-3) via next hop 10.1.1.5, which is reachable via the SR-MPLS Anycast SID 16100 assigned to ABR-1 and ABR-2.

   ■ **Received Label 19001:** This is the BGP labeled unicast label 19001 for 10.0.4.1

Note   CLI outputs for the second next hop route 10.0.4.2/32 are not included in the verification tasks because they are similar to those for 10.0.4.1/32.

Output 7-53   *SR-MPLS L3VPN Full-Mesh Configuration: BGP IPv4 LU RIB for 10.0.4.1/32 on PE-1 (IOS XR)*

```
RP/0/0/CPU0:PE-1#show bgp ipv4 labeled-unicast 10.0.4.1/32
BGP routing table entry for 10.0.4.1/32
Versions:
  Process           bRIB/RIB  SendTblVer
  Speaker                 28          28
    Local Label: 19001
Last Modified: Jul 17 09:49:09.410 for 3d18h
Paths: (1 available, best #1)
  Not advertised to any peer
  Path #1: Received by speaker 0
  Not advertised to any peer
  Local
    10.1.1.5 (metric 20) from 10.0.3.254 (10.0.4.1)
      Received Label 19001
      Origin IGP, metric 0, localpref 100, valid, internal, best, group-best,
labeled-unicast
      Received Path ID 1, Local Path ID 1, version 28
      Originator: 10.0.4.1, Cluster list: 10.0.3.254, 10.0.1.5, 10.0.1.254, 10.0.1.7
      Label-Index: 3001
```

Similarly to Output 7-53, Output 7-54 provides the BGP labeled unicast route information of the next hop route 10.0.4.1/32 for the BGP subnet 10.2.10.128/28 executed on router PE-2. The relevant details from this output are as follows:

■ **Paths (1 available, best #1, table default):**

   ■ **10.1.1.5 (metric 20) from 10.0.3.254 (10.0.3.254):** This is the BGP labeled unicast path to 10.0.4.1 (on PE-3) via next hop 10.1.1.5, which is reachable via the SR-MPLS Anycast SID 16100 assigned to ABR-1 and ABR-2.

   ■ **mpls labels in/out 19001/19001:** This is the BGP labeled unicast label 19001 for the address 10.0.4.1/32.

Output 7-54   *SR-MPLS L3VPN Full-Mesh Configuration: BGP IPv4 LU RIB for 10.0.4.1/32 on PE-2 (IOS XE)*

```
PE-2#show bgp ipv4 unicast 10.0.4.1/32
BGP routing table entry for 10.0.4.1/32, version 213
Paths: (1 available, best #1, table default)
```

```
Multipath: iBGP
Net local label from SRGB
  Not advertised to any peer
  Refresh Epoch 1
  Local
    10.1.1.5 (metric 20) from 10.0.3.254 (10.0.3.254)
      Origin IGP, metric 0, localpref 100, valid, internal, best
      sr-labelindex 0xBB9
      Originator: 10.0.4.1, Cluster list: 10.0.3.254, 10.0.1.5, 10.0.1.254, 10.0.1.7
      mpls labels in/out 19001/19001
      rx pathid: 0x1, tx pathid: 0x0
      Updated on Jul 18 2023 11:43:39 UTC
PE-2#
```

The following outputs executed in Metro 1, Core 1, and Metro 2 show the FIB route details for the next hop route 10.0.4.1/32.

Note   Outputs for the second next hop route 10.0.4.2/32 are excluded to keep these outputs concise.

Output 7-55 and Output 7-56 provide FIB details from routers PE-1 and PE-2 in Metro 1:

- **via 10.1.1.5/32:** This is the BGP path to 10.0.4.1 (PE-3) with next hop 10.1.1.5.

  - **recursion-via-/32:** IOS XR always recurses via /32 for labeled paths (that is, BGP labeled unicast).

  - **next hop 10.1.1.5/32 via 16100/0/21:** Next hop 10.1.1.5 (SR-MPLS Anycast SID from ABR-1 and ABR-2) is reachable via SR-MPLS with label 16100.

  - **next hop 192.168.3.1/32 Gi0/0/0/0   labels imposed {16100 19001}:** This is the full label stack, with IGP path via next hop 192.168.3.1/32 (on P-5) and SR-MPLS Anycast SID 16100 assigned to ABR-1 and ABR-2 and next hop 10.0.4.1 (on PE-3) with the BGP labeled unicast label 19001.

Output 7-55   *SR-MPLS L3VPN Full-Mesh Configuration: FIB Details for 10.0.4.1/32 on PE-1 (IOS XR)*

```
RP/0/0/CPU0:PE-1#show cef 10.0.4.1/32 detail

10.0.4.1/32, version 1369, labeled SR, internal 0x1000001 0x80 (ptr 0xa141565c) [1],
  0x0 (0xa13f7a80), 0xa08 (0xa1756420)
  Updated Jul 17 09:49:09.327
  Prefix Len 32, traffic index 0, precedence n/a, priority 4
```

```
gateway array (0xa134e37c) reference count 18, flags 0x78, source rib (7), 0
backups
                [7 type 5 flags 0x8441 (0xa1772558) ext 0x0 (0x0)]
 LW-LDI[type=5, refc=3, ptr=0xa13f7a80, sh-ldi=0xa1772558]
 gateway array update type-time 1 Jul 13 09:33:20.297
LDI Update time Jul 13 09:33:20.297
LW-LDI-TS Jul 13 09:33:20.297
  via 10.1.1.5/32, 3 dependencies, recursive [flags 0x6000]
  path-idx 0 NHID 0x0 [0xa17cabf8 0x0]
  recursion-via-/32
  next hop 10.1.1.5/32 via 16100/0/21
   local label 19001
   next hop 192.168.3.1/32 Gi0/0/0/0    labels imposed {16100 19001}


  Load distribution: 0 (refcount 7)


  Hash  OK  Interface            Address
   0     Y   recursive            16100/0
RP/0/0/CPU0:PE-1#
```

Output 7-56 shows IOS XE FIB details for the next hop route 10.0.4.1/32 on router PE-2:

- **recursive via 10.1.1.5 label 19001-(local:19001):** This is the BGP path to 10.0.4.1 (on PE-3) with the BGP labeled unicast label 19001 and next hop 10.1.1.5.

  - **nexthop 192.168.3.5 GigabitEthernet2 label 16100-(local:16100):** This is the IGP path to 10.1.1.5 via next hop 192.168.3.5 (on P-5) and SR-MPLS Anycast SID 16100 assigned to ABR-1 and ABR-2.

Output 7-56 *SR-MPLS L3VPN Full-Mesh Configuration: FIB Details for 10.0.4.1/32 on PE-2 (IOS XE)*

```
PE-2#sh ip cef 10.0.4.1/32 detail
10.0.4.1/32, epoch 2
  sr local label info: global/19001 [0x12]
  1 RR source [no flags]
  recursive via 10.1.1.5 label 19001-(local:19001)
    nexthop 192.168.3.5 GigabitEthernet2 label 16100-(local:16100)
PE-2#
```

The next stage of these FIB verifications is conducted in Core 1, where t. The output from ABR-1 in Output 7-57 provides the FIB details for the next hop route 10.0.4.1/32:

- **via 10.0.1.7/32:** This is the BGP path to 10.0.4.1 (on PE-3) with next hop 10.0.1.7. (BGP multipath is not configured, and the next hop 10.0.1.7 is the lower neighbor IP address.)

■ **next hop 10.0.1.7/32 via 16007/0/21:** This is the next hop 10.0.1.7 from ABR-3 via SR-MPLS label 16007.

■ **next hop 192.168.1.0/32 Gi0/0/0/2   labels imposed {16007 19001}:** This is the full label stack, with IGP path via next hop 192.168.1.0/32 (on P-1) and SR-MPLS label 16007 and next hop 10.0.4.1 (on PE-3) with the BGP labeled unicast label 19001.

Output 7-57   *SR-MPLS L3VPN Full-Mesh Configuration: FIB Details for 10.0.4.1/32 on ABR-1 (IOS XR)*

```
RP/0/0/CPU0:ABR-1#show cef 10.0.4.1/32 detail


10.0.4.1/32, version 15088, labeled SR, internal 0x5000001 0x80 (ptr 0xa1415d78)
  [1], 0x0 (0xa13f7c38), 0xa08 (0xa17566e0)
 Updated Jul 26 07:21:29.055
 Prefix Len 32, traffic index 0, precedence n/a, priority 4
  gateway array (0xa134e980) reference count 9, flags 0x78, source rib (7), 0
  backups
               [4 type 5 flags 0x8441 (0xa1772418) ext 0x0 (0x0)]
  LW-LDI[type=5, refc=3, ptr=0xa13f7c38, sh-ldi=0xa1772418]
  gateway array update type-time 1 Jul 26 07:21:29.055
 LDI Update time Jul 26 07:21:29.055
 LW-LDI-TS Jul 26 07:21:29.055
   via 10.0.1.7/32, 3 dependencies, recursive [flags 0x6000]
    path-idx 0 NHID 0x0 [0xa17cb170 0x0]
    recursion-via-/32
    next hop 10.0.1.7/32 via 16007/0/21
     local label 19001
     next hop 192.168.1.0/32 Gi0/0/0/2    labels imposed {16007 19001}


    Load distribution: 0 (refcount 4)


    Hash  OK  Interface              Address
     0    Y   recursive              16007/0
RP/0/0/CPU0:ABR-1#
```

Output 7-58 displays the FIB details for the next hop route 10.0.4.1/32 on the IOS XE router ABR-2:

■ **recursive via 10.0.1.7 label 19001-(local:19001):** This is the BGP path to 10.0.4.1 (on PE-3) with the BGP labeled unicast label 19001 and next hop 10.0.1.7.

■ **nexthop 192.168.1.8 GigabitEthernet3 label 16007-(local:16007):** This is the IGP path to 10.0.1.7 (on ABR-3) via next hop 192.168.1.8 (on P-2) and SR-MPLS label 16007.

Output 7-58 *SR-MPLS L3VPN Full-Mesh Configuration: FIB Details for 10.0.4.1/32 on ABR-2 (IOS XE)*

```
ABR-2#show ip cef 10.0.4.1/32 detail
10.0.4.1/32, epoch 2
  sr local label info: global/19001 [0x12]
  recursive via 10.0.1.7 label 19001-(local:19001)
    nexthop 192.168.1.8 GigabitEthernet3 label 16007-(local:16007)
ABR-2#
```

Finally, in Metro 2, the output from ABR-3 in Output 7-59 presents FIB details for the next hop route 10.0.4.1/32:

- **via 192.168.4.1/32, GigabitEthernet0/0/0/0:** The route is learned via OSPF over the interface GigabitEthernet0/0/0/0.

  - **next hop 192.168.4.1/32:** This is the IGP (OSPF) path to 10.0.4.1 via next hop 192.168.4.1 (on PE-3).

  - **labels imposed {ImplNull}:** ABR-3 is the PHP router and performs a label lookup and pop before forwarding the traffic.

Output 7-59 *SR-MPLS L3VPN Full-Mesh Configuration: FIB Details for 10.0.4.1/32 on ABR-3 (IOS XR)*

```
RP/0/0/CPU0:ABR-3#show cef 10.0.4.1/32 detail

10.0.4.1/32, version 537, labeled SR, internal 0x1000001 0x81 (ptr 0xa1415058) [1],
  0x0 (0xa13f7dc8), 0xa20 (0xa175644c)
 Updated Jul 26 07:19:28.546
 local adjacency 192.168.4.1
 Prefix Len 32, traffic index 0, precedence n/a, priority 1
  gateway array (0xa134ee6c) reference count 3, flags 0x68, source rib (7), 0
  backups
             [3 type 4 flags 0x8401 (0xa1772818) ext 0x0 (0x0)]
  LW-LDI[type=1, refc=1, ptr=0xa13f7dc8, sh-ldi=0xa1772818]
  gateway array update type-time 1 Jul 24 15:01:54.243
 LDI Update time Jul 24 15:01:54.243
 LW-LDI-TS Jul 24 15:01:54.243
   via 192.168.4.1/32, GigabitEthernet0/0/0/0, 9 dependencies, weight 0, class 0
 [flags 0x0]
   path-idx 0 NHID 0x0 [0xa18a86e8 0xa18a8740]
   next hop 192.168.4.1/32
   local adjacency
   local label 19001      labels imposed {ImplNull}
```

```
   Load distribution: 0 (refcount 3)

   Hash  OK  Interface              Address
   0     Y   GigabitEthernet0/0/0/0   192.168.4.1
RP/0/0/CPU0:ABR-3#
```

The FIB output for the next hop route 10.0.4.1/32 from router ABR-4 is presented in Output 7-60:

■ **nexthop 192.168.4.3 GigabitEthernet2:** This is the IGP (OSPF) path to 10.0.4.1 via next hop 192.168.4.3 (on PE-3).

Output 7-60   *SR-MPLS L3VPN Full-Mesh Configuration: FIB Details for 10.0.4.1/32 on ABR-4 (IOS XE)*

```
ABR-4#show ip cef 10.0.4.1/32 detail
10.0.4.1/32, epoch 2
  sr local label info: global/19001 [0x1B]
  nexthop 192.168.4.3 GigabitEthernet2
ABR-4#
```

A traceroute between the customer routers CE-1 and CE-2 provides a quick end-to-end verification that the customer subnets are reachable. The traceroute output from Output 7-61 confirms end-to-end reachability and that the label stack matches the FIB outputs from the previous commands.

Output 7-61   *SR-MPLS L3VPN Full-Mesh Configuration: Traceroute Between CE-1 and CE-2*

```
RP/0/0/CPU0:CE-1#traceroute 10.2.10.129 source 10.1.10.129

Type escape sequence to abort.
Tracing the route to 10.2.10.129

 1   10.1.10.0 19 msec <--------------------------------------------PE-1
 2   192.168.3.1 [MPLS: Labels 16100/19001/24002 Exp 0] 59 msec <---P-5
 3   192.168.3.11 [MPLS: Labels 19001/24002 Exp 0] 69 msec  <-------ABR-2
 4   192.168.1.8 [MPLS: Labels 16007/19001/24002 Exp 0] 49 msec <---P-2
 5   192.168.1.33 [MPLS: Labels 16007/19001/24002 Exp 0] 49 msec <--P-3
 6   192.168.1.39 [MPLS: Labels 19001/24002 Exp 0] 59 msec <--------ABR-3
 7   192.168.4.1 [MPLS: Label 24002 Exp 0] 69 msec <----------------PE-3
 8   10.2.10.1 59 msec  *  59 msec
RP/0/0/CPU0:CE-1#
```

As mentioned previously, the commands shown in this section are by no means all that can be used for verification of SR-MPLS L3VPN full-mesh services but should be sufficient for explanation purposes.

SR-MPLS L3VPN Hub-and-Spoke Service

In this section, we outline the configuration and verification tasks for setting up a standard L3VPN hub-and-spoke overlay network using an SR-MPLS transport network. Direct communication between spokes is not enabled; instead, spoke-to-spoke communication occurs through the hub site CE router. Hub-to-spoke communication is facilitated by using import and export route-target values, which will be detailed later.

SR-MPLS L3VPN Hub-and-Spoke Configuration

The reference network in Figure 7-16 is based on a single PE–CE interface and a single VRF instance hub site. In Metro 1, the hub site consists of the CE-1 router dual-homed to PE-1 and PE-2, and in Metro 2, the Spoke Site 1 router CE-2 is dual attached to PE-3 and PE-4, and the Spoke Site 2 router CE-3 is single attached to PE-5. The dual-attached hub site router CE-1 is set up in a unipath active/standby scenario via the PE routers PE-1 and PE-2 using a BGP local preference, with the active path set to a BGP local preference of 200 and the backup link set to a BGP local preference of 150. To improve convergence times in the event that the active PE–CE path fails, BGP PIC Edge has also been configured.

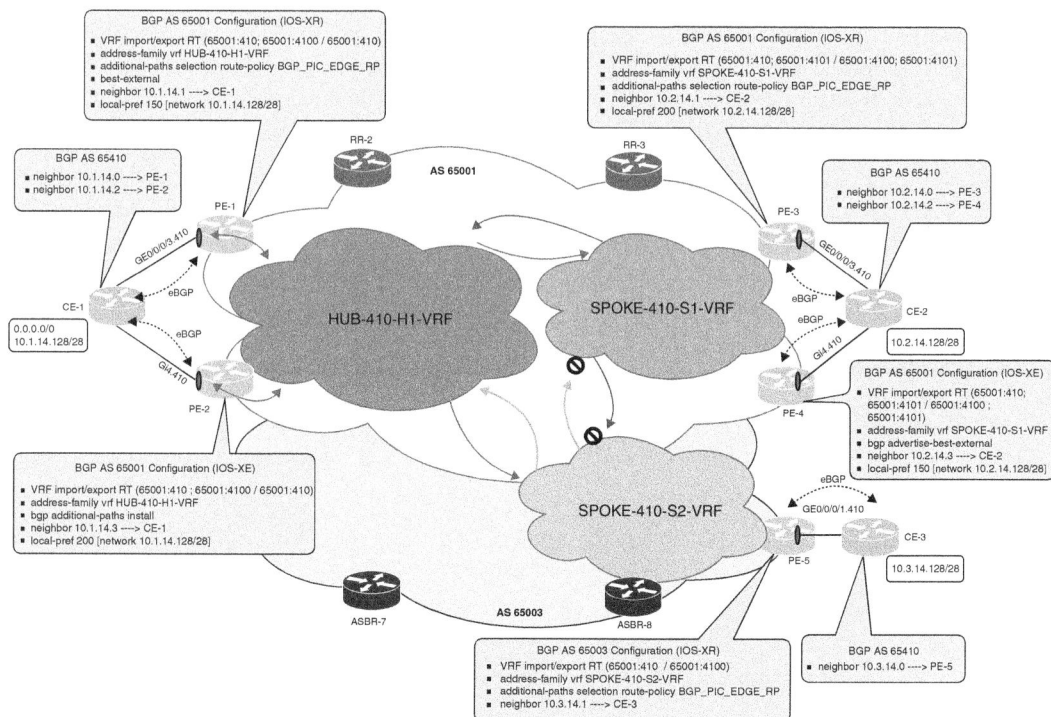

Figure 7-16 *SR-MPLS L3VPN Hub-and-Spoke Configuration Tasks*

To provision this L3VPN hub-and-spoke service, the following attributes are applicable to the service configuration:

- Hub site network 10.1.14.128/28 (on CE-1) is dual attached to PE-1 and PE-2 via the VRF instance HUB-410-H1-VRF.

- The hub site VRF instance HUB-410-H1-VRF is configured with export route target 65000:410 and import route targets 65000:410 and 65000:4100.

- Spoke Site 1 network 10.2.14.128/28 (CE-2) is dual attached via the routers PE-3 and PE-4 with the VRF instance SPOKE-410-S1-VRF and configured with export route targets 65000:4100 and 65000:4101; the import route targets configured are 65000:410 and 65000:4101. The reason for the import/export route target 65000:4101 is to import the backup paths of the CE-2 spoke site from the peer PE router.

- Spoke Site 2 network 10.3.14.128/28 from router CE-3 is single attached to PE-5 via the VRF instance SPOKE-410-S2-VRF and configured with export route target 65000:4100 and import route target 65000:410.

In the reference network shown in Figure 7-16, the desired behavior is for communication to be possible between the spoke sites only via the central hub site router CE-1, facilitated by router CE-1 advertising a default route toward the two spoke sites. The label allocation mode on the hub site PE routers has been left set to the default per-prefix label allocation mode as this will have the inter-spoke site traffic routed toward the hub site CE-1 first before it is routed back to the destination spoke site router. If these label allocation modes are set to the per-VRF label allocation mode, the PE routers will make an IP forwarding lookup for the next hop and route the traffic directly to the destination spoke site router without it first reaching the hub site router.

Config 7-39 shows the service configuration for the hub site VRF instance HUB-410-H1-VRF on router PE-1. The attached hub site router, CE-1, is generating the route 10.1.14.128/28 together with a default route toward the spoke sites, allowing them to reach the CE-1 subnet 10.1.14.128/28 as well as allowing spoke-to-spoke communication via the hub site router CE-1.

Config 7-39 *SR-MPLS L3VPN Hub-and-Spoke Configuration: Hub Site Configuration on PE-1 (IOS XR)*

```
!
vrf HUB-410-H1-VRF
 address-family ipv4 unicast
  import route-target
   65001:410
   65001:4100
  !
  export route-target
   65001:410
```

```
 !
 !
!
interface GigabitEthernet0/0/0/3
 description Connected_to_CE-1
 cdp
 !
interface GigabitEthernet0/0/0/3.410
 description Connected_to_CE-1
 vrf HUB-410-H1-VRF
 ipv4 address 10.1.14.0 255.255.255.254
 encapsulation dot1q 410
 !
route-policy SID($SID)
  set label-index $SID
end-policy
 !
route-policy PASS_RP
  pass
end-policy
 !
route-policy BGP_ADD_PATH_RP
  set path-selection all advertise
end-policy
 !
route-policy BGP_LOC-PREF_RP($LP)
  set local-preference $LP
end-policy
 !
route-policy BGP_PIC_EDGE_RP
  set path-selection backup 1 install
end-policy
 !
router bgp 65001
 bgp router-id 10.0.3.1
 address-family ipv4 unicast
  maximum-paths ibgp 2
  network 10.0.3.1/32 route-policy SID(2001)
  allocate-label all
  !
 address-family vpnv4 unicast
  additional-paths selection route-policy BGP_PIC_EDGE_RP
  !
```

```
neighbor-group IBGP-RR-NG
 remote-as 65001
 description *** iBGP peering to RR ***
 update-source Loopback0
 address-family ipv4 labeled-unicast
  !
 address-family vpnv4 unicast
  !
 !
neighbor 10.0.3.254
 remote-as 65001
 use neighbor-group IBGP-RR-NG
 description *** iBGP session to METRO-1 RR ***
 !
vrf HUB-410-H1-VRF
 rd 65001:4101
 address-family ipv4 unicast
  advertise best-external
  !
 neighbor 10.1.14.1
  remote-as 65410
  address-family ipv4 unicast
   route-policy BGP_LOC-PREF_RP(150) in
   route-policy PASS_RP out
   as-override
   site-of-origin 65410:1
   !
```

Config 7-40 shows the service configuration for the hub site VRF instance HUB-410-H1-VRF on the peer router PE-2. This router is configured as the active path to the hub site, based on the higher local preference value of 200 implemented with the configuration set local-preference 200.

Config 7-40 *SR-MPLS L3VPN Hub-and-Spoke Configuration: Hub Site Configuration on PE-2 (IOS XE)*

```
!
ip vrf HUB-410-H1-VRF
 rd 65001:4102
 route-target export 65001:410
 route-target import 65001:410
 route-target import 65001:4100
!
```

```
interface GigabitEthernet4
 description Connected_to_CE-1
 no ip address
 negotiation auto
 cdp enable
!
interface GigabitEthernet4.410
 description Connected_to_CE-1
 encapsulation dot1Q 410
 ip vrf forwarding HUB-410-H1-VRF
 ip address 10.1.14.2 255.255.255.254
!
router bgp 65001
 bgp router-id 10.0.3.2
 bgp log-neighbor-changes
 neighbor 10.0.3.254 remote-as 65001
 neighbor 10.0.3.254 update-source Loopback0
 !
 address-family ipv4
  network 10.0.3.2 mask 255.255.255.255
  segment-routing mpls
  neighbor 10.0.3.254 activate
  neighbor 10.0.3.254 additional-paths receive
  neighbor 10.0.3.254 send-label
  maximum-paths ibgp 2
 exit-address-family
 !
 address-family vpnv4
  neighbor 10.0.3.254 activate
  neighbor 10.0.3.254 send-community both
 exit-address-family
 !
 address-family ipv4 vrf HUB-410-H1-VRF
  bgp additional-paths install
  neighbor 10.1.14.3 remote-as 65410
  neighbor 10.1.14.3 activate
  neighbor 10.1.14.3 as-override
  neighbor 10.1.14.3 soo 65410:1
  neighbor 10.1.14.3 route-map BGP_LOC-PREF_RP in
 exit-address-family
!
route-map BGP_LOC-PREF_RP permit 10
 set local-preference 200
!
```

In Metro 2, Spoke Site 1 router CE-2 is attached to the VRF instance SPOKE-410-S1-VRF on both PE-3 and PE-4. Config 7-41 shows the configuration for router PE-3, with the active path to Spoke Site 1 configured due to the higher local preference applied with the route policy BGP_LOC-PREF_RP(200).

Config 7-41   *SR-MPLS L3VPN Hub-and-Spoke Configuration: Spoke Site 1 Configuration on PE-3 (IOS XR)*

```
!
vrf SPOKE-410-S1-VRF
 address-family ipv4 unicast
  import route-target
   65001:410
   65001:4101
  !
  export route-target
   65001:4100
   65001:4101
  !
 !
!
interface GigabitEthernet0/0/0/3
 description Connected_to_CE-2
 cdp
!
interface GigabitEthernet0/0/0/3.410
 description Connected_to_CE-2
 vrf SPOKE-410-S1-VRF
 ipv4 address 10.2.14.0 255.255.255.254
 encapsulation dot1q 410
!
route-policy SID($SID)
  set label-index $SID
end-policy
!
route-policy PASS_RP
  pass
end-policy
!
route-policy BGP_LOC-PREF_RP($LP)
  set local-preference $LP
end-policy
!
route-policy BGP_PIC_EDGE_RP
```

```
  set path-selection backup 1 install
end-policy
!
router bgp 65001
 bgp router-id 10.0.4.1
 address-family ipv4 unicast
  maximum-paths ibgp 2
  network 10.0.4.1/32 route-policy SID(3001)
  allocate-label all
 !
 address-family vpnv4 unicast
  additional-paths selection route-policy BGP_PIC_EDGE_RP
 !
 neighbor-group IBGP-RR-NG
  remote-as 65001
  description *** iBGP peering to RR ***
  update-source Loopback0
  address-family vpnv4 unicast
  !
 !
 neighbor 10.0.1.7
  remote-as 65001
  update-source Loopback0
  address-family ipv4 labeled-unicast
  !
 !
 neighbor 10.0.1.8
  remote-as 65001
  update-source Loopback0
  address-family ipv4 labeled-unicast
  !
 !
 neighbor 10.0.4.254
  remote-as 65001
  use neighbor-group IBGP-RR-NG
  description *** iBGP session to METRO-2 RR ***
  update-source Loopback0
 !
 vrf SPOKE-410-S1-VRF
  rd 65001:4103
  address-family ipv4 unicast
  !
```

```
 neighbor 10.2.14.1
  remote-as 65410
  address-family ipv4 unicast
   route-policy BGP_LOC-PREF_RP(200) in
   route-policy PASS_RP out
   as-override
   site-of-origin 65410:2
  !
```

Config 7-42 shows the relevant configuration for the IOS XE router PE-4, with connectivity to Spoke Site 1.

Config 7-42   *SR-MPLS L3VPN Hub-and-Spoke Configuration: Spoke Site 1 Configuration on PE-4 (IOS XE)*

```
!
ip vrf SPOKE-410-S1-VRF
 rd 65001:4104
 route-target export 65001:4100
 route-target export 65001:4101
 route-target import 65001:410
 route-target import 65001:4101
!
interface GigabitEthernet4
 description Connected_to_CE-2
 no ip address
 negotiation auto
 cdp enable
!
interface GigabitEthernet4.410
 description Connected_to_CE-2
 encapsulation dot1Q 410
 ip vrf forwarding SPOKE-410-S1-VRF
 ip address 10.2.14.2 255.255.255.254
!
router bgp 65001
 bgp router-id 10.0.4.2
 bgp log-neighbor-changes
 neighbor 10.0.1.7 remote-as 65001
 neighbor 10.0.1.7 update-source Loopback0
 neighbor 10.0.1.8 remote-as 65001
 neighbor 10.0.1.8 update-source Loopback0
```

```
neighbor 10.0.4.254 remote-as 65001
neighbor 10.0.4.254 update-source Loopback0
neighbor 10.2.14.3 remote-as 65400
!
address-family ipv4
 bgp advertise-best-external
 network 10.0.4.2 mask 255.255.255.255
 segment-routing mpls
 neighbor 10.0.1.7 activate
 neighbor 10.0.1.7 send-label
 neighbor 10.0.1.8 activate
 neighbor 10.0.1.8 send-label
 no neighbor 10.0.4.254 activate
 neighbor 10.2.14.3 activate
 neighbor 10.2.14.3 as-override
 neighbor 10.2.14.3 soo 65410:2
 neighbor 10.2.14.3 route-map BGP_LOC-PREF_RP in
 maximum-paths ibgp 2
exit-address-family
!
address-family vpnv4
 neighbor 10.0.4.254 activate
 neighbor 10.0.4.254 send-community both
exit-address-family
!
address-family ipv4 vrf SPOKE-410-S1-VRF
 bgp advertise-best-external
 neighbor 10.2.14.3 remote-as 65410
 neighbor 10.2.14.3 activate
 neighbor 10.2.14.3 as-override
 neighbor 10.2.14.3 soo 65410:2
 neighbor 10.2.14.3 route-map BGP_LOC-PREF_RP in
 exit-address-family
!
route-map BGP_LOC-PREF_RP permit 10
 set local-preference 150
!
```

In Metro 3, the Spoke Site 2 router CE-3 is single attached to the VRF instance SPOKE-410-S2-VRF on PE-5 (IOS XR), as shown in Config 7-43.

Config 7-43 *SR-MPLS L3VPN Hub-and-Spoke Configuration: Spoke Site 2 Configuration on PE-5 (IOS XR)*

```
vrf SPOKE-410-S2-VRF
 address-family ipv4 unicast
  import route-target
   65001:410
  !
  export route-target
   65001:4100
  !
 !
!
interface GigabitEthernet0/0/0/3
 description Connected_to_CE-3
 cdp
!
interface GigabitEthernet0/0/0/3.410
 description Connected_to_CE-3
 vrf SPOKE-410-S2-VRF
 ipv4 address 10.3.14.0 255.255.255.254
 encapsulation dot1q 410
!
route-policy SID($SID)
  set label-index $SID
end-policy
!
route-policy PASS_RP
  pass
end-policy
!
route-policy BGP_PIC_EDGE_RP
  set path-selection backup 1 install
end-policy
!
!
router bgp 65003
 bgp router-id 10.0.5.1
 address-family ipv4 unicast
  maximum-paths ibgp 2
  network 10.0.5.1/32 route-policy SID(4001)
  allocate-label all
 !
 address-family vpnv4 unicast
```

```
    additional-paths selection route-policy BGP_PIC_EDGE_RP
 !
 address-family l2vpn evpn
 !
 neighbor 10.0.5.2
  remote-as 65003
  update-source Loopback0
  address-family ipv4 labeled-unicast
  !
  address-family vpnv4 unicast
  !
 !
 neighbor 10.0.5.3
  remote-as 65003
  update-source Loopback0
  address-family ipv4 labeled-unicast
  !
  address-family vpnv4 unicast
  !
 !
 vrf SPOKE-410-S2-VRF
  rd 65003:410
  address-family ipv4 unicast
  !
  neighbor 10.3.14.1
   remote-as 65410
   address-family ipv4 unicast
    route-policy PASS_RP in
    route-policy PASS_RP out
    as-override
   !
  !
 !
!
```

The L3VPN hub site VRF instance configuration tasks include the configuration of the VRF instance HUB-410-H1-VRF and import/export route targets, as well as assignment of the PE–CE interfaces to the specific VRF instances. Spoke Site 1 is configured with the VRF instance SPOKE-410-S1-VRF, and Spoke Site 2 is provisioned with the VRF instance SPOKE-410-S2-VRF. These are the specific tasks:

- **Import/export route target 65001:410:** Include this route target on routers PE-1 and PE-2 allowing the hub site router CE-1 routes to be imported into the remote spoke site VRF instances. The peer hub site PE router will also import the hub site CE-1 routes because BGP PIC Edge is configured for the VRF instance HUB-410-H1-VRF.

■ **Import route target 65001:4100:** Import both the spoke site CE-2 and CE-3 routes from the remote spoke sites.

■ **Import/export route target 65001:4101:** Configure this route target on routers PE-3 and PE-4 because the Spoke Site 1 router CE-2 is dual attached and BGP PIC Edge functionality is configured for the VRF instance SPOKE-410-S1-VRF between these PE routers.

■ **Import route target 65001:410:** Import the hub site CE-1 routes into the VRF instance SPOKE-410-S1-VRF on routers PE-3 and PE-4 for Spoke Site 1.

■ **Import route target 65001:410:** Import the hub site CE-1 routes into the VRF instance SPOKE-410-S2-VRF on router PE-4 for Spoke Site 2.

The hub site is configured in a unipath active/standby scenario for the PE–CE links between CE-1 and PE-1/PE-2. The BGP PIC Edge and BGP best-external features allow for faster convergence in the event that the active path fails. These configurations are highlighted in Config 7-44 for PE-1 and Config 7-45 for PE-2, which show the following:

■ The ingress routes learned across the eBGP neighborship CE-1–PE-2 are matched with the route policy BGP_LOC-PREF_RP, and the BGP local preference is set to 200.

■ The ingress routes learned across the eBGP neighborship CE-1–PE-1 are matched with the route policy BGP_LOC-PREF_RP, and the BGP local preference is set to 150.

■ On the IOS XR router PE-1, BGP PIC Edge is configured explicitly together with the BGP best-external feature with the command **advertise best-external.**

■ On the IOS XE router PE-2, BGP PIC Edge is enabled through the command **bgp additional-paths install.**

The Spoke Site 1 is also configured in a unipath active/standby scenario for the PE–CE links between CE-2 and PE-3/PE-4 together with BGP PIC Edge and the BGP best-external feature:

■ The ingress routes learned across the eBGP neighborship CE-2–PE-3 are matched by the route policy BGP_LOC-PREF_RP, and the BGP local preference is set to 200.

■ The ingress routes BGP learned across the eBGP neighborship CE-2–PE-4 are matched by the route policy BGP_LOC-PREF_RP, and the BGP local preference is set to 150.

Config 7-44 *SR-MPLS L3VPN Hub-and-Spoke Configuration: BGP PIC Edge and BGP Best-External on PE-1 (IOS XR)*

```
<snip>
!
route-policy BGP_LOC-PREF_RP($LP)
  set local-preference $LP
end-policy
!
route-policy BGP_PIC_EDGE_RP
  set path-selection backup 1 install
end-policy
!
router bgp 65001
<snip>
 !
 address-family vpnv4 unicast
  additional-paths selection route-policy BGP_PIC_EDGE_RP
 !
!
 vrf HUB-410-H1-VRF
  rd 65001:4101
  address-family ipv4 unicast
   advertise best-external
  !
  neighbor 10.1.14.1
   remote-as 65410
   address-family ipv4 unicast
    route-policy BGP_LOC-PREF_RP(150) in
    route-policy PASS_RP out
    as-override
    site-of-origin 65410:1
   !
  !
<snip>
```

Config 7-45 shows the route map IOS XE configuration example for router PE-2.

Config 7-45 *SR-MPLS L3VPN Hub-and-Spoke Configuration: BGP PIC Edge and BGP Best External on PE-2 (IOS XE)*

```
<snip>
router bgp 65001
<snip>
 !
address-family ipv4 vrf HUB-410-H1-VRF
  bgp additional-paths install
```

```
  neighbor 10.1.14.3 remote-as 65410
  neighbor 10.1.14.3 activate
  neighbor 10.1.14.3 as-override
  neighbor 10.1.14.3 soo 65410:1
  neighbor 10.1.14.3 route-map BGP_LOC-PREF_RP in
 exit-address-family
!
route-map BGP_LOC-PREF_RP permit 10
 set local-preference 200
!
<snip>
```

SR-MPLS L3VPN Hub-and-Spoke Verification

The verification tasks for the hub-and-spoke configuration you have just seen involve several valuable service verification commands that help ensure that the SR-MPLS L3VPN hub-and-spoke service is properly configured and operating as intended.

Figure 7-17 shows the verification commands used in this section and focuses on the subnet 10.3.14.128/28 advertised into the spoke VRF instance SPOKE-410-S2-VRF from the router CE-3 and imported into the hub site VRF instance HUB-410-H1-VRF.

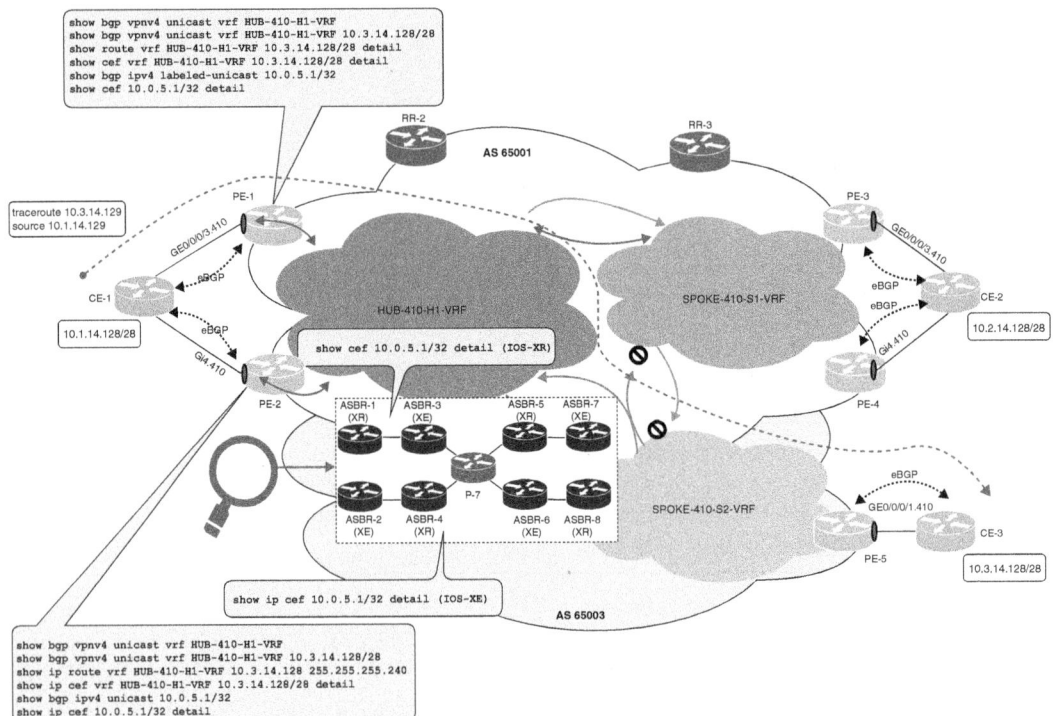

Figure 7-17   *SR-MPLS L3VPN Hub-and-Spoke Verification Tasks*

The command **show bgp vpnv4 unicast vrf HUB-410-H1-VRF** in Output 7-62 was collected on router PE-1 for the central hub site VRF instance. The subnets originating from the customer CE routers (CE-1, CE-2, and CE-3) are confirmed, and the IP subnet 10.3.14.128/28 originating from CE-3 will be the focus of the verification tasks. This subnet 10.3.14.128/28 has only a single next hop 10.0.5.1 (on PE-5) in Metro 3 (AS 65003).

Output 7-62 *SR-MPLS L3VPN Hub-and-Spoke Configuration: BGP VPNv4 RIB on PE-1 (IOS XR)*

```
RP/0/0/CPU0:PE-1#show bgp vpnv4 unicast vrf HUB-410-H1-VRF
<snip>
Status codes: s suppressed, d damped, h history, * valid, > best
              i - internal, r RIB-failure, S stale, N Nexthop-discard
Origin codes: i - IGP, e - EGP, ? - incomplete
   Network            Next Hop         Metric LocPrf Weight Path
Route Distinguisher: 65001:4101 (default for vrf HUB-410-H1-VRF)
*>i0.0.0.0/0          10.0.3.2              0    200      0 65410 i
*                     10.1.14.1                 150      0 65410 i
*>i10.1.14.128/28     10.0.3.2              0    200      0 65410 i
*                     10.1.14.1             0    150      0 65410 i
*>i10.2.14.128/28     10.0.4.1              0    200      0 65410 i
* i                   10.0.4.2              0    150      0 65410 i
*>i10.3.14.128/28     10.0.5.1                   100      0 65003 65410 i

Processed 4 prefixes, 7 paths
RP/0/0/CPU0:PE-1#
```

The command **show bgp vpnv4 unicast vrf HUB-410-H1-VRF** in Output 7-63 is from the IOS XE router PE-2.

Output 7-63 *SR-MPLS L3VPN Hub-and-Spoke Configuration: BGP VPNv4 RIB on PE-2 (IOS XE)*

```
PE-2#show bgp vpnv4 unicast vrf HUB-410-H1-VRF
BGP table version is 157, local router ID is 10.0.3.2
Status codes: s suppressed, d damped, h history, * valid, > best, i - internal,
              r RIB-failure, S Stale, m multipath, b backup-path, f RT-Filter,
              x best-external, a additional-path, c RIB-compressed,
              t secondary path, L long-lived-stale,
Origin codes: i - IGP, e - EGP, ? - incomplete
RPKI validation codes: V valid, I invalid, N Not found

     Network          Next Hop         Metric LocPrf Weight Path
Route Distinguisher: 65001:4102 (default for vrf HUB-410-H1-VRF)
 *bi  0.0.0.0         10.0.3.1                 150      0 65410 i
 *>                   10.1.14.3                200      0 65410 i
```

```
*>   10.1.14.128/28   10.1.14.3                  0    200      0 65410 i
*bi                   10.0.3.1                   0    150      0 65410 i
*bi  10.2.14.128/28   10.0.4.2                   0    150      0 65410 i
*>i                   10.0.4.1                   0    200      0 65410 i
*>i  10.3.14.128/28   10.0.5.1                        100      0 65003 65410 i
PE-2#
```

In Output 7-64, from the IOS XR router PE-1, the BGP VPNv4 route 10.3.14.128/28 originated from router CE-3 displays the following relevant information:

- **Paths: (1 available, best #1):** The output confirms that the subnet is available across one path only.

  - **Path #1:**

    - **10.0.5.1 (metric 20) from 10.0.3.254 (10.0.3.254):** PE-5 is the BGP next hop (10.0.5.1).

    - **Received Label 24009:** Router PE-5 has allocated a VPNv4 label 24009 for the route 10.3.14.128/28 from the router CE-3.

    - **Extended community: RT:65001:4100:** Route target 65001:4100 is applied to the subnet via PE-5, which allows the subnet to be imported into the central hub site VRF instance.

Output 7-64 *SR-MPLS L3VPN Hub-and-Spoke Configuration: BGP VPNv4 RIB for 10.3.14.128/28 on PE-1 (IOS XR)*

```
RP/0/0/CPU0:PE-1#show bgp vpnv4 unicast vrf HUB-410-H1-VRF 10.3.14.128/28
BGP routing table entry for 10.3.14.128/28, Route Distinguisher: 65001:4101
Versions:
  Process            bRIB/RIB   SendTblVer
  Speaker                  103          103
Last Modified: Aug  1 10:18:10.410 for 1d23h
Paths: (1 available, best #1)
  Not advertised to any peer
  Path #1: Received by speaker 0
  Not advertised to any peer
  65003 65410
    10.0.5.1 (metric 20) from 10.0.3.254 (10.0.3.254)
      Received Label 24009
      Origin IGP, localpref 100, valid, internal, best, group-best,
  import-candidate, imported
      Received Path ID 0, Local Path ID 1, version 103
      Extended community: RT:65001:4100
      Source AFI: VPNv4 Unicast, Source VRF: default, Source Route
  Distinguisher: 65003:410
RP/0/0/CPU0:PE-1#
```

Output 7-65 displays similar information for the BGP VPNv4 route 10.3.14.128/28 on the IOS XE PE router PE-2:

- **Paths (1 available, best #1, table HUB-410-H1-VRF):** The output confirms that the subnet is available from a single path.

  - **65003 65410, imported path from 65003:410:10.3.14.128/28:** The update with the route distinguisher 65003:410 is imported into the VRF instance, and the appended BGP AS 65003 and AS 65410 are included.

  - **10.0.5.1:** The next hop for router PE-5 in the global routing table, is learned via BGP labeled unicast.

  - **Extended Community: RT:65001:4100:** Route target 65001:4100 is applied to the subnet via PE-5, which allows the subnet to be imported into the central hub site VRF instance.

  - **mpls labels in/out nolabel/24009:** Router PE-5 has allocated a VPNv4 label 24009 for the route 10.3.14.128/28 from router CE-3.

Output 7-65 *SR-MPLS L3VPN Hub-and-Spoke Configuration: BGP VPNv4 RIB for 10.3.14.128/28 on PE-2 (IOS XE)*

```
PE-2#show bgp vpnv4 unicast vrf HUB-410-H1-VRF  10.3.14.128/28
BGP routing table entry for 65001:4102:10.3.14.128/28, version 157
Paths: (1 available, best #1, table HUB-410-H1-VRF)
  Additional-path-install
  Flag: 0x100
  Advertised to update-groups:
     27
  Refresh Epoch 1
  65003 65410, imported path from 65003:410:10.3.14.128/28 (global)
    10.0.5.1 (metric 20) (via default) from 10.0.3.254 (10.0.3.254)
      Origin IGP, localpref 100, valid, internal, best
      Extended Community: RT:65001:4100 , recursive-via-host
      mpls labels in/out nolabel/24009
      rx pathid: 0, tx pathid: 0x0
      Updated on Aug 1 2023 10:18:12 UTC
PE-2#
```

Figure 7-18 presents an overview of the BGP VPNv4 route 10.3.14.128/28 from the router CE-3 advertised via the PE-5 router in Metro 3.

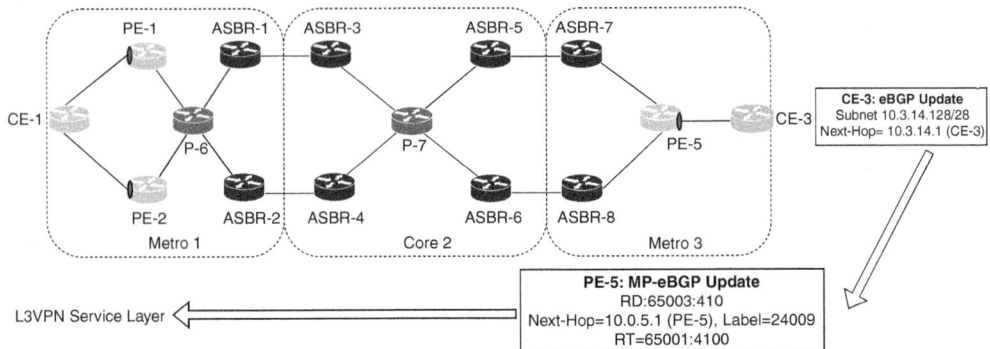

Figure 7-18 *SR-MPLS L3VPN Hub and Spoke: L3VPN Service Layer Overview on 10.3.14.128/28*

Output 7-66 shows output of the command **show route vrf HUB-410-H1-VRF 10.3.14.128/28 detail** on router PE-1 (IOS XR), which provides RIB details for the subnet 10.3.14.128/28 and confirms this received subnet's details:

- **10.0.5.1, from 10.0.3.254:** The active BGP path is via the next hop 10.0.5.1 (on PE-5).

- **Label: 0x5dc9 (24009):** Router PE-5 has allocated a VPNv4 label 24009 for the route 10.3.14.128/28 from router CE-3.

Output 7-66 *SR-MPLS L3VPN Hub-and-Spoke Configuration: RIB Details for 10.3.14.128/28 on PE-1 (IOS XR)*

```
RP/0/0/CPU0:PE-1#show route vrf HUB-410-H1-VRF 10.3.14.128/28 detail

Routing entry for 10.3.14.128/28
  Known via "bgp 65001", distance 200, metric 0
  Tag 65003, type internal
  Installed Aug  1 10:18:10.385 for 1d23h
  Routing Descriptor Blocks
    10.0.5.1, from 10.0.3.254
      Nexthop in Vrf: "default", Table: "default", IPv4 Unicast,
  Table Id: 0xe0000000
      Route metric is 0
      Label: 0x5dc9 (24009)
      Tunnel ID: None
      Binding Label: None
      Extended communities count: 0
      Source RD attributes: 0x0000:65003:410
      NHID:0x0(Ref:0)
<snip>
RP/0/0/CPU0:PE-1#
```

Output 7-67 shows the IOS XE command **show ip route vrf HUB-410-H1-VRF 10.3.14.128 255.255.255.240** executed on router PE-2, which displays the same RIB details for the subnet 10.3.14.128/28 that are displayed for router PE-1 in Output 7-66:

- **10.0.5.1 (default), from 10.0.3.254, recursive-via-host:** This is the BGP path via next hop 10.0.5.1 (on PE-5), and the next hop is resolved via host routes (in a process called host recursion).

- **MPLS label: 24009:** Router PE-5 has allocated a VPNv4 label 24009 for the route 10.3.14.128/28.

Output 7-67   *SR-MPLS L3VPN Hub-and-Spoke Configuration: RIB Details for 10.3.14.128/28 on PE-2 (IOS XE)*

```
PE-2#show ip route vrf HUB-410-H1-VRF 10.3.14.128 255.255.255.240


Routing Table: HUB-410-H1-VRF
Routing entry for 10.3.14.128/28
  Known via "bgp 65001", distance 200, metric 0
  Tag 65003, type internal
  Last update from 10.0.5.1 1d23h ago
  Routing Descriptor Blocks:
  * 10.0.5.1 (default), from 10.0.3.254, 1d23h ago, recursive-via-host
      opaque_ptr 0x7FE1A6F67C38
    Route metric is 0, traffic share count is 1
      AS Hops 2
      Route tag 65003
      MPLS label: 24009
      MPLS Flags: MPLS Required
PE-2#
```

Output 7-68 shows the FIB details displayed with the command **show cef vrf HUB-410-H1-VRF 10.3.14.128/28 detail** for the target subnet 10.3.14.128/28 on router PE-1 (IOS XR):

- **via 10.0.5.1/32, recursive:** The active BGP path is via router PE-5 with the next hop 10.0.5.1.

  - **recursion-via-/32:** IOS XR always recurses via /32 for labeled paths (that is, VPNv4 next hops).

  - **next hop 10.0.5.1/32 via 20001/0/21:** The next hop 10.0.5.1 (on PE-5) is learned via BGP labeled unicast, with label 20001.

  - **next hop 192.168.3.3/32 Gi0/0/0/1   labels imposed {18005 20001 24009}:** This is the full label stack, with an IGP path via next hop 192.168.3.3/32 (on P-6) and SR-MPLS label 18005 for ASBR-1. The next hop 10.0.5.1 (on PE-5) with the BGP labeled unicast label 20001. The service VPNv4 label is 24009.

■ **next hop 192.168.3.3/32 Gi0/0/0/1   labels imposed {18006 20001 24009}:** This is the full label stack, with an IGP path via next hop 192.168.3.3/32 (on P-6) and SR-MPLS label 18006 for ASBR-2. The next hop 10.0.5.1 (on PE-5) with the BGP labeled unicast label 20001. The service VPNv4 label is 24009.

Output 7-68   *SR-MPLS L3VPN Hub-and-Spoke Configuration: FIB Details for 10.3.14.128/28 on PE-1 (IOS XR)*

```
RP/0/0/CPU0:PE-1#show cef vrf HUB-410-H1-VRF 10.3.14.128/28 detail

10.3.14.128/28, version 31, internal 0x5000001 0x0 (ptr 0xa1416264) [1], 0x0 (0x0),
  0x208 (0xa17561b8)
 Updated Aug  1 10:18:10.404
 Prefix Len 28, traffic index 0, precedence n/a, priority 3
  gateway array (0xa134fca4) reference count 2, flags 0x2038, source rib (7), 0
  backups
               [1 type 1 flags 0x48441 (0xa1772798) ext 0x0 (0x0)]
  LW-LDI[type=0, refc=0, ptr=0x0, sh-ldi=0x0]
  gateway array update type-time 1 Aug  1 10:18:10.404
 LDI Update time Aug  1 10:18:10.404
   via 10.0.5.1/32, 3 dependencies, recursive [flags 0x6000]
    path-idx 0 NHID 0x0 [0xa17cbfa8 0x0]
    recursion-via-/32
   next hop VRF - 'default', table - 0xe0000000
    next hop 10.0.5.1/32 via 20001/0/21
     next hop 192.168.3.3/32 Gi0/0/0/1   labels imposed {18005 20001 24009}
     next hop 192.168.3.3/32 Gi0/0/0/1   labels imposed {18006 20001 24009}


   Load distribution: 0 (refcount 1)

   Hash  OK  Interface               Address
   0     Y   recursive               20001/0
RP/0/0/CPU0:PE-1#
```

Output 7-69 shows the output of the command **show ip cef vrf HUB-410-H1-VRF 10.3.14.128/28 detail**, which gives the IOS XE router PE-2 FIB details for the target subnet 10.3.14.128/28:

■ **recursive via 10.0.5.1 label 24009:** Router PE-5 with next hop 10.0.5.1 has allocated the VPNv4 label 24009 for the route 10.3.14.128/28.

   ■ **recursive via 10.0.3.5 label 20001-(local:20001):** This is the BGP path to 10.0.5.1 (on PE-5) with the BGP labeled unicast label 20001 and next hop 10.0.3.5 (on ASBR-1).

   ■ **nexthop 192.168.3.7 GigabitEthernet1 label 18005-(local:18005):** This is the IGP path via next hop 192.168.3.7 (on P-6) and SR-MPLS label 18005.

■ **recursive via 10.0.3.6 label 20001-(local:20001):** This is the BGP path to 10.0.5.1 (on PE-5) with the BGP labeled unicast label 20001 and the next hop 10.0.3.6 (on ASBR-2).

■ **nexthop 192.168.3.7 GigabitEthernet1 label 18006-(local:18006):** This is the IGP path via next hop 192.168.3.7 (on P-6) and SR-MPLS label 18006.

Output 7-69 *SR-MPLS L3VPN Hub-and-Spoke Configuration: FIB Details for 10.3.14.128/28 on PE-2 (IOS XE)*

```
PE-2#show ip cef vrf HUB-410-H1-VRF 10.3.14.128/28 detail
10.3.14.128/28, epoch 0, flags [rib defined all labels]
  recursive via 10.0.5.1 label 24009
    recursive via 10.0.3.5 label 20001-(local:20001)
      nexthop 192.168.3.7 GigabitEthernet1 label 18005-(local:18005)
    recursive via 10.0.3.6 label 20001-(local:20001)
      nexthop 192.168.3.7 GigabitEthernet1 label 18006-(local:18006)
PE-2#
```

Figure 7-19 provides an L3VPN service layer overview of the BGP VPNv4 route 10.3.14.128/28 from the router CE-3 propagated via the PE-5 router in Metro 3 together with the BGP labeled unicast transport layer for next hop reachability (BGP Prefix SIDs) of router PE-5 (10.0.5.1/32).

Note The SR-MPLS transport layer is excluded from the diagram Figure 7-19.

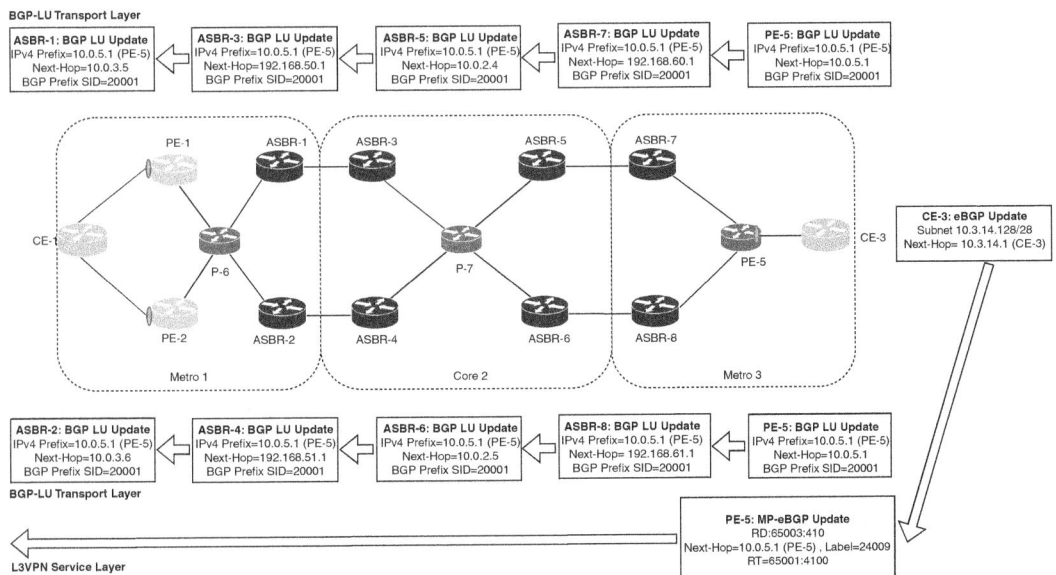

Figure 7-19 *SR-MPLS L3VPN Hub and Spoke: BGP LU Transport Layer Overview on 10.0.5.1/32*

Output 7-70 shows the command **show bgp ipv4 labeled-unicast 10.0.5.1/32** executed on router PE-1 and provides the BGP labeled unicast route information for the next hop route 10.0.5.1/32 for the L3VPN subnet 10.3.14.128/28:

- Paths (2 available, best #1):

  - Path #1:

    - **10.0.3.5 (metric 20) from 10.0.3.254 (10.0.3.5):** This is the BGP path to 10.0.5.1 (on PE-5) with next hop 10.0.3.5 (on ASBR-1).

    - **Received Label 20001:** This is the BGP labeled unicast label 20001 for 10.0.5.1.

  - Path #2:

    - **10.0.3.6 (metric 20) from 10.0.3.254 (10.0.3.6):** This is the BGP path to 10.0.5.1 (on PE-5) with next hop 10.0.3.6 (on ASBR-2).

    - **Received Label 20001:** This is the BGP labeled unicast label 20001 for 10.0.5.1.

Output 7-70 *SR-MPLS L3VPN Hub-and-Spoke Configuration: BGP IPv4 LU RIB for 10.0.5.1/32 on PE-1 (IOS XR)*

```
RP/0/0/CPU0:PE-1#show bgp ipv4 labeled-unicast 10.0.5.1/32


BGP routing table entry for 10.0.5.1/32
Versions:
  Process           bRIB/RIB  SendTblVer
  Speaker                 21          21
    Local Label: 20001
Last Modified: Jul 13 09:33:20.410 for 3w0d
Paths: (2 available, best #1)
  Not advertised to any peer
  Path #1: Received by speaker 0
  Not advertised to any peer
  65002 65003
    10.0.3.5 (metric 20) from 10.0.3.254 (10.0.3.5)
      Received Label 20001
      Origin IGP, localpref 100, valid, internal, best, group-best, multipath,
  labeled-unicast
      Received Path ID 1, Local Path ID 1, version 21
      Originator: 10.0.3.5, Cluster list: 10.0.3.254
      Label-Index: 4001
  Path #2: Received by speaker 0
  Not advertised to any peer
  65002 65003
```

```
   10.0.3.6 (metric 20) from 10.0.3.254 (10.0.3.6)
     Received Label 20001
     Origin IGP, metric 0, localpref 100, valid, internal, multipath,
   labeled-unicast
     Received Path ID 2, Local Path ID 0, version 0
     Originator: 10.0.3.6, Cluster list: 10.0.3.254
     Label-Index: 4001
RP/0/0/CPU0:PE-1#
```

Like Output 7-70, from router PE-1, Output 7-71 executed on router PE-2 displays the BGP labeled unicast route information of the next hop route 10.0.5.1/32 for the L3VPN subnet 10.3.14.128/28:

- **Paths (2 available, best #1, table default):**

    - **10.0.3.5 (metric 20) from 10.0.3.254 (10.0.3.254):** This is the BGP path to 10.0.5.1 (on PE-5) with next hop 10.0.3.5 (on ASBR-1).

    - **mpls labels in/out 20001/20001:** This is the BGP labeled unicast label 20001.

    - **10.0.3.6 (metric 20) from 10.0.3.254 (10.0.3.254):** This is the BGP path to 10.0.5.1 (on PE-5) with next hop 10.0.3.6 (on ASBR-2).

    - **mpls labels in/out 20001/20001:** This is the BGP labeled unicast label 20001.

Output 7-71 *SR-MPLS L3VPN Hub-and-Spoke Configuration: BGP IPv4 LU RIB for 10.0.5.1/32 on PE-2 (IOS XE)*

```
PE-2#show bgp ipv4 unicast 10.0.5.1/32
BGP routing table entry for 10.0.5.1/32, version 199
Paths: (2 available, best #1, table default)
Multipath: iBGP
Net local label from SRGB
  Not advertised to any peer
  Refresh Epoch 1
  65002 65003
    10.0.3.5 (metric 20) from 10.0.3.254 (10.0.3.254)
      Origin IGP, localpref 100, valid, internal, multipath, best
      sr-labelindex 0xFA1
      Originator: 10.0.3.5, Cluster list: 10.0.3.254
      mpls labels in/out 20001/20001
      rx pathid: 0x1, tx pathid: 0x0
      Updated on Jul 18 2023 11:43:39 UTC
  Refresh Epoch 1
  65002 65003
```

```
10.0.3.6 (metric 20) from 10.0.3.254 (10.0.3.254)
  Origin IGP, metric 0, localpref 100, valid, internal, multipath(oldest)
  sr-labelindex 0xFA1
  Originator: 10.0.3.6, Cluster list: 10.0.3.254
  mpls labels in/out 20001/20001
  rx pathid: 0x2, tx pathid: 0
  Updated on Jul 18 2023 11:43:39 UTC
PE-2#
```

Now we will scrutinize the FIB details for the next hop route to 10.0.5.1/32 that pertain to the L3VPN subnet 10.3.14.128/28. To accomplish this, we will use a sequence of commands, starting in Metro 1, proceeding to Core 2, and concluding in Metro 3.

The first set of verifications is from the router PE-1 in Metro 1, where the command **show cef 10.0.5.1/32 detail** provides the following FIB details (see Output 7-72):

- **via 10.0.3.5/32:** This is the BGP path to 10.0.5.1 (on PE-5) with next hop 10.0.3.5 (on ASBR-1).

  - **recursion-via-/32:** IOS XR always recurses via /32 for labeled paths (that is, BGP labeled unicast).

  - **next hop 10.0.3.5/32 via 18005/0/21:** Next hop 10.0.3.5 (on ASBR-1) is reachable via SR-MPLS, with the label 18005.

  - **next hop 192.168.3.3/32 Gi0/0/0/1 labels imposed {18005 20001}:** This is the full label stack, with the IGP path via the next hop 192.168.3.3/32 (on P-6) and SR-MPLS label 18005 and the next hop 10.0.5.1 (on PE-5) with the BGP labeled unicast label 20001.

- **via 10.0.3.6/32:** This is the BGP path to 10.0.5.1 (on PE-5) with next hop 10.0.3.6 (on ASBR-2).

  - **recursion-via-/32:** IOS XR always recurses via /32 for labeled paths (that is, BGP labeled unicast).

  - **next hop 10.0.3.6/32 via 18006/0/21:** Next hop 10.0.3.6 (on ASBR-2) is reachable via SR-MPLS, with the label 18006.

  - **next hop 192.168.3.3/32 Gi0/0/0/1 labels imposed {18006 20001}:** This is the full label stack, with the IGP path via next hop 192.168.3.3/32 (on P-6) and SR-MPLS label 18006 and next hop 10.0.5.1 (on PE-5) with the BGP labeled unicast label 20001.

Output 7-72   *SR-MPLS L3VPN Hub-and-Spoke Configuration: FIB Details for 10.0.5.1/32 on PE-1 (IOS XR)*

```
RP/0/0/CPU0:PE-1#show cef 10.0.5.1/32 detail


10.0.5.1/32, version 1508, labeled SR, internal 0x1000001 0x80 (ptr 0xa1415bd4) [1],
  0x0 (0xa13f7ad0), 0xa08 (0xa19d0238)
 Updated Aug  1 10:18:10.405
 Prefix Len 32, traffic index 0, precedence n/a, priority 4
  gateway array (0xa134e2f0) reference count 24, flags 0x78, source rib (7), 0
  backups
                [9 type 5 flags 0x441 (0xa1772698) ext 0x0 (0x0)]
  LW-LDI[type=5, refc=3, ptr=0xa13f7ad0, sh-ldi=0xa1772698]
  gateway array update type-time 5 Jul 17 09:48:39.279
 LDI Update time Jul 17 09:48:39.279
 LW-LDI-TS Jul 17 09:48:39.279
   via 10.0.3.5/32, 3 dependencies, recursive, bgp-multipath [flags 0x6080]
    path-idx 0 NHID 0x0 [0xa17caeb4 0x0]
    recursion-via-/32
    next hop 10.0.3.5/32 via 18005/0/21
     local label 20001
     next hop 192.168.3.3/32 Gi0/0/0/1    labels imposed {18005 20001}
   via 10.0.3.6/32, 3 dependencies, recursive, bgp-multipath [flags 0x6080]
    path-idx 1 NHID 0x0 [0xa17cb058 0x0]
    recursion-via-/32
    next hop 10.0.3.6/32 via 18006/0/21
     local label 20001
     next hop 192.168.3.3/32 Gi0/0/0/1    labels imposed {18006 20001}


    Load distribution: 0 1 (refcount 9)


    Hash  OK  Interface              Address
    0     Y   recursive              18005/0
    1     Y   recursive              18006/0
RP/0/0/CPU0:PE-1#
```

Output 7-73 shows the command **show ip cef 10.0.5.1/32 detail** from the IOS XE router PE-2 in Metro 1 and provides similar FIB details to Output 7-72:

- **recursive via 10.0.3.5 label 20001-(local:20001):** This is the BGP path to 10.0.5.1 (on PE-5) with the BGP labeled unicast label 20001 and next hop 10.0.3.5 (on ASBR-1).

  - **nexthop 192.168.3.7 GigabitEthernet1 label 18005-(local:18005):** This is the IGP path to 10.0.3.5 via next hop 192.168.3.7 (on P-6) and SR-MPLS label 18005.

- **recursive via 10.0.3.6 label 20001-(local:20001):** This is the BGP path to 10.0.5.1 (on PE-5) with the BGP labeled unicast label 20001 and next hop 10.0.3.6 (on ASBR-2).

    - **nexthop 192.168.3.7 GigabitEthernet1 label 18006-(local:18006):** This is the IGP path to 10.0.3.6 via next hop 192.168.3.7 (on P-6) and SR-MPLS label 18006.

Output 7-73 *SR-MPLS L3VPN Hub-and-Spoke Configuration: FIB Details for 10.0.5.1/32 on PE-2 (IOS XE)*

```
PE-2#show ip cef 10.0.5.1/32 detail
10.0.5.1/32, epoch 2, per-destination sharing
  sr local label info: global/20001 [0x12]
  1 RR source [no flags]
  recursive via 10.0.3.5 label 20001-(local:20001)
    nexthop 192.168.3.7 GigabitEthernet1 label 18005-(local:18005)
  recursive via 10.0.3.6 label 20001-(local:20001)
    nexthop 192.168.3.7 GigabitEthernet1 label 18006-(local:18006)
PE-2#
```

Remaining in Metro 1, the output from ASBR-1 in Output 7-74 provides FIB information for the next hop route 10.0.5.1/32:

- **via 192.168.50.1/32:** This is the BGP path to 10.0.5.1 (on PE-5) with next hop 192.168.50.1 (on ASBR-3).

    - **next hop 192.168.50.1/32 via 24000/0/21:** The next hop 192.168.50.1 (on ASBR-3) is a local adjacency, with local label 24000.

    - **next hop 192.168.50.1/32 Gi0/0/0/2   labels imposed {ImplNull 20001}:** This is the full label stack, with next hop 192.168.50.1/32 (on ASBR-3) with ImpNull and next hop 10.0.5.1 (on PE-5) with the BGP labeled unicast label 20001.

Output 7-74 *SR-MPLS L3VPN Hub-and-Spoke Configuration: FIB Details for 10.0.5.1/32 on ASBR-1 (IOS XR)*

```
RP/0/0/CPU0:ASBR-1#show cef 10.0.5.1/32 detail
10.0.5.1/32, version 7452, labeled SR, internal 0x5000001 0x80 (ptr 0xa1416cc8) [1],
  0x0 (0xa13f7b48), 0xa08 (0xa1756604)
 Updated Jul 17 09:48:38.181
 Prefix Len 32, traffic index 0, precedence n/a, priority 4
  gateway array (0xa134ee6c) reference count 21, flags 0x78, source rib (7), 0
  backups
              [8 type 5 flags 0x8441 (0xa1772418) ext 0x0 (0x0)]
  LW-LDI[type=5, refc=3, ptr=0xa13f7b48, sh-ldi=0xa1772418]
```

```
  gateway array update type-time 1 Jul  6 19:17:19.231
 LDI Update time Jul  6 19:17:19.231
 LW-LDI-TS Jul  7 04:57:24.036
  via 192.168.50.1/32, 5 dependencies, recursive, bgp-ext [flags 0x6020]
   path-idx 0 NHID 0x0 [0xa17cb88c 0x0]
   recursion-via-/32
   next hop 192.168.50.1/32 via 24000/0/21
    local label 20001
    next hop 192.168.50.1/32 Gi0/0/0/2    labels imposed {ImplNull 20001}


   Load distribution: 0 (refcount 8)


   Hash  OK  Interface                 Address
    0    Y   recursive                 24000/0
RP/0/0/CPU0:ASBR-1#
```

The output from the IOS XE router ASBR-2 in Output 7-75 provides similar FIB details for the next hop route 10.0.5.1/32:

- **recursive via 192.168.51.1 label 20001-(local:20001):** This is the BGP path to 10.0.5.1 (on PE-5) with the BGP labeled unicast label 20001 and next hop 192.168.51.1 (on ASBR-4).

  - **attached to GigabitEthernet3:** Reachable via interface Gi3 to ASBR-4.

Output 7-75 *SR-MPLS L3VPN Hub-and-Spoke Configuration: FIB Details for 10.0.5.1/32 on ASBR-2 (IOS XE)*

```
ASBR-2#show ip cef 10.0.5.1/32 detail
10.0.5.1/32, epoch 2
  sr local label info: global/20001 [0x12]
  recursive via 192.168.51.1 label 20001-(local:20001)
    attached to GigabitEthernet3
ASBR-2#
```

The output from **show ip cef 10.0.5.1/32 detail** on the IOS XE router ASBR-3 in Output 7-76 provides FIB details for the next hop route 10.0.5.1/32 in Core 2. On ASBR-3, there are two paths available: via ASBR-5 and ASBR-6. This behavior was applied via the configuration of maximum-paths ibgp 2 under bgp address-family ipv4:

- **recursive via 10.0.2.4 label 20001-(local:20001):** This is the BGP path to 10.0.5.1 (on PE-5) with the BGP labeled unicast label 20001 and next hop 10.0.2.4 (on ASBR-5).

  - **nexthop 192.168.2.1 GigabitEthernet2 label 17004-(local:17004):** This is the IGP path to 10.0.2.4 via next hop 192.168.2.1 (on P-7) and the SR-MPLS label 17004.

■ **recursive via 10.0.2.5 label 20001-(local:20001):** This is the BGP path to 10.0.5.1 (on PE-5) with the BGP labeled unicast label 20001 and next hop 10.0.2.5 (on ASBR-6).

■ **nexthop 192.168.2.1 GigabitEthernet2 label 17004-(local:17004):** This is the IGP path to 10.0.2.5 via next hop 192.168.2.1 (on P-7) and the SR-MPLS label 17005.

Output 7-76 *SR-MPLS L3VPN Hub-and-Spoke Configuration: FIB Details for 10.0.5.1/32 on ASBR-3 (IOS XE)*

```
ASBR-3#show ip cef 10.0.5.1/32 detail
10.0.5.1/32, epoch 2, per-destination sharing
  sr local label info: global/20001 [0x12]
  recursive via 10.0.2.4 label 20001-(local:20001)
    nexthop 192.168.2.1 GigabitEthernet2 label 17004-(local:17004)
  recursive via 10.0.2.5 label 20001-(local:20001)
    nexthop 192.168.2.1 GigabitEthernet2 label 17005-(local:17005)
ASBR-3#
```

Much as with the ASBR-3 router, there are two paths available on the IOS XR router ASBR-4, as shown in Output 7-77:via ASBR-5 and ASBR-6. This behavior was applied using the configuration of **maximum-paths ibgp 2** under bgp address-family ipv4:

■ **via 10.0.2.4/32:** This is the BGP path to 10.0.5.1 (on PE-5) with next hop 10.0.2.4 (on ASBR-5).

■ **recursion-via-/32:** IOS XR always recurses via /32 for labeled paths (that is, BGP labeled unicast).

■ **next hop 10.0.2.4/32 via 17004/0/21:** The next hop 10.0.2.4 (on ASBR-5) is reachable via SR-MPLS, with label 17004.

■ **next hop 192.168.2.3/32 Gi0/0/0/1   labels imposed {17004 20001}:** This is the full label stack, with the IGP path via next hop 192.168.2.3/32 (on P-7) and SR-MPLS label 17004 and next hop 10.0.5.1 (on PE-5) with the BGP labeled unicast label 20001.

■ **via 10.0.2.5/32:** This is the BGP path to 10.0.5.1 (on PE-5) with next hop 10.0.2.5 (on ASBR-6).

■ **recursion-via-/32:** IOS XR always recurses via /32 for labeled paths (that is, BGP labeled unicast).

■ **next hop 10.0.2.5/32 via 17005/0/21:** The next hop 10.0.2.5 (on ASBR-6) is reachable via SR-MPLS, with label 17004.

■ **next hop 192.168.2.3/32 Gi0/0/0/1   labels imposed {17005 20001}:** This is the full label stack, with the IGP path via next hop 192.168.2.3/32 (on P-7) and SR-MPLS label 17005 and next hop 10.0.5.1 (on PE-5) with the BGP labeled unicast label 20001.

Output 7-77   *SR-MPLS L3VPN Hub-and-Spoke Configuration: FIB Details for 10.0.5.1/32 on ASBR-4 (IOS XR)*

```
RP/0/0/CPU0:ASBR-4#show cef 10.0.5.1/32 detail
10.0.5.1/32, version 13895, labeled SR, internal 0x5000001 0x80 (ptr 0xa14154b8)
  [1], 0x0 (0xa13f7990), 0xa08 (0xa19fb058)
 Updated Aug  6 03:27:20.241
 Prefix Len 32, traffic index 0, precedence n/a, priority 4
  gateway array (0xa134e7dc) reference count 3, flags 0x78, source rib (7), 0
  backups
                [2 type 5 flags 0x8441 (0xa17724d8) ext 0x0 (0x0)]
  LW-LDI[type=5, refc=3, ptr=0xa13f7990, sh-ldi=0xa17724d8]
  gateway array update type-time 1 Aug  6 03:27:20.241
 LDI Update time Aug  6 03:27:20.241
 LW-LDI-TS Aug  6 03:27:20.241
   via 10.0.2.4/32, 5 dependencies, recursive, bgp-multipath [flags 0x6080]
    path-idx 0 NHID 0x0 [0xa17cad9c 0x0]
    recursion-via-/32
    next hop 10.0.2.4/32 via 17004/0/21
     local label 20001
     next hop 192.168.2.3/32 Gi0/0/0/1    labels imposed {17004 20001}
   via 10.0.2.5/32, 5 dependencies, recursive, bgp-multipath [flags 0x6080]
    path-idx 1 NHID 0x0 [0xa17ca93c 0x0]
    recursion-via-/32
    next hop 10.0.2.5/32 via 17005/0/21
     local label 20001
     next hop 192.168.2.3/32 Gi0/0/0/1    labels imposed {17005 20001}


    Load distribution: 0 1 (refcount 2)


    Hash  OK  Interface              Address
    0     Y   recursive              17004/0
    1     Y   recursive              17005/0
RP/0/0/CPU0:ASBR-4#
```

The next set of outputs captured in Core 2 is for the exit ASBR routers, ASBR-5 (see Output 7-78) and ASBR-6 (see Output 7-79), which provide FIB details for the next hop route 10.0.5.1/32.

Output 7-78 shows the output on IOS XR router ASBR-5:

- **via 192.168.60.1/32:** This is the BGP path to 10.0.5.1 (on PE-5) with next hop 192.168.60.1 (on ASBR-7).

  - **recursion-via-/32:** IOS XR always recurses via /32 for labeled paths (that is, BGP labeled unicast).

- **next hop 192.168.60.1/32 via 24008/0/21:** Next hop 192.168.60.1 (on ASBR-7) is a local adjacency, with local label 24008.

- **next hop 192.168.60.1/32 Gi0/0/0/1   labels imposed {ImplNull 20001}:** This is the full label stack, with next hop 192.168.60.1/32 (on ASBR-7) with ImpNull and next hop 10.0.5.1 (on PE-5) with the BGP labeled unicast label 20001.

Output 7-78   *SR-MPLS L3VPN Hub-and-Spoke Configuration: FIB Details for 10.0.5.1/32 on ASBR-5 (IOS XR)*

```
RP/0/0/CPU0:ASBR-5#show cef 10.0.5.1/32 detail


10.0.5.1/32, version 12814, labeled SR, internal 0x5000001 0x80 (ptr 0xa1415fa8)
 [1], 0x0 (0xa13f7b70), 0xa08 (0xa175644c)
 Updated Aug  1 10:19:57.415
 Prefix Len 32, traffic index 0, precedence n/a, priority 4
  gateway array (0xa134eb24) reference count 3, flags 0x78, source rib (7), 0
  backups
               [2 type 5 flags 0x8441 (0xa1772418) ext 0x0 (0x0)]
  LW-LDI[type=5, refc=3, ptr=0xa13f7b70, sh-ldi=0xa1772418]
  gateway array update type-time 1 Aug  1 10:19:57.335
 LDI Update time Aug  1 10:19:57.335
 LW-LDI-TS Aug  1 10:19:57.335
   via 192.168.60.1/32, 5 dependencies, recursive, bgp-ext [flags 0x6020]
    path-idx 0 NHID 0x0 [0xa17cbd78 0x0]
    recursion-via-/32
    next hop 192.168.60.1/32 via 24008/0/21
     local label 20001
     next hop 192.168.60.1/32 Gi0/0/0/1   labels imposed {ImplNull 20001}


    Load distribution: 0 (refcount 2)


    Hash  OK  Interface              Address
    0     Y   recursive              24008/0
RP/0/0/CPU0:ASBR-5#
```

The FIB output for next hop route 10.0.5.1/32 from ASBR-6 (IOS XE) is shown in Output 7-79:

- **recursive via 192.168.61.1 label 20001-(local:20001):** This is the BGP path to 10.0.5.1 (on PE-5) with the BGP labeled unicast label 20001 and next hop 192.168.61.1 (on ASBR-8).

- **attached to GigabitEthernet2:** Reachable via interface Gi2 to ASBR-8.

Output 7-79 *SR-MPLS L3VPN Hub-and-Spoke Configuration: FIB Details for 10.0.5.1/32 on ASBR-6 (IOS XE)*

```
ASBR-6#show ip cef 10.0.5.1/32 detail
10.0.5.1/32, epoch 2
  sr local label info: global/20001 [0x12]
  recursive via 192.168.61.1 label 20001-(local:20001)
    attached to GigabitEthernet2
ASBR-6#
```

Finally, Output 7-80, captured in Metro 3 for the IOS XE router ASBR-7 shows FIB details for the next hop route 10.0.5.1/32:

- **nexthop 192.168.5.1 GigabitEthernet1:** This is the IGP (IS-IS) path to 10.0.5.1 via next hop 192.168.5.1 (on PE-5).

Output 7-80 *SR-MPLS L3VPN Hub-and-Spoke Configuration: FIB Details for 10.0.5.1/32 on ASBR-7 (IOS XE)*

```
ASBR-7#show ip cef 10.0.5.1/32 detail
10.0.5.1/32, epoch 2
  sr local label info: global/20001 [0x1B]
  nexthop 192.168.5.1 GigabitEthernet1
ASBR-7#
```

Output 7-81, captured on IOS XR router ASBR-8, provides FIB details for the next hop route 10.0.5.1/32:

- **via 192.168.5.3/32, GigabitEthernet0/0/0/0:** This route is learned via IS-IS over the interface GigabitEthernet0/0/0/0.

  - **next hop 192.168.5.3/32:** This is the IS-IS next hop.

  - **local label 20001   labels imposed {ImplNull}:** ASBR-8, which is the PHP router, performs a label lookup and then pops the label before forwarding the traffic.

Output 7-81 *SR-MPLS L3VPN Hub-and-Spoke Configuration: FIB Details for 10.0.5.1/32 on ASBR-8 (IOS XR)*

```
RP/0/0/CPU0:ASBR-8#show cef 10.0.5.1/32 detail
10.0.5.1/32, version 12021, labeled SR, internal 0x1000001 0x83 (ptr 0xa1415800)
  [1], 0x0 (0xa13f7968), 0xa20 (0xa1756108)
 Updated Jul  7 04:56:50.986
 local adjacency 192.168.5.3
 Prefix Len 32, traffic index 0, precedence n/a, priority 1
  gateway array (0xa134ebb0) reference count 3, flags 0x68, source rib (7), 0
  backups
```

```
                   [3 type 4 flags 0x8401 (0xa1772298) ext 0x0 (0x0)]
  LW-LDI[type=1, refc=1, ptr=0xa13f7968, sh-ldi=0xa1772298]
  gateway array update type-time 1 Jul  7 04:56:39.236
 LDI Update time Jul  7 04:56:39.236
 LW-LDI-TS Jul  7 04:56:39.236
   via 192.168.5.3/32, GigabitEthernet0/0/0/0, 9 dependencies, weight 0, class 0
 [flags 0x0]
    path-idx 0 NHID 0x0 [0xa189b9a8 0xa189bab0]
    next hop 192.168.5.3/32
    local adjacency
    local label 20001       labels imposed {ImplNull}


    Load distribution: 0 (refcount 3)


    Hash  OK  Interface              Address
    0     Y   GigabitEthernet0/0/0/0  192.168.5.3
RP/0/0/CPU0:ASBR-8#
```

A traceroute between the customer hub site router CE-1 and the spoke site router CE-3 provides a quick end-to-end verification that the customer subnets are reachable between the hub site and the spoke site. The traceroute output in Output 7-82 confirms the end-to-end reachability and shows that the label stack matches the FIB outputs from the previously executed commands.

Output 7-82   *SR-MPLS L3VPN Hub-and-Spoke Configuration: Traceroute Between CE-1 (Metro 1) and CE-3 (Metro 3)*

```
RP/0/0/CPU0:CE-1#traceroute 10.3.14.129 source 10.1.14.129
Type escape sequence to abort.
Tracing the route to 10.3.14.129


 1   10.1.14.0 9 msec <----------------------------------------------PE-1
 2   192.168.3.3 [MPLS: Labels 18006/20001/24009 Exp 0] 89 msec <----P-6
 3   192.168.3.15 [MPLS: Labels 20001/24009 Exp 0] 119 msec <--------ASBR-2
 4   192.168.51.1 [MPLS: Labels 20001/24009 Exp 0] 79 msec <---------ASBR-4
 5   192.168.2.3 [MPLS: Labels 17005/20001/24009 Exp 0] 109 msec <---P-7
 6   192.168.2.6 [MPLS: Labels 20001/24009 Exp 0] 99 msec <---------ASBR-6
 7   192.168.61.1 [MPLS: Labels 20001/24009 Exp 0] 79 msec <---------ASBR-8
 8   192.168.5.3 [MPLS: Label 24009 Exp 0] 79 msec <----------------PE-5
 9   10.3.14.1 79 msec
RP/0/0/CPU0:CE-1#
```

As mentioned at the beginning of this section, communication is possible between the spoke site routers CE-2 and CE-3 but only via the central hub site (CE-1). This is due to the fact that the hub site advertises a default route toward both of the spoke sites.

A traceroute between CE-3 and CE-2 verifies that the spoke site subnets are reachable via the hub site router CE-1. The traceroute output in Output 7-83 confirms the end-to-end reachability.

Output 7-83 *SR-MPLS L3VPN Hub-and-Spoke Configuration: Traceroute Between CE-3 (Metro 3) and CE-2 (Metro 2)*

```
RP/0/0/CPU0:CE-3#traceroute 10.2.14.129 source 10.3.14.129
Type escape sequence to abort.
Tracing the route to 10.2.14.129

 1  10.3.14.0 0 msec <---------------------------------------------PE-5
 2  192.168.5.0 [MPLS: Labels 18002/20 Exp 0] 89 msec <--------------ASBR-7
 3  192.168.60.0 [MPLS: Labels 18002/20 Exp 0] 79 msec <-------------ASBR-5
 4  192.168.2.5 [MPLS: Labels 17003/18002/20 Exp 0] 89 msec <--------P-7
 5  192.168.2.2 [MPLS: Labels 18002/20 Exp 0] 79 msec <-------------ASBR-4
 6  192.168.51.0 [MPLS: Labels 18002/20 Exp 0] 89 msec <------------ASBR-2
 7  192.168.3.14 [MPLS: Labels 18002/20 Exp 0] 79 msec <------------P-6
 8  10.1.14.2 [MPLS: Label 20 Exp 0] 69 msec <---------------------PE-2
 9  10.1.14.3 79 msec <--------------------------------------------CE-1
10  10.1.14.0 79 msec <--------------------------------------------PE-1
11  192.168.3.1 [MPLS: Labels 16100/19001/24003 Exp 0] 209 msec <----P-5
12  192.168.3.11 [MPLS: Labels 19001/24003 Exp 0] 179 msec<---------ABR-2
13  192.168.1.8 [MPLS: Labels 16007/19001/24003 Exp 0] 129 msec <----P-2
14  192.168.1.33 [MPLS: Labels 16007/19001/24003 Exp 0] 149 msec <---P-3
15  192.168.1.39 [MPLS: Labels 19001/24003 Exp 0] 149 msec <--------ABR-3
16  192.168.4.1 [MPLS: Label 24003 Exp 0] 139 msec <----------------PE-3
17  10.2.14.1 139 msec
RP/0/0/CPU0:CE-3#
```

While the commands mentioned in this section are not exhaustive for configuration and verification of SR-MPLS L3VPN hub-and-spoke services, they should suffice for the purposes of explanation.

SR-MPLS L3VPN Extranet Service

This section describes the configuration and verification tasks for an L3VPN extranet service overlay network traversing an SR-MPLS transport network. In most cases, an L3VPN full-mesh or hub-and-spoke service site belongs to an entity (company, enterprise, or department) and serves users within that entity, and it is therefore referred to as an *intranet*. However, communications between different VPNs are sometimes required, such as between an external intercompany service or shared-service VPN and a limited subset of networks; these VPNs are referred to as *extranets*. A site can therefore be associated with more than one VPN—that is, both its intranet and one or more extranet VPNs. As with an L3VPN hub-and-spoke service, communication is achieved through the use of import and export route target values, and export map or import map policies may be used for more granular extranet access control.

SR-MPLS L3VPN Extranet Configuration

The two previously discussed L3VPN intranets—the full-mesh service and the hub-and-spoke service—are used to create the extranet service in the L3VPN extranet network shown in Figure 7-20. From Spoke Site 2 in the L3VPN hub-and-spoke service, a subnet attached to the Spoke Site 2 router (CE-3) in Metro 3 can communicate with a subnet attached to the router CE-1 in the L3VPN full-mesh service in Metro 1.

The CE-1 router is attached to the VRF instance FULL-400-VRF, which is dual-homed via the PE-1 and PE-2 routers. CE-1 is set up in a unipath active/standby scenario via the PE routers using BGP local preference, with the active path set to a BGP local preference of 200 and the backup link set to a BGP local preference of 150. BGP PIC Edge has also been configured to improve convergence when the more preferred PE–CE link fails:

- The subnet 10.1.10.144/28 will be exported to all the sites attached to the VRF instance FULL-400-VRF in the full-mesh service with an attached route target of 65001:400.

- This subnet 10.1.10.144/28 will also be exported to Spoke Site 2 router CE-3 in Metro 3 with an additional attached route target of 65001:4002.

- Spoke Site 2 router CE-3 will learn this additional extranet subnet 10.1.10.144/28 via its router PE-5, as it will be imported into the VRF instance SPOKE-410-S2-VRF.

- CE-1 will learn only this extranet subnet 10.3.14.144/28 originated by Spoke Site 2 router CE-3.

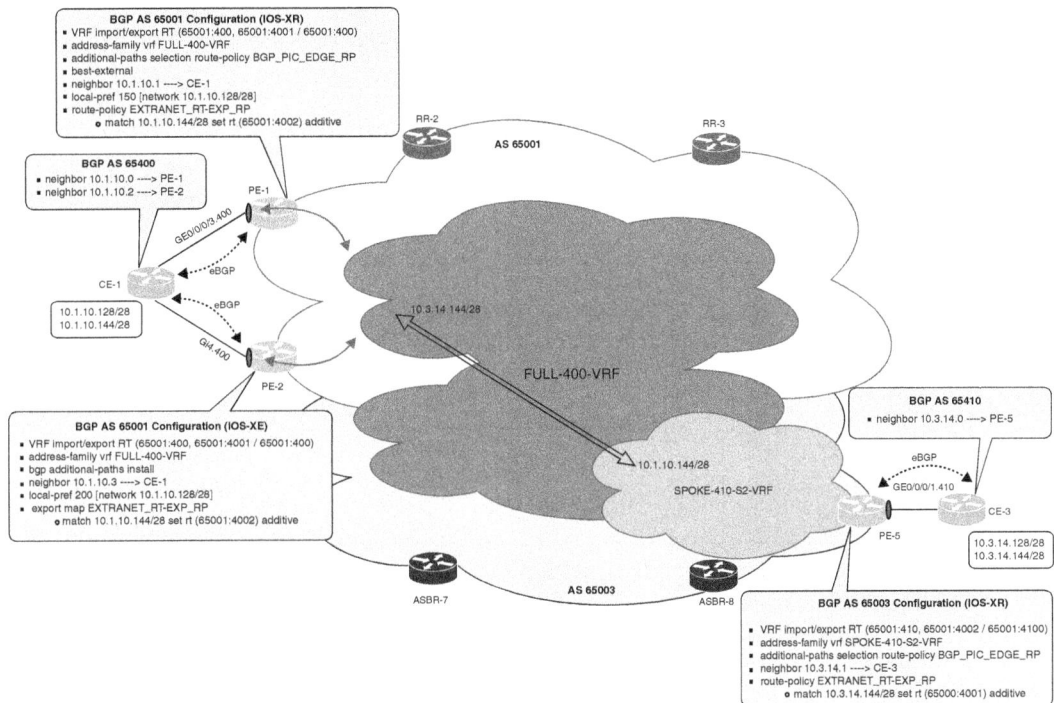

BGP AS 65001 Configuration (IOS-XR)
- VRF import/export RT (65001:400, 65001:4001 / 65001:400)
- address-family vrf FULL-400-VRF
- additional-paths selection route-policy BGP_PIC_EDGE_RP
- best-external
- neighbor 10.1.10.1 ----> CE-1
- local-pref 150 [network 10.1.10.128/28]
- route-policy EXTRANET_RT-EXP_RP
  ○ match 10.1.10.144/28 set rt (65001:4002) additive

BGP AS 65400
- neighbor 10.1.10.0 ----> PE-1
- neighbor 10.1.10.2 ----> PE-2

10.1.10.128/28
10.1.10.144/28

BGP AS 65001 Configuration (IOS-XE)
- VRF import/export RT (65001:400, 65001:4001 / 65001:400)
- address-family vrf FULL-400-VRF
- bgp additional-paths install
- neighbor 10.1.10.3 ----> CE-1
- local-pref 200 [network 10.1.10.128/28]
- export map EXTRANET_RT-EXP_RP
  ○ match 10.1.10.144/28 set rt (65001:4002) additive

BGP AS 65410
- neighbor 10.3.14.0 ----> PE-5

10.3.14.128/28
10.3.14.144/28

BGP AS 65003 Configuration (IOS-XR)
- VRF import/export RT (65001:410, 65001:4002 / 65001:4100)
- address-family vrf SPOKE-410-S2-VRF
- additional-paths selection route-policy BGP_PIC_EDGE_RP
- neighbor 10.3.14.1 ----> CE-3
- route-policy EXTRANET_RT-EXP_RP
  ○ match 10.3.14.144/28 set rt (65000:4001) additive

Figure 7-20 *SR-MPLS L3VPN Extranet Configuration Tasks*

Note Only extranet-related configurations are shown in the following examples.

As you can see in Config 7-46, router PE-1 uses the route policy EXTRANET_RT-EXP_ RP to match the 10.1.10.144/28 subnet to be exported and sets the export route target to 65001:4002. The **set extcommunity rt ($AS:$COM) additive** command allows the route target to be set in addition to the configured route target 65001:400 for the subnet 10.1.10.144/28, thereby allowing the subnet to be imported into the other L3VPN full-mesh sites for the VRF instance FULL-400-VRF. Import route target 65001:4001 allows the extranet subnet 10.3.14.144/28 from PE-5 to be imported into the VRF instance FULL-400-VRF on both PE-1 and PE-2.

Config 7-46 *SR-MPLS L3VPN Extranet Additional Configurations on PE-1 (IOS XR)*

```
!
vrf FULL-400-VRF
 address-family ipv4 unicast
  import route-target
   65001:400
   65001:4001
  !
```

```
   export route-policy EXTRANET_RT-EXP_RP(EXTRANET_EXP_PS, 65001, 4002)
   export route-target
    65001:400
   !
  !
 !
prefix-set EXTRANET_EXP_PS
  10.1.10.144/28
end-set
!
route-policy EXTRANET_RT-EXP_RP($PS, $AS, $COM)
  if destination in $PS then
    set extcommunity rt ($AS:$COM) additive
  endif
end-policy
!
```

The configuration on router PE-2 (IOS XE), is very similar. In Config 7-47, you can see that an export map EXTRANET_RT-EXP_RP matches the 10.1.10.144/28 subnet and sets the export route target to 65001:4002.

Config 7-47   *SR-MPLS L3VPN Extranet Additional Configurations on PE-2 (IOS XE)*

```
!
ip vrf FULL-400-VRF
 rd 65001:402
 export map EXTRANET_RT-EXP_RP
 route-target export 65001:400
 route-target import 65001:400
 route-target import 65001:4001
!
ip prefix-list EXTRANET_EXP_PS seq 5 permit 10.1.10.144/28
!
route-map EXTRANET_RT-EXP_RP permit 10
 match ip address prefix-list EXTRANET_EXP_PS
 set extcommunity rt 65001:4002 additive
!
```

As mentioned previously, the extranet route target 65001:4002 is included with the subnet 10.1.10.144/28, together with the L3VPN full-mesh route target 65001:400, as shown in Output 7-84 for PE-1.

Output 7-84 *SR-MPLS L3VPN Extranet: Route Policy Setting Route Targets to Additive on PE-1 (IOS XR)*

```
RP/0/0/CPU0:PE-1#show bgp vpnv4 unicast vrf FULL-400-VRF 10.1.10.144/28
BGP routing table entry for 10.1.10.144/28, Route Distinguisher: 65001:401
Paths: (2 available, best #1)
 Not advertised to any peer
  Path #1: Received by speaker 0
  Not advertised to any peer
  65400
    10.0.3.2 (metric 30) from 10.0.3.254 (10.0.3.2)
      Received Label 21
      Origin IGP, metric 0, localpref 200, valid, internal, best, group-best,
import-candidate, imported
      Received Path ID 0, Local Path ID 1, version 122
      Extended community: SoO:65400:1 RT:65001:400 RT:65001:4002
      Originator: 10.0.3.2, Cluster list: 10.0.3.254
      Source AFI: VPNv4 Unicast, Source VRF: default, Source Route
Distinguisher: 65001:402
  Path #2: Received by speaker 0
  Advertised to peers (in unique update groups):
    10.0.3.254
  65400
    10.1.10.1 from 10.1.10.1 (192.168.1.118)
      Origin IGP, metric 0, localpref 150, valid, external, best-external, backup,
add-path
      Received Path ID 0, Local Path ID 3, version 122
      Extended community: SoO:65400:1 RT:65001:400 RT:65001:4002
RP/0/0/CPU0:PE-1#
```

Config 7-48 shows the extranet-related configurations displayed for the router PE-5 where the route policy EXTRANET_RT-EXP_RP matches subnet 10.3.14.144/28 to be exported and sets the export route target to 65001:4001. In this case, the **set extcommunity rt ($AS:$COM) additive** command is required to allow this subnet to be imported into the hub site VRF instance for the L3VPN hub-and-spoke service. If this is not a requirement, then additive can be excluded from the configuration, and the subnet will only be imported into the VRF instance FULL-400-VRF on PE-1 and PE-2. The import route target 65001:4002 allows the extranet subnet 10.1.10.144/28 from the hub site to be imported into the VRF instance SPOKE-410-S2-VRF on PE-5.

Config 7-48   *SR-MPLS L3VPN Extranet Additional Configurations on PE-5 (IOS XR)*

```
!
vrf SPOKE-410-S2-VRF
 address-family ipv4 unicast
  import route-target
   65001:410
   65001:4002
  !
 export route-policy EXTRANET_RT-EXP_RP(EXTRANET_EXP_PS, 65001, 4001)
  export route-target
   65001:4100
  !
 !
!
prefix-set EXTRANET_EXP_PS
  10.3.14.144/28
end-set
!
route-policy EXTRANET_RT-EXP_RP($PS, $AS, $COM)
  if destination in $PS then
    set extcommunity rt ($AS:$COM) additive
  endif
end-policy
!
```

SR-MPLS L3VPN Extranet Verification

This section highlights several valuable commands for service verification that can help you ensure that the extranet service is set up and operating properly. It provides details on the steps required to verify the previously provisioned L3VPN extranet service. Figure 7-21 provides an overview of the commands used to verify this extranet service based on an SR-MPLS transport service. The Spoke Site 2 router CE-3 is attached to router PE-5 and accesses the VRF instance SPOKE-410-S2-VRF that is provisioned on this PE router. A subnet on CE-3 requires access to an extranet service subnet 10.1.10.144/28 attached to the CE-1 router. The CE-1 router is dual-homed to PE-1 and PE-2 via the VRF instance FULL-400-VRF and originates the extranet subnet 10.1.10.144/28. The PE routers apply an additional route target community to allow the importation of 10.1.10.144/28 into the VRF instance SPOKE-410-S2-VRF at PE-5 and learned on CE-3 as an extranet service.

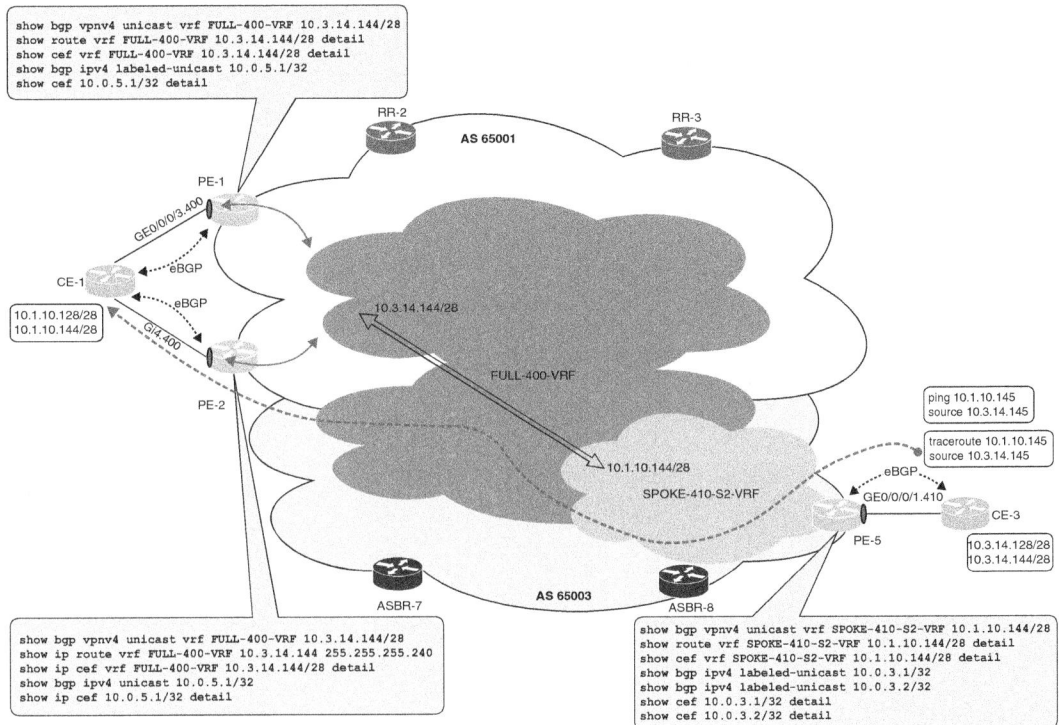

The figure contains the following text boxes:

```
show bgp vpnv4 unicast vrf FULL-400-VRF 10.3.14.144/28
show route vrf FULL-400-VRF 10.3.14.144/28 detail
show cef vrf FULL-400-VRF 10.3.14.144/28 detail
show bgp ipv4 labeled-unicast 10.0.5.1/32
show cef 10.0.5.1/32 detail
```

```
10.1.10.128/28
10.1.10.144/28
```

```
ping 10.1.10.145
source 10.3.14.145
```

```
traceroute 10.1.10.145
source 10.3.14.145
```

```
10.3.14.128/28
10.3.14.144/28
```

```
show bgp vpnv4 unicast vrf FULL-400-VRF 10.3.14.144/28
show ip route vrf FULL-400-VRF 10.3.14.144 255.255.255.240
show ip cef vrf FULL-400-VRF 10.3.14.144/28 detail
show bgp ipv4 unicast 10.0.5.1/32
show ip cef 10.0.5.1/32 detail
```

```
show bgp vpnv4 unicast vrf SPOKE-410-S2-VRF 10.1.10.144/28
show route vrf SPOKE-410-S2-VRF 10.1.10.144/28 detail
show cef vrf SPOKE-410-S2-VRF 10.1.10.144/28 detail
show bgp ipv4 labeled-unicast 10.0.3.1/32
show bgp ipv4 labeled-unicast 10.0.3.2/32
show cef 10.0.3.1/32 detail
show cef 10.0.3.2/32 detail
```

Other figure labels: RR-2, RR-3, AS 65001, PE-1, GE0/0/0/3.400, CE-1, eBGP, eBGP, G/4.400, 10.3.14.144/28, FULL-400-VRF, PE-2, 10.1.10.144/28, SPOKE-410-S2-VRF, eBGP, GE0/0/0/1.410, CE-3, PE-5, ASBR-7, AS 65003, ASBR-8

Figure 7-21 *SR-MPLS L3VPN Extranet Verification Tasks*

To view the BGP VPNv4 extranet route 10.3.14.144/28 from the Metro 3 router CE-3 in more detail on router PE-1 (IOS XR), you can use the command **show bgp vpnv4 unicast vrf FULL-400-VRF 10.3.14.144/28**. The output, as shown in Output 7-85, displays the following relevant information:

- **Paths (1 available, best #1):** The output confirms that the subnet is available across one path only.

- **Path #1:**

  □ **10.0.5.1 (metric 20) from 10.0.3.254 (10.0.3.254):** PE-5 is the BGP next hop (10.0.5.1).

  □ **Received Label 24010:** Router PE-5 has allocated the VPNv4 label 24010 for the extranet route 10.3.14.144/28 from router CE-3.

  □ **Extended community: RT:65001:4001 RT:65001:4100:** BGP route target 65001:4001 is applied to the subnet via PE-5 to allow importation into the VRF instance FULL-400-VRF on PE-1. The route target 65001:4100 is part of the hub-and-spoke configuration.

Output 7-85   *SR-MPLS L3VPN Extranet: BGP VPNv4 RIB for 10.3.14.144/28 on PE-1(IOS XR)*

```
RP/0/0/CPU0:PE-1#show bgp vpnv4 unicast vrf FULL-400-VRF 10.3.14.144/28
BGP routing table entry for 10.3.14.144/28, Route Distinguisher: 65001:401
<snip>
Paths: (1 available, best #1)
  Not advertised to any peer
  Path #1: Received by speaker 0
  Not advertised to any peer
  65003 65410
    10.0.5.1 (metric 20) from 10.0.3.254 (10.0.3.254)
      Received Label 24010
      Origin IGP, localpref 100, valid, internal, best, group-best,
import-candidate, imported
      Received Path ID 0, Local Path ID 1, version 129
      Extended community: RT:65001:4001 RT:65001:4100
      Source AFI: VPNv4 Unicast, Source VRF: default, Source Route
  Distinguisher: 65003:410
RP/0/0/CPU0:PE-1#
```

Similarly, on the IOS XE router PE-2, the command **show bgp vpnv4 unicast vrf FULL-400-VRF 10.3.14.144/28** displays the relevant information for the extranet route 10.3.14.144/28 (see in Output 7-86):

- **Paths (1 available, best #1, table FULL-400-VRF):** The subnet is available across a single path (PE-5).

  - **65003 65410, imported path from 65003:410:10.3.14.144/28:** The update with the route distinguisher 65003:410 is imported into the VRF instance with the appended BGP AS 65003 and AS 65410.

  - **10.0.5.1:** The next hop for router PE-5 in the global routing table, is learned via BGP labeled unicast.

  - **Extended Community: RT:65001:4001 RT:65001:4100:** The BGP route target 65001:4001 is applied to the subnet via PE-5 to allow importation into the VRF instance FULL-400-VRF on PE-2. The route target 65001:4100 is part of the hub-and-spoke configuration.

  - **mpls labels in/out nolabel/24010:** Router PE-5 has allocated the VPNv4 label 24010 for the route 10.3.14.144/28 from router CE-3.

Output 7-86   *SR-MPLS L3VPN Extranet: BGP VPNv4 RIB for 10.3.14.144/28 on PE-2 (IOS XE)*

```
PE-2#show bgp vpnv4 unicast vrf FULL-400-VRF 10.3.14.144/28
BGP routing table entry for 65001:402:10.3.14.144/28, version 28
Paths: (1 available, best #1, table FULL-400-VRF)
  Additional-path-install
  Advertised to update-groups:
     28
  Refresh Epoch 1
  65003 65410, imported path from 65003:410:10.3.14.144/28 (global)
    10.0.5.1 (metric 20) (via default) from 10.0.3.254 (10.0.3.254)
      Origin IGP, localpref 100, valid, internal, best
      Extended Community: RT:65001:4001 RT:65001:4100 , recursive-via-host
      mpls labels in/out nolabel/24010
      rx pathid: 0, tx pathid: 0x0
      Updated on Aug 8 2023 08:12:27 UTC
PE-2#
```

On the Metro 3 PE-5 (IOS XR) router, the BGP VPNv4 extranet route 10.1.10.144/28 from the Metro 1 CE-1 router displays the following relevant information (see Output 7-87):

- **Path: (2 available, best #2):** The output confirms that the subnet is available across two paths, and the second path is the preferred one.

  - **Path #1:**

    - **10.0.3.1 (metric 10) from 10.0.5.2 (10.0.5.2):** PE-1 is the BGP next hop (10.0.3.1).

    - **Received Label 24008:** Router PE-1 has allocated the VPNv4 label 24008 for the extranet route 10.1.10.144/28 from router CE-1.

    - **Origin IGP, metric 150, localpref 100, backup:** A MED of 150 (backup path) was set on egress by RR-2 based on the extranet route 10.1.10.144/28 having BGP local preference of 150. (Refer to the route reflector RR-2 configuration details in Config 7-24 for more details.)

    - **Extended community: SoO:65400:1 RT:65001:400 RT:65001:4002:** BGP route target 65001:4002 is applied to the subnet via the route policy EXTRANET_RT-EXP_RP on PE-1 to allow importation into the VRF instance SPOKE-410-S2-VRF on PE-5.

  - **Path #2:**

    - **10.0.3.2 (metric 10) from 10.0.5.2 (10.0.5.2):** PE-2 is the BGP next hop (10.0.3.2).

    ☐ **Received Label 21:** Router PE-2 has allocated VPNv4 label 21 for the extranet route 10.1.10.144/28 from router CE-1.

    ☐ **Origin IGP, metric 50, localpref 100, best:** A MED of 50 (best path) was set on egress by RR-2 based on the extranet route 10.1.10.144/28 having a BGP local preference not equal to 150. In this case, it was the BGP local preference 200. (Refer to the route reflector RR-2 configuration details in Config 7-24 for more details.)

    ☐ **Extended community: SoO:65400:1 RT:65001:400 RT:65001:4002:** BGP route target 65001:4002 is applied to the subnet via the route map EXTRANET_RT-EXP_RP on PE-2 to allow importation into the VRF instance SPOKE-410-S2-VRF on PE-5.

Output 7-87 *SR-MPLS L3VPN Extranet: BGP VPNv4 RIB for 10.1.10.144/28 on PE-5 (IOS XR)*

```
RP/0/0/CPU0:PE-5#show bgp vpnv4 unicast vrf SPOKE-410-S2-VRF 10.1.10.144/28
BGP routing table entry for 10.1.10.144/28, Route Distinguisher: 65003:410
<snip>
Paths: (2 available, best #2)
  Not advertised to any peer
  Path #1: Received by speaker 0
  Not advertised to any peer
  65001 65400
    10.0.3.1 (metric 10) from 10.0.5.2 (10.0.5.2)
      Received Label 24008
      Origin IGP, metric 150, localpref 100, valid, internal, backup, add-path,
    imported
      Received Path ID 0, Local Path ID 2, version 296
      Extended community: SoO:65400:1 RT:65001:400 RT:65001:4002
      Source AFI: VPNv4 Unicast, Source VRF: default, Source Route
    Distinguisher: 65001:401
  Path #2: Received by speaker 0
  Not advertised to any peer
  65001 65400
    10.0.3.2 (metric 10) from 10.0.5.2 (10.0.5.2)
      Received Label 21
      Origin IGP, metric 50, localpref 100, valid, internal, best, group-best,
    import-candidate, imported
      Received Path ID 0, Local Path ID 1, version 299
      Extended community: SoO:65400:1 RT:65001:400 RT:65001:4002
      Source AFI: VPNv4 Unicast, Source VRF: default, Source Route
    Distinguisher: 65001:402
RP/0/0/CPU0:PE-5#
```

Output 7-88 shows the output of running the command **show route vrf FULL-400-VRF 10.3.14.144/28 detail** on router PE-1 (IOS XR). It provides the RIB details for the subnet 10.3.14.144/28:

- **10.0.5.1, from 10.0.3.254:** The active BGP path is via the next hop 10.0.5.1 (on PE-5).

- **Label: 0x5dca (24010):** Router PE-5 has allocated the VPNv4 label 24010 for the extranet route 10.3.14.144/28 from router CE-3.

Output 7-88   *SR-MPLS L3VPN Extranet: RIB Details for 10.3.14.144/28 on PE-1 (IOS XR)*

```
RP/0/0/CPU0:PE-1#show route vrf FULL-400-VRF 10.3.14.144/28 detail

Routing entry for 10.3.14.144/28
  Known via "bgp 65001", distance 200, metric 0
  Tag 65003, type internal
  Installed Aug  8 08:09:33.922 for 2d20h
  Routing Descriptor Blocks
    10.0.5.1, from 10.0.3.254
      Nexthop in Vrf: "default", Table: "default", IPv4 Unicast, Table Id: 0xe0000000
      Route metric is 0
      Label: 0x5dca (24010)
      Tunnel ID: None
      Binding Label: None
      Extended communities count: 0
      Source RD attributes: 0x0000:65003:410
      NHID:0x0(Ref:0)
  Route version is 0x1 (1)
<snip>
RP/0/0/CPU0:PE-1#
```

Output 7-89 shows the output of the command **show ip route vrf FULL-400-VRF 10.3.14.144 255.255.255.240**, which provides RIB details for the subnet 10.3.14.144/28 from the IOS XE–based router PE-2:

- **10.0.5.1 (default), from 10.0.3.254, 2d20h ago, recursive-via-host:** This is the BGP path via next hop 10.0.5.1 (on PE-5), and the next hop is resolved via host routes (in a process called host recursion).

- **MPLS label: 24010:** Router PE-5 has allocated a VPNv4 label 24010 for the route 10.3.14.144/28.

Output 7-89   *SR-MPLS L3VPN Extranet: RIB Details for 10.3.14.144/28 on PE-2 (IOS XE)*

```
PE-2#show ip route vrf FULL-400-VRF 10.3.14.144 255.255.255.240


Routing Table: FULL-400-VRF
Routing entry for 10.3.14.144/28
  Known via "bgp 65001", distance 200, metric 0
  Tag 65003, type internal
  Last update from 10.0.5.1 2d20h ago
  Routing Descriptor Blocks:
  * 10.0.5.1 (default), from 10.0.3.254, 2d20h ago, recursive-via-host
      opaque_ptr 0x7FE1A6F670B0
      Route metric is 0, traffic share count is 1
      AS Hops 2
      Route tag 65003
      MPLS label: 24010
      MPLS Flags: MPLS Required
PE-2#
```

Output 7-90 shows the reverse direction, from router PE-5, and displays RIB details for the subnet 10.1.10.144/28, including the two paths via PE-1 and PE-2:

- **Number of pic paths 1:** BGP PIC Edge is configured, and one path is a backup path.

- **10.0.3.1, from 10.0.5.2, BGP backup path:** The backup BGP path is via next hop 10.0.3.1 (on PE-1), based on the BGP MED of 150.

- **Label: 0x5dc8 (24008):** Router PE-1 has allocated the VPNv4 label 24008 for the extranet route 10.1.10.144/28 from router CE-1.

- **10.0.3.2, from 10.0.5.2:** The active BGP path is via next hop 10.0.3.2 (on PE-2), based on the BGP MED of 50.

- **Label: 0x15 (21):** Router PE-2 has allocated the VPNv4 label 21 for the extranet route 10.1.10.144/28 from router CE-1.

Output 7-90   *SR-MPLS L3VPN Extranet: RIB Details for 10.1.10.144/28 on PE-5 (IOS XR)*

```
RP/0/0/CPU0:PE-5#show route vrf SPOKE-410-S2-VRF 10.1.10.144/28 detail


Routing entry for 10.1.10.144/28
  Known via "bgp 65003", distance 200, metric 50
  Tag 65001
  Number of pic paths 1 , type internal
```

```
Installed Aug  9 05:56:14.986 for 1d23h
Routing Descriptor Blocks
  10.0.3.1, from 10.0.5.2, BGP backup path
    Nexthop in Vrf: "default", Table: "default", IPv4 Unicast, Table Id: 0xe0000000
    Route metric is 150
    Label: 0x5dc8 (24008)
    Tunnel ID: None
    Binding Label: None
    Extended communities count: 1
      SoO:65400:1
    Source RD attributes: 0x0000:65001:401
    NHID:0x0(Ref:0)
  10.0.3.2, from 10.0.5.2
    Nexthop in Vrf: "default", Table: "default", IPv4 Unicast, Table Id: 0xe0000000
    Route metric is 50
    Label: 0x15 (21)
    Tunnel ID: None
    Binding Label: None
    Extended communities count: 1
      SoO:65400:1
    Source RD attributes: 0x0000:65001:402
    NHID:0x0(Ref:0)
<snip>
RP/0/0/CPU0:PE-5#
```

The next task is to verify the FIB for the target subnet 10.3.14.144/28 on the router PE-1, using the command **show cef vrf FULL-400-VRF 10.3.14.144/28 detail**, as demonstrated in Output 7-91, which provides the following relevant information:

- **via 10.0.5.1/32, recursive:** Router PE-5 is the active BGP path with next hop 10.0.5.1.

  - **recursion-via-/32:** IOS XR always recurses via /32 for labeled paths (that is, VPNv4 next hops).

  - **next hop 10.0.5.1/32 via 20001/0/21:** The next hop 10.0.5.1 (on PE-5) is learned via BGP labeled unicast with the label 20001, which is resolvable through two SR-MPLS paths:

    - **next hop 192.168.3.3/32 Gi0/0/0/1   labels imposed {18005 20001 24010}:** This is the full label stack, with the IGP path via next hop 192.168.3.3/32 (on P-6) and the SR-MPLS label 18005 for ASBR-1. The next hop 10.0.5.1 (on PE-5) with the BGP labeled unicast label 20001. The service VPNv4 label is 24010.

    - **next hop 192.168.3.3/32 Gi0/0/0/1   labels imposed {18006 20001 24010}:** This is the full label stack, with the IGP path via next hop 192.168.3.3/32 (on P-6) and the SR-MPLS label 18006 for ASBR-2. The next hop 10.0.5.1 (on PE-5) with the BGP labeled unicast label 20001. The service VPNv4 label is 24010.

Output 7-91   *SR-MPLS L3VPN Extranet: FIB Details for 10.3.14.144/28 on PE-1 (IOS XR)*

```
RP/0/0/CPU0:PE-1#show cef vrf FULL-400-VRF 10.3.14.144/28 detail
10.3.14.144/28, version 279, internal 0x5000001 0x0 (ptr 0xa14177b8) [1], 0x0 (0x0),
  0x208 (0xa1756604)
Updated Aug  8 08:09:33.942
Prefix Len 28, traffic index 0, precedence n/a, priority 3
  gateway array (0xa134fca4) reference count 4, flags 0x2038, source rib (7), 0
  backups
              [1 type 1 flags 0x40441 (0xa1772798) ext 0x0 (0x0)]
  LW-LDI[type=0, refc=0, ptr=0x0, sh-ldi=0x0]
  gateway array update type-time 1 Aug  1 10:18:10.405
LDI Update time Aug  6 02:54:50.154
  via 10.0.5.1/32, 3 dependencies, recursive [flags 0x6000]
   path-idx 0 NHID 0x0 [0xa17cbfa8 0x0]
   recursion-via-/32
   next hop VRF - 'default', table - 0xe0000000
   next hop 10.0.5.1/32 via 20001/0/21
    next hop 192.168.3.3/32 Gi0/0/0/1    labels imposed {18005 20001 24010}
    next hop 192.168.3.3/32 Gi0/0/0/1    labels imposed {18006 20001 24010}


   Load distribution: 0 (refcount 1)


   Hash  OK  Interface             Address
   0     Y   recursive             20001/0
RP/0/0/CPU0:PE-1#
```

As shown in Output 7-92, you can use the command **show ip cef vrf FULL-400-VRF 10.3.14.144/28 detail** to examine the FIB route information for the target subnet 10.3.14.144/28 on PE-2 (IOS XE):

■ **recursive via 10.0.5.1 label 24010:** Router PE-5 with next hop 10.0.5.1 has allocated the VPNv4 label 24010 for the route 10.3.14.144/28.

  ■ **recursive via 10.0.3.5 label 20001-(local:20001):** This is the BGP path to 10.0.5.1 (on PE-5) with the BGP labeled unicast label 20001 and next hop 10.0.3.5 (on ASBR-1).

    □ **nexthop 192.168.3.7 GigabitEthernet1 label 18005-(local:18005):** This is the IGP path via next hop 192.168.3.7 (on P-6) and the SR-MPLS label 18005.

  ■ **recursive via 10.0.3.6 label 20001-(local:20001):** This is the BGP path to 10.0.5.1 (on PE-5) with the BGP labeled unicast label 20001 and next hop 10.0.3.6 (on ASBR-2).

    □ **nexthop 192.168.3.7 GigabitEthernet1 label 18006-(local:18006):** This is the IGP path via next hop 192.168.3.7 (on P-6) and the SR-MPLS label 18006.

Output 7-92   *SR-MPLS L3VPN Extranet: FIB Details for 10.3.14.144/28 on PE-2 (IOS XE)*

```
PE-2#show ip cef vrf FULL-400-VRF 10.3.14.144/28 detail
10.3.14.144/28, epoch 0, flags [rib defined all labels]
  recursive via 10.0.5.1 label 24010
    recursive via 10.0.3.5 label 20001-(local:20001)
      nexthop 192.168.3.7 GigabitEthernet1 label 18005-(local:18005)
    recursive via 10.0.3.6 label 20001-(local:20001)
      nexthop 192.168.3.7 GigabitEthernet1 label 18006-(local:18006)
PE-2#
```

In the reverse direction, the FIB details for the target subnet 10.1.10.144/28 are displayed on router PE-5 with the command **show cef vrf SPOKE-410-S2-VRF 10.1.10.144/28 detail** (see Output 7-93). The following information is provided:

- **via 10.0.3.1/32, recursive, backup:** Router PE-1 is the backup BGP path with next hop 10.0.3.1.

  - **recursion-via-/32:** IOS XR always recurses via /32 for labeled paths (that is, VPNv4 next hops).

  - **next hop 10.0.3.1/32 via 18001/0/21:** The next hop 10.0.3.1 (on PE-1) is learned via BGP labeled unicast, with label 18001.

    - **next hop 192.168.5.0/32 Gi0/0/0/0   labels imposed {ImplNull 18001 24008}:** This is the full label stack, directly connected with an implicit null label via next hop 192.168.5.0/32 (on ASBR-7). The next hop 10.0.3.1 (on PE-1) is with the BGP labeled unicast label 18001. The service VPNv4 label is 24008.

    - **next hop 192.168.5.2/32 Gi0/0/0/1   labels imposed {ImplNull 18001 24008}:** This is the full label stack, directly connected with an implicit null label via next hop 192.168.5.2/32 (on ASBR-8). The next hop 10.0.3.1 (on PE-1) is with the BGP labeled unicast label 18001. The service VPNv4 label is 24008.

- **via 10.0.3.2/32, recursive:** Router PE-2 is the active BGP path with next hop 10.0.3.2.

  - **recursion-via-/32:** IOS XR always recurses via /32 for labeled paths (that is, VPNv4 next hops).

  - **next hop 10.0.3.2/32 via 18002/0/21:** Next hop 10.0.3.2 (on PE-2) is learned via BGP labeled unicast, with the label 18002.

    - **next hop 192.168.5.0/32 Gi0/0/0/0   labels imposed {ImplNull 18002 21}:** This is the full label stack, directly connected with an implicit null label via next hop 192.168.5.0/32 (on ASBR-7). The next hop 10.0.3.2 (on PE-2) is with the BGP labeled unicast label 18002. The service VPNv4 label is 21.

    - **next hop 192.168.5.2/32 Gi0/0/0/1   labels imposed {ImplNull 18002 21}:** This is the full label stack, directly connected with an implicit null label via next hop 192.168.5.2/32 (on ASBR-8). The next hop 10.0.3.2 (on PE-2) is with the BGP labeled unicast label 18002. The service VPNv4 label is 21.

Output 7-93   *SR-MPLS L3VPN Extranet: FIB Details for 10.1.10.144/28 on PE-5 (IOS XR)*

```
RP/0/0/CPU0:PE-5#show cef vrf SPOKE-410-S2-VRF 10.1.10.144/28 detail
10.1.10.144/28, version 79, internal 0x5000001 0x0 (ptr 0xa1417358) [1], 0x0 (0x0),
 0x208 (0xa19d06e8)
 Updated Aug  9 05:56:15.007
 Prefix Len 28, traffic index 0, precedence n/a, priority 3
  gateway array (0xa134fb00) reference count 4, flags 0x102038, source rib (7), 0
  backups
               [1 type 1 flags 0x48441 (0xa1772558) ext 0x0 (0x0)]
  LW-LDI[type=0, refc=0, ptr=0x0, sh-ldi=0x0]
  gateway array update type-time 1 Aug  8 07:55:41.085
 LDI Update time Aug  8 07:55:41.085
  via 10.0.3.1/32, 3 dependencies, recursive, backup [flags 0x6100]
    path-idx 0 NHID 0x0 [0xa17cc37c 0x0]
    recursion-via-/32
    next hop VRF - 'default', table - 0xe0000000
    next hop 10.0.3.1/32 via 18001/0/21
      next hop 192.168.5.0/32 Gi0/0/0/0   labels imposed {ImplNull 18001 24008}
      next hop 192.168.5.2/32 Gi0/0/0/1   labels imposed {ImplNull 18001 24008}
  via 10.0.3.2/32, 5 dependencies, recursive [flags 0x6000]
    path-idx 1 NHID 0x0 [0xa17cc264 0x0]
    recursion-via-/32
    next hop VRF - 'default', table - 0xe0000000
    next hop 10.0.3.2/32 via 18002/0/21
      next hop 192.168.5.0/32 Gi0/0/0/0   labels imposed {ImplNull 18002 21}
      next hop 192.168.5.2/32 Gi0/0/0/1   labels imposed {ImplNull 18002 21}


    Load distribution: 0 (refcount 1)

    Hash  OK  Interface               Address
    0     Y   recursive               18002/0
RP/0/0/CPU0:PE-5#
```

Note   The FIB and RIB verification details for the BGP labeled unicast routes 10.0.3.1/32 (on PE-1) and 10.0.3.2/32 (on PE-2) are excluded from this section for the sake of brevity. The BGP labeled unicast route 10.0.5.1/32 for the router PE-5 is discussed earlier in this chapter, in the section "SR-MPLS L3VPN Hub-and-Spoke Verification."

Output 7-94 shows an ICMP ping executed from router CE-3 with source IP address 10.3.14.145 to the router CE-1 destination IP address 10.1.10.129. It verifies that reachability is not possible because IP address 10.1.10.129 is not part of the extranet service.

Output 7-94 *SR-MPLS L3VPN Extranet: ICMP Ping from CE-3 to CE-1 Fails*

```
RP/0/0/CPU0:CE-3#ping 10.1.10.129 source 10.3.14.145

Type escape sequence to abort.

Sending 5, 100-byte ICMP Echos to 10.1.10.129, timeout is 2 seconds:

.....

Success rate is 0 percent (0/5)

RP/0/0/CPU0:CE-3#
```

Output 7-95 shows an ICMP ping from router CE-3 source IP address 10.3.14.145 to the CE-1 destination IP address 10.1.10.145, which verifies that reachability is possible as this IP address is indeed part of the extranet service.

Output 7-95 *SR-MPLS L3VPN Extranet: ICMP Ping from CE-3 to CE-1 Succeeds*

```
RP/0/0/CPU0:CE-3#ping 10.1.10.145 source 10.3.14.145

Type escape sequence to abort.

Sending 5, 100-byte ICMP Echos to 10.1.10.145, timeout is 2 seconds:

!!!!!

Success rate is 100 percent (5/5), round-trip min/avg/max = 69/81/89 ms

RP/0/0/CPU0:CE-3#
```

A traceroute from router CE-3 with source IP address 10.3.14.145 to router CE-1 with IP address 10.1.10.145 verifies the reachability of the extranet service (see Output 7-96).

Output 7-96 *SR-MPLS L3VPN Extranet: Traceroute to CE-1 Extranet Service in Metro 1*

```
RP/0/0/CPU0:CE-3#traceroute 10.1.10.145 source 10.3.14.145

Type escape sequence to abort.
Tracing the route to 10.1.10.145

1  10.3.14.0 0 msec <----------------------------------------PE-5
2  192.168.5.0 [MPLS: Labels 18002/21 Exp 0] 79 msec <---------ASBR-7
3  192.168.60.0 [MPLS: Labels 18002/21 Exp 0] 79 msec <--------ASBR-5
4  192.168.2.5 [MPLS: Labels 17003/18002/21 Exp 0] 79 msec <---P-7
5  192.168.2.2 [MPLS: Labels 18002/21 Exp 0] 79 msec <---------ASBR-4
6  192.168.51.0 [MPLS: Labels 18002/21 Exp 0] 79 msec <--------ASBR-2
7  192.168.3.14 [MPLS: Labels 18002/21 Exp 0] 259 msec ß-------P-6
8  10.1.10.2 [MPLS: Label 21 Exp 0] 69 msec <------------------PE-2
9  10.1.10.3 79 msec <----------------------------------------CE-1
RP/0/0/CPU0:CE-3#
```

Route Target Constraint

As service providers begin to converge their networks and scale out both the number of PE routers and the L3VPN and L2VPN services, the impacts of service scaling impact begin to take on a higher priority. For example, as VRF instances (L3VPN) or EVIs

(L2VPN) are deployed across multiple PE routers, these PE routers advertise and receive routes from all other PE routers within the core network. In most service configuration cases, a specific customer instance—either L3VPN or L2VPN—will not be required across all PE routers; however, these routes will still be advertised to and received from all the PE routers across the network. A PE router that receives routes for a service that it is not participating in will silently drop these routes. In the simplified network topology shown in Figure 7-22, router PE-1 is configured with the following VRF instances:

- FULL-500-VRF

- FULL-501-VRF

- FULL-503-VRF

Based on the other PE router service configurations, PE-1 will also receive routes for VRF instance FULL-502-VRF configured on PE-2 and PE-3 and for the VRF instance FULL-504-VRF configured on PE-3 and PE-4, and all these routes will be dropped upon receipt by PE-1.

Now let's focus on the two route reflectors, RR-1 and RR-2, in Figure 7-22. There is no requirement for RR-1 to learn the routes for VRF instance FULL-504-VRF from RR-2 because none of the RR-1 clients have been configured for this service. Similarly, for RR-2, there is no requirement to learn routes for VRF instance FULL-503-VRF from RR-1 because none of the RR-2 clients have been configured for this service.

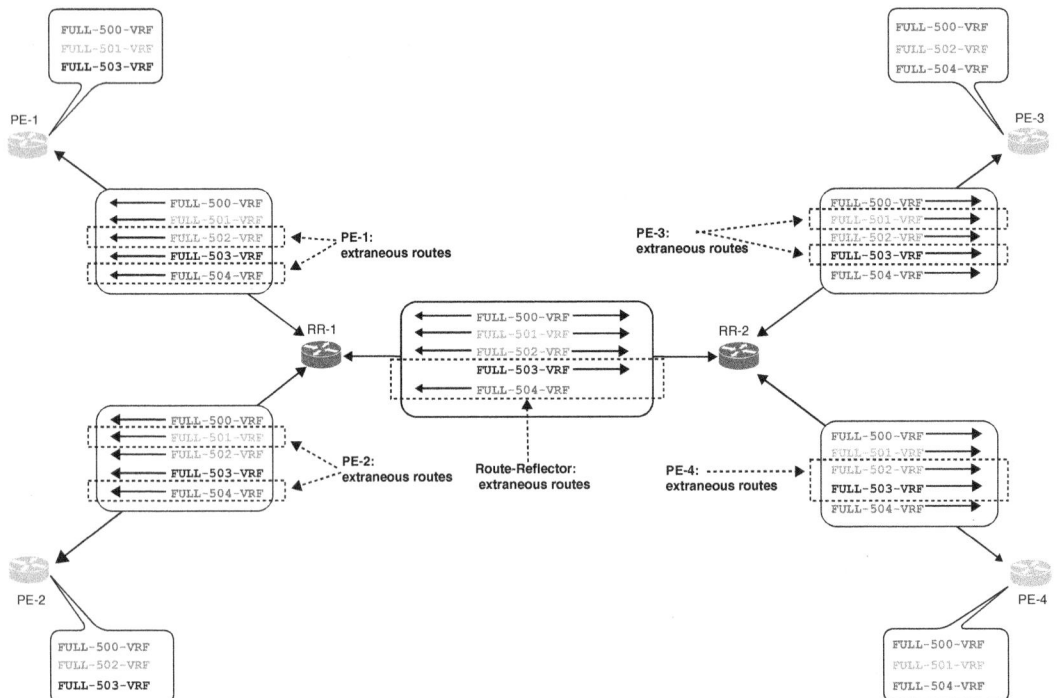

Figure 7-22 *Route Target Constraint: Route Reflector and PE Router Extraneous Routes*

In smaller networks and topologies, these additional routes may not have a significant performance impact on route reflectors and PE routers. However, as both the number of PE routers and the configured services increase, the processing and propagation of these additional extraneous routes can add additional unnecessary CPU cycles, memory consumption, and utilization impacts on both route reflectors and PE routers. The solution is to use BGP Constraint Route Distribution, described in RFC 4684.

Figure 7-23 displays the BGP Route Target Constraint (RTC) NLRI updates advertised from the various PE routers, together with the subsequent route reflector egress filters that permit only the required routes to be propagated toward the respective PE routers.

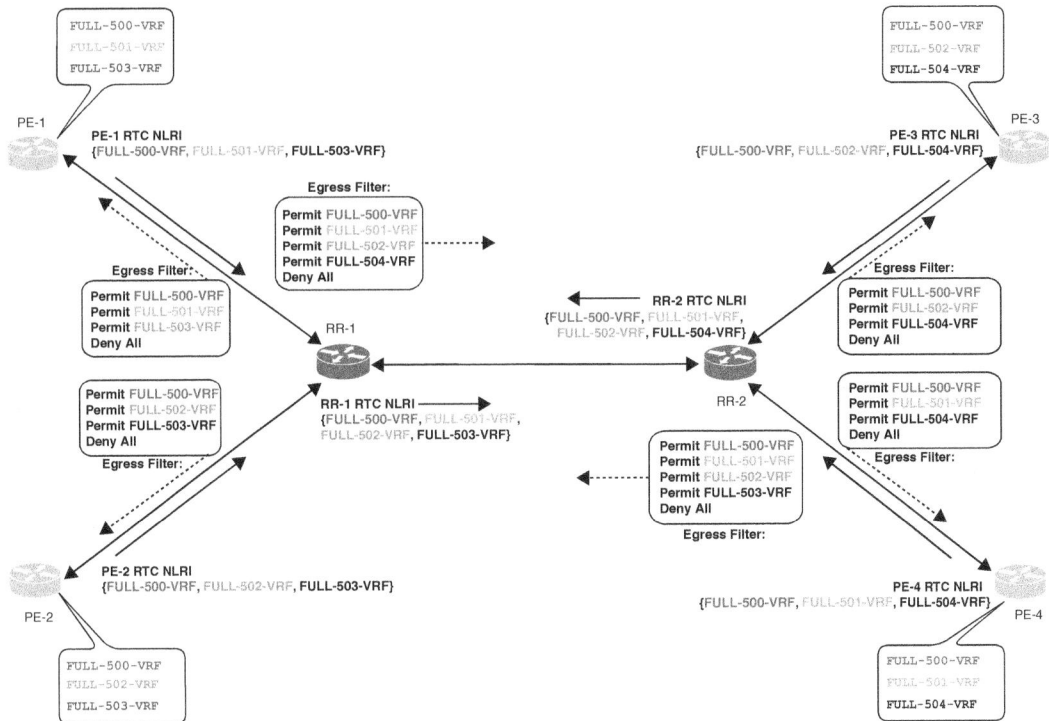

Figure 7-23 *Route Target Constraint: Route Reflector and PE Router RTC Route Exchange*

As described in detail earlier in this chapter, BGP route targets are used for distribution control of routes into VRF instances. By allowing the PE routers to exchange route-targets for routes they are interested in receiving from their peers, they effectively prevent unnecessary routes being advertised to themselves by these peers. These required route targets, known as *route target memberships*, are advertised via BGP UPDATE messages that propagate these route target memberships. This BGP Constrained Route Distribution capability allows BGP peer routers to advertise their route target membership and the restriction of VPN route advertisements based on the received peer route target memberships, whether for VPNv4/v6 or EVPN routes.

The packet capture shown in Example 7-4 describes the format of a BGP Route Target Constraint NLRI UPDATE message:

■ **Address family identifier (AFI): IPv4 (1):** This indicates IPv4 unicast.

■ **Subsequent address family identifier (SAFI): Route Target Filter (132):** This indicates a Route Target Constraint.

■ **Network Layer Reachability Information (NLRI):**

   ■ **MP Reach NLRI 65000:65000:501/96:** This output has the following format; AS number : route target / prefix length.

   ■ **Prefix Length: 96:** The prefix length is 12 bytes.

   ■ **Originating AS: 65000:** The originating autonomous system (AS) is 4 bytes in length.

   ■ **Community Prefix: 65000:501:** The BGP route target length is 8 bytes.

Example 7-4   *Route Target Constraint: VPNv4 Packet Capture*

```
<snip>
Border Gateway Protocol - UPDATE Message
    Type: UPDATE Message (2)
    Withdrawn Routes Length: 0
    Total Path Attribute Length: 52
    Path attributes
        Path Attribute - MP_REACH_NLRI
            Flags: 0x90, Optional, Extended-Length, Non-transitive, Complete
            Type Code: MP_REACH_NLRI (14)
            Length: 34
            Address family identifier (AFI): IPv4 (1)
            Subsequent address family identifier (SAFI): Route Target Filter (132)
            Next hop: fc00:0:105::1
                IPv6 Address: fc00:0:105::1
            Number of Subnetwork points of attachment (SNPA): 0
            Network Layer Reachability Information (NLRI)
                MP Reach NLRI 65000:65000:501/96
                    Prefix Length: 96
                    Originating AS: 65000
                    Community Prefix: 65000:501
        Path Attribute - ORIGIN: IGP
        Path Attribute - AS_PATH: empty
        Path Attribute - LOCAL_PREF: 100
<snip>
```

Output 7-97, Output 7-98, and Output 7-99 provide three examples of Route Target Constraint values from router PE-1.

In Output 7-97, for the Route Target Constraint value 65000:2:65000:501, the origin autonomous system number (ASN) is 65000, the route target is 65000:501, and the decimal value 2 (transitive two-octet AS-specific) indicates the route target attribute type and subtype.

Output 7-97   *Route Target Constraint: Example 65000:2:65000:501*

```
RP/0/RP0/CPU0:PE-1# show bgp ipv4 rt-filter
BGP router identifier 172.19.0.10, local AS number 65000
<snip>
*> 65000:2:65000:501/96
                    0.0.0.0                         32768 i
* i                 fc00:0:107::1            100     0 i
<snip>
```

In Output 7-98, for the Route Target Constraint value 65000:258: 172.19.0.11:502, the origin ASN is 65000, the route target is 172.19.0.11:502, and the decimal value 258 (transitive IPv4-address-specific) indicates the route target attribute type and subtype.

Output 7-98   *Route Target Constraint: Example 65000:258:172.19.0.11:502*

```
RP/0/RP0/CPU0:PE-1# show bgp ipv4 rt-filter
BGP router identifier 172.19.0.10, local AS number 65000
<snip>
*> i65000:258:172.19.0.11:502/96    fc00:0:107::1    100     0 i
<snip>
```

In Output 7-99, for the Route Target Constraint value 65000:1538: 00fc.0001.0200, the origin ASN is 65000, the route target is 00fc.0001.0200 (EVPN RT-4), and the decimal value 1538 (transitive EVPN) indicates the route target attribute type and subtype.

Output 7-99   *Route Target Constraint: Example 65000:1538:00fc.0001.0200*

```
RP/0/RP0/CPU0:PE-1#show bgp ipv4 rt-filter
BGP router identifier 172.19.0.10, local AS number 65000
*> 65000:1538:00fc.0001.0200/96
                    0.0.0.0                         32768 i
* i                 fc00:0:107::1            100     0 i
RP/0/RP0/CPU0:PE-1#
```

Route Target Constraint Configuration and Verification

This section provides a concise overview of setting up and validating Route Target Constraint on both a PE router and route reflectors. The RTC configurations presented here were configured on the SRv6 reference network in Appendix A, in the section "SRv6 Reference Network."

Config 7-49 highlights in the Route Target Constraint address family configured with address-family ipv4 rt-filter on router PE-1. These same configurations are replicated across router PE-2 in Metro 1 as well as on PE-3 and PE-4 in Metro 2.

Note The BGP RTC configuration is applicable for both VPNv4 and VPNv6 address families, as well as for the EVPN address family.

Config 7-49 *Route Target Constraint Configuration on PE-1*

```
!
router bgp 65000
 bgp router-id 172.19.0.10
 <snip>
 address-family vpnv4 unicast
  vrf all
   segment-routing srv6
    locator MAIN
    alloc mode per-vrf
  !
  !
 !
 address-family vpnv6 unicast
 !
 address-family ipv4 rt-filter
 !
 address-family l2vpn evpn
 !
 neighbor-group IBGP-RR1-NG
  remote-as 65000
  description *** iBGP peering to METRO-1 RR ***
  update-source Loopback0
  address-family vpnv4 unicast
  !
  address-family vpnv6 unicast
  !
  address-family ipv4 rt-filter
  !
  address-family l2vpn evpn
  !
```

Config 7-50 highlights the Route Target Constraint address family configured on RR-1 in Metro 1 and is applicable to RR-2 in Metro 2 of the SRv6 reference network (see Appendix A, in the section "SRv6 Reference Network").

Config 7-50 *Route Target Constraint Configuration on RR-1*

```
!
router bgp 65000
 bgp router-id 172.19.0.12
 <snip>
 address-family vpnv4 unicast
 !
 address-family vpnv6 unicast
 !
 address-family ipv4 rt-filter
 !
 address-family l2vpn evpn
 !
 neighbor-group IBGP-PE-NG
  remote-as 65000
  description *** iBGP peering to METRO-1 PE ***
  update-source Loopback0
  address-family vpnv4 unicast
   route-reflector-client
  !
  address-family vpnv6 unicast
   route-reflector-client
  !
  address-family ipv4 rt-filter
   route-reflector-client
  !
  address-family l2vpn evpn
   route-reflector-client
  !
 !
 neighbor-group IBGP-RR-NG
  remote-as 65000
  description *** iBGP peering to RR ***
  update-source Loopback0
  address-family vpnv4 unicast
  !
 address-family vpnv6 unicast
  !
  address-family ipv4 rt-filter
  !
 address-family l2vpn evpn
  !
```

The following verification outputs executed on RR-1 in Metro 1 show some commands that are useful in the verification of the Route Target Constraint feature.

The command **show bgp ipv4 rt-filter summary** in Output 7-100 executed on RR-1 displays the received RTC filter list from the route reflector clients and peers (PE-1, PE-2, and RR-2). For example, the route reflector client PE-1 (fc00:0:105::1) has advertised 16 route targets of interest based on its configured services.

Output 7-100 *Route Target Constraint: Summary Output on RR-1*

```
RP/0/RP0/CPU0:RR-1#show bgp ipv4 rt-filter summary
BGP router identifier 172.19.0.12, local AS number 65000
<snip>


BGP is operating in STANDALONE mode.


Process      RcvTblVer   bRIB/RIB   LabelVer   ImportVer   SendTblVer   StandbyVer
Speaker           237        237        237         237          237            0


Neighbor        Spk    AS MsgRcvd MsgSent   TblVer  InQ OutQ  Up/Down  St/PfxRcd
fc00:0:105::1     0 65000   15953   16255      237    0    0   1d21h          16
fc00:0:106::1     0 65000   16016   16181      237    0    0   1d21h          17
fc00:0:207::1     0 65000   16210   16081      237    0    0   1w3d           18


RP/0/RP0/CPU0:RR-1#
```

The route targets that the PE-1 router is interested in can be listed with the command **show bgp ipv4 rt-filter neighbors fc00:0:105::1 rt-filter.** You can see in Output 7-101 that the router PE-1 is interested in 16 route targets, which encompass both VPNv4 and EVPN services configured on the router. For example, RT:65000:503 is for the VPNv4 VRF instance FULL-503-VRF, and RT:65000:10205 is for the EVPN EVI 205, while EVPN ES Import:00fc.0001.0200 is for the bundle-ether 200 Ethernet segment route Type 4 route used for EVPN multi-homed Ethernet segment auto-discovery and the designated forwarder election procedure.

Output 7-101 *Route Target Constraint: Neighbor PE-1 RTC Table on RR-1*

```
RP/0/RP0/CPU0:RR-1#show bgp ipv4 rt-filter neighbors fc00:0:105::1 rt-filter

BGP neighbor is fc00:0:105::1
 Remote AS 65000, local AS 65000, internal link, Dynamic
 Description: *** iBGP session to METRO-1 PE ***
 Remote router ID 172.19.0.10
 Cluster ID 172.19.0.12
  BGP state = Established, up for 1d21h
  NSR State: None
```

```
  TCP open mode: passive only
<snip>

 For Address Family: RT Constraint
  BGP neighbor version 237
  Update group: 0.2 Filter-group: 0.3  No Refresh request being processed
  RT constraint nbr enabled for VPN updates:
  Route-Reflector Client
  AF-dependent capabilities:
    Graceful Restart capability advertised
      Local restart time is 120, RIB purge time is 600 seconds
      Maximum stalepath time is 360 seconds
    Graceful Restart capability received
      Remote Restart time is 120 seconds
      Neighbor did not preserve the forwarding state during latest restart
  Route refresh request: received 0, sent 0
  16 accepted prefixes, 16 are bestpaths
  Exact no. of prefixes denied : 0.
  Cumulative no. of prefixes denied: 0.
  Prefix advertised 38, suppressed 0, withdrawn 2
  AIGP is enabled
  An EoR was received during read-only mode
  Last ack version 237, Last synced ack version 0
  Outstanding version objects: current 0, max 4, refresh 0
  Additional-paths operation: None
  Send Multicast Attributes
  RT-Table with total RTs: 16
   RT:65000:1  RT:65000:100  RT:65000:102  RT:65000:200  RT:65000:201  RT:65000:300
   RT:65000:500  RT:65000:501  RT:65000:503  RT:65000:510  RT:65000:5001
   RT:65000:5100  RT:65000:10205  RT:65000:20205  EVPN ES Import:00fc.0001.0200
   EVPN ES Import:00fc.0001.0300

<snip>
RP/0/RP0/CPU0:RR-1#
```

To view the full Route Target Constraint table, you can use the command **show bgp ipv4 rt-filter wide**. In Output 7-102, the output of this command displays the various BGP RTC routes for the configured services in the SRv6 reference network. As mentioned at the beginning of this section, these routes take the following format, using 65000:2:65000:501/96 as an example:

■ **65000:** The originating AS is 4 bytes in length.

■ **2:** This is the route target attribute type and subtype in decimal (transitive 2-Octet AS-specific).

- **65000:501:** The BGP route target is 8 bytes in length.

- **/96:** The prefix length is 12 bytes.

Output 7-102 *Route Target Constraint: show bgp ipv4 rt-filter Output on RR-1*

```
RP/0/RP0/CPU0:RR-1#show bgp ipv4 rt-filter wide
BGP router identifier 172.19.0.12, local AS number 65000
<snip>


Status codes: s suppressed, d damped, h history, * valid, > best
              i - internal, r RIB-failure, S stale, N Nexthop-discard
Origin codes: i - IGP, e - EGP, ? - incomplete
   Network              Next Hop            Metric LocPrf Weight Path
*>i65000:2:65000:1/96   fc00:0:105::1              100  32768 i
* i                     fc00:0:205::1              100      0 i
*>i65000:2:65000:100/96 fc00:0:105::1              100  32768 i
* i                     fc00:0:205::1              100      0 i
*>i65000:2:65000:101/96 fc00:0:106::1              100  32768 i
* i                     fc00:0:206::1              100      0 i
*>i65000:2:65000:102/96 fc00:0:105::1              100  32768 i
* i                     fc00:0:106::1              100  32768 i
* i                     fc00:0:205::1              100      0 i
*>i65000:2:65000:200/96 fc00:0:105::1              100  32768 i
* i                     fc00:0:106::1              100  32768 i
* i                     fc00:0:205::1              100      0 i
*>i65000:2:65000:201/96 fc00:0:105::1              100  32768 i
* i                     fc00:0:106::1              100  32768 i
* i                     fc00:0:205::1              100      0 i
*>i65000:2:65000:210/96 fc00:0:106::1              100  32768 i
* i                     fc00:0:206::1              100      0 i
*>i65000:2:65000:300/96 fc00:0:105::1              100  32768 i
* i                     fc00:0:106::1              100  32768 i
* i                     fc00:0:205::1              100      0 i
*>i65000:2:65000:500/96 fc00:0:105::1              100  32768 i
* i                     fc00:0:106::1              100  32768 i
* i                     fc00:0:205::1              100      0 i
*>i65000:2:65000:501/96 fc00:0:105::1              100  32768 i
* i                     fc00:0:206::1              100      0 i
*>i65000:2:65000:503/96 fc00:0:105::1              100  32768 i
* i                     fc00:0:106::1              100  32768 i
*>i65000:2:65000:504/96 fc00:0:205::1              100      0 i
*>i65000:2:65000:510/96 fc00:0:105::1              100  32768 i
* i                     fc00:0:106::1              100  32768 i
* i                     fc00:0:205::1              100      0 i
*>i65000:2:65000:3000/96 fc00:0:106::1             100  32768 i
* i                     fc00:0:206::1              100      0 i
```

```
*>i65000:2:65000:5001/96        fc00:0:105::1                  100  32768 i
* i                             fc00:0:106::1                  100  32768 i
*>i65000:2:65000:5002/96        fc00:0:206::1                  100      0 i
*>i65000:2:65000:5100/96        fc00:0:105::1                  100  32768 i
* i                             fc00:0:106::1                  100  32768 i
*>i65000:2:65000:10205/96       fc00:0:105::1                  100  32768 i
* i                             fc00:0:106::1                  100  32768 i
* i                             fc00:0:205::1                  100      0 i
*>i65000:2:65000:20205/96       fc00:0:105::1                  100  32768 i
* i                             fc00:0:106::1                  100  32768 i
*>i65000:258:172.19.0.11:502/96 fc00:0:106::1                  100  32768 i
* i                             fc00:0:205::1                  100      0 i
*>i65000:1538:00fc.0001.0200/96 fc00:0:105::1                  100  32768 i
* i                             fc00:0:106::1                  100  32768 i
*>i65000:1538:00fc.0001.0300/96 fc00:0:105::1                  100  32768 i
* i                             fc00:0:106::1                  100  32768 i
*>i65000:1538:00fc.0001.0350/96 fc00:0:205::1                  100      0 i
*>i65000:1538:00fc.0002.0250/96 fc00:0:205::1                  100      0 i


Processed 24 prefixes, 51 paths
RP/0/RP0/CPU0:RR-1#
```

The route reflector RR-1 uses update group 0.1, as shown in Output 7-103, for both of the PE routers, PE-1 and PE-2. Each of these neighbors then uses a dedicated filter group. For example, the neighbor PE-1 (fc00:0:105::1) uses the filter group 0.2, and the neighbor PE-2 (fc00:0:106::1) uses the filter group 0.4. These per-PE router filter groups list all the route targets that each PE router is interested in.

Output 7-103 *Route Target Constraint: BGP Update Group Output on RR-1*

```
RP/0/RP0/CPU0:RR-1# show bgp vpnv4 unicast update-group

Update group for VPNv4 Unicast, index 0.1:
  Attributes:
    Neighbor sessions are IPv6
    Internal
    Common admin
    First neighbor AS: 65000
    Send communities
    Send GSHUT community if originated
    Send extended communities
    Route Reflector Client
```

```
      4-byte AS capable
      Send AIGP
      Send multicast attributes
      Extended Nexthop Encoding
      Minimum advertisement interval: 0 secs
   Update group desynchronized: 0
   Sub-groups merged: 7
   Number of refresh subgroups: 0
   Messages formatted: 341, replicated: 523
   All neighbors are assigned to sub-group(s)
     Neighbors in sub-group: 0.2, Filter-Groups num:2
       Neighbors in filter-group: 0.4(RT num: 17)
         fc00:0:106::1
       Neighbors in filter-group: 0.2(RT num: 16)
         fc00:0:105::1
<snip>
RP/0/RP0/CPU0:RR-1#
```

The route reflector RR-1 then filters the advertised prefixes to the neighbor routers, PE-1 and PE-2, based only on the route targets that these routers are interested in. In Output 7-104, the output of the command **show bgp vpnv4 unicast update-group 0.1 filter-group 0.2** displays the route targets for which router PE-1 is looking to receive routes from RR-1.

Output 7-104   *Route Target Constraint: BGP Filter Group 0.2 (PE-1) Output on RR-1*

```
RP/0/RP0/CPU0:RR-1#show bgp vpnv4 unicast update-group 0.1 filter-group 0.2

Update group for VPNv4 Unicast, index 0.1:
  Attributes:
    Neighbor sessions are IPv6
    Internal
    Common admin
    First neighbor AS: 65000
    Send communities
    Send GSHUT community if originated
    Send extended communities
    Route Reflector Client
    4-byte AS capable
    Send AIGP
    Send multicast attributes
    Extended Nexthop Encoding
    Minimum advertisement interval: 0 secs
```

```
Update group desynchronized: 0
Sub-groups merged: 7
Number of refresh subgroups: 0
Messages formatted: 341, replicated: 523
All neighbors are assigned to sub-group(s)
  Neighbors in sub-group: 0.2, Filter-Groups num:2
   Neighbors in filter-group: 0.2(RT num: 16)
     fc00:0:105::1
    Msg elems created : 42, Msg elems queued : 42, Msg elems deleted : 42
    Last update walk: prefixes (adv/wdn/skp/sup) : 0/0/1/0
    Total updates: prefixes (adv/wdn/non-optim) : 42/10/47
    Flags : 0x1, Nbr Cnt:1     Extended community:
     RT:65000:1  RT:65000:100  RT:65000:102  RT:65000:200  RT:65000:201
  RT:65000:300
   RT:65000:500  RT:65000:501  RT:65000:503  RT:65000:510  RT:65000:5001
   RT:65000:5100  RT:65000:10205  RT:65000:20205  EVPN ES Import:00fc.0001.0200
   EVPN ES Import:00fc.0001.0300
RP/0/RP0/CPU0:RR-1#
```

The output of the command **show bgp vpnv4 unicast update-group 0.1 filter-group 0.4**, presented in Output 7-105, shows the route targets that router PE-2 is looking to receive routes for from RR-1.

Output 7-105 *Route Target Constraint: BGP Filter Group 0.4 (PE-2) Output on RR-1*

```
RP/0/RP0/CPU0:RR-1#show bgp vpnv4 unicast update-group 0.1 filter-group 0.4

Update group for VPNv4 Unicast, index 0.1:
  Attributes:
    Neighbor sessions are IPv6
    Internal
    Common admin
    First neighbor AS: 65000
    Send communities
    Send GSHUT community if originated
    Send extended communities
    Route Reflector Client
    4-byte AS capable
    Send AIGP
    Send multicast attributes
    Extended Nexthop Encoding
    Minimum advertisement interval: 0 secs
```

```
Update group desynchronized: 0
Sub-groups merged: 7
Number of refresh subgroups: 0
Messages formatted: 341, replicated: 523
All neighbors are assigned to sub-group(s)
  Neighbors in sub-group: 0.2, Filter-Groups num:2
    Neighbors in filter-group: 0.4(RT num: 17)
     fc00:0:106::1
    Msg elems created : 30, Msg elems queued : 33, Msg elems deleted : 33
    Last update walk: prefixes (adv/wdn/skp/sup) : 1/0/0/0
    Total updates: prefixes (adv/wdn/non-optim) : 34/5/41
    Flags : 0x1, Nbr Cnt:1     Extended community:
       RT:65000:101  RT:65000:102  RT:65000:200  RT:65000:201  RT:65000:210
    RT:65000:300  RT:65000:500  RT:65000:502  RT:65000:503  RT:65000:510
    RT:65000:3000  RT:65000:5001  RT:65000:5100  RT:65000:10205  RT:65000:20205
    EVPN ES Import:00fc.0001.0200  EVPN ES Import:00fc.0001.0300
RP/0/RP0/CPU0:RR-1#
```

In conclusion, the BGP RTC feature provides an efficient mechanism for advertising route target membership information to peer routers, which in turn use the route target membership information to limit and filter routes being advertised back to originating routers. This filtering of additional extraneous routes reduces unnecessary CPU cycles, memory consumption, and bandwidth utilization impacts on both the route reflectors and PE routers throughout network.

Summary

This chapter explores a range of Layer 3 VPN services that are implemented over an SRv6 transport network. It demonstrates how to configure and troubleshoot these services on Cisco IOS XR routers, specifically using Version 7.8.2. It covers these services:

- L3VPN full-mesh service

- L3VPN hub-and-spoke service

- L3VPN extranet service

This chapter also delves into configuring and verifying these same Layer 3 VPN services, but with SR-MPLS as the underlying transport mechanism. It shows how to use routers running both Cisco IOS XR and IOS XE to set up and diagnose the various services.

Finally, this chapter discusses the BGP Route Target Constraint (RTC) functionality and its importance in optimizing the distribution of route target membership information among peer routers. This data is crucial for peers to fine-tune the routes they advertise to the routers from which the routes originated. The RTC feature is particularly beneficial for enhancing the efficiency of provider edge (PE) routers and route reflectors in large-scale network environments.

References and Additional Reading

L3VPN

- RFC 9252: BGP Overlay Services Based on Segment Routing over IPv6 (SRv6), https://datatracker.ietf.org/doc/rfc9252/

- RFC 4364: BGP/MPLS IP Virtual Private Networks (VPNs), https://datatracker.ietf.org/doc/rfc4364/

Route Target Constraint

- RFC 4360: BGP Extended Communities Attribute, https://datatracker.ietf.org/doc/html/rfc4360

- RFC 4684: Constrained Route Distribution for Border Gateway Protocol/MultiProtocol Label Switching (BGP/MPLS) Internet Protocol (IP) Virtual Private Networks (VPNs), https://datatracker.ietf.org/doc/html/rfc4684

Chapter 8

Service Assurance

Service providers offer a plethora of network services to end users today. A poor customer service experience can create the perception of inferior service quality, drive customer churn, and potentially have a financial impact. Similarly, with large enterprise networks, a poor customer service experience could negatively impact business efficiency and may result in a financial impact.

Service assurance is a set of procedures and processes designed to improve customer experience, maximize customer satisfaction, and reduce customer churn. Through the effective implementation of service assurance processes, a provider of end-user services can detect and resolve network faults, identify network quality issues, and monitor end-user contractual service-level agreements (SLAs). Service assurance covers multiple areas, including KPI monitoring, fault event management, network and service performance management, network traffic management, customer experience management, and trouble ticket management.

This chapter describes a subset of the tools and protocols service providers use in their service assurance processes and procedures. This chapter is structured into two main sections:

- **Transport:** Performance management in segment routing (SR) infrastructure is a critical aspect of modern network operations, ensuring that data packets are efficiently routed through a network using a simplified, scalable, and agile approach. Performance management in this context involves monitoring, measuring, and optimizing network performance by analyzing traffic flow, latency, error rates, and bandwidth utilization across predefined segments. Network administrators want to ensure that the SR infrastructure is not only delivering data with high precision and reduced complexity but also maintaining the quality of service (QoS) and meeting the SLAs required by various applications and services. This chapter offers a succinct exploration of performance measurement as it pertains to segment routing. It refrains from providing in-depth information, acknowledging that many of the tools being used today are in their infancy and subject to evolution during their development phase. The discussion touches on Segment-Routing Data Plane Monitoring (SR-DPM) and the Path Tracing (PT) mechanism.

- **Services:** L3VPN and L2VPN overlay services inherently lack built-in service assurance capabilities, necessitating the implementation of supplementary protocols in conjunction with these services to ascertain whether they fulfill the agreed-upon SLAs.

  - **L2VPN Service Assurance:** This section delves into the setup and validation of Connectivity Fault Management (CFM), which is used for fault management, as well as Y.1731, which provides both performance and fault management for Layer 2 services. The service assurance discussed in this section is specific to the Ethernet layer conveyed over L2VPN overlay services.

  - **L3VPN Service Assurance:** This section examines a widely recognized and established performance measurement tool from Cisco, known as IPSLA, which is employed for assessing packet delay, jitter, and loss. This section also briefly explores router implementations of Two-Way Active Measurement Protocol (TWAMP) and TWAMP Light, which offer capabilities for measuring packet delay, jitter, and loss akin to those provided by IPSLA.

Although this chapter does not cover all the tools available today, it does provide a brief roadmap of existing as well as upcoming strategies for the implementation of active SLA monitoring for both SR-MPLS and SRv6 transport services together with L2VPN and L3VPN overlay services.

Transport

This section describes two transport-related service assurance mechanisms designed to detect potential network faults and quality issues. The first mechanism, known as Segment Routing Data Plane Monitoring (SR-DPM), is used as a detection mechanism for traffic blackholes and path divergence in SR-MPLS networks. The second service assurance mechanism discussed here, known as Path Tracing (PT), involves using PT probes to provide full visibility of the paths taken by the PT probe packets. These PT probes encounter the same path and forwarding table behavior as normal customer traffic and can provide operators with extremely accurate real-time network status as well as historical data via an external time-series database. The Path Tracing feature forms part of a broader service assurance initiative known as Segment Routing Performance Measurement (SR-PM), which is an umbrella term for various components and tools that a network operator can deploy for network performance measurements.

Note   TWAMP Light is a simplified version of TWAMP (described in RFC 5357) that focuses on measuring network performance between endpoints. It was initially included as an appendix in RFC 5357 that did not provide enough detail to ensure consistent interoperability across different implementations. To resolve these shortcomings, RFC 8762 introduced Simple Two-Way Active Measurement Protocol (STAMP), which clarifies and builds on the concepts of TWAMP and has the capability to interoperate with a TWAMP Light device. This allows for a more straightforward and standardized approach to network performance measurement, facilitating easier deployment and consistent interpretation of results across various platforms and devices.

The SR-PM feature set encompasses the following:

■ **Link delay measurement:** One-way and two-way delay measurement can be performed across a single link between the TWAMP Light querier and TWAMP Light responder function configured on the routers. This allows for the measurement of these delay values and computation of delay metrics. (Figure 8-1 shows a one-way link delay measurement scenario.) These computed delay metrics can then be propagated network-wide via an IGP extension, such as IS-IS or OSPF TLV traffic engineering extensions, as described in RFC 7810. In addition, these delay metrics are also made available to the network operator via telemetry sensor data for visualization and additional processing. Because time stamp accuracy is key in link delay measurement, Precision Time Protocol (PTP) must be configured on routers that are specifically providing one-way delay measurements. The actual querier and responder frames generated by the routers are based on RFC 5357.

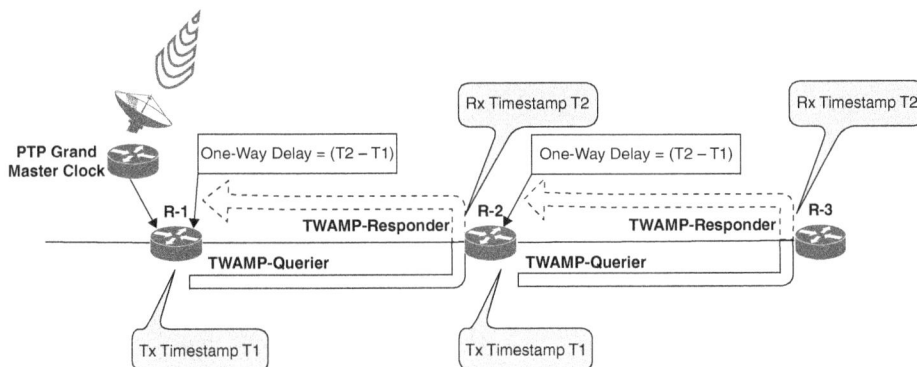

Figure 8-1   *Performance Measurement: One-Way Link Delay*

■ **End-to-end SR policy delay measurement:** One-way and two-way delay measurement can be performed across an end-to-end path between the TWAMP Light querier and TWAMP Light responder functions configured on the routers. Figure 8-2 shows an example of a one-way end-to-end policy delay measurement scenario across the SR policy path to router R-6 via router R-4. The delay values of the traversed path are dynamically computed and made available both to the traffic engineering function and as streamed telemetry data for further analysis by the network operator.

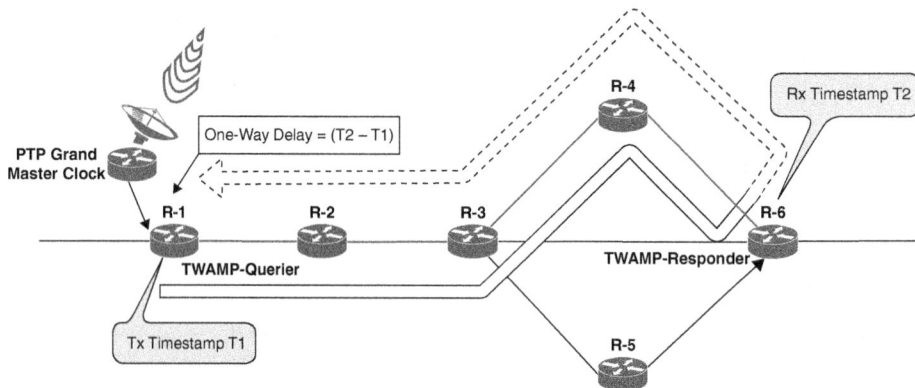

Figure 8-2 *Performance Measurement: One-Way End-to-End Policy Delay Measurement*

■ **End-to-end delay measurement of any endpoint:** One-way and two-way delay measurement can be performed across an end-to-end path to any IPv4 and IPv6 endpoint, whether these are located in the global routing table or within a VRF instance. The TWAMP Light querier and TWAMP Light responder functionality configured on the applicable routers facilitate these measurements and provide delay measurements via streamed telemetry sensor data. Figure 8-3 shows a one-way end-to-end delay measurement between VRF instances configured on the querier and responder nodes. In addition, the feature can simplify a network operator's service assurance toolkit by reducing the requirement for external TWAMP probes or devices.

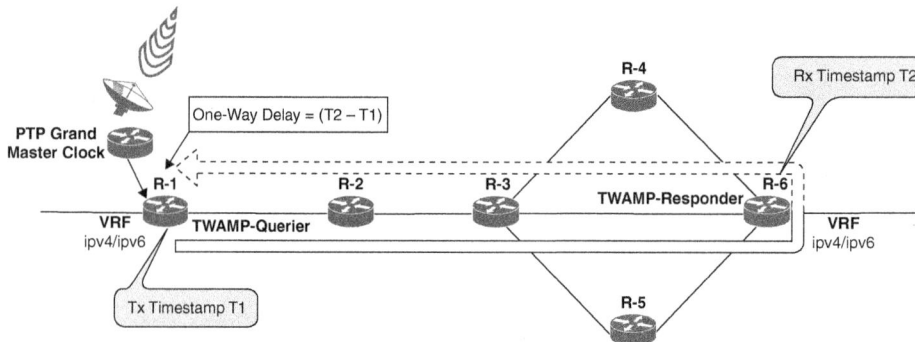

Figure 8-3 *Performance Measurement: One-Way End-to-End Delay Measurement of Any Endpoint*

■ **End-to-end SR policy liveness detection:** A network operator can use TWAMP Light performance measurement (PM) probes to verify the liveness of an SR policy endpoint or candidate path (see Figure 8-4). In a similar fashion to how the delay measurements are implemented, the TWAMP Light querier and TWAMP Light responder functionality on the routers facilitate these measurement:; The headend node initiates the PM probes and inserts them into the forwarding plane using the same label stack or SRv6 SID list as the SR policy. Upon receipt at the end node, the PM probes are time stamped, switched in the forwarding plane, and returned to the headend node. A returned PM probe received at the headend node provides confirmation of the liveness of the SR policy endpoint or candidate path, and a loss of liveness can rapidly trigger a re-optimization to another candidate path.

Note The term *liveness* is not specifically a reference to whether an end node is alive or dead but rather refers to the validity or existence of the SR policy candidate path or endpoint.

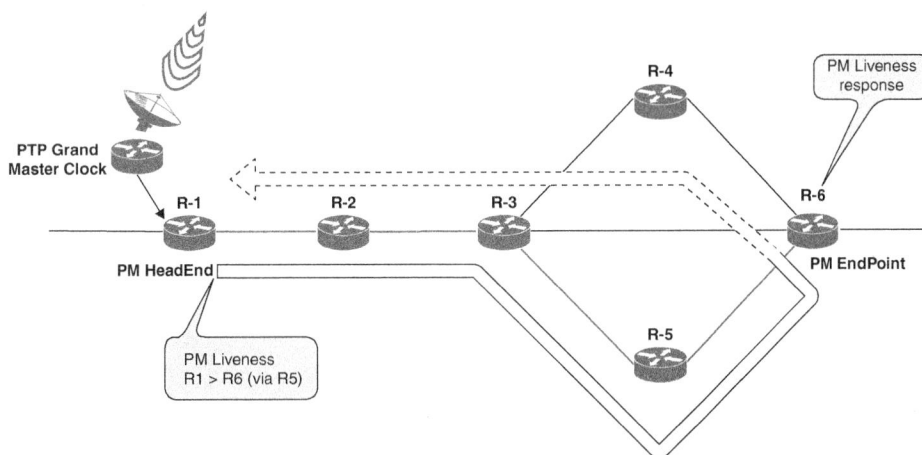

Figure 8-4 *Performance Measurement: End-to-End SR Policy Liveness Detection*

■ **Path Tracing:** Path Tracing (PT) is a powerful tool in the PM toolkit that answers a question that many network operators face in their networks today "What is the exact path taken by specific packets through my network?" In fact, this is an issue that's been around for many years and has been exacerbated with the proliferation of equal-cost multipathing (ECMP) routing, which is prevalent in most modern networks. Keep in mind that Path Tracing is a relatively new feature, and at this writing, not all of the functionality is available; some functionalities are still roadmap items commencing with SRv6 before addressing SR-MPLS–enabled networks.

Segment Routing Data Plane Monitoring (SR-DPM)

As mentioned earlier in this chapter, SR-DPM is used as a detection mechanism for both traffic blackholes and path divergence in SR-MPLS networks. With traffic blackholing, a router starts to drop network traffic toward a route or multiple routes, usually due to Forwarding Information Base (FIB) inconsistencies related to flapping routes, configuration errors, or even router hardware programming problems. Traffic blackholing can be hard to detect and troubleshoot, especially if the issues are transient in nature. Figure 8-5 illustrates a blackhole scenario where service traffic flowing between router CE-1 and router CE-2 encounters a faulty FIB entry for the Prefix SID of ABR-4 (16008) on router P-4 that causes traffic to be dropped.

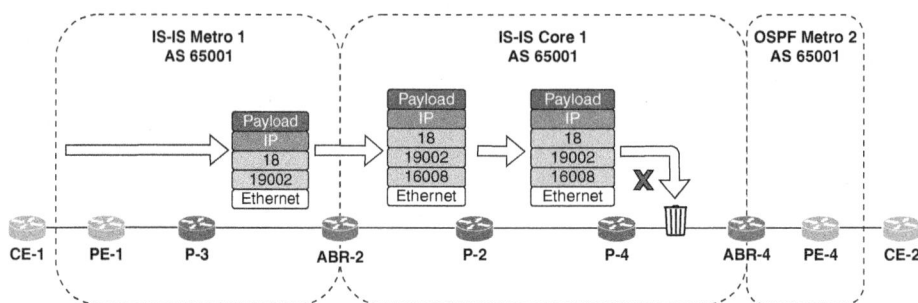

Figure 8-5   *SR-MPLS: Traffic Blackhole Example*

With path divergence, on the other hand, network traffic does not flow across the intended path based on the control plane metrics or packet label stack; rather, it is diverted through another path. In many cases, the diverted traffic could still reach its destination if a receiving node along the diversion path is able to interpret the label stack and forward the traffic onward. So, although the traffic is able to reach the destination and is not blackholed, this situation is not ideal because the diverged path may impact traffic SLAs and other service assurance targets. Path divergence occurrences are difficult to proactively detect and resolve and may result in negative customer satisfaction with the service offering.

Figure 8-6 shows a hypothetical example of path divergence, where upon reaching router P-3, a packet should be forwarded via router P-4 to ABR-4 (Prefix SID 16008) along the intended traffic path; instead, router P-3 pops the label 16008 and forwards the packet to ABR-3 along the diverged path. Router ABR-3 has label 19002 in its forwarding table because this is the BGP Prefix SID for router PE-4, and so ABR-3 is able to forward the packet on to router PE-4. Although the packet reaches its destination, it did not pass via the intended traffic path.

IS-IS Metro 1
AS 65001

IS-IS Core 1
AS 65001

OSPF Metro 2
AS 65001

Payload
IP
18
19002
16008
Ethernet
P-3

Payload
IP
18
19002
Ethernet
ABR-3

diverged traffic path

Payload
IP
18
19002
16008
Ethernet

Payload
IP
18
19002
Ethernet

intended traffic path

high-metric

CE-1   PE-1   P-3   ABR-2   P-2   P-4   ABR-4   PE-4   CE-2

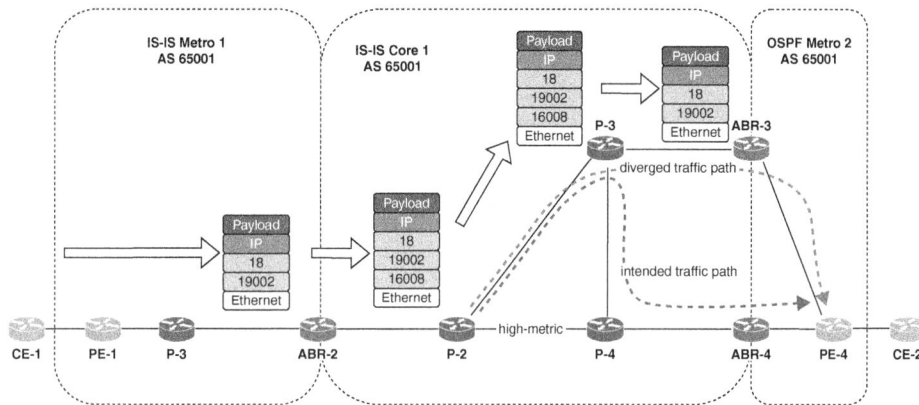

Figure 8-6   *SR-MPLS: Path Divergence Example*

Data Plane Monitoring (DPM) is a per-device data plane health detection mechanism that allows each device to validate its own data plane as well those of its immediate neighbors. By allowing DPM to be localized per device, the data plane health detection mechanism is distributed throughout the network, thereby negating any scale limitations of other end-to-end monitoring tools. Each device verifies all its attached neighbor links and destination prefixes through crafted label-switched path (LSP) echo packets. DPM runs continuously in the background, detecting faults that can either be logged to a syslog server or streamed to a telemetry collector.

Once DPM has been activated on a device, its functionality is divided into two stages:

■ **Stage 1: Adjacency verification and validation:** The crafted LSP echo requests are forwarded out each interface to all directly adjacent peer routers.

■ **Stage 2: Prefix reachability verification:** DPM verifies that each destination prefix in the routing table is reachable from both the initiating router and its downstream neighbors. This stage confirms the state of the control plane and forwarding path from the initiating router's perspective.

SR-DPM Configuration and Verification

Config 8-1 shows a basic configuration of DPM, where the only required configuration line is **mpls oam dpm**, although in this configuration example, the interval has been configured to occur every 10 minutes. The default DPM verification interval is 30 minutes, with a packet rate limit of 50 pps.

Note   DPM configuration is not required on the adjacent routers for this monitoring to work. However, best practice is to deploy DPM on all routers in the domain in order to reap the benefits of this monitoring service.

Config 8-1   *SR-MPLS: DPM Configuration*

```
!
mpls oam
 dpm
  interval 10
  !
 !
```

Once DPM has been configured on a router or after each configured DPM interval has elapsed, the events described in the following sections occur.

Stage 1: Adjacency Verification and Validation

In the example shown in Figure 8-7, DPM is configured on the router P-2 and immediately initiates the adjacency verification stage. In order for router P-2 to verify the adjacency to router ABR-2, it forwards a crafted LSP echo request packet out across the direct link toward router ABR-2. The captured packet in Example 8-1 provides the details of this crafted LSP echo request packet upon transmission from router P-2:

■ **MPLS Header:** The MPLS header displays the label 18, which is the Adjacency SID label used to reach router P-2 from router ABR-2. The packet is constructed with two labels, where the outer label 24001 is the router P-2 Adjacency SID label for router ABR-2. (This label is not shown in the packet capture because it was popped before transmission toward ABR-2.)

■ **IPv4 Src/Dst:** Source address 192.168.1.8 is the configured IP address for interface Gi0/0/0/0 of router P-2, and the destination IP address is always 127.0.0.1.

■ **Protocol:** UDP port 3503 is used.

■ **Target FEC Stack:** An LSP echo packet consists of a Target FEC Stack (TFS) TLV as well as a Downstream Mapping TLV.

  ■ **Type:** FEC type is Generic, which means it represents any IP control plane, whether SR-MPLS, LSP, or BGP.

  ■ **IPv4 Prefix:** This can be either the interface address or a loopback address. In this case, it is the configured IP address of interface Gi0/0/0/0 on router P-2.

■ **Detailed Downstream Mapping (DDSMAP):** The DDSMAP TLV contains the transit node interface and/or router ID details. In the case of the packet capture, this is the egress interface Gi0/0/0/0 on router P-2.

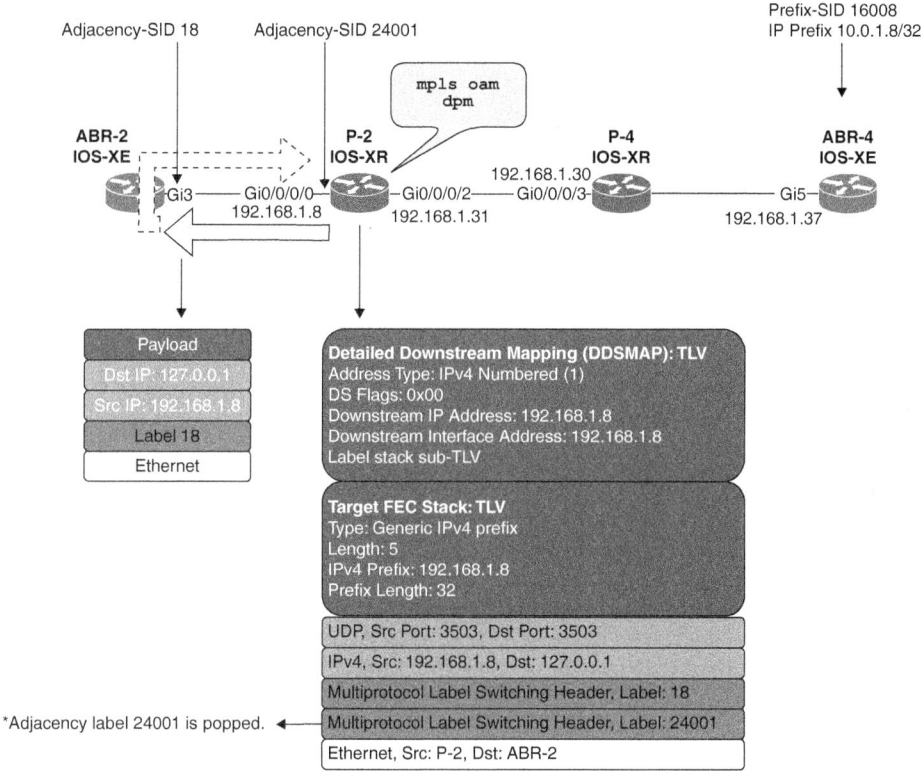

Figure 8-7 *SR-MPLS DPM Adjacency Verification Echo Packet Initiated*

Example 8-1 *SR-MPLS: DPM LSP Echo Packet*

```
Ethernet II, Src: RealtekU_08:30:ce (52:54:00:08:30:ce), Dst: RealtekU_1f:85:e1
  (52:54:00:1f:85:e1)
MultiProtocol Label Switching Header, Label: 18, Exp: 0, S: 1, TTL: 2
Internet Protocol Version 4, Src: 192.168.1.8, Dst: 127.0.0.1
User Datagram Protocol, Src Port: 3503, Dst Port: 3503
Multiprotocol Label Switching Echo
    Version: 1
    Global Flags: 0x0001
    Message Type: MPLS Echo Request (1)
    Reply Mode: Reply via an IPv4/IPv6 UDP packet (2)
<snip>
    Vendor Private
        Type: Vendor Private (64512)
        Length: 12
      Vendor Id: ciscoSystems (9)
      Value: 0001000400000004
    Target FEC Stack
```

```
        Type: Target FEC Stack (1)
        Length: 12
        FEC Element 1: Generic IPv4 prefix
            Type: Generic IPv4 prefix (14)
            Length: 5
            IPv4 Prefix: 192.168.1.8
            Prefix Length: 32
            Padding: 000000
Detailed Downstream Mapping
    Type: Detailed Downstream Mapping (20)
    Length: 24
    MTU: 0
    Address Type: IPv4 Numbered (1)
    DS Flags: 0x00
        0000 00.. = MBZ: 0x00
        .... ..0. = Interface and Label Stack Request: False
        .... ...0 = Treat as Non-IP Packet: False
    Downstream IP Address: 192.168.1.8
    Downstream Interface Address: 192.168.1.8
<snip>
```

Once router ABR-2 receives the LSP echo packet, it verifies that label 18 is the Adjacency SID for the interface Gi3 toward router P-2, pops the label, and forwards the echo packet back to router P-2, as shown in Figure 8-8. Upon receipt of the LSP echo packet, router P-2 verifies ownership of the IPv4 prefix in the Target FEC Stack TLV, and it ensures that the downstream interface address in the Detailed Downstream Mapping TLV is indeed the ingress interface where the echo packet is expected.

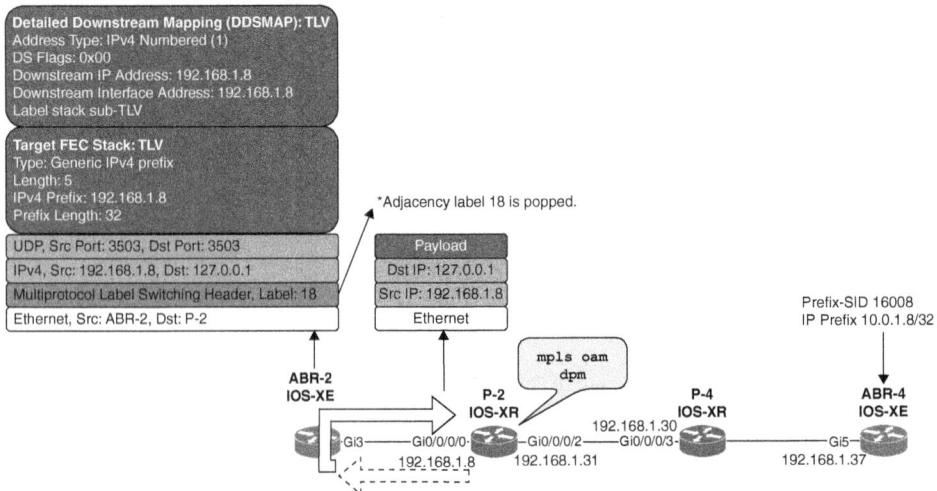

Figure 8-8 *SR-MPLS DPM Adjacency Verification Echo Packet Returned*

Stage 2: Prefix Reachability Verification

After the adjacency validation stage, DPM begins the FIB entry validation stage, where it determines whether all its FIB entries are correctly programmed. Figure 8-9 is a verification example of one such prefix—in this case the Prefix SID 16008 for router ABR-4 (10.0.1.8), where router P-2 validates both its own ingress and egress traffic forwarding path toward router ABR-4. Router P-2 forwards a crafted LSP echo toward the upstream neighbor router ABR-2, which in turn forwards the packet back through router P-2, egressing interface Gi0/0/0/2 toward router P-4.

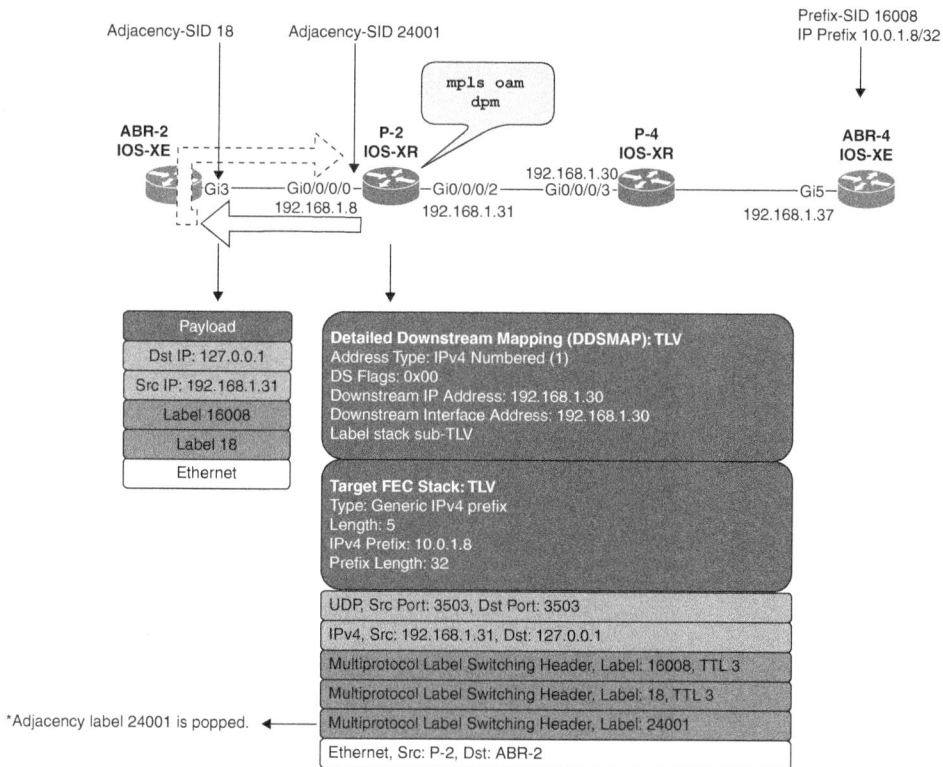

Figure 8-9   *SR-MPLS DPM Prefix Verification Echo Packet Initiated*

The Adjacency SID label 24001 toward router ABR-2 in the LSP echo is popped before being forwarded out the interface Gi0/0/0/0 toward the upstream router ABR-2, which in turn forward the packet back out interface Gi3 toward router P-2 based on the Adjacency SID 18. Router P-2 receives its own initiated LSP echo packet with Prefix SID 16008 and forwards the packet out the interface Gi0/0/0/2 toward the downstream router P-4, as shown in Figure 8-10.

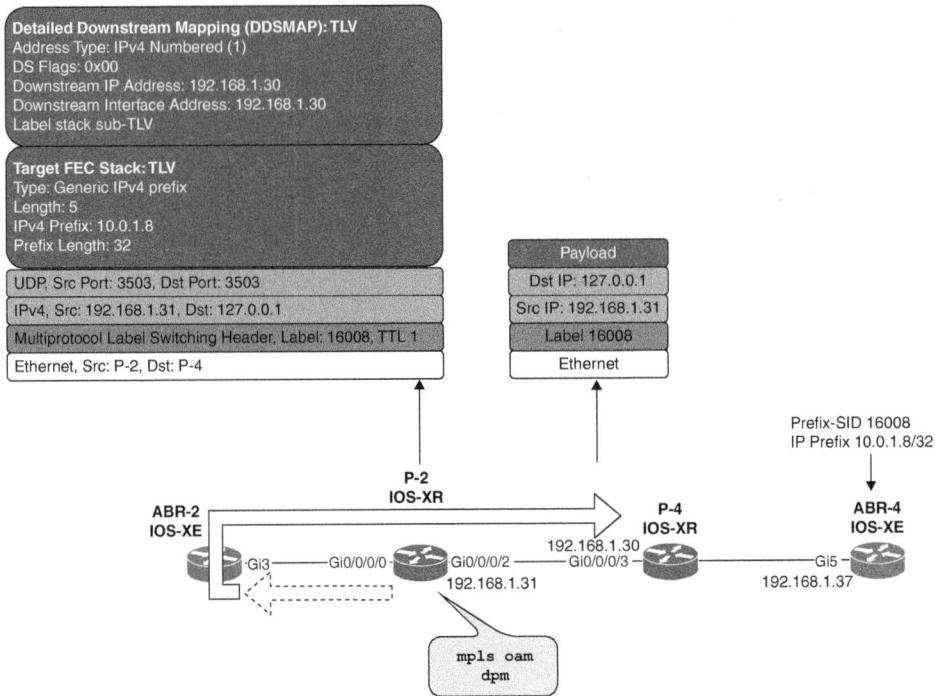

Figure 8-10 *SR-MPLS DPM Prefix Verification Echo Packet Forwarded*

On receipt of the packet, the downstream router P-4 examines the ingress LSP echo packet as the TTL will have expired and verifies the following:

■ From the Target FEC Stack TLV, it verifies reachability to the IPv4 prefix 10.0.1.8 of router ABR-4.

■ From the Detailed Downstream Mapping TLV, it verifies that the downstream interface address is indeed the interface on which it received the LSP echo and that it is the intended downstream node. In this example, router P-4 has the IPv4 address 192.168.1.30 configured on its local interface Gi0/0/0/3.

After router P-4 has verified the details of the downstream neighbor ABR-4, it returns a standard MPLS echo reply to router P-2, as shown in the packet capture in Example 8-2, which contains the following relevant information:

■ **IPv4 Src/Dst:** IP source address 192.168.1.30 is the interface Gi0/0/0/3 configured IP address on router P-4, and the destination IP address is 192.168.1.31 on router P-2.

■ **Detailed Downstream Mapping (DDSMAP):** The DDSMAP TLV contains the downstream IP address and downstream interface address 192.168.1.37 for interface Gi5 on router ABR-4.

■ **Return Code 8:** According to RFC 8029, the return code 8 means "label switched at stack-depth," indicating that the label operation is either a swap or a pop.

Example 8-2 *SR-MPLS: MPLS Echo Reply Packet*

```
Ethernet II, Src: RealtekU_1a:a5:93 (52:54:00:1a:a5:93), Dst: RealtekU_1c:fa:a6
  (52:54:00:1c:fa:a6)
Internet Protocol Version 4, Src: 192.168.1.30, Dst: 192.168.1.31
User Datagram Protocol, Src Port: 3503, Dst Port: 3503
Multiprotocol Label Switching Echo
    Version: 1
    Global Flags: 0x0001
    Message Type: MPLS Echo Reply (2)
    Reply Mode: Reply via an IPv4/IPv6 UDP packet (2)
    Return Code: Label switched at stack-depth RSC (8)
    Return Subcode: 1
    Sender's Handle: 0x3fa8b3ea
    Sequence Number: 1
    Timestamp Sent: Nov  2, 2023 11:57:31.978420172 UTC
    Timestamp Received: Nov  2, 2023 11:57:30.364124949 UTC
    Vendor Private
        Type: Vendor Private (64512)
        Length: 12
        Vendor Id: ciscoSystems (9)
        Value: 0001000400000004
    Detailed Downstream Mapping
        Type: Detailed Downstream Mapping (20)
        Length: 24
        MTU: 1500
        Address Type: IPv4 Numbered (1)
        DS Flags: 0x00
            0000 00.. = MBZ: 0x00
            .... ..0. = Interface and Label Stack Request: False
            .... ...0 = Treat as Non-IP Packet: False
        Downstream IP Address: 192.168.1.37
        Downstream Interface Address: 192.168.1.37
<snip>
```

After router P-2 receives the MPLS echo reply packet from router P-4, DPM processes the details. If it identifies any forwarding anomalies, it generates log messages to allow service assurance monitoring applications to act on these anomalies. The DPM process continues this verification cycle for all the local nodes, interfaces, and prefixes in the forwarding table.

The CLI command **show mpls oam dpm summary** in Output 8-1 provides a summary of the SR-DPM status from the last run on the router P-2. The following details are highlighted in the output:

- **DPM Validation Start Time:** This is the time interval when the LSP echo packets were initiated.

- **Interfaces Total/Eligible/Validated/Error(s):** On router P-2, there are six interfaces. One of them is the MgmtEth0 interface, and another is configured and in an up state but has no IS-IS adjacencies. This leaves four valid interfaces, based on information gleaned from the DPM property requests mentioned later in this list.

- **Prefix Total/Validated/Error(s):** Router P-2 has nine Prefix SIDs in the forwarding table.

- **Echo Request(s)/Retry/Response(s):** This is the total number of DPM LSP echo packets that were initiated.

- **Property Request(s)/Responses(s)/Error(s):** DPM property requests are the internal process requests to IS-IS to obtain all the IS-IS adjacency information for use by the DPM process.

- **Interval:** On router P-2, the DPM interval is set to 10 minutes, although the default is 30 minutes.

Output 8-1   *SR-MPLS DPM Summary on P-2*

```
RP/0/RP0/CPU0:P-2#show mpls oam dpm summary


MPLS OAM DPM Summary
-----------------------
Validation Status:                         Complete
DPM Validation Start Time:                 Nov  3 08:48:13.628
Interfaces Total/Eligible/Validated/Error(s): 6/4/4/0
Prefix Total/Validated/Error(s):           9/9/0
Echo Request(s)/Retry/Response(s):         32/0/32
Property Request(s)/Responses(s)/Error(s): 6/6/2
Interval:                                  10 minutes
DPM Echo Rate Limit:                       50 packet(s) per second
Collaborators:
                  Connected    Registered
                  ---------    ----------
SysDB             Y            Y
IM                Y            Y
RIB-V4            Y            Y
LSPV-Server       Y            -


Last DPM Fault: N/A
RP/0/RP0/CPU0:P-2#
```

The output of the CLI command **show mpls oam dpm adjacency**, shown in Output 8-2, is the result of the DPM property requests to the IS-IS process and displays the valid and adjacent interfaces from where the LSP echo packets are to be forwarded. The output matches the line Interfaces Total/Eligible/Validated/Error(s) from the CLI command **show mpls oam dpm summary.**

Output 8-2 *SR-MPLS DPM Adjacency on P-2*

```
RP/0/RP0/CPU0:P-2#show mpls oam dpm adjacency
Interface Name   Local Address   Outgoing Address Valid/Total Adj ISIS IPV4
  EXCLUDED Last Known Failure
---------------- ---------------- ---------------- ---------------- ---- ---- ------
   -- --------------------
Gi0/0/0/0        192.168.1.8      192.168.1.9      1/1              Y    Y    N
  N/A
Gi0/0/0/1        192.168.1.3      192.168.1.2      1/1              Y    Y    N
  10/29/23 04:28:21.446
Gi0/0/0/2        192.168.1.31     192.168.1.30     1/1              Y    Y    N
  10/29/23 04:28:21.411
Gi0/0/0/3        192.168.1.32     192.168.1.33     1/1              Y    Y    N
  10/29/23 04:28:21.402
Gi0/0/0/4        192.168.222.1    0.0.0.0          -/-              Y    Y    Y
  N/A
Mg0/RP0/CPU0/0   192.168.1.12     0.0.0.0          -/-              N    Y    Y
  N/A
RP/0/RP0/CPU0:P-2#
```

The prefixes being validated by DPM are listed with the CLI command **show mpls oam dpm prefix**, as shown in Output 8-3. The output from this command matches the line Prefix Total/Validated/Error(s) from the CLI command **show mpls oam dpm summary**. This example shows nine Prefix SIDs in IS-IS Core 1 from the SR-MPLS reference network in the Appendix A, "Reference Diagrams and Information."

Output 8-3 *SR-MPLS DPM Prefix on P-2*

```
RP/0/RP0/CPU0:P-2#show mpls oam dpm prefix
Prefix/Len       Prefix SID      Validation Status   Errors           Last Known
  Failure
---------------- ---------------- -------------------- ---------------- -------------
   ---------
10.0.1.1/32      16001           Complete            0                N/A
10.0.1.3/32      16003           Complete            0                N/A
10.0.1.4/32      16004           Complete            0                N/A
10.0.1.5/32      16005           Complete            0                N/A
10.0.1.6/32      16006           Complete            0                N/A
10.0.1.7/32      16007           Complete            0                N/A
10.0.1.8/32      16008           Complete            0                N/A
10.0.1.254/32    16254           Complete            0                N/A
10.1.1.5/32      16100           Complete            0                N/A
RP/0/RP0/CPU0:P-2#
```

As mentioned previously, the DPM process runs continuously in the background, and any detected faults are logged via syslog or streamed to a telemetry collector, and the operator is alerted to investigate further. Output 8-4 shows an example of a syslog error message that alerts the operator that the DPM process on router P-2 has received an MPLS echo reply with the return code value set to 4. RFC 8029 defines return code 4 as follows:

> Check the FEC label mapping that describes how traffic received on the LSP is further switched or which application it is associated with. If no mapping exists, set FEC-return-code to Return 4, "Replying router has no mapping for the FEC at stack-depth".

Output 8-4   *SR-MPLS DPM Syslog Message*

```
RP/0/RP0/CPU0:Oct 14 02:25:59.706 UTC: lspv_dpm[1150]: %ROUTING-LSPV_DPM-4-FAULT_
  NOTIFICATION : prefix:[10.0.1.8], sid[16008], upstream link:[ALL], downstream
  link:[ALL]. Output code:[F] - no FEC mapping
```

DPM is a relatively easily deployable detection mechanism for tracking both traffic blackholes and path divergence in SR-MPLS networks. DPM makes use of LSP echo packets to verify the Prefix SIDs of the originating router's forwarding table. It logs any forwarding path inconsistencies and notifies the operator via syslog logging directly on the router or via telemetry. Because DPM need only be configured on the originator device, the neighbor devices don't require a DPM configuration. The only requirement is that MPLS echo request and reply functionality must be supported.

Path Tracing (PT)

Increasing network bandwidth demand is a constant factor that network operators face when providing services—from mobile services to subscriber Internet access to traditional L2VPN/L3VPN business services. A provider can allocate additional bandwidth relatively inexpensively and easily by adding more inter-router links. In addition to meeting increased network bandwidth needs, operators can provide end-to-end path resiliency via other routers. In fact, most networks today are being deployed in this manner, using a routing strategy known as equal-cost multipathing (ECMP). ECMP is becoming an important design criterion in today's networks, allowing an easy path to upgrading network bandwidth and also providing network resiliency. ECMP enables a transmitting router to load balance traffic over multiple links. For example, in Figure 8-11, router R-1 is forwarding ingress traffic toward router R-13 across five ECMP paths.

Although traffic load balancing can occur on a per-packet basis, this is no longer the norm as it can lead to packets arriving out of order at the destination due to network or router delays (for example, because of device queue buffering delays on specific links). Per-flow traffic load balancing is the result of a hash computation across key fields from the packet header conducted by the router. The router can then use the hash information to determine the egress interface from which to forward the packet. For instance, on Cisco ASR 9000 routers, each incoming packet is subject to a 32-bit CRC (cyclic redundancy check) hash calculation based on header fields, with the specific fields selected depending on the type of packet. The hash calculation fields are platform and configuration dependent, but here is an example of some possibilities:

- **IPv4**: For IPv4 packets, the fields Source IP, Destination IP, Source Port (TCP/UDP only), Destination Port (TCP/UDP only), and Router ID are included in the calculation.

- **IPv6**: For IPv6 packets, the fields Source IP, Destination IP, Source Port (TCP/UDP only), Destination Port (TCP/UDP only), and Router ID are included in the calculation.

- **L2**: For L2 packets, the fields DMAC, SMAC, Source IP, Destination IP, and Router ID are included in the calculation.

From a calculated hash, a certain number of bits can be used to identify the path over which the packet is forwarded. For instance, if the platform is designed to support IGP paths with up to 32-way non-recursive options, then 5 bits from the calculated hash will be used.

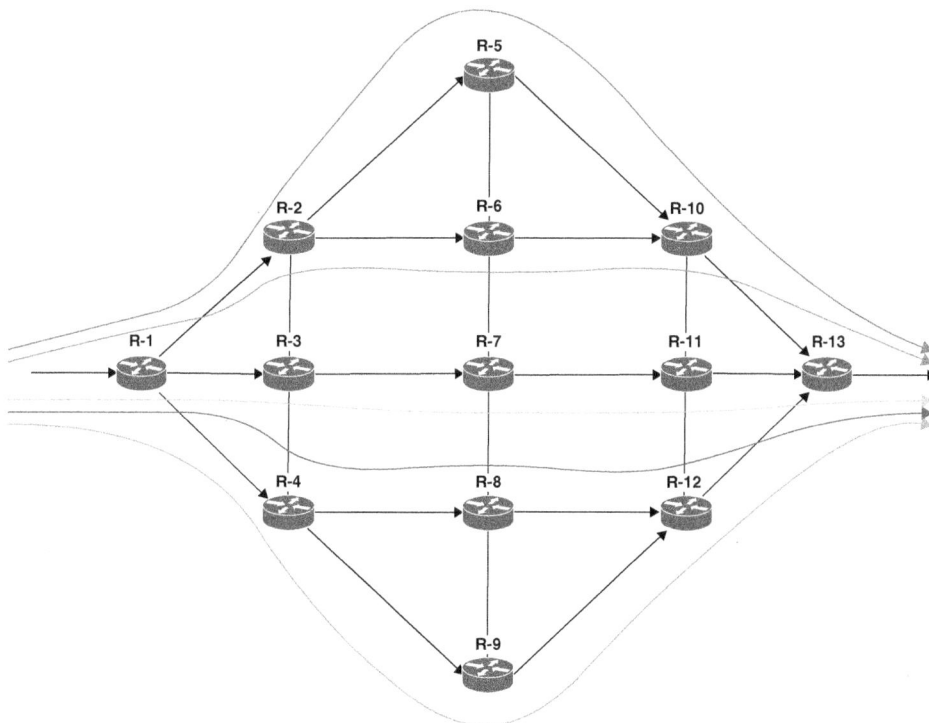

Figure 8-11   *Equal-Cost Multipathing (ECMP)*

ECMP plays an important role when designing, provisioning, and deploying modern networks. The deployment of ECMP in large-scale networks has intensified one of the long-standing challenges facing service providers and network operators: the ability to expeditiously detect and troubleshoot issues in networks with multiple ECMP paths. Figure 8-12 illustrates the potential challenges in networks with multiple ECMP paths, from traffic flows following unexpected ECMP paths to the actual discarding of specific traffic flows or even transient latency discrepancies between the various ECMP paths.

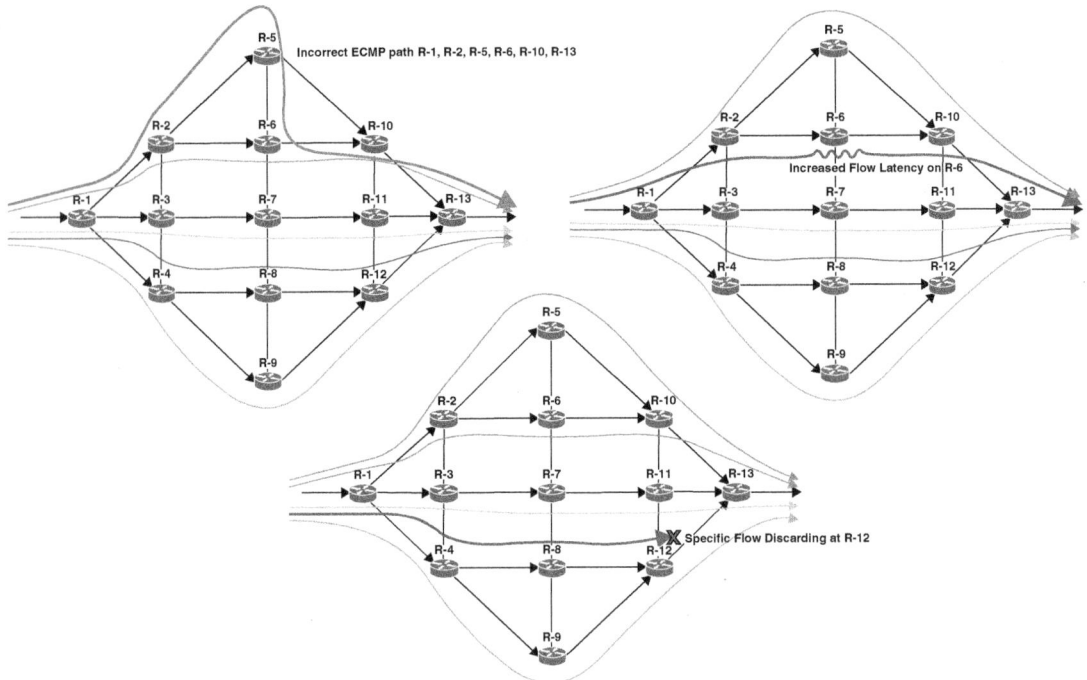

Figure 8-12 *ECMP Path Anomalies, Flow Discarding, and Increased Flow Latency*

Until recently, it was extremely difficult, if not impossible, for service providers and network operators to know through which ECMP paths customer traffic flows traversed their networks. Recently, however, Path Tracing, which the IETF is in the process of standardizing, has become a solution that allows network operators to monitor all ECMP paths across their networks in a more deterministic manner. PT packets are subjected to the same router forwarding behavior as normal customer traffic: They are forwarded via a router's hardware forwarding path and not punted to a CPU for additional processing. A PT probe packet is subjected to the same QoS requirements as regular traffic and is able to efficiently provide egress interface information, an accurate time stamp, and load information at each router hop. This collected data is then forwarded to an off-network application for correlation and analysis, allowing network operators to manage and monitor the health status of the networks under their control.

Path Tracing is designed to be extremely hardware efficient in terms of how packets are handled along the forwarding path. Each transit router records 3 bytes of data in the PT header within the IPv6 packet before forwarding it on to the next transit router. The data included by all the participating transit nodes is known as Midpoint Compressed Data (MCD) and includes the following:

- **12-bit interface ID:** An egress interface ID is used for path identification.

- **8-bit truncated time stamp:** The Precision Time Protocol (PTP) plays a fundamental role in the validity and accuracy of these time stamps.

- **4-bit load:** The egress interface load is expressed on a logarithmic scale.

The MCD is included in the Hop-by-Hop options header of the IPv6 packet with the option type set to 0x32 for PT.

So, at a high level, Path Tracing involves the following concepts, which are visualized in Figure 8-13:

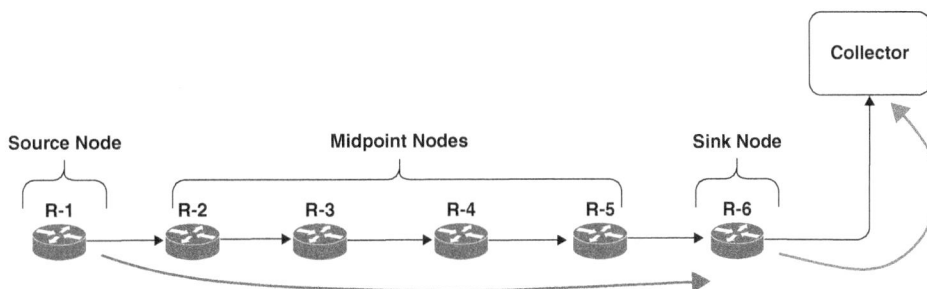

Figure 8-13 *Path Tracing Solution Overview*

- **Source node:** This is the device that will initiate the PT probe IPv6 packets and include the Hop-by-Hop header with the HbH-PT option set. All the bits in the HbH-PT Midpoint Compressed Data (MCD) field are initially set to 0, and a Destinations option header is included with the DOH-PT set; this header includes a 64-bit time stamp, session ID, egress interface ID, and egress interface load.

- **Midpoint nodes:** These are the transit nodes and routers that collect and include 3 bytes of MCD into the PT probes on the egress interfaces. This is done in hardware at line rate, and the MCD is pushed into the probe packets' MCD stack.

- **Sink node:** The sink node is the destination node for the PT probes, whose function is to include a receive 64-bit time stamp, an ingress interface ID, and the ingress interface load in the Destinations option header with DOH-PT set. The sink node encapsulates this information within an IPv6 header with the destination set to the regional collector (RC), where the data is included into a time-series database for analysis and visualization.

Let's take a closer look at the Path Tracing probes by starting with the PT probe initiator, which is the source node, and delve into the details of the PT IPv6 packet. The PT probe packet format shown in Figure 8-14 is based on the IETF draft draft-filsfils-ippm-path-tracing-01, which notes a significant header change compared to the previous drafts. This header change impacts both the source and sink node packet formats.

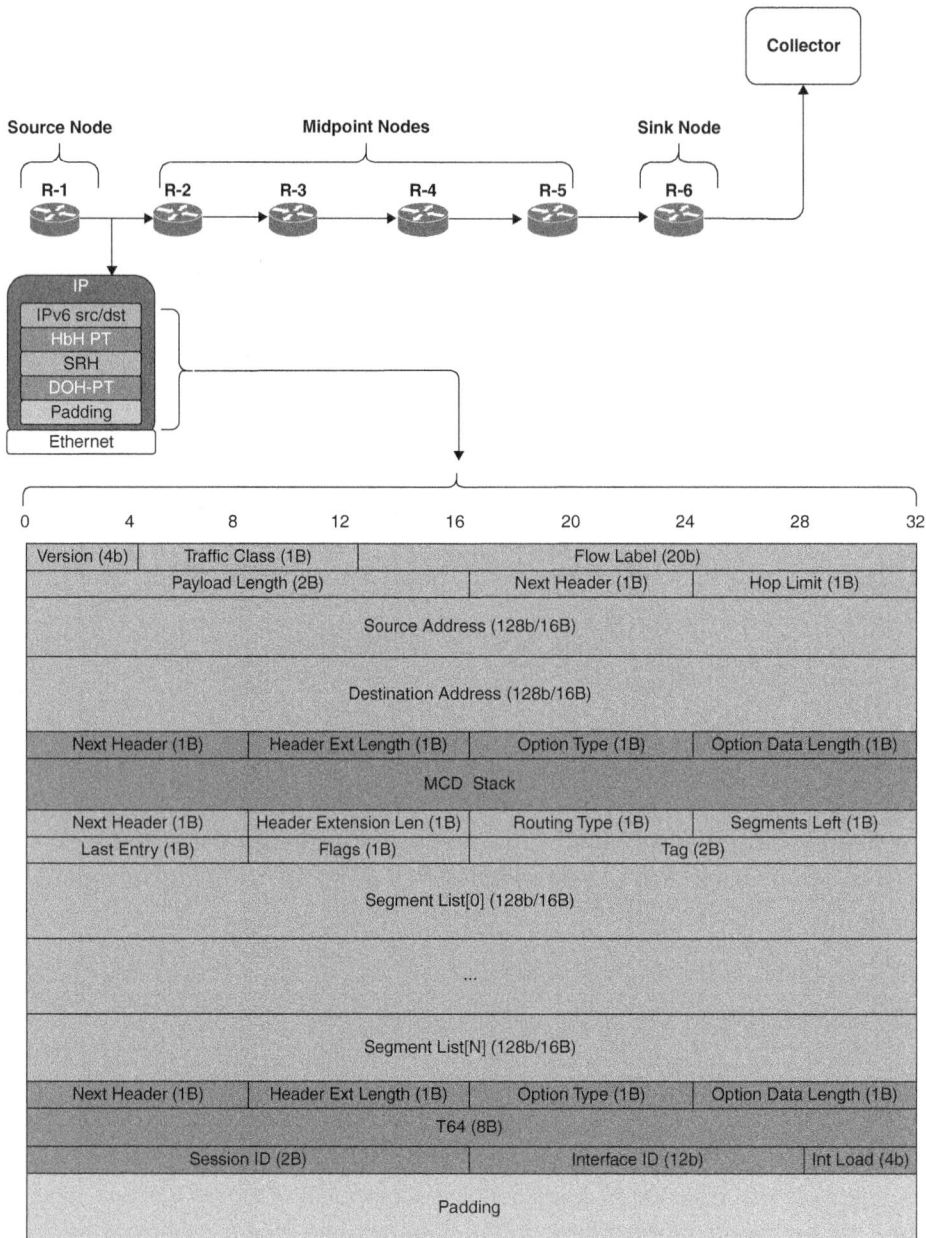

Figure 8-14 *Path Tracing Probe Packet Format: Source Node*

These are the relevant Path Tracing probe packet IPv6 header fields:

■ **Next Header:** This field is set to 0, indicating that the Hop-by-Hop (HbH) options header follows the IPv6 header.

- **IPv6 Source Address:** This is the source node's IPv6 address.

- **IPv6 Destination Address:** This is the sink node's IPv6 address or the first segment in the segment list.

These are the fields in the Hop-by-Hop (HbH) options header:

- **Next Header:** This field is set to 43, indicating that the Routing header follows the HbH header.

- **Option Type:** The three highest-order bits are set to 001.

  - **00:** This indicates that the HbH header is to be ignored by nodes that are not configured for or supporting Path Tracing.

  - **1:** This indicates that the HbH header data is to be inserted by nodes that support Path Tracing.

- **Option Data Length:** This is the length, in bytes, of the MCD stack.

- **Midpoint Compressed Data (MCD):** All bits are set to 0 in the MCD stack.

The segment routing header (SRH) is inserted if more than one SRv6 SID is required:

- **Next Header:** This field is set to 60, indicating that the IPv6 Destinations options header follows.

- **Routing Type:** This is set to 4 for the SRH.

- **Segment List:** (Optional) This is the reverse-order list of the IPv6 addresses (segments).

These are the fields in the IPv6 Destinations Option Header for Path Tracing (DOH-PT):

- **Next Header:** This field is set to 59, indicating that the IPv6 No Next header follows.

- **Option Type:** The three highest-order bits are set to 000.

  - **00:** This indicates that the DOH-PT is to be ignored by nodes that are not configured or that do not support Path Tracing.

  - **0:** This indicates that the DOH-PT fields are not to be modified in transit.

- **Option Data Length:** This is the length, in bytes (12 bytes), of the DOH-PT.

- **T64:** This is a 64-bit time stamp set by the source node.

- **Session ID:** This is a 2-byte session ID set by the source node for session correlation.

- **Interface ID (SRC.OIF):** This is the egress interface ID (12 bits).

- **Interface Load (SRC.OIL):** This is the egress interface load (4 bits).

Now let's look at the details of a PT IPv6 packet after it is processed by a midpoint node. Figure 8-15 shows the PT IPv6 probe packet after egressing router R-3.

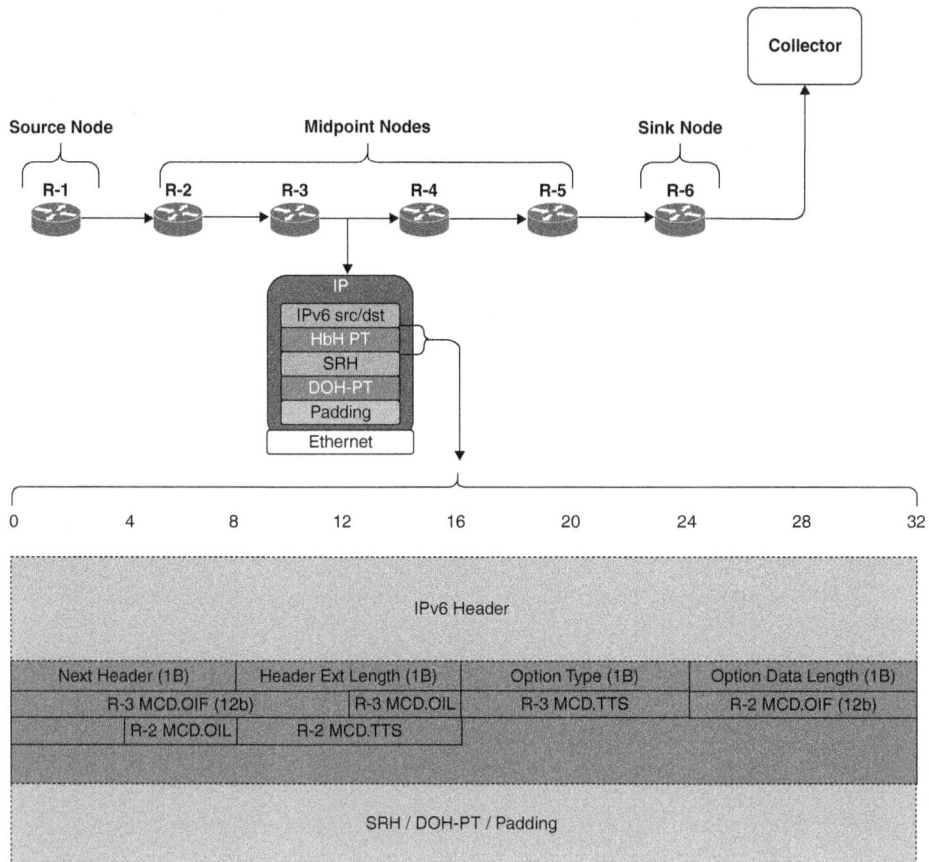

Figure 8-15 *Path Tracing Probe Packet Format: Midpoint Node*

As mentioned previously, Path Tracing is designed to be extremely hardware efficient, specifically in the way that probe packets are handled by the midpoint transit nodes. The following 3 bytes of data are included in the HbH header:

- **MCD OIF:** This is a 12-bit user-configured egress interface ID.

- **MCD OI:** This is a 4-bit egress interface load expressed in logarithmic scale.

- **MCD TTS:** This is an 8-bit truncated time stamp.

The midpoint node shifts the already inserted MCD stack by 3 bytes to the right and appends the MCD at the start of the stack.

Finally, the PT probe packets arrive at the sink node, whose function is to encapsulate these packets with a new IPv6 header whose destination is set to that of the regional collector (RC). The sink node also appends a new Destinations option header with DOH-PT set and includes in the new IPv6 header a 64-bit receipt time stamp, an ingress interface

ID, and the ingress interface load. Once this packet reaches the RC, the data is included in a time-series database for analysis. Figure 8-16 shows the IPv6 encapsulated PT probe being forwarded to the RC.

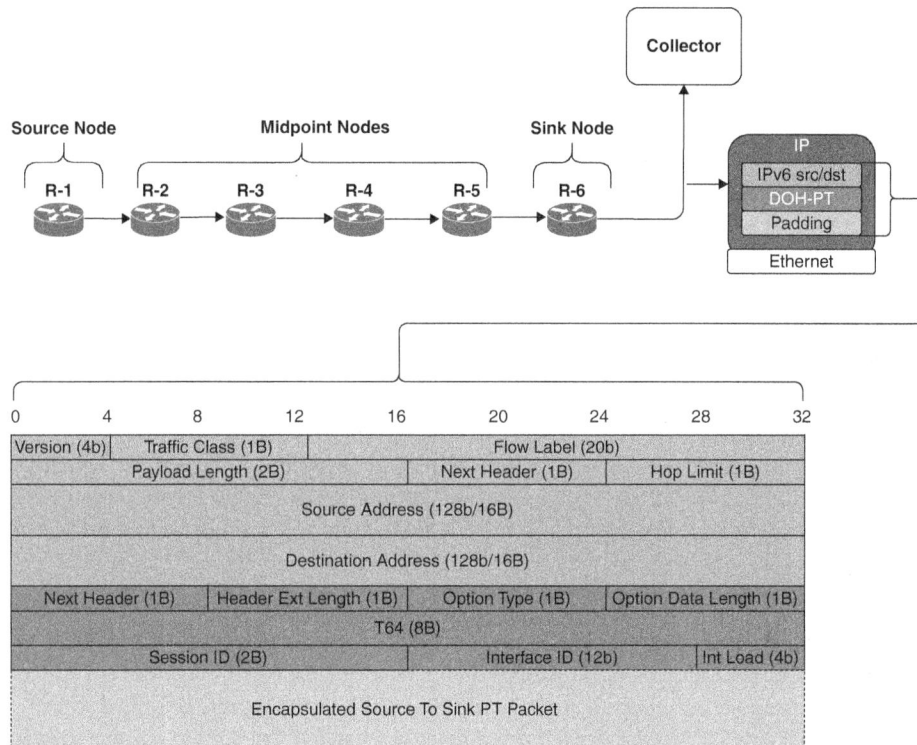

Figure 8-16 *Path Tracing Probe Packet Format: Sink Node*

The PT probe packet is encapsulated with an IPv6 header before being routed onto the regional collector:

- **Next Header:** This field is set to 60, indicating that the IPv6 Destinations header is next.

- **IPv6 Source Address:** This is the sink node's IPv6 address.

- **IPv6 Destination Address:** This is the regional collector's IPv6 address.

These are the fields in the IPv6 Destinations Option Header for Path Tracing (DOH-PT):

- **Next Header:** This field is set to 41, indicating that an encapsulated IPv6 header will follow because this is the encapsulated PT probe with the captured MCD.

- **T64 (SNK.T64):** This is a 64-bit time stamp set by the sink node.

- **Session ID:** This is set to zero.

- **Interface ID (SNK.IIF):** This is the ingress interface ID (12 bits).

- **Interface Load (SNK.IIL):** This is the ingress interface load (4 bits).

Finally, the source-to-sink Path Tracing probe packet is appended into an encapsulating IPv6 header with all the sink and midpoint nodes' collected data. It is then forwarded to the RC, where the data is included in a time-series database for analysis and visualization.

In summary, Path Tracing is a relatively new feature, and much of its functionality is not yet available for various router platforms as of this writing. However, network operators who are embarking on migrating current networks to SRv6/SR-MPLS or building green-field SRv6/SR-MPLS transport networks should understand the service assurance capabilities that Path Tracing will provide in the overall monitoring and management of the transport networks under their control.

Services

As you have already seen, service assurance is a set of procedures and processes designed to measure and monitor the SLAs of services that have been sold to customers. A service provider's adherence to SLAs drives positive customer experiences, maximizes customer satisfaction, and reduces customer churn, which in turn has an impact on the service provider's reputation for quality services as well as minimizing potential SLA penalties, which could have negative impacts on the service provider's finances.

The most effective way to measure and monitor SLAs is for traffic to be sent through the same service data forwarding path as customer traffic, to see if it is subjected to delay, packet drops, or suboptimal traffic paths. L3VPN and L2VPN overlay services have no embedded service assurance features, and therefore additional protocols need to be deployed alongside overlay services in order to verify whether the service actually meets the contracted SLAs.

L2VPN Service Assurance

Ethernet Operations, Administration, and Maintenance (OAM) is a suite of protocols and tools that allow a network operator to enable a fully FCAPS-capable network. FCAPS is an ISO Telecommunications Management Network model and framework for the management of networks. FCAPS refers to the following capabilities:

- **F:** Fault management

- **C:** Configuration management

- **A:** Accounting

- **P:** Performance management

- **S:** Security management

> **Note**   For more information on OAM fault management, see the Metro Ethernet Forum (MEF) specifications MEF 30.1 and MEF 35.1.

The ability to add OAM capabilities to a network platform is a key differentiator that allows a service provider network to be classed as carrier grade.

Ethernet OAM consists of multiple building blocks, as shown in Figure 8-17. This section discusses two of them in some detail: Connectivity Faulty Management (CFM), which is used for fault management, and Y.1731, which is used for both performance and fault management in an FCAPS-capable network. CFM is defined by both IEEE 802.1ag and Y.1731. The ITU-T Y.1731 protocol is effectively a superset of the CFM 802.1ag standard, in that it includes the features supported in the 802.1ag standard as well as additional extensions. The focus in this section is on the Y.1731 Performance Monitoring (PM) extension, which includes mechanisms for the measurement of frame delay, frame delay variation (jitter), and frame loss.

> **Note**   It is important to understand that the service assurance covered in this chapter pertains to the Ethernet layer carried over the L2VPN service and does not apply to any SR-MPLS or SRv6 functions.

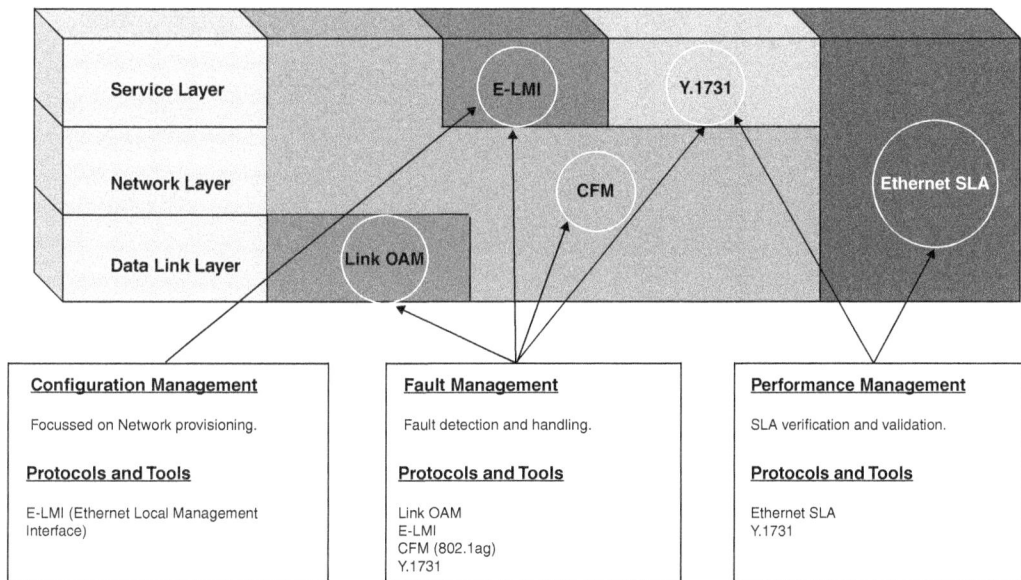

Figure 8-17 *Ethernet OAM Building Blocks*

Ethernet Connectivity Fault Management (CFM)

CFM is a family of protocols that provides the capability to detect, verify, isolate, and report end-to-end Ethernet connectivity faults. The IEEE standardized CFM in 2007 as part of IEEE 802.1ag-2007. CFM uses regular Ethernet frames that travel in-band with customer traffic, and any device that cannot interpret the CFM messages forwards them as normal data frames. The CFM frames are distinguishable via the Ether-Type (0x8902) and the multicast destination MAC (DMAC) address.

Conceptually, CFM consists of the following:

- **Maintenance domains (MDs):** CFM maintenance domains are the service provider, operator, and/or customer operational boundaries. They can be nested or can touch but cannot overlap. There can be up to eight levels (0–7); the higher the MD level, the wider the span. Figure 8-18 provides a conceptional overview that included maintenance domain endpoints and maintenance domain intermediate points within a Layer 2 bridged environment. Because maintenance domains may be nested, network administration responsibilities for a given end-to-end service can be allocated among multiple independent owners/operators of the services.

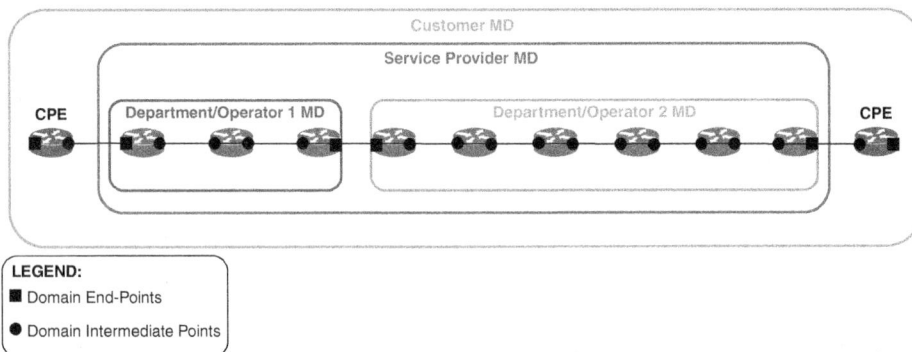

Figure 8-18   *CFM Functions: Maintenance Domains (MDs)*

- **Maintenance associations (MAs):** A CFM maintenance association is used to monitor a specific service instance within a CFM maintenance domain and can traverse multiple nested CFM maintenance domains. A CFM maintenance association is defined at the edge of the domain through a set of maintenance endpoints (MEPs).

- **Maintenance endpoints (MEPs):** A MEP denotes the boundaries of a CFM maintenance domain and can detect the presence of other MEPs within a CFM MA, as well as any local and remote associated connectivity failures. A MEP is identified through a configured MEP ID (1–8191). Figure 8-19 shows the relationships between the MEPs and maintenance intermediate points (MIPs) in various CFM maintenance domains.

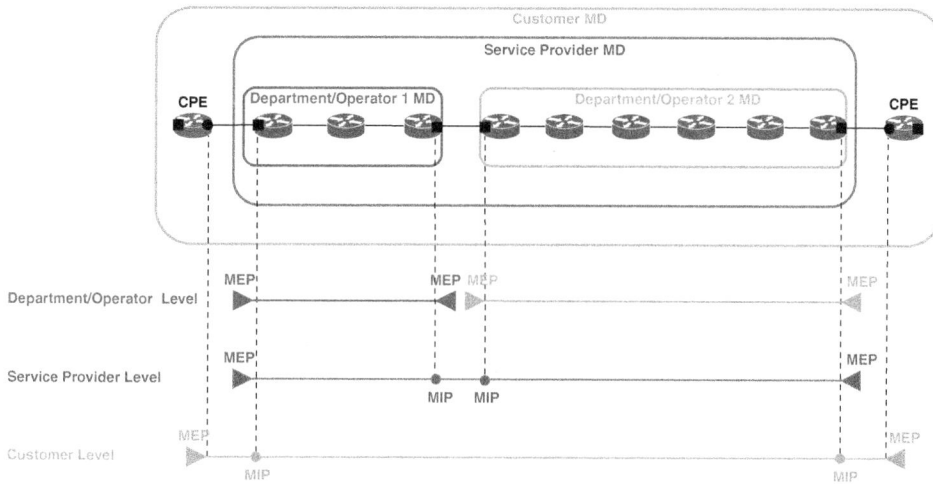

Figure 8-19   *CFM Functions: MEPs and MIPs*

- **Maintenance intermediate points (MIPs):** MIPs are internal to CFM maintenance domains and are created automatically through network functions such as bridge domains. They enable the discovery of paths between MEPs and faults by responding to CFM protocol messages (refer to Figure 8-19).

- **UP and DOWN MEPs:** CFM PDUs generated by an UP MEP are forwarded toward the L2 bridge function and not directly into the access-circuit where the MEP has been configured. UP MEPs are commonly used for end-to-end maintenance associations rather than across single links.

  CFM PDUs generated by a DOWN MEP are forwarded directly into the access circuit where the MEP has been configured. DOWN MEPs are mostly used for maintenance associations across single links. Figure 8-20 indicates the area UP/DOWN MEPs monitor on a router, bridge, or switch.

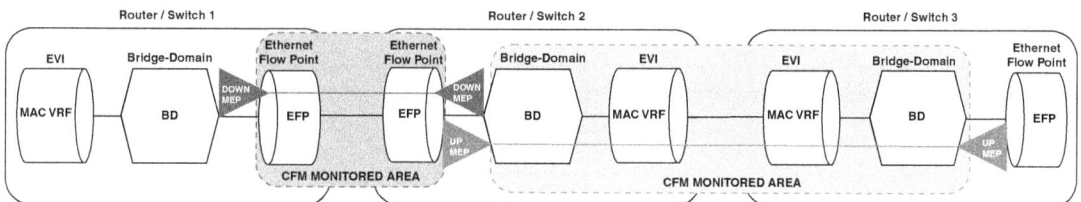

Figure 8-20   *CFM Functions: UP/DOWN MEPs*

CFM is a family of three protocols used in Ethernet OAM functionality:

- **Continuity Check Message (CCM):** The CCM protocol is used for fault detection, notification, and recovery and consists of per-MA unidirectional multicast packets that are transmitted at configurable periodic intervals by the MEPs. CCM frames transport the status of the router or switch interface on which the MEP is configured

and are catalogued into the CCM database by the MIPs along the same CFM maintenance association level before finally being terminated by the remote MEPs.
Figure 8-21 shows a CCM packet traversing a CFM maintenance association level
before terminating at the remote MEP.

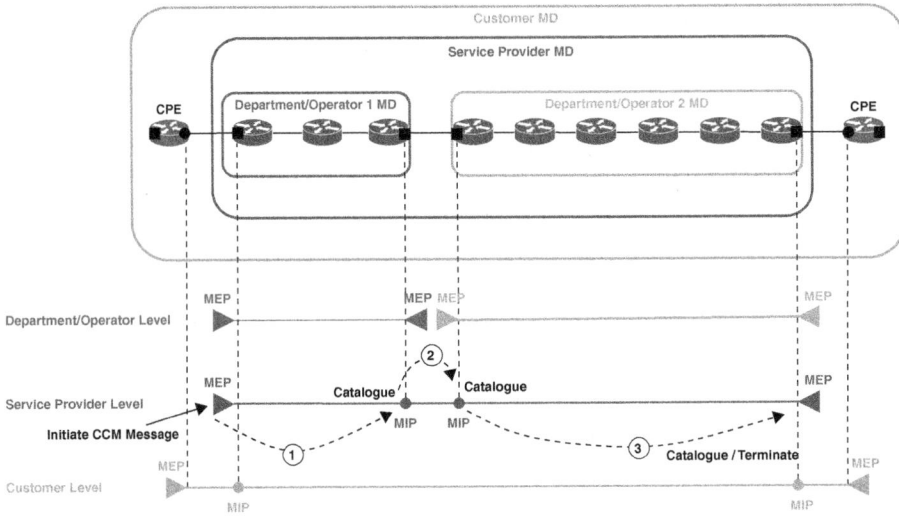

Figure 8-21   *CFM Functions: Continuity Check Message (CCM)*

■ **Loopback Protocol:** Loopback Protocol is used for fault verification, much like an
ICMP echo request. A MEP can send a unicast Loopback Message (LBM) to another
MEP or MIP in the same maintenance association, as shown in Figure 8-22. Upon
receiving the LBM, the receiving MEP/MIP replies with a unicast Loopback Reply
(LBR) to the originating MEP.

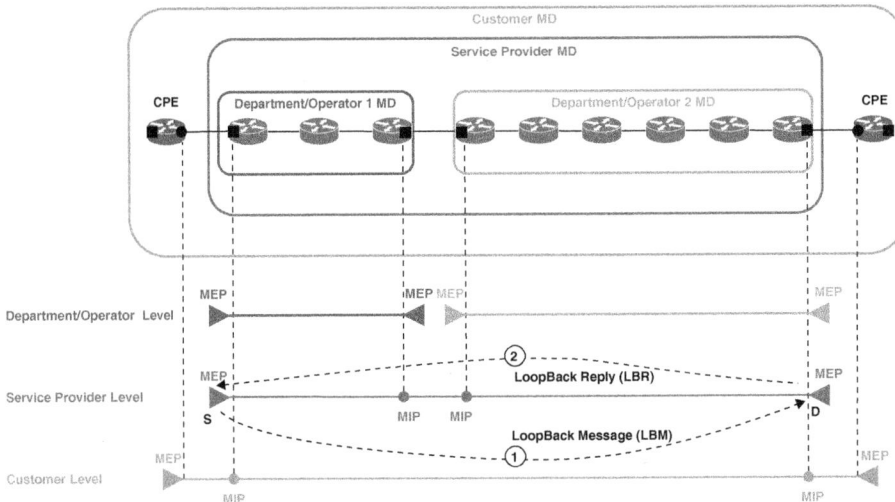

Figure 8-22   *CFM Functions: Loopback Message (LBM)*

■ **Linktrace Protocol:** This Ethernet traceroute protocol is used for path discovery and fault isolation, much the same way that traceroutes are used in IP networks for path discovery. The originating MEP transmits multicast Linktrace Messages (LTMs) to discover the MIPs along a path within the same maintenance association that terminates with a MEP. Each MIP along the path, together with the destination MEP, returns a unicast Linktrace Reply (LTR) to the originating MEP upon receiving the multicast LTM frames. Figure 8-23 shows the CFM LTM behavior through the maintenance association.

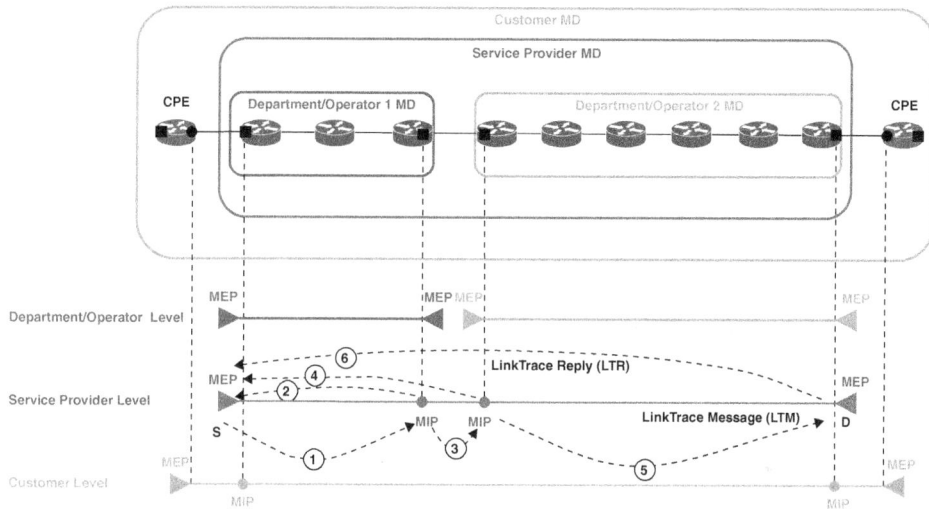

Figure 8-23   *CFM Functions: Linktrace Message (LTM)*

Ethernet CFM Configuration and Verification

The CFM CLI configuration shown in Config 8-2 is an example from the router PE-1 in the SRv6 reference network in Appendix A. It includes the following relevant information:

Note   The configuration presented in Config 8-2 serves solely as an illustrative example for explanatory purposes.

■ **domain ELAN-L1-DMN level 1:** A CFM maintenance domain name and level are initially configured. The per-service CFM maintenance associations will be hosted under this level 1 domain.

■ **service ELAN-200-L1-SVC bridge group ELAN-BG bridge-domain 200-BD:** Within the CFM maintenance domain level, the per-service CFM maintenance associations are configured and associated for each service (that is, per customer bridge domain).

- □ **maximum-meps 20:** This is an optional configuration to limit the number of peers MEPs learned in the CFM MA.

- □ **continuity-check interval 1m loss-threshold 3:** This is the time interval at which CCMs are transmitted (60 s) and sets the threshold limit for when a MEP is declared down (3 × 60 s).

- □ **continuity-check loss auto-traceroute:** This is an optional configuration to automatically trigger a CFM linktrace when reachability to a peer MEP has been lost.

- □ **continuity-check archive hold-time 10:** This is an optional configuration to archive (in minutes) peer MEP information when reachability to the peer MEP has been lost.

- □ **log continuity-check errors:** This is a useful optional configuration for logging CFM error events.

- □ **log continuity-check mep changes:** This is a useful optional configuration for logging CFM events.

- ■ **mep domain ELAN-L1-DMN service ELAN-200-L1-SVC mep-id 11:** This configuration creates the MEP under the interface and associates the specific MEP with a MEP ID number (1–8190).

Config 8-2 *Ethernet CFM: Maintenance Domain/Association and MEP Configuration*

```
!
ethernet cfm
 domain ELAN-L1-DMN level 1
  service ELAN-200-L1-SVC bridge group ELAN-BG bridge-domain 200-BD
   maximum-meps 20
   continuity-check interval 1m loss-threshold 3
   continuity-check loss auto-traceroute
   continuity-check archive hold-time 10
   log continuity-check errors
   log continuity-check mep changes
  !
 !
interface Bundle-Ether200.2000 l2transport
 encapsulation dot1q 2000
 ethernet cfm
  mep domain ELAN-L1-DMN service ELAN-200-L1-SVC mep-id 11
  !
 !
!
```

The output of the commands **show ethernet cfm local meps domain ELAN-L1-DMN service ELAN-200-L1-SVC** in Output 8-5 and **show ethernet cfm peer meps domain ELAN-L1-DMN service ELAN-200-L1-SVC** in Output 8-6 are useful for verifying local and remote MEPs for each CFM maintenance domain and maintenance association. The CLI command shown in Output 8-5, when run on router PE-1, reveals the configured MEP ID 11 associated with domain ELAN-L1-DMN (MD) at Level 1, which corresponds to the service ELAN-200-L1-SVC (MA):

- **ID 11:** This is the configured MEP ID.

- **Interface BE200.200:** This indicates that the MEP is applied to the subinterface BE200.2000 as per the applied configuration.

- **(State) (Up):** This indicates the state of the local interface.

- **Dir Up:** This indicates that the local MEP is configured as an UP MEP.

- **MEPs/Err 1/0:** This indicates that one remote MEP and zero errors have been detected.

- **RD N:** This indicates that no remote defects have been received from remote MEPs. If output says RD Y instead, you can view the CLI command with the word **detail** at the end to get additional details with regard to the received error condition.

Output 8-5 *Ethernet CFM: Per-Maintenance Domain and Per-Maintenance Association Local MEP Verification*

```
RP/0/RP0/CPU0:PE-1#show ethernet cfm local meps domain ELAN-L1-DMN
   service ELAN-200-L1-SVC

Defects (from at least one peer MEP):
 A - AIS received             I - Wrong interval
 R - Remote Defect received   V - Wrong level
 L - Loop (our MAC received)  T - Timed out
 C - Config (our ID received) M - Missing (cross-check)
 X - Cross-connect (wrong MAID) U - Unexpected (cross-check)
 P - Peer port down           F - CSF received


Domain ELAN-L1-DMN (level 1), Service ELAN-200-L1-SVC
   ID Interface (State)        Dir MEPs/Err RD Defects AIS
----- ----------------------- --- -------- -- ------- ---
   11 BE200.2000 (Up)          Up  1/0      N
RP/0/RP0/CPU0:PE-1#
```

The CLI command in Output 8-6 from router PE-1 provides the remote peer MEP:

- **St >:** The state is okay, and the peer MEP is not signaling any remote errors.

- **ID 12:** The remote peer MEP ID is configured as 12 on router PE-3.

- **Mac Address:** The remote peer MEP interface MAC address is specified.

- **Port Up:** The remote peer MEP interface state is signaled as Up.

- **CcmRcvd 2:** This is the number of CCM messages received from the peer MEP.

Output 8-6   *Ethernet CFM: Per-Maintenance Domain and Per-Maintenance Association Peer MEP Verification*

```
RP/0/RP0/CPU0:PE-1#show ethernet cfm peer meps domain ELAN-L1-DMN service
  ELAN-200-L1-SVC

Flags:
> - Ok                        I - Wrong interval
R - Remote Defect received    V - Wrong level
L - Loop (our MAC received)   T - Timed out
C - Config (our ID received)  M - Missing (cross-check)
X - Cross-connect (wrong MAID) U - Unexpected (cross-check)
* - Multiple errors received  S - Standby


Domain ELAN-L1-DMN (level 1), Service ELAN-200-L1-SVC
Up MEP on Bundle-Ether200.2000 MEP-ID 11
====================================================================================
St    ID MAC Address     Port    Up/Downtime   CcmRcvd SeqErr  RDI Error
-- ----- --------------- ------- ------------ --------- ------ ----- -----
>     12 0050.d14c.bbd0  Up      00:01:15           2       0     0     0
RP/0/RP0/CPU0:PE-1#
```

In Output 8-7, the interface on the remote PE-3 router where MEP ID 12 was configured is administratively shut down, as indicated by Port Down in the received CCM messages on PE-1.

Output 8-7   *Ethernet CFM: Peer MEP Interface Shutdown Verification*

```
RP/0/RP0/CPU0:PE-1#show ethernet cfm peer meps domain ELAN-L1-DMN service
  ELAN-200-L1-SVC

Flags:
> - Ok                        I - Wrong interval
R - Remote Defect received    V - Wrong level
L - Loop (our MAC received)   T - Timed out
```

```
C - Config (our ID received)    M - Missing (cross-check)
X - Cross-connect (wrong MAID)  U - Unexpected (cross-check)
* - Multiple errors received    S - Standby


Domain ELAN-L1-DMN (level 1), Service ELAN-200-L1-SVC
Up MEP on Bundle-Ether200.2000 MEP-ID 11

================================================================================
St    ID MAC Address   Port    Up/Downtime   CcmRcvd SeqErr   RDI Error
--  ----- -------------- ------- ----------- --------- ------ ----- -----
 >    12 0050.d14c.bbd0 Down    00:02:23            4       0     0     0
RP/0/RP0/CPU0:PE-1#
```

Output 8-8 illustrates a successful instance of using a CFM Loopback Message (LBM) for pinging the remote peer MEP 12 located on the PE-3 router.

Output 8-8   *Ethernet CFM: LBM-to-Peer MEP Verification*

```
RP/0/RP0/CPU0:PE-1#ping ethernet cfm domain ELAN-L1-DMN service ELAN-200-L1-SVC
  mep-id 12 source mep-id 11 interface Bundle-Ether200.2000

Type escape sequence to abort.
Sending 5 CFM Loopbacks, timeout is 2 seconds -
Domain ELAN-L1-DMN (level 1), Service ELAN-200-L1-SVC
Source: MEP ID 11, interface Bundle-Ether200.2000
Target: 0050.d14c.bbd0 (MEP ID 12):
  Running (5s) ...
Success rate is 100.0 percent (5/5), round-trip min/avg/max = 1/1/1 ms
Out-of-sequence: 0.0 percent (0/5)
Bad data: 0.0 percent (0/5)
Received packet rate: 1.3 pps
RP/0/RP0/CPU0:PE-1#
```

Finally, Output 8-9 shows a CFM traceroute originated from MEP ID 11 on PE-1 toward the remote peer MEP ID 12 on PE-3.

Hop 1 is where the CFM linktrace (traceroute) is initiated from the interface BE200.200 (0023.053b.b3e8) on router PE-1.

Hop 2 is from where the CFM linktrace response is received with the egress interface MAC address 0050.d14c.bbd0 on router PE-3. At Hop 2, the reference to PE-1 refers to the previous node along the path hosting the previous MEP/MIP responder.

Output 8-9   *Ethernet CFM: Linktrace Message (LTM) to Peer MEP Verification*

```
RP/0/RP0/CPU0:PE-1#traceroute ethernet cfm domain ELAN-L1-DMN service
  ELAN-200-L1-SVC mep-id 12 source mep-id 11 interface Bundle-Ether200.2000

Type escape sequence to return to prompt.

Traceroutes in domain ELAN-L1-DMN (level 1), service ELAN-200-L1-SVC
Source: MEP-ID 11, interface Bundle-Ether200.2000
==============================================================================
Traceroute at 2023-09-02 18:02:32 to 0050.d14c.bbd0,
TTL 64, Trans ID 1957610155:

  Running (7s) ...

Hop Hostname/Last           Ingress MAC/name         Egress MAC/Name          Relay
--- ------------------      --------------------     ---------------------    -----
  1 PE-1                     0023.053b.b3e8 [Ok]                               FDB
      0000-0023.053b.b3e8    BE200.2000
  2 PE-2                                              0050.d14c.bbd0 [Ok]      Hit
      PE-1                                            BE200.2000               MEP
Replies dropped: 0

RP/0/RP0/CPU0:PE-1#
```

ITU-T Y.1731 Performance Measurement

Ethernet loss measurement (ETH-LM) in Y.1731 is possible only in point-to-point networks through the use of actual data traffic flowing in the network. The reliance of Y.1731 loss measurement on the underlying data traffic can be a disadvantage because there may not always be consistent data flow. Therefore, an alternative loss measurement mechanism was defined and standardized for measuring traffic loss. This alternative measurement uses synthetic CFM frames and measures the loss of the synthetic frames rather than measuring the loss of actual data traffic. This Ethernet loss measurement is known as synthetic loss measurement (SLM) and is the Ethernet loss measurement mechanism discussed later, in the section "ITU-T Y.1731 Performance Measurement Configuration and Verification."

Figure 8-24 provides a high-level overview of the performance monitoring and measurement tools available with the ITU-T Y.1731 protocol.

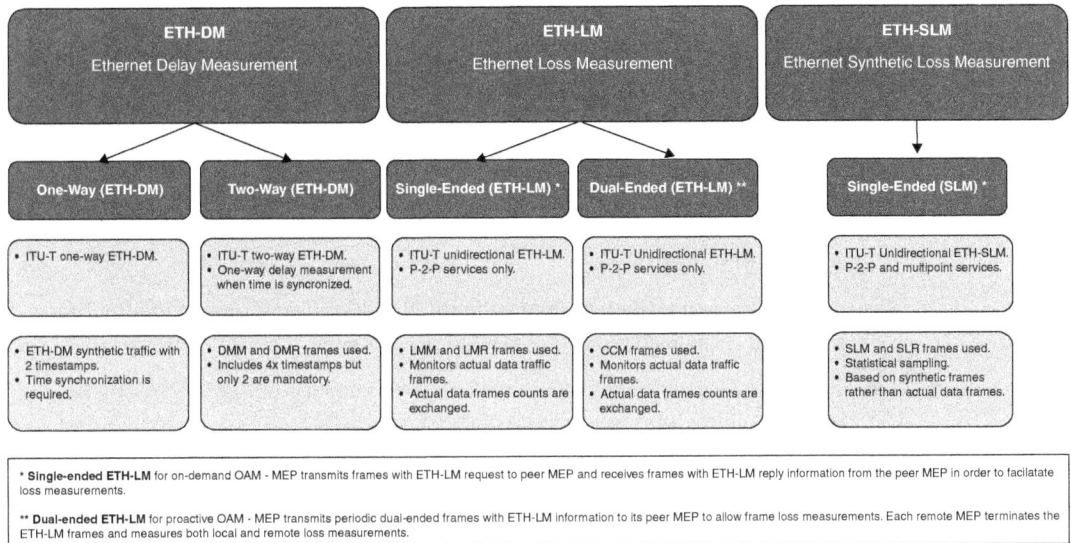

Figure 8-24 *ITU-T Y.1731 Performance Monitoring Overview*

This section focuses on the following Performance Monitoring extension mechanisms:

- **Two-way delay measurement:** This mechanism is used to measure frame delay and jitter (also known as delay variance) between two MEPs. Packets are transmitted from the initiator MEP and measure delay and jitter in both directions. The results may be combined to give round-trip delay and jitter values. The delay measurement mechanism can be summarized as follows:

  - Delay measurement uses delay measurement messages (DMMs) and delay measurement replies (DMRs).

  - Frame delay measurements and frame delay variations (jitter) can be obtained from these messages.

  - The source MEP sends a DMM with the time stamp t1 to the destination peer MEP, which receives this DMM at time stamp t2.

  - The destination MEP replies with a DMR at time stamp t3 to the source MEP, which receives this DMR at time stamp t4.

  - Delay measurement is calculated at the source MEP:

    - ☐ The round-trip time (RTT) can be approximately calculated as t4 – t1 or accurately as (t2 – t1) + (t4 – t3) if the remote MEP includes the t2 and t3 values in the DMR.

    - ☐ For the calculation of one-way delay in the source-to-destination (SD) or destination-to-source (DS) direction, there is a requirement that the clocks be synchronized, although this is not necessary for the RTT calculation.

■ **Synthetic loss measurement (SLM):** SLM determines frame loss between two MEPs by using synthetic frames transmitted from the initiator MEP and measuring the loss of these frames. This measurement can be treated as a statistical sample as it is synthetic in nature and used to approximate the frame loss ratio of normal data traffic. The SLM mechanism briefly encompasses the following:

- ■ The Loss Measurement or Frame Loss Ratio (FLR) is measured by the source MEP initiating SLM frames and the destination MEP replying with synthetic loss reply (SLR) frames

- ■ The FLR is measured over point-to-point, multipoint, and point-to-multipoint EVCs and is calculated over a configured measurement period.

- ■ TxFCf is a four-octet field that transports the number of SLM frames initiated from the source MEP toward the destination MEP.

- ■ TxFCb is a four-octet field that transports the number of SLR frames initiated from the destination MEP toward the source MEP.

- ■ TxFCf and TxFCb sequence numbers are used to track the synthetic frames sent in each direction.

- ■ When an SLR frame is received, the sequence numbers are compared to those from the last SLR received, and any loss in either direction can be determined.

- ■ FLR is expressed as a percentage and defined as:

$$\frac{NumFramesTX - NumFramesRX}{NumFramesTX} = \frac{Lost}{Sent}$$

ITU-T Y.1731 Performance Measurement Configuration and Verification

This section uses the same router PE-1 that is used for the CFM configuration in the earlier section "Ethernet CFM Configuration and Verification."

The first Y.1731 PM configuration we discuss here is an example of a single-ended delay measurement configuration (see Config 8-3). The Ethernet SLA configuration consists of the following building blocks:

■ **profile {*profile-name*} type cfm-delay-measurement:** Configure a descriptive profile name and select the PDU type (in this case, cfm-delay-measurement).

- ■ **probe:** Select the probe transmission pattern and properties.

  - □ **send burst:** Select the number of bursts per run, the number of PDUs per burst, and the PDU interval.

  - □ **priority:** Select the CoS (QoS) value (in this case, COS 0).

  - □ **packet size:** Select a probe frame size, in bytes.

- ■ **schedule:** Set the probe test run schedule to weekly or daily at a given time. The schedule can also be every hour/minute.

- **statistics:** Specify the statistics to be collected:

  - □ **measure:** Select round-trip delay, jitter, or various one-way options.

  - □ **aggregate:** Collected statistics can be aggregated into bins. For example, the results can be aggregated into 10 bins of width 10, meaning that the first bin will contain results in a range of 0 to 10 ms, the second bin will contain results in the range 10 to 20 ms, and the tenth bin will contain results in the range 90 ms and greater.

  - □ **buckets size:** The bucket contains n*probes, and statistics are calculated per bucket size every 1 hour, as shown in Config 8-3.

  - □ **buckets archive:** Results are archived for 24 hours on the router configured through the CLI command **buckets archive 24**.

- **sla operation profile DELAY-BE-L1 target mep-id 12:** Apply the configured PM profile under the previously configured CFM MEP configuration with a specific responder MEP ID as the peer target.

Config 8-3   *ITU-T Y.1731: Delay and Jitter Measurement Configuration*

```
!
ethernet sla
 profile DELAY-BE-L1 type cfm-delay-measurement
  probe
   send burst every 10 seconds packet count 10 interval 1 seconds
   priority 0
   packet size 128
  !
  schedule
   every 1 hours for 1 hours
  !
  statistics
   measure round-trip-delay
    aggregate bins 10 width 10
    buckets size 1 probes
    buckets archive 24
   !
   measure round-trip-jitter
    aggregate bins 10 width 10
    buckets size 1 probes
    buckets archive 24
   !
  !
 !
```

```
interface Bundle-Ether200.2000 l2transport
 encapsulation dot1q 2000
 ethernet cfm
  mep domain ELAN-L1-DMN service ELAN-200-L1-SVC mep-id 11
   sla operation profile DELAY-BE-L1 target mep-id 12
  !
 !
```

When verifying the configured delay measurement profile, the CLI command **show ethernet sla operations detail profile DELAY-BE-L1** executed in Output 8-10 provides an overview of the previously configured delay measurement profile DELAY-BE-L1 from Config 8-3. This important information is shown:

- **Profile 'DELAY-BE-L1':** This is the configured profile name.

- **Probe type 'cfm-delay-measurement':** This is the configured probe type (cfm-delay-measurement).

  - **burst sent:** This field displays the configured probe burst interval with the packet count and schedule.

  - **packets padded:** This field displays the configured packet size of 128 bytes with pattern 0x00000000, which can be modified and changed to any user-selected pattern via the CLI command **packet size 128 test pattern hex 0xabcd1234**, for example.

  - **packets use priority value of 0:** The operator can configure various probe CoS values to measure configured QoS behavior across the network. For example, the operator can verify whether voice traffic with Expedited Forwarding (EF) CoS markings are within the expected delay parameters.

- **Measures RT Delay:** This is the round-trip delay measurement, with results stored into the configured bins (in this case, 10 bins that are each 10 ms wide).

- **Measures RT Jitter:** This is the round-trip jitter measurement with results stored in the configured bins (in this case, 10 bins that are each 10 ms wide).

Output 8-10 *ITU-T Y.1731: Delay and Jitter Measurement Profile Overview*

```
RP/0/RP0/CPU0:PE-1#show ethernet sla operations detail profile DELAY-BE-L1


Source: Interface BE200.2000, Domain ELAN-L1-DMN
Destination: Target MEP-ID 12
================================================================================
Profile 'DELAY-BE-L1'
Probe type 'cfm-delay-measurement':
    burst sent every 10s, each of 10 packets sent every 1s
    packets padded to 128 bytes with pattern 0x00000000
```

```
     packets use priority value of 0
Measures RT Delay: 10 bins 10ms wide; 1 probes/bucket; 14 of 24 archived
Measures RT Jitter (interval 1): 10 bins 10ms wide; 1 probes/bucket; 14 of 24
  archived
Scheduled to run every 1hr first at 00:07:58 UTC for 1hr (360 bursts)
    last run at 08:07:58 CEST Thu 07 September 2023
RP/0/RP0/CPU0:PE-1#
```

The next set of useful information to be obtained is the actual round trip delay and jitter measurement statistics. The output of the CLI command **show ethernet sla statistics brief profile DELAY-BE-L1** in Output 8-11 provides a brief overview of the measurement statistics aggregated per bucket. Here we ignore the results of the first bucket because that was when both the CFM MEP and performance management configurations were applied and the buckets results are incomplete or invalid. Here we focus is on the second bucket:

- **Bucket started:** This is the time each bucket is started. As per the configuration, a probe is scheduled every 60 minutes for a duration of 60 minutes, and each statistics bucket contains 1 probe.

- **Results:** This is the aggregated per-bucket result for both RT-Delay and RT-Jitter.

- **Info:** This is additional information, including the packet count, which in this case is 3600 packets (60 pps × 60 minutes).

Note that the archive period configured for these statistics is 24, which means the statistics will wrap after 24 buckets (24 hours).

Output 8-11 *ITU-T Y.1731: Delay and Jitter Measurement Statistics Brief Verification*

```
RP/0/RP0/CPU0:PE-1#show ethernet sla statistics brief profile DELAY-BE-L1

Source: Interface BE200.2000, Domain ELAN-L1-DMN
Destination: Target MEP-ID 12
================================================================================
Profile 'DELAY-BE-L1', packet type 'cfm-delay-measurement'
Scheduled to run every 1hr first at 00:07:58 UTC for 1hr


Round Trip Delay
~~~~~~~~~~~~~~~~~
1 probes per bucket


No breached stateful thresholds.
```

	Results (ms)				Info	
Bucket started	-------------------------------------				--------------------	
(CEST)	Min	Max	Mean	SD	Suspect	Result Count
-----------------	--------	--------	--------	--------	-------	------------
18:21 06 Sep 2023	0.000	0.000	0.000	0.000	Yes	0
19:07 06 Sep 2023	0.082	0.094	0.086	0.001		3600
20:07 06 Sep 2023	0.082	0.094	0.086	0.001		3600
21:07 06 Sep 2023	0.082	0.096	0.086	0.001		3600
22:07 06 Sep 2023	0.082	0.094	0.086	0.001		3600
23:07 06 Sep 2023	0.083	0.094	0.086	0.001		3600
00:07 07 Sep 2023	0.083	0.096	0.086	0.001		3600
01:07 07 Sep 2023	0.082	0.095	0.086	0.001		3600
02:07 07 Sep 2023	0.082	0.095	0.086	0.001		3600
03:07 07 Sep 2023	0.082	0.095	0.086	0.001		3600
04:07 07 Sep 2023	0.082	0.095	0.086	0.001		3600
05:07 07 Sep 2023	0.083	0.094	0.086	0.001		3600
06:07 07 Sep 2023	0.082	0.095	0.086	0.001		3600
07:07 07 Sep 2023	0.082	0.094	0.086	0.001		3600
08:07 07 Sep 2023	0.082	0.095	0.086	0.001		1920 *

* indicates probe is in progress

Round Trip Jitter
~~~~~~~~~~~~~~~~~~
1 probes per bucket

No breached stateful thresholds.

	Results (ms)				Info	
Bucket started	-------------------------------------				--------------------	
(CEST)	Min	Max	Mean	SD	Suspect	Result Count
-----------------	--------	--------	--------	--------	-------	------------
18:21 06 Sep 2023	0.000	0.000	0.000	0.000	Yes	0
19:07 06 Sep 2023	0.000	0.010	0.001	0.001		3599
20:07 06 Sep 2023	0.000	0.010	0.001	0.001		3600
21:07 06 Sep 2023	0.000	0.011	0.001	0.001		3600
22:07 06 Sep 2023	0.000	0.010	0.001	0.001		3600
23:07 06 Sep 2023	0.000	0.010	0.001	0.001		3600
00:07 07 Sep 2023	0.000	0.012	0.001	0.001		3600
01:07 07 Sep 2023	0.000	0.011	0.001	0.001		3600
02:07 07 Sep 2023	0.000	0.011	0.001	0.001		3600
03:07 07 Sep 2023	0.000	0.010	0.001	0.001		3600
04:07 07 Sep 2023	0.000	0.009	0.001	0.001		3600

```
05:07 07 Sep 2023        0.000       0.010      0.001      0.001            3600
06:07 07 Sep 2023        0.000       0.011      0.001      0.001            3600
07:07 07 Sep 2023        0.000       0.009      0.001      0.001            3600
08:07 07 Sep 2023        0.000       0.011      0.001      0.001            1920 *


* indicates probe is in progress


RP/0/RP0/CPU0:PE-1#
```

Finally, the CLI command **show ethernet sla statistics detail profile DELAY-BE-L1**, as shown in Output 8-12, displays output similar to the output in Output 8-11 but with more details about the delay and jitter measurement statistics and a per-bin statistical range. Once again, the results of the first bucket can be ignored as that was when both the CFM MEP and performance management configurations were applied. The focus here is on the second bucket, from the time stamp 19:07:58. The output is self-explanatory, although an observation can be made that the aggregated statistic bin widths could be resized to microseconds rather than milliseconds with the CLI command **aggregate bins 10 width usec 1000** if required.

Output 8-12 *ITU-T Y.1731: Delay and Jitter Measurement Statistics Detailed Verification*

```
RP/0/RP0/CPU0:PE-1#show ethernet sla statistics detail profile DELAY-BE-L1


Source: Interface BE200.2000, Domain ELAN-L1-DMN
Destination: Target MEP-ID 12
================================================================================
Profile 'DELAY-BE-L1', packet type 'cfm-delay-measurement'
Scheduled to run every 1hr first at 00:07:58 UTC for 1hr


Round Trip Delay
~~~~~~~~~~~~~~~~~
1 probes per bucket


No stateful thresholds.


Bucket started at 18:21:16 CEST Wed 06 September 2023 lasting 1hr
    Pkts sent: 0
    Min: 0.000ms; Max: 0.000ms; Mean: 0.000ms; StdDev: 0.000ms


    Results suspect due to a probe starting mid-way through a bucket
    Results suspect due to a probe ending prematurely: 'CFM' detected the 'warning'
  condition 'Failed to determine MAC Address.  No Peer MEP with the requested
  MEP-ID found'
```

```
    Bins:
    Range           Samples   Cum. Count   Mean
    -----------     -----------  -----------  ----
     0 to 10 ms   0   (0.0%)   0   (0.0%)    -
    10 to 20 ms   0   (0.0%)   0   (0.0%)    -
    20 to 30 ms   0   (0.0%)   0   (0.0%)    -
    30 to 40 ms   0   (0.0%)   0   (0.0%)    -
    40 to 50 ms   0   (0.0%)   0   (0.0%)    -
    50 to 60 ms   0   (0.0%)   0   (0.0%)    -
    60 to 70 ms   0   (0.0%)   0   (0.0%)    -
    70 to 80 ms   0   (0.0%)   0   (0.0%)    -
    80 to 90 ms   0   (0.0%)   0   (0.0%)    -
    > 90     ms   0   (0.0%)   0   (0.0%)    -

Bucket started at 19:07:58 CEST Wed 06 September 2023 lasting 1hr
    Pkts sent: 3600; Lost: 0 (0.0%); Corrupt: 0 (0.0%);
                 Misordered: 0 (0.0%); Duplicates: 0 (0.0%)
    Result count: 3600
    Min: 0.082ms, occurred at 19:09:13 CEST Wed 06 September 2023
    Max: 0.094ms, occurred at 19:37:27 CEST Wed 06 September 2023
    Mean: 0.086ms; StdDev: 0.001ms

    Bins:
    Range           Samples       Cum. Count     Mean
    -----------   -------------   -------------   -----
     0 to 10 ms  3600 (100.0%)   3600 (100.0%)   0.086ms
    10 to 20 ms   0   (0.0%)     3600 (100.0%)    -
    20 to 30 ms   0   (0.0%)     3600 (100.0%)    -
    30 to 40 ms   0   (0.0%)     3600 (100.0%)    -
    40 to 50 ms   0   (0.0%)     3600 (100.0%)    -
    50 to 60 ms   0   (0.0%)     3600 (100.0%)    -
    60 to 70 ms   0   (0.0%)     3600 (100.0%)    -
    70 to 80 ms   0   (0.0%)     3600 (100.0%)    -
    80 to 90 ms   0   (0.0%)     3600 (100.0%)    -
    > 90     ms   0   (0.0%)     3600 (100.0%)    -

<snip>

Round Trip Jitter
~~~~~~~~~~~~~~~~~~
1 probes per bucket

No stateful thresholds.
```

```
Bucket started at 18:21:16 CEST Wed 06 September 2023 lasting 1hr
    Pkts sent: 0
    Min: 0.000ms; Max: 0.000ms; Mean: 0.000ms; StdDev: 0.000ms

    Results suspect due to a probe starting mid-way through a bucket
    Results suspect due to a probe ending prematurely: 'CFM' detected the 'warning'
    condition 'Failed to determine MAC Address.  No Peer MEP with the requested
    MEP-ID found'

    Bins:
    Range             Samples   Cum. Count  Mean
    -----------     -----------  ----------  ----
     0 to 10 ms  0   (0.0%)   0   (0.0%)    -
    10 to 20 ms  0   (0.0%)   0   (0.0%)    -
    20 to 30 ms  0   (0.0%)   0   (0.0%)    -
    30 to 40 ms  0   (0.0%)   0   (0.0%)    -
    40 to 50 ms  0   (0.0%)   0   (0.0%)    -
    50 to 60 ms  0   (0.0%)   0   (0.0%)    -
    60 to 70 ms  0   (0.0%)   0   (0.0%)    -
    70 to 80 ms  0   (0.0%)   0   (0.0%)    -
    80 to 90 ms  0   (0.0%)   0   (0.0%)    -
    > 90     ms  0   (0.0%)   0   (0.0%)    -

Bucket started at 19:07:58 CEST Wed 06 September 2023 lasting 1hr
    Pkts sent: 3600; Lost: 0 (0.0%); Corrupt: 0 (0.0%);
                 Misordered: 0 (0.0%); Duplicates: 0 (0.0%)
    Result count: 3599
    Min: 0.000ms, occurred at 19:08:01 CEST Wed 06 September 2023
    Max: 0.010ms, occurred at 19:37:28 CEST Wed 06 September 2023
    Mean: 0.001ms; StdDev: 0.001ms

    Bins:
    Range             Samples      Cum. Count    Mean
    -----------     -------------  -------------  ----
     0 to 10 ms  3599 (100.0%)   3599 (100.0%)  0.001ms
    10 to 20 ms     0   (0.0%)   3599 (100.0%)    -
    20 to 30 ms     0   (0.0%)   3599 (100.0%)    -
    30 to 40 ms     0   (0.0%)   3599 (100.0%)    -
    40 to 50 ms     0   (0.0%)   3599 (100.0%)    -
    50 to 60 ms     0   (0.0%)   3599 (100.0%)    -
    60 to 70 ms     0   (0.0%)   3599 (100.0%)    -
    70 to 80 ms     0   (0.0%)   3599 (100.0%)    -
    80 to 90 ms     0   (0.0%)   3599 (100.0%)    -
    > 90     ms     0   (0.0%)   3599 (100.0%)    -

<snip>
```

Now we will look at another Y.1731 PM configuration—in this case, the SLM configuration shown in Config 8-4, which consists of the following Ethernet SLA configuration building blocks:

- **profile** {*profile-name*} **type cfm-synthetic-loss-measurement**: Configure a descriptive profile name and select the PDU type **cfm-synthetic-loss-measurement**.

  - **probe**: Select the probe transmission pattern and properties:

    - **send burst**: Set the number of bursts per run, the number of PDUs per burst, and the PDU interval.

    - **priority**: Select the CoS (QoS) value (which is COS 0 in this example).

    - **synthetic loss calculation packets**: Configure the number of synthetic packets to use for each FLR calculation.

      - **packet size**: Select a probe frame size, in bytes, and optionally a packet test pattern, in hex.

  - **schedule**: Set the probe period test run schedule to weekly or daily at a given time. The schedule can also be every hour/minute.

  - **statistics**: Specify the statistics to be collected.

    - **measure**: Select one-way-loss-sd or one-way-loss-ds (where s = source and d = destination).

    - **aggregate**: Collected statistics can be aggregated into bins. For example, the results can be aggregated into 10 bins of width 10, meaning that the first bin will contain results in the range 0 to 10%, the second bin will contain results in the range 10% to 20%, and so on.

    - **buckets size**: The bucket contains *n**probes, and statistics are calculated per bucket size (every 1 hour).

    - **buckets archive**: Results are archived for 24 hours on the router configured using the CLI command **buckets archive 24**.

- **sla operation profile LOSS-BE-L1 target mep-id 12**: Apply the configured SLM profile under the previously configured CFM MEP configuration with a specific responder MEP ID as the peer target.

This configuration creates and schedules an SLM probe that functions as follows: Every hour (the length of the probing period), send a burst every 15 seconds with a frame count of 10 and a 1-second interval. The SLM packet size is 128 bytes, configured with a test pattern 0xabdc1234 and marked with the CoS Best-Effort value 0. The FLR will be calculated for every 20 packets (that is, for every 2 bursts—or every 30 seconds).

Config 8-4   *ITU-T Y.1731: SLM Configuration*

```
!
ethernet sla
 profile LOSS-BE-L1 type cfm-synthetic-loss-measurement
  probe
   send burst every 15 seconds packet count 10 interval 1 seconds
   priority 0
   synthetic loss calculation packets 20
   packet size 128 test pattern hex 0xabdc1234
  !
 schedule
   every 1 hours for 1 hours
  !
  statistics
   measure one-way-loss-sd
    aggregate bins 10 width 10
    buckets size 1 probes
    buckets archive 24
   !
   measure one-way-loss-ds
    aggregate bins 10 width 10
    buckets size 1 probes
    buckets archive 24
   !
  !
 !
interface Bundle-Ether200.2000 l2transport
 encapsulation dot1q 2000
 ethernet cfm
  mep domain ELAN-L1-DMN service ELAN-200-L1-SVC mep-id 11
   sla operation profile DELAY-BE-L1 target mep-id 12
   sla operation profile LOSS-BE-L1 target mep-id 12
  !
 !
!
```

The CLI command **show ethernet sla operations detail profile LOSS-BE-L1**,executed in Output 8-13, provides an overview of the configured SLM profile Loss-BE-L1 from Config 8-4:

- **Profile 'LOSS-BE-L1':** This is the configured profile name.

- **Probe type 'cfm-synthetic-loss-measurement':** This is the configured probe type (cfm-synthetic-loss-measurement).

- **burst sent:** This is the configured burst count with the packet count and schedule.

- **packets padded:** This is the configured packet size, 128 bytes, with pattern 0xabdc1234.

- **packets use priority value of 0:** This is the configured CoS value.

- **Frame Loss Ratio calculated every 30s:** The FLR is calculated for every 20 packets (that is, for every 2 bursts, or every 30 seconds).

- **Measures OW Loss SD:** This is the measured one-way source-to-destination loss, with results stored in the configured bins (10 bins that are 10% wide).

- **Measures OW Loss DS:** This is the measured one-way destination-to-source loss, with results stored in the configured bins (10 bins that are 10% wide).

- **Scheduled to run every 1hr:** The configuration is scheduled to run every hour, with 240 bursts (240 bursts × 10 packets = 2400 packets).

Output 8-13   *ITU-T Y.1731: Synthetic Loss Measurement (SLM) Profile Overview*

```
RP/0/RP0/CPU0:PE-1#show ethernet sla operations detail profile LOSS-BE-L1


Source: Interface BE200.2000, Domain ELAN-L1-DMN
Destination: Target MEP-ID 12
================================================================================
Profile 'LOSS-BE-L1'
Probe type 'cfm-synthetic-loss-measurement':
    burst sent every 15s, each of 10 packets sent every 1s
    packets padded to 128 bytes with pattern 0xabdc1234
    packets use priority value of 0
    Frame Loss Ratio calculated every 30s
Measures OW Loss SD: 10 bins 10% wide; 1 probes/bucket; 22 of 24 archived
Measures OW Loss DS: 10 bins 10% wide; 1 probes/bucket; 22 of 24 archived
Scheduled to run every 1hr first at 00:07:58 UTC for 1hr (240 bursts)
    last run at 14:07:58 CEST Sat 09 September 2023
RP/0/RP0/CPU0:PE-1#
```

The verification CLI command **show ethernet sla statistics brief profile LOSS-BE-L1** in Output 8-14 provides an overview of the FLR statistics. Again, the results of the first bucket are ignored, and we focus on the second bucket:

- **Bucket started:** This is the actual time each bucket is started. As per the configuration, a probe period is scheduled every 60 minutes, with a duration of 60 minutes, and each statistics bucket contains one probe period.

- **Results (%):** This is the aggregated per-bucket result for One-way Frame Loss (Source->Dest) and One-way Frame Loss (Dest->Source), with the FLR calculated for every 20 packets, which is every 2 bursts (or 30 seconds).

■ **Info:** This is additional information, including the packet count, which in this case is 2400 packets (240 bursts × 10 packets = 2400 packets).

Because the archive period configured for these statistics is 24, these statistics will wrap after 24 buckets (24 hours).

Output 8-14 *ITU-T Y.1731: SLM Measurement Statistics Brief Verification*

```
RP/0/RP0/CPU0:PE-1#show ethernet sla statistics brief profile LOSS-BE-L1


Source: Interface BE200.2000, Domain ELAN-L1-DMN
Destination: Target MEP-ID 12
================================================================================
Profile 'LOSS-BE-L1', packet type 'cfm-synthetic-loss-measurement'
Scheduled to run every 1hr first at 00:07:58 UTC for 1hr
Frame Loss Ratio calculated every 30s


One-way Frame Loss (Source->Dest)
~~~~~~~~~~~~~~~~~~~~~~~~~~~~~~~~~~
1 probes per bucket


No breached stateful thresholds.


                        Results (%)                    Info
Bucket started       -----------------------   ----------------------------
(CEST)                Min     Max  Overall  Suspect       Sent       Lost
-----------------    ------- ------- -------  -------  -----------  ----------
16:59 08 Sep 2023    0.000   0.000                     Yes            0          0
17:07 08 Sep 2023    0.000   0.000   0.000                         2400          0
18:07 08 Sep 2023    0.000   0.000   0.000                         2400          0
19:07 08 Sep 2023    0.000   0.000   0.000                         2400          0
20:07 08 Sep 2023    0.000   0.000   0.000                         2400          0
21:07 08 Sep 2023    0.000   0.000   0.000                         2400          0
22:07 08 Sep 2023    0.000   0.000   0.000                         2400          0
23:07 08 Sep 2023    0.000   0.000   0.000                         2400          0
00:07 09 Sep 2023    0.000   0.000   0.000                         2400          0
01:07 09 Sep 2023    0.000   0.000   0.000                         2400          0
02:07 09 Sep 2023    0.000   0.000   0.000                         2400          0
03:07 09 Sep 2023    0.000   0.000   0.000                         2400          0
04:07 09 Sep 2023    0.000   0.000   0.000                         2400          0
05:07 09 Sep 2023    0.000   0.000   0.000                         2400          0
06:07 09 Sep 2023    0.000   0.000   0.000                         2400          0
07:07 09 Sep 2023    0.000   0.000   0.000                         2400          0
08:07 09 Sep 2023    0.000   0.000   0.000                         2400          0
09:07 09 Sep 2023    0.000   0.000   0.000                         2400          0
10:07 09 Sep 2023    0.000   0.000   0.000                         2400          0
```

```
11:07 09 Sep 2023    0.000   0.000   0.000              2400          0
12:07 09 Sep 2023    0.000   0.000   0.000              2400          0
13:07 09 Sep 2023    0.000   0.000   0.000              2400          0
14:07 09 Sep 2023    0.000   0.000   0.000               320          0 *


* indicates probe is in progress

One-way Frame Loss (Dest->Source)
~~~~~~~~~~~~~~~~~~~~~~~~~~~~~~~~~~~
1 probes per bucket

No breached stateful thresholds.


                         Results (%)                    Info
Bucket started       -----------------------  -------------------------------
(CEST)                 Min    Max  Overall  Suspect      Sent        Lost
----------------     ------- ------- -------  -------  -----------  -----------
16:59 08 Sep 2023    0.000   0.000            Yes            0          0
17:07 08 Sep 2023    0.000   0.000   0.000              2400          0
18:07 08 Sep 2023    0.000   0.000   0.000              2400          0
19:07 08 Sep 2023    0.000   0.000   0.000              2400          0
20:07 08 Sep 2023    0.000   0.000   0.000              2400          0
21:07 08 Sep 2023    0.000   0.000   0.000              2400          0
22:07 08 Sep 2023    0.000   0.000   0.000              2400          0
23:07 08 Sep 2023    0.000   0.000   0.000              2400          0
00:07 09 Sep 2023    0.000   0.000   0.000              2400          0
01:07 09 Sep 2023    0.000   0.000   0.000              2400          0
02:07 09 Sep 2023    0.000   0.000   0.000              2400          0
03:07 09 Sep 2023    0.000   0.000   0.000              2400          0
04:07 09 Sep 2023    0.000   0.000   0.000              2400          0
05:07 09 Sep 2023    0.000   0.000   0.000              2400          0
06:07 09 Sep 2023    0.000   0.000   0.000              2400          0
07:07 09 Sep 2023    0.000   0.000   0.000              2400          0
08:07 09 Sep 2023    0.000   0.000   0.000              2400          0
09:07 09 Sep 2023    0.000   0.000   0.000              2400          0
10:07 09 Sep 2023    0.000   0.000   0.000              2400          0
11:07 09 Sep 2023    0.000   0.000   0.000              2400          0
12:07 09 Sep 2023    0.000   0.000   0.000              2400          0
13:07 09 Sep 2023    0.000   0.000   0.000              2400          0
14:07 09 Sep 2023    0.000   0.000   0.000               320          0 *


* indicates probe is in progress


RP/0/RP0/CPU0:PE-1#
```

In Output 8-15, the CLI command **show ethernet sla statistics detail profile LOSS-BE-L1** provides details on the FLR measurement statistics including a per-bin statistic. Once again, we ignore the results of the first bucket because that was when both the CFM MEP and SLM configurations were applied. We focus on the second bucket, from the time stamp 17:07:58. The results are aggregated into 10 bins with a width of 10%, which means the first bin will contain results that showed loss of 0 to 10% calculated from 2 bursts (20 packets), the second bin will contain results that showed loss of 10% to 20%, and so on. These FLR percentage statistics are calculated and displayed for one-way source-to-destination (SD) and one-way destination-to-source (DS) flows.

Output 8-15 *ITU-T Y.1731: SLM Measurement Statistics Detailed Verification*

```
RP/0/RP0/CPU0:PE-1#show ethernet sla statistics detail profile LOSS-BE-L1


Source: Interface BE200.2000, Domain ELAN-L1-DMN
Destination: Target MEP-ID 12
================================================================================
Profile 'LOSS-BE-L1', packet type 'cfm-synthetic-loss-measurement'
Scheduled to run every 1hr first at 00:07:58 UTC for 1hr
Frame Loss Ratio calculated every 30s


One-way Frame Loss (Source->Dest)
~~~~~~~~~~~~~~~~~~~~~~~~~~~~~~~~~~~
1 probes per bucket


No stateful thresholds.


Bucket started at 16:59:03 CEST Fri 08 September 2023 lasting 1hr
    Pkts sent: 0
    Min: 0.000%; Max: 0.000%; Mean; 0.000%; StdDev: 0.000%;

    Results suspect due to a probe starting mid-way through a bucket
    Results suspect due to a probe ending prematurely: 'CFM' detected the 'warning'
condition 'Failed to determine MAC Address.  No Peer MEP with the requested
MEP-ID found'

    Bins:
    Range           Count  Cum. Count  Mean
    -----------    ----------  ----------  ----
      0 to  10%  0    (0.0%)  0    (0.0%)    -
     10 to  20%  0    (0.0%)  0    (0.0%)    -
     20 to  30%  0    (0.0%)  0    (0.0%)    -
     30 to  40%  0    (0.0%)  0    (0.0%)    -
     40 to  50%  0    (0.0%)  0    (0.0%)    -
     50 to  60%  0    (0.0%)  0    (0.0%)    -
     60 to  70%  0    (0.0%)  0    (0.0%)    -
```

```
      70 to  80%  0   (0.0%)   0   (0.0%)      -
      80 to  90%  0   (0.0%)   0   (0.0%)      -
      90 to 100%  0   (0.0%)   0   (0.0%)      -


Bucket started at 17:07:58 CEST Fri 08 September 2023 lasting 1hr
    Pkts sent: 2400; Lost: 0 (0.0%); Corrupt: 0 (0.0%);
                     Misordered: 0 (0.0%); Duplicates: 0 (0.0%)
    Result count: 120
    Min: 0.000%, occurred at 17:07:58 CEST Fri 08 September 2023
    Max: 0.000%, occurred at 17:07:58 CEST Fri 08 September 2023
    Mean: 0.000%; StdDev: 0.000%; Overall: 0.000%


    Bins:
    Range             Count     Cum. Count     Mean
    -----------    ------------  ------------   ------
      0 to  10%  120 (100.0%)  120 (100.0%)  0.000%
     10 to  20%    0   (0.0%)  120 (100.0%)     -
     20 to  30%    0   (0.0%)  120 (100.0%)     -
     30 to  40%    0   (0.0%)  120 (100.0%)     -
     40 to  50%    0   (0.0%)  120 (100.0%)     -
     50 to  60%    0   (0.0%)  120 (100.0%)     -
     60 to  70%    0   (0.0%)  120 (100.0%)     -
     70 to  80%    0   (0.0%)  120 (100.0%)     -
     80 to  90%    0   (0.0%)  120 (100.0%)     -
     90 to 100%    0   (0.0%)  120 (100.0%)     -


<snip>


One-way Frame Loss (Dest->Source)
~~~~~~~~~~~~~~~~~~~~~~~~~~~~~~~~~~~
1 probes per bucket


No stateful thresholds.


Bucket started at 16:59:03 CEST Fri 08 September 2023 lasting 1hr
    Pkts sent: 0
    Min: 0.000%; Max: 0.000%; Mean; 0.000%; StdDev: 0.000%;


    Results suspect due to a probe starting mid-way through a bucket
    Results suspect due to a probe ending prematurely: 'CFM' detected the 'warning'
    condition 'Failed to determine MAC Address.  No Peer MEP with the requested
    MEP-ID found'
```

```
 Bins:
 Range              Count   Cum. Count  Mean
 ----------    ----------   ----------  ----
   0 to  10%   0   (0.0%)   0   (0.0%)    -
  10 to  20%   0   (0.0%)   0   (0.0%)    -
  20 to  30%   0   (0.0%)   0   (0.0%)    -
  30 to  40%   0   (0.0%)   0   (0.0%)    -
  40 to  50%   0   (0.0%)   0   (0.0%)    -
  50 to  60%   0   (0.0%)   0   (0.0%)    -
  60 to  70%   0   (0.0%)   0   (0.0%)    -
  70 to  80%   0   (0.0%)   0   (0.0%)    -
  80 to  90%   0   (0.0%)   0   (0.0%)    -
  90 to 100%   0   (0.0%)   0   (0.0%)    -

Bucket started at 17:07:58 CEST Fri 08 September 2023 lasting 1hr
 Pkts sent: 2400; Lost: 0 (0.0%); Corrupt: 0 (0.0%);
                 Misordered: 0 (0.0%); Duplicates: 0 (0.0%)
 Result count: 120
 Min: 0.000%, occurred at 17:07:58 CEST Fri 08 September 2023
 Max: 0.000%, occurred at 17:07:58 CEST Fri 08 September 2023
 Mean: 0.000%; StdDev: 0.000%; Overall: 0.000%

 Bins:
 Range              Count    Cum. Count    Mean
 ----------    -----------   ------------  ------
   0 to  10% 120 (100.0%)   120 (100.0%)   0.000%
  10 to  20%   0   (0.0%)   120 (100.0%)     -
  20 to  30%   0   (0.0%)   120 (100.0%)     -
  30 to  40%   0   (0.0%)   120 (100.0%)     -
  40 to  50%   0   (0.0%)   120 (100.0%)     -
  50 to  60%   0   (0.0%)   120 (100.0%)     -
  60 to  70%   0   (0.0%)   120 (100.0%)     -
  70 to  80%   0   (0.0%)   120 (100.0%)     -
  80 to  90%   0   (0.0%)   120 (100.0%)     -
  90 to 100%   0   (0.0%)   120 (100.0%)     -

<snip>
RP/0/RP0/CPU0:PE-1#
```

Ethernet Operations, Administration, and Maintenance (OAM) is a well-known and comprehensive suite of protocols that provide network operators with tools they need to effectively implement service assurance processes for L2VPN services over both SR-MPLS and SRv6 transport networks. Thanks to Ethernet OAM, a provider of end-user services can detect and resolve network faults, identify network quality issues, and monitor customers' SLAs based on their key performance indicators (KPIs).

L3VPN Service Assurance

This section discusses the service assurance performance measurement feature IPSLA as well as the standardized performance measurement feature TWAMP (described in RFC 5357).

IPSLA and TWAMP

IPSLA is a Cisco performance measurement feature developed in the early 2000s for deployment on Cisco routers and switches. Configuration of IPSLA on network devices allows for the active measurement of packet delay, jitter, and loss, and results can be extracted either via the CLI or through Simple Network Management Protocol (SNMP). These measurements are configured between network endpoints acting as senders and responders, as shown in Figure 8-25, using various configured operations, such as:

- UDP jitter

- UDP echo

- UDP path echo

- TCP connect

- ICMP jitter

- ICMP echo

- ICMP path echo

With the IPSLA feature, all the operational configurations are made on the IPSLA sender node, and the target configurations are deployed on the IPSLA responder node. In the initial phase, the sender communicates with the responder using the IPSLA control protocol, and the responder listens on the configured UDP ports for the operational test packets and responds to the test packets by inserting inbound and outbound time stamps into the response packets. When an operation has been completed, the results can be extracted from the sender via the CLI or SNMP.

After Cisco's IPSLA feature had been in use for a time, the IETF then standardized a performance measurement feature known as One-Way Active Measurement Protocol (OWAMP) (RFC 4656) with the aim of measuring network metrics such as one-way loss, one-way latency, one-way jitter, and so on. However, OWAMP did not provide round-trip or two-way network metrics. In 2008, the IETF introduced Two-Way Active Measurement Protocol (TWAMP) (RFC 5357), which added two-way or round-trip measurement capabilities.

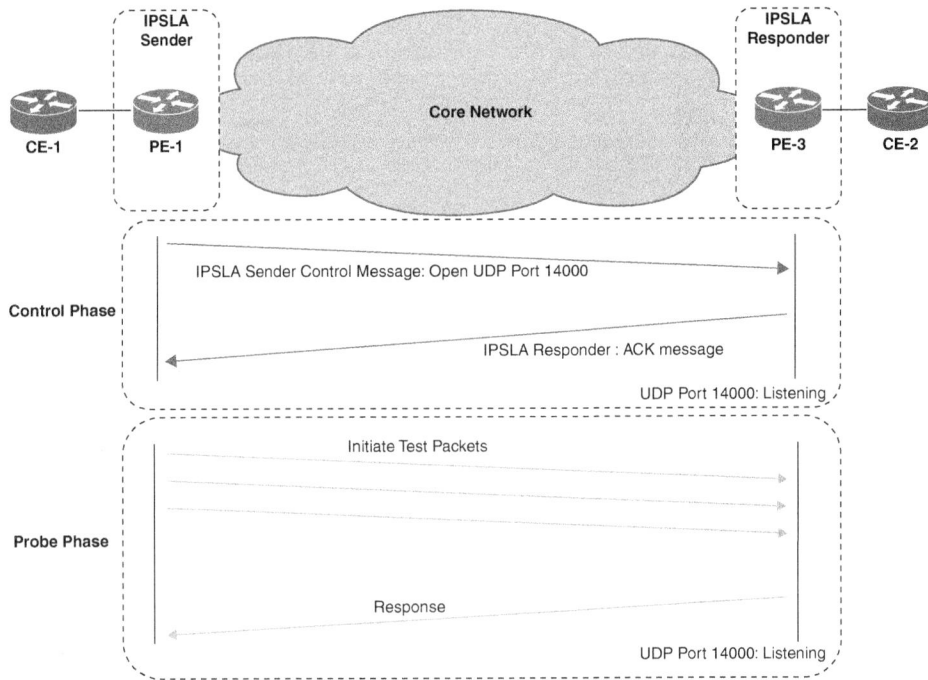

Figure 8-25 *IPSLA Sender and Responder High-Level Overview*

The TWAMP architecture consists of the following (see Figure 8-26):

- Controller
  - **Control client:** This is an endpoint function that sets up the TWAMP test sessions, starts the TWAMP sessions, and terminates these sessions when required.
  - **Session sender:** This is the transmitter of the TWAMP test packets to the reflector endpoint.
- Responder
  - **Server:** This is an endpoint function that manages the incoming TWAMP sessions on the configured TCP ports.
  - **Session reflector:** This endpoint reflects the received TWAMP test packets back to the sender endpoint.

The control client opens a TWAMP-Control session to TCP port 862 on the server and is responsible for the test initiation and test termination, along with any additional parameter negotiation with the server end device.

The TWAMP-Test packet streams are UDP packets transmitted by the session sender toward the session reflector. The session reflector transmits a response packet for each request received from the session sender with the required information in order to facilitate the two-way metric calculations performed by the session sender.

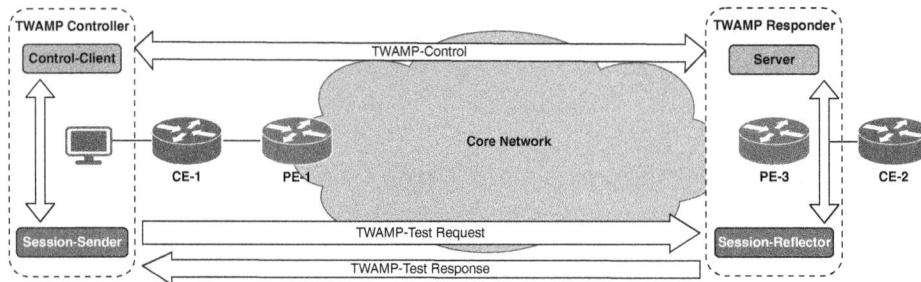

Figure 8-26   *TWAMP Architectural Overview*

The appendix section of RFC 5357 mentions TWAMP Light (see Figure 8-27), which has a simpler architecture than TWAMP because the TWAMP-Control protocol has been eliminated. To achieve this simplification, the TWAMP Light test session parameters are configured at both the transmit and receive end devices, effectively removing the control client and server components from the TWAMP architecture. Take note,

Note   Because TWAMP Light was only mentioned in the appendix of RFC 5357, it lacks the detailed specifications necessary to avoid issues with interoperability. Consequently, RFC 8762 formalized and expanded upon TWAMP Light, creating Simple Two Way Active Measurement Protocol (STAMP). STAMP offers the advantage of being both extendable and compatible with earlier TWAMP Light implementations.

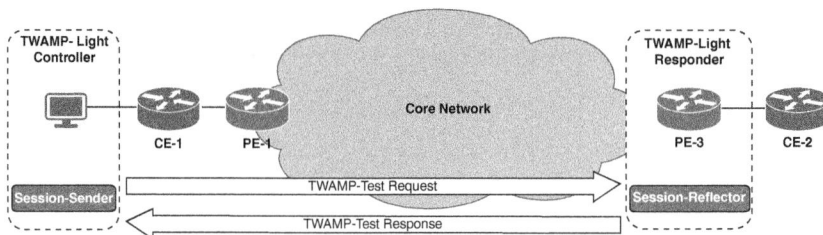

Figure 8-27   *TWAMP Light Architecture Overview*

IPSLA Configuration and Verification

As mentioned at the start of this section, the IPSLA performance measurement feature has been deployable on Cisco devices for many years. It is well known and widely used by many operators and enterprises. This section shows a subset of the available IPSLA operations deployed across an L3VPN full-mesh service overlay network provisioned across an SR-MPLS transport network (see Figure 8-28). This section is based on the SR-MPLS reference network shown in Appendix A.

This section shows IPSLA sender functionality provisioned on router PE-1 in IS-IS Metro 1 and routers PE-3 and PE-4 in OSPF Metro 2 configured as IPSLA responders. The IPSLA performance measurement configuration examples use the VRF instance FULL-400-VRF that was configured in Chapter 7, "L3VPN Service Deployment: Configuration and Verification Techniques." This section addresses both UDP echo and UPD jitter operations.

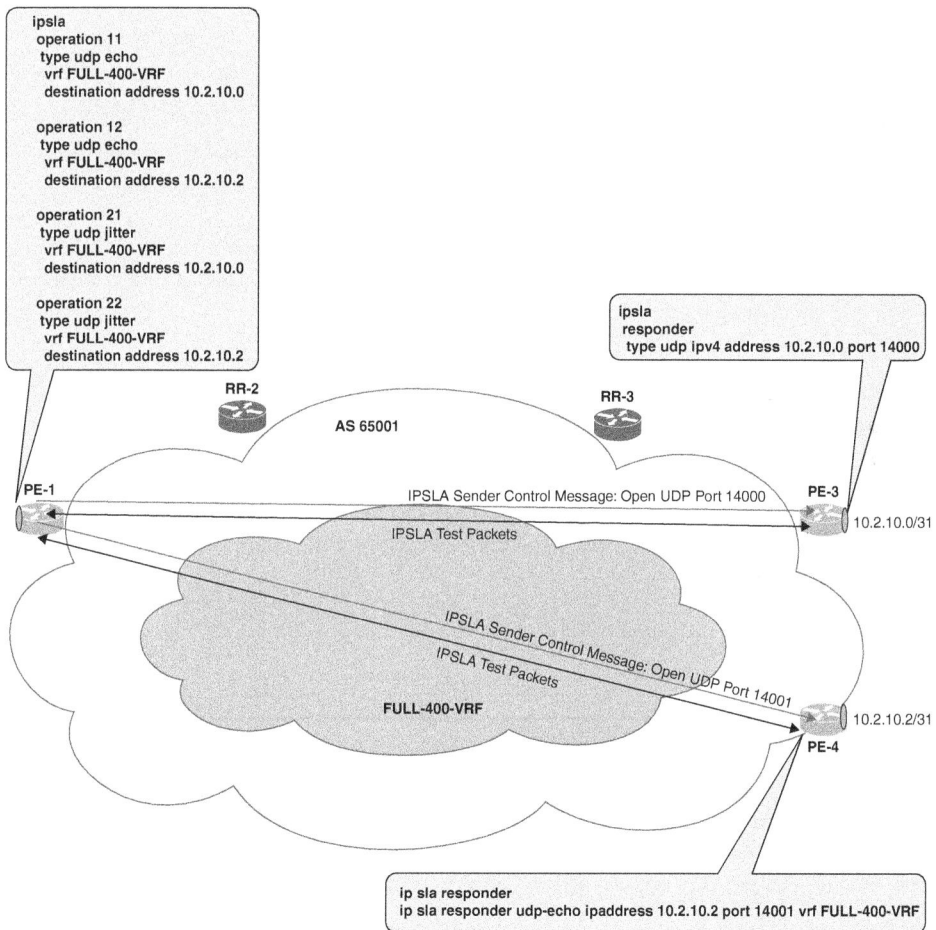

Figure 8-28 *IPSLA Configuration Tasks*

The IPSLA operation can be divided into three configuration components:

- IPSLA operation types

    - ICMP (echo, path-echo, path-jitter)

    - UDP (echo, jitter)

    - MPLS (lsp-ping, lsp-trace)

    - HTTP

    - TCP-Connect

- IPSLA reaction

    - It is possible to configure an event in order to trigger an action type (syslog action or SNMP trap action), such as a timeout, a connection loss, a round-trip time (RTT) rising or falling past the configured threshold values, and so on.

    - The configured action type event could be a syslog message, SNMP traps, or both that take place when a configured threshold or event is triggered.

- IPSLA scheduling

    - It is possible to schedule an IPSLA operation by defining its start time, operation lifetime, and age-out values.

Config 8-5 shows the IPSLA operational UDP echo type operation 11 and operation 12 targeting responders configured on router PE-3 and PE-4, respectively, and UDP jitter type operation 21 and operation 22 targeting the same responders. The operational IPSLA type configurations consist of the following building blocks:

- **operation {*operation-number*}**: This is a number assigned to the operational type in order to allow referencing by the IPSLA reaction and scheduling of configuration components.

    - **type {*operation-type*}**: Both UDP Echo and UDP jitter are configured in this example.

        - **vrf:** The L3VPN full-mesh VRF instance FULL-400-VRF is the VPN in which the operation is configured.

        - **destination address:** This is the IP address of the IPSLA responders. In this configuration, the IP address 10.2.10.0 is Gi0/0/0/3.400 on Router PE-3, and 10.2.10.2 is Gi4.400 on router PE-4.

        - **statistics:** The RTT statistics for the UDP echo operation are calculated over a 60-minute period and stored in 24 buckets, allowing a 24-hour historical overview. The UDP jitter operation collects RTT statistics, packet loss statistics, and jitter values over a 60-minute period and stores them in 24 buckets, allowing a 24-hour historical overview.

☐ **tos:** This is the Type of Service (ToS) value for the test packets. The configured ToS value is 184 (EF Expedited Forwarding), which is usually used for voice packet QoS marking.

☐ **datasize:** This is the test packet payload size, in bytes.

☐ **destination port:** This is the remote UDP port that the IPSLA responder will keep open for the incoming test packets.

☐ **frequency:** This is the rate at which the test packets are generated by the IPSLA sender.

Config 8-5 *IPSLA Sender Operation: UDP Echo and Jitter Configuration on PE-1 (IOS XR)*

```
ipsla
 operation 11
  type udp echo
   vrf FULL-400-VRF
   destination address 10.2.10.0
   statistics hourly
    buckets 24
   !
   timeout 1000
   tos 184
   datasize request 256
   destination port 14000
   frequency 10
  !
 !
 operation 12
  type udp echo
   vrf FULL-400-VRF
   destination address 10.2.10.2
   statistics hourly
    buckets 24
   !
   timeout 1000
   tos 184
   datasize request 256
   destination port 14001
   frequency 10
  !
 !
```

```
operation 21
 type udp jitter
  vrf FULL-400-VRF
  destination address 10.2.10.0
  statistics hourly
   buckets 24
   !
  timeout 1000
  tos 184
  datasize request 256
  destination port 14000
  frequency 10
 !
 !
operation 22
 type udp jitter
  vrf FULL-400-VRF
  destination address 10.2.10.2
  statistics hourly
   buckets 24
   !
  timeout 1000
  tos 184
  datasize request 256
  destination port 14001
  frequency 10
 !
 !
```

The IPSLA responder configuration on router PE-3 (IOS XR) is shown in Config 8-6.

Config 8-6   *IPSLA Responder Configuration on PE-3 (IOS XR)*

```
!
ipsla
 responder
  type udp ipv4 address 10.2.10.0 port 14000
  !
 !
!
```

The IPSLA responder configuration on router PE-4 (IOS XE) is documented in Config 8-7.

Config 8-7 *IPSLA Responder Configuration on PE-4 (IOS XE)*

```
!
ip sla responder
ip sla responder udp-echo ipaddress 10.2.10.2 port 14001 vrf FULL-400-VRF
!
```

The second component in the IPSLA operation configuration task is the configuration of the reaction component. The IPSLA reaction component deals with how each of the configured IPSLA operation components react to specific events as well as the configured event actions that take place. The configuration in Config 8-8 shows the IPSLA reaction component for the UDP echo type operation 11 and operation 12 and the UDP jitter type operation 21 and operation 22.

For the UDP echo type operation 11 and operation 12, the configuration is as follows:

- **reaction operation {***operation-number***}:** This is a reference to the configured IPSLA components. Operation 11 has the IPSLA target on router PE-3, and operation 12 has the IPSLA target on router PE-4.

  - **react connection-loss:** This triggers an action when a loss event is detected:

    - □ **action logging:** Syslog and SNMP traps are generated. The additional configuration **snmp-server traps ipsla** allows SNMP traps to be generated.

    - □ **threshold type immediate:** For a connection-loss event, the threshold is set to an immediate reaction.

  - **react rtt:** This triggers an action for round-trip time (RTT):

    - □ **action logging:** Syslog and SNMP traps are generated. The additional configuration snmp-server traps ipsla allows SNMP traps to be generated.

    - □ **threshold type immediate:** When the upper threshold or lower threshold limit is exceeded, an immediate reaction is triggered.

    - □ **threshold lower-limit {***lower-threshold***} upper-limit {***upper-threshold***}:** When the monitored RTT upper threshold of 70 ms is exceeded or when the monitored value falls below the lower threshold value of 50 ms, a notification is triggered.

For the UDP jitter type operation 21 and operation 22, the configuration is as follows:

- **reaction operation {***operation-number***}:** This is a reference to the configured IPSLA components. Operation 21 has the IPSLA target on router PE-3, and operation 22 has the IPSLA target on router PE-4.

  - **react jitter-average:** This triggers an action if the round-trip jitter exceeds the configured threshold values:

    - □ **action logging:** Syslog and SNMP traps are generated. The additional configuration snmp-server traps ipsla allows IPSLA-related SNMP traps to be generated.

□ **threshold type immediate:** When the upper threshold or lower threshold limit is exceeded, an immediate reaction is triggered.

□ **threshold lower-limit** {*lower-threshold*} **upper-limit** {*upper-threshold*}: When the monitored jitter average upper threshold of 15 ms is exceeded or when the monitored value falls below the lower threshold value of 11 ms, a notification is triggered.

Config 8-8   *IPSLA Sender Reaction: UDP Echo and Jitter Reaction Configuration on PE-1 (IOS XR)*

```
!
ipsla
 reaction operation 11
  react connection-loss
   action logging
   threshold type immediate
  !
  react rtt
   action logging
   threshold type immediate
   threshold lower-limit 50 upper-limit 70
  !
 !
 reaction operation 12
  react connection-loss
   action logging
   threshold type immediate
  !
  react rtt
   action logging
   threshold type immediate
   threshold lower-limit 50 upper-limit 70
  !
 !
 reaction operation 21
  react jitter-average
   action logging
   threshold type immediate
   threshold lower-limit 11 upper-limit 15
 !
 !
 reaction operation 22
  react jitter-average
```

```
  action logging
  threshold type immediate
  threshold lower-limit 11 upper-limit 15
 !
!
```

The third and final component in the IPSLA operation configuration task is the scheduling component, shown in Config 8-9. In this configuration example, all the IPSLA operations are configured with **start-time now**, which means these operations start simultaneously. If a device reloads, there is potential for increased CPU performance impact when other restarting protocols and processes are also competing for device resources. Therefore, an alternative option could be to start the operations sequentially with the command **start-time after hh:mm:ss**, with each operation scheduled at a different start time.

Config 8-9   *IPSLA Sender Scheduling Configuration on PE-1 (IOS XR)*

```
!
schedule operation 11
 start-time now
 life forever
 !
schedule operation 12
 start-time now
 life forever
 !
schedule operation 21
 start-time now
 life forever
 !
!
schedule operation 22
 start-time now
 life forever
 !
!
```

The output of the CLI command **show ipsla statistics 11** in Output 8-16 provides the RTT statistics from UDP echo type operation 11, which are as follows:

- **RTT values:**

    - **RTTAvg:** Average round-trip time

    - **RTTMin:** Minimum round-trip time

- **RTTMax:** Maximum round-trip time

- **NumOfRTT:** Number of round-trip time samples

- **RTTSum:** Sum of all round-trip time samples

- **RTTSum2:** Sum of the square of the samples used for standard deviation calculation

Output 8-16 *IPSLA Operation 11 UDP Echo Statistics on PE-1 (IOS XR)*

```
RP/0/RP0/CPU0:PE-1#show ipsla statistics 11

Entry number: 11
    Modification time: 11:48:23.349 UTC Mon Nov 20 2023
    Start time        : 11:48:23.326 UTC Mon Nov 20 2023
    Number of operations attempted: 102
    Number of operations skipped  : 10
    Current seconds left in Life  : Forever
    Operational state of entry    : Active
    Operational frequency(seconds): 10
    Connection loss occurred      : FALSE
    Timeout occurred              : FALSE
    Latest RTT (milliseconds)     : 73
    Latest operation start time   : 12:06:54.405 UTC Mon Nov 20 2023
    Next operation start time     : 12:07:04.405 UTC Mon Nov 20 2023
    Latest operation return code  : OK
    RTT Values:
        RTTAvg  : 73        RTTMin: 73        RTTMax : 73
        NumOfRTT: 1         RTTSum: 73        RTTSum2: 5329
RP/0/RP0/CPU0:PE-1#
```

The output of the CLI command **show ipsla statistics 21** in Output 8-17 provides the RTT, packet loss, and jitter statistics from UDP jitter type operation 21, which are as follows:

- Packet loss values:

  - **PacketLossSD:** Packets lost from the source (sender) to the destination (responder)

  - **PacketLossDS:** Packets lost from the destination (responder) to the source (sender)

- Jitter values:

  - **MinOfPositivesSD:** Minimum value of positive jitter from the source (sender) to the destination (responder)

  - **MaxOfPositivesSD:** Maximum value of positive jitter from the source (sender) to the destination (responder)

- **NumOfPositivesSD:** Number of positive jitter packets

- **SumOfPositivesSD:** Sum of positive jitter packets

- **Sum2PositivesSD:** Sum of the square of the samples used for standard deviation calculation

Similarly, for NegativesSD, the values in Output 8-17 provide the negative jitter from the source (sender) to the destination (responder), and PositivesDS and NegativesDS are the values from the destination (responder) to the source (sender).

Output 8-17 *IPSLA Operation 21 UDP Jitter Statistics on PE-1 (IOS XR)*

```
RP/0/RP0/CPU0:PE-1#show ipsla statistics 21

Entry number: 21
    Modification time: 11:48:23.349 UTC Mon Nov 20 2023
    Start time       : 11:48:23.327 UTC Mon Nov 20 2023
    Number of operations attempted: 40
    Number of operations skipped  : 10
    Current seconds left in Life  : Forever
    Operational state of entry    : Active
    Operational frequency(seconds): 10
    Connection loss occurred      : FALSE
    Timeout occurred              : FALSE
    Latest RTT (milliseconds)     : 148
    Latest operation start time   : 11:56:34.449 UTC Mon Nov 20 2023
    Next operation start time     : 11:56:44.449 UTC Mon Nov 20 2023
    Latest operation return code  : OK
    RTT Values:
      RTTAvg  : 148       RTTMin: 95        RTTMax : 185
      NumOfRTT: 10        RTTSum: 1481      RTTSum2: 226423
    Packet Loss Values:
      PacketLossSD        : 0         PacketLossDS : 0
      PacketOutOfSequence: 0          PacketMIA    : 0
      PacketLateArrival  : 0          PacketSkipped: 0
      Errors             : 0          Busies       : 0
      InvalidTimestamp   : 0
    Jitter Values :
      MinOfPositivesSD: 7         MaxOfPositivesSD: 66
      NumOfPositivesSD: 3         SumOfPositivesSD: 85
      Sum2PositivesSD : 4549
      MinOfNegativesSD: 1         MaxOfNegativesSD: 29
      NumOfNegativesSD: 6         SumOfNegativesSD: 69
      Sum2NegativesSD : 1417
      MinOfPositivesDS: 12        MaxOfPositivesDS: 15
```

```
    NumOfPositivesDS: 2          SumOfPositivesDS: 27
    Sum2PositivesDS : 369
    MinOfNegativesDS: 9          MaxOfNegativesDS: 63
    NumOfNegativesDS: 5          SumOfNegativesDS: 110
    Sum2NegativesDS : 4574
    JitterAve: 18       JitterSDAve: 17      JitterDSAve: 19
    Interarrival jitterout: 0           Interarrival jitterin: 0
  One Way Values :
    NumOfOW: 6
    OWMinSD : 8         OWMaxSD: 59         OWSumSD: 249
    OWSum2SD: 12087     OWAveSD: 41
    OWMinDS : 111       OWMaxDS: 138        OWSumDS: 759
    OWSum2DS: 96417     OWAveDS: 126
RP/0/RP0/CPU0:PE-1#
```

Another useful IPSLA command is **show ipsla statistics aggregated 11**, shown in Output 8-18, which displays three buckets of aggregated hourly statistics of the configured 24 statistics buckets.

Output 8-18   *IPSLA Operation 11 UDP Echo Aggregated Statistics on PE-1 (IOS XR)*

```
RP/0/RP0/CPU0:PE-1#show ipsla statistics aggregated 11

Entry number: 11
Hour Index: 0
    Start Time Index: 14:55:24.770 UTC Mon Nov 20 2023
    Number of Failed Operations due to a Disconnect     : 0
    Number of Failed Operations due to a Timeout        : 2
    Number of Failed Operations due to a Busy           : 0
    Number of Failed Operations due to a No Connection  : 0
    Number of Failed Operations due to an Internal Error: 37
    Number of Failed Operations due to a Sequence Error : 0
    Number of Failed Operations due to a Verify Error   : 0
    RTT Values:
      RTTAvg  : 129      RTTMin: 26         RTTMax : 885
      NumOfRTT: 321      RTTSum: 41500      RTTSum2: 10207350
Hour Index: 1
    Start Time Index: 15:55:24.770 UTC Mon Nov 20 2023
    Number of Failed Operations due to a Disconnect     : 0
    Number of Failed Operations due to a Timeout        : 0
    Number of Failed Operations due to a Busy           : 0
    Number of Failed Operations due to a No Connection  : 0
  Number of Failed Operations due to an Internal Error : 0
```

```
    Number of Failed Operations due to a Sequence Error : 0
    Number of Failed Operations due to a Verify Error   : 0
    RTT Values:
      RTTAvg  : 118        RTTMin: 19         RTTMax : 605
      NumOfRTT: 359        RTTSum: 42539      RTTSum2: 8570141
Hour Index: 2
    Start Time Index: 16:55:24.770 UTC Mon Nov 20 2023
    Number of Failed Operations due to a Disconnect      : 0
    Number of Failed Operations due to a Timeout         : 1
    Number of Failed Operations due to a Busy            : 0
    Number of Failed Operations due to a No Connection   : 0
    Number of Failed Operations due to an Internal Error : 0
    Number of Failed Operations due to a Sequence Error  : 0
    Number of Failed Operations due to a Verify Error    : 0
    RTT Values:
      RTTAvg  : 117        RTTMin: 26         RTTMax : 935
      NumOfRTT: 359        RTTSum: 42046      RTTSum2: 8661142
<snip>
RP/0/RP0/CPU0:PE-1#
```

The output of the command **show ipsla statistics aggregated 21** in Output 8-19 displays three buckets of aggregated hourly statistics for the UDP jitter operations of the configured 24 statistics buckets.

Output 8-19 *IPSLA Operation 21 UDP Jitter Aggregated Statistics on PE-1 (IOS XR)*

```
RP/0/RP0/CPU0:PE-1#show ipsla statistics aggregated 21

Entry number: 21
Hour Index: 0
    Start Time Index: 14:55:24.789 UTC Mon Nov 20 2023
    Number of Failed Operations due to a Disconnect      : 0
    Number of Failed Operations due to a Timeout         : 2
    Number of Failed Operations due to a Busy            : 0
    Number of Failed Operations due to a No Connection   : 0
   Number of Failed Operations due to an Internal Error: 37
    Number of Failed Operations due to a Sequence Error  : 0
    Number of Failed Operations due to a Verify Error    : 0
    RTT Values:
      RTTAvg  : 144        RTTMin: 17         RTTMax : 991
      NumOfRTT: 3203       RTTSum: 461768     RTTSum2: 161189472
    Packet Loss Values:
      PacketLossSD      : 0          PacketLossDS : 0
      PacketOutOfSequence: 0         PacketMIA    : 7
```

```
        PacketLateArrival   : 0        PacketSkipped: 0
        Errors              : 39       Busies      : 0
        InvalidTimestamp    : 0
      Jitter Values :
        MinOfPositivesSD: 1            MaxOfPositivesSD: 507
        NumOfPositivesSD: 945          SumOfPositivesSD: 24581
        Sum2PositivesSD : 3655233
        MinOfNegativesSD: 1            MaxOfNegativesSD: 43
        NumOfNegativesSD: 1859         SumOfNegativesSD: 23551
        Sum2NegativesSD : 413187
        MinOfPositivesDS: 1            MaxOfPositivesDS: 509
        NumOfPositivesDS: 935          SumOfPositivesDS: 17710
        Sum2PositivesDS : 2101952
        MinOfNegativesDS: 1            MaxOfNegativesDS: 193
        NumOfNegativesDS: 1190         SumOfNegativesDS: 13660
        Sum2NegativesDS : 509652
        JitterAve: 16       JitterSDAve: 17     JitterDSAve: 14
        Interarrival jitterout: 0             Interarrival jitterin: 0
      One Way Values :
        NumOfOW: 1043
        OWMinSD : 0         OWMaxSD: 912        OWSumSD: 178949
        OWSum2SD: 53065995  OWAveSD: 171
        OWMinDS : 69        OWMaxDS: 579        OWSumDS: 165333
        OWSum2DS: 34509419  OWAveDS: 158
Hour Index: 1
      Start Time Index: 15:55:24.789 UTC Mon Nov 20 2023
      Number of Failed Operations due to a Disconnect      : 0
      Number of Failed Operations due to a Timeout         : 0
      Number of Failed Operations due to a Busy            : 0
      Number of Failed Operations due to a No Connection   : 0
      Number of Failed Operations due to an Internal Error: 0
      Number of Failed Operations due to a Sequence Error : 0
      Number of Failed Operations due to a Verify Error    : 0
      RTT Values:
        RTTAvg  : 139      RTTMin: 18        RTTMax : 850
        NumOfRTT: 3576     RTTSum: 499739    RTTSum2: 163064441
      Packet Loss Values:
        PacketLossSD      : 0        PacketLossDS : 0
        PacketOutOfSequence: 0       PacketMIA    : 14
        PacketLateArrival  : 0       PacketSkipped: 0
        Errors             : 0       Busies      : 0
        InvalidTimestamp   : 0
      Jitter Values :
        MinOfPositivesSD: 1            MaxOfPositivesSD: 480
        NumOfPositivesSD: 1029         SumOfPositivesSD: 28234
```

```
   Sum2PositivesSD : 4447680
   MinOfNegativesSD: 1           MaxOfNegativesSD: 36
   NumOfNegativesSD: 2117        SumOfNegativesSD: 27246
   Sum2NegativesSD : 475686
   MinOfPositivesDS: 1           MaxOfPositivesDS: 402
   NumOfPositivesDS: 1003        SumOfPositivesDS: 19010
   Sum2PositivesDS : 2099504
   MinOfNegativesDS: 1           MaxOfNegativesDS: 285
   NumOfNegativesDS: 1342        SumOfNegativesDS: 15274
   Sum2NegativesDS : 589594
   JitterAve: 16         JitterSDAve: 17      JitterDSAve: 14
   Interarrival jitterout: 0             Interarrival jitterin: 0
 One Way Values :
   NumOfOW: 1158
   OWMinSD : 0          OWMaxSD: 705          OWSumSD: 185910
   OWSum2SD: 54129492   OWAveSD: 160
   OWMinDS : 68         OWMaxDS: 473          OWSumDS: 175864
   OWSum2DS: 34177162   OWAveDS: 151
Hour Index: 2
   Start Time Index: 16:55:24.789 UTC Mon Nov 20 2023
   Number of Failed Operations due to a Disconnect    : 0
   Number of Failed Operations due to a Timeout       : 1
   Number of Failed Operations due to a Busy          : 0
   Number of Failed Operations due to a No Connection : 0
   Number of Failed Operations due to an Internal Error: 0
   Number of Failed Operations due to a Sequence Error : 0
   Number of Failed Operations due to a Verify Error  : 0
   RTT Values:
   RTTAvg  : 143        RTTMin: 17           RTTMax : 999
   NumOfRTT: 3562       RTTSum: 511474       RTTSum2: 175542546
   Packet Loss Values:
   PacketLossSD      : 0         PacketLossDS : 8
   PacketOutOfSequence: 0        PacketMIA    : 20
   PacketLateArrival : 8         PacketSkipped: 0
   Errors            : 1         Busies       : 0
   InvalidTimestamp  : 0
   Jitter Values :
   MinOfPositivesSD: 1           MaxOfPositivesSD: 476
   NumOfPositivesSD: 1041        SumOfPositivesSD: 28654
   Sum2PositivesSD : 3996838
   MinOfNegativesSD: 1           MaxOfNegativesSD: 33
   NumOfNegativesSD: 2059        SumOfNegativesSD: 26932
   Sum2NegativesSD : 477414
   MinOfPositivesDS: 1           MaxOfPositivesDS: 528
   NumOfPositivesDS: 999         SumOfPositivesDS: 19471
```

```
    Sum2PositivesDS : 2335067
    MinOfNegativesDS: 1          MaxOfNegativesDS: 221
    NumOfNegativesDS: 1376       SumOfNegativesDS: 15480
    Sum2NegativesDS : 569038
    JitterAve: 16        JitterSDAve: 17     JitterDSAve: 14
    Interarrival jitterout: 0            Interarrival jitterin: 0
  One Way Values :
    NumOfOW: 1150
    OWMinSD : 0          OWMaxSD: 675        OWSumSD: 185479
    OWSum2SD: 53473969   OWAveSD: 161
    OWMinDS : 69         OWMaxDS: 714        OWSumDS: 184885
    OWSum2DS: 41036269   OWAveDS: 160
<snip>
RP/0/RP0/CPU0:PE-1#
```

In the reaction component configuration in Config 8-8, the CLI configuration line **action logging** allows any threshold-exceeding events to be logged to the router's syslog, as shown in Output 8-20. The log message indicates that UDP echo operation 11 has exceeded the configured RTT upper-limit threshold of 70 ms, with a measurement of 217 ms at the time interval 12:03:06.134. Then, at time interval 12:03:25.897, the monitored RTT value has fallen below the lower threshold value of 50 ms with a measurement of 33 ms.

Output 8-20   *IPSLA Syslog Triggered Event for Operation 11 on PE-1 (IOS XR)*

```
RP/0/RP0/CPU0:Nov 21 12:03:06.134 UTC: ipsla_sa[256]: %MGBL-IPSLA-5-THRESHOLD_SET :
  Monitor element has exceeded the threshold condition. Op:11, TargetAddr:10.2.10.0,
  MonElem:RTT(Type:immediate,Lower:50,Upper:70, LastVal:217)

RP/0/RP0/CPU0:Nov 21 12:03:25.897 UTC: ipsla_sa[256]: %MGBL-IPSLA-5-THRESHOLD_CLEAR
  : Monitor element has reset the threshold reaction. Op:11, TargetAddr:10.2.10.0,
  MonElem:RTT(Type:immediate,Lower:50,Upper:70, LastVal:33)
```

The log message displayed in Output 8-21 indicates that the UDP jitter operation 21 has exceeded the configured Jitter Average upper-limit threshold of 15 ms, with a measurement of 38 ms at the time interval 12:03:26.408. Then, at the time interval 12:03:56.196, the Jitter Average value fell below the lower threshold value of 11 ms, with a measurement of 8 ms.

Output 8-21   *IPSLA Syslog-Triggered Event for Operation 21 on PE-1 (IOS XR)*

```
RP/0/RP0/CPU0:Nov 21 12:03:26.408 UTC: ipsla_sa[256]: %MGBL-IPSLA-5-THRESHOLD_SET :
  Monitor element has exceeded the threshold condition. Op:21, TargetAddr:10.2.10.0,
  MonElem:JitterAvg(Type:immediate,Lower:11,Upper:15, LastVal:38)

RP/0/RP0/CPU0:Nov 21 12:03:56.196 UTC: ipsla_sa[256]: %MGBL-IPSLA-5-THRESHOLD_CLEAR
  : Monitor element has reset the threshold reaction. Op:21, TargetAddr:10.2.10.0,
  MonElem:JitterAvg(Type:immediate,Lower:11,Upper:15, LastVal:8)
```

In conclusion, network operators have deployed the IPSLA performance measurement feature on Cisco platforms for many years, and IPSLA is therefore well known and understood. A potential disadvantage in the deployment of IPSLA, especially in large-scale network deployments, is the possibility of overprovisioning multiple concurrent IPSLA operations and the increased testing frequencies potentially having a negative impact on devices. All test results need to be captured into a database on the device itself and subsequently polled via SNMP, with any threshold triggers logged either locally or pushed out as SNMP traps. Provisioning additional IPSLA operations may lead to the overburdening of SNMP resources both on devices and on the polling infrastructure. Network operators need to be cognizant of any potential IPSLA operation deployment and device overburdening by following a deployment strategy that will provide the performance measurements required for customer SLAs together with a reduction in network device and SNMP infrastructure impact.

TWAMP Light Configuration and Verification

This section describes a simple TWAMP Light deployment. TWAMP Light is minimally described in the appendix section of RFC 5357 as having a simpler architecture than TWAMP, with the TWAMP Control protocol eliminated. For the purposes of this section, the TWAMP controller is implemented using the Python tool twampy in lieu of a dedicated "shadow" CPE device. Figure 8-29 shows the TWAMP Light configurations used in this deployment example.

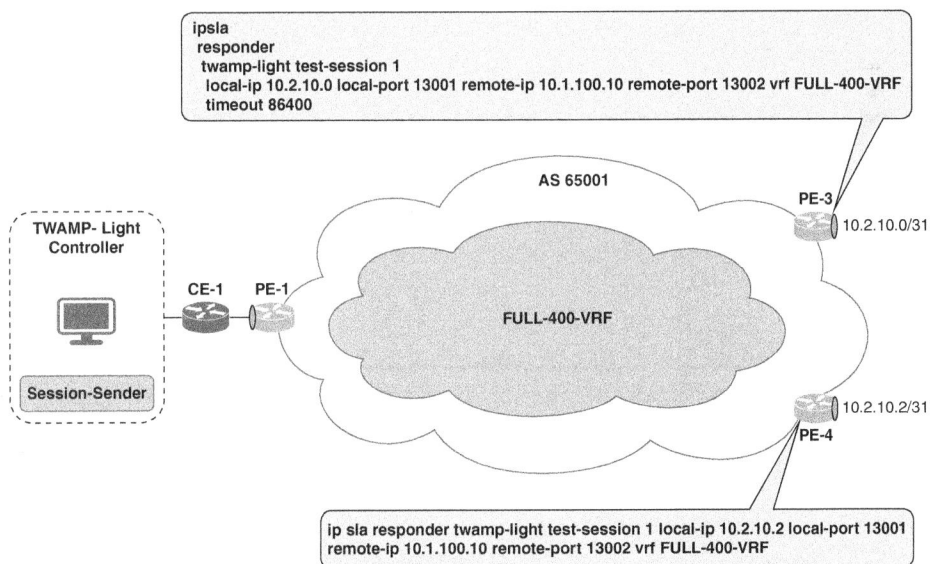

Figure 8-29 *TWAMP Light Configuration Tasks*

The IPSLA TWAMP Light responder configuration on the IOS XR router PE-3 is detailed in Config 8-10. In this example, the UDP ports are configured, thereby removing the requirement for the TWAMP Control session.

Config 8-10   *IPSLA TWAMP Light Responder Configuration on PE-3 (IOS XR)*

```
!
ipsla
 responder
  twamp-light test-session 1
   local-ip 10.2.10.0 local-port 13001 remote-ip 10.1.100.10 remote-port 13002 vrf
FULL-400-VRF
   timeout 86400
  !
 !
!
```

Config 8-11 is the IPSLA TWAMP Light responder configuration on the IOS XE router PE-4 for the same VRF instance FULL-400-VRF.

Config 8-11   *IPSLA TWAMP Light Responder Configuration on PE-4 (IOS XE)*

```
!
ip sla responder twamp-light test-session 1 local-ip 10.2.10.2 local-port 13001
  remote-ip 10.1.100.10 remote-port 13002 vrf FULL-400-VRF
!
```

The twampy Python script command line help option is shown in Output 8-22 for reference purposes.

Output 8-22   *TWAMP Light Sender Usage*

```
cisco@twampy-host~$ python3 twampy.py sender --help
usage: twampy.py sender [-h] [-l filename] [-q | -v | -d] [--tos type-of-service]
  [--dscp dscp-value] [--ttl time-to-live] [--padding bytes] [--do-not-fragment]
                         [-i msec] [-c packets]
                         [remote-ip:port] [local-ip:port]


options:
  -h, --help          show this help message and exit
  -q, --quiet         disable logging
  -v, --verbose       enhanced logging
  -d, --debug         extensive logging

Debug Options:
  -l filename, --logfile filename
                      Specify the logfile (default: <stdout>)
```

```
IP socket options:
  --tos type-of-service
                       IP TOS value
  --dscp dscp-value    IP DSCP value
  --ttl time-to-live   [1..128]
  --padding bytes      IP/UDP mtu value
  --do-not-fragment    keyword (do-not-fragment)


TWL sender options:
  remote-ip:port
  local-ip:port
  -i msec, --interval msec
                       [100,1000]
  -c packets, --count packets
                       [1..9999]
```

In the twampy example Output 8-23, the TWAMP Light **sender** argument is used with the UDP size 128 bytes and a transmitted count of 100 packets with an interval of 20 ms toward the destination IP address 10.2.10.0 and destination port 13001 with source IP address 10.1.100.10 and source port 13002. When the script completes, the output provides basic packet delay, jitter, and loss statistics.

Output 8-23   *TWAMP Light Sender Output Example*

```
cisco@twampy-host:~$ python3 twampy.py sender --padding 128 -c 100 -i 20
   10.2.10.0:13001 10.1.100.10:13002

================================================================================
Direction        Min        Max        Avg        Jitter      Loss
--------------------------------------------------------------------------------

  Outbound:        0us     629.20ms   210.61ms    19.15ms     0.0%
  Inbound:       1.15sec    2.73sec    2.09sec    12.67ms     0.0%
  Roundtrip:     91.39ms    2.77sec    2.08sec    23.00ms     0.0%

--------------------------------------------------------------------------------

                                            Jitter Algorithm [RFC1889]
================================================================================
```

The CLI command **show ipsla twamp session** in Output 8-24 is used to verify that the TWAMP Light responder session status is active on the IOS XR router PE-3 and that the IP and port addresses match those being used by the twampy Python tool.

Output 8-24   *IPSLA TWAMP Light Responder Verification on PE-3 (IOS XR)*

```
RP/0/RP0/CPU0:PE-3#show ipsla twamp session
***** TWAMP Sessions *****
No records matching query found
***** TWAMP-LIGHT Sessions *****
Session status: Active
Recvr Addr: 10.2.10.0
Recvr Port: 13001
Sender Addr: 10.1.100.10
Sender Port: 13002
Sender VRF Name: FULL-400-VRF
Session ID: 1
Mode: Unauthenticated
Number of Packets Received: 1200
Session timeout: 86400
Number of Packets Sent: 1200

RP/0/RP0/CPU0:PE-3 #
```

Similarly, the CLI command **show ip sla twamp-light session** in Output 8-25 verifies the status of the TWAMP Light responder session on the IOS XE router PE-4.

Output 8-25   *IPSLA TWAMP Light Responder Verification on PE-4 (IOS XE)*

```
PE-4#show ip sla twamp-light session
Session ID: 1
Status: Active
Local Addr: 10.2.10.2
Local Port: 13001
Remote Addr: 10.1.100.10
Remote Port: 13002
VRF: FULL-400-VRF
Test packet received: 1220
Test packet sent: 1220

PE-4#
```

Note   While the Python tool twampy used in the verifications for TWAMP Light in the SR-MPLS reference network is sufficient for the purposes of testing and explanations in this book, operators of large-scale networks need to deploy commercially available TWAMP controller and monitoring software.

Summary

Service assurance is a set of procedures and processes designed to improve customer experience, maximize customer satisfaction, and reduce customer churn. Service assurance–related tools and protocols allow network operators to operate and manage the networks under their management effectively while providing visibility into potential SLA-impacting events, with the ability to react and mitigate any network anomalies that may impact a network operator's service reputation and potentially the bottom line. Providing effective service assurance mechanisms within large networks can be a complex and potentially expensive undertaking.

This chapter covers existing and well-understood tools such as Y.1731, IPSLA, TWAMP, and TWAMP Light in the context of services transported across SR-MPLS and SRv6 core networks. Network operators can safely migrate existing IP or MPLS transport networks to SR-MPLS– or SRv6-based designs and continue using these existing management tools. However, these tools do have limitations. As network deployment scale starts to increase or more services with different SLA requirements are migrated onto the transport networks, the cost of managing the various SLAs may increase dramatically, or feature support may not be available on all devices, thereby reducing the overall effectiveness of these tools. Many of these tools and protocols were conceived and designed 20 years ago, and although they still perform admirably, there are newer tools being developed to address the challenges posed by these new transport networks. Cisco is actively working on new standards and tools in the service assurance area, as described briefly at the beginning of this chapter. For example, the Segment Routing Performance Measurement (SR-PM) initiative addresses the new challenges and demands brought about by ever-evolving networks.

References and Additional Reading

Transport

- RFC 7810: IS-IS Traffic Engineering (TE) Metric Extensions, https://datatracker.ietf.org/doc/html/rfc7810

- RFC 7471: OSPF Traffic Engineering (TE) Metric Extensions, https://datatracker.ietf.org/doc/html/rfc7471

- RFC 5357: A Two-Way Active Measurement Protocol (TWAMP), https://datatracker.ietf.org/doc/html/rfc5357

- RFC 8762: Simple Two-Way Active Measurement Protocol, https://datatracker.ietf.org/doc/html/rfc8762

- RFC 9503: Simple Two-Way Active Measurement Protocol (STAMP) Extensions for Segment Routing Networks, https://datatracker.ietf.org/doc/rfc9503

SR Data Plane Monitoring (SR-DPM)

- RFC 8029: Detecting Multiprotocol Label Switched (MPLS) Data-Plane Failures, https://datatracker.ietf.org/doc/html/rfc8029#page-17

Path Tracing (PT)

- IETF Draft: draft-filsfils-ippm-path-tracing-01 Path Tracing in SRv6 networks, https://datatracker.ietf.org/doc/draft-filsfils-ippm-path-tracing/01/

- RFC 8200: Internet Protocol, Version 6 (IPv6) Specification, https://datatracker.ietf.org/doc/html/rfc8200#section-4.3

Services

L2VPN Service Assurance

- MEF 30.1: Service OAM Fault Management Implementation Agreement Phase, https://www.mef.net/resources/mef-30-1-service-oam-fault-management-implementation-agreement-phase-2/

- MEF 35.1 Service OAM Performance Monitoring Implementation Agreement, https://www.mef.net/resources/mef-35-1-service-oam-performance-monitoring-implementation-agreement/

- CFM IEEE 802.1ag: IEEE Standard for Local and Metropolitan Area Networks Virtual Bridged Local Area Networks, Amendment 5: Connectivity Fault Management

- Y.1731: OAM Functions and Mechanisms for Ethernet-Based Networks, https://www.itu.int/rec/T-REC-G.8013-202306-I/en

L3VPN Service Assurance

- RFC 4656: A One-way Active Measurement Protocol (OWAMP), https://datatracker.ietf.org/doc/html/rfc4656

- RFC 5357: A Two-Way Active Measurement Protocol (TWAMP), https://datatracker.ietf.org/doc/html/rfc5357

- RFC 8762: Simple Two-Way Active Measurement Protocol, https://datatracker.ietf.org/doc/html/rfc8762

- RFC 9503: Simple Two-Way Active Measurement Protocol (STAMP) Extensions for Segment Routing Networks, https://datatracker.ietf.org/doc/rfc9503

- twampy Python tool, https://github.com/nokia/twampy

Chapter 9

High Availability and Fast Convergence

The topics of high availability and fast convergence within both service provider and enterprise networks cover a vast range of technologies, features, design options, and configuration options, many of which are well beyond the scope of this book. This chapter discusses a few well-known technologies that network operators can readily employ in any segment routing network they plan on deploying.

This chapter and other parts of this book discuss the following high availability and fast convergence features and technologies:

- **Failure detection:** Bidirectional Forwarding Detection (BFD) provides failure detection.

- **Topology-Independent Loop-Free Alternate (TI-LFA):** TI-LFA is used to precalculate backup paths, enabling rapid transition to alternative paths in the event of primary route failure.

- **Microloops:** These temporary routing loops can occur in IP networks during the convergence process following a topology change, such as link up/down events or configuration changes.

- **Anycast SID:** As discussed in Chapter 4, "Segment Routing in Detail," in the sections "SR-MPLS Anycast SID," and "SRv6 Anycast SID," where the Anycast SID provides high availability in the event of node failure.

- **BGP Prefix Independent Convergence (PIC) Edge:** BGP PIC Edge is a BGP fast-convergence feature designed to address various network failure scenarios. It is particularly useful in situations where devices managing a large number of routes might otherwise experience unacceptably high convergence times.

■ **IS-IS Unreachable Prefix Announcement (UPA):** As discussed in the section "Unreachable Prefix Announcement (UPA)" in Chapter 4, IS-IS UPA enables BGP PIC Edge functionality in SRv6 networks when summarization is deployed.

The network convergence mechanism can be divided into a set of discrete times:

■ **Failure event detection time:** Ideally, a network device can rapidly detect and react to link, peer node, or routing protocol failures. Devices that are physically connected to one another generally have fast failure detection times, and the loss of a physical interface or connection is generally detected immediately. However, there may be multiple hops between devices, such as when inter-device connectivity is provided by third-party services (for example, L2VPN connectivity). In these scenarios, physical failures may no longer be solely relied upon for failure detection, necessitating the use of other detection mechanisms, such as BFD.

■ **Network event information propagation time:** This is the rapidity with which a detected failure event is propagated throughout the network

■ **Topology update and repair path computation time:** This is the speed at which all network devices calculate repair paths after processing received network updates.

■ **Routing Information Base (RIB)/Forwarding Information Base (FIB) update time:** This is the time it takes network devices to download repair path information to the local hardware FIB tables.

Network convergence depends on all these measures of events during which traffic is lost:

Convergence Time = Failure Detection Time + Event Propagation Time + Path Computation Time + RIB/FIB Update Time

Fast Reroute (FRR) or BGP PIC mechanisms can switch traffic onto precomputed backup paths in the event that a network failure is detected while the event propagation, path computation, and RIB/FIB update events are being processed. Traffic loss in this case is equal to the failure event detection time.

BFD Failure Detection Mechanism

Bidirectional Forwarding Detection (BFD) is a lightweight protocol for the detection of link, protocol, or device failures that involves the use of lightweight bidirectional hello messages between device endpoints. BFD is a UDP-based protocol and can detect failures within less than 50 ms of the event occurrence. Many of today's routers have the ability to offload the generation of BFD hello packets from the general CPU to hardware silicon; for example, on Cisco ASR 9000 routers, the offload function is handled by a line card's individual network processing units (NPUs), allowing for increased deployment scale at very aggressive configured detection timer values.

BFD gives network operators a standardized method for link, protocol, or device failure detection throughout their networks. Protocols such as Link Aggregation Control Protocol (LACP) and routing protocols (for example, BGP, IS-IS, OSPF) have their own failure detection mechanisms that use protocol-specific hello or keepalive packets, but they cannot achieve failure detection in the sub-second ranges as BFD can. BFD offers a standardized rapid failure detection method far in excess of what these routing protocols are capable of.

The BFD protocol (RFC 5880) can be provisioned to run over any data-link protocol, whether across physical or logical interfaces (LAG). It has two defined operating modes and an echo function:

- **BFD async mode:** BFD endpoints transmit UDP control packets at preconfigured intervals toward the remote endpoint device. Receipt of those BFD packets at the endpoint confirms the operational state of the BFD control plane. If a configured interval period passes without an endpoint receiving a BFD control packet, the endpoint will take down the BFD session and inform the upper layer routing protocol of the failure, triggering a reconvergence event.

- **BFD demand mode:** In this mode, an endpoint with an established BFD session can request that the remote endpoint cease the transmission of BFD control packets through setting the demand (D) bit in the BFD control packets. When an endpoint needs to verify connectivity, it initiates a sequence of BFD control packets. If there is no response, the BFD session is terminated, triggering a reconvergence event. Be aware that the BFD demand operating mode is currently not supported on IOS XR or IOS XE platforms

- **BFD echo:** This function verifies only the bidirectional forwarding path between the local endpoint and the remote endpoint. To achieve this, the local endpoint sends BFD echo packets with its own local IP address as the destination IP address, causing the remote endpoint to loop these packets back to the local node. If BFD echo packets are not received by the local node, the BFD session is taken down, triggering a reconvergence event. Since the BFD echo packets are now being used for failure detection, the transmission of the BFD control packets is reduced to a 2-second interval rate.

Most Cisco products support BFD async mode with the echo function enabled by default. The BFD protocol comes in two versions, version 0 and version 1, where the latter supports BFD echo and is the default version used with all the newest IOS XE and IOS XR implementations. Figure 9-1 provides a high-level overview of two peers, routers R-1 and R-2, operating with a BFD async implementation without echo enabled, and routers R-3 and R-4 operating with BFD async and echo enabled.

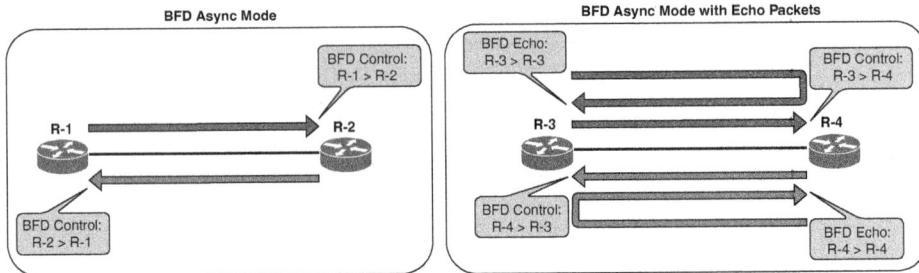

Figure 9-1   *BFD Async Mode and Async Mode with Echo Packets*

This chapter does not describe the implementation and verification of BFD directly across physical interfaces for static routes, HSRP, or dynamic routing protocols. Rather, it details the various BFD mechanisms over Link Aggregation Group (LAG), or bundle, interfaces. These are a few variations of BFD over LAG interfaces (RFC 7130) that you should be aware of:

- **BFD over VLAN over Bundle (BVLAN):** The initial BFD over Bundle support was an IPv4 BFD session across individual bundle subinterfaces and is no longer supported.

- **BFD over Bundle (IETF BoB):** This flavor is also known as micro-BFD and can be configured in a Cisco or IETF variant for inter-vendor interoperability and operates as a single-hop session. The client process for the BoB implementation is called bundlemgr, and in the event that a failure is detected, the bundlemgr process is immediately notified and tears down the bundle interface. Each bundle member link runs its own BFD session. The advantage of this is that, upon detecting a failure, the complete bundle interface can be torn down via the bundlemgr process. An example of when this would occur is when **bundle minimum-active links {***minimum_value***}** are configured, and the minimum active link number is breached.

- **BFD over Logical Bundle (BLB):** This BFD implementation is a replacement of the BVLAN option, where BFD sessions can run across the main bundle interface or per VLAN subinterface, if configured. BLB also operates as a single-hop session, much as with the BoB implementation, but it operates as a BFD multipath (MP) flavor, where the requirement is for Layer 3 IP address reachability rather than actual bundle members' links and member states. The BLB control packets use only one selected bundle interface member link (based on a LAG hash algorithm) to the remote endpoint. BLB's actual clients are therefore the routing protocols under which it is configured, such as BGP, IS-IS, OSPF, or even static routes. In addition, because BLB is a multipath implementation, it does not support the BFD echo function.

The BFD single-hop (SH) sessions were briefly introduced earlier as BFD sessions between directly attached endpoints, but for the sake of completeness, there are also BFD implementations known as BFD multi-hop (MH) and BFD multipath (MP). In a BFD multi-hop implementation, the BFD sessions are enabled between endpoints that are not directly connected but that are separated across multiple Layer 3 hops. BFD multipath refers to the possibility of an asymmetrical return path, meaning the transmit path and the receive path may differ. Configuring BFD under the BGP routing protocol or with Generic Routing Encapsulation (GRE) tunnels are examples of where BFD multi-hop and BFD multipath sessions can be established.

Next, we will look at BFD packet captures to better understand the subtle differences between the BoB and BLB implementations. The IPv6 BoB control packet shown in Example 9-1 was captured between router PE-1 and router P-5 from the SRv6 reference network in Appendix A, "Reference Diagrams and Information." Example 9-2 shows an IPv4 BLB packet that was captured between an IOS XE router and an IOS XR router.

BFD BoB (RFC 7130) control packets use a dedicated multicast destination MAC address 01:00:5E:90:00:01, and the destination UDP port is set to 6784.

BFD BLB uses the resolved destination MAC address, and the destination UDP port is set to 3784 (RFC 5881).

> **Note**   The actual BFD configuration from the packet capture in Example 9-1 is shown later on, in Config 9-1.

Example 9-1 contains the following highlighted information:

- **Ethernet II Src: Cisco_3b:ec:83 (68:79:09:3b:ec:83):** This is the egress interface MAC address.

- **Ethernet II Dst: IPv4mcast_90:00:01 (01:00:5e:90:00:01):** This is a dedicated multicast MAC address, per RFC 7130.

- **IPv6 Src: fe80::1002:** This is an operator-configured IPv6 link-local source address.

- **IPv6 Dst: fe80::1001:** This is an operator-configured IPv6 link-local destination address.

- **Traffic Class: 0xc0:** The router sets the IPv6 traffic class to CS6.

- **User Datagram Protocol, Src Port: 49152:** The BFD UDP source port is set to 49152.

- **User Datagram Protocol, Dst Port: 6784:** The BFD UDP destination port is set to 6784, per RFC 7130.

- **BFD control message:**

  - **Protocol Version: 1:** By default, IOS XR runs the version 1 BFD control header.

  - **Diagnostic Code:** This specifies the router's previous session state change reason (for example, BFD failure detection time exceeded).

- **Session State: Up:** This is the router's BFD session status view.

- **Message Flags:**

  - **Poll:** The poll (P) bit is used to notify the peer router of any BFD parameter changes.

  - **Final:** The final (F) bit is set when responding to BFD control packets with the P bit set.

  - **Control Plane Independent:** The control plane independent (C) bit is set in this packet capture because the BFD implementation is independent of the control plane (route processors [RPs]). This means that BFD is associated with the router line card, as opposed to the route processor. With the C bit set to 1, the BFD session can continue to operate and detect failures even if the control plane is restarting. This is useful in scenarios where the data plane needs to continue forwarding traffic even if the control plane is experiencing a reload or restart. (See RFC 5882 for more details.)

  - **Authentication Present:** The authentication (A) bit is set if authentication is configured.

  - **Demand:** The demand (D) bit is set if the demand mode is used. (This is currently not supported with IOS XR and IOS XE platforms.)

  - **Multipoint:** The multipoint (M) bit is for future use.

- **Detect Time Multiplier:** The configured multiplier value (3 in this case) multiplied by the negotiated interval timer (50 ms) equals the failure detection time (150 ms).

- **My Discriminator:** The transmitting router generates a unique discriminator value that is used to differentiate between multiple BFD sessions between two routers.

- **Your Discriminator:** The transmitting router reflects the peer router's My Discriminator value.

- **Desired Min TX Interval:** This is the router's desired minimum interval for BFD control packet transmission—in this case, 50,000 us.

- **Required Min RX Interval:** This is the router's minimum interval for BFD control packet reception—in this case, 50,000 us.

- **Required Min Echo Interval:** This is the router's minimum interval between received BFD echo packets that the router is configured for. In this example, echo packets with IPv6 BoB mode are not supported.

Example 9-1 *BFD BoB IETF Mode Control Packet*

```
Ethernet II, Src: Cisco_3b:ec:83 (68:79:09:3b:ec:83), Dst: IPv4mcast_90:00:01
  (01:00:5e:90:00:01)
Internet Protocol Version 6, Src: fe80::1002, Dst: fe80::1001
    0110 .... = Version: 6
    .... 1100 0000 .... .... .... .... ...= Traffic Class: 0xc0 (DSCP: CS6, ECN:
  Not-ECT)
        .... 1100 00.. .... .... .... ....= Differentiated Services Codepoint: Class
  Selector 6 (48)
        .... .... ..00 .... .... .... ....= Explicit Congestion Notification: Not
  ECN-Capable Transport (0)
    .... 0000 0000 0000 0000 0000 = Flow Label: 0x00000
    Payload Length: 32
    Next Header: UDP (17)
    Hop Limit: 255
    Source Address: fe80::1002
    Destination Address: fe80::1001
User Datagram Protocol, Src Port: 49152, Dst Port: 6784
BFD Control message
    001. .... = Protocol Version: 1
    ...0 0000 = Diagnostic Code: No Diagnostic (0x00)
    11.. .... = Session State: Up (0x3)
    Message Flags: 0xc8, Control Plane Independent: Set
        0... .. = Poll: Not set
        .0.. .. = Final: Not set
        ..1. .. = Control Plane Independent: Set
        ...0 .. = Authentication Present: Not set
        .... 0. = Demand: Not set
        .... .0 = Multipoint: Not set
    Detect Time Multiplier: 3 (= 150 ms Detection time)
    Message Length: 24 bytes
    My Discriminator: 0x83c1000b
    Your Discriminator: 0x83c10012
    Desired Min TX Interval:    50 ms (50000 us)
    Required Min RX Interval:   50 ms (50000 us)
    Required Min Echo Interval:   0 ms (0 us)
```

The packet in Example 9-2 was captured between an IOS XE router and an IOS XR router in the SR-MPLS reference network in Appendix A, "Reference Diagrams and Information.", where both routers are configured with the IPv4 BFD over Logical Bundle (BLB) implementation (as you'll see shortly, in Config 9-4). The router in this example is running IOS XE, and there are some differences from the previous BoB packet fields that are highlighted in the example:

■ **Ethernet II Src: Cisco-Li_ed:27:c0 (00:1e:e5:ed:27:c0):** This is the egress interface MAC address.

- **Ethernet II Dst: Cisco_61:d3:1f (00:26:ca:61:d3:1f):** This is the destination MAC address. Note the difference from the BoB implementation, where a multicast MAC address is used.

- **IPv4 Src: 192.168.3.1:** This is the operator-configured IP source address in this example.

- **IPv4 Dst: 192.168.3.0:** This is the operator-configured IP destination address in this example.

- **User Datagram Protocol, Src Port: 49152:** The BFD UDP source port is set to 49152.

- **User Datagram Protocol, Dst Port: 3784:** The BFD UDP destination port is set to 3784. Note the difference from the BoB implementation, where UDP port 6784 is used.

- **BFD control message flag:**

  - **Control Plane Independent:** The control plane independent (C) bit is not set in this packet capture because the BFD implementation is dependent on the control plane. Here you can see that BFD shares its fate with the route processor. (see RFC 5882 for details.)

Example 9-2 *BFD BLB Control Packet*

```
Ethernet II, Src: Cisco-Li_ed:27:c0 (00:1e:e5:ed:27:c0), Dst: Cisco_61:d3:1f
  (00:26:ca:61:d3:1f)
Internet Protocol Version 4, Src: 192.168.3.1, Dst: 192.168.3.0
    0100 .... = Version: 4
    .... 0101 = Header Length: 20 bytes (5)
    Differentiated Services Field: 0xc0 (DSCP: CS6, ECN: Not-ECT)
        1100 00.. = Differentiated Services Codepoint: Class Selector 6 (48)
        .... ..00 = Explicit Congestion Notification: Not ECN-Capable Transport (0)
    Total Length: 52
    <snip>
    Source Address: 192.168.3.1
    Destination Address: 192.168.3.0
User Datagram Protocol, Src Port: 49152, Dst Port: 3784
BFD Control message
    001. .... = Protocol Version: 1
    ...0 0000 = Diagnostic Code: No Diagnostic (0x00)
    11.. .... = Session State: Up (0x3)
    Message Flags: 0xc0
        0... .. = Poll: Not set
        .0.. .. = Final: Not set
```

```
    ..0. .. = Control Plane Independent: Not set
    ...0 .. = Authentication Present: Not set
    .... 0. = Demand: Not set
    .... .0 = Multipoint: Not set
Detect Time Multiplier: 3 (= 6000 ms Detection time)
Message Length: 24 bytes
My Discriminator: 0x00001001
Your Discriminator: 0x00010001
Desired Min TX Interval: 2000 ms (2000000 us)
Required Min RX Interval: 2000 ms (2000000 us)
Required Min Echo Interval:    0 ms (0 us)
```

BFD BoB Configuration

This section initially focuses on the IPv6 BFD over Bundle (BoB) implementation configured between the PE-1 and P-5 routers as shown in Figure 9-2 from the SRv6 reference
network in Appendix A, "Reference Diagrams and Information." The core links in the
SRv6 reference network were originally configured directly on physical interfaces; in the
following section, they will need to be converted to Bundle-Ethernet interfaces.

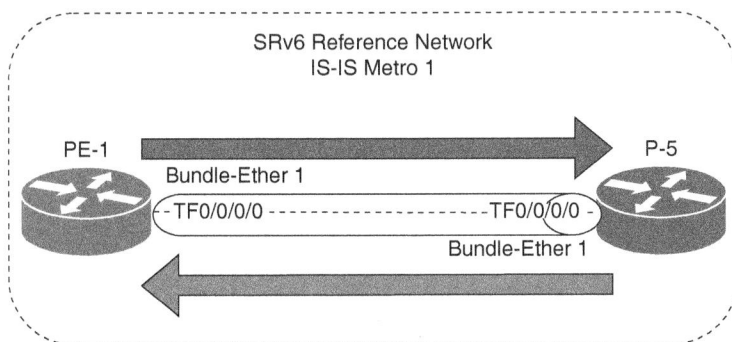

Figure 9-2 *BFD BoB Session Between PE-1 and P-5*

Note The different BFD configurations covered are platform and IOS version specific,
meaning that network operators must acquaint themselves with the nuances of BFD
implementation that pertain to their particular hardware and software versions when rolling
out BFD.

In this IPv6 BFD over Bundle (BoB) configuration section, the following restrictions apply:

- IPv6 BoB supports the IETF variant only.

- The IETF variant of IPv6 BoB does not support the echo function.

- The IETF variant of IPv6 BoB supports HW-Offload.

- HW-Offload does not support the echo function.

Config 9-1 and Config 9-2 show the initial LAG configurations between routers PE-1 and P-5 in IS-IS Metro 1. In this example, the interface TwentyFiveGigE0/0/0/0 has been allocated as a member of the Bundle-Ether1 interface on both routers.

Config 9-1   *Bundle-Ethernet Interface Configuration on PE-1 (IOS XR)*

```
!
interface Bundle-Ether1
 description Connected_to_P-5
 mtu 9216
 ipv6 address fe80::1001 link-local
!
interface TwentyFiveGigE0/0/0/0
 description Connected_to_P-5
 bundle id 1 mode active
!
```

The Bundle-Ethernet interface configuration on router P-5 is shown in Config 9-2.

Config 9-2   *Bundle-Ethernet Interface Configuration on P-5 (IOS XR)*

```
!
interface Bundle-Ether1
 description Connected_to_PE-1
 mtu 9216
 ipv6 address fe80::1003 link-local
!
interface TwentyFiveGigE0/0/0/0
 description Connected_to_PE-1
 bundle id 1 mode active
!
```

The next phase involves carrying out the BoB configuration tasks, as illustrated in Config 9-3 for router PE-1 and in Config 9-4 for router P-5, where the objective is to establish the fast failure detection mechanism for a Bundle-Ethernet interface. These are the important parts of Config 9-3 and Config 9-4:

- **bfd mode ietf:** This is the configuration option for choosing the IETF version of BFD.

- **bfd address-family ipv6 fast-detect:** This enables IPv6 BFD on the LAG interface.

- **bfd address-family ipv6 destination fe80::1003:** This is the IPv6 BFD session destination address, which is the link-local IPv6 address configured on adjacent routers (such as router P-5).

- **bfd address-family ipv6 minimum-interval 50:** This is the minimum interval period, in milliseconds, between the BFD async packets transmitted onto the Bundle-Ethernet interface member link. Note that BFD hardware offload supports a fixed number of interval timers for BFD sessions.

- **bfd address-family ipv6 multiplier 3:** This is the multiplier used with the previously described minimum interval in order to calculate the BFD control packet failure detection times. The BFD failure detection time in this configuration is 150 ms.

Depending on the hardware platform in use, you can configure the BFD hardware-offload functionality, thereby enabling the receipt and generation of BFD async packets to be offloaded from the line card general CPU to dedicated silicon for improved performance and scalability. On the ASR 9000 router family of products, the global command **hw-module bfd-hw-offload enable location** { *line-card-location* } together with a line card reload facilitates this functionality. By default, BFD is hardware offloaded on the Cisco 8000, NCS55xx, and NCS5xx platforms. For any potential restrictions, consult the configuration guide specific to each platform.

Config 9-3 *IETF BFD over Bundle-Ethernet Configuration on PE-1 (IOS XR)*

```
!
interface Bundle-Ether1
 description Connected_to_P-5
 bfd mode ietf
 bfd address-family ipv6 multiplier 3
 bfd address-family ipv6 destination fe80::1003
 bfd address-family ipv6 fast-detect
 bfd address-family ipv6 minimum-interval 50
 mtu 9216
 ipv6 address fe80::1001 link-local
!
```

The BFD peer configuration on router P-5 is shown in Config 9-4.

Config 9-4 *IETF BFD over Bundle-Ethernet Configuration on P-5 (IOS XR)*

```
!
interface Bundle-Ether1
 description Connected_to_PE-1
 bfd mode ietf
 bfd address-family ipv6 multiplier 3
 bfd address-family ipv6 destination fe80::1001
 bfd address-family ipv6 fast-detect
 bfd address-family ipv6 minimum-interval 50
 mtu 9216
 ipv6 address fe80::1003 link-local
!
```

BFD BoB Verification

Following the implementation of BFD configurations, a variety of helpful commands are available to aid in the operational verification and troubleshooting of BFD. The CLI command **show bfd ipv6 session** in Output 9-1 provides an overview of all IPv6 BFD sessions configured on the router. From the output, it is possible to ascertain the following information:

- **Interface: TF0/0/0/0 and BE1:** Because this is an IPv6 BoB implementation, both the Bundle-Ether1 interface and its member interfaces are displayed. In this case, there is a single member interface, TwentyFiveGigE0/0/0/0.

- **Dest Addr:** This is the IPv6 BFD session configured destination address; in this case, it is the link-local IPv6 address fe80::1003 of the router P-5.

- **H/W Yes:** BFD has been offloaded to dedicated hardware resources on the line card 0/0/CPU0.

- **Echo 0s(0s*0):** The BFD echo mode is not enabled.

- **Async 150ms(50ms*3):** Keep in mind that Interval Period × Multiplier = Failure Detection Time. With BoB, these outputs are applicable to the actual member interfaces.

- **State UP:** This is the status of the BFD session.

Output 9-1 *Global IPv6 BFD Session Overview on PE-1 (IOS XR)*

```
RP/0/RP0/CPU0:PE-1#show bfd ipv6 session
Interface          Dest Addr
                                        Local det time(int*mult)    State
H/W                NPU             Echo             Async
------------------ --------------- ---------------- --------------- ----------
TF0/0/0/0          fe80::1003
```

```
Yes                     0/0/CPU0          0s(0s*0)           150ms(50ms*3)      UP
BE1                     fe80::1003
No                      n/a               n/a                n/a                UP
---snip---
RP/0/RP0/CPU0:PE-1#
```

Output 9-2 shows the command **show bfd ipv6 session interface bundle-Ether 1 detail**, which provides insight into the BFD BoB functionality at the Bundle-Ether interface level, including the following pertinent information:

- **Session type: PR/V6/SH/BI/IB:** This field provides useful information about the BFD session implementation:

  - **PR:** This indicates that pre-routed single-path sessions are associated with physical interfaces and BFD over the Bundle-Ethernet interfaces.

  - **V6:** This indicates an IPv6 implementation.

  - **SH:** This indicates a BFD single-hop session.

  - **BI:** This indicates a bundle interface, in this case Bundle-Ether1.

  - **IB:** This indicates IETF BoB mode.

- **bundlemgr_distrib:** The bundle manager process is a client of BFD itself, and it therefore takes the physical interface link state and LACP status in conjunction with the BFD state when determining the functionality of a member interface's status.

Output 9-2   *BFD Bundle-Ethernet Session Details on PE-1 (IOS XR)*

```
RP/0/RP0/CPU0:PE-1#show bfd ipv6 session interface bundle-Ether 1 detail

I/f: Bundle-Ether1, Location: 0/RP0/CPU0
Dest: fe80::1003
Src: fe80::1001
 State: UP for 0d:5h:26m:13s, number of times UP: 1
 Session type: PR/V6/SH/BI/IB
Session owner information:
                          Desired                 Adjusted
 Client                   Interval   Multiplier Interval   Multiplier
 -------------------- --------------------- ---------------------
 bundlemgr_distrib     50 ms      3          0 ms      3
Session association information:
 Interface            Dest Addr / Type
 ------------------- ----------------------------------
 TF0/0/0/0            fe80::1003
                      BFD_SESSION_SUBTYPE_RTR_BUNDLE_MEMBER

RP/0/RP0/CPU0:PE-1#
```

Obtaining the BFD BoB session details per Bundle-Ethernet member involves using the command **show bfd ipv6 session interface TF0/0/0/0 detail**, as shown in Output 9-3:

- **Session type: PR/V6/SH/BM/IB:** This is similar to the previous output, but with a single difference:

  - **BM:** This is the bundle member interface, in this case the physical interface TF0/0/0/0.

- **Received parameters:** This section shows the peer router's configured interval period, multiplier value, and echo intervals, if supported.

- **Transmitted parameters:** This section shows the local router's configured interval period, multiplier value, and echo intervals, if supported.

- **Timer Values:** This section shows details of the negotiated timer values exchanged and agreed upon between local and peer routers. If there is a difference between these exchanged parameters, the negotiated and agreed values are based on the upper value.

- **Session owner information:**

  - **Client bundlemgr_distrib:** The bundle manager process is a client of BFD itself, and it therefore takes both the physical interface link state and LACP status together with the BFD state when determining the functionality of a member interface's status.

- **H/W Offload Info:** This field details the hardware-offload functionality for the specific session (for example, which line card and NPU it is offloaded to and whether the BFD control and/or BFD echo packets are offloaded to the NPU).

Output 9-3 *BFD Bundle-Ethernet Member Session Details on PE-1 (IOS XR)*

```
RP/0/RP0/CPU0:PE-1#show bfd ipv6 session interface TF0/0/0/0 detail

I/f: TwentyFiveGigE0/0/0/0, Location: 0/0/CPU0
Dest: fe80::1003
Src: fe80::1001
 State: UP for 0d:5h:27m:6s, number of times UP: 1
 Session type: PR/V6/SH/BM/IB
Received parameters:
 Version: 1, desired tx interval: 50 ms, required rx interval: 50 ms
 Required echo rx interval: 0 ms, multiplier: 3, diag: None
 My discr: 2147487763, your discr: 2210463750, state UP, D/F/P/C/A: 0/0/0/1/0
Transmitted parameters:
 Version: 1, desired tx interval: 50 ms, required rx interval: 50 ms
```

```
 Required echo rx interval: 0 ms, multiplier: 3, diag: None
 My discr: 2210463750, your discr: 2147487763, state UP, D/F/P/C/A: 0/0/0/1/0
Timer Values:
 Local negotiated async tx interval: 50 ms
 Remote negotiated async tx interval: 50 ms
 Desired echo tx interval: 0 s, local negotiated echo tx interval: 0 ms
 Echo detection time: 0 ms(0 ms*3), async detection time: 150 ms(50 ms*3)
Local Stats:
 Intervals between async packets:
   Tx: Number of intervals=6, min=1 ms, max=19 s, avg=5292 ms
       Last packet transmitted 19615 s ago
   Rx: Number of intervals=7, min=47 ms, max=14 s, avg=2981 ms
       Last packet received 19625 s ago
 Intervals between echo packets:
   Tx: Number of intervals=0, min=0 s, max=0 s, avg=0 s
       Last packet transmitted 0 s ago
   Rx: Number of intervals=0, min=0 s, max=0 s, avg=0 s
       Last packet received 0 s ago
 Latency of echo packets (time between tx and rx):
   Number of packets: 0, min=0 ms, max=0 ms, avg=0 ms
Session owner information:
                         Desired              Adjusted
  Client         Interval  Multiplier  Interval   Multiplier
  ------------------ --------------------- ---------------------
  bundlemgr_distrib  50 ms      3          50 ms      3
Session association information:
  Interface        Dest Addr / Type
  ------------------ ------------------------------------
  BE1              fe80::1003
                   BFD_SESSION_SUBTYPE_RTR_BUNDLE_INTERFACE

H/W Offload Info:
 H/W Offload capability : Y, Hosted NPU     : 0/0/CPU0
 Async Offloaded        : Y, Echo Offloaded : N
 Async rx/tx            : 14/16

RP/0/RP0/CPU0:PE-1#
```

In most scenarios, configuring a BoB implementation would be sufficient for fast failure detection, but in some instances, BoB is not supported. In such instances, a BFD over Logical Bundle (BLB) implementation may be configured.

BFD BLB Configuration

Figure 9-3 shows BFD over Logical Bundle (BLB) configured between routers PE-1 (IOS XR) and P-3 (IOS XE) from the SR-MPLS reference network in Appendix A, "Reference Diagrams and Information."

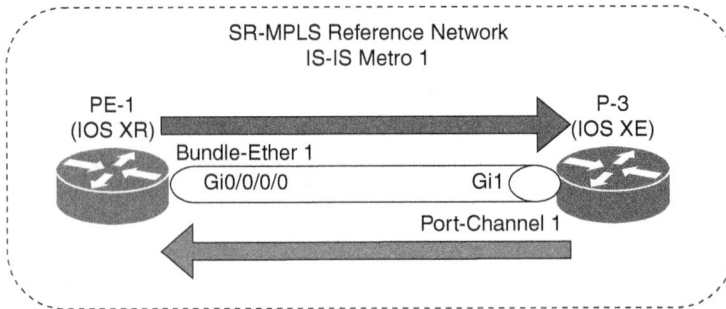

Figure 9-3   *BFD BLB Core Bundle-Ethernet Interface on PE-1 and P-3*

The following configuration examples are for BLB, and there is once again a requirement for LAG configurations between the routers PE-1 and P-3 in the IS-IS Metro 1 of the SR-MPLS reference network. In Config 9-5, the GigabitEthernet0/0/0/0 interface is designated as a member of the Bundle-Ether1 interface on the PE-1 router (an IOS XR router).

Config 9-5   *Bundle-Ethernet Interface Configuration on PE-1 (IOS XR)*

```
!
interface Bundle-Ether1
 description Connected_to_P-3
 ipv4 address 192.168.3.0 255.255.255.254
!
interface GigabitEthernet0/0/0/0
 description Connected_to_P-3
 bundle id 1 mode active
!
```

On router P-3 (an IOS XE router), the interface GigabitEthernet1 is allocated as a member of Port-channel1, as shown in Config 9-6.

Config 9-6   *Port-Channel Interface Configuration on P-3 (IOS XE)*

```
!
interface Port-channel1
 description Connected_to_PE-1
 ip address 192.168.3.1 255.255.255.254
```

```
!
interface GigabitEthernet1
 description Connected_to_PE-1
 channel-group 1 mode active
!
```

The BLB configuration tasks shown in Config 9-7 and Config 9-8 illustrate a typical use case where the requirement is for BFD over Bundle single-hop fast failure detection. Config 9-7 shows the relevant IOS XR BLB configurations on router PE-1, with the following information highlighted:

■ **bfd multipath include location 0/0/CPU0:** Multipath must be configured to allow BLB to operate. On a multi-line card chassis, the location can include one or more of these command lines.

■ **router isis METRO1 interface Bundle-Ether1 bfd fast-detect ipv4:** This line configures BFD BLB under the IS-IS protocol.

■ **router isis METRO1 interface Bundle-Ether1 bfd minimum-interval 2000:** This line configures the minimum interval period, in milliseconds, between the BFD async packets transmitted onto the Bundle-Ethernet interface member link.

■ **router isis METRO1 interface Bundle-Ether1 bfd multiplier 3:** This is the multiplier used with the minimum interval to calculate the BFD control packet failure detection times. The BFD failure detection time in this configuration is 6000 ms.

Config 9-7   *BFD over Logical Bundle Configuration on PE-1 (IOS XR)*

```
!
bfd
!
 multipath include location 0/0/CPU0
!
router isis METRO1
 interface Bundle-Ether1
  circuit-type level-2-only
  bfd minimum-interval 2000
  bfd multiplier 3
  bfd fast-detect ipv4
  point-to-point
  address-family ipv4 unicast
  !
 !
!
```

The router P-3 (an IOS XE router) BLB configurations from Config 9-8 are as follows:

- **bfd-template single-hop SH-BFD:** The BFD template SH-BFD is configured in this example, allowing this configuration to be implemented over multiple interfaces.

- **interval min-tx 2000 min-rx 2000 multiplier 3:** The BFD interval time and multiplier value are configured for this template.

- **bfd template SH-BFD:** The BFD template SH-BFD is applied under the Port-channel1 interface.

- **isis bfd:** This implements BFD support for the IS-IS routing protocol across the Port-channel1 interface.

Config 9-8 *BFD over Logical Bundle Configuration on P-3 (IOS XE)*

```
!
bfd-template single-hop SH-BFD
 interval min-tx 2000 min-rx 2000 multiplier 3
!
interface Port-channel1
 ip address 192.168.3.1 255.255.255.254
 ip router isis METRO1
 bfd template SH-BFD
 isis circuit-type level-2-only
 isis network point-to-point
 isis bfd
!
```

BFD BLB Verification

The BFC BLB operational verification and troubleshooting commands are similar to those described previously for IPv6 BFD BoB. The **show bfd session** command in Output 9-4 provides the status overview of all IPv4 BFD sessions configured on router PE-1. In this example, note the following details:

- **Interface BE1:** This is an IPv4 BLB implementation because the BFD session is active on the Bundle-Ether1 interface rather than on all members of the Bundle-Ethernet interface.

- **Dest Addr:** This is the BFD IPv4 session destination address, which is not explicitly configured because the BLB implementation is configured under the IS-IS routing protocol interface in this example.

- **Echo 0s(0s*0):** BFD echo mode is not enabled.

- **Async 6s(2s*3):** Keep in mind that Interval Period × Multiplier = Failure Detection Time.

- **H/W No:** BFD is not offloaded to dedicated hardware resources.

- **State UP:** The status of the BFD session is Up.

Output 9-4 *BFD Global IPv4 Session on PE-1 (IOS XR)*

```
RP/0/RP0/CPU0:PE-1#show bfd session
Interface          Dest Addr          Local det time(int*mult)     State
                                      Echo             Async   H/W  NPU
------------------ ---------------- ---------------- ---------------- ----------
BE1                192.168.3.1      0s(0s*0)         6s(2s*3)          UP
                                                              No    n/a
RP/0/RP0/CPU0:PE-1#
```

The BFD BLB session details are retrieved with the command **show bfd session interface bundle-ether 1 detail**, as shown in Output 9-5:

- **Session type: SW/V4/SH/BL:** This field provides useful information about the BFD session implementation.

  - **SW:** This indicates a switched session, or multipath, and is associated with the BLB implementation.

  - **V4:** This indicates an IPv4 implementation.

  - **SH:** This indicates a BFD single-hop session.

  - **BL:** This indicates a BLB implementation.

- **Received parameters:** This section shows the peer router's configured interval period, multiplier value, and echo intervals, if supported.

- **Transmitted parameters:** This section shows the local router's configured interval period, multiplier value, and echo intervals, if supported.

- **Timer Values:** This section shows details of the negotiated timer values exchanged and agreed upon between local and peer routers. If there is a difference between these exchanged parameters, the negotiated and agreed values are based on the upper value.

- **MP download state: BFD_MP_DOWNLOAD_ACK:** This indicates a multipath session.

- **Session owner information:**

  - **Client isis-METRO1:** This indicates that the IS-IS protocol process is a client of BFD.

Output 9-5 *BFD Bundle-Ethernet Session Detail on PE-1 (IOS XR)*

```
RP/0/RP0/CPU0:PE-1#show bfd session interface bundle-ether 1 detail

I/f: Bundle-Ether1, Location: 0/0/CPU0
Dest: 192.168.3.1
Src: 192.168.3.0
 State: UP for 0d:8h:36m:3s, number of times UP: 1
 Session type: SW/V4/SH/BL
Received parameters:
 Version: 1, desired tx interval: 2 s, required rx interval: 2 s
 Required echo rx interval: 0 ms, multiplier: 3, diag: None
 My discr: 4097, your discr: 65537, state UP, D/F/P/C/A: 0/0/0/0/0
Transmitted parameters:
 Version: 1, desired tx interval: 2 s, required rx interval: 2 s
 Required echo rx interval: 0 ms, multiplier: 3, diag: None
 My discr: 65537, your discr: 4097, state UP, D/F/P/C/A: 0/0/0/1/0
Timer Values:
 Local negotiated async tx interval: 2 s
 Remote negotiated async tx interval: 2 s
 Desired echo tx interval: 0 s, local negotiated echo tx interval: 0 ms
 Echo detection time: 0 ms(0 ms*3), async detection time: 6 s(2 s*3)
Label:
 Internal label: 24014/0x5dce
Local Stats:
 Intervals between async packets:
   Tx: Number of intervals=100, min=1662 ms, max=1999 ms, avg=1825 ms
       Last packet transmitted 791 ms ago
   Rx: Number of intervals=100, min=1509 ms, max=2001 ms, avg=1785 ms
       Last packet received 1065 ms ago
 Intervals between echo packets:
   Tx: Number of intervals=0, min=0 s, max=0 s, avg=0 s
       Last packet transmitted 0 s ago
   Rx: Number of intervals=0, min=0 s, max=0 s, avg=0 s
       Last packet received 0 s ago
 Latency of echo packets (time between tx and rx):
   Number of packets: 0, min=0 ms, max=0 ms, avg=0 ms
MP download state: BFD_MP_DOWNLOAD_ACK
State change time: Jan 21 02:25:11.987
Session owner information:
                          Desired               Adjusted
  Client          Interval  Multiplier  Interval  Multiplier
  ----------------  ----------  ----------  ----------  ----------
  isis-METRO1        2 s        3          2 s        3

RP/0/RP0/CPU0:PE-1#
```

As shown in Output 9-6, on router P-3 (IOS XE), the command **show bfd neighbors** provides a status overview of the IPv4 BFD sessions on this specific router. In this output, note the following details:

- **NeighAddr:** 192.168.3.0 is the source address of the router PE-1.

- **LD/RD:** The local discriminator (LD) and remote discriminator (RD) match the My discr: 65537 and your discr: 4097 values on the PE-1 router.

- **RH/RS:** The remote heard (RH) and remote state (RS) indicate that a BFD control packet has been received from the peer router, and the session state is Up.

- **State Up:** The BFD state is Up.

- **Int:** The BFD session is seen on the Port-channel1 interface.

Output 9-6 *BFD Global Session Verification on P-3 (IOS XE)*

```
P-3#show bfd neighbors

IPv4 Sessions
NeighAddr                       LD/RD         RH/RS     State     Int
192.168.3.0                     4097/65537    Up        Up        Po1
P-3#
```

The per-interface command **show bfd neighbors interface port-channel 1 details** provides additional relevant output regarding this BLB session, as shown from router P-3's perspective in Output 9-7:

- **MinTxInt: 2000000, MinRxInt: 2000000, Multiplier:3:** These are the interval timer and multiplier configured on the local router.

- **Received MinRxInt: 2000000, Received Multiplier:3:** These are the interval timer and multiplier received from the peer router.

- **Registered protocols: ISIS CEF:** These protocols are registered with BFD.

- **Last Packet:** Information from the BFD control packet is received from the peer router PE-1. (Refer to Example 9-1 for an explanation of the message flags in this output.)

Output 9-7 *BFD Port Channel Session Detail on P-3 (IOS XE)*

```
P-3#show bfd neighbors interface port-channel 1 details

IPv4 Sessions
NeighAddr                       LD/RD         RH/RS     State     Int
192.168.3.0                     4097/65537    Up        Up        Po1
```

```
Session state is UP and not using echo function.
Session Host: Hardware
OurAddr: 192.168.3.1
Handle: 2
Local Diag: 0, Demand mode: 0, Poll bit: 0
MinTxInt: 2000000, MinRxInt: 2000000, Multiplier: 3
Received MinRxInt: 2000000, Received Multiplier: 3
Holddown (hits): 0(0), Hello (hits): 2000(0)
Rx Count: 1978, Rx Interval (ms) min/max/avg: 1459/1999/2039
Tx Count: 1993, Tx Interval (ms) min/max/avg: 1574/1998/2010
Elapsed time watermarks: 0 0 (last: 0)
Registered protocols: ISIS CEF
Template: SH-BFD
Uptime: 01:00:28
Last packet: Version: 1            - Diagnostic: 0
             State bit: Up         - Demand bit: 0
             Poll bit: 0           - Final bit: 0
             C bit: 1
             Multiplier: 3         - Length: 24
             My Discr.: 65537      - Your Discr.: 4097
             Min tx interval: 2000000 - Min rx interval: 2000000
             Min Echo interval: 0
P-3#
```

Topology-Independent Loop-Free Alternate (TI-LFA)

In the early 2000s, network operators and product vendors came to the realization that as traffic loss–sensitive data services such as voice over IP (VoIP) and IPTV became more prevalent across IP networks, routing protocol convergence times during failure conditions were not able to provide adequate fast reroute times. Routing protocols such as IS-IS and OSPF were then configured with shorter hello intervals to allow for faster network convergence, but in many cases, these modifications led to increased CPU utilization and, potentially, additional network instability. Fundamentally, any type of convergence computation carried out in response to a detected failure condition will be insufficiently fast.

The pursuit of rapid network convergence has given rise to several fast reroute mechanisms. For instance, RSVP-TE and its fast reroute (FRR) capabilities offer a solution but also add considerable complexity for operators who are not concerned with the traffic engineering (TE) component of RSVP-TE. A mechanism known as IP Fast Reroute (IPFRR) allows a router, also known as a point of local repair (PLR), to preprogram a Loop-Free Alternate (LFA) path onto which it can rapidly switch traffic in the event of a link or peer router failure. This IPFRR mechanism allows networks to achieve sub-50 ms convergence times by switching traffic onto the precomputed paths in the event of network failure detection.

In Figure 9-4, the link between routers P-1 and P-3 is protected by a precomputed backup path from router P-1 to router P-3 via router P-4. IPFRR can calculate the LFA paths either on a per-link or per-prefix basis. In the per-link-based LFA computation, all the prefixes routed via the protected link will share the preprogrammed LFA path. The per-prefix calculation computes an LFA path for each prefix, potentially resulting in multiple preprogrammed LFA paths. The LFA calculation, as per RFC 5286, is based on the following formula:

> Distance(Neighbor, Destination) < Distance(Neighbor, PLR) + Distance(PLR, Destination)

Where the following is applicable in the formula:

- Distance is the shortest interior gateway protocol (IGP) metric between routers. For example, the shortest distance from router P-1 to router ABR-3 has a metric of 30.

- PLR is the point of local repair. For the link between routers P-1 and P-3 to destination ABR-3, P-1 is the PLR.

- Neighbor is the adjacent neighbor router to the PLR.

- Destination is the endpoint the LFA calculation is based on.

When applying the LFA calculation in Figure 9-4, where P-1 is the PLR, ABR-3 is the destination, and router P-2 is the evaluated neighbor:

> Distance(P-2, ABR-3) < Distance(P-2, P-1) + Distance(P-1, ABR-3)

This is the result:

> 45 < 10 + 30

This is a failure. Router P-2 is therefore not an LFA candidate for the destination ABR-3.

In the next iteration of the LFA calculation, P-1 is the PLR, ABR-3 is the destination, and router P-4 is the evaluated neighbor:

> Distance(P-4, ABR-3) < Distance(P-4, P-1) + Distance(P-1, ABR-3)

This is the result:

> 25 < 30 + 30

This is a success. Router P-4 is an LFA candidate for the destination ABR-3.

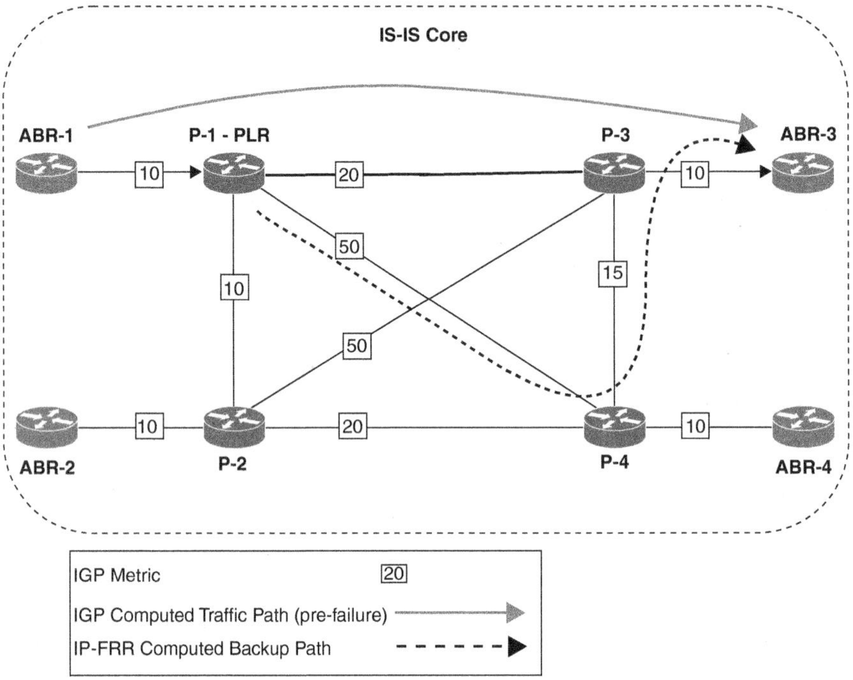

Figure 9-4   *IP Fast Reroute Loop-Free Alternate Pre-Failure*

IPFRR has disadvantages, as you can see in Figure 9-4, where the precomputed backup path is suboptimal in that once the IGP has converged, the traffic will be rerouted onto the path with the lower end-to-end metric. The precomputed LFA backup path to router ABR-3 in this example has a metric of 75 (50 + 15 + 10), while in Figure 9-5, the traffic flows over the post-convergence IGP path with a metric of 55 (10 + 20 + 15 + 10). To summarize, in the event of a link failure between routers P-1 and P-3, traffic will flow across the suboptimal path until the IGP has converged.

Another disadvantage of IPFRR is that it is dependent on the network topology and most likely will not be able to provide an LFA path for all destinations without traffic passing over the protected link. This disadvantage led to the development of the Remote Loop-Free Alternate (RLFA) FRR feature (RFC 7490). RLFA can be used in network topologies when a local LFA path is not available and is achieved by locating the candidate RLFA router, which is able to reach protected prefixes without passing over the protected link. The PLR establishes a label-switched path (LSP) via a targeted LDP (tLDP) session to the RLFA router, over which traffic can be tunneled when a failure event occurs. Once again, the LFA calculation applies when determining the candidate RLFA router:

Distance(Remote-Neighbor, Destination) < Distance(Remote-Neighbor, PLR) + Distance(PLR, Destination)

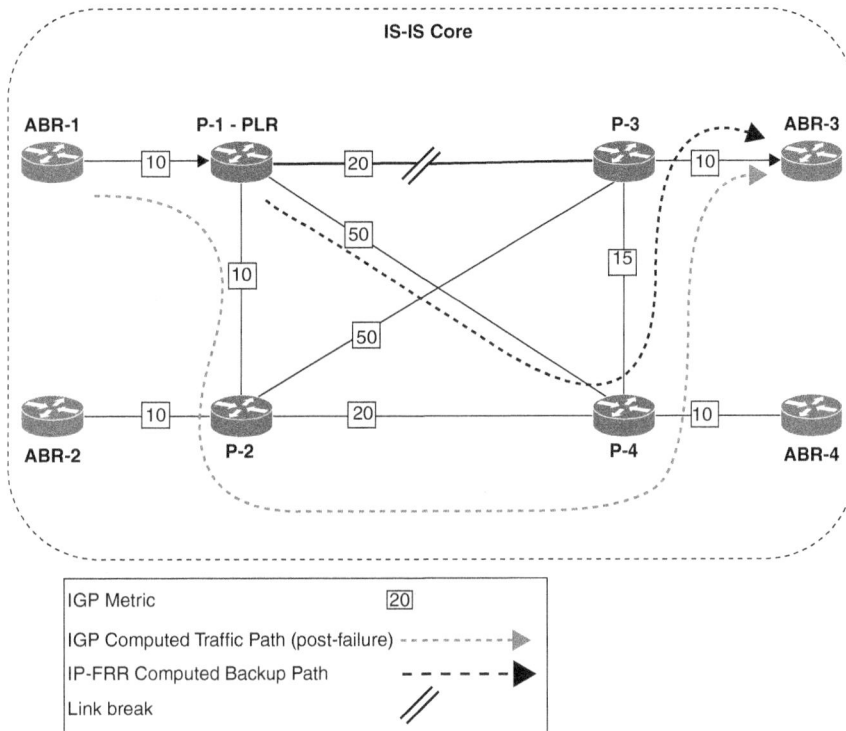

Figure 9-5   *IP Fast Reroute Loop-Free Alternate Post-Failure*

In order for the PLR router to determine the possible candidate RLFA routers, the P-space and Q-space are determined, where:

- **P-space:** This is the set of routers that are reachable from the PLR without the traffic traversing the protected link.

- **Extended P-space:** This is the set of routers that are reachable from the PLR's neighbors without the traffic traversing the protected link. It increases the selection of candidate RLFA routers.

- **Q-space:** This is the set of routers that can reach the destination without the traffic traversing the protected link.

- **PQ node:** This is the RLFA router that lies within both the P-space and the Q-space.

In the network shown in Figure 9-6, router P-1 has no local LFA protecting the destination ABR-3 from a link failure between routers P-1 and P-3. If P-1 forwards traffic to P-2, a portion of the traffic is forwarded back to router P-1 due to the ECMP path on R-2 toward ABR-3 causing a traffic loop situation. The deployment of the RLFA feature on router P-1 will allow for the location of potential candidate RLFA routers to overcome this scenario.

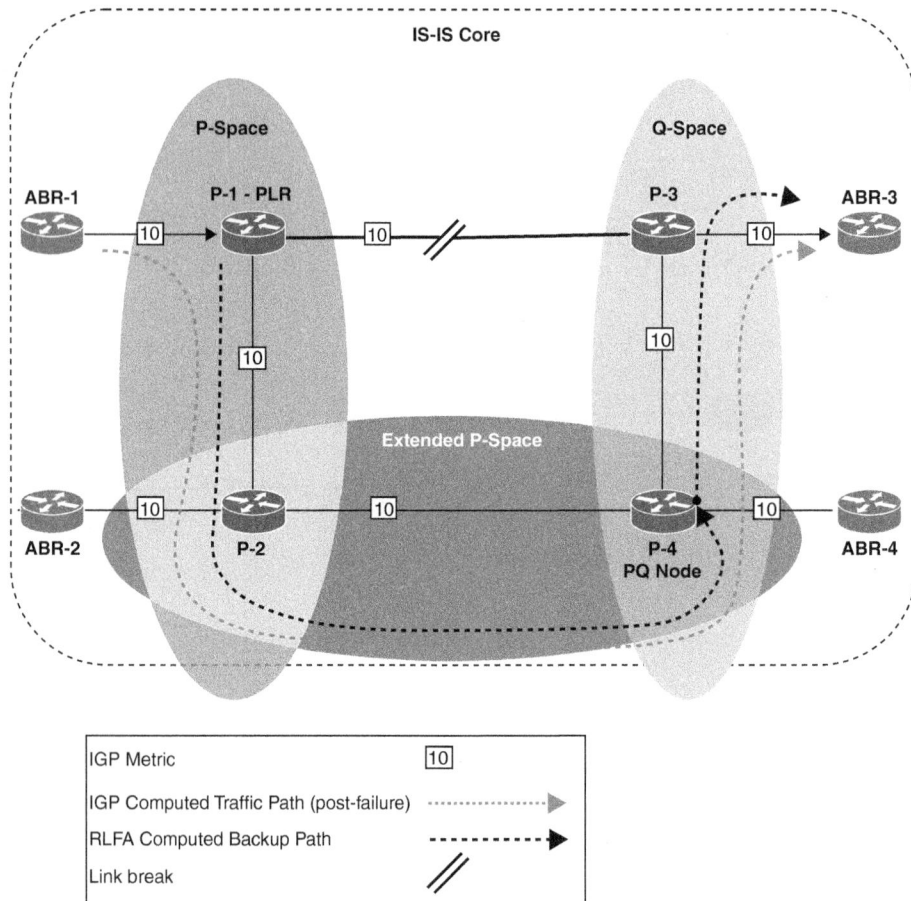

Figure 9-6 *Remote LFA Fast Reroute Overview*

The PLR router P-1 calculates the Q-space for the protected link P-1 to P-3 toward the destination ABR-3. The Q-space routers will include routers P-4 and P-3, which are able to reach the destination without the traffic traversing the protected link. The PLR router P-1 will also calculate the P-space for the protected link P-1 to P-3 toward the destination ABR-3, and in this case, the router P-2 is a candidate as it is reachable from the PLR without the traffic traversing the protected link. In addition, the extended P-space is calculated, which in this case is the set of routers that are reachable from the PLR's neighbor router P-2, without the traffic traversing the protected link. This extended P-space will therefore also include the router P-4. Finally, any routers contained within the area where the extended P-space and the Q-space merge are known as PQ routers. In this example, the router P-4 fits the profile and therefore is the selected PQ router. Router P-1 establishes a tLDP session to router P-4, over which traffic can be tunneled to the destination on ABR-3 when a failure event occurs. RLFA substantially increases the LFA protection in a network compared to the use of local LFA only, but it does require that RLFA candidate routers allow for the termination of tLDP sessions, and it cannot provide 100% protection coverage.

The emergence of segment routing has brought about an enhanced LFA feature that greatly eases a network operator's ability to deploy comprehensive network availability mechanisms. This feature, known as Topology-Independent Loop-Free Alternate (TI-LFA), can be implemented as part of the Day 0 SR configurations in a network rollout. With TI-LFA, the repair path to protect a destination against the failure is also the post-convergence path when the failure occurs, and it is therefore the shortest path to the destination once the failure event has occurred in the topology. The TI-LFA PLR encodes this post-convergence path as a list of segments, or a label stack; in the event that the FRR mechanism is activated, the appropriate label stack is pushed onto the repaired traffic.

TI-LFA provides 100% LFA protection coverage for link, router, and shared risk link group (SRLG) failures. An example of an SRLG is network circuits sharing a single fiber or fiber duct; if the fiber or fiber duct is compromised, all network circuits are impacted simultaneously. TI-LFA mitigates the potential of suboptimal backup paths by calculating an LFA path that the IGP protocol will also ultimately converge to. The major benefit of the precomputed TI-LFA backup path following the IGP post-convergence path is that the network operator will already have designed the post-convergence paths with the correct traffic dimensions factored in.

TI-LFA can be configured on a per-PLR basis, and it can include several LFA protection selections:

- Link protection
- Node protection
- SRLG protection

Next, we will look at TI-LFA configuration and verification in both SR-MPLS and SRv6 networks.

Link Protection Configuration

The TI-LFA link protection configuration for IOS XR routers in the SR-MPLS reference network are implemented using the configuration commands shown in Config 9-9.

Config 9-9   *TI-LFA Link Protection: SR-MPLS (IOS XR)*

```
!
router isis CORE1
!
 interface GigabitEthernet0/0/0/1
  address-family ipv4 unicast
   fast-reroute per-prefix
   fast-reroute per-prefix ti-lfa
  !
 !
```

The command **show isis fast-reroute summary** in Output 9-8 is useful for providing a network-wide summary overview of the FRR state from the perspective of the PLR router. From the output, you can see that there is a single medium priority route that is unprotected: The router ABR-2 is directly attached to router P-2, and there are no alternate paths that could be used as backup paths. By default, the IOS XR routers set originated /32 routes (usually the loopback interface) with a medium priority designation and the remainder to low priority, but there is an option to associate a user-defined tag to an IS-IS interface, which is then matched on peer routers in order to set their RIB import priority. IS-IS can be configured to select which route priority the TI-LFA mechanism will use for LFA computation. Although this behavior is not discussed in the following configuration tasks, it is useful in cases where the IGP route scale is large, and the operator would prefer to prioritize protected prefix computation.

Output 9-8   *TI-LFA Protection Summary on P-2 (IOS XR)*

```
RP/0/RP0/CPU0:P-2#show isis fast-reroute summary

IS-IS CORE1 IPv4 Unicast FRR summary

                          Critical   High       Medium     Low        Total
                          Priority   Priority   Priority   Priority
Prefixes reachable in L2
  All paths protected     0          0          9          12         21
  Some paths protected    0          0          0          0          0
  Unprotected             0          0          1          0          1
  Protection coverage     0.00%      0.00%      90.00%     100.00%    95.45%
RP/0/RP0/CPU0:P-2#
```

The TI-LFA link protection configuration for IOS XR routers in the SRv6 reference network is implemented using the same commands that are used for the SR-MPLS routers, but in this case these configuration commands are issued under the IPv6 address family, as shown in Config 9-10.

Config 9-10   *TI-LFA Link Protection (IOS XR)*

```
!
router isis CORE_1
!
interface GigabitEthernet0/0/0/0
  address-family ipv6 unicast
   fast-reroute per-prefix
   fast-reroute per-prefix ti-lfa
  !
 !
```

For IOS XE routers in the SR-MPLS reference network, the TI-LFA link protection configuration may be enabled for all interfaces under the IS-IS global router configuration, as shown in Config 9-11. In this example, IS-IS Level 2 is selected because the router is functioning as an IS-IS Level 2 device only.

Config 9-11 *TI-LFA Link Protection: Global Configuration (IOS XE)*

```
!
router isis CORE1
 fast-reroute per-prefix level-2 all
 fast-reroute ti-lfa level-2
 !
```

Alternatively, the IOS XE TI-LFA link protection configuration may be enabled for selected interfaces, as shown in Config 9-12.

Config 9-12 *TI-LFA Link Protection: Interface Configuration (IOS XE)*

```
!
interface GigabitEthernet1
 isis fast-reroute protection level-2
 isis fast-reroute ti-lfa level-2
 !
```

Link Protection Verification: SR-MPLS

Now we will examine various TI-LFA link protection scenarios within SR-MPLS networks, including zero-segment, single-segment, and double-segment cases. In this section, the TI-LFA verification focuses on the IOS XR router P-2 in the SR-MPLS network shown in Figure 9-7. Note the following in this configuration:

- **PLR:** Router P-2 is the PLR.

- **Repair node:** Router P-5 is adjacent to the PLR.

- **Destination:** Router ABR-4 has the IP address 10.0.1.8/32 and Prefix SID 16008.

- **Protected link:** {P-2 > P-1} via GigabitEthernet0/0/0/1 is the protected link.

- **Post-convergence path:** {P-5 > P-4 > ABR-4} via GigabitEthernet0/0/0/4 is the post-convergence path.

- **P-space:** P-5 is in the P-space because router P-2 can forward traffic to it without passing over the {P-2 > P-1} protected link.

- **Q-space:** P-5 is in the Q-space because it can forward traffic to the destination 10.0.1.8/32 without passing over the {P-2 > P-1} protected link.

- **Segments = 0:** Router P-2 can forward traffic directly to P-5 without an additional SID.

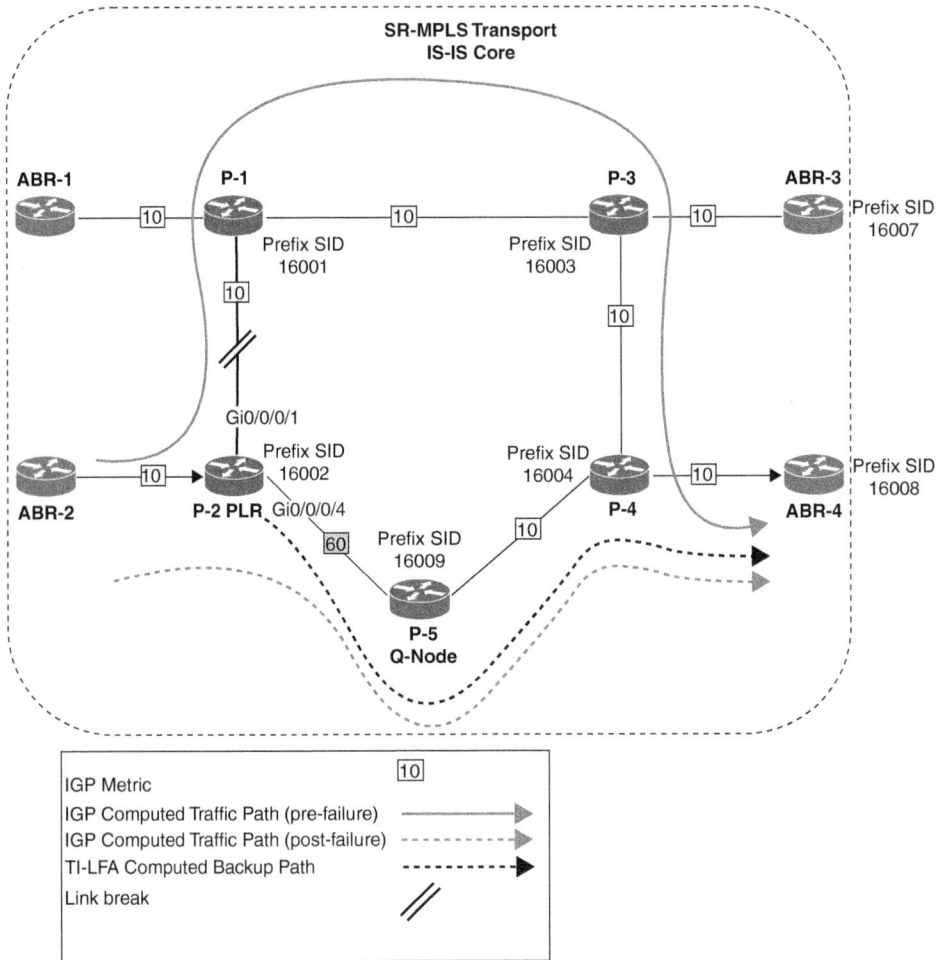

Figure 9-7   *Adjacent Zero-Segment TI-LFA Repair Node: SR-MPLS*

The **show route 10.0.1.8/32** command in Output 9-9 displays the protected link as GigabitEthernet0/0/0/1 with a metric of 40; the backup link is via GigabitEthernet0/0/0/4 with a metric of 80.

Output 9-9   *Zero-Segment TI-LFA RIB Backup Path: SR-MPLS on P-2 (IOS XR)*

```
RP/0/RP0/CPU0:P-2#show route 10.0.1.8/32

Routing entry for 10.0.1.8/32
  Known via "isis CORE1", distance 115, metric 40, labeled SR, type level-2
  Installed Feb 18 03:32:45.086 for 01:10:24
```

```
   Routing Descriptor Blocks
      192.168.1.101, from 10.0.1.8, via GigabitEthernet0/0/0/4, Backup (Local-LFA)
        Route metric is 80
      192.168.1.2, from 10.0.1.8, via GigabitEthernet0/0/0/1, Protected
        Route metric is 40
   No advertising protos.
RP/0/RP0/CPU0:P-2#
```

The TI-LFA backup path is shown in Output 9-10. This is a zero-segment TI-LFA backup path because the traffic is forwarded via the direct neighbor router P-5 with no additional SIDs; only the destination Prefix SID 16008 is required.

Output 9-10 *Zero-Segment TI-LFA IS-IS Fast Reroute Detail: SR-MPLS on P-2 (IOS XR)*

```
RP/0/RP0/CPU0:P-2#show isis ipv4 fast-reroute 10.0.1.8/32 detail

L2 10.0.1.8/32 [40/115] Label: 16008, medium priority
   Installed Feb 18 03:32:45.086 for 01:12:01
     via 192.168.1.2, GigabitEthernet0/0/0/1, Label: 16008, P-1, SRGB Base: 16000,
   Weight: 0
      Backup path: LFA, via 192.168.1.101, GigabitEthernet0/0/0/4, Label: 16008,
   P-5, SRGB Base: 16000, Weight: 0, Metric: 80
        P: No, TM: 80, LC: No, NP: Yes, D: Yes, SRLG: Yes
      src ABR-4.00-00, 10.0.1.8, prefix-SID index 8, R:0 N:1 P:0 E:0 V:0 L:0, Alg:0
RP/0/RP0/CPU0:P-2#
```

The FIB output from the command **show cef 10.0.1.8/32** in Output 9-11 verifies that no additional SIDs are required for traffic that may be forwarded across the TI-LFA computed backup path in the event that the protected link {P-2 > P-1} fails.

Output 9-11 *Zero-Segment TI-LFA FIB Backup Path: SR-MPLS on P-2 (IOS XR)*

```
RP/0/RP0/CPU0:P-2#show cef 10.0.1.8/32

10.0.1.8/32, version 2950, labeled SR, internal 0x1000001 0x8110 (ptr 0xe899c48)
  [1], 0x600 (0xe262698), 0xa28 (0x22cc8178)
 Updated Feb 18 03:32:45.090
 remote adjacency to GigabitEthernet0/0/0/1
 Prefix Len 32, traffic index 0, precedence n/a, priority 1
  gateway array (0xe0ccbe0) reference count 18, flags 0x500068, source rib (7), 0
  backups
             [7 type 5 flags 0x8401 (0xf4c5608) ext 0x0 (0x0)]
  LW-LDI[type=5, refc=3, ptr=0xe262698, sh-ldi=0xf4c5608]
```

```
  gateway array update type-time 1 Feb 18 03:32:45.089
 LDI Update time Feb 18 03:32:45.089
 LW-LDI-TS Feb 18 03:32:45.090
   via 192.168.1.101/32, GigabitEthernet0/0/0/4, 9 dependencies, weight 0, class 0,
 backup (Local-LFA) [flags 0x300]
    path-idx 0 NHID 0x0 [0x1be075b0 0x0]
    next hop 192.168.1.101/32
    remote adjacency
      local label 16008      labels imposed {16008}
   via 192.168.1.2/32, GigabitEthernet0/0/0/1, 8 dependencies, weight 0, class 0,
 protected [flags 0x400]
    path-idx 1 bkup-idx 0 NHID 0x0 [0xde77af0 0x0]
    next hop 192.168.1.2/32
     local label 16008      labels imposed {16008}


   Load distribution: 0 (refcount 7)


   Hash  OK  Interface               Address
   0     Y   GigabitEthernet0/0/0/1  remote
 RP/0/RP0/CPU0:P-2#
```

If the PLR router in Figure 9-7 is IOS XE based, the commands shown next may be used
to verify the TI-LFA behavior. Output 9-12 verifies that the route to router ABR-4 has a
repair path via the interface GigabitEthernet4 with a metric of 80, and the forwarding SID
is 16008.

Output 9-12   *Zero-Segment TI-LFA RIB Backup Path: SR-MPLS on P-2 (IOS XE)*

```
P-2#show ip route repair-paths 10.0.1.8 255.255.255.255
Routing entry for 10.0.1.8/32
  Known via "isis", distance 115, metric 40, type level-2
  Redistributing via isis CORE1
  Last update from 192.168.1.2 on GigabitEthernet1, 00:19:35 ago
 SR Incoming Label: 16008
  Routing Descriptor Blocks:
  * 192.168.1.2, from 10.0.1.8, 00:19:35 ago, via GigabitEthernet1, prefer-non-
  rib-labels, merge-labels
      Route metric is 40, traffic share count is 1
      MPLS label: 16008
      MPLS Flags: NSF
      Repair Path: 192.168.1.101, via GigabitEthernet4
     [RPR]192.168.1.101, from 10.0.1.8, 00:19:35 ago, via GigabitEthernet4,
  prefer-non-rib-labels, merge-labels
```

```
      Route metric is 80, traffic share count is 1
      MPLS label: 16008
      MPLS Flags: NSF
P-2#
```

And much as with the IOS XR router, the FIB output from the command **show ip cef 10.0.1.8 internal** in Output 9-13 confirms that no additional SIDs are required for traffic that may be forwarded across the TI-LFA computed backup path {P-5 > P-4 > ABR-4} via interface GigabitEthernet4 in the event that the protected link {P-2 > P-1} fails.

Output 9-13 *Zero-Segment TI-LFA FIB Backup Path: SR-MPLS on P-2 (IOS XE)*

```
P-2#show ip cef 10.0.1.8 internal
10.0.1.8/32, epoch 2, RIB[I], refcnt 6, per-destination sharing
  sources: RIB, LTE
  feature space:
    IPRM: 0x00028000
    Broker: linked, distributed at 4th priority
    LFD: 10.0.1.8/32 1 local label
    sr local label info: global/16008 [0x1B]
        contains path extension list
        sr disposition chain 0x7FE146CE4AC0
          label 16008
          FRR Primary
            <primary: TAG adj out of GigabitEthernet1, addr 192.168.1.2>
        sr label switch chain 0x7FE146CE4AC0
          label 16008
          FRR Primary
            <primary: TAG adj out of GigabitEthernet1, addr 192.168.1.2>
  ifnums:
    GigabitEthernet1(7): 192.168.1.2
    GigabitEthernet4(10): 192.168.1.101
  path list 7FE116577230, 41 locks, per-destination, flags 0x4D [shble, hvsh, rif,
hwcn]
    path 7FE141432B28, share 1/1, type attached nexthop, for IPv4, flags [has-rpr]
      MPLS short path extensions: [rib | prfmfi | lblmrg | srlbl] MOI flags = 0x21
label 16008
      nexthop 192.168.1.2 GigabitEthernet1 label [16008|16008]-(local:16008), IP adj
out of GigabitEthernet1, addr 192.168.1.2 7FE1414F1BA0
        repair: attached-nexthop 192.168.1.101 GigabitEthernet4 (7FE141432BF8)
    path 7FE141432BF8, share 1/1, type attached nexthop, for IPv4, flags [rpr,
rpr-only]
```

```
      MPLS short path extensions: [rib | prfmfi | lblmrg | srlbl] MOI flags = 0x1
label 16008
      nexthop 192.168.1.101 GigabitEthernet4 label 16008-(local:16008), repair, IP
adj out of GigabitEthernet4, addr 192.168.1.101 7FE1414F1740
output chain:
  label [16008|16008]-(local:16008)
  FRR Primary (0x80007FE141483B78)
    <primary: TAG adj out of GigabitEthernet1, addr 192.168.1.2 7FE1414F1970>
    <repair:  TAG adj out of GigabitEthernet4, addr 192.168.1.101 7FE1414F1510>
P-2#
```

In the TI-LFA example shown in Figure 9-8, the repair node is in the extended P-space as well as in the Q-space. Note the following about the network shown in this figure:

- **PLR:** Router P-2 is the PLR.

- **Repair node:** Router P-4 is the PQ node.

- **Destination:** Router ABR-3 has IP address 10.0.1.7/32 and Prefix SID 16007.

- **Protected link:** {P-2 > P-1} via GigabitEthernet0/0/0/1 is the protected link.

- **Post-convergence path:** {P-5 > P-4 > P-3 > ABR-3} via GigabitEthernet0/0/0/4 is the post-convergence path.

- **P-space:** P-5 is a P-space router because P-2 can forward traffic to P-5 without passing over the {P-2 > P-1} link.

- **Extended P-space:** P-4 is in the extended P-space of P-2 because router P-5 can forward traffic to it without passing over the {P-2 > P-1} protected link.

- **Q-space:** P-4 is in the Q-space because it can forward traffic to the destination 10.0.1.7/32 without passing over the {P-2 > P-1} protected link.

- **Segments = 1:** Router P-2 can forward traffic to router ABR-3 along the backup path by pushing an additional segment Prefix SID 16004.

The command in Output 9-14 shows that the protected link is GigabitEthernet0/0/0/1 with a metric of 30, and the backup path is via GigabitEthernet0/0/0/4 to the repair node 10.0.1.4 (P-4). Router P-4 can reach the destination without passing over the protected link {P-2 > P-1}.

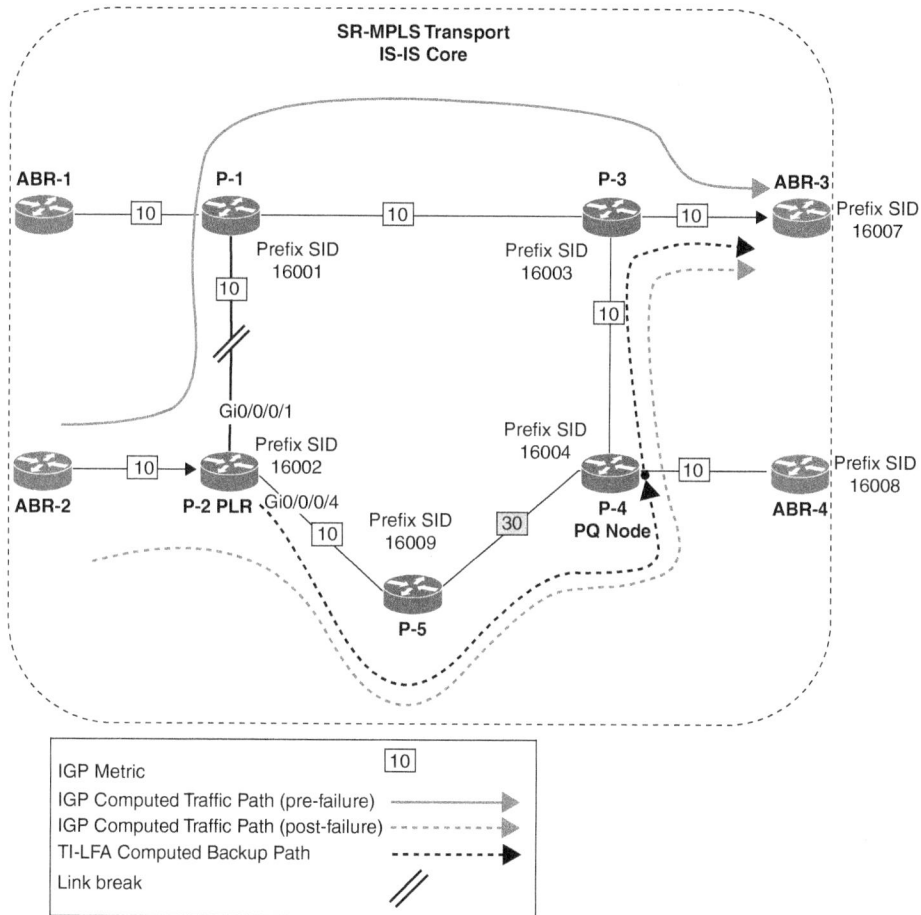

Figure 9-8 *Single-Segment TI-LFA PQ Node: SR-MPLS*

Output 9-14 *Single-Segment TI-LFA RIB Backup Path: SR-MPLS on P-2 (IOS XR)*

```
RP/0/RP0/CPU0:P-2#show route 10.0.1.7/32


Routing entry for 10.0.1.7/32
  Known via "isis CORE1", distance 115, metric 30, labeled SR, type level-2
  Installed Feb 20 11:00:22.427 for 01:22:45
  Routing Descriptor Blocks
    192.168.1.101, from 10.0.1.7, via GigabitEthernet0/0/0/4, Backup (TI-LFA)
      Repair Node(s): 10.0.1.4
      Route metric is 60
    192.168.1.2, from 10.0.1.7, via GigabitEthernet0/0/0/1, Protected
      Route metric is 30
  No advertising protos.
RP/0/RP0/CPU0:P-2#
```

Output 9-15 shows the TI-LFA backup path details. This is a single-segment TI-LFA backup path because the traffic is forwarded to router P-4 with initial Prefix SID 16004, and then it is forwarded on to the destination router ABR-3 with the Prefix SID 16007.

Output 9-15 *Single-Segment TI-LFA IS-IS Fast Reroute Detail: SR-MPLS on P-2 (IOS XR)*

```
RP/0/RP0/CPU0:P-2#show isis ipv4 fast-reroute 10.0.1.7/32 detail

L2 10.0.1.7/32 [30/115] Label: 16007, medium priority
   Installed Feb 20 11:00:22.426 for 01:43:20
      via 192.168.1.2, GigabitEthernet0/0/0/1, Label: 16007, P-1, SRGB Base: 16000,
   Weight: 0
         Backup path: TI-LFA (link), via 192.168.1.101, GigabitEthernet0/0/0/4 P-5,
   SRGB Base: 16000, Weight: 0, Metric: 60
            P node: P-4.00 [10.0.1.4], Label: 16004
         Prefix label: 16007
         Backup-src: ABR-3.00
         P: No, TM: 60, LC: No, NP: No, D: No, SRLG: Yes
      src ABR-3.00-00, 10.0.1.7, prefix-SID index 7, R:0 N:1 P:0 E:0 V:0 L:0, Alg:0
RP/0/RP0/CPU0:P-2#
```

The command in Output 9-16 shows that an additional SID is required for traffic that may be forwarded across the TI-LFA computed backup path to reach the repair node P-4 with Prefix SID 16004 in the event that the protected link {P-2 > P-1} fails, before being forwarded on to the final destination at router ABR-3 with Prefix SID 16007.

Output 9-16 *Single-Segment TI-LFA FIB Backup Path: SR-MPLS on P-2 (IOS XR)*

```
RP/0/RP0/CPU0:P-2#show cef 10.0.1.7/32

10.0.1.7/32, version 602, labeled SR, internal 0x1000001 0x8110 (ptr 0xe69ed20) [1],
   0x600 (0xd99c020), 0xa28 (0x22c1d8c8)
 Updated Feb 20 11:00:22.430
 remote adjacency to GigabitEthernet0/0/0/1
 Prefix Len 32, traffic index 0, precedence n/a, priority 1
  gateway array (0xd803f78) reference count 12, flags 0x500068, source rib (7), 0
  backups
              [5 type 5 flags 0x8401 (0xeba0888) ext 0x0 (0x0)]
  LW-LDI[type=5, refc=3, ptr=0xd99c020, sh-ldi=0xeba0888]
  gateway array update type-time 1 Feb 20 11:00:22.429
 LDI Update time Feb 20 11:00:22.430
 LW-LDI-TS Feb 20 11:00:22.430
   via 192.168.1.101/32, GigabitEthernet0/0/0/4, 10 dependencies,
  weight 0, class 0, backup (TI-LFA) [flags 0xb00]
```

```
    path-idx 0 NHID 0x0 [0xfd3a470 0x0]
    next hop 192.168.1.101/32, Repair Node(s): 10.0.1.4
    remote adjacency
     local label 16007      labels imposed {16004 16007}
   via 192.168.1.2/32, GigabitEthernet0/0/0/1, 8 dependencies, weight 0, class 0,
  protected [flags 0x400]
    path-idx 1 bkup-idx 0 NHID 0x0 [0xd5b1be0 0x0]
    next hop 192.168.1.2/32
     local label 16007      labels imposed {16007}


    Load distribution: 0 (refcount 5)


    Hash  OK  Interface             Address
    0     Y   GigabitEthernet0/0/0/1   remote
 RP/0/RP0/CPU0:P-2#
```

For IOS XE–based PLR routers, the commands discussed next may be used to verify the TI-LFA behavior. Output 9-17 confirms that the route to router ABR-3 has a TI-LFA repair tunnel MPLS-SR-Tunnel5 to the repair node P-4. From there, it can reach the destination router ABR-3 without traversing the protected link {P-2 > P-1}.

Output 9-17   *Single-Segment TI-LFA RIB Backup Path: SR-MPLS on P-2 (IOS XE)*

```
P-2#show ip route repair-paths 10.0.1.7 255.255.255.255
Routing entry for 10.0.1.7/32
  Known via "isis", distance 115, metric 30, type level-2
  Redistributing via isis CORE1
  Last update from 192.168.1.2 on GigabitEthernet1, 00:02:35 ago
 SR Incoming Label: 16007
  Routing Descriptor Blocks:
  * 192.168.1.2, from 10.0.1.7, 00:02:35 ago, via GigabitEthernet1,
 prefer-non-rib-labels, merge-labels
     Route metric is 30, traffic share count is 1
     MPLS label: 16007
     MPLS Flags: NSF
     Repair Path: 10.0.1.4, via MPLS-SR-Tunnel5
   [RPR]10.0.1.4, from 10.0.1.7, 00:02:35 ago, via MPLS-SR-Tunnel5, merge-labels
     Route metric is 40, traffic share count is 1
     MPLS label: 16007
     MPLS Flags: NSF
  P-2#
```

The **show isis fast-reroute ti-lfa tunnel** command in Output 9-18 provides an overview of the IS-IS TI-LFA tunnels from the perspective of the PLR router, with the tunnel MP5 to the endpoint router P-4 (10.0.1.4) being the repair path for the destination (10.0.1.7/32).

Output 9-18   *Single-Segment TI-LFA Tunnels: SR-MPLS on P-2 (IOS XE)*

```
P-2#show isis fast-reroute ti-lfa tunnel


Tag CORE1:
Fast-Reroute TI-LFA Tunnels:


Tunnel  Interface  Next Hop       End Point       Label    End Point Host
MP2     Gi1        192.168.1.2    10.0.1.1        16001    P-1
                                  10.0.1.5        16005    ABR-1
MP3     Gi1        192.168.1.2    10.0.1.4        16004    P-4
MP4     Gi1        192.168.1.2    10.0.1.3        16003    P-3
MP5     Gi4        192.168.1.101  10.0.1.4        16004    P-4


P-2#
```

Finally, Output 9-19 verifies that an additional SID 16004 is required for traffic that would be forwarded across the repair tunnel MPLS-SR-Tunnel5 to the repair node P-4 in addition to the SID 16007 to reach the destination router ABR-3.

Output 9-19   *Single-Segment TI-LFA FIB Backup Path: SR-MPLS on P-2 (IOS XE)*

```
P-2#show ip cef 10.0.1.7 internal
10.0.1.7/32, epoch 2, RIB[I], refcnt 6, per-destination sharing
  sources: RIB, LTE
  feature space:
    IPRM: 0x00028000
    Broker: linked, distributed at 4th priority
    LFD: 10.0.1.7/32 1 local label
    sr local label info: global/16007 [0x1B]
        contains path extension list
        sr disposition chain 0x7F7BA1126458
          label 16007
          FRR Primary
            <primary: TAG adj out of GigabitEthernet1, addr 192.168.1.2>
        sr label switch chain 0x7F7BA1126458
          label 16007
          FRR Primary
```

```
           <primary: TAG adj out of GigabitEthernet1, addr 192.168.1.2>
ifnums:
  GigabitEthernet1(7): 192.168.1.2
  MPLS-SR-Tunnel5(21)
path list 7F7B6CC6E9B8, 25 locks, per-destination, flags 0x4D [shble, hvsh, rif,
hwcn]
  path 7F7B71E43488, share 1/1, type attached nexthop, for IPv4, flags [has-rpr]
    MPLS short path extensions: [rib | prfmfi | lblmrg | srlbl] MOI flags = 0x21
label 16007
    nexthop 192.168.1.2 GigabitEthernet1 label [16007|16007]-(local:16007), IP adj
out of GigabitEthernet1, addr 192.168.1.2 7F7B6EB8E8E8
      repair: attached-nexthop 10.0.1.4 MPLS-SR-Tunnel5 (7F7B71E43558)
  path 7F7B71E43558, share 1/1, type attached nexthop, for IPv4, flags [rpr,
rpr-only]
    MPLS short path extensions: [rib | lblmrg | srlbl] MOI flags = 0x1 label 16007
    nexthop 10.0.1.4 MPLS-SR-Tunnel5 label 16007-(local:16007), repair,
IP midchain out of MPLS-SR-Tunnel5 7F7BA9F82CB8
output chain:
  label [16007|16007]-(local:16007)
  FRR Primary (0x80007F7B710FAA60)
    <primary: TAG adj out of GigabitEthernet1, addr 192.168.1.2 7F7B6EB8E6B8>
    <repair:  TAG midchain out of MPLS-SR-Tunnel5 7F7BA9F82A88
              label 16004
              TAG adj out of GigabitEthernet4, addr 192.168.1.101 7F7B6EB8EF78>
P-2#
```

Example 9-3 shows an ICMP packet captured on the link {P-2 > P-5} immediately after the protected link {P-2 > P-1} went down. The imposed SIDs 16004 and 16007 indicate the single-segment repair tunnel MPLS-SR-Tunnel5 being used to forward the ICMP frame to router ABR-3.

Example 9-3 *Single-Segment TI-LFA Failure Event Packet: SR-MPLS*

```
Ethernet II, Src: RealtekU_10:ce:2e (52:54:00:10:ce:2e), Dst: RealtekU_02:43:88
  (52:54:00:02:43:88)
MultiProtocol Label Switching Header, Label: 16004, Exp: 0, S: 0, TTL: 254
MultiProtocol Label Switching Header, Label: 16007, Exp: 0, S: 1, TTL: 254
Internet Protocol Version 4, Src: 10.0.1.6, Dst: 10.0.1.7
    0100 .... = Version: 4
    .... 0101 = Header Length: 20 bytes (5)
    Differentiated Services Field: 0x00 (DSCP: CS0, ECN: Not-ECT)
        0000 00.. = Differentiated Services Codepoint: Default (0)
        .... ..00 = Explicit Congestion Notification: Not ECN-Capable Transport (0)
```

```
   Total Length: 100
   Identification: 0x397d (14717)
   000. .... = Flags: 0x0
       0... .... = Reserved bit: Not set
       .0.. .... = Don't fragment: Not set
       ..0. .... = More fragments: Not set
   ...0 0000 0000 0000 = Fragment Offset: 0
   Time to Live: 255
   Protocol: ICMP (1)
   Header Checksum: 0xb563 [validation disabled]
   [Header checksum status: Unverified]
   Source Address: 10.0.1.6
   Destination Address: 10.0.1.7
Internet Control Message Protocol
```

The next TI-LFA scenario is one where the P-space and Q-space do not overlap and provides an example of the double-segment TI-LFA backup path behavior. Figure 9-9 shows this double-segment backup path where the P node and Q node are located on separate routers. Note the following about the network shown in this figure:

■ **PLR:** Router P-2 is the PLR.

■ **Repair node:** Router P-3 is the Q node.

■ **Destination:** Router ABR-3's IP address is 10.0.1.7/32, and its Prefix SID is 16007.

■ **Protected link:** {P-2 > P-1} via GigabitEthernet0/0/0/1 is the protected link.

■ **Post-convergence path:** {P-5 > P-4 > P-3 > ABR-3} via GigabitEthernet0/0/0/4 is the post-convergence path.

■ **P-space:** P-4 is in the P-space because the router P-2 can forward traffic to P-4 without passing over the {P-2 > P-1} link.

■ **Q-space:** P-3 is in the Q-space because it can forward traffic to the destination 10.0.1.7/32 without passing over the {P-2 > P-1} protected link.

■ **Segments = 2:** Router P-2 can forward traffic to router ABR-3 along the backup path by pushing two additional SIDs—the Prefix SID 16004 and router P-4's Adjacency SID 21—toward router P-3.

In this double-segment example, the command **show route 10.0.1.7/32** in Output 9-20 displays the protected link as GigabitEthernet0/0/0/1 with a metric of 30, and the backup link is via GigabitEthernet0/0/0/4 to the repair nodes 10.0.1.4 (P-4) and 10.0.1.3 (P-3). The router P-4 is required to reach the destination without passing over the protected link {P-2 > P-1}, and it does so by forwarding the traffic directly out the interface with its adjacent node, router P-3.

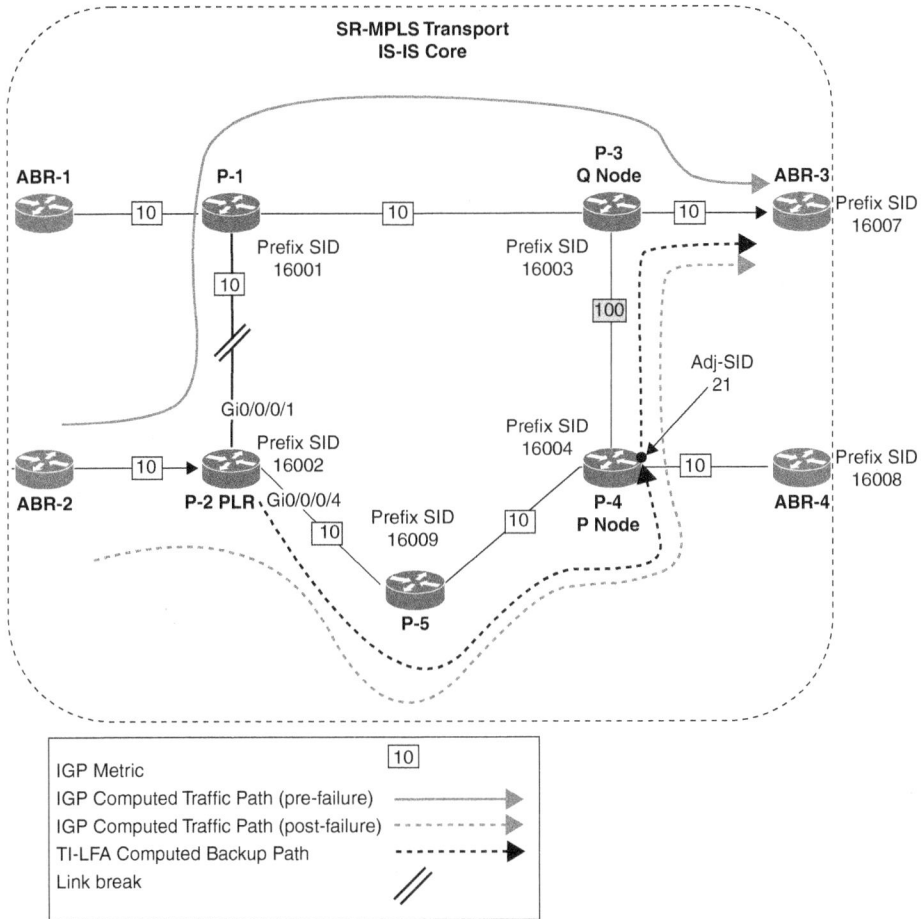

Figure 9-9   *Double-Segment TI-LFA P Node and Q Node: SR-MPLS*

Output 9-20   *Double-Segment TI-LFA RIB Backup Path: SR-MPLS on P-2 (IOS XR)*

```
RP/0/RP0/CPU0:P-2#show route 10.0.1.7/32


Routing entry for 10.0.1.7/32
  Known via "isis CORE1", distance 115, metric 30, labeled SR, type level-2
  Installed Feb 24 00:26:06.978 for 00:59:35
  Routing Descriptor Blocks
    192.168.1.101, from 10.0.1.7, via GigabitEthernet0/0/0/4, Backup (TI-LFA)
      Repair Node(s): 10.0.1.4, 10.0.1.3
      Route metric is 130
    192.168.1.2, from 10.0.1.7, via GigabitEthernet0/0/0/1, Protected
      Route metric is 30
  No advertising protos.
RP/0/RP0/CPU0:P-2#
```

The command in Output 9-21 shows the TI-LFA backup path. This is a double-segment TI-LFA backup path because the traffic is forwarded to the P node P-4 with the initial Prefix SID 16004. Traffic is then forwarded using the Adjacency SID 21 toward the Q node P-3, and finally it is forwarded on to the destination router ABR-3 with the Prefix SID 16007.

Output 9-21   *Double-Segment TI-LFA IS-IS Fast Reroute Detail: SR-MPLS on P-2 (IOS XR)*

```
RP/0/RP0/CPU0:P-2#show isis ipv4 fast-reroute 10.0.1.7/32 detail

L2 10.0.1.7/32 [30/115] Label: 16007, medium priority
   Installed Feb 24 00:26:06.978 for 01:13:09
      via 192.168.1.2, GigabitEthernet0/0/0/1, Label: 16007, P-1, SRGB Base: 16000,
   Weight: 0
      Backup path: TI-LFA (link), via 192.168.1.101, GigabitEthernet0/0/0/4 P-5,
   SRGB Base: 16000, Weight: 0, Metric: 130
           P node: P-4.00 [10.0.1.4], Label: 16004
           Q node: P-3.00 [10.0.1.3], Label: 21
           Prefix label: 16007
           Backup-src: ABR-3.00
        P: No, TM: 130, LC: No, NP: No, D: No, SRLG: Yes
      src ABR-3.00-00, 10.0.1.7, prefix-SID index 7, R:0 N:1 P:0 E:0 V:0 L:0, Alg:0
RP/0/RP0/CPU0:P-2#
```

The FIB details in Output 9-22 show that two additional labels are required for traffic that may be forwarded across the TI-LFA computed backup path to reach the P node P-4 with Prefix SID 16004. The Adjacency SID 21 is used to traverse the link interface Gi2 to reach the Q node P-3 in the event that the protected link {P-2 > P-1} fails, and then traffic is forwarded to the final destination, router ABR-3, with the Prefix SID 16007.

Output 9-22   *Double-Segment TI-LFA FIB Backup Path: SR-MPLS on P-2 (IOS XR)*

```
RP/0/RP0/CPU0:P-2#show cef 10.0.1.7/32

10.0.1.7/32, version 237, labeled SR, internal 0x1000001 0x8110 (ptr 0xe899d20) [1],
   0x600 (0xe02b140), 0xa28 (0x22c254b8)
 Updated Feb 24 00:26:06.992
 remote adjacency to GigabitEthernet0/0/0/1
 Prefix Len 32, traffic index 0, precedence n/a, priority 1
   gateway array (0xde93df8) reference count 12, flags 0x500068, source rib (7), 0
   backups
               [5 type 5 flags 0x8401 (0xf4c4b88) ext 0x0 (0x0)]
   LW-LDI[type=5, refc=3, ptr=0xe02b140, sh-ldi=0xf4c4b88]
   gateway array update type-time 1 Feb 24 00:26:06.992
```

```
LDI Update time Feb 24 00:26:06.992
LW-LDI-TS Feb 24 00:26:06.992
  via 192.168.1.101/32, GigabitEthernet0/0/0/4, 9 dependencies, weight 0, class 0,
  backup (TI-LFA) [flags 0xb00]
    path-idx 0 NHID 0x0 [0xfd2f510 0x0]
    next hop 192.168.1.101/32, Repair Node(s): 10.0.1.4, 10.0.1.3
    remote adjacency
     local label 16007      labels imposed {16004 21 16007}
  via 192.168.1.2/32, GigabitEthernet0/0/0/1, 6 dependencies, weight 0, class 0,
  protected [flags 0x400]
    path-idx 1 bkup-idx 0 NHID 0x0 [0xdc40be0 0x0]
    next hop 192.168.1.2/32
     local label 16007      labels imposed {16007}

    Load distribution: 0 (refcount 5)

    Hash  OK  Interface               Address
    0     Y   GigabitEthernet0/0/0/1  remote
RP/0/RP0/CPU0:P-2#
```

Now we will look at IOS XE commands that are similar to those used in the previous examples and that can be used to verify the TI-LFA behavior when the PLR router is running IOS XE.

The CLI command **show ip route repair-paths 10.0.1.7 255.255.255.255** in Output 9-23 indicates that the route to router ABR-3 has a TI-LFA repair tunnel via MPLS-SR-Tunnel3 to the repair node P-3, and from there it can reach the destination router ABR-3 without traversing the protected link {P-2 > P-1}.

Output 9-23   *Double-Segment TI-LFA RIB Backup Path: SR-MPLS on P-2 (IOS XE)*

```
P-2#show ip route repair-paths 10.0.1.7 255.255.255.255
Routing entry for 10.0.1.7/32
  Known via "isis", distance 115, metric 30, type level-2
  Redistributing via isis CORE1
  Last update from 192.168.1.2 on GigabitEthernet1, 00:04:59 ago
 SR Incoming Label: 16007
  Routing Descriptor Blocks:
  * 192.168.1.2, from 10.0.1.7, 00:04:59 ago, via GigabitEthernet1,
  prefer-non-rib-labels, merge-labels
      Route metric is 30, traffic share count is 1
      MPLS label: 16007
      MPLS Flags: NSF
```

```
    Repair Path: 10.0.1.3, via MPLS-SR-Tunnel3
   [RPR]10.0.1.3, from 10.0.1.7, 00:04:59 ago, via MPLS-SR-Tunnel3, merge-labels
    Route metric is 120, traffic share count is 1
    MPLS label: 16007
    MPLS Flags: NSF
P-2#
```

In this double-segment example scenario, the command **show isis fast-reroute ti-lfa tunnel** in Output 9-24 shows an overview of the IS-IS TI-LFA tunnels from the PLR router. Router P-2 initiates the tunnel MP3 via the P node P-4 with SID 16004 and the Adjacency SID 21 to reach the Q node P-3.

Output 9-24 *Double-Segment TI-LFA Tunnels: SR-MPLS on P-2 (IOS XE)*

```
P-2#show isis fast-reroute ti-lfa tunnel

Tag CORE1:
Fast-Reroute TI-LFA Tunnels:

Tunnel  Interface  Next Hop        End Point       Label      End Point Host
MP1     Gi1        192.168.1.2     10.0.1.1        16001      P-1
                                   10.0.1.5        16005      ABR-1
MP2     Gi1        192.168.1.2     10.0.1.3        16003      P-3
                                   10.0.1.4        24003      P-4
MP3     Gi4        192.168.1.101   10.0.1.4        16004      P-4
                                   10.0.1.3        21         P-3

P-2#
```

The FIB details in Output 9-25 show that two SIDs, 16004 and 21, are required for traffic that would be forwarded across the repair tunnel MPLS-SR-Tunnel3 via the P node P-4 to the repair Q node P-3, and the SID 16007 would be needed to reach the original destination router ABR-3.

Output 9-25 *Double-Segment TI-LFA FIB Backup Path: SR-MPLS on P-2 (IOS XE)*

```
P-2#show ip cef 10.0.1.7 internal
10.0.1.7/32, epoch 2, RIB[I], refcnt 6, per-destination sharing
  sources: RIB, LTE
  feature space:
    IPRM: 0x00028000
    Broker: linked, distributed at 4th priority
```

```
   LFD: 10.0.1.7/32 1 local label
   sr local label info: global/16007 [0x1B]
      contains path extension list
      sr disposition chain 0x7F9E09FF6018
        label 16007
        FRR Primary
          <primary: TAG adj out of GigabitEthernet1, addr 192.168.1.2>
      sr label switch chain 0x7F9E09FF6018
        label 16007
        FRR Primary
          <primary: TAG adj out of GigabitEthernet1, addr 192.168.1.2>
ifnums:
  GigabitEthernet1(7): 192.168.1.2
  MPLS-SR-Tunnel3(19)
path list 7F9E35460FC8, 23 locks, per-destination, flags 0x4D [shble, hvsh, rif,
hwcn]
  path 7F9E09F00D60, share 1/1, type attached nexthop, for IPv4, flags [has-rpr]
    MPLS short path extensions: [rib | prfmfi | lblmrg | srlbl] MOI flags = 0x21
label 16007
    nexthop 192.168.1.2 GigabitEthernet1 label [16007|16007]-(local:16007), IP adj
out of GigabitEthernet1, addr 192.168.1.2 7F9E04C700E0
      repair: attached-nexthop 10.0.1.3 MPLS-SR-Tunnel3 (7F9E09F00E30)
  path 7F9E09F00E30, share 1/1, type attached nexthop, for IPv4, flags [rpr,
rpr-only]
    MPLS short path extensions: [rib | lblmrg | srlbl] MOI flags = 0x1 label 16007
    nexthop 10.0.1.3 MPLS-SR-Tunnel3 label 16007-(local:16007), repair,
IP midchain out of MPLS-SR-Tunnel3 7F9E04C6F3C0
output chain:
  label [16007|16007]-(local:16007)
  FRR Primary (0x80007F9E39484040)
    <primary: TAG adj out of GigabitEthernet1, addr 192.168.1.2 7F9E04C6FEB0>
    <repair:  TAG midchain out of MPLS-SR-Tunnel3 7F9E04C6F190
             label 21
             label 16004
             TAG adj out of GigabitEthernet4, addr 192.168.1.101 7F9E04C70310>
P-2#
```

Example 9-4 shows an ICMP packet captured on the link {P-2 > P-5} after the protected link {P-2 > P-1} went down and illustrates the double-segment behavior. The imposed SIDs 16004, 21, and 16007 indicate that the repair tunnel MPLS-SR-Tunnel3 is being used to forward the ICMP frame to router ABR-3.

Example 9-4 *Double-Segment TI-LFA Failure Event Packet: SR-MPLS*

```
Ethernet II, Src: RealtekU_10:ce:2e (52:54:00:10:ce:2e), Dst: RealtekU_02:43:88
  (52:54:00:02:43:88)
MultiProtocol Label Switching Header, Label: 16004, Exp: 0, S: 0, TTL: 254
MultiProtocol Label Switching Header, Label: 21, Exp: 0, S: 0, TTL: 254
MultiProtocol Label Switching Header, Label: 16007, Exp: 0, S: 1, TTL: 254
Internet Protocol Version 4, Src: 10.0.1.6, Dst: 10.0.1.7
    0100 .... = Version: 4
    .... 0101 = Header Length: 20 bytes (5)
    Differentiated Services Field: 0x00 (DSCP: CS0, ECN: Not-ECT)
    Total Length: 100
    Identification: 0xf916 (63766)
    000. .... = Flags: 0x0
    ...0 0000 0000 0000 = Fragment Offset: 0
    Time to Live: 255
    Protocol: ICMP (1)
    Header Checksum: 0xac75 [validation disabled]
    [Header checksum status: Unverified]
    Source Address: 10.0.1.6
    Destination Address: 10.0.1.7
Internet Control Message Protocol
```

At this point, you should have an understanding of zero-segment, single-segment, and double-segment TI-LFA link protection scenarios that you may encounter in SR-MPLS networks. The basic commands presented in this section are intended to serve as a starting point for verifying and troubleshooting TI-LFA on platforms operating either IOS XR or IOS XE operating systems.

Link Protection Verification: SRv6

This section discusses SRv6 TI-LFA link protection verification based on the IOS XR operating system, beginning with the zero-segment TI-LFA example shown in Figure 9-10. Note the following about the network shown in this figure:

- **PLR:** Router P-2 is the PLR.

- **Repair node:** Router P-5 is adjacent to the PLR.

- **Destination:** Router ABR-4 END SID fc00:0:202:: is the destination.

- **Protected link:** {P-2 > P-1} via GigabitEthernet0/0/0/2 is the protected link.

- **Post-convergence path:** {P-5 > P-4 > ABR-4} via GigabitEthernet0/0/0/4 is the post-convergence path.

- **P-space:** P-5 is in the P-space because the PLR router can forward traffic to it without passing over the {P-2 > P-1} protected link.

- **Q-space:** P-5 is in the Q-space because it can forward traffic to the destination END SID fc00:0:202:: without passing over the {P-2 > P-1} protected link.

- **Segments = 0:** Router P-2 can forward traffic directly to P-5 without the insertion of an SRH.

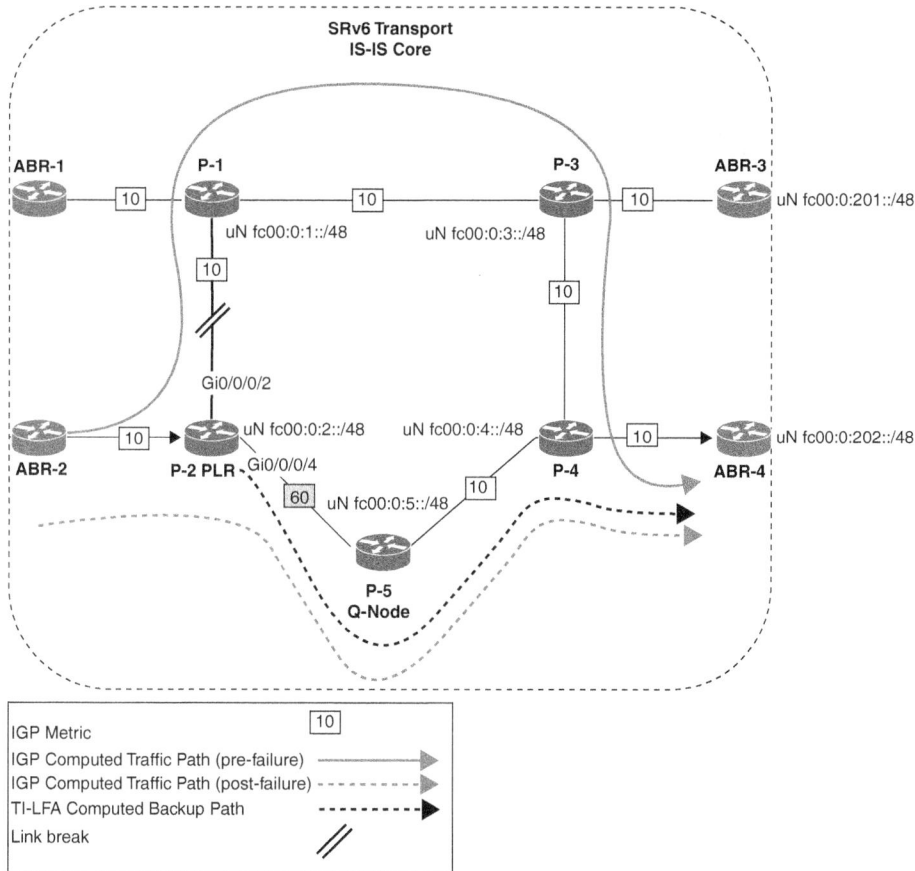

Figure 9-10 *Adjacent Zero-Segment TI-LFA Repair Node: SRv6*

The command **show route ipv6 fc00:0:202::/48** in Output 9-26 verifies that the protected link is GigabitEthernet0/0/0/2 with a metric of 41 for END SID fc00:0:202:: with a backup link via GigabitEthernet0/0/0/4 with a metric of 81.

Output 9-26   *Zero-Segment TI-LFA RIB Backup Path: SRv6 on P-2 (IOS XR)*

```
RP/0/RP0/CPU0:P-2#show route ipv6 fc00:0:202::/48


Routing entry for fc00:0:202::/48
  Known via "isis CORE_1", distance 115, metric 41, SRv6-locator, type level-2
  Installed Mar  1 12:07:32.633 for 00:23:14
  Routing Descriptor Blocks
    fe80::42:acff:fe15:e002, from ::, via GigabitEthernet0/0/0/2, Protected
      Route metric is 41
    fe80::42:acff:fe16:a03, from ::, via GigabitEthernet0/0/0/4, Backup (Local-LFA)
      Route metric is 81
  No advertising protos.
RP/0/RP0/CPU0:P-2#
```

The backup path shown in Output 9-27 indicates that this is a zero-segment TI-LFA backup path because the traffic is forwarded via the direct neighbor router P-5 without the insertion of an SRH header.

Output 9-27   *Zero-Segment TI-LFA IS-IS Fast Reroute Detail: SRv6 on P-2 (IOS XR)*

```
RP/0/RP0/CPU0:P-2#show isis ipv6 fast-reroute fc00:0:202::/48 detail


L2 fc00:0:202::/48 [41/115] Label: None, low priority
   Installed Mar 01 12:07:32.633 for 00:29:50
     via fe80::42:acff:fe15:e002, GigabitEthernet0/0/0/2, P-1, Weight: 0
      Backup path: LFA, via fe80::42:acff:fe16:a03, GigabitEthernet0/0/0/4, P-5,
Weight: 0, Metric: 81
       P: No, TM: 81, LC: No, NP: Yes, D: Yes, SRLG: Yes
     src ABR-4.00-00, ::
RP/0/RP0/CPU0:P-2#
```

Finally, the command in Output 9-28 verifies the FIB of the PLR router, which is able to forward traffic over the TI-LFA backup path to the direct repair node (Q node) P-5 without the requirement of additional SIDs.

Output 9-28   *Zero-Segment TI-LFA FIB Backup Path: SRv6 on P-2 (IOS XR)*

```
RP/0/RP0/CPU0:P-2#show cef ipv6 fc00:0:202::/48


fc00:0:202::/48, version 513, internal 0x1000001 0x220 (ptr 0x86eb5770) [1], 0x400
  (0x8765bda8), 0x0 (0x0)
 Updated Mar  1 12:07:32.637
 local adjacency to GigabitEthernet0/0/0/2
```

```
Prefix Len 48, traffic index 0, precedence n/a, priority 2
 gateway array (0x874c6318) reference count 7, flags 0x500000, source rib (7), 0
 backups
                [8 type 3 flags 0x8401 (0x87572e88) ext 0x0 (0x0)]
 LW-LDI[type=3, refc=1, ptr=0x8765bda8, sh-ldi=0x87572e88]
 gateway array update type-time 1 Mar  1 12:07:32.636
LDI Update time Mar  1 12:07:32.637
LW-LDI-TS Mar  1 12:07:32.637
  via fe80::42:acff:fe15:e002/128, GigabitEthernet0/0/0/2, 2 dependencies,
 weight 0, class 0, protected [flags 0x400]
   path-idx 0 bkup-idx 1 NHID 0x20004 [0x89b3f2a0 0x0]
   next hop fe80::42:acff:fe15:e002/128
  via fe80::42:acff:fe16:a03/128, GigabitEthernet0/0/0/4, 4 dependencies, weight 0,
 class 0, backup (Local-LFA) [flags 0x300]
   path-idx 1 NHID 0x20005 [0x872bff20 0x0]
   next hop fe80::42:acff:fe16:a03/128
   local adjacency


   Load distribution: 0 (refcount 8)


   Hash  OK  Interface            Address
    0    Y   GigabitEthernet0/0/0/2  fe80::42:acff:fe15:e002
RP/0/RP0/CPU0:P-2#
```

This second SRv6 TI-LFA example, shown in Figure 9-11 involves a single segment, where the repair node is located both in the extended P-space and the Q-space. Note the following about the network shown in this figure:

- **PLR:** Router P-2 is the PLR.

- **Repair node:** The PQ node P-4 is the repair node.

- **Destination:** Router ABR-3 with END SID fc00:0:201:: is the destination.

- **Protected link:** {P-2 > P-1} via GigabitEthernet0/0/0/2 is the protected link.

- **Post-convergence path:** {P-5 > P-4 > P-3 > ABR-3} via GigabitEthernet0/0/0/4 is the post-convergence path.

- **P-space:** P-5 is a P-space router because P-2 can forward traffic to P-5 without passing over the {P-2 > P-1} link.

- **Extended P-space:** P-4 is in the extended P-space of P-2 because router P-5 can forward traffic to it without passing over the {P-2 > P-1} protected link.

- **Q-space:** P-4 is in the Q-space because it can forward traffic to the destination END SID fc00:0:201:: without passing over the {P-2 > P-1} protected link.

■ **Segments = 1:** Router P-2 can forward traffic to router ABR-3 along the backup path via the PQ node P-4 with SID fc00:0:4:: by inserting an additional SRH (H.Insert.red) with the ABR-3 locator address stored in the segment list. The H.Insert.red headend behavior steers traffic into the fast reroute SRv6 policy on the PLR. This H.Insert.red behavior is discussed in more detail in Chapter 3, "What Is Segment Routing over IPv6 (SRv6)?" in the section "IPv6 Segment Routing Header (SRH) (RFC 8754)."

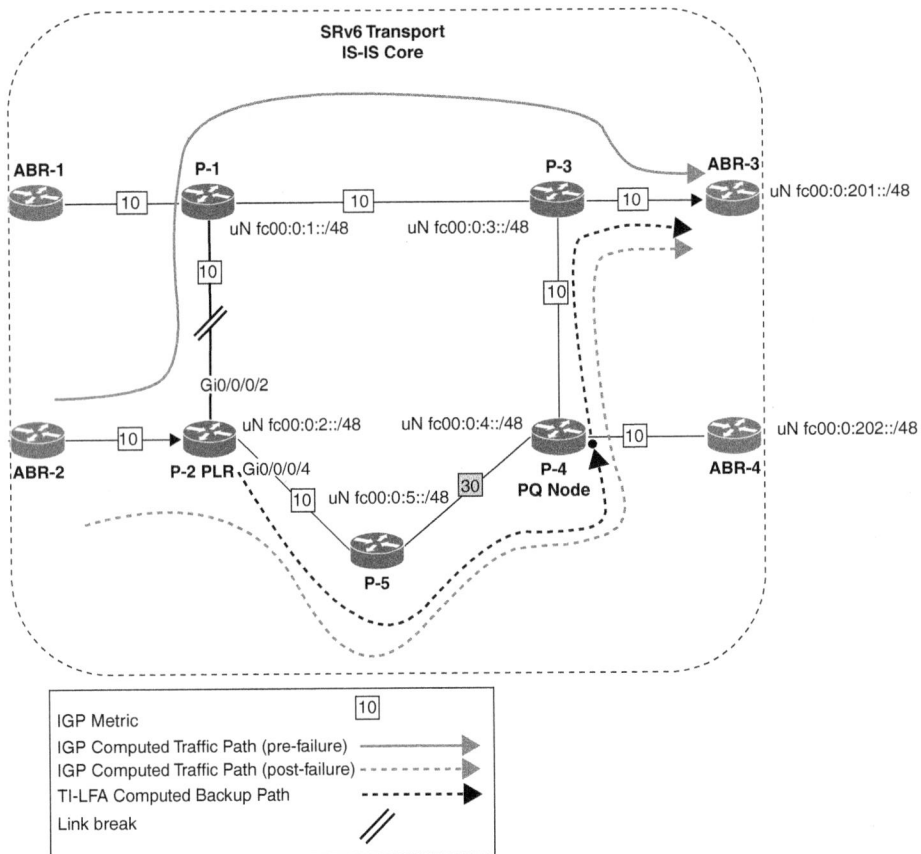

Figure 9-11 *Single-Segment TI-LFA PQ Node: SRv6*

The command **show route ipv6 fc00:0:201::/48 detail** in Output 9-29 confirms that the protected link is GigabitEthernet0/0/0/2 with a metric of 31, and the backup link is via GigabitEthernet0/0/0/4 to the repair node P-4 with SID fc00:0:4::. As indicated in the output, the PLR router inserts an SRH (H.Insert.Red) allowing router P-4 to look up the next segment and forward the traffic to the destination END SID fc00:0:201:: without passing over the protected link {P-2 > P-1}.

Output 9-29 *Single-Segment TI-LFA RIB Backup Path: SRv6 on P-2 (IOS XR)*

```
RP/0/RP0/CPU0:P-2#show route ipv6 fc00:0:201::/48 detail

Routing entry for fc00:0:201::/48
  Known via "isis CORE_1", distance 115, metric 31, SRv6-locator, type level-2
  Installed Mar  2 06:50:47.998 for 00:00:40
  Routing Descriptor Blocks
    fe80::42:acff:fe15:e002, from ::, via GigabitEthernet0/0/0/2, Protected
      Route metric is 31
      Label: None
      Tunnel ID: None
      Binding Label: None
      Extended communities count: 0
      Path id:1       Path ref count:0
      NHID:0x20003(Ref:53)
      Backup path id:65
    fe80::42:acff:fe16:a03, from ::, via GigabitEthernet0/0/0/4, Backup (Local-LFA)
      Route metric is 61
      Label: None
      Tunnel ID: None
      Binding Label: None
      Extended communities count: 0
      Path id:65           Path ref count:1
      NHID:0x20005(Ref:44)
      SRv6 Headend: H.Insert.Red [f3216], SID-list {fc00:0:4::}
  Route version is 0x17 (23)
  No local label
  IP Precedence: Not Set
  QoS Group ID: Not Set
  Flow-tag: Not Set
  Fwd-class: Not Set
  Route Priority: RIB_PRIORITY_NON_RECURSIVE_LOW (8) SVD Type RIB_SVD_TYPE_LOCAL
  Download Priority 2, Download Version 763
  No advertising protos.
RP/0/RP0/CPU0:P-2#
```

Output 9-30 shows a single-segment TI-LFA backup path example with the command
show isis ipv6 fast-reroute fc00:0:201::/48 detail. The backup path behavior is TI-LFA
(link) from the PLR interface GigabitEthernet0/0/0/4 toward router P-5 via the P node P-4
with the SID: fc00:0:4::.

Output 9-30   *Single-Segment TI-LFA IS-IS Fast Reroute Detail: SRv6 on P-2 (IOS XR)*

```
RP/0/RP0/CPU0:P-2#show isis ipv6 fast-reroute fc00:0:201::/48 detail

L2 fc00:0:201::/48 [31/115] Label: None, low priority
   Installed Mar 02 07:42:36.843 for 03:36:07
      via fe80::42:acff:fe15:e002, GigabitEthernet0/0/0/2, P-1, Weight: 0
         Backup path: TI-LFA (link), via fe80::42:acff:fe16:a03,
  GigabitEthernet0/0/0/4 P-5, Weight: 0, Metric: 61
            P node: P-4.00 [::], SRv6 SID: fc00:0:4:: uN (PSP/USD)
            Backup-src: ABR-3.00
         P: No, TM: 61, LC: No, NP: No, D: No, SRLG: Yes
      src ABR-3.00-00, ::
RP/0/RP0/CPU0:P-2#
```

The FIB verification command in Output 9-31 confirms the TI-LFA backup path via interface GigabitEthernet0/0/0/4 and shows that this single-segment TI-LFA backup path example requires the insertion of an SRH, based on the field SRv6 H.Insert.Red SID-list {fc00:0:4::}.

Output 9-31   *Single-Segment TI-LFA FIB Backup Path: SRv6 on P-2 (IOS XR)*

```
RP/0/RP0/CPU0:P-2#show cef ipv6 fc00:0:201::/48

fc00:0:201::/48, version 1108, SRv6 Headend, internal 0x1000001 0x220
  (ptr 0x87158df8) [1], 0x400 (0x881c8b68), 0x0 (0x89980628)
 Updated Mar  2 07:42:36.846
 local adjacency to GigabitEthernet0/0/0/2

 Prefix Len 48, traffic index 0, precedence n/a, priority 2
  gateway array (0x88034708) reference count 1, flags 0x500000, source rib (7), 0
  backups
               [2 type 3 flags 0x8401 (0x880e06c8) ext 0x0 (0x0)]
  LW-LDI[type=3, refc=1, ptr=0x881c8b68, sh-ldi=0x880e06c8]
  gateway array update type-time 1 Mar  2 07:42:36.846
 LDI Update time Mar  2 07:42:36.847
 LW-LDI-TS Mar  2 07:42:36.847
   via fe80::42:acff:fe15:e002/128, GigabitEthernet0/0/0/2, 14 dependencies,
  weight 0, class 0, protected [flags 0x400]
    path-idx 0 bkup-idx 1 NHID 0x20003 [0x89aa92a0 0x0]
    next hop fe80::42:acff:fe15:e002/128
   via fe80::42:acff:fe16:a03/128, GigabitEthernet0/0/0/4, 14 dependencies,
  weight 0, class 0, backup (Local-LFA) [flags 0xb00]
    path-idx 1 NHID 0x20005 [0x87e2cf20 0x0]
    next hop fe80::42:acff:fe16:a03/128
    local adjacency
```

```
   SRv6 H.Insert.Red SID-list {fc00:0:4::}

   Load distribution: 0 (refcount 2)

   Hash  OK  Interface                 Address
   0     Y   GigabitEthernet0/0/0/2    fe80::42:acff:fe15:e002
RP/0/RP0/CPU0:P-2#
```

Example 9-5 shows an ICMP packet captured on the link {P-2 > P-5} immediately after the protected link {P-2 > P-1} went down. In this single-segment example, the IPv6 destination address is the END SID fc00:0:4:: of the repair node P-4, and the inserted SRH contains the final segment END SID fc00:0:201:: of router ABR-3.

Example 9-5 *Single-Segment TI-LFA Failure Event Packet: SRv6*

```
Ethernet II, Src: 02:42:ac:16:0a:02 (02:42:ac:16:0a:02), Dst: 02:42:ac:16:0a:03
  (02:42:ac:16:0a:03)
Internet Protocol Version 6, Src: fc00:0:102::1, Dst: fc00:0:4::
    0110 .... = Version: 6
    .... 0000 0000 .... .... .... .... .... = Traffic Class: 0x00 (DSCP: CS0,
  ECN: Not-ECT)
    .... 0000 0000 0000 0000 0000 = Flow Label: 0x00000
    Payload Length: 84
    Next Header: Routing Header for IPv6 (43)
    Hop Limit: 59
    Source Address: fc00:0:102::1
    Destination Address: fc00:0:4::
    Routing Header for IPv6 (Segment Routing)
        Next Header: ICMPv6 (58)
        Length: 2
        [Length: 24 bytes]
        Type: Segment Routing (4)
        Segments Left: 1
        Last Entry: 0
        Flags: 0x00
        Tag: 0000
        Address[0]: fc00:0:201::
Internet Control Message Protocol v6
```

In the TI-LFA scenario in Figure 9-12, the P-space and Q-space do not overlap, so this is a double-segment TI-LFA backup path. Note the following about the network shown in this figure:

- **PLR:** Router P-2 is the PLR.

- **Repair node:** Router P-3 is the Q node.

- **Destination:** Router ABR-3 with END SID fc00:0:201:: is the destination.

- **Protected link:** {P-2 > P-1} via GigabitEthernet0/0/0/2 is the protected link.

- **Post-convergence path:** {P-5 > P-4 > P-3 > ABR-3} via GigabitEthernet0/0/0/4 is the post-convergence path.

- **P-space:** P-4 is in the P-space because router P-2 can forward traffic to P-4 without passing over the {P-2 > P-1} link.

- **Q-space:** P-3 is in the Q-space because it can forward traffic to the END SID fc00:0:201:: without passing over the {P-2 > P-1} protected link.

- **Segments = 2:** Router P-2 can forward traffic to router ABR-3 along the backup path via the P node P-4 with its Adjacency SID fc00:0:4:e001::, allowing the traffic to be forwarded out across the link {P-4 > P-3} to the repair Q node P-3. The PLR router will also have inserted an SRH (H.Insert.Red) with the ABR-3 locator address stored in the segment list, allowing the packet to reach its destination.

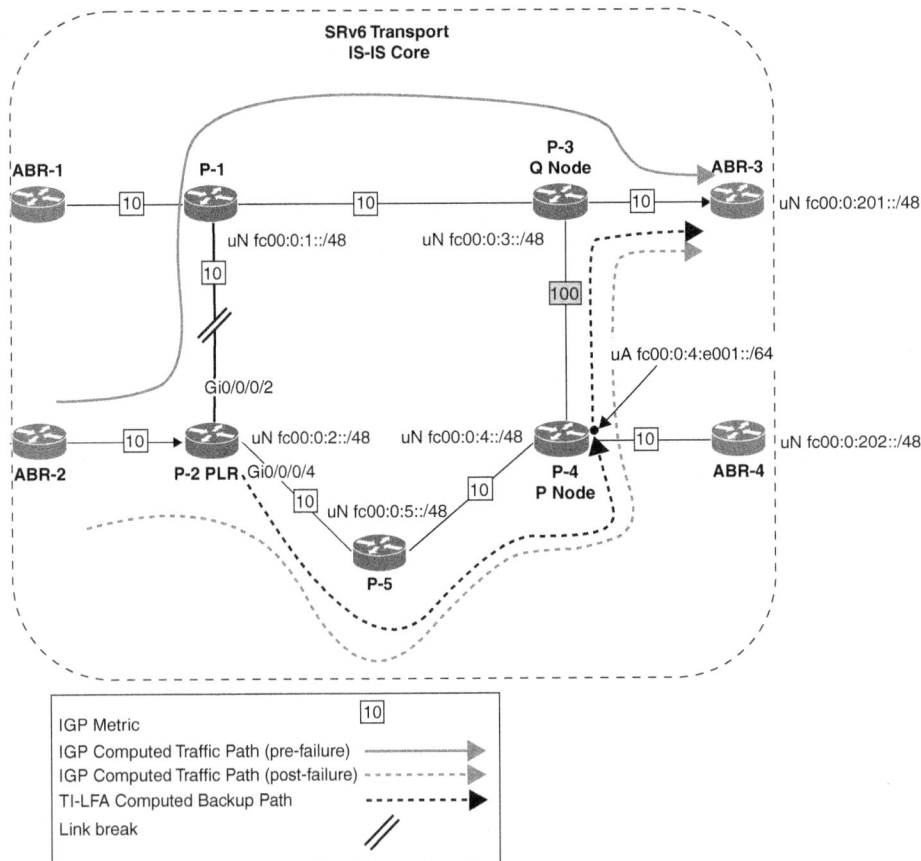

Figure 9-12 *Double-Segment TI-LFA P Node and Q Node: SRv6*

Output 9-32 confirms the protected link as GigabitEthernet0/0/0/2 with a metric of 31, and the backup link egresses GigabitEthernet0/0/0/4 via router P-5 toward the P node P-4. In this double-segment scenario, the IPv6 destination address is Adjacency SID fc00:0:4:e001:: on P-4, which allows the traffic to be forwarded out the link {P4 > P3} toward the repair Q node P-3. The PLR router will also have inserted an SRH (H.Insert. Red) so the repair Q node P-3 can perform a lookup of the next segment and forward the traffic to its destination END SID fc00:0:201::. With SR-MPLS, you saw two SIDs for double-segment backup paths; with SRv6, you see a single SID with two uSIDs—0x0004 being the global uSID of P-4 (End) and 0xe001 being the local uSID of P-4 (End.X) toward P-3.

Note   A full-length SID would require two segments in the segment list of the SRH.

Output 9-32   *Double-Segment TI-LFA RIB Backup Path: SRv6 on P-2 (IOS XR)*

```
RP/0/RP0/CPU0:P-2#show route ipv6 fc00:0:201::/48 detail

Routing entry for fc00:0:201::/48
  Known via "isis CORE_1", distance 115, metric 31, SRv6-locator, type level-2
  Installed Mar  2 12:12:06.933 for 00:03:56
  Routing Descriptor Blocks
    fe80::42:acff:fe15:e002, from ::, via GigabitEthernet0/0/0/2, Protected
      Route metric is 31
      Label: None
      Tunnel ID: None
      Binding Label: None
      Extended communities count: 0
      Path id:1        Path ref count:0
      NHID:0x20003(Ref:51)
      Backup path id:65
    fe80::42:acff:fe16:a03, from ::, via GigabitEthernet0/0/0/4, Backup (Local-LFA)
      Route metric is 131
      Label: None
      Tunnel ID: None
      Binding Label: None
      Extended communities count: 0
      Path id:65               Path ref count:1
      NHID:0x20005(Ref:41)
      SRv6 Headend: H.Insert.Red [f3216], SID-list {fc00:0:4:e001::}
  Route version is 0x2a (42)
  No local label
```

```
   IP Precedence: Not Set
   QoS Group ID: Not Set
   Flow-tag: Not Set
   Fwd-class: Not Set
   Route Priority: RIB_PRIORITY_NON_RECURSIVE_LOW (8) SVD Type RIB_SVD_TYPE_LOCAL
   Download Priority 2, Download Version 1194
   No advertising protos.
RP/0/RP0/CPU0:P-2#
```

The double-segment backup path example detailed in Output 9-33 indicates that the backup path behavior is TI-LFA (link) via the PLR interface GigabitEthernet0/0/0/4 toward router P-5. As mentioned previously, a single SID with two uSIDs is used, with the P node P-4 reachable with Node SID fc00:0:4:: (uSID 0x0004) and the repair Q node P-3 reachable via the Adjacency SID fc00:0:4:e001:: (uSID 0xe001) of router P-4.

Output 9-33 *Double-Segment TI-LFA IS-IS Fast Reroute Detail: SRv6 on P-2 (IOS XR)*

```
RP/0/RP0/CPU0:P-2#show isis ipv6 fast-reroute fc00:0:201::/48 detail

L2 fc00:0:201::/48 [31/115] Label: None, low priority
   Installed Mar 02 12:12:06.932 for 00:04:18
      via fe80::42:acff:fe15:e002, GigabitEthernet0/0/0/2, P-1, Weight: 0
         Backup path: TI-LFA (link), via fe80::42:acff:fe16:a03,
GigabitEthernet0/0/0/4 P-5, Weight: 0, Metric: 131
            P node: P-4.00 [::], SRv6 SID: fc00:0:4:: uN (PSP/USD)
            Q node: P-3.00 [::], SRv6 SID: fc00:0:4:e001:: uA (PSP/USD)
            Backup-src: ABR-3.00
         P: No, TM: 131, LC: No, NP: No, D: No, SRLG: Yes
      src ABR-3.00-00, ::
RP/0/RP0/CPU0:P-2#
```

The PLR router FIB verification command **show cef ipv6 fc00:0:201::/48** in Output 9-34 confirms the TI-LFA backup path via interface GigabitEthernet0/0/0/4. It also shows that this is a double-segment TI-LFA backup path example and requires the insertion of an SRH, as shown by the field SRv6 H.Insert.Red SID-list {fc00:0:4:e001::}, where the Adjacency SID fc00:0:4:e001:: causes traffic to be forwarded out the {P-4 > P-3} link toward the Q node P-3.

Output 9-34 *Double-Segment TI-LFA FIB Backup Path: SRv6 on P-2 (IOS XR)*

```
RP/0/RP0/CPU0:P-2#show cef ipv6 fc00:0:201::/48

fc00:0:201::/48, version 1194, SRv6 Headend, internal 0x1000001 0x220
  (ptr 0x87158df8) [1], 0x400 (0x881c8b68), 0x0 (0x899804c8)
```

```
Updated Mar  2 12:12:06.936
local adjacency to GigabitEthernet0/0/0/2


Prefix Len 48, traffic index 0, precedence n/a, priority 2
 gateway array (0x88034280) reference count 1, flags 0x500000, source rib (7), 0
 backups
                [2 type 3 flags 0x8401 (0x880e04e8) ext 0x0 (0x0)]
 LW-LDI[type=3, refc=1, ptr=0x881c8b68, sh-ldi=0x880e04e8]
 gateway array update type-time 1 Mar  2 12:12:06.936
LDI Update time Mar  2 12:12:06.936
LW-LDI-TS Mar  2 12:12:06.936
  via fe80::42:acff:fe15:e002/128, GigabitEthernet0/0/0/2, 12 dependencies,
 weight 0, class 0, protected [flags 0x400]
   path-idx 0 bkup-idx 1 NHID 0x20003 [0x89aa92a0 0x0]
   next hop fe80::42:acff:fe15:e002/128
  via fe80::42:acff:fe16:a03/128, GigabitEthernet0/0/0/4, 12 dependencies,
 weight 0, class 0, backup (Local-LFA) [flags 0xb00]
   path-idx 1 NHID 0x20005 [0x87e2cf20 0x0]
   next hop fe80::42:acff:fe16:a03/128
   local adjacency
   SRv6 H.Insert.Red SID-list {fc00:0:4:e001::}


   Load distribution: 0 (refcount 2)


   Hash  OK  Interface                 Address
   0     Y   GigabitEthernet0/0/0/2    fe80::42:acff:fe15:e002
RP/0/RP0/CPU0:P-2#
```

Example 9-6 illustrates the TI-LFA double-segment behavior through an ICMP packet captured on the link {P-2 > P-5} after the protected link {P-2 > P-1} went down. The IPv6 destination address is fc00:0:4:e001::, and the inserted SRH contains the final segment END SID fc00:0:201:: of router ABR-3.

Example 9-6 *Double-Segment TI-LFA Failure Event Packet: SRv6*

```
Ethernet II, Src: 02:42:ac:16:0a:02 (02:42:ac:16:0a:02), Dst: 02:42:ac:16:0a:03
  (02:42:ac:16:0a:03)
Internet Protocol Version 6, Src: fc00:0:102::1, Dst: fc00:0:4:e001::
    0110 .... = Version: 6
    .... 0000 0000 .... .... .... .... .... = Traffic Class: 0x00 (DSCP: CS0,
  ECN: Not-ECT)
    .... 0000 0000 0000 0000 0000 = Flow Label: 0x00000
    Payload Length: 84
```

```
    Next Header: Routing Header for IPv6 (43)
    Hop Limit: 59
    Source Address: fc00:0:102::1
    Destination Address: fc00:0:4:e001::
    Routing Header for IPv6 (Segment Routing)
        Next Header: ICMPv6 (58)
        Length: 2
        [Length: 24 bytes]
        Type: Segment Routing (4)
        Segments Left: 1
        Last Entry: 0
        Flags: 0x00
        Tag: 0000
        Address[0]: fc00:0:201::
Internet Control Message Protocol v6
```

We have looked at various TI-LFA link protection scenarios that you may encounter on SRv6 networks. These examples show a few useful verification commands to help you understand the TI-LFA link protection mechanism on IOS XR–based platforms. Next, we will look at the configuration and verification tasks for TI-LFA node protection.

Node Protection Configuration

In the previous examples, TI-LFA is configured for link protection only on the PLR router since there is no requirement for protecting against node failures. The PLR router in Figure 9-13 is now configured for TI-LFA node protection. In addition, direct links between router P-2 and P-3 and between ABR-3 and ABR-4 are included in the following examples.

The configuration tasks illustrated in Config 9-13 may be applied directly under the IS-IS instance global address family or under the IS-IS interface address family to override the configuration on the IS-IS instance. This TI-LFA node protection is implemented with a tiebreaker index value, which allows a protection preference to be selected if additional tiebreakers are configured, such as the shared risk link group (SRLG) tiebreaker described later in this chapter, in the section "SRLG Protection: Configuration."

Config 9-13 *TI-LFA Node Protection Global: SR-MPLS (IOS XR)*

```
!
router isis CORE1
 address-family ipv4 unicast
  fast-reroute per-prefix tiebreaker node-protecting index 100
```

```
!
interface GigabitEthernet0/0/0/2
  address-family ipv4 unicast
   fast-reroute per-prefix
   fast-reroute per-prefix tiebreaker node-protecting index 200
   fast-reroute per-prefix ti-lfa
  !
 !
```

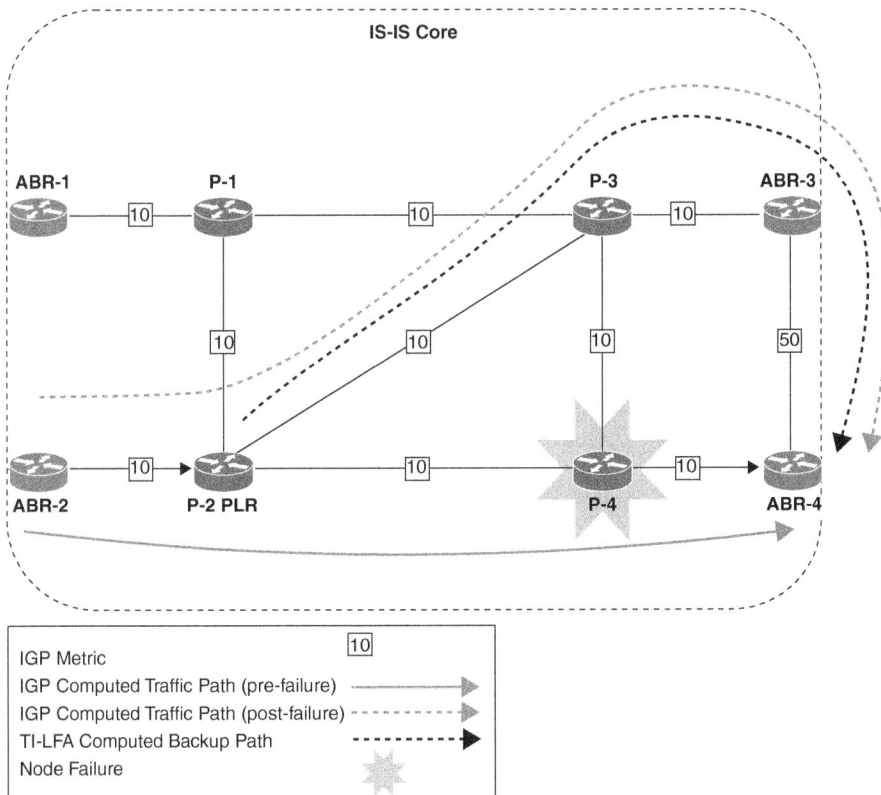

Figure 9-13 *TI-LFA Node Protection*

For SRv6-enabled routers, the TI-LFA node protection is configured the same way as for the SR-MPLS nodes except that in this case, it is under the IPv6 address family, as shown in Config 9-14.

Config 9-14   *TI-LFA Node Protection Global: SRv6 (IOS XR)*

```
!
router isis CORE_1
 address-family ipv6 unicast
  fast-reroute per-prefix tiebreaker node-protecting index 100
!
interface GigabitEthernet0/0/0/0
  address-family ipv6 unicast
   fast-reroute per-prefix
   fast-reroute per-prefix tiebreaker node-protecting index 200
   fast-reroute per-prefix ti-lfa
  !
 !
```

TI-LFA supports four tiebreakers that can be configured depending on the operator's requirements:

■ **node-protecting:** TI-LFA node protection is configured on the IS-IS instance, on the IS-IS interface, or on both.

■ **srlg-disjoint:** TI-LFA SRLG protection is configured on the IS-IS instance, on the IS-IS interface, or on both.

■ **lc-disjoint:** TI-LFA line card protection is configured on the IS-IS instance, on the IS-IS interface, or on both.

■ **default:** TI-LFA default protection is configured on the IS-IS interface only and refers to link protection only.

With the IOS XE routers in the SR-MPLS reference network, the TI-LFA node protection tiebreaker configuration may be enabled for all interfaces in the IS-IS global router configuration, as shown in Config 9-15.

Config 9-15   *TI-LFA Node Protection Tiebreaker Global (IOS XE)*

```
!
router isis CORE1
 fast-reroute per-prefix level-2 all
 fast-reroute tie-break level-2 node-protecting 100
 fast-reroute ti-lfa level-2
 !
```

Another configuration alternative could be to configure the TI-LFA node protection directly on an interface, as demonstrated in Config 9-16.

Config 9-16   *TI-LFA Link Protection Interface (IOS XE)*

```
!
interface GigabitEthernet2
 fast-reroute tie-break level-2 node-protecting 100
!
```

Next, we will carry out checks to confirm the TI-LFA node protection setup provisioned on router P-2 in the SR-MPLS reference network.

Node Protection Verification: SR-MPLS

The PLR router P-2 in Figure 9-14 has been configured with TI-LFA node protection on the interface GigabitEthernet0/0/0/2. The destination IPv4 prefix of interest is 10.0.1.8/32, located at router ABR-4. The TI-LFA node protection path is {P-2 > P-3 > ABR-3 > ABR-4}.

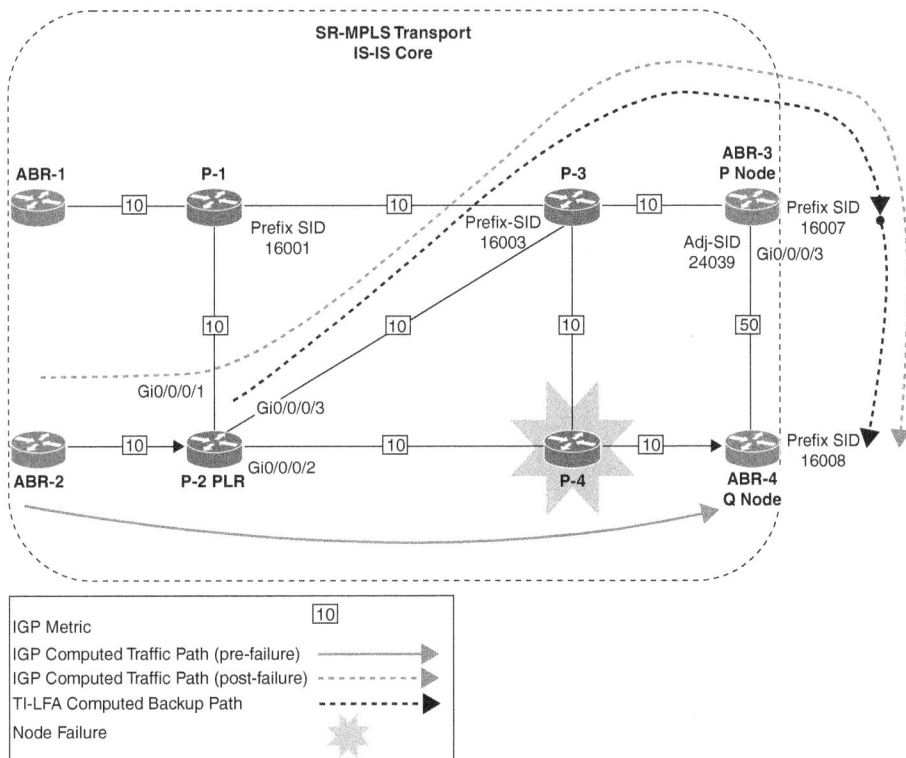

Figure 9-14   *TI-LFA Node Protection: SR-MPLS*

The CLI command **show route 10.0.1.8/32** in Output 9-35 displays the protected link toward router ABR-4 via interface GigabitEthernet0/0/0/2, and the TI-LFA backup path egresses via interface GigabitEthernet0/0/0/3 toward the repair nodes ABR-3 (P node) and ABR-4 (Q node).

Output 9-35 *TI-LFA Node Protection RIB Backup Path: SR-MPLS on P-2 (IOS XR)*

```
RP/0/RP0/CPU0:P-2#show route 10.0.1.8/32

Routing entry for 10.0.1.8/32
  Known via "isis CORE1", distance 115, metric 20, labeled SR, type level-2
  Installed Feb 25 04:19:57.641 for 01:07:04
  Routing Descriptor Blocks
    192.168.1.33, from 10.0.1.8, via GigabitEthernet0/0/0/3, Backup (TI-LFA)
      Repair Node(s): 10.0.1.7, 10.0.1.8
      Route metric is 70
    192.168.1.30, from 10.0.1.8, via GigabitEthernet0/0/0/2, Protected
      Route metric is 20
  No advertising protos.
RP/0/RP0/CPU0:P-2#
```

Output 9-36 confirms that the TI-LFA backup path is a double-segment example since the traffic is forwarded to the P node ABR-3 with the initial Prefix SID 16007 to avoid traversing the protected node P-4. The Adjacency SID 24039 on ABR-3 allows the traffic to be forwarded directly out the interface GigabitEthernet0/0/0/3 toward the Q node ABR-4. The output provides an indication that TI-LFA node protection is being used for this particular prefix through the Backup path: TI-LFA (node) field.

Output 9-36 *TI-LFA Node Protection IS-IS Fast Reroute Detail: SR-MPLS on P-2 (IOS XR)*

```
RP/0/RP0/CPU0:P-2#show isis ipv4 fast-reroute 10.0.1.8/32 detail

L2 10.0.1.8/32 [20/115] Label: 16008, medium priority
   Installed Feb 25 04:19:57.640 for 01:08:06
     via 192.168.1.30, GigabitEthernet0/0/0/2, Label: 16008, P-4, SRGB Base: 16000,
   Weight: 0
       Backup path: TI-LFA (node), via 192.168.1.33, GigabitEthernet0/0/0/3 P-3,
   SRGB Base: 16000, Weight: 0, Metric: 70
         P node: ABR-3.00 [10.0.1.7], Label: 16007
         Q node: ABR-4.00 [10.0.1.8], Label: 24039
         Prefix label: ImpNull
         Backup-src: ABR-4.00
       P: No, TM: 70, LC: No, NP: Yes, D: No, SRLG: No
     src ABR-4.00-00, 10.0.1.8, prefix-SID index 8, R:0 N:1 P:0 E:0 V:0 L:0, Alg:0
RP/0/RP0/CPU0:P-2#
```

The FIB forwarding confirmation in Output 9-37 indicates that two SIDs are required for traffic that may be forwarded across the backup path in order to reach the P node at ABR-3 with Prefix SID 16007 and using Adjacency SID 24039 to egress the interface GigabitEthernet0/0/0/3 to reach the Q node ABR-4.

Output 9-37   *TI-LFA Node Protection FIB Backup Path: SR-MPLS on P-2 (IOS XR)*

```
RP/0/RP0/CPU0:P-2#show cef 10.0.1.8/32


10.0.1.8/32, version 246, labeled SR, internal 0x1000001 0x8110 (ptr 0xe816b70) [1],
  0x600 (0xdb370b0), 0xa28 (0x22c1d1e0)
 Updated Feb 25 04:19:57.644
 remote adjacency to GigabitEthernet0/0/0/2
 Prefix Len 32, traffic index 0, precedence n/a, priority 1
  gateway array (0xd948d60) reference count 3, flags 0x500068, source rib (7), 0
  backups
                [2 type 5 flags 0x8401 (0xf4c4a08) ext 0x0 (0x0)]
  LW-LDI[type=5, refc=3, ptr=0xdb370b0, sh-ldi=0xf4c4a08]
  gateway array update type-time 1 Feb 25 04:19:57.644
 LDI Update time Feb 25 04:19:57.651
 LW-LDI-TS Feb 25 04:19:57.651
   via 192.168.1.33/32, GigabitEthernet0/0/0/3, 14 dependencies, weight 0, class 0,
 backup (TI-LFA) [flags 0xb00]
    path-idx 0 NHID 0x0 [0x22bac0f0 0x0]
    next hop 192.168.1.33/32, Repair Node(s): 10.0.1.7, 10.0.1.8
    remote adjacency
     local label 16008     labels imposed {16007 24039}
   via 192.168.1.30/32, GigabitEthernet0/0/0/2, 6 dependencies, weight 0, class 0,
 protected [flags 0x400]
    path-idx 1 bkup-idx 0 NHID 0x0 [0xd6df090 0x0]
    next hop 192.168.1.30/32
     local label 16008     labels imposed {16008}


    Load distribution: 0 (refcount 2)


    Hash  OK  Interface               Address
    0     Y   GigabitEthernet0/0/0/2  remote
RP/0/RP0/CPU0:P-2#
```

> **Note**   Because many of these example outputs are repetitive, the IOS XE–based router TI-LFA node and SRLG protection verification commands are combined in the section "SRLG Protection Verification: SR-MPLS," later in this chapter.

Node Protection Verification: SRv6

In this section, you will see how to perform basic verifications to ensure that the TI-LFA node protection is properly configured in the SRv6 reference network. The PLR router P-2 from the SRv6 reference network in Figure 9-15 has been configured with TI-LFA node protection on the interface GigabitEthernet0/0/0/1. The destination locator being verified is the END SID fc00:0:202:: of router ABR-4. The TI-LFA node protection path is {P-2 > P-3 > ABR-3 > ABR-4}.

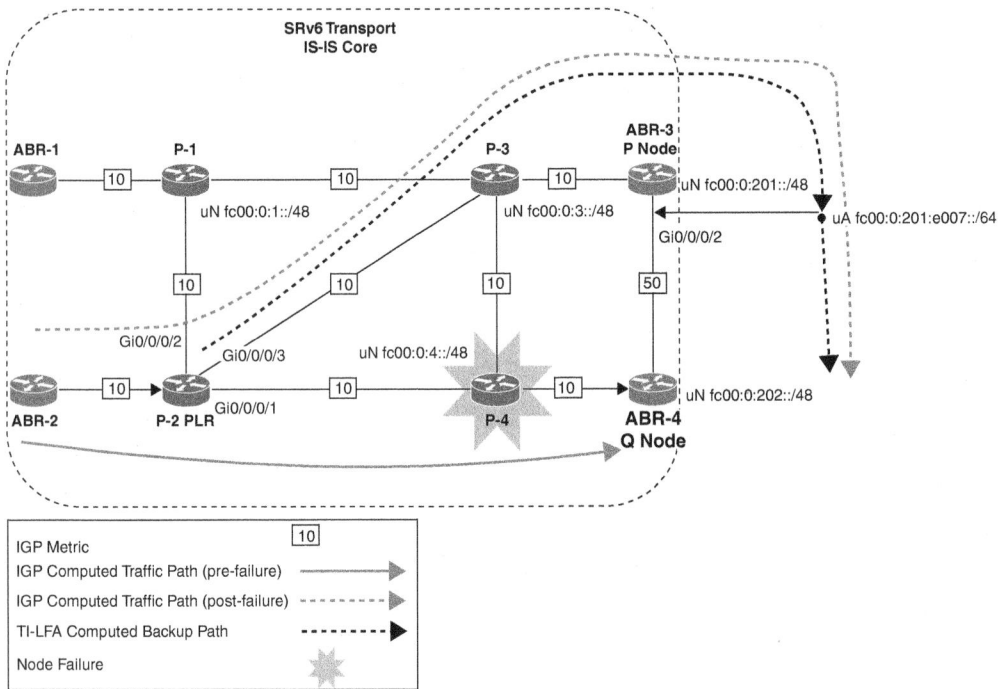

Figure 9-15   *TI-LFA Node Protection: SRv6*

The TI-LFA node protection verification outputs are similar to those of the SRv6 double-segment TI-LFA link protection example (refer to Figure 9-12), so in this section, we only need to examine the command **show isis ipv6 fast-reroute fc00:0:202::/48 detail** (see Output 9-38). This output indicates the backup path behavior as TI-LFA (node) via the PLR interface GigabitEthernet0/0/0/3. In this case, a single SID with two uSIDs is used; the P node ABR-3.00 is reachable with Node SID fc00:0:201:: (uSID 0x0201), and the repair Q node ABR-4.00 is reachable via the Adjacency SID fc00:0:201:e007:: (uSID 0xe007) of router ABR-3.

Output 9-38   *TI-LFA Node Protection ISIS Fast Reroute Detail: SRv6 on P-2 (IOS XR)*

```
RP/0/RP0/CPU0:P-2#show isis ipv6 fast-reroute fc00:0:202::/48 detail

L2 fc00:0:202::/48 [21/115] Label: None, low priority
    Installed Mar 03 03:37:22.657 for 00:24:19
      via fe80::42:acff:fe16:802, GigabitEthernet0/0/0/1, P-4, Weight: 0
      Backup path: TI-LFA (node), via fe80::42:acff:fe16:902, GigabitEther-
net0/0/0/3 P-3, Weight: 0, Metric: 71
```

```
      P node: ABR-3.00 [::], SRv6 SID: fc00:0:201:: uN (PSP/USD)
      Q node: ABR-4.00 [::], SRv6 SID: fc00:0:201:e007:: uA (PSP/USD)
      Backup-src: ABR-4.00
    P: No, TM: 71, LC: No, NP: Yes, D: No, SRLG: Yes
  src ABR-4.00-00, ::
RP/0/RP0/CPU0:P-2#
```

As you have seen, the TI-LFA node protection mechanism requires that the backup path not traverse the neighboring node. In this example, the double-segment TI-LFA behavior allows the bypass of router P-4 using the protection path {P-2 > P-3 > ABR-3 > ABR-4}.

SRLG Protection Configuration

In the previous example, TI-LFA is configured for node protection on the PLR router P-2. This section describes the protection of a set of interfaces with an identified shared failure risk, known as a shared risk link group (SRLG). The term SRLG as originally used with optical networks, in which separate networks could be impacted by a single failure event when sharing a common risk factor. An example of a risk factor could be that the optical cables are laid within the same conduits, making it possible for them to be damaged by an external event. Figure 9-16 identifies the interfaces GigabitEthernet0/0/0/2 and GigabitEthernet0/0/0/3 on the PLR router as being part of the same SRLG.

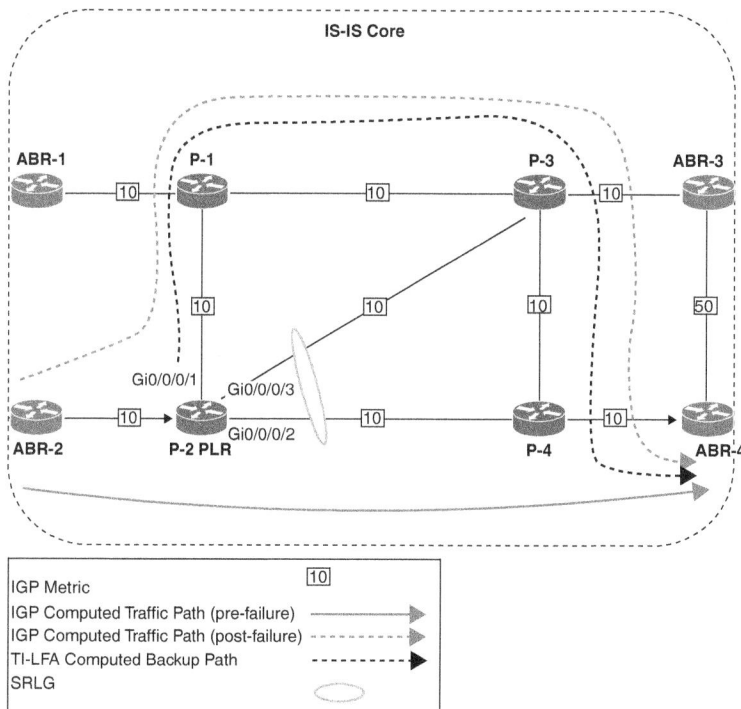

Figure 9-16 *TI-LFA SRLG Protection*

The commands for SRLG configuration in Config 9-17 provide an illustration of a straightforward arrangement for IOS XR routers, where interfaces GigabitEthernet0/0/0/2 and GigabitEthernet0/0/0/3 are both associated with a risk identified by the network operator.

Config 9-17   *Shared Risk Link Group Definition (IOS XR)*

```
srlg
 interface GigabitEthernet0/0/0/2
  name SRLG-1
 !
 interface GigabitEthernet0/0/0/3
  name SRLG-1
 !
 name SRLG-1
  value 100
 !
!
```

Config 9-18 displays the SRLG tiebreaker configured on the interfaces GigabitEthernet0/0/0/2 and GigabitEthernet0/0/0/3. Note that the command may also be configured directly under the global IS-IS process, which applies to all interfaces on the IS-IS instance, with the per-interface SRLG defining which interfaces are sharing the same identified risk.

Config 9-18   *TI-LFA SRLG Enabled per Interface (IOS XR)*

```
!
router isis CORE1
 !
 interface GigabitEthernet0/0/0/2
  address-family ipv4 unicast
   fast-reroute per-prefix
   fast-reroute per-prefix tiebreaker srlg-disjoint index 100
   fast-reroute per-prefix ti-lfa
  !
 !
 interface GigabitEthernet0/0/0/3
  address-family ipv4 unicast
   fast-reroute per-prefix
   fast-reroute per-prefix tiebreaker srlg-disjoint index 100
   fast-reroute per-prefix ti-lfa
  !
 !
```

For IOS XE–based routers, the SRLG configurations can be implemented as shown in Config 9-19.

Config 9-19   *Shared Risk Link Group Definition (IOS XE)*

```
!
interface GigabitEthernet2
srlg gid 100
!
interface GigabitEthernet3
srlg gid 100
!
```

In IOS XE, TI-LFA SRLG may be configured directly under the IS-IS instance, and the configuration will apply to all IS-IS Level 2 interfaces, as shown in Config 9-20.

Config 9-20   *TI-LFA SRLG Protection Enabled Globally (IOS XE)*

```
!
router isis CORE1
 fast-reroute per-prefix level-2 all
 fast-reroute tie-break level-2 srlg-disjoint 150
 fast-reroute ti-lfa level-2
!
```

In IOS XE, the SRLG tiebreaker configuration can be applied directly under a specific interface, thereby disabling all other tiebreakers, as shown in Config 9-21.

Config 9-21   *TI-LFA SRLG Protection Enabled per Interface (IOS XE)*

```
!
interface GigabitEthernet2
 srlg gid 100
 isis network point-to-point
 isis fast-reroute tie-break level-2 srlg-disjoint 150
!
```

SRLG Protection Verification: SR-MPLS

Now we will conduct verifications to validate the setup of TI-LFA SRLG protection on both IOS XR and IOS XE routers in the SR-MPLS reference network. The PLR router P-2 in Figure 9-17 has been configured with the TI-LFA SRLG tiebreaker under both interfaces GigabitEthernet0/0/0/2 and GigabitEthernet0/0/0/3. Once again, the destination IPv4 prefix of interest is 10.0.1.8/32, located at the router ABR-4. The protected interface GigabitEthernet0/0/0/2 and the potential protection path interface GigabitEthernet0/0/0/3 are both now part of the same SRLG named SRLG-1, with a configured index value of 100.

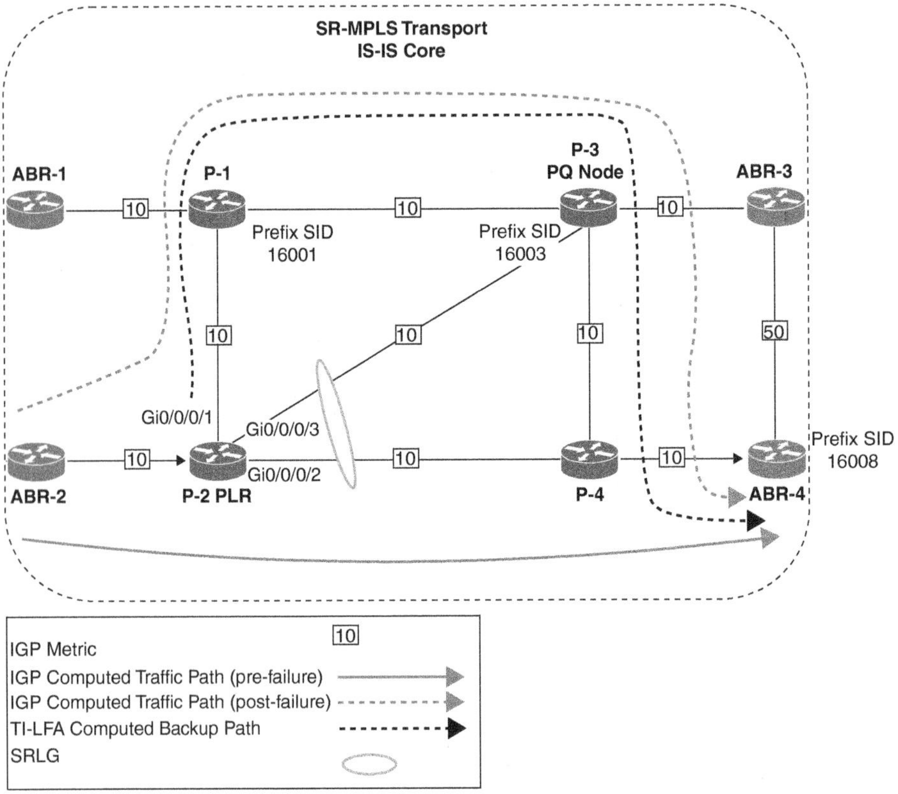

Figure 9-17 *TI-LFA SRLG Protection: SR-MPLS*

With the SRLG configuration, the protected link to router ABR-4 via interface GigabitEthernet0/0/0/2 now has the TI-LFA backup path via interface GigabitEthernet0/0/0/1 to the repair node P-3 (PQ node) before being forwarded on via router P-4 to the destination at router ABR-4. The RIB details in Output 9-39 indicate the repair node as P-3, reachable via interface GigabitEthernet0/0/0/1.

Output 9-39 *TI-LFA SRLG Protection RIB Backup Path: SR-MPLS on P-2 (IOS XR)*

```
RP/0/RP0/CPU0:P-2#show route 10.0.1.8/32

Routing entry for 10.0.1.8/32
  Known via "isis CORE1", distance 115, metric 20, labeled SR, type level-2
  Installed Feb 27 09:51:35.992 for 1d00h
```

```
Routing Descriptor Blocks
   192.168.1.30, from 10.0.1.8, via GigabitEthernet0/0/0/2, Protected
     Route metric is 20
   192.168.1.2, from 10.0.1.8, via GigabitEthernet0/0/0/1, Backup (TI-LFA)
     Repair Node(s): 10.0.1.3
     Route metric is 40
  No advertising protos.
RP/0/RP0/CPU0:P-2#
```

The TI-LFA backup path viewed with the command **show isis ipv4 fast-reroute 10.0.1.8/32 detail** in Output 9-40 shows the TI-LFA backup path via the interface GigabitEthernet0/0/0/1 to the PQ node P-3 with the SID 16003 before being forwarded on to the destination ABR-4 through the router P-4. This output also provides an indication that TI-LFA SRLG protection is being used for this prefix, as shown with Backup path: TI-LFA (srlg) in the output.

Output 9-40 *TI-LFA SRLG Protection IS-IS Fast Reroute Detail: SR-MPLS on P-2 (IOS XR)*

```
RP/0/RP0/CPU0:P-2#show isis ipv4 fast-reroute 10.0.1.8/32 detail

L2 10.0.1.8/32 [20/115] Label: 16008, medium priority
   Installed Feb 25 08:04:44.731 for 00:06:11
     via 192.168.1.30, GigabitEthernet0/0/0/2, Label: 16008, P-4, SRGB Base: 16000,
  Weight: 0
       Backup path: TI-LFA (srlg), via 192.168.1.2, GigabitEthernet0/0/0/1 P-1,
  SRGB Base: 16000, Weight: 0, Metric: 40
         P node: P-3.00 [10.0.1.3], Label: 16003
         Prefix label: 16008
         Backup-src: ABR-4.00
       P: No, TM: 40, LC: No, NP: No, D: No, SRLG: Yes
     src ABR-4.00-00, 10.0.1.8, prefix-SID index 8, R:0 N:1 P:0 E:0 V:0 L:0, Alg:0
RP/0/RP0/CPU0:P-2#
```

The FIB details in Output 9-41 confirm that an additional SID is required for traffic that may be forwarded across the TI-LFA computed backup path in order to reach the destination ABR-4 with Prefix SID 16008. The traffic will egress interface GigabitEthernet0/0/0/1 via router P-1 to the PQ node P-3 using SID 16003 before traversing router P-4 to the destination ABR-4 with SID 16008.

Output 9-41   *TI-LFA SRLG Protection FIB Details: SR-MPLS on P-2 (IOS XR)*

```
RP/0/RP0/CPU0:P-2#show cef 10.0.1.8/32


10.0.1.8/32, version 274, labeled SR, internal 0x1000001 0x8110 (ptr 0xe816b70) [1],
  0x600 (0xdb370b0), 0xa28 (0x22c1d2b0)
 Updated Feb 25 08:04:44.740
 remote adjacency to GigabitEthernet0/0/0/2
 Prefix Len 32, traffic index 0, precedence n/a, priority 1
  gateway array (0xd9487f0) reference count 3, flags 0x500068, source rib (7), 0
  backups
               [2 type 5 flags 0x8401 (0xf4c4b88) ext 0x0 (0x0)]
  LW-LDI[type=5, refc=3, ptr=0xdb370b0, sh-ldi=0xf4c4b88]
  gateway array update type-time 1 Feb 25 08:04:44.740
 LDI Update time Feb 25 08:04:44.740
 LW-LDI-TS Feb 25 08:04:44.740
   via 192.168.1.30/32, GigabitEthernet0/0/0/2, 6 dependencies, weight 0, class 0,
 protected [flags 0x400]
    path-idx 0 bkup-idx 1 NHID 0x0 [0xd6df270 0x0]
    next hop 192.168.1.30/32
     local label 16008      labels imposed {16008}
   via 192.168.1.2/32, GigabitEthernet0/0/0/1, 17 dependencies, weight 0, class 0,
 backup (TI-LFA) [flags 0xb00]
    path-idx 1 NHID 0x0 [0x22bab3d0 0x0]
    next hop 192.168.1.2/32, Repair Node(s): 10.0.1.3
    remote adjacency
     local label 16008      labels imposed {16003 16008}


   Load distribution: 0 (refcount 2)


   Hash  OK  Interface              Address
    0     Y   GigabitEthernet0/0/0/2    remote
RP/0/RP0/CPU0:P-2#
```

In some instances, it might make sense to combine the TI-LFA node and SRLG protection, as demonstrated in Figure 9-18.

In the example shown in Config 9-22, both the TI-LFA node and SRLG protection options are configured. If it is feasible, the router will integrate the two protection modes. However, in cases where both modes are possible but cannot be applied simultaneously, the tiebreaker rule comes into effect. Under this rule, the option with the higher index value is given preference.

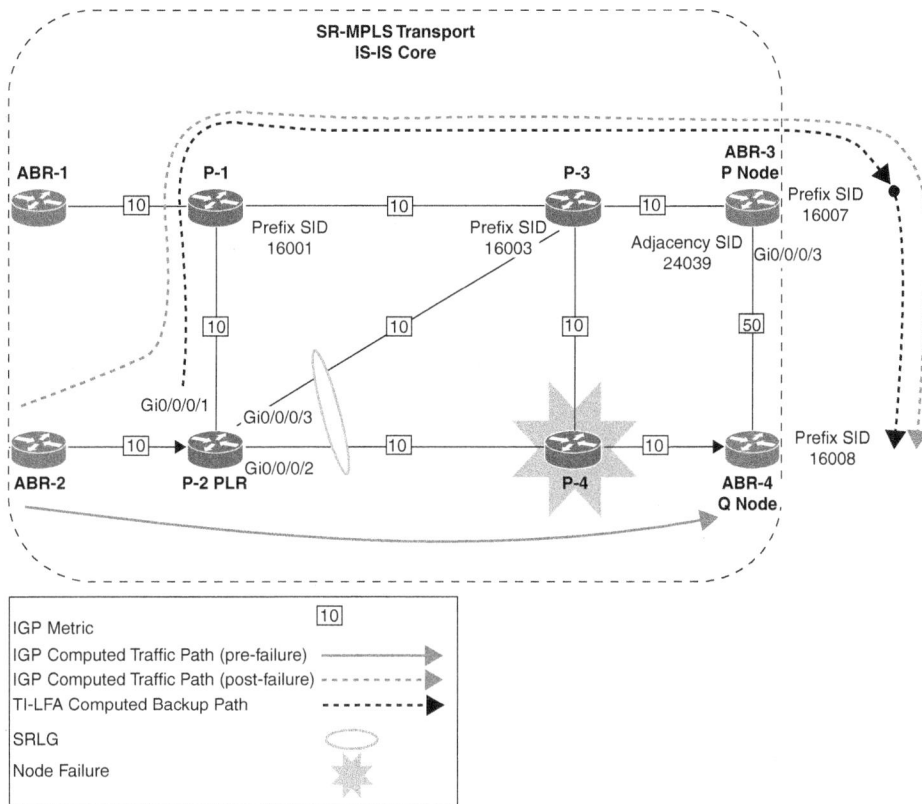

Figure 9-18 *TI-LFA SRLG and Node Combined Protection: SR-MPLS*

Config 9-22 *TI-LFA SRLG and Node Combined Protection: SR-MPLS (IOS XR)*

```
!
router isis CORE1
!
 interface GigabitEthernet0/0/0/2
  address-family ipv4 unicast
   fast-reroute per-prefix
   fast-reroute per-prefix tiebreaker node-protecting index 200
   fast-reroute per-prefix tiebreaker srlg-disjoint index 100
   fast-reroute per-prefix ti-lfa
  !
 !
```

In Output 9-42, the command **show isis ipv4 fast-reroute 10.0.1.8/32 detail** displays the TI-LFA backup path via the interface GigabitEthernet0/0/0/1 to the P node ABR-3 with SID 16007 and then egresses the interface GigabitEthernet0/0/0/1 (of router ABR-3) using the Adjacency SID 24039 to reach the Q node and destination ABR-4. From this output, it is apparent that both the TI-LFA node and SRLG protection are being used for this prefix with the Backup path: TI-LFA (node+srlg) field, as highlighted in the output.

Output 9-42 *TI-LFA SRLG and Node Combined Protection IS-IS Fast Reroute Detail: SR-MPLS on P-2 (IOS XR)*

```
RP/0/RP0/CPU0:P-2#show isis ipv4 fast-reroute 10.0.1.8/32 detail

L2 10.0.1.8/32 [20/115] Label: 16008, medium priority
   Installed Feb 25 08:22:18.901 for 03:21:23
      via 192.168.1.30, GigabitEthernet0/0/0/2, Label: 16008, P-4, SRGB Base: 16000,
   Weight: 0
         Backup path: TI-LFA (node+srlg), via 192.168.1.2, GigabitEthernet0/0/0/1 P-1,
   SRGB Base: 16000, Weight: 0, Metric: 80
            P node: ABR-3.00 [10.0.1.7], Label: 16007
            Q node: ABR-4.00 [10.0.1.8], Label: 24039
            Prefix label: ImpNull
            Backup-src: ABR-4.00
         P: No, TM: 80, LC: No, NP: Yes, D: No, SRLG: Yes
      src ABR-4.00-00, 10.0.1.8, prefix-SID index 8, R:0 N:1 P:0 E:0 V:0 L:0, Alg:0
RP/0/RP0/CPU0:P-2#
```

When the PLR is an IOS XE router and configured for both TI-LFA node and SRLG protection, the verification commands shown next would be applicable. The command **show ip route repair-paths 10.0.1.8 255.255.255.255** in Output 9-43 displays the TI-LFA backup path for the destination router ABR-4 as being set up via the MPLS-SR-Tunnel6.

Output 9-43 *TI-LFA SRLG and Node Combined Protection RIB Backup Path: SR-MPLS on P-2 (IOS XE)*

```
P-2#show ip route repair-paths 10.0.1.8 255.255.255.255
Routing entry for 10.0.1.8/32
   Known via "isis", distance 115, metric 20, type level-2
   Redistributing via isis CORE1
   Last update from 192.168.1.30 on GigabitEthernet2, 00:04:05 ago
   Routing Descriptor Blocks:
   * 192.168.1.30, from 10.0.1.8, 00:04:05 ago, via GigabitEthernet2, merge-labels
        Route metric is 20, traffic share count is 1
        MPLS label: 16008
        MPLS Flags: NSF
        Repair Path: 10.0.1.8, via MPLS-SR-Tunnel6
     [RPR]10.0.1.8, from 10.0.1.8, 00:04:05 ago, via MPLS-SR-Tunnel6, merge-labels
        Route metric is 90, traffic share count is 1
        MPLS label: implicit-null
        MPLS Flags: NSF
P-2#
```

Output 9-44 from the PLR router provides an overview of the IS-IS TI-LFA repair path tunnels that have been set up. The repair path to ABR-4 will use tunnel MP6, egressing the local interface GigabitEthernet1 via router P-1 toward the P-node ABR-3 with Prefix SID 16007. Using the Adjacency SID 24039, the traffic will egress ABR-3 directly out the interface Gi0/0/0/3 toward the destination at router ABR-4.

Output 9-44   *TI-LFA SRLG and Node Combined Protection Tunnels: SR-MPLS on P-2 (IOS XE)*

```
P-2#show isis fast-reroute ti-lfa tunnel

Tag CORE1:
Fast-Reroute TI-LFA Tunnels:

Tunnel   Interface   Next Hop       End Point       Label     End Point Host
MP2      Gi1         192.168.1.2    10.0.1.1        16001     P-1
                                    10.0.1.5        16005     ABR-1
MP4      Gi1         192.168.1.2    10.0.1.3        16003     P-3
MP3      Gi2         192.168.1.30   10.0.1.3        16003     P3
MP6      Gi1         192.168.1.2    10.0.1.7        16007     ABR-3
                                    10.0.1.8        24039     ABR-4
MP1      Gi2         192.168.1.30   10.0.1.3        16003     P-3
                                    10.0.1.254      16254     RR-1

PE-2#
```

In Output 9-45, the command **show isis rib 10.0.1.8 255.255.255.255**, which is used for local IS-IS RIB verification, offers a comprehensive view of the repair path information for the 10.0.1.8/32 route as observed from the PLR. The repair path for 10.0.1.8/32 via the MPLS-SR-Tunnel6 provides both node and SRLG protection, as indicated in the output. The P-node ABR-3 is reachable with the Prefix SID 16007, and the Adjacency SID 24039 on ABR-3 allows traffic to be forwarded directly to the Q-node ABR-4.

Output 9-45   *TI-LFA SRLG and Node Combined Protection ISIS RIB: on SR-MPLS P-2 (IOS XE)*

```
P-2#show isis rib 10.0.1.8 255.255.255.255

IPv4 local RIB for IS-IS process CORE1

IPV4 unicast topology base (TID 0, TOPOID 0x0) =================
Repair path attributes:
    DS - Downstream, LC - Linecard-Disjoint, NP - Node-Protecting
    PP - Primary-Path, SR - SRLG-Disjoint
```

```
10.0.1.8/32  prefix attr X:0 R:0 N:1  source router id: 10.0.1.8  prefix SID
  index 8 - Bound
  [115/L2/20] via 192.168.1.30(GigabitEthernet2), from 10.0.1.8, tag 0
    prefix attr: X:0 R:0 N:1
    source router id: 10.0.1.8
      SRGB: 16000, range: 8000 prefix-SID index: 8, R:0 N:1 P:0 E:0 V:0 L:0
    label: 16008
            (installed)
    repair path: 10.0.1.8(MPLS-SR-Tunnel6) metric:90 (DS,NP,SR)
      next-hop: 192.168.1.2 (GigabitEthernet1)
      TI-LFA node/SRLG-protecting, node-protecting
      SRGB: 16000, range: 8000 prefix-SID index: 8, R:0 N:1 P:0 E:0 V:0 L:0
      label: implicit-null
      P node: ABR-3[10.0.1.7], label: 16007
      Q node: ABR-4[10.0.1.8], label: 24039
      repair source: ABR-4
P-2#
```

Finally, Output 9-46 shows the PLR router FIB details for the protected prefix, obtained with the command **show ip cef 10.0.1.8 internal**. It shows the protected link {P-2 > P-4} via interface GigabitEthernet2 with a repair path via MPLS-SR-Tunnel6, which egresses GigabitEthernet1 toward the neighbor router P-1. Traffic toward the destination router ABR-4 will have the additional SIDs 16007 and 24039 imposed during the link, node, or SRLG failure event until the IGP has converged.

Output 9-46 *TI-LFA SRLG and Node Combined Protection FIB Backup Path: SR-MPLS on P-2 (IOS XE)*

```
P-2#show ip cef 10.0.1.8 internal
10.0.1.8/32, epoch 2, RIB[I], refcnt 6, per-destination sharing
  sources: RIB, LTE
  feature space:
    IPRM: 0x00028000
    Broker: linked, distributed at 4th priority
    LFD: 10.0.1.8/32 1 local label
    sr local label info: global/16008 [0x1B]
        contains path extension list
        sr disposition chain 0x7FC6F45D08C8
          label 16008
          FRR Primary
            <primary: TAG adj out of GigabitEthernet2, addr 192.168.1.30>
        sr label switch chain 0x7FC6F45D08C8
          label 16008
```

```
        FRR Primary
            <primary: TAG adj out of GigabitEthernet2, addr 192.168.1.30>
ifnums:
  GigabitEthernet2(8): 192.168.1.30
  MPLS-SR-Tunnel6(22)
path list 7FC75FD63950, 5 locks, per-destination, flags 0x49 [shble, rif, hwcn]
  path 7FC7600B97C8, share 1/1, type attached nexthop, for IPv4, flags [has-rpr]
    MPLS short path extensions: [rib | lblmrg | srlbl] MOI flags = 0x21 label
16008
    nexthop 192.168.1.30 GigabitEthernet2 label [16008|implicit-null]
(ptr:0x7FC6F45D08C8)-(local:16008), IP adj out of GigabitEthernet2, addr
192.168.1.30 7FC6F2137290
      repair: attached-nexthop 10.0.1.8 MPLS-SR-Tunnel6 (7FC7600B96F8)
  path 7FC7600B96F8, share 1/1, type attached nexthop, for IPv4, flags [rpr,
rpr-only]
    MPLS short path extensions: [rib | lblmrg | srlbl] MOI flags = 0x1 label
implicit-null
    nexthop 10.0.1.8 MPLS-SR-Tunnel6, repair, IP midchain out of MPLS-SR-Tunnel6
7FC6F4406F88
output chain:
  label [16008|implicit-null](ptr:0x7FC6F45D08C8)-(local:16008)
  FRR Primary (0x80007FC756FAFE90)
    <primary: TAG adj out of GigabitEthernet2, addr 192.168.1.30 7FC6F2137060>
    <repair: TAG midchain out of MPLS-SR-Tunnel6 7FC6F4406D58
            label 24039
            label 16007
            TAG adj out of GigabitEthernet1, addr 192.168.1.2 7FC6F21374C0>
P-2#
```

SRLG Protection Verification: SRv6

This section shows a fundamental check of the TI-LFA SRLG protection performed on
the PLR router P-2 in the SRv6 reference network. The SRv6 PLR router in Figure 9-19 has
been configured with the TI-LFA SRLG tiebreaker on interfaces GigabitEthernet0/0/0/1
and GigabitEthernet0/0/0/3. Both the protected interface GigabitEthernet0/0/0/1 and
the potential protection path interface GigabitEthernet0/0/0/3 are now part of the same
SRLG, named SRLG-1, with configured index value 100.

The destination locator being verified is fc00:0:202:: of router ABR-4, and so the TI-LFA
SRLG protection path is {P-1 > P-3 > P-4 > ABR-4}.

The command in Output 9-47 confirms that both interfaces GigabitEthernet0/0/0/1 and
GigabitEthernet0/0/0/3 are configured as part of the same SRLG.

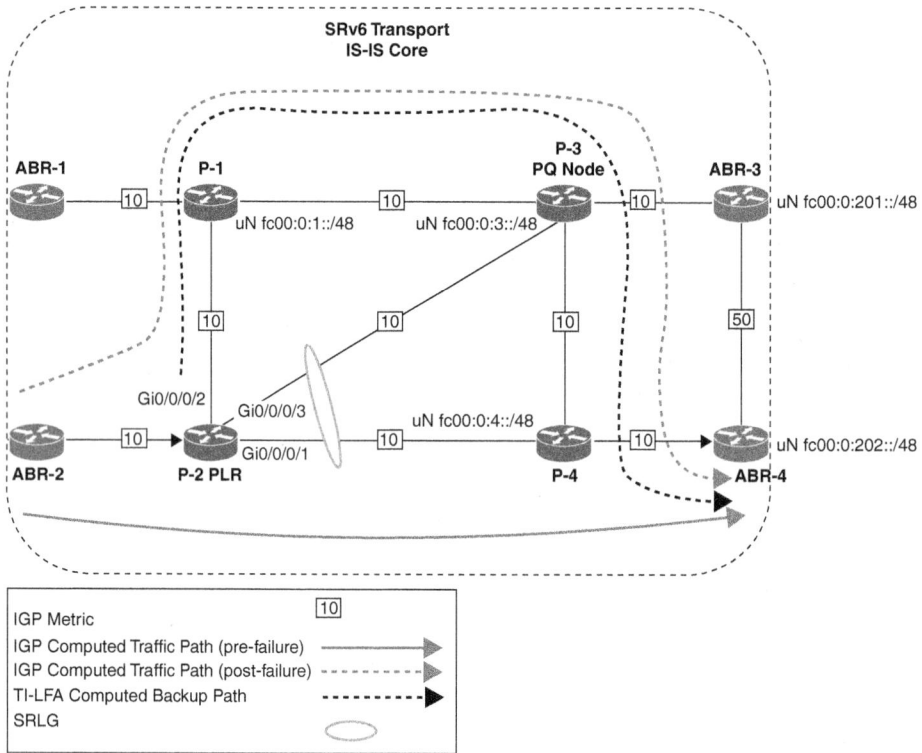

Figure 9-19 *TI-LFA SRLG Protection: SRv6*

Output 9-47 *SRLG Interface on P-2 (IOS XR)*

```
RP/0/RP0/CPU0:P-2#show srlg name SRLG-1


SRLG : SRLG-1
Value : 100


Interface:
 GigabitEthernet0/0/0/1
 GigabitEthernet0/0/0/3


RP/0/RP0/CPU0:P-2#
```

In Output 9-48, The command **show isis ipv6 fast-reroute fc00:0:202::/48 detail** issued from the PLR router displays the backup path behavior as TI-LFA (srlg) via interface GigabitEthernet0/0/0/2 toward router P-1. The repair PQ node P-3 is reachable with its Node SID fc00:0:3::, and it will forward the protected traffic over the shortest path {P-3 > P-4 > ABR-4}.

Output 9-48 *TI-LFA SRLG Protection IS-IS Fast Reroute Detail: SRv6 on P-2 (IOS XR)*

```
RP/0/RP0/CPU0:P-22#show isis ipv6 fast-reroute fc00:0:202::/48 detail

L2 fc00:0:202::/48 [21/115] Label: None, low priority
   Installed Mar 03 05:12:21.271 for 00:05:05
      via fe80::42:acff:fe16:802, GigabitEthernet0/0/0/1, P-4, Weight: 0
         Backup path: TI-LFA (srlg), via fe80::42:acff:fe15:e002, GigabitEther-
   net0/0/0/2 P-1, Weight: 0, Metric: 41
            P node: P-3.00 [::], SRv6 SID: fc00:0:3:: uN (PSP/USD)
            Backup-src: ABR-4.00
         P: No, TM: 41, LC: No, NP: No, D: No, SRLG: Yes
      src ABR-4.00-00, ::
RP/0/RP0/CPU0:P-2#
```

Finally, Figure 9-20 shows a scenario where both TI-LFA node and SRLG protection are configured on the PLR router.

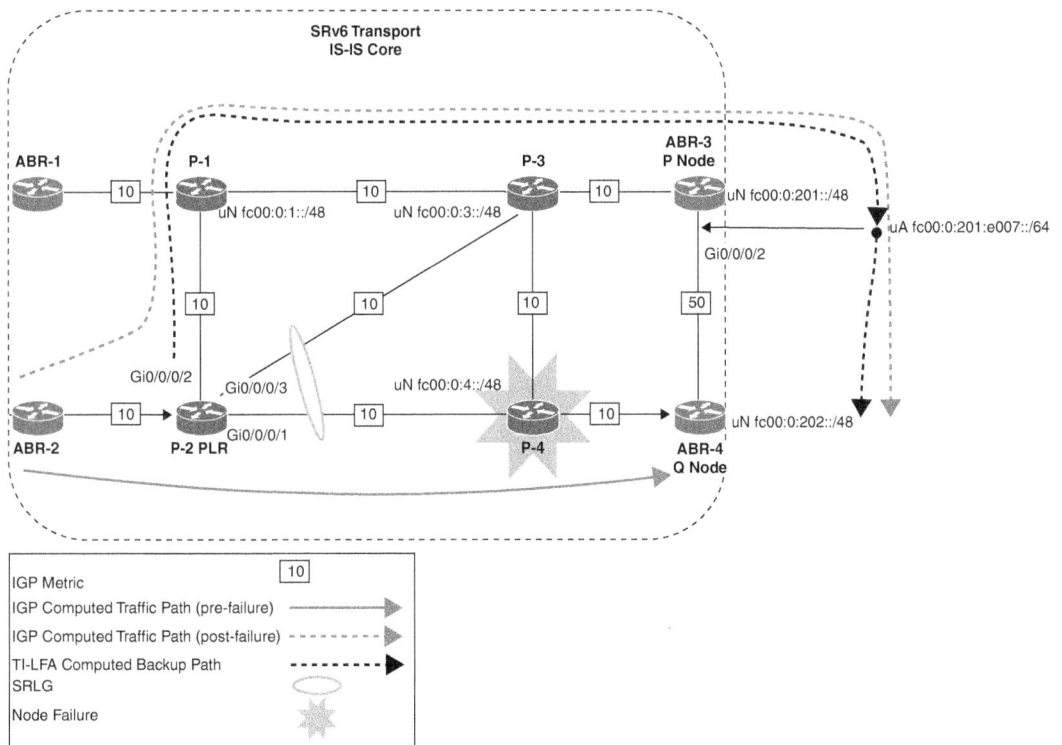

Figure 9-20 *TI-LFA SRLG and Node Protection: SRv6*

If both TI-LFA node and SRLG protection are needed, they can be set up as shown in Config 9-23. If both options are possible simultaneously, the PLR router will combine the two protection modes. However, if both protection modes are possible but cannot be applied simultaneously, the tiebreaker rule will apply, with the higher index value taking precedence.

Config 9-23   *TI-LFA SRLG and Node Combined Protection: SRv6 (IOS XR)*

```
!
router isis CORE_1
!
interface GigabitEthernet0/0/0/1
  address-family ipv6 unicast
   fast-reroute per-prefix
   fast-reroute per-prefix tiebreaker node-protecting index 200
   fast-reroute per-prefix tiebreaker srlg-disjoint index 100
   fast-reroute per-prefix ti-lfa
  !
 !
```

With the combined TI-LFA SRLG and node protection scenario, the command **show isis ipv6 fast-reroute fc00:0:202::/48 detail** in Output 9-49 reveals that the TI-LFA backup path is routed via the interface GigabitEthernet0/0/0/1. A single SID with two uSIDs is used in this double-segment scenario, with the P node ABR-3 reachable with Node SID fc00:0:201:: (uSID 0x201) and the repair Q node ABR-4 reachable via the Adjacency SID fc00:0:201:e007:: (uSID 0xe007) of router ABR-3. The output specifically indicates that both TI-LFA node and SRLG protections are in effect for this prefix, as evidenced by the Backup path: TI-LFA (node+srlg) field.

Output 9-49   *TI-LFA SRLG and Node Combined Protection IS-IS Fast Reroute Detail: SRv6 on P-2 (IOS XR)*

```
RP/0/RP0/CPU0:P-2#show isis ipv6 fast-reroute fc00:0:202::/48 detail
L2 fc00:0:202::/48 [21/115] Label: None, low priority
   Installed Mar 03 06:22:13.633 for 00:00:56
     via fe80::42:acff:fe16:802, GigabitEthernet0/0/0/1, P-4, Weight: 0
      Backup path: TI-LFA (node+srlg), via fe80::42:acff:fe15:e002,
GigabitEthernet0/0/0/2 P-1, Weight: 0, Metric: 81
        P node: ABR-3.00 [::], SRv6 SID: fc00:0:201:: uN (PSP/USD)
        Q node: ABR-4.00 [::], SRv6 SID: fc00:0:201:e007:: uA (PSP/USD)
        Backup-src: ABR-4.00
      P: No, TM: 81, LC: No, NP: Yes, D: No, SRLG: Yes
     src ABR-4.00-00, ::
RP/0/RP0/CPU0:P-2#
```

As mentioned at the beginning of this section, segment routing has allowed for the development of TI-LFA as an improvement over the classic LFA fast reroute technology. TI-LFA allows for 100% protection coverage with sub-50 ms network convergence in the event of link or node failure. Another important benefit of TI-LFA is that the LFA path follows the IGP post-convergence path, which reduces the risk of transient congestion or suboptimal routing occurring. Network operators also benefit from the ease of deployment and operability of TI-LFA. They can implement the feature as part of the Day 0 SR configurations in network rollouts or even deploy it incrementally if required.

Microloop Avoidance

Microloops are transient routing loops that can occur in IP networks during the convergence process after a topology change, such as link up and down events or even configuration changes to IGP metrics. These loops are typically short-lived but can cause significant packet loss and increased latency while the network stabilizes. Microloops arise because various routers in the network may update their routing tables at slightly different times, leading to temporary inconsistencies in the forwarding paths. For example, if one router updates its path to a destination before another router has had a chance to do so, packets may be forwarded in a loop between these routers until the network converges to a stable state. The advent of FRR mechanisms with potential network repair times of sub-50 ms also highlights microloops that were masked by the previously slower IGP convergence times. The resultant impact on the traffic could be increased jitter and delay, out-of-sequence packets, or even worse, actual loss of packets.

SR Microloop Avoidance offers extensive network coverage for preventing microloops. In addition to reacting to local events, this feature is also activated upon receiving IGP updates from non-local events. During the IGP convergence computation, the router may identify potential microloops along the new path to the destination. If possible microloop conditions are detected, the router will install an explicit SR path using a segment list to steer the traffic through a repair node. After a delay period, during which the network topology is expected to have converged, the explicit SR path is removed, and the traffic resumes following the post-failure computed IGP path.

Figure 9-21 shows what happens when a local failure occurs and the Microloop Avoidance feature is not configured. The following numerals correspond to the numerals in the figure:

1. **Pre-failure state:** Initially the traffic flows across the path from the source router ABR-2 to the destination router ABR-4 via the path {P-2 > P-1 > P-3 > P-4} due to a lower metric cost of 50. Output 9-50 from the PLR router P-2 displays the FIB entry to locator fc00:0:202:: (ABR-4) via interface GigabitEthernet0/0/0/2.

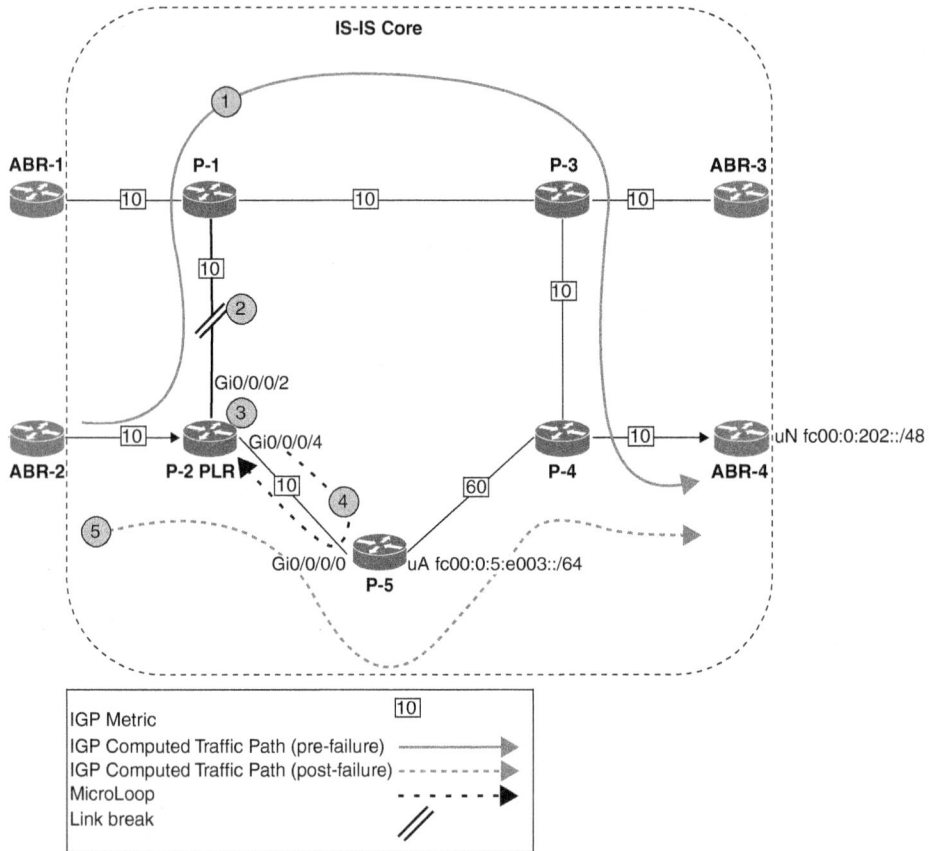

Figure 9-21   *Local Failure Without Microloop Avoidance*

Output 9-50   *Pre-Failure FIB Entry to ABR-4 from P-2*

```
RP/0/RP0/CPU0:P-2#show cef ipv6 fc00:0:202::/48
Fri Jul 26 02:56:53.378 UTC
fc00:0:202::/48, version 744, internal 0x1000001 0x220 (ptr 0x86fbad88) [1],
  0x400 (0x877ad978), 0x0 (0x0)
 Updated Jul 26 02:50:54.619
 local adjacency to GigabitEthernet0/0/0/1

 Prefix Len 48, traffic index 0, precedence n/a, priority 2
  gateway array (0x87617fc8) reference count 8, flags 0x0, source rib (7), 0 backups
              [9 type 3 flags 0x8401 (0x876c43c8) ext 0x0 (0x0)]
  LW-LDI[type=3, refc=1, ptr=0x877ad978, sh-ldi=0x876c43c8]
  gateway array update type-time 1 Jul 26 02:50:54.619
```

```
LDI Update time Jul 26 02:50:54.619
 LW-LDI-TS Jul 26 02:50:54.619
   via fe80::42:acff:fe15:7a03/128, GigabitEthernet0/0/0/2, 11 dependencies,
   weight 0, class 0 [flags 0x0]
     path-idx 0 NHID 0x20007 [0x873d1f20 0x0]
     next hop fe80::42:acff:fe15:7a03/128
     local adjacency


   Load distribution: 0 (refcount 9)


   Hash  OK  Interface              Address
     0    Y   GigabitEthernet0/0/0/2  fe80::42:acff:fe15:7a03
RP/0/RP0/CPU0:P-2#
```

The command **show cef ipv6 fc00:0:202::/48** in Output 9-51 is from the adjacent
router P-5 and displays the FIB entry to locator fc00:0:202:: (ABR-4) via interface
GigabitEthernet0/0/0/0 toward router P-2

Output 9-51 *Pre-Failure FIB Entry to ABR-4 from P-5*

```
RP/0/RP0/CPU0:P-5#show cef ipv6 fc00:0:202::/48
Fri Jul 26 03:41:20.672 UTC
fc00:0:202::/48, version 203, internal 0x1000001 0x220 (ptr 0x86fd69c0) [1], 0x400
  (0x8804dc78), 0x0 (0x0)
 Updated Jul 26 02:51:04.570
 local adjacency to GigabitEthernet0/0/0/0

 Prefix Len 48, traffic index 0, precedence n/a, priority 2
  gateway array (0x87eb9580) reference count 12, flags 0x0, source rib (7), 0
  backups
               [13 type 3 flags 0x8401 (0x87f668e8) ext 0x0 (0x0)]
  LW-LDI[type=3, refc=1, ptr=0x8804dc78, sh-ldi=0x87f668e8]
  gateway array update type-time 1 Jul 26 02:33:54.289
 LDI Update time Jul 26 02:33:54.290
 LW-LDI-TS Jul 26 02:51:04.570
   via fe80::42:acff:fe15:a403/128, GigabitEthernet0/0/0/0, 7 dependencies,
   weight 0, class 0 [flags 0x0]
     path-idx 0 NHID 0x20002 [0x87cb3938 0x0]
     next hop fe80::42:acff:fe15:a403/128
     local adjacency


   Load distribution: 0 (refcount 13)


   Hash  OK  Interface              Address
     0    Y   GigabitEthernet0/0/0/0  fe80::42:acff:fe15:a403
RP/0/RP0/CPU0:P-5#
```

2. **Failure event:** A link break event occurs on the path {P-2 > P-1}.

3. **IGP convergence:** The IGP process on router P-2 converges to the post-convergence path, which passes via router P-5 toward the destination router ABR-4. Output 9-52 from the PLR router now displays the FIB entry to locator fc00:0:202:: (ABR-4) via interface GigabitEthernet0/0/0/4 toward router P-5.

Output 9-52   *Post-Failure FIB Entry to ABR-4 from P-2*

```
RP/0/RP0/CPU0:P-2#show cef ipv6 fc00:0:202::/48
Fri Jul 26 04:02:33.354 UTC
fc00:0:202::/48, version 827, internal 0x1000001 0x220 (ptr 0x86fbad88) [1], 0x400
  (0x877ad978), 0x0 (0x0)
 Updated Jul 26 04:02:23.949
 local adjacency to GigabitEthernet0/0/0/4

 Prefix Len 48, traffic index 0, precedence n/a, priority 2
  gateway array (0x87616da8) reference count 9, flags 0x0, source rib (7), 0 backups
                [10 type 3 flags 0x8401 (0x876c3c48) ext 0x0 (0x0)]
  LW-LDI[type=3, refc=1, ptr=0x877ad978, sh-ldi=0x876c3c48]
  gateway array update type-time 1 Jul 26 04:02:23.949
 LDI Update time Jul 26 04:02:23.949
 LW-LDI-TS Jul 26 04:02:23.949
   via fe80::42:acff:fe15:a402/128, GigabitEthernet0/0/0/4, 10 dependencies,
  weight 0, class 0 [flags 0x0]
    path-idx 0 NHID 0x20006 [0x873d2118 0x0]
    next hop fe80::42:acff:fe15:a402/128
    local adjacency

    Load distribution: 0 (refcount 10)

    Hash  OK  Interface                 Address
    0     Y   GigabitEthernet0/0/0/4    fe80::42:acff:fe15:a402
RP/0/RP0/CPU0:P-2#
```

4. **Microloop event:** Traffic received on P-5 from P-2 destined to ABR-4 is forwarded back out to router P-2 because this path has a lower metric cost of 50 compared to the direct path via router P-4, which has a metric cost of 70. Router P-2 once again forwards the traffic back to P-5, thereby instantiating the microloop event. The post-failure output from router P-5 in Output 9-53 shows the FIB entry for fc00:0:202:: (ABR-4) still forwarding via interface GigabitEthernet0/0/0/0 toward router P-2.

Output 9-53 *Post-Failure FIB Entry to ABR-4 from P-5*

```
RP/0/RP0/CPU0:P-5#show cef ipv6 fc00:0:202::/48
Fri Jul 26 04:02:33.355 UTC
fc00:0:202::/48, version 235, internal 0x1000001 0x220 (ptr 0x86fd69c0) [1], 0x400
  (0x8804dc78), 0x0 (0x0)
 Updated Jul 26 03:59:15.426
 local adjacency to GigabitEthernet0/0/0/0

 Prefix Len 48, traffic index 0, precedence n/a, priority 2
  gateway array (0x87eb9580) reference count 12, flags 0x0, source rib (7), 0
  backups
                [13 type 3 flags 0x8401 (0x87f668e8) ext 0x0 (0x0)]
  LW-LDI[type=3, refc=1, ptr=0x8804dc78, sh-ldi=0x87f668e8]
  gateway array update type-time 1 Jul 26 02:33:54.289
 LDI Update time Jul 26 02:33:54.290
 LW-LDI-TS Jul 26 03:59:15.426
   via fe80::42:acff:fe15:a403/128, GigabitEthernet0/0/0/0, 7 dependencies,
  weight 0, class 0 [flags 0x0]
    path-idx 0 NHID 0x20002 [0x87cb3938 0x0]
    next hop fe80::42:acff:fe15:a403/128
    local adjacency

   Load distribution: 0 (refcount 13)

   Hash  OK  Interface                 Address
   0     Y   GigabitEthernet0/0/0/0    fe80::42:acff:fe15:a403
RP/0/RP0/CPU0:P-5#
```

5. **Full convergence:** At this point, all routers will have converged to the post-convergence path, and the microloop event will have cleared, allowing traffic to reach the destination on ABR-4.

The deployment of SR Microloop Avoidance on router P-2 allows it to forward traffic across the post-convergence path using a segment list by forwarding the traffic via {P-5 > P-4} toward the destination at router ABR-4. Thanks to the SR Microloop Avoidance feature configured on the PLR router P-2, the SRv6 H.Insert.red headend behavior (with SRH) can be observed using the command **show cef ipv6 fc00:0:202::/48**, as shown in Output 9-54. The IPv6 destination address is set to the Adjacency SID fc00:0:5:e003:: (P-5), and the final IPv6 destination address fc00:0:202:: (ABR-4) is stored in the segment list of the inserted SRH. Once the configured delay period has elapsed, the PLR router (P-2) updates the RIB table and forwards the traffic normally along the post-failure IGP-computed path.

Output 9-54   *Microloop Avoidance Behavior Post-Failure FIB Entry to ABR-4 from P-2*

```
RP/0/RP0/CPU0:P-2#show cef ipv6 fc00:0:202::/48
Fri Jul 26 04:28:18.541 UTC
fc00:0:202::/48, version 880, SRv6 Headend, internal 0x1000001 0x220 (ptr
  0x86fbad88) [1], 0x400 (0x877ad978), 0x0 (0x8975c638)
 Updated Jul 26 04:28:14.929
 local adjacency to GigabitEthernet0/0/0/4

 Prefix Len 48, traffic index 0, precedence n/a, priority 2
  gateway array (0x87617a58) reference count 8, flags 0x0, source rib (7), 0 backups
                [9 type 3 flags 0x8401 (0x876c4188) ext 0x0 (0x0)]
  LW-LDI[type=3, refc=1, ptr=0x877ad978, sh-ldi=0x876c4188]
  gateway array update type-time 1 Jul 26 04:28:14.929
 LDI Update time Jul 26 04:28:14.929
 LW-LDI-TS Jul 26 04:28:14.929
   via fe80::42:acff:fe15:a402/128, GigabitEthernet0/0/0/4, 8 dependencies,
  weight 0, class 0 [flags 0x0]
    path-idx 0 NHID 0x20006 [0x873d2118 0x0]
    next hop fe80::42:acff:fe15:a402/128
    local adjacency
    SRv6 H.Insert.Red SID-list {fc00:0:5:e003::}

   Load distribution: 0 (refcount 9)

   Hash  OK  Interface                 Address
   0     Y   GigabitEthernet0/0/0/4    fe80::42:acff:fe15:a402
RP/0/RP0/CPU0:P-2#
```

SR Microloop Avoidance not only provides local protection but allows for remote microloop protection. The following remote microloop events are illustrated in Figure 9-22:

Note   In this example, router P-3 functions as the PLR, and no microloop protection is configured on routers P-1, P-2, and P-5.

1. **Pre-failure state:** Initially the traffic flows across the IGP computed path from the source router ABR-2 to the destination router ABR-4 via the path {P-2 > P-1 > P-3 > P-4} due to the lower metric cost of 50.

2. **Failure event:** A link break event occurs between routers P-3 and P-4.

3. **IGP convergence:** The RIB on router P-3 and P-1 has converged to the post-convergence path {P-2 > P-5 > P-4} and then goes on to the destination router ABR-4. The RIB on routers P-2 and P-5 has not yet converged.

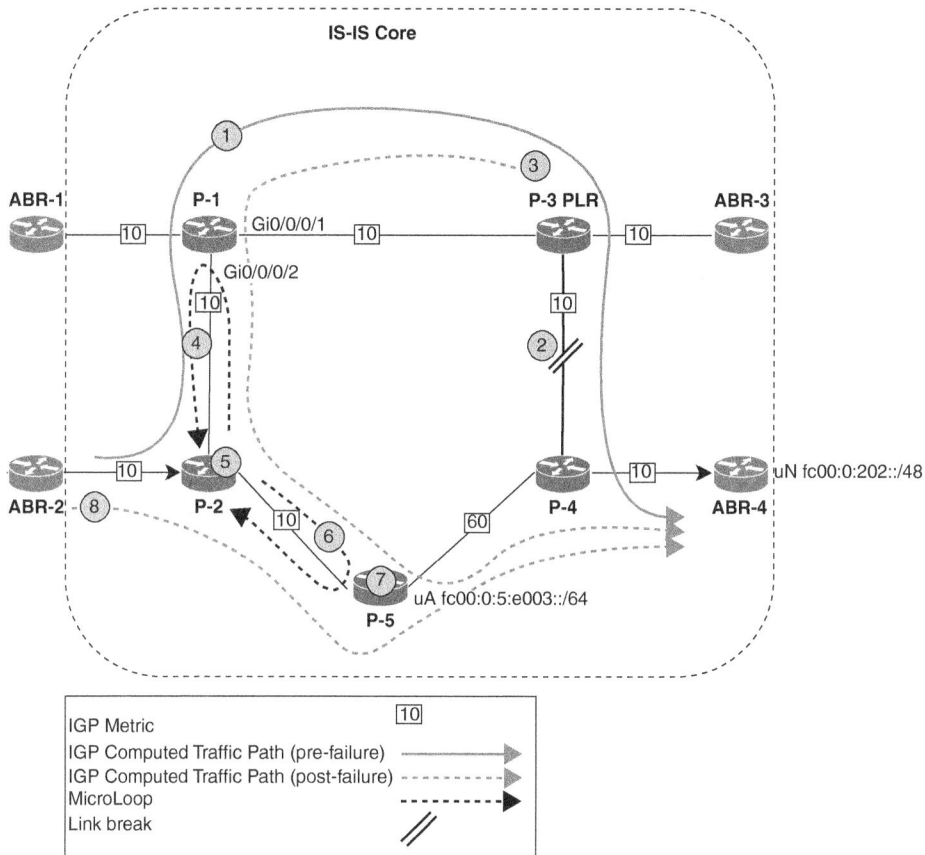

Figure 9-22 *Remote Failure Without Microloop Avoidance*

4. Microloop event: Traffic received on P-2 and destined for ABR-4 is forwarded on to router P-1 as this path has a lower metric cost of 40. Router P-1 forwards the traffic back to P-2, triggering the microloop event.

5. IGP convergence: The RIB on router P-2 converges to the post-convergence path via the path {P-5 > P-4} to the destination router ABR-4; router P-5 has not yet converged.

6. Microloop event: Traffic received on P-2 and destined for ABR-4 is now forwarded on to router P-5 because this is the post-failure convergence path. Because router P-5 has not yet converged, it returns the traffic back to P-2 via its pre-failure IGP computed path, thus creating a microloop event.

7. Full convergence: At this point, router P-5 will have converged to the post-convergence path, and the microloop event is cleared.

8. Post-failure state: Traffic from ABR-2 can reach the destination on ABR-4 via the post-convergence path.

If SR Microloop Avoidance is configured on the non-PLR router P-1, then during an IGP convergence computation event, P-1 determines that microloops are possible along the new path to the destination between itself and router P-2 and between routers P-2 and P-5. In this case, P-1 installs an explicit SR path by using a segment list and forwards the traffic via {P-2 > P-5 > P-4} toward the destination at router ABR-4. The SRv6 H.Insert. red headend behavior is visible in Output 9-55. The IPv6 destination address is set to the Adjacency SID fc00:0:5:e003:: (P-5), and the IPv6 destination address fc00:0:202:: (ABR-4) is stored in the segment list of the inserted SRH. Similarly, once router P-2 receives the IGP event and is configured with SR Microloop Avoidance, it also calculates that microloops are possible along the path via router P-5. P-2 also uses a segment list to forward traffic through router P-5 using the Adjacency SID fc00:0:5:e003::, and P-5 then forwards the traffic to the destination IPv6 address fc00:0:202::.

Output 9-55   *Microloop Avoidance Behavior Post-Failure FIB Entry to ABR-4 from P-1*

```
RP/0/RP0/CPU0:P-1#show cef ipv6 fc00:0:202::/48
Fri Jul 26 07:35:27.513 UTC
fc00:0:202::/48, version 781, SRv6 Headend, internal 0x1000001 0x220 (ptr
  0x86ec3168) [1], 0x400 (0x87f36858), 0x0 (0x8975d948)
 Updated Jul 26 07:35:23.269
 local adjacency to GigabitEthernet0/0/0/2


 Prefix Len 48, traffic index 0, precedence n/a, priority 2
  gateway array (0x87da06b8) reference count 2, flags 0x0, source rib (7), 0 backups
                [3 type 3 flags 0x8401 (0x87e4d008) ext 0x0 (0x0)]
  LW-LDI[type=3, refc=1, ptr=0x87f36858, sh-ldi=0x87e4d008]
  gateway array update type-time 1 Jul 26 07:35:23.265
 LDI Update time Jul 26 07:35:23.269
 LW-LDI-TS Jul 26 07:35:23.269
   via fe80::42:acff:fe15:7a02/128, GigabitEthernet0/0/0/2, 9 dependencies,
  weight 0, class 0 [flags 0x0]
    path-idx 0 NHID 0x20008 [0x87b99d28 0x0]
    next hop fe80::42:acff:fe15:7a02/128
    local adjacency
    SRv6 H.Insert.Red SID-list {fc00:0:5:e003::}


    Load distribution: 0 (refcount 3)


    Hash  OK  Interface                Address
    0     Y   GigabitEthernet0/0/0/2   fe80::42:acff:fe15:7a02
RP/0/RP0/CPU0:P-1#
```

The impact of microloops becomes more apparent with faster repair times such as those that are possible when TI-LFA is configured. Therefore, the configuration of the Microloop Avoidance feature is recommended across all routers. The configuration **microloop avoidance segment-routing** enables both local and SR Microloop Avoidance, and the command **microloop avoidance rib-update-delay 5000** sets the duration for which a potential explicit SR path using a segment list is used for traffic forwarding before the IGP process updates the RIB table. Config 9-24 is for IOS XR–based routers. When these routers are configured for SRv6, Microloop Avoidance must be configured under **address-family ipv6 unicast**.

Config 9-24   *Microloop Avoidance (IOS XR)*

```
!
router isis CORE1
 address-family ipv4 unicast
  microloop avoidance segment-routing
  microloop avoidance rib-update-delay 5000
!
```

The SR Microloop Avoidance configuration for IOS XE–based routers is similar to the configuration for IOS XR–based routers, as shown in Config 9-25.

Config 9-25   *Microloop Avoidance (IOS XE)*

```
!
router isis CORE1
 microloop avoidance segment-routing
 microloop avoidance rib-update-delay 5000
!
```

In conclusion, Microloop Avoidance and TI-LFA are two distinct mechanisms used for different purposes; however, it is recommended to configure both TI-LFA and the SR Microloop Avoidance feature.

BGP PIC Edge

In the section "Topology-Independent Loop-Free Alternate (TI-LFA)," earlier in this chapter, the focus is on fast convergence for IGPs within a network through a mechanism known as IP Fast Reroute (IPFRR)—and specifically TI-LFA in SR-based networks. With these fast reroute mechanisms, it is possible for most network deployments to achieve sub-50 ms IGP convergence. On the other hand, BGP can be slow to converge because it was originally designed to provide a stable Internet using a distance-vector routing protocol approach. As described in Chapter 6, "L2VPN Service Deployment: Configuration and Verification Techniques," and Chapter 7, "L3VPN Service Deployment: Configuration and Verification Techniques," these overlay services use BGP as the control plane, and the underlay transport network is based on either SR-MPLS or SRv6. Using BGP as the overlay control plane protocol allows for the transport of a large number of routes, which can increase the chances of slower route convergence during network events. So, is there an FRR-like mechanism for BGP, and if so, in what use cases would it be applicable? There is such a mechanism, and it is called Prefix Independent Convergence (PIC). PIC has two functional modes:

■ **PIC Core:** BGP reacts to core network event failures where the IGP reconverges to alternate paths toward the BGP next hops.

■ **PIC Edge:** BGP reacts to edge node (PE router) or edge link failures where BGP next hops will change.

Although BGP PIC Core is not the focus of this section, it is worth mentioning the actual BGP behavior that occurs when a core network event occurs. BGP PIC Core is active by default in most current IOS XR and IOS XE versions. Figure 9-23 shows router PE-1's BGP FIB entries for routes learned from router PE-2. This is a non-hierarchical FIB, and each BGP FIB entry has its own output interface information (OIF) pointer. When an IGP convergence event occurs, the forwarding plane must update the output interface for each BGP prefix entry individually. Depending on the scale of the routes, this process can take several seconds, potentially leading to a level of delay that negatively impacts customer services.

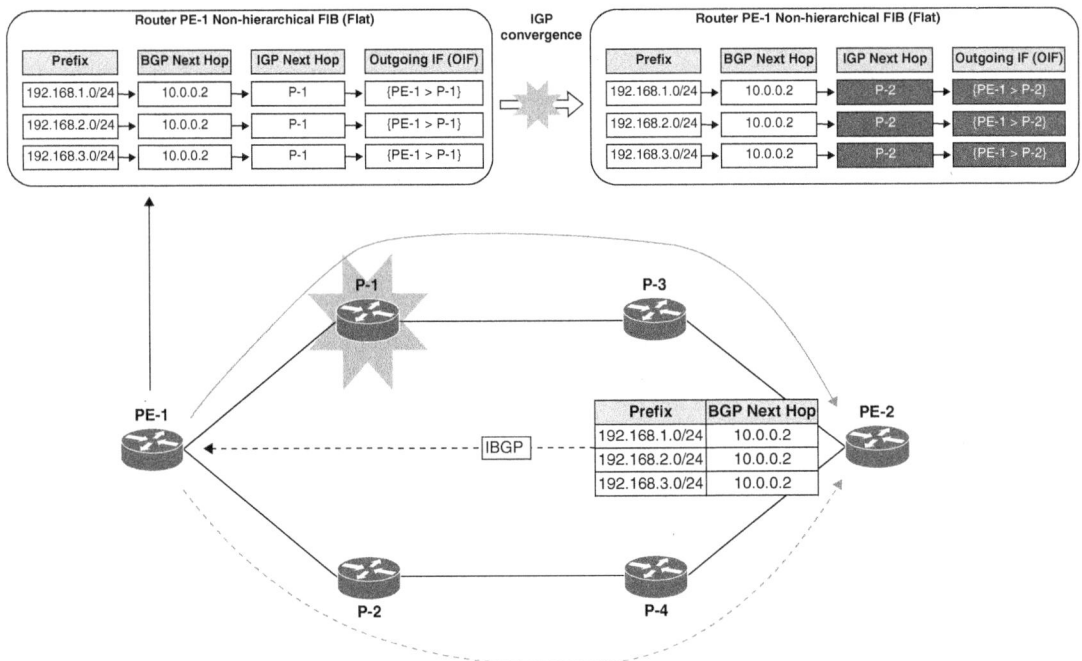

Figure 9-23 *BGP Core Non-Hierarchical FIB*

Since IOS XR and most IOS XE routers today support the BGP PIC Core feature by default, a hierarchical FIB is in place, where all BGP prefixes with the same next hop share a single IGP index that points to an outgoing interface adjacency. In the event of an IGP convergence event, as shown in Figure 9-24, instead of modifying each BGP prefix's index, only the shared IGP index pointer is modified; this significantly improves BGP convergence times to potentially sub-second times.

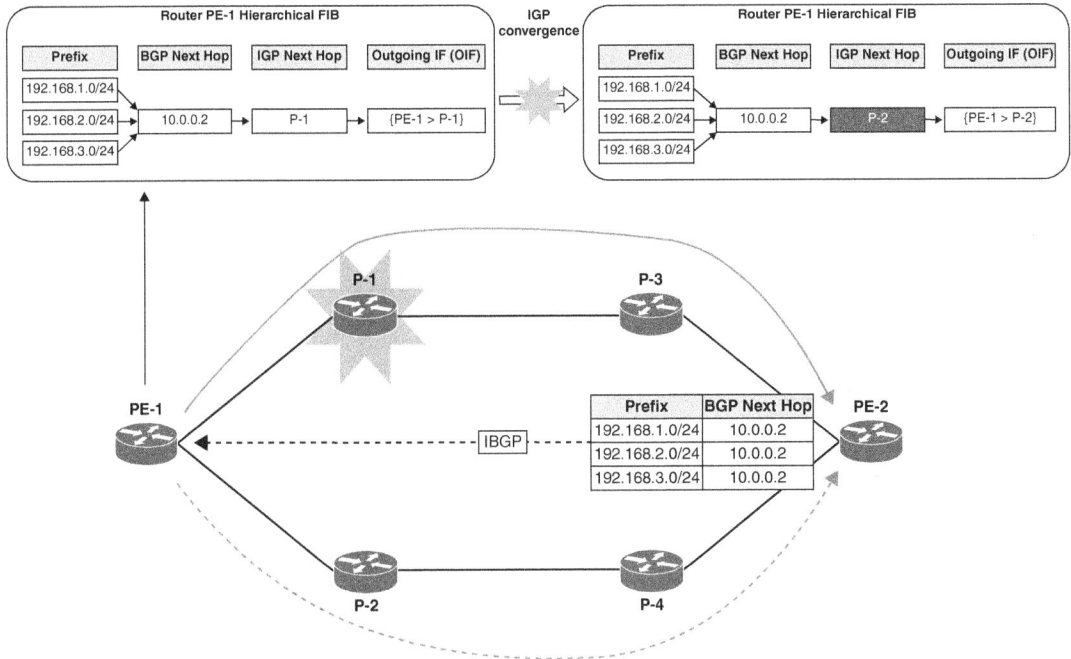

Figure 9-24 *BGP PIC Core Hierarchical FIB*

The BGP PIC Edge mechanism allows for fast routing convergence in the following circumstances:

■ **Edge node failure in which the BGP next hop is changed or deleted:** This situation is depicted in Figure 9-25. Invalidation and updating of BGP next hops is carried out by the periodic BGP scanner process running every 60 seconds, potentially leading to increased convergence delays when edge node failures occur. To mitigate this periodic scanner process, with both IOS XR and IOS XE, by default, once the RIB is modified, the router immediately informs the BGP process of any next hop prefix deletions or modifications. This IGP event–driven mechanism is known as BGP Next-Hop Tracking (BGP NHT), and it provides BGP fast reroute in the case where an alternate path exists for the IGP-learned BGP next hop. By default, BGP retains only the best path for a learned prefix based on the best path algorithm. However, with the BGP PIC mechanism, if a backup path is available, it is also retained. In Figure 9-25, the BGP process on router PE-1 registers the installed BGP next hops with the RIB. If router PE-2 suffers a node failure, the RIB on PE-1 immediately notifies BGP that a next hop address has been deleted. With IOS XR, RIB notifications are classified as follows:

■ **Critical:** A BGP next hop is either deleted or added to the RIB. This critical next hop trigger delay value is configurable and by default is 3000 ms (except with VPNv4 and VPNv6 address families, where it is 0 ms)

■ **Non-Critical:** The IGP metric to a BGP next hop has been modified in the RIB. The non-critical next hop trigger delay value is also configurable and by default is 10,000 ms.

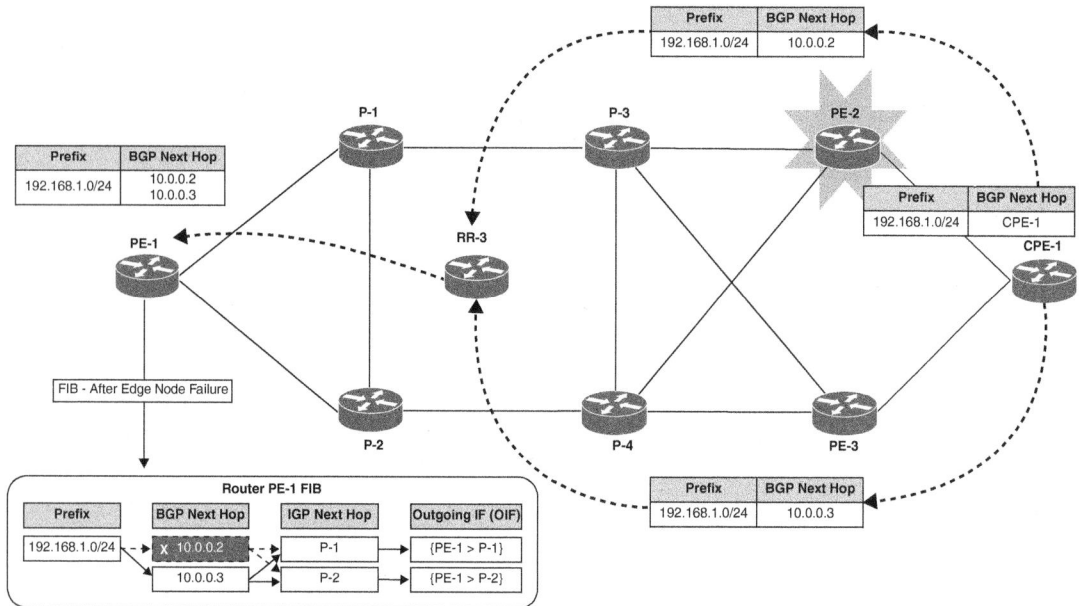

Figure 9-25 *BGP PIC Edge Node Failure*

■ **Edge node link failure:** In this condition, a PE router that sets next-hop-self for pre- fixes being advertised toward the overlay service route reflectors experiences a link failure on the link where it learns external prefixes. This edge access link failure does not result in the deletion of the BGP next hop route in the IGP, and hence the failure does not trigger IGP fast convergence and the subsequent BGP NHT. For the BGP PIC Edge mechanism to work effectively, two conditions must be met: First, a back- up PE router must be available, and second, in the event of a failure, traffic reaching the primary PE device must be encapsulated or tunneled to the backup PE device to avoid looping back to the primary (active) PE router. In Figure 9-26 the following conditions exist prior to the event occurrence:

■ Router PE-1 has a primary path for the prefix 192.168.1.0/24 via next hop 10.0.0.2 of PE-2 (iBGP).

■ Router PE-1 has a backup path for the prefix 192.168.1.0/24 via next hop 10.0.0.3 of PE-3 (iBGP).

■ Router PE-2 has a primary path for the prefix 192.168.1.0/24 direct via next hop CPE-1 (eBGP).

■ Router PE-2 has a backup path for the prefix 192.168.1.0/24 via next hop 10.0.0.3 of PE-3 (iBGP).

- Router PE-3 has a primary path for the prefix 192.168.1.0/24 via next hop 10.0.0.2 of PE-2 (iBGP).

- Router PE-3 has a backup path for the prefix 192.168.1.0/24 direct via next hop CPE-1 (eBGP).

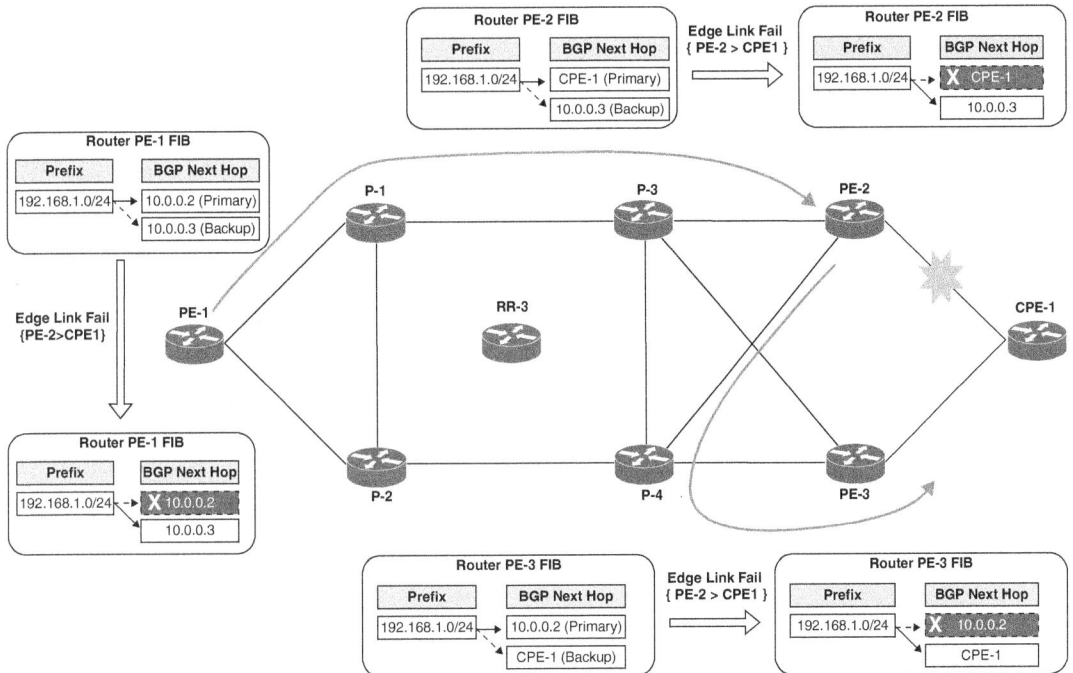

Figure 9-26 *BGP PIC Edge Link Failure*

Immediately following the external access link failure on the path {PE-2 > CPE-1}, any in-transit traffic from PE-1 reaching router PE-2 needs to be tunneled toward the backup router PE-3. The reason this traffic needs to be tunneled or encapsulated is so that the traffic is forwarded directly onto the egress interface toward CPE-1; otherwise, router PE-3 will perform a lookup and forward this traffic back to router PE-2, causing a loop event until BGP routing convergence has occurred. Once the next hop for the routes learned across the path {PE-2 > CE-1} has been withdrawn by PE-2, router PE-1 immediately updates its IGP index to point to the next hop of the backup router PE-3 for the prefixes learned from CE-1.

BGP PIC Edge has two operational methods that a network operator can provision, as shown in Figure 9-27. Although Figure 9-27 shows an SRv6 network, these operational methods are applicable to SR-MPLS networks as well:

- **Unipath:** A forwarding edge router forwards traffic via a primary next hop, with the backup next hop taking over in the event of a failure condition. This is also known as an active/backup service.

■ **Multipath (with backup):** A forwarding edge router load balances traffic via multiple active next hops and is colloquially known as an active/active service. Each multipath acts as a backup for the other multipath in the event of a failure; if both multipaths fail, the backup path is used.

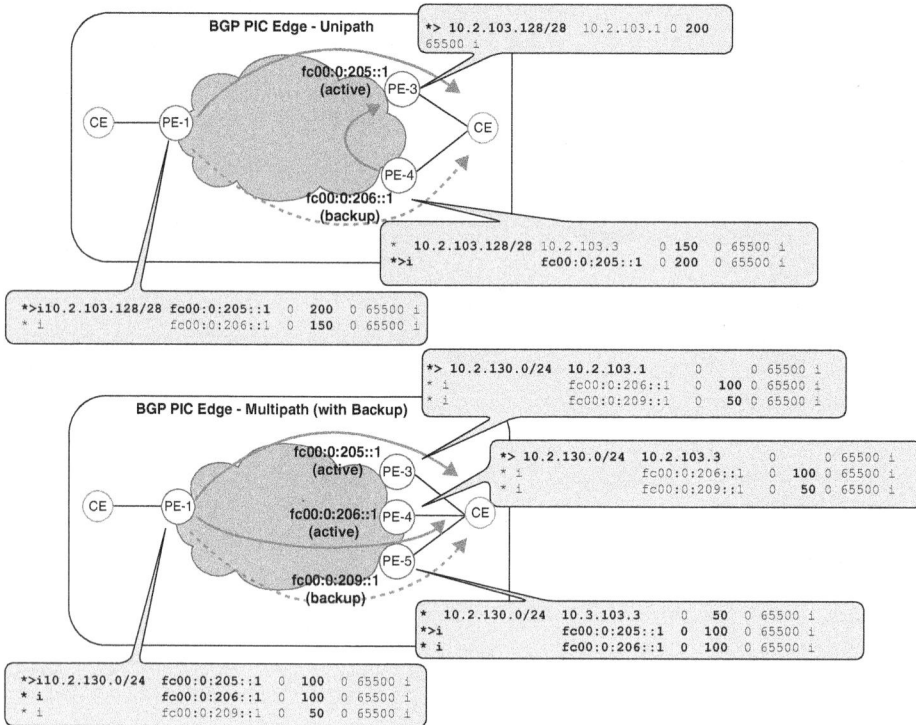

Figure 9-27 *BGP PIC Edge Unipath and Multipath (with Backup) Overview*

The following configuration and verification sections describe how BGP PIC Edge is configured and how it behaves in both SR-MPLS and SRv6 transport networks.

BGP PIC Edge Configuration: SR-MPLS

The configuration tasks in this section build on the SR-MPLS L3VPN full-mesh overlay service setup detailed in Chapter 7, in the section "SR-MPLS: L3VPN Overlay Service." Because the BGP PIC Edge configuration and verification for IOS XR and IOS XE routers are extensively covered there, they are only summarized here. It should be noted that the BGP PIC Edge multipath with backup feature is fully supported on IOS XR routers and is discussed in detail later in this chapter, in the section "BGP PIC Edge Multipath Verification: SRv6." However, this functionality is not completely available on IOS XE routers; therefore, the discussion on BGP PIC Edge multipath with backup is not extended in this SR-MPLS context.

In the SR-MPLS reference network in Figure 9-28, the VRF instance FULL-400-VRF is configured for unipath active/backup behavior for the PE–CE access links between CE-2 and both PE-3 and PE-4. The BGP PIC Edge and BGP best external features are additionally configured with the following behavior:

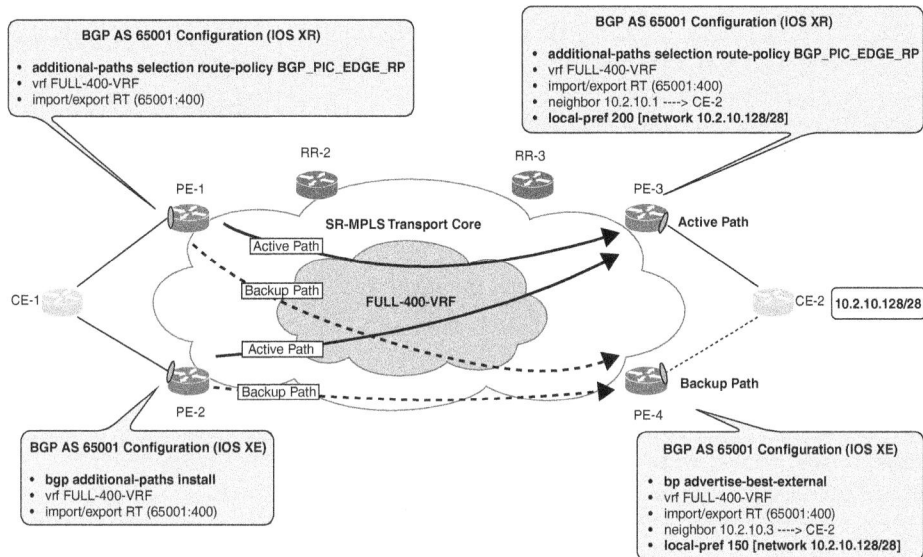

BGP AS 65001 Configuration (IOS XR)

- additional-paths selection route-policy BGP_PIC_EDGE_RP
- vrf FULL-400-VRF
- import/export RT (65001:400)

BGP AS 65001 Configuration (IOS XR)

- additional-paths selection route-policy BGP_PIC_EDGE_RP
- vrf FULL-400-VRF
- import/export RT (65001:400)
- neighbor 10.2.10.1 ----> CE-2
- local-pref 200 [network 10.2.10.128/28]

BGP AS 65001 Configuration (IOS XE)

- bgp additional-paths install
- vrf FULL-400-VRF
- import/export RT (65001:400)

BGP AS 65001 Configuration (IOS XE)

- bp advertise-best-external
- vrf FULL-400-VRF
- import/export RT (65001:400)
- neighbor 10.2.10.3 ----> CE-2
- local-pref 150 [network 10.2.10.128/28]

Figure 9-28 *BGP PIC Edge Unipath: SR-MPLS*

- Ingress route 10.2.10.128/28 is learned across the eBGP neighborship {CE-2 > PE-3} and is matched with a BGP route policy that sets the BGP local preference to 200.

- This same route is also learned across the eBGP neighborship {CE-2 > PE-4} and is matched with a BGP route policy that sets the BGP local preference to 150.

- The preferred path to this subnet is via the higher BGP local preference 200. Therefore, router PE-4 normally sends a BGP withdrawal update toward the RR and withdraws its path toward the subnet learned via the eBGP neighborship with router CE-2.

- Configuring BGP best external under the router BGP VRF instance on router PE-4 allows the subnet to be advertised and to no longer be withdrawn.

- The **additional-paths selection route-policy PIC_EDGE_RP** configuration on IOS XR PE routers allows the path via the backup router PE-4 to be programmed into the FIB as a backup path.

- The **bgp additional-paths install** configuration on IOS XE PE routers allows the path via the backup router PE-4 to be programmed into the FIB as a backup path.

- Unlike in the example configurations for the SRv6 configured PE routers, the VRF allocation mode remains as the default per-prefix allocation mode because the per-CE node allocation mode is not yet supported with BGP PIC Edge in IOS XE.

The router output in Output 9-56 verifies that the per-CE node allocation mode is not supported on IOS XE–based devices when the command **bgp advertise-best-external** is configured.

Output 9-56 *BGP PIC Edge per-CE Node Label Allocation Mode Unsupported: Best External (IOS XE)*

```
PE-4 (config)#mpls label mode vrf FULL-400-VRF protocol bgp-vpnv4 per-ce
% Cannot configure per-CE label mode for VRF FULL-400-VRF (address family ipv4),
  please remove Advertise Best External path configuration before changing the
  label mode
PE-4(config)#
```

Similarly, the output in Output 9-57 verifies that the per-CE node allocation mode is not supported on IOS XE–based devices when the command **bgp additional-paths install** is configured.

Output 9-57 *BGP PIC Edge per-CE Node Label Allocation Mode Unsupported: BGP Additional Paths (IOS XE)*

```
PE-4(config)#mpls label mode vrf FULL-400-VRF protocol bgp-vpnv4 per-ce
% Can not configure label mode for vrf FULL-400-VRF (address family ipv4),
  since additional-paths is configured in that VRF
PE-4(config)#
```

BGP PIC Edge unipath is enabled on the IOS XR routers through the route policy BGP_ PIC_EDGE_RP, as shown in Config 9-26. This route policy is then applied within the BGP VPNv4 address family configuration.

Config 9-26 *BGP PIC Edge Unipath on PE-1 and PE-3 (IOS XR)*

```
!
route-policy BGP_PIC_EDGE_RP
  set path-selection backup 1 install
end-policy
!
router bgp 65001
 address-family ipv4 unicast
  allocate-label all
 !
 address-family vpnv4 unicast
  additional-paths selection route-policy BGP_PIC_EDGE_RP
 !
```

For IOS XE routers, BGP PIC Edge unipath is enabled using the configuration command **bgp additional-paths install**, as shown in Config 9-27.

Config 9-27   *BGP PIC Edge Unipath on PE-2 (IOS XE)*

```
!
router bgp 65001
 address-family ipv4 vrf FULL-400-VRF
  bgp additional-paths install
  exit-address-family
 !
```

The backup path for the route 10.2.10.128/28 is advertised by the IOS XE router PE-4 with the **bgp advertise-best-external** command, as in Config 9-28. It is important to note that using the **bgp advertise-best-external** command also implicitly enables BGP PIC Edge on IOS XE routers.

Config 9-28   *BGP PIC Edge Unipath Configuration on PE-4 (IOS XE)*

```
!
router bgp 65001
 address-family ipv4 vrf FULL-400-VRF
  bgp advertise-best-external
  exit-address-family
 !
```

BGP PIC Edge Verification: SR-MPLS

This section focuses on the verification of the BGP PIC Edge unipath feature across routers using both IOS XR and IOS XE. The BGP PIC Edge verification tasks in this section focus on the unipath verification commands for the prefix 10.2.10.128/28 originating from the CE router CE-2 into the VRF instance FULL-400-VRF. Figure 9-29 shows the SR-MPLS transport network along with basic verification commands to ensure that the BGP PIC Edge mechanism is functioning as expected.

Note   The verification commands in this section are based on the SR-MPLS reference network provided in Appendix A.

The BGP VPNv4 route displayed with the command **show bgp vpnv4 unicast vrf FULL-400-VRF 10.2.10.128/28** on PE-1 in Output 9-58 illustrates the following relevant information as it pertains to BGP PIC Edge:

- **Paths: (2 available, best #1):** The output shows that the subnet is accessible via two paths, and the first path is identified as the preferred one.

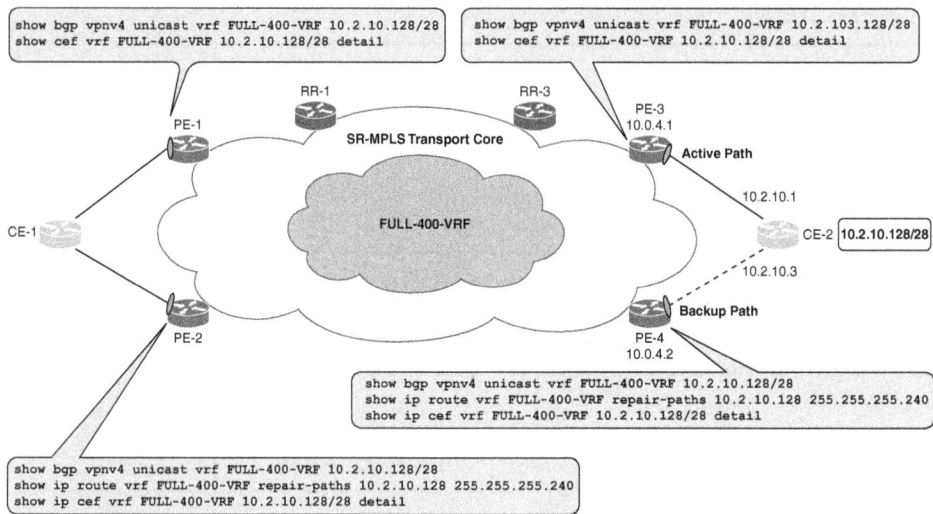

Figure 9-29 *BGP PIC Edge Unipath Verification: SR-MPLS*

- Path #1:

  - **10.0.4.1 (metric 20) from 10.0.3.254 (10.0.4.1):** PE-3 is the BGP next hop 10.0.4.1 and is learned via BGP labeled unicast.

  - **Received Label 24005:** Router PE-3 has allocated a VPNv4 label 24005 for the route 10.2.10.128/28 from CE-2.

  - **localpref 200, best:** The BGP local preference 200 ensures that this path via PE-3 is the best path for traffic forwarding.

- Path #2:

  - **10.0.4.2 (metric 20) from 10.0.3.254 (10.0.4.2):** PE-4 is the BGP next hop 10.0.4.2 and is learned via BGP labeled unicast.

  - **Received Label 20:** Router PE-4 has allocated a VPNv4 label 20 for the route 10.2.10.128/28 from router CE-2.

  - **localpref 150, backup, add-path,:** BGP local preference attribute of 150 applied to the subnet via PE-4 together with the BGP PIC Edge **additional-paths selection route-policy BGP_PIC_EDGE_RP** configuration on router PE-1 ensures that this path via PE-4 is the backup path in the event of a failure on PE-3.

Output 9-58 *BGP PIC Edge Unipath BGP VPNv4 RIB on PE-1 (IOS XR)*

```
RP/0/RP0/CPU0:PE-1#show bgp vpnv4 unicast vrf FULL-400-VRF 10.2.10.128/28

BGP routing table entry for 10.2.10.128/28, Route Distinguisher: 65001:401
```

```
Versions:
  Process              bRIB/RIB  SendTblVer
  Speaker                   323         323
Last Modified: Mar 21 11:13:14.031 for 00:00:19
Paths: (2 available, best #1)
  Not advertised to any peer
  Path #1: Received by speaker 0
  Not advertised to any peer
  65400
    10.0.4.1 (metric 20) from 10.0.3.254 (10.0.4.1)
      Received Label 24005
      Origin IGP, metric 0, localpref 200, valid, internal, best, group-best,
  import-candidate, imported
      Received Path ID 0, Local Path ID 1, version 323
      Extended community: SoO:65400:2 RT:65001:400
      Originator: 10.0.4.1, Cluster list: 10.0.3.254, 10.0.4.254
      Source AFI: VPNv4 Unicast, Source VRF: default, Source Route
  Distinguisher: 65001:403
  Path #2: Received by speaker 0
  Not advertised to any peer
  65400
    10.0.4.2 (metric 20) from 10.0.3.254 (10.0.4.2)
      Received Label 20
      Origin IGP, metric 0, localpref 150, valid, internal, backup, add-path,
  imported
      Received Path ID 0, Local Path ID 4, version 261
      Extended community: SoO:65400:2 RT:65001:400
      Originator: 10.0.4.2, Cluster list: 10.0.3.254, 10.0.4.254
      Source AFI: VPNv4 Unicast, Source VRF: default, Source Route
  Distinguisher: 65001:404
RP/0/RP0/CPU0:PE-1#
```

The BGP VPNv4 verification command executed on router PE-2 in Output 9-59 displays details similar to the output from the router PE-1 for the route 10.2.10.128/28:

- **Paths: (2 available, best #2, table FULL-400-VRF):** The output shows that the subnet is accessible via two paths, and the second path is identified as the preferred one.

- **Path #1:**

  - **10.0.4.2:** PE-4 is the BGP next hop 10.0.4.2 and is learned via BGP labeled unicast.

  - **localpref 150, backup/repair:** A BGP local preference of 150 is applied to the subnet on PE-4. In combination with the BGP PIC Edge on router PE-2, this ensures that the path via PE-4 becomes the repair path in the event of an access link failure on PE-3.

- **mpls labels in/out nolabel/20:** Router PE-4 has allocated a VPNv4 label 20 for the route 10.2.10.128/28 from router CE-2.

- **Path #2:**

  - **10.0.4.1:** PE-3 is the BGP next hop 10.0.4.1 and is learned via BGP labeled unicast.

  - **localpref 200, best:** The BGP local preference attribute 200 ensures that this path via PE-3 is the best path for traffic forwarding.

  - **mpls labels in/out nolabel/24005:** Router PE-3 has allocated a VPNv4 label 24005 for the route from router CE-2.

Output 9-59   *BGP PIC Edge Unipath BGP VPNv4 RIB on PE-2 (IOS XE)*

```
PE-2#show bgp vpnv4 unicast vrf FULL-400-VRF 10.2.10.128/28
BGP routing table entry for 65001:402:10.2.10.128/28, version 783
Paths: (2 available, best #2, table FULL-400-VRF)
  Additional-path-install
  Advertised to update-groups:
    2
  Refresh Epoch 1
  65400, imported path from 65001:404:10.2.10.128/28 (global)
    10.0.4.2 (metric 20) (via default) from 10.0.3.254 (10.0.3.254)
      Origin IGP, metric 0, localpref 150, valid, internal, backup/repair
      Extended Community: SoO:65400:2 RT:65001:400
      Originator: 10.0.4.2, Cluster list: 10.0.3.254, 10.0.4.254 ,
recursive-via-host
      mpls labels in/out nolabel/20
      rx pathid: 0, tx pathid: 0
      Updated on Mar 21 2024 10:40:31 UTC
  Refresh Epoch 1
  65400, imported path from 65001:403:10.2.10.128/28 (global)
    10.0.4.1 (metric 20) (via default) from 10.0.3.254 (10.0.3.254)
      Origin IGP, metric 0, localpref 200, valid, internal, best
      Extended Community: SoO:65400:2 RT:65001:400
      Originator: 10.0.4.1, Cluster list: 10.0.3.254, 10.0.4.254 ,
recursive-via-host
      mpls labels in/out nolabel/24005
      rx pathid: 0, tx pathid: 0x0
      Updated on Mar 21 2024 11:13:14 UTC
PE-2#
```

For the sake of brevity, only the RIB details **show ip route vrf FULL-400-VRF repair-paths 10.2.10.128 255.255.255.240** from router PE-2 in Output 9-60 is discussed:

- **10.0.4.1 (default), from 10.0.3.254, recursive-via-host:** The active BGP path uses next hop 10.0.4.1 on router PE-3. Because BGP PIC Edge is configured on PE-2, recursion through a summary or default route is disabled, and iBGP next hops are resolved using host routes instead.

- **MPLS label: 24005:** Router PE-3 has allocated a VPNv4 label 24005 for the route 10.2.10.128/28.

- **[RPR]10.0.4.2 (default), from 10.0.3.254, recursive-via-host:** The BGP repair path uses next hop 10.0.4.2 on router PE-4. With BGP PIC Edge configured on PE-2, recursion through a summary or default route is disabled, and iBGP next hops are resolved through host routes instead.

- **MPLS label: 20:** Router PE-4 has allocated a VPNv4 label 20 for the route 10.2.10.128/28.

Output 9-60   *BGP PIC Edge Unipath RIB Backup Path on PE-2 (IOS XE)*

```
PE-2#show ip route vrf FULL-400-VRF repair-paths 10.2.10.128 255.255.255.240


Routing Table: FULL-400-VRF
Routing entry for 10.2.10.128/28
  Known via "bgp 65001", distance 200, metric 0
  Tag 65400, type internal
  Last update from 10.0.4.1 00:11:40 ago
  Routing Descriptor Blocks:
  * 10.0.4.1 (default), from 10.0.3.254, 00:11:40 ago, recursive-via-host
      opaque_ptr 0x7F5C38C46770
      Route metric is 0, traffic share count is 1
      AS Hops 1
      Route tag 65400
      MPLS label: 24005
      MPLS Flags: MPLS Required
    [RPR]10.0.4.2 (default), from 10.0.3.254, 00:11:40 ago, recursive-via-host
      opaque_ptr 0x7F5C38C46398
      Route metric is 0, traffic share count is 1
      AS Hops 1
      Route tag 65400
      MPLS label: 20
      MPLS Flags: MPLS Required
PE-2#
```

Output 9-61 shows the FIB details from router PE-1, viewed with the command **show cef vrf FULL-400-VRF 10.2.10.128/28 detail**, and includes the following relevant FIB information:

- **via 10.0.4.1/32:** Router PE-3 is the active BGP path with next hop 10.0.4.1.

  - **next hop 10.0.4.1/32 via 19001/0/21:** PE-3 is the BGP next hop 10.0.4.1 and is learned via BGP labeled unicast,. with Prefix SID 19001.

■ **next hop 192.168.3.1/32 BE1   labels imposed {16100 19001 24005}:** This output displays the imposed label stack. Initially we see the IGP path via next hop 192.168.3.1/32 (on P-5). The imposed labels are the SR-MPLS Anycast SID 16100 assigned by the routers ABR-1 and ABR-2, the BGP Prefix SID 19001 from router PE-3 and finally the VPNv4 label 24005.

■ **via 10.0.4.2/32, backup:** Router PE-4 is the backup BGP path with next hop 10.0.4.2.

   ■ **next hop 10.0.4.2/32 via 19002/0/21:** PE-4 is the BGP next hop 10.0.4.2 and is learned via BGP labeled unicast, with Prefix SID 19002.

   ■ **next hop 192.168.3.1/32 BE1   labels imposed {16100 19002 20}:** This output displays the imposed label stack. Initially we see the IGP path via next hop 192.168.3.1/32 (on P-5). The imposed labels are the SR-MPLS Anycast SID 16100 assigned by the routers ABR-1 and ABR-2, the BGP Prefix SID 19002 from router PE-4 and finally the VPNv4 label 20.

Output 9-61   *BGP PIC Edge Unipath FIB Detail on PE-1 (IOS XR)*

```
RP/0/RP0/CPU0:PE-1#show cef vrf FULL-400-VRF 10.2.10.128/28 detail

10.2.10.128/28, version 139, internal 0x5000001 0x30 (ptr 0xe829408) [1], 0x600
  (0xe159268), 0xa08 (0xfe280a8)
 Updated Mar 23 09:21:49.740
 Prefix Len 28, traffic index 0, precedence n/a, priority 3
  gateway array (0xdfc22d0) reference count 4, flags 0x100038, source rib (7), 0
  backups
               [5 type 1 flags 0x441 (0xf4c4d68) ext 0x0 (0x0)]
  LW-LDI[type=1, refc=1, ptr=0xe159268, sh-ldi=0xf4c4d68]
  gateway array update type-time 5 Mar 23 09:48:22.758
 LDI Update time Mar 23 09:48:22.758
 LW-LDI-TS Mar 23 09:48:22.758
   via 10.0.4.1/32, 5 dependencies, recursive [flags 0x6000]
    path-idx 0 NHID 0x0 [0xe334e20 0x0]
    recursion-via-/32
    next hop VRF - 'default', table - 0xe0000000
    next hop 10.0.4.1/32 via 19001/0/21
     next hop 192.168.3.1/32 BE1         labels imposed {16100 19001 24005}
   via 10.0.4.2/32, 4 dependencies, recursive, backup [flags 0x6100]
    path-idx 1 NHID 0x0 [0xe336b68 0x0]
    recursion-via-/32
```

```
    next hop VRF - 'default', table - 0xe0000000
    next hop 10.0.4.2/32 via 19002/0/21
    next hop 192.168.3.1/32 BE1            labels imposed {16100 19002 20}


    Load distribution: 0 (refcount 5)


    Hash  OK  Interface            Address
    0     Y   recursive            19001/0
RP/0/RP0/CPU0:PE-1#
```

Output 9-62 verifies the IOS XE router PE-2 FIB details for the target subnet 10.2.10.128/28:

- **recursive via 10.0.4.1 label 24005:** Router PE-3 with next hop 10.0.4.1 has allocated a VPNv4 label 24005 for the route 10.2.10.128/28.

  - **recursive via 10.1.1.5 label 19001-(local:19001):** The BGP path to 10.0.4.1 (PE-3) has the BGP Prefix SID 19001 and the next hop 10.1.1.5 (ABR-1 and ABR-2).

  - **nexthop 192.168.3.5 GigabitEthernet2 label 16100-(local:16100):** The IGP path via next hop 192.168.3.5 (P-5) and SR-MPLS Anycast SID 16100 is assigned to routers ABR-1 and ABR-2.

- **recursive via 10.0.4.2 label 20 , repair:** The backup/repair path via PE-4 with next hop 10.0.4.2 has allocated a VPNv4 label 20 for the route 10.2.10.128/28.

  - **recursive via 10.1.1.5 label 19002-(local:19002):** The BGP path to 10.0.4.2 (PE-4) has the BGP Prefix SID 19002 and the next hop 10.1.1.5 (ABR-1 and ABR-2).

  - **nexthop 192.168.3.5 GigabitEthernet2 label 16100-(local:16100):** The IGP path via next hop 192.168.3.5 (P-5) and SR-MPLS Anycast SID 16100 is assigned to routers ABR-1 and ABR-2.

Output 9-62 *BGP PIC Edge Unipath FIB Detail on PE-2 (IOS XE)*

```
PE-2#show ip cef vrf FULL-400-VRF 10.2.10.128/28 detail
10.2.10.128/28, epoch 2, flags [rib defined all labels]
  recursive via 10.0.4.1 label 24005
    recursive via 10.1.1.5 label 19001-(local:19001)
      nexthop 192.168.3.5 GigabitEthernet2 label 16100-(local:16100)
  recursive via 10.0.4.2 label 20, repair
    recursive via 10.1.1.5 label 19002-(local:19002)
      nexthop 192.168.3.5 GigabitEthernet2 label 16100-(local:16100)
PE-2#
```

Moving on to the active egress router PE-3, the VPNv4 FIB command from Output 9-63 shows the following relevant information for the IPv4 subnet 10.2.10.128/28:

- **Paths: (2 available, best #2):** The output shows that the subnet is accessible via two paths, and the second path is identified as the preferred one.

- **Path #1:**

  - **10.0.4.2 (metric 3) from 10.0.4.254 (10.0.4.2):** Router PE-4 is the BGP next hop 10.0.4.2 and is learned via BGP labeled unicast.

  - **Received Label 20:** Router PE-4 has allocated a VPNv4 label 20 for the route learned from CE-2.

  - **localpref 150, backup, add-path:** The BGP local preference attribute 150 applied by router PE-4 combined with the BGP PIC Edge configuration on router PE-3 ensures that the path via PE-4 is the backup path.

- **Path #2:**

  - **10.2.10.1 from 10.2.10.1 (192.168.1.124):** Router CE-2 is the eBGP next hop 10.2.10.1.

  - **localpref 200, external, best:** The BGP local preference is set to 200 for all routes learned over this eBGP path and is the best path for the subnet 10.2.10.128/28.

Output 9-63 *BGP PIC Edge Unipath VPNv4 RIB on PE-3 (IOS XR)*

```
RP/0/RP0/CPU0:PE-3#show bgp vpnv4 unicast vrf FULL-400-VRF 10.2.10.128/28

BGP routing table entry for 10.2.10.128/28, Route Distinguisher: 65001:403
Versions:
  Process           bRIB/RIB  SendTblVer
  Speaker                 48          48
    Local Label: 24005
Last Modified: Mar 23 09:21:49.498 for 00:06:01
Paths: (2 available, best #2)
  Advertised to peers (in unique update groups):
    10.0.4.254
  Path #1: Received by speaker 0
  Not advertised to any peer
  65400
    10.0.4.2 (metric 3) from 10.0.4.254 (10.0.4.2)
      Received Label 20
      Origin IGP, metric 0, localpref 150, valid, internal, backup, add-path,
  imported
      Received Path ID 0, Local Path ID 2, version 48
```

```
     Extended community: SoO:65400:2 RT:65001:400
     Originator: 10.0.4.2, Cluster list: 10.0.4.254
     Source AFI: VPNv4 Unicast, Source VRF: default, Source Route
  Distinguisher: 65001:404
  Path #2: Received by speaker 0
  Advertised to peers (in unique update groups):
    10.0.4.254
  65400
    10.2.10.1 from 10.2.10.1 (192.168.1.124)
     Origin IGP, metric 0, localpref 200, valid, external, best, group-best,
  import-candidate
     Received Path ID 0, Local Path ID 1, version 37
     Extended community: SoO:65400:2 RT:65001:400
RP/0/RP0/CPU0:PE-3#
```

The verification command **show bgp vpnv4 unicast vrf FULL-400-VRF 10.2.10.128/28**
on the backup egress IOS XE router PE-4 in Output 9-64 shows the BGP PIC Edge
behavior on this device. It includes the following information:

- **Paths: (2 available, best #1, table FULL-400-VRF):** The output shows that the subnet is accessible via two paths, and the second path is identified as the preferred one.

- **Advertise-best-external:** The BGP best external feature configured on PE-4 allows
  the propagation of the external route and implicitly enables the BGP PIC Edge
  feature.

- **Path #1:**

  - **10.0.4.1:** PE-3 is the BGP next hop 10.0.4.1 and is learned via BGP labeled unicast.

  - **localpref 200, best:** The BGP local preference attribute 200 ensures that this path
    via PE-3 is the best path for traffic forwarding.

  - **mpls labels in/out 20/24005:** Router PE-3 has allocated a VPNv4 label 24005 for
    the route from router CE-2.

- **Path #2:**

  - **10.2.10.3 (via vrf FULL-400-VRF):** The eBGP next hop 10.2.10.3 of router CE-2
    in the VRF instance FULL-400-VRF.

  - **localpref 150, backup/repair, advertise-best-external:** The BGP local preference
    attribute 150 applied to the subnet on PE-4 in combination with BGP PIC Edge
    ensures that this path is the backup/repair path.

  - **mpls labels in/out 20/nolabel:** Router PE-4 has allocated VPNv4 label 20 for the
    route 10.2.10.128/28 from router CE-2.

Output 9-64   *BGP PIC Edge Unipath VPNv4 RIB on PE-4 (IOS XE)*

```
PE-4#show bgp vpnv4 unicast vrf FULL-400-VRF 10.2.10.128/28
BGP routing table entry for 65001:404:10.2.10.128/28, version 32
Paths: (2 available, best #1, table FULL-400-VRF)
  Advertise-best-external
  Flag: 0x100
  Advertised to update-groups:
     1
  Refresh Epoch 1
  65400, imported path from 65001:403:10.2.10.128/28 (global)
    10.0.4.1 (metric 3) (via default) from 10.0.4.254 (10.0.4.254)
      Origin IGP, metric 0, localpref 200, valid, internal, best
      Extended Community: SoO:65400:2 RT:65001:400
      Originator: 10.0.4.1, Cluster list: 10.0.4.254 , recursive-via-host
      mpls labels in/out 20/24005
      rx pathid: 0, tx pathid: 0x0
      Updated on Mar 23 2024 09:21:50 UTC
  Refresh Epoch 1
  65400
    10.2.10.3 (via vrf FULL-400-VRF) from 10.2.10.3 (192.168.1.124)
      Origin IGP, metric 0, localpref 150, valid, external, backup/repair,
advertise-best-external
      Extended Community: SoO:65400:2 RT:65001:400 , recursive-via-connected
      mpls labels in/out 20/nolabel
      rx pathid: 0, tx pathid: 0
      Updated on Mar 23 2024 09:21:50 UTC
PE-4#
```

Output 9-65 shows the egress router PE-3's FIB details, displayed with the command **show cef vrf FULL-400-VRF 10.2.10.128/28 detail:**

■ **via 10.0.4.2/32, backup:** The Router PE-4 is the backup BGP path with the next hop 10.0.4.2.

   ■ **next hop 10.0.4.2/32 via 19002/0/21:** Router PE-4 is the next hop 10.0.4.2 and is learned via BGP labeled unicast, with Prefix SID 19002.

   ■ **local label 24005:** VPNv4 label 24005 is allocated for the route 10.2.10.128/28.

   ■ **next hop 192.168.4.0/32 Gi0/0/0/0   labels imposed {19002 20}:** This output displays the imposed label stack. Initially we see the IGP path via next hop 192.168.4.0/32 (on ABR-3). The imposed labels are the BGP Prefix SID 19002 (on PE-4) and finally the VPNv4 label 20.

   ■ **next hop 192.168.4.2/32 Gi0/0/0/0   labels imposed {19002 20}:** This output displays the imposed label stack. Initially we see the IGP path via next hop

192.168.4.2/32 (on ABR-4). The imposed labels are the BGP Prefix SID 19002 (on PE-4) and finally the VPNv4 label 20.

■ **via 10.2.10.1/32, bgp-ext:** Router CE-2 is the active eBGP path with next hop 10.2.10.1.

    ■ **next hop 10.2.10.1/32 via 10.2.10.1/32:** The eBGP next hop 10.2.10.1 from router CE-2

    ■ **local label 24005:** VPNv4 label 24005 is allocated for the route 10.2.10.128/28.

    ■ **next hop 10.2.10.1/32 Gi0/0/0/3.400 labels imposed {None}:** On the egress interface to router CE-2, the label stack is popped, and IPv4 traffic is routed out to subnet 10.2.10.128/28.

Output 9-65 *BGP PIC Edge Unipath FIB Detail on PE-3 (IOS XR)*

```
RP/0/RP0/CPU0:PE-3#show cef vrf FULL-400-VRF 10.2.10.128/28 detail

10.2.10.128/28, version 20, internal 0x1000001 0x30 (ptr 0xe8048e8) [1], 0x600
  (0xdb27608), 0xa08 (0xfe01658)
 Updated Mar 23 09:21:49.659
 Prefix Len 28, traffic index 0, precedence n/a, priority 3
  gateway array (0xd9907f0) reference count 9, flags 0x100078, source rib (7), 0
  backups
                [7 type 4 flags 0x8441 (0xf4c4b28) ext 0x0 (0x0)]
  LW-LDI[type=1, refc=1, ptr=0xdb27608, sh-ldi=0xf4c4b28]
  gateway array update type-time 1 Mar 23 09:21:49.659
 LDI Update time Mar 23 09:21:49.695
 LW-LDI-TS Mar 23 09:21:49.695
   via 10.0.4.2/32, 5 dependencies, recursive, backup [flags 0x6100]
    path-idx 0 NHID 0x0 [0xdd05b68 0x0]
    recursion-via-/32
    next hop VRF - 'default', table - 0xe0000000
    next hop 10.0.4.2/32 via 19002/0/21
     local label 24005
     next hop 192.168.4.0/32 Gi0/0/0/0   labels imposed {19002 20}
     next hop 192.168.4.2/32 Gi0/0/0/1   labels imposed {19002 20}
   via 10.2.10.1/32, 3 dependencies, recursive, bgp-ext [flags 0x6020]
    path-idx 1 NHID 0x0 [0xe8049c0 0x0], Internal 0xd73c640
    next hop 10.2.10.1/32 via 10.2.10.1/32
     local label 24005
     next hop 10.2.10.1/32 Gi0/0/0/3.400 labels imposed {None}
```

```
    Load distribution: 0 (refcount 7)

    Hash  OK  Interface            Address
    0     Y   recursive            10.2.10.1
RP/0/RP0/CPU0:PE-3#
```

The final verification is the FIB details for the target subnet 10.2.10.128/28 on repair router PE-4. Output 9-66 shows this verification, using the command **show ip cef vrf FULL-400-VRF 10.2.10.128/28 detail:**

- **recursive via 10.0.4.1 label 24005:** The active router PE-3 (10.0.4.1) has allocated a VPNv4 label 24005 for the route 10.2.10.128/28.

  - **nexthop 192.168.4.4 GigabitEthernet1 label 19001-(local:19001):** The IGP path is via the next hop 192.168.4.4 (ABR-4). The next hop 10.0.4.1 (PE-3) is allocated the BGP prefix SID 19001.

  - **nexthop 192.168.4.6 GigabitEthernet2 label 19001-(local:19001):** The IGP path is via the next hop 192.168.4.6 (ABR-3). The next hop 10.0.4.1 (PE-3) is allocated the BGP prefix SID 19001.

- **recursive via 10.2.10.3, repair:** The Backup/repair path is reachable via the egress interface to the next hop 10.2.10.3 of router CE-2.

  - **attached to GigabitEthernet3.400:** Egress interface to router CE-2

Output 9-66 *BGP PIC Edge Unipath FIB Detail on PE-4 (IOS XE)*

```
PE-4#show ip cef vrf FULL-400-VRF 10.2.10.128/28 detail
10.2.10.128/28, epoch 2, flags [rib defined all labels]
  dflt local label info: other/20 [0x2]
  recursive via 10.0.4.1 label 24005-(local:20)
    nexthop 192.168.4.4 GigabitEthernet1 label 19001-(local:19001)
    nexthop 192.168.4.6 GigabitEthernet2 label 19001-(local:19001)
  recursive via 10.2.10.3, repair
    attached to GigabitEthernet3.400
PE-4#
```

BGP PIC Edge Configuration: SRv6

The BGP PIC Edge configuration in this section is based on the SRv6 L3VPN full-mesh overlay service described in Chapter 7, in the section "SRv6 with the LVPN Overlay Service." Recall that BGP PIC Edge is configured for certain prefixes from the CE-1 router dual-homed to PE-1 and PE-2 in IS-IS Metro 1 as well as for CE-3 dual-homed to PE-3 and PE-4 in IS-IS Metro 2. These prefixes learned from the CE-1 and CE-3 routers are configured in an active/backup setup:

■ Network 10.1.103.128/28 (CE-1) attached to VRF instance FULL-500-VRF with per-CE allocation mode via PE-1 and PE-2

■ Network 10.2.103.128/28 (CE-3) attached to VRF instance FULL-500-VRF with per-CE allocation mode via PE-3 and PE-4

This section focuses on the prefix 10.2.103.128/28 from router CE-3. The configuration tasks for BGP PIC Edge unipath are detailed in Chapter 7, and this section briefly recaps them as an introduction to BGP PIC Edge. The focus is on the multipath with backup scenario, and configuration and verification tasks are discussed later. In Figure 9-30, the IP route 10.2.103.128/28, originating from router CE-3, is available on both ingress routers PE-1 and PE-2 in an active/backup unipath scenario. The path via router PE-3 is the active path, and the path through PE-4 is the backup path. The following points are applicable for this BGP PIC Edge configuration:

■ The ingress route 10.2.103.128/28 learned across the eBGP neighborship {CE-3 > PE-3} is matched with a BGP route policy that allows the BGP local preference to be set to 200.

■ The ingress route is also learned across the eBGP neighborship {CE-3 – PE-4} and is matched with a BGP route policy that allows the BGP local preference to be set to 150.

■ The path to this route is now preferred via the higher BGP local preference of 200, and router PE-4 normally sends a BGP withdrawal update toward the RR and withdraws its path toward the subnet learned via the eBGP neighborship with router CE-3.

■ By configuring BGP best external under the router BGP VRF instance on router PE-4, the route is advertised and is therefore no longer withdrawn. Together with the **additional-paths selection route-policy PIC_EDGE_RP** configuration on all the PE routers, this means the path via the backup router PE-4 is added to the router's FIB entries as a backup path.

■ In these example configurations, the SRv6 allocation mode is explicitly configured with per-CE allocation mode under the VRF instance FULL-500-VRF, which activates BGP PIC resilient per-CE SID (DX4/DX6) allocation protection. (This is described in more detail in the section "BGP PIC Edge Unipath Verification: SRv6," later in this chapter.)

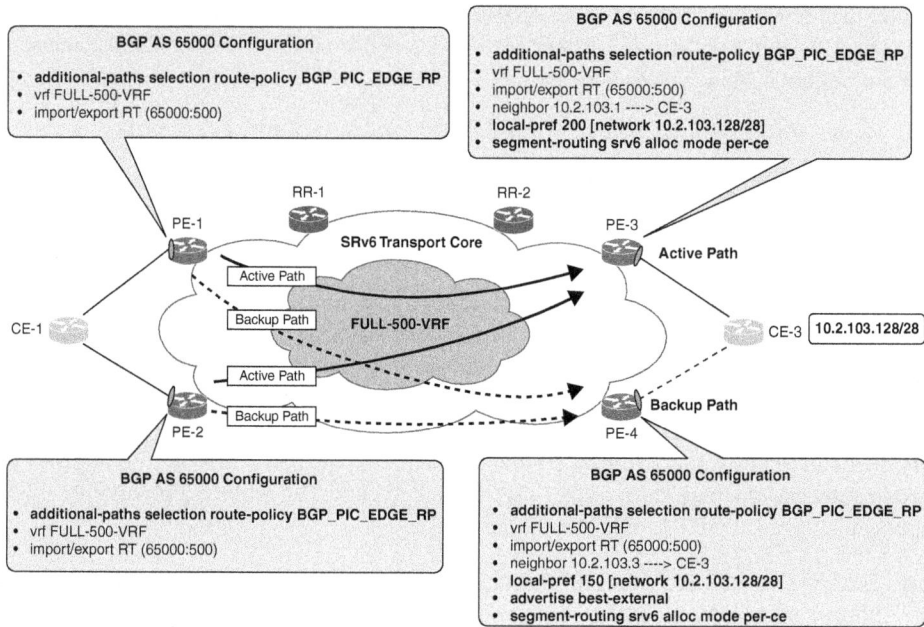

BGP AS 65000 Configuration

- additional-paths selection route-policy BGP_PIC_EDGE_RP
- vrf FULL-500-VRF
- import/export RT (65000:500)

BGP AS 65000 Configuration

- additional-paths selection route-policy BGP_PIC_EDGE_RP
- vrf FULL-500-VRF
- import/export RT (65000:500)
- neighbor 10.2.103.1 ----> CE-3
- local-pref 200 [network 10.2.103.128/28]
- segment-routing srv6 alloc mode per-ce

BGP AS 65000 Configuration

- additional-paths selection route-policy BGP_PIC_EDGE_RP
- vrf FULL-500-VRF
- import/export RT (65000:500)

BGP AS 65000 Configuration

- additional-paths selection route-policy BGP_PIC_EDGE_RP
- vrf FULL-500-VRF
- import/export RT (65000:500)
- neighbor 10.2.103.3 ----> CE-3
- local-pref 150 [network 10.2.103.128/28]
- advertise best-external
- segment-routing srv6 alloc mode per-ce

Figure 9-30 *BGP PIC Edge Unipath: SRv6*

BGP PIC Edge unipath is enabled on the routers PE-1 and PE-2 via the route policy BGP_PIC_EDGE_RP, as shown in Config 9-29, and then applied under the BGP VPNv4 address family.

Config 9-29 *BGP PIC Edge Unipath on PE-1 and PE-2 (IOS XR)*

```
!
route-policy BGP_PIC_EDGE_RP
  set path-selection backup 1 install
end-policy
!
router bgp 65000
address-family vpnv4 unicast
  vrf all
    segment-routing srv6
    !
  !
  additional-paths selection route-policy BGP_PIC_EDGE_RP
  !
!
```

The following configurations are applicable on the egress router PE-3, as shown in Config 9-30:

- An ingress route policy applies a BGP local preference of 200 to routes learned from router CE-3.

- The route-policy BGP_PIC_EDGE_RP enables BGP PIC Edge unipath.

- The SRv6 per-CE allocation mode is explicitly configured under the VRF instance FULL-500-VRF.

Config 9-30   *BGP PIC Edge Unipath on PE-3 (IOS XR)*

```
!
route-policy BGP_PIC_EDGE_RP
  set path-selection backup 1 install
end-policy
!
route-policy BGP_LOC-PREF_RP($LP)
  set local-preference $LP
end-policy
!
router bgp 65000
 address-family vpnv4 unicast
  vrf all
   segment-routing srv6
   !
  !
  additional-paths selection route-policy BGP_PIC_EDGE_RP
 !

 vrf FULL-500-VRF
  rd auto
  address-family ipv4 unicast
   segment-routing srv6
    alloc mode per-ce
   !
  !
  neighbor 10.2.103.1
   remote-as 65500
   address-family ipv4 unicast
    route-policy BGP_LOC-PREF_RP(200) in
    route-policy PASS_RP out
   !
```

The backup egress router PE-4 is configured according to the settings shown in Config 9-31:

- An ingress route policy applies a BGP local preference of 150 to routes learned from router CE-3.

- The route policy BGP_PIC_EDGE_RP enables BGP PIC Edge unipath.

- BGP best external is configured on router PE-4 to allow route 10.2.103.128/28 via the eBGP path to be advertised even though the preferred path is via router PE-3 due to the BGP local preference of 200.

- The SRv6 per-CE allocation mode is explicitly configured under the VRF instance FULL-500-VRF.

Config 9-31   *BGP PIC Edge Unipath on PE-4 (IOS XR)*

```
!
route-policy BGP_PIC_EDGE_RP
  set path-selection backup 1 install
end-policy
!
route-policy BGP_LOC-PREF_RP($LP)
  set local-preference $LP
end-policy
!
router bgp 65000
 address-family vpnv4 unicast
  vrf all
   segment-routing srv6
    !
  !
  additional-paths selection route-policy BGP_PIC_EDGE_RP
 !
 vrf FULL-500-VRF
  rd auto
  address-family ipv4 unicast
   advertise best-external
   segment-routing srv6
    alloc mode per-ce
   !
  !
  neighbor 10.2.103.3
   remote-as 65500
   address-family ipv4 unicast
    route-policy BGP_LOC-PREF_RP(150) in
    route-policy PASS_RP out
   !
```

In the BGP PIC Edge multipath with backup example shown in Figure 9-31, the IPv4 route 10.2.130.0/24 that originated from router CE-3 is available on both routers PE-1 and PE-2 in a multipath active/active scenario with an additional backup path, also known as a multipath protect path, via router PE-5. The following points are relevant for this BGP PIC Edge configuration:

■ The ingress route 10.2.130.0/24 learned across the two eBGP neighborships {CE-3 > PE-3} and {CE-3 > PE-4} is advertised into the overlay service network with the default BGP local preference of 100.

■ The same route learned across the eBGP neighborship {CE-3 > PE-5} is matched with an ingress BGP route policy on PE-5 that sets the BGP local preference to 50.

■ The paths to this route are preferred via both the routers PE-3 and PE-4, and the path via router PE-5 with the lower BGP local preference is the backup path.

■ Configuring **advertise best-external** under the router BGP VRF instance on router PE-5 means that route 10.2.130.0/24 will continue to be advertised and will no longer be withdrawn. The **additional-paths selection route-policy PIC_EDGE_RP** configuration with the addition of **multipath-protect** in the route policy for all PE routers ensures that the multipath is protected by the backup path via router P-5 and added to all the PE router FIB entries as a backup path.

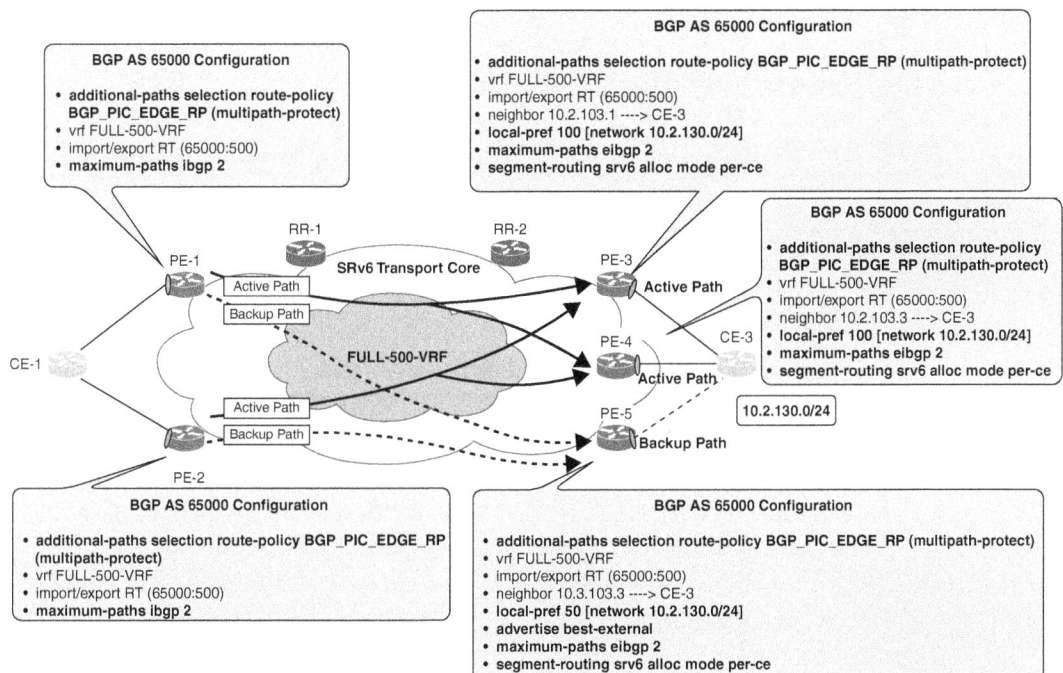

Figure 9-31 *BGP PIC Edge Multipath with Backup: SRv6*

BGP PIC Edge multipath with backup is enabled on routers PE-1 and PE-2 via the route policy BGP_PIC_EDGE_RP, as shown in Config 9-32, and then applied under the BGP VPNv4 address family. If both BGP PIC Edge unipath and multipath scenarios exist in the network, the configuration **set path-selection backup 1 install multipath-protect** suffices for both scenarios. The BGP multipath behavior is then enabled with the configuration line **maximum-paths ibgp 2** under the VRF instance FULL-500-VRF.

Config 9-32   *BGP PIC Edge Multipath with Backup on PE-1 and PE-2 (IOS XR)*

```
!
route-policy BGP_PIC_EDGE_RP
  set path-selection backup 1 install multipath-protect
end-policy
!
router bgp 65000
address-family vpnv4 unicast
  vrf all
    segment-routing srv6
    !
  !
  additional-paths selection route-policy BGP_PIC_EDGE_RP
 !
 vrf FULL-500-VRF
  rd auto
  address-family ipv4 unicast
   maximum-paths ibgp 2
   segment-routing srv6
   !
  !
```

On the active egress routers PE-3 and PE-4, the following configurations from Config 9-33 are applicable:

- The route policy BGP_PIC_EDGE_RP with the additional **multipath-protect** configuration in the route policy enables BGP PIC Edge multipath on the routers PE-3 and PE-4.

- The BGP multipath behavior is enabled with the configuration line **maximum-paths eibgp 2** under the VRF instance FULL-500-VRF. The preferred path is via the eBGP neighborship with CE-3, but there is a backup path via the alternate multipath PE router (PE-3 or PE-4) as well as the additional backup path via router PE-5.

- The SRv6 per-CE allocation mode is explicitly configured under the VRF instance FULL-500-VRF.

Config 9-33   *BGP PIC Edge Multipath with Backup on PE-3 and PE-4 (IOS XR)*

```
!
route-policy BGP_PIC_EDGE_RP
  set path-selection backup 1 install multipath-protect
end-policy
!
router bgp 65000
 address-family vpnv4 unicast
  vrf all
   segment-routing srv6
   !
  !
  additional-paths selection route-policy BGP_PIC_EDGE_RP
 !
 vrf FULL-500-VRF
  rd auto
  address-family ipv4 unicast
   maximum-paths eibgp 2
   segment-routing srv6
    alloc mode per-ce
   !
  !
```

On the backup egress router PE-5, the following configurations made in Config 9-34 are applicable:

- An ingress route policy sets routes from router CE-3 to the less preferred BGP local preference 50.

- The route policy BGP_PIC_EDGE_RP with the additional **multipath-protect** configuration in the route policy enables BGP PIC Edge multipath.

- BGP best external is configured to allow route 10.2.130.0/24 via the eBGP path to be advertised even though the preferred multipaths are via routers PE-3 and PE-4 due to the BGP local preference of 100.

- The BGP multipath behavior is under the VRF instance FULL-500-VRF with the configuration line **maximum-paths eibgp 2**.

- The SRv6 per-CE allocation mode is explicitly configured under the VRF instance FULL-500-VRF.

Config 9-34 *BGP PIC Edge Multipath with Backup on PE-5 (IOS XR)*

```
route-policy BGP_PIC_EDGE_RP
  set path-selection backup 1 install multipath-protect
end-policy
!
route-policy BGP_LOC-PREF_RP($LP)
  set local-preference $LP
end-policy
!
router bgp 65000
 address-family vpnv4 unicast
  vrf all
   segment-routing srv6
   !
  !
 additional-paths selection route-policy BGP_PIC_EDGE_RP
 !
 vrf FULL-500-VRF
  rd auto
  address-family ipv4 unicast
   maximum-paths eibgp 2
   advertise best-external
   segment-routing srv6
    alloc mode per-ce
  !
  neighbor 10.3.103.3
   remote-as 65500
   address-family ipv4 unicast
    route-policy BGP_LOC-PREF_RP(50) in
    route-policy PASS out
   !
  !
 !
!
```

BGP PIC Edge Unipath Verification: SRv6

This section discusses several useful commands that can be used to ensure that the BGP PIC Edge unipath operational method is configured and functioning correctly. This section examines the BGP PIC Edge unipath active/backup verification commands for the prefix 10.2.103.128/28, which originates from router CE-3, into the VRF instance FULL-500-VRF. Figure 9-32 provides an overview of the commands used for verification in this section.

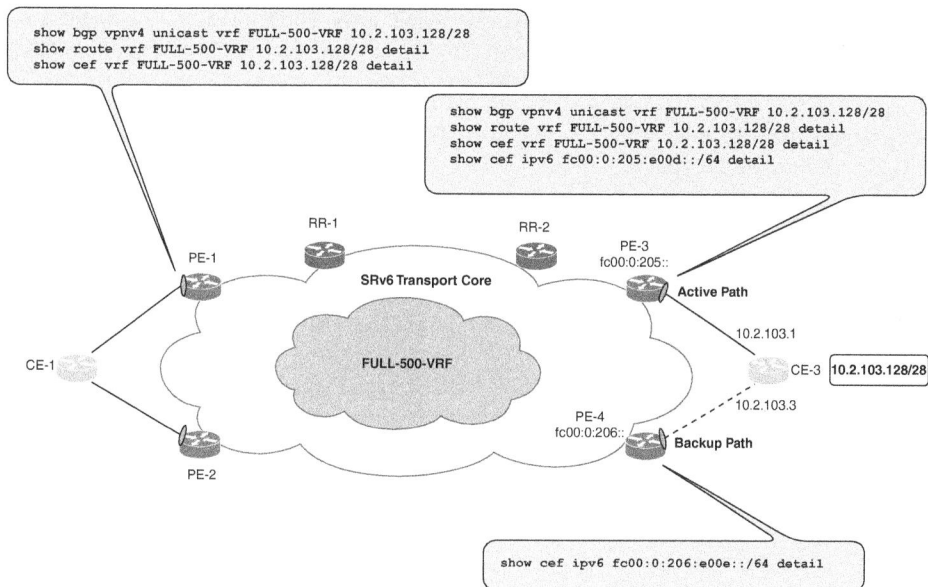

Figure 9-32 *BGP PIC Edge Unipath Verification: SRv6*

The command **show bgp vpnv4 unicast vrf FULL-500-VRF 10.2.103.128/28** executed on the ingress router PE-1 in Output 9-67 displays the following relevant BGP VPNv4 information for the IP subnet 10.2.103.128/28:

- **Paths: (2 available, best #1):** The output shows that the subnet is accessible via two paths, and the first path is identified as the preferred one.

- **Path #1:**

  - **fc00:0:205::1 (metric 61) from fc00:0:107::1 (172.19.0.19):** Router PE-3 is the BGP next hop fc00:0:205::, with BGP router ID 172.19.0.19.

  - **Received Label 0xe00d0:** The received label is 0xe00d0. Its most significant 16 bits, 0xe00d, is the SRv6 uSID with uDX4 endpoint behavior instantiated on PE-3 for the L3 adjacency toward CE-3.

  - **localpref 200, best:** The BGP local preference is set to 200, and this is therefore the active (best) path.

  - **Sid:fc00:0:205:::** This is the PE-3 remote Node SID (uN) from the configured SRv6 locator MAIN.

  - **Behavior:61:** The endpoint behavior is End.DX4 with NEXT-CSID (0x003D) because of the per-CE SID allocation under the VRF instance FULL-500-VRF.

- **Path #2:**

  - **fc00:0:206::1 (metric 61) from fc00:0:107::1 (172.19.0.20):** Router PE-4 is the BGP next hop fc00:0:206::, with BGP router ID 172.19.0.20.

- **Received Label 0xe00e0:** The received label is 0xe00e0. Its most significant 16 bits, 0xe00e, is the SRv6 uSID with uDX4 endpoint behavior instantiated on PE-4 for the L3 adjacency toward CE-3.

- **localpref 150, backup:** The BGP local preference is set to 150, and this is therefore the backup path.

- **Sid:fc00:0:206:::** This is the PE-4 remote Node SID (uN) from the configured SRv6 locator MAIN.

- **Behavior:61:** The endpoint behavior is End.DX4 with NEXT-CSID (0x003D) because of the per-CE SID allocation under the VRF instance FULL-500-VRF.

Output 9-67   *BGP PIC Edge Unipath VPNv4 RIB on PE-1 (IOS XR)*

```
RP/0/RP0/CPU0:PE-1#show bgp vpnv4 unicast vrf FULL-500-VRF 10.2.103.128/28
BGP routing table entry for 10.2.103.128/28, Route Distinguisher: 172.19.0.10:2
Versions:
  Process           bRIB/RIB  SendTblVer
  Speaker              387         387
Last Modified: Mar 16 08:20:08.021 for 20:02:45
Paths: (2 available, best #1)
  Not advertised to any peer
  Path #1: Received by speaker 0
  Not advertised to any peer
  65500
    fc00:0:205::1 (metric 61) from fc00:0:107::1 (172.19.0.19)
      Received Label 0xe00d0
      Origin IGP, metric 0, localpref 200, valid, internal, best, group-best,
  import-candidate, imported
      Received Path ID 0, Local Path ID 1, version 387
      Extended community: RT:65000:500
      Originator: 172.19.0.19, Cluster list: 172.19.0.12, 172.19.0.21
      PSID-Type:L3, SubTLV Count:1
       SubTLV:
        T:1(Sid information), Sid:fc00:0:205::, Behavior:61, SS-TLV Count:1
         SubSubTLV:
          T:1(Sid structure):
      Source AFI: VPNv4 Unicast, Source VRF: default, Source Route
  Distinguisher: 172.19.0.19:2
  Path #2: Received by speaker 0
  Not advertised to any peer
  65500
    fc00:0:206::1 (metric 61) from fc00:0:107::1 (172.19.0.20)
      Received Label 0xe00e0
      Origin IGP, metric 0, localpref 150, valid, internal, backup, add-path,
  imported
```

```
      Received Path ID 0, Local Path ID 4, version 387
      Extended community: RT:65000:500
      Originator: 172.19.0.20, Cluster list: 172.19.0.12, 172.19.0.21
      PSID-Type:L3, SubTLV Count:1
       SubTLV:
        T:1(Sid information), Sid:fc00:0:206::, Behavior:61, SS-TLV Count:1
         SubSubTLV:
          T:1(Sid structure):
      Source AFI: VPNv4 Unicast, Source VRF: default, Source Route
   Distinguisher: 172.19.0.20:1
RP/0/RP0/CPU0:PE-1#
```

The command **show route vrf FULL-500-VRF 10.2.103.128/28 detail** executed on router PE-1, as shown in Output 9-68, provides the RIB output for subnet 10.2.103.128/28, confirming the BGP PIC Edge backup path via router PE-4:

- **Number of pic paths 1:** The subnet 10.2.103.128/28 has a backup BGP PIC Edge path via router PE-4.

- **fc00:0:205::1, from fc00:0:107::1:** Router PE-3 is the BGP next hop fc00:0:205::.

  - **SRv6 Headend: H.Encaps.Red [f3216], SID-list {fc00:0:205:e00d::}:** fc00:0:205:e00d:: is the destination SID allocated to the route 10.2.103.128/28 by router PE-3.

- **fc00:0:206::1, from fc00:0:107::1, BGP backup path:** Router PE-4 is the BGP PIC Edge backup path with the next hop fc00:0:206::.

  - **SRv6 Headend: H.Encaps.Red [f3216], SID-list {fc00:0:206:e00e::}:** fc00:0:206:e00e:: is the destination SID allocated to the route 10.2.103.128/28 by router PE-4.

Output 9-68 *BGP PIC Edge Unipath RIB Details on PE-1 (IOS XR)*

```
RP/0/RP0/CPU0:PE-1#show route vrf FULL-500-VRF 10.2.103.128/28 detail

Routing entry for 10.2.103.128/28
  Known via "bgp 65000", distance 200, metric 0
  Tag 65500
  Number of pic paths 1 , type internal
  Installed Mar 16 08:20:08.094 for 20:23:48
  Routing Descriptor Blocks
    fc00:0:205::1, from fc00:0:107::1
      Nexthop in Vrf: "default", Table: "default", Ipv6 Unicast,
   Table Id: 0xe0800000
```

```
          Route metric is 0
          Label: None
          Tunnel ID: None
          Binding Label: None
          Extended communities count: 0
          Source RD attributes: 0x0001:44051:1245186
          NHID:0x0(Ref:0)
          SRv6 Headend: H.Encaps.Red [f3216], SID-list {fc00:0:205:e00d::}
       fc00:0:206::1, from fc00:0:107::1, BGP backup path
          Nexthop in Vrf: "default", Table: "default", Ipv6 Unicast,
       Table Id: 0xe0800000
          Route metric is 0
          Label: None
          Tunnel ID: None
          Binding Label: None
          Extended communities count: 0
          Source RD attributes: 0x0001:44051:1310721
          NHID:0x0(Ref:0)
          SRv6 Headend: H.Encaps.Red [f3216], SID-list {fc00:0:206:e00e::}
<snip>
RP/0/RP0/CPU0:PE-1#
```

Output 9-69 uses the command **show cef vrf FULL-500-VRF 10.2.103.128/28 detail** to view router PE-1's FIB table. This output provides the following relevant information:

- **via fc00:0:205::/128:** Router PE-3 is the BGP next hop fc00:0:205::.

  - **next hop fc00:0:205::/128 via fc00:0:200::/40:** The BGP next hop is learned via the summarized network route for the IS-IS Metro 2 SRv6 locator set in the global routing table.

  - **SRv6 H.Encaps.Red SID-list {fc00:0:205:e00d::}:** fc00:0:205:e00d:: is the destination SID allocated to the route 10.2.103.128/28 by router PE-3.

- **via fc00:0:206::/128 , backup:** Router PE-4 is the BGP PIC Edge backup path via next hop fc00:0:206::.

  - **next hop fc00:0:206::/128 via fc00:0:200::/40:** The BGP next hop is learned via the summarized network for the IS-IS Metro 2 SRv6 locator set in the global routing table.

  - **SRv6 H.Encaps.Red SID-list {fc00:0:206:e00e::}:** fc00:0:206:e00e:: is the destination SID allocated to the route 10.2.103.128/28 by router PE-4

Output 9-69 *BGP PIC Edge Unipath FIB Details on PE-1 (IOS XR)*

```
RP/0/RP0/CPU0:PE-1#show cef vrf FULL-500-VRF 10.2.103.128/28 detail
10.2.103.128/28, version 287, SRv6 Headend, internal 0x5000001 0x30 (ptr 0x8709d7c0)
 [1], 0x0 (0x0), 0x0 (0x89abf4c8)
Updated Mar 16 08:20:08.097
Prefix Len 28, traffic index 0, precedence n/a, priority 3
 gateway array (0x89c1faa0) reference count 3, flags 0x102010, source rib (7), 0
 backups
              [1 type 3 flags 0x40441 (0x875f09e8) ext 0x0 (0x0)]
 LW-LDI[type=0, refc=0, ptr=0x0, sh-ldi=0x0]
 gateway array update type-time 1 Mar 16 08:20:08.097
LDI Update time Mar 17 10:24:29.234

 Level 1 - Load distribution: 0
 [0] via fc00:0:205::/128, recursive

  via fc00:0:205::/128, 16 dependencies, recursive [flags 0x6000]
   path-idx 0 NHID 0x0 [0x86ebe400 0x0]
   next hop VRF - 'default', table - 0xe0800000
   next hop fc00:0:205::/128 via fc00:0:200::/40
   SRv6 H.Encaps.Red SID-list {fc00:0:205:e00d::}

 Load distribution: 0 1 (refcount 1)

 Hash  OK  Interface           Address
  0    Y   GigabitEthernet0/0/0/0   fe80::42:acff:fe16:8002
  1    Y   GigabitEthernet0/0/0/2   fe80::42:acff:fe16:8103

  via fc00:0:206::/128, 16 dependencies, recursive, backup [flags 0x6100]
   path-idx 1 NHID 0x0 [0x86ebe400 0x0]
   next hop VRF - 'default', table - 0xe0800000
   next hop fc00:0:206::/128 via fc00:0:200::/40
   SRv6 H.Encaps.Red SID-list {fc00:0:206:e00e::}

RP/0/RP0/CPU0:PE-1#
```

The next part of the BGP PIC Edge verification is conducted on the egress router PE-3, which is the primary path for subnet 10.2.103.128/28. The command executed on the egress router PE-3 in Output 9-70 displays the following relevant BGP VPNv4 information for the IPv4 subnet 10.2.103.128/28:

■ **Resilient per-CE nexthop set ID: 1:** Due to the per-CE allocation mode configuration, the received IPv4 packets is forwarded directly to the nh-set-id=1 (there is no IPv4 lookup) in the VRF instance FULL-500-VRF under normal forwarding circumstances. But under a primary PE–CE access link failure situation, a lookup takes place on any traffic received from the core, allowing this traffic to be forwarded back into the core and toward the backup path via router PE-4. This situation persists until BGP has fully converged on the ingress PE routers and these routers forward traffic via the updated next hop.

- **Paths: (2 available, best #1):** The output shows that the subnet is accessible via two paths, and the first path is identified as the preferred one.

- **Path #1:**

  - **10.2.103.1 from 10.2.103.1 (172.19.0.22):** Router CE-3 is the BGP next hop 10.2.103.1, with BGP router ID 172.19.0.22.

  - **localpref 200, external, best:** The BGP local preference is set to 200. This is the eBGP session to CE-3 and is therefore the BGP PIC Edge active (best) path.

- **Path #2:**

  - **fc00:0:206::1 (metric 21) from fc00:0:207::1 (172.19.0.20):** Router PE-4 is the BGP next hop fc00:0:206::, with BGP router ID 172.19.0.20.

  - **Received Label 0xe00e0:** The received label is 0xe00e0. Its most significant 16 bits, 0xe00e, is the SRv6 uSID with uDX4 endpoint behavior instantiated on PE-4 for the L3 adjacency toward CE-3.

  - **localpref 150, internal, backup:** The BGP local preference is set to 150 and is learned via iBGP. This is the BGP PIC Edge backup path via router PE-4.

  - **Sid:fc00:0:206:::** This is the PE-4 remote Node SID (uN) from the configured SRv6 locator MAIN.

  - **Behavior:61:** The endpoint behavior is End.DX4 with NEXT-CSID (0x003D) because of the per-CE SID allocation under the VRF instance FULL-500-VRF.

Output 9-70   *BGP PIC Edge Unipath VPNv4 RIB on PE-3 (IOS XR)*

```
RP/0/RP0/CPU0:PE-3#show bgp vpnv4 unicast vrf FULL-500-VRF 10.2.103.128/28

BGP routing table entry for 10.2.103.128/28, Route Distinguisher: 172.19.0.19:2
Versions:
  Process           bRIB/RIB  SendTblVer
  Speaker              108        108
    SRv6-VPN SID: fc00:0:205:e00d::/64
    Gateway Array ID: 1, Resilient per-CE nexthop set ID: 1
Last Modified: Mar 16 08:27:36.131 for 1d02h
Paths: (2 available, best #1)
  Advertised to peers (in unique update groups):
    fc00:0:207::1
  Path #1: Received by speaker 0
```

```
   Advertised to peers (in unique update groups):
     fc00:0:207::1
   65500
     10.2.103.1 from 10.2.103.1 (172.19.0.22)
       Origin IGP, metric 0, localpref 200, valid, external, best, group-best,
   import-candidate
       Received Path ID 0, Local Path ID 1, version 108
       Extended community: RT:65000:500
   Path #2: Received by speaker 0
   Not advertised to any peer
   65500
     fc00:0:206::1 (metric 21) from fc00:0:207::1 (172.19.0.20)
       Received Label 0xe00e0
       Origin IGP, metric 0, localpref 150, valid, internal, backup, add-path,
   imported
       Received Path ID 0, Local Path ID 2, version 108
       Extended community: RT:65000:500
       Originator: 172.19.0.20, Cluster list: 172.19.0.21
       PSID-Type:L3, SubTLV Count:1
        SubTLV:
         T:1(Sid information), Sid:fc00:0:206::, Behavior:61, SS-TLV Count:1
          SubSubTLV:
           T:1(Sid structure):
       Source AFI: VPNv4 Unicast, Source VRF: default, Source Route
   Distinguisher: 172.19.0.20:1
   RP/0/RP0/CPU0:PE-3#
```

The **show route vrf FULL-500-VRF 10.2.103.128/28 detail** command executed on router PE-3 in Output 9-71 details the RIB output for subnet 10.2.103.128/28, confirming the BGP PIC Edge backup path via router PE-4:

- **Number of pic paths 1:** The subnet 10.2.103.128/28 has a backup BGP PIC Edge path via router PE-4.

- **fc00:0:206::1, from fc00:0:207::1, BGP backup path:** Router PE-4 is the BGP PIC Edge backup path with the next hop fc00:0:206::.

  - **SRv6 Headend: H.Encaps.Red [f3216], SID-list {fc00:0:206:e00e::}:** fc00:0:206:e00e:: is the destination SID allocated to the route 10.2.103.128/28 by router PE-4.

- **10.2.103.1, from 10.2.103.1, BGP external:** This is the active path via the router CE-3 with the eBGP next hop 10.2.103.

Output 9-71   *BGP PIC Edge Unipath RIB Details on PE-3 (IOS XR)*

```
RP/0/RP0/CPU0:PE-3#show route vrf FULL-500-VRF 10.2.103.128/28 detail

Routing entry for 10.2.103.128/28
  Known via "bgp 65000", distance 20, metric 0
  Tag 65500
  Number of pic paths 1 , type internal and external
  Installed Mar 16 08:27:35.935 for 1d22h
  Routing Descriptor Blocks
    fc00:0:206::1, from fc00:0:207::1, BGP backup path
      Nexthop in Vrf: "default", Table: "default", IPv6 Unicast,
  Table Id: 0xe0800000
      Route metric is 0
      Label: None
      Tunnel ID: None
      Binding Label: None
      Extended communities count: 0
      Source RD attributes: 0x0001:44051:1310721
      NHID:0x0(Ref:0)
      SRv6 Headend: H.Encaps.Red [f3216], SID-list {fc00:0:206:e00e::}
    10.2.103.1, from 10.2.103.1, BGP external
      Route metric is 0
      Label: None
      Tunnel ID: None
      Binding Label: None
      Extended communities count: 0
      NHID:0x0(Ref:0)
      Path Grouping ID: 65500
<snip>
RP/0/RP0/CPU0:PE-3#
```

The subnet details from the FIB table of router PE-3, as shown in Output 9-72, provide the following relevant information:

- **via fc00:0:206::/128, backup:** Router PE-4 is the BGP PIC Edge backup path via next hop fc00:0:206::.

  - **next hop fc00:0:206::/128 via fc00:0:206::/48:** The BGP next hop is learned via the SRv6 locator for router PE-4.

    - **SRv6 H.Encaps.Red SID-list {fc00:0:206:e00e::}:** fc00:0:206:e00e:: is the destination SID allocated to the route 10.2.103.128/28 by router PE-4. In the event of an access link failure, router PE-3 does a lookup in the VRF instance FULL-500-VRF and forwards any traffic received from the core back into the core and toward the backup path via router PE-4. As mentioned previously, this persists until BGP has converged on the ingress PE routers.

- **via ::ffff:10.2.103.1/128, bgp-ext:** This is the active eBGP path to router CE-3.

  - **next hop ::ffff:10.2.103.1/128 via 10.2.103.1/32:** The BGP next hop IPv4 address of router CE-3 is mapped to IPv6.

  - **GigabitEthernet0/0/0/3.500 10.2.103.1:** Egress traffic to the destination subnet on CE-3 is forwarded out the interface GigabitEthernet0/0/0/3.500.

Output 9-72 *BGP PIC Edge Unipath FIB Details on PE-3 (IOS XR)*

```
RP/0/RP0/CPU0:PE-3#show cef vrf FULL-500-VRF 10.2.103.128/28 detail

10.2.103.128/28, version 28, SRv6 Headend, internal 0x1000001 0x30 (ptr 0x871b8268)
  [1], 0x0 (0x0), 0x0 (0x89c25260)
 Updated Mar 16 08:27:35.938
 Prefix Len 28, traffic index 0, precedence n/a, priority 3
  gateway array (0x89d210a8) reference count 3, flags 0x102010, source rib (7), 0
  backups
                [1 type 3 flags 0x48441 (0x877099c8) ext 0x0 (0x0)]
  LW-LDI[type=0, refc=0, ptr=0x0, sh-ldi=0x0]
  gateway array update type-time 1 Mar 16 08:20:08.055
 LDI Update time Mar 16 08:20:08.063

  Level 1 - Load distribution: 0
  [0] via ::ffff:10.2.103.1/128, recursive


   via fc00:0:206::/128, 6 dependencies, recursive, backup [flags 0x6100]
    path-idx 0 NHID 0x0 [0x86fd09b0 0x0]
    next hop VRF - 'default', table - 0xe0800000
    next hop fc00:0:206::/128 via fc00:0:206::/48
    SRv6 H.Encaps.Red SID-list {fc00:0:206:e00e::}

   via ::ffff:10.2.103.1/128, 7 dependencies, recursive, bgp-ext [flags 0x6020]
    path-idx 1 NHID 0x0 [0x871c2a88 0x0], Internal 0x89cea0b0
    next hop ::ffff:10.2.103.1/128 via 10.2.103.1/32


    Load distribution: 0 (refcount 1)


    Hash  OK  Interface               Address
    0     Y   GigabitEthernet0/0/0/3.500 10.2.103.1

RP/0/RP0/CPU0:PE-3#
```

The IPv6 FIB output in Output 9-73 on router PE-3 provides some details of the SID fc00:0:205:e00d::/64 for the subnet 10.2.103.128/28. As you may recall, this SID is used by the ingress PE routers to forward the L3VPN traffic to the destination. The backup path, indicated as::ffff:0.0.0.0/128 and backup, signifies that in the event of a local access link failure, router PE-3 performs a lookup in the VRF instance FULL-500-VRF routing table to determine the traffic's destination, which in this case is the backup router PE-4.

Output 9-73   *BGP PIC Edge Unipath IPv6 FIB Details: on PE-3 (IOS XR)*

```
RP/0/RP0/CPU0:PE-3#show cef ipv6 fc00:0:205:e00d::/64 detail

fc00:0:205:e00d::/64, version 439, SRv6 Endpoint uDX4, internal 0x1000001 0x0
  (ptr 0x86fced98) [1], 0x0 (0x0), 0x0 (0x89c251b0)
 Updated Mar 16 08:20:08.049
 Prefix Len 64, traffic index 0, precedence n/a, priority 0
 gateway array (0x87ed8240) reference count 1, flags 0x102010, source rib (7), 0
  backups
                [1 type 3 flags 0x48441 (0x87f814c8) ext 0x0 (0x0)]
 LW-LDI[type=0, refc=0, ptr=0x0, sh-ldi=0x0]
 gateway array update type-time 1 Mar 16 08:20:08.049
LDI Update time Mar 16 08:20:08.053


 Level 1 - Load distribution: 0
 [0] via ::ffff:10.2.103.1/128, recursive

  via ::ffff:0.0.0.0/128, 0 dependencies, weight 0, class 0, backup [flags 0x100]
   path-idx 0 NHID 0x0 [0x8752a300 0x0]
   next hop VRF - 'FULL-500-VRF', table - 0xe0000004
   next hop ::ffff:0.0.0.0/128


  via ::ffff:10.2.103.1/128, 7 dependencies, recursive [flags 0x6000]
   path-idx 1 NHID 0x0 [0x871c2a88 0x0], Internal 0x89cea0b0
   next hop VRF - 'FULL-500-VRF', table - 0xe0000004
   next hop ::ffff:10.2.103.1/128 via 10.2.103.1/32
  Load distribution: 0 (refcount 1)


  Hash  OK  Interface             Address
  0     Y   GigabitEthernet0/0/0/3.500 10.2.103.1

RP/0/RP0/CPU0:PE-3#
```

If an access link failure causes router PE-3 to redirect traffic to the backup router PE-4, the traffic is sent using the SID fc00:0:206:e00e:: (refer to Output 9-72). The router PE-4 IPv6 FIB details displayed with the command **show cef ipv6 fc00:0:206:e00e::/64 detail** in Output 9-74 confirm that the traffic exits directly through interface

GigabitEthernet0/0/0/4.500 on PE-4. This setup ensures that traffic does not loop back to router PE-3 during the time BGP takes to reconverge.

Output 9-74   *BGP PIC Edge Unipath IPv6 FIB Backup on PE-4 (IOS XR)*

```
RP/0/RP0/CPU0:PE-4#show cef ipv6 fc00:0:206:e00e::/64 detail


fc00:0:206:e00e::/64, version 571, SRv6 Endpoint uDX4, internal 0x1000001 0x0
  (ptr 0x86ebdaf8) [1], 0x0 (0x0), 0x0 (0x89c2d5d0)
 Updated Mar 15 10:00:37.888
 Prefix Len 64, traffic index 0, precedence n/a, priority 0
  gateway array (0x87da5848) reference count 1, flags 0x102010, source rib (7), 0
  backups
                [1 type 3 flags 0x48441 (0x87e4f168) ext 0x0 (0x0)]
  LW-LDI[type=0, refc=0, ptr=0x0, sh-ldi=0x0]
  gateway array update type-time 1 Mar 15 10:00:37.888
 LDI Update time Mar 15 10:00:37.888


  Level 1 - Load distribution: 0
  [0] via ::ffff:10.2.103.3/128, recursive

  via ::ffff:0.0.0.0/128, 0 dependencies, weight 0, class 0, backup [flags 0x100]
   path-idx 0 NHID 0x0 [0x87418210 0x0]
   next hop VRF - 'FULL-500-VRF', table - 0xe0000003
   next hop ::ffff:0.0.0.0/128


  via ::ffff:10.2.103.3/128, 6 dependencies, recursive [flags 0x6000]
   path-idx 1 NHID 0x0 [0x870b1448 0x0], Internal 0x89dc90b0
   next hop VRF - 'FULL-500-VRF', table - 0xe0000003
   next hop ::ffff:10.2.103.3/128 via 10.2.103.3/32
  Load distribution: 0 (refcount 1)


   Hash  OK  Interface                 Address
   0     Y   GigabitEthernet0/0/0/4.500 10.2.103.3

RP/0/RP0/CPU0:PE-4#
```

BGP PIC Edge Multipath Verification: SRv6

The verification tasks in this section address the BGP PIC Edge multipath (with backup) behavior, and the verification commands focus on the prefix 10.2.130.0/24 originated from router CE-3 into the VRF instance FULL-500-VRF. Figure 9-33 provides a high-level network overview with the commands for validating this functionality.

```
show bgp vpnv4 unicast vrf FULL-500-VRF 10.2.130.0/24
show route vrf FULL-500-VRF 10.2.130.0/24 detail
show cef vrf FULL-500-VRF 10.2.130.0/24 detail
```

```
show bgp vpnv4 unicast vrf FULL-500-VRF 10.2.130.0/24
show route vrf FULL-500-VRF 10.2.130.0/24 detail
show cef vrf FULL-500-VRF 10.2.130.0/24 detail
show cef ipv6 fc00:0:205:e00d::/64 detail
```

```
show cef ipv6 fc00:0:209:e005::/64 detail
```

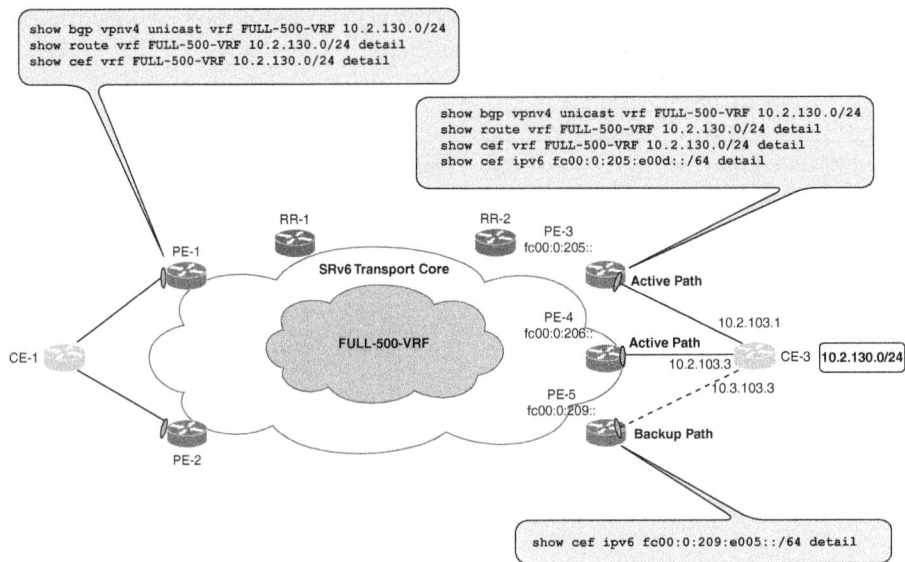

Figure 9-33 *BGP PIC Edge Multipath Verification: SRv6*

The BGP VPNv4 RIB details in Output 9-75 executed via the command **show bgp vpnv4 unicast vrf FULL-500-VRF 10.2.130.0/24** on the ingress router PE-1 display the following relevant multipath information for the IPv4 subnet 10.2.130.0/24:

■ **Paths: (3 available, best #1):** The output shows that the subnet is accessible via three paths, and the first path is identified as the preferred (best) one.

■ **Path #1:**

   ■ **fc00:0:205::1 (metric 61) from fc00:0:107::1 (172.19.0.19):** Router PE-3 is the BGP next hop fc00:0:205::, with BGP router ID 172.19.0.19.

   ■ **Received Label 0xe00d0:** The received label is 0xe00d0. Its most significant 16 bits, 0xe00d, is the SRv6 uSID with uDX4 endpoint behavior instantiated on PE-3 for the L3 adjacency toward CE-3.

   ■ **localpref 100, best, multipath:** The BGP local preference is set to the default value of 100, designating this as the overall best path, and due to the **maximum-paths ibgp 2** configuration, it forms a multipath with path #2.

   ■ **Sid:fc00:0:205:::** This is the PE-3 remote Node SID (uN) from the configured SRv6 locator MAIN.

   ■ **Behavior:61:** The endpoint behavior is End.DX4 with NEXT-CSID (0x003D) because of the per-CE SID allocation under the VRF instance FULL-500-VRF.

■ **Path #2:**

   ■ **fc00:0:206::1 (metric 61) from fc00:0:107::1 (172.19.0.20):** Router PE-4 is the BGP next hop fc00:0:206::, with BGP router ID 172.19.0.20.

- **Received Label 0xe00e0:** The received label is 0xe00e0. Its most significant 16 bits, 0xe00e, is the SRv6 uSID with uDX4 endpoint behavior instantiated on PE-4 for the L3 adjacency toward CE-3.

- **localpref 100, multipath, backup:** The BGP local preference is set to the default value of 100. This path is designated as a backup path due to the standard BGP best path algorithm (in this case, the BGP router ID), and because of the **maximum-paths ibgp 2** configuration, it forms a multipath with path #1.

- **Sid:fc00:0:206:::** This is the PE-4 remote Node SID (uN) from the configured SRv6 locator MAIN.

- **Behavior:61:** The endpoint behavior is End.DX4 with NEXT-CSID (0x003D) because of the per-CE SID allocation under the VRF instance FULL-500-VRF.

- **Path #3:**

  - **fc00:0:209::1 (metric 61) from fc00:0:107::1 (172.19.0.26):** Router PE-5 is the BGP next hop fc00:0:209::, with BGP router ID 172.19.0.26.

  - **Received Label 0xe0050:** The received label is 0xe0050. Its most significant 16 bits, 0xe005, is the SRv6 uSID with uDX4 endpoint behavior instantiated on PE-5 for the L3 adjacency toward CE-3.

  - **localpref 50, backup(protect multipath):** The BGP local preference is set to 50 on PE-5, making this path the backup (protect) path for multipath via routers PE-3 and PE-4.

  - **Sid:fc00:0:209:::** This is the PE-5 remote Node SID (uN) from the configured SRv6 locator MAIN.

  - **Behavior:61:** The endpoint behavior is End.DX4 with NEXT-CSID (0x003D) because of the per-CE SID allocation under the VRF instance FULL-500-VRF.

Output 9-75   *BGP PIC Edge Multipath VPNv4 RIB on PE-1 (IOS XR)*

```
RP/0/RP0/CPU0:PE-1#show bgp vpnv4 unicast vrf FULL-500-VRF 10.2.130.0/24
BGP routing table entry for 10.2.130.0/24, Route Distinguisher: 172.19.0.10:2
Versions:
  Process           bRIB/RIB  SendTblVer
  Speaker               412         412
Last Modified: Mar 18 23:39:58.021 for 00:00:39
Paths: (3 available, best #1)
  Not advertised to any peer
  Path #1: Received by speaker 0
  Not advertised to any peer
  65500
    fc00:0:205::1 (metric 61) from fc00:0:107::1 (172.19.0.19)
      Received Label 0xe00d0
      Origin IGP, metric 0, localpref 100, valid, internal, best, group-best,
  multipath, import-candidate, imported
```

```
      Received Path ID 0, Local Path ID 1, version 389
      Extended community: RT:65000:500
      Originator: 172.19.0.19, Cluster list: 172.19.0.12, 172.19.0.21
      PSID-Type:L3, SubTLV Count:1
       SubTLV:
        T:1(Sid information), Sid:fc00:0:205::, Behavior:61, SS-TLV Count:1
         SubSubTLV:
          T:1(Sid structure):
      Source AFI: VPNv4 Unicast, Source VRF: default, Source Route
  Distinguisher: 172.19.0.19:2
  Path #2: Received by speaker 0
  Not advertised to any peer
  65500
    fc00:0:206::1 (metric 61) from fc00:0:107::1 (172.19.0.20)
    Received Label 0xe00e0
    Origin IGP, metric 0, localpref 100, valid, internal, multipath, backup,
  add-path, import-candidate, imported
      Received Path ID 0, Local Path ID 10, version 389
      Extended community: RT:65000:500
      Originator: 172.19.0.20, Cluster list: 172.19.0.12, 172.19.0.21
      PSID-Type:L3, SubTLV Count:1
       SubTLV:
        T:1(Sid information), Sid:fc00:0:206::, Behavior:61, SS-TLV Count:1
         SubSubTLV:
          T:1(Sid structure):
      Source AFI: VPNv4 Unicast, Source VRF: default, Source Route
  Distinguisher: 172.19.0.20:1
  Path #3: Received by speaker 0
  Not advertised to any peer
  65500
    fc00:0:209::1 (metric 61) from fc00:0:107::1 (172.19.0.26)
    Received Label 0xe0050
    Origin IGP, metric 0, localpref 50, valid, internal, backup(protect
  multipath), add-path, imported
      Received Path ID 0, Local Path ID 12, version 412
      Extended community: RT:65000:500
      Originator: 172.19.0.26, Cluster list: 172.19.0.12, 172.19.0.21
      PSID-Type:L3, SubTLV Count:1
       SubTLV:
        T:1(Sid information), Sid:fc00:0:209::, Behavior:61, SS-TLV Count:1
         SubSubTLV:
          T:1(Sid structure):
      Source AFI: VPNv4 Unicast, Source VRF: default, Source Route
  Distinguisher: 172.19.0.26:1
  RP/0/RP0/CPU0:PE-1#
```

The RIB details from the command **show route vrf FULL-500-VRF 10.2.130.0/24 detail** on router PE-1 in Output 9-76 describe subnet 10.2.130.0/24, where the BGP multipath is via routers PE-3 and PE-4 and the BGP PIC Edge backup path is via router PE-5:

- **Number of pic paths 1:** The subnet 10.2.130.0/24 has a backup BGP PIC Edge path via router PE-5.

- **fc00:0:205::1, from fc00:0:107::1, BGP multi path:** Router PE-3 is the BGP next hop fc00:0:205:: and is a BGP multipath.

  - **SRv6 Headend: H.Encaps.Red [f3216], SID-list {fc00:0:205:e00d::}:** fc00:0:205:e00d:: is the destination SID allocated to the route 10.2.130.0/24 by router PE-3.

- **fc00:0:206::1, from fc00:0:107::1, BGP multi path:** PE-4 is the BGP next hop fc00:0:206:: and is a BGP multipath.

  - **SRv6 Headend: H.Encaps.Red [f3216], SID-list {fc00:0:206:e00e::}:** fc00:0:206:e00e:: is the destination SID allocated to the route 10.2.130.0/24 by router PE-4.

- **fc00:0:209::1, from fc00:0:107::1, BGP backup path:** PE-5 is the BGP PIC Edge backup path with the next hop fc00:0:209::.

  - **SRv6 Headend: H.Encaps.Red [f3216], SID-list {fc00:0:209:e005::}:** fc00:0:209:e005:: is the destination SID allocated to the route 10.2.130.0/24 by router PE-5.

Output 9-76 *BGP PIC Edge Multipath RIB Details on PE-1 (IOS XR)*

```
RP/0/RP0/CPU0:PE-1#show route vrf FULL-500-VRF 10.2.130.0/24 detail

Routing entry for 10.2.130.0/24
  Known via "bgp 65000", distance 200, metric 0
  Tag 65500
  Number of pic paths 1 , type internal
  Installed Mar 18 23:39:57.816 for 00:02:15
  Routing Descriptor Blocks
    fc00:0:205::1, from fc00:0:107::1, BGP multi path
      Nexthop in Vrf: "default", Table: "default", IPv6 Unicast,
Table Id: 0xe0800000
      Route metric is 0
      Label: None
      Tunnel ID: None
      Binding Label: None
      Extended communities count: 0
      Source RD attributes: 0x0001:44051:1245186
      NHID:0x0(Ref:0)
```

```
     SRv6 Headend: H.Encaps.Red [f3216], SID-list {fc00:0:205:e00d::}
  fc00:0:206::1, from fc00:0:107::1, BGP multi path
     Nexthop in Vrf: "default", Table: "default", IPv6 Unicast,
  Table Id: 0xe0800000
     Route metric is 0
     Label: None
     Tunnel ID: None
     Binding Label: None
     Extended communities count: 0
     Source RD attributes: 0x0001:44051:1310721
     NHID:0x0(Ref:0)
     SRv6 Headend: H.Encaps.Red [f3216], SID-list {fc00:0:206:e00e::}
  fc00:0:209::1, from fc00:0:107::1, BGP backup path
     Nexthop in Vrf: "default", Table: "default", IPv6 Unicast,
  Table Id: 0xe0800000
     Route metric is 0
     Label: None
     Tunnel ID: None
     Binding Label: None
     Extended communities count: 0
    Source RD attributes: 0x0001:44051:1703937
     NHID:0x0(Ref:0)
     SRv6 Headend: H.Encaps.Red [f3216], SID-list {fc00:0:209:e005::}
<snip>
RP/0/RP0/CPU0:PE-1#
```

In the FIB table of router PE-1, the command **show cef vrf FULL-500-VRF 10.2.130.0/24 detail** from Output 9-77 includes the following relevant information:

- **via fc00:0:205::/128 , bgp-multipath:** Router PE-3 forms part of the multipath with a BGP next hop fc00:0:205::.

  - **next hop fc00:0:205::/128 via fc00:0:200::/40:** The BGP next hop is learned via the summarized network route for the IS-IS Metro 2 SRv6 locator set in the global routing table.

  - **SRv6 H.Encaps.Red SID-list {fc00:0:205:e00d::}:** fc00:0:205:e00d:: is the destination SID allocated to the route 10.2.130.0/24 by router PE-3.

- **via fc00:0:206::/128 , bgp-multipath:** Router PE-4 forms part of the multipath with a BGP next hop fc00:0:206::.

  - **next hop fc00:0:206::/128 via fc00:0:200::/40:** The BGP next hop is learned via the summarized network for the IS-IS Metro 2 SRv6 locator set in the global routing table.

  - **SRv6 H.Encaps.Red SID-list {fc00:0:206:e00e::}:** fc00:0:206:e00e:: is the destination SID allocated to the route 10.2.130.0/24 by router PE-4.

- **via fc00:0:209::/128 , backup:** Router PE-5 is the BGP PIC Edge backup path via next hop fc00:0:209::.

  - **next hop fc00:0:209::/128 via fc00:0:200::/40:** The BGP next hop is learned via the summarized network for the IS-IS Metro 2 SRv6 locator set in the global routing table.

  - **SRv6 H.Encaps.Red SID-list {fc00:0:209:e005::}:** fc00:0:209:e005:: is the destination SID allocated to the route 10.2.130.0/24 by router PE-5.

Output 9-77 *BGP PIC Edge Multipath FIB Details on PE-1 (IOS XR)*

```
RP/0/RP0/CPU0:PE-1#show cef vrf FULL-500-VRF 10.2.130.0/24 detail
10.2.130.0/24, version 312, SRv6 Headend, internal 0x5000001 0x30 (ptr 0x8709d6c8)
  [1], 0x0 (0x0), 0x0 (0x8a3930a8)
 Updated Mar 18 23:39:57.819
 Prefix Len 24, traffic index 0, precedence n/a, priority 3
  gateway array (0x89c1fd58) reference count 1, flags 0x102010, source rib (7), 0
  backups
                [1 type 3 flags 0x48441 (0x875efcc8) ext 0x0 (0x0)]
  LW-LDI[type=0, refc=0, ptr=0x0, sh-ldi=0x0]
  gateway array update type-time 1 Mar 18 23:39:57.819
 LDI Update time Mar 18 23:39:57.826


 Level 1 - Load distribution: 0 1
  [0] via fc00:0:205::/128, recursive
  [1] via fc00:0:206::/128, recursive
  via fc00:0:205::/128, 17 dependencies, recursive, bgp-multipath [flags 0x6080]
    path-idx 0 NHID 0x0 [0x86ebe400 0x0]
    next hop VRF - 'default', table - 0xe0800000
    next hop fc00:0:205::/128 via fc00:0:200::/40
    SRv6 H.Encaps.Red SID-list {fc00:0:205:e00d::}


   Load distribution: 0 1 (refcount 1)


   Hash  OK  Interface             Address
   0     Y   GigabitEthernet0/0/0/0  fe80::42:acff:fe16:8002
   1     Y   GigabitEthernet0/0/0/2  fe80::42:acff:fe16:8103


  via fc00:0:206::/128, 17 dependencies, recursive, bgp-multipath [flags 0x6080]
    path-idx 1 NHID 0x0 [0x86ebe400 0x0]
    next hop VRF - 'default', table - 0xe0800000
    next hop fc00:0:206::/128 via fc00:0:200::/40
    SRv6 H.Encaps.Red SID-list {fc00:0:206:e00e::}


   Load distribution: 0 1 (refcount 1)
```

```
Hash  OK  Interface              Address
0     Y   GigabitEthernet0/0/0/0  fe80::42:acff:fe16:8002
1     Y   GigabitEthernet0/0/0/2  fe80::42:acff:fe16:8103

via fc00:0:209::/128, 17 dependencies, recursive, backup [flags 0x6100]
path-idx 2 NHID 0x0 [0x86ebe400 0x0]
next hop VRF - 'default', table - 0xe0800000
next hop fc00:0:209::/128 via fc00:0:200::/40
SRv6 H.Encaps.Red SID-list {fc00:0:209:e005::}
```

RP/0/RP0/CPU0:PE-1#

The egress router BGP PIC Edge multipath verification tasks are executed solely on router PE-3 in this section, as the outputs of PE-4 are expected to be similar. Additional commands need to be executed on the backup router PE-5 as well. The VPNv4 RIB of the egress router PE-3 in Output 9-78 displays the following information for the IP subnet 10.2.130.0/24:

- **Resilient per-CE nexthop set ID: 1:** Due to the **alloc mode per-ce** configuration, the received IPv4 packets are forwarded directly to the nh-set-id=1 (no IPv4 lookup) in the VRF instance FULL-500-VRF under normal forwarding circumstances. But under an access link failure situation, a lookup is forced to take place on any traffic received from the core, allowing this traffic to be forwarded back into the core and toward the backup multipath via router PE-4. This situation may persist until BGP has fully converged on the ingress PE routers and these routers forward traffic via the updated next hop on PE-4 or if the access link on PE-4 has also failed, via router PE-5.

- **Paths: (3 available, best #1):** The subnet 10.2.130.0/24 is available across three paths, and the first path is the preferred (best).

- **Path #1:**

  - **10.2.103.1 from 10.2.103.1 (172.19.0.22):** Router CE-3 is the BGP next hop 10.2.103.1 with BGP router ID 172.19.0.22.

  - **localpref 100, external, best, multipath:** The BGP local preference is set to 100 which is the default. This route is available via the eBGP session to CE-3 and will be the preferred path.

- **Path #2:**

  - **fc00:0:206::1 (metric 21) from fc00:0:207::1 (172.19.0.20):** Router PE-4 is the BGP next hop fc00:0:206::, with BGP router ID 172.19.0.20.

  - **Received Label 0xe00e0:** The received label is 0xe00e0. Its most significant 16 bits, 0xe00e, is the SRv6 uSID with uDX4 endpoint behavior instantiated on PE-4 for the L3 adjacency toward CE-3.

- **localpref 100, internal, multipath, backup:** The BGP local preference is set to 100, which is default. This route is available via iBGP and is the BGP PIC Edge multipath backup path, so it acts as a backup path for path #1.

- **Sid:fc00:0:206:::** This is the PE-4 remote Node SID (uN) from the configured SRv6 locator MAIN.

- **Behavior:61:** The endpoint behavior is End.DX4 with NEXT-CSID (0x003D) because of the per-CE SID allocation under the VRF instance FULL-500-VRF.

- Path #3:

  - **fc00:0:209::1 (metric 21) from fc00:0:207::1 (172.19.0.26):** PE-5 is the BGP next hop fc00:0:209::, with BGP router ID 172.19.0.26.

  - **Received Label 0xe0050:** The received label is 0xe0050. The most significant 16 bits, 0xe005, is the SRv6 uSID with uDX4 endpoint behavior instantiated on PE-5 for the L3 adjacency toward CE-3.

  - **localpref 50, internal, backup(protect multipath):** The BGP local preference is set to 50 on PE-5 and is learned via iBGP. This path is the BGP PIC Edge backup of the multipath, so PE-5 acts as a backup path for path #1 and path #2.

  - **Sid:fc00:0:209:::** This is the PE-5 remote Node SID (uN) from the configured SRv6 locator MAIN.

  - **Behavior:61:** The endpoint behavior is End.DX4 with NEXT-CSID (0x003D) because of the per-CE SID allocation under the VRF instance FULL-500-VRF.

Output 9-78   *BGP PIC Edge Multipath VPNv4 RIB Detail on PE-3 (IOS XR)*

```
RP/0/RP0/CPU0:PE-3#show bgp vpnv4 unicast vrf FULL-500-VRF 10.2.130.0/24


BGP routing table entry for 10.2.130.0/24, Route Distinguisher: 172.19.0.19:2
Versions:
  Process           bRIB/RIB  SendTblVer
  Speaker                131         131
    SRv6-VPN SID: fc00:0:205:e00d::/64
    Gateway Array ID: 1, Resilient per-CE nexthop set ID: 1
Last Modified: Mar 18 23:39:58.131 for 01:11:53
Paths: (3 available, best #1)
  Advertised to peers (in unique update groups):
    fc00:0:207::1
  Path #1: Received by speaker 0
  Advertised to peers (in unique update groups):
    fc00:0:207::1
  65500
    10.2.103.1 from 10.2.103.1 (172.19.0.22)
      Origin IGP, metric 0, localpref 100, valid, external, best, group-best,
multipath, import-candidate
```

```
             Received Path ID 0, Local Path ID 1, version 110
             Extended community: RT:65000:500
        Path #2: Received by speaker 0
       Not advertised to any peer
        65500
          fc00:0:206::1 (metric 21) from fc00:0:207::1 (172.19.0.20)
          Received Label 0xe00e0
          Origin IGP, metric 0, localpref 100, valid, internal, multipath, backup,
       add-path, import-candidate, imported
             Received Path ID 0, Local Path ID 2, version 110
             Extended community: RT:65000:500
             Originator: 172.19.0.20, Cluster list: 172.19.0.21
             PSID-Type:L3, SubTLV Count:1
              SubTLV:
              T:1(Sid information), Sid:fc00:0:206::, Behavior:61, SS-TLV Count:1
                SubSubTLV:
                 T:1(Sid structure):
             Source AFI: VPNv4 Unicast, Source VRF: default, Source Route
       Distinguisher: 172.19.0.20:1
        Path #3: Received by speaker 0
       Not advertised to any peer
        65500
          fc00:0:209::1 (metric 21) from fc00:0:207::1 (172.19.0.26)
          Received Label 0xe0050
          Origin IGP, metric 0, localpref 50, valid, internal, backup(protect
       multipath), add-path, imported
             Received Path ID 0, Local Path ID 4, version 131
             Extended community: RT:65000:500
             Originator: 172.19.0.26, Cluster list: 172.19.0.21
             PSID-Type:L3, SubTLV Count:1
              SubTLV:
              T:1(Sid information), Sid:fc00:0:209::, Behavior:61, SS-TLV Count:1
                SubSubTLV:
                 T:1(Sid structure):
             Source AFI: VPNv4 Unicast, Source VRF: default, Source Route
        Distinguisher: 172.19.0.26:1
       RP/0/RP0/CPU0:PE-3#
```

Output 9-79 shows the subnet's FIB details, obtained with the command **show cef vrf FULL-500-VRF 10.2.130.0/24 detail** from router PE-3. This output provides the following information:

- **via fc00:0:206::/128 , bgp-multipath, backup:** Router PE-4 forms part of the multipath with a BGP next hop fc00:0:206:: and is backup for the path via interface GigabitEthernet0/0/0/3.500.

- **next hop fc00:0:206::/128 via fc00:0:206::/48:** The BGP next hop is learned via the SRv6 locator for router PE-4.

- **SRv6 H.Encaps.Red SID-list {fc00:0:206:e00e::}:** fc00:0:206:e00e:: is the destination SID allocated to the route 10.2.130.0/24 by router PE-4.

- **via fc00:0:209::/128 , backup:** Router PE-5 is the BGP PIC Edge backup path via next hop fc00:0:209::.

  - **next hop fc00:0:209::/128 via fc00:0:209::/48:** The BGP next hop is learned via the SRv6 locator for router PE-5.

  - **SRv6 H.Encaps.Red SID-list {fc00:0:209:e005::}:** fc00:0:209:e005:: is the destination SID allocated to the route 10.2.130.0/24 by router PE-5. In the event of a local access link failure on both multipath routers, router PE-3 will do a lookup in the VRF instance FULL-500-VRF and forward any traffic received from the core back into the core and toward the backup path via router PE-5 until BGP has converged on the ingress PE routers.

- **via ::ffff:10.2.103.1/128, bgp-ext, bgp-multipath:** This is the active eBGP path to router CE-3.

  - **next hop ::ffff:10.2.103.1/128 via 10.2.103.1/32:** The BGP next hop IPv4 address of router CE-3 is mapped to IPv6.

  - **GigabitEthernet0/0/0/3.500 10.2.103.1:** Egress traffic to the destination subnet 10.2.130.0/24 on CE-3 is forwarded out the interface GigabitEthernet0/0/0/3.500.

Output 9-79 *BGP PIC Edge Multipath FIB Details on PE-3 (IOS XR)*

```
RP/0/RP0/CPU0:PE-3#show cef vrf FULL-500-VRF 10.2.130.0/24 detail

10.2.130.0/24, version 59, SRv6 Headend, internal 0x1000001 0x30 (ptr 0x871b8078)
  [1], 0x0 (0x0), 0x0 (0x8a2230a8)
 Updated Mar 18 23:39:57.805
 Prefix Len 24, traffic index 0, precedence n/a, priority 3
  gateway array (0x89d21b88) reference count 1, flags 0x102810, source rib (7), 0
  backups
               [1 type 3 flags 0x48441 (0x87709668) ext 0x0 (0x0)]
  LW-LDI[type=0, refc=0, ptr=0x0, sh-ldi=0x0]
  gateway array update type-time 1 Mar 18 23:39:57.806
 LDI Update time Mar 18 23:39:57.812

  Level 1 - Load distribution: 0 1
  [0] via fc00:0:206::/128, recursive
  [1] via ::ffff:10.2.103.1/128, recursive
```

```
via fc00:0:206::/128, 6 dependencies, recursive, bgp-multipath, backup
[flags 0x6180]
  path-idx 0 NHID 0x0 [0x86fd09b0 0x0]
  next hop VRF - 'default', table - 0xe0800000
  next hop fc00:0:206::/128 via fc00:0:206::/48
  SRv6 H.Encaps.Red SID-list {fc00:0:206:e00e::}


  Load distribution: 0 1 (refcount 1)


  Hash  OK  Interface              Address
  0     Y   GigabitEthernet0/0/0/0  fe80::42:acff:fe16:4d02
  1     Y   GigabitEthernet0/0/0/2  fe80::42:acff:fe16:5102

via fc00:0:209::/128, 4 dependencies, recursive, backup [flags 0x6100]
  path-idx 1 NHID 0x0 [0x86fd0e88 0x0]
  next hop VRF - 'default', table - 0xe0800000
  next hop fc00:0:209::/128 via fc00:0:209::/48
  SRv6 H.Encaps.Red SID-list {fc00:0:209:e005::}
    SRv6  SID-list {}


via ::ffff:10.2.103.1/128, 7 dependencies, recursive, bgp-ext, bgp-multipath
[flags 0x60a0]
  path-idx 2 NHID 0x0 [0x871c2a88 0x0], Internal 0x89cea0b0
  next hop ::ffff:10.2.103.1/128 via 10.2.103.1/32


  Load distribution: 0 (refcount 1)


  Hash  OK  Interface              Address
  4     Y   GigabitEthernet0/0/0/3.500 10.2.103.1

RP/0/RP0/CPU0:PE-3#
```

Although this is a repetition of Output 9-73, it is worth mentioning that the IPv6 FIB output from router PE-3 for the SID fc00:0:205:e00d::/64 displayed in Output 9-80 is applicable for the IP subnet 10.2.130.0/24. The backup path in the output is designated by via ::ffff:0.0.0.0/128 and backup. The output indicates that for router PE-3 to forward traffic to PE-4 or PE-5 in the event of a local access link failure, it must do a lookup in the VRF instance FULL-500-VRF before making a forwarding decision.

Output 9-80 *BGP PIC Edge Multipath IPv6 FIB Detail on PE-3 (IOS XR)*

```
RP/0/RP0/CPU0:PE-3#show cef ipv6 fc00:0:205:e00d::/64 detail

fc00:0:205:e00d::/64, version 439, SRv6 Endpoint uDX4, internal 0x1000001 0x0
  (ptr 0x86fced98) [1], 0x0 (0x0), 0x0 (0x89c251b0)
 Updated Mar 16 08:20:08.050
 Prefix Len 64, traffic index 0, precedence n/a, priority 0
  gateway array (0x87ed8240) reference count 1, flags 0x102010, source rib (7), 0
  backups
              [1 type 3 flags 0x48441 (0x87f814c8) ext 0x0 (0x0)]
  LW-LDI[type=0, refc=0, ptr=0x0, sh-ldi=0x0]
  gateway array update type-time 1 Mar 16 08:20:08.050
 LDI Update time Mar 16 08:20:08.054

 Level 1 - Load distribution: 0
  [0] via ::ffff:10.2.103.1/128, recursive

    via ::ffff:0.0.0.0/128, 0 dependencies, weight 0, class 0, backup [flags 0x100]
     path-idx 0 NHID 0x0 [0x8752a300 0x0]
     next hop VRF - 'FULL-500-VRF', table - 0xe0000004
     next hop ::ffff:0.0.0.0/128

   via ::ffff:10.2.103.1/128, 7 dependencies, recursive [flags 0x6000]
     path-idx 1 NHID 0x0 [0x871c2a88 0x0], Internal 0x89cea0b0
     next hop VRF - 'FULL-500-VRF', table - 0xe0000004
     next hop ::ffff:10.2.103.1/128 via 10.2.103.1/32

   Load distribution: 0 (refcount 1)

   Hash  OK  Interface                 Address
   0     Y   GigabitEthernet0/0/0/3.500 10.2.103.1

RP/0/RP0/CPU0:PE-3#
```

If traffic is forwarded from router PE-3 or PE-4 to the multipath backup router PE-5, it is encapsulated with the SID fc00:0:209:e005::, as shown in Output 9-79. The command **show cef ipv6 fc00:0:209:e005::/64 detail** from router PE-5 in Output 9-81 indicates that this traffic is directly routed out the interface GigabitEthernet0/0/0/3.500. This behavior prevents any packet-looping condition from occurring while BGP is converging after access link failures on both the access links of routers PE-3 and PE-4.

Output 9-81   *BGP PIC Edge Multipath IPv6 FIB Backup on PE-5 (IOS XR)*

```
RP/0/RP0/CPU0:PE-5#show cef ipv6 fc00:0:209:e005::/64 detail

fc00:0:209:e005::/64, version 354, SRv6 Endpoint uDX4, internal 0x1000001 0x0
  (ptr 0x86ebca00) [1], 0x0 (0x0), 0x0 (0x89a58470)
 Updated Mar 18 23:39:57.777
 Prefix Len 64, traffic index 0, precedence n/a, priority 0
  gateway array (0x87d98888) reference count 1, flags 0x102010, source rib (7), 0
  backups
                [1 type 3 flags 0x48441 (0x87e450c8) ext 0x0 (0x0)]
  LW-LDI[type=0, refc=0, ptr=0x0, sh-ldi=0x0]
  gateway array update type-time 1 Mar 18 23:39:57.777
 LDI Update time Mar 18 23:39:57.780

 Level 1 - Load distribution: 0
  [0] via ::ffff:10.3.103.3/128, recursive

  via ::ffff:0.0.0.0/128, 0 dependencies, weight 0, class 0, backup [flags 0x100]
   path-idx 0 NHID 0x0 [0x87410288 0x0]
   next hop VRF - 'FULL-500-VRF', table - 0xe0000003
   next hop ::ffff:0.0.0.0/128


  via ::ffff:10.3.103.3/128, 5 dependencies, recursive, bgp-multipath
  [flags 0x6080]
   path-idx 1 NHID 0x0 [0x8709e440 0x0], Internal 0x89b431a8
    next hop VRF - 'FULL-500-VRF', table - 0xe0000003
    next hop ::ffff:10.3.103.3/128 via 10.3.103.3/32


  Load distribution: 0 (refcount 1)


  Hash  OK  Interface                 Address
   0    Y   GigabitEthernet0/0/0/3.500 10.3.103.3

RP/0/RP0/CPU0:PE-5#
```

By now the reader will have an understanding of BGP PIC Edge operational methods and configurations as applied to both SR-MPLS and SRv6 networks. In the SR-MPLS network we addressed only the BGP PIC Edge unipath option on IOS XR and IOS XE routers. While in the SRv6 network, both BGP PIC Edge unipath and the multipath (with backup) options were discussed.

Summary

This chapter details various high availability and fast convergence mechanisms for segment routing networks. The chapter begins with a focus on Bidirectional Forwarding Detection (BFD) for fast failure detection, including its specialized forms: BFD over Bundle (BoB), also known as micro-BFD, and BFD over Logical Bundle (BLB), both intended for use with Link Aggregation Group (LAG) interfaces.

This chapter also discusses the traditional Loop-Free Alternate (LFA) approach and its limitations. With the introduction of segment routing, an improved method called Topology-Independent Loop-Free Alternate (TI-LFA) was developed to overcome the constraints of classic LFA. This chapter presents configuration and verification commands for several TI-LFA protection schemes, including link, node, and shared risk link group (SRLG) protection.

This chapter also covers microloops. A microloop is a phenomenon that has always existed in IP networks during link up/down events and IGP metric changes, but it was previously obscured by slower interior gateway protocol (IGP) convergence. This chapter describes the SR Microloop Avoidance mechanism, which is a configuration strategy for preventing microloops.

Finally, this chapter covers BGP Prefix Independent Convergence (PIC) as a fast reroute (FRR) mechanism. It focuses on how BGP PIC Core responds to core network incidents and how BGP PIC Edge deals with failures at edge nodes or links. The chapter provides insights into BGP PIC Edge's unipath and multipath setups with backup solutions, complete with the relevant commands for both SR-MPLS and SRv6 transport networks.

References and Additional Reading

BFD Failure Detection Mechanism

- RFC 7810: IS-IS Traffic Engineering (TE) Metric Extensions, https://datatracker.ietf.org/doc/html/rfc7810

- RFC 5880: Bidirectional Forwarding Detection (BFD), https://datatracker.ietf.org/doc/html/rfc5880

- RFC 5882: Generic Application of Bidirectional Forwarding Detection (BFD), https://datatracker.ietf.org/doc/html/rfc5882

- RFC 7130: Bidirectional Forwarding Detection (BFD) on Link Aggregation Group (LAG) Interfaces, https://datatracker.ietf.org/doc/html/rfc7130

Topology-Independent Loop-Free Alternate (TI-LFA)

- RFC 5286: Basic Specification for IP Fast Reroute: Loop-Free Alternates, https://datatracker.ietf.org/doc/rfc5286/

- RFC 7490: Remote Loop-Free Alternate (LFA) Fast Reroute (FRR), https://datatracker.ietf.org/doc/html/rfc7490

- IETF Draft: draft-ietf-rtgwg-segment-routing-ti-lfa-17 Topology Independent Fast Reroute using Segment Routing, https://datatracker.ietf.org/doc/draft-ietf-rtgwg-segment-routing-ti-lfa/17/

Microloop Avoidance

- RFC 8333: Micro-loop Prevention by Introducing a Local Convergence Delay, https://datatracker.ietf.org/doc/html/rfc8333

Chapter 10

Business Opportunities

While the previous chapters provide detailed technical information about segment routing (SR), this chapter explores the business opportunities that emerge from adopting this innovative technology. No company will invest in a technology if its business cannot benefit in some way. This chapter discusses various topics to help build a bridge between engineering, operations, marketing, finance, and product management. It can help stakeholders and leadership identify relevant benefits in their areas, effectively communicate, and justify the investment in a transformation where silos are torn down and barriers are identified and addressed in a timely manner for a successful transition to SR.

Networks and associated IT systems are implemented differently across network service providers and large enterprises, tailored to offer the desired services to internal and external customers. Likewise, network service providers adhere to different standards and frameworks, and each organization's history and decisions influence to what extent standards and frameworks are adopted. We appreciate that organizational structures, processes, terminologies, services, and other aspects vary significantly across network service providers, and this chapter attempts to be descriptive without using any specific standard, framework, or terminology.

Echoing the insights from earlier technical chapters—such as Chapter 2, "What Is Segment Routing over MPLS (SR-MPLS)?" and Chapter 3, "What Is Segment Routing over IPv6 (SRv6)?" —this chapter highlights substantial opportunities and advantages of SRv6 compared to SR-MPLS.

Note Given that not all organizations will prioritize SRv6 transformation work items or perceive the benefits the same way, there is no universal blueprint that fits all possible scenarios. Consequently, the topics in this chapter are presented with different perspectives in mind.

The introduction of SRv6 technology presents a unique opportunity for network service providers. By harnessing its full potential, providers can gain a significant market edge or at least ensure that they remain competitive with their network service offerings over the coming decade. The improved performance, greater scale, network simplification, and new service options associated with SRv6 allow for the convergence of multiple networks into one. This consolidation ideally results in just one network to purchase, build, operate, support, power, cool, and host, thereby leading to substantial reductions in capital expenditures (CapEx) and operational expenditures (OpEx). The benefits extend to potential organizational optimizations, avoided costs for redundancy and scale-related spare capacity in multiple networks, simpler and improved service-level management (SLM), fewer integration points, and the convergence of operation support systems (OSS), business support systems (BSS), and IT systems in general. These factors can multiply the business opportunity related to the introduction of SRv6.

However, the advantages of SRv6 are not limited to consolidation and optimization. You may recall the transition from Asynchronous Transfer Mode (ATM)–based services to IP technology and its profound market impact two to three decades ago. Similarly, SR protocol options enable the transportation of new services over IP. Leased line and optical point-to-point services can now be offered over IP, reducing the need for optical network-based services to be exposed to customers. This shift simplifies the optical network stack, reducing the requirements for its OSS, BSS, and related IT systems to implement, test, support, and maintain. Instead, the IP services stack can incorporate these as additional service flavors, potentially reducing the cost of offering traditional leased line or optical services and enabling providers to offer these services at more competitive prices. Network service providers currently relying on third-party leased line or optical point-to-point services may even consider offering such services themselves, using their SR network. SRv6 allows for simplified chaining of network connectivity services with additional services such as Network Address Translation (NAT), firewalls, deep packet inspection (DPI), intrusion prevention systems (IPSs), and services offered on virtual machines or containers within data centers or clouds, reducing complexity and costs.

Network service providers operating single IP networks and requiring relatively simple IP or VPN connectivity services can also benefit from the introduction of SRv6. Although traditional MPLS VPN transport networks have been around for two decades, the networking industry is less likely to invest in significant developments or address known limitations due to its maturity, and so the transition to SRv6 is the next logical step. With device generations increasingly focusing their feature support around SRv6 and reducing legacy features to remove complexity and costs, it's worth evaluating investment in SRv6 for the coming decade.

The introduction of SRv6 represents a tremendous opportunity for network service providers. Those who thoroughly analyze and leverage its full potential can undergo a true transformation, benefiting their business and customers for years to come. A detailed analysis may even reveal the business benefits associated with SRv6 as justification for an early network lifecycle. The following sections delve into how simplification, convergence, and standardization can lead to new business and enrich existing services.

Technological Opportunities and Benefits

Before we dive into CapEx and OpEx opportunities, this section provides background information on selected opportunities. Some of these opportunities are not directly related to SR as a technology but rather to the fact that a new network may be built, or a new technology may be introduced.

Fewer Protocols

Figure 10-1 shows network technology–specific protocol stacks (though it omits protocols that are in common across all technologies).

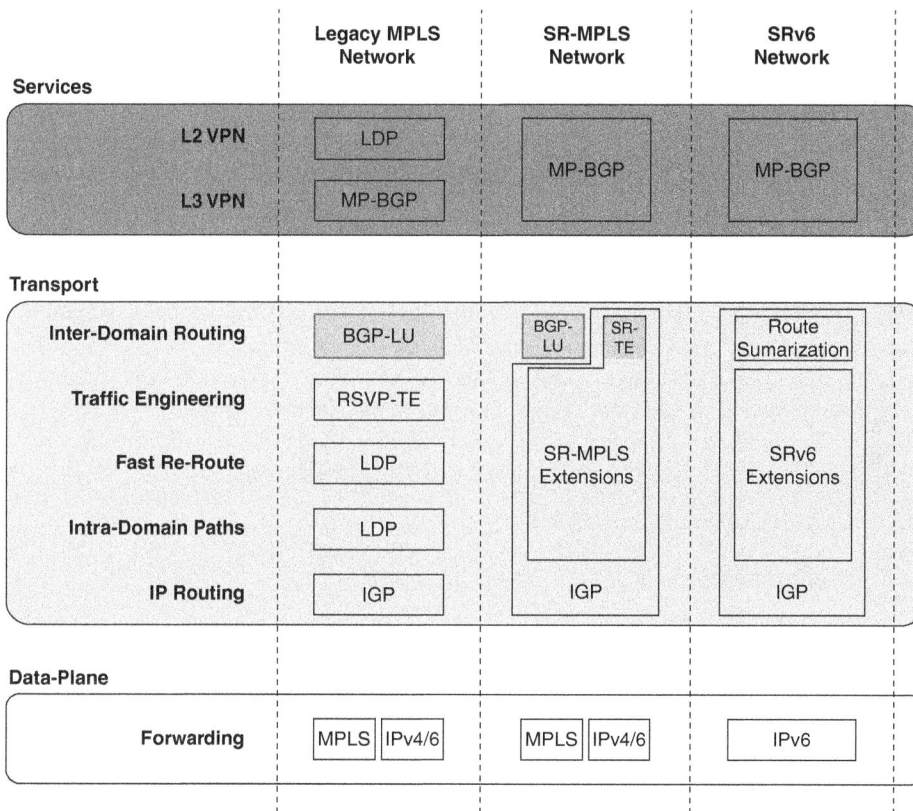

Figure 10-1   *Comparison of MPLS, SR-MPLS, and SRv6 Protocols*

Legacy MPLS networks require around six (6) specific protocols to provide VPN services. Label Distribution Protocol (LDP) is used to exchange labels for endpoints participating in L2VPN services, and Multi-Protocol BGP (MP-BGP) handles the exchange of L3VPN services–related network information. Transport across networks or network domains is facilitated by another BGP flavor, called Border Gateway Protocol Labeled Unicast (BGP-LU). L2VPN and L3VPN services with bandwidth commitments rely on the capabilities of Resource Reservation Protocol Traffic Engineering (RSVP-TE), which reserves bandwidth on all links along a desired traffic path. Interior gateway protocols (IGPs) such as Intermediate System-to-Intermediate System (IS-IS) and Open Shortest Path First (OSPF) are used to exchange topology information within the transport network. While Multiprotocol Label Switching (MPLS) is used to transport VPN traffic, most control protocols leverage pure IP transport.

SR-MPLS–based networks have a smaller protocol stack (4). LDP is not required on the services layer in next-generation networks because MP-BGP (EVPN) can be used to provide L2VPN services. SR-MPLS–specific IGP extensions serve traffic engineering, fast reroute, and intra-domain paths; in legacy MPLS networks, these functions were provided through LDP and RSVP-TE. Optionally, IGP extension can be leveraged for inter-domain routing to replace BGP-LU—for instance, using static or controller-based SR-TE policies.

The protocol stack of SRv6-based networks is significantly simpler, with only three protocols (3) required to provide VPN services. MP-BGP exchanges information related to Layer 2 and Layer 3 VPN services across all participating endpoints. No BGP-LU is required for inter-domain routing. The IPv6 data plane and IPv6 segment routing header (SRH) allow for the interconnection of networks through the use of route summarization and traffic engineering via additional segments in the IPv6 and SRH packet headers. An important operational advantage of deploying SRv6 in a network, as opposed to MPLS, lies in the elimination of label stacks. This move prevents label stack overflows in P nodes and enhances the scalability of PE nodes, thereby mitigating the operational risks involved with scaling up existing network segments and integrating new ones.

Fewer protocols also means the following:

- Less code running

- Fewer configurations to create and change

- Less knowledge required to build and operate a network

- Fewer potential defects and interoperability issues

Therefore, fewer protocols can positively influence network stability, streamline troubleshooting, and lead to shorter mean time to repair (MTTR) when incidents occur.

Network service providers implementing a multi-vendor strategy in their network can benefit from fewer interoperability issues because fewer protocols are required to peer between different vendors. However, SRv6 is early in its lifecycle, and related standards are maturing still. Vendors have made differing levels of progress in implementing SRv6 across platforms and potentially may have interpreted standards slightly differently.

Consequently, network service providers implementing a multi-vendor SRv6 network need to carefully assess the status of the preferred vendors, compare available features, and plan a thorough integration test phase.

More QoS Options

Figure 10-2 presents a comparison of the quality of service (QoS) options available with MPLS and SRv6. Legacy MPLS- and SR-MPLS–based networks are constrained to using the 3 experimental bits in the MPLS label, which offer a total of 8 QoS classes shared by both transport network internal traffic and customer traffic. In contrast, SRv6 QoS relies on the Traffic Class field (8 bit) in the IPv6 header, in which 6 differentiated services bits provide 64 QoS classes for more differentiated and advanced service offerings.

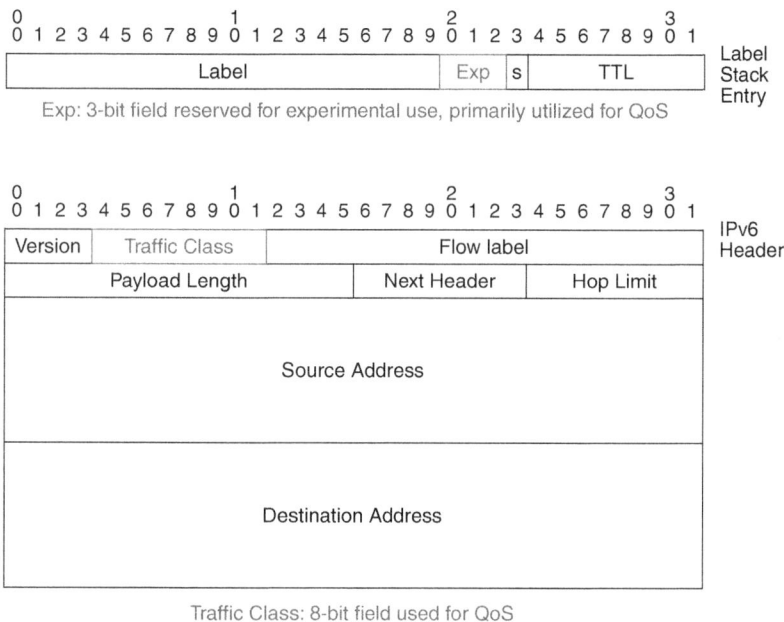

Figure 10-2   *MPLS Label and IPv6 Header*

Network service providers offering transport network services often struggle with aligning their QoS design to what their customers require. QoS classes of customers can overlap with transport network internal traffic classes, which can lead to customer traffic filling up queues that critical internal transport network protocols may rely on, resulting in incidents or outages in a worst-case scenario. This problem is usually avoided by re-marking the ingress traffic and deprioritizing customer traffic transported within VPN services or native IP transport networks, as Figure 10-3 shows. However, the consequence is that customer traffic is no longer handled with the intended priority across the transport network.

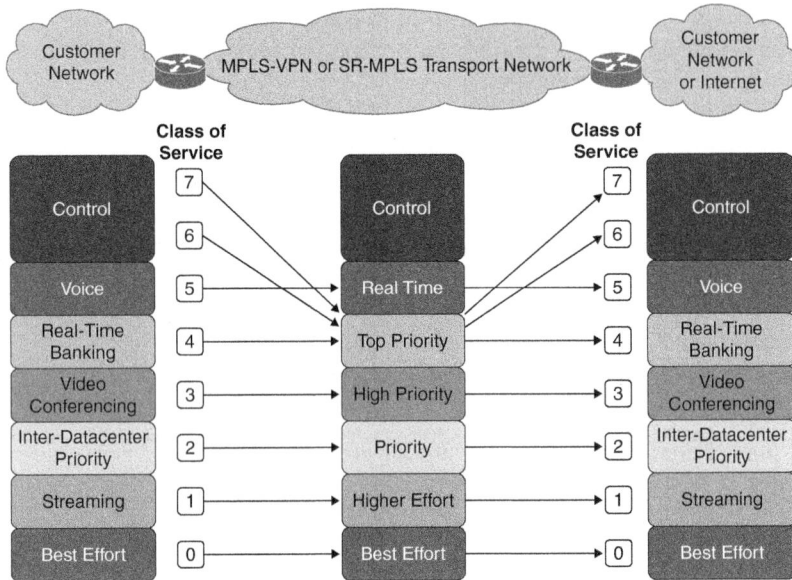

Figure 10-3   *Limited QoS Mapping Options in MPLS based Networks*

With the 64 possible QoS traffic classes allowed in the IPv6 header, SRv6 is able to overcome these challenges faced in MPLS-based networks. Customer traffic can be mapped to separate classes that correspond to the customer's traffic classification while not overlapping with transport network internal classes. Figure 10-4 illustrates one possible example, where the customer QoS classes have slightly less priority than any internal transport network traffic.

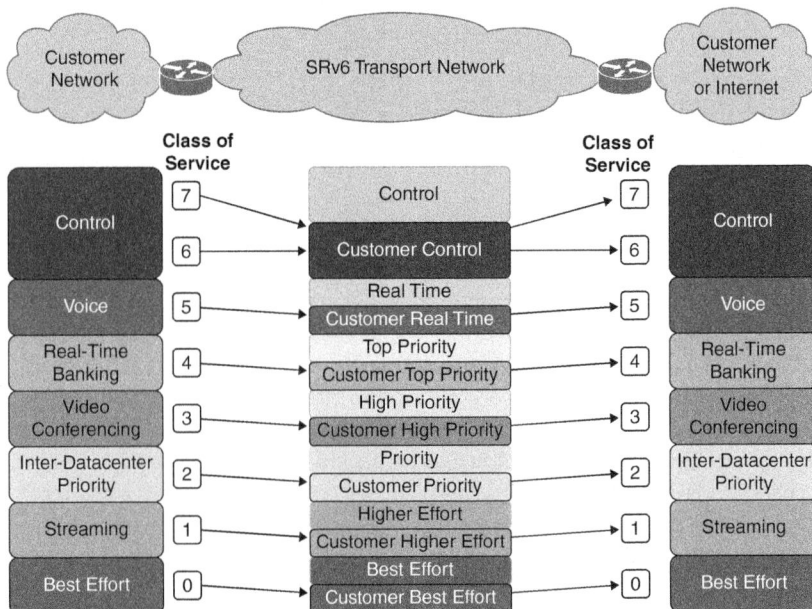

Figure 10-4   *QoS Mapping to Separate Classes in an SRv6 Transport Network*

It would even be possible to offer finer-grained QoS profiles to differentiate low- and high-revenue customers and monetize special QoS requirements. This could provide a competitive advantage for SRv6-based VPN service offerings over those using MPLS-VPN or SR-MPLS transport networks.

SR from the Access Network to the Data Center Network

A user in a customer network that connects to an application in a data center may pass many different network domains, as shown in Figure 10-5.

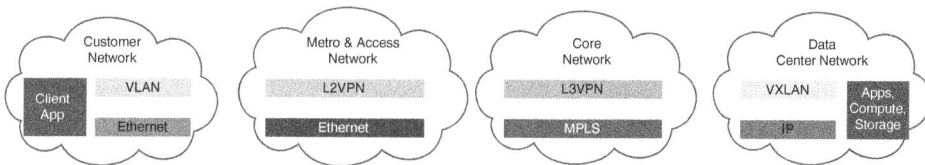

Figure 10-5   *Complex End-to-End Service*

Every domain provides a transport service that needs to be designed, provisioned, operated, and maintained individually. Table 10-1 focuses on the boundary between the core network and the data center network, where hundreds to thousands of connections are common.

Table 10-1   *Handoff Between Transport and Data Center Network Domains*

Network Domain	Customer Network	Metro and Access Transport Network	Core Transport Network	Data Center Network
Traffic separation	VLAN	VPN		VXLAN
QoS	IPv4/IPv6 IP Precedence (IPP) and Differentiated Services Code Point (DSCP) values (64 classes) Ethernet 802.1Q/p class of service (8 classes)	SRv6—IPv6 QoS field (64 classes) SR-MPLS—Label experimental bits (8 classes) Ethernet 802.1Q/p class of service (8 classes)		IPv4/IPv6 IPP and DSCP values (64 classes) Ethernet 802.1Q/p class of service (8 classes)
Traffic engineering	N/A	RSVP-TE or SR-TE		N/A

QoS capabilities can vary from one network domain to another, potentially requiring mappings between the domains along the path from the customer equipment and the services hosted in a data center. Such mappings need to be designed, implemented, tested, and maintained, and they may end up being a compromise with suboptimal mappings.

With SRv6, separate domains can become segments of an end-to-end service. Figure 10-6 shows three different options for how SR could be applied for unification across domains:

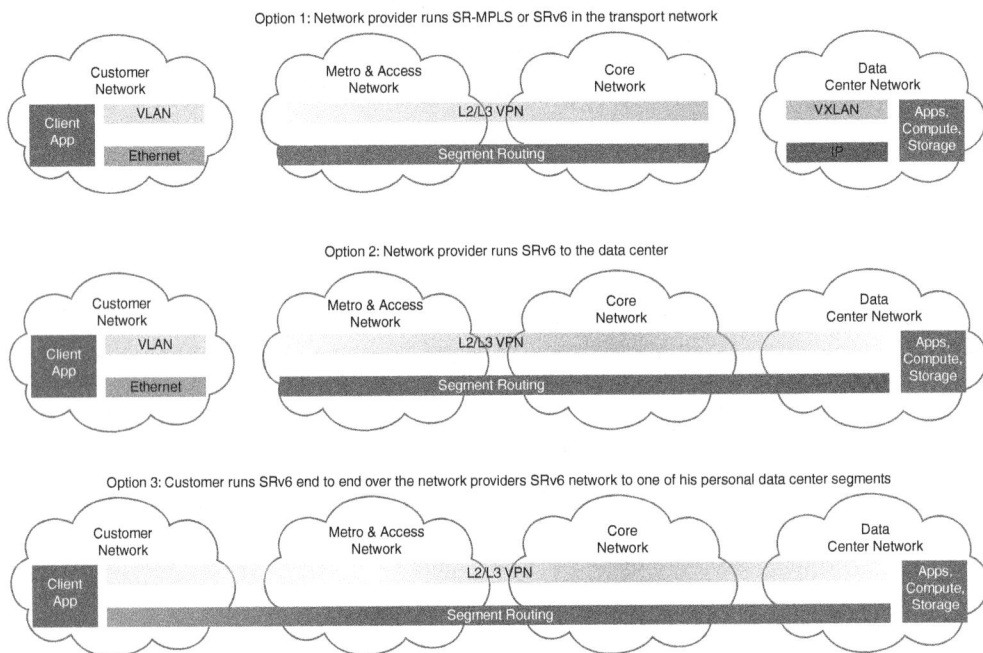

Figure 10-6 *End-to-End Service Options*

- **Option 1: Network service providers run SR-MPLS or SRv6 in the access, metro, and core network domains, simplifying the transport network:** Network and IT designs, configurations, tests, deployments, and management converge into a single domain, making engineering, operations, and support simpler and more cost-effective. Customer sites and data centers remain separate from network technology, IT, and operational perspectives.

- **Option 2: Network providers run SRv6 to the data center:** This option expands SR beyond the transport network to directly connect segments with cloud-native network functions (CNFs), virtual network functions (VNFs), or any applications running in containers or virtual machines (VMs) in the data center. By eliminating the need to map VPNs to Virtual Extensible LAN (VXLAN) at the core/data center boundary, this option simplifies the overall network architecture and minimizes potential points of failure. This direct and dynamic connectivity across transport and data center networks enables a unified team and IT architecture to manage and operate connectivity services end-to-end, enhancing agility and adaptability to changing business requirements. Furthermore, it enhances opportunities for developing and deploying microservices and cloud-native applications that are crucial for customers on their digital transformation journeys. This option works with SRv6 but not with SR-MPLS, as MPLS is typically not used within data centers.

■ **Option 3: Customer runs SRv6 end-to-end over the network provider's SRv6 network to one of their personal data center segments:** SR can be extended to segregate traffic within customer networks. When distinct VPNs represent different organizational segments—such as IT, finance, human resources, and marketing—or different security layers—such as intranet, office network, management network, or manufacturing—there is an opportunity to streamline VPN service configurations. Instead of managing numerous VPN services for each traffic category, network segments can be overlaid on a shared transport service to mirror the organizational structure or adhere to security concepts.

In a provider-managed scenario, where the network service provider takes full responsibility for managing a customer's network, a unified IT architecture can be implemented to control everything from the customer network to the data center network. Different applications, departments, or customers can be segmented, and services can be chained so that selected traffic passes through desired optional services, such as an intrusion prevention system (IPS), firewalls, or network address translation (NAT).

Customers may choose to independently use SRv6 to build VPNs that segregate various traffic categories over an SRv6-based VPN or even a plain IPv6 transport network service. Such a customer-managed scenario can reduce the number of services to procure and is transparent to the customer's transport network service provider. It allows the customer to leverage its IT infrastructure to manage and orchestrate these segments across its sites and data centers. The enhanced independence, increased flexibility, and closer integration of VPNs with clients and data center applications streamline network management and also have the potential to bolster security.

Traffic Engineering and Network Slicing

The flexibility of SR takes traditional traffic engineering a step further. Flexible Algorithm is an enhancement that provides virtual network topologies on a given network. Multiple flexible algorithms (flex algos) can be defined, each considering specific link attributes or metrics. The resulting virtual topologies are also referred to as network slices, and links may be missing or paths may be preferred using different criteria in one network slice than in the others. There is an N:1 mapping of services to flex algos; that is, one or multiple L3VPN or L2VPN services can use the same flex algo. Figure 10-7 provides two examples of how slicing-based network services could benefit customers and perhaps help generate extra revenue as a value-added service option:

■ **Encryption:** Highly confidential traffic of banking customers is transported over a flex algo with a virtual topology consisting of encrypted links only.

■ **Premium redundancy:** Mission-critical traffic from hospitals can fall back to mobile- or satellite-based backup paths, and other traffic cannot, thanks to a flex algo topology that includes mobile- and satellite-based network links.

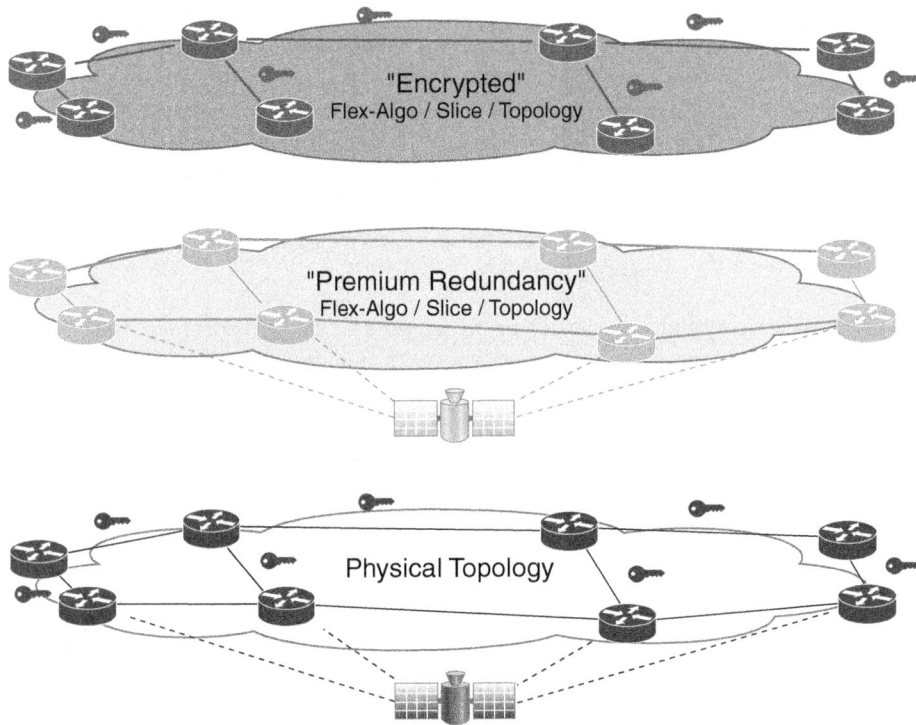

Figure 10-7   *Network Slicing Using a Flex Algo*

Here are some additional examples of where flex algos and traffic engineering may be useful:

- **Minimal latency:** Delay-sensitive applications prefer a path with the lowest possible latency. Standard optical fibers allow light to travel at approximately 200,000 km per second, which means about 1 ms delay every 200 km. One flex algo can use link delay measurements to offer a delay-optimized topology to such applications. Other non-delay-sensitive traffic follows the default flex algo topology, which balances traffic across paths with equal costs to ensure load sharing across links and nodes.

- **Disjoint paths:** A network can be split into two logical networks using two flex algos, which makes it possible to redundantly connect services or customers to both flex algos, which in turn ensures redundant paths over separate physical resources in the network.

- **Distribute load:** A primary path with increased traffic can lead to possible congestion situations that need to be mitigated. SR-TE can be used to mimic an equal-cost path over a longer distance until the primary path is built out.

Technically, network nodes and links can be configured with an affinity—that is, with attributes or capabilities that should be considered or avoided by one or multiple flex algo topology views. Flex algos work in combination with fast convergence features such as TI-LFA to provide failover within the specific topology in less than 50 ms upon link or node failures.

Flex algos can be created, modified, or deleted without impacting any other provisioned flex algos.

Refer to the following sections for more details:

- See the section "IGP Flexible Algorithm (Flex Algo) (RFC 9350)" in Chapter 2, "What Is Segment Routing over MPLS (SR-MPLS)?" for additional details on flex algos.

- See the section "Topology-Independent Loop-Free Alternate (TI-LFA)" in Chapter 9, "High Availability and Fast Convergence," for more information on TI-LFA.

Scale

SR is streamlined and works with minimal protocols, and with SRv6 we have seen a reduction to three protocols (as described earlier, in the section "Fewer Protocols"). Therefore, we would expect SR-MPLS and SRv6 to scale higher than traditional MPLS-VPN networks. Table 10-2 provides a qualitative and hardware-independent view of the improved scale.

Table 10-2   *SR Scalability Considerations*

Network Domain	Legacy MPLS/VPN	SR-MPLS	SRv6
Number of protocols	6	4	3
	(LDP, MP-BGP/ BGP-LU, RSVP-TE, IGP, MPLS, IPv4/6)	(MP-BGP/BGP-LU, IGP with SR-MPLS extensions, MPLS, IPv4/6)	(MP-BGP, IGP with SRv6 extensions, IPv6)
Max nodes per network domain	Thousands	Tens of thousands	Hundreds of thousands, thanks to the IPv6 route summarization in the underlay[1]
Number of IP routes	Today's MPLS-VPN scale	Improved scale compared to legacy MPLS/VPN, thanks to deterministic labels	Factors higher, thanks to IPv6 route summarization[1]
Number of VPN routes	Today's MPLS-VPN scale	Unchanged, no improvement, same scale as legacy MPLS/VPN	Similar scale as legacy MPLS/VPN

Network Domain	Legacy MPLS/VPN	SR-MPLS	SRv6
Traffic engineering tunnel states in network	State per tunnel on each node	0 state on transit nodes Tunnel state in the headend only	0 state on transit nodes Tunnel state in the headend only
Encapsulation overhead per user packet[2]	4 bytes per transport label and 4 bytes for the VPN service label	4 bytes per transport label and 4 bytes for the VPN service label	$0,\ if\ n = 0$ $40,\ if\ 1 \leq n \leq 6$ $40 + 8 + 16 \times \left\lceil \frac{(n-6)}{6} \right\rceil,\ if\ n > 6$ Where n equals the number of segments to pass through

[1] SRv6 allows summarization, as described in the section "Summarization" in Chapter 3.

[2] See Figure 3-47 in Chapter 3 for more details.

The reduction of the protocol stack in SR could potentially reduce device CPU or memory requirements, but these requirements are also network design, hardware, and software implementation dependent, which is why Table 10-2 does not try to provide a qualitative comparison of the required CPU and memory hardware resources.

Routed Optical Networks

Routed optical networks (RONs) converge the IP and the optical transport network to simplify and optimize network engineering and operations. This has become a feasible option only recently, thanks to the scalability of SR and advancements in newer generations of hardware technologies. Cisco includes new optics, private line emulation (PLE), and IT applications that enhance operational efficiency in its comprehensive RON product portfolio. The following sections look at these benefits in detail.

> **Note**   While this section outlines RON business benefits at the network layer, there are undoubtedly more technical facets that optical network specialists could delve into. However, those facets are beyond the scope of this book.

Benefit 1: Simplified Long-Distance Connectivity

New powerful, coherent optics allow high-speed connections up to a range of 80 km to 120 km over dark fiber without any additional amplification, as illustrated in Figure 10-8.

The potential distance is heavily determined by various factors, including the selected hardware versions (ZR or ZR+), their respective transmission power, the sensitivity of the receiver, and the chosen modulation scheme, which dictates the bandwidth that the links provides.

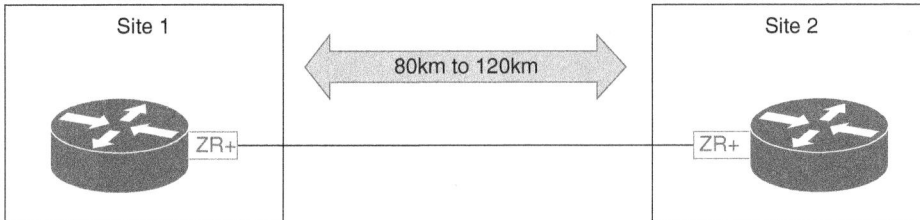

Figure 10-8 *Simplified Long-Distance Connection*

As a result of this simplification, the effort to establish and manage long-distance connections between IP network nodes or data centers becomes similar to the effort required when connecting nodes within a building. The form factor of such optics is the same as for standard optics used in IP networks, which allows similar port densities.

Benefit 2: Easier and Cost-Effective Scaling

Wavelength and modulation are configurable with ZR and ZR+ optics. This allows a simple passive multiplexer to combine the signals of multiple ZR(+) optics onto a single optical fiber, as illustrated in Figure 10-9. An organization can simply buy two ZR(+) optics to add another 400 Gbps connection between two network nodes.

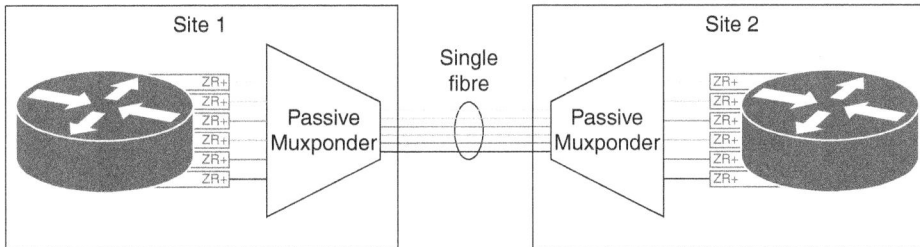

Figure 10-9 *Simplified Long-Distance Connection Scaling*

IP network teams can establish additional links more quickly without involving the optical transport network services. Less equipment involved also means less rack space, less power consumption, less cooling, and fewer potential error sources to consider when troubleshooting issues.

Benefit 3: Simplified Redundancy

Aligning an optical transport network (OTN) and an IP network (IPN) is initially and in the long term a critical area to engineer so that no single point of failure is introduced that could disconnect parts of the network and cause serious outages. Imagine a digger damaging an underground cable in a poorly aligned OTN and IPN redundancy situation, as shown in Figure 10-10. The digger will split the network into two parts, despite the redundant IPN links that should back up one another.

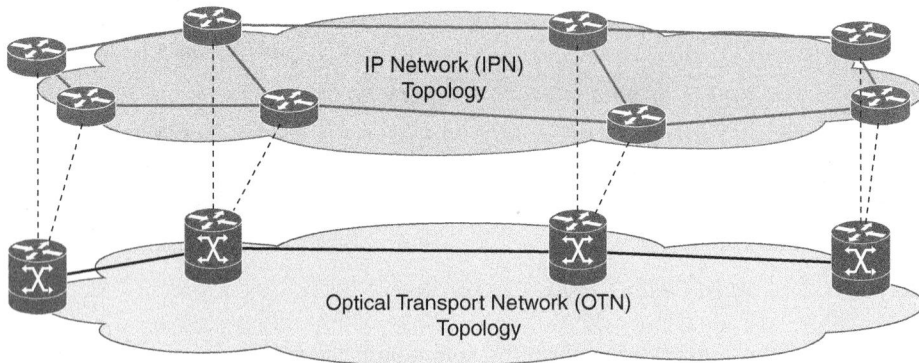

Figure 10-10 *Poor IPN and OTN Redundancy Alignment*

OTN and IPN designers must work together to mitigate the impact of OTN link failures. Figure 10-11 shows an imaginary scenario with perfectly aligned optical and IP networks. In this scenario, a single optical link outage will not cause redundant IPN links to fail.

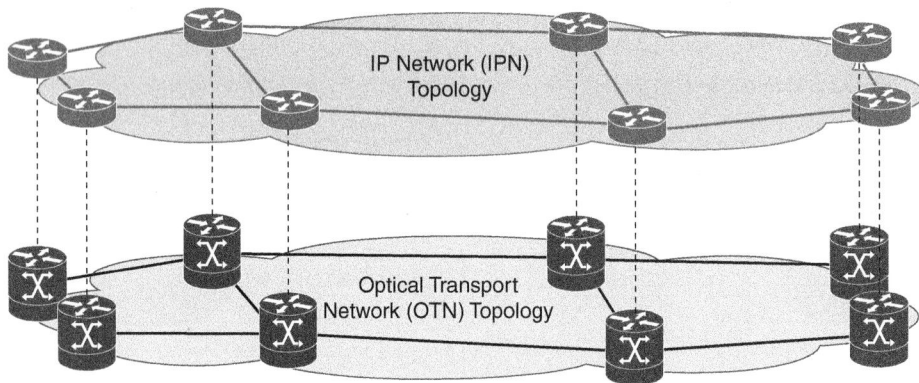

Figure 10-11 *Perfectly Aligned IPN and OTN Redundancy*

It can be challenging for IPN and OTN teams to exchange the latest information about where optical fiber is laid throughout a country wide, city, or even a building to ensure that redundant fiber is thoroughly physically separated. Figure 10-12 shows an example of a RON architecture where redundancy across the IP and optical networks is considered only once during the network build phase. IPN links may use dark fiber, which removes complexity and reduces capital investment and operational costs, as discussed earlier, in the section "Benefit 2: Easier and Cost-Effective Scaling."

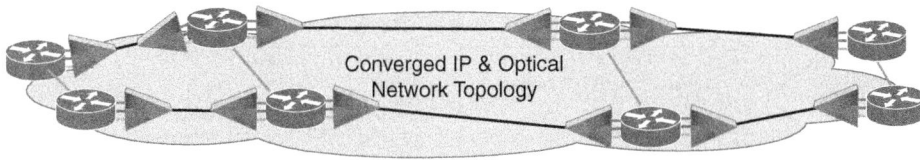

Figure 10-12 *Converged IP and Optical Networks*

With such a design, the OTN and IPN do not react and converge separately when a link failure occurs. A single set of features detect failures and redirect traffic over a redundant path, leading to fewer lines of code running, a lower probability of defects, reduced testing effort, and, importantly, no interference between the two networks during convergence. Network service providers that consider this RON approach for the IP transport network and PLE for the bulk of their optical service offering can reduce the costs in the OTN significantly. While IP networks converge comparably with optical networks—typically within 50 ms—there are higher-bandwidth and special wavelength service offerings that exceed what PLE can provide. However, in general, the optical IT and operational costs would benefit from the reduced number of optical services that need to be planned and managed on a daily basis.

Private Line Emulation

Are you interested in providing optical transport services over your IP network (IPN)? Private line emulation (PLE) enables you to deliver these services without the necessity of procuring, provisioning, managing, and monitoring an optical network. Prior to delving into PLE in more detail, let's look at some simplified diagrams that provide a basic understanding about optical transport network technologies.

Optical networks multiplex different wavelengths over a single fiber, as shown in Figure 10-13. Endpoints are connected through a specific wavelength.

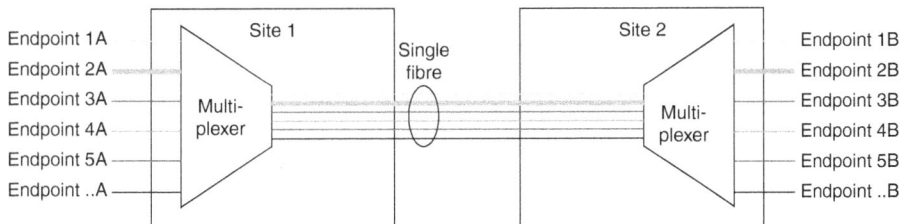

Figure 10-13 *Optical Networks Summary: DWDM*

Reconfigurable optical add/drop multiplexers (ROADMs) enable the addition, termination, and traversal of wavelengths. Figure 10-14 shows how the connection between endpoints 2A and 2B passes through Site 3, while the wavelength for endpoint 4A is dropped and diverted to the locally connected endpoint 4C.

Reconfigurable Optical Add/Drop Multiplexer (ROADM)
→ Add, drop, or pass through wavelengths on a given fibre.

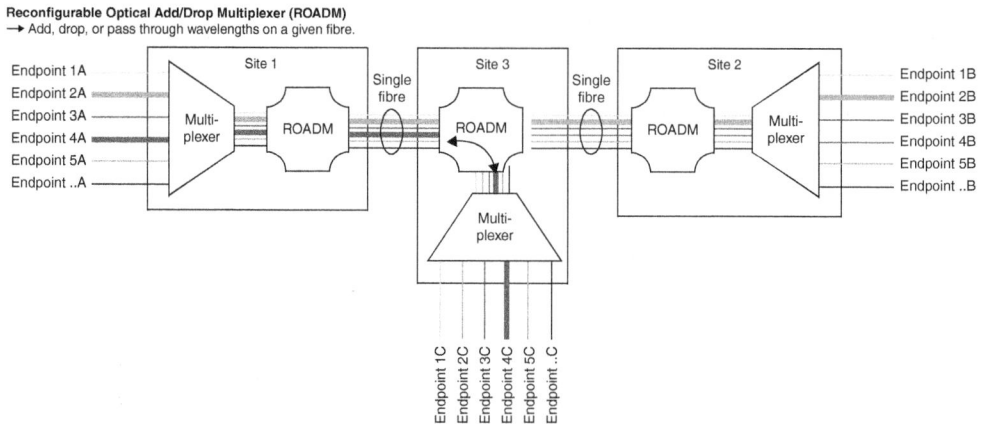

Figure 10-14 *Optical Networks Summary: ROADM*

Optical transport network (OTN) switches provide the ability to switch wavelengths or multiplex multiple optical connections over a given wavelength to increase spectral efficiency by using the latest generation high-capacity wavelengths and electrical multiplexing to fully utilize each wave within a fiber. Figure 10-15 provides an example where the OTN switch in Site 3 maps one wavelength to another to interconnect endpoints 2A and 4B since the same wavelength is not available between Site 1 and Site 3 as well as between Site 3 and Site 2.

Optical Transport Network (OTN)
→ Add, drop, pass through or change wavelengths. Some OTN switches allow multiplexing multiple connections over a given wavelength.

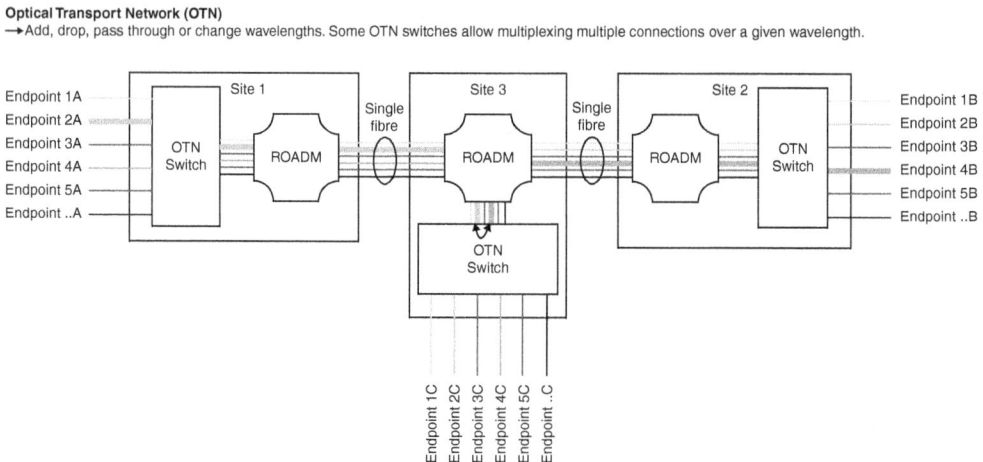

Figure 10-15 *Optical Networks Summary: OTN*

PLE makes it possible to offer leased line and optical wavelength services over an SR-MPLS or SRv6 transport network. Inbound bit streams are packetized, transported over the IP transport network (IPN), and serialized outbound on the remote end—fully bit transparent to both connected customer endpoints. With IP connectivity as the requirement, PLE-based services can be made accessible in remote locations, where optical infrastructure or additional wavelengths are uneconomical or simply not available. PLE could complement and geographically extend an existing OTN service offering to all sites with an IPN footprint while providing potentially substantial savings.

Figure 10-16 shows two options for offering PLE services. PLE CPEs can be deployed to the network edge or the customer premises (endpoints 3B and 5B), as shown for Site 2, or PLE-capable line cards can offer PLE services, as shown at Sites 1 and 3. Situations requiring wavelength swapping, as depicted for the OTN switch in Site 3 in Figure 10-15, are not relevant because the data is transported as packets over the IP network. The required and often less complex IP network stack, along with PLE-capable devices, is more cost-effective than the OTN infrastructure with OTN CPEs, transponders/mux-ponders, and OTN switches. As the number of hops increases end-to-end and more OTN infrastructure can be omitted, the business case for PLE becomes increasingly compelling.

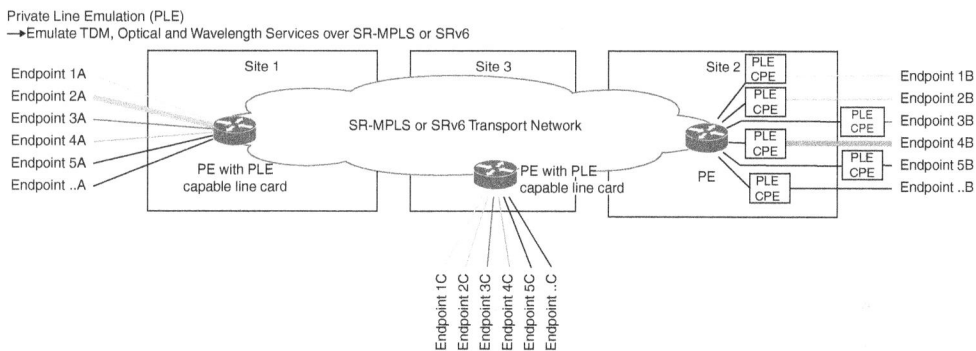

Figure 10-16   *PLE Summary*

Note   Figures 10-13 through 10-16 are simplified examples and optical network products may offer additional variants.

PLE can support a wide variety of networking protocols, such as Ethernet, OTN, Synchronous Optical Network (SONET), Synchronous Digital Hierarchy Network (SDH), and Fibre Channel (FC) services in a storage area network (SAN). At this writing, the following PLE payload types are supported:

- **Ethernet:** 1 Gigabit Ethernet and 10 Gigabit Ethernet
- **OTN:** OTU2 and OTU2e
- **SONET:** OC-48 and OC-192
- **SDH:** STM-16 and STM-64
- **Fibre Channel (FC):** FC1, FC2, FC4, FC8, FC16, and FC32

Similarly to services providing constant bandwidth that require adequate capacity on transport links in OTN, SONET, or SDH network or SANs, PLE service bandwidths need to fit the links that make up the transport network. PLE connections, characterized as elephant flows in the IPN, operate by selecting one of the most optimal paths during connection establishment. All packets associated with a PLE connection strictly adhere to that selected path for the duration of the connection, thereby guaranteeing sequential arrival at the remote end. Bandwidths up to 32 Gbps are reasonable, given 400 Gigabit Ethernet and 800 Gigabit Ethernet links in the transport network, and higher-bandwidths offering are best provided through traditional wavelength OTN services.

Storage networks can benefit from implementing FC over PLE. Figure 10-17 illustrates the process of replacing separate Fibre Channel infrastructure and transport services between data centers.

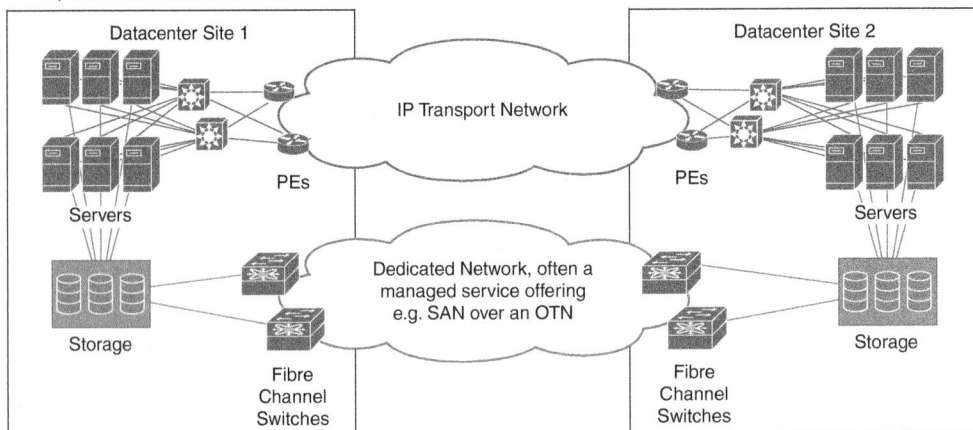

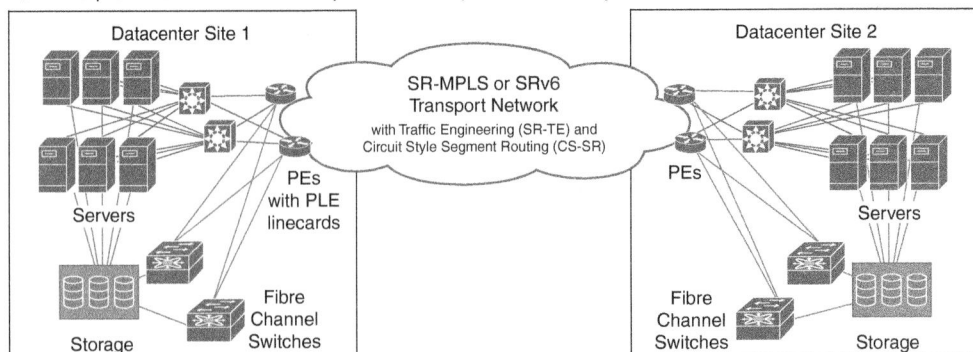

Figure 10-17 *PLE Benefits for Storage Networks*

Companies using SONET or SDH may prefer PLE to interconnect SONET/SDH nodes over retrofitting and migrating those technologies to a new OTN. The following list compares the bit-transparent PLE services with traditional Ethernet pseudowires and L2VPN transport services:

- **Transparency:** Bit-transparent PLE services offer full transparency, whereas L2 protocol transparency is not always provided on Ethernet pseudowires. Packets belonging to the customer may be interpreted by the transport network infrastructure, such as Link Aggregation Control Protocol (LACP), Local Link Discovery Protocol (LLDP), or Cisco Discovery Protocol (CDP).

- **Encryption:** The customer's Media Access Control Security (MACsec) or other L2 encryption works over PLE.

- **MTU:** Ethernet pseudowires need to align to the expected frame MTU, while PLE doesn't know what a frame is, and the customer's MTU is irrelevant for the transport network.

- **Synchronous Ethernet:** Synchronous Ethernet is only possible via PLE.

- **Precision Time Protocol (PTP):** Customers with a mobile network can run PTP and even SyncE over PLE. Class B, Class C, and so on are all possible via PLE.

- **More traffic with PLE:** Ethernet pseudowires only transmit traffic when there are inbound frames, whereas every PLE connection results in constant traffic.

- **Bandwidth options:** Ethernet pseudowires can be configured with Circuit Style Segment Routing (CS-SR) for any bandwidth. PLE options are documented earlier in this section.

Table 10-3 *PLE Complements the IP Transport Service Portfolio*

Service overlay	Private line emulation (PLE)	EVPN-VPWS
	▪ Bit transparent	▪ Ethernet only
	▪ Encrypted payloads	▪ No special hardware required
	▪ Fibre Channel	▪ Supports both connection-oriented and connectionless modes
Underlay transport	Circuit Style Segment Routing (CS-SR)	Segment routing
	▪ Bidirectional path with bandwidth guarantees	▪ Scale and simplicity
	▪ End-to-end path protection and restoration	
	Connection-Oriented	**Connectionless**

In addition to having PLE-capable endpoints, an IP transport network must consider the following points to offer such services:

■ **SR-MPLS or SRv6:** PLE is agnostic to the data plane and can run over SR-MPLS or SRv6.

■ **Capacity:** PLE-related bandwidth guarantees and constant bit rates need to be available in the network. While the percentages depend a lot on the offered services, 20% network capacity for PLE and 80% for traditional IP services is a common assumption to begin with.

■ **Capacity planning:** Every PLE connection results in a constant bit rate in the network. Capacity forecasts are paramount because oversubscription-, failure-, or congestion-related packet drops cause PLE-based connections to drop. There needs to be sufficient capacity to guarantee the bandwidth for all primary and backup paths across the SR-MPLS/SRv6 transport network. Ideally the capacity planning tooling allows for ingesting actual traffic data to ease the simulation of growth or the impact of different scenarios, such as link, node, or building failures.

■ **Segment Routing for Traffic Engineering (SR-TE):** Traffic engineering is used to guarantee bandwidth on the primary and the backup path via a CS-SR policy that is applied by a path computation element (PCE). The PCE can be either a special function of selected Cisco routers in the network or a separate application running in the network management infrastructure.

■ **Highest-priority traffic:** PLE relies on guaranteed bandwidth, where any missing packets or significant jitter will lead to reception errors on the remote end, bringing down a PLE-based connection. Therefore, PLE traffic should be treated with higher priority than voice traffic, as occasional packet loss or increased jitter doesn't typically cause voice calls to drop but rather degrades the voice quality. Only the network vital control traffic should have higher priority than the PLE traffic in the network.

■ **Limited load balancing:** The constant bit rates are packetized and transported in a single, long living flow in each direction between two PLE endpoints. Routers with multiple equal-cost multi-path (ECMP) options to reach a remote PLE endpoint decide on one path when the flow is established, and no further load balancing happens thereafter. Such flows are also widely referred to as elephant flows, and the limited load balancing needs to be considered in the SR-MPLS/SRv6 transport network design and capacity planning.

■ **Overhead:** The PLE encapsulation and packetization add overhead through extra header information of about 10% to a constant bit stream. For example, a 10 Gigabit Ethernet bit-transparent connection would result in an 11 Gbps flow in each direction, which in turn would require a 25 Gigabit Ethernet interface from the PLE-capable CPE toward the core transport network.

■ **Constant bit rate:** Today, there is no idle suppression available for PLE. Such suppression would reduce the transport network utilization when there is no real information transported over a PLE connection.

The benefits of offering PLE services on top of an SR-MPLS or SRv6 transport network can be summarized as follows:

- **Cost savings:** Only a more compact and SR-MPLS/SRv6 transport network–focused OTN needs to be built and operated, provided that with PLE possible bandwidths and associated constraints match the desired service offering. PLE-capable CPEs or line cards are cheaper than transponders and muxponders, reconfigurable optical add/drop multiplexers (ROADMs), or OTN switches.

- **Accessible:** PLE services can be offered in remote locations where the availability of fibers and wavelengths is limited.

- **Easier:** Breakouts to extract one customer from a given wavelength (64 or 96 wavelengths per fiber are common today) to connect their sites or changes in wavelengths on the path within the OTN are not applicable to PLE. Wavelengths are not relevant for the packetized bit stream, and the desired wavelength is a configuration on the customer equipment and the transponder connected to the PLE-capable CPE or line card at the transport network edge.

- **Stable and simple:** The configuration of a potentially necessary underlying compact OTN, with fewer links and wavelengths, can be more static, focusing on providing connectivity to the SR-MPLS/SRv6 transport network rather than on providing connectivity directly to customers.

- **Additional redundancy:** Planning for IPN redundancy and failure scenarios over an OTN requires a comprehensive understanding of the optical network to prevent redundant IP network links from unexpectedly using the same optical network resources. The primary and backup paths within a CS-SR policy should traverse different IPN and OTN links. Current IPNs typically switch over to backup paths in less than 50 ms. In rare double-failure scenarios, where both the primary and backup paths are unavailable, PLE-related CS-SR policies can be configured to dynamically select any remaining path.

- **Pay as you grow:** Instead of using more expensive OTN switches, it is more cost-effective and easier to add PLE endpoints and build out additional IPN core capacity.

You may remember the ATM/SDH/SONET-to-IP transition that occurred about two decades ago. PLE will certainly evolve further and augment or even challenge optical transport networks in the coming years.

Integrated Visibility

Network service monitoring and assurance must evolve to manage the consolidation-related growth in customer numbers, service endpoints, and application diversity and support new features, such as the sophisticated path selection options provided by flex algos. As with basic utilities such as water and electricity, customers expect voice, TV, music streaming, and Internet access to always be available. With steadily decreasing customer tolerance for outages and the growing risk of negative publicity in the news or on social media, it's more critical than ever before to handle incidents with utmost efficiency.

While converging multiple networks into a single network involves a significant investment, customers may not recognize the value because they do not see changes in their
VPN service, which still transports packets from one site to another, and the applications in the data center they use daily. However, the implementation of new technology
can offer a unique opportunity to enhance customer experience to a differentiated level.
With modernized and converged IT systems, customer dashboards can display network
health status, service usage information, potential congestion, and service performance
indicators by using delay, jitter, and drop measurements across the entire network. This
enhanced visibility is no longer a complex or resource-intensive task. The data model
based customer's service intent description can be extended to consistently configure
not just the network but also visibility features, such as customer dashboards and probe
measurements.

While Chapter 8, "Service Assurance," provides an introduction to service assurance
and details on related SR network–level features, the following sections describe several
cornerstones to optimizing the assurance IT stack and enhancing the customer experience
with integrated visibility.

Intent-Driven Configuration of Visibility Features

Any new network should be provisioned via a modern fulfillment solution that processes
intent-based service fulfillment requests, where data models structure and describe the
service intent, and fulfillment systems calculate the necessary configuration changes to
activate the desired service. With this approach, fulfillment engineers and software devel-
opers can concentrate on mapping the data model–based intent to actual configurations,
eliminating the need for writing complex scripts or source code with numerous condi-
tional statements for all possible service modification or removal scenarios. The intent-
and data model–based configuration methodology is widely used to configure transport
network nodes, links, routing protocols, QoS, and other protocols—collectively known
as the *underlay*—and to provision customer services by setting up VPNs, links, QoS,
and routing protocols to connect the customer premises equipment—referred to as the
overlay.

Visibility features should adhere to the same approach, with dashboard updates and
probe configuration changes in response to any service intent changes. Agreed SLAs
could be included in the intent description, directly influencing the analytics and online
dashboards that customers access to visualize their service usage, service quality, and
SLA compliance. While some network service providers prefer to enable visibility by
default, others may only configure it for the underlay and manage additional visibility for
the overlay as an option on the customer service–describing data models. This approach
allows providers to offer enhanced network service experiences as a paid service option.
Network operations teams also have the flexibility to establish this visibility on demand,
such as to monitor potential service impacts during a migration window or to gather
more information regarding a customer complaint.

Cisco's Network Service Orchestrator (NSO) is a prime example of an intent-based
fulfillment system capable of configuring visibility features using an intent- and data
model–based approach.

Intent-/Model-Based Assurance

Traditional assurance systems, where humans write rules to enrich and correlate events, are labor intensive and seldom able to manage all possible fault scenarios and event permutations. Assurance systems can also benefit from a data model–based intent description. Similarly to the fulfillment systems that calculate the required configuration changes, an assurance application can correlate events because it understands the desired service elements and their dependencies. For example, a service intent may include the configuration of service elements such as physical links, logical links, and BGP settings for overlay services. An intent-based assurance system can represent these dependencies in a graphical manner in order to simplify and accelerate the work of network operations teams performing service health checks or troubleshooting the root causes of incidents.

Besides the commonly displayed degraded service status, related events, and probable failure reason that traditional assurance systems would normally display, network operations teams troubleshooting a degraded service also have a view of the service elements that are functioning normally. Figure 10-18 shows the view that a network operations team would have of an L2VPN service at the network edge.

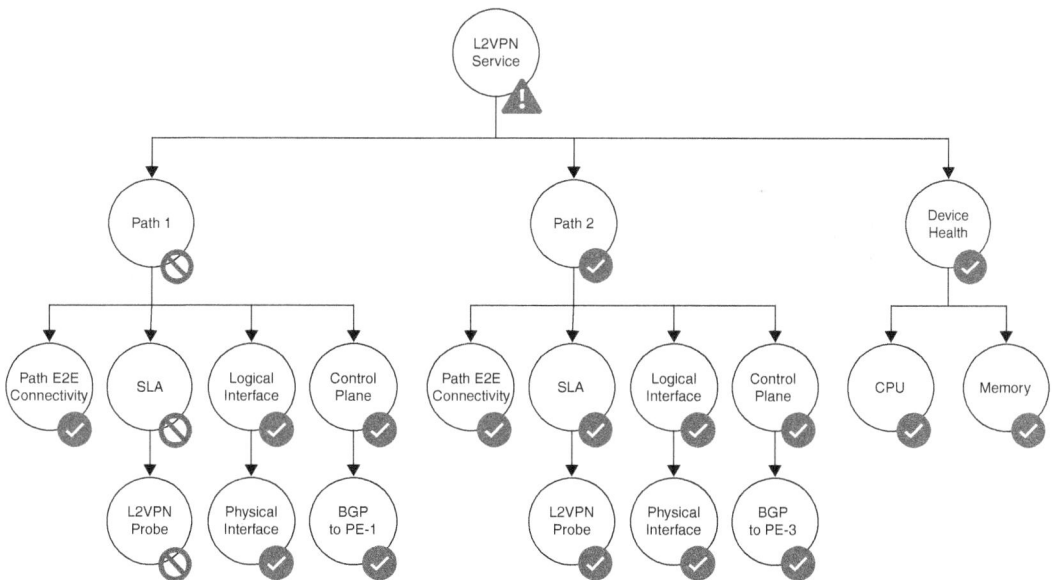

Figure 10-18 *Intent-/Model-Based Assurance*

Instead of just getting an SLA probe threshold breach alert, the network operations team member on duty is immediately provided with more information related to the service, including the following:

- The customer's service is fully operational via path 2.
- There is limited redundancy via the degraded path 1.

- The edge devices are healthy.

- Path 1 is generally okay and provides connectivity, but the quality is degraded.

Traditional, non-data-model and non-intent-aligned assurance systems typically fail to provide such an overview, and valuable time may be lost verifying the status of other non-impacted areas while trying to rapidly resolve an incident.

The IETF has described the intent- and model-based assurance approach in RFC 9417, which discusses service assurance for intent-based networking, and RFC 9418, which refines dependencies, subservices, health levels, and more.

Cisco's Crosswork product family is an excellent example of a modern intent-based and data model–driven assurance solution. It merges multiple applications into a common framework consisting of the Crosswork Network Controller (CNC), which combines both resource and service assurance; the Skylight component, which manages active network service monitoring; and the Network Insights application, which provides an understanding of how other network operators perceive the managed network in the Internet.

High-Precision Probing

Business customers are increasingly demanding bandwidth at low latency with little jitter, and so it is important to consider the measurement and visualization of key performance indicators (KPIs) to verify that associated aggressive service-level agreements (SLA) are met when providing services on an SR network. To use an analogy, we can compare a network with a road transportation system, where the transported IP packets are vehicles using that road system. It wouldn't be possible to view all vehicle traffic congestion if you sampled the traffic situation on highways and the queue lengths in front of traffic lights only a few times a day. Red traffic lights may cause no significant delays during the night, they may cause minimal traffic congestion during the day, and they might lead to gridlock traffic jams during rush hour. A shipping company may prepare all deliveries overnight, with most trucks leaving the warehouses just when the truck's night driving ban ends, at 5 a.m. As a result, the queues by traffic intersections in the neighborhood of the warehouses grow significantly, impacting the travel times of all other vehicles passing the same way. If you sample the road status doing a test drive every 15 minutes, you may not experience the peak traffic and intersection queues during those periods. However, if you were to do a test drive every minute, you would likely see that the road is fully congested with trucks that sit in traffic for a couple of minutes as a result. This is very similar to packets traversing an IP transport network, but in this context, the trucks causing the congestion are called microbursts, and the couple of test drives per hour are multiple probes per second.

Microbursts, which are usually undetected by network operations, can fill up queues, add delay, increase jitter, and cause packet loss in transport networks. Figure 10-19 visualizes the impact that packet loss, delay, and jitter can have on TCP flows. A drop rate of

2% leads to 80% less throughput. A delay of 5 ms or jitter of 1 ms leads to 10% lower throughput.

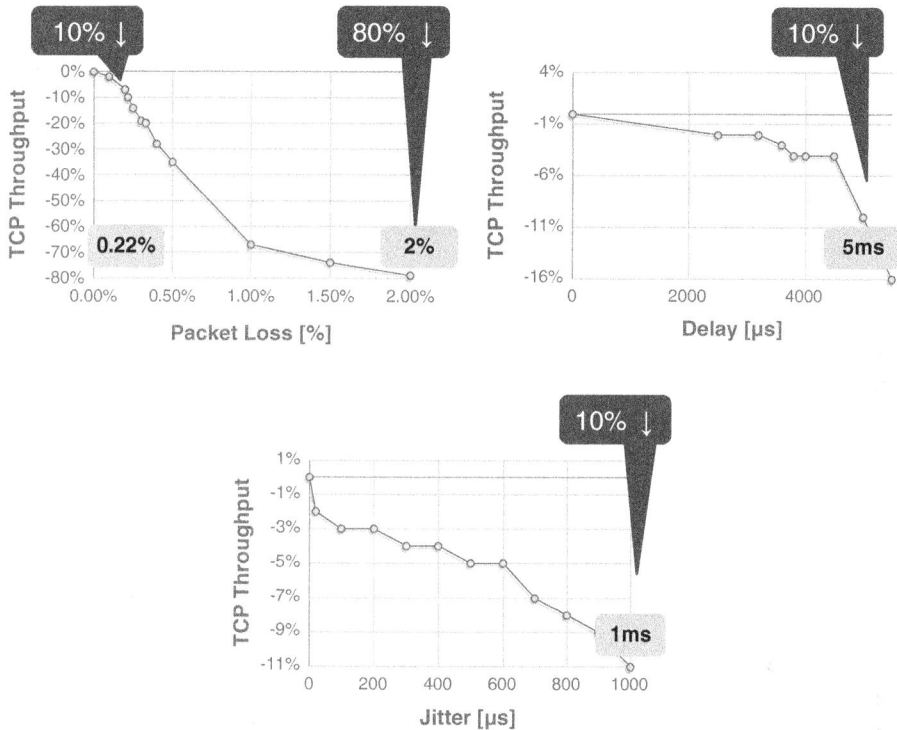

Figure 10-19   *Network Quality/Microburst Impact on TCP Throughput*

A tool to measure anything should be at least 10 times more accurate than the measurements taken to provide results with an appropriate precision and resolution. For example, if you want to measure delays of 0.5 ms, the solution used needs a precision of 50 us or better.

There are some widely used settings that many organizations use to start with, such as measuring standard services with 10 probes per second (that is, every 100 ms) and measuring synchronous or time-sensitive signaling traffic carrying services with 20 probes per second (that is, every 50ms), with microseconds precision. High-precision probing makes it possible to recognize even a few "trucks" queuing up within the IP transport network, as Figure 10-20 illustrates.

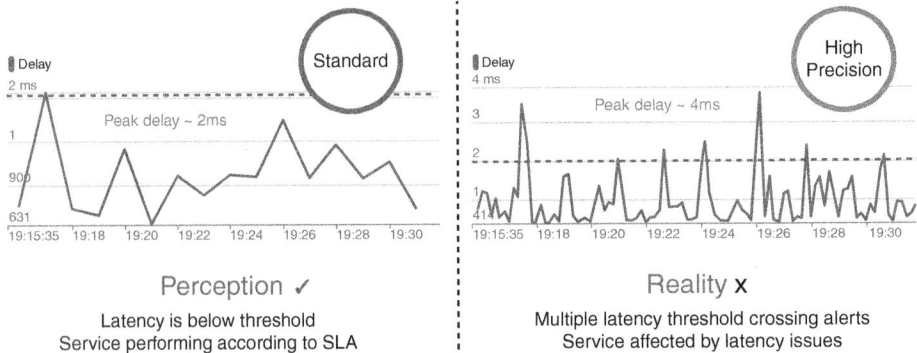

Figure 10-20   *Value of High-Precision Probing*

The higher sampling rate on the right-hand side of the figure uncovers the reality that the maximum wait time in front of the traffic lights is exceeded a couple of times. This kind of precise monitoring becomes significantly more crucial with a converged SR network, where applications that used to have their distinct networks with individual SLAs now coexist and compete for resources within a single shared network.

Note that this issue persists even when there are no packet drops in a network, and all nodes and links have spare capacity. In our analogy, even though no cars or trucks are dropped, wide junctions and multi-lane roads can still become congested, slowing down incoming traffic from other directions for several minutes. Accurate measurements support informed network design and planning decisions, such as prohibiting trucks on certain lanes (or introducing priority queuing), increasing the number of lanes (or adding links), or adjusting traffic light timing (or improving existing queuing configurations). While link bandwidth and device utilization are important, the key planning indicators are understanding how well KPIs, SLAs, and, consequently, customer expectations are met and whether there is a positive or negative trend. Traffic bursts may be systematically overlooked, microbursts may go unnoticed, and a link with a 50% average utilization over 30 seconds may already impact SLAs.

Another advantage of active probing is the ability to verify all possible paths through a network, including paths that might typically be avoided due to being narrow (low-bandwidth network links), passing through slow-speed areas (long delay), subject to tolls (expensive satellite links), or based on gravel (unstable microwave links under certain weather conditions). However, the number of probes can exponentially increase, requiring a well-designed hierarchical probing structure with an assurance application that comprehends the network intent to programmatically combine probe results into an end-to-end view. Network equipment vendors, such as Cisco Systems, have recognized the need for high-precision probing at scale, leading to recent developments in hardware and software that offer probing at an unprecedented scale.

High-precision probing ensures that customer expectations are met over any path and for any QoS class at any given time.

Path Tracing

Navigation applications recommend routes based on various factors such as speed limits and road types. More advanced navigation systems may even consider real-time traffic information, including actual speed, traffic queue times, or traffic jams reported by navigation applications in other vehicles or anonymous geolocation and movement data from mobile phones within the vehicles. Path Tracing (PT) is a new solution that draws parallels to our vehicle navigation analogy. However, instead of measuring actual traffic, PT sends synthetic probes through all possible equal-cost paths between network edges. It then records a time stamp, the egress interface ID, and egress link usage for every hop along the path.

PT focuses on the underlay transport network, and when the PT probes traverse all the equal-cost paths between network edges, as indicated for router PE-1 in Figure 10-21, PT provides well-structured measurement data that is easier to process and predestined to serve the path computation element (PCE) function and assurance systems in SR networks.

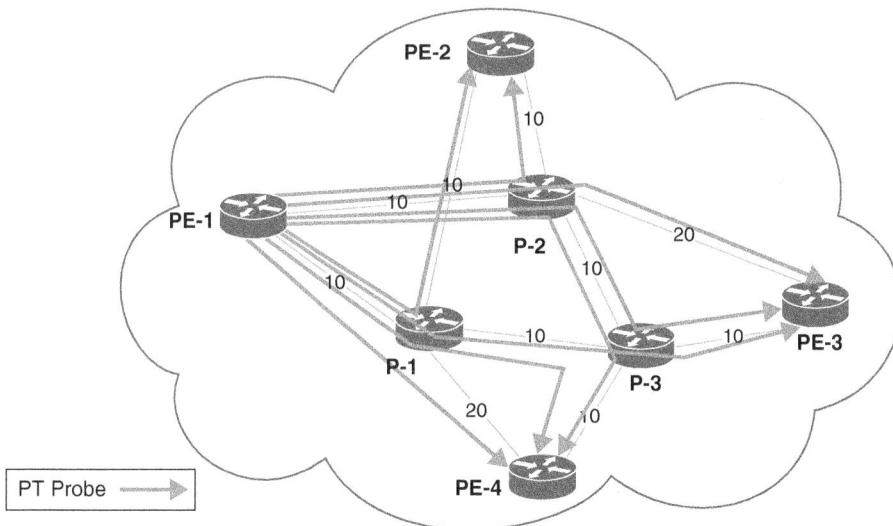

Figure 10-21   *PE-1–Originated PT Probes*

The PT design is very performance oriented. Measurements happen at line rate in hardware, which stamps just 3 bytes per hop in a fixed header section of 40 bytes overall, and only the receiving edge reports all the measurement records added by all hops for the entire path. Other protocols with similar intentions require more bytes per hop. For instance, In Situ Operations, Administration, and Maintenance (IOAM) requires 20 bytes per hop, and Inband Flow Analyzer (IFA) implementations require 32 bytes per hop. In addition, packet header structure and length changes on every hop make a hardware-based recording of the measurements at line rate much harder. The delay measurement precision is configurable and makes it possible to measure delay and jitter in microseconds.

PT telemetry data allows for the extraction of similar information and is likely to augment the operational processes and dashboards discussed in the earlier section "High-Precision Probing" in the future.

PT traffic is forwarded like any other traffic in the network and encounters unexpected and inefficient paths as any traffic when the actual forwarding doesn't match the optimal route determined by the routing protocol. An abrupt loss of path data, which can be caused by packet drops or a metric change that renders the path no longer one of the preferred equal-cost paths, leads to the affected probes capturing the anomalous event. These anomalies are eventually flagged and alerted by an analytics application.

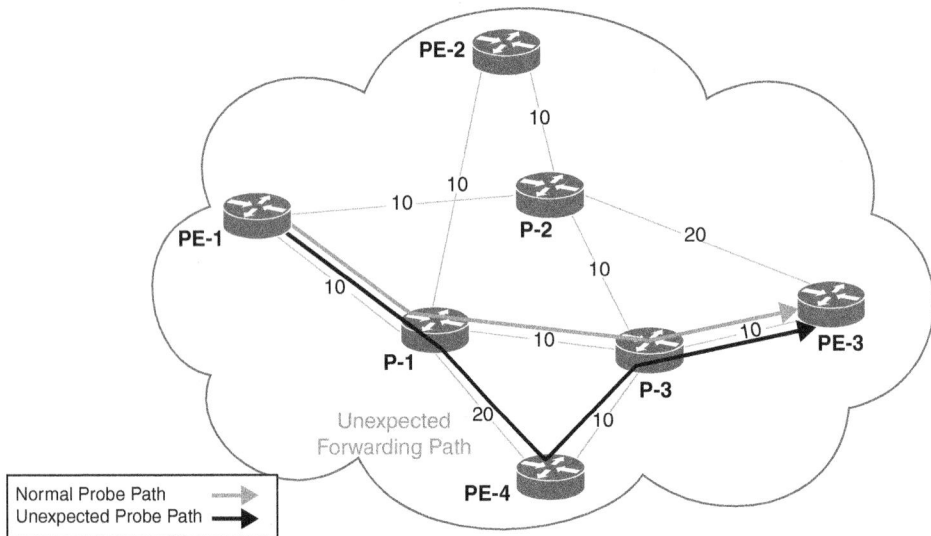

Figure 10-22 *Unexpected Path*

Systematically verifying all possible equal-cost paths between the edges of a transport network may sound like too many probes and a lot of resources being consumed. It is, however, more efficient to systematically probe all possible paths through a network using PT rather than, for example, evaluating actual traffic representing IPFIX records for the following reasons:

■ Sampling actual traffic flows on the different network nodes by using IPFIX requires many flows to be sampled, and it's still not ensured that all possible equal-cost paths are covered.

■ Flow records from different nodes need to be stored and correlated to provide an end-to-end network view, which consumes memory, storage, and CPU power, while flows sampled on one node may not correlate with those sampled on other nodes, and the correlation may fail in many cases. PT displays the information of all nodes in a path in a single record and doesn't require such correlation.

■ To correlate flows across nodes, IPFIX records need to include many parameters, which can lead to a single flow record exceeding 300 bytes. PT requires 100 times less data, at 3 bytes per hop.

PT is defined in IETF drafts for SRv6 and SR-MPLS. It is already widely supported in the industry, and first implementations are available for SRv6. Refer to the section "Path Tracing (PT)" in Chapter 8 for more technical details on PT.

Path tracing is a very resource- and cost-efficient option for monitoring all equal-cost paths through an SR network to detect forwarding inconsistencies, to provide valuable input into network capacity planning, and to enable automation around, for example, traffic engineering.

New Hardware Generation

Implementing any new solution with the latest hardware allows network service providers to take advantage of the newest developments, such as lower power consumption and smaller form factors with similar or higher performance.

The power consumption of a network device is influenced by several factors, one of which is the physical hardware architecture. While fixed-chassis configurations may offer less flexibility, they often provide certain advantages over modular chassis. For example, the absence of hardware modules reduces inter-module communication-related latency and also decreases the number of components, such as microchips, involved in information exchange, thereby reducing the need for buffering. These advantages can lead to more efficient power usage in fixed-chassis configurations.

Figure 10-23 shows two Cisco router models from different hardware generations. The earlier model, the ASR 9901, offers 456 Gbps throughput with a typical power consumption of 850 W, or approximately 186 W per 100 Gbps. In contrast, the newer 8202-32FH-M router, based on Cisco's Silicon One processor family, provides 12.8 Tbps throughput at 575 W, or 4.5 W per 100 Gbps, representing a power reduction of over 97%!

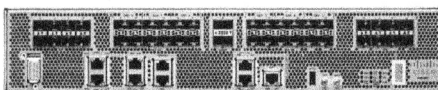

Cisco ASR9901 previous generation router (42 ports)

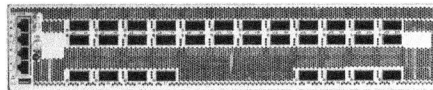

Cisco 8202-32FH-M Silicon One based new generation router (32 ports)

Figure 10-23 *New Hardware Generations*

CapEx Savings

SR-related direct and indirect savings result mainly from new service options and the increased scale of SR together with recent hardware developments. Table 10-4 provides an overview of potential CapEx savings, including the benefits explored earlier in this chapter. Because every network service provider is different, and market prices are constantly changing, the potential savings can vary, which is why Table 10-4 uses only qualitative impact ratings, as follows:

0:          No anticipated saving

$:   Typical saving of up to 10%

$$:   A significant saving of up to 25%

$$$:   Unfair market advantage

- $:   No saving; rather, additional costs are expected

This qualitative impact rating scale allows you to focus your review when comparing an investment in SR with a traditional network upgrade or lifecycle.

Table 10-4   *CapEx: SR Technology-Related Savings Overview*

Savings Category	Short Term	Long Term	Explanation
Less physical space	$$$	$$$	SR technology scale and newer generations of hardware can reduce the required rack space, power, backup power, and cooling capacity to be built by over 90% per 1 Tbps. (See the earlier section "New Hardware Generation" for details.)
Fewer racks			
Less power capacity			
Less backup power capacity			
Less cooling capacity			

Savings Category	Short Term	Long Term	Explanation
Fewer nodes Fewer links	$$	$$	Particularly when the scale of the SR technology and newer generations of hardware enable the convergence of multiple networks into one, fewer network nodes, fewer transport links, and less spare capacity are needed to handle failure and growth scenarios. Consequently, engineering will require fewer labs, fewer tests to be automated, and fewer protocols to be simulated at the targeted performance and scale.
Less spare capacity	$	$	
Lower lab costs	$	$	
Lower IT fulfillment costs	$	$$	
Lower IT assurance costs	$	$$	Requiring only a single fulfillment system for a converged network provides huge savings potential. Furthermore, SRv6 requires fewer protocols to be configured, which simplifies the processes of adding, modifying, and removing network elements and service configurations. The same principle applies to the assurance framework, which benefits from having one network and fewer protocols to monitor.
Lower IT integration costs	$$	$$$	
Lower security costs	$	$	A single network can significantly reduce the IT integration costs because less integration effort is required than is the case across multiple networks. Security monitoring and measures such as firewalls (FWs), intrusion detection systems (IDSs), intrusion prevention systems (IPSs), or thread detection systems can focus on a single converged network. The reduction in the number of protocols slightly decreases the attack surface.
Lower long-distance link costs Lower scaling costs	$$	$$	New optics support longer distances and simplify the process of laying long-distance links. Such optics also allow for the reduction of requirements and costs of an underlying optical network infrastructure, as detailed in the section "Routed Optical Networks," earlier in this chapter.
Lower hardware costs	$	$$	Vendors offer new technologies, often with attractive conditions, in order to drive market adoption, which can provide good short-term savings. Once a technology shift happens in the market, hardware and software supporting the legacy capabilities may become significantly more expensive, further improving the potential long-term savings.

Savings Category	Short Term	Long Term	Explanation
Faster service introduction	$	$$	The reduced number of protocols and the lower complexity cuts the development, testing, and rollout or migration efforts in both the short and long terms. Refer to the section "Fewer Protocols," earlier in this chapter, for an overview.
			Especially when SRv6 service chaining capability is used to configure services from the CPE over the transport network to the data center, it simplifies the combination of traditionally separate domains, such as access, transport, data center, or cloud services. Connectivity from a port on a CPE to a container behind a firewall in the cloud can be one with a common SRv6-based service configuration.
			Refer to the section "SR from the Access Network to the Data Center Network," earlier in this chapter, for further details.
			New SRv6 technology implementation issues and technical knowledge gaps can reduce the short-term savings.
Lower-wavelength and leased line service offering costs	$$	$$	The infrastructure required to offer leased line and optical wavelength services with bandwidths up to 32 Gbps can be optimized by using private line emulation. See the section "Private Line Emulation," earlier in this chapter, for more details.
Lower transit network integration costs	$	0	This saving is only applicable to SRv6. Disjoint SRv6 network nodes can be connected over any IPv6 network, providing additional SRv6 network design options. For instance, an SRv6 network could be built over third-party transit IPv6 network services. The flexibility to use any intermediate IPv6 network can also be advantageous for working out economical migration scenarios, with SRv6 implemented gradually with minimized service impact, step by step, in an existing IPv6 network.
			Refer to the section "Migration Paths from MPLS to SRv6" in Chapter 5, "Migrating to Segment Routing," for a detailed overview of integration and migrations options.
Lower multi-vendor integration costs	- $	$	The reduced number of protocols (see the earlier section "Fewer Protocols") may positively impact multi-vendor integration efforts in the future. However, SRv6 is early in its technology lifecycle, related IETF drafts are still maturing, and vendor-specific implementation status and interpretations need to align, with potential additional short- and mid-term cost implications.

Savings Category	Short Term	Long Term	Explanation
Simplified traffic engineering Economic service options	$	$	SR provides simpler mechanisms to implement traffic engineering. Here are a few examples: ■ Sensitive traffic is forwarded over encrypted links, while other traffic uses alternative higher-bandwidth and lower-cost links. ■ Voice traffic can use third-party network-based backup paths in failure scenarios, and other traffic is dropped. ■ Important business traffic can transfer high-cost satellite backup paths in failure scenarios. Refer to the earlier section "Traffic Engineering and Network Slicing" for details.
Lower development process automation costs Avoided risk	$$	$$$	Multiple networks offering (slightly) different services and teams following specific development and release processes using labs with different topologies and test data are significant cost factors. Having too many different setups may prevent a thorough development process and test automation. The following formula provides a simplified view of this challenge: $n * f * s * l * v$ = Automation Effort, where: n = number of networks f = features in each network s = services in each network l = variations in lab topologies or test data v = involved vendors A single consolidated network and service portfolio with a well-defined lab and testing strategy makes the process and testing automation tangible: $f * s$ = Automation Effort, where: f = features in each network s = services in each network Efforts driving factors may be removed, and a thorough process and test automation can allow any change to flow through the process in hours. Successfully executed automated end-to-end tests provide the highest confidence and reduce the risk associated with software upgrades, feature refinements, and any other change. See Chapter 11, "Organizational Considerations" for more background discussions and details on organizational and process aspects.

OpEx Savings

The composition of hardware, software, and features within any network drive operational and support costs over the entire network lifecycle. Most business cases consider these costs to far exceed the initial network buildout investment. Table 10-5 supports SR network investment discussions from an OpEx perspective. Some savings are already familiar because they are also CapEx relevant and are mentioned in the previous section. The qualitative ratings are the same as described earlier, in the section "Capex Savings," and allow investment comparisons between SR and other options (for example, maintain the status quo or continue with the "normal" network lifecycle, with design, features, and offered services remaining the same).

Table 10-5   *OpEx: SR Technology-Related Savings Overview*

Savings Category	Short Term	Long Term	Explanation
Lower power costs Lower cooling costs Lower CO_2 footprint	$$$	$$$	SR technology scale and newer generations of hardware can reduce the required power and cooling consumption by over 90% per Tbps, as detailed in the earlier section "New Hardware Generation." Hint: Service intent allows for calculating and visualizing the power consumption and CO_2 footprint per VPN service or per network edge, which may be a competitive advantage that attracts customers or improves energy savings in the network design and capacity planning activities.
Faster service restoration	$	$$	The reduced number of protocols and the lower complexity improves the average incident resolution time. New SRv6 technology–related troubles and knowledge ramp-up can impact the short-term savings.
Lower cost per packet/byte	$	$	SR can reduce the user traffic encapsulation overhead, as outlined in the earlier section "Scale," which is particularly relevant for satellite and radio network operators.
Lower wavelength and leased line service offering costs	$$	$$	The infrastructure required to offer leased line and optical wavelength services with bandwidths up to 32 Gbps can be optimized by using private line emulation. See the earlier section "Private Line Emulation" for details.

Savings Category	Short Term	Long Term	Explanation
Simplified traffic engineering	$	$	SR provides simple mechanisms to optimize and maximize network resource utilization. Refer to the earlier section "Traffic Engineering and Network Slicing" for details.
Lower multi-vendor testing costs	$	$	The reduced number of protocols (see the earlier section "Fewer Protocols") may positively impact multi-vendor integration testing efforts, such as when new software is released or new service flavors are introduced.
Lower operation efforts and costs	$$	$$	The deployment of a unified, converged network, made possible by SR technology and advancements in hardware, results in benefits as follows:
Less spare capacity	$$	$$	
Simpler capacity planning	$	$	▪ There is a single network to license and for which to procure support services.
Lower licensing costs	$$	$$	▪ There is less spare capacity for handling failure and growth scenarios to license, operate, and procure support for.
Lower support costs	$$	$$	
Lower lab costs	$	$	▪ Capacity planning efforts are reduced. ▪ There is a smaller IT stack to license and for which to procure support services.
Lower testing costs	$	$	
Lower marketing costs	$	$	▪ There is less lab infrastructure to maintain and license.
Fewer spare parts	$	$	▪ Fewer tests and less test data need to be maintained.

▪ There are fewer simulators and other test equipment to license and for which to procure support services.

▪ There is a single converged network services portfolio to maintain.

▪ Focusing on a converged network service offering reduces marketing efforts.

▪ There is a single network to secure, monitor and assure, inventory, and automate, and fewer spare parts are needed.

Savings Category	Short Term	Long Term	Explanation
Lower labor costs One operations team	0	$$$	The reduced number of protocols and the lower complexity reduces the training requirements and all associated costs.
			In some cases, the SR technology scale and newer generations of hardware can reduce the number of networks, associated processes, and team staffing requirements. The convergence itself and associated discussions can cause additional costs, resulting in minimal short- and mid-term savings.
Lower maintenance costs	$	$	Network slicing may be used to ease network maintenance by resiliently moving traffic over to another slice, freeing up the network nodes that require maintenance and mitigating any potential service impact.
			With only one network, it's easier to justify automation efforts for operational tasks. Software updates and end-to-end service testing can be thoroughly automated, reducing maintenance windows and related efforts and minimizing risk with such activities.

Business Case Guidance

Public studies and reports suggest possible savings, but you may need to know more precisely what type of savings your organization will realize. This section provides a template and guidance for network operators considering investing in SR. To simplify the creation of your business case, all tables are available in a Microsoft Excel file named "Segment-Routing-Business-Case-Template.xlsx", which can be found on the companion website. The Excel file includes sample data. Please update the cells with a yellow background to create your own business case. Refer to the introduction for more information on how to access the companion website.

Table 10-6 provides an overview of today's networks that a converged SR network may replace in the future. Examples of CapEx are a normal annual network refresh (typically 5% to 15% of the installed base), potentially planned extensions of the current network, or like-for-like replacement projects for legacy networks. Examples of OpEx are licenses, support subscriptions, maintenance, operational and support labor costs for network management, testing, and new software release deployments. The rows highlighted in light blue at the bottom represent the sum of CapEx and OpEx, as well as the annual total cost of ownership (TCO). If identifying the network and IT cost figures proves challenging, an annual company report can assist in deriving them. In instances where the annual report does not differentiate between networks and departments, a percentage-based split across the different networks can be useful.

Table 10-6 *Business Case: Current Plan*

Year	Y0	Y1	Y2	Y3	Y4	Y5	Y6	Y7	Y8	Y9	Y10
Network 1 CapEx											
OpEx											
Network 2 CapEx											
OpEx											
Network 3 CapEx											
OpEx											
Network *n* CapEx											
OpEx											
Annual Sum, Current Plan CapEx											
OpEx											
TCO											

Table 10-7 shows a possible plan, where a converged network and IT stack is built in the first two years, Y0 and Y1, and existing network services are migrated in the following years. During the phase-out period, when network services are being migrated to the converged network, the legacy networks should have lower CapEx. This is because maintenance may be deferred, and operational efforts decrease with the reducing number of active services.

Table 10-7 *Business Case: Converged Network Plan*

Year	Y0	Y1	Y2	Y3	Y4	Y5	Y6	Y7	Y8	Y9	Y10
New converged network CapEx											
OpEx											
Network 1 CapEx					Phase out	Out of service					
OpEx											
Network 2 CapEx						Phase out	Out of service				
OpEx											
Network 3 CapEx							Phase out	Out of service			
OpEx											
Network n CapEx								Phase out	Out of service		
OpEx											
Annual Sum, Converged Network CapEx											
OpEx											
TCO											

Costs from similar networks that were built in the past and that are currently operational can serve as initial assumptions for the two "New converged network" lines at the top of Table 10-7. Utilize Table 10-8 and Table 10-9 to offset these known costs with the anticipated benefits and savings. You can begin by filling in the known initial and annual CapEx of similar networks in Table 10-8 and then proceed with considering the expected markup/markdown, while marking those that are not expected to have any effect with either a 0 or N/A (for "not applicable").

Table 10-8   *Business Case: Refining Known CapEx*

From Savings Overview				Expected Costs Markup / Markdown	
0 : No anticipated saving					
$: Typical saving of up to 10%					
$$: A significant saving of up to 25%					
$$$: Unfair market advantage					
Savings Category	**Short Term**	**Long Term**		**Initial CapEx**	**Annual CapEx**
Known initial CapEx and annual CapEx of similar networks					
1 Less physical space	$$$	$$$			
Fewer racks					
Less power capacity					
Less backup power capacity					
Less cooling capacity					
2 Fewer nodes	$$	$$			
Fewer links					
Less spare capacity					
3 Lower long-distance link costs	$$	$$			
Lower scaling costs					
4 Lower hardware costs	$	$$			
5 Faster service introduction	$$	$$			
6 Lower wavelength and leased line service offering costs	$$	$$			
7 Lower transit network integration costs	$	0			
8 Lower multi-vendor integration costs	- $	$			
9 Simplified traffic engineering	$	$			
Economic service options					

From Savings Overview			Expected Costs Markup / Markdown	
0	:	No anticipated saving		
$	:	Typical saving of up to 10%		
$$	:	A significant saving of up to 25%		
$$$	:	Unfair market advantage		

Savings Category	Short Term	Long Term	Initial CapEx	Annual CapEx
10 Lower IT fulfillment costs	$$	$$		
11 Lower IT assurance costs	$$	$$		
12 Lower IT integration costs	$$$	$$$		
13 Lower security costs	$	$		
14 Lower lab costs	$	$		
15 Lower development process automation costs	$$	$$$		
Estimated Converged Network CapEx				

You can continue with the average annual OpEx of similar previous networks and consider the saving factors that apply to the given situation, marking those that are not expected to have any effect with a 0 or N/A.

Table 10-9 *Business Case: Refining Known OpEx*

From Savings Overview			Expected Costs Markup / Markdown	
0	:	No anticipated saving		
$	:	Typical saving of up to 10%		
$$	:	A significant saving of up to 25%		
$$$	:	Unfair market advantage		

Savings Category	Short Term	Long Term	Short Term annual OpEx	Long Term annual OpEx
Known annual OpEx of similar networks				
1 Less power consumption Lower cooling costs Lower CO_2 footprint	$$$	$$$		
2 Faster service restoration	$	$$		
3 Lower cost per packet/byte	$	$		

From Savings Overview			Expected Costs Markup / Markdown	
0 : No anticipated saving				
$: Typical saving of up to 10%				
$$: A significant saving of up to 25%				
$$$: Unfair market advantage				
Savings Category	**Short Term**	**Long Term**	**Short Term annual OpEx**	**Long Term annual OpEx**
4 Lower wavelength and leased line service offering costs	$$	$$		
5 Simplified traffic engineering	$	$		
6 Lower multi-vendor testing costs	$	$		
7 Lower operation efforts and costs	$$	$$		
8 Less spare capacity	$$	$$		
9 Simpler capacity planning	$	$		
10 Lower licensing costs	$$	$$		
11 Lower support costs	$$	$$		
12 Lower lab costs	$	$		
13 Lower testing costs	$	$		
14 Lower marketing costs	$	$		
15 Fewer parts	$	$		
16 Lower labor costs/one operations team	0	$$$		
17 Lower maintenance costs	$	$		
Estimated Converged Network OpEx				

Another OpEx contributor to be considered is a single- or multi-vendor strategy. SR technology is relatively young and early in its lifecycle. Important IETF drafts are maturing, and vendors have progressed their implementations to different degrees. A single-vendor strategy may therefore benefit the business case by avoiding long-term efforts and costs associated with additional vendors. You can extend the CapEx and OpEx tables (Tables 10-8 and 10-9, respectively) with rows representing the following considerations in the event that a multi-vendor strategy is mandatory.

- CapEx
  - Building and testing the network and all services for additional vendors
  - Additional migration scenarios

- Building automation for additional vendors

- IT integration efforts (for example, fulfillment, assurance, inventory) for additional vendors

- **OpEx**

  - Maintaining team knowledge on hardware and software of additional vendors

  - Interoperability issues related troubleshooting

  - Support for additional vendors

  - Monitoring field notices, security alerts, and software updates from multiple vendors

  - Additional hardware and software families to maintain and upgrade

  - Spare parts for additional vendors' hardware

If the evaluation process for building a converged SR network is at a stage where information is not yet available or it is challenging for other reasons, you could consider two alternative options:

- Engage vendors because they are eager to help estimate converged network costs and benefits

- Update the CapEx and OpEx of current networks with the savings indicated in reports, such as the one from ACG Research listed at the end of this chapter.

Now, utilize the result rows from the bottom of Tables 10-8 and 10-9 to populate the two "New Converged Network" lines at the top of Table 10-7.

Next, fill in Table 10-10 to compare the current plan in Table 10-6 with the converged network plan in Table 10-7. This comparison will offer initial insights into the commercial advantages of converging networks.

Table 10-10 *Business Case: Opportunity Analysis*

Year	Y0	Y1	Y2	Y3	Y4	Y5	Y6	Y7	Y8	Y9	Y10
	CapEx										
Current plan											
Converged network plan											
Improvement [%]											
	OpEx										
Current plan											
Converged network plan											
Improvement [%]											

Year	Y0	Y1	Y2	Y3	Y4	Y5	Y6	Y7	Y8	Y9	Y10
	TCO										
Current plan											
Converged network plan											
Improvement [%]											

Figure 10-24 provides an example of a graphical view for a business case. The Microsoft Excel business case template we have provided - a file named "Segment-Routing-Business-Case-Template.xlsx", which can be found on the companion website - also includes Table 10-10 and Figure 10-24.

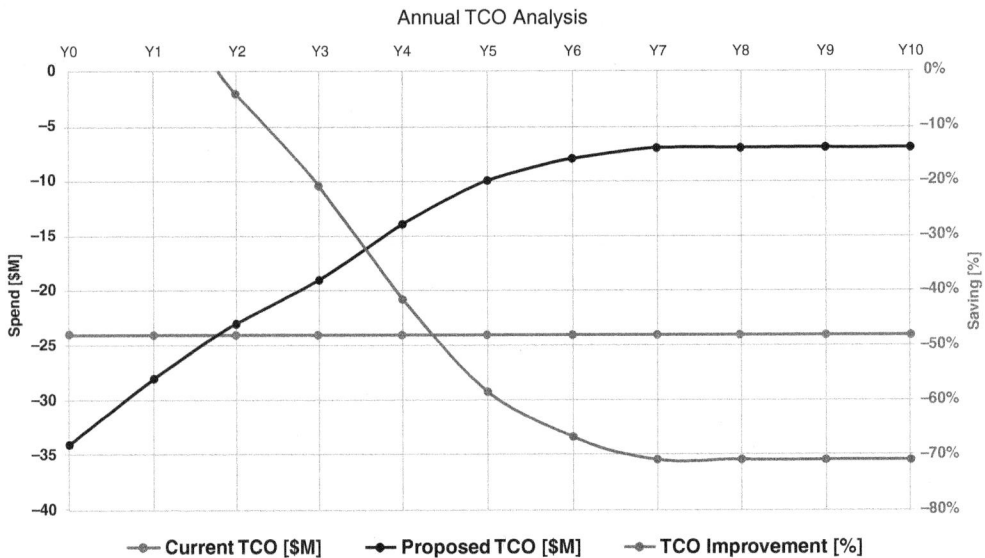

Figure 10-24 *Business Case: Annual TCO Analysis*

Note This graph uses illustrative template data. You can update the Microsoft Excel file to display your own TCO analysis.

CapEx and OpEx typically increase temporarily during the build of the network and the migration phase but are more than offset in subsequent years as the different networks are phased out.

Summary

This chapter describes the general business benefits of segment routing (SR), discusses CapEx and OpEx savings, and provides guidance and a template to help build a business case for investing into new technology and hardware that converge multiple networks into one.

Simplicity prevails. Complexity drives costs. SR allows IP/MPLS and IPv6 networks to be run with reduced complexity and improved scale. SR moves intelligence to the network edges, eliminating resource-consuming signaling protocols and simplifying the transport network by offering unparalleled programmability for IP networks. A converged network, routed optical network (RON), and SR-enabled circuit-style services using private line emulation (PLE) maximize asset utilization, which helps to offer competitive and profitable network services in the market. Table 10-11 summarizes the key aspects of a converged network approach versus maintaining or building separate networks.

Table 10-11   *SR-Enabled Converged Network Summary*

Converged SR Network	Separate Networks
Single solution to buy, operate, support, power, cool, host, and so on	*N* solutions to buy, operate, support, power, cool, host, and so on
Hardware, links, ports, and services that provide direct value to end customers	Hardware, links, and ports that often serve other networks offering links and ports (again) to their customers
One network with spare capacity to cover peak, growth, and failure scenarios	Bandwidth reservations to cover peaks, growth, and failure scenarios in *N* networks
Single SLA for end customer services	Accumulation of SLAs when services span multiple networks
One network that converges on failure	Accumulation of network convergence times for services that span a combination of networks
Single automated framework for provisioning, operation, and monitoring	Multiple separate IT stacks with various levels of automation and integration
Common integration point for higher-level service catalogues and automation workflows	Distinct integrations with the IT stack of each network

Chapter 11, "Organizational Considerations," discusses further factors in areas like strategy, organization, and processes for successful migration to SR. It also augments the thoughts about OpEx presented in this chapter.

References and Additional Reading

More QoS Options

- RFC 3032: MPLS Label Stack Encoding, https://datatracker.ietf.org/doc/html/rfc3032
- RFC 8200: Internet Protocol, Version 6 (IPv6) Specification, https://datatracker.ietf.org/doc/html/rfc8200

Routed Optical Networks

- Cisco Routed Optical Networking Portfolio, https://www.cisco.com/go/ron

Private Line Emulation

- IETF Draft Private Line Emulation over Packet Switched Networks, https://datatracker.ietf.org/doc/html/draft-ietf-pals-ple
- Cisco Routed Optical Networking Solution Guide, Release 2.0, https://www.cisco.com/c/en/us/td/docs/optical/ron/2-0/solution/guide/b-ron-solution-20/m-ple-configuration.html
- Routed Optical Networking [white paper], https://www.cisco.com/c/en/us/products/collateral/routed-optical-networking/routed-optical-networking-wp.html
- IETF Draft: Circuit Style Segment Routing Policies, https://datatracker.ietf.org/doc/html/draft-ietf-spring-cs-sr-policy

Intent-Driven Configuration of Visibility Features

- Cisco Crosswork Network Services Orchestrator, https://www.cisco.com/go/nso

Intent-/Model-Based Assurance

- RFC 9417: Service Assurance for Intent-Based Networking Architecture, https://datatracker.ietf.org/doc/html/rfc9417
- RFC 9418: A YANG Data Model for Service Assurance, https://datatracker.ietf.org/doc/html/rfc9418
- Cisco Crosswork Network Automation, https://www.cisco.com/go/crosswork

Path Tracing

- SRv6 Path Tracing in 90 Seconds, https://www.segment-routing.net/path-tracing

- IETF Draft: Path Tracing in SRv6 Networks, https://datatracker.ietf.org/doc/html/draft-filsfils-ippm-path-tracing

- RFC 9486: IPv6 Options for In Situ Operations, Administration, and Maintenance (IOAM), https://datatracker.ietf.org/doc/html/rfc9486

- RFC 9197: Data Fields for In Situ Operations, Administration, and Maintenance (IOAM), https://datatracker.ietf.org/doc/html/rfc9197#section-4.5

- IETF Draft: Inband Flow Analyzer, https://datatracker.ietf.org/doc/html/draft-kumar-ippm-ifa

- RFC 7011: Specification of the IP Flow Information Export (IPFIX) Protocol for the Exchange of Flow Information, https://datatracker.ietf.org/doc/html/rfc7011

- IETF Draft: Path Tracing in SRv6 Networks, https://datatracker.ietf.org/doc/html/draft-filsfils-spring-path-tracing

- IETF Draft: Path Tracing in SR-MPLS Networks, https://datatracker.ietf.org/doc/html/draft-filsfils-spring-path-tracing-srmpls

New Hardware Generation

- Cisco ASR 9901 Router Data Sheet, https://www.cisco.com/c/en/us/products/collateral/routers/asr-9000-series-aggregation-services-routers/datasheet-c78-740540.html

- Cisco 8000 Series Routers Data Sheet, https://www.cisco.com/c/en/us/products/collateral/routers/8000-series-routers/datasheet-c78-742571.html#Physicalcharacteristics

Business Case Guidance

- ACG Research: TCO Benefits of Converged 5G Ready IP Transport, https://www.acgcc.com/reports/

Organizational Considerations

After reviewing the promising business case for segment routing (SR) in Chapter 10, "Business Opportunities," you are now ready to evaluate how the introduction of SR will affect your organization. The potential impacts can vary greatly, depending on the number of networks converging and migrating to a new SR-based IP transport network, as well as the complexity of traditional non-IP services that may migrate to SR using new capabilities such as private line emulation (PLE). Just as the transition from Time-Division Multiplexing (TDM)–based services to IP/MPLS networks posed challenges in the mid-2000s, SR may impact more than just network engineering or operation teams. Departments that take care of marketing, sales, customer relationship management, and product and service portfolio management, along with any business partners and resellers will need to adapt to varying degrees.

Network service providers adhere to a variety of standards and frameworks, each shaped by an organization's unique history and set of decisions. This chapter serves as a guide, outlining important considerations and potential pitfalls for those leading the transformation to a programmable SR network and offering strategies to circumvent those pitfalls before they hinder progress. Given the considerable diversity in organizational structures, processes, terminologies, services, and other aspects across network service providers, this chapter is descriptive and deliberately avoids adherence to any specific standard, framework, or terminology, allowing for broad applicability and flexibility.

Throughout this book, the term *domain* refers to a segment of a network. This chapter expands on that concept, discussing how forming an SR domain can affect various areas, such as personnel, network infrastructure, IT frameworks, processes, service offerings, and development activities.

Although each network service provider follows its own unique path to SR, this chapter categorizes the various paths into the two scenarios, shown in Figure 11-1, to examine impacts and assist in navigating potential challenges.

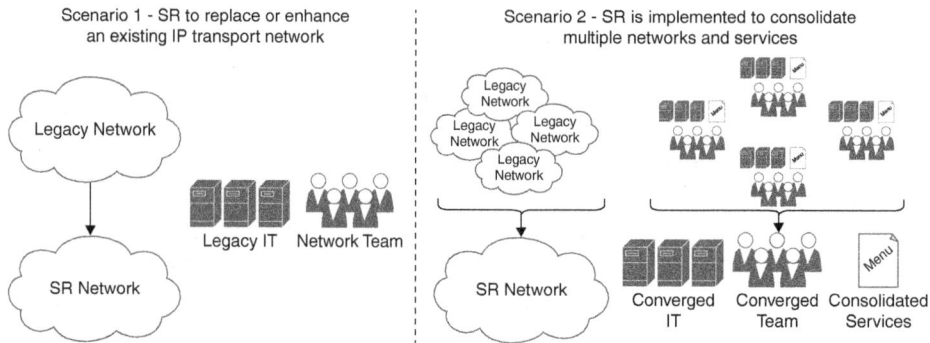

Figure 11-1   *Two Scenarios for Implementing SR*

The following areas are relevant in Scenario 1, where SR is introduced as a new technology to replace or enhance an existing IP transport network:

- **Knowledge:** The network architecture, engineering, and operation teams need to familiarize themselves with the SR technology.

- **Migration strategy:** A review of the current infrastructure for feature support, scalability, and anticipated remaining lifetime supports the choice between migrating to SR-MPLS versus SRv6.

- **IT evolution and gap awareness:** Applications involved in automating network resource and service configurations, along with monitoring and assurance systems, need adjustments to handle SR technology specifics. An assessment can provide an overview on the adaptions required to manage a new SR network. In the absence of viable options, establishing a new SR IT stack could be seen as a strategic move to modernize and phase out legacy systems.

Each of these points is discussed in greater detail later in this chapter.

When implementing SR to merge various networks and services, as in Scenario 2, the impact is potentially even greater. It's not just about combining networks; it's about fusing teams, processes, IT systems, and operational domains into a single entity. Alongside the still-relevant focus areas just listed for the first scenario, the more complex Scenario 2 calls for thoughtful evaluation of several additional considerations.

- **IT evolution and gap awareness (extension):** In Scenario 2, IT systems from various departments need to be consolidated. Separate workflow automation, fulfillment, inventory, IP address management, backup, and other systems must be converged to maximize simplicity, efficiency, and business benefits.

- **Domain definitions:** Consolidating teams and their operational domains demands a strategic approach to guarantee that the newly formed entity overseeing the SR network domain operates efficiently and effectively. This process includes evaluating and, if needed, redefining domains, roles, authorities, and responsibilities, as well as potentially consolidating physical network locations. Thorough preparation paves the way for a smoother transition for all affected teams and domains.

- **Team organization and transformation:** The merging of teams involves not only the blending of different skill sets but also the integration of diverse backgrounds and varying approaches to work, communication, and decision making. It also introduces significant uncertainty, raising questions about team composition. Developing a clear strategy for the team's evolution and maintaining open communication are essential to preserve motivation and ensure continuity throughout the transformation.

- **Existing and new processes:** Reviewing existing processes to pinpoint those affected by the transition to the new SR network domain is crucial for defining the overall transition scope. By simultaneously capturing the efficiency and effectiveness of existing processes, it is possible to identify potential templates for any new processes required in the SR domain.

- **Network services portfolio consolidation:** Merging network service portfolios is pivotal in consolidating multiple networks. Services often vary widely across networks, with some potentially offering numerous manual configuration options. Developing a service model that consolidates all services from the affected legacy networks demands considerable effort and will help determine which variants should be phased out to establish a standardized service definition. Although unlikely, it may be possible for the service modeling process to reveal a comprehensive model that encapsulates all service options from the merging networks. Regardless of the details, harmonizing the service portfolio is essential in order to streamline automation, assurance, testing, migration, and operations of the converged SR network.

- **Development and release methodology:** Individuals forming the new SR domain team will bring a variety of experiences from their previous roles, where they might have used Agile, Waterfall, DevOps, or a blend of these and other methodologies. They are likely comfortable with a variety of practices, artifacts, lab environments, processes, and tools. The integration of network services does more than just merge these different professional experiences; it also consolidates engineering and operational responsibilities, risks, and accountability within a unified domain. To effectively navigate the complexities of the SR domain and ensure both superior quality and efficient operations, a well-defined and robust development and release methodology is crucial.

- **Change management across domains:** When converging organizations, there is a need for a comprehensive change management strategy that addresses all levels of the affected domains in the organization. This strategy should include communication plans to keep all stakeholders informed, a common overall roadmap to align domains, training programs to upskill employees where necessary, and feedback mechanisms to address any concerns and challenges that may arise. Such a central change management strategy is critical to help domains and their employees transition to new ways of working, to foster acceptance of the new organizational structure, and to ensure that the combined entity can achieve its desired synergies and performance objectives.

The subsequent sections of this chapter delve into all these aspects in detail.

Scenario 1: Replacing or Enhancing a Legacy Network with SR

Every journey to SR needs to consider at least the three areas shown in Figure 11-2.

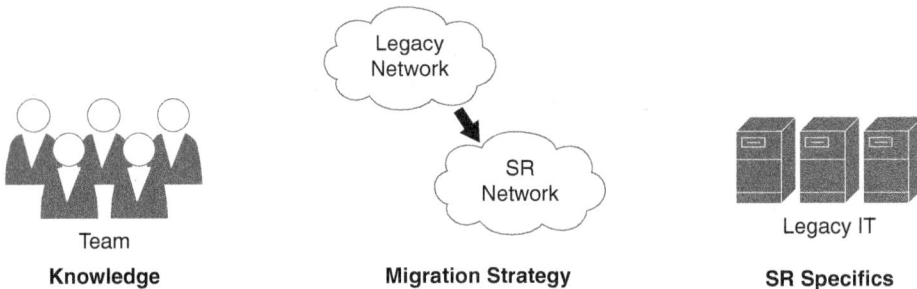

Figure 11-2   *Scenario 1: Replacing or Enhancing a Legacy Network with SR*

The following subsections explore these areas in greater detail and offer ideas to simplify the transition to SR.

Knowledge

What type of SR knowledge is essential for various roles within the organization? Who is tasked with making investment decisions? Who will fill which roles in the upcoming months, and who must possess substantial SR knowledge? This section aims to address these questions by identifying the key actors responsible for introducing SR within a service provider's network and discussing potential sources of knowledge. The actors and the sequence in which they require SR knowledge have been greatly simplified to serve as an introductory guide. To prevent redundancy, Scenario 2, which involves a more comprehensive transition to SR, is visually distinguished in Figure 11-3 by gray highlighting on the Scenario 2–relevant stakeholders and key tasks.

Let's now look at the reasoning for the required knowledge and the type of expertise needed by the actors at each chronological phase:

- **Network architects:** Faced with lifecycle challenges such as software or hardware nearing end-of-life or scaling issues, these professionals are tasked with finding suitable alternatives or successor technologies. They evaluate SR capabilities, identify network elements that lack SR support (such as load balancers and NAT), assess the impact on existing infrastructure, explore new service opportunities or enhancements using SR, and develop strategies for seamless SR migration to maintain service continuity. All these elements are then integrated into a target architecture, which serves as a baseline to evaluate the transition's impact on interfacing networks and existing IT systems.

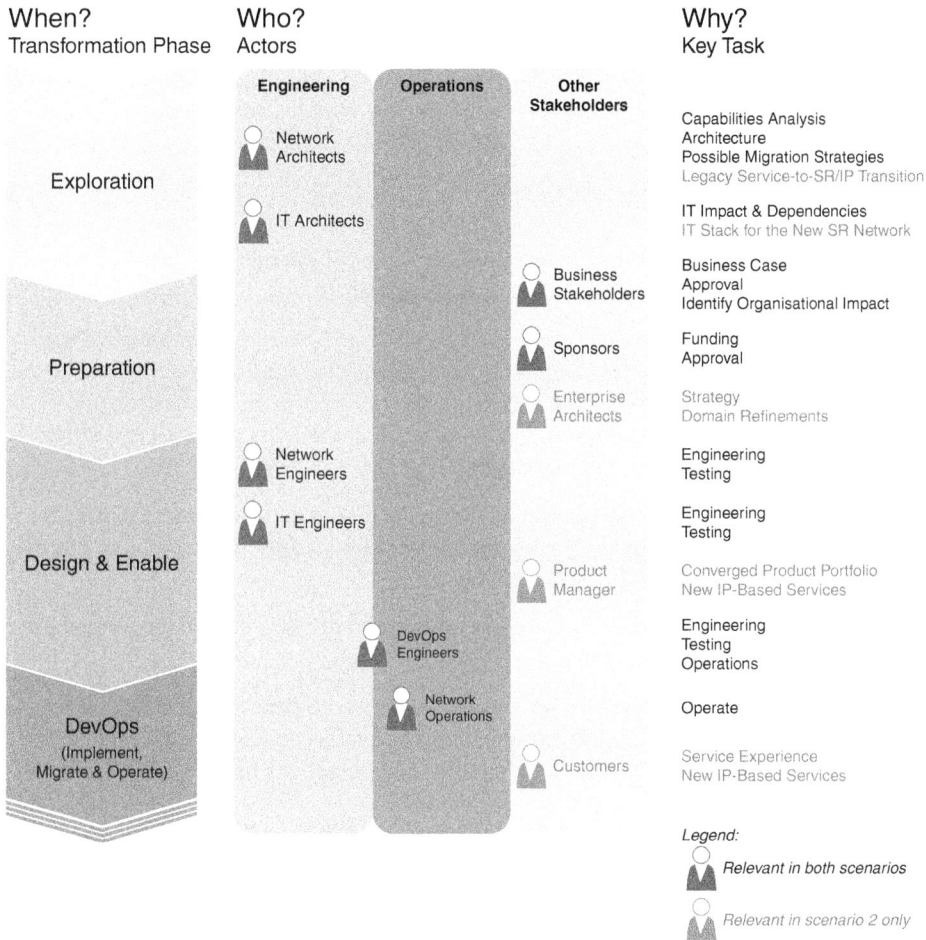

Figure 11-3 *SR Knowledge: Who Needs It, When, and Why*

- **IT architects:** IT specialists are engaged to assess the impact of introducing SR on the overall IT infrastructure. In Scenario 2, these experts must reach consensus on selecting the most suitable IT applications from the existing suite to oversee the new SR network. If current options prove inadequate, the IT architects may need to agree on the implementation of new IT systems, aiming to both modernize the framework and systematically retire outdated platforms.

- **Business stakeholders:** Business stakeholders must, at a high level, assess the various options—along with their benefits and impacts—identified by the architects. Collaboratively, they will craft a business case, refine the preferred solution, and define the commitments required from all affected parties. It is crucial that business stakeholders and architects reach and document consensus on the selected solution before proceeding with the transformation; their documentation serves as a reference point. Concurrently, business stakeholders should consider necessary organizational changes, such as restructuring for efficiency and evaluating the workforce's medium- and long-term prospects. Establishing strategic supplier partnerships to bridge resource and expertise gaps can be important, as it requires additional resources for engineering efforts, and existing personnel need to operate and, potentially, perform reduced maintenance on the current networks until their migration to SR has been completed.

- **Sponsors:** Sponsors need to review, agree, and approve the business case and confirm their buy-in to begin this transformational journey.

- **Enterprise architects:** In Scenario 2, the enterprise architecture team is tasked with outlining the evolution of existing network domains over time, considering the new SR network domain. They should define domain boundaries, authorities, responsibilities, and rules of interaction, using the inputs and thoughts provided in section "Domain Definitions," later in this chapter.

- **Network, IT, and DevOps engineers:** During the design and enablement phase, these engineers receive training to sharpen their skills so they are prepared to effectively contribute to the SR transformation.

- **Product managers:** Product managers collaborate to define a unified, converged network services product portfolio.

- **Network operations:** Following the design phase, rigorous testing, and rollout— adhering to a methodology like the one detailed in the section "Development and Release Methodology," later in this chapter— the operations team members then assume responsibility.

- **Customers:** In Scenario 2, customers may gain access to new SR and IP-based connectivity services that have the potential to enhance their existing infrastructure and perhaps reduce costs related to connectivity services.

Table 11-1 provides a selection of resources for acquiring essential knowledge or obtaining assistance of experts for a successful transition to SR. Keep in mind that implementing an SR network with a single vendor can streamline the learning curve and lessen the impact on actors across all phases, ultimately enhancing both timelines and quality.

Table 11-1   *SR Knowledge Sources*

Actors	Sources	Experienced Assistance
Network architects	This book	Cisco Professional Services
Network engineers	Cisco Live sessions	Cisco Customer Success Services
DevOps engineers	Cisco trainings	
Network operations	Cisco website	
Product managers		

Actors	Sources	Experienced Assistance
IT architects IT engineers	Cisco Automation Developer Days	Cisco Professional Services Cisco Customer Success Services Cisco Training Partners
Business stakeholders Sponsors	Mobile World Congress MPLS World Congress	Cisco Sales and Account Teams Cisco Professional Services
Enterprise architects	tmforum online resources around Open Digital Architecture (ODA), Operational Domain Management (ODM), and OpenAPI	Cisco Professional Services Cisco Customer Success

Migration Strategy

As network service providers enhance their essential knowledge, they must concurrently navigate the complexities of defining their migration strategy. This section explores the decision-making process, addressing considerations such as the potential construction of a new network and deciding between SR-MPLS and SRv6.

Various technical and non-technical factors play roles in determining the optimal migration strategy. Figure 11-4 outlines technical aspects and integrates a few business considerations for evaluating potential paths to SR.

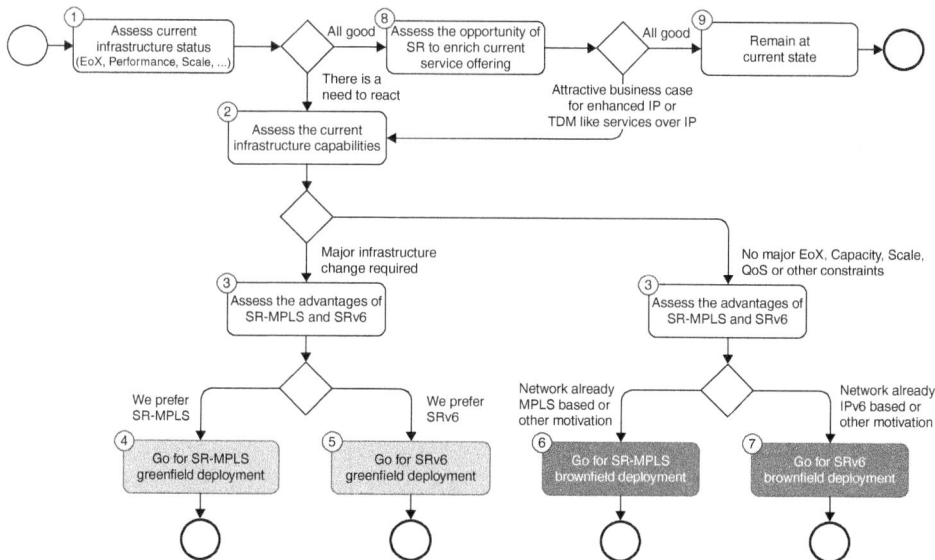

Figure 11-4 *Choosing the Best Migration Strategy*

The following list offers additional explanations, where the list numbers correspond to the numbers in Figure 11-4:

① The need to evaluate a potential network evolution is often driven by factors like hardware or software approaching end-of-life, performance issues, insufficient scalability, quality of service limitations, or general network constraints.

② Once agreement is reached that action is required, a summary of the current infrastructure's shortcomings is drawn up. The section "Migration Paths from MPLS to SRv6" in Chapter 5, "Migrating to Segment Routing," offers technical guidance on deciding whether to upgrade an existing network using a brownfield deployment model or establish a new SR network, following a greenfield deployment model. In some cases, it might be necessary to evaluate both models as the associated financial implications may influence the decision.

③ SR-MPLS and SRv6 offer advantages, such as fewer protocols, enhanced QoS options, wider coverage into the data center and access network areas, advanced traffic engineering, and network slicing opportunities, as well as increased scale. For further details, see the section "SR-MPLS or SRv6" in Chapter 3, "What Is Segment Routing over IPv6 (SRv6)?" and the section "Technological Opportunities and Benefits" in Chapter 10, "Business Opportunities." In a brownfield deployment model, the choice between SR-MPLS and SRv6 may be influenced by the network protocols currently in use and the organization's existing knowledge.

④ The SR-MPLS greenfield migration strategy, which involves the transition of services to a newly built network, is discussed in Chapter 5, in the section "Building a New SR-MPLS Network."

⑤ Similarly, two strategies for migrating services to a newly built SRv6 greenfield network are described in Chapter 5, in the sections "Building a New SRv6 Network Using SRv6 IWG" and "Building a New SRv6 Network Using Inter-AS Option A."

⑥ The section "Enabling SR-MPLS in an Existing Network (Coexistence)" in Chapter 5 describes a SR-MPLS brownfield migration strategy in which SR is introduced into an existing MPLS network.

⑦ Connecting capable PE devices to a new SRv6 core is a possible brownfield migration strategy detailed in Chapter 5, in the section "SRv6 Network Using Dual-Connected PE Devices."

⑧ Even if the existing infrastructure is in good condition, market demands for additional services may exceed the capabilities of that infrastructure. Expanding the existing network services product portfolio to attract more customers or adding value to increase revenue could be a necessary adjustment to maximize the potential of the infrastructure.

⑨ If the existing infrastructure and current service portfolio are both in good shape, then there may be no immediate need for action.

It is quite usual to have several feasible strategies. When this happens, crafting business case variants for the possible migration strategies is a sensible approach to enable stakeholders to reach a consensus on the preferred deployment model and migration strategy.

IT Evolution and Gap Awareness

This section discusses the impacts of introducing SR on the IT stack and how they can differ significantly between the two scenarios. Figure 11-5 shows one of many ways to represent a typical domain architecture for running an IP network. It emphasizes the components that require evaluation in Scenario 1, where SR is used to enhance or replace an existing IP transport network. A description of each component's purpose is provided later in this chapter, in the section "Domain Architecture Blueprint."

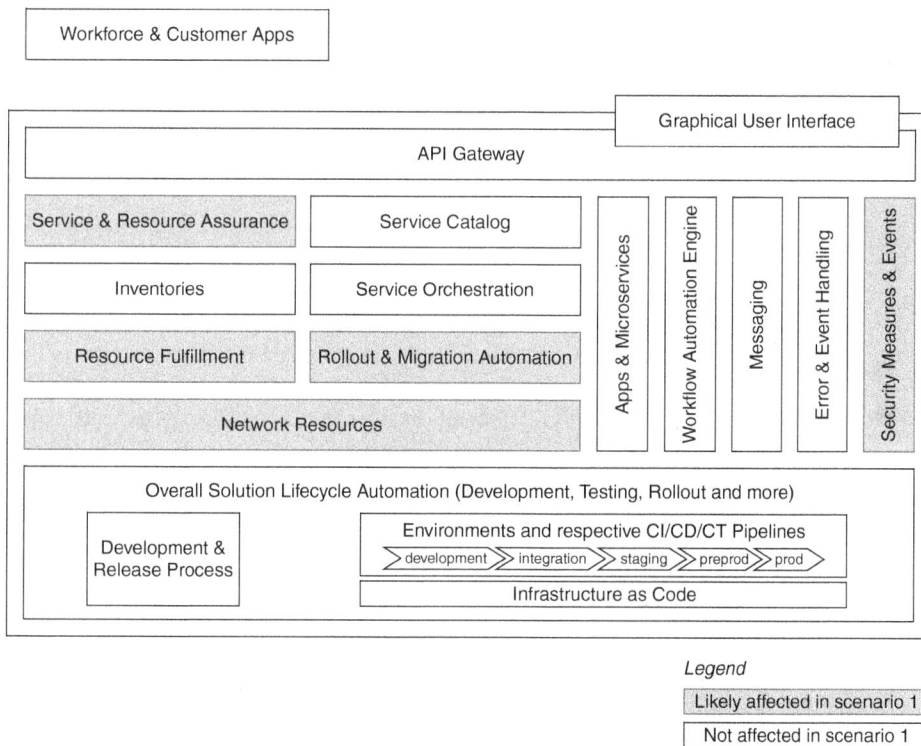

Figure 11-5 *Evaluating SR Readiness in a Typical Domain Architecture*

Table 11-2 summarizes the impacts for Scenario 1 and a variant of Scenario 1, which is anticipated to offer a substantial increase in scale. For Scenario 2, where multiple networks converge and a new SR network domain may be created, the effects are far reaching, and every architecture component should be examined. The table is extensive and does not provide a one-size-fits-all or clear-cut recommendation for all scenarios and network service provider–specific journeys. Nevertheless, some proposals might resonate and be relevant, leading to specific discussions about purpose, investment, and associated business benefits. As a result, additional IT architecture components might be included in the journey toward SR. The order of the rows aligns with Figure 11-5, starting from the top with the impacted components listed first, followed by the remaining components proceeding downward.

Table 11-2   *Impact Evaluation in a Typical Domain Architecture*

Architecture Component	Scenario 1 Enhance or Replace Network...	Scenario 1 ...at Increased Scale	Scenario 2 Converge Networks
Service and resource assurance	Change in protocol stacks and in how SRv6-provisioned services will require correlation rules to be reviewed and modified.	With the expanded scale and density of network services, network operations teams will encounter a surge in events. Therefore, it is important not only to consider SR technology support but to review the scalability and efficiency of the assurance IT application stack. Using the same event correlation and incident management capabilities as in the current network could lead to potential bottlenecks. Modern assurance applications use data models to define relationships between service building blocks, such as physical interfaces, logical interfaces, and routing protocols. This can significantly improve event correlation while reducing associated administrative overhead (for example, overhead related to the creation and maintenance of traditional rules to correlate or enrich events). Furthermore, these data models enable a well-organized visual representation of the status of all building blocks for any given service within a service health dashboard. This provides the on-duty network operator with a clear perspective on which building blocks are functioning correctly and which require attention, thus reducing manual verifications and troubleshooting and ultimately shortening the time required to restore services. It is easier to systematically evaluate the quality of network services and provide each customer with service usage and quality dashboards when integrating the assurance application stack with an intent-based resource fulfillment solution as referred to later in this table. Refer to Chapter 10 for more details.	

Architecture Component	Scenario 1	Scenario 1	Scenario 2
	Enhance or Replace Network...	...at Increased Scale	Converge Networks
Resource fulfillment	The current setup may be sufficient and may only require the addition of SR-specific changes to continue with the network services configurations.	Although manual or script-based network administration can be adapted for SR-based network service configurations and may be sufficient up to a certain point, it is more effective and scalable to employ an intent-based approach, where a well-structured intent description is automatically translated into the minimal configuration changes needed for a desired modification. Besides reducing manual labor and scripting efforts, an intent-based approach also handles a wider range of modification scenarios. Cisco's Network Service Orchestrator (NSO) is a prime example of an intent-based fulfilment system capable of configuring SR using an intent- and data model–based approach.	
Rollout and migration automation	The current setup may be sufficient and may only require the addition of SR-specific changes to continue with the rollout and migration of network resources and services.	With an increase in scale, an investment in automation or upgrade of existing automation may be warranted. This could lead to smoother interactions between the field workforce and automated processes. For instance, a web-based app, accessible on field workers' laptops or mobile devices while on-site, could enable them to initiate or advance a rollout or migration. Automated feedback or alerts on failed process steps could expedite issue identification and resolution, significantly reducing the overall rollout or migration effort and duration. A rollout and migration dashboard could enable planners to organize and monitor high-volume activities.	
Security measures and events	A security evaluation of the SR-MPLS or SRv6 technology is required. In the case of SRv6, for example, source routing is prone to spoofing attacks, and paths might be controllable without proper network precautions. Different SR-MPLS or SRv6 implementations among domains and vendors might introduce further vulnerabilities. These vulnerabilities must be countered with the correct security design, configuration, testing, and continual compliance monitoring.		

Architecture Component	Scenario 1 Enhance or Replace Network...	Scenario 1 ...at Increased Scale	Scenario 2 Converge Networks
Workforce and customer apps	N/A	In light of a substantial change and investment, this may be the ideal time to explore how tailored information and interaction methods could be provided to field workers, network operations staff, and business stakeholders to increase overall productivity. Consideration should also be given to whether customers would notice an enhanced service experience that goes beyond just faster packet delivery from A to B. Offering customers insights into network service utilization, availability, and performance could be a strategy to differentiate offered network services from those of competitors.	
Graphical user interface	N/A	N/A	As networks converge, the process will include the refinement of existing network domains or the establishment of additional domains. The SR domain adopting an API-first approach, coupled with integrating user-friendly GUIs, will streamline the evolution within the domain and improve interactions for customers.
API gateway	N/A	N/A	
Service catalog	N/A	N/A	As different services from various network domains converge, it is essential to assess whether one of their available service catalogs and orchestration would suffice to create a standard for the SR domain in the future.
Service orchestration	N/A	N/A	
Inventories	N/A	N/A	As diverse network domains converge, it is essential to assess whether one of their available inventories could also suffice to create a standard for the SR domain in the future.
Network resources	Network resources forming a new SR network are either enhanced or newly introduced to support SR. Additionally, connecting network resources may need to be upgraded or modified to ensure seamless integration with a new SR network.		

Architecture Component	Scenario 1 Enhance or Replace Network...	Scenario 1 ...at Increased Scale	Scenario 2 Converge Networks
Solution lifecycle automation	N/A	N/A	The merging of networks and services also concentrates the engineering and operations workload, duties, risks, and accountability on fewer teams, possibly down to just one team within an organization. To guarantee superior quality and efficient operation, it is essential to devise a well-thought-out development and release process, along with a suite of highly automated environments for development, integration, and comprehensive stakeholder testing of the overall solution. More guidance is provided in the section "Development and Release Methodology," later in this chapter.
Apps and microservices	N/A	N/A	When setting up a new domain, it can be beneficial to elect a preferred framework for developing applications and microservices, which can facilitate interactions with other domains or provide domain internal functions.
Workflow automation engine	N/A	N/A	It may be advantageous to specify a preferred workflow automation engine for a new SR domain to automate any processes across different IT applications or manual activities that staff seek to "outsource."
Messaging	N/A	N/A	A preferred communication mechanism between domain components can streamline application-to-application communication.
Error and event handling	N/A	N/A	Establishing a common error and event-handling framework can simplify the network and application monitoring.

N/A = Not applicable to the scenario. Existing elements should remain unaffected and continue to be used as is.

Upon thoroughly examining Table 11-2, stakeholders may provide feedback highlighting further considerations and benefits that could enrich the SR business case.

Scenario 2: Consolidating Networks and Services

The complexity of consolidating networks, services, teams, and IT systems is undeniably a recurring theme throughout this book. However, as described in Chapter 10, a successful network service consolidation can be exceptionally rewarding, offering substantial benefits when carried out with precision and foresight. Figure 11-6 provides a simplified illustration of the process where a legacy domain is nominated to become the future SR transport network domain, or a new domain is simply established. The outcome of this journey is the centralization of transport network services. Legacy domains may continue to exist but with more concentrated focus on specific customer services, which may include managing the mobile radio network services, providing data center services, providing residential Internet services, or delivering specific business-to-business services such as managed voice or various software as a service (SaaS) offerings, to name a few.

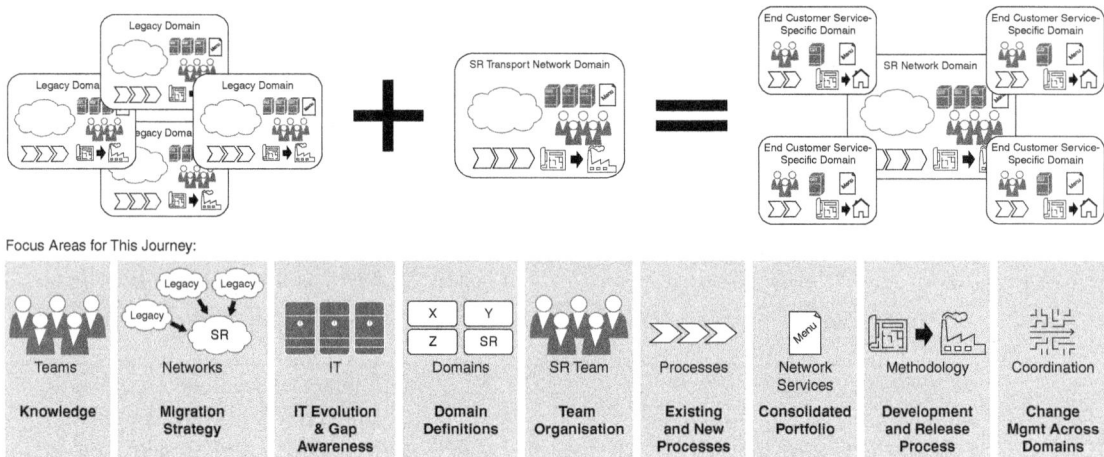

Figure 11-6 *Scenario 2: SR to Converge Networks, Services, and More*

The initial three focus areas—knowledge, network migration strategy, and IT evolution—have already been discussed. The following subsections address the remaining six areas and elaborate on key considerations for transforming to a consolidated SR network.

Domain Definitions

No single IT application stack and team can fully master the expertise required for the development, testing, and management of the multitude of services and platforms within a network services provider organization. Therefore, segmenting an organization into domains is a common approach. These domains usually correspond to services or service families and concentrate specialized knowledge and IT functions that are critical for managing, monitoring, and assuring services and platforms. This focused approach streamlines tool investments to best fit domain-specific requirements, often improving the effectiveness and precision of tools and granting domains a measure of autonomy and independence. Nonetheless, not every IT function warrants a domain-specific design and implementation. Applications that serve general needs, such as DNS, administrative user authentications, source code repositories, or security event analysis, are typically standardized and may be centralized within a shared services domain, as depicted at the bottom of the simplified domain overview in Figure 11-7.

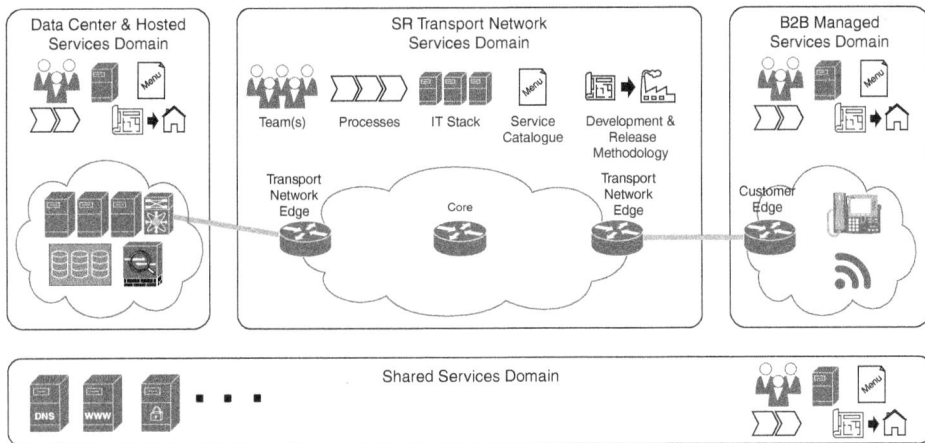

Figure 11-7   *Domains and Their Boundaries Within an Organization*

Figure 11-7 showcases examples of organizational domains, featuring a data center with associated hosted services, an innovative SR transport network service, B2B managed services, and a domain for shared services. The precision with which these domain definitions, objectives, boundaries, roles, and responsibilities are established directly contributes to smoother and more efficient operations within an organization.

When connecting and chaining services across domain boundaries, both shared and conflicting interests can surface at the connections of these domains, as shown in these examples:

- **Shared interests:**
  - **Data integrity and security:** Ensuring data consistency, accuracy, and security across domains is mutually beneficial. Domain architects responsible for data governance collaborate to determine the authoritative source of data. They establish which domains will hold copies and which will query data directly from the data mastering domain. At domain boundaries, as well as within domains, it is optimal to secure data by using authenticated and encrypted connections.
  - **Standardization:** Typically, domains share an interest in the standardization of processes, protocols, and interfaces, allowing for the simplification of both integration and maintenance efforts.

- **Conflicting interests:**

  - **Autonomy:** Individual domains often strive for autonomy, which may lead to conflicts at boundary points such as APIs, edge routers, or interfaces, particularly concerning configuration, monitoring, and lifecycle management. For instance, a domain that consumes an API might favor minimal changes and maximum stability, whereas the domain offering an API may aim to rapidly evolve its services and the APIs through which they are accessed. Disagreements may also arise around the features and configurations of edge routers and interfaces, and there may be reluctance to transfer configuration ownership and monitoring duties to another domain. Establishing a clear API contract to manage expectations on both sides, adopting a balanced and standardized configuration approach, and implementing dual monitoring by both domains during a transition period could be viable solutions to these challenges.

  - **Data authority:** Conflicting claims to ownership of data can lead to tensions between domains, especially when the data in question is mission critical, highly valuable, or sensitive. Establishing a highly reliable messaging framework for data sharing across domains can ease stakeholders to agree on primary data ownership and how other domains are notified of changes.

  - **Prioritization:** Each domain may operate with its own set of priorities, potentially leading to misalignments with the objectives or timelines of other domains. Regular coordination meetings, as described later in this chapter, in the section "Domain Organization and Transformation," are essential for aligning priorities and expeditiously addressing inter-domain dependencies.

  - **Resource allocation:** Competition for limited resources at the domain boundaries can result in conflicts regarding allocation of resources (for example, physical ports, forwarding capacity, memory for features), project timelines, or technology investments. For example, a domain that consumes services may have ambitious plans necessitating capacities and functionalities that exceed what the providing domain currently offers or has in its roadmap. Establishing regular inter-domain discussions, as detailed later in this chapter, in the section "Domain Organization and Transformation," will help to address and preempt these potential points of contention.

Balancing these shared and conflicting interests requires effective communication, collaboration, and governance structures that align the objectives and operations of the various domains for the benefit of the overall organization.

The initial foundational step in defining a domain is the establishment of clear lines of demarcation. The service access point (SAP) definition can be used to describe the interface through which one domain connects to another. A SAP delineates a service offering, such as a 10 Gigabit Ethernet interface, along with a range of available options, such as supported VPN topologies, routing protocols, quality of service (QoS) profiles, and redundancy configurations to meet high availability demands, all underpinned by an associated service-level agreement (SLA). Considering the conflicting interests mentioned earlier, stakeholders within a domain may prefer that a service be configured, monitored, and managed their way or even within their domain. Figure 11-8 presents two distinct approaches to defining SAPs.

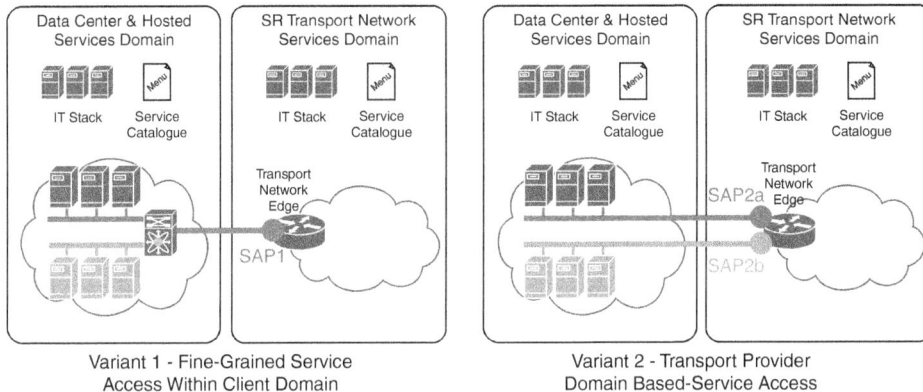

Figure 11-8   *Domain Boundary: Shared and Conflicting Interests*

The first variant allows the Data Center and Hosted Services domain full control over establishing its internal IP connectivity. This autonomy necessitates that the domain possess the necessary expertise to engineer and operate the IP transport network edge together with associated hardware, licenses, and IT infrastructure. In addition, the domain must exchange information to configure the local endpoints in order to success-fully establish connectivity with the SR Transport Network Services domain.

Conversely, the second variant delegates the responsibility for granular connectivity to the SR Transport Network Services domain. This approach requires that the SR Transport Network domain offer user-friendly graphical and API interfaces, enabling the Data Center and Hosted Services domain to manage its connectivity needs effectively. The attractiveness of the SR transformation's business case is enhanced in the second vari-ant, particularly with an increasing number of domains abandoning their individual IP transport edge infrastructure and IT responsibilities in favor of adopting the services offered by the SR Transport Network Services domain. This strategic move concentrates operational processes, know-how, and tools into a single domain, and it also brings net-work service providers closer to embracing the innovative possibilities of SRv6. Detailed insights into these opportunities are provided in Chapter 10, in the section "SR from the Access Network to the Data Center Network," which examines the benefits of extending SR connectivity directly to services and workloads within the data center domain.

Domain Architecture Blueprint

An organization's distinct network and IT configuration are shaped by historical choices between developing systems internally or sourcing them from suppliers. Figure 11-7 illus-trates both domain-specific and shared IT stacks. However, a critical question remains: What constitutes an essential part of each domain and its IT stack? The domain concept allows the introduction of a blueprint for a standardized structure that every domain can embrace, allowing shared foundational products and services to provide domain-specific IT functions. This alignment not only fosters synergies in expertise and reduces licensing costs but streamlines development, maintenance, and operational efforts, among other benefits. The architecture view presented in Figure 11-9 is the culmination of years of experience and numerous customer projects.

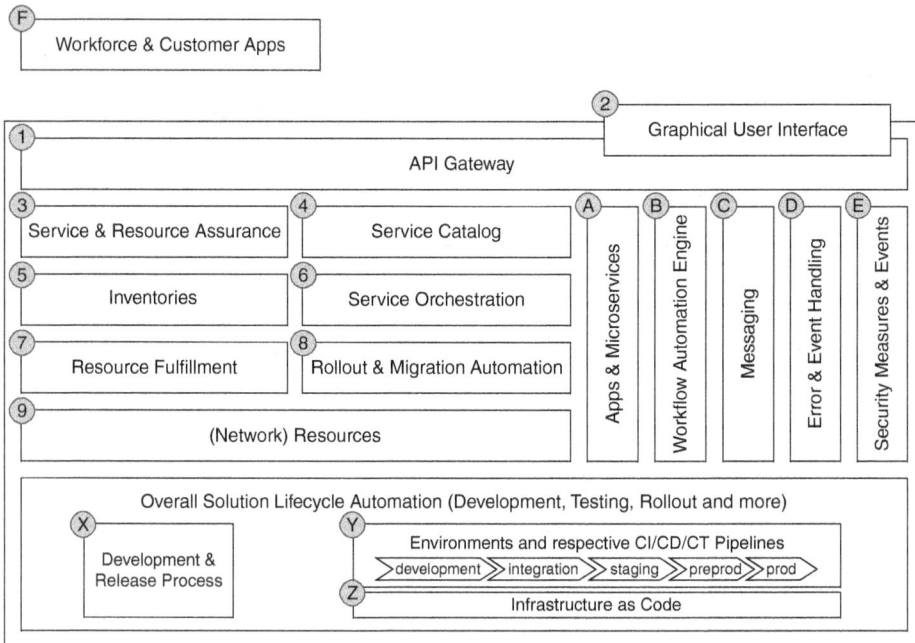

Figure 11-9   *Domain Architecture Blueprint*

The diagram is merely a blueprint, and not every component is required for each domain within an organization. However, this blueprint is invaluable for identifying potential gaps, facilitating careful planning, and setting realistic expectations. Domain architects can use this diagram as a template, adding existing components and applications to visually represent the current state, as shown in the example in Figure 11-10. Blank areas indicate components that are currently unavailable or areas identified as weak spots; these areas can be assessed to determine the necessity of action and to set appropriate priorities and implementation timelines. Some components may be implemented by taking advantage of the multi-tenant capabilities of applications offered as a shared service by other domains. For further guidance on assessing whether a component should be built internally within the domain or if it is more beneficial to acquire the desired functionality by leveraging a shared service from another domain, see the section "Domain Responsibilities and Their Architectural Implications," later in this chapter.

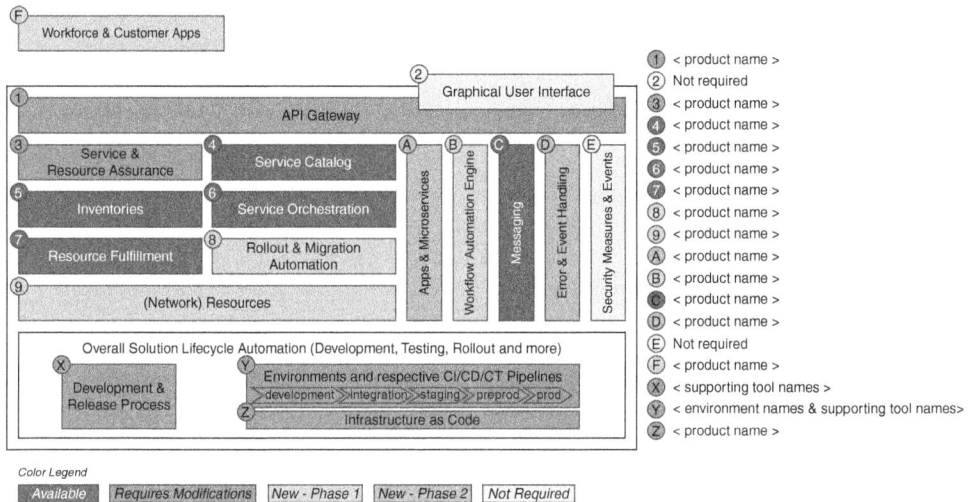

Figure 11-10 *Domain Architecture Example*

Now that the purpose of the architecture blueprint has been discussed, the following subsections examine the components of this blueprint in greater detail. The following overview corresponds to the alphanumeric labels shown in Figures 11-9 and 11-10.

Tip Business stakeholders can inherit and expand the following list to quantify the estimated benefits, introducing or enhancing an existing component together with potential CapEx and OpEx investments. These insights can subsequently be integrated into the overall business case, as detailed in Chapter 10.

① API Gateway and ② Graphical User Interface

The domain blueprint outlines the graphical and API interfaces at the top, marking them as essential entry points for other domains or customers to manage the services they use, whether initiating, modifying, canceling, or monitoring the services' status, utilization, and performance. Direct interactions with domain internal components can negatively affect the domain's ability to perform maintenance, implement evolutionary changes, or manage component lifecycles. Such direct interactions create external dependencies that require careful coordination and can potentially cause delays when planning changes. By channeling access through the domain's API gateway or graphical interface, domains can return alerts when performing maintenance work or, where possible, mask API changes from other domains that have not yet transitioned to the updated API versions of revised components.

A central entry point, such as an API gateway, serves not only as an entrance point but also as a critical security boundary for a domain. It ensures that inbound API calls are authenticated before being routed to internal components, which may be particularly beneficial when accessing component APIs with less stringent security standards. This gateway can offer throttling to safeguard domain components from overload, perform slight data transformations to accommodate API changes, manage load balancing to augment capacity, and support logging and security analysis, underlining the multifaceted value that API gateways provide.

Moreover, it can sometimes be advantageous for outbound API requests to pass through a domain's API gateway as well. This approach enables a domain to present a unified front to other domains by emanating from a single source. In addition, it allows for adaptation to different data naming conventions or swift API modifications of external domains, facilitating smoother cross-domain interactions and integrations. Figure 11-11 illustrates three different scenarios in which a component from one domain communicates with a component in another domain.

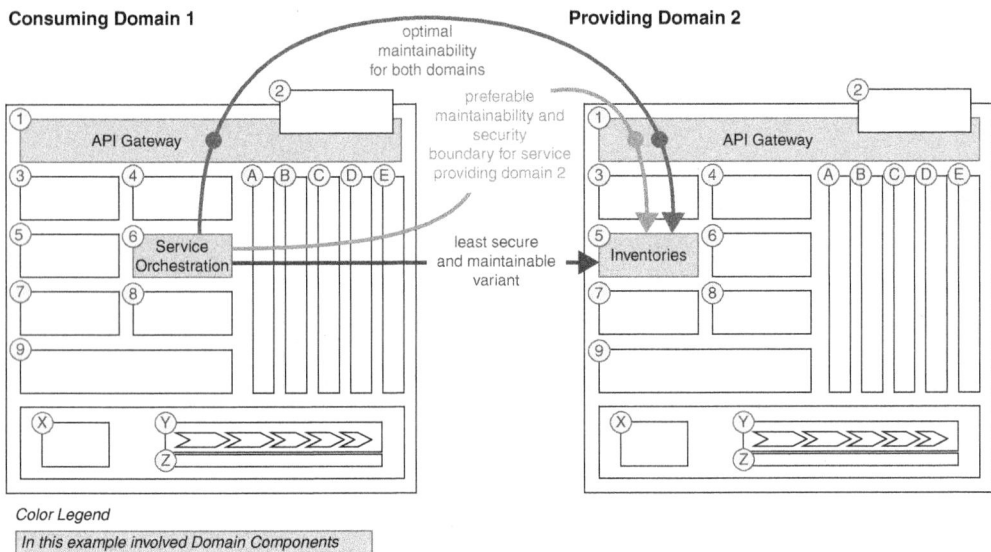

Figure 11-11   *Streamlining Inter-Domain Communication with API Gateways*

External graphical user interfaces should rely exclusively on external APIs, avoiding the implementation of specialized APIs or direct access to domain internal component APIs. This approach minimizes complexity and serves as a model for other domains and customers, demonstrating the expected method of consuming domain services via APIs.

③ Service and Resource Assurance

Service assurance focuses on the performance and availability of services that a domain offers to its customers or other domains. It involves monitoring services to detect, diagnose, and resolve issues that affect the user experience. Service assurance ensures that services meet the agreed-upon quality standards and service-level agreements (SLAs). Resource assurance is concerned with the health and performance of the physical and virtual infrastructure resources, such as servers, network devices, storage systems, and software applications. Resource assurance activities include monitoring these resources for utilization, capacity, failures, and other operational metrics to prevent service degradation or outages.

Ideal monitoring practices integrate service and resource assurance to assess the service health accurately. By considering the service relevance and potential impact of resource events, a more holistic evaluation of service health can be achieved. Modern assurance applications employ data models to define the relationships between service and resource elements, such as physical and logical interfaces, routing protocols, and probes that measure latency, jitter, or drop rates. This data model approach not only enhances event correlation but reduces the administrative burden—for example, by eliminating the need to create and maintain complex rules for event correlation or enrichment.

Furthermore, these data models are well organized and can facilitate a structured visual representation of the status of all service elements on a service health dashboard. For an on-duty network operator, this translates into a clear view of which elements are operating as expected and which ones need attention, thereby streamlining the verification process and shortening the time required to troubleshoot and restore services.

Last but not least, assurance products with artificial intelligence (AI) capabilities are becoming increasingly popular for detecting anomalies and patterns across solution components or over time in the vast data lakes of events and metrics that domains typically deal with today.

④ Service Catalog

A domain must transparently declare the services it provides to its customers and other domains—a task for which service catalogs are designed. These catalogs are crucial for listing new and existing services and also for detailing any updates, showing possible up- and downgrade paths, and indicating when services are phased out. They typically include information on pricing, available service options, and associated SLAs. Moreover, catalogs should be user-centric, offering built-in functionality or clear instructions that enable customers to easily order, access, or modify services.

⑤ Inventories

Inventories serve a multitude of use cases, ranging from financial to operational. Financially, they help clarify a domain's assets, cataloging hardware, software, and licenses to manage cost and investment. Operationally, inventories are crucial for lifecycle management, tracking hardware and software versions that are approaching end-of-life, and identifying licenses that are nearing expiration. In addition, inventories play a critical role in documenting the physical and logical layout of a domain's resources, detailing the locations of physical components, their interconnections, the types of connections, and the allocation of logical resources such as IP addresses.

While financial and lifecycle inventories often aid business functions and processes in a semi-automated manner, technical inventory aspects are deeply integrated with various operational systems. They support ⑥ service orchestration by determining which services are available on specific devices at particular sites, assist in ⑦ resource fulfillment by identifying available ports on devices within sites, and contribute to ③ service and resource assurance by informing on whether to generate alerts based on the operational status of resources, such as whether a port is not yet in service or is undergoing maintenance. These examples highlight just a few of the ways inventories underpin the efficiency and effectiveness of domain operations.

⑥ Service Orchestration

The array of services a domain offers is analogous to a musical symphony, where various service elements, provided by different components within the domain, work in concert to fulfill a customer's service request. Take, for instance, a SaaS order, which may trigger a sequence of activities. These activities may include initializing and launching a container, installing and configuring the application, establishing network connectivity, setting up backup processes, activating assurance and monitoring systems, updating the customer service dashboard with the new service details, and informing the billing system of the service change. Communication with the customer is also crucial, both for providing updates on the progress of intermediate steps and for announcing the completion of the service setup. All these tasks may be streamlined and automated through the use of process or workflow applications, which enhance efficiency and also ensure consistency and reliability in service delivery.

⑦ Resource Fulfillment

Resource fulfillment represents the practical execution layer where services desired by other domains or customers are configured on physical or virtual components. Modern resource fulfillment systems operate on a data model–driven basis, allowing service intent to be defined abstractly. These systems automatically calculate the minimal configuration changes needed to enable, modify, or terminate a service on the relevant resources. By automating these processes, there is a significant reduction in manual labor and scripting and also an enhanced capability to manage a broader spectrum of service modifications with greater efficiency.

⑧ Rollout and Migration Automation

Automating labor-intensive activities, such as high-volume rollouts or migrations that require field technicians to go on-site and teams to perform many steps in various IT systems, can lead to substantial savings. Over the past two decades, applications supporting these activities have evolved. They provide detailed instructions for the field force regarding locations to visit, resources to touch, and tasks to perform, and they now also offer an interactive experience where the field force can initiate and monitor automated updates to the correct software and configuration. Furthermore, these systems prepare adjacent components to interface with newly installed resources, verify connectivity and health, and instantly communicate any issues, such as suboptimal link quality or incorrect wiring, back to the technicians. Along with this real-time feedback, technicians receive guidance on resolving any potential issues, and the operational state is continuously monitored, providing status updates throughout the process. This continuous monitoring and guidance should conclude with a satisfying confirmation: "Rollout complete. Well done! You can move on."

Automation as described here typically involves a (B) workflow automation engine, (7) resource fulfillment systems, and various (A) apps and microservices, all of which are accessible either through the domain's (1) API gateway or a (2) graphical user interface on a mobile device or laptop. In addition, a specialized rollout and migration dashboard could be used to help planners organize and monitor these high-volume operations.

(9) (Network) Resources

Ultimately, it is physical or virtual resources that provide the services offered by a domain. Given the network-centric focus of this book, these resources likely encompass various types of networking hardware, including routers, switches, and firewalls, among others. Homologation—that is, restricting the types of resources used and the software they run—can lead to desirable simplifications. By standardizing on a few types of resources, there are fewer variations to manage and consider in engineering, testing, and automation activities, reducing complexity and potential errors.

(A) Apps and Microservices

Often, there is a requirement to create customized applications to support various internal or external functions of a domain. By standardizing on a common framework and centralizing the provision of underlaying computational and application resources, a domain can enhance long-term operability and harness synergies. This approach helps avoid the pitfalls of individual teams or personnel pursuing their unique solutions, which often lead to continuity issues when those individuals leave or transition to different roles within the organization.

(B) Workflow Automation Engine

A workflow typically consists of a series of activities, some of which can be automated, and others that may require manual intervention and confirmation upon completion. These activities can vary in duration, with some even spanning weeks, exemplifying the unique characteristics of workflows. All stakeholders—whether field personnel, customers, or other domains—benefit from a well-designed workflow. Such a workflow streamlines the user experience by adopting a business process view and abstracts technical complexities of the underlying components. When we discussed (8) rollout and migration automation, we documented an application of such a workflow automation engine. Similar to the case for (A) apps and microservices, standardizing on a single workflow automation engine is advantageous because it allows for the realization of synergies and simplifies operations over the long term.

Ⓒ Messaging

To optimize communication between applications within a domain, it is beneficial to designate a preferred method and mechanism for communication. Messaging systems facilitate reliable one-to-one or one-to-many messaging, providing a robust infrastructure for information exchange. Asynchronous messaging is often favored because it reduces tight coupling between applications. This means that if one component is under maintenance or temporarily experiencing high load, other applications can wait for a response without immediately failing the operation that triggered the message or re-sending requests until the recipient is ready to process them. Such an approach improves system resilience and also enhances scalability by allowing components to process messages at their own pace, thus accommodating fluctuating workloads and preventing bottlenecks.

Ⓓ Error and Event Handling

Error and event handling typically involves interfacing with individual application logs and event streams, which are often integrated with Ⓒ messaging frameworks. Rather than allowing each application to escalate errors or critical events in its own unique manner, a more effective strategy is to channel these notifications through a centralized system. This approach allows for the aggregation and routing of error and event information to assurance systems and other interested applications within the domain. By consolidating error and event handling, the domain can facilitate more coherent monitoring, quicker response times, and streamlined issue resolution, thereby improving the overall reliability and operational efficiency of the domain.

Ⓔ Security Measures and Events

In defining a domain, the inclusion of security enforcement resources is obligatory. Firewalls, along with intrusion detection and prevention systems, play a vital role in safeguarding domain components. ① API gateways offer additional protection against threats to service interfaces, and web application firewalls help to shield ② graphical user interfaces from vulnerabilities. Beyond these protective measures, security monitoring applications are essential for the thorough examination of logs and events across all domain components to detect potential threats. At the heart of these security efforts lies the security operations center (SOC), which is paramount in ensuring uninterrupted and secure services. A well-equipped SOC is instrumental in preventing security breaches that could compromise the domain's reputation and also the reputation of the entire organization.

Ⓕ Workforce and Customer Apps

Creativity flourishes with accessibility. By providing smooth and well-documented APIs, a domain greatly simplifies the process for both customers and its own workforce to imagine and implement more effective ways to integrate the domain's services into their daily routines and the tools they use.

Solution Lifecycle Automation

To ensure superior quality and efficient operations within a domain, establishing a robust development and release process is essential. Such a process should be underpinned by a suite of highly automated environments tailored for development, integration, and rigorous testing by all stakeholders, ensuring excellent domain services.

(X) Process facilitating components are crucial for accurately documenting desired changes, such as new features or improvements, and effectively coordinating these changes. They make it possible to define, organize, and monitor work items, manage dependencies, and oversee the assignments and progress of other domains, teams, and individual contributors.

(Y) Development, testing, and release automating components are instrumental in maintaining a repository of designs, source code, and configuration templates. These components are at the forefront of automating the testing, which includes acceptance testing to verify new functionalities and regression testing to ensure that existing features remain unaffected by changes. Simulators replicate customer or inter-domain interactions with the domain's services, and emulators replicate other domains' components, facilitating early-stage development and testing before integrating.

(Z) Environments automating components play a pivotal role in ensuring that development and testing environments can be quickly reinitialized or updated. This capability is vital for setting the stage for acceptance tests and other verifications, allowing for consistent and reliable test outcomes across test cycles.

> **Note** For a more detailed discussion of these components and their roles in a development and release methodology, see the section "Development and Release Methodology," later in this chapter.

Domain Responsibilities and Their Architectural Implications

While the previous section, "Domain Architecture Blueprint," outlines a potential domain architecture, it leaves some key questions unanswered: How do we ascertain the need to build and operate a component within the domain? Under what conditions can a domain component be based on a shared service from another domain? Clarifying a domain's responsibilities can help in finding answers to these questions.

The responsibilities of a domain within an organization's architecture can vary depending on the specific context, business objectives, and operational model. The first 10 responsibilities a domain may consider have a technical character. Integration of specific components into the domain architecture is required for these responsibilities to be managed effectively:

1. **Service delivery:** Ensuring reliable and efficient delivery of services that fall within the domain's scope

2. **Service management:** Ordering, modifying, terminating, and monitoring services

3. **Resource management:** Managing the physical and virtual resources required to provide the domain's services, including hardware and software

4. **Incident and problem management:** Identifying, responding to, and resolving incidents and problems that affect the domain's services

5. **Performance management:** Monitoring and optimizing the performance of services and underlying infrastructure to meet the standards and expectations of customers and consuming domains

6. **Capacity management:** Planning, monitoring, and optimizing the domain's capacity to handle current and future demands, both during normal operations and in failure scenarios

7. **Security and compliance:** Maintaining the security of the domain's services and data together with ensuring compliance with relevant regulations and organizational policies

8. **Change management:** Implementing processes for managing changes in the domain, including updates, enhancements, and decommissioning of the offered service portfolio and underlying resources

9. **Quality assurance:** Establishing quality standards and processes to ensure that the domain's services meet specifications and user requirements

10. **Documentation and knowledge management:** Retaining detailed documentation of services, configurations, and processes and managing the knowledge within the domain

Responsibilities 11 to 17 may be addressed by processes and shared services offered throughout the organization:

11. **Business alignment:** Aligning the domain's services and projects with the broader business goals and strategies of the organization

12. **Continuity planning:** Ensuring that the domain has plans and capabilities in place for business continuity and disaster recovery

13. **Cost management:** Controlling costs associated with the domain's services, including budgeting, forecasting, and cost optimization efforts

14. **Stakeholder communication:** Communicating with stakeholders to keep them informed about service status, changes, and other relevant information

15. **Innovation and improvement:** Continuously seeking ways to innovate and improve the domain's services and operations

16. **Collaboration and integration:** Collaborating within and across domains

17. **Vendor management:** Managing relationships with vendors and third-party service providers that are involved in the domain's operations

Once the domain responsibilities are reviewed and clearly defined, it becomes possible to determine whether and how to integrate components that provide the respective functionality within the domain. The remainder of this section introduces a potential build-versus-buy decision-making framework that can be adapted to specific needs, starting with Table 11-3, which suggests possible criticality levels. Determining a component's criticality creates a common understanding of its importance to a domain and the potential impact in the event of problems. High-criticality components, which are essential for the core functionality and performance of the domain, may warrant a domain-specific build to ensure flexibility, availability, and performance. Conversely, low-criticality components, which have less impact on the domain, might be more cost-effectively and efficiently bought as services. An evaluation of the availability and suitability of shared services then leads to a recommendation on whether to build a component within a domain or to use a shared service from another domain.

Finally, this section provides an illustrative example of how to document this decision-making process for all responsibilities and components within a domain.

Table 11-3 *Assessing Component Criticality to a Domain*

Criticality Level	Description	Sample Failure
Service functionality relevant	The domain's services may fail or degrade if the component malfunctions or is unavailable.	Service availability, resiliency, and performance might suffer in the event of a network component breakdown.
Service operability relevant	A failure in a component that is critical to service operability won't directly impact service consumers. Nonetheless, it can affect the visibility of services and resources, thereby hindering operability, supportability, SLA compliance reporting, or the security of the domain services.	An assurance application failure can leave network operations without visibility and impair the observability functions available to customers and service-consuming domains.
Service modifications relevant	When components that are critical to service modifications fail, customers and other domains are unable to order, change, or terminate existing services.	If the API gateway experiences an outage, it would inhibit customers and other domains from carrying out service management activities.
Service lifecycle relevant	These components facilitate the development of new services, as well as the evolution, enhancement, and bug fixing of existing services and their underlying resources.	The unavailability of a source code repository or automated pipelines could cause delays in the scheduled delivery of an upcoming release.

There may be an option to build a component by leveraging a shared service from another domain or even a public service. Table 11-4 explores the availability options for such components.

Table 11-4 *Availability of Components as Shared Services by Other Domains*

Shared Service Availability	Description
Not available	This component, or its functionality, is not provided as a shared service by any other domain.
Available but with limitations	A component can be provided as a shared service by another domain, but this arrangement may come with constraints. For instance, it may lack tenant capabilities that allow for a domain-specific, isolated view and administration. In addition, the offered functionality might not fully meet the domain's expectations due to its lack of specialization. Examples include service orchestration, resource fulfillment, and assurance components, which may require extensive tailoring to align with the domain-specific technology. However, even with customization, they might still fall short of the accuracy and performance achieved by a solution tailored to the domain's technological requirements.
Available	Another domain provides this component as a shared service, with all the necessary capabilities included.

After you have categorized domain relevance and assessed various shared services availability options, it's time to decide whether to build or buy. Table 11-5 offers recommendations on whether to build a component internally within a domain or to use a shared service from another domain. The criticality levels are displayed on the left, and recommendations are provided for each shared service availability option represented in the columns. Note that there is no strict differentiation between "available" and "available with limitations"; instead, guidance is provided to help domain architects decide whether to build a component within the domain or leverage a shared service.

Table 11-5 *To Build or Borrow: Recommendations for Domain Components*

Criticality Level	Shared Service Availability		
	Not Available	**Available with Limitations**	**Available**
Critical: Service functionality relevant	**Build** within the domain.	**Build** within the domain to minimize external dependencies for critical service functionality.	
Major: Service operability relevant		This recommendation hinges on the domain's priorities. If temporary downtime of a shared service is tolerable, and limited network visibility and SLA transparency are deemed acceptable, then adopting a **shared component** from another domain may be a practical choice. Conversely, if such limitations are unacceptable, **building** a dedicated component within the domain may be preferable.	

Criticality Level	Shared Service Availability		
	Not Available	Available with Limitations	Available
		In any case, it is crucial to carefully evaluate potential limitations of a shared component to prevent any disadvantageous long-term effects or inefficiencies in operating the domain.	
Major: Service modiwfications relevant		A multi-tenant-capable **shared component** may be used if it is acceptable to avoid modifying or deploying services during unavailability. Otherwise, building a dedicated component within the domain could be the preferred approach. However, it is vital to consider any limitations of a shared component to avoid long-term issues.	
Moderate: Service lifecycle relevant		Employ a tenant-capable **shared component** from another domain, making certain to address any service limitations to avoid long-term consequences and **build only** what is required specifically for the domain.	

Publicly accessible services via the Internet may also be considered for providing certain component functionalities. However, factors such as connectivity, manageability, long-term service availability, the impact of public service changes on the domain, data confidentiality, and licensing concerns must be thoroughly assessed when considering the use of a public service within a domain.

Let's return to the key question raised at the beginning of this section: How do we decide whether to build and operate a component within the domain or to leverage a shared service? Table 11-6 applies the discussed build-versus-buy decision framework and offers a sample overview that describes how responsibilities are covered and components are provisioned within a domain.

Table 11-6 *Domain Component Sourcing: Example for a New SR Transport Network Domain*

Addressed Responsibilities	Architecture Component	Shared Service Availability	Criticality Level	Guided Example Conclusion
Service management	① API gateway	Available	Major: Service modifications relevant	Build component using and customizing a shared service.

Addressed Responsibilities	Architecture Component	Shared Service Availability	Criticality Level	Guided Example Conclusion
	② Graphical user interface	Not available	Major: Service modifications relevant	Build, because it's not available, perhaps on a companywide shared framework.
	④ Service catalog	Available	Major: Service modifications relevant	Build component using and customizing a shared service.
	⑥ Service orchestration	Available	Major: Service modifications relevant	Build component using and customizing a shared service.
Service delivery	⑨ (Network) Resources	Not available	Critical: Service functionality relevant	Build component within the domain.
Service management Resource management	⑤ Inventories	Available but with limitations	Major: Service operability relevant	Build component within the domain, as the specifics of SR technology are likely to incur unforeseen customization expenses and expose limitations of a shared service.
	⑦ Resource fulfillment	Available but with limitations	Major: Service modifications relevant	Build component within the domain, as the specifics of SR technology are likely to incur unforeseen customization expenses and expose limitations of a shared service.

Addressed Responsibilities	Architecture Component	Shared Service Availability	Criticality Level	Guided Example Conclusion
	(8) Rollout and migration automation	Available	Major: Service modifications relevant	Build component using and customizing a shared service.
	(A) Apps and microservices	Available	Major: Service modifications relevant	Build component using and customizing a shared service.
	(B) Workflow automation engine	Available	Major: Service modifications relevant	Build component using and customizing a shared service.
	(C) Messaging	Available	Major: Service operability relevant	Build component using and customizing a shared service.
	(F) Workforce and customer apps	Not available	Major: Service modifications relevant	Evaluate whether available (A) apps and microservices and (2) graphical user interface are sufficient for workforce and customer applications or whether specific apps need to be built.
Service management Resource management Incident and problem management Performance management Capacity management	(3) Service and resource assurance	Available but with limitations	Major: Service operability relevant	Build, as the specifics of SR technology are likely to incur unforeseen customization expenses and expose limitations of a shared service.

Addressed Responsibilities	Architecture Component	Shared Service Availability	Criticality Level	Guided Example Conclusion
Change management Quality assurance Documentation and knowledge management	Ⓧ Ⓨ Ⓩ Solution lifecycle automation	Available	Moderate: Service lifecycle relevant	Leverage shared service for documentation, source code management, environment automation, testing, and additional functions.
Incident and problem management	Ⓓ Error and event handling	Not available	Major: Service operability relevant	Evaluate whether benefits justify the investment into building the component within the domain.
Security and compliance	Ⓔ Security measures and events	Available but with limitations	Major: Service operability relevant	Evaluate whether limitations are acceptable for the domain to leverage the available shared service.

Now that the technical domain architecture has been outlined, the next section shifts focus to the people aspect, delving into the organizational transformation.

Domain Organization and Transformation

A team needs to concentrate on its domain's scope and responsibilities. Domain leadership should foster regular interactions between domains, while those in managing roles are responsible for coordinating the synchronization of plans, roadmaps, and interdependencies both within their own domain and across domains. Furthermore, it is vital to facilitate consistent communication between domain architects and component engineering teams to share and maintain knowledge throughout the organization. Regular inter-domain meetings between architects are essential to maintain a unified architectural vision and service operations across the network service provider. Component leads should proactively communicate upcoming changes to their teams and counterparts in other domains to ensure accurate and timely information flow. While this approach may appear straightforward, two key questions persist: How can domains be structured to enhance such coordination and effective communication? Within the realm of transport network services and in the midst of an SR transformation, which critical roles should be defined, and what should their responsibilities and expectations be? Figure 11-12 presents a potential domain organization model, with the intention of facilitating discussions and enabling network service providers to customize it according to their preferred terminology, organizational framework, and distinct role-naming conventions and definitions.

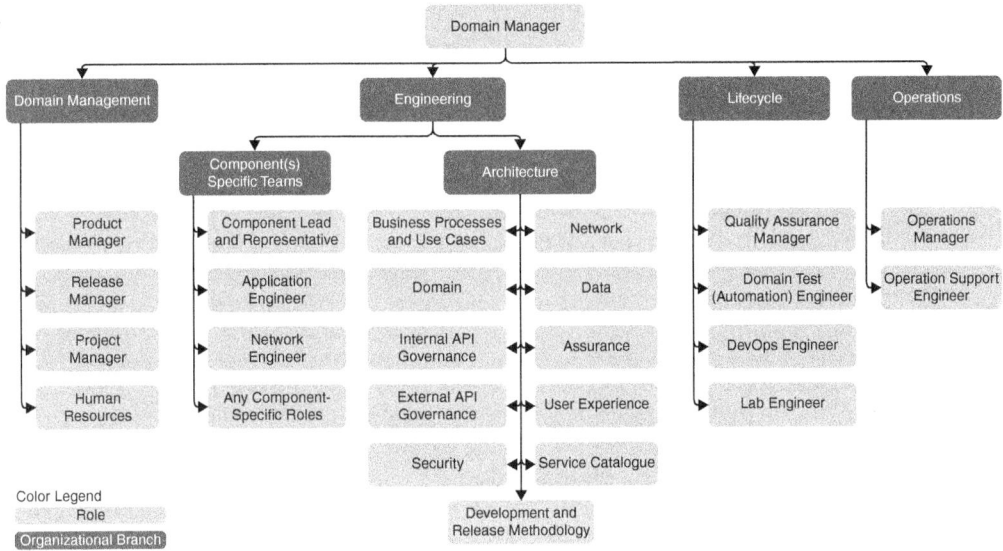

Figure 11-12 *Domain Organization: Key Roles*

Table 11-7 provides a comprehensive description of the relevance and functions of all the roles depicted in Figure 11-12.

Table 11-7 *Roles Within a Domain*

Role	Description
Domain Managing Roles	
Domain manager	This role encompasses the oversight of all operations within a domain, including managing financial aspects such as budgeting and cost control, coordinating staffing requirements, and ensuring high-level strategic alignment with other domains.
Product manager	Product managers are responsible for managing the lifecycle of services products that the domain offers to customers and other domains, including their creation, updating, and retirement. This role ensures that products are economically viable and meet the needs of customers and other domains efficiently, simultaneously aligning on budget and resources with the domain manager.

Role	Description
Project manager	This role is responsible for the planning, execution, and closure of major feature and change requests that entail numerous dependencies and substantial effort. The individuals in this position are tasked with managing a detailed schedule, ensuring the timely delivery of all dependencies, and effectively coordinating various activities to meet project milestones and deadlines.
Release manager	In domains that consist of many components, it is essential to track and test how different versions of these components work together. This awareness helps prevent the deployment of untested combinations into the production environment. Release managers work in tandem with product and project managers as well as component leads to coordinate changes and ensure that everything is tested in harmony. They also engage with customers and other domains that use these services, not just to keep them informed about upcoming releases but also to ensure that friendly customers and affected partner domains test and perhaps even approve an upcoming new release in a staging environment prior to deployment into production.
Human resources manager	This role is responsible for overseeing the staffing aspects of the domain, encompassing a range of activities including the onboarding process, performance management, structuring compensation and benefits, managing employee relations, ensuring adherence to policies and compliance with regulations, addressing training and development needs, and upholding health and safety standards.
Engineering Roles	
IT architect	IT architects typically shoulder a breadth of responsibilities that are crucial to the domain's long-term success and operational efficiency. Their coverage spans a diverse set of areas, including but not limited to the following: ■ **End-to-end domain process and use case definitions:** This entails the analysis of business requirements and the extraction of both functional and non-functional requirements. Architects guide the individual components within their domain, ensuring that they address their requirements and their components' contributions to the domain processes and use cases. ■ **Domain architecture:** This involves detailing the composition of the domain, clarifying the function of each component, and defining the communication pathways between them, whether internal or crossing domain boundaries.

Role	Description
IT architect	■ **Internal API governance:** Architects define strategies for intra-domain communication, determining how components should interact for various interaction patterns and communication needs—whether synchronously or asynchronously, in one-to-one or one-to-many relationships.
	■ **External API governance, strategy, and management:** This includes several sub-areas:
	■ **Inter-domain API strategy:** Architects outline how the domain will handle external communication, accommodating various interaction patterns and communication needs.
	■ **API catalog:** Architects provide guidance on the creation and maintenance of a comprehensive catalog of user-friendly APIs that are process oriented, well documented, and testable at any time, which is crucial for preventing inefficient and frustrating experiences for API consumers.
	■ **API contracts:** Clearly defined contracts set expectations concerning API availability, resiliency, maintenance schedules, versioning, and life-cycle management. These contracts specify how changes to the API, whether backward compatible or not, will be communicated. They also outline the time frames permitted for consumers to adjust to these changes. In addition, contracts may set forth expectations for consumers to validate new API releases, ensuring that they meet their requirements before they are deployed into the production environment.
	■ **API security:** Architects define supported authentication and encryption methods, required role-based access control mechanisms, and data security measures. They also incorporate protection mechanisms such as throttling, anomaly detection, and integration with a security operations center (SOC) for cautious security monitoring.
	■ **API administration and support:** Architects provide guidance on how API consumers can obtain access, request enhancements, or report issues.
	■ **Data architecture:** This critical function involves determining the data needs of various components within the domain, identifying authoritative sources for data, and establishing protocols for how data updates are requested, captured, and distributed. It ensures that all components have access to accurate, up-to-date data and that there is a clear understanding of how data flows and is managed both within a single domain and across multiple domains. Data architecture also addresses concerns such as data governance, quality, privacy, and security, establishing a comprehensive framework for data utilization and stewardship.

Role	Description
IT architect	■ **Assurance:** Maintaining transparency regarding the health and quality of both resources and services is paramount for a domain's integrity and reliability. Proactive monitoring and regular quality checks are essential for identifying and resolving issues before they impact customers or other domains. It is important to prevent situations where customers or interconnected domains are the first to notice and report problems, as this can significantly erode trust and satisfaction with the services provided by the domain.
	■ **User experience:** For domains that offer graphical user interfaces or apps, IT architects should provide principal guidance on the desired user experience. This encompasses the design principles, wireframe templates, accessibility, usability, and interactive elements that contribute to a seamless and engaging experience for the end user.
	■ **Service catalog:** In collaboration with network architects, IT architects are responsible for defining a domain's service catalog. This catalog details the services available, including descriptions of each service and guidance for how users and other domains can request, modify, or discontinue these services. The service catalog serves as a comprehensive resource, ensuring clarity and ease of access for service consumers.
	■ **Security:** IT architects are responsible for defining and maintaining the security aspects of the overall domain architecture and the services it provides.
	■ **Development and release methodology:** IT architects are instrumental in delineating the methodologies for development and release processes. They define the lifecycle stages—from conceptualization, design, and development to testing and deployment—ensuring that changes are systematically validated and verified before being introduced into the production environment. Their role is crucial in implementing best practices that minimize risks and align with organizational standards for quality and performance.
	While this list of responsibilities for IT architects is comprehensive, it doesn't cover everything. To effectively manage the wide range of responsibilities, some organizations establish specialized roles tailored to specific areas of expertise (for instance, roles such as data architect, API architect, and security architect). Figure 11-12 outlines such suggested positions.
	IT architects are responsible for creating and maintaining an IT high-level design (HLD) for the domain. This pivotal document encompasses all applicable areas previously outlined and serves as a foundational reference for the domain's components and teams.

Role	Description
Network architect	Essential in domains that revolve around network services, network architects determine the future direction of the network. They strategize on the introduction of new services, define how connections with other networks will be established, and plan the migration path for existing networks or services that customers and other domains use as they transition to newer generations of network technology and services.
	Network architects create and maintain a network HLD, which outlines the overarching structure of the network, its redundancy, the capacity it provides, and the services it facilitates. This document serves as a foundational reference for network engineers as they develop the detailed network low-level design (LLD) and inherit specific testing requirements. It also guides IT architects in absorbing IT requirements that may include automation of network changes and service updates. Ultimately, the insights and directives from the network HLD are carried forward by IT component-specific teams, which integrate them into their own component LLD, development, and testing activities.
Component lead and representative	Subject matter experts (SMEs) are designated individuals—usually one or two per component—who bring in-depth understanding of their specific areas. An SME acts as the primary point of contact for questions concerning their component(s), thereby optimizing communication with architects and other teams. This focused approach reduces the need for communication and frequent meetings involving the broader team. SMEs are instrumental during the design phase for new changes, working closely with their team to relay expectations and steer the implementation process. To ensure wide-ranging expertise and encourage collaborative knowledge-sharing, teams may periodically rotate these responsibilities among members.
	SMEs are responsible for ensuring that component-specific LLDs are kept up-to-date. These documents articulate the functions of the components, as well as how use cases and specific requirements are addressed. Furthermore, SMEs take the lead in defining and reviewing acceptance criteria and overseeing the planning and execution of component testing.
Application engineer	Application engineers are tasked with the development and maintenance of applications, ensuring that their functionality, reliability, and performance are in line with user needs and business requirements. They are also accountable for creating and automating unit tests for their components. These unit tests are essential for confirming that every use case and requirement is met, thereby guaranteeing that the component contributes effectively to the overall domain operation.

Role	Description
Network engineer	Network engineers are tasked with maintaining the network LLD, specifying target configurations and migration details and establishing precise testing procedures and validation steps. A key part of their role involves automating these network tests to confirm that the expected network services are not only performing to standard but functioning correctly whenever required. This meticulous approach ensures the reliability and efficiency of the network infrastructure.
Lifecycle Roles	
Quality assurance manager	Quality assurance managers define the criteria for quality gates and methodically review the test coverage for each component as well as for the domain as a whole. This involves a careful examination of the testing outcomes to ensure that they meet the established standards. The individuals in this position are responsible for the final sign-off on new releases, confirming their readiness to progress further toward the production environment.
Domain test (automation) engineer	In domains that consist of many components, it is challenging to clearly define responsibility and accountability for verifying the overall domain services. Domain test engineers step in and play a critical role in this regard, methodically reviewing the network services provided by the domain. This includes the APIs available through the API gateway and any graphical user interfaces to manage tasks such as ordering, modifying, terminating, or monitoring these domain services. They create automated test suites that simulate the actions of customers or other domains, sending API requests or network traffic to identify any unexpected responses or behaviors. When the domain's services have external dependencies and require interaction with other domains, these engineers design and implement mocks to emulate both the expected and unexpected responses from these external domains during the early stages of development and integration testing. After completing a test cycle for a new release, they document the results, thereby providing a transparent and accountable report of the expected domain's service quality with an upcoming release. This documentation is an essential input for the quality assurance manager's role, as previously discussed, and contributes to the decision-making process for release sign-off and a production rollout.
DevOps engineer	This role is responsible for a combination of software development (Dev) and IT operations (Ops) practices. DevOps engineers promote a culture of collaboration between the traditionally siloed development and operations teams. They aim to shorten the development lifecycle, ensuring high-quality releases with a focus on automation. They cleverly integrate and use tools to streamline repetitive tasks and boost efficiency. Such recurring tasks include compiling code, configuring servers and applications, performing unit or overall domain service tests, conducting vulnerability and best practices scans on code, and establishing or reinitializing development and testing environments.

Role	Description
Lab engineer	People in this supportive role are responsible for building and maintaining labs, as well as the associated tools.
Operation Roles	
Operations manager	This role is responsible for managing daily service operations, including planning staff shifts, coordinating maintenance windows, escalating issues as needed, and ensuring effective problem management. In addition, there is a continuous commitment to working with the team to improve operational efficiency and productivity.
Operation support engineer	These engineers are responsible for operating the service. At times, it is practical for technical engineering staff to fulfill multiple roles, including overseeing the operation of domain services in the production environment. For example, software engineers who work on key components or network engineers might also take on support roles in operations. However, the allocation of dual roles must be carefully evaluated, as expecting team members to support domain services on a shift work model could inhibit their ability to focus on the engineering tasks that are essential for developing upcoming releases.

Not every role is necessary for each domain within an organization, yet this table can be useful in identifying potential gaps. It is common for certain roles to be shared among multiple individuals and sometimes for a single person to take on several different roles.

In the development of a new feature or migration, architects play a key role in clarifying architectural questions, mapping out inter-domain and component dependencies, and drafting a high-level design that sets the stage for component-specific teams to deliver their contribution to the overall solution. Under the leadership of a project manager, representatives from all affected components, as well as one or more architects who provide the required architectural expertise, prepare the finer details for component teams to develop and tests the feature or migration. A domain test engineer would be tasked with verifying the overall domain service or migration functionality. Meanwhile, a DevOps engineer would enhance existing pipelines to consider new source code. A lab engineer would adjust the existing laboratory environment to accommodate any changes, and, finally, an operation support engineer would be responsible for monitoring the development process, providing operational feedback, and communicating forthcoming changes to the operations team at an early stage. In summary, a successful and efficient implementation of new functions or migrations hinges on the collaboration of multiple roles and expertise. One effective approach is the formation of a virtual team, or squad, as depicted in Figure 11-13.

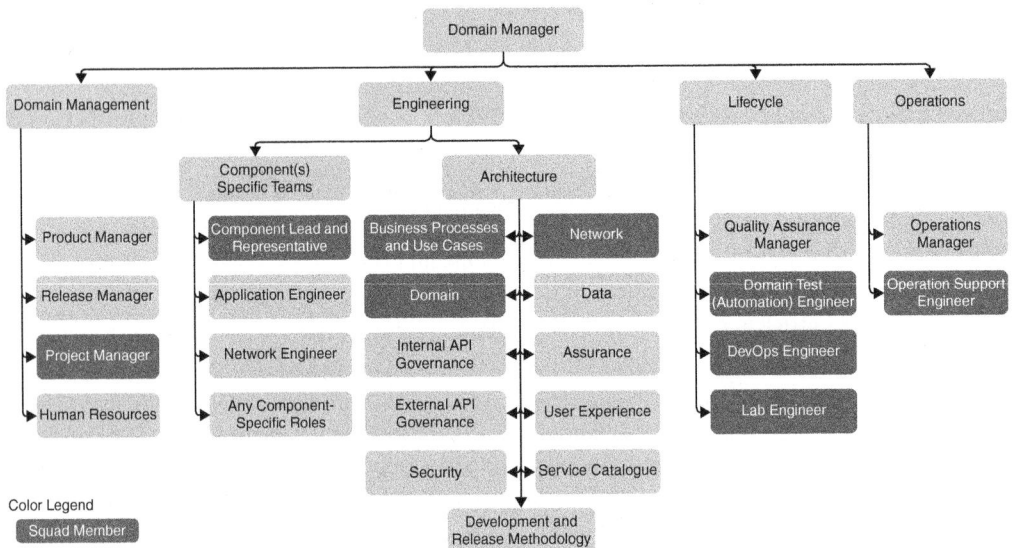

Figure 11-13 *Feature or Migration Squad*

Provided that there is sufficient staffing for all essential roles, it is possible to establish multiple squads that can simultaneously progress through the development of features and migrations. While virtually assigning representatives to squads, it is crucial to maintain stable, component-specific teams for two main reasons:

■ Component teams share expertise, uphold best practices, ensure consistency, and leverage synergies for their component across the various features and migrations they support.

■ Component teams provide a platform for junior members to join and develop their skills. Such members may not have the opportunity to be directly assigned to a feature or migration squad.

Having explored the potential structure of a domain organization and its effective operation on new features or migrations, we now turn our attention to the potential challenges associated with transitioning from the current organizational structure to the desired one. In the context of consolidating multiple transport network services and teams into a unified SR network service team, it is essential to recognize that migrating and merging teams requires not just combining different skill sets but harmonizing a variety of backgrounds and distinct approaches to work, communication, and decision making. Plus, such a transformation can bring considerable uncertainty. Questions may arise about team composition: Who will be part of the new team taking care of the converged SR network? What will it mean for those not selected?

The diverse organizational structures prevent us from offering detailed, one-size-fits-all recommendations. However, at a high level, establishing a strategy and maintaining transparent communication are critical to encouraging team motivation and guaranteeing continuity during the extensive multi-year transformation process. It is important to provide introductory training on the new technology across the organization. Rather than selecting only the most standout individuals, consider a more holistic approach: Define a core team and rotate members from existing teams into and out of the SR domain, especially while the legacy networks are still in operation and have not fully transitioned to the new SR network. It may be beneficial to select the most effective existing team as a whole and guide its evolution into the SR domain rather than assemble a completely new team.

Existing and New Processes

As part of building the new converged SR domain, it is beneficial to review all existing processes of the legacy domains, assessing them for efficiency, effectiveness, and potential redundancy. This thorough evaluation lays the groundwork for establishing standardized procedures within the new SR domain that draw on the best practices of legacy processes while eliminating any identified inefficiencies. Adjustments to existing processes affected by the SR transformation must be carefully managed to preserve operational continuity. It is essential to strike a delicate balance between maintaining ongoing operations and introducing the changes necessary for the new SR domain.

A converged SR domain may also consolidate various customer segments, each with different maintenance windows expectations and SLAs. While business customers may allow maintenance work over the weekends, customers transporting mobile traffic will prefer maintenance to be performed between 3 a.m. and 6 a.m. on weekdays. To accommodate this diversity, change processes can benefit from additional automation that shortens change windows for increased service availability.

Periodic reviews by process owners are necessary to maintain efficiency and make refinements as required. These refinements may include accelerating process steps, enhancing operational workflows, and increasing the scope of task automation, particularly for procedures that are currently slow or labor intensive. Aim to automate processes wherever economically feasible and ensure that they are capable of interfacing seamlessly with other domains through domain-specific APIs.

End-to-end process definitions across domains are often managed by an enterprise architecture team. These teams typically consist of domain representatives who ensure that processes are well documented, accessible to everyone involved in the process implementation, and operate efficiently and effectively.

Service Portfolio Consolidation

Merging the network service portfolio plays a significant role in the convergence of multiple networks into a single, unified SR network. It is common for services to differ greatly between legacy networks, with some perhaps offering a multitude of manually adjusted service configuration options. The consolidation of these services into a unified SR-based service portfolio requires significant efforts. Creating models of network services and their options can shed light on which specific variants should be discontinued and transitioned to a more standardized service definition. In rare instances, the service modeling activity might uncover a service model that encompasses all options from all networks involved. No matter the specifics, harmonizing the portfolio is essential to streamline various activities—including automation, assurance, testing, migration, and operations—for the converged SR network over the coming years. In essence, this is a strategic move to significantly cut operational costs (OpEx) in the long term.

Development and Release Methodology

In recent years, there has been a significant shift in network operations, moving away from traditional command-line interface (CLI)–based network changes toward automation solutions that are engineered and rigorously tested as part of the development process. This transition can represent a major cultural change for many network operations teams, as it emphasizes automation, consistency, and reliability over manual interventions. By automating the development process of the network and IT systems, an organization can ensure that changes are thoroughly vetted and aligned with best practices before deployment, ultimately leading to more stable and predictable network environments. Such an approach enhances operational efficiency and also fosters a culture of continuous improvement and collaboration.

According to the Oxford dictionary, a *methodology* is a set of methods and principles used to perform a particular activity. This section provides methods and principles to prepare for and ease the automation of the development and release processes, which can be integrated into preferred frameworks such as Agile, Waterfall, DevOps, or others. It begins by describing a clear flow for managing changes and introducing new capabilities within the SR domain. Subsequently, it outlines the necessary environments and offers an analysis of the tooling involved. However, before exploring these topics, Table 11-8 first summarizes the principles that the proposed methodology is based on.

Table 11-8   *Methodology Principles*

Principle	Description	Desired Benefit
Simplicity Transparency	To effectively manage a domain, it is crucial to have a clear understanding of the status of each new feature, change, or bug fix, as well as the components they rely on in a well-defined development and release process. A feature's status should be readily identifiable, whether it's in the backlog, scheduled for upcoming sprints, under design and development, or in the stakeholder acceptance testing phase. Furthermore, it should be clear which specific component releases will incorporate related changes and how they will align with the broader domain release schedule.	Clear position of each change within the development and release process ensures transparency. Clear ownership at each stage of the process accelerates progress and promotes efficiency. Enhanced coordination within the domain and with external stakeholders streamlines the management of dependencies and the harmonization of schedules.

Principle	Description	Desired Benefit
Fail early Predictable delivery	The methodology aims to identify potential failures as early as possible in the development cycle. This is why acceptance tests are integrated into the development activities. The goal is to uncover any scaling, performance, security, redundancy, or operational issues well in advance rather than discovering them later, possibly just a few weeks before a scheduled production rollout. Late-stage identification of such issues typically leads to significant delays, potentially requiring the release to cycle back to a development status and disrupt the timeline for upcoming releases. Such delays can be frustrating for everyone involved—team members, customers, and other domains awaiting the new release—and they may negatively affect the domain's reputation.	Application and network engineering teams reliably achieve their objectives, delivering expected results on schedule.
One lab design, built multiple times	Network and IT architects collaborate to create a well-defined lab design that undergoes extensive review, ensuring consensus that it faithfully represents the production environment and facilitates the verification of all acceptance criteria. This comprehensive approach streamlines the lab design and setup, simplifies documentation, reduces the need for discussions, and eases environment and test automation, test data definition, tooling, and many other tasks.	Engineering teams can automate the processes of building and reinitializing environments, as well as solution testing, just once, and then efficiently reuse these automations multiple times across all lab environments driving consistency and quality.
Automation first	Everyone in the domain should attempt to identify and implement automation for tasks that are performed frequently and whose automation would result in a significant reduction of time and efforts.	By encouraging the automation of repetitive and manual tasks, the workplace becomes more attractive to talent, fostering innovation and job satisfaction. This shift not only enhances employee engagement but also leads to lower OpEx for the business, driving overall efficiency and profitability.
Universal	The methodology must be flexible and apply universally, whether it applies to updating network configuration templates, automation scripts, application source code, or external libraries.	Engineering and operation across different roles, disciplines, and components within the domain are easier and consistent.

Overall, these principles are defined to streamline alignment among teams, domains, and stakeholders; increase throughput to manage the aggregated workload within the new converged SR network domain; and, ultimately, reduce time to market while enhancing quality.

Process with a Clear Flow

The process in this section is designed to address the full spectrum of features and changes within a domain. The simplified development and release process in Figure 11-14 spans the entire development and release cycle—from the initial identification of a feature or change; through design, development, and testing at various stages of maturity; to the final rollout in production. Throughout this process, all involved teams align their efforts toward a unified definition of the feature or change. Moreover, the process provides clear guidance on how and when external parties, such as customers and other domains, can conduct testing on both upcoming releases and the existing production release.

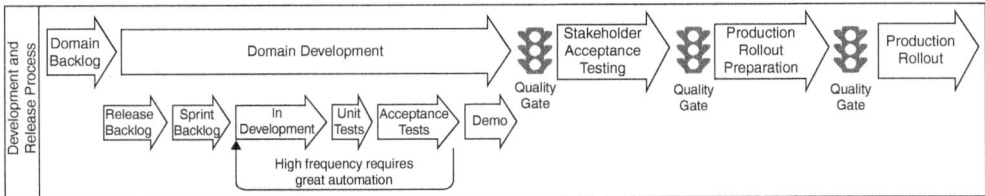

Figure 11-14 *Key Phases in the Development and Release Process*

Table 11-9 provides a description of each phase in the process.

Table 11-9 *Key Phases in the Development and Release Process*

Stage	Description	Outcomes
Domain backlog	Business stakeholders along with engineering and operation teams identify and submit requests for features and changes. These requests are routinely reviewed and prioritized. To enhance their clarity, descriptions, affected components, and external dependencies are reviewed in discussions with architects and the leads of impacted components.	Transparent domain backlog and prioritization
	Architects do preparatory work and may begin to update high-level designs (HLDs), documenting what the component teams will address at a later stage before the request reaches the sprint backlog stage.	HLD updates
	Based on their priority, these requests are eventually selected for the release backlog and scheduled for inclusion in an upcoming release.	

Stage	Description	Outcomes
Release backlog	Component teams primarily source their work from the domain backlog but also have the freedom to introduce their own specific features and changes. Such contributions are subsequently evaluated and ranked in consideration of the team's limited bandwidth and release schedule constraints. To ensure comprehensive traceability, component leads document detailed subtasks under the main domain request to outline all the required work items. These subtasks are then considered according to their urgency and, when deemed appropriate, included in the sprint backlog to be addressed in the forthcoming sprint.	Transparent release backlog and prioritization
Sprint backlog	Component leads prepare low-level design (LLD) updates and establish precise guidelines that direct the documentation of each request or change within their teams.	Up-to-date documentation
In development	Once the sprint starts, the team proceeds to develop the requested feature or change, refines the LLD, and implements automated unit tests to verify that their component functions as intended.	Network configurations, scripts, source code, software releases, and so on Component LLD draft
Unit tests	Development has concluded, and final unit tests are expected to finalize the process shortly.	Component LLD release Automated unit tests Unit test results
Acceptance tests	Domain testers are responsible for verifying that the entire domain's functionality or updates operate as planned. They achieve this by designing and conducting acceptance tests, which are implemented in an automated fashion whenever it is economically feasible.	Automated acceptance tests Acceptance test results
Demo	Domain testers present a demonstration of the upcoming release to all members in the domain to showcase new features and gather feedback.	Early insight into an upcoming release

Stage	Description	Outcomes
Quality gate	The quality assurance manager reviews all component LLD updates, unit test results, acceptance test outcomes, and demo feedback and then consults with the product manager and component leads to assess whether the components are ready for release. If required, the quality assurance manager may request the removal of specific features or changes from the component releases that yield unsatisfactory results.	Domain release health assessment, with a continue/stop decision
Stakeholder testing	The release manager schedules a change window for the upcoming domain release and coordinates subsequent testing with friendly customers and affected partner domains.	Stakeholder feedback Acceptance test results
Quality gate	The quality assurance manager evaluates the results of stakeholder testing and, if necessary, may request refinement or removal of any features or changes from the component releases that do not meet expectations.	Domain release health assessment, with a continue/stop decision
Production rollout preparation	After the release manager collaborates with the operations manager to identify a suitable change window for the production rollout, the pre-production environment is upgraded a few days before the production rollout to conduct a final verification of the release in preparation for the production deployment. Note: While broader IT stack integration tests are commonly performed during this phase, this proposed process suggests that these tests are successfully completed much earlier, during the acceptance tests phase or, at the latest, as part of the stakeholder testing phase.	Acceptance test results
Quality gate	The quality assurance manager evaluates the results of stakeholder testing and, if necessary, may request refinement or removal of any features or changes from the component releases that do not meet the expectations.	Domain release health assessment, with a continue/stop decision
Production rollout	A change window applies the change in production.	Results of non-intrusive acceptance tests

The high-level overview provided is expected to be widely accepted, yet it lacks the required details concerning ownership, specifically who is accountable for a feature or change at different stages of the process. Additional details are required to equip teams with a precise understanding of their roles in delivering value and participating in the process. In accordance with the roles outlined earlier in this chapter, in the section "Domain Responsibilities and Their Architectural Implications," the example in Figure 11-15 offers a next level of detail, assigns clear ownership for each feature or change at every phase, and sets the stage for tooling solutions that can effectively illustrate the current status in the delivery process. This kind of visual representation is crucial for domain and team ceremonies, where leadership assesses progress and makes strategic interventions when needed.

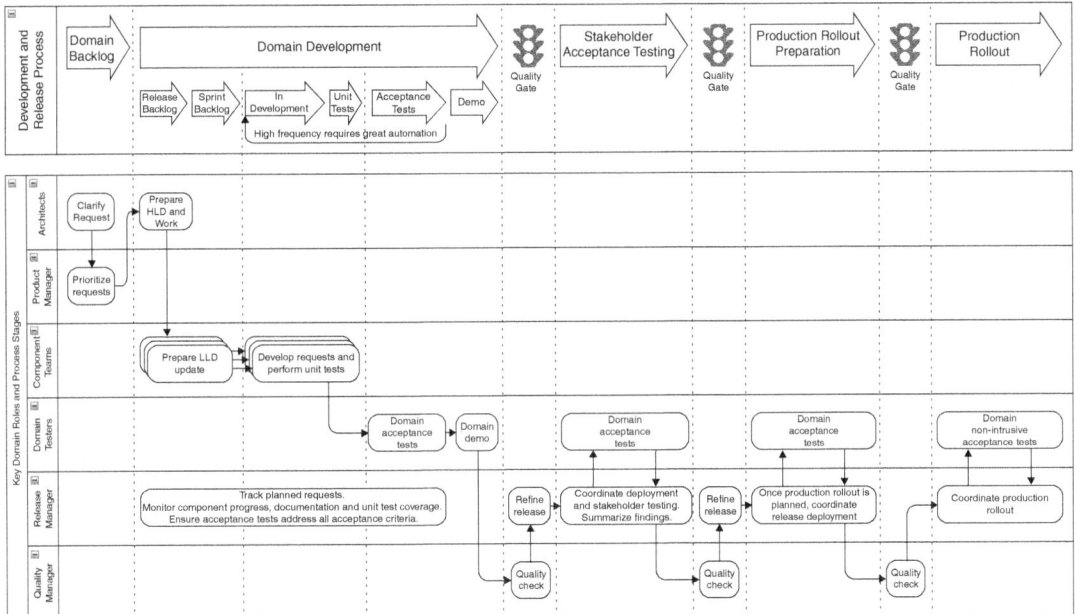

Figure 11-15   *Defining the Development and Release Process: The Next Level*

While ownership of a feature or change is clearly defined in this process, larger features may require the assembly of squads that bring together diverse roles and expertise. These squads aim to manage complex tasks and facilitate—or at least streamline—the transfer of ownership. This approach is further illustrated in Figure 11-13, in section "Domain Organization and Transformation."

Environments

Lab environments are instrumental in supporting the delivery methodology and its associated development and release processes. This section provides guidance on important considerations and acknowledges that not every suggested environment is mandatory in every case. Despite common management reservations about investing in additional lab environments, the insights from this section enable a clear articulation of the value and necessity of such investments during strategic discussions. There are circumstances in which advanced simulators for mobile network or satellite operators may be prohibitively expensive. In such cases, sharing testing resources across multiple lab environments may be the only feasible strategy. Nevertheless, even significant investments in multiple labs can rapidly yield returns through efficiency gains while reducing risks and issues.

Each phase of the development and release process maps to a corresponding environment, as illustrated in Figure 11-16.

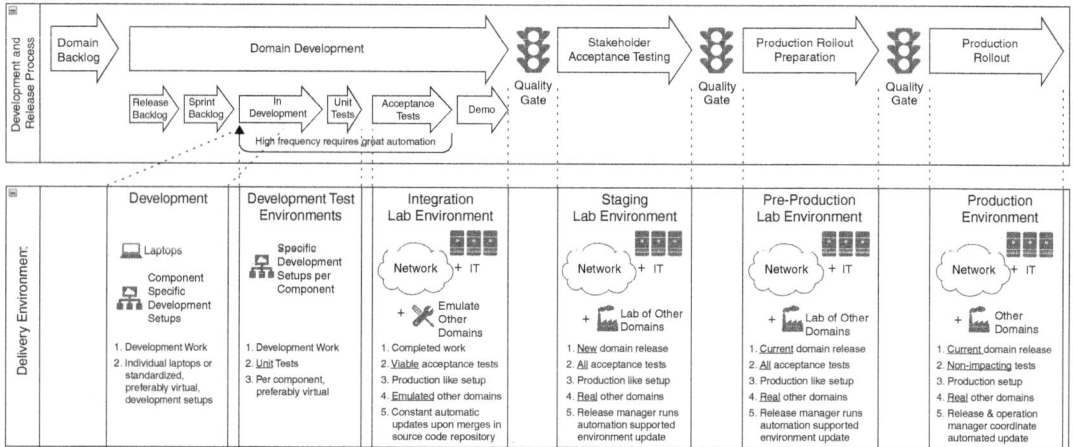

Figure 11-16 *Optimizing Flow: Key Environments for Development and Release Efficiency*

Considering the methodology principle "One lab design, built multiple times" outlined in Table 11-8 at the beginning of this section, network and IT architects work together to develop a well-defined lab design. This collaborative effort ensures consensus that the lab is a true representation of the production environment and supports the validation of all foreseeable acceptance criteria. Serving as the foundation for constructing the integration, staging, and pre-production lab environments, this unified design streamlines documentation and also optimizes environment administration and testing. It requires much less effort to automate the processes of building or reinitializing environments, as well as executing test cases and evaluating their results, when the automation is created just once and then applied across all environments. Moreover, this uniformity allows for the use of very similar, if not identical, test data and the near-identical setup of tooling, which together further accelerate the development process. A thorough exploration of what can be common may uncover additional advantages and opportunities for this approach to alleviate pain points and further boost organizational efficiency.

Table 11-10 summarizes the purpose and characteristics of the environments, as well as the potential impacts on a domain that chooses to omit one of these environments.

Table 11-10   *The Contribution of Each Environment and the Implications of Skipping One*

Environment	Purpose Summary and Description	Implications of Skipping
Development	Developers and network engineers have the option to create a personalized workspace for developing code and network configurations. Depending on the requirements, they can use their own laptops, a dedicated cloud service, or specialized lab infrastructure, particularly when access to real hardware is required.	Engineers commonly assert that bypassing the opportunity to test and develop in an isolated environment can significantly reduce their efficiency and effectiveness.
Development test	The output from developers and network engineers undergoes initial testing in an automated development test environment. Unit tests are run to verify that the developed code and configurations will support domain features or changes for the first time.	Engineering and development practices vary widely, with personalized development environments designed for individual efficiency and effectiveness often resulting in inconsistencies across and within teams. These can pose significant challenges during later component integration.
Integration	When developing a new domain release, it is essential to test tightly coupled components together both early and frequently.	Frequent integration testing of in-development components often disrupts the environment. Using later-stage environments for such testing requires pausing ongoing development when a domain release is subject to stakeholder testing, thereby hindering the development activities. Furthermore, there is a risk that stakeholders may observe instability during uncoordinated testing periods—even when they are not intended to access the environment—which could negatively affect the perceived quality of upcoming domain releases.

Environment	Purpose Summary and Description	Implications of Skipping
Staging	While engineering progresses using the previous environments, key stakeholders, such as friendly customers and other domains, perform testing against the candidate for an upcoming domain release in the staging environment. This testing determines whether the new release will have a positive, neutral or negative impact on the stakeholders.	If stakeholders are to use a prior environment to verify an upcoming release instead, engineering activities for future releases must be temporarily suspended. This is necessary because the integration environment needs to be updated to reflect the upcoming release and must be dedicated solely to verification efforts. Such measures are crucial to maintain stability and secure positive feedback from stakeholders. If, instead, stakeholders are to use the subsequent pre-production environment for verification, the situation becomes more complex. Updating this environment—which is crucial for in-depth analysis and reproduction of issues with the current domain release in production—would disrupt operations. It would also hinder the domain's ability to verify any hot fixes before deploying them into the production environment.

Environment	Purpose Summary and Description	Implications of Skipping
Pre-production	Friendly customers and other domains can use this environment to further develop their solutions and verify compatibility with the domain's current production release. In parallel, the operation teams use this isolated environment to diagnose and resolve issues encountered in production, as well as to rigorously test hot fixes, ensuring that they effectively rectify the problems before they are rolled out into the live production environment.	For stakeholders, customers, and other domains, the absence of this environment would force them to verify their own development progress against the production environment, which is often undesirable. For operations, there would be collision of interests when production issues need to be analyzed. Either the development work would need to halt in the integration environment, or the stakeholder verification of an upcoming release in the staging environment might need to be rescheduled. Either way, production issues hit the progress related to the engineering of an upcoming domain release, thereby frustrating everyone involved and requiring rescheduling to handle the encountered delay.
Production	The production environment runs the current domain release.	Skipping this environment is not an option.

Occasionally, additional lab environments are necessary. For instance, a demo lab may be essential for staff training sessions or for conducting proof of concepts (PoC). Dedicated integration labs can be particularly valuable in scenarios where partners are responsible for delivering major components to the domain's architecture, especially if their development process and release schedule do not easily align with those of the domain.

Table 11-11 summarizes the key factors to consider when preparing and constructing a suite of environments that effectively support the overall development and release process.

Table 11-11 *Considerations in Lab Environment Preparation and Construction*

Consideration	Description	Typical Owners
Lab blueprint	A blueprint is a common lab design that is used for constructing the integration, staging, and preproduction environments and that enables the verification of all foreseeable acceptance criteria.	Architects

Consideration	Description	Typical Owners
Lab automation	It is vital to embrace the automation first methodology principle, as detailed in Table 11-8, by implementing tools to automate acceptance testing in each lab environment. These are several examples of tools to consider:	Architects Domain managers Product managers DevOps engineers
	■ **Test automation framework:** Cisco's Customer Experience Test Automation Manager (CXTM), for instance, uses natural language for test definition, allowing non-developers to automate testing with ease. It delivers a consolidated view of different domains and their labs, features both an API and a web-based user interface, and is not tied to any specific vendor. In addition, it supports a wide variety of protocols—including REST, SOAP, and UI—for interactions with IT, network, and testing tools, and it offers extensibility to integrate seamlessly with various tools, such as those mentioned next.	
	■ **Fiber cut simulator:** Integrated into each network link under testing, this tool automates the verification of link failure impact by simulating fiber cuts and restorations via API calls.	
	■ **AC power switch:** This switch is used for controlling the power supply to components, allowing the simulation of power outages with API calls.	
	■ **DC power switch:** This is similar to an AC power switch but is typically more expensive to procure and install. This switch is specifically for shutting off DC-powered components.	
	■ **Traffic and protocol simulators:** These simulators are designed to generate a range of traffic loads and emulate various protocols. Some may allow you to mimic protocol misbehaviors for testing the system's responses and robustness. On the receiving end, delay, jitter, and packet loss can be measured, which enables the assessment of service quality and recovery time after a link or component failure.	
	■ **Fiber switch:** Embedded into links, this switch facilitates the simulation of field engineers rewiring an optical link from one device to another via an API call.	

Consideration	Description	Typical Owners
	Beyond test automation support tools, which are vital for managing high-volume, repetitive test cycles with consistent, reproducible outcomes and detailed test result reporting, additional tools exist to streamline and expedite the development and release process, including this type of tools:	
	■ **Environment initialization:** Tools that streamline the reinitialization and deployment of desired configurations, applications, and test data into environments enhance the consistency and reproducibility of acceptance test run results. Cisco's Customer Experience (CX) service team offers infrastructure as code (IaC) solutions that can be tailored to various needs.	
Naming and IP addressing concept	It is important to establish a solid naming and IP addressing scheme across all lab environments. Host name patterns should reflect the lab environment, designated by specific letters (for example, *d* for development, *i* for integration, *s* for staging, *pp* for pre-production, and *p* for production). While general IP addresses may remain identical throughout all lab environments, management IP addresses should be unique to each individual lab.	Architects Network engineers
Mapping to other domain labs	While a new domain, its IT, and its network infrastructure can be developed within the proposed lab environments, seamless interfacing and close collaboration with the labs of connected domains—and, where applicable, customers—are critical. Engaging in discussions to harmonize development and release methodologies is crucial. Clarifying the purpose of each lab environment, the types of releases deployed, and the nature of testing conducted aids in defining how to interconnect lab environments across domains and, potentially, with customers.	Architects
Lab investment	Obtaining the necessary budget to establish the desired lab environments requires comprehensive discussions within the management team to promote mutual recognition of the strategic value and long-term advantages of these labs. The domain manager and product manager work in tandem to secure the essential financial backing needed to build the envisioned lab setups.	Domain managers Product managers

Consideration	Description	Typical Owners
Migrating to the new development and release methodology	Domains transitioning from a setup with fewer lab environments require careful planning and budget for the expansion to the desired set of lab environments.	Domain managers Product managers
Migration tests	While the automation first methodology principle, as detailed in Table 11-8, promotes the automation of tests, applying this to migration use cases may not always be economically or practically justifiable. Fiber switches available on the market can facilitate API-driven simulations of field service workers rerouting optical fibers between device ports. However, the investment in automating these migration tests is warranted only if there is a significant volume of migrations.	Domain testers

With the environments clarified, the next section explains how changes to components leverage and flow through these environments.

Domain Releases: A Symphony of Component Builds and Release Candidates

Network engineers may adjust templates for network components, and software engineers may update source code or the binaries of the frameworks they use, introducing additional capabilities to collectively enhance the value of domain services. Figure 11-17 illustrates the convergence of three different components.

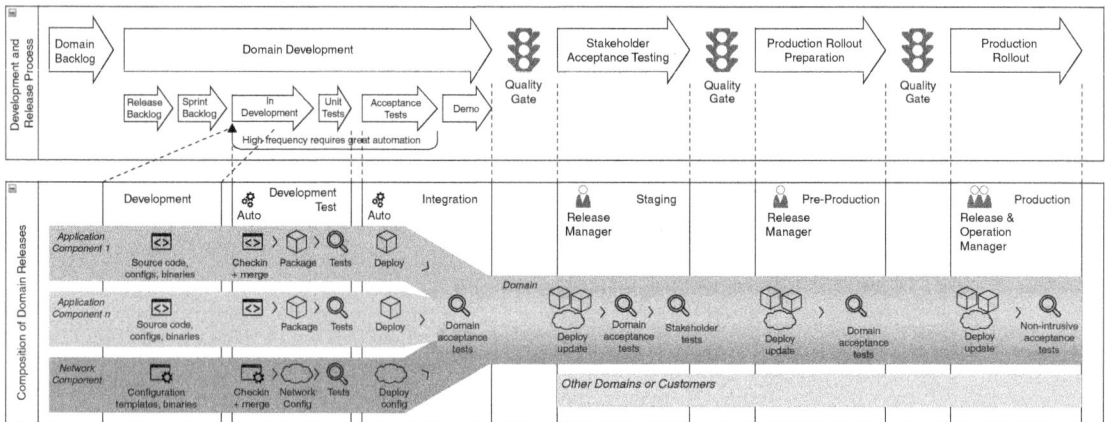

Figure 11-17   *Component Builds and Release Candidates Join Up to Domain Releases*

In the development environment, technology specialists define and customize components. When changes are committed to the source code repository, they trigger automation in the development test environment. This leads to the automated build and packaging of software applications or the updating of network components to match network configuration template changes. The process includes component-specific unit tests to confirm their contribution to the domain's expected features.

After network and software engineers validate their work through unit test results and deem their components functional, they merge their changes with what others may work on for the upcoming release. This merge triggers another round of development test environment automation, assembling application components and updating network configurations, followed by a fresh set of unit tests. The integration environment automation then recognizes this upcoming release preparation type of output from the development test environment and installs it to run comprehensive acceptance tests on all components within the domain, ensuring that the domain's services function as intended. Domain test engineers define and automate these tests in parallel with component development.

Upon successful acceptance testing, the teams may agree that there is sufficient value to move a step further towards production by producing release candidate builds for all components. As with previous builds, the release candidates undergo unit tests in the development test environment and acceptance tests in the integration environment before they become available for stakeholder testing. Once all testing has passed, the release manager coordinates a maintenance window and testing schedule with external domains and friendly customers to validate the upcoming domain release and its individual component release candidates in the staging environment. If stakeholders encounter no significant issues, the release and operations manager schedule a change window for production deployment. Prior to this deployment, the pre-production environment receives an update, setting the stage for the final update to the production environment.

Tooling: Embracing Automation for Environment and Process Efficiency

Development and release automation is not represented by a single pipeline but rather by multiple pipelines, each customized for a specific process phase and environment. Figure 11-18 presents an overview of the key delivery automation functions, each aligned with the specific purposes of the delivery environments within the domain.

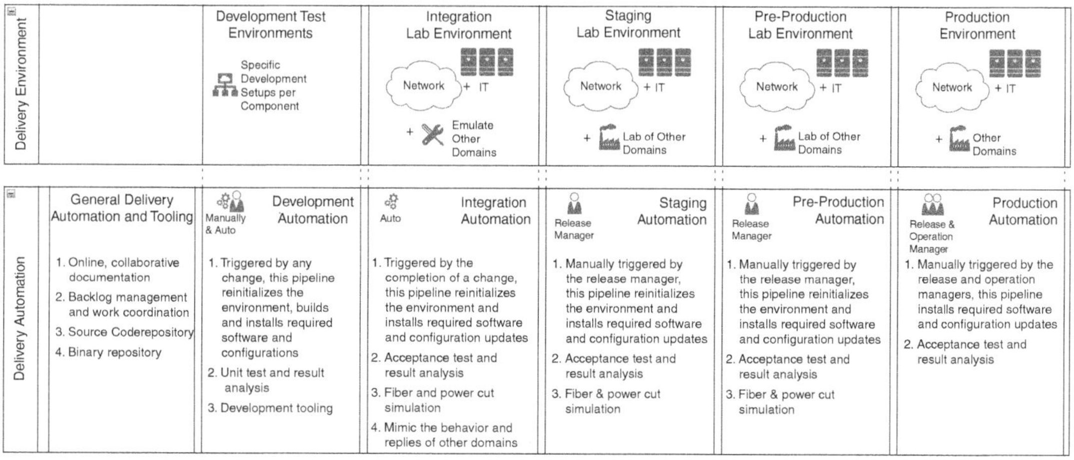

Figure 11-18 *Delivery Automation*

The following sections provide an overview of a selection of the automation tools mentioned in Figure 11-18.

Tooling: Source of Truth

A common repository should serve as the definitive source of truth for all source code, scripts, customizations for application components, configuration templates for network components, and automations for acceptance tests that verify domain services. If a change is not present in the source code repository, it is not part of the component, and it is not part of the domain's solution. The previous section demonstrated how various components are developed and tested individually before they are integrated and tested thoroughly. But how do you understand or determine whether a change is incorporated into this set of environments and associated automation? The answer again lies in the source code repository. Such a repository manages multiple versions of the same source code, script, and so on, allowing concurrent work and facilitating the merging of changes from different contributors once their work is complete. This is supported by a concept involving branches, which is depicted in Figure 11-19, where branches are created for various purposes and represent different engineering stages.

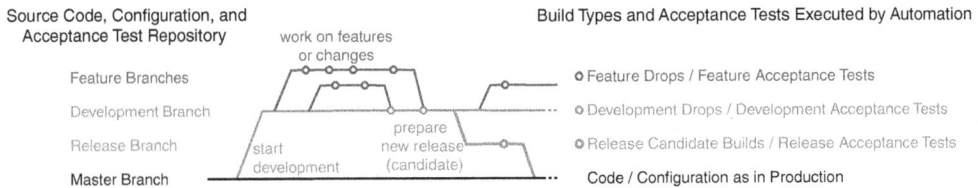

Figure 11-19   *Source Code Repository: Synchronizing Work on Configurations, Code, and Tests*

The master branch typically reflects what is currently deployed in the production environment. When initiating work on a new release, a development branch is spawned. Team members then branch off to create feature branches for specific features or changes. When changes are pushed to the source code repository, the development test environment automation tools, called *development pipelines*, spring into action. These component-specific pipelines manage tasks such as code quality analysis, and they build, package, and deploy software applications, or they update network configurations. After all these tasks, they initiate unit testing and automated analysis and reporting of results. This activity is depicted in Figure 11-20 for two components: Component 1 and Component n.

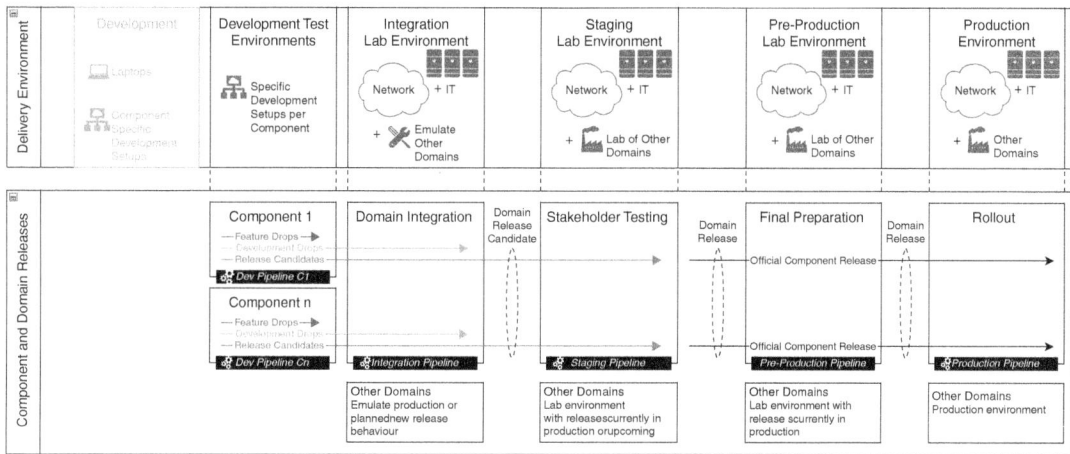

Figure 11-20 *Mapping Branches to Environments*

Once work is completed and a feature drop has successfully passed all unit tests, the team can merge changes back into the development branch, confirming the completion of the feature or change. This merge triggers the development automation pipeline again. It builds and packages application-type development drops or updates network configurations in the development test environment. However, this package is distinct from previous feature drops, signaling to the integration pipeline, once the development pipeline completes, that the package is based on the development branch and is ready for integration and acceptance testing with all domain components in the integration environment.

When a set of development drops is deemed ready for production, each component team creates a release branch. This branch allows for final adjustments, thorough documentation, and tagging of the release candidate in preparation for the domain release.

Domain testers follow a similar process with their test automation, branching off to integrate new feature and change-related test updates, ensuring that the domain's acceptance criteria are met. Working on tests activates both the development and integration automation pipelines, as described earlier. The resulting builds and development acceptance test results form the baseline for the quality assurance manager to authorize the release manager to proceed with stakeholder tests.

After the release candidates pass stakeholder and acceptance tests in the staging environment, the quality assurance manager approves them for production deployment. At this time, they may be elected as official component releases for the domain. Component teams then tag the release drop in the source code repository accordingly and merge the release branch into the master branch. Following this, the release and operations manager work in tandem to schedule the deployment into the production environment and into the pre-production environment a few days prior.

Table 11-12 provides an overview with guidance and examples on how to name the branches in a source code repository.

Table 11-12 *Considerations for Source Code Repositories*

Consideration	Description	Typical Owners
Branch naming	**Master branch:** Commonly, this branch is named *master* and reflects what is currently deployed in the production environment.	IT architects Component leads
	Development branch: Some may prefer a new development branch to be created for each development cycle. Others prefer a persistent branch named *development*, used continuously over the years.	
	Feature branch: The names of feature branches should correspond to the features or work items listed in a planning and scheduling tool, incorporating the identifiers used within that tool. An example would be feature-SR-1234-NewFeatureX.	
	Release branch: A release branch is typically named after the upcoming planned release version it represents, with distinctions made between major (1.x to 2.x), minor (1.1.x to 1.2.x), and bug fix (1.1.1 to 1.1.2) types of updates. For instance, a branch might be named release-1.1.3.	
Consistency	Coordinating efforts within a domain becomes more manageable when the following elements are standardized across all components: ■ Branch naming conventions ■ Source code repository structures (where applicable)	IT architects Component leads

Now that there is clarity on how to store and maintain source code, scripts, configurations, and more, it is time to review how binary-type artifacts are handled.

Tooling: Binary Repository

Development, engineering, and automation tools depend on and produce a variety of artifacts that require secure storage. Typical artifacts include software and libraries used in application development, as well as builds and packages generated by the dev pipeline. A binary repository is ideally suited for this task, offering a centralized location where all automation pipelines can store and retrieve binary files. Table 11-13 provides an overview of key aspects to consider when using a binary repository in a domain.

Table 11-13 *Considerations for Binary Repositories*

Consideration	Description	Typical Owners
Package naming	**Feature drops:** The names of feature drops should directly relate to the feature or work item entries in project management tools, including the associated identifiers and the commit ID that initiated the build. An example naming convention is *<component name>-<feature branch name>-<YYYYMMDD>-<BuildId>*.zip, leading to package names such as network_configuration-feature-SR-1234-New-FeatureX-20240331-01.zip.	IT architects Component leads
	Development drops: Packages resulting from merges or commits to the development branch must be named to clearly reflect the state at the time of creation. A possible naming convention is *<component name>-<development branch name>-<YYYYMMDD>-<BuildId>*.zip, resulting in package names like network_configuration-development-20240331-01.zip.	
	Release candidate drops: These packages are named to correspond with the targeted release version, differentiating between major (1.x to 2.x), minor (1.1.x to 1.2.x), and bug fix (1.1.1 to 1.1.2) updates. An example naming convention could be *<component name>-<release branch name>-<YYYYMMDD>-<BuildId>*.zip, which would produce package names like network_configuration-release-1.1.0-20240331-01.zip.	
Consistency	Coordinating efforts within a domain becomes more manageable when the following elements are standardized across all components: ■ Package naming conventions ■ Binary repository structures (where applicable)	IT architects Component leads

With the storage and maintenance of software images, libraries, and other binary files clarified, the next step is to examine their integration into the automation landscape.

Tooling: Pipelines

Armed with insights from the earlier section "Process with a Clear Flow" and an understanding of the supporting environments, you are now in a position to more effectively allocate automation tasks to pipelines. This strategic alignment ensures that the inputs and outputs of automation efforts support the roles of team members in every process phase.

Pipelines (refer to Figure 11-20) should consider the following purpose and key aspects:

- **Environment specific:** Define pipelines per environment.

- **Clear hand-offs:** Describe the pipeline input parameters and the pipeline outputs that may serve as inputs to the next environment's pipeline. Define and agree on the transient data to be retained for planning and quality management purposes, such as enabling comparisons of acceptance test results with those from previous test iterations.

- **Quality outputs:** Optimize outputs to accelerate quality gate reviews and change board decisions.

- **Different pipeline triggers:** While some pipelines are triggered automatically (for example, check-ins of new source code, automated test case, or new router configuration), others are activated manually (for example, release manager ensuring stability in the staging and pre-production environments and only triggering the pipeline during a change window that has been agreed upon with stakeholders).

Table 11-14 provides a high-level overview of the tasks performed by each pipeline.

Table 11-14 *An Overview of Automation Pipelines*

Pipeline Name	Number of Instances	Trigger	Main Tasks	Key Outputs
Development test	One per component	Source code, script, configuration, test case, or any other change occurs in the source code repository.	1. Package the component (for example, zip all network configurations or build an application package). 2. Perform code security analysis for software application type components. 3. Unit test the component. 4. Communicate to relevant stakeholders.	1. Binary artifacts 2. Unit test results
Integration	One for the entire domain	The development test pipeline uploads a development or a release candidate built into the binary repository.	1. Update environment with desired packages and configurations. 2. Execute acceptance tests. 3. Communicate to relevant stakeholders.	1. Binary artifacts 2. Acceptance test results

Pipeline Name	Number of Instances	Trigger	Main Tasks	Key Outputs
Staging	One for the entire domain	The release manager identifies the specific component releases for deployment and manually initiates the staging pipeline, possibly through a user-friendly interface that displays recently tested combinations of release candidate packages in the integration environment.	1. Update environment with desired packages and configurations. 2. Execute acceptance test. 3. Communicate to relevant stakeholders.	1. Binary artifacts 2. Acceptance test results
Pre-production	One for the entire domain	The release manager identifies the specific component releases for deployment and manually initiates the pre-production pipeline, possibly through a user-friendly interface that displays recently tested combinations of release candidate packages in the staging environment.	1. Update environment with desired packages and configurations. 2. Execute acceptance test. 3. Communicate to relevant stakeholders.	1. Binary artifacts 2. Acceptance test results
Production	One for the entire domain	The release and operation manager identify the specific component releases for deployment and manually initiate the production pipeline, possibly through a user-friendly interface that displays recently tested combinations of release candidate packages in the pre-production environment. There may be further options where the pipeline may begin with updating pilot production sites in a first run.	1. Update environment with desired packages and configurations. 2. Conduct non-intrusive acceptance tests that do not generate garbage data or impact the service's performance. 3. Communicate to relevant stakeholders.	1. Binary artifacts 2. Production acceptance test results

Pipelines could automatically notify relevant stakeholders, as Table 11-15 suggests.

Table 11-15 *Enhancing Transparency and Process Efficiency with Pipeline Notifications*

Development Test Pipeline	Integration Pipeline	Staging Pipeline	Pre-Production Pipeline	Production Pipeline
Engineers receive immediate feedback on the impact of their updates in the source code repository, whether positive or negative. Component leads are kept informed about the latest changes and statuses.	Engineers receive immediate feedback on the impact of their updates in the source code repository, whether positive or negative. Component leads are kept informed about the latest changes and statuses. Project managers monitor the progress of large features or significant changes through pipeline notifications.	Release managers keep track of the domain release deployment and testing progress. Quality assurance managers use the details in pipeline notifications to oversee and ensure the quality standards of the planned domain release.	Release managers keep track of the domain release deployment and testing progress. Quality assurance managers use the details in in pipeline notifications to oversee and ensure the quality standards of the planned domain release.	Release managers keep track of the domain release deployment progress. Operations managers stay informed about domain release rollout progress through pipeline notifications.

Change Management Across Domains

Transforming an organization requires careful management, as the shift described in this chapter inevitably raises numerous questions and a great deal of uncertainty that must be addressed and managed effectively. It is sensible to establish a dedicated governance team responsible for overseeing the transformation from an organizational and technical perspective, serving as a central point of contact for any inquiries, concerns, or suggestions.

Maintaining daily operations while undergoing a significant transformation presents a considerable challenge. This is why it is often beneficial to bring in external experts—individuals experienced with similar transitions, network architects and engineers knowledgeable about new SR technologies being introduced, or IT architects who can provide fresh perspectives. These professionals can assist in determining the optimal target solution and provide extra capacity to handle the high workload that arises from simultaneously running the current business, defining the new solution, and orchestrating the migration from the current state to the desired state.

Change management should address the following key considerations from an organizational perspective as well as a technical perspective:

- Prepare
  - Assess what to change and the impact it will have.
  - Create the target architecture.
  - Build a business case for the investment.
  - Identify stakeholders and determine their roles and responsibilities.
- Plan
  - Create a plan that outlines the steps required to achieve the change.
  - Map out the steps to the target architecture.
  - Define success metrics and how they will be measured.
  - Establish a communication strategy to keep everyone informed.
  - Identify and mitigate potential risks and resistance.
- Implement
  - Enable leadership to drive and support the change.
  - Communicate the change effectively at all levels of the organization.
  - Maintain focus and avoid implementing numerous changes simultaneously.
  - Train and equip employees with the skills and knowledge they need.
- Manage
  - Support employees through the transition by providing clear directions.
  - Address concerns and feedback.
  - Monitor the progress of the change.
  - Promote the change with rewards, recognitions, and success stories.
- Sustainability
  - Embed the change into the organization's culture and practices.
  - Continue to improve and refine.

Figure 11-21 provides an example for discussion when defining a change governance team. A core team, primarily comprising members from domains most affected by the SR transformation, will typically handle the majority of tasks and meet frequently. In addition, they will run regular alignment sessions with an extended change governance team that includes representatives from less affected neighboring domains.

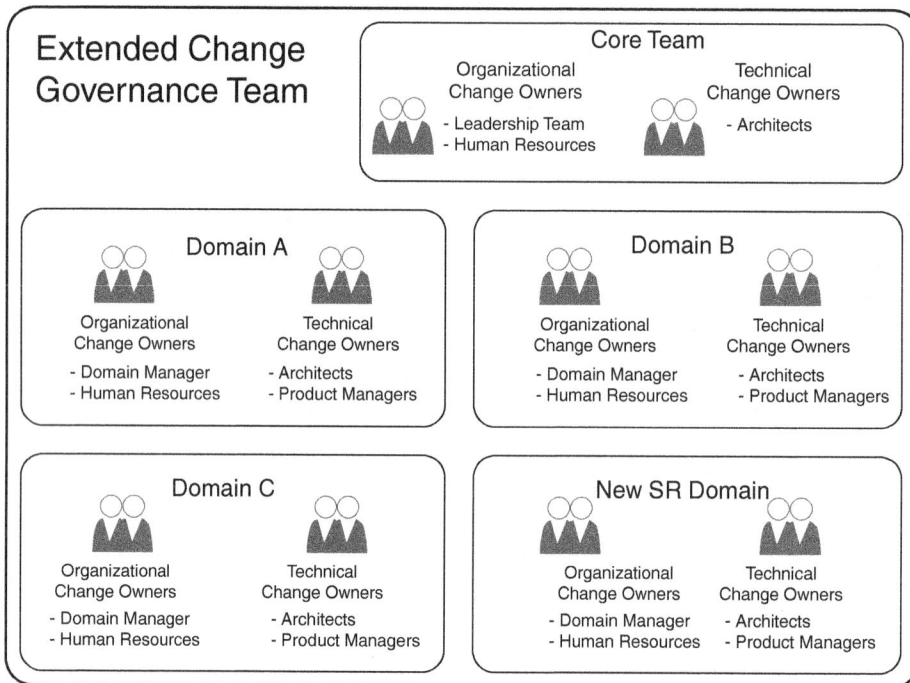

Figure 11-21 *Streamlining the Transformation with a Dedicated Change Governance Team*

Ultimately, change management is about people. Successfully guiding and equipping individuals to navigate change requires empathy, clear communication, and the ability to adapt to distinct circumstances. These elements are essential for a successful transformation and the realization of organizational goals.

Summary

This chapter outlines organizational considerations in two scenarios: Scenario 1, where segment routing (SR) is introduced as a new technology to replace or enhance an existing IP transport network, and Scenario 2, where SR is deployed to consolidate various networks, services, and teams. The generic examples provided here can be tailored to the specific situation, terminology, and preferences of a network service provider. They help to prevent the oversight of critical elements and support the multi-year transformation to SR, particularly in the complex context of Scenario 2.

Introducing SR presents an excellent opportunity to modernize the legacy network and IT infrastructure. Developing an architectural blueprint for the SR domain is crucial for identifying the necessary actions. It is essential to strike the right balance between being cautious—making no changes or only minimal ones to ensure continuity and minimize resistance among affected teams—and being assertive in implementing significant changes. A change governance team with broad support can assess this balance, justify and advocate for bold changes, and govern their implementation. This approach ultimately secures the business case and leads to an optimal reduction in operational expenses.

References and Additional Reading

Knowledge

- Cisco Live conferences, www.ciscolive.com
- Cisco trainings, www.cisco.com/go/training
- Cisco professional services, www.cisco.com/go/services

IT Evolution and Gap Awareness

- Cisco Crosswork Network Services Orchestrator, https://www.cisco.com/go/nso

Reference Diagrams and Information

The reference networks in this appendix serve various sections throughout the book. Centralizing this information helps avoid repetitive explanations across different chapters.

SR-MPLS Reference Network

Figure A-1 shows the SR-MPLS reference network, which is a foundational framework for executing configuration tasks necessary for building and troubleshooting L3VPN services.

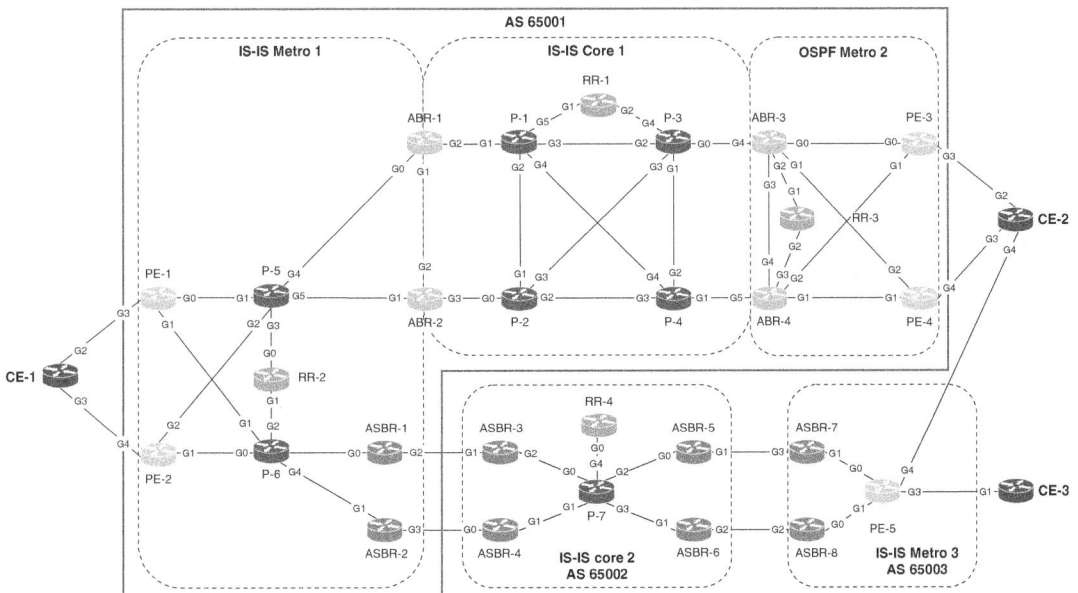

Figure A-1 *SR-MPLS Reference Network*

Naming and addressing details for the SR-MPLS reference network are listed in Table A-1.

Table A-1   *SR-MPLS Reference Network Nodes*

Domain	Host Name	Management IP	IS-IS NSAP	IPv4 Loopback	SR-MPLS SID
Core 1	P-1	192.168.1.11/24	49.0001.0001.0000.0001.00	10.0.1.1/32	16001
Core 1	P-2	192.168.1.12/24	49.0001.0001.0000.0002.00	10.0.1.2/32	16002
Core 1	P-3	192.168.1.13/24	49.0001.0001.0000.0003.00	10.0.1.3/32	16003
Core 1	P-4	192.168.1.14/24	49.0001.0001.0000.0004.00	10.0.1.4/32	16004
Core 1	ABR-1	192.168.1.15/24	49.0001.0001.0000.0005.00	10.0.1.5/32	16005
Core 1	ABR-2	192.168.1.16/24	49.0001.0001.0000.0006.00	10.0.1.6/32	16006
Core 1	ABR-3	192.168.1.17/24	49.0001.0001.0000.0007.00	10.0.1.7/32	16007
Core 1	ABR-4	192.168.1.18/24	49.0001.0001.0000.0008.00	10.0.1.8/32	16008
Core 1	RR-1	192.168.1.19/24	49.0001.0001.0000.0254.00	10.0.1.254/32	16254
Core 2	P-7	192.168.1.21/24	49.0002.0002.0000.0001.00	10.0.2.1/32	17001
Core 2	ASBR-3	192.168.1.22/24	49.0002.0002.0000.0002.00	10.0.2.2/32	17002
Core 2	ASBR-4	192.168.1.23/24	49.0002.0002.0000.0003.00	10.0.2.3/32	17003
Core 2	ASBR-5	192.168.1.24/24	49.0002.0002.0000.0004.00	10.0.2.4/32	17004
Core 2	ASBR-6	192.168.1.25/24	49.0002.0002.0000.0005.00	10.0.2.5/32	17005
Core 2	RR-4	192.168.1.26/24	49.0002.0002.0000.0254.00	10.0.2.254/32	17254
Metro 1	PE-1	192.168.1.111/24	49.0003.0003.0000.0001.00	10.0.3.1/32	18001
Metro 1	PE-2	192.168.1.112/24	49.0003.0003.0000.0002.00	10.0.3.2/32	18002
Metro 1	P-5	192.168.1.113/24	49.0003.0003.0000.0003.00	10.0.3.3/32	18003
Metro 1	P-6	192.168.1.114/24	49.0003.0003.0000.0004.00	10.0.3.4/32	18004
Metro 1	ASBR-1	192.168.1.115/24	49.0003.0003.0000.0005.00	10.0.3.5/32	18005
Metro 1	ASBR-2	192.168.1.116/24	49.0003.0003.0000.0006.00	10.0.3.6/32	18006
Metro 1	ABR-1	N/A	49.0003.0003.0000.0007.00	N/A	N/A
Metro 1	ABR-2	N/A	49.0003.0003.0000.0008.00	N/A	N/A
Metro 1	RR-2	192.168.1.117/24	49.0003.0003.0000.0254.00	10.0.3.254/32	18254
Metro 1	CE-1	192.168.1.118/24	N/A	N/A	N/A
Metro 2	PE-3	192.168.1.121/24	49.0004.0004.0000.0001.00	10.0.4.1/32	19001

Domain	Host Name	Management IP	IS-IS NSAP	IPv4 Loopback	SR-MPLS SID
Metro 2	PE-4	192.168.1.122/24	49.0004.0004.0000.0002.00	10.0.4.2/32	19002
Metro 2	RR-3	192.168.1.123/24	49.0004.0004.0000.0254.00	10.0.4.254/32	19254
Metro 2	CE-2	192.168.1.124/24	N/A	N/A	N/A
Metro 3	PE-5	192.168.1.131/24	49.0005.0005.0000.0001.00	10.0.5.1/32	20001
Metro 3	ASBR-7	192.168.1.132/24	49.0005.0005.0000.0002.00	10.0.5.2/32	20002
Metro 3	ASBR-8	192.168.1.133/24	49.0005.0005.0000.0003.00	10.0.5.3/32	20003
Metro 3	CE-3	192.168.1.134/24	N/A	N/A	N/A

SRv6 Reference Network

Figure A-2 shows the SRv6 reference network, which is an essential framework for carrying out configuration tasks required for building and troubleshooting both EVPN-based L2VPN and L3VPN services.

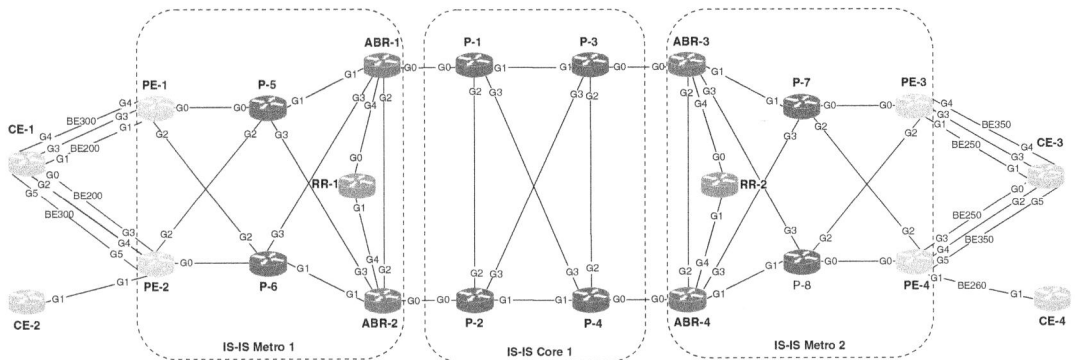

Figure A-2 *SRv6 Reference Network*

Note   CE routers CE-1 and CE-3 have multiple interfaces connecting to their PE routers. These additional interfaces were added to accommodate various configuration combinations, as the CE routers support both L2VPN and L3VPN services.

Table A-2 provides naming and addressing details for the SRv6 reference network.

Table A-2   *SRv6 Reference Network Nodes*

Domain	Host Name	Management IP	IS-IS NSAP	IPv6 Router Loopback	SRv6 Locator
Core 1	P-1	172.19.0.2	49.0000.0000.0000.0001.00	fc00:0:1::1/128	fc00:0:1::/48
Core 1	P-2	172.19.0.3	49.0000.0000.0000.0002.00	fc00:0:2::1/128	fc00:0:2::/48
Core 1	P-3	172.19.0.4	49.0000.0000.0000.0003.00	fc00:0:3::1/128	fc00:0:3::/48
Core 1	P-4	172.19.0.5	49.0000.0000.0000.0004.00	fc00:0:4::1/128	fc00:0:4::/48
Metro 1	ABR-1	172.19.0.6	49.0001.0001.0000.0001.00	fc00:0:101::1/128	fc00:0:101::/48
Metro 1	ABR-2	172.19.0.7	49.0001.0001.0000.0002.00	fc00:0:102::1/128	fc00:0:102::/48
Metro 1	P-5	172.19.0.8	49.0001.0001.0000.0003.00	fc00:0:103::1/128	fc00:0:103::/48
Metro 1	P-6	172.19.0.9	49.0001.0001.0000.0004.00	fc00:0:104::1/128	fc00:0:104::/48
Metro 1	PE-1	172.19.0.10	49.0001.0001.0000.0005.00	fc00:0:105::1/128	fc00:0:105::/48
Metro 1	PE-2	172.19.0.11	49.0001.0001.0000.0006.00	fc00:0:106::1/128	fc00:0:106::/48
Metro 1	RR-1	172.19.0.12	49.0001.0001.0000.0007.00	fc00:0:107::1/128	fc00:0:107::/48
Metro 1	CE-1	172.19.0.13	N/A	N/A	N/A
Metro 1	CE-2	172.19.0.14	N/A	N/A	N/A
Metro 2	ABR-3	172.19.0.15	49.0002.0002.0000.0001.00	fc00:0:201::1/128	fc00:0:201::/48
Metro 2	ABR-4	172.19.0.16	49.0002.0002.0000.0002.00	fc00:0:202::1/128	fc00:0:202::/48
Metro 2	P-7	172.19.0.17	49.0002.0002.0000.0003.00	fc00:0:203::1/128	fc00:0:203::/48
Metro 2	P-8	172.19.0.18	49.0002.0002.0000.0004.00	fc00:0:204::1/128	fc00:0:204::/48
Metro 2	PE-3	172.19.0.19	49.0002.0002.0000.0005.00	fc00:0:205::1/128	fc00:0:205::/48
Metro 2	PE-4	172.19.0.20	49.0002.0002.0000.0006.00	fc00:0:206::1/128	fc00:0:206::/48
Metro 2	RR-2	172.19.0.21	49.0002.0002.0000.0007.00	fc00:0:207::1/128	fc00:0:207::/48
Metro 2	CE-3	172.19.0.22	N/A	N/A	N/A
Metro 2	CE-4	172.19.0.23	N/A	N/A	N/A

SR Migration Reference Network

Figure A-3 shows the SR migration reference network, which is a framework for performing configuration tasks crucial for transitioning services from SR-MPLS to SRv6.

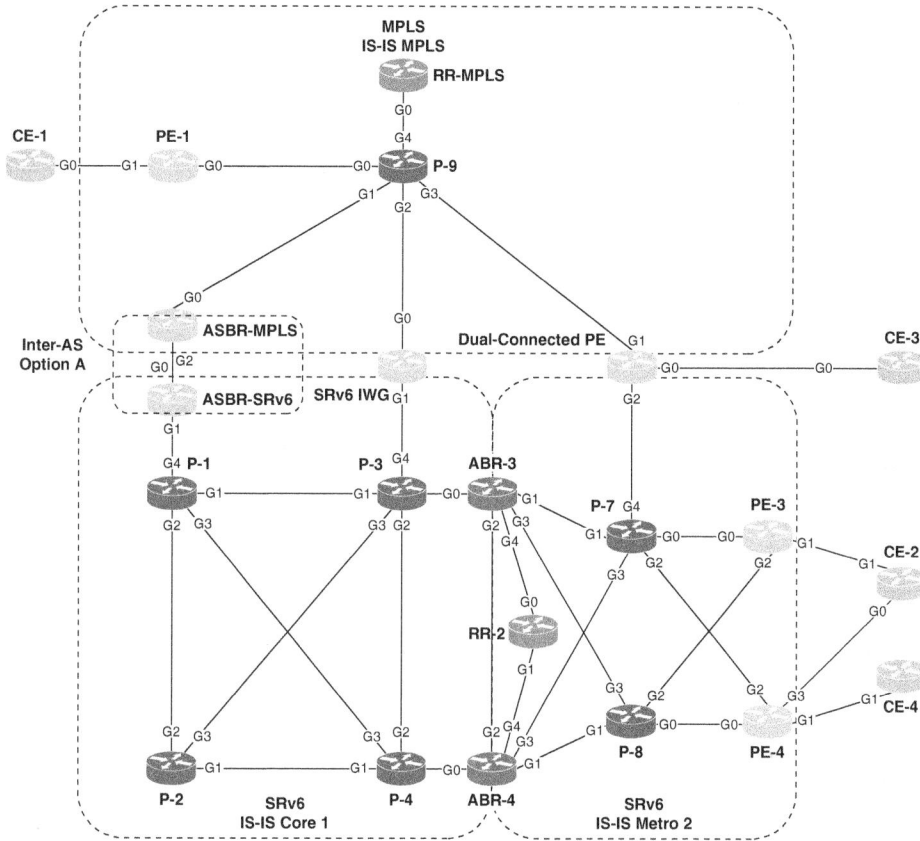

Figure A-3 *SR Migration Reference Network*

Naming and addressing details for the SR migration reference network are shown in Table A-3.

Table A-3 *SR Migration Reference Network Nodes*

Domain	Host Name	Management IP	IS-IS NSAP	IPv4 Loopback/ IPv6 Loopback	SR-MPLS SID/ SRv6 Locator
Core 1	P-1	172.19.0.2	49.0000.0000.0000.0001.00	fc00:0:1::1/128	fc00:0:1::/48
Core 1	P-2	172.19.0.3	49.0000.0000.0000.0002.00	fc00:0:2::1/128	fc00:0:2::/48
Core 1	P-3	172.19.0.4	49.0000.0000.0000.0003.00	fc00:0:3::1/128	fc00:0:3::/48
Core 1	P-4	172.19.0.5	49.0000.0000.0000.0004.00	fc00:0:4::1/128	fc00:0:4::/48
Core 1	ASBR-SRv6	172.19.0.24	49.0000.0000.0000.0007.00	fc00:0:7::1/128	fc00:0:7::/48

Domain	Host Name	Management IP	IS-IS NSAP	IPv4 Loopback/ IPv6 Loopback	SR-MPLS SID/ SRv6 Locator
Core 1 Mpls	SRv6-IWG	172.19.0.25	49.0001.0001.0000.0008.00	10.0.0.8/32 fc00:0:8::1/128	16008 fc00:0:8::/48
Metro 2 Mpls	Dual-Connected PE	172.19.0.26	49.0002.0002.0000.0009.00	10.0.0.9/32 fc00:0:209::1/128	16009 fc00:0:209::/48
Metro 2	ABR-3	172.19.0.15	49.0002.0002.0000.0001.00	fc00:0:201::1/128	fc00:0:201::/48
Metro 2	ABR-4	172.19.0.16	49.0002.0002.0000.0002.00	fc00:0:202::1/128	fc00:0:202::/48
Metro 2	P-7	172.19.0.17	49.0002.0002.0000.0003.00	fc00:0:203::1/128	fc00:0:203::/48
Metro 2	P-8	172.19.0.18	49.0002.0002.0000.0004.00	fc00:0:204::1/128	fc00:0:204::/48
Metro 2	PE-3	172.19.0.19	49.0002.0002.0000.0005.00	fc00:0:205::1/128	fc00:0:205::/48
Metro 2	PE-4	172.19.0.20	49.0002.0002.0000.0006.00	fc00:0:206::1/128	fc00:0:206::/48
Metro 2	RR-2	172.19.0.21	49.0002.0002.0000.0007.00	fc00:0:207::1/128	fc00:0:207::/48
Metro 2	CE-3	172.19.0.22	N/A	N/A	N/A
Metro 2	CE-4	172.19.0.23	N/A	N/A	N/A
MPLS	P-9	172.19.0.27	49.0001.0001.0000.0007.00	10.0.0.7/32	16007
MPLS	PE-1	172.19.0.29	49.0001.0001.0000.0001.00	10.0.0.1/32	16001
MPLS	RR-MPLS	172.19.0.28	49.0001.0001.0000.0003.00	10.0.0.3/32	16003
MPLS	ASBR-MPLS	172.19.0.30	49.0001.0001.0000.0006.00	10.0.0.6/32	16006

Index

Symbols

* wildcard, 1112

A

ABR (area border router), 5, 38, 39, 224
acceptance test, 1085, 1087
active-active mode, 425
active-backup mode, 426
address family, BGP, 84
adjacency, IS-IS, verification, 265–266
adjacency segment, 226
Adjacency SID, 47–49, 226
Adj-SID sub-TLV, 59–61, 68–69
algorithm. *See also* Flex Algo
  operator-defined, 74–75
  SPF (Shortest Path First), 56, 73–74, 220
Angstrom era, ONLINE
anycast, set, 219
anycast SID, 45, 47, 219
  SR-MPLS, 254–255
    configuration, 254–256
    verification, 256–257
  SRv6, 270–271

configuration, 271
use case, 272–282
verification, 272
architecture, SPRING, 40–41
area
  IS-IS, 222
  OSPF, 224
ASBR (autonomous system border router), 5, 20
assembler code, 34–35
assurance, intent-/model-based, 1019–1020. *See also* service assurance
automation, 1065, 1097–1098
  pipeline, 1098, 1101–1104
  solution lifecycle, 1067
  test, 1094

B

backup path, 19
base format, 108
BD (bridge domain), 447
BFD (Bidirectional Forwarding Detection), 857–859. *See also* BLB (BFD over Logical Bundle); BoB (BFD over Bundle)

async mode, 859–860

BLB, 861

    configuration, 872–874

    packet capture, 863–865

    verification, 874–883

BoB, 861

    configuration, 865–868

    packet capture, 863

    verification, 868–871

demand mode, 859

echo, 859–860

over LAG interfaces, 860

packet capture, 861–862

SH (single-hop) sessions, 860–861

BG (bridge group), 447

BGP. *See also* **MP-BGP (Multiprotocol Border Gateway Protocol)**

address families, 84

-free core, 1

L3VPN, Flex Algo, 318–322

Link-State Extensions for SRv6, 201–205

MP_REACH_NLRI path attribute, 608–609

multiprotocol, 17

NHT (next hop tracking), 220

operational complexity, 22

PIC (Prefix Independent Convergence), 292–293

PIC Edge, 945–948

    multipath verification, SRv6, 981–995

    unipath configuration, SR-MPLS, 948–951

    unipath configuration, SRv6, 962–970

    unipath verification, SR-MPLS, 951–962

    unipath verification, SRv6, 970–981

Prefix SID, 324, 609–610

    configuration, 324–326

    enabling in an SR-MPLS network, 376–383

    verification, 327–328

protocol ID, 96

proxy Prefix SID, 383–387

RR (route reflector), 6

UPDATE message, 83–84, 86–87, 96–98, 186, 187–188, 190, 191, 203–204

    for SRv6 L2 services, 192–193

    for SRv6 L3 services, 194–195, 196–198

BGP Link-State extensions for SR, 87–95

BGP Peering SID, 50–52

BGP Prefix SID, 49–50, 85–87

BGP-LU (BGP Labeled Unicast), 220

inter-AS, 343

    configuration, 344–345

    data forwarding, 349–350

    design, 343

    verification, 345–348

intra-AS

    design, 330

    with Prefix SID, 328–330

binary repository, 1100–1101

Binding Segment SID, 52–53

BLB (BFD over Logical Bundle), 860, 861

configuration, 872–874

packet capture, 863–865

verification, 874–883

BoB (BFD over Bundle), 860, 861

configuration, 865–868

packet capture, 863

verification, 868–871

broadcast domain, EVPN, 444

brownfield deployment, 354

coexistence migration strategy, 356–357

IPv6 backhaul strategy, 356–357

SR-MPLS, 358–360

    enabling and preferring on P1, P2, and PE-1, 363–365

enabling on P2, P3, and PE-3,
    360–363

BVLAN (BFD over VLAN over Bundle),
    860

C

CCM (Continuity Check Message), 809–
    810

CE (customer edge) router, 5, 6

CFM (Ethernet Connectivity Fault
    Management), 808

    CCM (Continuity Check Message),
        809–810

    configuration, 811–812

    Linktrace Protocol, 811

    Loopback Protocol, 810

    MA (maintenance association), 808

    MD (maintenance domain), 808

    MEP (maintenance endpoint), 808–809

    MIP (maintenance intermediate point),
        809

    PDUs, 809

    verification, 813–816

change management, 1104–1106

CI/CD/CT (continuous integration/
    continuous delivery/continuous
    testing), 1101

Cilium, ONLINE

CML (Cisco Modeling Lab), ONLINE

code, assembler, 34–35

coexistence brownfield strategy, 356–357

collision, label, 43

command/s

    containerlab deploy, ONLINE

    containerlab inspect, ONLINE-ONLINE

    debug lacp packets, 483

    help sr localsid, ONLINE-ONLINE

    hw-module, 240

    hw-module bfd-hw-offload enable
        location, 867

microloop avoidance rib-update-delay
    5000, 942–943

pcap trace, ONLINE-ONLINE

ping, 249, 254, 270, 349, 423, 635, 676,
    767, ONLINE-ONLINE, ONLINE-
    ONLINE, ONLINE-ONLINE,
    ONLINE-ONLINE, ONLINE-
    ONLINE

ping ethernet cfm domain service, 815

segment-routing mpls sr-prefer, 361

service vpp status, ONLINE-ONLINE

service vpp stop, ONLINE-ONLINE

show bfd ipv6 session, 868–869

show bfd ipv6 session interface bundle-
    Ether 1 detail, 869

show bfd ipv6 session interface TF0/0/0/0
    detail, 870–871

show bfd neighbors, 877

show bfd neighbors interface port-
    channel 1 details, 877–878

show bfd session, 875

show bfd session interface bundle-ether 1
    detail, 875–876

show bgp ipv4 labeled-unicast, 347, 348,
    377–378, 379–381, 713, 740–741

show bgp ipv4 rt-filter, 771, 774

show bgp ipv4 rt-filter neighbors,
    774–775

show bgp ipv4 unicast, 328, 348,
    713–714

show bgp ipv4 vpn, ONLINE-ONLINE

show bgp l2vpn evpn bridge-domain,
    446, 521–522, 525–527, 537, 540,
    549–550, 568–569

show bgp l2vpn evpn bridge-domain
    200-BD, 527–529

show bgp l2vpn evpn bridge-domain
    200-BD received-sids wide, 523–524

show bgp l2vpn evpn bridge-domain
    VPWS:300, 594–599

show bgp l2vpn evpn rd, 458–461, 464,
    467–469, 470, 523, 601

show bgp l2vpn evpn route-type, 530

show bgp l2vpn evpn route-type
    ethernet-segment, 530–532, 600

show bgp l2vpn evpn summary, 518–519

show bgp segment-routing srv6,
    ONLINE-ONLINE

show bgp summary, ONLINE-ONLINE

show bgp vpnv4 uni vrf, ONLINE-
    ONLINE

show bgp vpnv4 unicast, 741–742

show bgp vpnv4 unicast advertised
    summary, 408–409

show bgp vpnv4 unicast vrf, 626,
    628–630, 646–647, 649–650,
    651–652, 655, 659–661, 663,
    667–668, 670, 673–674, 702–703,
    704–705, 705–706, 733–735,
    758–759, 760, 951–953, 954,
    958–960, 971–973, 976–977,
    982–984, 989–990

show bgp vpnv4 unicast vrf local-sids,
    627, 647–648, 663–664, 671

show bgp vpnv4 unicast vrf received-sids,
    627–628, 648, 664, 671

show bgp vrf, 276, 320–321, 409–410,
    420–421

show bgp vrf nexthop-set, 634, 650, 667

show bgp vrf-db table, 566–567, 656

show bgp vrf-db table all, 519–521, 594

show bpg vpnv4 unicast vrf, 665–666

show bundle bundle-Ether 200, 478, 484

show bundle bundle-Ether 250, 481, 482

show bundle bundle-Ether 300, 575–576

show cef, 887–888, 892–893, 898–899,
    926

show cef detail, 714–715, 716, 717–718,
    743, 744–745, 747, 748, 749–750

show cef ipv6, 904–905, 908–909,
    912–913, 937–940, 942

show cef ipv6 detail, 980–981, 993–994

show cef vrf, 276, 279

show cef vrf detail, 632–633, 654,
    669–670, 675, 709–711, 738, 764,

766, 955–957, 960–962, 974–975,
    979, 986–988, 991–992

show ethernet cfm local meps domain
    service, 813

show ethernet cfm peer meps domain
    service, 814–815

show ethernet sla operations detail
    profile, 820–821, 827–828

show ethernet sla statistics brief profile,
    821–823, 829–830

show ethernet sla statistics detail profile,
    823–825, 831–834

show evpn ethernet-segment, 494, 580

show evpn ethernet-segment interface
    BE200 carving detail, 496–498

show evpn ethernet-segment interface
    BE300 carving detail, 581–582

show evpn ethernet-segment interface
    Bundle-Ether260 detail, 538–539

show evpn evi, 498, 583–584

show evpn evi ead, 584–585

show evpn evi inclusive-multicast detail,
    502–503

show evpn evi vpn 200 mac, 501–502

show evpn evi vpn 205 mac, 560–561

show evpn evi vpn-id 200 detail,
    499–500

show evpn summary, 493–494

show interfaces brief, 477–478, 483,
    574–575, ONLINE-ONLINE

show ip cef detail, 715, 717, 718, 744,
    745–746, 749

show ip cef internal, 889–890, 894–895,
    900–901, 930–931

show ip cef vrf, ONLINE-ONLINE

show ip cef vrf detail, 711, 739, 765, 957

show ip ospf database, 234

show ip route repair-paths, 888–889, 893,
    899–900, 928, 954–955

show ip route vrf, 737, 762

show ip route vrf repair-paths, 709

show ipsla statistics 11, 843–844

show ipsla statistics 21, 844–846

show ipsla statistics aggregated 11, 846–847

show ipsla statistics aggregated 21, 847–850

show ipsla twamp session, 854

show ipv6 cef, ONLINE-ONLINE

show ipv6 route isis, ONLINE-ONLINE

show isis adjacency, 265–266

show isis database, 233, 247, 265, 272, 288, 291, 299, 309–310

show isis fast-reroute summary, 884

show isis fast-reroute ti-lfa tunnel, 894, 900, 929

show isis flex-algo, 308

show isis ipv4 fast-reroute detail, 887, 892, 898, 904, 918, 925, 927–928, 933–934, 934

show isis ipv6 fast-reroute detail, 908, 912

show isis neighbor, ONLINE-ONLINE

show isis rib, 929–930

show isis srv6 locators det, ONLINE-ONLINE

show l2vpn bridge-domain bd-name 200-BD detail, 508–510

show l2vpn bridge-domain bd-name detail, 563–565

show l2vpn bridge-domain brief, 508, 511, 544

show l2vpn forwarding bridge-domain ELAN-BG:200-BD mac-address location 0/RP0/CPU0, 510–511

show l2vpn forwarding bridge-domain ELAN-BG:210-BD mac-address location 0/RP0/CPU0, 545

show l2vpn forwarding xconnect detail location, 591

show l2vpn mac-learning, 512

show l2vpn mac-learning mac all location, 511

show l2vpn xconnect group VPWS-XC, 589–591

show lacp, 479–480, 576–577

show lacp bundle-Ether 250, 481, 482

show memif, ONLINE-ONLINE

show mpls forwarding, 362, 364, 374

show mpls oam dpm adjacency, 797

show mpls oam dpm prefix, 797

show mpls oam dpm summary, 795–796

show route, 891, 896–897, 917–918, 924–925

show route 10.0.1.8/32, 886–887

show route ipv6, 280–281, 282, 289, 290, 291–292, 300, 311–312, 903–904

show route ipv6 detail, 906–907, 911–912

show route vrf, 278

show route vrf detail, 631–632, 653–654, 668–669, 674–675, 708, 736, 761, 762–763, 973–974, 977–978, 985–986

show segment-routing srv6 capabilities-parameters, ONLINE-ONLINE

show segment-routing srv6 locator, ONLINE-ONLINE, ONLINE-ONLINE

show segment-routing srv6 locator MAIN detail, ONLINE-ONLINE

show segment-routing srv6 locator MAIN sid, 513–514, 546–547

show segment-routing srv6 sid, 503–504, 586, ONLINE-ONLINE, ONLINE-ONLINE

show segment-routing srv6 sid detail, 633, 634–635, 656

show segment-routing traffic-eng policy, 274–275

show slrg name, 932

show sr localsids, ONLINE-ONLINE, ONLINE-ONLINE

show sr policies, ONLINE-ONLINE

show sr steering-policies, ONLINE-ONLINE

show trace, ONLINE-ONLINE, ONLINE-ONLINE, ONLINE-ONLINE

systemctl restart frr, ONLINE-ONLINE

traceroute, 249, 312, 342, 362–363, 364–365, 375–376, 382, 383, 412, 423, 645, 677, 718–719, 750–751, 767

traceroute ethernet cfm domain service, 816

compiler, 34

Containerlab, ONLINE-ONLINE

Linux SRv6 lab deployment, ONLINE-ONLINE

topology definition, ONLINE, ONLINE-ONLINE

containerlab deploy command, ONLINE

containerlab inspect command, ONLINE-ONLINE

CONTINUE operation, 41

control plane, 10, 87–88

MPLS, 205–207

show isis database, 257

SR-MPLS, 207–209, 243–244

SRv6, 209–210, 257

traceroute, 254

VPP (Vector Packet Processor), ONLINE-ONLINE

converged SR domain, 1083

development and release process, 1084–1086

environments, 1089–1096

key phases, 1086–1089

service portfolio consolidation, 1083–1084

convergence, 878–879. *See also* Microloop Avoidance

calculating, 858

failure event detection time, 858

IPFRR (IP Fast Reroute), 878–881

microloops, 935

network event information propagation time, 858

RIB/FIB update time, 858

RLFA (Remote Loop-Free Alternate), 880–882

topology update and repair path computation time, 858

CPU (central processing unit), 33, 35, ONLINE

ISA (instruction set architecture), 35

program counter, 35

CSC MPLS network migration, 434–435

D

DARPA (Defense Advanced Research Projects Agency), 28

data plane, 10

MPLS, 205–207

segment routing, 36–37

SONiC (Software for Open Networking in the Cloud), ONLINE

SR-MPLS, 41–42, 207–209

SRv6, 209–210

VPP (Vector Packet Processor), ONLINE-ONLINE

database, label switching, 43, 44. *See also* FIB (Forwarding Information Base); RIB (Routing Information Base)

debug lacp packets command, 483

deployment model

brownfield, 354

greenfield, 354

dev pipeline, 1098

development and release process, 1084

automation, 1097–1098

domain releases, 1096–1097

key phases, 1086–1089

lab environments, 1089–1096

testing, 1097

development test, 1091

Dijkstra SPF algorithm, 224

disaggregation, SONiC (Software for Open Networking in the Cloud), ONLINE-ONLINE

domain, 1043. *See also* converged SR domain

architecture blueprint, 1059–1061

API gateway and graphical user interface, 1061–1062

apps and microservices, 1065

error and event handling, 1066

inventories, 1063–1064

messaging, 1066

network resources, 1065

resource fulfillment, 1064

rollout and migration automation, 1064–1065

security measures and events, 1066

service and resource assurance, 1062–1063

service catalog, 1063

service orchestration, 1064

solution lifecycle automation, 1067

workflow automation engine, 1065

workforce and customer apps, 1066

availability of components as shared services by other domains, 1070

boundaries, 1056–1058, 1059

component criticality, 1069

component sourcing, 1071–1074

converged SR, 1083

development and release methodology, 1084–1086

service portfolio consolidation, 1083–1084

key roles, 1075–1082

organization and transformation, 1074–1075

recommendations for components, 1070–1071

responsibilities, 1067–1069

SAP (service access point), 1058–1059

segment routing, 38

squads, 1082

teams, 1082–1083

downstream on-demand, 11

DPDK, ONLINE-ONLINE

dual-homed greenfield strategy, 356

E

ECMP (equal-cost multipath), 25, 38, 798–800

EFP (Ethernet flow point), 447

E-LAN, 472–473

port-active multihomed service

access circuit configuration, 474–477

access circuit verification, 477–484

BGP configuration, 514–518

BGP verification, 518–533

EVPN configuration, 484–491

EVPN verification, 491–504

L2VPN configuration, 504–507

L2VPN verification, 507–514

route types and usage, 473

single-homed service, 533–534

BGP configuration, 520–547

BGP verification, 547–551

EFP configuration, 534–535

EFP verification, 535

EVPN configuration, 535–536

EVPN verification, 536–542

L2VPN configuration, 542–543

L2VPN verification, 543–547

E-Line

all-active BGP

configuration, *591–593*

verification, 593–601

all-active EFP (access circuit)

configuration, 571–574

verification, 574–577

all-active EVPN

configuration, 577–579

verification, 579–586

all-active L2VPN

configuration, 586–588

verification, 588–591

BGP route types and usage, *570–571*

End behavior, SRv6, **113–114**

End.B6.Encaps behavior, **142–143**

End.B6.Encaps.Red behavior, **143–144**

End.B6.Insert behavior, **144–145**

End.B6.Insert.Red behavior, **145–146**

End.DT2M behavior, SRv6, **122–123**

End.DT2U behavior, SRv6, **120–121**

End.DT4 behavior, SRv6, **116–117**

End.DX2 behavior, SRv6, **119**

End.DX4 behavior, SRv6, **117–118**

endpoint behaviors, **141**

SID (segment identifier), 1113

SRv6 policy, 141, 146

uSID (micro SID), 149–150

endpoint node, **126**

endpoint/egress node, **38**

end-to-end QoS, MPLS (Multiprotocol Label Switching), **21–22**

End.X behavior, SRv6, **114–115**

EPE (egress peer engineering), **41**

ES (Ethernet segment), **445, 447–449**

ESI (Ethernet segment identifier), **445, 449–450**

Ethernet CFM (Connectivity Fault Management). *See* CFM (Ethernet Connectivity Fault Management)

Ethernet OAM (Operations, Administration, and Maintenance), **806–807**

Ethernet tag ID, **450–452**

EVC (Ethernet virtual circuit), **447**

EVI (EVPN instance), **444, 445–447**

EVPN (Ethernet VPN), **212, 215, 440–441**

aliasing, 444

benefits, 443–444

BGP routes, 452–454

broadcast domain, 444

E-LAN, 472–473

port-active MHD BGP configuration, 514–518

port-active MHD BGP verification, 518–533

port-active MHD EVPN configuration, 484–491

port-active MHD EVPN verification, 491–504

port-active MHD L2VPN configuration, 504–507

port-active MHD L2VPN verification, 507–514

port-active multihomed service, 474–484

route types and usage, 473

SHD BGP configuration, 520–547

SHD BGP verification, 547–551

SHD EFP configuration, 534–535

SHD EFP verification, 535

SHD EVPN configuration, 535–536

SHD EVPN verification, 536–542

SHD L2VPN configuration, 542–543

SHD L2VPN verification, 543–547

single-homed service, 533–534

E-Line

all-active BGP configuration, 591–593

all-active BGP verification, 593–601

all-active EFP configuration, 571–574

all-active EFP verification, 574–577

all-active EVPN configuration, 577–579

all-active EVPN verification, 579–586

all-active L2VPN configuration, 586–588

all-active L2VPN verification, 588–591

BGP route types and usage, 570–571

ES (Ethernet segment), 445, 447–449

ESI (Ethernet segment identifier), 445, 449–450

Ethernet tag ID, 445, 450–452

E-Tree, 551–552

BGP configuration, 565

BGP verification, 565–569

EFP (access circuit) configuration, 553–555

EFP (access circuit) verification, 555–556

EVPN configuration, 556–559

EVPN verification, 559–561

L2VPN configuration, 561–563

L2VPN verification, 563–565

EVI (EVPN instance), 445–447

MAC VRF instance, 444

MEF 6.3, 441–442

Route Type 1

per-ESI Ethernet A-D route, 454–458

per-EVI Ethernet A-D route, 458–463

Route Type 2, 463–466

Route Type 3, 467–469, 512

Route Type 4, 470–472

VLAN services interfaces, 451–452

EVPN VPWS, 191–192, 199–200

extranet L3VPN

over SR-MPLS

configuration, 752–756

verification, 756–767

over SRv6

configuration, 657

verification, 662–677

F

F3216 format, 148

failure event detection time, 858

FEC (forwarding equivalence class), 11

FIB (Forwarding Information Base), 10

pre- and post-failure entries, 936–942

update time, 858

flat MPLS network migration, 429–430

Flex Algo, 73–78, 1005–1007

assigning to a BGP L3VPN service, 318–322

calculation of a path, 303

definition, 302

definition advertisement, 302

disjoint paths, 312–313

configuration, 313–315

verification, 315–318

installation of forwarding entries, 303

link attribute advertisement, 302–303

low-latency path, 304–305

configuration, 305–308

verification, 308–312

metrics, 78

prefix metric, 303

SID advertisement, 303

SR-MPLS configuration, 322–324

sub-sub-TLVs, 79–83

use cases, 304

Flexible Algorithm Definition sub-TLV, 78–79

Flow Label field, IPv6 header, 104–106

forwarding plane, 10

FRR (Fast Reroute), 18–19, 41, 858

FRR (Free Range Routing), ONLINE-ONLINE

    daemons, ONLINE-ONLINE

    IPv4 L3VPN service, ONLINE-ONLINE

    release 9.1, ONLINE-ONLINE

    SRv6 headend and endpoint support, ONLINE-ONLINE

    system architecture, ONLINE

    vytish, ONLINE-ONLINE

full-mesh L3VPN

    over SR-MPLS

        BGP label allocation modes, 701

        configuration, 689–700

        verification, 701–719

    over SRv6

        BGP configuration on PE-2, 624–625

        configuration, 610–622

        full-mesh verification, 625–636

        SRv6 configuration, 623–624

        VRF and interface configuration, 622

G

GRE over L3VPN, 26

greenfield deployment, 354

    dual-homed migration strategy, 356

    interworking migration strategy, 355–356

    SR-MPLS, 365

        BGP proxy Prefix SID, 383–387

        enabling LDP on the border node, 372–376

        enabling SRMS, 365–372

        enabling the BGP Prefix SID, 376–383

    SRv6

        building a new network using an IWG, 389–401

        building a new network using dual-connected PE devices, 413–424

        building a new network using inter-AS Option A, 401–413

GUA (global unicast address), 162, 164

H

hash, n-tuple, 25

headend behaviors, 132

header

    IPv6, 104

        Flow Label field, 104–106

        Next Header field, 106

        Traffic Class field, 104

    MPLS, 6–7

    segment routing, 36–37, 106–107, 125–127. *See also* SRH (segment routing header)

        fields, 124–125

        Penultimate Segment Pop, 127–128

        Ultimate Segment Pop, 129

        USD (Ultimate Segment Decapsulation), 130–132

help sr localsid command, ONLINE-ONLINE

H.Encaps behavior, 132–133

H.Encaps.L2 behavior, 135

H.Encaps.L2.Red behavior, 136–137

H.Encaps.Red behavior, 133–135

high-availability, 425, 857–858. *See also* BFD (Bidirectional Forwarding Detection); FRR (Fast Reroute); LFA (Loop-Free Alternate); TI-LFA

(Topology-Independent Loop-Free Alternate)

active-active, 425

active-backup, 426

BFD (Bidirectional Forwarding Detection), 857–859

    async mode, 859–860

    BLB, 861

    BoB, 861, 863

    demand mode, 859

    echo, 859–860

    over LAG interfaces, 860

    packet capture, 861–862

    SH (single-hop) sessions, 860–861

FRR (Fast Reroute), 858

LFA (Loop-Free Alternate), 879–880

load sharing, 426

TI-LFA (Topology-Independent Loop-Free Alternate), 883

high-level programming language, 33–34

high-precision probing, 1020–1023

H.Insert behavior, 138–140

hub-and-spoke L3VPN

  over SR-MPLS

    configuration, 719–732

    verification, 732–751

  over SRv6

    configuration, 636–645

    verification, 645–657

hw-module bfd-hw-offload enable location command, 867

hw-module command, 240

I

IGP (interior gateway protocol), 10

  link-state. *See* IS-IS; OSPF (Open Shortest Path First)

  PCE (path computation element), 211

  Prefix SID, 45–47

segments, 36

summarization, 220

IMIX (Internet Mix), ONLINE

integration test, 1080, 1091

intent-driven configuration, 1018

intent-/model-based assurance, 1019–1020

inter-AS BGP-LU, 341–342, 343

  configuration, 344–345

  data forwarding, 349–350

  design, 343

  verification, 345–348

inter-AS routing, 21

  Option A, 401–413

  Option C, 431–433

interface, loopback, 163–164

interface loopback address, SRv6, 237–238

interworking greenfield strategy, 355–356

intra-AS BGP-LU

  BGP Additional Path feature, 331–332

  configuration, 332–337

  design, 330

  with Prefix SID, 328–330

  verification, 337–341

IOS XE, 251–253

  advertising the BGP Prefix SID, 326

  assigning Prefix SID to Loopback0, 231

  BGP-LU session on ASBR-3, 344

  configuring anycast SID, 256

  enabling segment routing, 230

  enabling segment routing for IS-IS, 246

  enabling segment routing for OSPF, 250

  SR-MPLS IS-IS verification, 247–248

  verifying Prefix SID assignment, 236

  verifying the advertisement of the anycast SID, 257

IOS XR

  advertise the SRv6 locator, 307

advertising the BGP Prefix SID, 326

assigning an SRv6 locator to flex algo 128, 307

assigning link delay, 307

assigning Prefix SID to Loopback0, 231

BGP-LU session on ASBR-1, 344

Cisco EVC framework, 446–447

configuring anycast SID, 255–256

configuring anycast SRv6 locator on P-3, 271

configuring IS-IS on ABR-1, 263

configuring IS-IS on P-1, 262–263

configuring IS-IS on PE-1, 263–264

configuring IS-IS on RR-1, 264–265

enabling segment routing, 230

enabling segment routing for IS-IS, 246

enabling segment routing for OSPF, 250

enabling SRv6, 240

enabling UPA processing, 298

increasing the maximum number of UPAs, 297

modifying the UPA lifetime, 296

prefix tagging for UPA generation, 297

propagating UPAs from IS-IS to Level 1, 298

selectively generating UPAs, 297

SR-MPLS IS-IS verification, 247

SR-MPLS OSPF verification, 250–251

SRv6-TE policy and traffic steering using color, 273–274

summary route advertisement, 286

summary route for flex algo 128, 308

suppressing default route generation, 286

UPA announcement, 296

verifying Prefix SID assignment, 235

verifying the advertisement of the anycast SID, 257

IoT (Internet of things), 37

IP (Internet Protocol), 28

IPFRR (IP Fast Reroute), 878–881

iproute2, ONLINE-ONLINE, ONLINE, ONLINE, ONLINE-ONLINE

IPSLA, 834

configuration, 836–843

verification, 843–851

IPv6

backhaul brownfield strategy, 356–357

GUA (global unicast address), 162, 164

header

Flow Label field, 104–106

Next Header field, 106

Traffic Class field, 104

LLA (link local address), 162, 164–165

ULA (unique local address), 162

ISA (instruction set architecture), 35

IS-IS. See also SR-MPLS, IS-IS; SRv6, IS-IS

areas, 222

extensions for segment routing (RFC 8667), 53–54

Adj-SID sub-TLV, 59–61

Flex Algo sub-sub-TLVs, 79–83

LAN-Adj-SID sub-TLV, 61

Prefix-SID sub-TLV, 57–59

Router Capability TLV, 54–57

Segment Routing Algorithm sub-TLV, 55–56

SID/Label Binding TLV, 61–62

SID/Label sub-TLV, 63–64

SRLB sub-TLV, 56–57

extensions for SRv6, 175–176

segment routing over IPv6 capabilities, 180–183

segment routing over IPv6 locator, 176–180

SIDs, 183–186

levels, 222

LSP (label switched path), 179–180

overload bit, 223

route leaking, 223

route propagation, 223

router types, 222

routing, 222

verifying Prefix SID assignment, 235

ITU-T Y.1731 Performance Measurement

delay and jitter measurement

configuration, 818–820

verification, 820–825

SLM (synthetic loss measurement), 816

configuration, 826–827

verification, 827–834

L

L2VPN, 3, 27. *See also* **EVPN (Ethernet VPN)**

pseudowire, 11–12

service assurance, 806–807

CFM (Ethernet Connectivity Fault Management), 808–816. See also CFM (Ethernet Connectivity Fault Management)

ITU-T Y.1731 Performance Measurement. See ITU-T Y.1731 Performance Measurement

L3VPN, 2, 605–606

extranet

over SR-MPLS, configuration, 752–756

over SR-MPLS, verification, 756–767

over SRv6, 656

over SRv6, configuration, 657–662

over SRv6, verification, 662–677

Flex Algo, 318–322

full-mesh, over SR-MPLS

BGP label allocation modes, 701

configuration, 689–700

verification, 701–719

full-mesh, over SRv6

BGP configuration on PE-2, 624–625

configuration, 610–622

SRv6 configuration, 623–624

verification, 625–636

VRF and interface configuration, 622

GRE over, 26

hub-and-spoke, over SR-MPLS

configuration, 719–732

verification, 732–751

hub-and-spoke, over SRv6, 636

configuration, 636–645

verification, 645–657

interoperability, ONLINE-ONLINE

Cisco Catalyst 8000V Edge IPv4 L3VPN service, ONLINE-ONLINE

FRR IPv4 L3VPN service, ONLINE-ONLINE

over SR-MPLS, 677–679

configuration, 679–685

verification, 686–688

over SRv6, 608

BGP Prefix SID path attribute, 609–610

MP_REACH_NLRI path attribute, 608

NLRI, 608

service assurance, 834, 847–850

IPSLA, 834. See also IPSLA

TWAMP, 835–836. See also TWAMP (Two-Way Active Measurement Protocol); TWAMP Light

lab environment, 1089–1093

development, 1096–1097

preparation and construction, 1093–1096

label/s, 1, 7–9

allocation, 12–13

-based forwarding, 15–16

collisions, 43

POP operation, 14

PUSH operation, 14

service, 14, 16

space limitation, 20–21

SWAP operation, 14

LAG (link aggregation group), 25, 105

LAN-Adj-SID sub-TLV, 61

LDP (Label Distribution Protocol), 1, 12.
   See also **mLDP**

downstream on-demand, 11

enabling on the border node, 372–376

ID, 11

-IGP synchronization, 24

label/s

   allocation, 12–13

   -based forwarding, 15–16

   service, 14, 16

   space limitation, 20–21

neighbor discovery, 11–12

unsolicited downstream, 11

legacy network. *See also* **domain**

replacing or enhancing with SR

   IT evolution and gap awareness,
      1051–1056

   migration strategy, 1049–1051

   required knowledge and expertise,
      1046–1049

SR consolidation, 1056–1074

LER (label edge router), 5

levels, IS-IS, 222

LFA (Loop-Free Alternate), 878–880

LFIB (Label Forwarding Information
   Base), 10

Linktrace Protocol, 811

Linux SRv6/Linux kernel, ONLINE-
   ONLINE

Containerlab topology definition,
   ONLINE-ONLINE

hardware offloading, ONLINE-ONLINE

lab deployment, ONLINE-ONLINE

   Containerlab, ONLINE-ONLINE

   Layer 3 overlay services, ONLINE

   Linux IPv4 L3VPN service,
      ONLINE-ONLINE

   Linux IPv4/IPv6 L3VPN service,
      ONLINE-ONLINE

   Linux IPv6 L3VPN service,
      ONLINE-ONLINE

   Linux point-to-point L2VPN
      service, ONLINE-ONLINE

   overlay services VPN-1, ONLINE-
      ONLINE

   overlay services VPN-2, ONLINE-
      ONLINE

   overlay services VPN-3, ONLINE-
      ONLINE

   underlay connectivity, ONLINE-
      ONLINE

   underlay domain transport,
      ONLINE-ONLINE

network stack, ONLINE-ONLINE

RPD (routing policy database), ONLINE-
   ONLINE, ONLINE-ONLINE

SRv6 endpoint support, ONLINE-
   ONLINE

SRv6 headend support, ONLINE-
   ONLINE

SRv6 overlay services configuration,
   ONLINE-ONLINE

uA/End.X (NEXT-CSID) endpoint
   behavior, ONLINE

LLA (link local address), 162, 164–165

load sharing, 426

locator addressing scheme, SRv6,
   165–169

large-scale deployments, 170–172

small- and medium-scale deployments,
   169–170

uSID, 238–239

loopback interface, 163–164

Loopback Protocol, 810

LSA (link-state advertisement), 224

LSD (label switching database), 43, 44

LSP (label switched path), 21

   echo request packet, 790–791

   IS-IS, 179–180

   labels, 380

LSR (label switch router), 5

M

MA (maintenance association), 808

MAC VRF instance, 444

MCD (Midpoint Compressed Data), 800–801

MD (maintenance domain), 808

MEF (Metro Ethernet Forum), 441–442

message/s

   BGP Route Target Constraint, 770

   BGP UPDATE, 83–84, 86–87, 96–98, 186, 187–188, 190, 191, 203–204

      for SRv6 L2 services, 192–193

      for SRv6 L3 services, 194–195, 196–198

   SR-MPLS DPM syslog, 798

methodology, 1084

metrics, Flex Algo, 78

Microloop Avoidance, 935, 942–943

   local protection, 935–940

   remote protection, 940–941

microloop avoidance rib-update-delay 5000 command, 942–943

microloops, 935

migration test, 1096

migration to segment routing, 353–354. *See also* brownfield deployment; greenfield deployment

   coexistence brownfield strategy, 356–357

   deployment models

      brownfield, 354

      greenfield, 354

   dual-homed greenfield strategy, 356

   interworking greenfield strategy, 355–356

   IPv6 backhaul brownfield strategy, 356–357

   MPLS to SRv6, 427–429

      CSC MPLS network, 434–435

      flat MPLS network, 429–430

      MPLS network with inter-AS option C, 431–433

      unified MPLS network, 430–432

   SR-MPLS, 358

   SRv6, 387–389

      building a new network using an IWG, 389–401

      building a new network using dual-connected PE devices, 413–424

      building a new network using inter-AS Option A, 401–413

MIP (maintenance intermediate point), 809

mLDP, 3

MP_REACH_NLRI path attribute, 608–609

MP-BGP (Multiprotocol Border Gateway Protocol), 6, 17

   extension/s, 83–85

      BGP Link-State, 87–95

      BGP Link-State extensions for SR BGP Egress Peer Engineering (RFC 9086), 95–98

      BGP overlay services on SRv6, 186–201

      BGP Prefix SID, 85–87

MPLS (Multiprotocol Label Switching), 4, 6, 28, 440. *See also* LDP (Label Distribution Protocol)

   backbone routes, 5

   BGP-free core, 1

   CE (customer edge) router, 6

   control plane, 205–207

data plane, 205–207

FRR (fast reroute), 18–19

header, 6–7

L2VPN, 3, 27. *See also* L2VPN

L3VPN, 2, 26. *See also* L3VPN

label/s, 1, 7–9

   -based forwarding, 15–16

   POP operation, 14

   PUSH operation, 14

   service, 16

   space limitation, 20–21

   SWAP operation, 14

LDP (Label Distribution Protocol), 11, 12

   downstream on-demand, 11

   -IGP synchronization, 24

   unsolicited downstream, 11

LER (label edge router, 5

LSP (label switched path), 21

LSR (label switch router), 5

mLDP, 3

operational complexity, 22

pseudowire, 440

QoS, end-to-end, 21–22

RSVP-TE, 22–23

   limitations, 23–24

   tunnel, 22–23

services, 2

traffic protection, 18

Unified, 210

use cases, 3–4

VPN, 16–18, 20

VRF instance, 3, 5

MPLS TE (Traffic Engineering), 3–4

mVPN, 3

N

neighbor adjacency, LDP, 11

neighbor discovery, LDP (Label Distribution Protocol), 11–12

network, as a computer, 37

network event information propagation time, 858

Next Header field, IPv6 header, 106

NEXT operation, 41

NLRI, 201–203, 608

Node SID, 45–46, 226

nonrouted SID, 110–111

n-tuple hash, 25

O

open-source SRv6, ONLINE, ONLINE-ONLINE. *See also* **open-source SRv6 lab deployment**

FRR (Free Range Routing), ONLINE-ONLINE

   daemons, ONLINE-ONLINE

   release 9.1, ONLINE-ONLINE

   SRv6 headend and endpoint support, ONLINE-ONLINE

   system architecture, ONLINE

   vytish, ONLINE-ONLINE

Linux kernel, ONLINE-ONLINE

   hardware offloading, ONLINE-ONLINE

   network stack, ONLINE-ONLINE

   SRv6 endpoint support, ONLINE-ONLINE

   SRv6 headend support, ONLINE-ONLINE

   uA/End.X (NEXT-CSID) endpoint behavior, ONLINE

SONiC (Software for Open Networking in the Cloud), ONLINE-ONLINE

   cli, ONLINE

   container modules, ONLINE-ONLINE

   data plane, ONLINE

   disaggregation, ONLINE-ONLINE

   sonic-cfggen, ONLINE

system architecture, ONLINE-ONLINE

VPP (Vector Packet Processor), ONLINE-ONLINE

   data plane, ONLINE-ONLINE

   endpoint support, ONLINE-ONLINE

   headend support, ONLINE-ONLINE

   linux-cp control plane integration plug-in, ONLINE-ONLINE

   pps (packets per second), ONLINE-ONLINE

   vector packet processing graph, ONLINE-ONLINE

open-source SRv6 lab deployment

L3VPN interoperability, ONLINE-ONLINE

   Cisco Catalyst 8000V Edge IPv4 L3VPN service, ONLINE-ONLINE

   FRR IPv4 L3VPN service, ONLINE-ONLINE

Linux SRv6, ONLINE-ONLINE

   Containerlab, ONLINE-ONLINE

   Layer 3 overlay services, ONLINE

   Linux IPv4 L3VPN service, ONLINE-ONLINE

   Linux IPv4/IPv6 L3VPN service, ONLINE-ONLINE

   Linux IPv6 L3VPN service, ONLINE-ONLINE

   Linux point-to-point L2VPN service, ONLINE-ONLINE

   overlay services VPN-1, ONLINE-ONLINE

   overlay services VPN-2, ONLINE-ONLINE

   overlay services VPN-3, ONLINE-ONLINE

   underlay connectivity, ONLINE-ONLINE

   underlay domain transport, ONLINE-ONLINE

VPP (Vector Packet Processor), ONLINE-ONLINE

   basic setup, ONLINE-ONLINE

   IPv4 L3VPN service, ONLINE-ONLINE

   IPv6 L3VPN service, ONLINE-ONLINE

   point-to-point L2VPN service, ONLINE-ONLINE

   underlay connectivity, ONLINE-ONLINE

operator-defined algorithm, 74–75

optical transport network (OTN), 73–74

OSPF (Open Shortest Path First). *See also* **SR-MPLS, OSPF; SRv6, OSPF**

ABR (area border router), 224, 229

areas, 224

extensions for segment routing (RFC 8665), 64

   Adj-SID sub-TLV, 68–69

   Prefix Range TLV, 72–73

   Prefix-SID sub-TLV, 70–71

   Segment Routing Algorithm TLV, 65

   SID/Label Range TLV, 65–66

   SRLB TLV, 66–67

   SRMS Preference TLV, 67

LSA (link-state advertisement), 224

shortest path tree, 224

SPF (Shortest Path First) algorithm, 224

verifying Prefix SID assignment, 235

OSPFv3, 225

route filtering, 225

route summarization, 225

overlay, 1018

overload bit, IS-IS, 223

P

P router, 6

path attribute. *See also* BGP

BGP Prefix SID, 609–610

MP_REACH_NLRI, 608–609

path divergence, 788–789

pcap trace command, ONLINE-ONLINE

PCE (path computation element), 211

PE router, 5, 606, 767–768

RTC (route target constraint), 768–771

configuration, 771–774

memberships, 769

verification, 774–780

Penultimate Segment Pop, 127–128

per-ESI Ethernet A-D route, 454–458

per-EVI Ethernet A-D route, 458–463

PHP (penultimate hop popping), 39

PIC (Prefix Independent Convergence), 943, 944–945

PIC Edge

multipath verification, SRv6, 981–995

unipath

SR-MPLS, configuration, 948–951

SR-MPLS, verification, 951–962

SRv6, configuration, 962–970

SRv6, verification, 970–981

ping command, 249, 254, 270, 292, 349, 423, 635, 676, 767, ONLINE-ONLINE, ONLINE-ONLINE, ONLINE-ONLINE, ONLINE-ONLINE, ONLINE-ONLINE

ping ethernet cfm domain service command, 815

pipeline, 1101–1104

PLE (private line emulation), 1011–1017

PLR (point of local repair), 878–879

policy

segment routing, 38–40, 41, 52–53

SRv6, 126

End.B6.Encaps behavior, 142–143

End.B6.Encaps.Red behavior, 143–144

End.B6.Insert behavior, 144–145

End.B6.Insert.Red behavior, 145–146

endpoint behaviors, 141, 146

headend behaviors, 132, 140

H.Encaps behavior, 132–133

H.Encaps.L2 behavior, 135

H.Encaps.L2.Red behavior, 136–137

H.Encaps.Red behavior, 133–135

H.Insert behavior, 138–140

POP operation, 14

pps (packets per second), ONLINE-ONLINE

Prefix Attribute Flags sub-TLV, 178–179

prefix metric, Flex Algo, 303

Prefix Range TLV, 72–73

Prefix SID, 76–77, 226

BGP, 324

configuration, 324–326

enabling in an SR-MPLS network, 376–383

proxy, 383–387

verification, 327–328

verifying, 235–236

Prefix SID TLV, 95

Prefix-SID sub-TLV, 58–59, 70–71

primary path, 18

program counter, 35

protocol ID, BGP, 96

pseudowire, 3, 11–12, 27, 440

P-space, 881–882, 896–897

PT (Path Tracing), 784, 787, 798–801, 1023–1025

MCD (Midpoint Compressed Data), 800–801

probe packets, 801–806

PUSH operation, 14, 41

Q-R

QoS, end-to-end, 21–22

Q-space, 881–882, 896–897

RD (route distinguisher), 17

reachability

    SR-MPLS, verification, 248–249, 253–254

    SRv6, verification, 270

    UPA (Unreachability Prefix Announcement), 293–295

        configuration, 295–298

        verification, 298–301

resource assurance, 1062–1063

RFC 4385, 26, 27

RFC 4760, 84

RFC 5036, 11

RFC 5357, 785

RFC 6391, 26

RFC 6513, 3

RFC 6790, 26, 26

RFC 7432, 449, 454

RFC 7855, 40–41

RFC 8317, 552

RFC 8402, 87–88

RFC 8667, IS-IS extensions for segment routing, 53–57, 256

RFC 8668, 48, 93

RFC 8754, 123–132

RFC 8762, 785

RFC 8986, 107, 111

RFC 9085, 87–95

RFC 9086, 95–98

RFC 9252, 186–201

RFC 9350, 74

RFC 9352, 175–186

RFC 9356, 48

RFC 9417, 1020

RIB (Routing Information Base), 10, 12, 858

RLFA (Remote Loop-Free Alternate), 880–882

RONs (routed optical networks), 1008–1011

route filtering, OSPFv3, 225

route leaking, IS-IS, 223

route propagation, IS-IS, 223

route summarization. *See also* **summarization**

    OSPFv3, 225

    SRv6, 172–175

Route Type 1

    per-ESI Ethernet A-D route, 454–458

    per-EVI Ethernet A-D route, 458–463

Route Type 2, 463–466

Route Type 3, 467–469, 512

Route Type 4, 470–472

routed SID, 110–111

router

    area border, 5, 38, 224

    autonomous system border, 5, 20

    CE (customer edge), 5, 6

    IS-IS, 222

    label edge, 5

    label switch, 5

    P (provider), 6

    PE (provider edge), 5, 606, 767–768

    PLR (point of local repair), 878–879

    P-space, 881–882, 896–897

    Q-space, 881–882, 896–897

Router Capability TLV, 54–57

routing, inter-AS, 21

RPD (routing policy database), ONLINE-ONLINE, ONLINE-ONLINE

RR (route reflector), 6

    RTC (route target constraint), 768–771

        configuration, 771–774

        memberships, 769

verification, *774–780*

RSVP-TE, 22–23

limitations, 23–24

tunnel, 22–23

RT (route target), 17–18, 389, 390

RTC (route target constraint), 768–771

configuration, 771–774

memberships, 769

verification, 774–780

S

SAP (service access point), 1058–1059

scalability, 220

SDN (software-defined networking), 28–29

segements, 36

Segment Routing Algorithm sub-TLV, 55–56

Segment Routing Algorithm TLV, 65

Segment Routing Capability sub-TLV, 54–55

segment-routing mpls sr-prefer command, 361

sensors, IoT, 37

service assurance, 783, 1062–1063

L2VPN, 806–807

CFM (Ethernet Connectivity Fault Management), 808–816. *See also CFM (Ethernet Connectivity Fault Management)*

ITU-T Y.1731 Performance Measurement. See ITU-T Y.1731 Performance Measurement

L3VPN, 834

IPSLA, 834. See also IPSLA

TWAMP, 835–836. See also TWAMP (Two-Way Active Measurement Protocol); TWAMP Light

transport-related. *See* transport-related service assurance

service catalog, 1063

service chaining, 213

service label, 14, 16

service orchestration, 1064

service portfolio consolidation, 1083–1084

service provider/s

benefits of SRv6 adoption, 998–999

network evolution, 210–212

PE (provider edge) routers, 606. *See also* PE router

technological opportunities and benefits of SR

CapEx savings, 1026–1029

fewer protocols, 999–1001

integrated visibility, 1017–1018

more QoS options, 1001–1003

new hardware generation, 1025

OpEx savings, 1030–1032

PLE (private line emulation), 1011–1017

RONs (routed optical networks), 1008–1011

scale, 1007–1008

traffic engineering and network slicing, 1005–1007

unification across domains, 1003–1005

service vpp status command, ONLINE-ONLINE

service vpp stop command, ONLINE-ONLINE

show bfd ipv6 session command, 868–869

show bfd ipv6 session interface bundle-Ether 1 detail command, 869

show bfd ipv6 session interface TF0/0/0/0 detail command, 870–871

show bfd neighbors command, 877

show bfd neighbors interface port-channel 1 details command, 877–878

show bfd session command, 875

show bfd session interface bundle-ether 1 detail command, 875–876

show bgp ipv4 labeled-unicast command, 347, 348, 377–378, 379–381, 713, 740–741

show bgp ipv4 rt-filter command, 771, 774

show bgp ipv4 rt-filter neighbors command, 774–775

show bgp ipv4 unicast command, 328, 348, 713–714

show bgp ipv4 vpn command, ONLINE-ONLINE

show bgp l2vpn evpn bridge-domain 200-BD command, 527–529

show bgp l2vpn evpn bridge-domain 200-BD received-sids wide command, 523–524

show bgp l2vpn evpn bridge-domain command, 446, 521–522, 525–527, 537, 540, 549–550, 568–569

show bgp l2vpn evpn bridge-domain VPWS:300 command, 594–599

show bgp l2vpn evpn rd command, 458–461, 464, 467–469, 470, 523, 601

show bgp l2vpn evpn route-type command, 530

show bgp l2vpn evpn route-type ethernet-segment command, 530–532, 600

show bgp l2vpn evpn summary command, 518–519

show bgp segment-routing srv6 command, ONLINE-ONLINE

show bgp summary command, ONLINE-ONLINE

show bgp vpnv4 uni vrf command, ONLINE-ONLINE

show bgp vpnv4 unicast command, 741–742

show bgp vpnv4 unicast vrf command, 626, 628–630, 646–647, 649–650, 651–652, 655, 659–661, 663, 667–668, 670, 673–674, 702–703, 704–705, 705–706, 733–735, 758–759, 760, 951–953, 954, 958–960, 971–973, 976–977, 982–984, 989–990

show bgp vpnv4 unicast vrf local-sids command, 627, 647–648, 663–664, 671

show bgp vpnv4 unicast vrf received-sids command, 627–628, 648, 664, 671

show bgp vrf command, 276, 320–321, 409–410, 420–421

show bgp vrf nexthop-set command, 634, 650, 667

show bgp vrf-db table all command, 519–521, 594

show bgp vrf-db table command, 566–567, 656

show bpg vpnv4 unicast vrf command, 665–666

show bundle bundle-Ether 200 command, 478, 484

show bundle bundle-Ether 250 command, 481, 482

show bundle bundle-Ether 300 command, 575–576

show cef command, 887–888, 892–893, 898–899, 919, 926

show cef detail command, 714–715, 716, 717–718, 743, 744–745, 747, 748, 749–750

show cef ipv6 command, 904–905, 908–909, 912–913, 936–937, 937–940, 942

show cef ipv6 detail command, 980–981, 993–994

show cef vrf command, 276, 279

show cef vrf detail command, 632–633, 654, 669–670, 675, 709–711, 738, 764, 766, 955–957, 960–962, 974–975, 979, 986–988, 991–992 show ethernet cfm local meps domain service command, 813

show ethernet cfm peer meps domain service command, 814–815

show ethernet sla operations detail profile command, 820–821, 827–828

show ethernet sla statistics brief profile command, 821–823, 829–830

show ethernet sla statistics detail profile command, 823–825, 831–834

show evpn ethernet-segment command, 494, 580

show evpn ethernet-segment interface BE200 carving detail command, 496–498

show evpn ethernet-segment interface BE300 carving detail command, 581–582

show evpn ethernet-segment interface Bundle-Ether260 detail command, 538–539

show evpn evi command, 498, 540–542, 583–584

show evpn evi ead command, 501, 584–585

show evpn evi inclusive-multicast detail command, 502–503

show evpn evi vpn 200 mac command, 501–502

show evpn evi vpn 205 mac command, 560–561

show evpn evi vpn-id 200 detail command, 499–500

show evpn summary command, 493–494

show interfaces brief command, 477–478, 483, 574–575, ONLINE-ONLINE

show ip cef detail command, 715, 717, 718, 744, 745–746, 749

show ip cef internal command, 889–890, 894–895, 900–901, 930–931

show ip cef vrf command, ONLINE-ONLINE

show ip cef vrf detail command, 711, 739, 765, 957

show ip ospf database command, 234

show ip route repair-paths command, 888–889, 893, 899–900, 928, 954–955

show ip route vrf command, 737, 762

show ip route vrf repair-paths command, 709

show ipsla statistics 11 command, 843–844

show ipsla statistics 21 command, 844–846

show ipsla statistics aggregated 11 command, 846–847

show ipsla statistics aggregated 21 command, 847–850

show ipsla twamp session command, 854

show ipv6 cef command, ONLINE-ONLINE

show ipv6 route isis command, ONLINE-ONLINE

show isis adjacency command, 265–266

show isis database command, 233, 247, 257, 265, 272, 288, 291, 299, 309–310

show isis fast-reroute summary command, 884

show isis fast-reroute ti-lfa tunnel command, 894, 900, 929

show isis flex-algo command, 308

show isis ipv4 fast-reroute detail command, 887, 892, 898, 904, 918, 920–921, 925, 927–928, 933–934

show isis ipv6 fast-reroute detail command, 908, 912

show isis neighbor command, ONLINE-ONLINE

show isis rib command, 929–930

show isis srv6 locators det command, ONLINE-ONLINE

show l2vpn bridge-domain bd-name 200-BD detail command, 508–510

show l2vpn bridge-domain bd-name detail command, 563–565

show l2vpn bridge-domain brief command, 508, 511, 544

show l2vpn forwarding bridge-domain ELAN-BG:200-BD mac-address location 0/RP0/CPU0 command, 510–511

show l2vpn forwarding bridge-domain ELAN-BG:210-BD mac-address location 0/RP0/CPU0 command, 545

show l2vpn forwarding xconnect detail location command, 591

show l2vpn mac-learning command, 512

show l2vpn mac-learning mac all location command, 511

show l2vpn xconnect group VPWS-XC command, 589–591

show lacp bundle-Ether 250 command, 481, 482

show lacp command, 479–480, 576–577

show memif command, ONLINE-ONLINE

show mpls forwarding command, 362, 364, 374

show mpls oam dpm adjacency command, 797

show mpls oam dpm prefix command, 797

show mpls oam dpm summary command, 795–796

show route 10.0.1.8/32 command, 886–887

show route command, 891, 896–897, 917–918, 924–925

show route ipv6 command, 280–281, 282, 289, 290, 291–292, 300, 311–312, 903–904

show route ipv6 detail command, 906–907, 911–912

show route vrf command, 278

show route vrf detail command, 631–632, 653–654, 668–669, 674–675, 708, 736, 761, 762–763, 973–974, 977–978, 985–986

show segment-routing srv6 capabilities-parameters command, ONLINE-ONLINE

show segment-routing srv6 locator command, ONLINE-ONLINE, ONLINE-ONLINE

show segment-routing srv6 locator MAIN detail command, ONLINE-ONLINE

show segment-routing srv6 locator MAIN sid command, 513–514, 546–547

show segment-routing srv6 sid command, 503–504, 586, ONLINE-ONLINE, ONLINE-ONLINE

show segment-routing srv6 sid detail command, 633, 634–635, 656

show segment-routing traffic-eng policy command, 274–275

show slrg name command, 932

show sr localsids command, ONLINE-ONLINE, ONLINE-ONLINE

show sr policies command, ONLINE-ONLINE

show sr steering-policies command, ONLINE-ONLINE

show trace command, ONLINE-ONLINE, ONLINE-ONLINE, ONLINE-ONLINE

SID (segment identifier), 36–37, 42–43
  Adjacency, 47–49, 226
  allocation, 43–44, 115
  anycast, 45, 47, 219
  BGP Peering, 50–52
  BGP Prefix, 49–50, 85–87
  Binding Segment, 52–53
  block addressing considerations, 163
  compression, 161–162
  Node, 38–39
  Prefix, 45–47, 76–77
  SRv6, 107–108, 183–186
    End behavior, 113–114
    End.DT2M behavior, 122–123
    End.DT2U behavior, 120–121
    End.DT4 behavior, 116–117

End.DX2 behavior, 119

End.DX4 behavior, 117–118

endpoint behaviors, 1113

End.X behavior, 114–115

Locator field, 108–110

routed/nonrouted, 110–111

verification, 266–270

SID/Label Binding TLV, 61–62

SID/Label Range TLV, 65–66

SID/Label sub-TLV, 63–64

SID/Label TLV, 91

SLA (service-level agreement), 783–784, 806

SLM (synthetic loss measurement), 816

configuration, 826–827

verification, 827–834

SLRG (shared risk link group), 921. *See also* **TI-LFA (Topology-Independent Loop-Free Alternate), SLRG protection**

SmartNICs, ONLINE

software-defined networking, 28–29

SONiC (Software for Open Networking in the Cloud), ONLINE-ONLINE

cli, ONLINE

container modules, ONLINE-ONLINE

data plane, ONLINE

disaggregation, ONLINE-ONLINE

sonic-cfggen, ONLINE

system architecture, ONLINE-ONLINE

source code repository, 1098–1100

source node, 126

source routing, 35–36

source/ingress node, 38

SPF (Shortest Path First) algorithm, 56, 73–74, 220, 224

SPRING architecture, 40–41

SR (segment routing), 225. *See also* **SR-MPLS**

adjacency segment, 226

benefits, 212–214

BGP Link-State extensions, 87–95

business case guidance, 1032–1034, 1036–1037

opportunity analysis, 1037–1038

refining known CapEx, 1034–1035

refining known OpEx, 1035–1036

data plane, 36–37

domain, 38

enabling

on IOS XE, 230

on IOS XR, 230

endpoint/egress node, 38

EPE (egress peer engineering), 41

feature support, 215

header, 106–107

IETF standards, 39, 40

IS-IS extensions (RFC 8667), 53–54

Adj-SID sub-TLV, 59–61

Flex Algo sub-sub-TLVs, 79–83

LAN-Adj-SID sub-TLV, 61

Prefix-SID sub-TLV, 57–59

Router Capability TLV, 54–57

Segment Routing Algorithm sub-TLV, 55–56

SID/Label Binding TLV, 61–62

SID/Label sub-TLV, 63–64

SRLB sub-TLV, 56–57

network as a computer, 37

OSPF extensions (RFC 8665), 64

Adj-SID sub-TLV, 68–69

Prefix Range TLV, 72–73

Prefix-SID sub-TLV, 70–71

Segment Routing Algorithm TLV, 65

SID/Label Range TLV, 65–66

SRLB TLV, 66–67

SRMS Preference TLV, 67

policy, 38–40

policy/ies, 41, 52–53

replacing or enhancing a legacy network with. *See also* legacy network

   IT evolution and gap awareness, 1051–1056

   migration strategy, 1049–1051

   required knowledge and expertise, 1046–1049

SID (segment identifier), 36–37

source/ingress node, 38

SPRING architecture, 70–77

transit node, 38

SR-DPM (Segment Routing Data Plane Monitoring), 784, 788–789

adjacency verification and validation, 790–792

configuration, 789–790

prefix reachability verification, 793–798

SRGB (segment routing global block), 44–45, 226–227

reconfiguring, 229

verifying, 232–234

SRH (segment routing header), 36–37, 123–124, 125–127, 147

fields, 124–125

Penultimate Segment Pop, 127–128

Ultimate Segment Pop, 129

USD (Ultimate Segment Decapsulation), 130–132

uSID instruction, 147–148

SRLB (segment routing local block), 45, 227–228

reconfiguring, 229

verifying, 232–234

SRLB sub-TLV, 56–57

SRLB TLV, 66–67

SR-MPLS, 41

addressing, 227

anycast SID, 254–255

   configuration, 254–256

   verification, 256–257

building a new network, 365

   BGP proxy Prefix SID, 383–387

   enabling LDP on the border node, 372–376

   enabling SRMS, 365–372

   enabling the BGP Prefix SID, 376–383

configuration, 228–229

   assign the prefix SID, 230–231

   enable segment routing, 230

   reconfiguring the SRGB/SRLB, 229

control plane, 207–209, 243–244

data forwarding, 341–342

data plane, 41–42, 207–209

enabling in an existing network (coexistence), 358–360

   enabling and preferring on P1, P2, and PE-1, 363–365

   enabling on P2, P3, and PE-3, 360–363

Flex Algo, 322–324

IS-IS, 244–246

   configuration, 246

   verification, 247–249

L3VPN overlay service, 677–679

   BGP label allocation modes, 701

   configuration, 679–685

   extranet, configuration, 752–756

   extranet, verification, 756–767

   full-mesh, configuration, 689–700

   full-mesh, verification, 701–719

   hub-and-spoke, configuration, 719–732

   hub-and-spoke, verification, 732–751

   verification, 686–688

label, collisions, 43

LSD (label switching database), 43

migration to segment routing, 358

OSPF, 250

configuration, 250

verification, 250–253

Prefix SID, 45–47

reachability, verification, 248–249, 253–254

SID (segment identifier), 42–43

Adjacency, 47–49

allocation, 43–44

anycast, 47

BGP Peering, 50–52

BGP Prefix, 49–50

Binding Segment, 52–53

Node, 45–46

sub-TLVs, 57–61

SRGB (segment routing global block), 44–45

SRLB (segment routing local block), 45

verify the SRGB and SRLB, 232–234

verifying the Prefix SID assignment, 235–236

SRMS (segment routing mapping server), 365–372

SRMS Preference TLV, 67

SR-PM (Segment Routing Performance Measurement), 784

end-to-end delay measurement of any endpoint, 786

end-to-end SR policy delay measurement, 785–786

end-to-end SR policy liveness detection, 787

link delay measurement, 785

PT (Path Tracing), 787

SRv6, 29–30, 103, 213–214, 601, ONLINE-ONLINE

BGP link-state extensions, 201–205

building a new network

using an IWG, 389–401

using dual-connected PE devices, 413–424

using inter-AS Option A, 401–413

control plane, 209–210, 257

data plane, 209–210

endpoint node, 126

Flex Algo, 301. *See also* Flex Algo

hardware and software support, 214

interface loopback address, 237–238

IS-IS, 257–260

anycast SID, 270–271

anycast SID configuration, 271

anycast SID use case, 272–282

anycast SID verification, 272

configuration, 260–265

reachability verification, 270

summarization, 282–285

summarization configuration, 286–287

summarization verification, 287–292

UPA (Unreachability Prefix Announcement), 293–295

UPA configuration, 295–298

UPA verification, 298–301

verification, 265

verify the SIDs, 266–270

verifying IS-IS adjacency, 265–266

verifying the database, 266

IS-IS extensions (RFC 9352), 175–176

segment routing over IPv6 capabilities, 180–183

segment routing over IPv6 locator, 176–180

SIDs, 183–186

IWG (interworking gateway), 389–390

L3VPN overlay service, 608. *See also* full-mesh L3VPN

BGP Prefix SID path attribute, 609–610

extranet, configuration, 657–662

extranet, verification, 662–677

full-mesh, configuration, 610–625

full-mesh, verification, 625–636

hub-and-spoke, configuration,
636–645

hub-and-spoke, verification,
645–657

MP_REACH_NLRI path attribute,
608

NLRI, 608

locator addressing scheme, 165–169

large-scale deployments, 170–172

small- and medium-scale
deployments, 169–170

MP-BGP extensions, BGP overlay
services, 186–201

open-source. See open-source SRv6

policy, 126

End.B6.Encaps behavior, 142–143

End.B6.Encaps.Red behavior,
143–144

End.B6.Insert behavior, 144–145

End.B6.Insert.Red behavior,
145–146

endpoint behaviors, 141, 146

headend behaviors, 132, 140

H.Encaps behavior, 132–133

H.Encaps.L2 behavior, 135

H.Encaps.L2.Red behavior,
136–137

H.Encaps.Red behavior, 133–135

H.Insert behavior, 138–140

SID (segment identifier), 107–108

block addressing considerations,
163

compression, 161–162

End behavior, 113–114

End.DT2M behavior, 122–123

End.DT2U behavior, 120–121

End.DT4 behavior, 116–117

End.DX2 behavior, 119

End.DX4 behavior, 117–118

endpoint behaviors, 1113

End.X behavior, 114–115

Locator field, 108–110

routed/nonrouted, 110–111

source node, 126

SRH, 125–127

fields, 124–125

Penultimate Segment Pop,
127–128

Ultimate Segment Pop, 129

USD (Ultimate Segment
Decapsulation), 130–132

standards, 103

summarization, 172–175

transit node, 126

uSID (micro SID), 236, 239

allocation, 236–237

globally significant, 150–151

instruction extension, 147–150

locally significant, 150–151

locator addressing scheme,
238–239

routed/nonrouted, 151

uA endpoint variants, 156–160

uN endpoint variants, 152–155

verification, 241–242

uSID configuration, 239

enable SRv6 uSIDs, 239–240

modify SRv6 parameters, 240

VPNv6 services, 194–195

SRv6 BGP PeerNode SID TLV, 205

SRv6 End SID sub-TLV, 179

SRv6 End.X SID sub-TLV, 183–185

SRv6 Locator TLV, 177–178

SRv6 Service Data sub-sub-TLV, 188–189

SRv6 SID Information sub-TLV, 188

stakeholder testing, 1088

standards

segment routing, 39, 40

SRv6, 103

stitching RT, 390
sub-sub-TLV, 79–80
   Flex Algo, 79–83
   SRv6 IS-IS, 185–186
   SRv6 Service Data, 188–189
sub-TLV
   Adj-SID, 59–61, 68–69
   Flexible Algorithm Definition, 78–79
   IS-IS Flexible Algorithm Definition, 77–79
   LAN-Adj-SID, 61
   Prefix Attribute Flags, 178–179
   Prefix-SID, 58–59, 70–71
   Segment Routing Algorithm, 55–56
   Segment Routing Capability, 54–55
   SID/Label, 63–64
   SRLB, 56–57
   SRv6 End SID, 179
   SRv6 End.X SID, 183–185
   SRv6 Locator, 176–177
   SRv6 SID Information, 188
summarization, 220
   IS-IS, 172–175, 282–285
   OSPFv3, 225
SWAP operation, 14
synchronization, LDP–IGP, 24
systemctl restart frr command, ONLINE-ONLINE

T

tcpdump, ONLINE-ONLINE
TDP (Tag Distribution Protocol), 1. See also LDP (Label Distribution Protocol)
TE (traffic engineering), 35–36, 38, 41, 210, 213
teams, 1082–1083. See also domain
test/ing, 1067, 1080, 1086, 1088, 1097
   acceptance, 1085, 1087

   automation, 1094
   development, 1091
   integration, 1080, 1091
   migration, 1096
   stakeholder, 1088
   unit, 1079, 1087
TI-LFA (Topology-Independent Loop-Free Alternate), 883
   combined SRLG and node protection, 934
   link protection
      configuration, 883–885
      SR-MPLS verification, 885–902
      SRv6 verification, 902–914
   node protection
      configuration, 914–917
      SR-MPLS verification, 917–919
      SRv6 verification, 919–921
      tiebreakers, 916
   SLRG protection
      configuration, 921–923
      SR-MPLS verification, 923–931
      SRv6 verification, 931–948
time/timer, 857–858
   EVPN E-LAN port-active MHD EVPN, 491
   failure event detection, 858
   network event information propagation, 858
   topology update and repair path computation, 858
TLV (type length value), 53. See also ISIS; OSPF; sub-sub-TLV; sub-TLV
   L2 Bundle Member Attributes, 93
   Prefix Range, 72–73
   Prefix-SID, 95
   Router Capability, 54–57
   Segment Routing Algorithm, 65
   SID/Label, 91

SID/Label Binding, 61–62

SID/Label Range, 65–66

SRLB, 66–67

SRMS Preference, 67

SRv6 BGP PeerNode SID, 205

SRv6 Locator, 177–178

topology

definition, ONLINE

update and repair path computation time, 858

traceroute command, 249, 254, 312, 342, 362–363, 364–365, 375–376, 382, 383, 412, 423, 645, 677, 718–719, 750–751, 767

traceroute ethernet cfm domain service command, 816

traffic blackholing, 788

Traffic Class field, IPv6 header, 104

traffic load balancing, 798–799

transit node, 38, 126

transport-related service assurance

PT (Path Tracing), 784, 787, 798–801, 1023–1025

MCD (Midpoint Compressed Data), 800–801

probe packets, 801–806

SR-DPM (Segment Routing Data Plane Monitoring), 788–789

adjacency verification and validation, 790–792

configuration, 789–790

prefix reachability verification, 793–798

TTL (Time to Live), 7

tunnel, RSVP-TE, 22–23

TWAMP (Two-Way Active Measurement Protocol), 306–307, 835–836

TWAMP Light, 785

configuration, 851–853

verification, 853–854

U

ULA (unique local address), 162

Ultimate Segment Pop, 129

underlay connectivity, 1018

Linux SRv6, ONLINE-ONLINE

VPP (Vector Packet Processor), ONLINE-ONLINE

Unified MPLS, 210

unified MPLS network migration, 430–432

unit test, 1079, 1087

unsolicited downstream, 11

UPA (Unreachability Prefix Announcement), 293–295

configuration, 295–298

verification, 298–301

update packing, 190–191

USD (Ultimate Segment Decapsulation), 130–132

uSID (micro SID), 36–37, 147–149, 236, 239

allocation, 236–237

configuration, 239

endpoint behaviors, 149–150

F3216 format, 148

globally significant, 150–151

locally significant, 150–151

locator addressing scheme, 238–239

SRv6 configuration

enable SRv6 uSIDs, 239–240

modify SRv6 parameters, 240

verification, 241–242

uA endpoint variants, 156–160

uN endpoint variants, 152–155

V

VPLS (Virtual Private LAN Service), 440

VPN, 20

extranet, 657

intranet, 657

MPLS, operational complexity, 22

VRF (virtual routing and forwarding), 17–18

VPP (Vector Packet Processor), ONLINE-ONLINE

data plane, ONLINE-ONLINE

DPDK, ONLINE-ONLINE

endpoint support, ONLINE-ONLINE

headend support, ONLINE-ONLINE

lab deployment, ONLINE-ONLINE

basic setup, ONLINE-ONLINE

IPv4 L3VPN service, ONLINE-ONLINE

IPv6 L3VPN service, ONLINE-ONLINE

point-to-point L2VPN service, ONLINE-ONLINE

underlay connectivity, ONLINE-ONLINE

linux-cp control plane integration plug-in, ONLINE-ONLINE

pps (packets per second), ONLINE-ONLINE

vector packet processing graph, ONLINE-ONLINE

VPWS (Virtual Private Wire Service), 440

VRF (virtual routing and forwarding), 17–18, 605, 606

VRF instance, 3, 38, 5

vytish, ONLINE-ONLINE

W-X-Y-Z

wildcard, *, 1112